The Book of Film Biographies

The Book of Film Biographies

A Pictorial Guide of 1000 Makers of the Cinema

Robin Morgan and George Perry, Eds.

A Bob Adelman Book

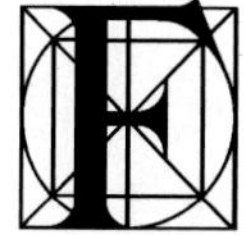

Fromm International Publishing Corporation
New York

First Fromm International Edition, 1997.

Published in the United States by Fromm International Publishing Corporation, New York.

LIBRARY OF CONGRESS CATALOGING-IN-PUBLICATION DATA

Morgan, Robin, 1953-
The book of film biographies: a pictorial guide/Robin Morgan &
George Perry, eds.
1st Fromm International ed.
p. cm.
Includes index
ISBN 0-88064-185-1
1. Motion picture actors and actresses - Biography - Dictionaries.
2. Motion picture producers and directors - Biography - Dictionaries.
3. Screenwriters - Biography - Dictionaries. I. Perry, George C.II. Title
PN1998.2M667 1997
791.43 '092' 2-dc21
[B]
97-37134
CIP

10 9 8 7 6 5 4 3 2 1
Printed in Scotland.

Contents

100 Glorious Years of Movies

The 20th century is the first to have been covered from start to finish by moving pictures, although the glossy, spectacular Spielbergian epics at its end bear little resemblance to the flickering, unsteady images produced by film pioneers at its beginning.

To celebrate the movie century we decided to compile our own list of 1000 people we felt had made the biggest contribution to the greatest development in man-made communication since the invention of the printing press.

This is a book for browsing through, for keeping near the television and the VCR, for consulting before a visit to the video store. Our main aim is to stimulate discussion, and controversy. There is no such thing as an objective, definitive list. We freely admit our selection is opinionated and biased. For instance, it is heavily weighted towards western cinema and Hollywood. Even so, you may find your favorite movie star has not been included. Yet some of the entries may seem bewildering or obscure, but have in our opinion deserved their selection. This is intended to be a work full of surprises. So, where is Johnny Depp? Why has Madonna not been included? Have we not realized how important Spyros Skouras was in the history of Hollywood? We make no apologies for such lapses. Someone else's list will always be different. Compiling it was great fun. A team of accomplished, professional film writers produced each entry, encapsulating in a few well-chosen words why that particular person had been chosen. We have offered a further challenge to debate, by providing lists of the 10 must-see movies across seven film genres. Every title is well-known, and as far as we are concerned they are the best of their kind.

As we have said. We enjoyed compiling this book, and in that spirit we hope you have the same pleasure reading it.

The Editors

ABBOTT & COSTELLO
US comedians (1895-1974 and 1906-59)

They were Hollywood's hottest box office property during the 1940s and early 1950s with matinee favourites such as *Buck Privates*, which grossed a then huge $10m. Famous for their unsophisticated slapstick, they provided baseball's Hall of Fame with the legendary "Who's on First?" routine, performed in *The Naughty Nineties* (45). William A Abbott, the straight man of the two, was born into a successful circus family. Louis Francis Cristillo did everything, from soda-fountain jerk to working on Warner's main lot before pairing with Abbott. The duo fashioned their first success in the Broadway revue Streets of Paris. After a decade their career went into decline with flops such as *Buck Privates Come Home* (47) before briefly reviving their flagging fortunes with *Abbott and Costello Meet Frankenstein* (48). Both experienced serious financial problems before Costello died of a heart attack; Abbott spent his last 10 years in a retirement home.

BIRT ACRES
British photographer, inventor and film maker (1854-1918)

An unfamiliar name, but that of a significant pioneer. In 1895 he collaborated with Robert William Paul (qv), building a camera that was a modified version of the Edison Kinetoscope, with which he proceeded to experiment. Historians differ on exact details of his contributions to the development of early British cinema, but he is widely credited, among other achievements, with holding the first public screening in Britain at the Royal Photographic Society in January 1896. The programme consisted of five films made by Acres, among them *The Derby* and *The Opening of the Kiel Canal* by Kaiser Wilhelm. He also made what Paul called their "first saleable film", The Oxford-Cambridge Boat Race, and was the first person to attempt the establishment of a public cinema, at the corner of Piccadilly Circus and Shaftesbury Avenue in March 1896, projecting films using his Kineopticon. The venue was destroyed by fire within a few weeks, but he continued his work and holds a respected place among those who advanced the technology and commercialisation of the motion picture.

KEN ADAM
British art director, production designer (1921-)

A Berliner who moved to Britain at the age of 13, Adam studied architecture before securing his first job as a draughtsman on *This Was A Woman* (48). He became an art director in the 1950s and production designer in the 1960s. Adam has regularly created spectacular and unique designs. He also produced memorable sets where a sense of jokiness and suspense are rolled into one, in particular *Goldfinger* (64) (with its dazzling Fort Knox interior), *Thunderball* (65), *You Only Live Twice* (67) and *The Spy Who Loved Me* (77), the latter securing him an Oscar nomination. He also received a nomination for *Around the World in 80 Days* (56) and won the Oscar for *Barry Lyndon* (75). His British awards include a Bafta for *Dr Strangelove* and a London Critics' Circle Award for *Addams Family Values* (93). His design of *Boys On The Side* (95), starring Whoopi Goldberg (qv), marked his seventh collaboration with the director Herbert Ross (qv). Five operas at the Royal Opera House, Covent Garden, were designed by Adam and exhibitions of his work can be found at the American Museum of the Moving Image in New York, the Cinémathèque in Paris and the Spoleto Museum in Italy.

ISABELLE ADJANI
French actress (1955-)

France's most feted modern female star has achieved iconic status in the manner of Arletty, Bardot or Moreau (qqv). Her screen performances began when she was 14 years old in a film made on her school holidays; at 17 she was appearing on French television. Her initial success, however, came on stage at the Comédie Française, where she became a hot ticket in Molière and Lorca roles. Ever a woman with her own agenda, she rejected a 20-year theatre contract to make the film that was to turn her into an international talking point and secure her first Oscar nomination, Truffaut's (qv) *The Story Of Adèle H* (75). Her portrayal of the driven daughter of Victor Hugo confirmed her as both a mature actress and a magnetic screen beauty, two sides of her talents that have been vying ever since. Cannes awards and Césars followed for *Possession* (81), *Quartet* (81), *One Deadly Summer* (83) and *Camille Claudel* (88) – another Oscar-nominated part, which she also co-produced. Adjani has a unique screen appeal, projecting a sense of wayward passion that makes her simultaneously a victim and a potential vixen.

PERCY ADLON
German producer, director and screenwriter (1935-)

Born in Munich, Adlon was an actor before establishing himself as a prodigious documentary film maker. In 1981 he wrote and directed his first theatrical feature, *Celeste*, an account of the last days of Marcel Proust as related by his maid. However, it was *Sugarbaby* (85), the story of an overweight mortician who seduces a subway driver, that launched Adlon's reputation worldwide. It also cemented his liaison with Marianne Sägebrecht, a Bavarian-Viennese cabaret performer who has appeared in three of his films. He went on to direct his first English-language picture, *Bagdad Cafe* (88), the extraordinary saga of a Bavarian tourist who takes over a Mojave desert diner. It is Adlon's juxtaposition of his characters – with themselves and the landscape – that gives his work such distinction. Whether pitting Sägebrecht against Jack Palance (qv) in *Bagdad Cafe*, or casting the singer k d lang as an androgynous drifter in *Salmonberries* (91), Adlon tests the rules. Furthermore, he bestows his films with a pictorial surrealism that makes them quite distinctive. He is married to the writer-producer Eleanore Adlon.

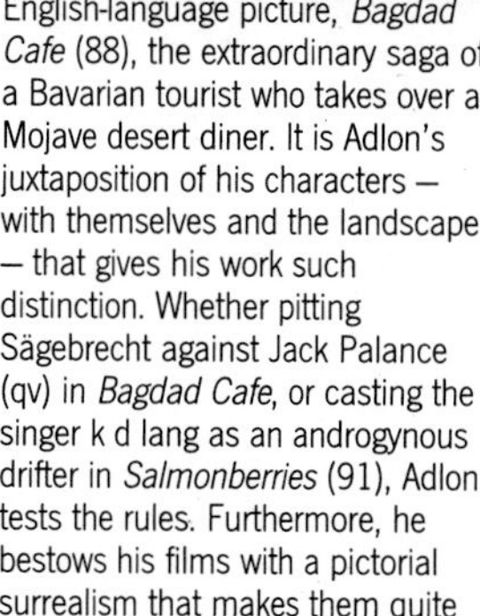

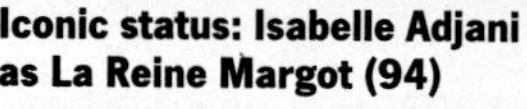

Iconic status: Isabelle Adjani as La Reine Margot (94)

RENEE ADOREE
French actress (1898-1933)

Clutching her beloved's abandoned boot in the first world war romance *The Big Parade* (25) as the American army marches past, Renée Adorée featured in a scene that the director King Vidor (qv) intended should "jerk a tear". A French critic, castigating the stereotype, said Adorée was dressed "like a burlesque miller's wife", but it was a moment of high poignancy. The petite brunette was born in a circus and christened Jeanne de la Fonte. She ventured to Hollywood after dancing at the Folies Bergère in Paris and acting in Australia. Her Gallic cuteness and jaunty sexuality gained her parts in boudoir romps such as *A Man's Mate* (24) and *Exchange of Wives* (25), but it was her role in *The Big Parade* that is remembered as her definitive performance. Ill-health impeded her career as a star and at the age of 35 she died from tuberculosis.

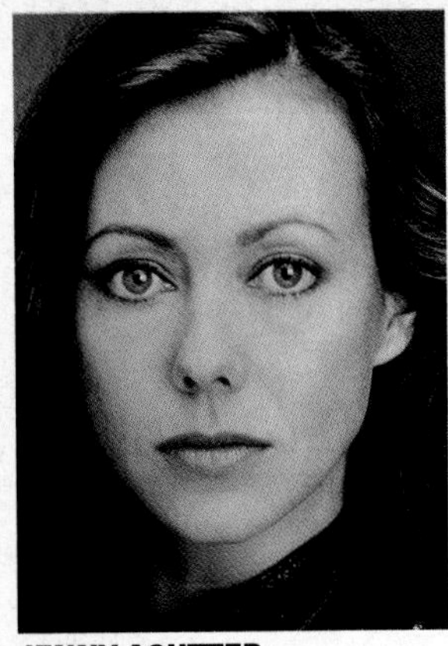

JENNY AGUTTER
British actress (1952-)

The careers of child actresses rarely survive adolescence, but Jenny Agutter's has been exceptional. She began acting at ballet school and appeared in the BBC television serial, The Railway Children. In 1972 it was successfully remade as a family film in which she played the eldest and most resourceful of three Edwardian children transplanted from London to Yorkshire. She won an Emmy in the following year for her role in a television film of Paul Gallico's The Snow Goose. She was also outstanding as a 16-year-old girl stranded with her small brother in the Australian outback in Nicholas Roeg's (qv) *Walkabout* (71). A Bafta award followed for her performance in Sidney Lumet's (qv) *Equus* (77), and in *An American Werewolf in London* (81) she played a sympathetic nurse. She has a natural, unforced beauty and a dancer's ability to move gracefully. Lately, she has divided her time between Los Angeles and London, but her film appearances have become sporadic.

ANOUK AIMEE
French actress (1932-)

In the 1950s and 1960s her air of vulnerable eroticism made her one of the most eye-catching actresses in international cinema. The daughter of actors, Françoise Sorya Dreyfus, took her first new name from the maid she played in her debut at 14 in *La Maison Sous La Mer* (46), later adding Aimée at the suggestion of director Marcel Carné (qv). Jacques Prévert (qv) was so enchanted with the willowy dance student that he wrote the tragic romance *Les Amants de Verone* (48) for her. Rank subsequently contracted her and, with her English debut in *Golden Salamander* (50) opposite Trevor Howard (qv), the teenager was tipped for stardom when marriage to the director Nico Papatakis and motherhood intervened. The pattern for her career was periodic success interspersed with unimportant roles and numerous marriages. Fellini's (qv) *La Dolce Vita* made Aimée a true star in 1960, after which other notable work included Jacques Demy's (qv) *Lola* (61), her only excursion into French New Wave, and Claude Lelouch's (qv) glossy *Un Homme et une Femme* (66), a worldwide hit that brought her an Oscar nomination. She was named best actress at Cannes for *Leap Into the Void* in 1980. Her fourth husband was the actor Albert Finney (qv).

ALAN ALDA
US actor, director and writer (1936-)

Frequently portraying a quintessentially decent and educated cynic, Alda's first success was the television series M*A*S*H (72-83), for which he won Emmy awards as best actor, writer and director. He made his film debut in 1963 in *Gone Are the Days*, but continues to work with distinction in television and on stage. He excels in contemporary moral dilemma or social comedy roles. Since *The Four Seasons* (81) he has written and directed as well as starred in his own films. He is the son of actor Robert Alda (1914-86), best known for playing Gershwin (qv) in *Rhapsody in Blue* (45).

ROBERT ALDRICH
US director, producer (1918-83)

After studying law and economics at the University of Virginia, he arrived in Hollywood in 1941 and began working his way up the RKO ladder, from production clerk to associate producer. His first feature film was *Big Leaguer* (53). His production company, Associates and Aldrich, was set up a year later and enabled him to produce the bulk of his subsequent work. Although no stranger to critical success (*The Big Knife* (55) and *Autumn Leaves* (56) won awards at film festivals in Venice and West Berlin), it was popular hits such as *Whatever Happened to Baby Jane?* (62) and *The Dirty Dozen* (67) that established his name. He exhibited a masterly control of tension, which often resulted in fraught atmospheres and a dark sense of impending violence. This was evident not only in the brutal *The Grissom Gang* (71) and his best film *Ulzana's Raid* (72), but also in the controversial *The Killing of Sister George* (68), which gained notoriety for its lesbian love scenes. His last films – including the coarse comedy *The Choirboys* (77) – were not typical of his compellingly abrasive style.

MARC ALLEGRET
French director (1900-73)

The son of a French pastor, he became companion-secretary to his uncle, the writer André Gide. Allégret (right) first achieved success as the director of *Fanny* (32), the second in the Marius trilogy, Marcel Pagnol's emotionally earthy account of rural life. His work after *Fanny, L'Arlesienne* (42) and *Le Bal du Comte d'Orgel* (69) were typical of his skill at decorating romantic melodramas.

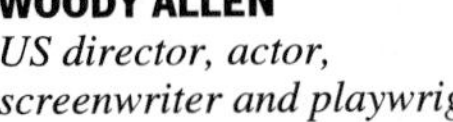

WOODY ALLEN
US director, actor, screenwriter and playwright (1935-)

Starting as an adolescent jokesm who supplied material for columnists and television shows, Allen finally let rip on stage with h by now familiar mixture of comic introspection, perpetual confusior and full-blown lust. As a

creenwriter and performer he ade his cinema debut with *'hat's New, Pussycat* (65), and ag-centred offerings such as *Play Again, Sam* (72), directed by erbert Ross (qv), found him a che market. It was, however, the ur-Oscar winner *Annie Hall* (77) at brought his artsy Manhattan gonising and hapless buffoonery a world audience. *Manhattan* 9) upped the quotient of urban ngst. His career has included self-onscious homages to Bergman v) (*Interiors* in 78) and xpressionism (*Shadows and Fog* 92). His controversial separation om Mia Farrow (who replaced ane Keaton (qv) on screen as len's favourite actress) has not opped his return to frivolity with *'anhattan Murder Mystery* (93) nd *Bullets Over Broadway* (94).

ESTOR ALMENDROS
panish cinematographer, 'rector (1930-92)

his teens he directed short films, udied philosophy and literature at e University of Havana, Cuba, nd made his home in New York here he studied film editing and nematography. Almendros moved Paris in the 1960s, where he ecame an important figure in the ench New Wave, working with hmer and Truffaut (qqv). The eak of his career is widely garded to be Terrence Malick's *ays of Heaven* (78), for which he on an Oscar for photography so nereal and other-worldly it hieved a mythical quality. He oved on to work on the box office nash *Kramer vs. Kramer* (79), t the 1980s saw his return to llaborate with Truffaut on *The ast Metro* (80) and Rohmer on *uline at the Beach* (83). His arkling work on the sickly remake *The Blue Lagoon* (80) proved to the film's only high point. In 88 his focus returned to Cuba en he co-wrote and co-directed a cumentary on Castro's rocky man rights record, *Nadie cuchaba (Nobody Listened).*

EDRO ALMODOVAR
panish director (1951-)

former telephone company nployee and leading light of

Madrid's avant-garde scene *(la movida)* in the 1970s, Almodóvar has become modern Spanish cinema's most successful and controversial export. His 10 feature films have stylishly set out to shock and unsettle, serving up murder, incest, fetishism and every permutation of sexuality in a flamboyant mix of the kitsch, camp, melodramatic and wickedly comic. This anarchic, taboo-busting approach has earned him an international cult following and even an Oscar nomination for *Women on the Edge of a Nervous Breakdown* (88). But a later film, *Kika* (93), which features a comic rape scene, was refused a certificate in America. No director since Ingmar Bergman (qv) has consistently provided such challenging roles for his favourite actresses: Victoria Abril in his later work, before that Carmen Maura.

ROBERT ALTMAN
US director, screenwriter and producer (1925-)

Born in Kansas City, Altman studied engineering at university and served as a pilot in the war. After a stint making industrial films, he entered television and learned his craft churning out up to two shows a week. He made his name in films with *M*A*S*H* (70) and followed with a wide variety of pictures – everything from sci-fi to westerns – which were invariably marked with a dark, satirical edge. Favouring naturalistic sound and lighting, Altman has been instrumental in inventing modern cinema. He is also a great "actor's director", which accounts for the large number of stars who have queued up to work for him for basic fees. Yet, while critically championed, Altman has failed to find lasting commercial success, although he worked his way back into the public eye with *The Player* (92) and *Short Cuts* (93), both of which earned him best director Oscar nominations.

ERIC AMBLER
British writer (1909-)

An eminent novelist specialising in espionage thrillers, several of Ambler's works have been adapted for the screen, including *The Mask of Dimitrios* (44), *Journey Into Fear* (42) and *Topkapi* (64) from The Light of Day. He has also been responsible for many outstanding original and adapted screenplays. He was nominated for an Oscar for his script of *The Cruel Sea* (53). After graduating from the University of London, Ambler initially worked as an engineer, then tried his hand on the stage and at writing advertising copy. When he joined Alexander Korda (qv) in 1938 he had already written four successful novels. Ambler's world of intrigue is scarcely glamorous, his heroes are often flawed and the work they do is shady and sordid.

DON AMECHE
US actor (1908-93)

A fixture in Twentieth Century Fox films from 1935 to the mid-1940s, Ameche was a dapper, slightly built and sophisticated light comedian who six times partnered Alice Faye (qv) in memorable musicals and led in two notable biopics – *The Story of Alexander Graham Bell* (39) and *Swanee River* (39). Intermittently busy in the 1950s, 1960s and 1970s, he returned to full activity with John Landis's (qv) *Trading Places* (83) and won an Oscar as best supporting actor in Ron Howard's (qv) *Cocoon* (85).

G M ANDERSON
US actor, director and producer (1882-1971)

Max Aronson from Little Rock, Arkansas, abandoned the life of a travelling salesman to become "Broncho Billy" Anderson. He was cast in *The Great Train Robbery* (03) and by 1907 he had worked at Vitagraph, Selig, where he also wrote and directed, and formed the Essanay company, home to Chaplin (qv) in 1915, with George K Spoor, adding producing to his considerable repertoire. He created the popular role of Broncho Billy in *The Bandit Makes Good* (07), a

successful two-reel western. It spawned some 400 shorts establishing him as the first identifiable screen cowboy hero. He made his last films in 1922, but in 1957 the Academy of Motion Pictures honoured him with a special Oscar for "contributions to the development of motion pictures as entertainment".

JUDITH ANDERSON
Australian actress (1898-1992)

Anderson, born in Adelaide, made her New York debut in 1918 and was created a Dame of the British Empire in 1960. She was renowned for her performances in work from Shakespeare to Eugene O'Neill when her career was at its height in the 1930s and 1940s. She was sought-after for heavy character parts and is for ever associated with her second screen role, the mad and malevolent Mrs Danvers, the sinister housekeeper of Manderley in Alfred Hitchcock's (qv) Oscar-winning *Rebecca* (40). Other notable appearances include the oppressed Big Mama to Burl Ives's Big Daddy in the screen adaptation of Tennessee Williams's *Cat on a Hot Tin Roof* (58).

LINDSAY ANDERSON
British director, critic (1923-94)

Born in India, the son of a Scottish major-general and educated at Cheltenham and Oxford, this self-proclaimed anarchist and John Ford (qv) fan first came to public prominence as a radical critic in the Oxford film magazine Sequence, which he co-founded. He began to produce social documentaries with Free Cinema, questioning perceived notions and winning an Oscar for *Thursday's Children* about the deaf before making his feature film debut with a powerful adaptation of David Storey's *This Sporting Life* (63), a Rugby League saga, which launched the film career of Richard Harris (qv). Other film highlights include *If. . .*(68), a gutsy satire of a rebellion within a British public school, which won a Golden Palm at Cannes, *Britannia Hospital* (82), a savage indictment of the health service, and *The Whales of August* (87), which united Bette Davis and Lillian Gish (qqv) and Glory Glory for television, a caricature of evangelism. The rest of his career was confined to the theatre, writing criticism and theorising.

DANA ANDREWS
US actor (1909-92)

He was a resolutely square-jawed hero who nevertheless managed to suggest a loser's emotional ambiguity. It worked well as the wrongly accused lynch victim in *The Ox-Bow Incident* (43) and the love-possessed cop in *Laura* (44). An accountant, he was trained as a singer and hired by Samuel Goldwyn (qv) as a supporting ▷

actor in westerns. He made some of his best movies for Twentieth Century Fox and his finest moments were as the airman trying to come to terms with civilian life in *The Best Years of Our Lives* (46), the fraught army officer in *A Walk in the Sun* (45) and the smalltown prosecutor uncovering corruption in *Boomerang!* (47). Despite his handsomely rigid face, he successfully played embittered and disillusioned roles. He was stalked by alcoholism, which resulted in banal subjects towards the end of his career, though he flickered into focus in *The Last Tycoon* (76).

JULIE ANDREWS
British actress (1935-)

Singing in London cabaret at the age of 12, Andrews made her New York stage debut in The Boy Friend and created the Broadway role of Eliza in My Fair Lady to rapturous applause and reviews. She lost the part in the film version because Rex Harrison (qv), jealous of the applause she had attracted on stage and afraid that her wonderful voice would further upstage him in the film, vetoed her in favour of Audrey Hepburnn (qv). Her first film, *Mary Poppins* (64), made her a star and won her the best actress Oscar for her embodiment of the wholesome, melodious and magical heroine. An equally fine performance as Maria in *The Sound of Music* (65) was Oscar-nominated and the film remains the most successful musical of all time. From the beginning she challenged the prim image created by those two films, but the perception has unfairly lingered; even 16 years later when she bared her breasts in *S.O.B.* (81) at the age of 46, it became an international media event. She has consistently delivered comic or solidly dramatic performances in *The Americanization of Emily* (64), *Thoroughly Modern Millie* (67), *Star!* (68) and several films with her second husband, Blake Edwards (qv), such as *10* (79), with Dudley Moore (qv), and *Victor/Victoria* (82). She emerged with credit from the screen adaptation of the stage play *Duet for One* (86) as a musician who is a victim of multiple sclerosis.

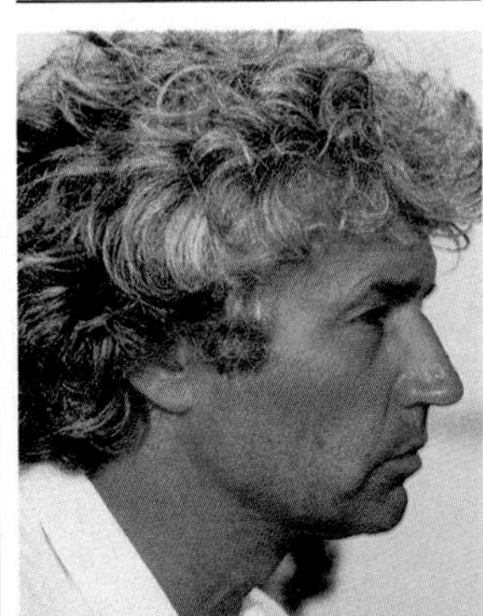

JEAN-JACQUES ANNAUD
French director, screenwriter (1943-)

Annaud made his feature debut with *Black And White In Color* (76), an amusing diversion about a gaggle of patriotic Frenchmen stationed at a remote trading post in West Africa. The comedy established Annaud as a director of promise when it won the Oscar for best foreign film. Since moving into the international arena with *Quest For Fire* (81), Annaud's films have carved a significant niche in the global marketplace. He made a credible adaptation of Umberto Eco's medieval mystery *The Name of the Rose* (86) with Sean Connery (qv). In 1992 he attracted much controversy with his (relatively) explicit adaptation of Marguerite Duras's autobiographical novel *The Lover.*

ANN-MARGRET
US actress, singer and dancer (1941-)

The vivacious, flame-haired "sex kitten" of 1960s American cinema, Swedish-born Ann-Margret Olsson was singing with a band in her teens when George Burns (qv) put her in his Las Vegas act. She was snapped up by Hollywood, making her debut as Bette Davis's (qv) innocent daughter in *Pocketful Of Miracles* (61). It was, however, her torrid singing performance at the 1962 Academy Awards that made her a star, with a six-picture deal including *Bye Bye Birdie* (63). She paired on and off-screen with Elvis Presley in *Viva Las Vegas* (64) and sang for President John F Kennedy

at his last birthday party. She plummeted from hot to has-been almost as rapidly as her ascent, but rebounded as a Vegas headliner. Her touching performance in *Carnal Knowledge* (71) won her new respect, her slithering in an ocean of baked beans in the rock opera Tommy (75) new oglers, and in the 1980s she was acclaimed for her dramatic TV work, notably in A Streetcar Named Desire. She survived a near-fatal stage fall in Las Vegas in 1972, which resulted in multiple injuries. She also had to cope with alcoholism and the long illness of her husband, the actor turned manager Roger Smith. *Grumpy Old Men* (94) with Walter Matthau and Jack Lemmon (qqv) demonstrated that she remains flagrantly seductive in her fifties.

OTTOMAR ANSCHUTZ
German pioneer (1846-1907)

A German photographer, born in Poland, Anschütz was greatly impressed by the sequential photographs of movement taken by Eadweard Muybridge. From 1882 Anschütz began to make sequences in a much sharper form. He went on to invent a viewing device called the Electrical Tachyscope in 1889 in which each of a sequence of transparencies was momentarily illuminated as it paused over a slit, and in 1893 he succeeded in projecting his simple moving pictures on a large screen at the Chicago World's Fair.

MICHELANGELO ANTONIONI
Italian director (1912-)

Antonioni clung obsessively to his dream of directing, which he realised at the age of 38 with *Cronaca di un Amore* (50). His piecemeal journey towards that goal included writing film reviews. He became Rossellini's (qv) script

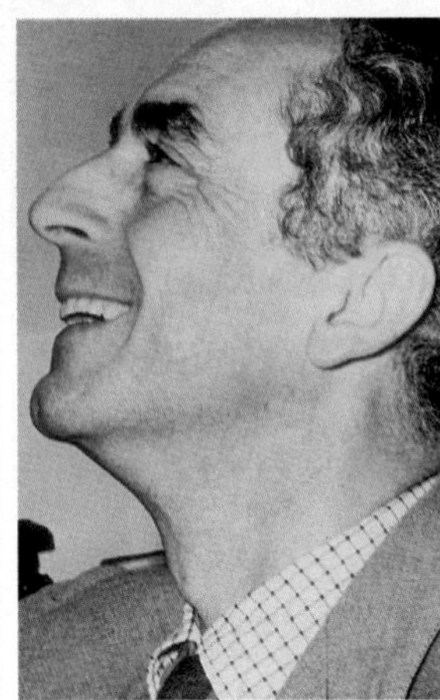

collaborator on *Una Pilota Ritorna* (42) and Marcel Carné's (qv) assistant on *Les Visiteurs du Soir* (42). After learning to direct on documentaries, he made *L'Avventura* (60), the first part of a trilogy that included *La Notte* (61) and *L'Eclisse* (62), which was hailed as an intoxicating Italian original. *Blow-Up* (66) – a lumpy mixture of the irritating and inspired that captured mid-1960s London – was his best known film for being made in Britain. In 1985 he was partially paralysed and his subsequent project *Beyond the Clouds* (95) required Wim Wenders's collaboration.

ROSCOE "FATTY" ARBUCKL
US comic actor (1887-1933)

A childhood of vaudeville appearances preceded parts in or and two reelers in 1907 and Arbuckle was hired as a Keystone Cop in 1913 by Mack Sennett (qv He featured in a series of Chaplin (qv) shorts and when the star left

ennett, Arbuckle won a meatier are of the spotlight paired with abel Normand (qv) in the jolly atty and Mabel films. Arbuckle's pularity spread. Soon, bids for s services were boosting his fees an astronomical level and ature films inevitably followed, tably the first incarnation of *ewster's Millions*. But 1921 ought a scandal and irreparable image after Arbuckle attended a rty where a girl died. An cusation of rape was suggested the girl's dying words and his ns were banned. He was tried ee times for manslaughter and ally acquitted for lack of idence in 1923. However, the blic was disgusted, the industry sowned him and his career was tually destroyed. This scandal d others in the film industry entually prompted Hollywood to t up the Hays Office to censor elf. As a star, Arbuckle s finished, although he ntinued to direct a string of films der the pseudonym William B odrich, including the first Eddie ntor (qv) films.

E ARDEN

actress (1912-90)

nice Quedens was the disputed queen of the "always a desmaid, never a bride" school 18-carat supporting actresses. e was instantly recognisable for chic appearance, elegant style d, most famously, her caustic screen tongue. Via summer ck, the regional theatre mpanies and Broadway, she gan her film career in 1937. She n a best supporting actress car nomination for *Mildred rce* (45) at Warner where, der contract during the 1940s, reached her peak. Arden casionally graced more serious e such as *The Dark at the Top of Stairs* (60), and was unafraid of sympathetic roles, such as the chy sister-in-law in *The Unfaithful*) or the spiteful friend in *The ce of the Turtle* (47). She oyed a successful TV and radio eer during the 1950s and 50s and in 1978 turned up as school principal in *Grease*.

ALAN ARKIN

US Actor (1934-)

Best regarded for his sensitive Oscar-winning portrayal of a deaf-mute in *The Heart Is a Lonely Hunter* (68) and the paranoid pacifist Yossarian in *Catch-22* (70), Arkin is a fine comedy actor and a master of the hang-dog expression, always leaving an indelible impression in otherwise unmemorable films. Born in New York, trained in Chicago, he earned a Tony for his Broadway appearance in Carl Reiner's (qv) Enter Laughing and went on to win a first Oscar nomination for his role as a dozy Soviet submariner in his debut film *The Russians Are Coming! The Russians Are Coming!* (66), a satire on cold war hysteria. A multi-talented individual, who recently played the laconic father-figures in *Coup de Ville* (90) and *Edward Scissorhands* (90), he has picked up awards as a theatre director and made his mark as an author, songwriter and musical performer.

HAROLD ARLEN

US composer (1905-86)

Hyman Arluck was the son of an up-state New York cantor and became a nightclub pianist at the age of 15 and a bandleader by 20. He wrote the music for *The Wizard Of Oz* (39) and won an Oscar for *Over The Rainbow*. He had begun with songs for Broadway revues by Earl Carroll, George White and the Cotton Club and his talent for melodic invention led to his scoring of films as diverse as *Cabin In The Sky* (43), *A Star Is Born* (54) and *The Country Girl* (54). He was regarded as one of the Syncopated Six composers – a sextet that included Jerome Kern and Irving Berlin (qqv), but he never quite achieved the musical comedy status he craved on Broadway.

RICHARD ARLEN

US actor (1899-1976)

To this day, Arlen is best known for his starring role in William Wellman's (qv) *Wings* (27), the first film to win the Oscar for best picture. None the less, he made 133 films, working right up to his death in 1976. Before his debut in 1920 he was a pilot with the Royal Canadian Flying Corps and worked as a messenger for a film laboratory when, following a minor traffic incident, he was spotted by Paramount Pictures and signed up as an extra. Seven years later in *Wings* he won ecstatic reviews as the volatile, tragic pilot. Later the rugged, athletic actor was the star of countless programmers and was a reliable supporting player in major features. He was married to the actress Jobyna Ralston, his *Wings* co-star.

ARLETTY

French actress (1898-1992)

If she had appeared in only one film, Marcel Carné's (qv) masterly *Les Enfants du Paradis* (45), her status as a screen legend would still have been secure. Léonie Bathiat was born in a working-class suburb of Paris. The daughter of a miner, she left school at 13 and worked in a factory, then found work as an artist's model and chorus girl. She was 32 before she made her first film and 40 when she played a prostitute in *Hôtel du Nord* (38), the first of her three films for Carné. Her husky, spat-out delivery made her a national institution, the epitome of a streetwise, earthy Parisienne. It was her third Carné role, as the emancipated courtesan Garance in *Les Enfants du Paradis*, that guaranteed her worldwide acclaim as luminously beautiful yet toughly sage. Scandal overtook her after the war when it emerged she had had an affair with a German officer. She never repeated her earlier success, withdrawing from film work when an accident in 1963 caused the gradual loss of her eyesight.

GEORGE ARLISS

British actor (1868-1946)

Earning the sobriquet "first gentleman of the screen" for his ability to portray notable historical figures, Arliss entered films at the advanced age of 53, repeating several of the impersonations that had made him famous on stage. He made his screen debut in 1921 in *The Devil*, a silent film adaptation of a Molnar play in which he had appeared. The same year he made *Disraeli*, co-starring with his wife Florence Arliss, and remains best known for repeating the role in the 1929 sound remake. If it looks like antiquated ham now, it brought him fame and an Oscar then. He is also remembered for his screen Voltaire, Cardinal Richelieu, Alexander Hamilton and Wellington, and was in the unlikely company of Bette Davis (qv), co-starring in *The Man Who Played God* (32).

GILLIAN ARMSTRONG

Australian director (1950-)

Armstrong made her mark internationally with *My Brilliant Career* (79), a tale of a woman buffeted between her compulsion to write and others' expectations of marriage. This role gave actress Judy Davis (qv) her international

start. Her ability to enhance psychological and emotional accuracy with a strong visual punch (her early study of costume and stage design have helped), Armstrong again placed Davis at the centre of *High Tide* (87), a film about a woman stumbling on the daughter she had abandoned long before. American efforts such as *Mrs Soffel* (84), in which a prison warden's wife, played by Diane Keaton (qv), falls for a convicted murderer, were less accomplished and raised suspicions of studio interference and directorial compromise. *Starstruck* (82), Armstrong's ironic ride through the business of stardom, was powered by an appealing, free-wheeling absurdity, while *The Last Days of Chez Nous* (93) also saw Armstrong back on Australian turf. She regained her place in American cinema with *Little Women* (94), in which resonances of *My Brilliant Career* were apparent.

LOUIS ARMSTRONG

US musician, actor (1900-71)

He learned the cornet during his time at the Waifs' Home in New Orleans, and from there freewheeled from band to band, working with Kid Ory, King Oliver and Fletcher Henderson. As early as 1926 Satchmo (a contraction of "satchel-mouth") was being heralded as "the world's greatest trumpet player" during a stint with Carroll Dickerson's orchestra. Wider popularity came through the Broadway revue Hot Chocolates, where he introduced the Fats Waller song Ain't Misbehavin'. ▷

ugely successful international urs followed and in 1936 he arred in *Pennies From Heaven* ongside Bing Crosby (qv), though popular consensus has it at the widening of his appeal incided with a subsidence of usical invention and depth. More m roles followed, including *Cabin the Sky* (43), *A Song Is Born* 8), *High Society* (56), nd 1957 saw the release of the ur-volume album Satchmo, A usical Biography. His acting pearances were largely nexceptional (he was often alled upon to play himself), ut his rough, desperate voice and arm trumpet playing have a meless beauty. His plaintive ndering of We Have All the Time the World, the love theme from *n Her Majesty's Secret Service* 9), was recently re-released on e back of an advertisement, to eat chart success.

EAN ARTHUR
S actress (1905-91)

thur's first film was *Cameo Kirby* 3) for John Ford (qv) and she as established as a silent player efore sound revealed her dry, musical, but appealingly husky ice. *The Whole Town's Talking* 5) with Ford was her calling card r a 10-year reign as a no-nsense, tomboyish girl-next-door roine, ideally suited for the social medy of Frank Capra (qv), who atured her in three Oscar nners: *Mr Deeds Goes to Town* 6), *You Can't Take It With You* 8) and *Mr Smith Goes to ashington* (39).After Columbia eased her from contract in the d-1940s she made only two ore films, *A Foreign Affair* (48) d her last, *Shane* (53).

OROTHY ARZNER
S director (1900-79)

e first woman admitted to the rectors' Guild of America, Arzner s for some time the only female ector at any big Hollywood udio. She drove ambulances in e first world war and rose rapidly m secretary to top film editor at ramount in the 1920s. After eatening to leave in 1927 she directed *Fashions For Women* (27). She directed 17 feature films and is now revered as a key figure by feminist and lesbian film makers. One of Arzner's better known films, *The Bride Wore Red* (37), is a typical Joan Crawford (qv) vehicle. The most feminist-angled of her films is *Christopher Strong* (33). Arzner also tackled Zola's tragedy *Nana* (34) and anti-Nazi propaganda in her final film, *First Comes Courage* (43). She later taught film at UCLA, where her students included Francis Ford Coppola (qv).

staire and Rogers (left) stablished dance in films

HAL ASHBY
US director, editor (1929-88)

Latterly feted for his cult romantic comedy *Harold and Maude* (71) and the much acclaimed drama *The Last Detail* (73), Ashby's life reads like a typical Tinseltown rags to riches to fadeout saga. Raised in a broken home in Utah and divorced four times, he ascended the dizzying Hollywood heights only to fall from critical grace as his lifestyle contributed to the liver cancer that cut his career short. Winning an Oscar for editing *In the Heat of the Night* (67), he made the sex comedy *Shampoo* (75) before graduating to more serious matters with a sentimental biography of Woody Guthrie, *Bound for Glory* (76), and a love story about a paraplegic Vietnam veteran, *Coming Home* (78), which was nominated for best picture and direction at the 1978 Oscars.

ANTHONY ASQUITH
British director (1902-68)

The son of the first Earl of Oxford and Asquith, the British prime minister from 1908 to 1916, and nicknamed "Puffin", he went into films as soon as he graduated from Oxford, going to America to learn the craft. Along with Bernard Shaw, H G Wells, Julian Huxley and other members of the London intelligentsia he co-founded the Film Society in 1925 which enabled banned works, some by Eisenstein (qv), to be shown to British audiences. His first film, the silent *Shooting Stars* (28) pioneered new techniques. He made several films in collaboration with the playwright Terence Rattigan including *The Way to the Stars* (45), *The Winslow Boy* (48) and *The Browning Version* (51), three adaptations of Shaw plays, and *The Importance of Being Earnest* (52). He portrayed the middle and upper classes with gentle satire, at its best in *The Demi-Paradise* (43). Despite his patrician background he was a staunch upholder of workers' rights and a prominent figure in film trade unionism.

FRED ASTAIRE
US actor, dancer (1899-1987)

Starting as a vaudeville dancer with his sister Adele at the age of seven, the Astaires graduated to Broadway and London's West End before Adele retired to marry. Fred's 1932 screen test produced the famous description "Can't act. Slightly bald. Can dance a little". He went on to establish dance as a cinematic form, most notably in a 10-film partnership with Ginger Rogers (qv), but also with Rita Hayworth, Judy Garland, Eleanor Powell, Cyd Charisse and Leslie Caron (qqv). His polished perfectionism and artless, untrained singing of many specially written songs has endeared him to successive generations in films from *Dancing Lady* (33) to *Finian's Rainbow* (68). He was also in demand as a dramatic actor, *On the Beach* (59), and was a best supporting actor Oscar nominee for *The Towering Inferno* (74). He was awarded a special Oscar in 1949 for his contribution to films and given an American Film Institute life achievement award in 1981.

MARY ASTOR
US actress (1906-87)

In spite of a career lasting from 1922 to 1965, Astor loathed Hollywood. She failed a screen test for D W Griffith (qv), was signed up by Famous Players, was dropped after six months, then re-signed a year later. She languished in minor films until John Barrymore (qv) cast her as Lady Margery opposite his *Beau Brummel* (24). Over the next two decades she excelled in a number of films, notably *Dodsworth* (36) and *The Maltese Falcon* (41), exhibited a fine instinct for comedy in *The Palm Beach Story* (42) and won an Oscar as best supporting actress for *The Great Lie* (41). Drink and a period in analysis caused her career to dip in the 1950s and she retired in mid-1960s.

RICHARD ATTENBOROUGH
British actor, director (1923-)

"Dickie" is perhaps British cinema's original "living legend", his extensive career mapping out the chequered history of the British film industry. The director of the exquisite literary drama *Shadowlands* (93) first appeared as a coward in *In Which We Serve* (42). Born in Cambridge and trained at Rada, his first big success was as Pinkie in the stage and film versions of Graham Greene's (qv) dramatic *Brighton Rock* (47). By acting in and co-producing *The Angry Silence* (60), he underwent a mid-career change of direction, pointedly illustrated by his chilling portrayal of the loathsome murderer Christie in *10 Rillington Place* (70). Active in many film industry, public and charitable causes, he is renowned for his tireless energy, enthusiasm and dedication. He has a love affair with the big picture, spectacularly portrayed in his epic Oscar-winning *Gandhi* (82), the anti-apartheid *Cry Freedom* (87) and his tribute to the little clown in *Chaplin* (92). His recent acting successes have included *Jurassic Park* (93) and *Miracle on 34th Street* (94). Knighted in 1976, he is now Lord Attenborough of Richmond upon Thames.

STEPHANE AUDRAN
French actress (1932-)

Best known to contemporary cinema audiences as the ▷

enigmatic Parisian chef who invades the austerity of two pious sisters with her sumptuous meals in *Babette's Feast* (87), Audran has been a star in France for more than 20 years, aided not only by a series of full roles, but also by her marriages to directors Jean-Louis Trintignant and Claude Chabrol (qqv). Chabrol directed her in *Les Biches* (68), in which she played a rich lesbian spiralling into despair, and *Violette Nozière* (77), in which a young girl poisoned her parents. She also had a high-profile part in *The Discreet Charm of the Bourgeoisie* (72), Buñuel's (qv) satirical jab at the middle class. The Berlin Festival awarded her best actress for *Les Biches*, while Bafta honoured her for *Just Before Nightfall* (71) and *The Discreet Charm of the Bourgeoisie*.

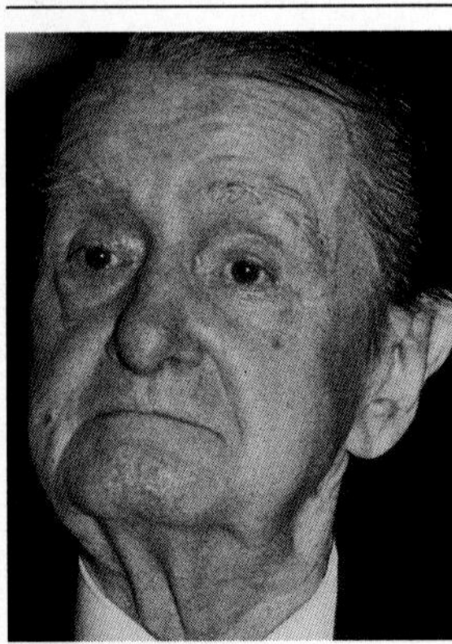

GEORGES AURIC
French composer (1899-1983)

The influential coterie of modern composers, Le Groupe des Six, dominated France's progressive musical scene in the early 1920s. Auric was a member, along with Durey, Honneger, Milhaud, Poulenc and Taillefere. Auric was responsible for more than 100 film scores, his first for Cocteau's (qv) *Le Sang d'un Poete* (30). Among his British film contributions were *Passport to Pimlico* (49), *The Lavender Hill Mob* (51) and *The Innocents* (61). In Hollywood he scored William Wyler's (qv) *Roman Holiday* (53) and John Huston's (qv) *Heaven Knows, Mr Allison* (57). One of his themes, from *Moulin Rouge* (52), became a chart-topper as the song Where Is My Heart?

CLAUDE AUTANT-LARA
French director (1903-)

He began as a designer, assisted René Clair (qv) on two films in the 1920s, made a documentary short in 1926 and experimented with wide-screen techniques in the same year. Autant-Lara made *Ciboulette* (33), his first feature, but it was not until the early 1940s that he gained recognition with several stylish and entertaining films, earning an international reputation with *Le Diable au Corps (The Devil in the Flesh)* in 1946. This story of an affair between a

17-year-old schoolboy, Gérard Philipe (qv), and a married woman, Micheline Presle, whose husband is away at the war, caused outrage and cemented Autant-Lara's image as an anti-Establishment figure. His film about the cowardice and hypocrisy of the French during the occupation, *A Pig Across Paris* (56), is much admired. He continued to court controversy, never more so than when he joined Le Pen's National Front and became a right-wing MEP. He was forced to resign after making anti-semitic remarks.

DANIEL AUTEUIL
French actor (1950-)

Born in Algeria to opera singer parents, this immensely subtle actor began his career in musical comedy, progressed to film comedies and broke through to meatier roles when he cut his hair and dyed it red to convince Claude Berri (qv) he should play the grotesque Ugolin in *Jean de Florette* and *Manon des Sources* (both 86). It was a hugely impressive performance. The role won him a César for best actor and a Bafta for best supporting actor. His most rewarding role since Ugolin has been as the emotionally stunted violin maker in *Un Coeur en Hiver* (92), opposite his then partner, Emmanuelle Béart (qv).

GENE AUTRY
US actor, singer (1907-)

Autry was the singing cowboy who never seemed to aspire to anything very much, except money. Bob Hope (qv) said: "Gene used to ride off into the sunset; now he owns it." Will Rogers (qv) so liked the singing radio telegrapher's voice he suggested Autry take it up as a career. From 1928 he sang on radio and began making records. After small singing roles in westerns he gained popularity in *Tumblin' Tumbleweeds* (35) with his horse Champion and sidekick Smiley Burnette. Thereafter came a string of movies and serials for Republic

Studios. When he joined the US air corps in 1942 his place was taken by Roy Rogers (qv). But he re-established himself in Hollywood after the war without difficulty, helped by radio and TV appearances. His famous quote: "I'm no great actor and I'm no great rider and I'm no great singer. But whatever it is I'm doing they like it."

GEORGE AXELROD
US screenwriter, director (1922-)

An actor in his native New York, Axelrod wrote several hundred scripts for radio and TV before achieving Broadway fame in the 1950s with his delightful satirical comedies The Seven Year Itch and Will Success Spoil Rock Hunter?, both of which were subsequently filmed. In the 1950s his screenwriting work included the Judy Holliday-Jack Lemmon (qqv) marital romp *Phffft!* (54) and an excellent adaptation of William Inge's comedy-drama *Bus Stop* (56), arguably Monroe's (qv) finest hour-and-a-half. After a charming adaptation of Truman Capote's *Breakfast At Tiffany's* (61), Axelrod shifted gear for the harrowing thriller *The Manchurian Candidate* (62), which he also co-produced. He subsequently lost his golden

touch and the work became patchier, although his directorial foray, the black comedy *Lord Love a Duck* (66), enjoys cult status.

DAN AYKROYD
Canadian actor, writer (1952-)

Dropping out of university in Ottawa, where he was studying criminology, Aykroyd became well-known on Canadian television with the irreverent Second City comedy group. Shortly after arriving in New York in 1975, he began working as a regular on Saturday Night Live, NBC's hugely successful comedy show. There he teamed up with a number of characters including, most famously, Jake and Elwood Blues, the Blues Brothers. Starring in a high-budget film spin off from these characters with John Belushi (qv) proved financially disappointing, but has since gained massive cult status on video. After Belushi died in 1982, Aykroyd continued to write screenplays and hit pay dirt in 1984 by co-writing (with Harold Ramis) and starring in the hit *Ghostbusters*. He netted an Oscar nomination for a small role in *Driving Miss Daisy* (89) and made his directing debut in 1991 with *Nothing But Trouble*. In 1993, *Coneheads* resurrected an old SNL sketch, although the film's failure in America meant that it only received a video release in Britain. For many years a talent on the verge of inspiration, Aykroyd has never quite fulfilled his promise.

LEW AYRES
US actor (1908-97)

A former dance band musician, Ayres played the war-destroyed Paul Baumer in *All Quiet on the Western Front* (30) and became a national idol as Dr Kildare in nine films over three years in the late 1930s and early 1940s. His star waned, though, when he declared himself a conscientious objector a the outbreak of the second world war. Hollywood found it hard to forgive, even though he served under fire as a medical orderly, and a boycott was only lifted for *The Dark Mirror* (46). As the befriending doctor of the mute girl in *Johnny Belinda* (48) he was nominated for an Oscar which made him, once again, a kindly force to be reckoned with. His bes part thereafter was as the America vice-president in Otto Preminger's (qv) *Advise and Consent* (62).

LAUREN BACALL
US actress (1924-)

After being spotted by Mrs Howar Hawks on the cover of Harper's Bazaar in 1943, Bacall was signe to Warner and made her first film, *To Have and Have Not*, with Humphrey Bogart (qv) in 1944. She was an immediate hit and th were married in 1945. Her combination of sexual allure, toughness and a distinctive husky voice was unique and set a new style of screen heroine. Her partnership with Bogart was successfully repeated in *The Big Sleep* (46), *Dark Passage* (47) an *Key Largo* (48), and off-screen the marriage was devoted. Bacall nursed Bogart through the cancer that killed him and her career in 1957. Disputes with Warner over unsuitable roles led to suspensior and fines. Lately, her greatest successes have been on Broadwa including Cactus Flower and Applause (a musical adaptation c All About Eve).

URT BACHARACH
S composer (1929-)

ıcharach has composed some of e most recognisable tunes likely be found in a lift, not least Walk ı By, Do You Know The Way To ın Jose? and I'll Never Fall In ve Again. The son of a wspaper columnist, he started t as a nightclub pianist, then ɔk to studying classical music. e was conductor-arranger for Vic ımone and Marlene Dietrich (qv) d, with lyricist Hal David, wrote a ımber of successful songs. He d David were nominated for the st song Oscar three years nning (1965-67) and in 1969 ɔn the award for Raindrops Keep llin' On My Head from *Butch ıssidy and the Sundance Kid.* For e latter film, Bacharach was also noured for best score. Since en, the composer has won a cond Oscar for the song Best at You Can Do from *Arthur* (81).

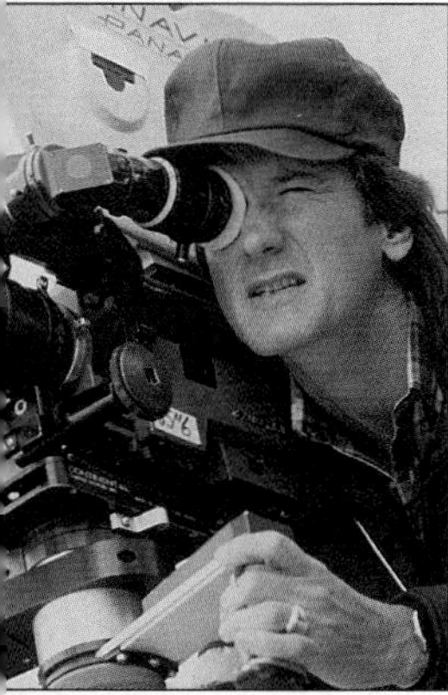

HN BADHAM
S director, producer (1939-)

rn in Britain, raised in Alabama, d a graduate of Yale, Badham rked his way into mainstream ɔllywood from the mail room at iversal. He began directing for evision and made his feature but in 1976 with *The Bingo Long aveling All-Stars & Motor Kings,* e adventures of an all-black seball team. It earned him *turday Night Fever* (77). His lectic choice of material, from e thought-provoking *Whose Life Is Anyway?* (81) to *The Assassin,* e 1993 remake of Besson's (qv) *kita*, results in films of popular peal but denies him a stinguishing stylistic stamp.

MICHAEL BALCON
British producer (1896-1977)

In 1919 Balcon began work as a regional distributor and established the Victory Motion Pictures company with Victor Saville (qv), a small company which provided shorts promoting the Anglo-American Oil Company. For *Woman to Woman* (23), the first feature he produced, he hired Hitchcock (qv) to work as writer, art director and assistant director. This association resulted in Hitchcock's first directing job, *The Pleasure Garden* (25). Balcon was director of production for Gaumont-British in 1931 and filled the same post at MGM-British from 1936. He then took charge of production at Ealing Studios, presiding during the post-war golden era over classics such as *Dead of Night* (45), *Kind Hearts and Coronets* (49), *The Lavender Hill Mob* (51) and *The Ladykillers* (55). After Ealing's demise he set up Bryanston Films in 1959 and acquired British Lion five years later. He was a prime driving force in the British film industry for four decades.

LUCILLE BALL
US actress, producer. (1911-89)

A performer from the age of 15, Ball (above) broke into Hollywood in 1933 as one of the scantily clad Goldwyn Girls. Her gifts slowly emerged through small appearances in numerous musicals and comedies and by the 1940s she had carved out a niche as a comedienne and useful support to jokers such as Bob Hope (qv). Her dramatic roles were few, but she was excellent in *Dance, Girl Dance* (40) and *The Big Street* (42). In partnership with Desi Arnaz, the Cuban bandleader and her husband from 1941, they devised and produced I Love Lucy, inspired by My Favourite Husband, their earlier radio programme. By 1960, after her divorce from Arnaz, the former RKO contract player had become president of Desilu Productions, a large entertainment company with holdings that included the old RKO studios. She starred in two more long-running series and the occasional film.

LUCIEN BALLARD
US cinematographer (1908-88)

Ballard first made his mark shooting interiors in black and white. He worked as a cutter and assistant cameraman at Paramount and became a director of photography on *Crime and Punishment* (35). Already established as a master of introspective, interior set-ups, he found a second life as a cinematographer who could colour

the outdoors, significantly the westerns of Budd Boetticher and Sam Peckinpah (qqv). His use of the widescreen was remarkable in *Ride the High Country* (62), while his telephoto lens in *The Wild Bunch* (69) enhanced its visual impact. He shot several films starring Merle Oberon (qv), his wife from 1945 to 1949, most importantly *The Lodger* (44).

MICHAEL BALLHAUS
German cinematographer (1935-)

One of the elite brigade of lighting cameramen, he first came to prominence with Fassbinder (qv) in the 1970s. Ballhaus is credited with intensifying the claustrophobic feel of Fassbinder's films, his trademark mobile camerawork and use of mirrors making the characters appear even more trapped within the frame. Since moving to America in the early 1980s he has worked with leading directors. An impressive range of films includes Scorsese's (qv) *The Color of Money* (86), *The Last Temptation of Christ* (88) and *The Fabulous Baker Boys* (89).

ANNE BANCROFT
US actress (1931-)

Although she won her Oscar for the dramatic portrayal of the mute Helen Keller's teacher in *The Miracle Worker* (62), she will always be remembered as the tantalising Mrs Robinson seducing the virginal Dustin Hoffman (qv) in Mike Nichols's (qv) Oscar-winning film *The Graduate* (67). Anna Maria Louise Italiano was born in New York and attended the Actors Studio, where her fiery temperament made her ideal to play women in adversity, such as the agonised wife in *The Pumpkin Eater* (64). She also produced some great cameos, such as dancing with Mel Brooks, her husband, (qv) in his *Silent Movie* (76). She was memorable in *84 Charing Cross Road* (87) and in *Torch Song Trilogy* (88).

VILMA BANKY
Hungarian actress (1898-1991)

A discovery of Samuel Goldwyn (qv), Banky arrived in Hollywood in 1925, having begun a European film career five years earlier in Austria. She landed roles in two of Rudolph Valentino's films, *The Eagle* (25) and *The Son Of The Sheik* (26) and immediately fascinated audiences with her exotic beauty. Her career continued through the the silent era with leads opposite such idols as Ronald Colman and Gary Cooper (qqv), and in 1927 she married another star, Rod La Rocque, a happy union until his death in 1969. Unable to make the transition to talkies (her Hungarian accent was too impenetrable) she retired gracefully.

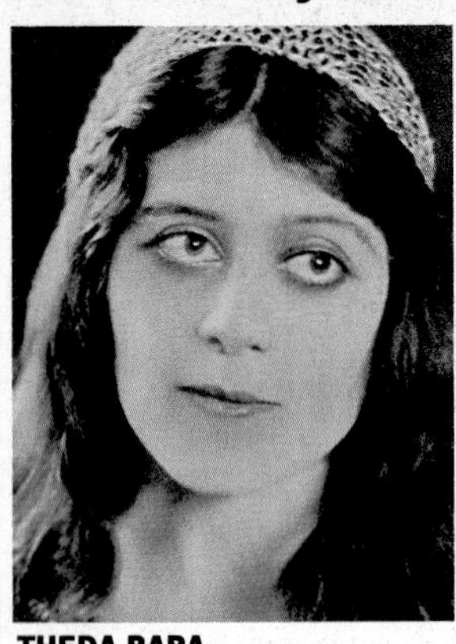

THEDA BARA
US actress (1890-1955)

After the virginal Mary Pickford (qv), Bara was a startling overdose of sexual fantasy. Her voluptuous roles with black-smudged eyes set in a hypnotic stare and breasts clad in coiled-snake bra cups made her famous. Born in Ohio and christened Theodesia Goodman, publicists claimed she was the love child of a French artist and his Arab mistress. Her screen name was an anagram of "Arab Death". She was famously called "The Vamp – the woman who does not care!". A shy girl, she always insisted that her seductive scenes were filmed on closed sets. She made 40 films such as *Serpent of the Nile* (16) and *The Tiger Woman* (17), though it was her first, *A Fool There Was* (15), which set the tone with its screen invitation "Kiss me, my fool!". As audiences grew more sophisticated, her exotic roles appeared increasingly absurd. She parodied herself in her last, *Madame Mystery* (26), a comedy short, and died nearly 30 years later.

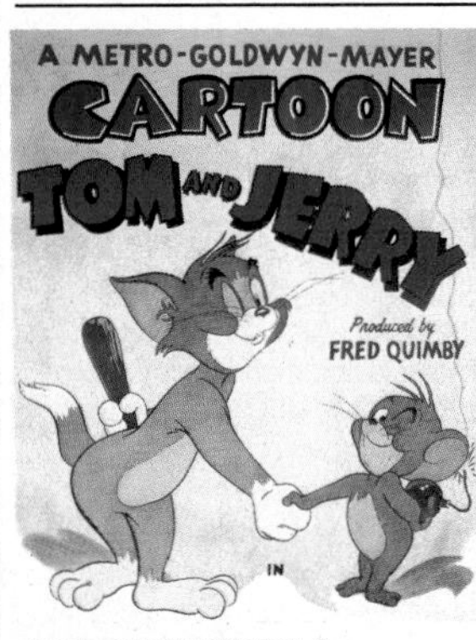

JOSEPH BARBERA & WILLIAM HANNA
US animators, producers (1911- and 1910-)

Hanna and Barbera are as inextricably linked as Tom and Jerry, their most beloved creations, whose capers in the eternal cat-and-mouse game have delighted audiences for more than 50 years. Hanna was a story editor and songwriter, Barbera a cartoonist when they teamed up in 1939 at the MGM shorts department under Fred Quimby, the producer. With Barbera drawing, Hanna directing and both writing, they came up with two characters born to fast-paced conflict. "I knew that no matter where you ran it," said Barbera, "the minute you saw a cat and mouse you knew it was a chase." The inventively battling duo first appeared in *Puss Gets the Boot* (40) and subsequently starred in more than 150 shorts, seven of them Oscar winners. When MGM closed its cartoon division in 1957, the partners formed Hanna-Barbera Productions, achieving a prodigious output of popular television cartoon series including The Flintstones, Yogi Bear, Top Cat, Huckleberry Hound and The Jetsons, ensuring Hanna-Barbera's place as the best-known names in animation after Disney.

JUAN ANTONIO BARDEM
Spanish director, producer (1922-)

A communist inspired by the Italian neo-realists, he hoped to create cinema with a social conscience in Spain. Bardem's first success came in collaboration with Berlanga (qv) on the hit films *That Happy Pair* (51) and *Welcome, Mr Marshall* (52), then as the director of *Death of a Cyclist* (55) about the moral bankruptcy of the ruling classes, which won the Critics' Award at Cannes. In 1955 his two-year-old film magazine Objectivo was shut by Franco and in 1956, during the filming of *Calle Mayor*, a critique of smalltown macho values, he was arrested on political charges, although released after a public outcry. In 1961 Uninci, the film production company he helped found, incurred official wrath for producing Buñuel's (qv) *Viridiana* (61), leading to a further clampdown.

BRIGITTE BARDOT
French actress (1934-)

Spotted by the young director Roger Vadim (qv) on the cover of Elle magazine, Bardot married him in 1952. In his directorial debut, *And Woman Was Created* (56), she launched a look that redefined sex appeal and inspired millions of imitators. Her nonchalant nudity, kittenish and childlike appearance and apparently uninhibited sensuality brought saturation press coverage of her private life. Divorce from Vadim in 1957 and brief liaisons and marriages, inflamed world opinion and upset the Catholic establishment. As an actress she won a following with Clouzot's (qv) *The Truth* (60), and among her English language films are *Viva Maria!* (65) with Jeanne Moreau (qv) and *Shalako* (68) with Sean Connery (qv). In Godard's (qv) *Contempt* (63) she appears with her real name, Camille Javal. After retiring, she started the Brigitte Bardot Foundation for the Protection of Distressed Animals in 1976. Awarded the French Legion of Honour in 1985, Bardot auctioned her jewellery for her foundation in 1987.

WILLIAM GEORGE BARKER
British pioneer (1867-1951)

In 1902 Barker, a colourful, energetic, former commercial traveller, bought two large houses on Ealing Green in west London and started making films in their gardens. In 1907 he built the first covered stage, greenhouse-style, which was soon followed by two more. Barker had begun making films as an amateur with a Lumière (qv) camera he had bought for £40 in 1896, and turned professional in 1901. He had a flair for

showmanship and his films were often adventurous and ambitious. He brought Sir Herbert Tree and his company to Ealing, paid him £1,000 borrowed from creditors, and made *Henry VIII* (11). In 1912 he made the first screen version of *Hamlet*, filming all 22 scenes in a day. His patriotic spectacle on the life of Queen Victoria, *Sixty Years A Queen* (13), is alleged to have made a then unprecedented profit of £35,000. His most famous film was *Jane Shore*, the epic of the war of the roses, which featured thousands of extras and came out in the same year as D W Griffith's (qv) *The Birth of a Nation* (15). His film career faltered with the rest of the British film industry during the first world war and when it ended he sold up and retired.

JEAN-LOUIS BARRAULT
French actor, theatre director (1910-94)

Barrault was essentially a man of the theatre, making his stage debut in 1931. His illustrious career saw him acting and directing at the Comédie-Française during the second world war and he formed a company with his wife, the distinguished actress Madeleine Renaud. (They died within a few months of each other.) Director of the Théatre de France from 1959, he was sacked for his left-wing sympathies during the May 1968 student uprisings in Paris, but held other top theatre posts. Barrault's film career was secondary, but not insubstantial. His first film, *Les Beaux Jours* (35), was for Marc Allégret (qv) and he worked for Sacha Guitry, Renoir and Christian-Jaque (qqv), playing Hector Berlioz for the latter in *La Symphonie Fantastique* (42). He earned his immortal place in cinema history for his performance in Marcel Carné's (qv) magnificent classic, *Les Enfants du Paradis* (45). As th[e] mime artist Debureau, tormented by his love for Arletty's (qv) Garance, he displayed his gifts to sublime and unforgettable effect.

Bardot (right) launched a loo[k] that redefined sex appeal an[d] inspired millions of imitators

ETHEL BARRYMORE
US actress (1879-1959)

As the product of a distinguished theatrical family, Barrymore was bound to do well. Not only was sh[e] called "the first lady of American theatre", she won an Oscar in 1944 and a Broadway theatre wa[s] named after her. The daughter of actors Maurice Barrymore and Georgiana Drew and the sister of Lionel and John Barrymore (qqv), she made her stage debut aged 1[…] – opposite John Drew, her uncle, who was one of the leading lights of his day. In 1914 she appeared in her first film, T*he Nightingale* (14), and in a number of silents i[n] the 1920s. *Rasputin and the Empress* (32) was her first talkie, which she co-starred with her brothers. However, theatre was he[r] first love. After a 12-year absence from the cinema she returned to snatch a best supporting actress Oscar for *None But the Lonely Heart* (44). From then on she enhanced many films with her domineering presence, winning a further three Oscar nominations.

JOHN BARRYMORE
US actor (1882-1942)

Remembered for outshining his actor-family (parents, brother and sister), and for a rich, deep delivery, Barrymore fiddled with comic swashbucklers, light romances and jolly romps before finding substance in *Dr Jekyll and Mr Hyde* (20). As Hamlet had established him on the stage, so Jekyll gave him new weight on celluloid. His interpretation of the role was so deep and detailed tha[t] he went from Jekyll to Hyde and back without make-up. Even whe[n] stranded by mediocrity, Barrymore's subdued power, ▷

The Barrymore clan: Ethel (left) and brothers John and Lionel (right)

playful energy and vocal boom gave life to the picture. For all his idol status – audiences flocked to see him in *Don Juan* (26) – he preferred meaty character parts. Though studios hurled him into pictures with the advent of sound, it was too late for a star hit by drinking, affairs, four failed marriages and a shaky memory.

LIONEL BARRYMORE
US actor, director (1878-1954)

Unlike his more flamboyant younger brother John (qv), Lionel was an ambitious, yet stolid character actor best noted for playing crusty old men in 15 Dr Kildare films, a nasty businessman in *It's a Wonderful Life* (46), a kindly uncle in *Key Largo* (48) and a cantankerous patriarch in *Duel in the Sun* (46). The first member of the Barrymore acting dynasty to take screen acting seriously, he was a leading Broadway thespian before joining the Biograph studio in 1909 to appear in some of D W Griffith's (qv) early masterpieces. Abandoning the theatre in 1923 to spend the next 27 years at MGM, he played 250 screen roles, picking up an Oscar as a lawyer worried about his daughter falling in love with a gangster in *A Free Soul* (31). Crippled by arthritis, he played Dr Gillespie in all 15 Kildare pictures in a wheelchair. He directed five films, wrote a novel and a symphony, as well as wielding the occasional paintbrush.

RICHARD BARTHELMESS
US actor (1895-1963)

A childhood spent working in theatres during breaks from school led Barthelmess to a part in *War Brides* (16). In the same year he won the male lead in *Snow White* and a succession of starring roles followed. He was charming in *The Valentine Girl* (17), stern in *For Valour* (17) and provided likeable support for George M Cohan in the comedy *Hit-the-Trail Holliday* (18). After appearing with Dorothy Gish in *The Hope Chest* (19), he was introduced to D W Griffith (qv) by her and worked with the director on several features under a three-year contract. When Griffith switched from Paramount to United Artists, Barthelmess appeared in *Way Down East* (20), Griffith's hugely popular first film for UA. It was with Inspiration, his own production company, that he gave his best performance in Henry King's (qv) masterpiece *Tol'able David* (21). Five years of efficient but unremarkable work ensued until he signed with First National and *The Patent Leather Kid* (27) shoved him back on top. He had to sing in the 1929 talkie, *Weary River* (though he was later dubbed), but his peak had passed. He quit films in 1942 after *The Spoilers*.

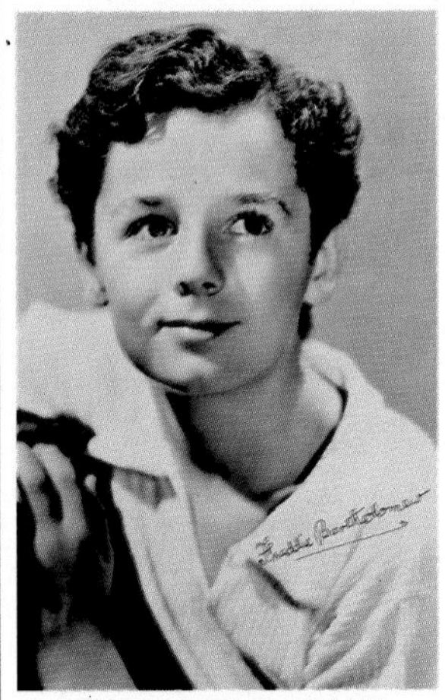

FREDDIE BARTHOLOMEW
British actor (1924-92)

The child actor took Hollywood by storm with an immaculate, well-bred snootiness that was the envied joy of parents and the derided butt of their offspring. Bartholomew's wavy locks were tousled with malice by Basil Rathbone (qv) as Mr Murdstone in *David Copperfield* (35), while Garbo (qv) fondled them with tender loving care for *Anna Karenina* (35). He was a natural for *Little Lord Fauntleroy* (36) and *The Devil Is a Sissy* (36), in which he co-starred with the unruly Mickey Rooney (qv). He could act, as he proved in *Captains Courageous* (37) in which he was the spoiled-rotten kid learning about life and death from Spencer Tracy (qv) playing a fisherman marked for tragedy. Even Tracy admitted himself upstaged "at times". The vogue for little-gent films died with the second world war. Bartholomew joined the American army airforce, made TV commercials and embarked on a career in advertising, making a significant impact on Madison Avenue.

RICHARD BASEHART
US actor (1914-84)

In spite of his strong masculine looks and cleft chin, Basehart was most at home in introspective roles and, due to an eclectic range of choices, managed to escape typecasting. The son of a newspaper editor, he started out as a radio announcer and reporter

until controversy surrounding one of his stories forced him to switch careers. He opted for the stage, making his Broadway debut in 1938. On winning the New York Critics' Award for his role in The Hasty Heart, he attracted the attention of Hollywood and made a considerable impact in *He Walked by Night* (48) as a killer on the run. Over the next 33 years he acted in a wide variety of films and particularly distinguished himself as the would-be suicide in *Fourteen Hours* (51), as the gentle acrobat in Fellini's (qv) *La Strada* (54) and as Ishmael in Huston's (qv) *Moby Dick* (56). He was also the star of the TV series Voyage to the Bottom of the Sea.

KIM BASINGER
US actress (1953-)

In childhood Basinger pursued ambitions to be a dancer and singer. She posed for Playboy on her arrival in New York in 1970 and modelling success ensued. Then small roles in films and on television encouraged her to make acting a career. Her first notable role was in the TV remake of From Here to Eternity. It was clear from her appearances in *Never Say Never Again* (83) and Blake Edwards's (qv) *The Man Who Loved Women* (83), that her beauty would carry her even if her acting talents could not. She came to full notoriety and public attention with *Nine ½ Weeks* (86) in which she and Mickey Rourke played sexual obsessives. She is, though, a remarkable example of the cult of celebrity, having ascended to the status of household name without the aid of blockbuster hits; *Batman* (89) was a rare box office smash for her. She is also famous for her extra-curricular activities – a supposed romance with the pop star Prince, marriage to the actor Alec Baldwin and the multi-million dollar lawsuit she lost after pulling out of the lead in Jennifer Lynch's *Boxing Helena* (93). So far her work has not matched her celebrity and her collaborations with Baldwin – the most recent, a remake of Sam Peckinpah's (qv) *The Getaway* (94) – have been tepid at best.

ALAN BATES
British actor (1934-)

A handsome leading man, convincing across the spectrum from hero to social misfit, Bates has avoided being stereotyped at the cost of international stardom. Appearing in some of the most notable and successful films of the past three decades, he has opted for good writing and "difficult" pictures. His debut was in *The Entertainer* (60), and he made a strong impression in *A Kind of Loving* (62), then attracted international attention in *Zorba the Greek* (64). Popular successes followed: *Georgy Girl* (66), *Far From the Madding Crowd* (67), *Women in Love* (69) and *The Go-Between* (71). He was nominated for the best actor Oscar for *The Fixer* (68). Stage and television work has continued alongside his Hollywood, British and continental films, from *King of Hearts* (66) to *102 Boulevard Haussmann* (90). Cameo roles in mainstream films from *The Rose* (79) to *Hamlet* (90) parallel more substantial contributions to such non-commercial projects as *A Day in the Death of Joe Egg* (72) and *We Think the World of You* (88).

ANNE BAXTER
US actress (1923-85)

Baxter was the granddaughter of the architect Frank Lloyd Wright. She made her Broadway debut in her early teens in Seen But Not Heard and moved from theatre to films in 1940, with 49 screen

appearances in 40 years. Long on quiet, sometimes enigmatic charm she gave several interesting performances working with front-rank directors such as Welles, Wilder, Hitchcock and Mankiewicz (qqv). Having won the supporting Oscar for *The Razor's Edge* (46), she gave Mankiewicz her most celebrated performance as the poisonous Eve Harrington to Bette Davis's (qv) Margo Channing in *All About Eve* (50), earning another Oscar nomination (20 years later she played the Davis role, taking over from Lauren Bacall (qv) in Applause, the Broadway musical version). A contract artist at Twentieth Century Fox for many years, she married actor John Hodiak, but they divorced after seven years. Baxter remarried and lived on a remote cattle station in Australia during the 1960s, later writing a successful book about her experiences there. She returned to acting on television in 1983, replacing Davis in the series Hotel until she died of a stroke in 1985.

WARNER BAXTER
US actor (1891-1951)

Today he is probably remembered best as the Broadway stage director who tells Ruby Keeler (qv) in *42nd Street* (33): "Sawyer, you're going out a youngster. But you've got to come back a star." In the 1930s he was popular with audiences as the Cisco Kid, a carefree, ladykilling Mexican bandido he played in a number of films beginning with *In Old Arizona* (29), for which he won an Oscar. His film career had begun in the first world war after experience in theatre and he ɔrked steadily through the silent a. One of his outstanding rformances was in John Ford's v) *The Prisoner of Shark Island* 6) as the doctor imprisoned for eating Lincoln's assassin. In the 940s his career declined lowing illness, but he recovered make a succession of cond-feature films such as *Crime octor* (43). He died of eumonia in 1951 after a botomy operation performed to lieve an arthritic condition.

ATHALIE BAYE
rench actress (1948-)

though she studied drama at the aris Conservatory after dancing ofessionally in America, it was aye's cover girl looks that brought er to the attention of film oducers. It was clear from the art that she was an actress who ould dig deep, at home with either e telling detail of character acting the broad emotional strokes of a ading role. Her stardom, though, as not been earned at the pense of her character work. A de-ranging actress, her depth of terpretation ensures her beauty is ot a key consideration; she articularly impressed in 1979 with *auve Qui Peut La Vie*, *La Balance* 2) and *Le Retour de Martin uerre* (82). As a whore in *La alance* she avoided stereotypes d brought the character to life. In *artin Guerre*, a plot later recycled r Jodie Foster (qv) in *Sommersby* 3), Baye supplied most of the m's ambiguity with her forceful straint.

NDRE BAZIN
rench critic, theorist 918-58)

azin was an unlikely revolutionary, left-wing Catholic who failed to d work as a teacher and pursued stead his passion for cinema, anging its direction. During the azi occupation he ran a club owing banned films; after the ar he was film critic for La arisien Liberé and founded La evue du Cinéma. In 1951 this urnal was transformed into Les ahiers du Cinéma, which was to come the most influential film blication of its time. In its pages,

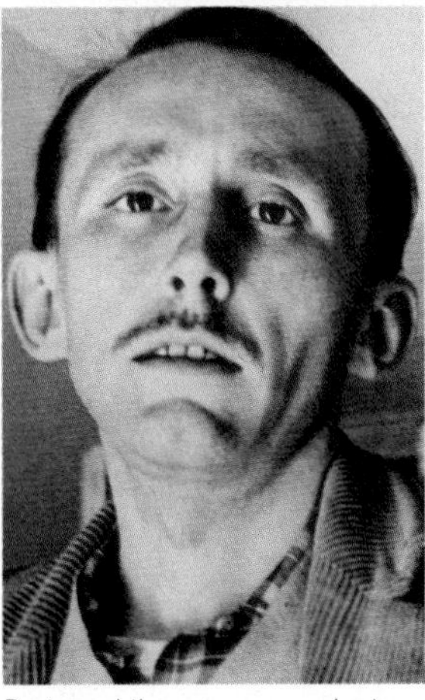

Bazin and the young men who in the 1960s were to form the New Wave of *auteur* directors — Bazin's protégé Truffaut, Chabrol, Godard, Rohmer, Rivette (qqv) — rejected the "well-made" period pieces of post-war French cinema and promoted a new, freewheeling kind of film that was a direct expression of its director's vision.

EMMANUELLE BEART
French actress (1965-)

Béart's fair and graceful beauty in the title role enhanced the romantic dimension of Claude Berri's (qv) internationally successful *Manon des Sources* (86). It was only her third film and in the dozen now to her credit she has demonstrated an ability and range placing her at the forefront of contemporary French screen actresses. Raised in virtual isolation by her mother, Béart went to Canada as a teenager and became interested in acting. She made her screen debut at the age of 19 in *L'Enfant Trouvé* (84) and has worked for prestige directors including Ettore Scola (qv). The only blip has been a lovely but unfortunate appearance in her first American film, the dud fantasy *Date With an Angel* (87). Her first decade's work include the contrast between her cool beauty and emotional turmoil as the deceptively passionate violinist of *Un Coeur en Hiver* (93) and Claude Chabrol's (qv) *L'Enfer* (94).

THE BEATLES
British band (1959-70)

They began their ascent in the basement nightclubs of Liverpool by way of Hamburg, where they made scratchy studio recordings. Originally it was a five-man group, John Lennon, Paul McCartney, George Harrison, Stuart Sutcliffe and Pete Best. Sutcliffe left and Best was dropped in favour of the more flamboyant Ringo Starr. The band's first single, Love Me Do, reached No 17 in Britain and No 1 in the American charts in 1962. Their second, Please Please Me, was the first of an uninterrupted string of No 1 hit singles and LPs throughout the 1960s. The band exerted tremendous influence way beyond music and were crucial in the development of an international sub-culture that swept the entertainment industry, not least Hollywood. Richard Lester's (qv) film *A Hard Day's Night* (64) captured the exhilaration of Beatlemania and was followed by the musical parody *Help!* (65), the psychedelic cartoon *Yellow Submarine* (68) and *A Magical Mystery Tour*, a hallucinogenic television film. In the band's declining days Michael Lindsay-Hogg directed them in the performance film *Let It Be* (70). McCartney has more recently produced and starred in *Give My Regards to Broad Street* (84).

WARREN BEATTY
US actor, director and producer (1937-)

If Beatty's screen power had approached that of his fabled libido, he would have been the biggest star in history. The son of a drama coach and Shirley MacLaine's (qv) brother, he served his apprenticeship in the theatre and made his film debut opposite Natalie Wood (qv) in *Splendor in the Grass* (61). As an actor his sex appeal outstripped his expressiveness, but his shrewdness made him a Hollywood power broker after he produced and starred in *Bonnie & Clyde*, the film event of 1967. The satire *Shampoo* (75) and the fantasy *Heaven Can Wait* (78) were his projects, the latter marking his directorial ▷

debut. The peak of his artistic endeavours was the sprawling romantic/political epic *Reds* (81), for which he received an Oscar for direction. The low point was the catastrophic and expensive flop, *Ishtar* (87), with Dustin Hoffman (qv). At the age of 54 he turned in a fine performance as the charming psychopathic mobster, *Bugsy* (91). Despite his achievements, Beatty is more famous for his espousal of liberal causes and his affairs with actresses from Joan Collins to Madonna (qqv), before marrying *Bugsy* co-star Annette Bening.

JACQUES BECKER
French director (1906-60)

The son of a wealthy Parisian industrialist, Becker served an eight-year apprenticeship before the second world war with Jean Renoir (qv). He made only 13 films, many of which are known outside France. His work was even held in esteem by the renegades of the New Wave, especially his masterpiece *Casque d'Or/Golden Marie* (52), a radiantly sensual tale with Simone Signoret (qv) and Serge Reggiani as doomed lovers in 1890s Paris. He is also admired for the charm of his lighter romantic comedies, such as *Edward and Caroline* (51), while *Touchez pas au Grisbi* (53) had an influence on future French gangster films. He was married to the actress Françoise Fabian and was the father of the film director Jean Becker.

WALLACE BEERY
US actor (1885-1949)

A classic, blundering giant with a plug-ugly mug, mischievous eyes and gravelly voice, Beery was cast in the mould of a lovable oaf — essentially vulnerable, but always a little dangerous. The son of a Kansas policeman and one of a clan of actors, he ran away from home to join the circus before making his way to New York where he was employed as a female impersonator. Entering films as an actor and director in 1913, he carried over his stage persona in a series of drag acts, then became a Keystone comedian, a muscle-brained heavy and lumbering hero,

like his over-the-hill boxer in the unashamed weepie, *The Champ* (31), for which he was awarded his only Oscar. In spite of his obvious limitations, he exhibited some versatility in roles as diverse as the desperate businessman in *Grand Hotel* (32), the social climber in *Dinner at Eight* (33), Long John Silver in *Treasure Island* (34) and the Mexican revolutionary Pancho Villa in *Villa Villa!* (34).

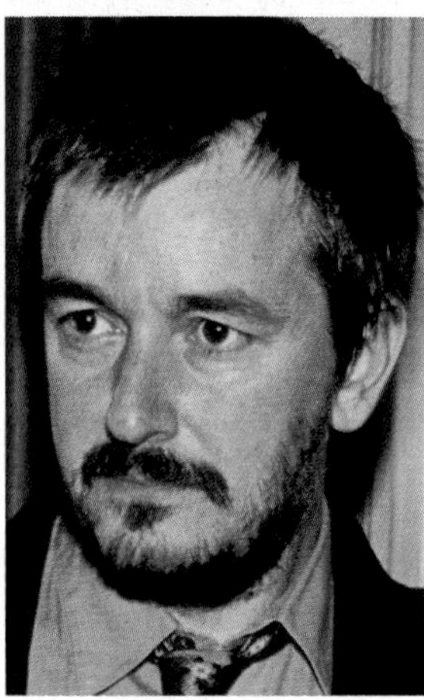

JEAN-JACQUES BEINEIX
French director (1946-)

With his debut feature *Diva* (81), made after a 10-year apprenticeship as an assistant director and screenwriter, Beineix gained international recognition, won a César and a devoted following among the young and hip. His next film, *Moon In The Gutter* (83), was a disappointment and the "designer" tag attached to his work began to look like an empty compliment. His fortunes revived with the Oscar-nominated *Betty Blue* (86), establishing Béatrice Dalle, its female lead, as an international favourite. It also demonstrated that Beineix could move out of the shadowy fantasy lands of his first two films into the more exposed terrain of a study of destructive love. A later work, *IP5* (92), was another critical dud and earned him the wrath of the French press, which accused him of working the film's star, Yves Montand (qv), literally to death. Beineix denied the charges vehemently.

MONTA BELL
US director, writer and producer (1891-1958)

As a newspaperman Bell rose to become editor of a Washington DC daily before being drawn to films in the early 1920s. He dabbled in acting, producing and directing, and became a friend of Chaplin (qv), who gave him a part in *The Pilgrim* (23). He became a fully-fledged director in 1924 and was soon established on the MGM lot, the most prestigious of Hollywood studios, where he directed Garbo (qv) in her American debut, *The Torrent* (26).

Many of his films no longer exist in viewable copies, but among those that do are *Upstage* (26) and *Man, Woman and Sin* (27), both of them rich in atmosphere and displaying a stylish wit. In 1929 Bell moved to New York, taking charge of production at the Astoria Studios in Queens, which were owned by Paramount. He occasionally directed talkies, but the sparkle of his silent films had disappeared.

JEAN-PAUL BELMONDO
French actor (1933-)

Belmondo's classical training in the theatre and nine supporting roles on film finally gave way to a rush of success. Perfectly in tune with the stylistic and thematic arrogance of the French New Wave, Belmondo was a natural choice for the restless, small-fry gangster in *A Bout de Souffle/Breathless* (59) who hurtles across Paris, the police on his tail. *Breathless* transformed Belmondo into France's leading male star. His reference, in character, to Bogart reflected his love of American gangsters. Though often reduced to walk-through acting in international puddings, he proved he could stretch in Louis Malle's (qv) *Le Voleur* (67), in which his energy gave way to thoughtfulness, and Jean-Pierre Melville's (qv) *Léon Morin, Priest* (61) as a radical cleric.

JOHN BELUSHI
US actor (1949-82)

His route on to Saturday Night Live, American TV's breeding ground for new comic talent, was by way of Chicago's Second City comedy group and Lemmings, an off-Broadway revue that earned him rave notices. Along with Bill Murray, Gilda Radner and Chevy Chase, Belushi was an SNL regular, teaming up with his friend Dan Aykroyd (qv) to create *The Blues Brothers* for the show, a movie (80) and an armful of albums. Unlike Aykroyd, Belushi found a role which fitted him immaculately: it was his first big performance, as a raucous scene-stealing slob in *National Lampoon's Animal House* (78), the seminal college kid comedy that spawned countless imitations. The rest of his too brief career was dogged by uncertainty and misjudgment. He only appeared in seven films, including Jack Nicholson's (qv) *Goin' South* (78), and *Continental Divide* (81), an unlikely romantic comedy. His last role was with Aykroyd again in the lacklustre *Neighbors* (81), which wasted both actors' talents. Belushi died of an overdose in 1982; the messy details of his life were picked over in Bob Woodward's voyeuristic book Wired. He was perhaps the most underused, underestimated and truly crazed comic actor of his generation.

Belmondo (above) was transformed by Breathless

ROBERT BENCHLEY
US writer, actor (1889-1945)

A journalist (Vanity Fair, Life, The New Yorker) and humorist, Benchley first made his cinematic mark with a succession (1928-45) of 10-minute comedy shorts with such titles as *The Sex Life of the Polyp* (28), *How to Sleep* (35) and *How to Take a Vacation* (41), which he wrote and appeared in. *How to Sleep* won an Oscar for best short subject (comedy), by which time he had embarked on a parallel career in feature films, as a comic support and a screenwriter. He was nominated for an Oscar as one of the co-writers of *Foreign Correspondent* (40). His roles, often as a bumbling lawyer, writer or pompous relative, include *Dancing Lady* (33), *China Seas* (35), *The Sky's the Limit* (43), and *Road to Utopia* (45). He featured in Disney's first film with live action, *The Reluctant Dragon* (41), touring the studio and meeting Disney. He was the writer Nathaniel Benchley's father and grandfather of Peter, the author of Jaws.

RICHARD BENJAMIN
US director, actor (1938-)

An affable, light-romantic leading man with a nice line in Jewish wholesomeness, Benjamin confounded his critics when he went behind the camera to direct and made a lucrative career at it. Trained at New York's High School of the Performing Arts, he landed a couple of films in the 1950s before establishing himself on Broadway in The Star-Spangled Girl in 1966. He achieved some success in two screen adaptations of Philip Roth novels, *Goodbye Columbus* (69) and *Portnoy's Complaint* (72), but was soon relegated to supporting roles. In 1982 he switched careers to direct *My Favorite Year* (82), a comedy with Peter O'Toole (qv) as a wayward matinee idol, and he has rarely acted since. In spite of the commercial success of *The Money Pit* (86), *Mermaids* (90) and *Made in America* (93), Benjamin has never fulfilled the artistic promise of his directorial debut. He has been married to actress Paula Prentiss since 1961, co-starring with her in the television sitcom He & She.

JOAN BENNETT
US actress (1910-90)

As she proved in *The Woman in the Window* (44) and *Scarlet Street*

(45), Bennett could be a *femme fatale* with a style that made men willing victims. She eloped at 16 with a millionaire and her third husband, the producer Walter Wanger, was briefly jailed for shooting Jennings Lang, her agent. She was the younger sister of Constance Bennett, their careers seesawing in rivalry until Joan went brunette to distinguish herself from her blonde sibling, and Constance's career finally dipped in salute. Her three most memorable films were *The Woman on the Beach* (47) for Jean Renoir (qv), *The Secret Beyond the Door* (48) for Fritz Lang (qv) and *The Reckless Moment* (49) for Max Ophuls (qv). She progressed to maternity in *Father of the Bride* (50) with grace.

ROBERT BENTON
US director, writer (1932-)

Two films, *Bonnie & Clyde* (67) and *Kramer vs Kramer* (79), had a significant effect on two of Hollywood's most popular genres, gangster films and domestic drama. The first, which Benton co-scripted with David Newman, not so much glamourised screen violence as raised the notion that Joe Public could become Robin Hood. The second, a disturbing child-custody drama starring Dustin Hoffman and Meryl Streep (qqv), which won five Oscars, established his directorial credentials and changed Hollywood's traditional aversion to divorce sagas. Born in Texas, where he trained as a painter, he did a stint in the army and a period as an art director at Esquire magazine, during which time he wrote articles, books and collaborated on scripts with Newman that ultimately resulted in *There Was a Crooked Man* (70), *What's Up, Doc?* (72) and *Superman* (78). He turned his hand to direction with a highly regarded civil war western, *Bad Company* (72). Other films include *Places in the Heart* (84), a Depression-era drama that won an Oscar for best original screenplay, and *Nobody's Fool* (94).

BRUCE BERESFORD
Australian director (1940-)

While studying philosophy at the University of Sydney, Beresford began working on amateur films and, after graduating, moved to London and a string of jobs. In spite of persevering with attempts to penetrate the British film industry, he met with no success and went to east Nigeria. He returned to London in 1966 and was appointed secretary to the British Film Institute's production board, soon taking over as head of production. A government financing initiative for the Australian cinema tempted him back to Sydney in 1971, where he made the excessively vulgar comedy *The Adventures of Barry McKenzie*,

featuring Barry Humphries. Beresford was also responsible for its appalling sequel, but things took a better turn with the more intelligent and promising satire *Don's Party* (76). It won him an important award from the American Film Institute, but what impressed the rest of the world was his terse military drama, *Breaker Morant* (80). Between that and the Oscar triumph of *Driving Miss Daisy* (89) stands a body of work, fascinating mainly in its inconsistency and eclecticism. Nevertheless, Beresford was a key figure in the renaissance of Australian cinema in the late 1970s.

CANDICE BERGEN
US actress (1946-)

An incandescent beauty, Bergen is equally adept at comedy and drama and was a star in the late 1960s and early 1970s. She was unable, however, to sustain her high profile, although her career has benefited from several upswings. The daughter of Edgar Bergen, the ventriloquist, she was born in Beverly Hills, educated in Switzerland and modelled for Revlon. Playing a college lesbian in her first film, *The Group* (66), she received terrible reviews, but redeemed herself in *Getting Straight* (70), *Soldier Blue* (70) and *Carnal Knowledge* (71). She was particularly effective in Herbert Ross's (qv) *T R Baskin* (71), in which she played a smalltown girl at sea in Chicago – before suffering a career relapse. In 1979 she came back with a bang as Burt Reynolds's (qv) eccentric former wife in *Starting Over* and was nominated for an Oscar as best supporting actress. She then played the photo-journalist Margaret Bourke-White in *Gandhi* (82). She enjoyed another career boost playing the title role in the CBS sitcom Murphy Brown, a series that took several well-publicised pot shots at the American Establishment. She is Louis Malle's (qv) widow.

INGMAR BERGMAN
Swedish director (1918-)

After a strict Lutheran upbringing, Bergman, then a student, escaped into theatre work, moving to film as a script doctor in 1941. He went on to create a formidable body of work, one of the most singular achievements of the modern cinema. Not incapable of a lighter touch, as *Smiles of a Summer Night* (55) shows, his characteristic work is an intense, demanding exploration of the human soul and psyche, especially the female psyche. All have been starkly beautiful and committedly acted by his troupe of regulars – Max von Sydow, Liv Ullmann (qqv), Harriet Andersson, Gunnar Bjornstrand and Bibi Andersson. *The Seventh Seal* (57), his medieval allegory of man's struggle with mortality, won him prizes at Cannes and by the late 1950s he was an art house god. However, by the time he made *The Silence* (63), audiences were turning away from his uncompromising style to the easier-going pleasures of American movies and the French New Wave. His next films were more intimate studies of psychological crisis. *Persona* (66), a complex portrait of an actress who stops speaking mid-performance, shows him at full stretch. In 1976, charged with income tax fraud, his career seemed in decline. In 1983, though, he charmed audiences and won the Oscar for *Fanny And Alexander,* a mature recreation of his childhood that many regard as his best work.

INGRID BERGMAN
Swedish actress (1915-82)

A luminous beauty with a saintly image and an air of inner strength, Bergman lost public favour after scandalising the world by leaving her first husband and child for the Italian director Roberto Rossellini (qv) in 1949. She had left Sweden in 1936 at David O Selznick's (qv) invitation, and exchanged national fame for international superstardom through roles in such films as *Casablanca* (42), *For Whom the Bell Tolls* (43), *Gaslight* (44, best actress Oscar), *Notorious* (46) and *Joan of Arc* (48). The public's adoration of her diminished when she ran off with Rossellini, who directed her in *Stromboli* (50), and married him the same year. Condemned in America, they worked in Europe. *Anastasia* (56), made in Britain, proved to be her return ticket to Hollywood and a second Oscar for best actress. The rehabilitation was confirmed in *Indiscreet* (58) and *The Inn of the Sixth Happiness* (58). She won another Oscar as best supporting actress for *Murder on the Orient Express* (74), when she began battling the cancer that killed her. She continued to work and was nominated for a best actress Oscar for Ingmar Bergman's (qv) *Autumn Sonata* (78). The actress Isabella Rossellini is her daughter.

ELISABETH BERGNER
British actress (1898-1986)

Elfin faced and gauzily blonde, Bergner was a superb exponent of the twee. Born in an area of Poland annexed by Russia, she was educated at the Vienna Conservatoire and, after a German film career cut short by Hitler's rise to power, came to Britain and made *Catherine The Great* (34) for Alexander Korda (qv) and was Oscar nominated for *Escape Me Never* (35); reports said she was paid the then enormous fee of £20,000 for playing the yearning waif. She starred in *A Stolen Life* (39) with Michael Redgrave (qv), but two-faced women were beyond her range. J M Barrie, whose whimsy matched hers, wrote the play The Boy David for her. In 1938 she became a British citizen and after the early 1940s her career was confined to the occasional stage and film role.

BUSBY BERKELEY
US choreographer, director (1895-1976)

William Berkeley Enos attended a military academy before becoming a top Broadway dance director. Brought to Hollywood by Samuel Goldwyn (qv) in 1930 to stage the musical numbers for the Eddie Cantor (qv) vehicle *Whoopee!,* he went on to join Warner and transform the screen musical. He was innovative, dazzlingly imaginative, vulgar, erotic and magical. He combined the precision of military drill with adventurous camerawork, which turned bevies of beautiful young women into kaleidoscopic mazes of water lilies, violins and jigsaw puzzles. It was an indulgence of the American Dream for Depression-weary audiences and gave them such gloriously over-the-top numbers as By a Waterfall (*Footlight Parade,* 33), Lullaby of Broadway (*Gold Diggers of 1935,* 35) and the rare socially conscious reminder, such as My

Forgotten Man *(Gold Diggers of 1933,* 33*)*. Later, at MGM, his exuberant routines for Judy Garland and Mickey Rooney (qqv) were simpler. Although he directed a number of films, he remains revered for his dance direction. With the demise of the musical he settled, with his sixth wife, for retirement.

LUIS GARCIA BERLANGA
Spanish director (1921-)

The most accessible of the anti-Franco directors, Berlanga's work skilfully delivers a bitter social and political critique in a popular style. In his early collaborations with his schoolfriend Bardem (qv), *Welcome, Mr Marshall* (51) and *That Happy Pair* (51) and later with the scriptwriter Rafael Azcona on the Oscar-nominated *Placido* (61) and award-winning *El Verdugo* (63), he created a form of Spanish film that was contemporary – neo-realism with a twist – yet, with its black humour and tragic perspective, rooted in his national

traditions. His characters tend to be social underdogs who have their dreams of self-betterment grimly thwarted; chillingly so in his most accomplished film, *El Verdugo,* when the hero must garrotte a political prisoner to secure the apartment that comes with his job as town executioner. Freed from censorship in the 1970s, Berlanga's work developed an

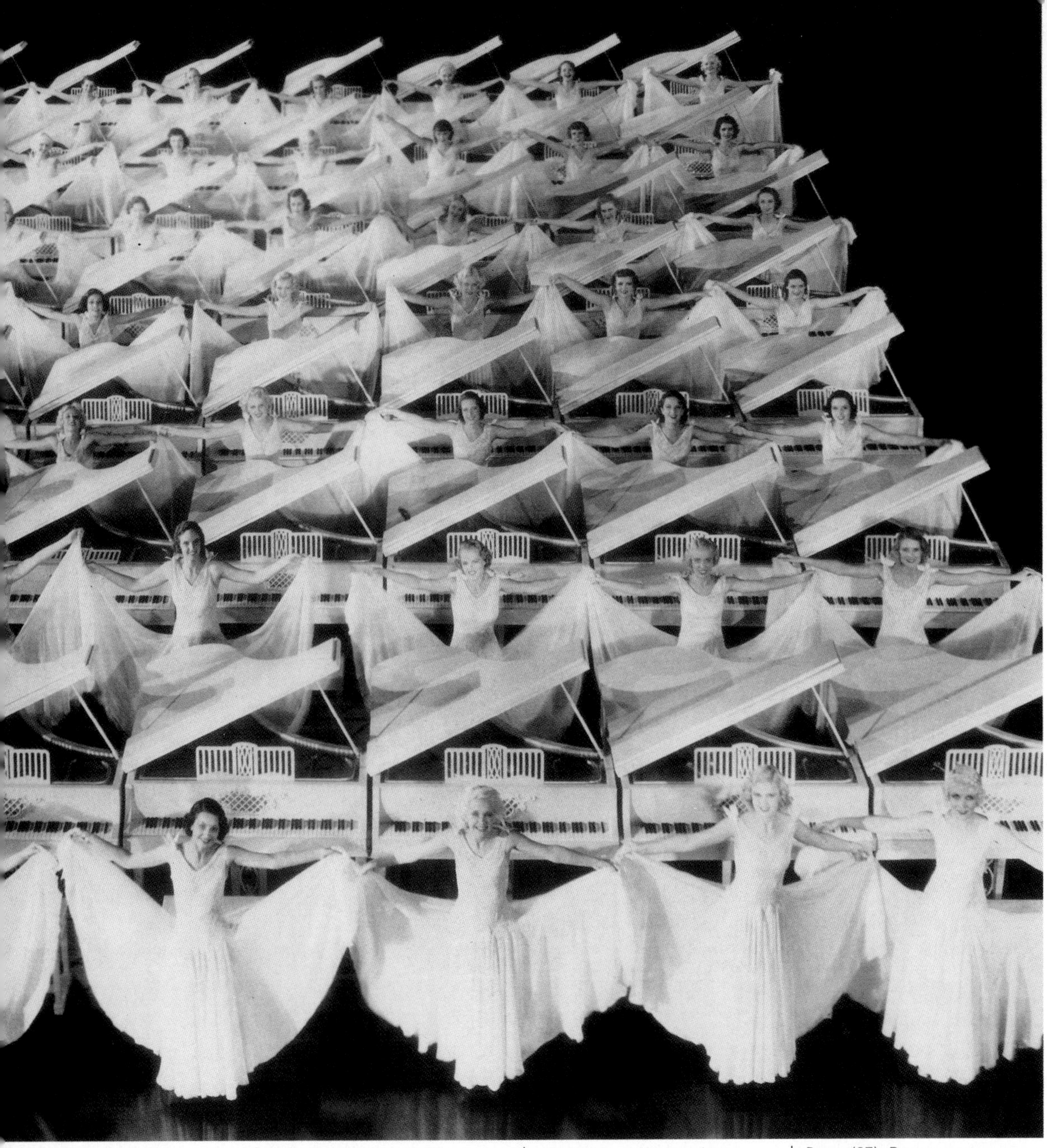

Indulgence: Berkeley's Gold Diggers of 1935 (left) had 50-plus pianos in one scene

erotic strain, notably with *Life Size* (77), about a man who becomes obsessed with an inflatable doll. He has also edited a collection of literary erotica. He topped the box office again in Spain in 1985 with *The Heifer*, an absurdist comedy about a bullfight, set in the Spanish civil war.

IRVING BERLIN
US composer (1888-1989)

Israel Baline, a cantor's son, went from Siberia to New York's East Side when he was five. He grew up to become America's most popular composer – on Broadway, on radio, on records and in Hollywood. Although a musical genius, he could not read a note and was only able to compose in F sharp, transposing to another key with a specially adapted piano. He ushered in the talkie era when Al Jolson (qv) spoke a few ad-libbed words before singing Blue Skies in *The Jazz Singer* (27). He also wrote White Christmas, the biggest-selling song hit of all time, first sung by Bing Crosby (qv) in *Holiday Inn* (42). He scored the Astaire-Rogers (qqv) films *Top Hat* (35) and *Follow the Fleet* (36), and his Broadway musicals Annie Get Your Gun and Call Me Madam were made into blockbuster films. The two most compendious collections of Berlin songs on film are in *Alexander's Ragtime Band* (38) and *Blue Skies* (46). He was an astute businessman and fought to retain his copyrights. He also had an astonishing ear for popular vernacular, which is why his songs appealed to generations of listeners and filmgoers.

PANDRO S BERMAN
US producer (1905-96)

Because he produced a number of Astaire and Rogers (qqv) musicals, including *The Gay Divorcee* (34), *Swing Time* (36) and *Shall We Dance* (37), Berman was instinctively linked to exuberance and technical triumph. Though he had a deep affection for the musical, he also set up dramas including *The Hunchback of Notre Dame* (39) with Charles Laughton (qv), *The Blackboard Jungle* (55) and *Sweet Bird of Youth* (62).

ELMER BERNSTEIN
US composer (1922-)

Still in demand in his seventies, Bernstein must be the only person in motion pictures who has collaborated with Cecil B DeMille and Martin Scorsese (qqv). Juilliard trained, a former dancer and concert pianist, Bernstein arrived in Hollywood from New York radio in 1950 and rapidly established his reputation for versatility. His *oeuvre* has encompassed adventure, prestige drama and zany comedy. He has scored 200 pictures, many of them evoked by a few bars of his music: the splashy *The Magnificent Seven* (60), the jaunty theme of *The Great Escape* (63) or the

haunting simplicity of *To Kill A Mockingbird* (62). In 1991 he adapted Bernard Herrmann's (qv) 1962 *Cape Fear* score for Scorsese's remake in homage to the composer who was his early hero and mentor. He has recorded selections of his and Herrmann's work with the Royal Philharmonic Orchestra and received an Oscar for his *Thoroughly Modern Millie* (67) score and the Emmy for television's The Making of a President.

CLAUDE BERRI
French director, producer (1934-)

A former actor in Chabrol's (qv) *Les Bonnes Femmes* (60) and Zinnemann's (qv) *Behold A Pale Horse* (64), Berri received an Oscar for his directorial debut short *Le Poulet* (64). His reputation for sensitive and humorous observation is best realised in his early, most personal films *Le Vieil Homme Et L'Enfant* (66), inspired by his childhood under Nazi occupation, and *Mezel Tov où Le Mariage* (68), in which as writer, director and star he drew appealingly on his experience of Jewish immigrant family life. His dubious *Un Moment D'Egarement* (77) was treated to the 1984 Hollywood remake *Blame It on Rio*. Later efforts attracted such stars as Deneuve, Trintignant and Depardieu (qqv), but were emptier. Then his ambitious two-part epic adapted from Marcel Pagnol, *Jean de Florette* and *Manon des* ▷

Sources (86), secured his international standing. Its triumph encouraged him to mount the most expensive French film yet made, the ploddingly worthy adaptation of Zola's *Germinal* (93). Among his many productions is Roman Polanski's (qv) *Tess* (79).

BERNARDO BERTOLUCCI
Italian director (1942-)

The son of a distinguished poet and film critic, Bertolucci was a published poet and amateur film maker while still in his teens. He abandoned his university studies at the age of 19 to work with Pasolini (qv) and scored his first directorial success at 22 with *Before the Revolution* (64). His slim but impressive portfolio of films, from *The Conformist* (70) onwards, all shot by Vittorio Storaro (qv), has established him as an unpredictable maestro who can veer from the intimate savagery of *Last Tango in Paris* (72) to the epic lyricism of *The Last Emperor* (87), which won nine Oscars. There is an intellectual coolness to his approach and a visual intensity that is often compared with opera. He is an unrivalled creator of sensuous textures, eloquent compositions and haunting images. When he is on form, this stylishness is a key component, as in *The Conformist*, a chilling study of a cowardly pre-war fascist, where the empty modishness of the oppressive 1930s settings underlines the moral bankruptcy of the new social order the protagonist aspires to fit into. The increasingly lavish scale and budgets of his recent films have not brought corresponding critical success. He married the British director Clare Peploe in 1979.

LUC BESSON
French director, producer and screenwriter (1959)

Heavily inspired by the stylistic arrogance and designer gloss of 1980s commercials and pop videos, Besson has gone on to shape the visual ideas of a new generation of eager young directors. He is held up as a style warrior and role model. Hailed in Paris at the age of 25 for his first film, *Le Dernier Combat* (84), he next made *Subway* (85) and acquired an international audience. Though *Subway* gave proof of his detailed use of the big screen and his stunning visual clout, the relentless, prowling camera and giddy swirl of images tended to overwhelm the narrative. With his next film, *The Big Blue* (88), a bigger budget unleashed considerable indulgence and stranded the plot between endless underwater blackness and the predictable kookiness of Rosanna Arquette. *Leon* (94) was an accomplished and unusual crime film and *The Fifth Element* (97), a futuristic fantasy, revealed his style at its most extreme.

Billy Bitzer (above left) with the director D W Griffith

BILLY BITZER
US cinematographer (1872-1944)

Johann Gottlob Wilhelm Bitzer (aka George William Bitzer), was one of cinema's most innovative and influential artists. After training as an electrical engineer, he joined the Magic Introduction Company in 1894 where he helped develop the Mutoscope machine, which used a flurry of images to suggest motion. For 12 years from 1896 he shot newsreel footage, but his best known and most outstanding achievements arose from a partnership with D W Griffith (qv), which began in 1908 on *A Calamitous Elopement*. Bitzer invented and honed myriad techniques that have now seeped into cinematic convention, including the flashback, split-screen shot, matte shot and soft-focus. The collaboration with Griffith lasted 16 years, during which time he helped finance *The Birth of a Nation* (15). Advancing technology, however, left the once revolutionary cinematographer feeling anachronistic. He turned to drink, his work thinned out and he never achieved the recognition he so rightly merited.

J STUART BLACKTON
British/US pioneer (1875-1941)

Born in Sheffield, South Yorkshire, he emigrated to the United States in 1885 and became an illustrator for the New York World. During an interview with Thomas Alva Edison (qv), the inventor suggested that he photograph some of Blackton's drawings. Blackton decided to experiment and purchased a Kinetograph camera. With Albert E Smith and William T Rock he established the Vitagraph Company in 1897 with a rooftop studio in Manhattan. Their first film was *The Burglar on the Roof*, with Blackton appearing before the camera. During the Spanish-American war of 1898 they made fake newsreels as well as genuine films, moving to Brooklyn and the first enclosed film studio in the world. Blackton developed stop motion cinematography to animate his cartoons. He was an extraordinary creative power in American cinema and wrote, produced, directed and acted in hundreds of films. He pioneered propaganda, two- and three-reel comedies and theatrical adaptations, and starred in the *Happy Hooligan* series, the first comic strip spin-off. His career dwindled after the first world war. In 1926 Vitagraph was taken over by Warner and Blackton lost his fortune in the Wall Street crash.

MEL BLANC
US voice artist (1908-89)

Although one of the most omnipresent figures in 20th-century entertainment, Blanc was a household voice. Altogether, he voiced some 3,000 cartoons in his 60-year career, including those featuring Porky Pig, Tweetie Pie, Sylvester, the Road Runner, Daffy Duck, Speedy Gonzales, Woody Woodpecker, Barney Rubble and, most famously, Bugs Bunny (qv). He entered showbusiness as a tuba player, later playing violin and bass for the NBC Radio Orchestra. In 1933 he and his bride Estelle Rosenbaum provided voices on a daily radio show in Portland, Oregon, prompting Blanc to try his luck with Warners cartoon unit. It took him 18 months to land his first audition, but following his portrayal of a drunken bull in *Picador Porky* (37) he articulated a further 850 cartoons for Warner over a 50-year period. Later "the man of 1,000 voices" hosted his own radio show, produced a number of hit records and worked for everybody from CBS to Hanna-Barbera (qv). Although he cited Bugs Bunny as his favourite creation, Blanc was allergic to carrots.

Mel Blanc (right): known as the "man of 1,000 voices"

ERNARD BLIER
rench actor (1916-89)

orn in Buenos Aires of French arents, Blier was educated at the aris Conservatory and made his m debut in *Troix-six-neuf* (37). He as taken prisoner by the Germans 1942 and after the war opeared in various stage oulevard comedies. He oecialised in character roles, aying ordinary workers in various ettings. He showed his versatile amatic prowess in *Dedée 'Anvers* (48) and particularly *Quai es Orfèvres* (47), a classic of the

rime genre. Blier won acclaim for is role as a country teacher in *'Ecole buissoniere* (49), which olidified his career as a leading ctor in French and foreign films. s he became more portly and alding, he took roles as a police spector, most notably Javert in *es Misérables* (57) and *Le Dossier oir* (57). He appeared in more an 200 films and was the father f director Bertrand Blier (qv).

BERTRAND BLIER
French director (1939-)

Son of the actor Bernard Blier (qv), he served a lengthy apprenticeship as assistant to numerous directors before making his second and breakthrough feature, *Les Valseuses* (74), based on his own novel. Both crude and lyrical, the lewd and criminal odyssey of ne'er-do-wells established his cynical, bourgeoise-bating flair and made a star of Gérard Depardieu (qv), who has since become a regular collaborator. Satirical and arguably sexist, Blier's commercial and frequently cruel *oeuvre* is characterised by polished, provoking explorations of sexual relationships, notably in his light-hearted Oscar-winning *Preparez Vos Mouchoirs* (78), the black *ménage à trois* comedy *Tenue du Soirée* (86) – Depardieu's drag debut – and *Trop Belle Pour Toi* (89), in which Depardieu as the car salesman turns from his stunning wife (Carole Bouquet) to his plain receptionist (Josiane Balasko).

JOAN BLONDELL
US actress (1909-79)

In the 1930s, Blondell's likeable, brassy glamour was constantly contained in cynical, fast-talking broads snapping out put-downs with the best of them, including James Cagney (qv), with whom she went to Hollywood to film their stage show as *Sinners' Holiday* (30). She was born to a vaudeville couple and toured the world until she won a Dallas beauty contest. For 10 years she worked at Warner, becoming known as The Warner Sister for her omnipresence

"either as girl reporter or girl detective", she complained. Her work on the Busby Berkeley (qv) extravaganza *Dames* (34) and on *Bullets or Ballots* (36) refined her ability to suggest a vulnerability beneath a hard-boiled exterior, as in *A Tree Grows In Brooklyn* (45), her Oscar-nominated *The Blue Veil* (51) and *The Cincinnati Kid* (65). She was three times married – to the cameraman George Barnes (1933-35), actor Dick Powell (qv) (1936-45) and the producer Mike Todd (qv) (1947-50).

CLAIRE BLOOM
British actress (1931-)

London-born Bloom trained for the stage at the Guildhall and Central schools, turning professional at the age of 15. A film contract with Rank began inauspiciously with a minor stage adaptation, *The Blind Goddess* (48). On her return from a season at Stratford-on-Avon, where she played Ophelia to Paul Scofield's Hamlet, the studio dropped her. When she was 19, Charles Chaplin (qv) invited her to America to test for the ballerina in *Limelight* (52). Since then, the serenely beautiful and very English actress has proved durable on both sides of the Atlantic. She excels at acerbic, elegant middle-class wives and mothers, most recently in Joanna Trollope's A Village Affair. The novelist Philip Roth is her third husband, after Rod Steiger (qv) and Broadway producer Hillard Elkins. Her recent roles include an Italian countess in the American TV soap, As The World Turns.

DON BLUTH
US animator (1938-)

Bluth claims he was six years old when he dreamed of animating for Disney. Eleven years later he was hired to "fill in the bits" on the studio's *Sleeping Beauty* (59) and stayed for 18 months. After a spell in Argentina, he returned to America and got his degree in English literature. By 1971 he was back at Disney working on *Robin Hood* (73). He stayed for eight years, but became disenchanted with the studio's unbending regime. With Gary Goldman and 14 other artists he set up his own production company making *The Secret of NIMH* (82), a critical success but a commercial disappointment. With Steven Spielberg (qv) as executive producer, his next picture, *An American Tail* (86), was a box-office hit. That year, Bluth moved to Dublin to make his films for half the price of Disney's. While instrumental in getting animation back on its feet in the late 1980s, his subsequent features could not compete with Disney's new era.

BUDD BOETTICHER
US director (1916-)

Trained as a matador and hired as consultant for *Blood and Sand* (41), he made low-budget films, including the supposedly autobiographical *The Bullfighter and the Lady* (51) and a

surprisingly vicious thriller, *The Killer Is Loose* (56). Teaming with Randolph Scott (qv) for some laconic, hard-hitting westerns, the Chicago-born director spent most of his career making saddle-up classics such as *The Tall T* (57) and *Ride Lonesome* (59). He also collaborated with Audie Murphy, but his great achievement was a non-western, *The Rise and Fall of Legs Diamond* (60), which was a minor masterpiece. Eight years of his life was eaten up trying to make *Arruza* (72), a documentary about the real-life bullfighter. Boetticher ran out of money, his wife ran out on him, he had a nervous breakdown and was briefly jailed.

DIRK BOGARDE
British actor (1921-)

An extra in *Come on George* (39), his first full role following wartime service was in *Esther Waters* (48). Handsome and versatile, he played a cop killer in *The Blue Lamp* (50), but in the Doctor series and *A Tale of Two Cities* (58) he became popular as a romantic lead or hero. More complex roles, in *Victim* (61), *The Servant* (63) and *Accident* (67) added range to the matinee idol status he resented. Bogarde restricted his appearances, living on the Continent for many years. Notable performances in *The Fixer* (68) and *The Damned* (69) were capped with a *tour de force* as Von Aschenbach in *Death in Venice* (71) followed by *The Night Porter* (74) and *Despair* (79). His last elegaic performance was in Bertrand Tavernier's (qv) *These Foolish Things* (90). In 1992 he was knighted.

HUMPHREY BOGART
US actor (1899-1957)

A tough guy whose influence and enduring popularity are out of proportion to his comparatively few films as a leading man, Bogart made his film debut in 1930. He came to notice in *The Petrified Forest* (36), repeating the title role he played on Broadway. He was thereafter usually cast either as a villainous gangster or a battling attorney. His clipped vocal manner and "stone face" were the result of a first world war incident that almost severed his upper lip. John Huston (qv), who directed *The Maltese Falcon* (41), made him a star and his status was consolidated with *Casablanca* (42), *To Have and Have Not* (44) – on which he met Lauren Bacall (qv), his third wife – *The Big Sleep* (46), *The Treasure of the Sierra Madre* and *Key Largo* (48). He extended his range in *In a Lonely Place* (50), *The African Queen* (51), *The Caine Mutiny* and *Sabrina* (54), but fighting cancer and nursed by Bacall, he died at home in his sleep.

PETER BOGDANOVICH
US director, writer (1939-)

Bogdanovich had a background in film journalism, with creditable monographs of Ford, Hitchcock, Welles (qqv) and others. He entered production with Roger Corman (qv) in the mid-1960s and his first directorial work was *Targets* (68), which starred Boris Karloff (qv). His next three films succeeded as wistful recollections of an American past, the elegiac paean to smalltown Texas, *The Last Picture Show* (71), the screwball Hawksian tribute *What's Up, Doc?* (72) and the picaresque back roads adventures of a salesman and his young daughter, *Paper Moon* (73). Bogdanovich's career then faltered. His next films were marred by featuring his romantic partner Cybill Shepherd, and *Nickelodeon* (76), intended as a tribute to silent comedy, failed. He briefly returned to form in 1985 with *Mask*, starring Cher (qv) as the mother of a Californian youth with an "elephant man" facial deformity, but his talent is erratic and to a large extent still unfulfilled.

RAY BOLGER
US actor, dancer (1904-87)

He was a serviceable actor, but an outstanding dancer in the great American musical tradition. He took dancing lessons and appeared in amateur stage productions while doing a succession of conventional jobs. He turned professional in the early 1920s, touring with a small musical comedy company before going into vaudeville as one half of a dancing duo. Broadway beckoned, eventually making him a stage star, and he made his Hollywood debut in *The Great Ziegfeld* (36). His dancing with Anna Neagle (qv) in *Sunny* (41) elevated the limp enterprise; his rendering of Who in *Look for the Silver Lining* (49) was the picture's saving moment and he repeated his Broadway success in the title role of *Where's Charley?* (52), a musical version of Charley's Aunt. The films failed to capitalise on his gifts. He will always be remembered for his distinctive portrayal of Scarecrow in *The Wizard of Oz* (39).

Bolger (below with Doris Day): an outstanding dancer

WARNER BROS. Pictures Presents
DORIS DAY RAY BOLGER
in "APRIL IN PARIS"
Produced by William Jacobs
Directed by David Butler
Musical numbers staged and directed by LeRoy Prinz
Colour by TECHNICOLOR
A Warner Bros. Picture

Expelled from school for indiscipline, Bogart (right) abandoned Ivy League plans to study medicine

ROBERT BOLT
British screenwriter (1924-95)

A former teacher, Bolt (above right with Olivier (qv)) was an established playwright with Flowering Cherry and A Man For All Seasons when he was catapulted into the front ranks of cinema by the director David Lean (qv), for whom he scripted *Lawrence of Arabia* (62) and *Dr Zhivago* (65). The latter brought Bolt his first Oscar, a second came for his adaptation of *A Man for All Seasons* (66), directed by Fred Zinnemann (qv). The third Lean-Bolt project, *Ryan's Daughter* (70), flopped. But Bolt persevered, making his directing debut with *Lady Caroline Lamb* (72), a vehicle for Sarah Miles, his second wife and widow, who had starred as Ryan's daughter. He continued working with Lean, but their script for *The Bounty* was abandoned when Bolt had a heart bypass operation and stroke in 1979. He made a partial recovery, but Lean died in 1991 before they could complete their adaptation of Conrad's Nostromo. Bolt has been accused of being an out-of-step "middlebrow", yet this was his greatest strength: a talent for bringing broad historical sweeps and big ideas into focus through characters audiences could accept.

SERGEI BONDARCHUK
Ukrainian actor/director (1920-94)

Born in Ukraine during the traumatic early days of the revolution, Bondarchuk was considered to be one of Soviet cinema's most powerful exponents, first as a classic actor and then as a director who specialised in literary themes such as the monumental *War and Peace* (67). A semi-professional actor in his early teens, he was taught the Soviet version of the Stanislavsky method at the Rostov drama school. In the second world war he worked as an entertainer behind the lines with various Red Army ensembles. Studying under Pudovkin (qv) at Moscow's All-Union State Institute of Cinematography after the war, he made his screen debut playing a man twice his age in Gerasimov's *Young Guard* (48). Discovering he was in an ideal position to help in the rehabilitation of Soviet cinema in the post-Stalin years, he actively promoted Italian and British co-cultural productions, particularly *Waterloo* (70). Although accused of being part of the furniture during the days of perestroika by the younger generation, he managed to keep his desk at the studio.

JOHN BOORMAN
British director (1933-)

He worked as a dry cleaner, then a film critic before moving into television as an assistant film editor and later a documentary producer. Boorman's first feature, *Catch Us If You Can* (65), was a wacky pop film with the Dave Clark Five. His next was the tense thriller *Point Blank* (67), which is regarded as his finest work. His talent has proved erratic. For every resonant, complex work, such as the back-to-nature horror *Deliverance* (72), there has been a laughable indulgence, such as the sci-fi flop *Zardoz* (74). After the disappointing *Exorcist II: The Heretic* (77), Boorman rediscovered, through the epic Arthurian fantasy *Excalibur* (81), his inspiration and ambition. In 1982 he produced *Angel* for first-time director Neil Jordan (qv) and returned to directing with *The Emerald Forest* (85). His greatest latter-day commercial and critical success was the autobiographical home front comedy-drama *Hope and Glory* (87), which he followed with the misguided *Where the Heart Is* (90). However, he showed his belief in libertarianism in *Beyond Rangoon* (95).

This picture will move, delight and entertain you . . . beautifully played, superbly directed. Go and see it. You will love it.
Donald Zec, Daily Mirror
The best film to come out of America for many a long month.
Alan Brien, Evening Standard
A most moving film.
Paul Holt, Daily Herald
A picture to be seen not once but again and again.
Peter Burnup, News of the World
Compels the attention, touches the heart, haunts the memory.
Paul Dehn, News Chronicle
One of the most pleasing pictures I have seen.
Leonard Mosley, Daily Express
A film of beauty and truth and grand acting.
Maurice Wiltshire, Daily Mail
Brilliantly acted, directed and written.
Harris Deans, Sunday Dispatch
The best adult film yet made by an American studio.
Gerald Bowman, Evening News
HAROLD HECHT
and BURT LANCASTER
present
WINNER OF THE COVETED 'GRAND PRIX' INTERNATIONAL FILM FESTIVAL, CANNES 1955
MARTY
STARRING
ERNEST BORGNINE · BETSY BLAIR
Story and Screenplay by PADDY CHAYEFSKY
Directed by DELBERT MANN
Produced by HAROLD HECHT
Associate Producer PADDY CHAYEFSKY
UNITED ARTISTS
QUALITY PICTURES UA IN QUANTITY

RNEST BORGNINE
'S actor (1917-)

ne squat, broad face, piercing yes and tendency to grunt caused orgnine to be cast as a natural eavy, the most famous of which as his sadistic sergeant in *From lere to Eternity* (53). He also uccessfully fleshed out an edgy, ggressive villain in *Bad Day at lack Rock* (55). Borgnine, born to alian parents in Connecticut, went live in Milan until he was seven, hen he returned to Connecticut, ined the navy and then went to cting school in Hartford. Treading e boards in Virginia and ucceeding with his early thuggish m roles, he triumphed in *Marty* 55) and rightly scooped an Oscar s the lonely, sensitive Bronx utcher whose crippling insecurity ept him at a distance from girls. espite a wide body of work over e years, including *The Dirty ozen* (67) and *Escape From New ork* (81), *Marty* will go down as orgnine's greatest hit.

FRANK BORZAGE
US director (1894-1962)

Bittersweet romanticism (his detractors call it sentimentality) and consistency of style were the hallmarks of this first winner of the best director Oscar for *7th Heaven* (27), the poignant tale of a Paris "sewer rat" and the waif he rescues from degradation. A former bit player in theatre touring companies, Borzage went to

Hollywood at the age of 20 and appeared in westerns for Thomas Ince (qv). Graduating to direction at Mutual, he rapidly mastered his craft, pioneering the use of soft focus and impressing with his visual fluency. He made the transition to sound, winning a second Oscar for *Bad Girl* (31). Margaret Sullavan (qv) graced four of his best films, the last of which, the anti-Nazi drama *The Mortal Storm* (40), marked the end of his best period. A victim of McCarthyism, he made no films between 1948 and 1958, concluding his career with *The Big Fisherman* (59).

STEPHEN BOSUSTOW
Canadian animator (1911-81)

Born in British Columbia, Bosustow won his first art competition at 11 and became a professional animator in his early twenties. In 1934 he was signed by Disney and stayed there for seven years until instigating an artists' strike, after which he left to work for Hughes Aircraft as a design illustrator. A year later he set up his own company and produced Franklin D Roosevelt's 1944 re-election cartoon, *Hell-Bent for Election.* Then, in 1945, he and other ex-Disney animators set up United Productions of America to challenge the artistic stranglehold of Disney and cultivate a new form of animation. At UPA his artists were encouraged to adopt simpler styles and fresh techniques. Bosustow produced many of UPA's films, three of which, *Gerald McBoing Boing, When Magoo Flew* and *Mister Magoo's Puddle*

Jumper, won Oscars for best short cartoon. In 1961 he sold his share in UPA and formed Stephen Bosustow Productions, a company devoted to making educational films and travel shorts.

JOHN AND ROY BOULTING
British producers, directors (1913-85 and 1913-)

The Boulting twins worked turn and turn about, one producing while the other directed. They entered the industry in the 1930s and made their feature debut in 1939 with *Trunk Crime.* They overcame censorship problems with *Pastor Hall* (40), a film based on the Nazi persecution of Pastor Niemoller.

After their screen version of Robert Ardrey's pacifist play *Thunder Rock* (42), the brothers split: John to the RAF where he made *Journey Together* (45), a feature on aircrew training; Roy to the army and documentaries such as *Desert Victory* (43) and *Burma Victory* (45). They reunited after the war for *Fame Is the Spur* (47), the adaptation of Grahame Greene's (qv) novel *Brighton Rock* (47) and an adapted play, *The Guinea Pig* ▷

The 10 best comedies

Annie Hall (1977)
The best of Woody Allen, with Diane Keaton in the lead

Bringing Up Baby (1938)
Howard Hawks teams Cary Grant and Katharine Hepburn in screwball comedy

City Lights (1931)
At its peak, the genius of Charlie Chaplin's mime

The General (1927)
A Buster Keaton masterpiece, mixing comedy with American Civil War history

Kind Hearts and Coronets (1949)
Robert Hamer's urbane, black satire and the best of the Ealing comedies

Monsieur Hulot's Holiday (1953)
Jacques Tati's immortal character makes his debut

A Night at the Opera (1935)
The anarchic, zany Marx Brothers in their best film

The Producers (1968)
Mel Brooks never topped this outrageous backstage farce

Some Like It Hot (1959)
Monroe, Curtis and Lemmon in Billy Wilder's classic cross-dressing masterpiece

To Be or Not to Be (1942)
Jack Benny and Carole Lombard in Ernst Lubitsch's great wartime black comedy

(48), in which a working-class boy enters a public school. Later the Boultings specialised in comedies, including *Private's Progress* (56), *Lucky Jim* (57) and *I'm All Right Jack* (59), in which Peter Sellers (qv) appeared as a trade union shop steward. The brothers established a reputation for fine craftsmanship and occasional irreverence towards the system.

CLARA BOW
US actress (1905-65)

One of the earliest hyped and victimised Hollywood sex symbols, the "It Girl" is recalled less for her work than as a flapper off-screen, undone by sex and drug abuse scandals. She possessed genuine star power and a vivacious, contemporary quality that has worn better than the outdated style of many of her peers. Bow grew up in

poverty and at 16 was "discovered" in a beauty competition. Groomed by the producer B P Schulberg, she broke through in the mid-1920s, starring notoriously in Elinor Glyn's story *It* (27) as the definitive gold-digger conquering with sex, a role she reprised often. In a rare part as an innocent, she was the girl next door who pluckily goes to war driving an ambulance in William Wellman's (qv) Oscar-winning *Wings* (27). By the time she was 25, Bow had made nearly 50 pictures when the talkies' cruel exposure of her abrasive accent finished a career already severely damaged by lurid publicity and the mental breakdowns that plagued the rest of her reclusive life.

WILLIAM BOYD
US actor (1898-1972)

As Hopalong Cassidy, Boyd was the most benign of B-picture cowboys. A character created by pulp writer Clarence E Mulford, Hopalong (so called because he had a slight limp) never cocked a trigger in anger, his hair was a benediction in premature white and he did not drink, smoke or swear. Boyd had been a silent screen favourite of Cecil B DeMille (qv) with roles in *Volga Boatman* (26) and *The King of Kings* (27). Confusion with two other showbusiness William Boyds did him no good until, at the age of 40, he took on the name of

Hopalong. The limp soon vanished as 66 Cassidy-themed films ensued. TV re-runs, variety acts and ownership of the character trademark ensured Boyd's financial security. Married four times, the Ohio-born hero was the only good guy to wear black.

CHARLES BOYER
French actor (1897-1978)

With his French accent, spaniel eyes and continental charm, he was known as "The Great Lover" among English-speaking audiences, although he never uttered the line "Come with me to the casbah" in his best film *Algiers* (38). He studied philosophy at the Sorbonne and drama at the Paris Conservatory. He was always a French matinee idol and his first film, *L'Homme du Large* (20), brought him, by way of Germany, to MGM, which first employed him to make French versions of American films before starring him in *The Magnificent Lie* (31). Not an instant success, he was forced to make frequent excursions back and forth across the Atlantic until he established his credentials with *Private Worlds* (35) with Claudette Colbert (qv), *The Garden of Allah* (36), *All This, and Heaven Too* (40) *Cluny Brown* (46) with Jennifer Jones and Max Ophuls's (qqv) magnificent *Madame de. . .* (53). Advancing maturity restricted him to charming cameos in films such as *Around the World in 80 Days* (56). Given an Oscar for cementing Franco-American relations during the war, Boyer committed suicide two days after the death of his beloved British wife Pat Paterson.

KENNETH BRANAGH
British director, actor and writer (1960-)

After studying drama, Branagh won early acclaim for his performance in Another Country on the stage. He left the Royal Shakespeare Company to form the Renaissance Theatre Company, for whom he wrote, acted and directed. Promising roles on film, including *A*

Month in the Country (87), were followed by *Henry V* (89), which he adapted, directed and took the title role in. The subsequent features *Dead Again* (91), a tepid thriller, and *Peter's Friends* (92), a self-indulgent British buddy comedy, were sore disappointments. Both featured his wife and frequent co-star Emma Thompson (qv). Tellingly, it was not until his light, enjoyable film version of *Much Ado About Nothing* (93) that faith was restored. He was again to demonstrate his fluency with Shakespeare with his all-star *Hamlet* (97).

KLAUS MARIA BRANDAUER
Austrian actor (1944-)

Brandauer has had a colourful career in important Austrian/German films and a motley variety of British/American productions. He was catapulted into international film recognition with Istvan Szabo's stunning, Oscar-winning *Mephisto* (81), in which he played an actor on the horns of 1930s fascism. He was nominated for best supporting actor as Meryl Streep's (qv) feckless husband in Sydney Pollack's (qv) *Out of Africa* (85) and in 1990 directed *Georg Elser/Seven Minutes.*

MARLON BRANDO
US actor, director and producer (1924-)

Widely believed to be the finest exponent of film acting, the naturalism of his playing (he was a founder member of the Actors Studio and the most prominent champion of the Method) and characteristically mumbled delivery brought him fame first on Broadway in 1947 in A Streetcar Named Desire. Unconventional behaviour, perceived as rebelliousness, and youthful, brooding good looks added to his popular appeal in the 1950s. His first film was *The Men* (50) and he was Oscar-nominated for *Streetcar* (51), *Viva Zapata!* (52) and *Julius Caesar* (53). He had a vintage year in 1953-54 with *The Wild One, On the Waterfront* (his first Oscar) and *Désirée.* He set up a production company and made his directing debut with *One-Eyed Jacks* (61). The 1960s saw diminishing returns, from his self-indulgences in *Mutiny on the Bounty* (62) to *Queimada!* (70). He also bought an island retreat near Tahiti, the ▷

Brando and Vivien Leigh in A Streetcar Named Desire

Bounty location. *The Godfather* (72), which brought him his second Oscar (although he refused to accept it to highlight the problems of native Americans), and *Last Tango in Paris* (72) restored him to top status, but his form has been intermittent since. *The Missouri Breaks* (76), *Superman* (78) and *Apocalypse Now* (79) did nothing for his reputation and he took a long break until *A Dry White Season* (89), which brought a best supporting actor Oscar nomination. More recently he appeared in *Don Juan de Marco* (95). His personal life has been marked by scandal and tragedy, including the imprisonment of his son for voluntary manslaughter and the suicide of his daughter.

PIERRE BRASSEUR
French actor (1903-72)

Brasseur made more than 80 films and had an easy way with irony and wit, giving full vent to this quality in the screenplays of Jacques Prévert (qv). The most famous of these was *Quai des Brumes/Port of Shadows* (38), in which he brought as much force to the picture as Jean Gabin (qv), the film's star. The son of an actress, he trod the boards at 15 and graced the screen at 20. He learned his craft from Harry Baur, but only moved into the first division with *Quai des Brumes*. The creative variety in his life included poetry, a number of plays and an autobiography, Ma Vie Envrac. His name survives through his son, the actor Claude Brasseur.

ROBERT BRESSON
French director (1907-)

This enigmatic, solitary, consummate *auteur* of French cinema was a brilliant, prizewinning student who entered the industry in 1933 as the screenwriter on *C'était un Musicien* after a brief career as a painter. The tight construction and stylistic brevity of painting dominated Bresson's films from the start, as does a continuing obsession with the achievement of grace through death. Unusually embraced by both the Old Guard and New Wave, he chose to

enhance his sparse approach with the use of amateur actors. He directed *Les Anges du Péché* (42), his first big feature, after a year's internment as a prisoner of war in Germany, which provided material for *A Man Escaped* (56). His reputation was enhanced by *Diary of a Country Priest* (50), which won the International Prize at the Venice festival. *A Man Escaped* won him best director at Cannes, *Le Procés de Jeanne d'Arc* (62) the Cannes Special Jury Prize. His first film in colour, *Une Femme Douce* (69), the story of a pawnbroker keeping vigil over his suicidal wife, neatly combines use of voice-over and the triumph of spirituality over death. His seminal Notes sur le Cinématographie was published in 1975. He was made an officer of the *Légion d'honneur* in 1978.

JEFF BRIDGES
US actor (1949-)

An American favourite who can ooze introspection on screen, Bridges has created a catalogue of characters representing choice roles rather than commercial success. In Hollywood, stardom and meaty character acting rarely go hand in hand. With a face that suggests picket-fence contentment and boy-next-door romance, his fine performances often reveal his penchant for darkness, for the yawning gap between the possibility of the American Dream and the nasty grip of reality. In *Cutter's Way* (81) his character represented an America tortured by Vietnam; in *The Fabulous Baker Boys* (89) he suffered disillusion; and in Terry Gilliam's (qv) *The Fisher King* (91) the black hole of his life was filled by magic, courtesy of Robin Williams (qv). Nostalgia, *The Last Picture Show* (71), romance, *Against All Odds* (84), and psychological drama, *Fearless* (93), have all been embraced. His father is Lloyd, his brother Beau.

ALBERT R BROCCOLI
US producer (1909-96)

Universally known as "Cubby", Broccoli entered the film industry in the late 1930s as an assistant director. Fifteen years later he moved to Britain, formed Warwick Pictures with Irving Allen, a fellow American exile, and started with a trio of negligible Alan Ladd (qv) vehicles. The heist thriller *A Prize of Gold* (55) was a highlight, with Broccoli devoting most of his energy to jungle adventures. He finally realised a prestigious project with *The Trials of Oscar Wilde* (60). His master stroke, in partnership with Harry Saltzman until 1976, was the acquisition of the rights to and the production of the James Bond series. An international phenomenon since *Dr No* (62), Broccoli's Bond empire has endured for more than 30 years through 17 films and five screen Bonds, from Sean Connery (qv) to Pierce Brosnan. His sole non-007 venture since 1963 was the children's musical *Chitty Chitty Bang Bang* (68). In 1981 he received the coveted Irving G Thalberg (qv) award for production achievement.

PETER BROOK
British director (1925-)

In spite of being known to cinema audiences for his savage vision of the human condition contained in William Golding's *Lord of the Flies* (63) and *Marat/Sade* (66), his

reputation is primarily that of a critical theoretician of British theatre. Although film was central to Brook's thinking, particularly the realism of the French New Wave, he was forced by financial circumstances to turn to the theatre, even to making films of theatrical productions, such as *King Lear* (70). Born in London and educated at Oxford, he proclaimed his career intentions with an amateur film, *Sentimental Journey* (43), and quickly followed it with a dramatic *Dr Faustus. The Beggar's Opera* (53) was his first feature. Determined to bring the classics within the orbit of contemporary drama, he founded the experimental Centre for International Creation, where he established the primacy of improvisational workshops. Recently, he produced a surreal television epic based on the classic Indian saga The Mahabharata.

LOUISE BROOKS
US actress (1906-85)

A gifted and alluring star famed for her distinctively bobbed hair and enigmatic face, she has become an icon of the cinema. A trained dancer, she was a Ziegfeld Girl before making a number of formula flapper films as a contract player. She made her reputation in *A Girl in Every Port* (28) then, riding freight trains dressed as a boy in *Beggars of Life* (28), she seduced audiences with her sexy androgynous quality. She gave he most famous performance as Lulu the doomed, amoral femme fatale in *Pandora's Box* (28). It was the zenith of a career that collapsed largely through her intransigence. Humiliated by Harry Cohn (qv), who put her in the chorus line of a Grace Moore musical and made publicity capital out of her mighty fall, she retired in 1938. Alone and reclusive, she took to writing acute articles on film and published a highly regarded memoir, Lulu in Hollywood, in 1982.

MEL BROOKS
US director, writer and actor (1926-)

An ill wind blew Brooks a lot of good with *Blazing Saddles* (74). H first, caustically funny film, *The Producers* (68), with its Springtime For Hitler musical routine drew a word-of-mouth audience. But his parody western, *Blazing Saddles*, with cowboys breaking wind after a campfire diet of baked beans, was a universal smash. His work thereafter pastiched styles such as *Silent Movie* (76) and the Hitchcockian *High Anxiety* (77), but only *Young Frankenstein* (74) had any class. A former gag writer to Sid Caesar, facetiousness came to the fore with clodhoppers such as *History Of The World – Part 1* (81), *Spaceballs* (87) and *Life Stinks* (91). His work as producer-backer is more exciting than his personal material, from David Lynch's (qv) *The Elephant Man* (80) to David Cronenberg's (qv) *The Fly* (86). His most recent directorial stint was *Robin Hood: Men in Tights* (93), in which a camp Sherwood queen robbed old jokes to give to the new. He is married to the actress Anne Bancroft (qv).

RICHARD BROOKS
US director, screenwriter and producer (1912-92)

After a term as a sports writer in Philadelphia and a radio commentator in New York, Brooks moved to Los Angeles in 1941 to write for radio. He collaborated on screenplays before joining the marine corps in wartime. Later, he won acclaim for co-scripting *Key Largo* (48) with John Huston (qv) and made his directorial debut with *Crisis* (50), a leaden political thriller. He made *Blackboard Jungle* (55), a sensational exposé of New York's school system, for which his screenplay was nominated for an Oscar. Five years later he won the award for his screenplay of *Elmer Gantry*. While doggedly trying to make films of social significance, Brooks was, ironically, at his best when directing contemplative action-adventures, such as the westerns *The Professionals* (66) and *Bite the Bullet* (75). He also had a knack for drawing exceptional performances out of his stars, notably Elizabeth Taylor (qv) in *Cat on a Hot Tin Roof* (58) and Diane Keaton (qv) in *Looking for Mr Goodbar* (77). In the 1980s his career slowed to a standstill with a couple of flops. He was married to the actress Jean Simmons (qv) from 1960 to 1977.

CLARENCE BROWN
US director (1890-1987)

After assisting the director Maurice Tourneur, who was a huge influence on his work, he made his name with *The Eagle* (25) starring Rudolph Valentino (qv). At MGM, he became a respected director, working in particular with Greta Garbo (qv) on some of her best-loved films, including *Inspiration* (31) and *Anna Karenina* (35), earning himself a reputation as one of the few people who could keep the petulant star happy. His association with MGM stretched into the 1950s and his rural dramas, such as *The Yearling* (46) and *Intruder in the Dust* (49), kept him in favour. After his retirement from cinema in the mid-1950s, he founded the Clarence Brown Theatre for the Performing Arts at the University of Tennessee.

TOD BROWNING
US director (1882-1962)

When he was a boy Browning ran away from his Kentucky home to join a circus. It was an experience of bizarre carnival seesawing between the daring and the damaged that coloured all his movies, especially his most famous, *Dracula* (31), and his most notorious, *Freaks* (32). He began in cinema as an actor, but later became friendly with, and wrote for, Lon Chaney (qv), the horror star whose make-up was often as painful to apply as to observe. *The Unholy Three* (25) and *London After Midnight* (27) were two of their finest collaborations. After Chaney's death, Browning established himself as a nerve scrambler. *Freaks*, with its story of a circus's deformed exhibits wreaking revenge on a deceitful beauty, was disturbing and banned for many years. Undeterred, Browning made other notable grotesques, such as *Mark of the Vampire* (35) and *The Devil Doll* (36). As a manipulator of his own devils he and his rival, James Whale (qv), were masters of a genre they helped to create.

KEVIN BROWNLOW
British director, historian and restorer (1938-)

At the age of 18 he started to direct *It Happened Here* in partnership with Andrew Mollo, an ambitious

work that assumed a Nazi invasion of Britain. It took six years to make and was released in 1966. After a spell at Woodfall Films as a film editor he turned to writing books, including several on the silent cinema, led by the compendious The Parade's Gone By. In 1980 he and David Gill, his partner, made a television series on Hollywood before the talkies. He also spent several years restoring Abel Gance's (qv) magnificent, almost lost masterpiece *Napoleon* (27), which led to a series of great silent films with live orchestral accompaniments and newly struck prints. Thanks to his tireless work on the big screen and on television the silent cinema is still alive.

YUL BRYNNER
US actor (1915-85)

Who can forget the magnificent musical *The King And I* (56), when

Browning's Freaks proved too disturbing for censors and was banned for many years

Brynner revealed his shaved pate to a startled Deborah Kerr (qv)? Brynner certainly could not. Apart from the 4,625 stage performances he gave in 30 years, the Oscar-winning role in his second feature film guaranteed him international celebrity. Typical of his well-constructed persona, his history is shrouded in mystery, with alternative stories about his origins, which he often perpetuated, claiming him to be a son of Swiss and Mongolian parents in Sakhalin or Vladivostok. We do know that Taidje Khan Jr started out as a Parisian trapeze artiste and philosophy student, who emigrated to America where he established himself on TV before scoring his sensational hit as the King of Siam. Not one to sell his acting short, ▷

he relied on his image to carry him through a galaxy of powerful films, the best of which include Cecil B DeMille's (qv) *The Ten Commandments* (56), John Sturges's (qv) *The Magnificent Seven* (60) and Michael Crichton's (qv) *Westworld* (73). He died of cancer while working on an anti-smoking TV commercial.

JACK BUCHANAN
British actor, singer and dancer (1890-1957)

Born, bred and educated in Scotland, he made a career as the quintessential Englishman. Tall, dark and handsome, his debonair manner, neat dancing and pleasing voice made him a musical comedy star of the London stage, but he also acted in several largely forgotten silent films before a 1924 Broadway debut with Beatrice Lillie and Gertrude Lawrence in Charlot's Revue. Of his Hollywood films, *Monte Carlo* (30), in which he co-starred with Jeanette MacDonald (qv), remains a durable delight for aficionados, but the high spot was his return to the screen, after a 10-year absence, in *The Band Wagon* (53), one of the last great musicals. Sharing the honours with Fred Astaire (qv), his uninhibited

portrayal of an existential theatrical poseur is memorable, not least when he dons white tie and tails to croon and hoof I Guess I'll Have to Change My Plan with his co-star. He was ill when he made *Les Carnets du Major Thompson* (56), an ill-conceived disaster that marked the end for Buchanan and for Preston Sturges (qv), its once great director.

BUGS BUNNY
US rabbit (1938-)

In an industry dominated by a mouse, the wisecracking, streetwise, yet effortlessly urbane rabbit is the star of Warner's Looney Tunes. He began life in 1936 as Happy Rabbit and was a supporting character in *Porky's Hare Hunt*, starring Porky Pig. Tex Avery created his persona, although Mel Blanc (qv), his vocal coach, changed the name to Bugs Bunny in homage to Ben "Bugs" Hardaway, the rabbit's visual creator. Blanc also replaced the

character's best-known line from "Hey, what's cookin'?" to "Ehh, what's up, Doc?", and established the incomparable Bronx-Brooklyn accent. In 1960, Bugs augmented his global fame by bounding into his own half-hour slot on prime-time television. He is now the figurehead for Warner Family Entertainment.

LUIS BUNUEL
Spanish director, producer (1900-83)

His surrealist short, *Un Chien Andalou* (28) made with Salvador Dali, announced the arrival of a supreme maverick. Buñuel's dark humour and anarchic sensibility are quintessentially Spanish, yet he spent little time there after leaving for Paris in 1925, settling in Mexico in 1946 after stints in Hollywood as a dubber. *Viridiana* (61), the tale of a virginal novice's awakening to the world, which notoriously features a pastiche of Leonardo's Last Supper composed of beggars and lunatics, caused an outrage that shut the film's production company and ensured that it remained unscreened in Spain until 1974. Fetishism, prostitution, religious repression and hypocrisy are typical Buñuel subjects, delivered in a deceptively plain style that can suddenly veer off into dream sequences, fantasies, ruptured narratives and bizarre images. He was a subversive, whose genius exposed the ironies of human weakness without condemning it. He was awarded best foreign film Oscar for The *Discreet Charm of the Bourgeoisie* (72).

GEORGE BURNS
US actor (1896-96)

Perhaps the longest-lived link with vaudeville, and the grinning embodiment of a more innocent Hollywood, Nathan Birnbaum died within days of reaching his 100th birthday. Famous for his cigar chomping, witty asides and amusing, roguish charm with the ladies, Burns returned to the cinema screen for *The Sunshine Boys* (75) after a small gap of 35 years. Back in the days of vaudeville, he was originally part of a children's singing quartet before trying roller skating and then comedy. His first sizeable comic triumph came when he teamed up with Gracie Allen in 1925. They married and soon made America laugh through radio, television and films. *The Big Broadcast* films (32,36,37), *Love in Bloom* (35) and *College Swing* (38) were among the feature films. In *The Sunshine Boys*, which also

starred Walter Matthau (qv), Burns's life paralleled his role as the charismatic vaudevillian coaxed out of retirement. He won an Oscar for his role. In *Going in Style* (79), Burns played one of three stalwart pensioners in Queens who spit at the inevitability of old age.

ELLEN BURSTYN
US actress (1932-)

Edna Rae Gilhooley was a veteran of the chorus line, serial TV and the Actors Studio. She was nearly 40 when as Burstyn she made an impact on film in Peter Bogdanovich's (qv) *The Last Picture Show* (71), in which she played Cybill Shepherd's sexy, frustrated mother and received the first of five Oscar nominations. Her most haunting performance was as the despairing, discarded mistress in *The King of Marvin Gardens* (72). At her height in 1974 she won the Oscar as the weary, vulnerable widow travelling hopefully in *Alice Doesn't Live Here Any More* – a film she developed, produced and engaged director Martin Scorsese (qv) for – and on Broadway originated the Tony-winning role she reprised on film in *Same Time, Next Year* (78) with Alan Alda (qv). Within the narrow

range of roles available to a middle-aged actress she made a special mark with her portrayal of wounded but defiant women, holding her own even against the special effects excess of *The Exorcist* (73) as the agonised mother. She has served as an artistic director of the Actors Studio and as president of Actors' Equity.

RICHARD BURTON
British actor (1925-84)

With a beautiful voice and a darkly handsome presence, Richard Jenkins traded his fame as the greatest British stage actor after Olivier (qv) for more lucrative cinema stardom and the glamorous life as Elizabeth Taylor's (qv) husband. He met his first wife, actress Sibyl Williams, on his film debut in *The Last Days of Dolwyn* (49). Film and stage continued alongside television work until *Cleopatra* (63) moved him into film stardom. With or without Taylor, whom he divorced, remarried and redivorced, Burton shone, particularly in *The Spy Who Came in From the Cold* (65), *Who's Afraid of Virginia Woolf?* (66), *The Taming of the Shrew* (67) and *Anne of the Thousand Days* (69) – for which he was nominated for an Oscar. He was again nominated for *Equus* (77), but his final years – he died after *1984* (84) – were less noteworthy

TIM BURTON
US director (1960-)

In childhood he was an addict of cartoons and horror films. After studying animation on a Disney fellowship Burton went to work at the studio as an apprentice, winning attention in 1982 for *Vincent*, a tribute to his idol, Vincent Price (qv), who narrated. His 30-minute feature, *Frankenweenie*, about a dog monster, has never been released. His first live-action film, *Pee-Wee's Big Adventure* (85), indicated a quirkily original talent and was a success, helping him towards the profitable *Batman* (89) and *Batman Returns* (92). His masterpiece, however, is *Edward Scissorhands* (90), the fable about a lonely boy who leaves his fairy-tale castle to live in suburban America. It provided the last role for Price as the inventor who created him. Burton's subjects are broad and often strange. His *Ed Wood* (94) was about a legendarily bad film maker.

MICHAEL CACOYANNIS
Greek Cypriot director (1922-)

Cacoyannis first found international fame and Oscars with *Zorba the Greek* (64), , but his early promise shone through in *Stella* (54), which was Melina Mercouri's film debut, and *The Girl In Black* (56), with Ellie Lambetti. *Electra* (61) and *Iphigenia* (76) with Irene Papas were more emotionally sure of touch and landscape. Often working with the cameraman Walter Lassally (qv), he tried several projects after *Zorba* involving ancient epics, such as *The Trojan Women* (74) and *The Story of Jacob and Joseph* (74), but substance subsumed style.

NICOLAS CAGE
US actor (1964-)

Concerned that his most conspicuous connection to the film business would be his name – he is Francis Ford Coppola's (qv) nephew – he changed it for his second film. He dropped out of high school and made his debut on American television in 1981. Minor roles followed but it was with his uncle's *Rumble Fish* (83) that he first showed himself to be an actor worthy of attention. He worked in the family business twice more – on the ill-fated gangster film *The Cotton Club* (84) and the time-travel comedy *Peggy Sue Got Married* (86) – but earned acclaim for his work on the over-blown *Birdy* (84) and as the romantic lead opposite Cher (qv) in *Moonstruck* (87). His career took a refreshing diversion into the independent sector working with idiosyncratic directors in the Coen Brothers' (qv) *Raising Arizona* (87) and David Lynch's (qv) *Wild at Heart* (90). He topped those with an Oscar for his performance in *Leaving Las Vegas* (95).

JAMES CAGNEY
US actor, dancer (1899-1986)

He may have been stocky and unglamorous, but he was also the most versatile of stars. The swaggering, staccato bravado and explosive aggression that informed his memorable thugs transformed into the electric energy and charm of his song and dance men. Raised on New York's Lower East Side, he worked as a waiter, pool-room racker and female impersonator before acting. Warners hired him for *Sinners' Holiday* (31), a film version of his Broadway success Penny Arcade, and put him under contract. His vicious hoodlum in *The Public Enemy* (31), famously pulping a grapefruit into Mae Clarke's face, established him along with Edward G Robinson (qv) as the era's archetypal screen gangster. He also played Bottom in *A Midsummer Night's Dream* (35) and gave an Oscar-winning impersonation of George M Cohan in *Yankee Doodle Dandy* (42). He retired after a comic *tour de force* as a Coca-Cola sales executive in *One Two Three* (61), but came back 20 years later for a small role in *Ragtime* (81). He formed his own production company in 1942, was awarded the first American Film Institute life achievement award and received the American government's Freedom Medal, its highest civilian honour.

Cagney's great menace made him a hoodlum archetype

Caine as the unheroic Harry Palmer in The Ipcress File

SAMMY CAHN
US songwriter (1913-93)

Frank Sinatra said: "Sammy is the greatest!" From a man not noted for flattery, it was the highest accolade and in Cahn's world of lyricist-underdogs it was like a pat

on the head from God. Cahn won four Oscars for his songs, a career summed up by Three Coins In The Fountain, High Hopes and All The Way. A New Yorker, Samuel Cohen's ebullience survived through many collaborations (Jule Styne, Jimmy Van Heusen (qqv) and Saul Chaplin among them). His films always had a comic spin to the lyrics, from *Anchors Aweigh* (45) through to *Robin and the Seven Hoods* (64). Sinatra starred in both.

MICHAEL CAINE
British actor (1933-)

Probably Britain's most successful film star of the past three decades, Caine's cockney origins as Maurice Micklewright are anything but concealed. It was in *Zulu* (64) as an upper-class officer that he made his mark. As a cheerful Lothario in *Alfie* (66), opposite Olivier (qv) in *Sleuth* (72) and with Julie Walters in *Educating Rita* (83) he won Oscar nominations. Despite excellent work in such disparate films as *The Ipcress File* (65), *The Italian Job* (69), *Get Carter* (71) and *The Man Who Would Be King* (75), on which he met Shakira Baksh, his second wife, it was not until *Hannah and Her Sisters* (86) that Caine received an Oscar. Appearances in the undistinguished *The Swarm* (78) and *Jaws: The Revenge* (87) can be overlooked. Under-rated as an actor, he is famous for his pragmatic approach: "First of all I choose the great ones, and if none of those comes, I choose the mediocre ones, and if they don't come – I choose the ones that are going to pay the rent."

JAMES CAMERON
US director (1954-)

Born in Canada, he majored in physics before constructing sets for

low-budget Roger Corman (qv) films such as *Battle Beyond the Stars* (80). His first directing job was inauspicious, *Piranha II: The Spawning* (81). Directing his screenplay of *The Terminator* (84) he struck gold, providing a crucial career turn for Arnold Schwarzenegger (qv) and a shot in the arm for the stale sci-fi genre. The film was a masterly thriller, which recalled the paranoid menace of early 1970s films. *Terminator 2: Judgment Day* (91), the sequel, boasted a higher budget and superb special effects, but not the original's tautness. Cameron showed himself to be an action director *par excellence* with *Aliens* (86). *The Abyss* (89) was a breakthrough film in the use of computerised effects. He was reunited with Schwarzenegger for *Truer Lies* (94) and was responsible for the costliest epic of all time, *Titanic* (97).

JANE CAMPION
NZ director, writer (1955-)

With the release of *The Piano* (93) Campion has become an international cinema figure and feminist director. She graduated with a BA in anthropology from Victoria University in New Zealand and studied art in Sydney. She began film making at the Australian School of Film and Television in 1981 where she wrote and directed her first film, *Peel* (82), a short which won the Palme d'Or at Cannes (86). Her first big feature, *Sweetie* (89), won her the Georges Sadoul Prize, the LA Critics Award, and the Australian Critics' best film and best director award. But it was the lyrical, engrossing and often harrowing *An Angel at My Table* (90), based on the autobiography of the writer Janet Frame, that thrust Campion into the spotlight and won her seven prizes at the Venice Film Festival. *The Piano* (94), the story of Victorian female

subjugation as seen through the experiences of a deaf mute played by Holly Hunter (qv), was nominated for best film at the 1994 Academy Awards. Campion is an enigmatic workaholic who tries to keep her personal life firmly under wraps.

DYAN CANNON
US actress (1937-)

Superficially a bubbly blonde with a humorous streak, Cannon has talents that go considerably deeper which have been inadequately

fulfilled. Born of a Baptist father and a Jewish mother, Samille Diane Friesen left the University of Washington, where she studied anthropology, to become a model in Los Angeles. She had supporting roles in a couple of films and on TV before appearing on Broadway. For some years she lived with Cary Grant (qv), who was 35 years older, marrying him in 1965 (divorced 1968) and bearing his only child, a girl. She went back to films, being nominated for an Oscar for *Bob & Carol & Ted & Alice* (69), which established her a a leading actress. She was also nominated for *Heaven Can Wait* (78). She turned to direction with *Number One* (76), which dealt with children's curiosity concerning thei bodies and adult attitudes. In 199 she produced, directed, wrote and appeared in *The End of Innocence* a semi-autobiographical drama.

EDDIE CANTOR
US actor (1892-1964)

The singing comic with banjo eyes and a unique style, Edward Israel Iskowitz was born on New York's Lower East Side. A vaudeville and burlesque trouper from childhood, he became one of the brightest lights on Broadway in the Ziegfeld Follies and hit musicals. His first film was *Kid Boots* (26), but Cantc without sound was scarcely Cantor Ziegfeld's early sound revue, *Glorifying the American Girl* (29), provided a taste of Cantor's pizzaz and he excited with the screen version of *Whoopee!* (30), Samuel Goldwyn's (qv) first musical and the first to boast dance numbers staged by Busby Berkeley (qv). A

·ing of elaborate musical ·medies was subsequently ·ounted around him, notably *The ·d From Spain* (32), *Roman ·candals* (33), and *Ali Baba Goes · Town* (37). The rest were flimsy ·d contemporaries believed ·antor's electrifying presence was ·ver done justice on film. His ·30s radio programme enjoyed ·st popularity, contributing to his ·senchantment with repetitive ·ctures. He wrote four volumes of ·tobiography and received a ·ecial Oscar in 1956.

·AKIMA CANUTT
·S stuntman (1895-1986)

·os Edward Canutt found his way ·o small roles in 1920s cowboy ·ns by winning the rodeo world ·ampionship. In 1924 he began ·pearing in low-budget westerns. · also achieved recognition by ·ubling for stars such as John ·ayne, Clark Gable and Roy ·gers (qqv), and was in many of ·nema's most spectacular

·ments, for instance *Stagecoach* ·9), *Ben-Hur* (59) and *Spartacus* ·0). The 1930s brought him work · a second unit director. Once ·ain, he rose to the top. He ·urned to low-budget westerns in · 1940s as a director and won a ·ecial Oscar in 1966 for making · profession of stuntman safer.

·RANK CAPRA
·S director (1897-1991)

·s most famous films focused on · common man – ideally ·sonified by James Stewart or ·ry Cooper (qqv) – who through ·eer moral character and ·termination beat the odds. Capra ·s Hollywood's optimist, whose ·nerous lashings of sentiment, ·rried to comedy, elevated the ·otions of American audiences, ·eped in the Depression and war. · films were, he once said, a ·nk you note to America. One of ·ven children, Capra was born · poverty in Sicily until at six he ·ved to California. In 1925 he ·s employed by Mack Sennett (qv) to write gags for comedian Harry Langdon (qv), the latter hiring him as a director on his next three films. While Langdon's career declined, Capra's flourished when he was taken on by Harry Cohn (qv) at Columbia Pictures. Of his 51 films (including 11 documentaries), his most celebrated remain *It Happened One Night* (34), *Mr Deeds Goes to Town* (36) and *Mr Smith Goes to Washington* (39). *It's a Wonderful Life* (47) must go down in history as the ultimate "feelgood" film.

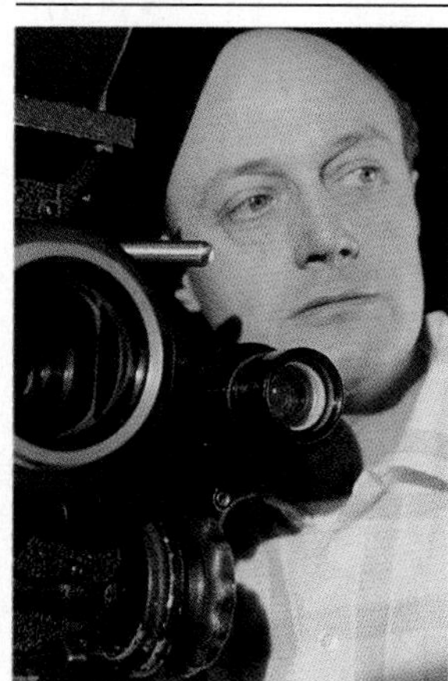

JACK CARDIFF
British cinematographer/ director, (1914-)

A giant of the British film industry, his inventive camerawork proved that every film requires more than a director to make it work. Although he has a number of directorial credits, most notably taking over *Young Cassidy* (65) when John Ford (qv) fell ill, his talent shines brighter as a cinematographer on such films as Powell and Pressburger's (qqv) *A Matter of Life and Death* (46) and *Black Narcissus* (47), for which he won an Oscar. He began acting at the age of four, became a camera assistant at 13 and worked on *Wings of the Morning* (37), Britain's first Technicolor film. Refining his skills on travelogues and Ministry of Information films during the second world war, it soon became apparent he had a unique style, infusing Technicolor's usual cool hues with saturated tonal contrasts to create bold, atmospheric compositions. Other notable films in his vast portfolio include Korda's (qv) *The Four Feathers* (39), Powell's *The Red Shoes* (48), Hitchcock's (qv) *Under Capricorn* (49), *Pandora and the Flying Dutchman* (51), Huston's (qv) *The African Queen* (51), plus *War and Peace* (56), *The Vikings* (58), *Death on the Nile* (78) and *Rambo: First Blood Part II* (85).

HARRY CAREY
US actor (1878-1947)

John Ford (qv) dedicated his film *The Three Godfathers* (49) "to the memory of Harry Carey – bright star of the early western sky".

Henry DeWitt Carey II was born in the Bronx and rehearsed for many roles in life, including writing his own melodramas. He joined Biograph in 1909 and appeared in many of D W Griffith's (qv) productions, before emerging as a western star with Ford on 26 productions, often playing a cowpoke called Cheyenne Harry. He was a jack-of-all-trades, often collaborating on the scripts, helping with production and even directing. Of his 90-odd films, which began with *Bill Sharkey's Last Game* (09) and ended with *So Dear To My Heart* (48), he won an Oscar nomination for best supporting actor in Capra's (qv) *Mr Smith Goes to Washington* (39).

HOAGY CARMICHAEL
US songwriter, actor (1899-1981)

He was the shirtsleeved bar room piano player who sang in an instantly recognisable casual and plaintive voice. Carmichael was responsible for many memorable song hits, the best known of which was Stardust, written in 1931. He came from Bloomington, Indiana (his first name was Hoagland), a drop-out lawyer who turned to jazz, performing and composing with his own band. From 1936 he was writing music for films, beginning with *Anything Goes.* Then he began playing small parts as a cafe pianist, memorably in *To Have and Have Not* (44) and *The Best Years of Our Lives* (46). His song In The Cool, Cool of the Evening from *Here Comes The Groom* (51) won an Oscar.

Capra shows how to make an entrance and stay in frame

MARCEL CARNE
French director (1909-96)

Born in Paris and the son of a cabinet-maker, Carné spent time as an insurance clerk and a film critic before Françoise Rosay introduced him to her husband Jacques Feyder (qqv), which led to his first job as assistant to chief cameraman Georges Périnal (qv) on *Les Nouveaux Messieurs* (28). In 1929 he was taken under the wing of René Clair (qv), who made him his assistant on *Sous Les Toits de Paris*. He co-directed until 1936, assisting Feyder on his important features: *Le Grand Jeu* (33), *Pension Mimosa* (34) and *La*

Kermesse héroïque (35). In 1936 he made his directorial debut with *Jenny*. Carné's best work was during his collaboration with poet-screenwriter Jacques Prévert (qv) in the 1930s and 1940s, which produced such instances of romantic fatalism as *Drôle de Drame/Bizarre, Bizarre* (37), *Quai des Brumes* (38) and *Le Jour se lève* (39). The partnership is best remembered for the seminal aesthetic masterpiece *Les Enfants du Paradis* (45). Carné abhorred location work and after his split with Prévert in 1948 his creativity stagnated despite directing consistently until 1976.

MARTINE CAROL
French actress (1922-67)

In a world where women stars were often guided if not dominated by their spouses, Carol's career was a case of husband knows worst. Maryse Mourer was ahead of Bardot and Moreau (qqv) as the love goddess of the 1950s, in films depicting her as a courtesan who got into period costumes only to slither out of them. *Caroline Chérie* (51) was the first of these under-dressed romps, but her then husband, Christian-Jaque (qv), the director, further exposed her in *Adorable Creatures* (52), *Lucrezia Borgia* (53), *Madame Du Barry* (54) and *Nana* (55). She was caught in a velvet trap and it took Max Ophuls (qv) to rescue her from typecasting by choosing her for *Lola Montès* (55), the woman whose affair with the King of Bavaria gained world notoriety and celebrity exploitation. Following a brief, disastrous foray to Hollywood she died of a heart attack.

LESLIE CARON
French actress, dancer (1931-)

Exuding a coquettish, gamine charm, Caron shone in a number of MGM musicals before establishing herself as a character actress. The daughter of a dancer, she studied ballet at 10 and by 16 was performing with Roland Petit's Ballet des Champs-Elysées, where she was spotted by Gene Kelly (qv). He cast her as his dancing partner in MGM's Oscar-winning musical *An American in Paris* (51) and Caron was an overnight star. In *Lili* (53), another MGM musical, she proved her durability and was nominated for best actress Oscar. She was teamed opposite Fred Astaire (qv) in *Daddy Long Legs* (55), another success, and then recreated her (London) stage role of *Gigi* (58) in the popular Oscar-winning film. Four years later, in the British kitchen sink drama *The L-Shaped Room* (62), she demonstrated greater depth as an actress and received another Oscar nomination. However, her subsequent film career failed to do her justice and she was reduced to supporting roles in a number of international productions. She was married to the British director Sir Peter Hall between 1956-1966.

JOHN CARPENTER
US director (1948-)

A leading figure in the sci-fi/horror scene of the 1970s, he made the Oscar-winning short, *The Resurrection of Broncho Billy* (70), while a graduate student. In 1974, he and Dan O'Bannon made the zany cult sci-fi comedy *Dark Star* (74) for $60,000. His next film, *Assault on Precinct 13* (76), was a bravura thriller that took its cue from Howard Hawks (qv), but it was *Halloween* (78) that earned him wide attention. An edgy, *Psycho*-style horror film it had a sparse, electronic score written by Carpenter. *The Fog* (8 showed his mastery of tension but the futuristic thriller *Escape From New York* (81) indicated h had lost his touch, a view endor by films that followed, even though they were notable for innovative special effects.

JOHN CARRADINE
JS actor (1906-88)

\ Hollywood regular from the mid-1930s to 1950, Carradine was a naverick character actor whose chief claim to fame is fathering (by hree marriages) five sons, three of hem actors: David, Keith and Robert. Strikingly tall and gaunt, he nainly played villains (Count Dracula three times) or the best riend of the leading actor. Far from being the conventional, gregarious ype, he had a reputation as a oner and an educated ham, who ecited Shakespeare as he stalked he streets. Notable films include *The Invisible Man* (33), *Bride of Frankenstein* (35), *Alexander's Ragtime Band* (38), *Stagecoach*, *The Hound of the Baskervilles* and *Drums Along the Mohawk* (39), *The Grapes of Wrath* (40) and *The Adventures of Mark Twain* (44). He ontinued to work through to the 980s: his final three films were *Monster in the Closet*, *Peggy Sue Got Married* and *The Tomb* (all 86).

EAN-CLAUDE CARRIERE
rench screenwriter (1931-)

ynonymous with a ceaseless olley of quality films during the st 30 years, Carrière has let his reativity roam free. A long-time ollaborator of Luis Buñuel (qv), he as able to move from realism to urrealism and back. Generally riting scripts that give full, emanding, sometimes bizarre oles to actors, he has capably travelled characters against the ackground of a particular period or place and linked the personal to the political, social or historical. Louis Malle's (qv) *Milou In May* (89), Philip Kaufman's (qv) *The Unbearable Lightness of Being* (88) and two films for Volker Schlöndorff (qv), *Circle of Deceit* (81) and *The Tin Drum* (79) are clear, classy examples. *Cyrano de Bergerac* (90) was a more recent illustration.

MADELEINE CARROLL
British actress (1906-87)

An early model of Alfred Hitchcock's (qv) deceptively cool, ladylike blondes, Carroll was one of Britain's favourite stars and most popular exports to 1930s' Hollywood. She was first invited to America for John Ford's (qv) family saga *The World Moves On* (34). It was after her performances in two Hitchcock espionage thrillers, memorably in *The 39 Steps* (35) handcuffed to Robert Donat (qv), that she returned to Hollywood a sophisticate to play high-grade romance and adventure opposite Gary Cooper, Tyrone Power and Henry Fonda (qqv). She was a consort for Ronald Colman (qv) in *The Prisoner of Zenda* (37), made a good musical with Dick Powell (qv) and several chic comedies with Fred MacMurray (qv). She played the title role to Bob Hope (qv) in *My Favorite Blonde* (42) and after her marriage – the second of four – to actor Sterling Hayden (qv), Carroll's sister was killed in the blitz, prompting her return to Britain to work for the Red Cross until the war's end. She made only three more films.

JOHN CASSAVETES
US director, actor and writer (1929-89)

Slim, dark and intense, he was a talented film and TV actor who earned a supporting Oscar nomination for *The Dirty Dozen* (67). It was as a director, though, that he made his contribution with *Shadows* (61), shot on a shoestring with a 16mm camera and a group of friends. In spite of its rough finish, it won an award at Venice and set the tone for his future films: improvisational, intimate, grittily realistic. First came *Too Late Blues* (62) and the under–rated *A Child is Waiting* (63). Later, he pursued an independent path, gaining polish and earning recognition for his low-key powerful dramas, generally starring Gena Rowlands (qv), his actress wife, and his friend Peter Falk. Effectively America's answer to cinéma vérité and the New Wave, his work includes *A Woman Under the Influence* (74) and *Gloria* (80).

ALBERTO CAVALCANTI
Brazilian director, writer (1897-1982)

An avant-garde set designer, he began directing and sometimes writing his own films in 1926. He made features and documentaries, and in 1942 was invited by Michael Balcon (qv) to be an associate producer and director at Ealing, bringing his documentary influence to bear on feature films that included *Went the Day Well?* (42), *Champagne Charlie* (44) and *Nicholas Nickleby* (47). He returned to Brazil in 1949, revitalising the film industry as head of Vera Cruz productions, but was sacked on suspicion of communism three years later. Back in Europe he worked with Brecht on the high quality film version of the playwright's *Herr Puntila and his Servant Matti* (55). Cavalcanti also directed features for French and British TV and taught at UCLA.

ANDRE CAYATTE
French director (1909-89)

Appreciated as a director who guided his films according to strong personal beliefs, Cayatte was no great stylist. A moralist who ripped into his targets, he may well be remembered for films that railed against the French judiciary, such as *Justice is Done* (50), *We Are All Murderers* (52), *Avant le Déluge* (54) and *Le Dossier Noir* (55), the first three of which won awards at

Venice or Cannes. Most memorable is his attack on capital punishment in *We Are All Murderers.* He also made a modern version of Romeo and Juliet entitled *Les Amants de Vérone* (49).

CLAUDE CHABROL
French director (1930-)

A passionate fan of Alfred Hitchcock (qv), he was a founder of the New Wave, making his directorial debut with *Le Beau Serge* (58), his sombre view of smalltown life. *Les Cousins* (59) followed, in which the decadence of urban Paris is described through the eyes of a rural peasant. His films tend to be dispassionate observations of manipulative outsiders whose disruptive activities violently explode the calm façade of petit bourgeois propriety. However, the innocent assumptions of the working class do not come off

unscathed in his lyrical *Les Bonnes Femmes* (60). He has made profitable excursions into the commercial market with such films as *Violette Nozière* (77) and over-blown epics such as *Madame Bovary* (91). His best films include *Les Biches* and *La Femme Infidèle* (both 68). He was formerly married to Stéphane Audran (qv).

LON CHANEY
US actor (1883-1930)

Known as "The Man of a Thousand Faces" for his ability to assume multiple personalities, he was the most famous silent screen star of early horror films such as *The Hunchback of Notre Dame* (23) and *The Phantom of the Opera* (25). Born in Colorado Springs to deaf-mute parents, he used mime to communicate. Working his way up from stage hand and vaudeville comic to playing bit parts, he drifted to Hollywood where his supreme skills and handy make-up box made ▷

Unmasked: Chaney horrifies in the Phantom of the Opera

him ideal for the cripple in *The Miracle Man* (19). He made 140 films before he died of throat cancer at the age of 47. He used a variety of techniques, including 70lb of padding for the Hunchback. Working for Universal, Paramount and MGM, his most productive collaboration was with the director Tod Browning (qv), his macabre soul mateHe died just one month before the release of his first talkie, a remake of *The Unholy Three* (30). A son, Creighton (Lon Chaney Jr), made a career out of repeating his father's horror roles.

CHARLIE CHAPLIN
British clown (1889-1977)

Born in London to a runaway father and mentally ill mother, Chaplin was sent to an orphanage. In 1906 he joined Fred Karno's company and, four years later in America, signed on with Keystone. Two-reelers established him as the Little Tramp, an international icon, whose dancing rhythms of comedy changed slapstick. *Easy Street*, *The Cure* and *The Immigrant* (all 17) were Dickensian in their exaggeration of character with social comment. He broadened that comment through a string of masterpieces, *The Gold Rush* (25), a special Oscar for *The Circus* (28), *City Lights* (31), *Modern Times* (36), *The Great Dictator* (40) and *Monsieur Verdoux* (47), taking sound hesitantly in his stride. He was involved in all aspects of production, once keeping a film crew idle for months on full pay while he thought out a problem. His involvement with women led to scandal and he fell foul of McCarthyism, was kicked out of America and exiled to Switzerland with Oona, his wife. He returned to America in 1972 to receive an honorary Oscar, but only on a one-month visa ("They are still afraid of me"). His film attempts to justify himself, *Limelight* (52) and *A King in New York* (57), were moderately successful but *The Countess From Hong Kong* (66) with Marlon Brando and Sophia Loren (qqv) was a disaster. However polished the rough diamond had become, he had cutting edges ("I wouldn't go back to America if Jesus Christ was president"). The legend still looms over all cinema because his artistic aspirations have to be measured against his remarkable achievements as pantomimist, director, producer and composer. He was knighted in 1975.

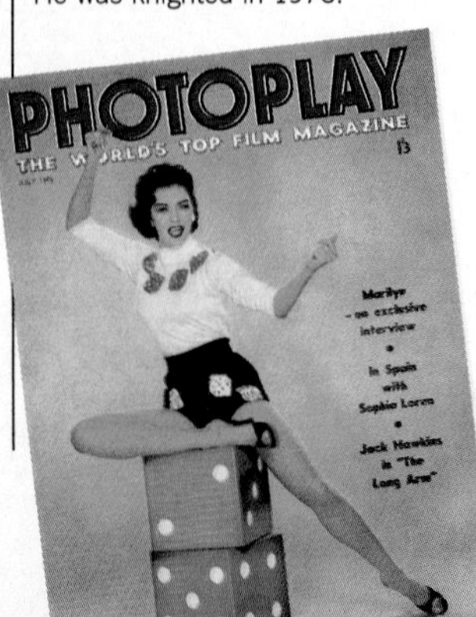

Chaplin, a comic genius who combined slapstick with acute satire, in Modern Times (36)

CYD CHARISSE
US dancer, actress (1921-)

Tula Ellice Finklea did not appear on film until 1943 when she performed under the name Lily Norwood. She had a background in ballet and was married to Nico Charisse, her ballet tutor. She signed to MGM in 1946 and was soon a regular player in its musicals and famous for her collaborations with Fred Astaire and Gene Kelly (qqv). Even after such triumphs as *Singin' in the Rain* (52), *The Band Wagon* (53), *Brigadoon* (54) and her best film *Silk Stockings* (57), Charisse could not survive the decline of the musical; in straight roles she was an actress of limited ability. Erratic cameos in the unremarkable *Warlords of Atlantis* (78) did little to keep her in the public eye.

PADDY CHAYEFSKY
US writer (1923-81)

A prolific, perceptive and passionate playwright, with many critically and commercially successful Broadway plays, notably The Tenth Man, to his credit. He owed his screenwriting career to TV, for which he wrote during the 1950s' flowering of original drama. One of his best films was *Marty* (55), a love story about two plain, lonely people, which won him the first of three Oscars. Also a writer of short stories, radio plays and novels, Chayefsky later displayed a new, cynical and satirical streak which brought him Oscars for *The Hospital* (71) and *Network* (76). He adapted his novel *Altered States* (80) for Ken Russell (qv) but, appalled by the mangling it received, disowned it and was credited as Sidney Aaron, which were his first names.

CHEN KAIGE
Chinese director (1952-)

Educated at the Beijing Film Academy, Chen graduated in 1982. His work subsequently marked a turnaround in the traditions of Chinese cinema, relying heavily on political stories and sumptuous visual design over the more literal and literary conventions of storytelling. His fir film, *Yellow Earth* (84), was a restrained portrait of Chinese culture. Chen's next two films, *Th Big Parade* (85) and *King of Children* (87), stirred ghosts of th cultural revolution, but it was his fourth feature, *Farewell My Concubine* (93), that brought hir into the international spotlight. It

ared the Palme d'Or at the 1993 nnes Film Festival with Jane mpion's (qv) *The Piano.* hough it is the weakest of en's films, it reinforced his sition as a master.

HER
S actress, singer (1946-)

ıer (Cherilyn Sarkisian) has ıded her sheepskin coat, bell-ıttoms, hit records and husband Sonny Bono for the solid gold of mainstream Hollywood. Initially dismissed by many who saw her as an out-of-time 1960s' hippie, she was given her first chance by Robert Altman (qv), who cast her in *Come Back to the Five and Dime, Jimmy Dean, Jimmy Dean* (82). Playing one of three ageing Dean fans who reunite to commemorate his death, Cher's vigorous, naturalistic style and expressive eyes coped easily with disillusion and the sadness of a woman disappointed by missed opportunities. Her propulsion into the big time with a series of credible performances enabled her to win the best actress award at Cannes for *Mask* (85), an Oscar nomination for *Silkwood* (83) and an Oscar for the romantic comedy *Moonstruck* (87). Starry vehicles such as *Suspect* (87) and *The Witches of Eastwick* (87) have kept her name in the forefront. She has even returned to pop without losing her big-screen authority.

MAURICE CHEVALIER
French actor-singer (1888-1972)

"Love the public as you would your mother," said the man whose straw boater, oo-la-la accent and pendulous lower lip were as recognisable as Chaplin's bowler and cane. He had been a cafe singer, rescued from obscurity by the famed Mistinguett to partner her in bed and on stage at the Folies Bergère. He was a Parisian success with songs such as Louise and silent film shorts such as *Trop Credule* (08). After Paramount Studios called (MGM turned him down), his most successful films in Hollywood were with Jeanette MacDonald (qv), notably *Love Me Tonight* (32), Rouben Mamoulian's (qv) enchanting comedy in which all the dialogue was in rhyme. He quit Hollywood after a row over billing with soprano Grace Moore, entertained German troops during the second world war (he denied collaboration) and returned to Hollywood for a series of musicals, including *Gigi* (58) singing Thank Heaven For Little Girls. At the 1958 Academy Awards he received a special Oscar "for his contribution to the world of entertainment for more than half a century".

CHRISTIAN-JAQUE
French director (1904-94)

Christian Maudet studied art and architecture and was a journalist and film critic before entering films as a poster and set designer. He assisted several directors and then directed *Le Bidon D'Or* (32), the first of a prolific output that made him one of France's most commercially successful film makers. His choice of material was eclectic, though he had a penchant for costume drama and is remembered internationally for the comedy swashbuckler *Fanfan la Tulipe* (52). His higher aspirations included a version of Zola's *Nana* (55) starring one of his five wives, the voluptuous, pre-Bardot idol Martine Carol (qv).

JULIE CHRISTIE
British actress (1941-)

A beautiful, strong-featured leading lady who has paralleled Alan Bates (qv) in her pursuit of the challenging and literary rather than the simply lucrative, Christie achieved fame quickly in *Billy Liar* (63), her third film. The same director, John Schlesinger (qv), put her in *Darling* (65), which won her the best actress Oscar. In *Doctor Zhivago* (65), *Fahrenheit 451* (66), *Far From the Madding Crowd* (67) and *Petulia* (68) she confirmed the stardom; in *The Go-Between*, *McCabe and Mrs Miller* (both 71) and *Don't Look Now* (73) she confirmed her acting qualities. Few films since, with the notable exceptions of *Shampoo* (75), *Heaven Can Wait* (78), *The Return of the Soldier* and *Heat and Dust* (both 83), have tempted her out of semi-retirement and away from a commitment to animal rights.

MICHAEL CIMINO
US director, screenwriter (1943-)

While there is some uncertainty surrounding Cimino's early career (his claim that he was a medical trainee with the Green Berets has been contested), he was definitely born in New York where he studied design and architecture before breaking into advertising and industrial film making. As a screenwriter, he co-wrote *Magnum Force* (73) for Clint Eastwood (qv) and made his directorial debut on Eastwood's *Thunderbolt and Lightfoot* (74). His second film as director, the harrowing Vietnam epic *The Deer Hunter*, swept the Oscars in 1978, although it was criticised in many quarters for being racist. However, Cimino's brutal, sweeping western *Heaven's Gate* (80) was a financial disaster, even though many critics recognised its artistic merit. Spectacularly behind schedule and 600% over budget, the film became a symbol of Hollywood profligacy and was the subject of Steven Bach's book Final Cut. His subsequent career has been no more auspicious, with *Year of the Dragon* (85) attacked for its unflattering portrayal of Asian-Americans and *The Sicilian* (87) running into legal trouble. In the 1990s many of Cimino's publicised projects were stillborn.

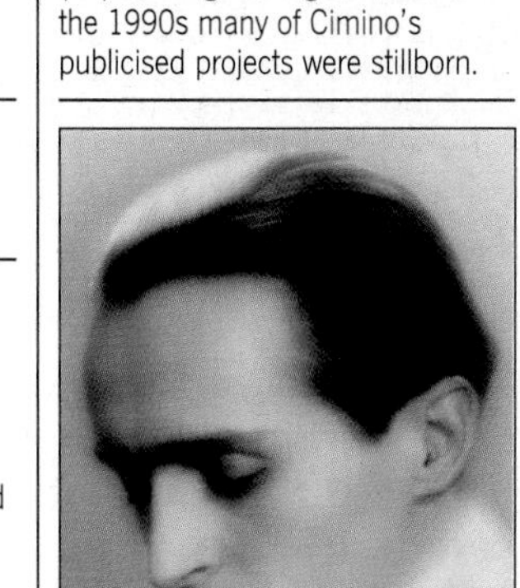

RENE CLAIR
French director (1898-1981)

René-Lucien Chomette was the precocious son of a Parisian soap merchant. He wrote and directed his own plays from the age of seven. In 1917 he volunteered to drive ambulances at the front where he was invalided out. Traumatised by his experiences he entered a Dominican monastery in 1918. He re-emerged after the armistice to write for the Paris ▷

newspaper L'Intransigent. In 1920 he changed his name to René Clair and began acting before decamping to Brussels to study cinema technique. He wrote and directed his first feature, *Paris qui dort* (24), a minor flirtation with the emerging avant-garde, but his career soared with the release of the masterly comedy, *Entr'acte* (24). Clair is credited with single-handedly reviving French cinema comedy after the first world war. A satirist of ironic originality, he presented a tragi-comic view of life. In 1935 he directed in Britain via Alexander Korda (qv), returning to France in 1938. When the Germans invaded he moved his family to America where he signed with Universal. The undistinguished *The Flame of New Orleans* (41), then *I Married a Witch* (42) and *It Happened Tomorrow* (44) precipitated his return to Paris in 1946 where he continued to work.

T E B CLARKE
British screenwriter (1907-89)

Thomas Ernest Bennett Clarke, or "Tibby" to those who knew him, was one of the greatest comedy writers in British film. Following a career as a journalist and novelist, he joined Ealing in 1943. His first original screenplay, *Hue and Cry* (47), set a tone for future Ealing comedies. Excelling at satirical, understated humour, he received his first Oscar nomination for *Passport to Pimlico* (49), but won it two years later for *The Lavender Hill Mob*. His other successes include *The Blue Lamp* (50), *The Titfield Thunderbolt* (53) and *Law and Disorder* (58). Following another Oscar nomination for his adaptation of D H Lawrence's *Sons and Lovers* (60), Clarke embarked on a number of unfinished Hollywood projects. By the 1970s he had become disillusioned with the business and turned out only two more films. His autobiography, This Is Where I Came In, was published in 1974.

JACK CLAYTON
British director (1921-95)

Born in Brighton, Clayton got a job at Denham Studios at the age of 14 as a teaboy. At the start of the

second world war he was a film editor with Warner, then served in the RAF film unit, eventually becoming its commanding officer. After the war he returned to Denham as an associate producer. His first fiction film was *The Bespoke Overcoat* (55), which won an award for short feature at the Venice Film Festival. His first full-length feature was the ground breaking *Room at the Top* (58), which opened up new horizons of realism for British cinema. He followed that with *The Innocents* (61), the atmospheric reinterpretation of Henry James's ghost story, The Turn Of The Screw. Clayton's films were few, but distinguished for their careful craftsmanship and respect for his actors. His glossy version of *The Great Gatsby* (74) was a box office disappointment. His last film, *The Lonely Passion of Judith Hearne* (87), displayed his touch.

RENE CLEMENT
French director (1913-96)

His first job in the industry was as a cameraman and his early work was documentary, apart from the Tati (qv) short *Soigne ton Gauche* (36). His eye-catching feature *La Bataille du Rail* (46) was in stark documentary style, using former resistance railwaymen to reconstruct their wartime sabotage exploits. His expertise with visual effects led Cocteau to use him as a technical adviser on *La Belle et la Bête* (46). This preoccupation and his meticulousness characterised Clément's work, from the conventional, such as *Les Maudits* (47), a U-boat thriller, to his most sensitive film, the classic *Jeux interdits* (52), a portrait of children in war that starred six-year-old Brigitte Fossey and won the foreign film Oscar. *Knave of Hearts* (54), Clément's English debut, was almost an aberration for its wit and light touch. One of his most entertaining later films is *Plein Soleil* (59), a Patricia Highsmith thriller with a star-making break for Alain Delon (qv) as Ripley.

MONTGOMERY CLIFT
US actor (1920-66)

Along with Marlon Brando (qv), Clift was an early member of the Actors Studio and a similarly intense performer. Handsome, sensitive and intelligent, he was persuaded to give up Broadway for Hollywood, and was nominated for an Oscar for his first screen role in *The Search* (48). Three other nominations followed, for *A Place in the Sun* (51), *From Here to Eternity* (53) and *Judgment at Nuremberg* (61). He specialised in introspective and self-doubting roles. Following a car accident in 1957, which scarred his good looks, there were stories of alcohol and drug abuse. In *The Misfits* (61) he co-starred with the similarly ill-starred Marilyn Monroe and Clark Gable (qqv). He played Sigmund Freud in *Freud* (62), during the making of which he underwent eye surgery. He died aged 45 of a heart attack.

GLENN CLOSE
US actress (1947-)

A stage actress, notable as the lead in the principal American production of Lloyd-Webber's Sunset Boulevard, Close is a 12th-generation New Englander whose background is in folk singing and theatre. Her film debut, *The World According to Garp* (82), won her a best supporting actress Oscar nomination as the mother of Robin Williams (qv). Further nominations followed for Lawrence Kasdan's (qv) *The Big Chill* (83), *The Natural* (84), as Robert Redford's (qv) childhood sweetheart, *Fatal Attraction* (87), as a deranged, rejected lover, and *Dangerous Liaisons* (88). *Maxie* (85) was a rare but successful comedy outing. Strikingly handsome, Close has also brought intelligence and a strong physical presence to such roles as Gertrude in *Hamlet* (90) and a Swedish opera singer – she is an accomplished lyric soprano – in *Meeting Venus* (91). She remains committed to Broadway.

HENRI-GEORGES CLOUZOT
French director (1907-77)

A painstaking worker dogged by poor health, he made relatively few films, but two of them – *The Wages of Fear* (53) and *Les Diaboliques* (54) – earned him an international reputation. He was a screenwriter from 1931 to 1933, when a stay in a sanitorium forced him out of films for five years. After the liberation he was suspended from film work for six months when *Le Corbeau*, his 1943 thriller about a poison pen writer tormenting a small town, was deemed anti-French (its production company was Nazi-backed). *Quai des Orfèvres* (47) established him as a master of suspense, but with *The Wages of Fear* and *Les Diaboliques* (both featuring his wife, Vera Clouzot), he demonstrated he was not only a solid craftsman, but also a sour dissector of the destructive power of human nature. Often compared to Hitchcock (qv) for his love of finding evil in the everyday, his vision is much bleaker. *Les Diaboliques*, with its heart-stopping bathroom scene, is cinema at its most sadistic, austere and relentless. Clouzot followed it with an acclaimed documentary on Picasso, but illness increasingly hampered his projects.

LEE J COBB
US actor (1911-76)

An imposing character actor, Cobb was a child prodigy violinist until he

broke a wrist. He ran away from home to act and after radio work his teens and youthful forays to Hollywood, settled into serious contemporary drama with New York's influential Group Theatre. Parallel to his gradual emergenc in film, Cobb created an impress body of work on Broadway, climactically, in 1949, originating the role of Willy Loman in Arthur Miller's Death of a Salesman wit performance that became theatr legend. Most familiar as a bellico big mouth, Cobb, with his hefty build and distinctive, deep voice, hit his stride on screen from his mid-thirties, appearing usually in key "heavy" support roles. He received an Oscar nomination fo his domineering patriarch Fyodor *The Brothers Karamazov* (58) an for *On the Waterfront* (54) as the inaptly named Friendly, the malevolent union racketeer. Another memorable portrayal car in *12 Angry Men* (57) as the bitte juror holding out for conviction. H Loman was filmed for TV in 196 and he appeared in the long-running western series The Virginian in the 1960s.

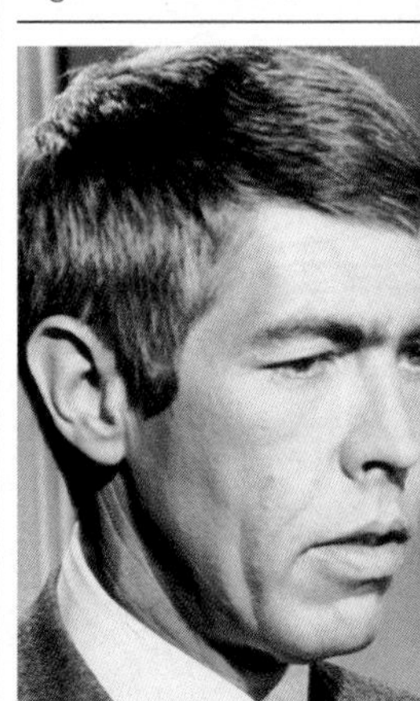

JAMES COBURN
US actor (1928-)

Tall, amiable, charming and threatening, Coburn looks like a man who would rather not use fi words where two would do. He d not disappoint in Sam Peckinpah (qv) *Pat Garrett and Billy the Kid* (73). Possessed of earnest introspection and an unsettling ambiguity, he was also cast by

Peckinpah in *Cross of Iron* (77), which filters the second world war through German eyes. Having been weaned on stage work, television commercials and live plays (he produced some strong support performances during the American golden age of live television drama), he emerged intact as a gunslinger in *The Magnificent Seven* (60). Proving equally at ease with frivolity, he romped through two Bond spoofs, *Our Man Flint* (66) and *In Like Flint* (67).

JEAN COCTEAU

French director, writer, actor (1889-1963)

He was a colossus of 20th-century French culture. Although primarily a poet, his manifold talent spread itself across publishing, theatre and cinema. His first film was *Le Sang d'un Poète* (30), an innovative, dreamlike statement which he directed, edited and narrated. He returned to a similar theme in his masterpiece *Orphée* (50), in which Jean Marais (qv) descends into the underworld, and its revisitation, *Le Testament d'Orphée* (60). He wrote and imposed his presence on *L'Eternel Retour* (43) and Bresson's (qv) *Les Dame du Bois de Boulogne* (45). In 1945 he directed *La Belle et la Bête*, an enchanting fairy story with Josette Day and Marais. He went on to write, direct and perform in *Eagle With Two Heads* and created a claustrophobic adaptation of his play, *Les Parents terribles* (both 48). Cocteau's imagery is idiosyncratic and persuasive. The most famous is the mirror through which his protagonist moves from one plane of existence to another, as though it were a penetrable membrane. Cocteau was the honorary president of the Cannes Film Festival and author of a manifesto on the art of the cinema.

La Belle et la Bête, which was directed by Jean Cocteau (inset) with Jean Marais

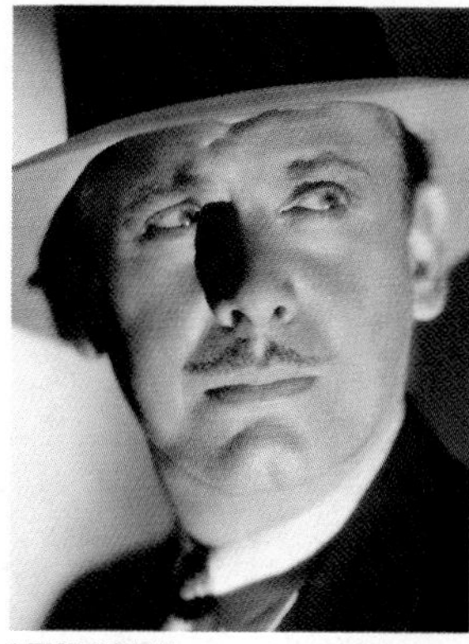

LEW CODY

US actor (1884-1934)

Born of French descent in Maine, Louis Joseph Coté was a smooth charmer, sometimes with honest intentions, or else a ne'er-do-well. He gave up medical studies to go into stock theatre and then vaudeville. He entered films with Thomas Ince's (qv) production company in 1915. *So This Is Marriage* (24), *Monte Carlo* (26) *and What a Widow* (30) all consolidated his leading man status. He married Mabel Normand (qv) after they filmed *Mickey* (18) together. Their union had a sense of sadness; both of them were doomed to die young, she first in 1930 from pneumonia and tuberculosis, and then he from heart disease.

JOEL & ETHAN COEN

US director, producer and screenwriters (1955- and 1958-)

The Coen brothers' partnership, forged in Super-8 film making when they were children, is unique in contemporary American cinema. Joel, the director, studied film at New York University and worked as an editor. Ethan, the producer, graduated in philosophy at Princeton before joining his brother to write screenplays. Their debut, *Blood Simple* (84), was an audacious *noir* homage made on a small budget that aroused extravagant admiration among cinéastes. It set the tone for their subsequent films: the frantic, odd-ball comedy *Raising Arizona* (87), the moody, labyrinthine gangster fable *Miller's Crossing* (90) and ▷

the bizarre view of studio-era Hollywood and artistic angst, *Barton Fink* (91), which won the grand prize at Cannes. *The Hudsucker Proxy* (94), was a visually dazzling, style-conscious project full of references to comic classics and *Fargo* (96) a droll account of a murder in wintry Minnesota.

HARRY COHN
US film mogul (1891-1958)

He was an autocratic despot with a love for films. As the all-powerful president of Columbia he guided it successfully through the talkies, the Depression and the onslaught of TV. He gauged the popular appeal of his films by the time it took him to get restless and "scratch his backside". The second son of an immigrant tailor, he was a pool hustler and song plugger, then Carl Laemmle's (qv) secretary at Universal before he and his brother Jack joined with Joseph Brandt to form Columbia. After Brandt's departure and Jack's failed attempt to secure control, he relegated his brother to the New York office. Said to be the founder of the "casting couch" and the "meanest man in Hollywood", Cohn was unstinting when it came to promoting Rita Hayworth (qv) and Kim Novak and kept many philanthropic activities secret. Combining his financial acumen with the popular sentiments of Frank Capra's (qv) homespun tales and the zany antics of the Three Stooges, in his time he produced many classics for Columbia, including *Platinum Blonde* (31) and *It Happened One Night* (34), for which posterity can be grateful.

CLAUDETTE COLBERT
US actress (1905-96)

Born in Paris, Claudette Lily Chauchoin arrived in New York at the age of six. She wanted to be a fashion designer, but instead turned to acting, making her stage debut in 1923. She played leads on Broadway from 1925-27 and entered films in Frank Capra's (qv) silent and unsuccessful *For the Love of Mike* (27). She blossomed in talkies such as Cecil B DeMille's (qv) *The Sign of the Cross* (32) bathing in asses' milk and as

Colbert came to Britain to star in The Planter's Wife

Cleopatra (34). Capra provided her with a comic hit and a best actress Oscar for *It Happened One Night* (34), with Colbert as a madcap heiress and Clark Gable (qv) as a hard-boiled newspaperman. Although she played dramatic roles with conviction, receiving an Oscar nomination for her American wartime housewife in *Since You Went Away* (44), she excelled in comedy as an attractive, witty, resourceful heroine. She was brilliant in Preston Sturges's (qv) sublime 1942 screwball masterpiece *The Palm Beach Story* and her ultimate hit was *The Egg and I* (47), in which a sophisticated New Yorker marries a chicken farmer. Exacting with lighting cameramen, she always insisted that her face be photographed from the left.

JOAN COLLINS
British actress, producer (1933-)

A beautiful leading lady and now the famously well-preserved survivor of three marriages and several career gaps, Collins went from Rada to film with barely a pause. From nymphette, as in *Lady Godiva Rides Again* (51) and *Cosh Boy* (53), in Britain she went to Hollywood and temptress roles in *Land of the Pharaohs* and *The Virgin Queen* (both 55), and thereafter flitted back and forth for the likes of *Sea Wife* (57), with

Richard Burton (qv), *Esther and the King* (60) and *The Road to Hong Kong* (62). Married to Anthony Newley, she gallantly co-starred in his *Can Heironymus Merkin Ever Forget Mercy Humppe and Find True Happiness?* (69). The 1970s brought diminished status via horror and exploitation films, notably *Tales from the Crypt* (72), *Alfie Darling* (75), *The Stud* (78) and *The Bitch* (79). Television revived her career, thanks mainly to Dynasty and mini-series, which she also produced. Most recently she co-starred with Steven Berkoff in his film *Decadence* (94).

RONALD COLMAN
British actor (1891-1958)

Born in Richmond, Surrey, he left school at 16 and worked for a steamship company. He was invalided out of the army in 1916 and became an actor. His handsome profile elevated him quickly to leading player and he moved to America, where Lillian Gish (qv) chose him to play opposite her in *The White Sister* (23). He quickly developed into a popular romantic lead and one of the great stars of the silent era. He

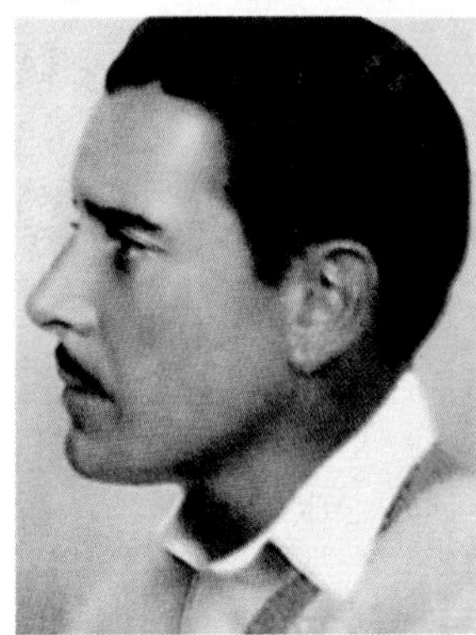

and Vilma Banky (qv) made a number of films together, the most popular of which was *Beau Geste* (26). His pleasant, well-modulated speaking voice and distinctive, clear diction made him a natural for the talkies when many of his contemporaries were forced into early retirement. In the 1930s he epitomised a gentlemanly hero in Ford's (qv) *Arrowsmith* (31), as Sydney Carton in *A Tale of Two Cities* (35), in Capra's (qv) romantic fantasy *Lost Horizon* (37) and in a dual role in *The Prisoner of Zenda* (37). Wartime audiences lapped up his performances as an amnesiac married to Greer Garson (qv) in *Random Harvest* (42) for which he was nominated for an Oscar. He finally won an Oscar in 1948 for *A Double Life*.

CHESTER CONKLIN
US actor (1888-1971)

Born in Oskaloosa, Iowa, this walrus-faced slapstick comedian always worked in the shadow of Chaplin (qv). He began his career in a variety of jobs, vaudeville and circus clowning before joining Mack

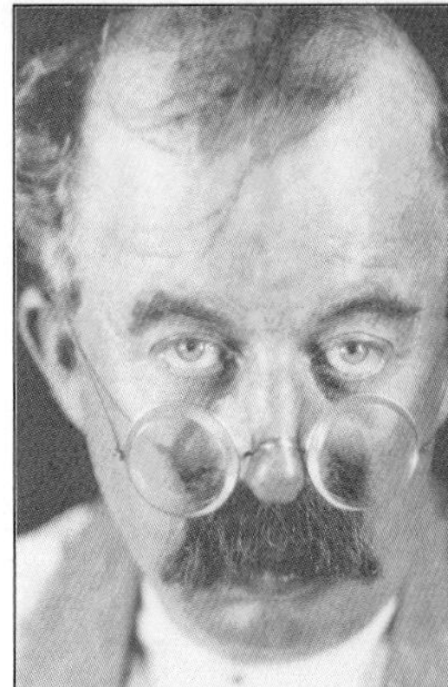

Sennett's (qv) Keystone Cops in 1913, where he was instantly recognisable. He worked with Ma Swain on the Ambrose-Walrus comedy shorts, produced the Sunshine Comedies at Fox and worked with W C Fields (qv), usually in supporting roles, until t 1950s, when his crude comedy routines had gone out of date. He was in Von Stroheim's (qv) *Greed* (24) and Chaplin's (qv) *The Grea Dictator* (40). At 77 he married h fourth wife, a 65-year-old resident of his old folk's nursing home.

EAN CONNERY
ritish actor (1930-)

ıe most durable (and the highest ıid) British star since the 1950s, ɔnnery retains his dignity even in s worst films. Tall (6ft 3in), uscular and charismatic, he ldom disguises his Scottish ogue, even when playing reigners. In fact, it is his souciance and lack of vanity that em to endear audiences. Born in dinburgh to a lorry driver and a eaning woman, Connery joined e navy at the age of 15 and did d jobs before drifting into acting. y the early 1960s he had ɔ-starred in a handful of minor ms when he was chosen to play)7 in *Dr No* (62), the first in the ɔpular James Bond series. In all, e played Bond incomparably in even films. His career seemed to e winding down in the early 980s when his role as an Irish ɔp in Brian De Palma's (qv) hit *he Untouchables* (87) won him an scar and re-established his ɔmmercial viability and star atus. Since then, he has starred the immensely successful *diana Jones and the Last rusade* (89) and *The Rock* (96).

CHARD CONTE
'S actor (1914-75)

ıe son of a barber, he emerged ɔm Jersey City and had various ckel-and-dime jobs before ɹdging towards showbusiness as performing waiter in Connecticut. ia Kazan (qv) saw him and gave him a scholarship to the Neighborhood Playhouse in New York. The result was an almost non-stop film career. Often looking most dangerous in silence, Conte will be remembered for *Call Northside 777* and *Cry of the City* (both 48). In the first, he plays a convicted killer whom crusader James Stewart (qv) wants to free; in the second, as a wounded gangster on the run, he is the epitome of squalid city life. He was the scheming Barzini in *The Godfather* (72).

GARY COOPER
US actor (1901-61)

He epitomised the stoical, handsome hero, the shy, awkward man of few words, who called himself Mr Average Joe American. Contrary to the popular image he was not just a monosyllabic hunk. Apart from his inspired Oscar-winning portrayal of the sheriff in *High Noon* (52), he proved equally adept at light comedy in Capra's (qv) *Mr Deeds Goes to Town* (36) and dramatic understatement in Borzage's (qv) *Farewell to Arms* (32). His performance so impressed Ernest Hemingway, its author, that he insisted Cooper play the hero of *For Whom the Bell Tolls* (43). Frank James Cooper was born in Montana of British parents and dubbed Gary after the city in Indiana. He studied agriculture and became a rancher before working as an extra in many silent westerns such as *The Thundering Herd* (25). He first gained star status in the talkies with *The Virginian* (29), followed by *Morocco* (30) opposite Marlene Dietrich (qv) and numerous other hits in a career that included some 95 films, finishing with *The Naked Edge* (61) alongside Deborah Kerr (qv). Knowing he was dying of cancer, the Academy awarded him a special Oscar in 1960.

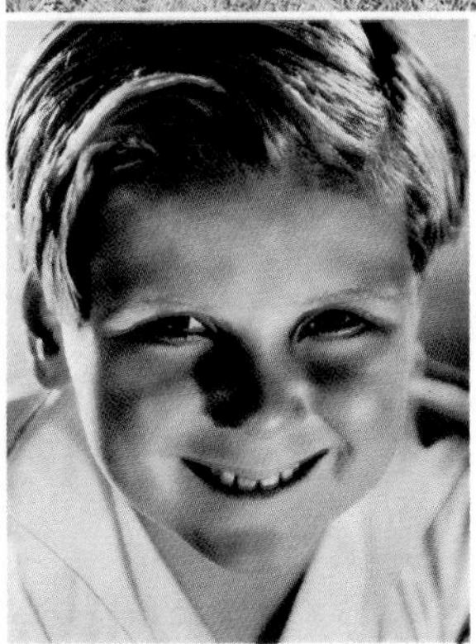

JACKIE COOPER
US actor (1921-)

Among the male stars of the 1930s, Cooper's cute-tough stance made him an acceptable film brat for the *Our Gang* series. He was nominated for the Oscar as *Skippy* (31), directed by Norman Taurog, his uncle, and was then a droll contrast to Wallace Beery (qv) in *The Champ* (31) and *The Bowery* (33). His Jim Hawkins in *Treasure Island* (34) was memorable casting. He became a television producer and played the Daily Planet editor in all four *Superman* films (78-87).

MERIAN C COOPER & ERNEST B SCHOEDSACK
US directors (Cooper 1893-1973, Schoedsack 1893-1979)

In the pioneering days of the cinema, few embraced its spirit so wholeheartedly as Cooper and Schoedsack. Making what they called "natural dramas", they forged the way for documentary film production, making up the rules as they went along. Following service in the first world war, they met in Poland. While working as a reporter, Cooper aided the Poles in their struggle against Russia, was imprisoned for spying and barely escaped with his life. Meanwhile, Schoedsack, posing as a newsreel cameraman, was helping Poles to escape. In 1925 they joined forces and braved hazardous mountain terrain to direct *Grass* (25), a chronicle of the migration of Persian nomads in search of grazing. The film was a great success and a landmark in documentary film making. In China they directed *Chang* (27), staging a spectacular elephant stampede. Subsequently, they brought their unique sense of derring-do to a number of exotic adventure films and collaborated on *The Four Feathers* (29) and their masterpiece, *King Kong* (33) (qv).

FRANCIS FORD COPPOLA
US director, writer and producer (1939-)

An influential producer of entrepreneurial spirit, he is a wildly erratic writer and director whose films swing between the epic and the intimate, huge success and abysmal failure. A UCLA film school graduate, he worked for Roger Corman (qv) in the early 1960s and was one of the group of directors dubbed the "movie brats" that included De Palma, Spielberg, Scorsese and George Lucas (qqv), whose *American Graffiti* (73) he produced. Coppola turned out to be the most recklessly ambitious and least consistent of the group. He dropped the name Ford in the 1970s, the decade of *The Conversation* (74), one of his best small-scale films, but later resumed it. His achievements remain the Oscar-winning and monumentally profitable *Godfather* trilogy, his Vietnam war epic, *Apocalypse Now* (79), and the cult film *Rumble Fish* (83). His Zoetrope studios, where he made the critically and commercially catastrophic *One From the Heart* (82), went bankrupt in 1990. He is the son of Carmine Coppola, the composer, the actress Talia Shire's brother and the actor Nicolas Cage's (qv) uncle.

ROGER CORMAN
US director, producer (1926-)

After running errands at Twentieth Century Fox he pursued a career as a literary agent before returning to film in 1953 as a writer and producer. His directing debut came two years later and began an apparently unstoppable roll of low-budget projects which he infused with a mischievous sense of humour and crafted with an economical hand. The best of these were the horror pictures he produced in the 1960s, particularly those adapted from the work of Edgar Allan Poe, many of which starred Vincent Price (qv). His influence was waning by the 1980s and none of the features he was involved in after *Battle Beyond the Stars* (80) found any kind of success. He is, however, regarded as one of the original motivating forces in the American cinema.

CONSTANTIN COSTA-GAVRAS
Greek director (1933-)

A rebel who moved from Greece to France where he was apprenticed to socially aware film directors, ▷

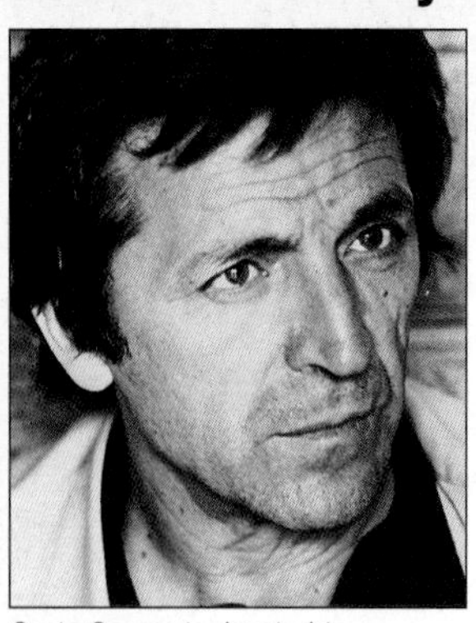

Costa-Gavras is devoted to combining the political and the personal in mainstream suspense. Only his debut, *The Sleeping Car Murders* (65), is the exception, a Hollywood-style atmospheric hunt for a killer. He made his name internationally with the Oscar-winning *Z* (68), a denunciation of the Greek junta. He was invited to direct *The Godfather* (72), but declined on the grounds that it glorified criminals. He did not make an American film until *Missing* (82), the quest by an American conservative father to discover the truth behind his activist son's disappearance in Chile, which won an Oscar for his screenplay. He has never duplicated the success of these, but has persisted in setting thrillers against such backdrops as the Palestinian troubles, the white supremacist movement in America and the investigation of war crimes.

KEVIN COSTNER
US actor, director and producer (1955-)

One of contemporary Hollywood's most bankable stars, it took Costner less than 10 years to rise from bit-part player, with one line in *Frances* (82) and as a corpse in *The Big Chill* (83), to a pre-eminent place in Hollywood's hierarchy. His breakthrough was *The Untouchables* (87), in which he played the gang-busting Eliot Ness, although the Oscar went to Sean Connery (qv). *No Way Out* (87) and two sympathetic roles in *Bull Durham* (88) and *Field of Dreams* (89) led to his debut as director, co-producer and leading man in *Dances With Wolves* (90), a labour of devotion which won seven Oscars and was a box-office smash. Further winning performances in *Robin Hood: Prince of Thieves, JFK* (both 91), co-starring with Whitney Houston in *The Bodyguard* (92), which he also co-produced, and Clint Eastwood's (qv) *A Perfect World* (93) have kept his status high, but *Wyatt Earp* (94) was a disappointment and *Waterworld* which, in production in 1995, threatened to be the costliest film ever.

JOSEPH COTTEN
US actor (1905-94)

After working on Broadway with Orson Welles (qv) and co-starring there with Katharine Hepburn (qv) in The Philadelphia Story, the tall, richly and quietly imposing leading man moved into films also courtesy of Welles, who featured him in his own first three films: *Citizen Kane* (41), *The Magnificent Ambersons* (42) and *Journey into Fear* (43). He worked again with Welles on *Othello* (52) and *Touch of Evil* (58) and finally in *F for Fake* (74). Although any career which also included distinguished roles in *Shadow of a Doubt* (43), *Gaslight* (44), *Portrait of Jennie* (48) and *The Third Man* (49) cannot be described as unsuccessful (he continued working until the 1980s, including the calamitous *Heaven's Gate* in 1981), the previous three decades had seen a considerable decline in the quality of the films in which he appeared.

TOM COURTENAY
British actor (1937-)

Courtenay was born in Hull and educated at University College, London, and Rada. He began acting at the Old Vic and came to notice in Billy Liar at the Cambridge Theatre in 1961. He entered films with *The Loneliness of the Long Distance Runner* (62). His sparse realism and impeccable northern credentials perfectly suited the gritty, working-class dramas of the time. *Billy Liar* followed (63) and Courtenay won a best supporting actor Oscar nomination for *Doctor Zhivago* (65) and was again nominated for *The Dresser* (83). A seemingly insecure man, he has never appeared comfortable with fame. He has recently had a stage renaissance, and won best actor awards, for his one-man *tour de force* of a Soviet dissident writer and alcoholic in Moscow Stations.

RAOUL COUTARD
French cinematographer, director (1924-)

A highly skilled and versatile technician, Coutard was instrumental in shaping the visual style of the French New Wave. A stills photographer for magazines such as Life, he graduated to film as a newsreel, documentary and combat cameraman, switching to feature films in 1959. He brought such techniques as hand-held cameras and rapid panning to bear on more than a dozen films with Jean-Luc Godard (qv), starting with *A Bout de Souffle* (60). He also worked with Truffaut (qv), notably on *Jules et Jim* (61), where he introduced stills and newsreel sequences into the flow of imagery. He subsequently demonstrated his ability with more conventional work for Costa-Gavras, Jacques Demy (qqv) and others. In 1970 he made *Hoa-Binh,* the first of three features he directed, but did not photograph. The tale of a North Vietnamese family destroyed by the war, it was a vivid evocation of a place where he had lived for some years. In 1986 he photographed *Max Mon Amour,* his penultimate assignment before his retirement.

NOEL COWARD
British director, writer and actor (1899-1973)

Coward came to films with a stage reputation for dangerous comedy

and clipped emotions, but spoke patriotically for Britain with *In Which We Serve* (42), which won him a special Oscar. He co-directed with David Lean (qv) and then re-wrote his play Still Life as *Brief Encounter* (45) for Lean, which bared emotions but not bodies. While his stage career flourished, his interest in films dwindled to notable cameos in *Around the World in 80 Days* (56) and *Bunny Lake is Missing* (65). Best of all was his imprisoned criminal mastermind for *The Italian Job* (69), a role nearly as joyous as the spymaster meeting Alec Guinness (qv) in a gents' lavatory in *Our Man in Havana* (60).

WES CRAVEN
US director (1939-)

Craven's fascination with dreams has produced significant film nightmares, notably the lucrative *Nightmare on Elm Street* series he originated in 1984, making the razor-fingered Freddy Krueger an anti-hero of the 1980s. Craven came to film from a background in philosophy and literature, abandoning teaching humanities to make his debut with a pornographic film. He established his reputation with the controversial cult film *Last House on the Left* (72), reputedly inspired by Bergman's (qv) *Virgin Spring* (60), an orgy of rape, torture and revenge. *The Hills Have Eyes* (78), the terrorising of an American family by flesh-eating backwoodsmen, is regarded by horror aficionados as the prime example of Craven's satire. He surrendered control of the *Nightmare* sequels to make other independent chillers until reclaiming Krueger in *Wes Craven's New Nightmare* (94).

JOAN CRAWFORD
US actress (1904-77)

Born in San Antonio, Texas, Crawford was at great pains to hide her chequered early life, which included stints as a fan dancer, waitress and porno flick actress. As Lucille Le Sueur she travelled as a dancer to Chicago and Detroit, ending up in New York where she was spotted by an MGM executive. The studio took her to Hollywood where she was signed to it for the next 18 years, making her screen debut as a chorus member in *Pretty Ladies* (25). Crawford went on to exemplify the quintessential film star. An awesome industry cat fighter, she fashioned herself through struggle, intrigue and a backbone of steel into the perfect embodiment of glamour, toughness and simmering sexuality. Her fan magazine heyday came with *Paid* (30), *Dance Fools Dance* and *Possessed* (both 31), *Letty Lynton* (32) and *Grand Hotel* (32). She appeared with Clark Gable (qv) in such hits as *Dancing Lady* (33), *Forsaking All Others* (34) and *Love*

Crawford fought for fame but died a miserable alcoholic

the Run (36). Her finest critical od ironically coincided with a in her star status from 1939 to 2, when she made such sics as *A Woman's Face* (41), glorious *Mildred Pierce* (45), for ch she won the best actress ar, and *Possessed* (47), for ch she was nominated. She fell of favour in the 1950s, but her eer revived again with Whatever ppened to *Baby Jane?* (62), in ch she starred with her arch- Bette Davis (qv). There owed more low budget horror s. Latterly she became a use and alcoholic. She was ried four times but died a ely woman in 1977.

ARLES CRICHTON
itish director (1910-)

his twenties he began working in British film industry as an tor on films such as *Things to me* (36) and *Elephant Boy* (37) ore his first directing job, the rt *The Young Veterans* (41). He s working for Ealing by 1944, nenting his reputation as an ute and light-handed comedy ector on such successful and luring movies as *Hue and Cry*), *The Lavender Hill Mob* (51) d *The Titfield Thunderbolt* (53). a result of his work during ing's golden age from the 1940s the early 1950s, he is now ognised as one of Britain's most portant post-war directors. In 88, John Cleese was keen to ng an Ealing flavour to his nedy *A Fish Called Wanda*, and ked Crichton to direct. It proved be an international success ically and commercially.

ICHAEL CRICHTON
director, screenwriter and oducer (1942-)

ctor, anthropologist, novelist, vel writer, biographer, film ector, producer, screenwriter and mputer wizard, Crichton is a wering 6ft 9in and enormously ccessful. A graduate of Harvard, had written several novels nder the pseudonym John nge) by the time he earned his). Before he was 30 years old e *Andromeda Strain* (71), the t book published under his own

name, was a bestseller and film. It inspired him to direct a television version of his novel Binary, which led to his directing such popular films as *Westworld* (73) and *Coma* (78). Credited with inventing the "techno-thriller", Crichton's greatest successes as a writer include *Rising Sun* (93), *Jurassic Park* (93) and *Disclosure* (94).

JOHN CROMWELL
US director (1888-1979)

He became a hit on Broadway as an actor, producer and director and left behind an impressive track record when he moved to Hollywood in 1928. Having acted in *The Dummy* (29), he soon dug himself in as a director and brought a starry gloss to many studio-bound films. *Of Human Bondage* (34) was the launch pad for Bette Davis (qv), who played a wonderfully over-cooked waitress; in his definitive version of *The Prisoner of Zenda* (37) Ronald Colman (qv) swashes and buckles like no other; and for *Abe Lincoln in Illinois* (40) Cromwell extracted a performance of subtle power from Raymond Massey.

DAVID CRONENBERG
Canadian director, screenwriter (1943-)

Shivers (75), *Rabid* (77) and *The Brood* (79) made him a cult hero among youthful admirers of gruesome horror films, but he broke through to mass popularity without softening his approach with *Scanners* (81), *Videodrome* (82) and *The Dead Zone* (83). His remake of *The Fly* (86) was notable for its compassion. His depth as a writer was underlined in *Dead Ringers* (88) and he was a popular

choice to adapt and direct William Burroughs's "unfilmable" book *Naked Lunch* (91). His skill with more mainstream material has not yet been established, and *Crash* (96) scandalised many pro-censorship campaigners.

Crosby made a career out of crooning and wisecracking

HUME CRONYN
Canadian actor, screenwriter (1911-)

Born in London, Ontario, the son of a politician, he is an alumnus of McGill University, Montreal, and the Mozarteum, Salzburg, Cronyn has enjoyed parallel careers in the theatre, where he has written, acted, directed and produced, and on the screen, making his debut in Hitchcock's (qv) *Shadow of a Doubt* (43)as the neighbour obsessed with murder stories. In the previous year he married the British actress Jessica Tandy (qv). Until her death in 1994 they were an enduring team on stage, television and on film. Cronyn, small and fiercely intelligent, has played a broad range of character roles, from loathsome villains, such as the power-crazed sadistic prison warden in *Brute Force* (47), to the feisty pensioner in *Cocoon* (85). He is perhaps at his finest in *Hamlet* (64), a record of Gielgud's (qv) Broadway production in which Burton (qv) plays the prince and Cronyn is Polonius, investing the

role with extraordinary depth. He appeared as Jessica Tandy's lover in one of her last films, *Camille* (95) a poignant farewell to a fine friendship.

BING CROSBY
US actor, singer (1903-77)

Harry Lillis Crosby ("Bing" came from a comic strip) started singing at Gonzaga University, Spokane, Washington. He joined the Paul Whiteman Orchestra and as one of the Rhythm Boys acquired national popularity through radio. Crosby crooned with the trio in *King Of Jazz* (30), a portmanteau of Whiteman numbers. He went solo and was signed by Mack Sennett (qv) to appear in featurettes. His radio show and recordings established him as America's top musical star and Paramount gave him roles that made the most of his easygoing persona and calculated ordinariness. In 1940 he was teamed with Bob Hope (qv) in the first of the Road films *(Road to Singapore, Zanzibar, Morocco, etc)* and in 1942 recorded the most popular song of all time, Irving Berlin's (qv) White Christmas for *Holiday Inn*. He won an Oscar portraying a priest in *Going My Way* (44). Crosby, with Sinatra and Presley (qqv) was one of the three great male vocalists of the century and although he had perfect pitch could not read a note. He died playing golf.

TOM CRUISE
US actor (1962-)

The former Thomas Cruise Mapother IV is now rated as Hollywood's most bankable star. Even his "flops", *Cocktail* (88) and *Far and Away* (92), made money. He started acting at high school, moved to New York and landed a bit part in Zeffirelli's *Endless Love* and a plum role in *Taps* (both 81). Since then he has powered his way past his fellow "Brat Packers": in *Legend* (85), *Top Gun* and *The Color of Money* (both 86), *Rain Man* (88), *A Few Good Men* (92), *The Firm* (93) and *Interview With a Vampire* (94). He received an Oscar nomination for his impassioned Vietnam veteran in *Born on the Fourth of July* (89). He emerged as an ideal hero for the 1980s: tough but clean-living, a hustler with a heart. His transformation from down-at-heel teenager into multi-millionaire screen idol before he was 30 years old is a yuppie version of the American dream, the acceptable face of modern narcissism.

BILLY CRYSTAL
US actor (1947-)

Raised in New York City, where his family owned the Commodore jazz label and store, Crystal showed a knack for stand-up comedy before entering college. He began by honing a stage act that illustrated his gifts for mimicry and satire. He came to national prominence on television in the early 1980s, notably in the series Soap and Saturday Night Live. His film career took off with *The Princess Bride* (87), which began his association with Rob Reiner (qv), the director. Crystal is a gifted comedy actor. His films include, *Throw Momma From The Train* (87), *When Harry Met Sally . . .* (89), *City Slickers* (91), *Mr Saturday Night*, also directing (92), and a cameo in the heavy metal music satire *This Is Spinal Tap* (84). He co-wrote the 1991 and 1992 Academy Awards television specials. A human rights activist, Crystal has co-hosted many Comic Relief benefits on HBO.

GEORGE CUKOR
US director (1899-1983)

Katharine Hepburn (qv) swore by, and sometimes at, Cukor, whose reputation for handling temperamental women stars was as legendary as it was legitimate. "Treat them as friends," was his much-quoted key to success with such edgy stars as Jean Harlow (qv) in *Dinner at Eight* (33), Joan Crawford (qv) in *A Woman's Face* (41) and Ingrid Bergman (qv) in *Gaslight* (44). Most of all, though, there was Hepburn, with whom he had many successes. He did not get on with some men, notably Clark Gable (qv) who, fearing his masculinity was under threat, had him fired from *Gone With the Wind*. Cukor won an Oscar for *My Fair Lady* (64), but it should have been earlier for coaxing Judy Garland (qv) to finish *A Star Is Born* (54).

JAMIE LEE CURTIS
US actress (1958-)

The daughter of Tony Curtis and the actress Janet Leigh (qqv), Curtis has repeatedly reshaped her career over a bumpy road to the top. Dropping out of college at 18, she took small TV roles before landing a regular part in the series Operation Petticoat, based on the 1959 comedy that starred her father. Her first film, *Halloween* (78), opened to enormous acclaim, launching Curtis on the next leg of her career. Displaying a talent for playing feisty heroines in situations of extreme peril, she was dubbed "The Queen of Scream" and appeared in a handful of low-budget horror films. Then, positioned on a downward path of exploitation, she exhibited an unexpected erotic attraction in *Trading Places* (83) and was an overnight sex symbol. Curtis fortified this image as an aerobics instructor in the ill-fated *Perfect* (85) before revealing a keen comedy instinct in *A Fish Called Wanda* (88). More recently, she starred with Arnold Schwarzenegger (qv) in *True Lies* (94).

TONY CURTIS
US actor (1925-)

The only Hollywood star to have a haircut named after him, Bernard Schwartz was the son of a former amateur actor from Hungary who became a tailor in the Bronx. Straightened out by a probation officer when he was 12, he spent the war serving in submarines and then attended the New York School of Dramatic Art. He established a reputation as a swashbuckling beefcake star in *The Prince Who Was a Thief* (51) after bit-part appearances prompted an avalanche of female fan mail, which persuaded Universal to recognise his potential. Forced to learn his trade on the set with the likes of Burt Lancaster (qv) in *Sweet Smell of Success* (57), he gained an Oscar nomination for his part as a racist convict chained to Sidney Poitier (qv) in *The Defiant Ones* (58). His best performances include Billy Wilder's (qv) sublime comedy *Some Like It Hot* (59), where he courted Marilyn Monroe (qv) by impersonating Cary Grant (qv), and his powerful portrayal of the schizophrenic *Boston Strangler* (68). In recent years he has been restricted to cameo appearances and excursions into TV.

MICHAEL CURTIZ
Hungarian director (1888-1962)

Born in Budapest, the son of a Jewish architect and an opera

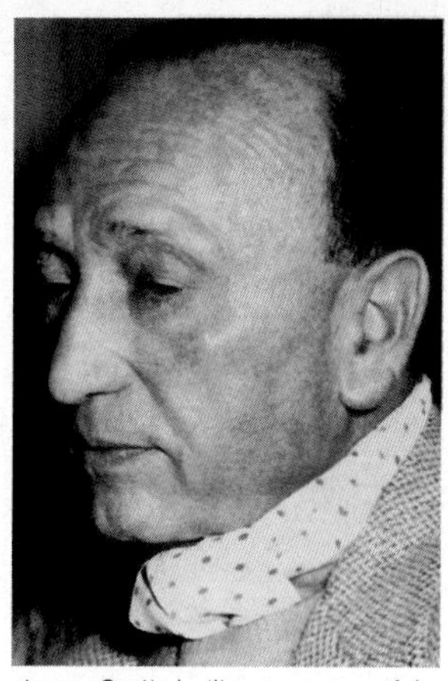

singer, Curtiz built up a successful career as a film maker in Hungary, Austria and Germany before moving to Hollywood in 1926 at the bidding of Harry Warner. He was to become one of Warner's most prolific directors, making more than 100 features between 1927 and 1953. His range encompassed *Captain Blood* (35), which established a swashbuckling persona for Errol Flynn (qv); the archetypal East Side drama, *Angels With Dirty Faces* (38); the historical pageantry of *The Private Lives of Elizabeth and Essex* (39); the patriotic musical biography, *Yankee Doodle Dandy* (42); the eternal espionage romance, *Casablanca* (42); and the noir-influenced *Mildred Pierce* (45). Curtiz was a polished studio director, a craftsman whose work entertained millions and is now grudgingly respected by historians. He was legendarily fierce on the set and employed an exotic vocabulary. David Niven (qv) called his memoirs after a Curtiz order heard during *Charge of the Light Brigade* (36), "Bring on the empty horses".

PETER CUSHING
British actor (1913-94)

An actor whose quiet English decency was dramatically at odds with his unsettling screen image, Cushing will for ever be joined at the hip to Hammer Films. So un-dangerous in reality that he seemed barely capable of assertion, he lived a life devoted to bookshops, contemplation and his beloved Kent coast. Instantly recognised for his bleak, skeletal looks, Cushing understood that he had been creatively strangled by the narrow noose of horror. He di appear in the Olivier (qv) *Hamlet* (48), but complained: "If I played Hamlet they'd call it a horror film He was good at gliding across the screen with sinister ease and was cornerstone of Hammer's succes He first stepped out in *The Curse of Frankenstein* (57) before bringing a telling ambiguity to the character in *The Revenge of Frankenstein* (58). By *Frankenste*

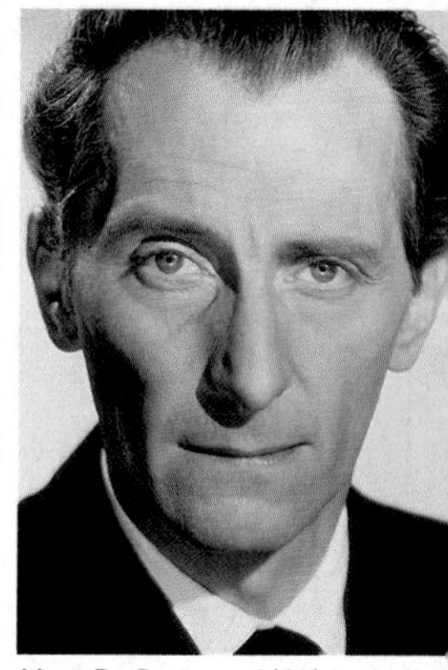

Must Be Destroyed (69) he had imbued the role with an icy arrogance. Eerily convincing as th prophetic doctor in *Dr Terror's House of Horrors* (64), he also excelled at Sherlock Holmes's lea determination in *The Hound of th Baskervilles* (59).

PAUL CZINNER
Hungarian director (1890-1972)

Czinner began as a theatre direct in Vienna, making one film before settling in Germany where the love drama, *Nju* (24), starring Elisabet Bergner (qv), set the tone for his career. He married Bergner and dedicated himself to enshrining he fragile talents, notably in *Der Träumende Mond* (32). He starre her as *Catherine the Great* (34) and allowed his camera to eclipse Olivier's (qv) Orlando in favour of her Rosalind in *As You Like It* (36) Bergner won an Oscar nominatio for his romantic weepie, *Escape M Never* (35). In the mid-1950s Czinner transferred his interests to capturing live opera and ballet performances on film.

Douglas Fairbanks Jr, Elisabeth Bergner, Czinner and Alexander Korda during filming of Catherine the Grea

ILLEM DAFOE
S actor (1955-)

:h his angular cheekbones, ense eyes and sepulchral tures, he has the ideal haunted k to play demented delinquents, umatised, angst-ridden ividuals and manic men with a ssion. His looks were used to ir best effect in his car-winning role as a good-guy geant in *Platoon* (86), the ually frustrated Messiah in *The st Temptation of Christ* (88), a mpaigning anti-racist FBI officer *Mississippi Burning* (88), evil carnate in *Wild at Heart* (90) and lrug dealer in *Light Sleeper* (92). rn in Wisconsin, he dropped out university and went to Paris with touring group Theatre X, before urning to New York's SoHo trict where he became an active ember of the Wooster Group, an perimental ensemble directed by wife Elizabeth Lecompte. He efly became a cult figure, but s lately been less prominent.

EBE DANIELS
S actress (1901-71)

aniels was making short films at e age of nine and continued to appear while at school. She became a leading lady of silent films first with Hal Roach (qv), for whom she made 200 two-reel comedies opposite Harold Lloyd (qv) and the droopy-moustached Harold "Snub" Pollard, and from 1919 under contract to Paramount. There she played leading roles of all kinds, but specialised in light, mischievous but sympathetic parts. Her first talking role in *Rio Rita* (29) also revealed her singing voice, later featured in *42nd Street* (33), in which she is the leading lady whose injury gives chorus girl Ruby Keeler (qv) her big break. In 1930 she married Ben Lyon, her co-star in *Alias French Gertie* (30) and several other films. They moved to England in 1936, establishing a successful light comedy career on radio and the stage with the wartime Hi Gang! and later Life with the Lyons. Subsequent films were radio show spin-offs.

Daniels' integrity made him Garbo's favourite cameraman

WILLIAM H DANIELS
US cinematographer (1895-1970)

His career spanned more than half a century (with almost 20 years spent at MGM). Flexible, sensitive and innovative, Daniels placed his camera at the service of the subject, the director's intention and the stars, never seeking to dominate or distort with imagery. An artist and craftsman of rare distinction who had worked on Von Stroheim's (qv) silents, he became known as Garbo's (qv) cameraman. He earned her total trust and enhanced her special quality in all her best films. Through the decades he fulfilled the visual requirements of material ranging from Shakespeare to comedy, drama, musicals, westerns, action-adventure and thrillers, and worked with many of Hollywood's foremost stars and directors. In 1948 he won a well-deserved Oscar for his work on Dassin's (qv) *The Naked City*.

JOE DANTE
US director (1948-)

A prominent director in the first wave of cine-literate American film makers, he graduated from the ▷

Philadelphia College of Art in 1968 and worked for a time as a film critic before becoming Roger Corman's (qv) trailer editor in 1973. It was under Corman's guidance that he broke into film making, directing his first feature, *Hollywood Boulevard*, in 1976 and editing another Corman production, Ron Howard's (qv) *Grand Theft Auto* (77). He scored his biggest directorial hit in 1984 with the mischievous horror-comedy *Gremlins*. The film embodies Dante's style. Littered with cinematic allusions – to Capra (qv) and 1950s sci-fi – it uses tension and expectation to comic and thrilling effect. Subsequent projects have been more interesting in their theory than the execution, though the warmth and inventiveness of *Matinee* (93) is impossible to deny. He remains an influential figure in Hollywood.

DANIELLE DARRIEUX
French actress (1917-)

Her father died when she was seven years old and her mother concentrated on her creative future. At the age of 14 she was a cello student at the Paris Conservatoire when her mother sent her to audition for *Le Bal* (31). She was a hit with audiences and producers and her enormous body of work saw her progress from uncertain introspectives to fashionable, knowing women. She became France's top female star in the 1930s. Because she entertained German troops during the war the French underground demanded her execution, but she survived to continue her film career. She appeared on stage, became known in the 1960s as a singer (on stage and record) and, in 1970, replaced Katharine Hepburn (qv) in the Broadway production of Coco. Her films include *Retour a l'Aube* (38), *Battements de Coeur* (39), *Adieu Chérie* (45), *Occupe-toi d'Amélie* (49), *L'Amant de Lady Chatterley* (55) and, more recently, *Quelques Jours avec moi* (87).

JULES DASSIN
US director, producer and screenwriter (1911-96)

Dassin's career as a director revealed a contradictory talent. Early films were notable for their stark realism and brutality and culminated in the hard-hitting prison drama *Brute Force* (47) and the ground-breaking New York thriller *The Naked City* (48).

Daves directs Glenn Ford in the classic 3:10 to Yuma

Blacklisted by McCarthyism, he was forced to work overseas, replicating New York in London for his atmospheric *Night and the City* (50). In France he directed the enormously popular *Rififi* (55), an ingenious heist thriller memorable for its prolonged silent burglary. He then directed a number of films with the Greek actress Melina Mercouri (qv), who became his wife in 1966. He worked with her on the successful *Never on Sunday* (60) and four years later starred her in *Topkapi*, another crime caper filmed in Istanbul. Although Dassin returned to America in 1961, he continued to regard Europe as his home.

DELMER DAVES
US director (1904-77)

Although he made only a few films, Daves was the first Hollywood director of westerns to have an empathy with his native American characters, having lived in his youth with the Hopi and Navajo tribes. Born in San Francisco and educated at Stanford University, he began his film career as a prop boy, then actor and scriptwriter until a stint as technical adviser on college films led to his co-writing *The Petrified Forest* (36) and directing the tensely dramatic *Destination Tokyo* (44). He was known as a meticulous stylist, famous for his use of sweeping crane shots to emphasise how his central characters were at odds with their environment – especially in *The Red House* (47) with Edward G Robinson (qv), *Dark Passage* (47) with Humphrey Bogart and Lauren Bacall (qqv), the notable western saga *Jubal* (56), *3:10 to Yuma* (57), with Glenn Ford (qv) fighting smalltown parochialism, and *Cowboy* (58).

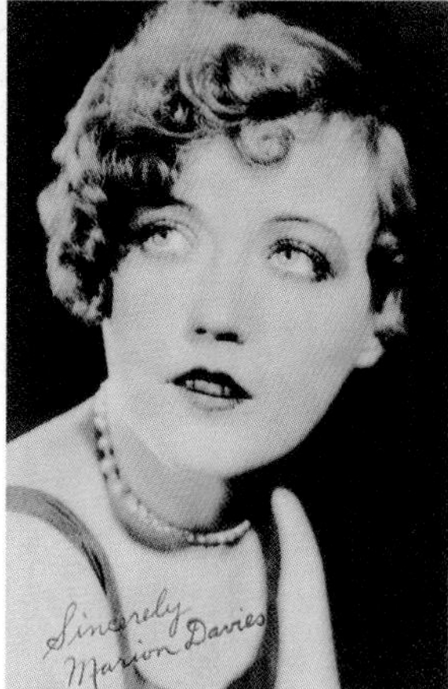

MARION DAVIES
US actress (1897-1961)

As the lover of the press tycoon William Randolph Hearst, it was Davies's fate to be the prototype for Susan Alexander, the mistress-wife of *Citizen Kane* (41). Even Orson Welles (qv) admitted the injustice. Davies was plucked from the Ziegfeld Follies by Hearst and established a light-hearted reputation in *Tillie the Toiler* (27), *The Patsy* (28) and *Blondie of the Follies* (32). Hearst then used Cosmopolitan Pictures to put her into a dramatic context with *Operator 13* (34), even though she was best in slapstick. The director King Vidor (qv) said: "She was the cleverest girl at being dumb I know." Warner put her into mediocrities that did neither she nor it much good. Her loyalty to Hearst was such that when he was in financial trouble she returned the jewels he had given her.

BETTE DAVIS
US actress (1908-89)

Ruth Elizabeth Davis was of patrician New England stock and went on to represent the tough, razor-sharp screen woman with a core of unvarnished femininity. Many of her most famous lines have passed into common usage. She began her stage career in George Cukor's (qv) production of Broadway in 1928 and two years later she won a contract from Universal, making her debut film *Bad Sister* (31). She was taken up by Warner and so began a long and illustrious association with the studio. Her celebrated roles, including Oscars for *Dangerous* (35) and *Jezebel* (38), were *Of Human Bondage (34), Marked Woman* (37), *The Old Maid* and *Dark Victory* (both 39), *The Letter* (40), *Now Voyager* (42), *Mr Skeffington* (44), *The Corn Is Green* (45) and *The Private Lives of Elizabeth and Essex* (39). She quarrelled incessantly with Jack Warner (qv) about pay and script quality, resulting in a long court battle. She left the studio in 1949 and created Margo Channing in *All About Eve* (50). In the 1960s Davis's career turned to low-budget horror, the most famous of which was *Whatever Happened to Baby Jane?* (62). She was president of the Academy in 1941 and co-founder of the Hollywood Canteen in 1946. Davis was nominated for 10 best actress Oscars and given the prestigious life achievement award by the American Film Institute in 1977. She died aged 81 after a series of strokes.

ENA DAVIS
actress (1957-)

r studying drama at Boston versity, Davis worked as a sgirl and model before landing nall part in *Tootsie* (82). She since been nominated for two ars, winning best supporting ess for her oddball dog trainer *he Accidental Tourist* (88), but ng the best actress award for sparky runaway in *Thelma and ise* (91). Her striking beauty slender figure should have cast her as a glamorous antic lead, but her height

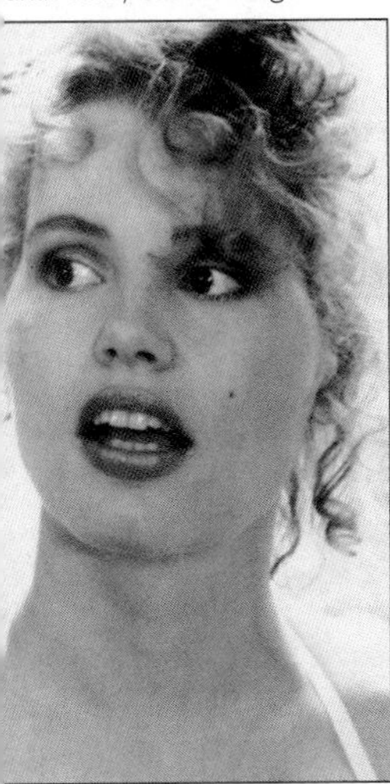

out 6ft) marked her out as an conventional star. Her career headed into uncharted territory ch, by Hollywood standards, es as eccentric, drawing on her nt for wisecracks and wacky tures. In *A League of their Own*) she eclipsed her team-mates, uding Madonna. She married f Goldblum (qv), her co-star in *e Fly* (86), in 1987, then the ector Renny Harlin, with whom made the disastrous pirate film *tthroat Island* (95).

DY DAVIS
stralian actress (1956-)

st lady of the contemporary stralian screen and a character tress recognised around the rld, Davis has often put her ractive features at the service of ceful, even defiant roles. She s two Oscar nominations, for *A ssage to India* (84) and *Husbands and Wives* (92), as well as awards for *My Brilliant Career* (79) and *Winter of Our Dreams* (81). She played opposite Colin Friels, her husband, in the D H Lawrence adaptation, *Kangaroo* (86), as she did in *High Tide* (87). Davis shone in *Barton Fink* (91) and *Husbands and Wives*, and redeemed the second-rate *Impromptu* (91), in which she played George Sand to Hugh Grant's Frédéric Chopin, but she has yet to establish bankable Hollywood status.

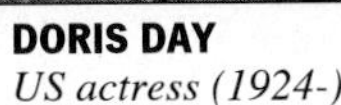

Entertainer Davis Jnr could also act tough, as in Reprieve

SAMMY DAVIS JR
US actor, singer, dancer (1925-90)

Blessed and cursed by the celebrity attached to his membership of Sinatra's (qv) "Rat Pack", Davis was a trouper born to vaudevillians, on stage from the age of two. The vicissitudes of the Depression motivated the boy to become an all-round entertainer, song-and-dance man, comic and musician. By the mid-1950s he was a solo nightclub and recording star when he lost an eye in a car crash. Rebounding with the dynamism for which he was famous, he entered films (apart from dancing in a couple of black pictures) in *The Benny Goodman Story* (56) and made more than 20 while remaining a television regular and concert headliner. He shone at his brightest as a showstopper in musicals: as Sportin' Life in *Porgy and Bess* (59) and preaching The Rhythm of Life in *Sweet Charity* (68). He performed a memorable swan song in the dance celebration *Tap* (89) before cancer claimed him. The second of his three wives was Swedish actress May Britt.

DORIS DAY
US actress (1924-)

Doris von Kappelhoff is famous for her roles as a vacuous heroine in 1950s' Warner musicals and the perpetual virgin of Universal's 1960s' sex comedies. Day went spectacularly out of fashion with the onset of the sexual revolution, but time has reappraised her as a fine actress with an acute sense of timing. Her screen image belied an incisive intelligence. Her career began as a singer with Bob Crosby's Chicago band in 1940 and a successful recording career led to her film debut in *Romance on the High Seas* (48), replacing Betty Hutton. She appeared with Bob Hope (qv) on a celebrated series of concert tours in 1948, formed Arwin Productions in 1955 and made *Pillow Talk* (59), which began her partnership with Rock Hudson (qv). Her best films include *Tea for Two* (50), *Lullaby of Broadway* and *On Moonlight Bay* (both 51), *April in Paris* (52), *Calamity Jane* (53), *The Pajama Game* (57), *Please Don't Eat the Daisies* (60) and *Lover Come Back* (62). She sued her lawyer in 1968 for embezzling a life's earnings. Married three times and nominated for an Oscar for *Pillow Talk*, she is devoted to animal rights.

DANIEL DAY-LEWIS
British actor (1957-)

The grandson of Sir Michael Balcon (qv) and son of poet laureate Cecil Day-Lewis and Jill Balcon, his actress wife, he was educated in a state primary school, followed by Bedales. His mother's connections won him the role as an upper-class delinquent in *Sunday Bloody Sunday* (71). Day-Lewis is an obsessive role preparer and reclusive depressive who was propelled to cinema stardom as the disabled Irish writer Christy Brown in *My Left Foot* (89), which won him a best actor Oscar and Bafta. Small parts in *Gandhi* (82) and *The Bounty* (84) led to his big break as a gay south London punk in the critical and cult success *My Beautiful Laundrette* (85). His rise was cemented with Merchant Ivory's (qqv) *A Room With a View* (85), as the pretentious Cecil Vyse. *The Unbearable Lightness of Being* (88) was not a commercial hit but brought him to American attention. *Stars and Bars* (88) was a resounding flop. After his brilliant performance in *My Left Foot*, Day-Lewis appeared in *Eversmile, New Jersey* (89), *The Last of the Mohicans* (92), *In the Name of the Father* and *The Age of Innocence* (both 93). He has now become an Irish citizen.

THE MOTION PICTURE EVENT YOU'VE BEEN WAITING FOR.

Its surface is barren.
Its true strength hidden.
Its foreboding desert conceals
the power to fold space,
to slow time, to send the mind
where the body cannot go.
It is the source of the
ultimate power.

It is the deadly battleground
where a young leader will emerge
to command an army of
six million warriors against
the tyrannical force that threatens
to enslave the universe.

It is the clash for the
greatest prize of all...

The planet called Dune.

DUNE

A world beyond your experience, beyond your imagination.

JAMES DEAN
US actor (1931-55)

The three films, *East of Eden* and *Rebel Without a Cause* (both 55) and *Giant* (56), on which his legendary reputation rests, spoke to and for the alienated and rebellious youth of the mid-1950s. Throughout the world young people identified with the intensity, the brooding good looks, the neurotic behaviour and the hesitant inarticulacy of his screen characters. It is a moot point whether his stardom would have endured had he lived, but his early and shocking death at the wheel of his Porsche guaranteed him screen immortality and a mythical status. Raised in the Midwest, he attended UCLA, followed by a period of acting with James Whitmore's theatre group. After bit parts in films and TV commercials, he went to New York where he attended classes at the Actors Studio. His performance as the Arab pederast in The Immoralist on Broadway led to a Warner contract followed by two Oscar nominations (one posthumous) and international idolatry. His pervasive influence inspired the play and film *Come Back to the 5 & Dime, Jimmy Dean, Jimmy Dean* (82), directed in both instances by Robert Altman (qv).

BASIL DEARDEN
British director (1911-71)

Dearden's "social problem" films included anti-German prejudice, *Frieda* (47); racism, *Sapphire* (59); homosexuality, *Victim* (61); and sectarian bias, *Life for Ruth* (62). He learned timing while co-directing with Will Hay (qv) such comedies as *The Goose Steps Out* (42), and his action scenes in *The Blue Lamp* (50) give real zip to a film that began a long-running police cliché. One of Britain's best heist films, *The League of Gentlemen* (59), shows him at his sharpest. His fault was that he was too accommodating. When he started at Ealing in the 1930s he used his real name, Basil Dear, but Basil Dean, the head of the studio, took exception and made him change it.

Dean in Fairmount, Indiana, to film East of Eden

OLIVIA DE HAVILLAND
US actress (1916-)

The sister of Joan Fontaine (qv), her debut was in Max Reinhardt's *A Midsummer Night's Dream* (35). She appeared opposite Errol Flynn (qv) in several action/romantic features, including *The Adventures of Robin Hood* and *Dodge City* (both 39), *The Private Lives of Elizabeth and Essex* (38) and *They Died With Their Boots On* (41). On loan from Warner, she won an Oscar nomination as Melanie in *Gone With the Wind* (39). Her demands for more such assertive roles brought her into conflict with the studio, resulting in a three-year legal battle. She returned with an Oscar-winning performance in *To Each His Own* (46), a nomination for *The Snake Pit* (48) and another Oscar for *The Heiress* (49), but then abandoned films for Broadway. Moving to France in the mid-1950s, she has since appeared only sporadically, most memorably in *The Light in the Piazza* (62) and *Hush . . . Hush, Sweet Charlotte* (65).

DINO DE LAURENTIIS
Italian producer (1919-)

At the age of 17 he enrolled at the Centro Sperimentale di Cinematografia in Rome and undertook a variety of industry related jobs before producing his first film. After war service he met his wife Silvana Mangano while producing *Bitter Rice* (49). With Carlo Ponti he formed the Ponti-De Laurentiis company at the start of the 1950s, producing two Oscar-winning features, including *La Strada* (54). When the company split in 1957, De Laurentiis built Dinocittà, a studio complex tailor-made for producing epics. But when the Italian film industry declined the studio folded. In the 1970s he moved to America where he quickly gained a reputation as a flamboyant producer. His production company, De Laurentiis Entertainment Group, collapsed under the weight of such box-office disasters as David Lynch's (qv) *Dune* (84). Since the company's bankruptcy he has been involved with a succession of small-time flops, apart from *Blue Velvet* (86) and *Body of Evidence* (93).

The 10 best thrillers

The Asphalt Jungle (1950)
Best of heist-that-goes-wrong plots, directed by John Huston

Double Indemnity (1944)
Stanwyck as a classic femme fatale in Wilder's great noir

The Godfather (1972)
Francis Ford Coppola's violent, epic study of a Mafia family

Goodfellas (1990)
A boy grows up to join the Mob in Scorsese's fine account

The Maltese Falcon (1941)
Humphrey Bogart as Hammett's Sam Spade in a timeless classic

Psycho (1960)
Hitchcock's terrifying Old-Dark-House horror spoof still chills

Scarface (1932)
Paul Muni as a Capone-like gangster changed public perceptions of crime

The Third Man (1949)
A British classic, Welles as drug runner in post-war Vienna

Touch of Evil (1958)
Mexican border-town sleaze with Welles as corrupt cop

Vertigo (1958)
Hitchcock's haunting enigma with Novak and Stewart

Adolph Zukor
AND
Jesse L. Lasky
Present the Mightiest
Dramatic
Spectacle of All the Ages
BY CECIL B. DeMILLE
The Ten
Commandments
STORY BY JEANIE MACPHERSON
A Paramount Production
(Famous Players-Lasky Corporation)

EORGES DELERUE
rench composer (1924-92)

elerue ranged across the ectrum of French cinema, but so scored *A Man for All Seasons* 6), *Women in Love* and *Anne of e Thousand Days* (both 69). His reer ended with a sizeable ntribution to the Hollywood ainstream. Although composing theatre, orchestra, television d ballet, he was best known as a n composer able to paint the oad brush strokes of big emotion well as the tiny nuances of aracter. Equally at home with neful sentiment and the jagged musical shapes required for character anxiety or danger, he wrote such diverse scores as *Hiroshima mon Amour* (59), *The Day of The Jackal* (73), *True Confessions* (81), *Silkwood* (83), *Salvador* and *Platoon* (both 86) and *Steel Magnolias* (89). He also completed *Day for Night* (73) and *The Last Metro* (80), two of Truffaut's (qv) later films.

ALAIN DELON
French actor, producer (1935-)

One of the most popular French stars of the 1960s and 1970s, Delon was ideal casting as the melancholy hit man in Melville's (qv) *Le Samourai* (67), as well as the disenchanted police commissioner in the same director's *Un Flic* (72). He also wielded guns in *The Sicilian Clan* (68) and *Borsalino* (70). Forays to Hollywood in the 1960s failed to establish him in the English-speaking markets. After he played the pilot in the disastrous *The Concorde – Airport '79* (79), his films were seldom seen outside France, although his turn as the homosexual Baron de Charlus in *Swann in Love* (84) drew praise. From 1964 Delon has been a successful producer and made his directorial debut with *Pour la Peau d'un Flic* (81).

DOLORES DEL RIO
Mexican actress (1905-83)

Her dark beauty and peasant sensuality could make male audiences feel tipsy, but she came from the Mexican aristocracy; her father was a leading banker. At 16 she married and moved to Hollywood where she made *Joanna* (25), a silent film that did not typecast her because of accent.

She was constantly in work, but never in anything that might have stretched her. Not even as the woman of mystery in *Journey Into Fear* (43), in which she co-starred with her ardent admirer Orson Welles (qv). Dissatisfied, she returned to Mexico to queen it over lucrative low-budget films, but found time to appear in John Ford's (qv) *The Fugitive* (47) and *Cheyenne Autumn* (64). Strangely, her best role was in an Elvis Presley (qv) film, *Flaming Star* (60), directed by Don Siegel (qv), which showed that behind her beauty there was a mind.

CECIL B DeMILLE
US director, producer (1881-1959)

Cecil Blount DeMille's name on a marquee meant more to filmgoers than those of the stars. He pioneered the feature film (and Hollywood as its capital), shaping stars and tastes. He co-founded the company that became Paramount, the biggest in films, with DeMille as director-general. He was a storyteller of shrewdness, sentiment, vulgarity and power in equal measures. He is remembered most for the scale and extravagance of his biblical and historical epics: *The Ten Commandments* (23 and 56), *Cleopatra* (34) and *Samson and Delilah* (49), but he worked in (or invented) every genre, from western, drama and saucy comedy to flag-waving Americana and rip-snorting adventure. As late as 1952 he won an Oscar for best picture for his circus saga *The Greatest Show on Earth.* He appeared as himself in Billy Wilder's (qv) *Sunset Boulevard* (50) and his vain and autocratic behaviour inspired the catchphrase "Ready when you are, Mr DeMille".

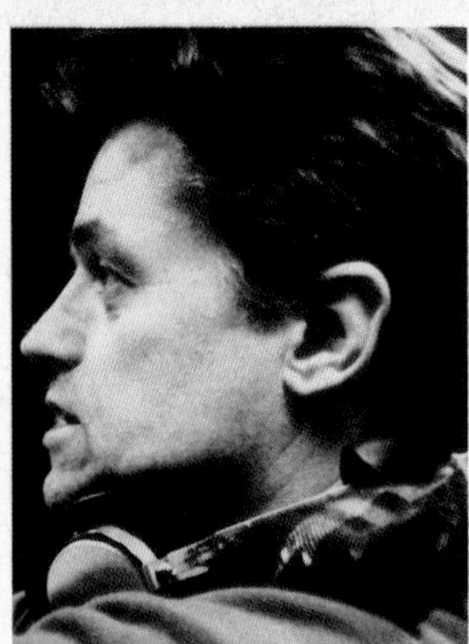

JONATHAN DEMME
US director (1944-)

One of the more versatile American directors, he is as adept at feature films, such as the terrifying Oscar-winner *Silence of the Lambs* (91), as he is with wickedly subversive documentaries, such as *Cousin Bobby* (92). He has a gift for fusing a heady concoction of black comedy with high drama to create excitingly visual, old-fashioned message films. Reared in Long Island and Miami, he was a film critic, salesman and maker of commercials before he met Roger Corman (qv) and made the sexploitation thriller *Caged Heat* (74). He went on to make the critically acclaimed *Crazy Mama* (75), which is a fusion of all his favourite things – extravagant music, exotic cultures, wild, wild women and bloody finales. In such comedies as *Melvin and Howard* (80) and *Something Wild* (86) he illustrates a passion for mannered eccentricity, but there is very little of his explosive energy in the mafia farce *Married to the Mob* (88) or the mainstream Hollywood Aids film *Philadelphia* (93).

JACQUES DEMY
French director (1931-90)

Demy was the most romantic auteur of the New Wave, dedicated to creating delight. His best work has a fairy-tale quality with its radiant women – Anouk Aimée, Catherine Deneuve, Jeanne Moreau (qqv) – luminous photography, elegant composition and music by Michel Legrand (qv), his regular collaborator. After work in animation, documentaries and shorts, his early feature, *Lola* (61), launched him internationally and boosted Aimée's stock. It revealed his love of Hollywood musicals, as did his most famous film *Les Parapluies de Cherbourg* (64), a mundane tale of young love lost rendered daring for being sung in its entirety (songs and recitative by Demy and Legrand). He was married to Agnès Varda (qv), one of France's foremost women directors, who paid tribute to his life in *Jacquot de Nantes* (91).

CATHERINE DENEUVE
French actress (1943-)

Catherine Dorléac was born in Paris, the younger sister of the actress Françoise Dorléac. Adopting the surname Deneuve, her mother's maiden name, her film debut was in *Les Collégiennes* (56). Breathtakingly beautiful, she quickly encapsulated the seductive, soiled heroine with a hint of innocence inhabiting a world of gamblers, criminals and soldiers of fortune. She most famously inspired Luis Buñuel's (qv) *Belle de Jour* (67), Polanski's (qv) *Repulsion* (65) and Demy's (qv) *Les Demoiselles de Rochefort* (67). She won her highest critical acclaim at home for Demy's *Les Parapluies de Cherbourg* (64). Her first Hollywood film was *The April Fools* (69). Known as much for her tangled romantic life as her films, in 1960 she began her infamous personal and professional relationship with Roger Vadim (qv), by whom she had a child. She also had a child by Marcello Mastroianni (qv) and was married to the British photographer David Bailey. She has been in more than 150 films, the most celebrated of which include a bisexual private eye, *Ecoute Voir . . .* (78), a Nazi schemer in *Le Dernier Métro* (80) and an amputee in *Tristana* (70). She has been the muse for the couture houses of Paris.

ROBERT DE NIRO
US actor (1943-)

He is considered to be the most versatile Method actor in contemporary cinema. His total immersion in a role is best exemplified by his excessive weight gain for his Oscar-winning portrayal of the ageing Jake La Motta in *Raging Bull* (80). He was born in New York and educated at the NY High School of Music and Art. He trained for the stage under Brando's (qv) influential teacher Stella Adler and in many off-Broadway productions. Cast in early independent productions by Brian De Palma and Roger Corman (qqv), it was his association with Martin Scorsese (qv), who put him in *Mean Streets* (73), that launched him into the critical spotlight. He won an Oscar for best supporting actor in *The Godfather Part II* (74) and a nomination for *The Deer Hunter* (78), but it was in his searing performance as the violently troubled *Taxi Driver* (76) that the star was born, popping up to play the saxophone in *New York, New York* (77) and brilliantly taking on the comic mantle of *The King of Comedy* (83). *Once Upon a Time in America* (84) and *Midnight Run* (88) enlarged his range, before the renewal of his Scorsese connection in *GoodFellas* (90) and *Cape Fear* (91), where his performance as the psychotic Max Cady almost tipped over into parody.He made a sound but unremarkable directorial debut with *A Bronx Tale* (93).

BRIAN DE PALMA
US director (1940-)

To some he is one of cinema's virtuosos, to others a heartless technician with nothing to say. The son of a surgeon, he enrolled as a physics undergraduate at Columbia University but transferred to drama and began making 16mm shorts, moving on to low-budget features. *Sisters* (72) ushered in his signature style: outlandish thrillers that rework Hitchcock but with a higher gore factor. In the 1980s he started raiding the gangster film for subjects, with *Scarface* (83) the result. But disaster struck with *The Bonfire of the Vanities* (90); *Carlito's Way* (93) has only partially restored his reputation. There is no better orchestrator of the set piece or manipulator of audiences; he shoots scenes calculated to assault the senses. Complexity of characterisation is not a prime concern; the more human a character, the better his chances of being blown away by the script – John Travolta's (qv) punk teenager with a conscience in *Carrie* (76), Sean Connery's (qv) crusty cop in *The Untouchables* (87). Intellectually he also offers few rewards, although his work is a buff's delight, awash with references to Hitchcock, Antonioni, Powell and Eisenstein (qqv).

GERARD DEPARDIEU
French actor (1948-)

A virtual one-man cinema industry who makes four to five films a year, his broad shoulders have propped up French film for two decades. His life is already the stuff of legend: a scamp from a working-class family who ran away to Paris and transformed himself from a near-illiterate delinquent with a speech impediment into France's most popular stage and screen actor in every genre imaginable. His breakthrough role as as a petty thug in *Les alseuses* (74); international ecognition came for the costume ramas *Jean de Florette* (86) and *yrano de Bergerac* (90). His ualities are seemingly at odds: a angerous presence always on the oint of erupting, he can also be elicate and tender, despite his ngainly frame. Cyrano was an eal role: a poetic soul in a rotesque body. International works nclude *Green Card* (90), *1492: he Conquest of Paradise* (92) and *ly Father the Hero* (94).

ITTORIO DE SICA
alian director, actor 1902-74)

smooth matinee idol on stage nd screen, De Sica first tried recting during the war and elivered a series of lightweight alian efforts. He found his own ch voice with *The Children Are Vatching Us* (42) about the orrupting effects of adults on hildhood purity. The human glow f this film was mirrored in *hoeshine* (46) and *Bicycle Thieves* 18), two Oscar winners that were ey components of Italian neo-alism. Both centred on touching les set in the collapse of post-war ome. Authentic, documentary-yle detail and non-professional ctors were offset by a soaring rical sense. De Sica continued to ct, but *The Garden of the Finzi-ontinis* (70) about the Fascist tranglehold on Jewish-Italian life on him his last Oscar.

NDRE DE TOTH
lungarian writer, editor and irector (1913-)

e entered films in 1931 while udying law at the University of Budapest, later directing several features. In the 1930s he worked in England for fellow Hungarian Alexander Korda (qv) and was assistant director on *The Four Feathers* (39) and *The Thief of Bagdad* (40). At the start of the war he went to Hollywood, but did not find film work until Korda used him on *The Jungle Book* (42). He made his Hollywood directing debut in 1944 with *None Shall Escape* and went on to make many distinctive thrillers and westerns, often with dark psychological motifs. Some of his films starred Veronica Lake (qv), to whom he was married from 1944 to 1952. He was a craftsman who understood writing, editing and directing and was more of an innovator than he was given credit for at the time. Although only having one eye he was responsible for the best of the films of the 1950s' 3-D craze, *House of Wax* (53). When asked how he did it he said "You only use one eye to look through a viewfinder."

DANNY DeVITO
US actor, director and producer (1944-)

In spite of his diminutive stature (5ft), DeVito packs an extraordinary punch in his comic creations and has become one of the most visible stars. Predominantly cast as two-timing creeps, lovable or otherwise, DeVito is at his best when venting his spleen on a co-star of comparable clout. He has been a fine sparring partner for Bette Midler and Billy Crystal (qv) and a successful foil to Arnold Schwarzenegger (qv). However, it is Michael Douglas (qv) who DeVito must thank for his rise, for casting him in an off-Broadway production of One Flew Over the Cuckoo's Nest. DeVito repeated his role (Martini) in the Oscar-winning film (75), but he turned down a television spin-off to play the loathsome Louie De Palma in the sitcom Taxi, which won him an Emmy. He then played the villain opposite Douglas in *Romancing the Stone* (84) and has not looked back. The same year he directed The Ratings Game for television, starring with Rhea Perlman, his wife – and embarked on a second career. He directed *The War of the Roses* (89) and was executive producer of *Pulp Fiction* (94).

THOROLD DICKINSON
British director (1903-84)

An Oxford graduate of fine intellect and sensibility, his most significant contribution to British cinema is as a teacher of film theory, which led to his appointment as the country's first professor of film at the University of London. He began his career as a sound editor and went on to film editing and assistant directing before making his first feature. His output was small but included two memorable features: *Gaslight* (40), starring Diana Wynyard and Anton Walbrook (qv) and far superior to MGM's version four years later, and *The Queen of Spades* (48). Based on Pushkin's story, with sets by Oliver Messel and mesmerising performances from Walbrook and Edith Evans (qv), it is a masterly, atmospheric evocation of this Russian tale. He is also noted for *Next of Kin* (42), an acclaimed war propaganda film.

WILLIAM DIETERLE
German director (1893-1972)

From a severely deprived childhood he took to acting in theatrical groups and began appearing in German silent films, including *Faust* (26). In 1923 he started to direct films in which he was starring. Hollywood beckoned in 1930 and Dieterle got himself a contract with Warner. A switch to RKO came in 1939 where he directed *All That Money Can Buy* (41), considered by many to be his greatest film. Despite his success, and panache with romantic dramas such as *Love Letters* (45), his liberal tendencies made him an enemy of McCarthyites, though he managed to escape the infamous blacklist. Before his retirement in 1965 he struggled through a number of poor quality films that did not deserve his notoriously meticulous attention.

MARLENE DIETRICH
German actress (1901-92)

"I can only say that she makes reason totter on her throne," wrote the critic James Agate of her first great success in *The Blue Angel* (30). The facts of Dietrich's life are mired in myth and lies. The daughter of a Prussian officer, she had been acting for some time when she was "discovered" by Sternberg (qv) and hit pay dirt with her seductive Lola Lola in *Blue Angel* on whose wings she flew to Paramount. She commanded a massive salary and made six more films with Sternberg, who placed her in ever more extravagant settings, costumes and ludicrous plots in *Morocco* (30), *Dishonored* (31), *Shanghai Express* and *Blonde Venus* (both 32), *The Scarlet Empress* (34) and *The Devil Is A Woman* (35). Marketed as Garbo's (qv) rival, she became a massive star, but suffered career vicissitudes from the late 1930s on. An anti-Nazi, she refused Hitler's offers of huge fees and her films were banned in Germany. In the war she toured battle zones, singing to US troops. In the 1950s she added cabaret to her armoury and made a fortune. In spite of Maximilian Schell's (qv) documentary *Marlene* (84), in which her taped utterances reveal her as a difficult and unpleasant woman, and being trashed in her daughter Maria Riva's biography, the legend remains after her lonely death in Paris.

HOWARD DIETZ
US lyricist, publicist (1896-1983)

He was from 1924 a member of the Round Table, the celebrated literary circle at the Hotel Algonquin in his native New York, having worked as a newspaperman and later in advertising. The two main reasons for which he should be remembered are that he devised Leo the Lion, the Metro-Goldwyn-Mayer trademark, and coined a studio motto, Ars Gratia Artis ("art for art's sake"), that spoke for his Columbia University education. The second is that he wrote That's Entertainment! with composer Arthur Schwartz, a song that has become the unofficial anthem of showbusiness. Dietz maintained a dual career as vice-president in charge of publicity at MGM from 1940 until 1957 and as the lyricist and librettist of several Broadway shows and a translator of operas. His best-known song was Dancing in the Dark, his most famous film *The Band Wagon* (53).

MATT DILLON
US actor (1964-)

Good looking and popular with both sexes as pin-up or role model for his naturalistic playing, Dillon entered films while still a high school student in Jonathan Kaplan's *Over the Edge* (79), as a rebellious youth. On the strength of this and similarly callow roles in *Little Darlings* and *My Bodyguard* (both 80), *Liar's Moon* (81) and three tales of teenagers in trouble adapted from stories by S E Hinton: *Tex* (82), *Rumble Fish* and *The Outsiders* (both 83), he almost constituted a one-man Brat Pack. He moved on to more rewarding, post-teen roles in *The Big Town* (87) and *Kansas* (88). The gangster spoof *Bloodhounds of Broadway* (89) gave his comic skills scope opposite Madonna and Rutger Hauer. As a gang leader attempting to quit drug taking in *Drugstore Cowboy* (89), he gave his strongest dramatic performance to date. His work in *Singles* (92) won popular and some critical favour. Given his maturing photogenic looks, screen presence and developing talent, it would seem fair to assume that his best work is still to come.

WALT DISNEY
US animator, producer and executive (1901-66)

An autocrat whose personality was at odds with the intoxicating abandon of his films and which led to an animators' strike in 1941, Disney was an obsessive whose demand for technical excellence led to *Steamboat Willie* (28), the first Mickey Mouse cartoon with sound. Disney himself supplied Mickey's voice. He had begun his creative life in a commercial art studio in Kansas City. It was there he met fellow artist Ub Iwerks (qv), who emerged as his collaborator throughout the golden years. These were made possible by the maestro's progress with two- and three-strip colour with the multiplane camera, which gave animation more credible perspective and action detail. The first Disney feature, *Snow White and the Seven Dwarfs* (37), had all the classic components: clearly defined, often eccentric characters, imaginative twists and turns, narrative, memorable songs and a pace to put gangster films to shame. All this meant that creativity was not concentrated on animation techniques. *Fantasia* (40), *Bambi* (42), *Lady and the Tramp* (55) and *101 Dalmatians* (61) followed, as did wartime propaganda films, live action outings (beginning with *Treasure Island* in 1950), nature documentaries and theme parks. Today, due to his organisation's shrewd marketing of its back catalogue, animation has been revived, with Disney still the yardstick against which it is judged. The 1994 feature *The Lion King* is the most financially successful cartoon in the history of cinema.

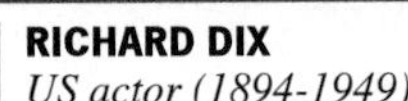

RICHARD DIX
US actor (1894-1949)

A star who once epitomised the wholesome all-American male, his subsequent typecasting was as an alcoholic and loser. Dix was an honourable gunslinger, crusading news reporter and, in DeMille's (qv) *The Ten Commandments* (23), the saintly hero. While studying medicine in Minnesota he caught the acting bug in a drama club and was soon appearing in repertory theatre. Two years after his Broadway debut, he made his first film and was an overnight star. In

Disney, the giant of animation and a perfectionist tyrant

the next decade he was a ubiquitous presence, first under contract to Samuel Goldwyn (qv), then to Paramount. For RKO he starred in the popular *Cimarron* (30). He was never to repeat this success. In the 1940s he played The Whistler in a succession of low-budget action adventures.

EDWARD DMYTRYK
US director (1908-)

Dmytryk was blighted by the anti-communist hysteria that engulfed Hollywood just as he began to achieve great things. Canadian-born to Ukrainian parents, he joined Paramount at 15, rising from messenger to leading editor. Columbia and then RKO gave him the opportunity to direct, churning out B films until his two propaganda dramas of 1943 became spectacular earners. He contributed to RKO's film noir cycle with *Murder My Sweet* (44) and *Crossfire* (47), which was an engrossing thriller dealing with anti-semitism, while *Till the End of Time* (46) was a fine war veterans' drama. In 1947 Dmytryk – briefly a Communist party member – was among the Hollywood 10 eventually blacklisted and jailed for refusing to co-operate with the House Un-American Activities Committee investigation into communist affiliations in the industry. He recanted and was released, moving to Britain where he made three films. In 1951 he went home, named names and was allowed to work again, to the lasting bitterness of many. His subsequent films were characterless, with few exceptions; *The Sniper* (52), *Broken Lance* (54) and the naval court martial drama *The Caine Mutiny* (54) still enjoy high repute. In his later years Dmytryk taught film at the University of Texas and at USC in Los Angeles.

ROBERT DONAT
British actor (1905-58)

The man who portrayed William Friese-Greene in *The Magic Box* (51) was a tall, soft-spoken and handsome Mancunian with an

gaging smile. One of his most nous roles was as Richard nnay in Hitchcock's (qv) *The 39 eps* (35) and the title role in *odbye Mr Chips* (39) – where he nvincingly aged 58 years on mera – for which he won the car. Born of Polish-British rents, who sent him for elocution sons to overcome a stammer, appeared in repertory when only , before making his debut in ndon as a distinguished classical tor some 14 years later. After rda (qv) featured him in *The vate Life of Henry VIII* (33), he nt to Hollywood to play *The unt of Monte Cristo* (34), only to ect the subsequent lure of nerican films for a successful reer in Britain. Suffering from ronic asthma and severe pressions, he refused more films an he made, giving an impression at he never fulfilled his potential. orking with an oxygen mask on *e Inn of the Sixth Happiness* 8), he died before it was released his apposite last screen words ging in the audience's ears: "We all not see each other again, I nk. Farewell."

ANLEY DONEN
S director (1924-)

rn in South Carolina, he became Broadway hoofer, making his but in 1940 as a chorus boy in l Joey, which coincidentally ited the career of Gene Kelly) as a song-and-dance star. He rked with Kelly on the oreography of the 1941 show st Foot Forward and went to llywood for the 1943 film rsion. He was the choreographer of several more musicals, including *Cover Girl* (44), *Holiday in Mexico* (46), *A Date With Judy* (48) and *Take Me Out to the Ball Game* (49), which he also co-wrote and, with Kelly, directed the finale. Still with Kelly, he co-directed *On The Town* (49), *Singin' in the Rain* (52) and *It's Always Fair Weather* (55). His solo musicals include *Seven Brides for Seven Brothers* (54) and *Funny Face* (57). From 1958 he worked mostly in Britain, directing glossy comedies adapted from the stage, such as *Indiscreet* (58) and *The Grass Is Greener* (60), and stylish, elaborately photographed thrillers, such as *Charade* (63) and *Arabesque* (66).

RICHARD DONNER
US director (1939-)

An off-Broadway actor before uprooting to California, his first directorial assignments – advertisements and documentaries – served as groundwork for his entry into television, directing episodes of such successful series as The Fugitive, Wanted Dead or Alive and The Twilight Zone. His work in the cinema was initially erratic and he had only completed three full-length features in 15 years by the time he scored his first international commercial success with *The Omen* (76). From there he moved to the record-breaking *Superman The Movie* (78) which cashed-in on the public's appetite for big-budget, special effects-packed blockbusters. A string of unsatisfying flops followed, during which time he also began producing. He was not to find commercial favour again until the *Lethal Weapon* trilogy began in 1987. In 1994 he made a film version of the comedy western television show Maverick, but it proved disappointing.

DIANA DORS
British actress (1931-84)

She was the quintessential good time girl-next-door of the 1940s and 1950s, later graduating to character roles with surprising aplomb. As the blonde bombshell of British cinema she was promoted as England's answer to

Marilyn Monroe (qv), but she was more posturing than provocative. Then, as the years and weight caught up with her, she personified the heart-of-gold neighbour and cheeky housekeeper. Even in her worst films (of which there were many) she lent a note of distinction, always ready with a conspiratorial wink. Her original name was Diana Fluck (the source of many jokes). She made her film debut at the age of 15 and evolved into a starlet before proving she could act in *Yield to the Night* (56), playing a murderess awaiting execution. It attracted the attention of Hollywood, where she was signed up by RKO. Two flops later she was back in Britain, appearing in a string of undistinguished dramas and comedies. She tried Hollywood again, with no more luck, before settling for a career as a character actress. With the exceptions of *The Amazing Mr Blunden* (72) and *Steaming* (84), her later films were uniformly dire.

KIRK DOUGLAS
US actor (1916-)

Issur Danielovitch Demsky, later Isidore Demsky, later still Kirk Douglas, was born in Amsterdam, New York, to Russian Jewish migrants. He worked hard to put himself through university and drama school and appeared on Broadway in 1941, just before his war service in the navy. His film career began after his discharge with *The Strange Love of Martha Ivers* (46) and he became, alongside Burt Lancaster (qv), the first of a new generation of rugged post-war male stars. He confirmed his position with the boxing drama *Champion* (49), for which he received an Oscar nomination. He specialised in ruthless, driven, self-centred but flawed heroes: *Ace in the Hole* (51), *The Bad and the Beautiful* (52) and as Van Gogh in *Lust for Life* (56). Importantly, he restored the writer Dalton Trumbo (qv), who had been ousted by the House Un-American Activities Committee, to favour with *Spartacus* (60), which Douglas also executive produced. A tireless campaigner for innumerable causes, he holds the Presidential Medal of Freedom, America's highest civilian honour. He is the actor Michael Douglas's (qv) father.

MELVYN DOUGLAS
US actor (1901-81)

A discerning actor who twice left Hollywood for Broadway, Douglas hit his stride as a leading man who shared the screen with Dietrich, Colbert, Crawford, Garbo (qqv) et al.His Broadway triumph with Tonight or Never propelled him to Hollywood, where he repeated the role on film. Despite holding his own against Garbo in *As You Desire Me* (32), he felt professionally uneasy and returned to Broadway. In Hollywood again he proved his ability with comic treats such as *Theodora Goes Wild* (36) with Irene Dunne (qv), and *Ninotchka* (39) with Garbo. After his second Broadway break in the 1950s, he gave cinema a parting shot, swapping stardom for character acting. It won him best supporting actor Oscars for *Hud* (63) and *Being There* (79).

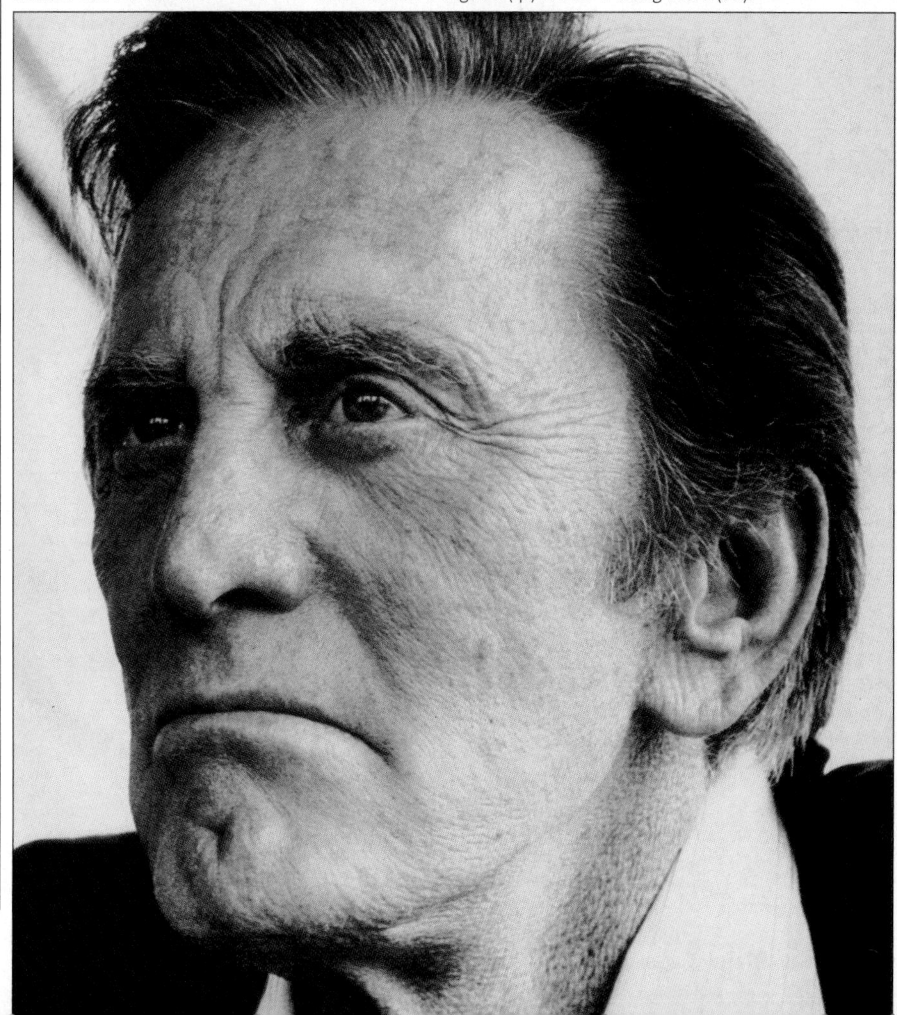

The tireless Kirk Douglas: an old block with a young chip

MICHAEL DOUGLAS
US actor, producer (1944-)

The son of Kirk Douglas (qv), he began as an assistant director, switching to acting, initially on stage and television, in the 1960s. Craggily handsome, he found success as co-producer of *One Flew Over the Cuckoo's Nest* (75), which won all five top Oscars. *Romancing the Stone* (84) and *Jewel of the Nile* (85) made him a star as a romantic action hero, but this perception was quickly altered. In 1987 *Fatal Attraction* and *Wall Street*, for which he won the best actor Oscar, signalled a rare skill at portraying morally ambiguous or challenged leading characters, confirmed in such box-office hits as *Black Rain* and *The War of the Roses* (both 89), *Basic Instinct* (92), *Falling Down* (93) and *Disclosure* (94). His admission of personal problems, suggesting that his real life was under strain from the pressures of success, has only added to his popular appeal.

ALEXANDER PETROVICH DOVZHENKO
Russian director (1894-1956)

Dovzhenko was not just a pioneer of early Soviet film, he was considered to be the celluloid poet of the revolution. His masterpiece *Earth* (30) is a prime example of the way he combined his communism with an intensely personal vision to create stirring lyrical films about the struggle to survive. The son of a Ukrainian peasant, he was largely self-taught. Before university he joined the Red Army, became a teacher and worked for a time as an ambassador. At the age of 32, encouraged by Lenin's vision of the cinema as the revolutionary art of the masses, he became obsessed with making films. His first controversial film, *Zvenigora* (27), so confused the local bureaucrats that they called in Eisenstein and Pudovkin (qqv) to okay the project. His next films, which included his overtly political *Arsenal* (29), the controversial *Earth* and Stalin's favourite, *Shchors* (39), won him promotion to head of the Kiev studios. He continued to work, writing some optimistic screenplays, which were completed by his wife Yulia Solntseva after he died of cancer.

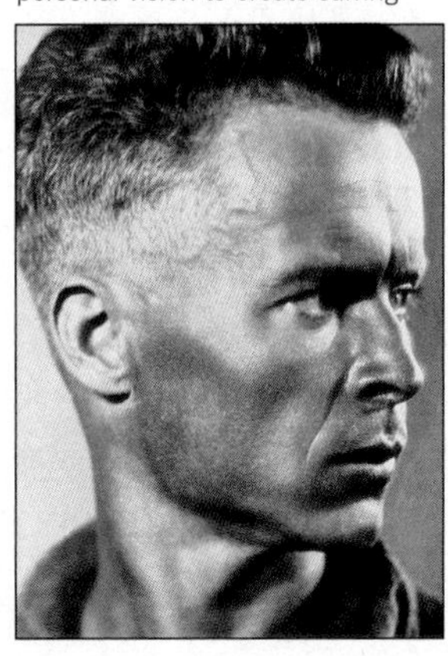

MARIE DRESSLER
Canadian actress (1869-1934)

The heavyweight Dressler called herself an "ugly duckling", though MGM boss Louis B Mayer (qv) declared her a swan, saying his three greatest stars were Garbo, Tracy (qqv) and Dressler. During the Depression she was a box office draw because audiences related to her personal circumstances. Trained as an opera singer, she went into stage drama but, unemployed, was rescued from suicide by Chaplin's (qv) *Tillie's Punctured Romance* (14), which set her pattern for weighty harridans. She suffered the slings and arrows of outrageous comedians but, teamed with Wallace Beery (qv) in *Min and Bill* (30), she won an Oscar as the gentler half of a waterfront couple. She and Beery reunited for *Tugboat Annie* (33), but she could also play the grande dame with grace, as in her performance with Jean Harlow (qv) in *Dinner at Eight* (33). It was Dressler who wrote "You're only as good as your last picture."

CARL THEODOR DREYER
Danish director, writer (1889-1968)

Acknowledged as Denmark's greatest film maker and as the creator of several masterpieces, Dreyer's career was always a struggle punctuated by long periods of inactivity when he was unable to raise finance. His films, even the acclaimed *The Passion of Joan of Arc* (28) and the witch-hunt story *Day of Wrath* (43), filmed during Denmark's Nazi occupation, were financial failures. This, combined with his obsessive attention to detail, alienated producers. Much of his work explored the dark, painful reaches of the human soul, though he was also capable of humour, as in *The Parson's Widow* (20). The Danish government recognised his achievements in 1952, giving him the management of Copenhagen's best cinema, which brought him financial security. He made two masterpieces before his death: *Ordet* (54) and *Gertrud* (64).

RICHARD DREYFUSS
US actor (1947-)

Born in Brooklyn and educated at Beverly Hills High, Dreyfuss made his stage debut at the age of 10 at the West Side Jewish Center, New York, and joined The Session, an influential comedy group in San Francisco. During the Vietnam war he was a conscientious objector and worked as a filing clerk at the Los Angeles County General hospital. His first film was a bit part in *The Graduate* (67). He came to screen prominence with *American Graffiti* (73), *The Apprenticeship of Duddy Kravitz* (74) and the blockbuster *Jaws* (75), which established his name. He looks unlike a traditional leading man. Short and stocky, he has never fitted into any stereotype. His career peaked with a best actor Oscar for *The Goodbye Girl* and his starring role in *Close Encounters of the Third Kind* (both 77). During the late 1970s he developed a drug problem and his life and career fell apart. He successfully underwent treatment and made *The Competition* (80), *Down and Out in Beverly Hills* (86), *Tin Men* (87), *Always* (89), *Postcards From the Edge* (90), *Lost in Yonkers* (93) and *Silent Fall* (95).

Faye Dunaway stays cool amid the brouhaha of Oscar fame

FAYE DUNAWAY
US actress (1941-)

Bonnie and Clyde (67) was one of the hottest, most imitated films of the 1960s. Dunaway's impact as Bonnie Parker, the sexy, naive, thrill-seeking moll, launched a look – lean, slinky and black bereted – and her career. It was her third picture after a stint at New York's Lincoln Center Repertory Company and off-Broadway. Her Oscar-nominated performance for Arthur Penn (qv) propelled her to star status, which she retained through much of the 1970s. As a tall, cool blonde she provided seductive chic in glossy mainstream films. A nervy intensity came to the fore with European directors. She was fascinating (and again Oscar-nominated) in *Chinatown* (74) and won an Oscar for her cold, neurotic television executive in *Network* (76). She was not well received, however, for her Joan Crawford (qv) in *Mommie Dearest* (81). Some of her best work has been on television playing Eva Peron and evangelist Aimee Semple McPherson.

IRENE DUNNE
US actress (1898-1990)

Despite graduating from the Chicago Musical College, Dunne failed her audition for the New York Metropolitan Opera and strayed into musical comedy. In less than a decade she had carved herself a niche as a reliable lead and was appearing in touring and Broadway productions of musical shows. A subsequent RKO contract led to her film debut in *Leathernecking* (30) and a prosperous career that anned more than two decades. ıe found success playing straight ˌes in heart-rending melodramas, ˌtty comedies and lively musicals ɔm *Magnificent Obsession* (35), ʳough *Theodora Goes Wild* (36), *Show Boat* (36). After *It Grows* *Trees* (52) she retired and came a political campaigner for e Republicans. Her only recent ɪnnection with the film industry ɜs in 1965 when she was ɔpointed to Technicolor's board.

JIMMY DURANTE
US comedian (1893-1980)

His nose typecast him as a comic almost from birth, so that his title for it – "Schnozzola" – became his nickname. The son of a fairground barker, he acquired his gravel voice, he said, trying to make himself heard on the vaudeville circuit. He alone was

responsible for the fractured English in his songs: "I don't just split infinitives, I mangle 'em." In his own New York nightclub he performed in his own mixed race trio. MGM signed him but gave him indifferent films such as *Broadway to Hollywood* (33) or *It Happened in Brooklyn* (47) about which Frank Sinatra (qv) said: "Durante can upstage anybody, me included." If his acting was negligible, his presence was palpable. Audiences loved him, even when his voice had faded. He always ended his act with the line: "Goodnight, Mrs Calabash, wherever you are!" – Mrs Calabash was his pet name for his late wife.

DEANNA DURBIN
US actress, singer (1921-)

The recipient of a special Oscar for "bringing to the screen the spirit and personification of youth", she was originally dropped by MGM in favour of Judy Garland (qv) after one musical short. Signed by

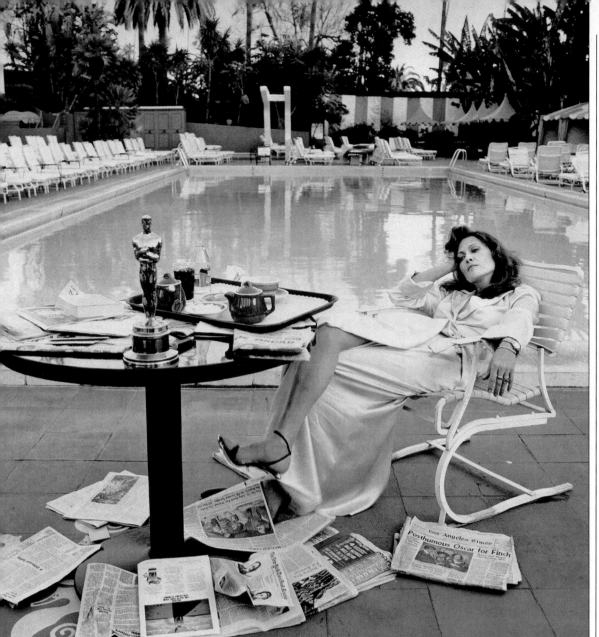

Universal, a studio on the verge of bankruptcy, she almost saved it with her box-office popularity. With a pretty face and a winningly precocious personality, she specialised in Pollyanna characters, reconciling her estranged parents in *Three Smart Girls* (36), her debut feature, and melting Leopold Stokowski into conducting her penurious father's orchestra in *100 Men and a Girl* (37). Her first screen kiss (from Robert Stack) in *First Love* (39) made headlines, but when the transition to adulthood – and straight roles – was complete, her career gradually declined. She retired after *Her Butler's Sister* (43), *Christmas Holiday* (44), *Something in the Wind* (47) and *For the Love of Mary* (48) because, she said: "I was the highest-paid star with the poorest material." After two failed marriages she settled in the south of France with Charles David, her third husband, who had directed her in *Lady on a Train* (45).

ROBERT DUVALL
US actor (1931-)

An unshowy actor who can hold a scene just by standing in shot, he finally won the Oscar he deserved for *Tender Mercies* (83). His boozing, defeated country singer, who puts himself back together after he meets a good woman, is one of many career highlights. The others include his counsellor in *The Godfather* (72), his surf-crazy colonel in *Apocalypse Now* (79) and his morally aware detective in *True Confessions* (81). More recent offerings, such as his poised southerner in *Rambling Rose* (91) and his grizzled Indian scout in *Geronimo: An American Legend* (93), also impress. Duvall trained at the Neighborhood Playhouse in New York and completed his share of stock and off-Broadway before striking a chord as Gregory Peck's (qv) innocent, retarded neighbour in *To Kill a Mocking Bird* (62). As a director he made *Angelo, My Love* (83), a quietly observant tale of contemporary gypsies.

JULIEN DUVIVIER
French director (1896-1967)

He directed his first feature in 1919, but it was not until the 1930s that he began emerging as a considerable talent, notably with *Pépé le Moko* and *Un Carnet de Bal* (both 37). In 1938 he made his Hollywood debut with the Strauss biography, *The Great Waltz*, and continued to work in ▷

America on big-budget productions until 1945 when he returned to Europe for such assignments as the direction of Vivien Leigh (qv) in *Anna Karenina* (47). *The Little*

World of Don Camillo (51) earned him a prize in Venice and he was to continue writing and directing up to his death. His work, particularly during the "poetic realism" phase, is an important element in the history of European cinema.

ALLAN DWAN
US director (1885-1981)

In today's climate of costly, state-of-the-art film making it is hard to comprehend that Dwan directed more than 400 films in 49 years. In his most productive stretch he was churning out two one-reelers a week. It was his pioneering method of production – driving into the wilderness, finding a subject and pointing the camera – that informed Peter Bogdanovich's (qv) reverential *Nickelodeon* (76). His output embraced the entire language of cinema, from one-reelers to CinemaScope. Following his contribution to the invention of the neon light, Dwan sold some stories to the Essanay studio and was hired as a scenario editor. Moving to the American Film Company, he stumbled into directing his first feature when the original director was too drunk.

Subsequently, he turned out a stream of one-reel westerns before switching to features. He is also credited with inventing the dolly shot, where the camera travels on wheels to follow the action. He was responsible for the crane sequence in *Intolerance* (16). During the 1940s and 1950s he concentrated on comedies and westerns (on remarkably low budgets) before directing his last big success, *Sands of Iwo Jima* (49), with John Wayne (qv). Dwan estimated he had worked on 1,850 pictures.

CLINT EASTWOOD
US actor, director (1930-)

A product of disruptive schooling and constantly in transit with his jobbing father, he had a string of physical jobs before joining the army special services in 1950. He then became a television actor in Hollywood, playing Rowdy Yates in Rawhide. The trio of spaghetti westerns he made with director Sergio Leone (qv) in the 1960s as The Man With No Name earned him international success. Back in America he began working with the director Don Siegel (qv), who was to be an important influence, and founded Malpaso Productions. *Dirty Harry* (71) landed him another instantly recognisable part. He directed and starred in *Play Misty for Me* (71) and *The Outlaw Josey Wales* (76) and endures beyond many other action heroes of his generation precisely because he sniffs out complex, stimulating projects. In 1985 he was decorated Chevalier des Arts et Lettres in France. His most magnificent work, *Unforgiven* (92), which questioned the myths of the western hero, won a best picture Oscar. He is an iconic figure; an actor and film maker of great intelligence.

NELSON EDDY
US singer, actor (1907-67)

A boy soprano, later an opera singer and singing star, he made his film debut in *Broadway to Hollywood* (33). He then achieved huge popularity as Jeanette MacDonald's (qv) screen partner in a series of operettas including *Naughty Marietta* (35), *Rose Marie*

(36), *Maytime* (37), *Sweethearts* (38), *Balalaika* (39), *Bitter Sweet* (40), *The Chocolate Soldier* (41) and *I Married an Angel* (42). Now regarded as high camp, the films were astonishingly successful on both sides of the Atlantic. Known as "America's Sweethearts", Eddy and MacDonald were not romantically involved off-screen (she was married to actor Gene Raymond). When their appeal waned with the war years the partnership ended. They each made only a handful of further films. Eddy concentrated on concerts, cabaret and recording.

THOMAS ALVA EDISON
US inventor (1847-1931)

"The Wizard of Menlo Park", after the New Jersey laboratory where he patented hundreds of inventions including the light bulb and the phonograph, Edison is usually given credit for "inventing" motion pictures. In fact William (W K L) Dickson, his Scottish assistant, built the Kinetophonograph in 1889, a projector that synchronised with a record. (The sprocketed celluloid film was provided by the photographic inventor George Eastman.) It was followed by a camera, the Kinetograph, and a viewer, the Kinetoscope. Dickson built the "Black Maria", the first film studio in the world, for Edison in 1892. Taking his cue from the Lumière brothers' (qv) Cinématographe, a camera-projector, Edison snapped up the rights to an American equivalent, the Vitascope, premiering a film show in New York in 1896. He bought out, teamed with or blocked rival producers with the formation in 1909 of the Motion Picture Patents Company, a monopoly that held until 1917.

BLAKE EDWARDS
US director (1922-)

William Blake McEdwards served the US Coastguard 1944-45 and created the successful NBC serie Richard Diamond, Private Detective. He directed his first screen feature *Bring Your Smile Along* in 1955 and has always been regarded as an unpredictal uneven renegade. Although his greatest success has been in comedies, most notably the Pink Panther series starring Peter Sell (qv), Edwards has consistently skipped genres. He loves the widescreen format, filling it with objects and colours. His reputati peaked in the early 1960s with *Operation Petticoat* (59), *Breakfa at Tiffany's* (61), *Days of Wine a Roses* (63) and *The Pink Panthe* (64). The failure of the big budge *Darling Lili* (70) led to Edwards's 1970s wilderness years with only *The Tamarind Seed* (74) gaining attention. His revival of the Pink Panther's mordant slapstick with *The Return Of The Pink Panther* (75), made him bankable again. The renewed series bankrolled *1* (79), a sleeper hit starring Dudle Moore (qv) and Julie Andrews (q

Eastwood relaxing in his mobile dressing room

Edwards's wife, in a comedy of sexual manners. He went on to make the frenzied black farce *S.O.B.* (81). Edwards continues to make films, although his career would seem to be in the doldrums.

SERGEI EISENSTEIN

Russian director (1898-1948)

Despite making only 14 films, he is one of the most innovative and pioneering directors in the history of cinema. His montage technique influenced Orson Welles, Godard, Brian De Palma and Oliver Stone (qqv). Born in Latvia and trained as an engineer, he spent time in a Red Army agitprop team and worked with Meyerhold and Mayakovsky before he concentrated on transforming cinema into a political weapon. His images in *Strike* (24) and *Battleship Potemkin* (25) and *October* (28) are not intended as historical documents but to convey the revolutionary spirit of the times. The same is true of his patriotic *Alexander Nevsky* (38), with its memorable ice battle against the Teutonic knights. He was troubled by interference and smallpox and several of his films were unfinished, notably *Bezhin Meadow* (37) and the third part of *Ivan the Terrible* (46), which had apparently been endorsed by Stalin after he had objected to Part II. He was appointed artistic head of Mosfilm in 1940 and died of a heart attack while working on a series of theoretical essays.

The master and the mouse: Eisenstein meets Mickey

MICHAEL EISNER

US mogul (1942-)

Chairman of the board and chief executive officer of Walt Disney, Eisner is one of Hollywood's top tycoons. Starting in television, he worked at CBS and ABC, leaving in 1976 to become president of Paramount at a time when the studio's profits soared with blockbusters that included *Saturday Night Fever* (77), *Star Trek – The Motion Picture* (79), *An Officer and a Gentleman* (82) and *Raiders of the Lost Ark* (81). In 1984 he moved to Disney with his key personnel and drove the company not merely to revived fortunes but, for the first time in its history, to number one at the box office. When Jeffrey Katzenberg (qv) ran the Walt Disney Studios (with its Hollywood, Touchstone and Walt Disney Pictures branches), Eisner backed the resurrection of animation, which yielded *Beauty and the Beast* (91), *Aladdin* (92) and *The Lion King* (94), the highest grossing animated features ever. In 1994, Katzenberg left acrimoniously, leaving Eisner in control of the film operation as well as the other realms of the empire. According to Forbes magazine, Eisner has earned a reputed $40m in a good year.

DANNY ELFMAN

US composer (1954-)

With Hollywood soundtracks relying more and more on pop compilations, it is ironic that Elfman has injected a fresh vitality into film music. Ironic, because he was the founder of Oingo Boingo, the Los Angeles rock band. It was the group's overt theatricality that attracted the attention of Tim Burton (qv), the director, who signed Elfman to compose the music for *Pee-wee's Big Adventure* (85). His eccentric score propelled the picture and Burton hired him to compose all of his films – with the exception of *Ed Wood* (94), the director's only box-office disappointment. In *The Nightmare Before Christmas* (92) Elfman not only wrote the music and the 10 songs but also sang the part of Jack Skellington, the film's protagonist. He is now in demand as a film composer and has written the theme tunes to such television fare as The Simpsons. He is currently at work on two more musicals and is planning to direct his first film.

DENHOLM ELLIOTT

British actor (1922-92)

Mixing an archetypal English smoothness and well-polished manners with a singular weirdness, which either lit up his face or lurked suggestively beneath the surface, Elliott could be seedy, squalid, dangerous, dark or jolly. With a crumpled face that seemed to move in different directions at one and the same time, he spent his life fleshing out intriguing support roles with his peculiar charisma. The first of such roles, often crucial to a film, came with *Dear Mr Prohack* (49). *The Heart of the Matter* and *The Cruel Sea* (both 53) made an impression and his sweaty, money-grubbing backstreet abortionist in *Alfie* (66) brought some welcome ballast to the film's relentless cheer. *Spy With a Cold Nose* (66) was a period spy spoof, while in *Trading Places* (83) he was

an impeccably English butler. Both films underlined his penchant for dry comedy. *Raiders of the Lost Ark* (81) and *Indiana Jones and the Last Crusade* (89) had him romping about, while *Defence of the Realm* (86) cast him again in a more typical, sinister role.

JULIUS J EPSTEIN

US screenwriter (1909-)

A New Yorker, he worked in radio as a publicist, became interested in writing stage plays and entered films in 1935 as a screenwriter. From 1939, and under contract at Warner with his twin brother Philip, he jointly wrote many top films, including *The Strawberry Blonde* (41), *The Man Who Came to Dinner* and *The Male Animal* (both 42) and *Arsenic and Old Lace* (44). Their most famous was *Casablanca* (42), for which they won an Oscar, with Howard Koch. The immortal line "Round up the usual suspects" occurred to them while they were driving along Santa Monica Boulevard in Los Angeles on their way to the studio. After his brother's death, Julius continued a solo career, occasionally producing, and was nominated for the script of *Pete 'n' Tillie* (72) and his last film, *Reuben, Reuben* (83).

EDITH EVANS

British actress (1888-1976)

Born in London and educated at St Michael's School, Chester Square, Evans was a milliner before making her stage debut in Troilus and Cressida in 1912. Her first film was *A Welsh Singer* (15). In between touring with the actress Ellen Terry and many successful classical roles, she made her sound debut in *The Queen of Spades* (48). She reprised Lady Bracknell, her most famous stage role, on film in *The Importance of Being Earnest* (52). She received best supporting actress Oscar nominations for *Tom Jones* (63), *The Chalk Garden* (64) and was nominated for best

actress for *The Whisperers* (66), which also won her many awards, although it received mixed reviews. She will be best remembered for her quivering indignation. She was made a DBE in 1946.

MAX FACTOR

US make-up expert (1877-1938)

He worked at the Russian Imperial Theatre as a wigmaster and make-up artist before emigrating to America in 1904. He revolutionised the art of screen make-up, pioneering what he called a system of "colour harmony". Essentially, it matched cosmetics to blend with a woman's individual colouring for a "natural" look, far removed from the heavy theatrical greasepaint to which the camera had proved so unsympathetic. He developed ▷

Julius Epstein and his brother won an Oscar for Casablanca

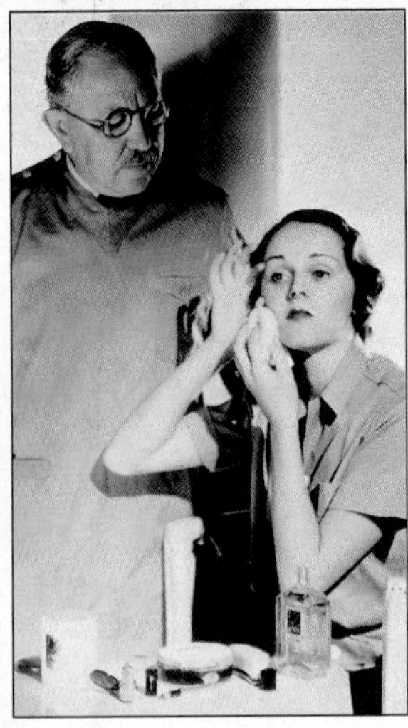

cosmetics to harmonise both with the face and the film stock. Factor famously classified women into seven types, ranging from light blonde to dark brunette, and pronounced the oval-shaped face to be the ideal. As well as developing products such as Panchromatic base, he formulated techniques for applying rouge and eye shadow so as to give "depth" and shape to the face. When he died, his products and methods were in use in the majority of film studios worldwide, while the marketing of his commercial make-up range allowed millions of women to try to emulate the look of their screen idols.

DOUGLAS FAIRBANKS
US actor (1883-1939)

He was the closest Hollywood ever came to giving America a monarch. Nobody brought as much fun to his public: the easy-going smile, the breezy swagger and the acrobatic grace were masculine poetry in motion. He started with a series of social comedies, such as *Manhattan Madness* (16), and went on to such swashbucklers as *The Mark of Zorro* (20), *Robin Hood* (22) and *The Thief Of Bagdad* (24), which he also wrote and produced. He expressed emotion in action. When America's favourite swashbuckler married its sweetheart, Mary Pickford (qv), the couple were revered like royalty and they entertained lavishly at Pickfair, their home. They teamed with Chaplin and D W Griffith (qqv) to form United Artists. Fairbanks never quite made the transition into sound; *The Taming of the Shrew* (29) shows him at his saucy, rumbustious best despite Pickford's final wink at the camera. After divorcing her he married Lady Sylvia Ashley. His last film was *The Private Life of Don Juan* (34).

DOUGLAS FAIRBANKS JR
US actor (1909-)

The son of Douglas (qv) and the Rhode Island heiress Anna Beth Sully, he was cast in a more classical mould than his swashbuckling father, who took little interest in his acting. Forced to carve his way through the Hollywood jungle, he became a bit-part actor and scriptwriter and had acted in a score of films when he married Joan Crawford (qv). Never a serious contender for his father's mantle, best filled by Errol Flynn (qv), it was not until he moved to Britain to play the conniving Grand Duke Peter in *Catherine the Great* (34) that he carved out a niche with parts ranging from handsome heroes and gentlemen gigolos to well-meaning weaklings and the archetypal black sheep, exemplified in his role in *The Prisoner of Zenda* (37). He served in the navy during the second world war. An avowed Anglophile and intimate of the royal family, he received an honorary knighthood for furthering Anglo-American amity. During the 1950s he hosted a theatrical series for American TV and in the 1960s hosted and acted in Douglas Fairbanks Presents for British TV. He retired to Florida with his second wife Mary Lee Hartford.

RAINER WERNER FASSBINDER
German director (1946-82)

He spent his childhood embroiled in the joys of moviegoing and began making short films after dropping out of school. He formed a theatrical company and first dabbled in full-length feature film production in 1969. The prolific nature of his work during those first few years might have been written off as youthful exuberance had the films not been so rich in texture. With such films as *Why Does Herr R Run Amok?* (70) and *The Bitter Tears of Petra von Kant* (72), Fassbinder quickly established his style – economical, political, dry, sometimes allegorical – and won resounding favour from international critics despite a lack of financial success. His favourite actress, Hanna Schygulla (qv),

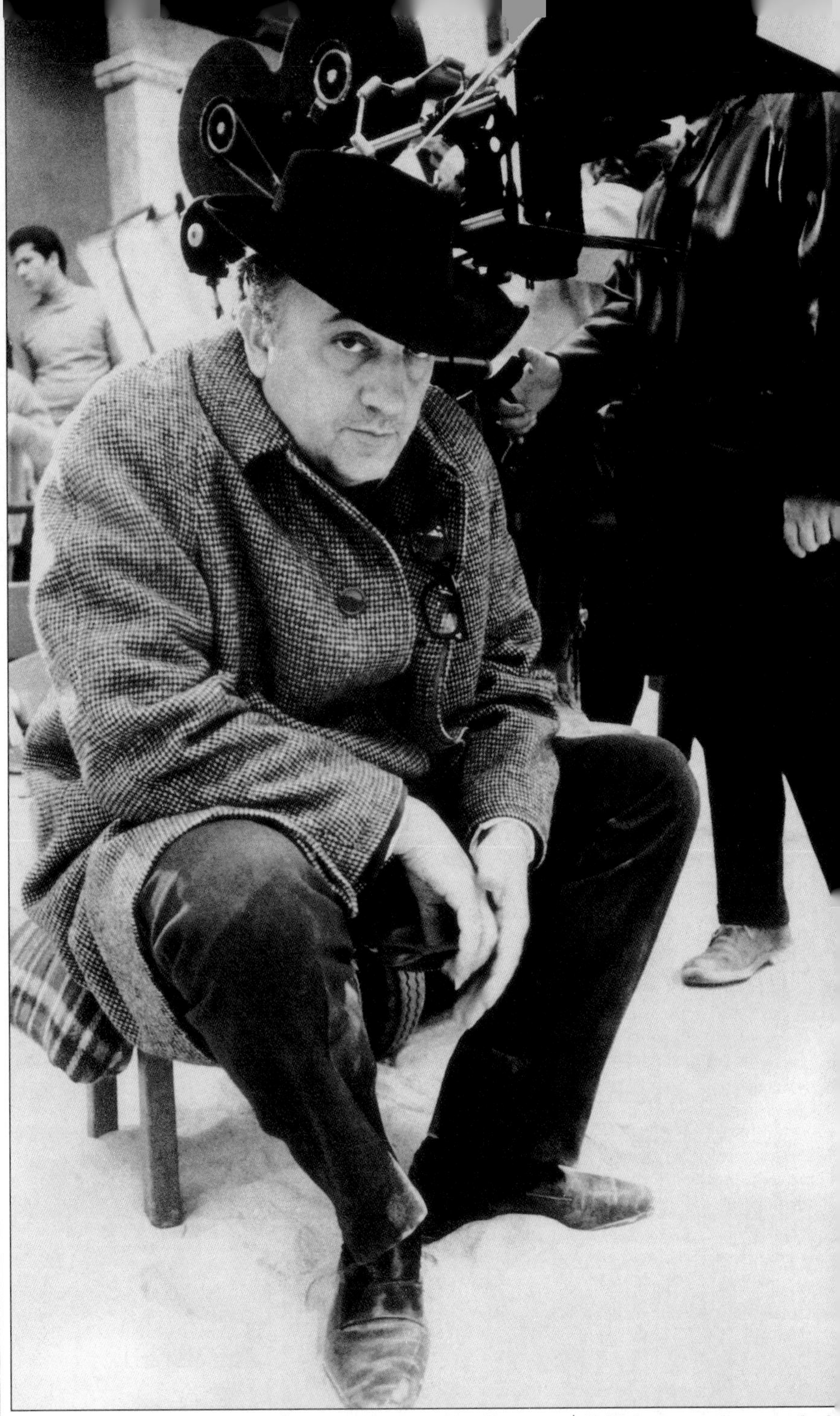

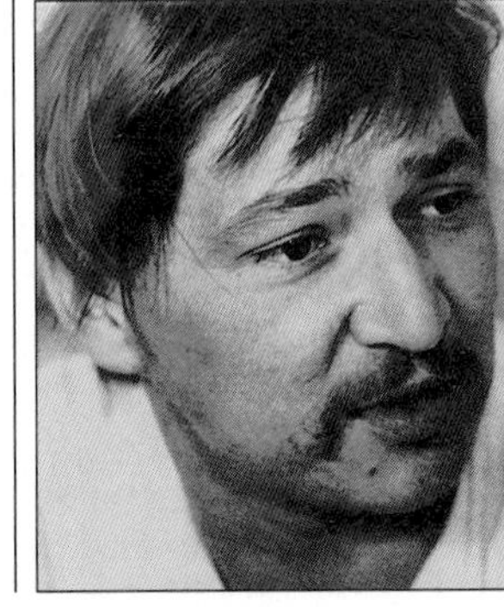

appeared in many of his films, including *The Marriage of Maria Braun* (79). He sometimes acted in his films, notably in *Fox and His Friends* (75), where his role as a lonely homosexual was thought to be a rare glimpse into his personal life. In 1982 he won the Berlin Festival's Golden Bear for *Veronika Voss*, but he died the same year. His talents embraced writing, art direction, editing and composing.

ALICE FAYE
US actress, singer (1912-)

The sassy leading lady of American musical films of the 1930s and early 1940s, Faye was a Broadway chorus girl in George White's Scandals when she was spotted by Rudy Vallee. He got her the female lead in George White's *Scandals* (35), the film of the show, when the leading lady walked out. She first combined comedy and the fu use of her contralto singing voice *Sing, Baby Sing* (36). Thereafter, i *On the Avenue, You Can't Have Everything, Wake Up and Live* anc *In Old Chicago* (all 37), and *Alexander's Ragtime Band* (38), *Rose of Washington Square* (39), *Lillian Russell* and *Tin Pan Alley* (both 40), *That Night in Rio* and *Weekend in Havana* (both 41), *Hello Frisco Hello* (42) and *The Gang's All Here* (43), she consolidated her position as the leading lady of musical films. Fox studio boss Darryl F Zanuck (qv), though, refused to allow her to sir on radio and introduced Betty

Fellini: ostentatious magical ringmaster of Italian cinema

able (qv) as a rival attraction. He owed Grable to eclipse Faye, who it her contract in 1945. She has ade only four films since.

:DERICO FELLINI
ılian director (1920-93)

counts of his childhood are ught with discrepancies (he was notorious and self-confessed liar), t it is known that he left his metown of Rimini in 1938 and came a proofreader and rtoonist in Florence. In Rome he ›rked as a reporter and met the ector Roberto Rossellini (qv), o asked Fellini to help him on *ɔen City* (45), his neo-realist count of the Nazis in Rome. ter a series of brief llaborations, he directed his own ature, *Luci del Varietà* (50). With *'itelloni* (53), an autobiographical ıdy of bored adolescents, he ceived critical and commercial claim. *La Strada*, a year later, on the Oscar for best foreign film. s most accomplished and st-loved films are *La Dolce Vita* 0) and *8½* (63). Their tentatiously poetic and luscious ages influenced generations of n makers, including Martin orsese (qv), and spawned the m Fellini-esque. He fell from vour during the 1970s, with the ception of *Amarcord* (73), which ve him his fourth Oscar, as his ›rk grew increasingly pretentious. s last jibes at the modern world, cluding *Ginger and Fred* (86), monstrated his love of cinema.

FERNANDEL
French actor (1903-71)

Reviled by the critics, the comic actor made many films between 1930 and 1950, most of them third-rate. In the 1950s the quality of his pictures improved and he became popular with English-speaking audiences. He went on to confound his critics to become a national institution and was made a member of the Legion of Honour. He was a child performer, then an amateur comedian and singer before turning to vaudeville in

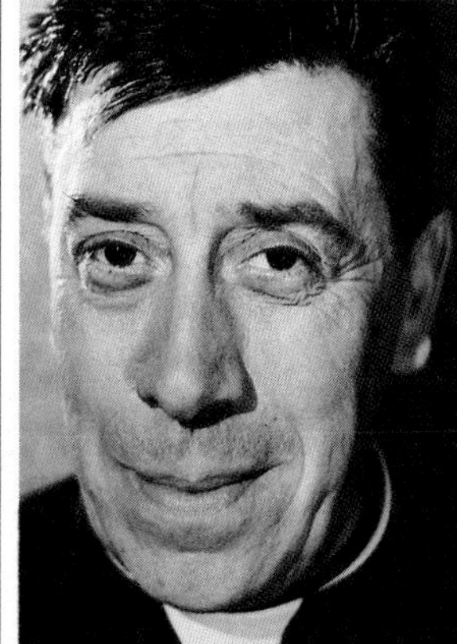

1922. Ironically, he established himself on screen in a dramatic role as the virtuous, backward grocer's son in *Le Rosier de Madame Husson* (31). Before long his lugubrious features and horse's grin steered him into a string of popular comedies. The most notable was the Don Camillo series in which he played an unconventional priest. Fernandel appeared in 150 films in one of the longest careers of any French star.

JOSE FERRER
US actor, director (1909-92)

A Puerto Rican, Ferrer (below left) first found fame on Broadway as a leading man and a director. Nominated for a best supporting actor Oscar as the Dauphin in *Joan of Arc* (48), he took the best actor award in the title role of *Cyrano de Bergerac* (50) and was nominated for his Toulouse-Lautrec in *Moulin Rouge* (52). Other characterisations include Sigmund Romberg in *Deep in My Heart* (54), Dreyfus in *I Accuse!* (58), which he also directed, and Herod in *The Greatest Story Ever Told* (65). Among his other acting/directorial credits are *The Cockleshell Heroes* (55) and the television/media satire *The Great Man* (56), which he co-wrote. After directing *State Fair* (62), he confined himself to acting. He was married to the actress Uta Hagen and the singer Rosemary Clooney.

LOUIS FEUILLADE
French director, writer (1873-1925)

Responsible for more than 700 films, most of which he also

scripted, Feuillade wrote a further 100 for other directors. He achieved prodigious numbers before feature-length films became commonplace and much of his output was in multi-episode serials. His greatest creations were fantastic adventures. In 1913 the first of his five Fantômas serials appeared, based on a series of novels by Pierre Souvestre and Marcel Allain. The hero was a master-criminal who specialised in bizarre disguise. In 1915 his *Les Vampires*, a 10-episode serial, featured a gang of jewel thieves led by Jean Aymé and Musidora, a glamorous villainess in black tights. In 1916 *Judex*, a cloaked nocturnal crusader battling against criminality, made his first appearance. After Feuillade's death he was forgotten, until the Cinémathèque Française held a post-war retrospective. New film-makers became aware of the breadth of his imagination and its undoubted influence on German expressionism of the 1920s.

JACQUES FEYDER
Belgian director (1885-1948)

Against parental wishes he became an actor in Paris, then switched to film, making short comedies during the first world war. An early feature was the exotic (and then record-breakingly expensive) *L'Atlantide* (21). Throughout the 1920s and 1930s he secured a reputation for craftsmanship and versatility. During a Hollywood sojourn he directed Garbo's (qv) last silent, *The Kiss* (29), and for Korda (qv) in Britain he made *Knight Without Armour* (37) with Robert Donat and Marlene Dietrich (qqv). His version of Zola's *Thérèse Raquin* (27) is lost. His three best-known films, *Le Grand Jeu* (34), *Pension Mimosas* (35) and *La Kermesse héroïque* (35), were made with Françoise Rosay (qv), his wife and the *grande dame* of French cinema. *La Kermesse*, a tale of invasion and occupation, won him best director at Venice, but later offended the Nazis, forcing Feyder into Swiss exile.

Jacques Feyder, director of Garbo's last silent

SALLY FIELD
US actress, producer (1946-)

A former teenage star of 1960s TV sitcoms, she was long pigeon-holed in light, lowbrow comedy – particularly during her relationship with sometime co-star Burt Reynolds (qv). Prestige directors would not even audition her, but after work at the Actors Studio and a well-received performance in the offbeat *Stay Hungry* (76) she was finally rewarded with the plum role of *Norma Rae* (79), winning the Oscar for her oppressed housewife-

textile worker turned union activist. Always in the shadow of more glamorous actresses, she re-emerged as a plucky young widow surviving the Depression in *Places in the Heart* (84), but was widely ridiculed for her excited outburst of gratitude ("You like me! You really like me!") when accepting her second Oscar. Her answer was to develop her own, unappreciated projects. In 1994, she topped the "most profitable" accountings as female lead in *Mrs Doubtfire* (93) and *Forrest Gump* (94).

GRACIE FIELDS
British actress (1889-1979)

Born in Rochdale, Lancashire, and known affectionately as "Our Gracie", she was a music hall entertainer at 13 and became the highest paid film actress in Britain during the Depression. With a voice like a yodelling song thrush, so memorably captured in the title song of the anti-mill closure film *Sing As We Go* (34), she symbolised an indomitable, fighting spirit to her largely working-class audience. She was an invaluable celebrity before the war with *Keep Smiling* (38) and *Shipyard Sally* (39) and so popular that parliament once adjourned to allow MPs to listen to her on the radio. She never conquered America, despite making three Hollywood films and being voted third after Shirley Temple and Clark Gable (qqv) in the Motion Picture Herald poll in 1937. She emigrated with Monty Banks, her second husband, when his Italian origins marked him as an alien during the war, and improved her fortunes with *Holy Matrimony* (43) and *Molly and Me* (45). She later lived on Capri with her third husband and became a DBE in 1979.

W C FIELDS
US comedian (1879-1946)

His name was William Claude Dukenfield and his comedy donated nothing to charity. It consistently hit a sour note dedicated to the proposition that you should *Never Give a Sucker an Even Break* (41). The son of a cockney immigrant, whose beatings and street brawls Fields blamed for his red, bulbous nose, he was a carnival juggler and vaudevillian before Broadway musicals gained him fame and roles in shorts such as *The Fatal Glass of Beer* (33). His slurring whine became familiar stock in trade for impersonators and his alcoholism was legendary. He wrote screenplays under names such as Mahatma Kane Jeeves, but it was his Mr Micawber in *David Copperfield* (35) that revealed a quality which had little to do with eccentricity. He starred opposite another original, Mae West (qv) in *My Little Chickadee* (40). He had a baroque turn of phrase and was an old-time trouper who always paid for routines he purloined from TV. He died on Christmas Day, a festival which, of course, he hated.

PETER FINCH
British actor (1916-77)

William Mitchell was born in London and went to live in Sydney, Australia, at the age of 10, where he roamed between a variety of dead-end jobs before making his first, forgettable film, *Mr Chedworth Steps Out* (39). After war service he worked in Australian theatre and in such adventure yarns as *Rats of Tobruk* (44) and *Eureka Stockade* (49). He was spotted by Laurence Olivier (qv) who persuaded him to appear with him in classical roles on the British stage. He subsequently had an affair with Vivien Leigh (qv), Olivier's wife. He suffered appalling stage fright and soon transferred to film, hopping between romantic lead and sinister heavy. Some of his best known roles are in *The Wooden Horse* (50), *The Heart of the Matter* (53), *Elephant Walk* (53), *The Dark Avenger* (55) and *The Nun's Story* (58). His work included Powell and Pressburger's (qqv) *The Battle of the River Plate* and *A Town Like Alice* (both 56), *In the Cool of the Day* (63), *The Pumpkin Eater* (64), *Judith* (65), *Far From the Madding Crowd* (67) and *Sunday Bloody Sunday* (71). His last feature was his most memorable, as the crazed newscaster in Sidney Lumet's (qv) *Network* (76), for which he won a posthumous Oscar.

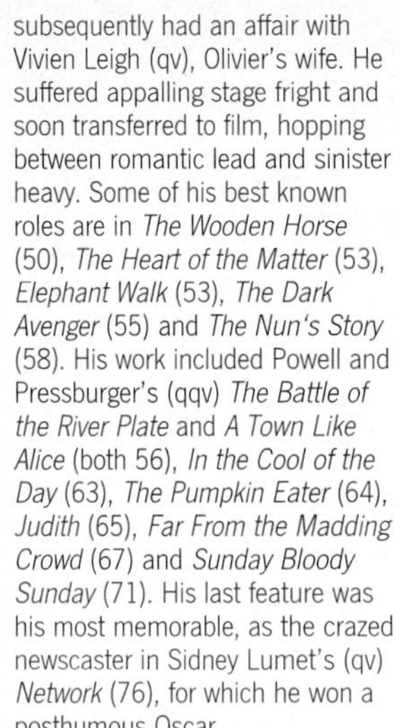

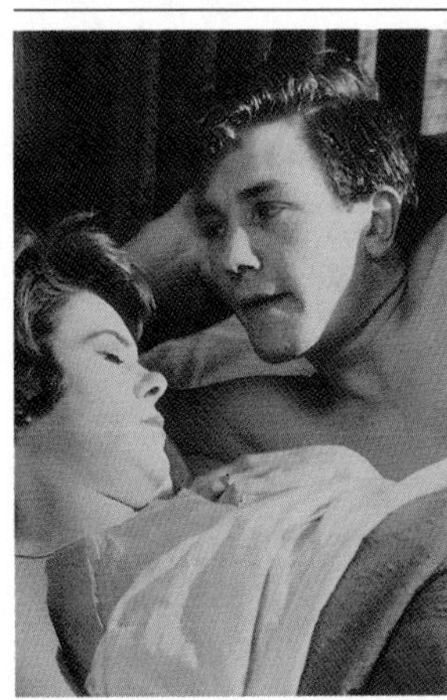

ALBERT FINNEY
British actor (1936-)

Finney's rough-hewn looks reflect the monosyllabic unease, the slow-burning intensity or the brute explosions that have characterised his work. After treading the boards in Birmingham and satisfying audiences with numerous Shakespearean roles, he first impressed in *Saturday Night and Sunday Morning* (60), supplying an electric charge of raging non-conformity and became a 1960s icon. He turned down the title role in Lean's (qv) *Lawrence of Arabia* (62), but remained aloft with *Tom Jones* (63), in which he embodied the jokey randiness of the hero. He starred in and directed *Charlie Bubbles* (67) and went on to attempt a musical, playing Daddy Warbucks in *Annie* (82). He excelled as the arrogant actor/manager in *The Dresser* (83) and the boozy diplomat in *Under the Volcano* (84). He turned in a distinguished performance as the desiccated schoolmaster in the remake of Terence Rattigan's *The Browning Version* (94).

TERENCE FISHER
British director (1904-80)

After editing a number of films, he finally made it to director at 44 and went on to create a British horror genre with Hammer. Even though his films lacked the visually rich expressionism of the German and American classics, Fisher employed colour in the service of character. Some of his Frankenstein and Dracula films are saturated in a wash of lurid reds, with deathly white skin thrown in for added scares. He delivered pictures with conveyor belt rapidity, *The Curse of Frankenstein* (57) and *Dracula* (58) among them. *Dracula – Prince of Darkness* (65) returned the vampire to eroticism, while *The Hound of the Baskervilles* (59) is considered by some to be the best-ever Sherlock Holmes film.

BARRY FITZGERALD
Irish actor (1888-1961)

Hollywood's favourite caricature of an Irishman, the diminutive Fitzgerald (5ft 3in) distinguished many films with his twinkling charm. William Joseph Shields retired from the civil service at 41 and joined Dublin's Abbey Theatre. There Sean O'Casey wrote The Silver Tassle for him, which led to his memorable role in Juno and the Paycock. His film debut was a repeat of his performance in the latter in Hitchcock's (qv) screen version in 1930. John Ford (qv) invited him to Hollywood to recreate his stage role in O'Casey's *The Plough and the Stars* (36). He worked with Ford again in *Four Men and a Prayer* (38) and *How Green Was My Valley* (41) before being hailed in Leo McCarey's (qv) *Going My Way* (44), in which he played the cranky Father Fitzgibbon to Bing Crosby's (qv) singing priest. He received the best supporting actor Oscar for the film. He won a contract at Paramount and remained in Hollywood until 1956.

ROBERT FLAHERTY
US director (1884-1951)

A discarded cigarette in the editing room destroyed his first film, but the second, *Nanook of the North* (22), was an engaging chronicle of the Eskimos' struggle for survival. The son of a miner and prospector he dug deep for his subjects, living with them to understand them better. The result was often haloed with a heroism about man against

nature. In the Hollywood marketplace, *Moana* (26) and *Tabu*, started in 1928 but not released until 1931, he over-shot footage and commercial considerations. His *Man of Aran* (34), *Elephant Boy* (37) and *Louisiana Story* (48) have a simpl and single-minded grandeur.

VICTOR FLEMING
US director (1883-1949)

His place in film history is dependent on his accreditation as the director of *Gone With the Winc* and *The Wizard of Oz* (both 39), but his reputation was built on action films with Gary Cooper, Clark Gable and Spencer Tracy (qqv). He utilised the appeal of his former girlfriend Clara Bow (qv) in *Mantrap* (26) and promoted Jean Harlow (qv) as the *Bombshell* (33 A former racing driver and stills photographer, he learned from D Griffith (qv), John Emerson and Allan Dwan (qv). During the first world war he accompanied President Wilson to Europe as his chief cameraman. After the war h

graduated to the director's chair with two Douglas Fairbanks (qv) films and established himself on works such as *The Virginian* (29), *Treasure Island* (34) and *Captains Courageous* (37). David O Selznick (qv) chose him to replace George Cukor (qv) on *Gone With the Wind*, for which Fleming won an Oscar. His last film was the critically abused *Joan of Arc* (48).

ERROL FLYNN
Australian actor (1909-59)

The swashbuckler who capered his way through a host of Boy's Own fantasies was born in Hobart, Tasmania. He wandered the Pacific doing odd jobs before appearing as Fletcher Christian in *In the Wake of the Bounty* (33). After a period in British repertory he was cast by Warner for *The Case of the Curious Bride* (35), which teamed him with director Michael Curtiz (qv). Flynn was not a great actor, but he had an athletic and attractive personality and stormed through such adventure classics as *Captain Blood* (35), *The Charge of the Light Brigade* (36), *The Adventures of Robin Hood* (38), *The Private Lives of Elizabeth and Essex* (39) with Bette Davis (qv), *The Sea Hawk* (40), *They Died With Their Boots On* (41) and *Objective Burma!* (45). He was also a notorious womaniser, whose reputation became seriously tarnished after charges of unlawful intercourse with two under-age girls in 1942. He was acquitted, but eventually sank into drink and sloth; his last films were lacklustre.

Flynn, romantic action hero and notorious party animal

HENRY FONDA
US actor (1905-82)

Like his friend James Stewart (qv), he was the quintessential nice guy exuding resolute decency and quiet charm in a range of films from comedy to westerns. He made more than 80 films and his unsympathetic roles can be counted on one hand. After appearing in The Farmer Takes a Wife on Broadway, he made his Hollywood debut in the film version in 1935. He returned to the theatre in the 1950s, notably in Two for the Seesaw, alternating stage and screen thereafter. His career highlights were numerous – with Bette Davis (qv) in *Jezebel* (38), Stanwyck (qv) in *The Lady Eve* (41) and as Wyatt Earp in *My Darling Clementine* (46). His navy service earned a presidential citation, his acting an AFI life achievement award, an honorary Oscar in 1978, and the best actor Oscar for his crotchety dying husband in *On Golden Pond* (81). Margaret Sullavan (qv) was the first of his five wives; the heiress Frances Brokaw, who committed suicide, was the second and mother of Jane (qv) and Peter.

JANE FONDA
US actress (1937-)

She was the pre-eminent American actress of the 1970s, although her outspoken opposition to the Vietnam war made her unpopular and earned her the name "Hanoi Jane". The daughter of Henry (qv) she grew up as Hollywood royalty, but under the shadow of her mother's suicide. After a conventional period as a pretty ingénue, she transformed into a 1960s sex kitten under the influence of Roger Vadim (qv), her first husband. *Barbarella* (68) made her an icon, but in the 1970s she embraced feminist, realist and political roles, playing a

cynical prostitute in *Klute* (71), the writer Lillian Hellman in *Julia* (77) and a determined newswoman in the nuclear accident thriller *The China Syndrome* (79). She received Oscars for *Klute* and *Coming Home* (78). After marrying Ted Turner, the media mogul, she announced her retirement from films in 1993.

JOAN FONTAINE
US actress (1917-)

The younger sister of Olivia de Havilland (qv), she began her acting career under the name Joan Burfield and made her film debut in *No More Ladies* (35). Although she had played leading roles opposite Fred Astaire (qv) in *A Damsel in Distress* (37) and Douglas Fairbanks Jr (qv) in *Gunga Din* (39), it was only as the heroine of *Rebecca* (40) that she achieved stardom and a best actress Oscar nomination. She won the award for *Suspicion* (41) and was again nominated for *The Constant Nymph* (42). Her 1940s roles, including *Jane Eyre* (43), leaned towards the genteel, but she matured into tougher, sometimes vicious characterisations in *Born to Be Bad* (50), *Flight to Tangier* (53), *Beyond a Reasonable Doubt* (56) and *Tender Is the Night* (62). Her husbands included the actor Brian Aherne, producer William Dozier and producer Collier Young.

BRYAN FORBES
British actor, writer and director (1926-)

Born in east London, John Clarke went to Rada, entering films as an actor in 1948 (after military service) in *The Small Back Room*. His eager, boyish looks won him war film roles such as *The Wooden Horse* (50), usually as a keen NCO (he says he was turned down for *The Cruel Sea* because he "wasn't officer material"). He began writing screenplays with *Cockleshell Heroes* (55). In 1959 he and Richard Attenborough (qv) formed Beaver Films. He directed *Whistle Down the Wind* (61), *The L-Shaped Room* (62) and *Seance on a Wet Afternoon* (64) and wrote and directed *King Rat* (65) in America. In 1969 he became head of production at Elstree, resigning two years later in spite of such artistic successes as *The Railway Children* (71). Several of his films, *The Raging Moon* (70), *The Stepford Wives* (74) and *International Velvet* (78) have featured Nanette Newman, his wife since 1954. He is the author of several best-selling books and has run a bookshop in Virginia Water, in London's leafy stockbroker belt.

GLENN FORD
US actor (1916-)

A versatile leading man, born in Canada, who has specialised in portraying decent, deep-thinking heroes, he made his mark on stage and screen – his first film was *Heaven With a Barbed Wire Fence* (39) – before war service. Two films, *Gilda* and, with Bette Davis (qv), *A Stolen Life* (both 46), ▷

proved pivotal in his transition to star. Westerns, thrillers, dramas and comedies have all allowed him to exhibit his range in such examples as *The Man From Colorado* (48), *The Big Heat* (53), *The Teahouse of the August Moon* (56), *3:10 to Yuma* and *Don't Go Near the Water* (both 57), *The Four Horsemen of the Apocalypse* (62) and *Midway* (76). He has also appeared regularly in television series, but has made fewer films since the 1970s. He has been married to three actresses: Eleanor Powell (qv), Kathryn Hays and Cynthia Hayward.

HARRISON FORD
US actor (1942-)

Ford has become an international star playing an introspective action man in the Oscar-nominated *Witness* (85), *Patriot Games* (92), *Clear and Present Danger* (94) and the Indiana Jones trilogy (81, 84 and 89). He first roamed Hollywood in a series of bit parts, often playing television cowboys

(The Virginian), before disenchantment set in and he took up carpentry. His appearance in George Lucas's (qv) *American Graffiti* (73) led to his launch pad in Lucas's *Star Wars* (77). Ridley Scott's (qv) *Blade Runner* (82) gave him a cult following. The business comedy *Working Girl* (88) and the action thriller *The Fugitive* (93) have maintained his status as the foremost of Hollywood's elite.

JOHN FORD
US director (1894-1973)

Whatever reappraisals are currently touted, his eye for the Monument Valley visual and his myth making are legendary. He made a string of films under the name Jack Ford, then went into Oscar territory with *The Informer* (35), the classic *Stagecoach* (39) and *The Grapes of Wrath* (40), which gave voice to John Steinbeck's anger. There was another Oscar for the Welsh sentiment of *How Green Was My Valley* (41), but more important was the re-invention of Wyatt Earp for *My Darling Clementine* (46). The cavalry sustained Ford's career with a series of outpost epics — the famous trilogy was *Fort Apache* (48), *She Wore a Yellow Ribbon* (49) and *Rio Grande* (50) — but it was the Irish comedy *The Quiet Man* (52) that won another Oscar. *The Searchers* (56) was a more compelling western than anything before and *Cheyenne Autumn* (64) was his valedictory western, atoning in some respects for his earlier representations of native Americans. Ford loved heroes and perceived himself as one.

CARL FOREMAN
US writer, producer (1914-84)

A prolific and accomplished writer, he was blacklisted at his peak by the House Un-American Activities Committee. He subsequently co-wrote the Oscar-winning screenplay for *The Bridge on the River Kwai* (57) without credit and establishe himself in the British film industry The son of Russian immigrants, Foreman attended law school anc was a newspaper reporter in Chicago before moving to Hollywood. After writing radio material for Bob Hope (qv), he joined Frank Capra and John Huston (qqv) making documentaries for the war effort. He then set up his own productic company with Stanley Kramer, fo whom he wrote some of his most memorable screenplays, includin *Champion* and *Home of The Bra* (both 49) and *The Men* (50), all with strong social themes. He wa writing *High Noon* (52) when he was blacklisted, but still secured Oscar nomination. In Britain he worked as a script consultant for Alexander Korda (qv), then collaborated with Michael Wilson, another banned Oscar nominee, *River Kwai*. Later he concentratec on producing, directing only one more film, *The Victors* (63). In 1970 he was awarded the CBE.

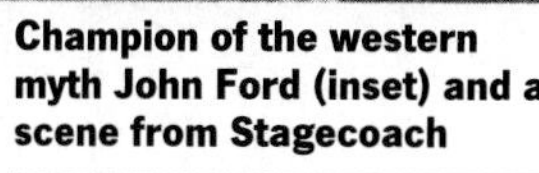

Champion of the western myth John Ford (inset) and a scene from Stagecoach

LOS FORMAN
Czechoslovakian director (1932-)

Banned by the Nazis, he graduated from Prague's Academy of Music and Dramatic Art and made his debut with *Black Peter* (63), which won first prize at the Locarno film festival. It was his charming comedy *The Firemen's Ball* (67), though, that brought him to the attention of critics and audiences. He lived as an expatriate in France in the late 1960s after Russia invaded Czechoslovakia, then moved to New York. He directed *Taking Off* (71) for Universal and formed part of the directorial team covering the 1972 Munich Olympics for the official film *Visions of Eight* (73), but it was *One Flew Over the Cuckoo's Nest* (75) that rocketed him into the big league, winning all five top Oscars; the first film to do so since *It Happened One Night* 41 years earlier. Forman directed the belated screen version of the hippie musical *Hair* (79) and successive films included *Ragtime* (81) and another Oscar triumph, *Amadeus* (84). Since then his only work of note, *Valmont* (89), was overshadowed by the delayed release of Stephen Frears's (qv) film *Dangerous Liaisons* (88), which was adapted from the same de Laclos text.

GEORGE FORMBY
British actor (1904-61)

With his toothy giggle and dazzling artistry on the ukelele (actually a hybrid instrument, the banjulele), he developed a simple-minded slapstick style that commended itself to a generation that needed cheering up during the Depression. The son of a Lancashire comedian, he worked the northern variety circuit as a youngster and made his first film appearance in a racing drama at the age of 11. His debut as a comedian was in 1934 in *Boots Boots*. Its success prompted Basil Dean at Ealing to sign him to appear in *No Limit* (35), the first of 11 films he made there. In the 1930s he and Gracie Fields (qv) were consistent top performers at the British box office. Formby left Ealing for Columbia, but his later work lacked simplicity and his good-natured, slightly risqué gormless charm. His film career came to a halt with *George in Civvy Street* (46), when it was found that the post-war audience had deserted him. The rest of his career was devoted to the stage.

BILL FORSYTH
British director, writer (1946-)

His films are celebrated for quirky humour and charm, but they are also melancholy and unsettling. After training at the National Film School he worked with the Glasgow Youth Theatre. Many of that theatre's aspirants featured in his debut, *That Sinking Feeling* (79), a comedy of unemployed teenagers staging a heist of kitchen sinks, which attracted attention at the Edinburgh and London film festivals. His most popular films were *Gregory's Girl* (80) and *Local Hero* (83), for which Forsyth received a Bafta for best direction. Hollywood beckoned, but proved an unfruitful environment for a film-maker whose gifts were not engaged by commercial or formulaic considerations. *Housekeeping* (87) did not fare well and his disenchantment increased after the failure of *Breaking In* (89). His most ambitious work, *Being Human* (89), in which Robin Williams (qv) plays five characters, went straight to video in Britain.

BOB FOSSE
US director, choreographer (1927-87)

He danced in a few 1950s films, notably *Kiss Me Kate* (53) and *My Sister Eileen* (55), and choreographed his first Broadway show, The Pajama Game in 1954 (winning the first of eight Tonys) followed by Damn Yankees in 1955, and their subsequent film versions. His heavily jazz-influenced dance style was cool and angular with athletic leaps and slides. The first film he directed was his Broadway success *Sweet Charity* (69), with Shirley MacLaine (qv). With his second, *Cabaret* (72), he and his star Liza Minnelli (qv) won Oscars. He was nominated for *Lenny* (74), a biography of the comedian Lenny Bruce, and in 1979 made *All That Jazz*, in which Roy Scheider played a chain-smoking dance director (clearly based on Fosse) who fantasises on his women and excessive existence before succumbing to a heart attack. Fosse eventually did just that a few years later in Washington DC during a revival of Sweet Charity. His three wives were all dancers: Mary-Ann Niles, Joan McCracken and Gwen Verdon.

JODIE FOSTER
US actress (1962-)

Brandy, her pushy mother, had her working in commercials by the age of three. At five she could read scripts and appeared in several television series. At 10 she made her film debut for Disney and was not quite 13 when she impressed as the young prostitute who

inspires De Niro's (qv) bloody crusade in *Taxi Driver* (76). It won her first Oscar nomination, but stamped her with an amoral image that largely prevailed from *Bugsy Malone* (76) to *The Hotel New Hampshire* (84). She was rescued by Oscars for her portrayal of a rape victim in *The Accused* (88) and an FBI agent confronting Hannibal Lecter in *The Silence of the Lambs* (91). She made her directing debut and starred in *Little Man Tate* (91). Recent films have included *Sommersby* (93) and the Oscar-nominated *Nell* (94). Tough and versatile, her precocious gifts and intellect (Yale graduate, fluent French speaker) have carried into adulthood. She has also coped well with a career low during the 1980s, the would-be presidential assassin John Hinckley's deranged devotion for her and gay militant attempts to "out" her.

JAMES FOX
British actor (1939-)

Born in London to a theatrical family, he first appeared on screen as a child in *The Miniver Story* and *The Magnet* (both 50) through Robin Fox, his agent father. Schooling intervened until *The Loneliness of the Long Distance Runner* (62) and *The Servant* (63), as Dirk Bogarde's (qv) closeted but decadent master. In an age when the working-class lad ruled, Fox managed to carve a niche by playing slightly down-at-heel, upper-class men. But a raft of odd choices followed, such as *Tamahine* (63) and *Those Magnificent Men in Their Flying* ▷

Machines (65), *Thoroughly Modern Millie* (67) and his best performance of this period as a dissolute gangster in *Performance* (70). Then he shocked everyone by disappearing into a religious sect for 10 years, just as suddenly re-emerging to continue his career with *Runners* (83), *Greystoke* and *A Passage To India* (both 84), *The Whistle Blower* (87), *The Russia House* (90) and as Sir Anthony Blunt in John Schlesinger's (qv) A Question of Attribution, which was made for BBC television.

MICHAEL J FOX
US actor (1961-)

Beginning as a juvenile in Canadian television, this short (5ft 4in), fresh-faced actor moved to California and success on American TV in the series Family Ties, making his film debut with *Midnight Madness* (80). The role of McFly in the time travel sci-fi hit *Back to the Future* (85) made him a star. That film and its sequels (89, 90) are still his best known work. Besides other winning light-romantic/comedy roles in *The Secret of My Success* (87) and *Doc Hollywood* (91), he has taken tougher roles in the cautionary tale about drugs, *Bright Lights, Big City* (88), the Vietnam drama *Casualties of War* (89), *The Hard Way* (91) and *For Love or Money* (93). He is married to actress Tracy Pollan, his Family Ties co-star.

FREDDIE FRANCIS
British director, cinematographer (1917-)

Now receiving wider recognition in his later years, Francis has been responsible for some memorable compositions, such as *The Elephant Man* (80), *The French Lieutenant's Woman* (81) and *Cape Fear* (91). He started as a clapper boy at 17 and was appointed director of photography for the Army Kinematograph Unit before rejoining the studios after the second world war as a camera operator on *Mine Own Executioner* (47), *Moulin Rouge* (53) and *Beau Brummell* (54). As a cinematographer, his compositional excellence and creative use of light flooded across such works as *Room at the Top* (59), *Saturday Night and Sunday Morning* (60) and *The Innocents* (61). His rich photography in *Sons and Lovers* (60) won him an Oscar, but in later years he directed a mixed bag of films, many for Hammer, including *Paranoiac* (63), *Dr Terror's House of Horrors* (65) and *Dracula Has Risen From the Grave* (68).

KAY FRANCIS
US actress (1903-68)

The daughter of the stage actress Katherine Clinton was spurred by love, in *Cynara* (32), and duty, in *British Agent* (34). The daughter of a Broadway actress, she made her elegant debut in *Gentlemen of the Press* (29). She established herself as one of the most glamorous stars, her perfect figure arrayed in high fashion, though Ernst Lubtisch's (qv) *Trouble in Paradise* (32) gave her a chance to sparkle. She worked with the best directors – King Vidor, Michael Curtiz, Frank Borzage (qqv) – and made dozens of films throughout the 1930s until the war heralded a decline popularity. Jack Benny's *Charley's Aunt* (41) was some compensation.

GEORGES FRANJU
French director (1912-87)

With his friend Henri Langlois he made a 16mm short in 1934, started a film magazine and formed a cinema club, before they founded the French Cinémathèque in 1937. It was 1949 before he began making the documentaries on which his reputation rests. The first and most notable was *Le Sang des Bêtes* (49), a vivid record of daily slaughter in an abbatoir, juxtaposed with everyday images of Parisian life. His features, of which

the best known is probably the Gothic melodrama *Les Yeux sans Visage* (59), are reasonably eclectic, but reflect a sombre world view and a cold beauty, influenced by German Expressionism, Feuillade (qv) – to whom he paid homage with *Judex* (63) – Cocteau (qv) and French poetic realism.

JOHN FRANKENHEIMER
US director (1930-)

An airforce film unit gave him his first taste of the technicalities of film making. While serving in the early 1950s he completed several short documentaries and later worked for CBS TV. He became a respected director before landing his first film, *The Young Stranger* (57). His next projects heralded an assured and accomplished talent. Two of his most famous films, *Birdman of Alcatraz* and *The Manchurian Candidate*, were released in 1962. Another sharp-edged thriller, *Seven Days in May* (64), confirmed his place in mainstream cinema as did *Seconds* (66). The period after these successes proved barren as he moved to Europe and began making films which eschewed tension for style. There was a briefly heartening change when he directed *French Connection II* (75), but there has been little since to indicate the magic still exists. The

violent pulp thriller *52 Pick-Up* (86) was a modest critical success, but his career has come full circle and he is back directing for TV.

SIDNEY FRANKLIN
US director, producer (1893-1972)

He entered films in 1913 and initially worked with his brother Chester Franklin on children's comedy shorts. After Chester was drafted for war service, Sidney developed skills as a craftsman and directed a number of polished features, such as *Her Night Of Romance* (25), *Quality Street* (27) and *The Last of Mrs Cheyney* (29) and *Wild Orchids* (29) with Garbo

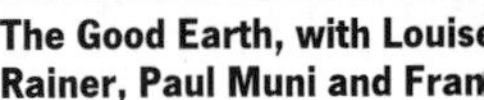

The Good Earth, with Louise Rainer, Paul Muni and Fran

(qv). At MGM under Irving Thalberg's (qv) wing he became renowned as an exponent of the stellar production values that characterised the studio's outpu He was regarded as the foremo "woman's picture" director wit *The Guardsman* (31), *The Barr of Wimpole Street* (34) and *The Good Earth* (37). After Thalberg death he became a producer a his *Mrs Miniver* (42) won the b picture Oscar. Late in his caree returned to directing with a rem of *The Barretts of Wimpole Stre* (57), after which he retired.

STEPHEN FREARS
British director (1941-)

Like so many of his generation, Frears made his name in televi and moved on to social comme films that denounced the Thatc years. He started out as writer/director on the short, *Th Burning* (67), directed the critic well received *Gumshoe* (72) an

ıade many strong television ıramas, such as England, Their ngland and Saigon – Year of the at. His cinema break came with ıe cult sleeper *My Beautiful aundrette* (85). The Joe Orton iography *Prick Up Your Ears* and ıe less successful *Sammy and ʼosie Get Laid* (both 87) put Frears n the Hollywood A-list of directors. is best known work to date is *ʼangerous Liaisons* (88) followed y the *The Grifters* (90), *Accidental lero* (92) and *The Snapper* (93).

RTHUR FREED
'S producer, lyricist '894-1973)

e had an uncanny instinct for ʼent, nurtured the careers of ıcente Minnelli, Gene Kelly and ıdy Garland (qqv) and was sponsible for the lion's share of e most visible musicals of the ʼ40s and 1950s. In collaboration th Nacio Herb Brown, the mposer, he was commissioned write the songs for MGM's ound-breaking *The Broadway elody* (29) and so helped to unch the film musical. He ntinued to turn out a prodigious mber of songs (including Singin' the Rain and You Are My Lucky ar) before being elevated to sociate producer on *The Wizard Oz* (39). Thereafter he produced catalogue of musical classics cluding *Meet Me in St Louis* (44), *ı the Town* (49), *An American in ris* (51), *Singin' in the Rain* (52) d *Gigi* (58). Such was his golden ıch, Freed was given carte ınche to make such experimental usicals as the all-black *Cabin in e Sky* (43) and the whimsical, ʼreal *Yolanda and the Thief* (45).

ORGAN FREEMAN
S actor (1937-)

ıree-time Oscar nominee and ıner of numerous theatre awards work ranging from Shakespeare Brecht, Freeman is one of only andful of black American actors ıave escaped stereotyping. He ıde his New York debut in 1968 ı was a familiar television ʼsonality in films from 1980, aking through as a charming, ʼchopathic pimp in *Street Smart*). Two years later he reprised award-winning off-Broadway role the chauffeur whose dignity and

patience were sorely tested while *Driving Miss Daisy* (89). He was then in demand for drama and adventure, from a civil war epic, *Glory* (89), to playing the Moorish sidekick to Kevin Costner's (qv) *Robin Hood: Prince of Thieves* (91). He also had the satisfaction of winning roles not written as black: Eastwood's (qv) ageing partner in *Unforgiven* (92) and the resigned inmate who is saved by Tim Robbins (qv) in *The Shawshank Redemption* (94). Freeman also directed a South African drama, *Bopha!* (93) and featured in many television films.

SAMUEL FULLER
US director (1911-)

A B-movie director who is hailed as an authentic American auteur by Godard and Wenders (qqv) for his two-fisted frontal assaults on the sensibilities, Fuller is considered to be an existentialist. On the other hand, he has also been dismissed as a fascist disciple of Senator Joe McCarthy. Variously a New York crime journalist, a hobo who jumped freight trains and a soldier in the second world war, his caustic vision often features amoral characters struggling to survive the asylum of life. This was best illustrated in his psychological horror yarn *Shock Corridor* (63). War and criminality are central themes, his hyperactive camera scurrying through the undergrowth of life. Each character is caught up in a violent rite of passage where established moral certainties are tested to breaking point, most powerfully exemplified in *Steel Helmet* (51) *Underworld USA* (61) and *The Big Red One* (80).

JEAN GABIN
French actor (1904-76)

Known for portraying tough-guy outsiders whose gruff demeanour still gave space to sensitivity and self-awareness, Gabin had a charisma and body of work so attractive that it made him a national hero. A dancer at the Folies-Bergère, he initially made the screen via the films of Julien Duvivier (qv), in particular *Maria Chapdelaine* (34), *La Bandera* and *Golgotha* (both 35) and *La Belle Equipe* (36). It was Duvivier's *Pépé le Moko* (36) that elevated him to star status. He electrified the screen as a gangster in hiding and

Gable was Hollywood's 'King' — on and off screen

built on this success with Renoir's (qv) *La Grande Illusion* (37), Carné's (qv) *Quai des Brumes* (38) and *Le Jour se lève* (39). Before joining the Free French navy during the second world war he faltered with two anaemic American films, *Moontide* (42) and *The Imposter* (44). Some post-war excellence was still to be found, particularly in *Touchez pas au Grisbi* (54) and *L'Affaire Dominici* (72).

CLARK GABLE
US actor (1901-60)

Known as the "King of Hollywood", he carved a unique niche in cinema history for his macho performance as Rhett Butler in *Gone With the Wind* (39). For the film connoisseur his last role, as the cowboy opposite Marilyn ▷

ırbo's melancholic look was nuine: she lived and died a ·eply unhappy woman

ınroe (qv) in *The Misfits* (61), will most remembered. Born in io, he made tyres and sold ties 'ore seeking his fortune as an :or. Turned down by Darryl F ıuck (qv) for looking like an ape, ·as not until he upstaged Leslie ·ward (qv) and pushed Norma earer (qv) around in *A Free Soul* ı) that he stamped his brand on cinema, helped by sizzling on-een romances with off-screen er Joan Crawford (qv). He ıfounded the critics with his car-winning comic turn in pra's (qv) *It Happened One ght* (34) and upset his female s by shaving off his moustache *Mutiny on the Bounty* (35). rried four times, his third wife role Lombard (qv) was killed in a ne crash in 1942.

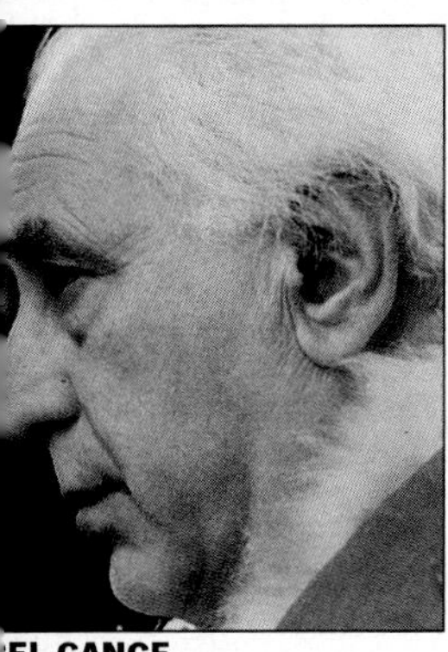

·EL GANCE

ench director, writer 389-1981)

cinematic significance was ›wn to few until, in 1981, his mmoth silent epic *Napoléon* ') was reissued in a restored sion by the historian Kevin ·wnlow (qv), with two new ·res, one by Carl Davis, the other Carmine Coppola. The publicity vated Gance to his rightful ition as one of the world's atest film makers. Fiercely ovative, he would try anything to e his films sweep and motion, ting his camera on cars, cranes, dges and even a trapeze. He › pioneered the wide-angle lens, spective sound and three-screen jection, the latter used to ·ctacular effect in *Napoléon*. His nt actors spoke written dialogue, ch was a rarity. His three sterpieces remain the anti-war *ccuse* (19), remade in 1938 ı lip-synched silent footage. *La ıe* (23) and *Napoléon*. He is still arded as the best screen grapher, with *Lucrezia Borgia* ·), *Beethoven* (36), *La Reine rgot* (53) and Marie Tudor in 55 for French TV.

ETA GARBO

edish actress (1905-90)

ın in Stockholm, Greta Lovisa stafsson had a deeply unhappy childhood from which, in spite of her success, she never emotionally recovered. After stage training and a few short films, her mentor Mauritz Stiller (qv) cast her in *Gösta Berling's Saga* (24). Spotted by MGM in 1925 she went to Hollywood where she made 10 silent films before talking in *Anna Christie* (30). Garbo dominated MGM in the 1930s with the classic *Mata Hari* (32), *Queen Christina* (33), *The Painted Veil* (34), *Anna Karenina* (35), *Ninotchka* (39) and *Two-Faced Woman* (41). She probably moved audiences most as *Camille* (37) giving up Robert Taylor (qv) and dying in consumptive glory. She overwhelmingly owed her success to cinematographer William Daniels (qv), whose lighting made an angular-featured, almost masculine woman into the embodiment of luminescent beauty. She left Hollywood in 1942 to become a recluse in New York. She never married; there is evidence she was a lesbian and it has been alleged that the photographer Cecil Beaton was the great love of her life. She saw out her days behind dark glasses walking in Central Park.

AVA GARDNER

US actress (1922-90)

One of the great love goddesses of the screen, she vividly fulfilled the rags-to-riches Hollywood dream. Born to poor North Carolina farmers, she was offered a film contract at 17 on the strength of a photograph. By the age of 21 she had made a dozen films and married Mickey Rooney (qv). She emerged as the embodiment of the dark, alluring siren in *The Killers* (46). Although she made more than 60 films and was seldom required to be anything more than a charismatic beauty, she received an Oscar nomination for her gutsy floozy in *Mogambo* (53) and was touching as the tragic gypsy film star in *The Barefoot Contessa* (54) and a Hemingway lost soul in *The Sun Also Rises* (57). Her second marriage, to bandleader Artie Shaw, also failed and her tempestuous third, to Frank Sinatra (qv), made many headlines. She worked less after the 1950s and retired to a colourful life in Spain before settling in London.

JOHN GARFIELD

US actor (1913-52)

Years before Scorsese and De Niro (qqv), Julius Garfinkle worked New York's mean streets as a gang member but found a way out with the left-inclined Group Theatre. In Hollywood he was typecast as a loner with a sawmill of chips on his shoulder in *They Made Me a Criminal* and *Dust Be My Destiny* (both 39), but for MGM he made *The Postman Always Rings Twice* (46) with Lana Turner (qv). He was the violinist discovered by Joan Crawford (qv) for *Humoresque* (46) and his liberal anger made him a convincing boxer victim in *Body and Soul* (47) and numbers racketeer in the brilliant *Force of Evil* (48). John Huston's (qv) *We Were Strangers* (49) showed him at his best as a Cuban rebel with a cause. The paranoid anti-communist taint of McCarthyism had the effect of undermining his career, but his tough-talking, slow-burn personality sparked fires in younger audiences that were not to be lit again until Marlon Brando (qv) took to the screen.

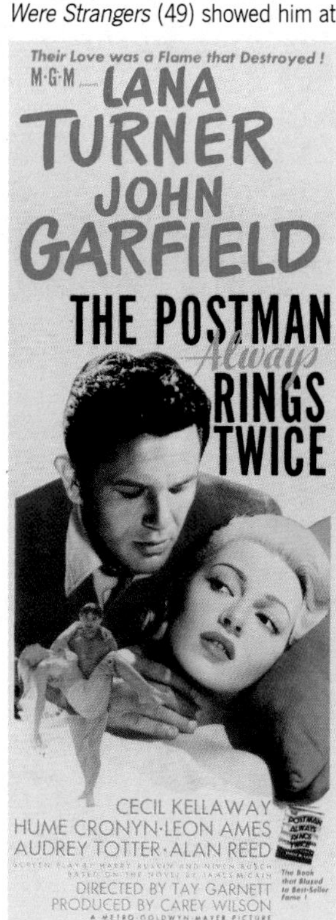

JUDY GARLAND

US actress, singer (1922-69)

The daughter of vaudevillians, Frances Gumm was a performer at three. Under contract to MGM in 1936, *The Wizard of Oz* (39) made her a star. The price was a lifelong cycle of pill taking and by the time of her tragic and premature death she had had five husbands including Vincente Minnelli (qv), numerous breakdowns, several suicide attempts, lawsuits and a reputation for unreliability. She was a great star of unique artistry and appeal, whether teamed with Mickey Rooney (qv) in *Babes in Arms* (39) and many others, or singing and dancing, *Meet Me in St Louis* (44), or acting, *Under the Clock* (45). Passionate, funny and vulnerable, her jittery edge betrayed her tremulous hold on herself. Her great ironic testament is Cukor's (qv) *A Star Is Born* (54), which represented her comeback after a long rough patch. As a small-time singer who rises to stardom and pays in personal tragedy, she gave a virtuoso performance.

LEE GARMES

US cinematographer (1898-1978)

After leaving high school he worked as a prop boy and painter's assistant at the Thomas H Ince (qv) studios. In the same year, 1916, he began working as an assistant cameraman on many shorts and features until 1924 when he became a lighting cameraman. His work was notable for its technical innovation. He expanded horizons, particularly in the use of dollies, and by the 1930s was widely recognised as a master craftsman of black and white photography. At the end of that decade he was also producing and directing features, though some of his work went uncredited. Most notable among his list of anonymous accomplishments was

his cinematography on *Gone With the Wind* (39), which occupied approximately the first third of the film. He worked on *The Secret Life of Walter Mitty* and *Nightmare Alley* (both 47), but his sole Oscar was won in 1932 for *Shanghai Express*.

JAMES GARNER

US actor (1928-)

His real surname is Bumgarner and he was born in Oklahoma. He won the Purple Heart in the Korean war and briefly attended the University of Oklahoma before drifting from carpet layer to travelling salesman. His first acting role was a non-speaking, uniformed appearance in The Caine Mutiny Court-Martial on Broadway in 1954, which led to television appearances and a few film parts. His break was the lead in the TV series Maverick. In the 1960s he played a succession of engaging, roguish film roles in *Move Over Darling* (63), *The Americanization of Emily* (64) and *Support Your Local Sheriff* (69). He had further success on television in The Rockford Files and was nominated for an Oscar for *Murphy's Romance* (85). His rugged, easy-going charm was evident again in *Maverick* (94) in which he reprised his most famous character.

TAY GARNETT
US director, writer (1894-1977)

William Tayler Garnett was a comedy writer for silent films from the early 1920s. He directed his first film, *Celebrity* (which he also helped to write) in 1928 and established a reputation with *Her Man* (30) and *One Way Passage* (32). Thereafter, his films (which he often co-wrote) depended on the quality of his leading players, as in *China Seas* (35) with Clark Gable and Jean Harlow (qqv), and *Seven Sinners* (40) with Marlene Dietrich and John Wayne (qqv). The most well known are *The Postman Always Rings Twice* (46), a quintessential *film noir*, with Lana Turner and John Garfield (qqv) and, by contrast, *A Connecticut Yankee in King Arthur's Court* (48) with Bing Crosby and Cedric Hardwicke (qqv). By the 1950s he was directing more for TV than film. His last pictures were made in 1972 but not released until 1977.

GREER GARSON
US actress (1908-96)

Born in Co Down, she worked in an advertising agency after taking a degree at the University of London, and became interested in amateur dramatics. Her first professional appearance was at the Birmingham Rep in 1932; two years later she was appearing on the London West End stage. Her first film, *Goodbye Mr Chips* (39) for MGM, won her an Oscar nomination. In 1942 she won the Oscar for her portrayal of a well-heeled housewife undergoing the rigours of the home front in *Mrs Miniver*, Hollywood's tribute to British wartime indomitability. It made her a big star and she confirmed her promise in *Random Harvest* (42) opposite Ronald Colman (qv). She co-starred several times with Walter Pidgeon (qv), who had played Mr Miniver, notably in *Blossoms in the Dust* (41), *Madame Curie* (43), *Mrs Parkington* (44) and *Julia Misbehaves* (48). A soft-spoken, red-headed beauty, Garson excelled in strong-willed feminine roles. She retired to Texas and then New Mexico in the 1950s and in 1992 funded the Greer Garson Theater on the campus of Southern Methodist University in Dallas.

JANET GAYNOR
US actress (1906-84)

For a transcendent period in the late 1920s, Laura Gainor was America's wide-eyed and waif-like silent screen darling. She started as an extra, graduated to two-reel westerns and joined Fox for her first feature, *The Johnstown Flood* (26). A handful of films later, *Seventh Heaven* (27) made her the first recipient of the best actress Oscar. It was followed by *Sunrise* (27), *Street Angel* (28) and a more successful teaming with the romantic lead Charles Farrell in *Christina* and *Lucky Star* (both 29). Her first sound picture was *Sunny Side Up* (29). She quarrelled with Fox, was suspended, but returned to make *Daddy Long Legs* (31), *Tess of the Storm Country* (32), *State Fair* (33) and *The Farmer Takes a Wife* (35) among others. She fell out of fashion in the late 1930s after making *Small Town Girl* (36) and *A Star Is Born* (37)..

BEN GAZZARA
US actor (1930-)

Biagio Gazzara was born to Sicilian immigrants on New York's Lower East Side. He was among the intense young anti-heroes to come out of the Actors Studio in the early 1950s. He enjoyed success on Broadway in A Hatful of Rain and Cat on a Hot Tin Roof, but watched others take those roles on film.

He made his screen debut as a terrifying military cadet in *The Strange One* (57), the screen version of Calder Willingham's End As a Man, which he had performed on stage. Two years later he featured to strong effect as an ambivalent suspect in *Anatomy of a Murder* (59), a success he found difficult to build on. Subsequently he was best known as a television star in the 1960s and for his collaborations with his friend John Cassavetes (qv), most notably as one of the titular *Husbands* (70). He starred with Gena Rowlands (qv) and Aidan Quinn in the Emmy award-winning television film An Early Frost, one of the first dramas to deal with Aids. Bilingual, he found a second home in Italy, where he made many films and directed *Oltre L'Oceano* (90).

RICHARD GERE
US actor (1949-)

Gere played rock, blues and country on different instruments with different bands before summer stock acting landed him the lead understudy in Grease in 1972. He went on to star in the London production, which led to *Baby Blue Marine* (76), *Looking For Mr Goodbar* (77), *Days of Heaven* (78) and *American Gigolo* (80). As a romantic lead he sailed through *An Officer And A Gentleman* (82) and spent the next few years embracing Tibetan Buddhism. He revived his iconic box-office appeal with *Pretty Woman* and *Internal Affairs* (both 90). Selective with work, which he increasingly seeks to control, he has had production roles in *Final Analysis* (92), *Sommersby* (92) and *Mr Jones* (93).

GEORGE GERSHWIN'S
MELODY FROM RHAPSODY IN BLU
FROM THE WARNER BROS FILM
"RHAPSODY IN BLUE"
THE STORY OF GEORGE GERSHWIN
MELODY from RHAPSODY IN BLUE
I GOT RHYTHM
THE MAN I LOVE
SOMEBODY LOVES ME
FASCINATING RHYTHM
LIZA
SUMMERTIME
EMBRACEABLE YOU
OH! LADY, BE GOOD
BIDIN' MY TIME
PRICE 2/- NET EACH
CHAPPELL

GEORGE GERSHWIN
US composer (1898-1937)

Born in Brooklyn, he first showed an interest in music at 12 and had his first hit, Swanee, in 1919. He wrote a string of Broadway hits, generally collaborating with Ira, his brilliant lyricist brother. Many of his sublime and enduring melodies found their way into almost 50 films. Standards such as Embraceable You, The Man I Love and Someone to Watch Over Me featured frequently, while his orchestral work, Rhapsody in Blue (the title of a 1945 biopic starring Robert Alda), was performed four times, first in *King of Jazz* (30). His opera Porgy and Bess was filmed in 1959, the stage hit Girl Crazy was made three times and he provided original scores for two Astaire (qv) vehicles, *A Damsel in Distress* (37), which yielded A Foggy Day, and *Shall We Dance?* (37). His score for *The Goldwyn Follies* (38) included Love is Here To Stay, sung again by Gene Kelly (qv) in *An American in Paris* (51). His death of a brain tumour at 39 was an incalculable loss to American music.

CEDRIC GIBBONS
US designer (1893-1960)

The designer of the Oscar, who went on to win the award 12 times (with 37 nominations), Gibbons began working in films with the Edison Studios in 1915 and was on the staff of MGM from its formation in 1924 until 1956. Elegance and luxury were the hallmarks of Gibbons's work, most frequently in collaboration or as supervising art director. Along with the costume designer (Gilbert) Adrian and lighting cameraman Rosson, Gibbons was reponsible the glossy sumptuousness associated with the studio's heyday. His Oscar-winning films were *The Bridge of San Luis Re* (29), *The Merry Widow* (34), *Pri*

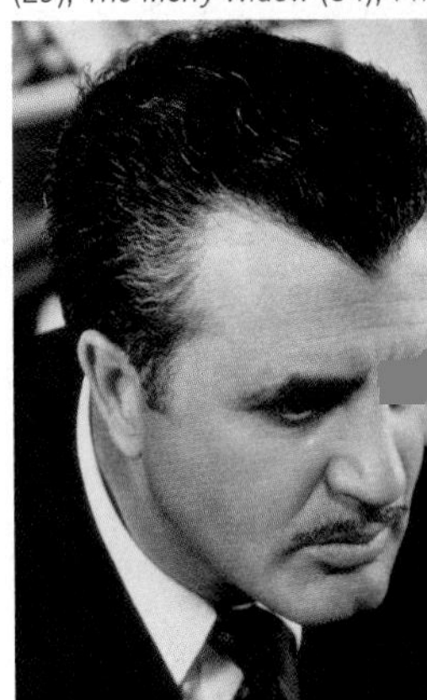

and Prejudice (40), *Blossoms in the Dust* (41), *Gaslight* (44), *The Yearling* (46), *Little Women* (49), *An American in Paris* (51) *The B and the Beautiful* (52), *Julius Caesar* (53) and *Somebody Up There Likes Me* (56). He received special award in 1950. He was married to the actress Dolores D Rio (qv).

MEL GIBSON
Australian actor, director (1956-)

Gibson was born in Peekskill, N York, the sixth of 11 children. At the age of 12 his Irish father an Australian mother took him to Australia where he graduated fr Sydney's National Institute of Dramatic Art before getting bit in minor films. A handsome charmer with a quick wit, he ha ade the transition from cult wild an to global superstar without mpromising a much-prized vate life shared with his wife byn and their five children in al Australia. He first came to n prominence as the road rrior in George Miller's futuristic tion picture *Mad Max* (79). It s only after the international

ccess of Peter Weir's (qv) i-war film *Gallipoli* (81) that he s invited to America and became op Hollywood action man. With proceeds of two *Mad Max* quels (81, 84) and three ney-spinning *Lethal Weapon* s (87, 89, 92) in the bank, he ved to be a phenomenal -office asset in Zeffirelli's *mlet* (90), directing himself in *Man Without a Face* (93) and *nspiracy Theory* (97).

HN GIELGUD
tish actor (1904-)

e of the great Shakespearean ors, Gielgud strayed into films in later years and became a ed character actor. The grand hew of the actress Ellen Terry, studied at Rada and made his ng debut at the Old Vic in 21. Achieving enormous success Richard of Bordeaux in 1932 he attracted acclaim for his nlet. On screen, he made an

John Gilbert with Garbo in The Flesh and the Devil

impression as the disenchanted music teacher in *The Good Companions* (33), was a charming Ashenden in Hitchcock's (qv) *The Secret Agent* (36) and was impressive as Disraeli in *The Prime Minister* (41). Later, he played Cassius in *Julius Caesar* (53) and was nominated for an Oscar as Louis VII in *Becket* (64). Then, following his remarkable performance as the dying writer in Resnais's (qv) *Providence* (76), he won the Oscar as Dudley Moore's (qv) acerbic manservant in *Arthur* (81). In Peter Greenaway's (qv) *Prospero's Books* (91) he realised his long-standing ambition of playing Prospero on screen, voicing all the characters in The Tempest. He was knighted in 1953.

JOHN GILBERT
US actor (1895-1936)

Nepotism landed him a regular role as an extra with the Thomas H Ince (qv) company from where he graduated to bigger parts, even leads, using the name Jack Gilbert. His talents were best displayed opposite Mary Pickford (qv) in *Heart o' the Hills* (19). Fox signed him on the strength of that role where he worked until his golden period at MGM began in the mid-1920s. There, his star escalated beyond all predictions; every film he graced became a commercial hit. The second half of the decade was effectively his, the best films being his collaborations with Garbo (qv), including *Flesh and the Devil* and *Anna Karenina* (both 27) and *Queen Christina* (33). There were rumours that the two were having an affair, heightening the audience's adoration. His appeal dipped with talkies, both because of his slightly high voice and the fact that the romances that had made him were falling from favour. He had also incurred the enmity of Louis B Mayer (qv). His final years were blurred by alcoholism.

LEWIS GILBERT
British director (1920-)

The maker of the Douglas Bader war biopic, *Reach for the Sky* (56), and the Queen's rumoured favourite films *Educating Rita* (83) and *Shirley Valentine* (88), Gilbert was a child actor who became a film maker in the RAF. His first feature, *The Little Ballerina* (47), was for children, and war epics such as *The Sea Shall Not Have Them* (54) followed. *The Greengage Summer* (61) was a successful study of the sweet and sour pain of growing up, but three James Bond films, *You Only Live Twice* (67), *The Spy Who Loved Me* (77) and *Moonraker* (79), released his talent for mechanistic exploitation. Nothing in his later films reached the tragi-comedy of *Alfie* (66) with Michael Caine (qv), although *Shirley Valentine* and *Stepping Out* (90) were about women realising their potential.

TERRY GILLIAM
US director, writer and animator (1940-)

Although an American, Gilliam first found fame in Britain as a member of Monty Python's Flying Circus on television and as a performer, animator, writer and eventually director in the series of five zany spin-off films they made. Born in Minneapolis and a political science graduate of Occidental College, Los

Angeles, he worked as a writer, illustrator and cartoonist before coming to London in 1967. His wicked, surreal humour has infused all his films, as have his extraordinary (and disturbing) visuals. His first non-Python film was *Time Bandits* (81), a history of the world as a children's fantasy, followed by the futuristic nightmare *Brazil* (85). His costly failure, *The Adventures of Baron Munchausen* (88), exacerbated industry unease with his ambitious flights of imagination which polarised audiences. He found redemption superbly with *The Fisher King* (90), starring Robin Williams and Jeff Bridges (qqv).

SIDNEY GILLIAT
British director, writer and producer (1908-94)

Educated at London University, he entered the film industry in the closing days of silents as a title writer on Hitchcock's (qv) *Champagne* (28). In the 1930s he wrote a number of Michael Balcon's (qv) successes, including *Rome Express* (32), *Friday the 13th* (33) and uncredited, *A Yank at Oxford* (38). In association with Frank Launder (qv) on Hitchcock's *The Lady Vanishes* (38), he formed a writing, producing and directing partnership. *Millions Like Us* (43), a propaganda film on women war workers, was the first feature they directed. The best of the team's later work, which Gilliat directed and Launder produced, included *Waterloo Road* (44) *The Rake's Progress* (45), *Green for Danger* (46), *London Belongs to Me* (48) and *State Secret* (50). In the 1950s the team moved into comedy with the St Trinians films featuring the nightmare schoolchildren devised by the cartoonist Ronald Searle.

ILLIAN GISH
JS actress (1893-1993)

aving one of the longest careers cinema history, Gish witnessed s birth and was still stealing cenes in her nineties. As an génue her fragile beauty was the erfect foil for the histrionics of her entor D W Griffith (qv). Making er acting debut at the age of five, ongside Dorothy, her younger ster, "Baby Lillian" was efriended by Gladys Smith, nother child star. Smith, having ecome Mary Pickford (qv), troduced the sisters to Griffith, ho cast them in *An Unseen nemy* (12). Three years later she ayed Elsie Stoneman in Griffith's ndmark *The Birth of a Nation* 5) . . . and a star was born. efore falling out with Griffith over oney, she starred in his asterworks *Intolerance* (16), *earts of the World* (18), *Broken ossoms* (19), *Way Down East* 0) and *Orphans of the Storm* 2). She was unforgettable in the ent classics *The Scarlet Letter* 6) and *The Wind* (28) and shone *The Night of the Hunter* (55) and *e Whales of August* (87). In later e she lectured extensively on her markable career.

AN-LUC GODARD
iss director, screenwriter 930-)

acted in shorts for Jacques ette and Eric Rohmer (qqv), de a couple of films and wrote Cahiers du Cinéma before king *Breathless* (60), his feature ut. Dedicated to the Monogram dio, it reflected his fascination American gangster B-movies brought together his innovative effective use of hand-held neras, jump cuts and other ices. *Le Petit Soldat* (60), ling with the brutality on both es of the Algerian war, was held for three years. It starred a Karina (qv), whom Godard rried (and divorced) and with om he made eight of his most essible films. Contemptuous of itional and commercial cinema, abandoned any concessions to ter *Weekend* (68), generally g film as a medium for left- g socio-political messages.

Gish in The Wind; her film career spanned 75 years

PAULETTE GODDARD
US actress (1905-90)

Chaplin's (qv) leading lady and then wife, Goddard was a stunning actress who never made superstar status. Marion Levee was born in New York. As an ex-Goldwyn Girl she married a rich industrialist, was divorced in 1931 and put herself and her wealth into Chaplin's *Modern Times* (36). Its success made them Hollywood's First Couple for almost a decade. She nearly won the Scarlett O'Hara role in *Gone With the Wind*, but made *The Young in Heart* (38) for Selznick (qv) as a consolation prize, followed by *The Women* (39) and *North West Mounted Police* (40). After the war she married Burgess Meredith (qv) and co-starred with him in one of her biggest successes, *The Diary of a Chambermaid* (46). *Unconquered* and *An Ideal Husband* (both 47), made by Korda (qv) in Britain, followed. She married Erich Maria Remarque in 1958 and retired.

WHOOPI GOLDBERG
US actress (1949-)

She is not only the most successful African-American actress in the history of Hollywood, but is also considered to be one of the highest-grossing women in contemporary cinema, helped in no small part by her Oscar nomination for Spielberg's (qv) *The Color Purple* (85) and the best supporting actress Oscar for *Ghost* (90). Caryn Johnson was educated at the New York High School for the Performing Arts and went on the stage at the age of eight, followed by numerous bit parts in Broadway musicals and Californian revues. Her first success was with her one-woman Spook Show, which toured Europe before triumphing on Broadway. When Spielberg chose her to play the lead in his adaptation of Alice Walker's story about an abused woman in segregated America, he launched a career that has eclipsed the reputation of every other black actress. A natural comic with a fine singing voice, she has dared to venture where many would have bombed, with *Clara's Heart* (88), *Sarafina!*, *The Player* and *Sister Act* (all 92), *Corrina, Corrina* (94) and *The Associate* (97).

JEFF GOLDBLUM
US actor (1952-)

His ascent began with school plays, a spell at New York's Neighborhood Playhouse and numerous bit parts on and off-Broadway. He was immaculately cast in *The Fly* (86), his biggest role to date, as the obsessive scientist who becomes a human fly, and was an alien in *Earth Girls Are Easy* (89), a patchy satire on Californian morals. He brought a detached intelligence to his roles in *Deep Cover* (92), as a drug-dealing lawyer, and in *Jurassic Park* (93), as a strange mathematician.

The 10 best westerns

High Noon (1952)
Gary Cooper stands alone in Fred Zinnemann's classic

My Darling Clementine (1946)
John Ford's vision of Wyatt Earp and Tombstone, with Henry Fonda

Once Upon a Time in the West (1968)
Sergio Leone's epic masterpiece, with Henry Fonda as a vicious hired gun

Red River (1948)
Cattle-drover John Wayne takes them to Missouri in Hawks's classic western

Rio Bravo (1959)
Wayne as beleaguered sheriff in riposte to High Noon

The Searchers (1956)
Wayne spends years seeking his niece abducted by Indians

Shane (1953)
Gunfighter Alan Ladd defends the homesteaders from vicious landgrabbers and goes his way

Stagecoach (1939)
Its passengers endure countless perils in Ford's classic masterpiece

Unforgiven (1992)
Clint Eastwood's ageing gunslinger emerges for one last job before the fade-out

Winchester '73 (1950)
A lost rifle is the basis of Anthony Mann's episodic study

REDFORD/HOFFMAN
"ALL THE PRESIDENT'S MEN"

LLIAM GOLDMAN
writer (1931-)

r Oberlin College and Columbia versity, he moved into writing, dling children's stories, plays novels. He is best known for screenplays, which have always n impeccably constructed and nished with original and distinct ances. One of his first, for *Butch ssidy and the Sundance Kid*), earned him an Oscar and ckly sealed his reputation in lywood as a writer who could k efficiently and produce a xtbook" script. He put such nts to use in the writing of his birational and popular insider's k at Hollywood, Adventures in

Screen Trade, in 1983. The 70s were important for two stigious projects, the Watergate ler *All the President's Men* ich won him a second eenwriting Oscar) and *Marathon n* (both 76), which were ased to commercial and critical cess. There have been some guided projects, but Goldman tinues to be recognised as one he industry's strongest writers.

RRY GOLDSMITH
composer (1929-)

anist of classical distinction, he died film composition with los Rozsa (qv) and, after a od in television (Gunsmoke and Man from UNCLE), scored h commercial films as *Von n's Express* (65), *Patton* (70) *The Boys From Brazil* (78). He an Oscar for his score for *The en* (76) and has admitted his ration of Stravinsky ("for the he moves rhythms around") Rozsa ("always himself, yet vant to the movie").

SAMUEL GOLDWYN
US producer (1882-1974)

In danger of being remembered for his verbal infelicities, such as "include me out" and "a verbal contract isn't worth the paper it's printed on", as much as for the films he brought to the screen. Shmuel Gelbfisz (later Samuel Goldfish) was born in Poland. He made his way via Britain to America and married the sister of performer/producer Jesse L Lasky, with whom he entered the film business. He had immediate success with *The Squaw Man* (14). Bought out by Lasky and Adolph Zukor (qv) in 1916, he teamed up with Edgar Selwyn to form the company name and later his own, Goldwyn, but was edged out. Not consulted over the merger creating MGM in 1924, he had formed Samuel Goldwyn Productions. He made his mark as an independent bringing together acting, directing and other talents for some of the cinema's most popular titles, including *Dodsworth* (36), *Stella Dallas* (26 and 37), *Wuthering Heights* (39), *The Little Foxes* (41), *The Best Years of Our Lives* (46), *The Secret Life of Walter Mitty* (47) and *My Foolish Heart* (49).

GONG LI
Chinese actress (1965-)

When China's film makers burst on to the world scene in the 1980s, they brought to international acclaim an actress who has adorned much of their best work. Gong made her film debut in Zhang Yimou's (qv) *Red Sorghum* (87) while still a student. She rapidly went on to star in numerous films in Hong Kong, Taiwan and mainland China. In Chen Kaige's (qv) Palme D'Or-winning *Farewell My Concubine* (93), she played an opportunistic prostitute, one of several characters she has portrayed from youth to old age. Her most fruitful collaboration has been with Zhang, for whom she starred as the exquisite, educated girl forced to become a nobleman's concubine in *Raise The Red Lantern* (91), a country woman battling bureaucracy in *The Story of Qiu Ju* (92) and an aristocrat enduring poverty, toil and tragedy in *To Live* (94). By 1995 they had

made six films together and were shooting a seventh, *Shanghai Triads*, when they ended their personal relationship as one of China's most fashionable and celebrated couples. Following the Chinese censors' fury when *To Live* was shown at the 1994 Cannes Film Festival without approval, she was temporarily forbidden to travel.

JOHN GOODMAN
US actor (1952-)

A character actor in demand as best friend, slob and criminal since the mid-1980s, Goodman translated his popularity in the TV series Roseanne into leading film roles. These included an uncouth Las Vegas entertainer succeeding to the British throne as *King Ralph* (91), the American baseball legend *The Babe* (92) and *Born Yesterday* (93), none of which were hits. He worked extensively in theatre before entering films in 1983. While playing comedy well, he was also a deceptively clownish bad cop in *The Big Easy* (86), a tenacious escaped convict in the Coen brothers' (qv) madcap *Raising Arizona* (87), Al Pacino's (qv) wisecracking partner in *Sea Of*

Love (89) and he stole *Arachnophobia* (90) as the proud pest exterminator. His most impressive success was as the bore next door who is not what he seems to John Turturro's (qv) hapless *Barton Fink* (92) made by the Coen brothers (qv).

RUTH GORDON
US actress (1896-1985)

Born in Wollaston, Massachusetts, she was a talented stage actress and writer who made forays into films, initially with a bit part in Albert Capellani's *Camille* (15). She returned to the New York stage working extensively with the producer Jeff Harris, by whom she had a child. In middle age she brought her particular brand of sugar-coated waspishness into vogue, appearing in *Two-Faced Woman* (41), *Edge Of Darkness* and *Action in the North Atlantic* (both 43). Two of her plays, *Over 21* (45) and *The Actress* (53), have also been filmed. She married Garson Kanin (qv) in 1942 and they became a notable comedy writing team for George Cukor, Spencer Tracy and Katharine Hepburn (qqv), responsible for *Adam's Rib* (49) and *Pat and Mike* (52). She returned for an autumnal heyday of sharp, manipulative old ladies in *Inside Daisy Clover* (65), *Whatever Happened to Aunt Alice?* (69), *Harold and Maude* (71) and *Any Which Way You Can* (80). Notoriously cranky on and off set, she was Mia Farrow's chilling neighbour in *Rosemary's Baby* (68) for which she won an Oscar. Her last was *Trouble With Spies* (87).

EDMUND GOULDING
British director (1891-1959)

He was one of MGM's greatest window-dressers for the 1930s. A born-in-a-trunk Londoner, he moved to America as an actor and playwright. In Hollywood, after writing novels and screenplays, he became a director noted for style and swank with *Grand Hotel* (32), a portmanteau film of linked stories starring almost all of MGM's celebrities. He complained he never had a completely free hand, but when he switched from MGM to Warner he was able to adjust with such Bette Davis (qv) vehicles as *Dark Victory* and *The Old Maid* (both 39). Essentially a studio man – "I hate locations" – at Twentieth Century Fox he gave Tyrone Power (qv) his best films as the seeker after truth in *The Razor's Edge* (46) and as the carnival "geek" in *Nightmare Alley* (47). However bizarre the role, he knew how to display stars to their advantage.

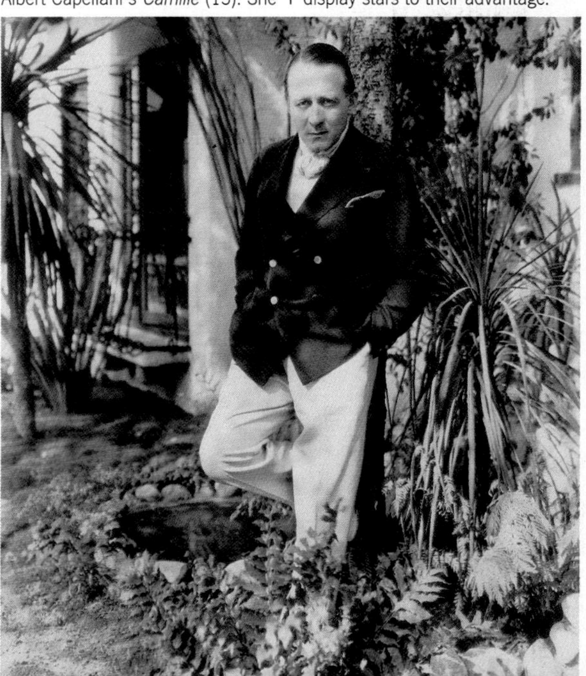

BETTY GRABLE
US actress (1916-73)

Blonde, curvaceous and a popular pin-up of the 1940s with famously admired legs, Grable was in films, initially in the chorus, from 1929. Samuel Goldwyn (qv) changed her name to Frances Dean in 1931, but RKO changed it back in 1932. Roles slowly improved and in 1937 she married former child star Jackie Coogan (qv). In 1940 she divorced and was signed by Darryl F Zanuck (qv) at Fox, who wanted to put pressure on Alice Faye (qv), his reigning musical leading lady. Grable replaced Faye in *Down Argentine Way* (40) and led in a string of musicals. In 1943 she married Harry James, the bandleader. Straight dramatic roles, as in *That Lady in Ermine* (48), were less notable. A forces' favourite, she continued to enjoy post-war success, but was being edged out by another rising star, Marilyn Monroe (qv), with whom she made *How To Marry a Millionaire* (53). *Three for the Show* (55) was her last film.

GLORIA GRAHAME
US actress (1924-81)

Whether they were acting with her on screen or gawping at her from the stalls, men were reined in by Grahame, whose come-hither looks, full voice and dark suggestiveness spelled sex. Often performing crucial roles, she shone in Fritz Lang's (qv) *Human Desire* (54), in which she slid inexorably towards disaster. *The Big Heat* (53), also shot through with Lang's dramatic darkness, had one memorable scene in which she had scalding coffee thrown in her face by Lee Marvin (qv). Having won best supporting actress Oscar for *The Bad and the Beautiful* (52), she rode high for a few years before offers dwindled. A late revival saw her in such films as *A Nightingale Sang in Berkeley Square* (79), *Melvin and Howard* (1980) and *The Nesting* (1981).

STEWART GRANGER
British actor (1913-93)

Tall, urbane and athletic, Granger was a 1950s matinee idol and one of Britain's most successful exports to Hollywood. James Stewart was born in London and invited to try his luck as a film extra by Michael Wilding, an actor friend. The easy money and glamour appealed to

him, so he enrolled at the Webber Douglas drama school and from necessity changed his name. After a short time in theatre, he was cast as the romantic interest in *So This Is London* (39) and became a star as the hero of *The Man in Grey* (43), which set the tone for Gainsborough costumers. He was much in demand and, along with James Mason, Margaret Lockwood (qqv) and Phyllis Calvert, became a staple ingredient of bodice-ripping British romances. In 1950 he married Jean Simmons (qv) and entered a new phase of his success – as the star of MGM's popular *King Solomon's Mines* (50). Contracted to MGM, he established himself as a hardy successor to Flynn and Fairbanks (qqv).

CARY GRANT
US actor (1904-86)

Witty, sophisticated and debonair, he was also irresistibly handsome with a trademark cleft chin and distinctive voice. His incomparable lightness of touch enriched many classic 1930s screwball comedies, while a contradictory suggestion of caddishness, as in Hitchcock's (qv) *Suspicion* (41) and *Notorious* (46), lent an extra dimension. His charisma was unimpaired by time, but he retired at 62 having wooed and won, on screen, virtually every Hollywood leading lady of note. He married five times, becoming a father for the first time at gone 60 with Dyan Cannon (qv), wife number four. Archibald Leach was born in Bristol and ran away from a broken home in his teens, joining a travelling vaudeville troupe that took him to America in 1920. Odd jobs followed, then a return to Britain and musical comedy, then back to America, stage musicals and a Paramount contract. *Blonde Venus* (32) with Dietrich (qv) and two films with Mae West (qv) began a star career that endured untarnished for 34 years. In 1970 he received a special Oscar.

Grant, Dunne and Asta the dog in The Awful Truth

PETER GREENAWAY
British director (1942-)

One of Britain's most original and controversial film makers, he trained as a painter at Walthamstow Art College in London. His work in the film industry began shortly afterwards, editing various documentaries over the course of the next 11 years. The late 1960s also saw the start of his experimentation in film. Some of his work from that period and the 1970s attracted approval and awards at various film festivals. His first full-length feature, the British Film Institute-funded mock-documentary *The Falls* (80), showed that a significant force in cinema was emerging. The acclaimed *The Draughtsman's Contract* (82) provided further vindication and brought the director to an international audience. His films are characterised by sumptuous design and photography, pulsating scores (many of them by the composer Michael Nyman), scatological detail and mechanical, perverse plotting. Much of his work is cold but innovative. His finest film is the lurid Jacobean-style thriller *The Cook, the Thief, His Wife and Her Lover* (89). His brutal parable, *The Baby of Macon* (93), was roundly savaged, but *The Pillow Book* (96) restored his reputation.

GRAHAM GREENE
British writer (1904-91)

William Golding described him as the ultimate chronicler of 20th-century man's consciousness and anxieties. As well as his prolific novels, he is credited with writing more screenplays, especially of h own stories, than any other write Central to his plots is the plight c the underdog, trapped within labyrinthine political contradictio This is best exemplified by Carol Reed's (qv) thriller *The Third Ma* (49), in which Joseph Cotten (qv searches for his friend Orson Welles (qv), only to discover he is his nemesis. Beginning with the *Orient Express* (34) and ending some 49 years later with *The Honorary Consul* (83), his stories include *This Gun for Hire* (42), a early film noir, the British gangst movie *Brighton Rock* (47), the eccentric tale of *Our Man in Havana* (59) and *The Comedian* (67), which attacked the despicable Duvalier regime. Born Berkhamsted and educated ther and at Oxford, he was a sub-edit on The Times and the Spectator' film critic, where he participated the debate on the state of British cinema. His diverse passions included travelling, Russian roulette, alcohol, drugs, psychoanalysis, communism, th British secret service, Third Worl liberation and Catholicism. His fi essays are collected in The Pleasure Dome.

JOHN GRIERSON
British documentarist (1898-1972)

Credited as being the founder of the documentary movement in t 1920s (and the first to use the word "documentary"), his philosophy was to "exploit the powers of natural observation, to build a picture of reality, to bring the cinema to its destiny as a social commentator, inspirator a art". There was no equivocation, but in the magnificent visual poe

ght Mail (36), fusing W H
den's verse with Benjamin
tten's music, art and
ertainment prove compatible.
me were screened in cinemas,
ny had to be shown in factory
nteens and public halls. Born in
otland and educated at Glasgow
iversity, he taught at Durham
iversity before visiting America
a Rockefeller Fellowship to
dy mass communication.
turning to Britain he set up a
n unit within the Empire
rketing Board to create a
mpany of socially conscious film
kers. The most notable of his
leagues was Paul Rotha (qv). In
39 he established the National
n Board of Canada.

VID WARK GRIFFITH
director (1875-1948)

first passion was for acting –
stumbled through a series of
upes and tours – before
ancial instability forced him to
ept menial jobs while touting
scripts around studios. He
nd minor success selling stories
Biograph and in 1909 began
ecting for them before becoming
ir general director. There he
ected more than 400 films (most
hem shorts) and joined the
ematographer Billy Bitzer (qv) in
innovative creative partnership.
his reputation grew, Griffith took
more ambitious films and, after
ving Biograph in 1913, went to
iance-Majestic as production
ef, laying the groundwork for his
l war epic *The Birth of a Nation*
). It was a landmark in film
tory, with its advanced cinematic
hniques, intricate editing,
ernating close-ups and long-shots
m varying camera angles.
hough a huge success it
acted controversy for dubious
racial politics. His next film, *Intolerance* (16), was constructed on an even larger canvas, although its scale and multi-threaded plotting made it indigestible and its commercial failure put him in debt. He continued to direct at a prolific rate and in 1919 joined Chaplin, Pickford and Fairbanks (qqv) to form United Artists. His first feature for UA was *Broken Blossoms* (19). During the making of *Way Down East* (20), financially his second most successful film, his star Lillian Gish (qv) sustained permanent damage to a hand that trailed in icy water during a frozen river sequence. Griffith worked in a wide variety of genres before the disaster of his last film *The Struggle* (31). He died 17 years later, lonely and bitter in a Hollywood hotel, a great film maker forgotten by the industry he once led.

ALEC GUINNESS
British actor (1914-)

On the London stage from 1934, he began his film career after wartime service in the Royal Navy with David Lean's (qv) *Great Expectations* (46). As Fagin in *Oliver Twist* (48) he established his credentials as Britain's most chameleon-like actor, playing eight roles in *Kind Hearts and Coronets* (49). Through the 1950s he was Disraeli in *The Mudlark* (50), was nominated for an Oscar for *The Lavender Hill Mob* (51) and starred in *Father Brown* (54), *The Ladykillers* (55) and *The Bridge on the River Kwai* (57), for which he won the best actor Oscar. He was nominated for co-writing *The Horse's Mouth* (58) and knighted in 1959. He has contributed notable character portrayals to such films as *Lawrence of Arabia* (62), *Doctor Zhivago* (65), *Cromwell* (70), the *Star Wars* trilogy (77, 80 and 83), *A Passage to India* (84) and *Little Dorrit* (88). He was awarded an honorary Oscar in 1970 for "advancing the art of screen acting".

SACHA GUITRY
French director, writer and actor (1885-1957)

He wrote more than 120 stage plays and often cast himself and ▷

Togged out: Guinness had his eyes on the top in The Card

one of his four wives as the lead players. He saw the screen as a means of recording his plays, including *Pasteur, Bonne Chance* (both 35), *Le Nouveau Testament* (36), *Les Perles de la Couronne* (37) and *Le Diable boiteux* (48). It is claimed he allowed only single takes in the three films he wrote for Michel Simon (qv), among them *Le Poison* (51). In *Si Versailles métait conté* (55) he played Louis XIV and in his well-received epic *Napoléon* (55) he was Talleyrand. The son of Lucien Guitry, a renowned French stage star, his reputation was blunted by alleged collaboration with the Nazis.

EDMUND GWENN
British actor (1875-1959)

His talent for encapsulating lovable, Pickwickian virtues interspersed with sentimental homily found its perfect vehicle as Kris Kringle (aka Santa Claus) in *Miracle on 34th Street* (47), for which he won an Oscar. A native of Glamorgan, he first appeared on stage in 1896. A few silent films were followed by early talkies, *The Skin Game* and *Hindle Wakes* (both 31). His first Hollywood film was *The Bishop Misbehaves* (35) followed by *Laburnum Grove* (36), *Parnell* (37) and *A Yank at Oxford* (38). Gwenn's saccharine level rose perceptively with permanent Hollywood residency and he was either used as a convivial dispenser of fortune cookie wisdom or mischievously by Hitchcock (qv) who made him an amiable hitman in *Foreign Correspondent* (40). His last batch of films included *Of Human Bondage* (46), *Life With Father* (47), *The Bigamist* (53) and *The Trouble With Harry* (55).

GENE HACKMAN
US actor (1931-)

Hollywood's busiest actor and one of its best, he lied about his age at 16 to join the marines for three years. Numerous dead-end jobs followed before he enrolled for training at California's Pasadena Playhouse, from where he progressed to steady work, mostly in comedies, on Broadway. His meteoric rise in films began with the Oscar-nominated Buck Barrow in *Bonnie and Clyde* (67), since when he has become a star. For every top-class film he makes, about three are unworthy of his excellence. Overwork resulted in heart surgery in 1990. A five-times Oscar nominee, he has twice won best actor, the first for Popeye Doyle in *The French Connection* (71), the role with which he is forever identified.

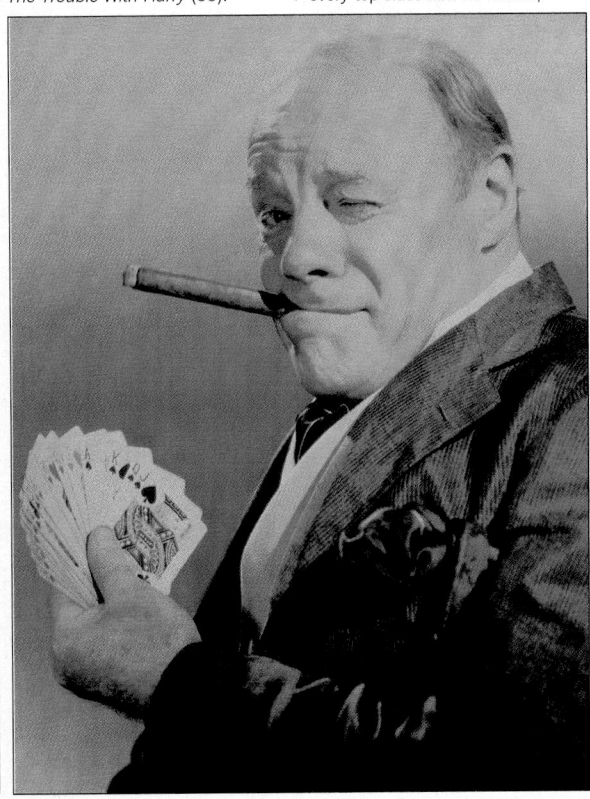

ROBERT HAMER
British director (1911-63)

He entered films as a clapper boy after graduating from Cambridge and by 1935 was a film editor. At Ealing, near the beginning of its great period under Michael Balcon (qv), his directorial debut was the Haunted Mirror sequence in the portmanteau ghost film *Dead of Night* (45). His first full-length feature, *It Always Rains on Sunday* (47), was an atmospheric East End of London drama about an escaped convict returning home. His finest work, however, was the urbane black comedy *Kind Hearts and Coronets* (49). Nothing he did consequently fulfilled the promise he had shown and he fought and lost a long battle with alcoholism.

MARVIN HAMLISCH
US composer (1944-)

Hamlisch was 29 years old when he ran up to the podium to collect an Oscar for his score for *The Sting* (73). A few minutes later he was back on stage accepting a second statuette for his music for *The Way We Were* (73) and before the evening was over he was clutching a third Oscar for his title song to the latter film. He is the only person to win three Oscars in one night. Over the next 15 years he received another seven nominations, confirming his reputation as one of the most popular and successful composer-songwriters in the business. At seven he was the youngest student ever admitted to the Juilliard School of Music, six months later he composed his first song and at eight he had performed his first public recital. He was 23 when he wrote the score for *The Swimmer* (68) and his skill at bringing a popular touch to incidental music has kept him in demand ever since. He won the Tony and the Pulitzer prize for his music for the 1976 Broadway musical A Chorus Line, filmed in 1985, and has received four Grammies.

IRENE HANDL
British actress (1901-87)

A stalwart of post-war British comedies, her bedraggled appearance belied a sharp intelligence; her novel, The Sioux, was a critically-praised bestseller. On screen she was best known as either a dumpy charlady, lady's maid or crook's mother, her voice swooping up and down in such classic comedies as *The Belles of Trinian's* (54). She was a specialis in outraged and bewildered innocence and her eccentric cameos were always worth lookin out for in B-movies. As the shop steward's wife with a mind of her own in Peter Sellers's (qv) *I'm All*

ght Jack (59), she was a balefully mic reason for him to commit nself to Marxism. Teamed with ny Hancock, also a comedian of nperament, for *The Rebel* (61), e defiantly faced him down. The t of her 73 screen appearances s in *Absolute Beginners* (86).

M HANKS
S actor (1956-)

nks was a comedy star for a cade before becoming one of llywood's top leading men in a n of hits and an Oscar-winning rformance as a courageous Aids tim in *Philadelphia* (93). A new e Jack Lemmon (qv), combining yishness, humour and sensitivity n an open, Everyman face, he rted in classical theatre, but ade his name in Bosom Buddies, elevision drag comedy. Being oed by a mermaid in *Splash* 4) launched him into variable medies, but ventures into drama ed to find an audience, although was named best actor by the s Angeles critics for *Punchline* 3). *Big* (88) earned him his first car nomination as a youngster pped in a man's body, but again tumbled into inferior material, during a low with *The Bonfire of Vanities* (90). His alcoholic eemed in *A League of Their vn* (92) stopped the rot and saw n in two 1993 landmarks: the ckbuster romantic comedy *eepless in Seattle* and *iladelphia*, for which he won the car. As *Forrest Gump* (94), the ndide-like simpleton progressing ough American history, he nfirmed his stature as a ntemporary box-office king and it ught him the Oscar for the ond year running.

Y (YIP) HARBURG
S lyricist (1896-1981)

e wordsmith of the songs in *The zard of Oz* (39), Harburg began ting poetry at New York City llege. After gaining a BSc he set an electrical appliance shop. at went bust, so he took out his se from a bottom drawer and s soon writing for Ziegfeld and l Carroll revues. His most fruitful off partnership was with nposer Harold Arlen (qv), while films range from *Babes in Arms* (39) to *Gay Purr-ee* (62). His stage musicals were all hits, which meant he could pick and choose in Hollywood; a mix 'n' match that led to the despairing steeliness of Brother, Can You Spare a Dime? for *The Gold Diggers of 1937* (36), the yearning simplicity of his Oscar-winning Over The Rainbow for *The Wizard of Oz* and Lydia, the Tattooed Lady for Groucho Marx (qv) in *At the Circus* (39).

CEDRIC HARDWICKE
British actor (1893-1964)

A deep-voiced leading man and character actor (latterly, often, an aristocrat or villain), Hardwicke was on the London stage and in films briefly before the first world war. By the early 1930s he was a success in both media, especially in the title role in *Dreyfus* (31) and as Charles II in *Nell Gwyn* (34), the year he was knighted. Thereafter, he worked mainly in Hollywood. Among his many memorable film roles are Livingstone in *Stanley and Livingstone* (39), Dr Arnold in *Tom Brown's School Days* and Mr Jones in *Victory* (both 40), as a Nazi (one of several he played) in *The Moon is Down* (43), Ralph Nickleby in *Nicholas Nickleby* (47), King Arthur in *A Connecticut Yankee in King Arthur's Court* (49), Edward IV in Olivier's (qv) *Richard III* (55) and alongside Mickey Rooney (qv) in *Baby Face Nelson* (57). He also acquitted himself well in a host of cameo and brief appearances until *The Pumpkin Eater* (64), in the year of his death.

DAVID HARE
British director, screenwriter (1947-)

One of the leading radicals of the British theatre during the 1970s, he has carried his political passions into cinema as a screenwriter and director – winning the Golden Bear at the Berlin Film Festival for his debut film *Wetherby* (85). David Rippon was born in Sussex, graduated from Cambridge and co-founded the experimental Portable Theatre. He went on to become resident dramatist at the Royal Court in London and the Nottingham Playhouse and the director of the Joint Stock Theatre Company. A socialist, who believes that the audience must make up its own mind, he challenges them to break with complacency. He wrote and directed *Paris by Night* (89) as a noirish thriller about

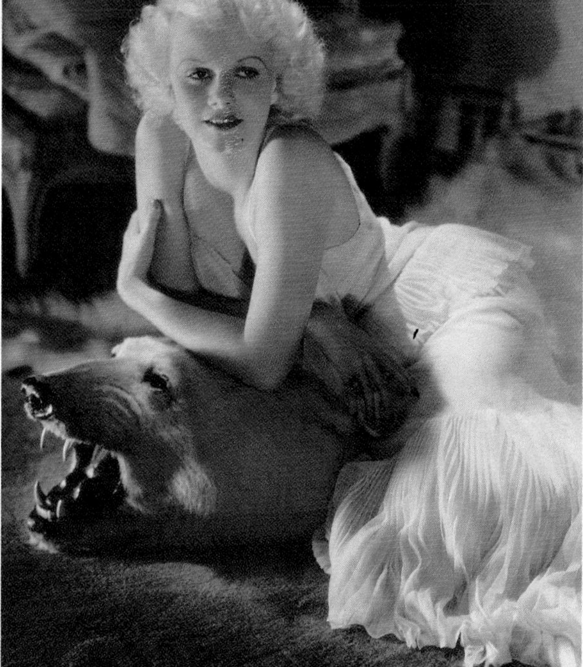

Thatcherism. *Strapless* (89) is a feminist allegory on the destruction of the National Health Service and *Damage* (92), directed by Malle (qv), a metaphor for incestuous post-modernist attitudes.

JEAN HARLOW
US actress (1911-37)

One of the screen's enduring icons, Harlean Carpenter was born in Kansas City, Missouri, and arrived in Los Angeles already married at 16. Her most spectacular early appearance is as the blonde who loses her skirt in a taxi door in Laurel & Hardy's (qv) short, *Double Whoopee* (28). Divorced in 1929, she became Jean Harlow and appeared in the Howard Hughes (qv) aviation epic *Hell's Angels* (30) as the blonde who needed to slip into something comfortable. She attracted attention in *The Public Enemy* and *Platinum Blonde* (both 31) and was then signed by MGM who skilfully built her into a comedy star, pitting her against such top leading men as Clark Gable, Spencer Tracy and Cary Grant (qqv). Her best films, *Red Dust* (32), *Dinner at Eight* (34), *China Seas* (35) and *Libeled Lady* (36), are classics. Harlow's private life was chequered; she was married three times (one husband, Paul Bern, was found dead one month after the wedding). While filming *Saratoga* (37) with Gable she became ill and died of a cerebral oedema at only 26. A double completed the film.

RICHARD HARRIS
Irish actor (1930-)

He trained at the London Academy of Music and Dramatic Art, making his theatre debut in The Quare Fellow for Joan Littlewood in 1956 and gaining London West End status with The Ginger Man. It was not until *This Sporting Life* (63), a Lindsay Anderson (qv) contribution to the bleak British new realism, that he made his mark in films, winning best actor at Cannes and an Oscar nomination. In truth, with a few exceptions – *The Red Desert* (64) for Antonioni (qv), *Camelot* (67) and *A Man Called Horse* (70) – his filmography outstrips the size of his achievements, which have too often been limited to dull performances in mediocre to poor films. He is perhaps more famous for his legendary hell-raising, boozing and brawling in public than as a star. That said, as an Irish farmer passionately protecting his threatened property in *The Field* (90), he gave a superb performance of Lear-like stature to match his huge frame and now extremely grizzled face.

REX HARRISON
British actor (1908-90)

Harrison enjoyed a long career personifying the elegant man-about-town. He will for ever be associated with his crowning, Oscar-winning role as the arrogant Professor Higgins who transformed a guttersnipe into a duchess for a bet in *My Fair Lady* (64), a part he originated on Broadway. He joined the Liverpool Repertory Theatre at 16 and entered films young, moving easily between Britain and Hollywood, stage and screen for more than 60 years. Vintage Harrison includes the husband caught between rival living and dead wives in *Blithe Spirit* and the debonair cad of *The Rake's Progress* (both 45), the spectral seaman of *The Ghost and Mrs Muir* (47) and the jealous conducter in *Unfaithfully Yours* (48). He made a mark as Caesar amid the frenzy

surrounding his *Cleopatra* (63) co-stars Elizabeth Taylor and Richard Burton (qqv). He was also noted for the amorous activity that prompted the nickname "Sexy Rexy": his six wives included actresses Lilli Palmer, Kay Kendall, Rachel Roberts and Elizabeth Harris. He was knighted in 1989.

RAY HARRYHAUSEN
US special effects expert (1920-)

His work in such films as *The Seventh Voyage of Sinbad* (58) has an imaginative magic that continues to impress. His creativity with Dynamation and Superdynamation, where actors were integrated with animated models, still dazzles. ▷

Harryhausen pioneered the art of special effects, often the key element in providing a fantasy world on screen. His prehistoric beast thawed out by an atom bomb in *The Beast From 20,000 Fathoms* (53), the octopus bursting to the surface in *It Came From Beneath the Sea* (55), the creatures of *The Three Worlds of Gulliver* (60) are examples of his stop-motion animation skill. As a boy he had experimented at home after seeing *King Kong* (33). His entry into the industry came with *Mighty Joe Young* (49), where he assisted Willis O'Brien with the effects. They went on to win an Oscar and Harryhausen's career received an auspicious start.

WILLIAM S HART
US cowboy (1865-1946)

Growing up in South Dakota, he learned to speak Sioux as a boy, worked as a hand on cattle trails and later became a close friend of Wyatt Earp. Hart honed his craft as a Shakespearean actor on Broadway, but did not make his first film until he was 49. Writing and starring in *The Bargain* (14), it catapulted him into an acting and directing career that lasted for 11 years. The call for more action-oriented westerns forced him to retire. In his most notable films – *Hell's Hinges* (16), *The Aryan* (17) and *The Toll Gate* (20) – he exemplified the tall, brooding loner later emulated by heroes from Randolph Scott to Clint Eastwood (qqv). In his later years he wrote western novels.

LAURENCE HARVEY
British actor (1927-73)

Laruska Mischa Skikne was born in Janiskis, Lithuania. He was educated in Johannesburg and served in the South African army before entering Rada in 1946. He sauntered around British theatre for a couple of years before making his film debut in *House of Darkness* (48). After *The Scarlet Thread* (51), *The Good Die Young* (54) and *I Am a Camera* (55), his portrayal of Joe Lampton in *Room at the Top* (59) made him fashionable. He went to Hollywood to make *The Alamo* (60), but gave his best performance as the brain-washed Raymond Shaw in Frankenheimer's

(qv) seminal classic *The Manchurian Candidate* (62). Harvey directed and produced *The Ceremony* (63). His films include *Butterfield 8* (60), *Walk on the Wild Side* (62), *The Running Man* (63), *Of Human Bondage* (64) and *Darling* (65). After a lifetime of ill-health he succumbed to cancer at the tragically young age of 45.

HENRY HATHAWAY
US director (1898-1985)

Born to a stage manager and an actress, he was a child actor for the American Film Company and prop boy for Universal. He entered the industry as an assistant director and after completing two years of military service had his first opportunity to direct in 1932. His early films were all low-budget westerns (the genre in which he would produce some of his best work), but within four years his name carried with it a guarantee of quality and efficiency. He worked with Paramount, then Twentieth Century Fox and was renowned for adhering to the strictures imposed by budget and shooting schedule. He adopted the use of real locations with *The House on 92nd Street* (45), *13 Rue Madeleine* (47) and *Call Northside 777* (48). His most outstanding work was *The Desert Fox* (51), but he could also bring a touch of class to more shaky projects. *Niagara* (53) was a tense drama featuring a somewhat incongruous Marilyn Monroe (qv) and he was as industrious as ever on *True Grit* (69), one of John Wayne's (qv) last films.

JACK HAWKINS
British actor (1910-73)

The most plausible exponent of the British stiff upper lip after his naval skipper in *The Cruel Sea* (53), he began on the stage and gained substantial parts in *A Shot in the Dark* (33) and *Death at Broadcasting House* (34). After war service in India he found a home at Ealing Studios and was brilliantly cast in *Mandy* (52) as an exasperated man in the story of a deaf girl. He was on the side of law in *The Long Arm* and *The Man in the Sky* (both 56), though more ambiguously upright as the mastermind of *The League of*

Gentlemen (60), Britain's best heist film. Howard Hawks (qv) put him into the *Land Of The Pharaohs* (55) sarcophagus and John Ford (qv) placed him in dramatic handcuffs for *Gideon's Day* (58). He was at his best as more overbearing characters, notably Alec Guinness's (qv) state prosecutor in *The Prisoner* (55). In 1966 he lost the use of his vocal cords after a cancer operation and others voiced him. It is typical of him that he continued to act.

HOWARD HAWKS
US director, screenwriter and producer (1896-1977)

Hawks claimed he was keen only on "fun and business". Despite this, he often wrote and produced the films he was directing. He leapt about from westerns, gangster thrillers and detective stories to screwball comedies and musicals, but certain themes kept surfacing. Men coping under threat and male kinship were key concerns. The narrative drive of films as diverse

as *Scarface* (32) and *Bringing Up Baby* (38) was the result of a lean, organised style in which gratuitous by-ways were banned and a central mood was powerfully sustained. His later films, such as *Rio Bravo* (59), revealed an appetite for moral contemplation. Hawks received his first break in the props department of the Famous Players-Lasky studios, going on to create a resonant body of work over more than 40 years, including *Twentieth Century* (34), *The Big Sleep* (46), *Red River* (48) and *Gentlemen Prefer Blondes* (53). He received an honorary Oscar in 1975.

WILL HAY
British comedian (1888-1949)

Although this much-loved star of British films made his mark in music hall, he was a brilliant *farceur* whose comic bent was far removed from the tradition of rapid-fire patter and the double entendre. Instead, helped by his deceptively stern and authoritative presence, he created a bumbling, irascible schoolmaster in a series of sketches. The character resurfaced on film in *Boys Will Be Boys* (35). His attention to details of

characterisation was well suited to the camera, and his films offered a series of crafty idlers or incompetent windbags trying to extricate themselves from self-created disasters or con themselves into positions of importance. He was generally accompanied and "assisted" by Graham Moffat, a cheeky, Bunterish youth, and Moore Marriott, a lively ancient. Hay's best film was *Oh Mr Porter* (37) in which, as the station master of a crumbling Northern Irish rural halt, he foils a gang of gun runners by insanely farcical means and the help of his usual pair of sidekicks Moffat and Marriott.

SESSUE HAYAKAWA
Japanese actor (1889-1973)

A member of a high-class family, he arrived in America in 1908 to study political science at the University of Chicago. After graduation he joined a Japanese theatre troupe in California and Thomas Ince (qv) signed him for

films. His first big hit was *The Typhoon* (14) and he quickly became established as an adept a[t] playing oriental heroes and suave villains in a restrained style and so shaped American perceptions of the Japanese in the early years of films. He founded his own production company, which made 20 films before he left Hollywood i[n] 1923. In Britain he made *The Great Prince Shan* and *Sen Yan's Devotion* (both 24). He remained i[n] Europe during the German occupation and made films in France. After the war he returned to Hollywood appearing in occasional character roles, most memorably as the camp commandant opposite Alec Guinness (qv) in David Lean's (qv) *The Bridge on the River Kwai* (57).

STERLING HAYDEN
US actor (1916-86)

He served as a mate on a schooner, but turned to modelling for extra money to buy his own boat. He made his film debut for Paramount in *Virginia* (41) at the age of 25 and was sold to the public as "The Most Beautiful Ma[n] in the Movies". He joined the marines in 1942 and then American special operations, serving as an undercover agent behind enemy lines in Yugoslavia. Hayden returned to films in 1947 after briefly joining the American Communist party. He dropped his image as an idol by playing a criminal in *The Asphalt Jungle* (50). In 1951 he was called before the House Un-American Activities Committee and avoided blacklistin[g]

y naming others. His two finest erformances were for Stanley ubrick (qv) in the pulp thriller *he Killing* (56) and in the dark atire *Dr Strangelove* (64). Perhaps ecause of the conflict between his 'holesome looks and aptitude in nsavoury roles, he was frequently addled with unpromising parts.

SUSAN HAYWARD
US actress (1918-75)

Edythe Marrener was a photographer's model who, as Susan Hayward, became a popular leading lady in the 1950s. Brought to Hollywood as a possible Scarlett O'Hara, she worked as a contract player, then ingénue in *Beau Geste* (39), *Reap the Wild Wind* (42) and *Deadline at Dawn* (46), before gaining recognition with her Oscar-nominated performance as an alcoholic in *Smash Up: The Story of a Woman* (47). She received four more nominations and stardom portraying fighters, survivors, tragedy queens and hard-luck women with guts, such as Jane Froman, a paralysed singer, in *With a Song in My Heart* (52), scandalous Rachel Jackson in *The President's Lady* (53) and Lillian Roth, the troubled fallen star, in *I'll Cry Tomorrow* (55). She won an Oscar for her role as a prostitute bound for the gas chamber in *I Want to Live* (58). Eventually tiring of melodramatic weepies, she played the Bette Davis (qv) role in the remake of *Stolen Hours* (63) and all but retired in 1964. She lost her long battle with a brain tumour at the age of 56.

RITA HAYWORTH
US actress (1918-87)

Hayworth was the quintessential "Love Goddess" of the 1940s. Talented, beautiful and boasting a torrent of (dyed) red hair, she was a pre-eminent pin-up of the second world war and one of the leading dancers of her day. A cousin of Ginger Rogers (qv) she followed in the Latin American dancing steps of her father and at 13 performed in Mexican nightclubs in Los Angeles. Spotted by a film executive, she was signed to Twentieth Century Fox and appeared in 25 films before her

breakthrough in Hawks's (qv) *Only Angels Have Wings* (39). She teamed up with Fred Astaire (qv) in the delightful *You'll Never Get Rich* (41) and *You Were Never Lovelier* (42) and scored as the *femme fatale* in *Gilda* (46), her most celebrated role. She changed her image by dyeing her hair blonde and cutting it short for her second husband Orson Welles's (qv) thriller *The Lady From Shanghai* (48). Although she starred in a number of musicals, her singing voice was usually dubbed, including her notorious rendering of Put the Blame on Mame in *Gilda*. She died of Alzheimer's disease aged 68.

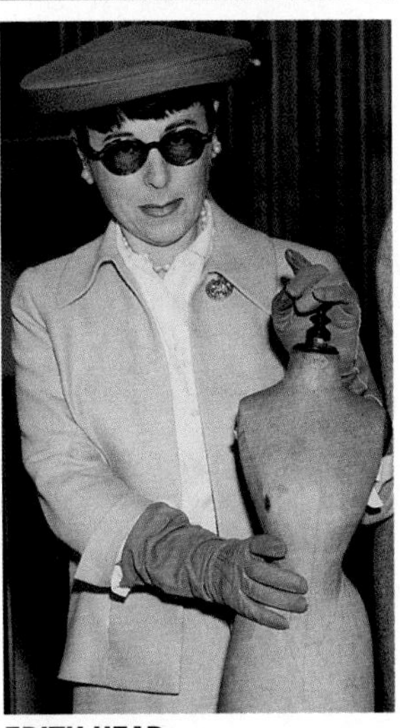

EDITH HEAD
US costume designer (1907-81)

A tough, opinionated workaholic, she was the most influential designer in Hollywood, with eight Oscars and 35 nominations. She bluffed her way into Paramount's wardrobe department and stayed for 44 years, creating such classic images as Jean Harlow's (qv) figure-hugging silk slip, Dorothy Lamour's (qv) jazzy sarong, Marlene Dietrich's (qv) severely tailored suit, the wasp-waisted gowns of Bette Davis (qv) and Elizabeth Taylor (qv) and the discreetly sexy yet respectable look of Hitchcock's (qv) blondes, particularly Grace Kelly (qv). Head's workload was phenomenal: Ingrid Bergman's (qv) espionage wardrobe for *Notorious* (46), Hedy Lamarr's (qv) extravagant peacock cape for *Samson and Delilah* (50) and for such films as *The Greatest Show on Earth* (52) and *The Man Who Shot Liberty Valance* (62). In 1967 she switched to Universal, dressing *Sweet Charity* (69), *Airport* (70), *The Sting* (73) and *The Man Who Would Be King* (75). In some 750 films through six decades she inspired fashion trends, designed Vogue patterns, airline uniforms and became a TV pundit offering chic advice. One of the first top figures to endorse equal rights in the industry, she was not pretty but she had style.

BEN HECHT
US writer (1893-64)

He was perhaps Hollywood's most versatile and prolific screenwriter, with some 70 films to his credit. His fingers tapped out scripts for films as diverse as von Sternberg's (qv) *Underworld* (for which he received an Oscar at the first ever Academy Awards in 1928) and the perennially successful newspaper comedy *The Front Page* (31), which had three further film adaptations. Reputed to have amassed a fortune, he apparently reviled the cheap vulgarity of his Hollywood paymasters, preferring to think of himself as a serious writer of plays and novels. The son of New York Jewish immigrants and raised in Wisconsin, he showed early promise on the piano but at 16 became a cub reporter then a war correspondent, crime reporter and budding novelist, before turning up broke in Hollywood. He wrote *Gunga Din* and *Wuthering Heights* (both 39), *Notorious* (46) and *Farewell to Arms* (57). He also collaborated, uncredited, on many films, including *Gone With the Wind* (39) and Hitchcock's (qv) *Rope* (48). His early life was recorded in his book A Child of the Century, filmed as *Gaily Gaily* (69) and starring Beau Bridges.

VAN HEFLIN
US actor (1910-71)

A boyish leading man who went on to become a rugged character actor, Heflin attended the Yale School of Drama but did not settle.

Working intermittently as a stage actor, Katharine Hepburn (qv), requested him for *A Woman Rebels* (36). He went on to win the Oscar as best supporting actor for *Johnny Eager* (42), which made him a leading man. He continued to work on stage and in film, but is best remembered for his intelligent and convincing performances in *The Strange Love of Martha Ivers* (46), *Act of Violence* (48) and *Madame Bovary* (49), *The Prowler* (51), *Shane* (53), *Patterns* (56) and *3:10 to Yuma* (57). Reduced to character roles in lesser films in the 1960s, he made a notable last bow with his appearance in *Airport* (70).

SONJA HENIE
Norwegian actress, ice skater (1910-69)

Triple Olympic gold medallist Henie translated her physical prowess into screen fame. She started skating at the age of eight, won her first world championship at 15 and at 17 claimed her first Olympic figure skating title. After her 1936 gold she was signed by Darryl F Zanuck (qv) to Twentieth Century Fox. She had musicals mounted around her which, typically, cast her as the belle of a winter resort winning the heart of Tyrone Power or Don Ameche (qqv) with her extravagant ice skating routines. When her speciality wore thin with audiences in the 1940s, she produced and starred in ice revues. The best of her films are *Thin Ice* (37) and *Sun Valley Serenade* (41).

PAUL HENREID
US actor, director (1908-92)

Born in Trieste while it was still Austrian, this patrician but somewhat stolid leading man of the 1940s began his career in Vienna. He made his first film in 1933, but moved to Britain in 1935 where he made a good impression with *Victoria the Great* (37), *Goodbye Mr Chips* (39) and *Night Train to Munich* (40). Moving to America that year, he quickly succeeded with *Now Voyager* (42) opposite Bette Davis (qv) and in *Casablanca* (42) with Ingrid Bergman (qv). He continued in leading roles, including *Of Human Bondage* (46) and *Last of the Buccaneers* (50), but then began directing as well as acting for cinema and television. *A Woman's Devotion* (56) and *Dead Ringer* (64) are his best known works as a director and *The Four Horsemen of the Apocalypse* (62) is his best late film as an actor. His last appearance was as a cardinal in *Exorcist II: The Heretic* (77).

JIM HENSON
US puppetmaster, director (1936-90)

At the age of 18 he worked as a puppeteer on the television show Sam and His Friends. He then studied theatre at the University ▷

Innovator: Henson with Phoebe Cates on the set of Labyrinth

of Maryland and became a professional puppeteer. In the late 1950s he began creating characters who would later form an integral part of his television series Sesame Street. He was also working with film and won an Oscar nomination for his short *Time Piece* (65). Four years later he dusted off his colourful cast of puppet characters, called them Muppets and scored a worldwide hit. Henson was both puppeteer and voice for a number of his characters. The irreverent series was his greatest achievement and bore four big-screen spin-offs, the best of which was the original, *The Muppet Movie* (79). Later puppet-animated features such as *The Dark Crystal* (82) suggested a more thoughtful form of storytelling. By the time of Henson's death from streptococcal pneumonia, his organisation was providing puppet animation for countless films. He was the foremost innovator of puppetry.

AUDREY HEPBURN
Swiss actress (1929-93)

The Belgian-born daughter of a Dutch aristocrat mother and an Anglo-Irish father, she endured the second world war in occupied Holland before training with the Ballet Rambert. After working as a photographic model, chorus girl and bit part film actress in Britain, she played Gigi on Broadway at the French novelist Colette's behest and found stardom. A graceful gamine who spoke in an alluringly hybrid Anglo-European accent, she showed Hollywood that leading ladies need not conform to glamorous stereotypes to win audiences. She was awarded the best actress Oscar for *Roman Holiday* (53). Memories of her lesser achievements – *Breakfast at Tiffany's* (61) and *My Fair Lady* (64) – obscure her better work, such as *The Nun's Story* (59). Her high style and class were enhanced by Givenchy in numerous films, notably the musical *Funny Face* (57), while her expressive eyes and radiant smile entranced fans until she retired in 1967. She came back in *Robin and Marian* (76), but spent her last years as Unicef's most eloquent ambassador, comforting Third World children even when suffering from the cancer that killed her.

KATHARINE HEPBURN
US actress (1907-)

The uncrowned Queen of Hollywood, winning 12 nominations and an unprecedented four Oscars, she has played everything from light comedy to high drama – most memorably as the feisty heroine of *Adam's Rib* (49), the psalm-singing spinster in *The African Queen* (51), and Eleanor of Aquitaine in *The Lion in Winter* (68). Born into a wealthy Connecticut family, she pursued a career in theatre before her aristocratic accent proved a winner in her debut film *A Bill of Divorcement* (32). Her first Oscar came a year later with *Morning Glory* (33). During the Depression her upper-class air was considered box office poison, but she survived to raise her banner with *The Philadelphia Story* (40). She picked up two more Oscars for *Guess Who's Coming to Dinner* (67) and *On Golden Pond* (81). Her love affair with Spencer Tracy (qv) was legendary. Replying to her taunt that he was too small, he said: "Don't worry Miss Hepburn, I'll soon cut you down to my size." She appeared in *Love Affair* (94), Warren Beatty's (qv) remake of *An Affair To Remember* (57).

CECIL HEPWORTH
British pioneer (1874-1953)

He was one of the most innovative figures in the British film industry, an inventor of projection devices and the author of Animated Photography, the first British manual on film. He began making fiction and documentary films in 1899, often appearing in them as an actor. His narrative for *Rescued by Rover* (05) is the most polished to that date, telling a coherent, properly edited story. He also experimented with synchronised sound long before the first world war. As the head of his own studio he was responsible for a wide range of films, the most famous of which was *Comin' Thro' the Rye* (16). The post-war British film industry crisis hit him hard and in 1924 he was bankrupted. His name is commemorated in a shopping centre at Walton-on-Thames, Surrey, which stands on the site of his studio.

BERNARD HERRMANN
US composer (1911-75)

Between 1955 and 1964 he composed for all of Hitchcock's (qv) films – including *Vertigo* (58), *North by Northwest* (59) and *Psycho* (60) – establishing a distinctive and powerful style that has been much emulated since. Able to create a portentous atmosphere with little gimmickry, he developed the violin as an effective dramatic tool, notably in the legendary shower scene in *Psycho*. At 20 he founded and conducted the New Chamber Orchestra and five years later was writing music for Orson Welles's (qv) Mercury Playhouse Theater. He wrote the impressionistic and innovative music for Welles's *Citizen Kane* (41), although that year the Oscar went to his score for *All That Money Can Buy* (41). He also contributed a memorable soundtrack to Welles's *The Magnificent Ambersons* (42). He received his fifth Oscar nomination for the atmospheric score to Scorsese's (qv) *Taxi Driver* (76). Herrmann also wrote ballet music, an opera, a symphony, a cantata and a violin concerto.

BARBARA HERSHEY
US actress (1948-)

It took some years for Hershey to be regarded as an actress of substance. A steady flow of mediocre films masked her talent. Yet she had seemed a fresh and perky prospect as far back as her teen years when she appeared in The Monroes television series and more emphatically in *Last Summer* (69). She made *Boxcar Bertha* (72) and *The Last Temptation of Christ* (88) for Martin Scorsese (qv) and worked with Woody Allen (qv) on *Hannah and Her Sisters* (86). Her hits include *Shy People* (87), *A World Apart* and *Beaches* (both 88), *The Public Eye* (91) and *Falling Down* (93). In 1973 she temporarily changed her surname to Seagull, after killing one by mistake, and had a son called Free by the actor David Carradine.

WERNER HERZOG
German director (1942-)

One of the most influential and controversial luminaries of the New German Cinema, he is full of daring ideas and strange philosophical motivation. He wrote his first script at 15, hawked it vainly round producers at 17 and began his association with Klaus Kinski (qv) when his family moved to Munich and shared a house with the oddball actor. He attended

Duquesne University in Pittsburgh on a Fulbright Scholarship studying film and television, and claims he worked as a rodeo rider and smuggler of TV sets across the Mexican border to finance his films. In 1964 he won the prestigious Carl Mayar prize for his first screenplay *Signs of Life*, which he directed in 1968. His international breakthrough, though, came with the compelling *Aguirre the Wrath of God* (72). Shot in the jungles of Peru the landscape and images are awe-inspiring, but the shoot almost killed everyone concerned. *The Enigma of Kasper Hauser* (74) preceded other works, including *Nosferatu The Vampyre* (79) and *Fitzcarraldo* (82). He has since concentrated on documentaries as the fortunes of the new German directors have generally declined.

CHARLTON HESTON
US director, actor (1923-)

Epics were made for Heston, the screen's greatest exponent of heroic, anguished martyrdom. Cecil B DeMille (qv) chose his Mount Rushmore profile for the circus boss in *The Greatest Show on Earth* (52) and as Moses in *The Ten Commandments* (56). He won an Oscar for *Ben-Hur* (59) and followed it with the mythic spectacular *El Cid* (61). His ambition went beyond the rugged. His clout allowed Orson Welles (qv) to make *Touch of Evil* (58), in which Heston played a Mexican detective; he helped Sam Peckinpah (qv) put together the studio-botched *Major Dundee* (65) and he was the love-blighted Norman knight in the magnificent *The War Lord* (65). When he outgrew historical epics he looked to the future: the last voice of reasoned humanity in *Planet of the Apes* (68) and as the hard-muscled survivor in *The Omega Man* (71) and *Soylent Green* (73). One of his silliest and best disaster films was *Earthquake* (74), though it was he, not special effects, that made the earth move. Recently he returned in cameos for *Wayne's World 2*, *Tombstone* and Schwarzenegger's (qv) *True Lies* (all 93).

GEORGE ROY HILL
US director (1922-)

A one-time performer, his most popular films starred Julie Andrews, Paul Newman and Robert Redford (qqv). After studying music at Trinity College, Dublin, he acted at the Abbey Theatre before distinguishing himself as a pilot in the second world war and in Korea. In the 1950s he directed a number of TV productions and Broadway plays until at 40 he made his first film, *Period of Adjustment* (62), an unsuccessful but engagingly acted adaptation of the Tennessee Williams play he had directed on stage. *Hawaii* (66) with Julie Andrews proved to be his first commercial triumph. After *Thoroughly Modern Millie* (67), again hit with Andrews, he cemented his reputation with *Butch Cassidy and the Sundance Kid* (69). The canny teaming of Newman and Redford in the title roles launched the buddy film. He repeated the formula to even greater success with *The Sting* (73), which won him an Oscar as best director.

WALTER HILL
US director (1942-)

His original ambition was to be a cartoonist, but after gaining an English degree at Michigan State University he wrote documentaries before becoming a second assistant director on *Bullitt* and *The Thomas Crown Affair* (both 68). It gave him a taste for directing and he shot his own screenplay, *Hard Times* (75). A rich period of stylised action films followed, including the minimalist chase thriller *The Driver* (78) and

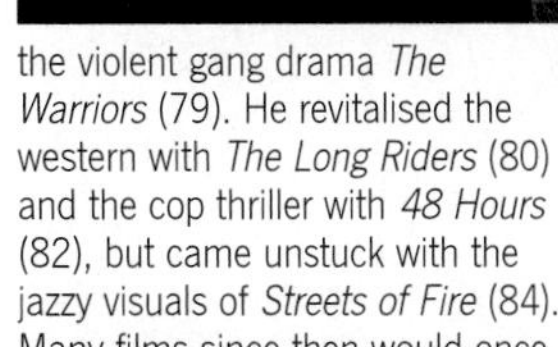

the violent gang drama *The Warriors* (79). He revitalised the western with *The Long Riders* (80) and the cop thriller with *48 Hours* (82), but came unstuck with the jazzy visuals of *Streets of Fire* (84). Many films since then would once

have been labelled B-movies, but *Geronimo: An American Legend* (93) was a sensitive and lyrical western that recalled his former glories. He is one of America's most consistently surprising and technically inspired directors.

ALFRED HITCHCOCK
British director (1899-1980)

The screen's master of suspense was born in Leytonstone, east London, and received a strict Jesuit education. He entered the film industry in 1920 as a title writer when Famous Players-Lasky opened a London studio and was soon assisting. His first two films, *The Pleasure Garden* (25) and *The Mountain Eagle* (26), now lost, were made in Germany, but it was his third, *The Lodger* (26), which

Hitchcock's suspense style is much admired — and emulated

brought him public attention. His Scotland Yard thriller *Blackmail* (29) was made first as a silent and then as Britain's first talkie. A stream of fine thrillers followed through the 1930s, including *The Man Who Knew Too Much* (34), *The 39 Steps* (35) and *The Lady Vanishes* (38), then he signed a Hollywood contract with David Selznick (qv) and their *Rebecca* (40) won the Oscar for best picture. His American films include the exceptional thrillers *Shadow of a Doubt* (43), *Notorious* (46), *Strangers on a Train* (51), *Rear Window* (54), *Vertigo* (58), *North by Northwest* (59), *Psycho* (60) and *The Birds* (63). He was knighted shortly before his death.

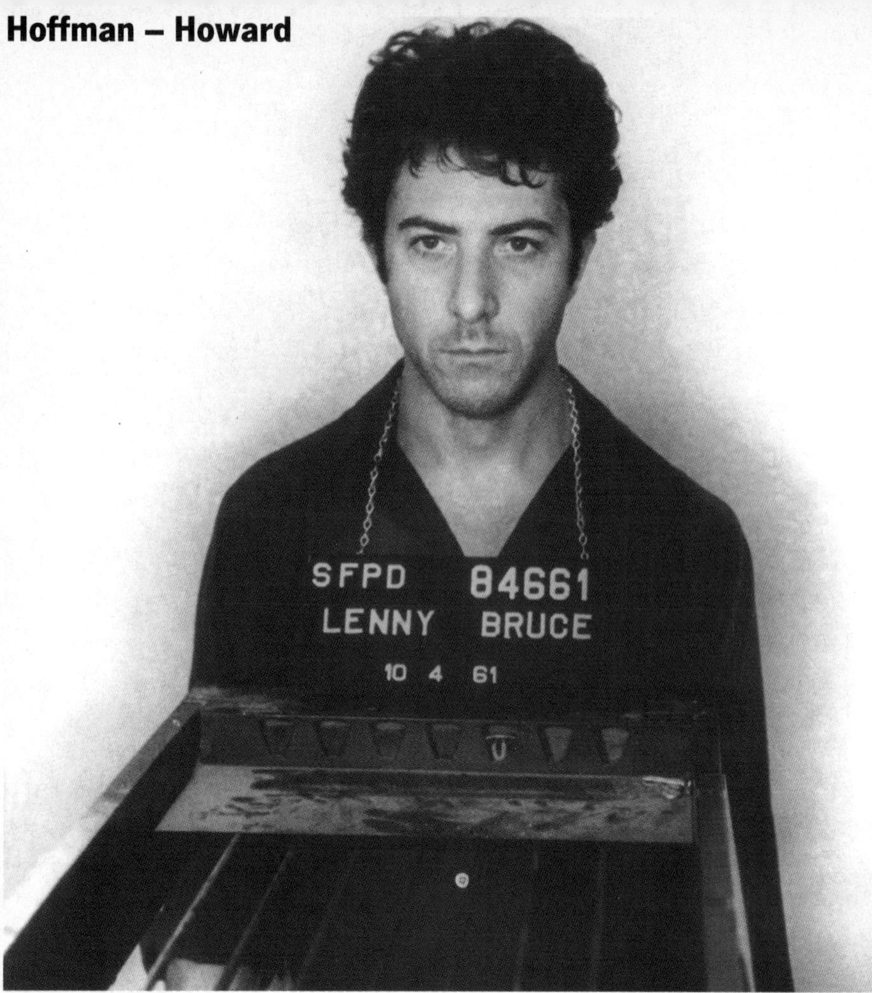

Arresting performer: Hoffman as Lenny Bruce in Lenny

DUSTIN HOFFMAN
US actor (1937-)

California-born, he trained at the Pasadena Playhouse and with Lee Strasberg, imbibing the Method at the Actors Studio. He scratched a living in the New York theatre for several years before director Mike Nichols (qv), flying in the face of typecasting convention, gave him the plum role of Benjamin Braddock, the 20-year-old Wasp in *The Graduate* (67). His success marked the emergence of a new breed of Hollywood star and he has since distinguished himself in an extraordinary variety of roles, from street bum Ratso Rizzo in *Midnight Cowboy* (69), through 121-year-old Jack Crabb in *Little Big Man* (70) and a virtuoso Lenny Bruce impersonation in *Lenny* (74), to his brilliantly deft cross-dressing Michael Dorsey in *Tootsie* (82). Serious minded and meticulous, he is a superlative character actor with leading man status, a six-time Oscar nominee and two-time winner, for *Kramer Vs. Kramer* (79) and *Rain Man* (88).

WILLIAM HOLDEN
US actor (1918-81)

Holden's career reflected his journey from youth to ravaged disillusionment. The handsome product of a wealthy family, William Beedle Jr was spotted in a Pasadena college production and contracted to Paramount. His first important role was *Golden Boy* (39). After wartime army service Billy Wilder (qv) explored a darker seam in him as the despairing screenwriter turned gigolo in *Sunset Boulevard* (50) and the cynical PoW in *Stalag 17* (53), for which Holden received the Oscar. By 1956 he was the number one box office star and the highest paid after a string of successes including *Sabrina* and *The Country Girl* (both 54) and *Love Is a Many-Splendored Thing* (55) and *Picnic* (56) opposite such actresses as Audrey Hepburn, Grace Kelly, Jennifer Jones (qqv) and Kim Novak. He was at his best playing sophisticated charmers and world-weary heels. Heavy drinking took a visible toll and his popularity fell sharply in the 1960s, but he had some fine moments – as the leader of *The Wild Bunch* (69) and the appalled newsman in *Network* (76). Known as "Golden Holden" for his wealth, he died after hitting his head on a table, the body lying undiscovered for days.

AGNIESZKA HOLLAND
Polish director (1948-)

Born in Warsaw and educated at Prague's celebrated FAMU film academy, she studied film making under Milos Forman (qv) and Ivan Passer. She made her co-directing debut in 1977 with *Screen Test* and wrote her first screenplay, *Without Anaesthesia*, for Andrzej Wajda (qv). Her first solo directorial feature *Provincial Actors* (79) won the International Critics Prize at Cannes. After the imposition of martial law in 1981, she emigrated to Paris. Her last Polish feature, *A Woman Alone* (82), is the grim tale of an unmarried mother's struggle for survival. *To Kill a Priest* (88), was loosely based on the story of a murdered priest who supported Solidarity. Holland has a recurring interest in the dispossessed of the second world war. Her West German film *Bitter Harvest* (85) explores the relationship between a prosperous farmer and the Jewish refugee he shelters. *Europa, Europa* (91), nominated for best foreign film Oscar, chronicles a Jewish boy's progress through war-torn Germany. She is married to the Czech director Laco Adamlk.

JUDY HOLLIDAY
US actress (1921-65)

Her squawky voice and blue-eyed stare as Billie Dawn, the culture-ravenous moll in *Born Yesterday* (50), won her an Oscar, but Holliday was no dumb blonde. She had worked back-stage for Orson Welles's (qv) Mercury Theater, and put her own comedy on stage when she formed a revue group with Betty Comden and Adolph Green. Her first film success was when she hijacked *Adam's Rib* (49), a comedy vehicle for Katharine Hepburn and Spencer Tracy (qqv). The Oscar did not release her from bird-brain roles, though she injected some poignancy into *The Marrying Kind* (52) and, as the voice of secretarial liberalism, into *The Solid Gold Cadillac* (56). *Full of Life* (56) was uneven but touching. The musical *Bells Are Ringing* (60), was her last film before her death from cancer at 43. Written by Comden and Green, she played a switchboard operator, the job she had had at the Mercury Theater.

STANLEY HOLLOWAY
British actor, singer (1890-1982)

He started out in music hall and the legitimate stage in 1919 and first appeared on screen in *The Rotters* (21). In *Champagne Charlie* (44), he was well suited to Alberto Cavalcanti's (qv) homage to the spontaneity of mid-Victorian music hall. He was primarily associated with the golden days of Ealing and such films as *Passport to Pimlico* (49), *The Lavender Hill Mob* (51) and *The Titfield Thunderbolt* (53). His triumphant contribution to *My Fair Lady* (64) as Alfred Doolittle reaffirmed his status as one of the screen's great comedy actors.

BOB HOPE
US comedian (1903-)

Known the world over as the wise-cracking coward with the ski jump nose who always lost Dorothy Lamour to Bing Crosby (qqv) in seven Road films, he was one of the top 10 money-spinning film stars of the 1940s and 1950s. Arriving in America when he was four years old from Eltham in south London, Leslie Townes Hope won a Chaplin (qv) impersonation contest

at the age of 10. He served his apprenticeship in vaudeville with song, patter and eccentric dancing. He starred on Broadway and then moved to Hollywood to appear in *The Big Broadcast of 1938* (38). Scoring his first screen success as a comedy coward in *The Cat and the Canary* (39), he followed it up with *The Road to Singapore* (40). Reaching a box office peak opposite Jane Russell (qv) in *The Paleface* (48), his film career began to wane during the late 1950s. Considered to be a national institution and a cultural ambassador, he entertained American troops in seven theatres of war from the second world war to the Gulf. His many honours include five special Oscars.

ANTHONY HOPKINS
British actor (1937-)

A Welsh-born leading man and character actor of phenomenal range, his greatest commercial success was achieved when he was 54. He made his stage debut in 1960 and concentrated on theatre work until the 1970s, although his first film was Lindsay Anderson's (qv) mid-length *The*

ıite Bus (67). He was notable in e Lion In Winter (68), Tony :hardson's (qv) *Hamlet* (69), *The oking Glass War* (70), *When ght Bells Toll* (71), *A Doll's House* 3) and *Young Winston* (72). In ıerica from 1974, initially to pear on Broadway in Equus, he ık many television and film leads d character roles including *Magic* 3), *The Elephant Man* (80), Bligh *The Bounty* (84) and *84 Charing oss Road* (87), before the role of nnibal Lecter in *The Silence of e Lambs* (91) won him the best tor Oscar. *Howards End* (92), *e Remains of the Day* and *adowlands* (both 93) and *The ad to Wellville* (94) have kept n at the top of his profession. He as knighted in 1993.

ENNIS HOPPER

S actor, director (1936-)

ırmerly an outrageous hell-raiser d a cult Method actor – he peared in *Rebel Without a Cause* 5) and *Giant* (56) – he became legend as a motorcycling druggie *Easy Rider* (69). Directed by him d co-authored with Peter Fonda, returned $40m on a $400,000 vestment, setting him up for a ounding bout with the critics when he produced, wrote, directed and starred in *The Last Movie* (71). Dismissed as the crazed ramblings of an egomaniac, it put his career on hold for at least a decade, although he did memorably appear in Wenders's (qv) *The American Friend* (77) and Coppola's (qv) *Apocalypse Now* (79). After cleaning up his act in the 1980s with the help of a drug programme, his cult status was elevated when he played a misfit in *Hoosiers* (86), a chilling psychopath in *Blue Velvet* (86), a militant in *True Romance* (93) and an evil genius in *Super Mario Bros* (93). He directed the well-received *Colors* (88), and *Catchfire* (91) using a pseudonym.

LENA HORNE

US singer, actress (1917-)

Strikingly attractive, with a rich voice, she found fame as a nightclub singer (beginning at the Cotton Club in Harlem). She was the first African American to sign a long-term Hollywood contract with MGM, but her roles were almost invariably as a guest singer whose scenes could be cut when the films were distributed in segregated areas. Her contribution to such films as *The Duke is Tops* (38), *Broadway Rhythm* (44), *Ziegfeld Follies* and *Till the Clouds Roll By* (both 46) and *Words and Music* (48) can be deduced from their titles, although she had proper parts in the all-black musicals *Cabin in the Sky* and *Stormy Weather* (both 43). Her friendship with the actor and singer Paul Robeson (qv) may account for her long absence from the screen, but in 1969 she was given a dramatic role opposite Richard Widmark (qv) in *Death of a Gunfighter*. Her only other film to date is a guest spot in the musical *The Wiz* (78).

EDWARD EVERETT HORTON

US actor (1886-1970)

He was one of the most distinctive and likeable character actors of the 1930s, with a lopsided smile and a world-weary manner. An alumnus of Columbia University where he

appeared in student revues, he made his screen debut in the silent era. The coming of sound made him and he was a regular in such Ernst Lubitsch (qv) comedies as *Trouble in Paradise* (32) and *Design for Living* (33). He was also a memorable Mad Hatter in *Alice In Wonderland* (33). An undisputed master of the double take, he was particularly brilliant as the twittering foil to Fred Astaire (qv) in *The Gay Divorcee* (34), *Top Hat* (35) and *Shall We Dance* (38). His was generally a one-joke character who saw a black lining in every cloud, making many a threadbare comedy shine.

WARNER-PATHE DISTRIBUTORS LTD. present
"A QUESTION OF LOYALTY" (A)
with DENNIS HOPPER · GERALD MOHR
Directed by WALTER DONIGER
Produced by ROY HUGGINS
A WARNER BROS. PICTURE

BOB HOSKINS

British actor (1942-)

A one-time labourer who entered fringe theatre in his twenties, he established himself in classical and avant-garde work at London's Royal Court, Royal Shakespeare Company and National Theatre. His breakthrough screen roles were as the tragic Arthur, the sheet music salesman in Dennis Potter's television serial Pennies From Heaven and an embattled gangster in *The Long Good Friday* (81). His ease with an American accent brought plenty of lucrative work with *The Cotton Club* (84), *Sweet Liberty* (86), *Who Framed Roger Rabbit* (88) and *Mermaids* (90). His biggest success came in Neil Jordan's (qv) dark story *Mona Lisa* (86) as an ex-con betrayed by love, for which he won best actor at Cannes and an Oscar nomination. He also co-wrote and directed *Raggedy Rawney* (89), a central European gypsy drama.

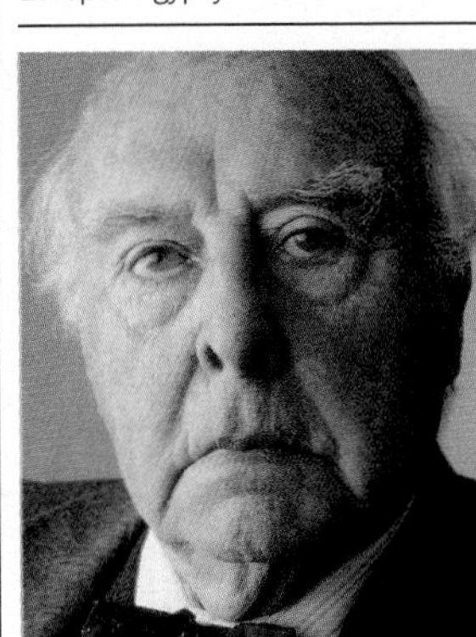

JOHN HOUSEMAN

US producer, actor (1902-88)

His top-drawer accent stemmed from an English mother and a public school education, but it was his Alsatian father who gave him a fluency in French and German and let him loose in the family grain business, which fell foul of the Depression. The arts beckoned and he directed the radical opera Four Saints in Three Acts. His roller-coaster partnership with Orson Welles (qv) resulted in them founding three theatre companies, but their liaison ended in acrimony when Houseman claimed a script credit for *Citizen Kane* (41), an assertion always denied by Welles. His work as a producer included high-quality films such as *Letter From an Unknown Woman* (48), *They Live by Night* (49), *The Bad and the Beautiful* (52), *Lust for Life* (56) and *All Fall Down* (62). Among his acting credits were *Seven Days In May* (64), *Paper Chase* (73) for which he won best supporting actor Oscar, and *Three Days of the Condor* (75). An off-Broadway theatre now carries his name.

LESLIE HOWARD

British actor, director (1893-1943)

Quintessentially the tolerant, pipe-smoking Englishman, Howard (who dropped his surname of Stainer) was the son of Hungarian immigrants. A stage actor before he went in to films, he achieved stardom in Hollywood in the 1930s playing opposite Bette Davis (qv) in *Of Human Bondage* (34) and *The Petrified Forest* (36), and with Norma Shearer (qv) in *Romeo and Juliet* (36). He also appeared as Sir Percy Blakeney in Korda's (qv) *The Scarlet Pimpernel* (35) and as Henry Higgins in *Pygmalion* (38), which he co-directed with Anthony Asquith (qv). After playing Ashley Wilkes in *Gone With the Wind* (39) he returned to Britain and made films such as *Pimpernel Smith* (41) *The First of the Few* (42) and *The Gentle Sex* (43) to boost wartime morale. He died when his airliner was shot down by the Germans between Lisbon and London.

RON HOWARD

US actor, director (1954-)

He is one of the few successful child actors to have established himself as an adult. Howard was born in Duncan, Oklahoma, the son of actors Rance and Jean Howard, and made his first public appearance at the age of 18 ▷

months. Two years later he made his first feature, *Frontier Woman* (56). In the ensuing years he appeared in more than 50 television shows, most notably The Andy Griffith Show and Happy Days. His film appearances have included *The Wild Country* (71), *American Graffiti* (73) and *The Shootist* (76). He began directing in the early 1980s and came to notice with *Night Shift* (82), his second feature. A Hollywood insider of considerable influence, he is best known for light comedy and his long association with the writers Lowell Ganz and Babaloo Mandel, who wrote many episodes of Happy Days. Howard's most noted features include *Splash* (84), *Cocoon* (85), *Willow* (88) and *Backdraft* (91). Many consider *Parenthood* (89) with Steve Martin (qv) to be his most closely observed and best film to date.

TREVOR HOWARD
British actor (1916-88)

With a career spanning 43 years in British and international films, few British actors have enjoyed such lasting success. In spite of making his name in David Lean's (qv) *Brief Encounter* (45) as the decent doctor in love with Celia Johnson (qv), his romantic career was short-lived. Soon he moved on to playing more authoritative figures, frequently army officers. Trained at Rada, he made his theatrical debut while still in college, but acted on stage for 10 years before making his film debut. After *Brief Encounter* he worked with Lean again on *The Passionate Friends* (49) and made a big impression as the acerbic intelligence officer in *The Third Man* (49). In *The Heart of the Matter* (53) he played the pitiful, emotionally impotent Scobie with unerring precision, but it was his moving portrayal of the miner in *Sons and Lovers* (60) that earned him an Oscar nomination. He was a splendid Captain Bligh to Brando's (qv) Fletcher Christian in *Mutiny on the Bounty* (62). In his later years he enlivened many a minor picture with his gruff and commanding presence.

JAMES WONG HOWE
US cinematographer (1899-1976)

Born in China, he moved to America with his family when he was five years old. A move to Los Angeles brought a variety of film industry jobs. In 1922 he got his first job as a director of photography, billed originally as James Howe. He was known as an industrious worker whose low-key lighting compositions (which gave rise to the nickname Low Key Hoe) were the result of painstaking attention to detail. He was also one of the pioneers of the deep focus technique. He achieved a high public profile with Oscars for *The Rose Tattoo* (55) and *Hud* (63). His only forays into directing, *Go, Man, Go* (54) and *The Invisible Avenger* (58, co-directed with John Sledge), were unremarkable, but he continued as director of photography until a year before his death, when he worked on *Funny Lady* (75). His photography defined the visual style of Warner's output in the 1940s.

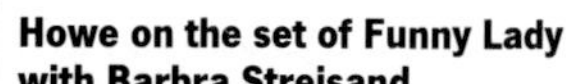
Howe on the set of Funny Lady with Barbra Streisand

Hudson was rebuilt to fit Hollywood's ideal of a man

ROCK HUDSON
US actor (1925-85)

Roy Scherer was a postman, naval aircraft mechanic and truck driver until an agent spotted his film potential. One of the most popular box office stars of the 1950s and 1960s, he is remembered for being among the first famous victims of Aids. A beefcake male pin-up with an amiably casual air, he was one of the last studio-manufactured stars. Universal capped his teeth, arranged a marriage, changed his name and taught him to speak, casting him in supporting, mostly western, roles until he received top billing in *The Lawless Breed* (52). A year later Douglas Sirk's (qv) glossy melodrama *Magnificent Obsession* made him a superstar for several years to come. His most weighty achievement (Oscar-nominated) was his performance as Elizabeth Taylor's (qv) cattle rancher husband in *Giant* (56), his most popular, a clutch of pleasing romantic comedies with Doris Day (qv), starting with *Pillow Talk* (59).

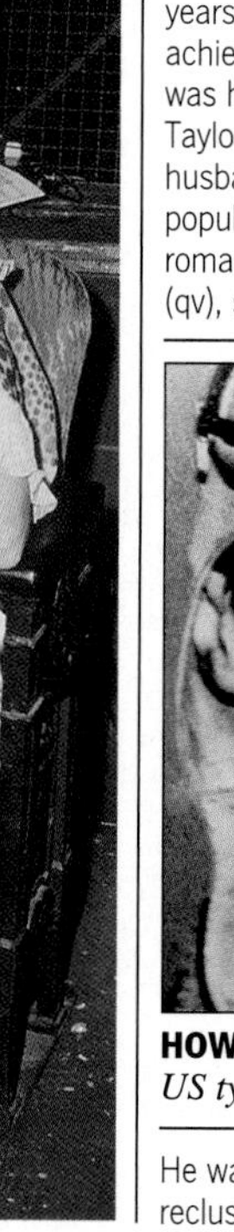

HOWARD HUGHES
US tycoon (1905-76)

He was possibly the best-known recluse in history. At 18 he inherited the Hughes Tool company and was soon ploughing its profits into film making. He directed the costly aviation epic *Hell's Angels* (30) and gave a small part to Jean Harlow (qv), whose career he boosted. He backed Lewis Milestone's (qv) *The Front Page* (31) and Howard Hawks's (qv) *Scarface* (32). In the mid-1930s he vanished from Hollywood, becoming in turn an airline pilot, aircraft designer and a record-breaking round-the-world flier. His notoriety increased when he directed Jane Russell (qv) in *The Outlaw* (43) and designed a cantilevered bra for her which she found unwearable. In 1946 he was nearly killed in an air crash, which changed him from playboy to recluse. In 1948 he acquired RKO and six years later had ploughed a once great studio into the ground, yet still managed to make $10m profit from its sale. In the mid-1960s he moved to a penthouse in the Desert Inn, Las Vegas. Only his close team of Mormon associates ever saw him and even Jean Peters, his wife, was not privileged. His eccentricity attracted much media speculation, the most bizarre being that of a fake diaries hoax by Clifford Irving. Several films have portrayed this strangest of Hollywood moguls, but the best was Jonathan Demme's (qv) *Melvin and Howard* (80).

JOHN HUGHES
US director, writer and producer (1950-)

A career as an advertising copywriter, after dropping out of the University of Arizona, preceded his editorship of the irreverent National Lampoon magazine in 1979. Three years later he was writing for Lampoon's film projects, including the slapstick comedy *National Lampoon's Vacation* (83). In 1984 he wrote and directed *Sixteen Candles*, an early blueprint for the sub-genre of teen comedy. A series of features similarly focusing on Chicagoan middle-class, disaffected adolescents followed, the most popular of which were *The Breakfast Club* (85) and *Pretty in Pink* (86). He gave the formula a welcome twist with the self-mocking *Ferris Bueller's Day Off* (86). There were many ill-conceived disasters, which may be linked to his reputed habit of writing a screenplay over a weekend, but the success of the two *Home Alone* comedies (90, 92), which he wrote and produced, are testimony to his skill.

HOLLY HUNTER
US actress (1958-)

She studied at the Carnegie Mellon University in New York and began a successful stage career, notably in four Beth Henley plays. She repeated her performance in The Miss Firecracker Contest in the 1989 film version. A diminutive (5ft 2in) southerner from Georgia, she is difficult to cast but usually makes an impact. Her best year – until her Oscar-winning performance as the mute heroine in *The Piano* (93) – was 1987 with *Broadcast News*, which attracted critics' awards and an Oscar nomination, and *Raising Arizona* with Nicolas Cage (qv). She has twice starred with Richard Dreyfuss (qv), in *Always* (89) and *Once Around* (91), and was nominated for an Oscar for *The Firm* (93) with Tom Cruise (qv).

ISABELLE HUPPERT
French actress (1955-)

Huppert epitomises the female star of the 1990s, less concerned with personal image than the quality of work in hand. She was born in Paris, specialised in Russian literature at the Paris Conservatoire and then moved to the Conservatoire National d'Art Dramatique. She made her screen debut at 16 in *Faustine et le Bel Eté* (71) and appeared in more than 15 films before she was 21. Two roles propelled her into international stardom, the guileless heroine of *The Lacemaker* (77) and the casual murderess of *Violette Nozière* (77). Huppert has often used her star status to get uncommercial projects off the ground, including Jean-Luc Godard's (qv) *Sauve qui Peut* (80), Joseph Losey's (qv) *The Trout* (82) and her sister Caroline's *Signé Charlotte* (84). Highlights of her career so far include *César et Rosalie* (72), *Les Valseuses* (74), the ill-fated *Heaven's Gate* (80), *Wings of the Dove* (81) and Hal Hartley's *Amateur* (94).

JOHN HURT
British actor (1940-)

Abandoning his studies as an artist (which included a spell at St Martin's School of Art), Hurt has gone on to be best known for his roles as tormented, driven outsiders. His debut was in *The Wild and the Willing* (62), but he found international fame as The Naked Civil Servant on television. He was a social leper in *The Elephant Man* (80) and brought some ballast to the glossy swirl of *Midnight Express* (78). The *Alien* burst from his stomach in 1979 and he paraded an alcohol-soaked conscience in the much-maligned *Heaven's Gate* (80). In *The Hit* (84) he captured the arrogance of an assassin, in *Scandal* (89) the corruptibility of Stephen Ward and in *Rob Roy* (94), a pompous aristo.

WILLIAM HURT
US actor (1950-)

Hurt combined good looks and intellect to effect in the 1980s when he was considered one of Hollywood's A-list men. Son of a diplomat and stepson of Henry Luce III, the publishing magnate, he gained recognition with New York's Circle Repertory Company and his film debut in Ken Russell's (qv) psychedelic *Altered States* (80). He made an impact in the first of four films for Lawrence

Kasdan (qv) as the lustful lawyer undone by Kathleen Turner's (qv) *femme fatale* in *Body Heat* (81) and reached a pinnacle (and an Oscar) with the bravura role of the imprisoned homosexual surviving on fantasy in *Kiss of the Spider Woman* (85). He received an Oscar nomination for *Children of a Lesser God* (86) and enjoyed another unequivocal hit in *Broadcast News* (87). A child support suit brought against him by a former companion exacerbated his image problem with a public that was always lukewarm to him. Since then he has had only one meaty role, as *The Doctor* (91).

ANJELICA HUSTON
US actress (1951-)

The daughter of John Huston (qv), she did not establish herself until she was 34 years old. Yet once in control of her career she displayed a commanding presence matched with a steely elegance. Born in Los Angeles while her father was away filming *The African Queen* (51), she spent her early childhood in Ireland. Against her will she was cast in the lead of her father's poorly received *A Walk With Love and Death* (69), an experience ▷

that sent her scurrying to New York to escape. She began a career as a model, moving to California where she met Jack Nicholson (qv), her lover for 17 years, and began taking bit parts in films. She won an Oscar as Nicholson's vindictive former fiancée in *Prizzi's Honor* (85), following it with increasingly interesting roles, notably in *The Dead* (87), *The Grifters* and *The Witches* (both 90). She was an unflappable Morticia in *The Addams Family* (91) and in *Addams Family Values* (93).

JOHN HUSTON
US director, writer and actor (1906-87)

The son of the actor Walter Huston, he wrote dialogue in Hollywood, collaborating on *Jezebel* (38) and *High Sierra* (41), graduating to directing with *The Maltese Falcon* (41). *Treasure of the Sierra Madre* (48) won him an Oscar and was followed by *Key Largo* (48), *The Asphalt Jungle* (50), *The Red Badge of Courage* and *The African Queen* (both 51), *Moulin Rouge* (52), *Beat the Devil* (53) and *Moby Dick* (56), all of which he co-wrote. Some criticised *The Unforgiven* (60), *The Misfits* (61) and *The Night of the Iguana* (64). *Fat City* and *The Life and Times of Judge Roy Bean* (both 72) and *The Man Who Would Be King* (75) saw him back in favour. His daughter Anjelica (qv) won best supporting actress Oscar in his *Prizzi's Honor* (85) and his son Tony scripted *The Dead* (87), his last film. As an actor he was most effective in *The Cardinal* (63), *Chinatown* (74) and *The Wind and the Lion* (75). He died on the location of his son Danny's first film as a director.

WALTER HUSTON
US actor (1884-1950)

He was born in Toronto where he studied drama, went into the theatre and moved to film acting and Hollywood in the 1920s when stage players were in demand for the talkies. He first impressed with his authoritative portrayal in the title role of D W Griffith's (qv) *Abraham Lincoln* (30), thereafter giving solid, reliable performances, particularly in William Wyler's (qv) *Dodsworth* (36), in which he repeated his Broadway role. In his son John's (qv) *The Treasure of the Sierra Madre* (48) he appeared as a grizzled gold prospector and won a best supporting actor Oscar, and he had a walk-on role in *The Maltese Falcon* (41), the younger Huston's directing debut.

PETER HYAMS
US director, cinematographer and writer (1943-)

Although best known for his direction of *2010* (84), the sequel to Kubrick's (qv) *2001: A Space Odyssey*, he has proved to be an excellent satirist of subjects drawn from his own experience, such as *Stay Tuned* (92). Born in New York and educated at Syracuse University, he began directing and penning television films in 1970. The best of them was Goodnight My Love, which inspired his feature debut *Busting* (74). Both have odd-couple cops running around firing from the lip. A fine craftsman with a flair for big picture style and action, he is one of the few directors who is his own screenwriter and cinematographer. Essentially allegorical, his tales concern individuals struggling against an oppressive system. In his best, *Capricorn One* (78), his heroes try to survive a bogus space mission. *Outland* (81) is a space age remake of *High Noon*. Recent films include *The Presidio* (88) and *Narrow Margin* (90).

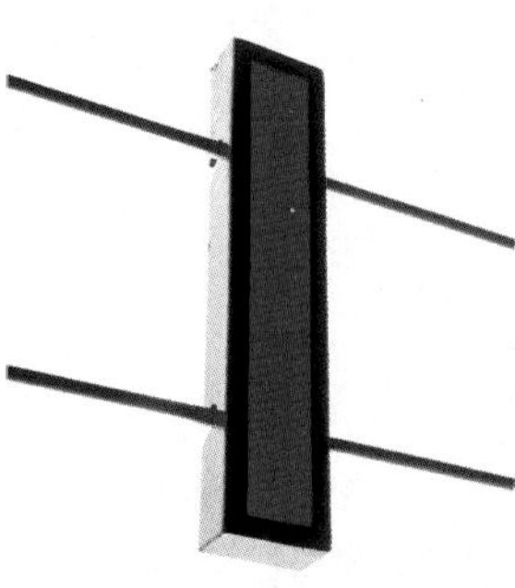

KON ICHIKAWA
Japanese director (1915-)

Although few of his films have been seen by western audiences, Ichikawa is admired universally. His early training was in animation and his debut was a puppet film, *A Girl at Dojo Temple* (46), which was confiscated and destroyed by

occupying American forces. Noted at first for the satirical humour of his work, he found a wider audience with darker subjects, such as the burial of the war dead in *The Burmese Harp* (56) and the horrors of war in *Fires on the Plain* (59), while *The Key* (59) was a study of sexual obsession. *Conflagration* (58) is another study of obsession, this time of purity. Though bleak, his later films do not lack humour. *My Enemy the Sea* (63) is relatively easy-going while *An Actor's Revenge* (63) is a dazzling exercise in ambiguity. He also makes documentaries, including *Tokyo Olympiad* (65). He has used animation in films such as *Being Two Isn't Easy* (62) and *Mr Poo* (53). His late works include *Princess From the Moon* (87) and *Noh Mask Murders* (91).

THOMAS H INCE
US producer, director and screenwriter (1882-1924)

The Ince brothers (the others were John and Ralph) grew up in a theatrical family and entered films separately. Thomas was the most successful and eventually became second only to Griffith (qv) in the hierarchy of the main silent period. He may also have founded the studio system. He turned to films in 1910 and was soon directing short films with Mary Pickford (qv) for Carl Laemmle's (qv) Imp Company. He then set up his own studio, which was run on factory lines. Ince's output was mainly westerns; he had own wild west show on the 20,000-acre lot of Inceville, as it was called. His great anti-war film was *Civilization* (16). After quarrelling with his partners he built a new studio at Culver City and dropped the western hero William S Hart (qv). Ince died on the yacht of William Randolph Hearst, apparently of "serious indigestion", but rumour had it that his host shot him for having an affair with Marion Davies (qv), Hearst's mistress.

REX INGRAM
Irish director (1892-1950)

Born in Dublin, the son of a clergyman, Reginald Ingram Montgomery Hitchcock read law at Trinity College before emigrating to America where he studied sculpture at Yale. After a fortuitous meeting with Edison's (qv) son Charles in 1913, he began a career as an actor, writer and set designer with the Edison company, later moving to Vitagraph, Fox and Universal. Badly wounded while in the Canadian Royal Air Corps during the first world war, he moved to Metro in 1920 where the screenwriter June Mathis insisted he direct her adaptation of *The Four Horsemen of the Apocalypse* (21), allowing him to set up his own production company with his wife Alice Terry. Triumphing with the likes of *The Prisoner of Zenda* (22) and *Scaramouche* (23), he worked for MGM in Europe after a dispute with Louis B Mayer (qv) over not being given *Ben-Hur* (25). When talkies came he retired to Morocco, then returned to America to pursue his writing and sculpture.

JAMES IVORY
US director (1928-)

The unlikely triumvirate of quiet, mannered Ivory, exuberant Indian producer Ismail Merchant (qv) and screenwriter Ruth Prawer Jhabvala (qv) is usually part of the marketing of their films, such as the global success *A Room With a View* (86), *Howards End* (92) and *The Remains of the Day* (93). Ivory had always been attracted beyond his homeland: *Venice: Theme and Variations* (57) and *The Delhi Way* (59) were two early documentaries. Living in India for some years, he met Merchant and, along with Jhabvala, they created several pictures about India and its East-West culture clash. They had an early commercial peak with *Shakespeare Wallah* (65), which prodded British imperialism. A hit-and-miss period followed until he directed *The Europeans* (79), which displayed sensitivity and beautifully framed shots. Films such as *Heat and Dust* (83), *The Bostonians* (84), *Maurice* (87) and *Jefferson in Paris* (95) all contained his sure, sustained control.

UB IWERKS
US animator (1901-71)

Instead of the Disney Organisation it might have been the Iwerks Organisation, because Iwerks was Walt's (qv) first partner. The two met while working as commercial artists in Kansas City. Disney's business drive soon left Iwerks behind, although they were reunited on *Alice in Cartoonland* (23). He worked with Disney on *Steamboat Willie* (28) and was responsible for drawing the first Mickey Mouse in *Plane Crazy* (28). His own studio flopped, so it was back to Disney to work on cartoons and as special effects supervisor on such part live-action features as *The Reluctant Dragon* (41) and *Song of the South* (46). His effects work on *20,000 Leagues Under the Sea* (54), as well as *Lady and the Tramp* (55), was the lighter end of a spectrum that darkened when he created effects for Hitchcock's (qv) *The Birds* (63). He won two Oscars for technical achievement. Art Babbitt, the Disney animator, said of him: "He could draw rings round Walt and that's what he did with Mickey Mouse."

Huston on the set of Moby Dick (right) which he co-wrote

GLENDA JACKSON
British actress (1936-)

Born in Birkenhead, Cheshire, she started in repertory theatre after a stint as a shop assistant and a scholarship to Rada. She had a small part in *This Sporting Life* (63), but it was her stage and subsequent screen portrayal of Charlotte Corday in Peter Brook's (qv) celebrated *Marat/Sade* (67) that brought her to prominence. Her role in Ken Russell's (qv) adaptation of D H Lawrence's

Women in Love (69) won her an Oscar. This was followed by *The Boy Friend, The Music Lovers* and *Sunday Bloody Sunday* (all 71) for which she was nominated. Known for portraying strong-willed, independent women, Jackson made a successful foray into feisty comedy roles and won her second Oscar for *A Touch of Class* (73). This was followed by *The Maids* (74), *Hedda* (75), *The Incredible Sarah* (76), *Stevie* (78), *Return of the Soldier* (81), *Beyond Therapy* (87) and *The Rainbow* (89). She lost interest in acting in the 1980s, becoming a Labour MP in 1992 and a minister in 1997.

MIKLOS JANCSO
Hungarian director (1921-)

He studied art and ethnography and completed a law degree before entering the Film Academy in Budapest. He is famed for his choreographic camera, tracking balletically, schematically and economically across the bleak Hungarian plains where most of his films, dealing in revolutionary warfare, were shot. His international reputation came when *The Round-Up* (65) was shown at Cannes. This visually striking account of torture, interrogation

and killing of peasants by Austro-Hungarian troops in 1848, with its detached tone and minimal dialogue, established his unique style. He made striking use of colour in *The Confrontation* (69), carrying it further in *Red Psalm* (71). *Private Vices – Public Virtues* (76) gained a wider audience, but betrayed his best work.

EMIL JANNINGS
Swiss actor (1884-1950)

In his time his range, gravity and power were unequalled by his contemporaries. Establishing himself in Max Reinhardt's Deutsches Theatre company in Berlin, he was encouraged by Ernst Lubitsch (qv) to try film, appearing in 27 silents, seven directed by Lubitsch. *Varieté* (25), in which he excelled as a jealous trapeze artist, was a success in America and he was signed to a three-year contract with Paramount. In Hollywood he starred in two tailor-made vehicles, *The Way of All Flesh* (27) and *The Last Command* (28), and became

the first actor to win an Oscar. In 1929 he starred opposite Marlene Dietrich (qv) in *The Blue Angel* (30), a talkie filmed in both German and English. While Dietrich went on to international stardom, Jannings, cursed by his poor command of English, remained in Germany. His subsequent films were poorly received when, in 1940, he was made head of the government-funded Ufa and appeared in propaganda films for the Nazis. Blacklisted by the allies, he retired to Austria in 1945.

DEREK JARMAN
British director, artist (1942-94)

Jarman's death from Aids robbed British cinema of an iconoclast who was simultaneously provocative, outrageous, derided and loved. Artist, film maker and author, his films were invariably made independently on minute budgets with a supportive network of friends, collaborators and admirers. They celebrate art, nature and homosexual eroticism and rail against social stagnation and the Establishment. His work includes a controversial vision of the Christian martyr *Sebastiane* (76), the anarchic *Jubilee* (78) and Shakespearean punk with *The Tempest* (79). Later films such as

Caravaggio (86) and *War Requiem* (89) were equally distinctive but arguably more accessible. *Blue* (93) is his remarkable valedictory. Made when Jarman was blind, the film is a blue screen with no images, accompanied by a chorus of voices reading his diary of illness and reflections on loss, anger and pain. It is a touching, courageous and contemplative work.

JIM JARMUSCH
US director (1953-)

He studied at Columbia University and at Cinémathèque Française in Paris before enrolling at NYU Film School, where he met veteran director Nicholas Ray (qv) and served as his teaching assistant. His directing debut was the 16mm feature *Permanent Vacation* (82), but it was the critically acclaimed *Stranger Than Paradise* (84) that brought him international respect and recognition, winning the Cannes Film Festival's Camera d'Or for best new director. The follow-up was *Down by Law* (86). He also acted in a selection of films made by his peers, including Alex Cox's *Straight to Hell* (87) and Aki Kaurismäki's *Leningrad Cowboys Go America* (89), and flirted with short films and pop videos. There was a muted reception to the portmanteau film *Mystery Train* (89), his first colour feature, but he made considerable progress with *Night On Earth* (92). He is a significant *auteur* of the American independent scene.

MAURICE JARRE
French composer (1924-)

Jarre (who once said: "If the audience is conscious of the music, it probably is not as interested in the film as it should be"), is the epic composer whose robust, often exotic melodies supported and occasionally carried the action. His themes are some of the most recognisable written for the cinema. Lara's Theme from *Doctor Zhivago* (65), his music for *The Longest Day* and *Lawrence of Arabia* (both 62) and *Ryan's Daughter* (70) are instantly recognisable. Jarre studied at the Paris Conservatoire before joining the orchestra of the Jean-Louis Barrault Theatre Company. He wrote his first score in 1951 for Jean Vilar's stage production of Le Prince de Hambourg. He wrote for a number of screen shorts before scoring his first feature in 1959. Despite working on more than 16[illegible] films, he is best known for his work with David Lean (qv), for whom he wrote four scores. His son is Jean-Michel Jarre, the composer.

HUMPHREY JENNINGS
British documentarist (1907-50)

An artist before he joined the GPO Film Unit, he was regarded with some suspicion by John Grierson (qv), the leader of the British documentary movement. His first truly personal film was *Spare Time* (39), but his talent was properly tested during the war. *London Can Take It* (40) expressed the blitz spirit, *Listen to Britain* (42) was a collage of sounds and images of a nation at war, *Words for Battle* (41) counterpointed the harmony of the countryside with scenes of military preparedness, ending with Olivier (qv) speaking the Gettysburg address as tanks rumble past Lincoln's statue in Parliament Square. Jennings made his masterpiece *Fires Were Started* (43) as a semi-feature, revealing the ordeal of London auxiliary firemen. The British cinema's most poetic voice, he was largely unfulfilled and died hunting for locations in Greece, leaving a small but precious oeuvre.

NORMAN JEWISON
Canadian director, producer (1926-)

A director of romantic comedies, topical thrillers and satire, he began with TV musical specials starring Judy Garland (qv) and Harry Belafonte. After naval service in the second world war he worked as a taxi driver, bought a ticket to Britain and joined the BBC as an actor and writer. He was then hired by CBS in America and progressed to feature films in the early 1960s. *The Cincinnati Kid* (65) with Steve McQueen and Edward G Robinson (qqv) was an early success followed by *In the Heat of the Night* (67), where racism is tightly

woven into a southern thriller. He brought out a romantic sparkle in Doris Day (qv) in *The Thrill of It All* (63) and *Send Me No Flowers* (64) and showed off his musical expertise with *Fiddler on the Roof* (71) and *Jesus Christ Superstar* (73). His career has veered between excellence and indifference and includes *Rollerball* (75), *A Soldier's Story* (84), *Moonstruck* (87), *In Country* (89) and *Other People's Money* (91).

RUTH PRAWER JHABVALA
US writer (1927-)

Born in Cologne, Germany, she moved to India in 1959 where she began her collaboration with director James Ivory and producer Ismail Merchant (qqv). Several of their screenplays have been adapted from her novels: *Heat and Dust* (83) was published in 1975 and the film was one of the team's finest achievements. Her other screenplays include *Shakespeare Wallah* (65), *Bombay Talkie* (70), *Roseland* (77), *Hullabaloo Over Georgie and Bonnie's Pictures* (78) and *The Bostonians* (84). She won Oscars for her screenplays of E M Forster's novels *A Room With a View* (86) and *Howards End* (92) and was nominated for *The Remains of the Day* (94).

ROLAND JOFFE
British director (1945-)

After directing at London's Young Vic, Old Vic and National Theatre and making a number of TV documentaries and dramas, Joffé, the grandson of Jacob Epstein, the sculptor, made his feature debut with *The Killing Fields* (84). The drama, based on the experiences of New York Times correspondent Sydney Schanberg and his translator Dith Pran in Cambodia's torment in the 1970s, won three Oscars. He received nominations for best picture and best director for *The Mission* (86), which won the Palme d'Or at Cannes. Since then he has found success and finance more elusive. *Fat Man and*

Little Boy (89), which starred Paul Newman (qv) developing the atomic bomb, was arresting but overlooked. After a lengthy and difficult production, *The City of Joy* (92) starring Patrick Swayze, his moving story of an American doctor in the slums of Calcutta, received a lukewarm reception.

CELIA JOHNSON
British actress (1908-82)

Her style was contained, well mannered and very British. She arrived on screen from the West End of London stage to play the captain's wife in the wartime naval drama *In Which We Serve* (42), with Noël Coward (qv), and moved a notch or two down the social scale for *This Happy Breed* (44), his study of inter-war dwellers in Clapham, south London. Her skill at suggesting repressed passion was remarkable in *Brief Encounter* (45), another association with Coward and directed by David Lean (qv). Lacking such fine vehicles, she never really reached those heights again, but always provided reliable, admired performances in films such as *I Believe in You* (51), *The Captain's Paradise* (53) and *A Kid for Two Farthings* (55). She was also memorable as the waspish headmistress in *The Prime of Miss Jean Brodie* (69), her last film.

NUNNALLY JOHNSON
US writer, producer and director (1897-1977)

A journalist and writer from 1932, he added production to screenwriting, which began with *A Bedtime Story* (33). At Twentieth Century Fox he wrote, mostly alone, *The Man Who Broke the Bank at Monte Carlo* (35), *Jesse James* and *Rose of Washington Square* (both 39) and, notably, *The Grapes of Wrath* (40), then *Tobacco Road* (41) and *The Moon Is Down* (43). He formed International Pictures, later absorbed by Universal, for whom he made *The Woman in the Window* (44) and *The Dark Mirror* (46). After *The Mudlark* (50), *The Long Dark Hall* and *The Desert Fox* (both 51), *My Cousin Rachel* (52) and *How to Marry a Millionaire* (53). He added directing to writing and producing with *Black Widow* (54), *The Man in the Gray Flannel Suit* (56) and *The Three Faces of Eve* (57). His career ended as the writer of widely different films,, including *Flaming Star* (60) and *The Dirty Dozen* (67).

AL JOLSON
US singer, actor (1886-1950)

Asa Yoelson was the son of a cantor in St Petersburg in Russia who emigrated to America. After a period in vaudeville specialising in black-face routines, he achieved stardom on the New York stage and made cinéma history singing, and uttering the words "You ain't heard nothin' yet" in *The Jazz Singer* (27), the first talkie. The financially ailing Warner studio paid him $75,000 plus a percentage, risking everything on the success of this schmaltzy story about a cantor's son who deserts the synagogue for the theatre, much like Jolson's life story. He and Warner made a fortune and did even better with *The Singing Fool* (28). For ever associated with hits such as Mammy and April Showers, his popularity declined with changing fashion, but revived when he entertained American troops in the 1940s. He gained a new audience through two biopics, *The Jolson Story* (46) and *Jolson Sings Again* (49), with songs dubbed by Jolson. Ruby Keeler (qv) was the third of his four wives.

CHUCK JONES
US animator (1912-96)

The man who created Bugs Bunny (qv), Porky Pig, Daffy Duck, Speedy Gonzalez, Wile E Coyote and others. Noted for their frenzied, surreal eccentricity, they appealed to the public because the streetwise heroes always overcame the wicked schemers. Educated at the Chouinard Art Institute in Los Angeles, he worked in a variety of jobs, including merchant seaman and artist, before entering the industry as an assembly line animator and going on to work at Warners in 1935. He won Oscars for *For Scentimental Reasons* (49) and *So Much, So Little* (50). He helped lead the successful strike against Disney, which he had joined in the early 1950s. When Warner closed its animation department in 1962, he produced Tom and Jerry cartoons for MGM, winning a third Oscar for *The Dot and the Line* (65). Director Joe Dante (qv) so admired Jones that he gave him a cameo appearance in his *Gremlins* (84).

JAMES EARL JONES
US actor (1931-)

A distinguished performer of stage and screen, Jones was born in Arkabutla, Missouri, the son of a boxer turned actor. Despite his many roles, he is best known for lending his resonant *basso profundo* to the malevolent villain Darth Vader in George Lucas's (qv) *Star Wars* series. He came to

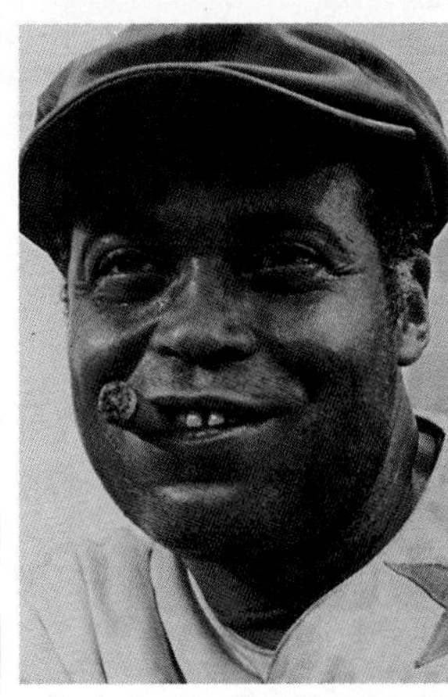

notice in the New York stage production of The Great White Hope, which earned him an Oscar nomination when he transferred it to the screen in 1970. Among his many and varied screen roles are his debut in *Dr Strangelove* (64), *The Comedians* (67), *A Piece of the Action* (77), *Conan the Barbarian* (82), *Matewan* (87), *Field of Dreams* (89), *The Hunt for Red October* (90), *Patriot Games* (92) *Sommersby* (93) and *Clear and Present Danger* (94). A campaigner for equal rights, Jones has received several civil liberties awards and citations.

JENNIFER JONES
US actress (1919-)

She made her debut as Phyllis Isley in *New Frontier* (39). David O Selznick (qv) signed her, changed her name and groomed her. Their first film was *The Song of Bernadette* (43) for which she won the best actress Oscar. She was nominated as best supporting actress for *Since You Went Away* (44) and as best actress in *Love Letters* (45) and *Duel in the Sun* (47). She married Selznick in 1949 after *Portrait of Jennie* (48) and before *Madame Bovary* (49) were made. She was nominated for a best actress Oscar for *Love Is a Many-Splendored Thing* (55), and featured strongly in *Carrie* and *Ruby Gentry* (both 52) and *Beat the Devil* (53). Her final films for Selznick were *A Farewell to Arms* (57) and *Tender is the Night* (62). He died in 1965 and she has since appeared only in *The Idol* (66), *Angel Angel Down We Go* (69) and *The Towering Inferno* (74).

QUINCY JONES
US musician, composer (1933-)

A musical guru of prodigious talent and influence, he is better known as a record industry executive, producer and songwriter. At the age of 10 he was singing in a gospel quartet in Seattle where he befriended Ray Charles, with whom he later toured the northwest. After studying at the Berklee School of Music in Boston, he played trumpet with Lionel Hampton before settling in Paris where he worked as a composer, conductor and arranger for six years. In 1963 he produced his first hit, It's My Party, and two years later worked with Sidney Lumet (qv) on the score for *The Pawnbroker* (65), the first of three successful collaborations. Other notable soundtracks include his sinister music for *In Cold Blood* and *In the Heat of the Night* (both 67). With *The Color Purple* (85) he fulfilled a long-standing ambition by producing the adaptation of the Alice Walker novel. He was the subject of a documentary, *Listen Up* (90), and is married to the actress Nastassja Kinski.

TOMMY LEE JONES
US actor (1946-)

He tasted acting while studying English at Harvard and then appeared on Broadway. His big break came with his electrifying performance as Gary Gilmore in the television film The Executioner's Song. His grim introspection held many scenes in *Coal Miner's Daughter* (80), *The River Rat* (84) and *The Big Town* (87), but *JFK* (91) secured him an eye-catching role. As the manhunter in *The Fugitive* (93), he had almost equal screen time with Harrison Ford (qv), winning the Oscar for best supporting actor. Later films include *The Client, Natural Born Killers* (94) and *Men in Black* (97).

NEIL JORDAN
Irish director, screenwriter (1950-)

The Crying Game (92), a powerful inter-racial bisexual love story set against the background of the Troubles in Northern Ireland, was nominated for six Academy Awards and won him the Oscar for best screenplay. Ever controversial, his stories have touched on many aspects of contemporary politics, including powerful roles for women and a horrific Aids allegory *Interview With the Vampire* (94). Born in Sligo and educated at Dublin University, where he read English and Irish history, he is a successful novelist and founder of the Irish Writers Co-operative. He began his remarkable cinematic career as a creative consultant on John Boorman's *(qv) Excalibur* (81). He has an excellent critical record, especially with subjects close to his heart, as in his surrealistic debut feature *Angel* (82), the adult fairy tale *The Company of Wolves* (84) and the extraordinary *Mona Lisa* (86). His American-produced *High Spirits* (88) and *We're No Angels* (89) received mixed receptions.

GUS KAHN
US songwriter (1886-1941)

He moved from Koblenz, Germany, to America at the age of four and spent his childhood in Chicago, where he first tasted success writing songs for vaudeville turns. It led to a career composing for stage and screen musicals. His most

notable early film assignments were *The Jazz Singer* (27), *Whoopee!* (30) and *Flying Down to Rio* (33), which were characterised by simplistic but effervescent compositions. His projects on Broadway and in Hollywood yielded partnerships with, among others, George Gershwin (qv), Walter Donaldson and Bronislaw Kaper, and he married Grace LeBoy, another occasional collaborator. His best songs were Pretty Baby, Yes Sir, That's My Baby, Makin' Whoopee and Flying Down to Rio. Despite being the subject of the film *I'll See You in My Dreams* (52), starring Danny Thomas and Doris Day (qv), Kahn remains less famous than his compositions.

MADELINE KAHN
US actress (1942-)

She is the most quirkily original and offbeat of comic actresses. She trained as an opera singer, appeared in cabaret and off-Broadway and won an international following among those who treasure her Lily Von Shtupp in Mel Brooks's (qv) *Blazing Saddles* (74) and her Trixie Delight, who tries to snare Ryan O'Neal in Peter Bogdanovich's (qv) *Paper Moon* (73). Her first impact on the screen was as O'Neal's disgruntled fiancée in *What's Up Doc?* (72). She enjoys continued success on Broadway and has been nominated four times for a Tony, winning it in 1992 for her Gorgeous Titelbaum in The Sisters Rosensweig. On TV she has had her own show, Oh Madeline, and won an Emmy for Wanted: The Perfect Guy.

HERBERT T KALMUS
US inventor (1881-1963)

A graduate of the Massachusetts Institute of Technology, Kalmus began experimenting with colour cameras in 1912. In 1915 he co-founded the Technicolor corporation. Early Technicolor was a two-colour (red and green) process seen for the first time in *The Gulf Between* (17). Few films used the process in the silent era, but it was used for brief sequences in *The Phantom of the Opera* (25), *Ben-Hur* (26) and other films. Douglas Fairbanks (qv) shot *The Black Pirate* (26) throughout in two-colour Technicolor and in the early 1930s a three-colour process was devised, initially used in the Disney cartoon, *Flowers and Trees* (33). The first full-length film was *Becky Sharp* (35). During the war the Monopack system was developed, obviating the need for a bulky camera capable of handling three separate reels of film. Kalmus was the father of natural colour in the cinema and for years the phrase "in glorious Technicolor" excited filmgoers until patents lapsed in 1949 and other processes ended Technicolor's near monopoly.

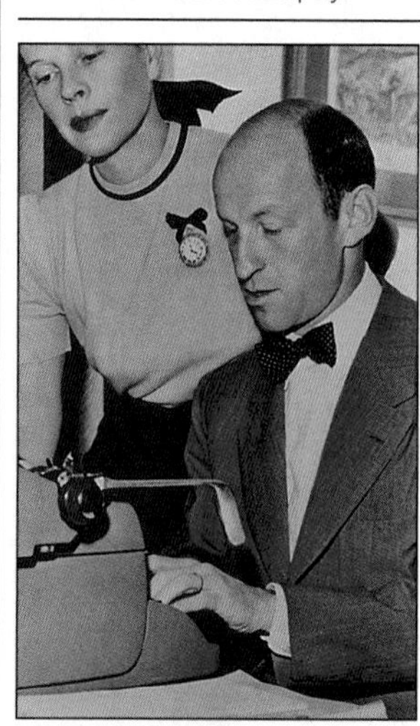

GARSON KANIN
US director (1912-)

Sam Goldwyn (qv) welcomed him to Hollywood after his brief but spectacular Broadway career as an actor and director with the words, "I hear you are a very clever genius". The Goldwyn tie-in was not lengthy ("he kept calling me Thalberg"), but Kanin soon established a reputation for urban comedies such as *The Great Man Votes* (38), with an alcoholic John Barrymore (qv), and *Bachelor Mother* (39), with Ginger Rogers (qv). He battled to blunt the censors' scissors and sneaked sophisticated writing past them. He won an Oscar for co-directing and editing the documentary on Europe's liberation, *The True Glory* (45), and was nominated for screenwriting Oscars for *A Double Life* (48) and the Hepburn-Tracy (qqv) comedy of the sexes, *Adam's Rib* (49). George Cukor (qv) filmed his play *Born Yesterday* (50) and won an Oscar for Judy Holliday (qv). Kanin's wife and frequent collaborator was the actress Ruth Gordon (qv).

ANNA KARINA
Danish actress (1940-)

Copenhagen-born beauty Hanne Karin Blarke Bayer was a successful model and fledgling actress in Denmark when she met Jean-Luc Godard (qv) at the age of 18 and embarked on the collaboration that made her an icon of the French New Wave. Godard's fascination with her was immediate, but she turned down the role that went to Jean Seberg (qv) in *Breathless* (60). She made her feature debut in Godard's *Le Petit Soldat* (60) and married him a year later. Although she worked with other directors, it was through his lens she was idealised as romantic, tender and impulsive. Their most important collaboration is *Pierrot le Fou* (65), the account of a love-hate relationship reflecting their own. After their split in 1967 she continued to work across Europe, writing and directing *Vivre Ensemble* (73), but it is her image from the 1960s that endures.

BORIS KARLOFF
British actor (1887-1969)

As *Frankenstein* (31) his menace was leavened to arouse pity as well as horror and he became one of the century's most potent icons. Born in Camberwell, south London, William Henry Pratt was obsessed with cricket, a preoccupation that lasted through Canadian repertory,

ɔrking as a labourer and reaching ɔllywood as a memorable scalper *The Last of the Mohicans* (20). ɔund suited the whispered threat his lisp in the melodrama *The ·iminal Code* (31), but it was *ankenstein* that made him a ɔusehold name. Variations on that eme were relentless, the best cluding *The Mummy* (32), *The ·ide of Frankenstein* (35) and the ıinese detective in the *Mr Wong* 7-40) series. The director Roger ɔrman (qv) gave him comic ɔrror with *The Raven* (63), while ·ter Bogdanovich (qv) paid ɔching tribute with *Targets* (68), which Karloff is the aged horror ar up against senseless slaughter.

AWRENCE KASDAN
S director, writer (1949-)

s plans to become an English acher were interrupted by his expected success copywriting evision ads. He emerged as a ɔllywood co-writer with *The mpire Strikes Back* (80), the cond and perhaps most ɔjoyable of the *Star Wars* trilogy, ıd he co-wrote the third, *Return of e Jedi* (83). He scripted *Raiders the Lost Ark* (81) for Steven ɔielberg (qv) and directed his own ɔtic thriller *Body Heat* (81), the st of many collaborations with the ·tor William Hurt (qv). He is best ɔown for *The Big Chill* (83), a ɔmedy about a reunion of friends. ıe *Accidental Tourist* (88) and *·and Canyon* (91) followed, but s sprawling *Wyatt Earp* (94) with ɔvin Costner (qv) did not impress.

EFFREY KATZENBERG
S mogul (1950-)

ıen he arrived as chairman of e Walt Disney Studios in 1984, the company was churning out anaemic efforts that cynically traded on Walt's (qv) name. Katzenberg, who had been chairman Barry Diller's sidekick at Paramount, found an ally in Michael Eisner (qv), the boss of the Walt Disney company. Through shrewdly re-releasing classic cartoons (theatrically and on video) Disney not only made quick, big bucks but also proved that

animation was viable again. *The Little Mermaid* (89), *Beauty and the Beast* (91) and *Aladdin* (92) spearheaded the revival and, with the classic Disney components of distinctive characters, inventive set-ups and the narrative grip of a gangster picture, saw off the blander opposition. His live-action romps include *Outrageous Fortune* (87), *Honey I Shrunk the Kids* (89) and *Pretty Woman* (90), one of Hollywood's biggest cash juggernauts. He left Disney after a fall-out with Eisner and set up The Dream Works with Steven Spielberg (qv). His legacy to Disney was *The Lion King* (94).

PHILIP KAUFMAN
US director, writer (1936-)

A Harvard Law School dropout, he made award-winning curiosities in the 1960s and *The Great Northfield Minnesota Raid* (72), a vivid western. He co-wrote *The Outlaw Josie Wales* (76) and *Raiders of the Lost Ark* (81), but was disappointed not to direct them. He had cult success with his remake of *The Invasion of the Body Snatchers* (78) and *The Wanderers* (79), his story of 1960s Bronx teenagers. He followed these with a prestigious adaptation of Tom Wolfe's *The Right Stuff* (83), which was nominated for eight Oscars. At his most successful mixing political, literary and human elements, his skilful adaptation of Milan Kundera's *The Unbearable Lightness of Being* (88) was also highly regarded. *Henry and June* (90), the fruit of his long fascination with Henry Miller, was the centre of a censorship controversy in America and eventually had a limited, indifferent release. He then seemed to bend to commercial considerations and made Michael Crichton's (qv) *Rising Sun* (93). Kaufman works in close collaboration with his wife Rose and producer son Peter, a trio known as "Pita Rosenphil".

DANNY KAYE
US actor (1913-87)

David Kaminski from Brooklyn was a stand-up comedian before he was 14, working in the resort hotels of the Catskills. During the 1930s he was a cabaret performer and appeared in a few two-reel shorts. He became a Broadway star in 1941 with his show-stopping, tongue-twisting number, Tchaikovsky, in the Kurt Weill musical Lady in the Dark, and was signed by Samuel Goldwyn (qv). His feature film debut was as a hypochondriac draftee in *Up in Arms* (44), followed by *Wonder Man* (45), *The Kid From Brooklyn* (46) and the most effective Goldwyn showcase for his zany talents, *The Secret Life of Walter Mitty* (47). His film career began to fade in the 1950s, although *Hans Christian Andersen* (52), with its array of hit songs, was a box office success. Kaye turned to TV in the 1960s as his film appearances became rare. He died while undergoing heart surgery.

ELIA KAZAN
US director (1909-)

Author of five novels, two (America America and The Arrangement) are partly autobiographical and were filmed in 1963 and 1969 respectively. The Turkish-born son of Greek parents, he was one of Broadway's most distinguished directors, mounting the works of America's foremost playwrights, including Tennessee Williams, whose *Baby Doll* (56) he filmed. He studied drama at Yale, began his career as an actor and, in 1947, co-founded the Actors Studio. Brando (qv), its most famous Method student, gained fame through *A Streetcar Named Desire* (51) directed by Kazan on stage and screen. A superlative director of actors and a star maker – James Dean and Warren Beatty (qqv) were among his protégés – his choice of material, such as *Gentleman's Agreement* (47) and *Pinky* (49), suggest a liberal and humane conscience. His image, though, was tarnished when he named names during the McCarthy witch-hunt in the early 1950s. His best director and best picture Oscars for *Gentleman's Agreement* and *On the Waterfront* (54) represent less than one-tenth of his Academy honours: 46 nominations and 16 wins.

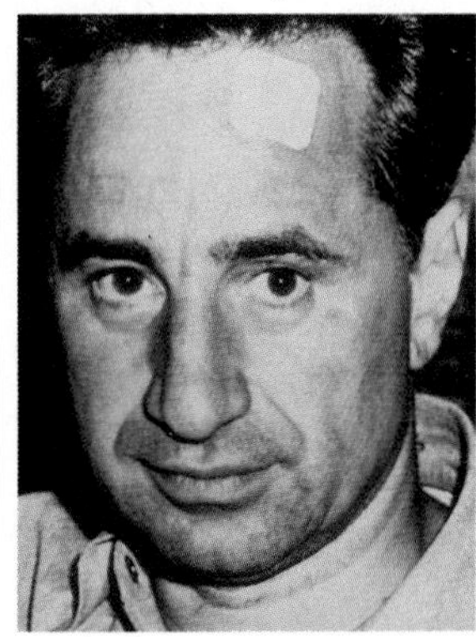

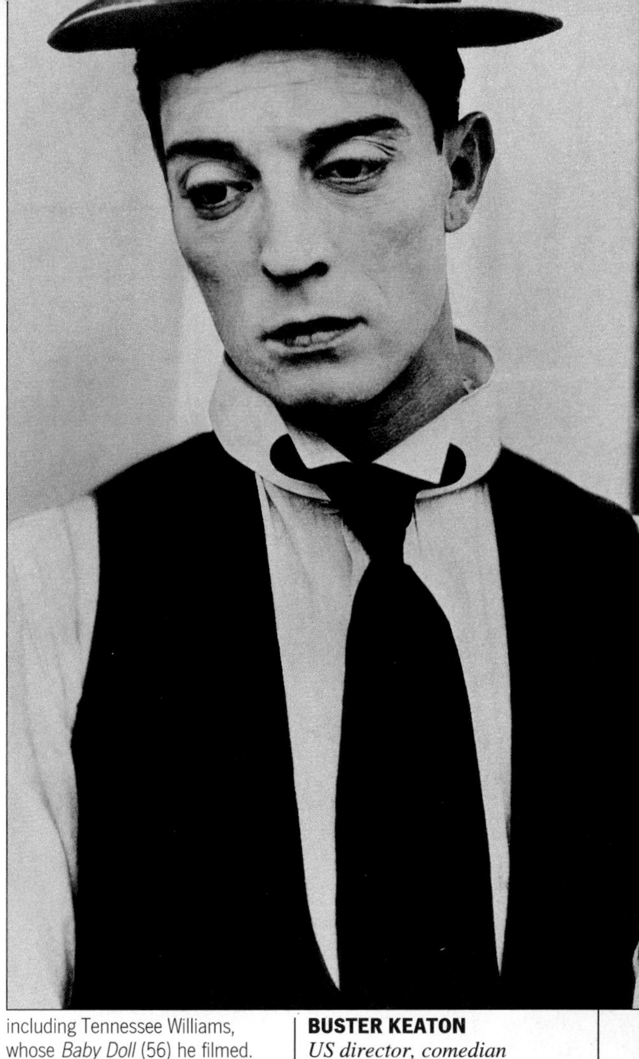

BUSTER KEATON
US director, comedian (1895-1966)

Joseph Francis Keaton (the magician Harry Houdini nicknamed him Buster at six months) joined his parents in The Three Keatons when he was three. A headliner at six, his rise in vaudeville led to an invitation to join Fatty Arbuckle (qv) in supporting roles until his feature debut in *One Week* (20). Known as the Great Stone Face for his deadpan expression and stoical perseverance, he is the most inventive of the silent clowns, best seen in *The Playhouse* (21), *The Navigator* (24) and *The General* (27), his crowning masterpiece. Apart from choreographing and performing all his routines, he also masterminded his surrealist scenarios. Unlike many vaudeville comedians who performed in films regardless of the background scenery, he made it integral to the cinematic continuity. His fortunes changed with a move to MGM, where he lost control over his productions. Mismanagement and a failed marriage were followed by a slide into alcoholism and poverty. During the 1950s renewed appreciation of his work and an appearance with his old rival Chaplin (qv) in *Limelight* (52) sparked a brief revival and a special Oscar in 1962. He died of cancer shortly after a receiving a tumultuous reception at the Venice Film Festival in 1966.

DIANE KEATON
US actress, director (1946-)

A witty and attractive leading lady, Diane Hall was long associated with Woody Allen (qv). Their collaboration began on Broadway in Play It Again, Sam in 1969. Outstanding as Kay Corleone in *The Godfather* trilogy (72, 74, 90) she played opposite Allen in *Play It Again, Sam* (72), *Sleeper* (73) and *Love and Death* (75), before winning the best actress Oscar and setting various trends as *Annie Hall* (77). Other Keaton/Allen films include *Interiors* (78), *Manhattan* (79), *Radio Days* (87) and (replacing Mia Farrow) *Manhattan Murder Mystery* (93). Besides an Oscar-nominated performance in *Reds* (81), she was outstanding in *Looking for Mr Goodbar* (77), *Baby Boom* (87) and *Marvin's Room* (1996). An enthusiastic, published photographer, she has directed for film and television including an episode of the cult series Twin Peaks.

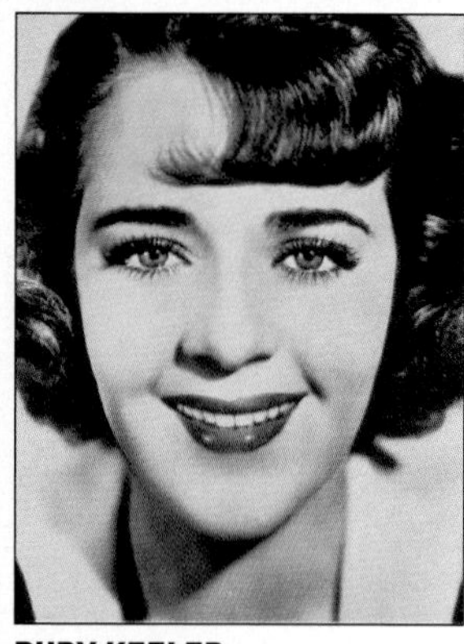

RUBY KEELER
US actress, dancer (1909-93)

So effective was her embodiment of the sweet chorus girl chosen to replace the star, Ethel Keeler seemed to dominate the musicals of the 1930s. Two men, the choreographer Busby Berkeley (qv) and her frequent leading man Dick Powell (qv), saw to it that she reigned brightly; a third, her husband Al Jolson (qv), that her career ended abruptly. At 13 she was a proficient tap dancer and a year later she made the chorus on Broadway. Jolson spotted her in Los Angeles and followed her to New York, where they married in 1928. Graduating to a Broadway star, she landed the lead in Warner's *42nd Street* (33) as the unknown who replaces Bebe Daniels (qv) at the 11th hour. Such was the success of the film that Keeler starred in several sunny Warner/Berkeley musicals. In 1937 Jolson fell out with Warner and took Keeler with him, after which she appeared in only two more films, divorcing Jolson in 1940. She returned in 1971, starring on Broadway in No No Nanette.

HARVEY KEITEL
US actor (1939-)

Born in New York and a product of the Actors Studio, Keitel joined the marines after school, then worked in summer stock before meeting the director Martin Scorsese (qv) in the early 1970s to form a lasting partnership. He came to prominence in Scorsese's *Mean Streets* (73) and international recognition in the same director's controversial *Taxi Driver* (76). After a disagreement with Francis Ford Coppola (qv) he was fired on location from the lead in *Apocalypse Now* (79) and replaced by Martin Sheen (qv). Highlights of his career include *Alice Doesn't Live Here Anymore* (75), *The Duellists* (77), *Bad Timing* (80), *Wise Guys* (86), *Last Temptation of Christ* (88), *Thelma & Louise* (91) and *The Bad Lieutenant* (92). He also acted in and part-financed Quentin Tarantino's (qv) *Reservoir Dogs* (92). He received a best supporting actor Oscar nomination for his role in the director Jane Campion's (qv) *The Piano* (93).

GENE KELLY
US dancer, actor, director and choreographer (1912-96)

A dancer from childhood, he took an economics degree and carved a multi-faceted Broadway career, becoming a star in Pal Joey before making his Hollywood debut at MGM in *For Me and My Gal* (42) at the age of 30. He established his imaginative and exuberant credentials as co-director, co-choreographer and star in three films with Stanley Donen (qv), including *Singin' in the Rain* (52). Virile and athletic, with a pleasingly husky singing voice, adequate acting ability and cocky charm, he ignited the screen in a host of memorable routines, including a *pas de deux* with himself in *Cover Girl* (44), partnering cartoon characters in *Invitation to the Dance* (56) — one of two musicals he directed — and the extended ballet in *An American in Paris* (51). He fared less well with non-musicals, directing six and acting in several. He danced with Astaire (qv) in *Ziegfeld Follies* (46) and remarked: "If I'm the Marlon Brando of dancing, Fred Astaire's Cary Grant."

GRACE KELLY
US actress (1928-82)

Kelly's brief but spectacular acting career encompassed 11 films. The daughter of a self-made millionaire politician, she was a successful model in New York while attending the American Academy of Dramatic Art. After theatre and TV work, she landed a small part in *Fourteen Hours* (51) and was cast as Gary Cooper's (qv) bride in *High Noon* (52). She was nominated for a supporting Oscar for *Mogambo* (53) opposite Clark Gable and Ava Gardner (qqv) and the next year won the Oscar for an atypically unglamorous role as Bing Crosby's (qv) bitter wife in *The Country Girl* (54). Her most memorable work is as Alfred Hitchcock's (qv) ideal — the cool blonde with passionate depths — in *Dial M for Murder* and *Rear Window* (both 54) and *To Catch a Thief* (55). After making *High Society* (56) she married Prince Rainier of Monaco. She died from a stroke while driving and injuries sustained in the resulting car crash.

JEROME KERN
US composer (1885-1945)

He was regarded as the first maestro of the native American musical by George Gershwin and Irving Berlin (qqv). His *Show Boat*, filmed twice (36, 51), bridged the gap between traditional European-based operetta and an indigenous musical theatre. The son of a New York furniture dealer, he went to Hollywood in 1930 to write original scores and songs. He won Oscars for The Way You Look Tonight from the film *Swing Time* (36) and The Last Time I Saw Paris from *Lady Be Good* (41), but between those high notes there was a flash-flood of songs that became a torrent – Ol' Man River, Smoke Gets in Your Eyes, Look for the Silver Lining, They Didn't Believe Me. Robert Walker (qv) played him in the biopic *Till The Clouds Roll By* (46), which included many of those tunes. He returned to New York with the intention of writing a musical, Annie Get Your Gun, but he died and Berlin took over.

DEBORAH KERR
British actress (1921-)

Despite her beach scene with Burt Lancaster (qv) in *From Here to Eternity* (53), Kerr was often cast as the well-bred woman, a nun, governess or spinster. In a career spanning 54 years, she has always dominated the screen and earned six best actress Oscar nominations. She appeared with the corps-de-ballet in Prometheus at Sadler's Wells in London before turning to acting. While her first film appearance in *Contraband* (40) was edited out, she made an impact in her next picture, *Major Barbara* (41). Such British successes as *The Life and Death of Colonel Blimp* (43) and *Black Narcissus* (47) opened the doors to Hollywood, where she thrived in ladylike roles. Of these, her portrayal of the no-nonsense governess in *The King and I* (56) is most fondly remembered. She was equally impressive in the weepy *An Affair to Remember* and *Heaven Knows Mr Allison* (both 57), *Separate Tables* (58), *The Sundowners* (60) and *The Assam Garden* (85). In 1994 she was awarded an honorary Oscar.

KRZYSZTOF KIESLOWSKI
Polish director (1941-96)

His *Camera Buff* (79), a bleak satire about artistic freedom versus the state, was the first of his films to attract critics in the West, while *Blind Chance* (82), initially suppressed under martial law, and *No End* (84) fell foul of the state for their pro-Solidarity stance. His thoughtful, moral films are refreshingly at odds with the mainstream. His main work to date is *The Ten Commandments*, a series of 10 films made for television of which *A Short Film About Killing* and *A Short Film About Love* (both 88) have been released in Britain, and *The Three Colours* trilogy (93, 94) based on the French flag. *Three Colours: Red* sadly was his last film, but it was a triumph of style and content.

HENRY KING
US actor, director (1888-1982)

He was one of Hollywood's most durable, constantly reliable film makers with a career that lasted to 1962 when he directed his last film, *Tender Is the Night*. His first landmark work was *Tol'able David* (21) with Richard Barthelmess (qv) as star, which revealed his love of American rural life. As a Fox contract director he turned out many notable films. However varied the subjects, they were fashioned with the immaculate craftsmanship that made him one of the finest, most consistent directors of the studio era. Among them were *Lloyds of London* (36), *In Old Chicago* and *Alexander's Ragtime Band* (both 38), *Jesse James* (39), *The Song of Bernadette* (43), *A Bell for Adano* (45), *Twelve O'Clock High* (49) and *The Gunfighter* (50), the latter two proving to be Gregory Peck's (qv) best films.

KING KONG
Skull Islander ape (1933)

Called the "Eighth Wonder of the World", he was discovered by an unscrupulous showman in 1933 who used a beautiful white woman as bait to capture the beast. He took Kong to New York where he escaped, kidnapped the woman and ran amok through the city before being spectacularly slain atop the Empire State Building by the airforce. A fanciful beauty and the beast fable, it inspired the most famous monster film of all time –

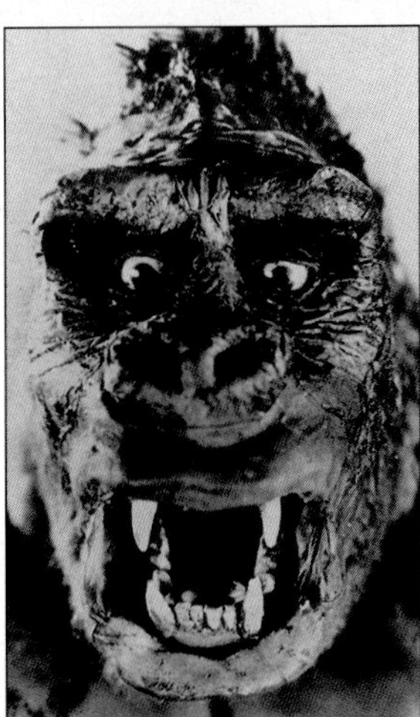

made by Merian C Cooper and Ernest B Schoedsack (qqv) with Robert Armstrong, Fay Wray (qv) and Bruce Cabot. Kong's real creator, though, was Willis O'Brien. Building 18in models and enlargements of the head, hand and foot, they combined stop-motion animation with live action, travelling mattes, front and back projections and optical printing.

BEN KINGSLEY
British actor (1943-)

His first film was *Fear Is the Key* (72), but for much of the 1970s he worked on stage with the Royal Shakespeare Company. He won the best actor Oscar for only his second feature, in the title role of *Gandhi* (82), but has had less opportunity to shine since. He has managed to keep a high profile, though, with his performances in *Betrayal* (83), *Turtle Diary* (85) and *Without a Clue* (88). His portrayal of Meyer Lansky in *Bugsy* (91) earned him an Oscar nomination for best supporting actor and he had a riveting central role in *Schindler's List* (93). With *Death and the Maiden* (95), acting almost entirely with his eyes as a man bound, gagged and tortured, he has added another role to his range of intense character studies.

KLAUS KINSKI
German actor (1926-91)

Nikolaus Günther Nakszynski, who was born in Zoppot, Poland, will be remembered as a wild eccentric whose *outré* celluloid life was mirrored by his bizarre off-screen antics. He rose to international prominence with the German New Wave and made his reputation as the chosen leading actor of the director Werner Herzog (qv), for whom he made his most celebrated films. His early life is shrouded in mystery, but he emerged in post-war Munich acting in a motley of films, including *Morituri* (48), *Decision Before Dawn* (51), *Ludwig II* (55), *Doctor Zhivago* (65) and *For a Few Dollars More* (66). He hooked up with Herzog for the awe-inspiring *Aguirre, Wrath of God* (73), in which he played a mad conquistador plotting, murdering and hectoring an expedition crew in the wilds of Peru. His two other Herzog films are *Nosferatu* (78) and *Fitzcarraldo* (82), in which he plays an Irish adventurer seeking to bring Verdi to the natives of the Amazon. Kinski never stopped working right up to his death. He was the father of the actresses Nastassja and Pola Kinski.

KEVIN KLINE
US actor (1947-)

Following a Catholic education from Benedictine monks, he studied drama at Indiana University and the Juilliard. He then toured with John Houseman's (qv) Acting Company for four years and, by the late 1970s, had won widespread acclaim and two Tony awards. Two productions of Hamlet balanced the demands of his burgeoning film career. He made his debut with a

volatile performance opposite Meryl Streep (qv) in *Sophie's Choice* (82), repeated his Tony-winning Broadway role as the Pirate King in the film version of *The Pirates of Penzance* (83) and went on to be praised in Lawrence Kasdan's (qv) *The Big Chill* (83). He played the newspaper editor Donald Woods in Richard Attenborough's (qv) apartheid drama *Cry Freedom* (87), but it was the British comedy *A Fish Called Wanda* (88) that made him a household name and brought him an Oscar for best supporting actor. He was beaten to the lead role in *Ghost* (90) by Patrick Swayze, but gave his best performance in *Grand Canyon* (91), which was more deserving of his talents. He was warm and funny as a presidential fraud in *Dave* (93) and is equally comfortable in comedy or drama.

Kinski and Cecilia Rivera in Aguirre, the Wrath of God

A London Film Production presented by

ALEXANDER KORDA and DAVID O. SELZNICK

JOSEPH COTTEN VALLI
ORSON WELLES
TREVOR HOWARD

CAROL REED'S PRODUCTION

THE THIRD MAN

Based on a Story by GRAHAM GREENE *Screenplay by* GRAHAM GREENE

Produced and Directed by **CAROL REED**

Distributed by BRITISH LION

BING CROSBY · DANNY KAYE
ROSEMARY CLOONEY · VERA-ELLEN
with DEAN JAGGER · Lyrics and Music by IRVING BERLIN
Produced by Robert Emmett Dolan · Directed by MICHAEL CURTIZ
Dances and Musical Numbers Staged by Robert Alton
Written for the screen by Norman Krasna, Norman Panama and Melvin Frank · A PARAMOUNT PICTURE

Storyteller: Krasna co-wrote the popular White Christmas

NDREI KONCHALOVSKY
ussian director, screenwriter '937-)

dissident casualty of the cold ar, he was attracted to Hollywood ter winning a jury prize at Cannes *Siberiade* (79) but has never ined the same critical acclaim thin commercial cinema, despite promising debut with *Maria's vers* (84). He made *Duet For e* (86) in Britain. Studying film the state school under Mikhail mm, he won a prize at Cannes r his graduation film, *The Boy d the Pigeon* (61). His debut ature, *The First Teacher* (65), owed he was more interested in aking poetic films about ordinary ople than the triumphs of Soviet bour programmes. Undaunted by iticisms of his masterpiece *Asya's appiness* (67), he had successes th *Uncle Vanya* (71), *Romance r Lovers* (74) and *Siberiade,* hich was withdrawn after his fection. The best of his American ms include the rural saga *Shy eople* (87) and his attack on alinism in *The Inner Circle* (91).

ALEXANDER KORDA
British producer, director (1893-1956)

A political exile from his native Hungary, where he had been a journalist then film producer and director, Korda arrived in Britain in 1930 after spells in Germany, France and the United States. He produced and directed *The Private Life of Henry VIII* (33), the most internationally successful British film to that date, which provoked such unwarranted optimism that several financial institutions had their fingers badly burned. He was responsible for a flow of distinguished films in the 1930s, including *The Ghost Goes West* (35), *Things to Come* (36), *Rembrandt* (36) and *Elephant Boy* (37). He built Denham studios, but was forced to relinquish control. During the war he made *Lady Hamilton* (41) in Hollywood and was knighted for services to Britain, which included a little discreet espionage. After the war *An Ideal Husband* (48), Powell and Pressburger's (qqv) *The Small Back Room* and Carol Reed's (qv) *The Third Man* (both 49), and Lean's (qv) *The Sound Barrier* (52) were among his successes.

ZOLTAN KORDA
Hungarian director (1895-1961)

The Four Feathers (39) epitomised his flair for exotic, entertaining cinema. Like many of his films it was produced by his older brother Alexander (qv) and designed by his younger brother Vincent. Korda served in the Austro-Hungarian army in the first world war before becoming a cameraman. In Britain he directed pictures for Alexander's London Films,

including *Sanders of the River* (35). Ill-health forced him to move to California, where he directed several pictures, including *Jungle Book* (42) and *The Macomber Affair* (47). Returning to London Films he directed and produced *Cry the Beloved Country* (51). In contrast to his earlier films, the picture combined simplicity and understated charm.

ERICH WOLFGANG KORNGOLD
Austro-Hungarian composer (1897-1957)

Born in Brno, Moravia, he was a child prodigy whose early cantata, Gold, moved Mahler to pronounce him a genius. He wrote songs, orchestral works and operas for the concert halls of Vienna and Berlin as well as theatre scores for the director Max Reinhardt. Reinhardt took him to Hollywood and Warner to score *A Midsummer Night's Dream* (35), which Korngold arranged from the music of Mendelssohn. Prevented by the Anschlüss from returning to Vienna to stage his fifth opera, he continued what became a long association with Warner, during which his rich melodies enhanced

many costume films, notably the Errol Flynn (qv) cycle. His scores for *The Private Lives of Elizabeth and Essex* (39) and *The Sea Hawk* (40) were nominated for Oscars and he won an Oscar for *The Adventures of Robin Hood* (38) and *Anthony Adverse* (36). Other notable scores include *Kings Row* (42) and *The Constant Nymph* (43).

NORMAN KRASNA
US writer, producer (1909-84)

Born in Queens, New York, his first job after NYU and law school was as film and drama critic, then drama editor on a variety of New York publications. His film career began when he was appointed publicity director for Warner. He started writing for Hollywood and Broadway in the 1930s. His early film work included the stories for *Fury* (36) and *You and Me* (38), both directed by Fritz Lang (qv). He wrote many Hollywood comedies and his reputation as one of the most appealing scriptwriters gathered momentum. In 1937 he produced his first feature, *Big City.* He directed three films: *Princess O'Rourke* (43), which won an Oscar for best original screenplay, *The Big Hangover* (50) and *The Ambassador's Daughter* (56). His best-known work, however, was *White Christmas* (54), which he co-wrote with Melvin Frank and Norman Panama.

The 10 best musicals

The Band Wagon (1953)
Classic backstage yarn with Fred Astaire, Cyd Charisse and Jack Buchanan

Cabaret (1972)
Bob Fosse's innovative adaptation of a Broadway hit

42nd Street (1933)
Most famous of the Busby Berkeley choreographic extravaganzas for Warners

Meet Me in St Louis (1944)
Hometown Americana is captivating in Vincent Minnelli's classic

On the Town (1949)
Three sailors go girl hunting on New York shore leave

Singin' in the Rain (1952)
Kelly's masterpiece; a dazzling musical satire on Hollywood's transition to talkies

Top Hat (1935)
Best of the Astaire-Rogers musicals, with sublime Berlin score and luxurious settings

The Umbrellas of Cherbourg (1964)
Jacques Demy's novel, haunting, romantic drama entirely in song

West Side Story (1961)
A dazzling transfer of a great stage musical to the screen

Yankee Doodle Dandy (1942)
James Cagney's tour de force in a landmark biography

Being the adventures of a young man whose principal interests are rape, ultra-violence and Beethoven.

STANLEY KUBRICK'S

CLOCKWORK ORANGE ⓧ

From Warner Bros A Warner Communications Company

Released by Columbia-Warner Distributors Ltd

Original Soundtrack recording on Warner Bros. K46127.

Stanley Kubrick with Tony Curtis and Laurence Olivier on the set of Spartacus (60)

'ERNER KRAUSS
erman actor (1884-1959)

a Germany beset by pessimism ter the first world war, Krauss as the embodiment of asochistic despair as various 'ant figures dominating a nihilistic orld. Two of his most famous les were as the showman ychiatrist in *The Cabinet of Dr aligari* (19) and Jack the Ripper in *'axworks* (24), both inhabiting an pressionist cinema of tilted gles and sinister silhouettes.

e was similarly at home with alistic melodramas, such as *yless Street* (25) – in which, as a utal butcher, he worked with arbo (qv) – and as the dream-unted chemistry professor in *ecrets of a Soul* (26). In *The Man 'ithout a Name* (32) he was an nnesiac told that he did not exist. efore he made the anti-semitic *ud Süss* (40) he was made an tor of the State by Adolf Hitler.

TANLEY KUBRICK
'S director (1928-)

film maker of international ature for more than 30 years, he as produced some of the nema's most innovative films. He an obsessive perfectionist whose endless takes have driven actors to despair. Born in New York, he started out as an apprentice photographer on Look magazine. In the early 1950s he made documentary shorts for RKO until a fateful meeting with producer James B Harris. The resulting partnership made *The Killing* (56), which gave them the power to acquire the rights to the novel *Paths of Glory* (57) and make one of the great anti-war films of all time. Kubrick was established. *Spartacus* (60) and *Lolita* (62) followed, then the masterpiece *Dr Strangelove* (64), *2001: A Space Odyssey* (68), *A Clockwork Orange* (71) – which he has banned from screening for fear it will spark imitative violence – *Barry Lyndon* (75), *The Shining* (80) and *Full Metal Jacket* (87). His only Oscar was for the special effects on *2001*. In 1997 he was shooting *Eyes Wide Shut* in secrecy.

AKIRA KUROSAWA
Japanese director (1910-)

Best known in the West for his rich and resonant *Kagemusha* (80) and *Ran* (85), his distinctive interpretation of King Lear, his

films have a style that reflects his depth of purpose, economy and humanity and his training as an artist. Having started his career as assistant to the director Kajiro Yamamoto, he has ranged from traditional to modern, East to West, with four of his films – *The Idiot* (51), *The Lower Depths* (57), Macbeth, which became *Throne of Blood* (57), and *Ran* – adapted from western literature. John Ford (qv) influenced *The Hidden Fortress* (58). In return, his Oscar-winning *Rashomon* (50) led to a remake as *The Outrage* (64), *Seven Samurai* (54) became *The Magnificent Seven* (60), and *Yojimbo* (61) inspired *A Fistful of Dollars* (64). A driven *auteur*, he attempted suicide when *Dodes' Ka-Den* (70) was a commercial failure. *Dersu Uzala* (75), which won an Oscar, gave him new confidence.

GREGORY LA CAVA
US director (1892-1952)

Remembered as the creator of a string of intelligent comedies in the 1930s, La Cava began as a political cartoonist and collaborator with Walter Lantz the animator. By the early 1920s he was making live-action comedy shorts and then features, including two silent films with W C Fields (qv), *So's Your Old*

Man (26) and *Running Wild* (27). Actors liked him and he drew apparently spontaneous performances from them. His best known films include *Symphony of Six Million* (32), *Gabriel Over the White House* (33), *What Every Woman Knows* (34), *She Married Her Boss* (35), *My Man Godfrey* (36), *Stage Door* (37), *5th Avenue Girl* (39) – almost a remake of *My Man Godfrey*, with Ginger Rogers (qv) replacing William Powell (qv) – and *The Primrose Path* (40). In a disagreement over the script of *One Touch of Venus* (48) he abandoned the film during production and was replaced by William A Seiter, who took sole credit. After an unsuccessful attempt to sue for breach of contract, La Cava never directed again.

ALAN LADD
US actor (1913-64)

Diminutive (5ft 5in) but gracefully athletic, he spent a discouraging decade in bit parts before many established leading men were called up for war service. Promoted zealously by Sue Carol, the agent he subsequently married, he found fame as serene hard men: the vengeful killer of *This Gun for Hire* (42) and a Dashiell Hammett loner in *The Glass Key* (42). His teaming with Veronica Lake (qv) in these and three other films proved one of the more striking, if reluctant, screen partnerships of the day. His 1950s heroes enjoyed less success until he took the title role as the mysterious lone gunman in George Stevens's (qv) classic western *Shane* (53). Troubled and losing ground rapidly after that, he attempted suicide in 1962 and died from alcohol and barbiturates after making his memorable swan-song as Nevada Smith in *The Carpetbaggers* (64). Alan Ladd Jr, his son, became a producer and studio executive.

CARL LAEMMLE
US mogul (1867-1939)

Born in Germany, the 10th of 13 children, he emigrated at 17 to America and in 1906 opened a nickelodeon. Forced out of independent distribution by Edison's (qv) monopoly, he went into production as the Independent Motion Picture Company (Imp). Laemmle is the inventor of the star system. Until then players' names were unknown, but he audaciously lured Florence Lawrence ("The Biograph Girl") to his studio, then Mary Pickford (qv), who was to become the highest-paid American actress. By 1912 Imp had absorbed other companies and emerged as Universal. In 1915 he opened Universal City in the San Fernando Valley. The lavish films made in his reign include Erich von Stroheim's (qv) extravagant *Foolish Wives* (22), *The Hunchback of Notre Dame* (23) with its huge outdoor set, and *The Phantom of the Opera* (25) with Lon Chaney (qv) and an opera house set. Known as Uncle Carl, he is said to have put more than 70 relatives on the payroll. Debts forced the sale of Universal in 1936.

VERONICA LAKE
US actress (1919-73)

The peekaboo blonde hair, over-dazed eyes and pert face marked her for fame with Alan Ladd ▷

(qv). Discovered after beauty contests and minor roles, the best in *Sullivan's Travels* (41), she teamed with Ladd in *This Gun for Hire* and *The Glass Key* (both 42). She was an enchantress in *I Married a Witch* (42), but was back with Ladd for *The Blue Dahlia* (46). She made headlines when her wartime hairdo was imitated by munitions girls, because the style risked being pulled into machinery, and when she was found working as a waitress in Manhattan. Married three times, she made a couple of comeback films.

HEDY LAMARR
US actress (1914-96)

Like her contemporaries Garbo and Dietrich (qqv), she was imported by Hollywood as a mystery woman. Her films were respectable successes, but her career fizzled out by the 1950s. Sometimes stranded by mediocrities such as *I Take This Woman* (40), in which Spencer Tracy (qv) is transfixed by her beauty, she went on to bring a spark to *The Heavenly Body* (43). She was well served by Clarence Brown, the director, and James Stewart (qqv) in the romantic comedy *Come Live With Me* (41), while she lit up *White Cargo* (42) as the seductress Tondelayo. The camp excess of *Samson and Delilah* (49) was her single sizeable hit. Discovered by Max Reinhardt when she was the window-dressing in many Austro-German films, she never equalled the impact of her 10-minute nude appearance in *Ecstasy* (33), all prints of which her first of six husbands tried unsuccessfully to buy up.

DOROTHY LAMOUR
US actress (1914-96)

A beauty queen and singer from New Orleans whose first marriage was to Herbie Kaye, the bandleader, she entered films in the mid-1930s and immediately became popular with her debut, in her trademark sarong, in *The Jungle Princess* (36). *The Hurricane* (37) confirmed this

exotic temptress image, which is now best remembered from her succession of appearances opposite Bob Hope and Bing Crosby (qqv) in the *Road to Singapore* (40), *Zanzibar* (41), *Morocco* (42), *Utopia* (46), *Rio* (47) and *Bali* (53). In *The Road to Hong Kong* (62) she was insultingly made second fiddle to Joan Collins (qv). These films were interspersed with similar duties in the likes of *Tropic Holiday* (38), *Moon Over Burma* (40), *Aloma of the South Seas* (41), *Rainbow Island* (44), *Masquerade in Mexico* (45) and *Donovan's Reef* (63). Dramatic roles underlined her suitability for light comedy and romance.

BURT LANCASTER
US actor (1913-95)

Raised in East Harlem, New York, he won an athletic scholarship to NYU, setting his sights predominantly on basketball. Later, he formed an acrobatic partnership with Nick Cravat, mostly performing in circuses. After serving in the second world war he auditioned for a Broadway role, starring in The Sound of Hunting, which led to an invitation to appear in Robert Siodmak's (qv) noir thriller *The Killers* (46). He was an imposing, memorable presence and made 10 films before the end of the decade. In 1948 he formed the Hecht-Lancaster production company with Harold Hecht, though all his recognition came from a combination of swashbuckling adventures and emotional dramas. His popular successes include *From Here to Eternity* (53), *Elmer Gantry* (60), for which he won a best actor Oscar, and *Birdman of Alcatraz* (62). His finest work was arguably for Luchino Visconti (qv) on *The Leopard* (63), the first

of many European films he made, and as an ageing criminal in Louis Malle's (qv) *Atlantic City* (80). He continued acting in films until 1990 when he suffered a stroke.

JOHN LANDIS
US director, screenwriter and actor (1950-)

He established himself as the prince of parody with the cult comedy *The Blues Brothers* (80). Born in Chicago and raised in Los Angeles, he dropped out of school to work in the Twentieth Century Fox post room and as a stuntman. After a successful debut with *Schlock* (73), he directed *The Kentucky Fried Movie* (77) and *National Lampoon's Animal House* (78), which earned $160m from a $3m investment. He sealed his success with *An American Werewolf*

in London (81), which won an Oscar for Rick Baker's lycanthropic transformation effects. A special effects explosion on *Twilight Zone – The Movie* (83) resulted in the death of the actor Vic Morrow and two children. His other notable films include *Trading Places* (83), *Amazon Women on the Moon* (87) and the vampire film *Innocent Blood* (92).

FRITZ LANG
Austrian director (1890-1976)

A former art and architecture student and an Austrian army officer in the first world war, the career of this prime exponent of German Expressionist techniques and images divides into German and American phases. His powerful sense of drama and detached examination of human psychology often serviced plots concerning the criminal and psychopathic, as in his first success, *The Spiders* (19), *Dr Mabuse* (22) and *M* (31), his classic study of a child murderer. Though Thea von Harbou, his wife and screenplay collaborator, chose to remain in Germany, the Jewish Lang fled for America where the New York skyline had inspired his futuristic allegory *Metropolis* (26). For 20 years he battled with Hollywood producers who interfered with his creative vision. MGM, for example, insisted on a white star, Spencer Tracy (qv), and a happy ending to *Fury* (36), his anti-lynching drama and first American film. He created a handful of works that make him one of the masters of *film noir* and crime melodrama.

Expressionist: Fritz Lang had a powerful sense of drama

HARRY LANGDON
US actor, comedian (1884-1944)

With his Mona Lisa smile and fusion of guile and oddness, Langdon was rated by Harold Lloyd (qv) as the funniest man of his time. His fame, though, was due to the decline of his peers – Lloyd and Keaton (qv) had lost their ingenuity and Chaplin (qv) was inactive. His unique style shone in three classics: *Tramp Tramp Tramp* and *The Strong Man* (both 26) and *Long Pants* (27). After 20 years of vaudeville and the circus, he was spotted by Mack Sennett (qv) in 1923. Under the guidance of the director Harry Edwards and gag writers Arthur Ripley and Frank Capra (qv), Langdon starred in 25 shorts before making any features. Deserting Sennett for Warner, he appropriated Edwards, Ripley and Capra and his career bloomed. As a director he succumbed to sentimentality. Sound brought obscurity and he died penniless.

JESSICA LANGE
US actress (1949-)

Lange rebounded from an unhapp debut in *King Kong* (76) to becom one of Hollywood's most bankabl stars in the 1980s. Born in Minnesota, she studied mime in Paris and modelled in New York before her discovery by Dino De Laurentiis (qv). She was Bob Fosse's (qv) angel of death in *All That Jazz* (79) and was a sensatic opposite Jack Nicholson (qv) in *Th Postman Always Rings Twice* (81)

er breakthrough came in 1982 ith a supporting Oscar for the ve interest in *Tootsie* and her first five best actress Oscar ominations for her performance s the tragic actress *Frances* (82). *Country* (84), *Sweet Dreams* 5) and *Music Box* (89) her uccess was curbed only by her eference for earnest material and otherhood. She won the Oscar r her manic-depressive in *Blue ky* (94) – a film made three years arlier but embroiled in a legal spute. She has three children by e dancer/actor Mikhail aryshnikov and the playwright/ tor Sam Shepard (qv).

NGELA LANSBURY
'S actress (1925-)

ansbury's career has spanned ore than 50 years of critical cclaim and commercial success. orn in London, the daughter of a mber merchant and an actress, ne emigrated to America in 1940 nd was naturalised 11 years later. ne was trained at the Weber ouglas School of Dramatic Art in ondon and the Feagin School of rama in Radio, New York. She ent straight in to films in *Gaslight* 4), which earned her a debut scar nomination for best upporting actress. *The Picture of orian Gray* (45) gained her a econd nomination and *The anchurian Candidate* (62) a third. ther notable films are *The Three usketeers* (48), *The Long Hot ummer* (58), *Bedknobs and roomsticks* (71) and *Death on the ile* (78). She voiced the animated *eauty and the Beast* (92) and ow stars in the popular TV series urder She Wrote.

HERRY LANSING
'S producer (1944-)

ne first woman after Alice Guy in 910 to head a leading studio, she ombines business sense with a oneering conscience. A former acher and actress in *Loving* and *o Lobo* (both 70), she joined GM as a script reader and mbed through the ranks to ecome vice-president of creative fairs. As production vice-president Columbia she guided *Kramer Vs ramer* and *The China Syndrome*

(both 79) to commercial success and in 1980 was appointed president of Twentieth Century Fox. However, wishing for more direct involvement with the film-making process, she formed Jaffe-Lansing in 1983 with Stanley R Jaffe, producing *Fatal Attraction* (87) and *The Accused* (88). In 1992 she became chairman of Paramount and continued to reveal a keen business sense with the success of *Indecent Proposal* (93) and *Forrest Gump* (94), which she nurtured in the face of opposition. It stands as her greatest triumph to date. She is married to William Friedkin, the director.

MARIO LANZA
US singer, actor (1921-59)

He made only seven films, yet the tenor is still popular 36 years after his death from a heart attack, due in part to his wildly fluctuating weight and addiction to alcohol and barbiturates. He had a magnificent voice and if his projected operatic and concert career had not been interrupted by wartime service he might not have entered films. His debut was *That Midnight Kiss* (49) opposite Kathryn Grayson, a partnership repeated in *The Toast of New Orleans* (50). The title role of *The Great Caruso* (51) was his apogee, although *Because You're Mine* (52) was another hit. Reportedly too fat to appear in *The Student Prince* (54), he provided the singing voice for Edmund Purdom. *Serenade* (56) and *The Seven Hills of Rome* (58) were less good and, to judge from *For the First Time* (59), things were not improving when he died.

WALTER LASSALLY
British cinematographer (1926-)

A refugee from Germany in the 1930s, Lassally has spurned the big studios for the attractions of independent production, as in Simon Callow's directing debut, *The Ballad of the Sad Café* (91), to which he brought an elegant, poetic grit. After early work as a clapper boy, his cinematography on industrial films shaped him for Lindsay Anderson's (qv) *Thursday's Children* (54) and Karel Reisz's (qv) *We Are the Lambeth Boys* (59). After *A Taste of Honey* (61)

and *The Loneliness of the Long Distance Runner* (62), he captured the panting excitement of *Tom Jones* (63) and won an Oscar for *Zorba the Greek* (64). His independent route led him to Germany for *Ansichten einer Clowns* (76) and *Die Frau Gegenüber* (78) and to Merchant-Ivory (qqv) for *Heat and Dust* (82) and *The Bostonians* (84).

CHARLES LAUGHTON
British actor (1899-1962)

Gassed in the first world war, he tried acting as a means of exercising his damaged vocal cords. He gained a scholarship to Rada, won the coveted gold medal and made his London West End debut in 1926, marrying the actress Elsa Lanchester in 1929. His official film career began with *Piccadilly* (29). He and Lanchester went to Broadway in 1931 for Payment Deferred and filmed it the

following year. He returned to Britain in 1933 to play the king in *The Private Life of Henry VIII* for Korda (qv), winning an Oscar. A string of celebrated roles on both sides of the Atlantic followed, including *The Barretts of Wimpole Street* (34), *Ruggles of Red Gap* and Captain Bligh in *Mutiny on the Bounty* (both 35), *Rembrandt* (36), *Jamaica Inn* and Quasimodo in *The Hunchback of Notre Dame* (both 39). He had a mesmeric voice and was a notable audience pleaser. An American citizen from 1950, his later roles included the title character in Lean's (qv) *Hobson's Choice* (54) and defending counsel in Wilder's (qv) *Witness for the Prosecution* (57). Laughton directed one film, *Night of the Hunter* (55), a Gothic fable of good versus evil and one of the most outstanding of the genre, but it failed at the box office. His talent as a director, suggested by this film, remained unfulfilled.

FRANK LAUNDER
British director, screenwriter (1907-97)

Launder brightened up many lusty young lives with the madcap adventures of *The Belles of St Trinian's* (54), which he produced with his lifelong collaborator Sidney Gilliat (qv). A former civil servant, born in Hitchin, Hertfordshire, he acted in Brighton repertory and wrote two plays before becoming a screenwriter with Gilliat. Writing intelligent scripts for some notable British hits, including Hitchcock's (qv) *The Lady Vanishes* (38) and Carol Reed's (qv) *Night Train to Munich* (40), the two worked with Gainsborough, scripting comedies for Max Miller, Stanley Lupino, Will Hay (qv) and the Crazy Gang.

Forming Individual Pictures in 1944, they made their directorial and screenwriting debut with *Millions Like Us* (43), a tribute to those fighting on the home front. Launder scored high success with the lively pairing of Alastair Sim and Margaret Rutherford (qqv) in *The Happiest Days of Your Life* (50), which opened the gates to the five St Trinian's farces.

LAUREL AND HARDY
British and US comedians (1890-1965 and 1892-1957)

Perhaps the best-loved comedy double act of all time, they created a world of childlike wonder and violence. The podgy daintiness of the tie-fiddling, finger-waving Hardy ("Another fine mess you've gotten us into") was wed to the wan clumsiness of a hair-rumpling, ▷

Laurel and Hardy in The Second Hundred Years (27)

bowler-tipping Laurel ("You know, Ollie, I've been thinking"). They seemed like two halves of the same ego. Laurel, from England, had toured in vaudeville with Fred Karno and made 75 films and Hardy, a southern gentleman, was a comic star in early silents. They had been together in *Lonely Dog* (17), but teamed properly in *Slipping Wives* and *Putting Pants on Philip* (both 27). *The Music Box* (32) won them an Oscar, but masterpieces such as *Way Out West* (37) went unrewarded though containing moments of magic conceived by Laurel, who received a special Oscar in 1960. Stan, the creative dynamo of the partnership, died in poverty.

DAVID LEAN
British director (1908-91)

An early passion for cinemagoing decided him on a film career. He worked his way up from tea boy to film editor – his credits include *Pygmalion* (38) and *The 49th Parallel* (42) – before co-directing *In Which We Serve* (42) with Noël Coward (qv), its author and star. He directed three more Coward scripts, notably *Brief Encounter* (45), a perfect evocation of stifling decency in middle-class Britain. *Great Expectations* (46) and *Oliver Twist* (48) followed. Superbly cast and brilliantly edited, they remain the finest of all screen Dickens. In the mid-1950s he switched to epics, which include *The Bridge on the River Kwai* (57), *Lawrence of Arabia* (62) – seven Oscars for each – and *A Passage to India.* Released in 1984, the year he was knighted, it regained the prestige he had lost with the failure of *Ryan's Daughter* (70). A meticulous craftsman, he is remembered for these sumptuous large-scale works, but it is in the intimate 1940s films that his best work is found. Internationally admired, he received the American Film Institute's Life Achievement Award in 1990.

BRUCE LEE
US actor (1940-73)

Born in California, he grew up in Hong Kong, where he had a minor martial arts film career under the name Li Siu Lung. Returning to America he resumed his acting career and landed occasional film and television work. By the time of his early death of brain oedema he had accumulated a worldwide fan club. The tragedy prompted studios and distributors to release hastily edited, mostly Green Hornet footage from TV to cash in on Lee's ever-expanding cult status. His films *Fists of Fury* (71), *Fist of Fury* (72) and his most accomplished and well-known *Enter the Dragon* (73) were re-released throughout the 1970s and Lee's popularity was assured. New action stars such as Jackie Chan and Jean-Claude Van Damme claim Lee has been an important influence. In 1993 he was the subject of a successful biopic, *Dragon: The Bruce Lee Story.* In the same year Brandon Lee, his son, was killed on the set of *The Crow,* dying at the same age as his father.

CHRISTOPHER LEE
British actor (1922-)

The recognisable face of Dracula, Lee has made more than 300 films since 1948, most in the traditional horror genre and a vast majority with modest budgets. Christopher Frank Caradini was the son of a lieutenant-colonel in the British Army, although he took his mother's maiden name and was educated at Wellington College. After distinguished war service with the RAF – he was decorated and mentioned in dispatches – he entered films with *Corridor of Mirrors* (48). From then on he worked consistently on such screen gems as *Moulin Rouge* (52), *The Private Life of Sherlock Holmes*

(70) and *The Man With the Golde Gun* (74). Tall, Dark and Gruesome, his autobiography, was published in 1977. A clever, erudi man, Lee has an encyclopaedic knowledge of opera and cricket.

SPIKE LEE
US director, writer, producer and actor (1957-)

A fiercely intense and talented *provocateur,* Lee wears the mantle of the angry young black man of contemporary American cinema. Son of a composer and a teacher, a graduate of Morehouse College and NYU Film School, he received extravagant acclaim for his first ar third features, the street-smart

She's Gotta Have It (86) and *Do the Right Thing* (89), a controversial study of racial tension. Ever cool to mainstream formulas and always the subject c debate, his jazz film *Mo' Better Blues* (90) and his inter-racial relationship story *Jungle Fever* (91 met with mixed receptions, which did not deter him from his most ambitious, powerful and meditativ biopic of *Malcolm X* (92). Making films addressed to black Americans, Lee is a seminal figure to a younger generation of black film makers. He is held in wary regard for his style, verve and uncompromising independence by the American industry.

MICHEL LEGRAND
French composer (1931-)

Legrand has enjoyed an international reputation ever since his collaborations with New Wave

m maker Jacques Demy (qv), ›st famously his haunting score › their entirely sung worldwide hit, ›s Parapluies de Cherbourg (64). ›e child prodigy son of film ›mposer Raymond Legrand, he ›s a student of the Paris ›nservatoire at the age of 11. A ›ger-songwriter and bandleader ›fore entering films, he is noted › the lush, romantic lyricism of › songs and scores, epitomised › his Oscars for The Windmills of ›ur Mind from *The Thomas Crown ›fair* (68), the score for *The ›mmer of '42* (71) and the songs ›d score for Barbra Streisand's ›v) *Yentl* (83). He has written for ›ench, British and American films, ›cluding *The Go-Between* (71), *›dy Sings the Blues* (72) and *›lantic City* (80). He also co-wrote ›d directed *Cinq Jours en Juin* ›9), based on his adolescence in ›ris in the second world war.

›RNEST LEHMAN
›S writer (1920-)

›former short story writer, his first ›oryline film credit was for *The ›side Story* (48). He adapted ›muel Taylor's play *Sabrina* (54) › Billy Wilder (qv), the story of a ›xer based on Rocky Graziano ›ayed by Paul Newman (qv) in *›omebody Up There Likes Me* (56) ›d his own short story for ›exander Mackendrick's (qv) ›nical view of a Broadway ›lumnist in *Sweet Smell of ›ccess* (57). His versatility is ›monstrated by his screenplays › Hitchcock's (qv) *North by ›orthwest* (59) and adaptations of blockbusting Broadway musicals such as *West Side Story* (61), *The Sound of Music* (65) and *Hello Dolly!* (69). His only attempt at directing was the undistinguished *Portnoy's Complaint* (72), which shows that writers are not always the best protectors of their work. Later he was responsible for the screenplay of Hitchcock's final film, *Family Plot* (76).

JANET LEIGH
US actress (1927-)

During the 1950s, alongside her then husband Tony Curtis (qv), Leigh was one of the most popular Hollywood stars. She entered films in 1947 with no previous acting experience and her performances and billing grew in stature as she matured. She was rarely given roles of substance and her early films, such as *Little Women* and *The Forsyte Saga* (both 49), capitalised on her sweet good looks. She was frequently featured in costume adventures, often opposite Curtis, but her most impressive appearances were in quite different films, such as *The Naked Spur* (53), *Pete Kelly's Blues* (55), *Touch of Evil* (58) and as the murder victim in the shower in *Psycho* (60). *The Manchurian Candidate* (62) and *An American Dream* (66) are also notable. She appears to have retired after appearing in *The Fog* (80) with Jamie Lee Curtis (qv), her daughter.

MIKE LEIGH
British director (1943-)

A celebrated improvisational theatre director who turned his unique rehearsing style to films, Leigh is an observant chronicler of the nuances of working-class life. He was born in Salford, Greater Manchester, and entered Rada in 1960. He began directing and writing his own plays at the Victoria Theatre, Stoke-on-Trent, in 1966 and went on to the Midland Arts Centre Theatre, Birmingham, and then the Royal Shakespeare Company. His principal stage works include the hit Abigail's Party. He began directing films with *Bleak Moments* (72), *High Hopes* (88), *Life Is Sweet* (90), *Naked* (93) and the excellent *Secrets and Lies* (95). A taciturn figure in the

industry, he has won many film festival and critical awards, including best director at Cannes in 1993 for *Naked*. He was awarded an OBE in 1993.

VIVIEN LEIGH
British actress (1913-67)

She was so heart-stoppingly beautiful it was possible to forgive her limitations as an actress. Born and raised in India, she arrived in Britain at the age of seven for a convent education. After attending Rada she made her film debut in *Things Are Looking Up* (34). A contract with Korda (qv) ensued and she met and married Laurence Olivier (qv) when they made *Fire Over England* (37). Visiting him in Hollywood when he was making *Wuthering Heights* (39), she caught David O Selznick's (qv) eye, landed the coveted role of Scarlett and won an Oscar for *Gone With the Wind* (39). She was memorably cast with Olivier in Korda's patriotic tribute to Nelson, *Lady Hamilton* (41), Sir Winston Churchill's favourite film, and returned to Britain to play opposite Claude Rains (qv) in Gabriel Pascal's excessive *Caesar and Cleopatra* (45). She won her second Oscar as Blanche in *A Streetcar Named Desire* (51). Tuberculosis and manic depression severely blighted her career. Her marriage to Olivier ended in 1960.

CLAUDE LELOUCH
French director, screenwriter (1937-)

At the age of 13 he directed his first short, *La Mal du Siècle* (50), which won a prize at the Cannes Amateur Festival. A professional from 1956, he continued making shorts and television commercials and directed his first feature in 1960 with the help of family money. However, he earned neither reputation nor commercial success until the worldwide popularity of *A Man and a Woman* (66). Voted best film at Cannes, it also won the foreign film Oscar and made a fortune. Focusing on a love affair between Jean-Louis Trintignant and

Anouk Aimée (qqv), conducted in the chic environs of Deauville to the strains of Francis Lai's insistent theme tune, it sums up Lelouch's style: technically accomplished, freewheeling and glossy. He has an eye for classy casting and had further success with *Vivre pour Vivre* (67), starring Yves Montand (qv) and Annie Girardot, and *A Man and a Woman: 20 Years Later* (86) with the original stars.

JACK LEMMON
US actor (1925-)

Born in Boston and a Harvard graduate, John Uhler Lemmon III played piano in a beer hall, served in the navy and performed on radio, television and Broadway before making his film debut in two Judy Holliday (qv) films. Establishing his star status with the best supporting Oscar for Ensign Pulver in *Mister Roberts* (55), he confirmed his diversity in Billy Wilder's (qv) *Some Like It Hot* (59), playing an alcoholic in *Days of Wine and Roses* (62) and in the legendary relationship with Walter

Matthau (qv) in *The Odd Couple* (68). He also directed Matthau in *Kotch* (71). After winning best actor Oscar for *Save the Tiger* (73), his dramatic range extended to playing a conscience-stricken engineer in *The China Syndrome* (79) and an American patriot who has to come to terms with his country's complicity with Chilean fascism in *Missing* (82), which won him best actor at Cannes. His later successes include *Dad* (89), *JFK* (91), *Glengarry Glen Ross* (92), *Short Cuts* and, with Matthau, *Grumpy Old Men* (both 93).

SERGIO LEONE
Italian director (1921-89)

Born to a screen star and a film pioneer, he began his film career as an assistant to such directors as Raoul Walsh and Fred Zinnemann (qqv). He served as assistant on *Quo Vadis* (51) and *Ben-Hur* (59) then second unit director and screenwriter. His directorial debut on *The Last Days of Pompeii* (59) was ignored in favour of co-director Mario Bonnard, but he received credit for *The Colossus of Rhodes*

(61). The spaghetti western *A Fistful of Dollars* (64) established him as a fierce, imaginative director with an impeccable mastery of tension. *For a Few Dollars More* (65) and *The Good, the Bad and the Ugly* (66) rejuvenated the western and made Clint Eastwood (qv) a star. After the financial failure of his big budget epic *Once Upon a Time in the West* (68), he shunned directing until his expansive gangster film *Once Upon a Time in America* (84) starring Robert De Niro and James Woods (qqv). It was incoherent in the studio's cut, but resonant and poetic in Leone's full version. One of the great directors, his cinema tended to be one of majesty and power.

MERVYN LeROY
US director (1900-87)

Effectively launching Warner's gangster cycle with *Little Caesar* (30) and lauded for his tough, uncompromising direction of *I Am a Fugitive From a Chain Gang* (32), it is hard to reconcile him as the director of *Gold Diggers of 1933* (33) and producer of *The Wizard of Oz* (39). A former actor and gag ▷

writer, LeRoy joined First National Pictures (part of Warner) in the 1930s and directed a number of programme fillers before making his name with *Little Caesar.* He directed the gritty *Five Star Final* (31) and *They Won't Forget* (37) and then, in 1938, switched to MGM where he made *Waterloo Bridge* (40), *Random Harvest* (42) and *Madame Curie* (43). In the 1950s he set up his own production company and replaced John Ford (qv) on *Mister Roberts* (55), followed by *No Time For Sergeants* (58) and *Gypsy* (62).

RICHARD LESTER
US director (1932-)

Although a TV director for CBS at the age of 20, he started in films in Britain with the surreal short *The Running Jumping and Standing Still Film* (60) starring Peter Sellers (qv). The mix of satire, slapstick, frantic cross-cutting, documentary inserts and pop music reflected the irreverence of the Beatles (qv) in *A Hard Day's Night* (64) and *Help!* (65). His love of the silent era was also a clear influence. Able to divide audiences and critics, Lester is perceived as either a stylistic maverick or a flashy, empty showman. His frenetic approach also affected *A Funny Thing Happened on the Way to the Forum* (66) and *The Three Musketeers* (74), but his romantic story *Petulia* (68) and historic romance *Robin and Marian* (76) were quieter in style and since then his influence has waned.

BARRY LEVINSON
US director, writer and producer (1942-)

Born and raised in Baltimore, the setting for his autobiographically inspired trio *Diner* (82), *Tin Men* (87) and *Avalon* (90), he was a stand-up comic, Emmy award-winning comedy writer and a screenwriter providing gags for

early mentor Mel Brooks (qv). He co-scripted the outrageous satire *. . . And Justice for All* (79) with his first wife Valerie Curtin before making his accomplished directorial debut with *Diner.* His directing successes include Redford's (qv) baseball vehicle *The Natural* (84), Robin Williams's (qv) *tour de force* in *Good Morning, Vietnam* (87), Dustin Hoffman's (qv) Oscar-winning autistic savant in *Rain Man* (88) – which also won Oscars for best picture, screenplay and direction – and Warren Beatty's (qv) *Bugsy* (91). The failure of his expensive fable *Toys* (92), a film he had dreamed of making for more than a decade, was a bitter setback, but he recovered with a hit adaptation of Michael Crichton's (qv) provocative *Disclosure* (95). Baltimore Pictures, his production company, has also developed the acclaimed *Quiz Show* (94), directed by Redford.

ALBERT LEWIN
US director, producer and screenwriter (1894-1968)

He directed only six films, but his literary elegance and painstaking

attention to detail singled him out as a film-maker of significance. Educated at Harvard, Lewin taught English and was film critic for the Jewish Tribune before joining MGM as a scriptwriter in 1924. There he worked as Irving Thalberg's (qv) personal assistant, later becoming a producer. After Thalberg's death in 1936 he joined Paramount and five years later was writing and directing his own films. Of these, the first two were the most successful. *The Moon and Sixpence* (42) was a faithful adaptation of Maugham's liberal biography of the painter Gauguin and *The Picture of Dorian Gray* (45) was a stylish version of the Oscar Wilde novel. After a heart attack and the box office failure of his later films, Lewin concentrated on writing screenplays.

JERRY LEWIS
US actor, director and producer (1926-)

In Martin Scorsese's (qv) *The King of Comedy* (83), he shed tomfoolery for the role of sweaty, anxious chat show host opposite Robert De Niro (qv). He is, however, renowned for his comic partnership with Dean Martin. Lewis sang on stage with his parents at the age of five and was performing as a stand-up comic at the age of 18. His career took off when he met Martin. Their act was based on contradiction: Martin was the self-assured singer Lewis the unco-ordinated, freewheeling loon. They moved into film with *My Friend Irma* (49). *Jumping Jacks* and *Sailor Beware* (both 52) are examples of his comic mania, with *That's My Boy* (51) and *Artists and Models* (55) mistakenly letting Lewis indulge himself. Committing himself to comedy after the split with Martin in 1956, he often wrote, produced and/or directed his films. *The Ladies' Man* (61) revealed a passion for the potential of cinema and *The Nutty Professor* (63) saw him push comedy to the limits. He appeared in the British film *Funny Bones* (94).

King of comedy? Lewis's humour is based on mania

VAL LEWTON
US producer, screenwriter (1904-51)

Trained in journalism at Columbia University, he was a prolific writer of novels and poetry with almost 20 books to his credit when he became a story editing assistant to David O Selznick (qv). In 1942 he graduated to producer at RKO, instituting the B-movie horror cycle that made his name. His films concentrated on psychodrama and resulted in such masterpieces of poetic horror as *Cat People* (42) and *I Walked With a Zombie* (43). Direction was shared between Jacques Tourneur (qv) and, especially, Mark Robson (qv), though he gave Robert Wise (qv) his first directing job with *The Curse of the Cat People* (44). The camera angles, eerily effective sound, atmospheric lighting and chilling content were dictated by Lewton. *Bedlam* (46), co-written with Robson and inspired by Hogarth's Rake's Progress, was his bid for the A-list, but though critically appreciated it failed at the box office. He produced five mediocre non-horror films and died prematurely of a heart attack.

MAX LINDER
French comedian (1883-1925)

A dapper dandy, his silent comedy relied on facial expression, which influenced Chaplin and Mack Sennett (qqv). "Chaplin called me his teacher," he once said, "but I am glad enough myself to take lessons from him." A native of Bordeaux, he was put under contract by distributor Charles Pathé (qv). His rich loafer at odds

with the world in *Max Wants a Divorce* and *Max in a Taxi* (both 17) became successful in Americ[a] and Europe. Gassed in the first world war, he had several nervous ɛakdowns and his attempts to ·rt a company in Hollywood were varted, although his Douglas 'rbanks's (qv) parody, *The Three ıst-Get-Theres* (22), was claimed. He returned to France a appointed man where he and wife committed suicide. aplin based the elegant aracter of *Monsieur Verdoux* (47) Linder. Fragments of his work re rediscovered in the 1960s.

ıATOLE LITVAK
ssian director (1902-74)

tagehand in his youth in St ersburg, he studied philosophy, ended drama school and later ed and directed for a stage ipe. In 1923 he became a set signer and assistant director for

Nordkino studios. Within a year he was writing scripts and had made his directorial debut with *Tatiana*. He worked for the next 10 years in Germany, France and Britain, including editing G W Pabst's (qv) controversial *The Joyless Street* (25). As the Nazis' popularity increased, the Jewish director left Germany to work for Pathé in Paris. His best film for them was *Mayerling* (36), which was an international success and his passport to Hollywood, where it is generally thought he produced some of his weakest work. He served in the American army during the war and worked with Frank Capra (qv) on *Why We Fight*, a series of films produced by the army. In 1948 he made his strongest film, *The Snake Pit*.

HAROLD LLOYD
US actor (1893-1971)

With Keaton and Chaplin (qqv), Lloyd was the third of the great clowns produced by the silent cinema. The personality he adopted in most of his films was more outgoing and jaunty than Keaton's and never resorted to pathos in the Chaplin manner. He was the all-American go-getter, triumphing over the odds whatever they were. He made his first film in 1912 as an extra. In 1914 Hal Roach (qv) engaged him to play a character called Willie Work. He moved briefly to Mack Sennett (qv) and, disillusioned, back to Roach who gave him a new character called Lonesome Luke, which had similarities to Chaplin's tramp.

Go-getter: Lloyd triumphing over the odds in Never Weaken

Lonesome featured in more than 100 shorts. Lloyd and Roach then devised the optimistic "glasses" character with his three-piece suit and straw hat. Lloyd was a natural athlete and often performed his own stunts, such as in *Safety Last* (23) in which he dangles from the hands of a clock high above a Los Angeles street. His right hand had been badly injured in an explosion in *Haunted Spooks* (20) and he wore a special glove to disguise the absence of fingers. He left Roach in 1923 and made several more silent features, including *The Kid Brother* (27) and *Speedy* (28). His appeal gently faded away in the sound era and he retired gracefully.

KEN LOACH
British director (1936-)

Britain's foremost left-wing feature film maker, his gritty stories are drawn from contemporary working-class life. He uses a combination of improvisation, cinéma vérité and abrasive realism to confront audiences with a recognisable political predicament. He was attracted to experimental theatre while reading law at Oxford. After two years in the RAF he rejected the law in favour of a repertory company and entered television in the 1960s distinguishing himself as a director on Z-Cars and The Wednesday Play. Cathy Come Home highlighted the plight of the homeless and his first feature, *Poor Cow* (68), led to *Kes* (69). After films on the mental health of *Family Life* (71), the cold war in *Fatherland* (86) and Northern Ireland in *Hidden Agenda* (90), he has won acclaim for *Riff-Raff* (91), *Raining Stones* (93) and *Ladybird Ladybird* (94) *Land and Freedom* (95) and *Carla's Song* (96).

MARGARET LOCKWOOD
British actress (1916-90)

Lockwood trained at Rada, was on the stage in her teens and made her film debut in *Lorna Doone* (35). She played opposite Maurice Chevalier (qv) in *The Beloved Vagabond* (36) and Hitchcock's (qv) *The Lady Vanishes* (38) made her a star. One of the top leading ladies of British films during the 1940s, she was often cast as a calculating beauty. Her hits include *The Stars Look Down* and *Night Train to Munich* (both 40), *Quiet Wedding* (41), *Alibi* (42), *The Man in Grey* (43), *The Wicked Lady* (45) as a glamorous highway robber and *Bedelia* (46). Successes became fewer and after *Cast a Dark Shadow* (55) she abandoned film to resume her stage career and make a new one in TV. She returned once, to general acclaim, as Cinderella's stepmother in *The Slipper and the Rose* (76).

MARCUS LOEW
US mogul (1870-1927)

One of the pioneers who created Hollywood, he was born in New York City, the son of Austrian immigrants. He left school at nine to support his impoverished family. After making a modest fortune in the fur business, he saw the opportunity in moving pictures and bought a chain of nickelodeons and leading vaudeville theatres for conversion to cinemas. In 1920 he acquired Metro Pictures, from which Samuel Goldwyn (qv) had just resigned. The following year Louis B Mayer Pictures joined the group and in 1924 a controlling interest in Goldwyn was acquired. Metro-Goldwyn-Mayer was born. Loew's Inc was the controlling company, running the most important studio in Hollywood from New York. Loew ended his life as one of America's richest men and MGM became the largest producer of films in the world.

GINA LOLLOBRIGIDA
Italian actress (1927-)

Even after Hollywood had replaced her carefree sensuality with its own

packaged glamour, Lollobrigida proved immensely popular in America, her enthusiasm and pin-up figure having entranced Europe for many years before. The daughter of a carpenter, she posed as a model in illustrated novels, competed in beauty contests and studied fine art. In 1946, her first year on screen, she appeared in *Aquila Nera, Elisir d'Amore* and *Lucia di Lammermoor. Fanfan la Tulipe* (52) and René Clair's (qv) *Les Belles de Nuit* (52) were shot through with her magnetic warmth and the French invented "lollobrigidienne" as a synonym for curvaceous. "La Lollo", as she became known, blossomed in John Huston's (qv) *Beat the Devil* (54) and ensnared Burt Lancaster and Tony Curtis (qqv) in *Trapeze* (56). She easily matched Sean Connery and Ralph Richardson (qqv) in *Woman of Straw* (64). Her more recent career has included photography and a return to the screen in the American television series Falcon Crest.

HERBERT LOM
British actor (1917-)

Best known for his role as the demented police inspector in the Pink Panther films, he has had a long and distinguished career as a versatile character actor. Herbert Charles Angelo Kuchacevich ze Schluderpacheru was born in Prague, where he began his stage and screen career. He arrived in Britain in 1939 after the German invasion to continue his training at the Old Vic. Ironically, his film debut was in *Mein Kampf My Crimes* (40), followed by *The Young Mr Pitt* (42), in which he played Napoleon, a part he was to repeat in King Vidor's (qv) *War and Peace* (56). His career includes *The Ladykillers* (55), *The Phantom of the Opera* (62), *Spartacus* (60) and *Murders in the Rue Morgue* (71). His first Panther film, *A Shot in the Dark* (64), led to *The Return of the Pink Panther* (75), *The Pink Panther Strikes Again* (76) and a raft of sequels.

CAROLE LOMBARD
US actress (1908-42)

Jane Peters was born in Fort Wayne, Indiana. Her divorced

mother moved her to Los Angeles where she was spotted by the Fox director Allan Dwan (qv). Not only one of Hollywood's most glamorous 1930s stars, she was also a sublime comedienne gifted with intelligence and personality. Dwan put her in *A Perfect Crime* (21) and her first lead came with *Marriage in Transit* (25). After *Hearts and Spurs* (25), a car crash and facial scarring delayed her career for two years. She made two-reelers for Mack Sennett (qv), transferred to Pathé and then Paramount, where her comic talents were recognised in *The Arizona Kid* and *Fast and Loose* (both 30) and *It Pays to Advertise* (31). She met her future husband Clark Gable (qv) on *No Man of Her Own* (32). *Bolero* and *Twentieth Century* (both 34) catapulted her to stardom. She became the highest paid star in Hollywood in 1937 and demanded straight roles. *Vigil in the Night* and *They Knew What They Wanted* (both 40) pleased the critics, but she returned to comedy for *Mr and Mrs Smith* (41). At the height of her fame she was killed in a plane crash near Las Vegas on a war bonds selling mission.

ANITA LOOS
US writer (1893-1981)

Her remarkable 40-year career as playwright, screenwriter and novelist began in her teens. She started with D W Griffith (qv) in 1912, writing *The New York Hat* for Mary Pickford (qv). Her material for several of Douglas Fairbanks's (qv) films, including *The Americano* (16), was instrumental in promoting her rise to popularity. She earned immortality for her 1925 novel Gentlemen Prefer Blondes, which became a play and two films, most famously with Marilyn Monroe (qv) in 1953. She also contributed her sardonic gifts to a variety of films, including *San Francisco* (36), *Saratoga* (37), the successful MGM version of Clare Boothe's play *The Women* (39) and the tear-jerking *Blossoms in the Dust* (41), starring Greer Garson (qv). She adapted Colette's Gigi for Broadway and was sent to London to look over Audrey Hepburn (qv) for the lead, thus proving herself a starmaker. She recorded her life in three autobiographies.

SOPHIA LOREN
Italian actress (1934-)

A lush, voluptuous Neapolitan beauty, Sofia Scicolone was the love goddess of the 1950s and 1960s and is still working 45 years after her debut. Born in Rome, but raised in poverty in Naples, she was discovered by the producer Carlo Ponti when she was a 15-year-old beauty contestant. She married him in 1957, split in 1962 and remarried in 1966. Under his tutelage she rose to stardom by the mid-1950s, when she went to Hollywood to partner such leading men as Cary Grant, Frank Sinatra and Charlton Heston (qqv) in the epics *The Pride and the Passion* (57) and *El Cid* (61), while forays to Britain included a comedy with Peter Sellers (qv) and Chaplin's (qv) last film. Most of her best work, however, was in Italy with Vittorio de Sica (qv), whose *Two Women* (60) won her a best actress Oscar; a rarity for a foreign language performance. De Sica teamed her in *Yesterday, Today and Tomorrow* (63) and *Marriage Italian Style* (64) with Marcello Mastroianni (qv), her leading man in 13 films, including Robert Altman's (qv) *Prêt à Porter* (94).

PETER LORRE
Hungarian actor (1904-64)

Few character actors cut such a distinctive figure. Short, furtive and bug-eyed, Lorre was equally adept at evincing pity or revulsion, most often cast as villains and perhaps best remembered as Sydney

…eter Lorre photographed …r Vanity Fair in 1936

…eenstreet's sidekick in eight …ns. A former bank clerk and …scure actor in Swiss, Austrian …d German theatre, he was …otted by Fritz Lang (qv) and cast … the grotesque child murderer in … (31). In just 12 lines of dialogue, … projected a universe of sinister …notions and the film made him a …r. After fleeing Nazi Germany for …tain in 1933, he played the …ntlemanly kidnapper to chilling …ect in Hitchcock's (qv) *The Man …ho Knew Too Much* (34). In …llywood he was a success as the …ental detective *Mr Moto* (1937- …) and created other indelible …aracters in *The Maltese Falcon* …1), *Casablanca* (42) and *Arsenic …d Old Lace* (44). He returned to …rmany to direct, script and star … *Der Verlorene* (51). He died of a …art attack after his return to …llywood and *The Raven* (63) with …ncent Price (qv).

JOSEPH LOSEY
US director (1909-84)

He jettisoned early medical ambitions to work in theatre as an actor and critic. By 1938 he was documentary supervisor for the Rockefeller Foundation and was directing shorts a year later. After service in the second world war he

returned to theatre and worked for a time with Brecht. As a director in Hollywood he won respect for his efficiency and speed. He was named as a one-time communist in 1951, blacklisted by the House Un-American Activities Committee and moved to Europe. In Britain he established himself with *The Servant* (63), *Accident* (67) and *The Go-Between* (71), three sharp social dramas scripted by the playwright Harold Pinter. Each focused on issues of class and morality, the latter two winning prizes at the Cannes Film Festival. He uprooted to France before directing the unsettling *Mr Klein* (77) and a screen adaptation of *Don Giovanni* (79), but his subsequent sporadic output was dull by comparison.

BESSIE LOVE
US actress (1898-1986)

Juanita Horton was born in Midland, Texas, and was at high

school when she entered films. Her bubbly beauty enlivened scores of films in the silent era, but serious stardom eluded her. She made her mark in film history in 1929 by singing and dancing in *The Broadway Melody*, the first MGM musical, which brought her an Oscar nomination. Appearances in more early musicals followed, including *The Hollywood Revue of 1929* (29), but after marriage she semi-retired. After her divorce in 1935 she moved to Britain and appeared in wartime films, later playing character parts, notably in *On Her Majesty's Secret Service* (69), as well as performing on stage. A memorable later role was as the telephone answering service operator in *Sunday Bloody Sunday* (71). She occasionally returned to America and also appeared in Warren Beatty's (qv) *Reds* (81).

MYRNA LOY
US actress (1905-93)

Her real name was Myrna Adele Williams and she was a cattleman's daughter from Montana. She trained as a dancer, making her first appearance at 12. At 18 she was in the chorus at Grauman's Chinese Theater in Hollywood. After a few unsuccessful forays into casting offices, she became typecast in exotic roles as a vamp. As such she might well have been forgotten, but in 1934 W S Van Dyke (qv) cast her as William Powell's (qv) witty, resourceful wife in the first of *The Thin Man* films and she was brilliant. As the top box office female star in 1936 she was elected "Queen of Hollywood" with Clark Gable (qv) as "King".

Together they made several films. She made her peacetime comeback as Fredric March's (qv) wife in William Wyler's (qv) Oscar-winning *The Best Years of Our Lives* (46). Astonishingly for such a fine actress she never even won an Oscar nomination, but was given an honorary award in 1991.

ERNST LUBITSCH
US director (1892-1947)

Few have matched the visual humour that became known as "the Lubitsch touch". His eminence was such that he received an Oscar in 1937 for his "25-year contribution to motion pictures". On stage as a teenager in his native Berlin he was acting in silent comedies by 1913 and soon directing. After dramatic successes featuring the actress Pola Negri (qv), he established himself as a master of satirical comedy, *The Oyster Princess* (19), and of costume drama, *Madame* ▷

Dubarry (19) and *Anna Boleyn* (20). His first American film was *Rosita* (23) with Mary Pickford (qv), and his silent hits included *The Marriage Circle* and *Forbidden Paradise* (both 24), *Kiss Me Again* and *Lady Windermere's Fan* (both 25). *The Love Parade* (29) was his first talkie, followed by *Monte Carlo* (30), *The Smiling Lieutenant* (31), *Trouble in Paradise* (32), *The Merry Widow* (34), *To Be or Not to Be* (42) and *Heaven Can Wait* (43). Heart attacks disrupted his final years and he handed over direction of *That Lady in Ermine* (48) to Preminger (qv) before he died.

GEORGE LUCAS
US director, producer (1944-)

While acknowledged as an influential, twice-nominated director, it is as a producer and founder of the special effects factory Industrial Light & Magic that established him as a phenomenon of contemporary cinema. After film school at the University of Southern California he was taken under the wing of Francis Ford Coppola (qv) and directed his gripping and intelligent sci-fi thriller, *THX-1138* (71). His autobiographical *American Graffiti* (73) was a hit but could not compare with the triumph of *Star Wars* (77). Nominated for 10 Oscars, it was the highest grossing film of its day. Turning his back on directing, Lucas produced moneymaking franchises with both the *Star Wars* sequels and Spielberg's (qv) Indiana Jones trilogy. More recently he has focused on television, special effects, video games and fine-tuning the digital technology to produce three *Star Wars* prequels and to reissue the originals.

BELA LUGOSI
US actor (1882-1956)

His chilling opening line in Tod Browning's (qv) 1931 film version of Bram Stoker's classic – "I am Drac-ula . . . I bid you welcome" – established him as the classic film monster. Béla Ferenc Blasko was born in Hungary, the son of a banker. He trained at the Budapest Academy before becoming an actor. Forced to leave Hungary in 1919 for his involvement as a union organiser in the 1918 communist revolution, he made

several films in Germany and America. He became the personification of screen evil; his prince of darkness could never be confused with the ghouls and zombies he played throughout the rest of his career, which included one deviation – opposite Greta Garbo (qv) in *Ninotchka* (39). Plagued by personal problems, he increasingly parodied himself, even signing autographs in a coffin, until financial and marital strains resulted in treatment for drug addiction. He died filming *Plan 9 From Outer Space* (56) and was buried in his Dracula cape. Martin Landau won an Oscar playing him in *Ed Wood* (94).

SIDNEY LUMET
US director (1924-)

He was a child actor and graduated from Columbia University. His directing career began in summer stock. After television he made his directorial debut with the powerful courtroom drama *12 Angry Men* (57), which won him an Oscar nomination. He moved on from there with some confidence, taking on such heavyweight projects as *A View From the Bridge* and *Long Day's Journey Into Night* (both 62). He is a significant director for three thought-provoking and controversial films – *Serpico* (73) and *Dog Day Afternoon* (75), his collaborations with Al Pacino (qv), and the Oscar-winning *Network* (76). His judgment failed him with *The Wiz* (78), an all-black update of *The Wizard of Oz*, and his only good film since is *Prince of the City* (81). *Running on Empty* (88) stands out from several mediocre post-1981 features.

LOUIS & AUGUSTE LUMIERE
French pioneers (1864-1948 and 1862-1954)

On December 28 1895 the Lumière brothers attracted a paying public in Paris to watch their films and cinema was born. But Louis, ever the inventor, regarded the new medium as so ephemeral that he returned to exploring advances in photography. The sons of a manufacturer of photographic supplies, they created the Cinématographe, which combined the functions of camera and projector. It was used to show Louis's early films, such as *La Sortie des Usines Lumière* (95) and *L'Arrivé d'un Train en Gare de la Ciotat* (95), in which a train hurtled towards the camera. Louis also directed the first fiction film, *L'Arroseur Arrosé* (95), in which a gardener is drenched. The brothers were soon sending news cameramen around the world. However, by the time Louis had abandoned cinema, audiences were becoming more discerning and competition from Gaumont and Pathé had arrived. Also on the horizon was the pioneer George Méliès (qv), whose fantasies were strikingly different from Louis's documentary approach. There are many founding fathers of the cinema, but the Lumières are often regarded as the most successful.

IDA LUPINO
US actress, director (1918-95)

She looked for one moment as if she would transcend Bette Davis (qv) in the affections of the pre-war public. A blonde, doll-like actress, she was born in London to stage parents (her father was the actor Stanley Lupino). She trained at Rada and was discovered by the producer Allan Dwan (qv) when he was seeking a nymph-like temptress for *Her First Affair* (33). Paramount starred her in *The Search for Beauty* (34) with Larry "Buster" Crabbe and *Paris in Spring* (35), but the studio loaned her to several other companies with limited success. Her roles got smaller and after several more lacklustre vehicles she asked to be released from her contract. She had limited success at Columbia with *The Lone Wolf Spy Hunt* and *The Lady and the*

Mob (both 39), but Warner rescued her in *They Drive by Night* (40) and suddenly Lupino had muscle. Some of her most notable performances include *The Hard Way* (43), *Hollywood Canteen* (44), *Pillow to Post* (45), *Deep Valley* (47), *Road House* (48) and *Lust for Gold* (49). She began directing with *Never Fear* and continued with *Outrage* (both 50), *Hard, Fast and Beautiful* (52) and *The Bigamist* (53). Her last film was *Deadhead Miles* (82).

DAVID LYNCH
US director, writer and producer (1946-)

He gained notoriety for graphic sexual violence on screen, but is essentially a conservative whose work both satirises and celebrates banal Americana. Mel Brooks (qv) once characterised him as "Jimmy Stewart from Mars". The son of an

agricultural scientist, he was a struggling artist when an experimental short won him a fellowship to the American Film Institute. Over a period of five years he made *Eraserhead* (77), a cult hit that attracted Brooks, who assigned him to *The Elephant Man* (80), which in turn led to the tortuous sci-fi disaster *Dune* (85). He won his second Oscar nomination and best picture from the American National Society of Film Critics for his controversial *Blue Velvet* (86). Featuring Dennis Hopper (qv) as a psychopath, the film is a landmark of 1980s' independent American cinema. His hot and nasty lovers-on-the-run picture *Wild at Heart* (90) won the Cannes Palme D'Or, while his soap noir Twin Peaks was the television phenomenon of 1990. Jennifer, his daughter, launched her directorial career with *Boxing Helena* (92).

LEO McCAREY
US director, producer and screenwriter (1898-1969)

An important influence on screen comedy, he was a qualified lawyer before becoming Tod Browning's (qv) assistant in 1920. He served

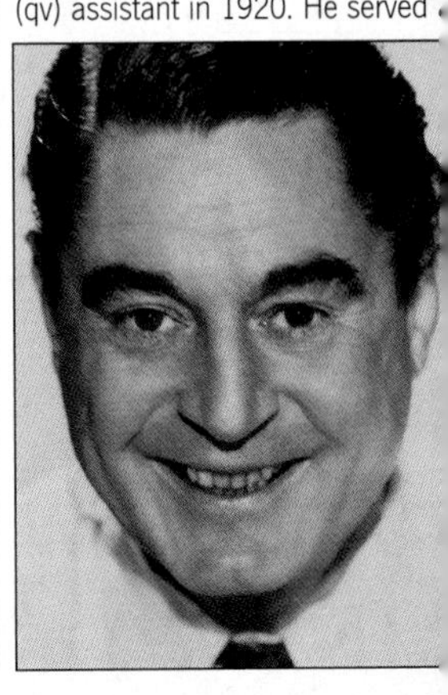

ck-of-all-trades apprenticeship en joined Hal Roach (qv) as a g writer, director and supervisor. e teamed Laurel with Hardy (qv), ur of whose silent shorts he rected. He continued as a force zany comedies with such stars The Marx Brothers (qv) in *Duck oup* (33), W C Fields, Harold oyd and Mae West (qqv) in *Belle the Nineties* (34). His *Ruggles of ed Gap* (35) with Charles ughton (qv) was a highlight and moved into the screwball genre, nning an Oscar for the Cary ant-Irene Dunne (qqv) vehicle *ne Awful Truth* (37). His ntimental streak informed the scar-winning script and direction *Going My Way* (44) and its quel *The Bells of St Mary's* (45), th starring Bing Crosby (qv). Wit d romance distinguished the ory line and direction of *Love fair* (39), which he remade as *An fair to Remember* (57), as usual -writing the updated screenplay.

VINSOR McCAY
S animator (1871-1934)

efore Disney (qv) there was cCay. Early animation was debted to him and even Walt, a ouch at giving others credit, knowledged his contribution. He ew the Little Nemo comic strip r the New York Herald, the hero eing his small son. He transferred e strip to film in 1905 and llowed it with *Gertie the Trained inosaur* (09). In the evenings cCay was a vaudeville performer d the dinosaur's adventures were nstructed to fit in with his act, a ghlight of which was Gertie eming to take an apple from his and and eat it. His "epic" was *he Sinking of the Lusitania* (18) elieved to be the first feature-ngth cartoon. It sank him and he turned to newspapers. His work as an inventive charm and clarity line that marks him down as a oneer and a considerable artist.

OEL McCREA
S actor (1905-90)

aying cowboy roles was ppropriate for the grandson of a agecoach driver. McCrea was aised in California and after raduating from Pomona State ollege he had his first taste of cting at the Pasadena Playhouse. e was in films from 1922 in small oles and as a horse wrangler. Tall

and clean-cut, he achieved his first lead in *The Silver Horde* (30) and became a reliable performer in a variety of films through the 1930s, ranging from outdoor action dramas such as *Come and Get It* (36) to the urban comedy *Three Blind Mice* (38). He excelled in Cecil B DeMille's (qv) western *Union Pacific* (39) and was Hitchcock's (qv) gauche newspaperman in *Foreign Correspondent* (40). He was brilliantly cast in Preston Sturges's (qv) two sublime comedies, *Sullivan's Travels* (41) and *The Palm Beach Story* (42). After the war he concentrated on westerns, reaching his apotheosis in Sam Peckinpah's (qv) elegiac *Ride the High Country* (62).

JEANETTE MacDONALD
US actress, singer (1901-65)

Moving from Broadway musicals to films, this attractive soprano was an immediate success from her debut in *The Love Parade* (29) opposite Maurice Chevalier (qv), with whom she also made *One Hour With You* and *Love Me Tonight* (both 32) and *The Merry Widow* (34). It was her screen partnership with Nelson Eddy (qv), though, that brought her popular success in eight operetta/musicals beginning with *Naughty Marietta* (35) and including *Rose Marie* (36), *Maytime* (37), *The Girl of the Golden West* and *Sweethearts* (both 38), *New Moon* and *Bitter Sweet* (both 40) and *I Married an Angel* (42). She had also sung through her tears in *San Francisco* (36), partnered Allan Jones in *The Firefly* (37), reconquered Broadway in *Broadway Serenade* (39) and sung opposite Gene Raymond, her husband, in *Smilin' Through* (41). *Cairo* (42) effectively ended her starring career and after a brief return for *Three Daring Daughters* (48) and *The Sun Comes Up* (49) she concentrated on singing.

ALEXANDER MACKENDRICK
British director (1912-93)

He was born in Boston, Massachusetts, to Scottish parents and trained as a commercial artist at the Glasgow School of Art. His first film work was on pre-war advertising shorts, switching to documentaries in 1939. He joined Ealing as a screenwriter and directed his first feature, the seminal Ealing comedy *Whisky Galore!*, in 1949 . His subsequent humorous triumphs at Ealing included *The Man in the White Suit* (51) and the delicious black comedy *The Ladykillers* (55). After Ealing's fadeout he made *Sweet Smell of Success* (57), the acutely observed study of Broadway cynicism, and a handful of other films before leaving the industry to teach in California. His output was limited, but always memorable.

VICTOR McLAGLEN
US actor (1886-1959)

A clergyman's son from Tunbridge Wells, Kent, he had the body of an ox and his John Ford (qv) roles exploited that physique with notable bluster. He had been a boxer, gold miner and music hall strong man in Australia before making several British films, such as *The Call of the Road* (20). In America he and Edmund Lowe established the bantering soldier characters Flagg and Quirt in *What Price Glory?* (26). Ford revived his fortunes with *The Lost Patrol* (34) and *The Informer* (35), for which he won an Oscar. He never touched the top again, though Ford came to the rescue with such films as *She Wore a Yellow Ribbon* (49). He had become a burlesque Irishman by this time and was a creature of whimsical extravagance in Ford's *The Quiet Man* (52).

SHIRLEY MacLAINE
US actress (1934-)

The elder half-sister of Warren Beatty (qv), she harboured showbusiness ambitions from an early age, joining chorus lines on Broadway. She was offered a film contract when the producer Hal Wallis (qv) saw her understudying in a Broadway show and made an auspicious debut in Hitchcock's (qv) *The Trouble With Harry* (55). Her film career bloomed and she won Oscar nominations for *Some Came Running* (59), Billy Wilder's (qv) *The Apartment* (60) and *Irma La Douce* (63). Her off-screen life was peppered with political activism, while the roles she took began to suggest that she was limited to playing kookie women. In the early 1970s she wrote about her travel experiences and sought out her roots in 1976 with A Gypsy in My Soul, a one-woman Broadway show. Though nominated for another Oscar for *The Turning Point* (77) she was not a winner until *Terms of Endearment* (83). Similar feisty roles followed in *Steel Magnolias* (89), *Postcards From the Edge* (90) *Used People* (92) and *Guarding Tess* (94). Her performances have still not lost the unpredictable energy that made her such a sparkling presence in the 1950s and 1960s.

NORMAN McLAREN
British animator (1914-87)

McLaren widened the parameters of his art, employing unusual and diverse types of music, experimenting with abstract form and drawing images directly on to celluloid. While studying interior design at the Glasgow School of Art he discovered animation. His 16mm documentary *Seven Till Five* (33), a day in the life of an art school, won him financial backing for *Camera Makes Whoopee* (35). That attracted the attention of the documentary film maker John Grierson (qv), who invited him to work at the GPO Film Unit in London. In 1938 he made his first professional animated film, *Love on the Wing*. In 1941 he followed Grierson to Canada, set up the animation department at the National Film Board and produced a series of outstanding films. With *Neighbors* (52), which won the Oscar for best documentary short, he developed pixillation, in which he photographed live actors on each frame of film to create an arresting robotic effect.

FRED MacMURRAY
US actor (1908-91)

Between 1934 and 1967 no more than two years passed without a film appearance by MacMurray, a former big band singer and one of cinema's best known comedy leading men. He also created memorable characters in *Double Indemnity* (44), *The Caine Mutiny* (54) and *The Apartment* (60). He made his film debut with *Girls Go Wild* (34) and was quickly playing leads, though rarely in big budget films. Contemporary comedy was varied with westerns, period pieces, adventure films and musicals, including *The Trail of the Lonesome Pine* (36), *True Confession* (37), *Dive Bomber* (41), *The Egg and I* (47), *There's Always Tomorrow* (56) and *Face of a Fugitive* (59). Then, thanks to the television series My Three Sons,

his career revived and he made a number of films for Disney (qv), including *The Absent-Minded Professor* (61), *Son of Flubber* (63), *Follow Me Boys!* (66) and *Charley and the Angel* (73). His last film was *The Swarm* (78).

STEVE McQUEEN
US actor (1930-80)

Sought after and highly paid, he was tough, supercool and given to sudden bursts of charm. Playing mostly action roles, his charismatic presence dominated the screen. A troubled man from a broken home, insecure and prone to violence, he was raised in an institution and became a drifter. He joined the marines but three years and a spell in a naval prison later he was drifting again before deciding to become an actor. Trained at New York's Neighborhood Playhouse

and the Actors Studio, he took over from Ben Gazzara (qv) on Broadway in Hatful of Rain, but his first film lead, in the sci-fi B-movie *The Blob* (58), went unnoticed. Stardom was established with *The Great Escape* (63) in which McQueen performed his own stunts as a PoW attempting a motorcycle getaway. Numerous hits included *The Cincinnati Kid* (65), *Bullitt* and the more sophisticated *The Thomas Crown Affair* (both 68). In 1977 he produced and starred in Ibsen's *An Enemy of the People*, revealing serious aspirations cut short by his death from cancer.

ANNA MAGNANI
Italian actress (1908-73)

A screaming woman who runs after a Nazi lorry laden with prisoners and is shot down in the street is one of international cinema's most indelible images. It is from Roberto Rossellini's (qv) *Rome, Open City* (45), the foundation of the neo-realist movement and the film that made Magnani a star after years as a bawdy nightclub singer and minor player in numerous Italian films. Half-Italian, half-Egyptian, illegitimate and raised in poverty by her grandmother, she had an earthy sensuality and passion. She was much prized for tragedy and comedy by such directors as Luchino Visconti, Jean Renoir (qqv) and her then lover Rossellini (qv), with whom she also made the grim *L'Amore* (48). Her film career was waning when Tennessee Williams created for her the lusty widow of *The Rose Tattoo* (55), which won her a best actress Oscar, and the shopkeeper looking for love in *The Fugitive Kind* (60). As the quality of her films declined she returned to stage and TV. Thousands attended her funeral.

NORMAN MAILER
US writer, film-maker (1923-)

Though best known as a novelist, his involvement in film stretches as far back as 1948 and his first novel, The Naked and the Dead, which was filmed 10 years later. *An American Dream* (66) showed Hollywood's blundering incomprehension of his work and caused Mailer to write, produce, direct and star in three features which gave full vent to his high-energy commitment and sizeable raft of ideas. *Wild 90* and *Beyond*

the Law (both 68) were initial stabs at directing and in *Maidstone* (71) he played Norman T Kingsley, a radical film-maker running for president. He gave his work the anti-style roughness of period underground films. He appeared in *The Year of the Woman* (73), *Town Bloody Hall* (79) and Jean-Luc Godard's (qv) *King Lear* (87) and then returned to directing with *Tough Guys Don't Dance* (87), which he skilfully adapted from his own play.

TERRENCE MALICK
US director (1943-)

Although he directed only two films, *Badlands* (73) and *Days of Heaven* (78), he enjoys cult status. Born in Ottawa, Illinois, the son of an oil company executive, he was raised in Texas and Oklahoma, before graduating from Harvard and Oxford. Working as a journalist on Newsweek and Life, he taught philosophy at the Massachusetts Institute of Technology before joining the American Film Institute. Although he is alleged to have worked on the screenplay of *Drive He Said* and *Dirty Harry* (both 71), his first acknowleged script was for *Pocket Money* (72). *Badlands*, based on the Starkweather-Fugate killing spree, was a haunting film about two sociopaths who are affected by the crude romanticism of popular culture. *Days of Heaven* is a visual poem about a torrid triangular relationship. Disillusioned by its lack of commercial success, he withdrew from films.

JOHN MALKOVICH
US actor (1953-)

A stage actor who entered films almost as an afterthought, he is a distinguished if mildly eccentric dramatic technician much loved by the critics. Born into a literary family, he took a drama degree at the University of Illinois and in 1976 co-founded the experimental theatre group Steppenwolf with the actor Gary Sinise, who later found fame in *Forrest Gump* (94). Malkovich formed links with playwrights and in 1982 won an Obie award for his performance in True West. He was offered *Places in the Heart* (84) which won him a best supporting actor Oscar. He made *The Killing Fields* (84), *Eleni* (85), *Making Mr Right*, *The Glass Menagerie* and *Empire of the Sun* (all 87), *Miles From Home* and *Dangerous Liaisons* (both 88), which was both a critical and commercial success. He went on to make the dire *The Sheltering Sky* (90), but came back as the psychotic assassin in Clint Eastwood's (qv) *In the Line of Fire* (93). He moves effortlessly between stage and cinema but has yet to fulfil his potential.

LOUIS MALLE
French director (1932-95)

He was one of the few French post-war directors to be successful in Europe and America. After the rbonne and film school he came Jacques Cousteau's sistant, co-directing *The Silent orld* (56). His directorial debut, e noir thriller *L'Ascenseur pour Echafaud* (57), launched Jeanne oreau (qv) with whom he also ade the award-winning *Les nants* (58). Moving coolly tween subjects and styles, his rly work encompasses studies of coholism, crime and a frolic arring Moreau and Bardot (qv) lled *Viva Maria* (65). His best n of the 1970s is *Lacombe icien* (74), about wartime llaboration. *Pretty Baby* (78), his ntroversial American debut, picted a child prostitute played Brooke Shields, but *Atlantic ty* (80), the rich portrait of an eing hoodlum, was much more ccessful. His most acclaimed ork is *Au Revoir les Enfants* 7), an autobiographical story of hoolboys in Nazi-occupied ance. Following the cool ception of *Damage* (92), he rned to an intimate record of a orkshop production of Uncle nya, *Vanya on 42nd Street* (94). e was married to the American tress Candice Bergen (qv).

AVID MAMET
'S writer, director (1947-)

ne of America's most celebrated aywrights and emerging film rectors, he has long been a arling of the critics for his heady, tellectual prose. Born in Chicago nd educated at Goddard College, ermont, where he became artist residence, his academic credits e among the most impressive in e film business. He began his eative career in the theatre with e influential Sexual Perversity in hicago, filmed as *About Last ight* (86), and came to theatrical ominence with Glengarry Glen oss. His directorial debut was the omplex, exciting thriller *House of ames* (87), followed by the afiosi conundrum *Things Change* 8) and *Homicide* (91). His reenplay credits include *The ostman Always Rings Twice* (81), *he Verdict* (82) and *Hoffa* (92).

OUBEN MAMOULIAN
'S director (1898-1987)

ducated in Moscow and London, e began as a theatre director,

visiting London on tour and staying to direct in the West End. He directed the first Porgy and Bess on Broadway in 1927. His cinema career began with the innovative early talkie, *Applause* (29). His fluid and rhythmic style was applied to everything, from the gangster film *City Streets* (31) through to *Silk Stockings* (57). In between he made *Dr Jekyll and Mr Hyde* (32), the musical comedy *Love Me Tonight* (32), Marlene Dietrich's (qv) *Song of Songs* and Garbo's (qv) *Queen Christina* (both 33). He directed Anna Sten in *We Live Again* (34), the first full-length Technicolor film *Becky Sharp* (35), the musicals *The Gay Desperado* (36) and *High Wide and Handsome* (37), William Holden (qv) in *Golden Boy* (39), Tyrone Power (qv) in *The Mark of Zorro* (40) and *Blood and Sand* (41), Gene Tierney and Henry Fonda (qqv) in *Rings on Her Fingers* (42) and Mickey Rooney (qv) in *Summer Holiday* (48).

HENRY MANCINI
US composer (1924-94)

As well as his *The Pink Panther* (64) theme and the ballad Moon River from *Breakfast at Tiffany's* (61), Mancini recorded more than 90 albums, received 20 Grammies from 72 nominations and four Oscars from 18 nominations. The son of Italian immigrants, he studied music at Juilliard before joining the Glenn Miller Orchestra as pianist and arranger. Appropriately, he broke into films as arranger of *The Glenn Miller Story* (54), for which he won his first Oscar nomination, and then worked on *The Benny Goodman Story* (56). He provided the poignant, percussive music for Orson Welles's (qv) *Touch of Evil* (58) and scored Peter Gunn for Blake Edwards (qv), beginning a partnership that was to embrace 26 films, including the soundtracks for *Days of Wine and Roses* (62), *The Great Race* (65) and *10* (79). He had a No 1 hit with his instrumental single Love Theme from Romeo and Juliet and wrote the unforgettable music for *Hatari!* (62), *Charade* (63) and *Two for the Road* (67).

JOSEPH L MANKIEWICZ
US director, screenwriter (1909-93)

A journalist who translated German silent film intertitles, he was the brother of Herman Mankiewicz, who wrote most of *Citizen Kane* (41). He guided the fated Taylor-Burton (qqv) *Cleopatra* (63) to screen success and was a film maker of exceptional wit and literacy, giving full value to the words. He drew first-rate performances from actors and his gifts are best exemplified in *A Letter to Three Wives* (49) and *All About Eve* (50), both of them Oscar winners for screenplay and direction. His range, however, was eclectic: *Five Fingers* (52) dealt with espionage in semi-documentary style, *Julius Caesar* (53) was restrained Shakespeare and he gave appropriate gusto to his only musical, *Guys and Dolls* (55). His share of failures included *The Barefoot Contessa* (54) and *Suddenly Last Summer* (59), which neither he nor Katharine Hepburn (qv) could rescue from Tennessee Williams's overwrought script.

ANTHONY MANN
US director (1906-67)

Mann made great westerns, but his arenas for conflict were men's minds. His heroes felt themselves tainted by the battles in which they were engaged. He developed his craft with some claustrophobic B-movies such as *T-Men* (48), but then opened out into the world of the frontier with *Winchester '73* (50), exploring a harder streak in James Stewart (qv) than had been seen before. *Bend of the River* (52) and *The Naked Spur* (53) followed,

testing character as much as pursuing action. He made the hagiographic *The Glenn Miller Story* (54) and the spectacular epic *El Cid* (61) and had modest success with *The Fall of the Roman Empire* (64) and *The Heroes of Telemark* (65). He died making *A Dandy in Aspic* (68), which was finished by Laurence Harvey (qv), its star.

JEAN MARAIS
French actor (1913-96)

A meeting with Jean Cocteau (qv) in 1937 changed his life. Rejected by the Paris Conservatory, Marais became a photographer's assistant before securing bit parts on stage. His dashing blond looks guaranteed him small roles in film, but his work with Cocteau (who wrote with Marais in mind) transformed him into an actor of substance. He made his name as a romantic hero in Delannoy's *L'Eternel Retour* (43) and moved on to a dual role in Cocteau's *La Belle et la Bête* (46). His popularity in France soared in Cocteau's *L'Aigle à deux Têtes* and *Les Parents Terribles* (both 48) and *Orphée* (50). *Le Gentleman de Cocody* (65) was one of the last films he made before he vanished, returning to grace the screen with mature character roles in *Ombre et Secrets* (83), *Parking* (85) and *Le Lien de Parenté* (86).

FREDRIC MARCH
US actor (1897-1975)

His family wanted him to be a banker, but after the University of Wisconsin and first world war army service he moved to New York in 1920 and turned to acting. He was an extra in films until 1926 and his first Broadway lead in The Devil in the Cheese. He was signed by Paramount and soon provided evidence of his emotional depth. He won an Oscar for his *Dr Jekyll and Mr Hyde* (32) and his best roles in the 1930s included Browning in *The Barretts of Wimpole Street* (34), Vronsky in *Anna Karenina* (35), Norman Maine in Wellman's (qv) *A Star Is Born* (37) and opposite Carole

Lombard (qv) in the comedy *Nothing Sacred* (37). He won his second Oscar for his memorable performance as a returning soldier in Wyler's (qv) *The Best Years of Our Lives* (46). He regularly alternated between theatre and film and won a New York Drama Critics award for Long Day's Journey into Night in 1956. In his later years his choice of roles remained astute and he closed his career with *The Iceman Cometh* (73)

GEORGE MARSHALL
US director (1891-1975)

With some 100 features and scores of one- and two-reelers to his credit, he was one of the most versatile of the leading studio directors. Born in Chicago, he was a railroad worker, professional baseball player and reporter before becoming an extra with Universal, where he became an all-round craftsman. After the second world war he worked for Pathé on Ruth Roland serials and Harry Carey (qv) westerns and then moved to Fox. Apart from directing Laurel and Hardy (qv), he worked with W C Fields (qv) on *You Can't Cheat an Honest Man* (39), Bob Hope (qv) in *The Ghost Breakers* (40) and ▷

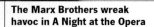

The Marx Brothers wreak havoc in A Night at the Opera

Monsieur Beaucaire (46), and set Dean Martin and Jerry Lewis (qv) on the road to success with *My Friend Irma* (49). His most memorable films include *Incendiary Blonde* (45) with Betty Hutton, *The Blue Dahlia* (46) with Alan Ladd and Veronica Lake (qqv), *Houdini* (53) with Tony Curtis (qv), the innovative musical *Red Garters* (54) and the droll western *The Sheepman* (58), with Glenn Ford and Shirley MacLaine (qqv).

HERBERT MARSHALL
British actor (1890-1966)

He epitomised the well-bred Englishman whose unflappable exterior masked deep, sensitive and occasionally passionate feelings. The son of an actor, he was assistant to a theatrical impresario before making the transition to acting in 1911. During the first world war he lost his right leg and disguised the handicap on film. In the 1920s he established himself in London and New York, made his screen debut in *Mumsie* (27) and followed it with the politically controversial *Dawn* (28). His American talkie debut was opposite Jeanne Eagels in *The Letter* (29). *Secrets of a Secretary* (31) with Claudette Colbert (qv) won him a part opposite Marlene Dietrich (qv) in *Blonde Venus* (32), followed by the finest of his sophisticated comedies, Ernst Lubitsch's (qv) *Trouble in Paradise* (32). He enjoyed amorous interludes with many leading ladies, including Gloria Swanson (qv). He was in the remake of *The Letter* (40) with Bette Davis (qv).

ENNY MARSHALL
S director (1942-)

ırn in the Bronx, Penny arscharelli's father was an dustrial film maker and her other a dance instructor. She tended the University of New exico and worked as a dance acher and actress in summer eatre productions during the id-1960s, The Danny Thomas our, then Saturday Night Live in e 1970s. She is known for her ft touch with emotional issues d light, social comedy. After acting in hit television shows she began directing with *Jumpin' Jack Flash* (86), a well-received spy comedy. She hit the jackpot with *Big* (88), a witty child inside a man's body scenario which grossed millions worldwide and made Tom Hanks (qv) a star. *Awakenings* (90) with Robin Williams and Robert De Niro (qqv) confirmed her critical reputation. *A League of Their Own* followed (92), but Marshall has yet to consolidate.

STEVE MARTIN
US actor, writer and comedian (1945-)

Born in Waco, Texas, his family moved to southern California when he was five years old. He graduated in theatre arts from UCLA and then wrote for the Smothers Brothers television show. He went on to perform his own material on Tonight, Saturday Night Live, in live stand-up comedy and on record, where his Wild and Crazy Guy routine was sharpened and extended. He made his film debut singing Maxwell's Silver Hammer in the dire *Sgt Pepper's Lonely Hearts Club Band* (78) and wrote and played the lead in *The Jerk* (79) directed by Carl Reiner (qv). Reiner was also responsible for other zany Martin films such as *Dead Men Don't Wear Plaid* (82), *The Man With Two Brains* (83) and *All of Me* (84). He is essentially a clown to whom the inexplicable occurs almost routinely, such as his conversations with a traffic sign in *L A Story* (91), but in a number of films he has revealed a capacity to play sensitive victims of circumstance: the 1930s travelling salesman in *Pennies From Heaven* (81), the fire chief in *Roxanne* (87), the suburban father in *Parenthood* (89) and the architect whose dream home is occupied by a woman claiming to be his wife in *Housesitter* (92).

LEE MARVIN
US actor (1924-87)

The hard man of American film for three decades, he came from a prosperous background in New York, joined the marines and was seriously wounded in the Pacific in 1944. He joined a theatre company, graduating from summer theatre to Broadway to TV, where Henry Hathaway (qv) discovered him. His break came in the war drama *Eight Iron Men* (52). He went from ubiquitous villain – most memorably throwing boiling coffee into Gloria Grahame's (qv) face in *The Big Heat* (53) – to hero, having consolidated his tough guy image in the TV series M Squad. He won an Oscar for *Cat Ballou* (65) as a drunken gunman and his evil, metal-nosed twin. It made him a top 10 star. He then led *The Dirty Dozen* (67), was remorselessly vengeful in the brutal *Point Blank* (67) and had an unlikely singing hit with I Was Born Under a Wandering Star from *Paint Your Wagon* (69). Latterly synonymous with undemanding but macho adventures, he had a last great role as the indomitable sergeant of *The Big Red One* (80).

THE MARX BROTHERS
US comedians (Chico 1891-1961, Harpo 1892-1964, Groucho 1895-1977, Zeppo 1901-79)

The most outrageously eccentric comedy team in Hollywood history, they made an art of anarchy. Groucho was a master of the cynical pun, Harpo a harp-playing mime artist who relished chaos, Chico a piano-playing flim-flam man who spoke in mock Italian and Zeppo was the straight man. Born in New York, the sons of a Jewish tailor, their mother Minna Schoenberg encouraged them to exploit their musical talents in vaudeville and then on Broadway where they developed their comedy act. Signed by Paramount, they reprised their show *The Cocoanuts* (29) and *Animal Crackers* (30) before completing their three finest films: *Monkey Business* (31), *Horse Feathers* (32) and their anti-war satire *Duck Soup* (33). After the latter flopped Thalberg (qv) signed them to MGM where they were teamed up with their celebrated foil Margaret Dumont. *A Night at the Opera* (35) was their most commercially successful film followed by *A Day at the Races* (37). Their last collaboration was *Love Happy* (49), although they appeared in separate sections of *The Story of Mankind* (57). Only Groucho continued in films, finishing with *Skidoo* (68).

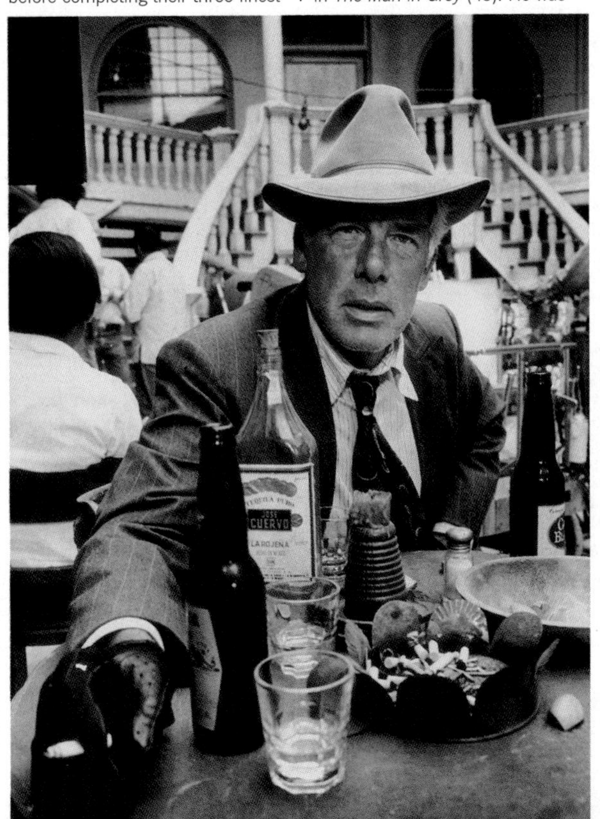

JAMES MASON
British actor (1909-84)

With his brooding good looks and mellifluous voice he was Britain's reigning box office star in the 1940s and remained in demand long after most of his contemporaries. After being ignominiously dismissed from his first film, *The Private Life of Don Juan* (34), he turned up in a series of "quota quickies" before making his mark as the sadistic aristocrat in *The Man in Grey* (43). He was equally impressive as the wounded IRA gunman in Carol Reed's (qv) *Odd Man Out* (47) and capitalised on his celebrity in America by moving there in 1947. In Hollywood he lost some of his edge, but excelled in *A Star Is Born* (54), *North by Northwest* (59) and *Lolita* (62). Even in old age, with his face set in a hangdog expression, he continued to secure leading roles, lending distinction to *Georgy Girl* (66), *Autobiography of a Princess* (75), *The Verdict* (82) and *The Shooting Party* (84).

MARCELLO MASTROIANNI
Italian actor (1923-96)

Italy's most famous actor internationally, Mastroianni was a draughtsman during the war, spent time in a German labour camp, escaped and hid in Venice. In Rome after the liberation he joined an amateur drama group and caught the attention of Visconti (qv). He won a reputation as an engaging actor in Italy, winning wider recognition in Visconti's *White Nights* (57). But it was as the world-weary, morally bankrupt journalist in Fellini's (qv) *La Dolce Vita* (60) that he gained fame. As a veteran of some 100 films, he distinguished himself as a skilled light comedian, romantic leading man and interpreter of serious roles. Nominated three times for an Oscar, his appearance in Robert Altman's (qv) *Prêt à Porter* (94) marked his third American film. Although married from 1950, he enjoyed several extra-marital liaisons and had a daughter by Catherine Deneuve (qv).

WALTER MATTHAU
US actor (1920-)

One of the cinema's most popular comic leading men, typically grouchy and acerbic, he studied journalism and played mostly villains in films, having established himself as a Broadway actor. Although his work was respected in his early films, it was only after Broadway success in The Odd Couple in 1965 that he moved to the top. He won an Oscar as best supporting actor in *The Fortune Cookie* (66) and other comedy successes followed: *The Odd Couple* and *The Secret Life of an American Wife* (68), *Cactus Flower* (69), *Plaza Suite, A New Leaf* and an Oscar nomination for *Kotch* (all 71), *Pete 'n' Tillie* (72), *The Front Page* (74), another Oscar nomination for *The Sunshine Boys* (75), *The Bad News Bears* (76), *House Calls* and *California Suite* (both 78), *Buddy Buddy* (81), *Grumpy Old Men* (93) and *IQ* (94). He has also done justice to straight dramatic roles, including *The Taking of Pelham One Two Three* (74) and *JFK* (91).

JESSIE MATTHEWS
British actress, dancer and singer (1907-81)

One of 11 children and born into poverty, she made her stage debut at the age of 10. As a teenager she was given a chorus line job by C B Cochran. A few unbilled parts in films followed and elocution lessons purged her cockney accent. She had wide eyes, prominent teeth and a spontaneous giggle and her dancing was breathtaking. After

Out of the Blue (31) and *There Goes the Bride* (32), Balcon (qv) signed her. She made an impact in *The Good Companions* (33) and *Friday the 13th* (33). Victor Saville's (qv) *Evergreen* (34) is the best of her 1930s musicals. She had a breakdown during filming and a Hollywood contract with MGM came to nothing. Her husband, Sonnie Hale, directed her in *Head over Heels* and *Gangway* (both 37) and *Sailing Along* (38), but his touch was pallid compared with Saville's. The war effectively ended her film career. Her marriage collapsed and an American tour was cancelled after a second breakdown. In 1963 she began playing Mrs Dale in the BBC radio soap. Her last years were spent modestly in suburbia.

CARL MAYER
Austrian screenwriter, director (1894-1944)

The co-author of *The Cabinet of Dr Caligari* (19), Mayer was one of the most potent figures in pre-Nazi German cinema. Thrown on the streets by a suicidal gambling father, his work contained several distorted father figures, of which Caligari was the first. His *Shattered* (21) was typical, about an obsessed railwayman and his love for a corrupted daughter, but it was the scripts for director F W Murnau (qv) that achieved status, especially with *The Last Laugh* (24). When the Nazis came to power he moved to Paris and wrote for Elisabeth Bergner (qv); *Ariane* (31) was one of his several likeable films. In Britain he worked as a consultant for Korda (qv), but he was no longer at the creative cutting edge and his word was seldom heeded. Like his father he was a gambler.

Hypnotic: Carl Mayer's Dr Caligari still horrifies today

LOUIS B MAYER
US mogul (1885-1957)

For years he was the highest paid man in America. A self-confident entrepreneur at an early age, Mayer was a scrap metal dealer in New Brunswick, Canada, and Boston before snapping up a

decaying cinema in Massachusetts. He made his first fortune from distributing *The Birth of a Nation* (15) in New England and his first serious attempt at production was with Anita Stewart in *Virtuous Wives* (18). After the creation of MGM he was driven by a commitment to his studio and its films. He was authoritarian, tyrannical, supportive of admirers but unyielding to those whose opposition he regarded as a personal attack. He not only signed up many stars (it was said MGM had "more stars than there are in the heavens") but also paid attention to production staff to ensure MGM films had an expensive shine. He was an instinctive populist, but his sure touch for common taste deserted him by 1951, the year he was ousted from MGM. A diehard Republican, he was a key figure in founding the Academy of Motion Picture Arts and Sciences in 1927 – an attempt by the moguls to bring the unions to heel, but now more associated with the Oscars.

GEORGES MELIES
French pioneer (1861-1938)

At school he excelled at art, but his father forced him into first working as a mechanic. He became an illusionist and illustrator in Paris and in 1888 bought Robert Houdin's theatre and showcased his imaginative craft. Inspired by the Lumière brothers (qv) he incorporated film into his magic show in 1896 and designed a camera. By 1897 he was making so many films that he used his theatre solely to screen them. The same year he built Europe's first film studio and started directing literary adaptations as well as special effects extravaganzas, including a version of *Cinderella* (99). His most famous work is the innovative *A Trip to the Moon* (02). He enjoyed international success before the public wearied of his magic experiments. In spite of this decline in popularity his most imaginative film, *The Conquest of the Pole* (12), was yet to come. He went back to magic in 1915.

Making magic: Méliès at work in Europe's first film studio

JEAN-PIERRE MELVILLE
French director, screenwriter (1917-73)

Influenced by American gangster novels and films, eight of his 13 productions dealt with criminals. The war delayed the start of his career, but in 1946 he formed his own company and made the impressive *Le Silence de la Mer* (49), a parable of the French resistance of which he was a member. He secured his reputation with *Les Enfants Terribles* (50), co-written with Cocteau (qv) from the latter's novel and brilliantly evoking the claustrophobic world of an obsessional teenage brother-sister relationship. Though not of the New Wave, he pre-dated its techniques ith his freewheeling location amera and jump-cutting in *Bob le lambeur* (55). Belmondo (qv) was ne sympathetic *Léon Morin Priest* 51), Alain Delon (qv) the cold-looded killer in *The Samurai* (67), which was perhaps the peak of Melville's romantic gangster films. Gestapo-occupied Lyon was the etting for *L'Armée des Ombres* 59), a compelling account of the wartime resistance.

ADOLPHE MENJOU
US actor (1890-1963)

He entered the film industry in 914, served in the first world war nd returned to the screen in 1921 n *The Sheik* and *The Three Musketeers*. He played the wealthy educer in Chaplin's (qv) first rama, *A Woman of Paris* (23) and was a roué in *The Marriage Circle* 24) and *The Ace of Cads* (26). He as the lover discarded by Marlene Dietrich (qv) in *Morocco* (30) and eceived an Oscar nomination as ne editor in *The Front Page* (31). Supporting roles included with Gary Cooper (qv) in *A Farewell to Arms* 32), Katharine Hepburn (qv) in everal films and Shirley Temple qv) in *Little Miss Marker* (34). His ast roles were in *Paths of Glory* 57) and the sour recluse weetened by *Pollyanna* (60).

WILLIAM CAMERON MENZIES
US director-designer (1896-1957)

Like Fritz Lang (qv), he trained as an architect; unlike Lang he was more concerned with how a film looked than with what it had to say, hence his futuristic sets for *Things to Come* (36), which he directed, and the dramatic panoramas of *Gone With the Wind* (39). He established the collaborative worth of production designers and his soaring designs won him an Oscar for *The Dove* (28). He worked on Douglas Fairbanks's (qv) and Alexander Korda's (qv) versions of *The Thief of Bagdad* (24 and 40 respectively), but his diligence could be expensive. A memo from David Selznick (qv) lamented that Menzies spent a year laying out pictorial ideas for *Gone With the Wind*. Typical of his production design is the sinister windmill sequence in Hitchcock's (qv) thriller *Foreign Correspondent* (40). Other than *Things to Come*, his directorial work was mediocre, though *Address Unknown* (44), about a hounded Nazi-American, is a B-movie thriller that alarms through its anger.

JOHNNY MERCER
US lyricist (1909-76)

Although he could not read music he wrote some of the most popular songs of the 1930s, 1940s and 1950s. He is probably best remembered for the words of Moon River from *Breakfast at Tiffany's* (61). He worked with some of the

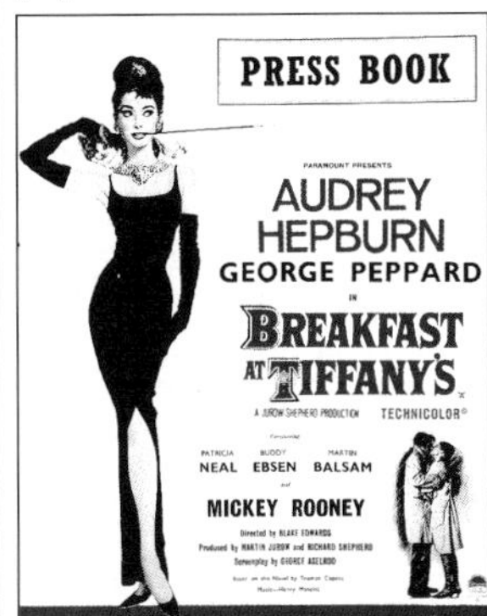

century's most celebrated composers, including Harold Arlen, Hoagy Carmichael, Jerome Kern, Henry Mancini, Harry Warren (qqv) and André Previn. He displayed a passion for word play and a capacity for absorbing local phrases. After writing Lazybones in 1933, his first hit song, he began his film career the same year and received 18 Oscar nominations, winning for On the Atchison Topeka and the Sante Fe (46), In the Cool, Cool, Cool of the Evening (51), Moon River and the title number from *Days of Wine and Roses* (62). He also wrote the lyrics to a number of film musicals including *You Were Never Lovelier* (42), *Seven Brides for Seven Brothers* (54) and *Daddy Long Legs* (55).

ISMAIL MERCHANT
Indian producer, director (1936-)

He was born in Bombay and was an MBA from New York University. With screenwriter Ruth Prawer Jhabvala and director James Ivory (qqv) he is responsible for *Shakespeare Wallah* (65), their very first success, *Roseland* (77), *Heat and Dust* (83), *The Bostonians* (84), *A Room With a View* (86), *Howards End* (92), *The Remains of the Day* (93) and *Jefferson in*

America (95). He also produced *The Deceivers* and *The Perfect Murder* (both 88) and *The Ballad of the Sad Cafe* (91). He returned to directing (he was nominated for a best director Oscar in 1960 for *The Creation of a Woman*) in 1994 with *In Custody*. An ideal producer, in that he mixes sharp deal-making instincts with a passion for and sensitivity towards cinema, he has ensured that Ivory's films have not remained exclusive. He has even found time for a cookbook, Ismail Merchant's Indian Cuisine.

Greek goddess: Mercouri was famous after Never on Sunday

MELINA MERCOURI
Greek actress (1923-94)

Fluent in four languages, she gave her definitive performance as a Piraeus prostitute in *Never on Sunday* (60), written and directed by Jules Dassin (qv), who became her second husband. Nominated for a best actress Oscar, she shared honours with Jeanne Moreau (qv) at the 1960 Cannes Festival. The daughter of a politician, she acted on stage from her mid-teens but her first film was *Stella* (55). Before *Never on Sunday* her best role was in Joseph Losey's (qv) *The Gypsy and the Gentleman* (58). *Topkapi* (64) preceded her divorce from Dassin in 1966, with whom she continued to work, though the results, including *10.30PM Summer* (66) and *Promise at Dawn* (70), were not well received. Politically active in opposition to the military government in Greece in the late 1960s, she was exiled. On her return in 1974 she went into politics, becoming a member of parliament and then a minister.

BURGESS MEREDITH
US actor (1908-)

Born in Cleveland, Ohio, he was a newspaper reporter before making his name on Broadway in Maxwell Anderson's Winterset in 1935, playing the role on film the following year. He appeared in *Idiot's Delight* (39), as George in *Of Mice and Men* (40) and Ernie Pyle in *The Story of GI Joe* (45). He wrote and appeared in Renoir's (qv) *The Diary of a Chambermaid* (46) with Paulette Goddard (qv), his then wife, and became renowned for playing wise

supporting characters. His left-wing connections brought him to the attention of the House Un-American Activities Committee, but he survived to appear in such films as *The Man on the Eiffel Tower* (49), which he also directed. In the 1960s he played the Penguin in the Batman television series, a role repeated in the 1966 film, and he was nominated for an Oscar for *The Day of the Locust* (75). He proved by his performance as Stallone's (qv) trainer in four *Rocky* films (76-90) that he could still stamp his authority on a work.

MICKEY MOUSE
US animated character (1927-)

Reputedly dreamed up by Disney (qv) and his wife, his first incarnation was as Mortimer Mouse and primitive. Ub Iwerks (qv), Disney's assistant, was responsible for the original drawings which depicted a jovial but blank-eyed mouse with huge ears. Although two silent shorts had been completed, the talkie *Steamboat Willie* (28) was the first to be released. Many short animated films followed featuring Mickey and such regulars as Minnie and Pegleg Pete. The arrival of Donald Duck in 1936 ended Mickey's sole reign, but his image has been retained as the generic symbol of the Disney empire. His role in *Fantasia* (40) comes during the Sorcerer's Apprentice sequence, but his fame is based more on his iconic status than mere film appearances.

TOSHIRO MIFUNE
Japanese actor (1920-)

Probably the West's most recognised Japanese actor, he was born in Tsingtao, China, to Japanese parents. He ventured into films after the end of the war. A flamboyant actor, he was impressive as a fearsome samurai warrior. Making his debut in *These Foolish Times* (46), he graduated to playing leads before beginning his long collaboration with Kurosawa (qv) in *Drunken Angel* (48). Critically acclaimed for playing the bandit-rapist in *Rashomon* (50), he followed it up as the elemental leader in *Seven Samurai* (54) and as the lone samurai in *Yojimbo* (61), which won him a best actor award at Venice. After making his directorial debut with *The Legacy of the Five Hundred Thousand* (64) and starring in his last Kurosawa film *Red Beard* (65), he moved to Hollywood for *Grand Prix* (66) and then co-starred in *Hell in the Pacific* (69). He also played Admiral Yamamoto in *Midway* (76).

BERNARD MILES
British actor (1907-91)

An actor of Dickensian eccentricity, he appeared in 45 films, bringing an irresistible earthiness to his roles. Shortly after his stage debut in 1930 he began to be seen regularly on the screen, although his Iago in the Old Vic's 1941 Othello established him as an actor of merit. A year later he triumphed as the chief petty officer who loses his wife in Noël Coward and David Lean's (qqv) *In Which We Serve* (42). He co-directed and wrote the wartime rural drama *Tawny Pipit*

(44) and was memorable as the faltering Joe Gargery in Lean's *Great Expectations* (46). His other notable performances include the down-at-heel clerk Newman Noggs in *Nicholas Nickleby* (47), the decrepit doorman in *The Smallest Show on Earth* (57) and the butler in *Heavens Above* (63). He is also renowned as the founder of London's Mermaid Theatre. He was made a life peer in 1979.

LEWIS MILESTONE
US director (1895-1980)

This once great director's decline can be traced from *All Quiet on the Western Front* (30) via *A Walk in the Sun* (46) to *The Halls of Montezuma* (51). The first is one of the most indignant anti-war films ever made, the second a poetic acceptance of battle, the third a jingoistic hymn to American arms. Hollywood may have changed the way the Ukrainian-born master looked at life, but a sense of irony was always present in his work, from *The Front Page* (31) to *The Strange Love of Martha Ivers* (46), a tongue-in-cheek film noir.

He described himself as an opportunist – *All Quiet on the Western Front*'s final butterfly scene came from watching his car's windscreen wipers during a storm – but he was an artist who, like his tracking shots, just went sideways. He certainly did not deserve Brando's (qv) tantrums on *Mutiny on the Bounty* (62).

RAY MILLAND
US actor (1907-86)

A prolific character actor and a leading man for many years, Reginald Truscott-Jones was born in Wales. He began in films in Britain and moved to Hollywood for the bulk of his long career, although he returned to Britain for *French Without Tears* (39). *Beau Geste* (39), *The Major and the Minor* (42) and *Ministry of Fear* (44) were among his notable films before *The Lost Weekend* (45) won him a best actor Oscar. *The Big Clock* and *So Evil My Love* (both 48), *The Thief* (52) and Hitchcock's (qv) *Dial M for Murder* (54) were his best. He began directing as well as acting with *A Man Alone* (55) followed by such interesting projects as *The*

Safecracker (58) and *Panic in the Year Zero!* (62). He graced Roger Corman's (qv) *The Premature Burial* (62) and *X – The Man With the X-Ray Eyes* (63). *Love Story* (70) revived his career and he made at least one film a year from 1972 to 1984. His last film was *The Sea Serpent* (86).

ANN MILLER
US actress, dancer (1923-)

A long-legged attractive Texan who married and divorced three millionaires, she began in Hollywood at 13 (her mother lied about her age to get her employed and reference books often make her four years older) and entranced producers with her high-octane personality. She began at RKO but reached her peak at MGM, always

as a second lead in acid-tongued roles. Her talents were largely relegated to enlivening now deservedly forgotten musicals, such as *Radio City Revels* (38), but she took her chances when they came: the ambitious Broadway climber deserting Astaire (qv) for stardom in *Easter Parade* (48), her zany anthropology student dancing up a storm in *On the Town* (49) and a memorable Bianca in *Kiss Me Kate* (53). Of her few non-musical roles the best was the ballet student daughter in Capra's (qv) *You Can't Take It With You* (38). She retired in 1956, but took over Mame from Angela Lansbury (qv) on Broadway and was a triumph on stage with Mickey Rooney (qv) in Sugar Babies in 1979.

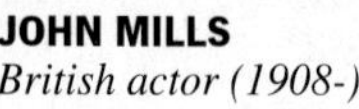

JOHN MILLS
British actor (1908-)

An endearing institution of the British cinema with more than 80 films to his credit, he has progressed from resolutely stiff-upper-lip heroes in the 1950s to the village idiot in *Ryan's Daughter* (70), for which he won an Oscar. He was born in Suffolk and worked as a clerk before joining a

London revue. After his first film appearance in *The Midshipmaid* (32), his fresh-faced charm appealed in such diverse roles as Shorty Blake in *In Which We Serve* (42), Pip in *Great Expectations* (46) and the title role in *Scott of the Antarctic* (48). He triumphed in *Tunes of Glory* (60) and increasingly became associated with memorable character parts, particularly opposite his daughter Hayley in *Tiger Bay* (59), as the world-weary officer in *King Rat* (65) and as the working-class father in *The Family Way* (67). He directed himself in *Sky West and Crooked* (65) and played the viceroy of India in *Gandhi* (82). His second wife is the playwright Mary Hayley Bell. He was knighted in 1977.

LIZA MINNELLI
US actress, singer (1946-)

Her debut, aged three, was in the final scene of *In the Good Old Summertime* (49). The daughter of Judy Garland and Vincente Minnelli (qqv), she had a difficult childhood and in adult life has fought

Liza Minnelli and her father Vincente at a Hollywood party

oholism and emotional
oblems. Her parents divorced
en she was five and she flitted
tween them, learning
owbusiness from two of its most
ebrated practitioners. She was
Broadway at the age of 17 and
n a Tony two years later. She
de a modest film debut as
ert Finney's (qv) American
retary in *Charlie Bubbles* (67)
d was nominated for an Oscar
The Sterile Cuckoo (69). She
n it for her Sally Bowles in Bob
sse's (qv) *Cabaret* (72). Her TV
ecials and stage shows have also
n awards. Her film career has
en sadly sporadic, considering
r talent, although Scorsese's (qv)
w York, New York (77) and
hur (81) are notable. Her most
ent role was as the dance
cher in *Stepping Out* (91).

NCENTE MINNELLI
S director (1903-86)

s films for MGM epitomise all
t was stylish yet affectingly
ocent about Hollywood in the
40s and 1950s. He was a set
d costume designer in Chicago
d New York, became art director
the Radio City Music Hall in
33 and then directed stage
sicals. He moved to film in the
40s, directing the first all-black
sical, *Cabin in the Sky* (43), as
ll as sequences for Judy Garland
), his wife, in *Ziegfeld Follies* and
the Clouds Roll By (both 46).
eir three films together included
et Me in St Louis (44). He went
to tackle a range of genres from
iable comedy, such as *Father of
e Bride* (50), to *Lust for Life* (56),
biography of Van Gogh, but he
l be best remembered for his
mptuously designed musical
owcases for Garland, Kelly and
taire (qqv), particularly *The Band
agon* (53). His films garnered 20
cars, six for *An American in
ris* (51) including best film.

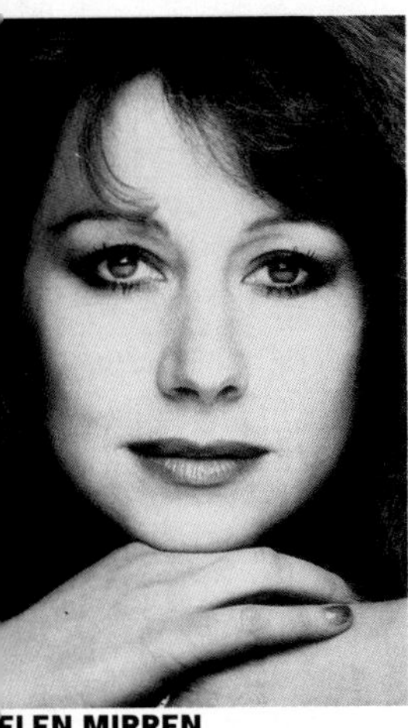

ELEN MIRREN
ritish actress (1945-)

ne of the most admired actresses
orking today, she was with the
ational Youth Theatre from
63-64 after convent school and
acher training college. She was a spellbinding talent, playing Cleopatra at the Old Vic by 1965. She has played all the leading classical roles, often returning to appear with the Royal Shakespeare Company. Her films include *O Lucky Man!* (73), *The Long Good Friday* (80), *Cal* (84) and *The Cook, the Thief, His Wife and Her Lover* (89). She attracted international acclaim for the award-winning television series Prime Suspect and was nominated for a best supporting actress Oscar for her Queen Charlotte in *The Madness of King George* (95).

ROBERT MITCHUM
US actor (1917-97)

As a sleepy eyed, nonchalant tough guy he has made more than 100 films, but only late in life received critical acknowledgment. After a restless youth, menial jobs and a boxing career, he found his way via local theatre into B-movies, making his name and receiving his only Oscar nomination for *The Story of GI Joe* (45). He played soldiers, adventurers, private eyes and was a handsome co-star for leading ladies from Loretta Young to Marilyn Monroe (qqv). His biggest hit was the medical melodrama *Not as a Stranger* (55); his most remarkable performance, the demented preacher of *The Night of the Hunter* (55). His own favourite was playing a marine trapped on a Japanese-held island with Deborah Kerr (qv) in *Heaven Knows Mr Allison* (57). His presence retained its potency, oozing menace in *Cape Fear* (62), weariness in *The Friends of Eddie Coyle* (73) or a fine Philip Marlowe in *Farewell My Lovely* (75). He also played the cuckold in *Ryan's Daughter* (70). He was married to his childhood sweetheart for more than 50 years.

TOM MIX
US actor (1880-1940)

He was the most popular cowboy star of the silent cinema. The son of a poor Pennsylvania lumber worker, Mix toured America with a wild west show and won the national riding and rodeo championship in 1909. Although his early studio publicity claimed he had fought in the Spanish-American war, the Boxer Rebellion and the Boer war, none of it was true. He started out rounding up cattle for the Selig company's *Ranch Life in the Great Southwest* (10), but he became an actor in *An Apache's Gratitude* (13), *Cactus Jake – Heartbreaker* (14) and *The Taming of Grouchy Bill* (16). The 100 or more one- and two-reel films he made as both actor and director were initially driven by humour, but soon turned to hair-raising action. After his arrival at Fox in 1917 he became a star, appearing in more than 60 westerns. On screen he never smoked, drank or fought without reason. He joined a circus after the advent of sound, but Universal lured him back for several westerns including *Destry Rides Again* (32) and *The Miracle Rider* (35). He then left films to found a circus and died in a car crash.

KENJI MIZOGUCHI
Japanese director (1898-1956)

In spite of a poverty stricken childhood in Tokyo and unstable teenage years (he left school at the age of 13 and his mother died when he was 17), he trained as an artist and newspaper designer and started a theatre group. He acted briefly in films before becoming an assistant director and then, in 1922, a director. His work has been acclaimed as among the most poetic and expressive in cinema history, characteristics typified by his most widely seen film, the haunting fable *Ugetsu Monogatari* (53). His other most significant films include *The Life of Oharu* (52), *Sansho Dayu* and *Chikamatsu Monogatari* (both 54). They all contain examples of his painstakingly and richly detailed frames and his interest in the psychology of Japanese women. Along with his countrymen Ozu and Kurosawa (qv), he is a master of Japanese cinema.

MARILYN MONROE
US actress (1926-62)

The ultimate screen goddess and an icon of the 20th century, Norma Jean Mortenson was born to an unmarried, unstable mother and raised in foster homes. She married, worked in a munitions factory, modelled for pin-ups, screen tested, was cast in a few bit parts and dropped by Twentieth Century Fox before she was 20. She struggled between studios in small roles before making a mark in *The Asphalt Jungle* (50), but her voluptuous sexuality and comedic instincts saw her rise meteorically, reaching her apotheosis as the definitive blonde siren in *Gentlemen Prefer Blondes* (53). Much of her subsequent material was banal, but her impact was spectacular. She is beloved as the innocent fantasy girl exacerbating *The Seven Year Itch* (55), the boisterously wooed "chantoosie" of *Bus Stop* (56), the wounded bombshell Sugar in *Some Like It Hot* (59) and the sad divorcee of *The Misfits* (61) – eerily the last film for Monroe, Gable and Clift (qqv). Her second husband was the baseball hero Joe DiMaggio, her third, the playwright Arthur Miller and her lovers included President John F Kennedy and reportedly his brother Robert. She was a relentless self-improver. Her death from a barbiturates overdose seemed the inevitable outcome to her unhappy life, guaranteeing that the legend will endure beyond that of any other Hollywood star.

YVES MONTAND
French actor (1921-91)

Born near Florence, the son of Jewish peasants, the family moved to Marseille when Mussolini came to power. Ivo Levi left school at 11 and had a succession of jobs until he was taken on as a music hall singer. He moved to the Moulin Rouge in Paris where he met his first lover Edith Piaf and appeared in *Etoile sans Lumière* (46). Marcel Carné (qv) spotted him and put him in *Les Portes de la Nuit* (46). In 1951 he married the actress Simone Signoret (qv) and his career took off with *La Salaire de la Peur* (53) followed by *Tempi Nostri* (53) and *Napoléon* (55). He went to Hollywood for *Let's Make Love* (60) with Monroe (qv) and *Grand Prix* (66) brought him fame outside France. Montand and Signoret were notable leftwingers and he began to take more parts with a political theme. Despite the fact that his flame flickered less brightly in Hollywood, he continued to be popular in France and his career there continued with *Jean de Florette* and *Manon des Sources* (both 86), which were his critical swan-song. When he died thousands lined the Paris streets.

ROBERT MONTGOMERY
US actor, director (1904-81)

He was a popular MGM leading man, playing opposite Norma Shearer, Greta Garbo, Joan Crawford and Myrna Loy (qqv). *Their Own Desire* (29), *The Divorcee* (30), *Inspiration* (31), *Forsaking All Others* (34) and *The Last of Mrs Cheyney* (37) were key films. Although popular with the public he fell foul of the studio by helping to found the Screen Actors Guild, becoming president for four terms. MGM then cast him in *Night Must Fall* (37) and the audience responded to him. He received an Oscar nomination for best actor, as he did for *Here Comes Mr Jordan* (41). In the war he was a naval lieutenant commander. His later films included John Ford's (qv) *They Were Expendable* (45), where he stood in for the director, and he directed *Lady in the Lake* and *Ride the Pink Horse* (both 47) and *Eye Witness* (50) among others. He also advised President Eisenhower on his TV appearances.

Flair and laughter: Montand (right) and (left) the Pythons

MONTY PYTHON
British actors, writers (1969-)

The Python team of John Cleese, Terry Jones, Eric Idle, Graham Chapman, Terry Gilliam (qv) and Michael Palin, are responsible for five ensemble films, of which two are reworkings of the TV series. Each has individual films, the most successful of which has been *A Fish Called Wanda* (88), for which Cleese received a best actor Bafta and a screenplay Oscar nomination. Palin also shone as K-k-k-Ken. The team's films are characteristically anarchic outings that harness the surreal sketch form of the TV shows to grander big-screen conventions, taking low-budget swipes at them along the way: the Arthurian saga which cannot stretch to horses, the biblical epic with a cast of dozens. *The Meaning of Life* (83) won a special jury prize at Cannes, but the team's most sustained act of cinema and the most pointedly funny – because it put forward serious arguments about the nature of faith – was *The Life of Brian* (79). Christian groups in Britain and America failed to see the joke and lobbied for it to be banned. It passed the British censors, although some local authorities refused to screen it.

COLLEEN MOORE
US actress (1900-88)

Such was her celebrity in the 1920s that her name adorned clothes and cosmetics and a doll was fashioned in her image. Although a siren of the silents, she was equally at home in serious roles and comedy and was one of the highest paid stars of her era. After her uncle, the editor of The

Chicago Examiner, helped manoeuvre D W Griffith's (qv) *Intolerance* (16) past the censor, the film maker agreed to take the aspiring actress under his wing. She became a star in *Flaming Youth* (23) and set the jazz age kicking. She continued to shock in *The Perfect Flapper* (24), *Naughty but Nice* (27) and *Synthetic Sin* (29). Her only sound film of significance was *The Power and the Glory* (33) in which she played Spencer Tracy's (qv) spurned wife. She later turned to writing and business, combining the two in her book, How Women Can Make Money in the Stock Market.

DUDLEY MOORE
British actor (1935-)

He made a rare transition from British television comedy to Hollywood celebrity after starring opposite Bo Derek in Blake Edwards's (qv) sex comedy *10* (79). He was dubbed the "sex thimble", a reference both to his height and his unlikely elevation to the ranks of lust object for female audiences. He was raised in Dagenham, London, and won an organ scholarship to Oxford University. He sprang to prominence in the influential satirical revue Beyond the Fringe in 1961 alongside Oxbridge graduates Alan Bennett, Jonathan Miller and Peter Cook. His friendship with Cook blossomed and they became a TV double act as well as playing the outrageously profane Derek & Clive on record. Many of his early film appearances, such as *The Wrong Box* (66) and the cult hit *Bedazzled* (67), were with Cook. Of

his later Hollywood roles only *Arthur* (81), in which he played a puerile playboy, repeated the popular success of *10*. In spite of an uneven film career, he has delivered notable performances in such films as *Crazy People* (90) and *Blame it on the Bellboy* (92) that have confirmed his unique comic presence in films.

ROGER MOORE
British actor (1927-)

He is best known for playing James Bond in seven films. His film career was interrupted by military service, but he resumed it with *Paper Orchid* (49) and moved to America for television work and films such as *The Last Time I Saw Paris* (54), *The King's Thief* (55) and *The Sins of Rachel Cade* (61). Worldwide exposure on TV in Ivanhoe, Maverick and particularly The Sain contributed to his being offered the

Bond films, from *Live and Let Die* (73) via *The Spy Who Loved Me* (77) to *A View to a Kill* (85). TV success in The Persuaders with Tony Curtis (qv) and lesser films alternated with Bond, including *Gold* (74), *The Wild Geese* (78) and *The Cannonball Run* (81). *Bullseye* (90) teamed him effectively with Michael Caine (qv).

AGNES MOOREHEAD
US actress (1906-74)

Orson Welles (qv) brought her to Hollywood, but Hollywood did not know what to do with her. Despite her presence as Kane's mother in *Citizen Kane* (41), her precise delivery and sharp features typecast her in shrewish roles. Welles protected her talents for another couple of films, *The Magnificent Ambersons* (42), for which she received an Oscar nomination, and *Journey into Fear* (43). She illuminated other films that could never touch those highs: *Jane Eyre* (44), in which she was reunited with Welles, the 100-plus-year-old woman in *The Last Moment* (47) and in the Gothic revival of *Hush . . . Hush, Sweet Charlotte* (64). She is probably best remembered as the waspish granny in the Bewitched TV series.

KENNETH MORE
British actor (1914-82)

A versatile star of memorable British films such as *Genevieve* (53), *Reach for the Sky* (56) and *The Admirable Crichton* (57). He was born in Gerrards Cross, Buckinghamshire, and tried fur trapping in Canada before beginning his film career in *Look Up and Laugh* (35). Small parts, interrupted by navy duty during the second world war, led to *Chance of a Lifetime* (49) in which he played an idealist engineer in a worker's co-operative. *Genevieve* brought him star status and he received the best actor award from Bafta for *Doctor in the House* (54) and an accolade from Venice for the film version of Terence Rattigan's *The Deep Blue Sea* (55). He was excellent as a starchy hero in *North West Frontier* (59), *Sink the Bismark!* (60) and *The Longest Day* (62), in which he marched up and down the Normandy beaches with a bulldog. His last appearance was in the Mark Twain send-up *The Spaceman and King Arthur* (79). He died from Parkinson's disease.

JEANNE MOREAU
French actress (1928-)

In the view of most directors and critics during the early 1960s, Moreau was head and shoulders above other actresses. Born in Paris, the daughter of a Lancashire chorus girl and a French barman, she stayed with her father when the marriage broke up in 1939. She studied at the Paris Conservatoire, moving on to an illustrious period at the Comédie Française and her first film role was in *Dernier Amour* (48). She struggled for 10 years to crack screen stardom, making a string of inferior films. Then *Les Liaisons Dangereuses* (59) brought her great attention, Antonioni's (qv) *La Notte* (61) followed and then a handful of films for Godard and Truffaut (qqv), including *Jules et Jim* (61). She flirted with films outside France, including Joseph Losey's (qv) *Eva* (62). She made many memorable films with the director Louis Malle (qv), most notably *Le Feu Follet* (63). *Lumière* (76), which she also directed, enhanced her reputation, followed by the much praised *L'Adolescente* (79). In recent years she has appeared with her customary distinction.

ENNIO MORRICONE
Italian composer (1928-)

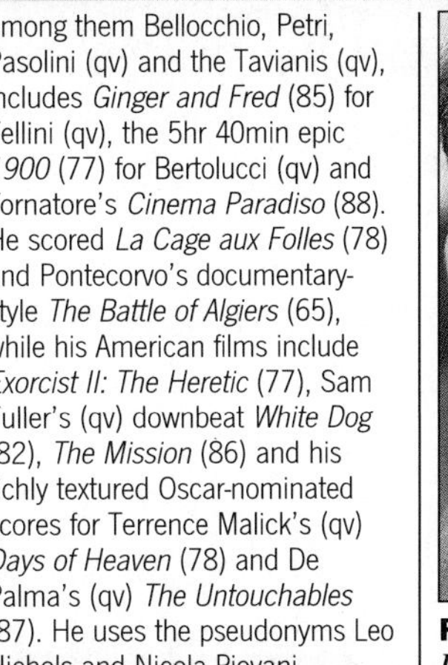

He studied music at the Santa Cecilia Conservatory in Rome and has worked on more than 350 original film scores since 1961. He came to prominence with his haunting music for Sergio Leone's (qv) spaghetti westerns, incorporating choruses, solo voices and whistling in *The Good, the Bad and the Ugly* (66). His work with prominent Italian directors, among them Bellocchio, Petri, Pasolini (qv) and the Tavianis (qv), includes *Ginger and Fred* (85) for Fellini (qv), the 5hr 40min epic *1900* (77) for Bertolucci (qv) and Tornatore's *Cinema Paradiso* (88). He scored *La Cage aux Folles* (78) and Pontecorvo's documentary-style *The Battle of Algiers* (65), while his American films include *Exorcist II: The Heretic* (77), Sam Fuller's (qv) downbeat *White Dog* (82), *The Mission* (86) and his richly textured Oscar-nominated scores for Terrence Malick's (qv) *Days of Heaven* (78) and De Palma's (qv) *The Untouchables* (87). He uses the pseudonyms Leo Nichols and Nicola Piovani.

PAUL MUNI
US actor (1895-1967)

He brought a perfectionist's zeal to the parts he played, even analysing the impact of make-up for each role. As a child actor in Austria he appeared on stage with his parents, had his first English-speaking role on Broadway aged 31 and was signed by Fox in 1929. Unhappy with his first two films, including *The Valiant* (29), which won him an Oscar nomination, he returned to Broadway before *Scarface* and *I Am a Fugitive From a Chain Gang* (both 32) launched him as a star. He appeared in many socially authentic dramas of the period for Warner, but it was his biopics that drew his biggest audiences. *The Story of Louis* ▷

The 10 best fantasies

Bride of Frankenstein (1935)
Best of all mad-scientist dramas, filled with extravagant wit

ET The Extra-Terrestrial (1982)
Spielberg's astonishing view of the power of childhood innocence

Fantasia (1940)
Walt Disney's pioneering, exciting mix of music and animation

Forbidden Planet (1956)
The Tempest restaged as a sci-fi outer-space adventure

Invasion of the Body Snatchers (1956)
Aliens have never replicated humans more terrifyingly

It's a Wonderful Life (1947)
Frank Capra's sentimental masterpiece uses a "what-if?" theme

Stairway to Heaven (A Matter of Life and Death) (1946)
Powell and Pressburger's singular vision of the celestial world

Star Wars (1977)
George Lucas's brilliant concept of a future world long ago

2001: A Space Odyssey (1968)
A masterpiece by Stanley Kubrick, as astronauts track alien life

The Wizard of Oz (1939)
Judy Garland never surpassed her role in this children's classic

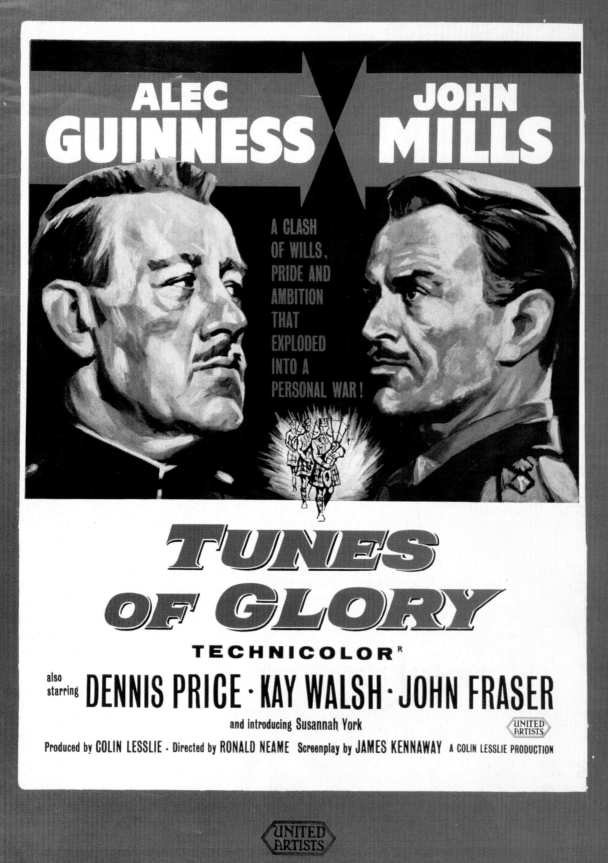

EXHIBITORS' CAMPAIGN BOOK

JOHN
MILLS

A CLASH
OF WILLS,
PRIDE AND
AMBITION
THAT
EXPLODED
INTO A
PERSONAL WAR!

TECHNICOLOR[R]

also starring DENNIS PRICE · KAY WALSH · JOHN FRASER

and introducing Susannah York

UNITED ARTISTS

Produced by COLIN LESSLIE · Directed by RONALD NEAME Screenplay by JAMES KENNAWAY A COLIN LESSLIE PRODUCTION

UNITED ARTISTS

Pasteur (36), for which he won an)scar, and *The Life of Emile Zola* 37) were high achievements. After ows over the roles he was offered e left Warner and demand for his skills withered, yet he managed to each beyond the easy sentiment of *The Last Angry Man* (59), his :nal film role.

'RIEDRICH WILHELM IURNAU
Jerman director (1889-1931)

Vhether letting his camera stare nblinkingly in *Schloss Vogelöd* 21) or giving it wings in *The Last augh* (24), he used it to heighten is films' illusion of reality. Vith Fritz Lang (qv) he was the re-eminent exponent of German xpressionism, having studied hilosophy at Heidelberg and vorked with Max Reinhardt in Berlin before he began directing 1919. Concentrating on the orror genre, he produced his nasterpiece, *Nosferatu* (22), naking the most of its natural ocations. Based on Bram Stoker's Dracula (and condemned by Stoker's widow for breach of opyright), it is a film of tmospheric intensity aided by the houlish figure of Max Schreck as ne count. Murnau followed it with hree more masterworks, all tarring Emil Jannings (qv), *The ast Laugh* and *Tartuffe* (26), ased on the Molière play, and *aust* (26). Lured to Hollywood in 927 he directed two more iumphs, the haunting, Oscar-inning *Sunrise* (27) and *Tabu* 31), with the documentary film-naker Robert Flaherty (qv), before s death in a car crash.

DDIE MURPHY
JS actor (1961-)

s a schoolboy in Brooklyn and ueens, New York, he began riting and performing stand-up omedy at local venues. He was ired by the Saturday Night Live elevision programme before he as 20 years old, establishing his opularity by creating a stream of utlandish characters. His film ebut in Walter Hill's (qv) comedy riller *48 HRS* (82) was explosive: reetwise and littered with bscenities. His best performance

came a year later in the snappy comedy *Trading Places* (83), though his biggest commercial success was as the rebellious detective Axel Foley in *Beverly Hills Cop* (84), which led to two lesser sequels. The concert film *Eddie Murphy Raw* (87) returned him to stand-up, but was marred by misogyny and homophobia. He has been a restless actor, perhaps frustrated that none of his roles, nor his appalling directorial debut *Harlem Nights* (89), have found success. He is one of cinema's startling comic talents and later films, *Boomerang* and *The Distinguished Gentleman* (both 92) and *The Nutty Professor* (96) suggest he is setting his sights on romantic comedies.

ALLA NAZIMOVA
Russian actress (1879-1945)

Crimean-born Nazimova was one of the most exotic émigrés to early Hollywood. A gifted violinist, she went from the St Petersburg Conservatory to theatre training with Stanislavsky in Moscow. At 25 she became the toast of Broadway in Ibsen. She made her film debut in 1916 and was built up as "The Woman of a Thousand Moods", while Hollywood was fascinated by stories of scandalous parties at The Garden Of Allah, her estate off Sunset Boulevard. She created vehicles for herself with the director Charles Bryant, her common law husband, which included *Camille* (21), Ibsen's *A Doll's House* (22) and Wilde's *Salome* (23). After 17 films she left Bryant and Hollywood in 1925 for the theatre, but returned for strong character roles including Tyrone Power's (qv) mother in *Blood and Sand* (41) and the marquesa in *The Bridge of San Luis Rey* (44). Her final part was in David O Selznick's (qv) *Since You Went Away* (44).

Neame between Peck and Rank on A Million Pound Note

ANNA NEAGLE
British actress (1904-86)

When still a chorus girl she was urged by Herbert Wilcox (qv), her mentor and later husband, into the decorous sauciness of *Nell Gwyn* (34) and *Peg of Old Drury* (35). She was then swathed in the muffling good taste of two Victoria films, *Victoria the Great* (37) and *Sixty Glorious Years* (38). After that came plucky British heroines, including *Nurse Edith Cavell* (39) and Amy Johnson in *They Flew Alone* (42). After teaming with Michael Wilding in the wartime weepie *Piccadilly Incident* (46), she won box office approval with a series of upper-class women in *The Courtneys of Curzon Street* (47), *Spring in Park Lane* (48) and *Maytime in Mayfair* (49). Then it was back to war with *Odette* (50) and *The Lady With the Lamp* (51).

RONALD NEAME
British director, cinematographer (1911-)

One of British cinema's most accomplished craftsmen who, during the brief golden age in the mid-1940s, was a key figure in some outstanding films. Neame's mother was the silent actress Ivy Close and his father the cinematographer Elwin Neame. He first went to Elstree as a camera assistant on Hitchcock's (qv) *Blackmail* (29), graduating by 1934 to cinematographer on such films as *Pygmalion* (38) and *In Which We Serve* (42). He then joined Noël Coward, David Lean (qqv) and Anthony Havelock-Allan to form the Cineguild production company and co-wrote the screenplays of *Blithe Spirit* and *Brief Encounter* (both 45) and *Great Expectations* (46). The first film he directed was *Take My Life* (47) and his others include *The Card* (52), *The Man Who Never Was* (56), *The Horse's Mouth* (59), *Tunes of Glory* (60) and *The Prime of Miss Jean Brodie* (69). Much of his later career was spent in Hollywood where he directed spectaculars such as *The Poseidon Adventure* (72).

POLA NEGRI
US actress (1894-1987)

She was born in Poland, trained as a dancer. She wrote and financed her first film in Warsaw in 1914, moving to Berlin in 1917 to work notably with Ernst Lubitsch (qv) in *The Eyes of the Mummy* and *Gypsy Blood* (both 18), *Madame DuBarry* (19), *Sappho* (21) and *Die Flamme* (22). Moving to Hollywood she had success with *Bella Donna* (23), *Lily of the Dust* and *Forbidden Paradise* (both 24), *East of Suez* and *Flower of Night* (both 25) and *Hotel Imperial* (27). Liaisons with Chaplin (qv) and (so she claimed) Rudolph Valentino (qv) kept her in the headlines, but after Valentino's death in 1926 her fame dimmed (a heavy accent also proved unattractive to talkie audiences). She moved back to Germany, where one of her successes, *Mazurka* (35), was a favourite of Hitler. She fled to France ahead of the advancing Nazis in 1941 and settled permanently in America. She retired after *Hi Diddle Diddle* (43), returning only for a cameo in *The Moon-Spinners* (64).

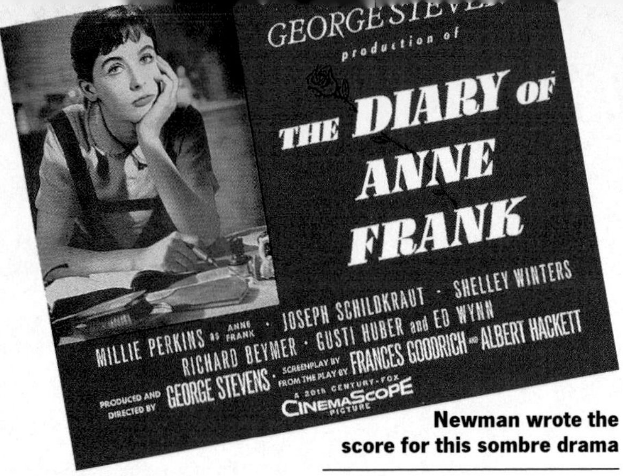

Newman wrote the score for this sombre drama

ALFRED NEWMAN
US composer (1901-70)

He dominated the scoring of film music for more than 25 years and won nine Oscars. He was born into a poor family in New Haven, Connecticut, but because of his talent at the piano he won a scholarship with Sigismond Stojowski in New York. Abandoning his studies at 14 to help his family, he was hired by the Strand theatre on Broadway as a pianist. He began his composing career with George White's Scandals of 1920. His big film break came when Irving Berlin (qv) contracted him as musical director on *Reaching for the Moon* (31). In 1933 Darryl F Zanuck (qv) set up Twentieth Century Pictures and in 1940 Newman became head of the Twentieth Century Fox music department. He was nominated for 45 Oscars, winning for, among others, *Alexander's Ragtime Band* (38), *Tin Pan Alley* (40), his favourite *The Song of Bernadette* (43), *Call Me Madam* (53), *The King and I* (56) and *Camelot* (67).

PAUL NEWMAN
US actor, director (1925-)

Although he won his first Oscar for *The Color of Money* (86), he is better remembered for his original playing of "Fast" Eddie Felson in *The Hustler* (61). Born into a prosperous Cleveland family, he served in the navy during the second world war before graduating in economics (he started a profitable laundry business at university) and going on to study the Method at the Actors Studio. His good looks enabled him to survive the disaster of *The Silver Chalice* (54), to succeed in *Somebody Up There Likes Me* (56) and as Billy the Kid in *The Left-Handed Gun* (58). Many hits followed: *Cat on a Hot Tin Roof* (58), *Hud* (63), *Cool Hand Luke* (67) and *Butch Cassidy and the Sundance Kid* (69). He directed Joanne Woodward (qv), his second wife, in *Rachel Rachel* (68) and their collaborations culminated in an Oscar nomination for *Mr & Mrs Bridge* (90). Active in liberal politics, the owner of a health food business and a motor racing team, he has endured as a star and won an eighth Oscar nomination for *Nobody's Fool* (94).

DUDLEY NICHOLS
US screenwriter (1895-1960)

A member of the screenwriting aristocracy, he left newspaper reporting in New York for Hollywood in 1929. During his career he also directed three films, including an ill-fated version of O'Neill's *Mourning Becomes Electra* (47). It was his screenplays, especially in collaboration with John Ford (qv), that won him laurels, particularly for the landmark western *Stagecoach* (39). Nichols was nominated for an Oscar for Ford's *The Long Voyage Home* (40), Howard Hawks's (qv) *Air Force* (43) and Anthony Mann's (qv) western *The Tin Star* (57). He worked for Renoir (qv) on *Swamp Water* (41) and *This Land is Mine* (43), adapted Graham Greene (qv) with *The Fugitive* (47) and tackled racism with *Pinky* (49). His talents also embraced lighter material, most memorably with his buoyant script for Hawks's screwball comedy *Bringing Up Baby* (38) and profitably for McCarey's (qv) *The Bells of St Mary's* (45). His last film was Cukor's (qv) spoof western *Heller in Pink Tights* (60).

Screwball words by Nichols for Grant and Hepburn

MIKE NICHOLS
US director (1931-)

Although *Who's Afraid of Virginia Woolf?* (66) won considerable

admiration, it was *The Graduate* (67) that clinched his reputation. Michael Igor Peschkowsky was born in Berlin and at the age of seven was a Jewish refugee from the Nazis. In America he was forced to seek scholarships to continue his education and did a variety of odd jobs, before enrolling with Lee Strasberg's Actors Studio. He joined the Second City group in Chicago, which included Alan Arkin (qv). It was not until his directorial successes on Broadway that he exploited his flair for getting the best out of actors. Given an $11m budget to direct Joseph Heller's *Catch-22* (70), he went on to make *Carnal Knowledge* (71), had a temporary lapse with *The Day of the Dolphin* (73) but returned to form with *Silkwood* (83). His other films include *Working Girl* (88), *Postcards From the Edge* (90), *Regarding Henry* (91) and *Wolf* (94) with Jack Nicholson (qv).

JACK NICHOLSON
US actor (1937-)

A fabled hellraiser and ladies ma Nicholson was the roaring new blood of 1970s cinema. Raised ir New Jersey he drifted into acting in his teens. He appeared in numerous Roger Corman (qv) cul films and produced and wrote others, including *Head* (68). He was the smalltown lawyer in *Easy Rider* (69), a performance that brought the first of eight Oscar nominations. He confirmed his stardom as a complex drifter in a work written for him, *Five Easy Pieces* (70), the first of many important performances that included *Chinatown* (74) and his Oscar-winning McMurphy in *One Flew Over the Cuckoo's Nes* (75). From the 1980s he interspersed leads with supportin roles such as the former astronau in *Terms of Endearment* (83), for which he received the best supporting Oscar, and he dominated *Batman* (89) as The Joker. He made his directorial debut with *Drive He Said* (71) an then made *Goin' South* (78).

EONARD NIMOY
'S actor, director (1931-)

: Spock, the half-Vulcan officer on e starship Enterprise with pointed ırs and curious haircut, is one of levision and cinema's most during icons. More than any her his character ensured the sting and worldwide popularity of e TV space adventure Star Trek. ne six films based on Gene oddenberry's creation, made etween 1979 and 1991, form one the most successful film series all time. Before Star Trek, he d played small roles in films and n TV. He has gained theatrical spectability for Vincent, his one-an show on Van Gogh. He rected *Star Trek III: The Search r Spock* (84), but subsequent on-outer space assignments such *Three Men and a Baby* (87) and *oly Matrimony* (94) are less than emorable. He called his itobiography I Am Not Spock.

AVID NIVEN
ritish actor (1909-83)

e knew the value of the man-bout-town image when he first ettled in Hollywood, playing tennis ith the right people, mixing with rol Flynn (qv) and many rlfriends. His autobiographies veal a Scottish survival course in hoolboy unhappiness which sent m into films where his throwaway arm was used to best effect, as *The Charge of the Light Brigade* 36) and *The Prisoner of Zenda* 37). He was contracted to Sam oldwyn (qv), but returned to itain to fight the Nazis. After ome unsatisfying American films e returned to London to play the ewildered pilot in *A Matter of Life and Death* (46) and Phileas Fogg in *Around the World in 80 Days* (56), but it was for the phoney major in *Separate Tables* (58) that he won his Oscar. He died from the disabling consequences of motor neurone disease.

Scandal ruined Mabel Normand's brilliant career

PHILIPPE NOIRET
French actor (1930-)

Born in Lille and in more than 100 films since the early 1960s, he has fleshed out an extraordinary range of roles with deep emotions and telling nuances. He employs his distinctive pear-shaped face to suggest introspection or buffoonery and his performances almost always exude humanity. Since the gloom of *Thérèse Desqueyroux* (62), where he was charismatic as an unexciting husband, he has embraced the crazy frivolity of *Zazie dans le Métro* (60) as a transvestite artist and given depth to his comically corrupt detective in *Le Cop* (84). He slotted in perfectly to the bittersweet jazz world of *Round Midnight* (86) and as an ageing, shuffling projectionist in *Cinema Paradiso* (88). Black humour proved no problem for him in *Tango* (93), where his indifference to murder was a comic treat.

NICK NOLTE
US actor (1934-)

A versatile leading man with a prickly reputation, he was born in Omaha, Nebraska, the son of an engineer and a mother from a distinguished academic family. In his youth he was a champion athlete and all-round rebel who was convicted of selling counterfeit draft cards and put on probation. He was taken to the theatre by a friend while at Pasadena City College and became hooked on acting. For 20 years he toured America in more than 150 summer stock productions until 1973 when in Los Angeles he was spotted for the television adaptation of Rich Man, Poor Man, which was a worldwide hit. *The Deep* (77) and *Who'll Stop the Rain?* (78) followed, but his big break came with *48 HRS* (82). After *Under Fire* (83) and *Teachers* (84) he became a top Hollywood star with *Down and Out in Beverly Hills* (86). *Three Fugitives* (89), *Q&A* and *Another 48 HRS* (*both* 90), *The Prince of Tides* and *Cape Fear* (both 91) and *Jefferson in Paris* (95) are notable.

MABEL NORMAND
US actress (1894-1930)

Pretty, vivacious and the best comedienne of the silent era, she also directed many of the successful shorts that bore her name (*Mabel's Adventures, Mabel's Stormy Love Affair* etc). She began at 16 with D W Griffith (qv) at Biograph, but it was Mack Sennett (qv) who realised her potential, lost his heart to her and took her to Keystone. There she co-starred with Chaplin (qv) and sometimes directed him. Their best-known collaboration was *Tillie's Punctured Romance* (14), after which she made several films with Fatty Arbuckle (qv). Sennett set up the Mabel Normand Feature Film Company and she made *Mickey* (18). She joined Goldwyn, then became addicted to drugs. In 1922 she was implicated in the scandal surrounding the murder of the director William Desmond Taylor. Sennett re-employed her but further scandals ensued and her image was irreparably damaged. She made a couple of shorts for Hal Roach (qv) in 1926, the year she married the already ill actor Lew Cody (qv) in a sad bid for stability. Four years later she died from drugs and tuberculosis.

ALEX NORTH
US composer (1910-91)

Classically trained, North contributed striking scores for a range of films from the epic to the offbeat, from *A Streetcar Named Desire* (51), *Daddy Long Legs* (55), *The Long Hot Summer* (58), *Spartacus* (60), *The Misfits* (61), *Cleopatra* (63) and *Cheyenne Autumn* (64) to *Who's Afraid of Virginia Woolf?* (66), *Pocket Money* (72), *Wise Blood* (79) and *Prizzi's Honor* (85). He even wrote a song for *Ghost* (90). Despite 15 Oscar nominations he had to wait until 1986 to receive an honorary lifetime achievement Oscar. His large catalogue of compositions includes three symphonies. He also collaborated with Benny Goodman and wrote ballet music for American choreographers.

RAMON NOVARRO
Mexican actor (1899-1968)

He was launched by MGM to replace Rudolph Valentino (qv), but he lacked the intensity and his irony was a poor substitute for strong-jawed passion. Nevertheless, he starred in some of the most popular romantic epics of the 1920s. Fleeing the Mexican troubles in 1914 he worked as a singing waiter in Los Angeles before turning to film extra work. He made an impact in the Mack Sennett (qv) comedy *A Small Town Idol* (21) and caught the attention of the director Rex Ingram (qv) who persuaded him to change his name (from Ramon Samaniegos) and cast him as Rupert of Hentzau in *The Prisoner of Zenda* (22). He was back to swashbuckling in *Scaramouche* (23), then starred in his most famous film, the spectacular *Ben-Hur* (26). He was also memorable in Lubitsch's (qv) *The Student Prince* (27). He was murdered in 1968.

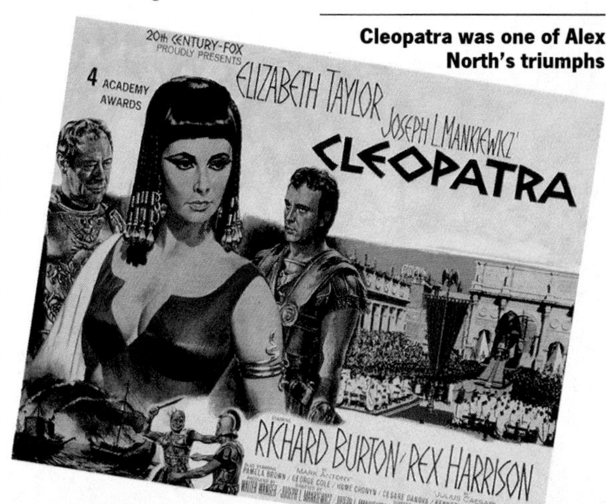

Cleopatra was one of Alex North's triumphs

PHILLIP NOYCE
Australian director (1950-)

At the University of Sydney he made short films with borrowed equipment. He won a prize at the 1974 Sydney Film Festival and made his first feature, *Backroads* (77), a 60-minute road film with racial overtones. His first main feature, *Newsfront* (78), recalled the rivalry between post-war newsreel companies and mixed social history with intense drama. Full international recognition came with his claustrophobic thriller *Dead Calm* (89), in which three people, one a homicidal maniac, are marooned at sea. He has since been much in demand in Hollywood where he has made such action thrillers as *Patriot Games* (92) and *Clear and Present Danger* (94). He is now the most internationally successful of the outstanding crop of film makers who emerged in the Australian New Wave of the late 1970s.

SVEN NYKVIST
Swedish cinematographer (1922-)

He has photographed more than 110 films and is one of the greatest exponents of his art. Visual simplicity is his hallmark. Known primarily as Ingmar Bergman's (qv) cinematographer – they have worked together on 22 films – Nykvist excels at natural, atmospheric lighting and at capturing the deeper emotions in his actors' faces. The son of a Lutheran missionary, he studied stills photography in Stockholm before discovering the moving image. Making his breakthrough on Bergman's *Sawdust and Tinsel* (53) after the original cameraman fell ill, he made some bold experiments on *The Silence* (63) and *Persona* (66) to create a lustrous, surreal effect. He won Oscars for his lighting of *Cries and Whispers* (72) and *Fanny and Alexander* (83) and has collaborated with Woody Allen, Louis Malle, Polanski, Tarkovsky (qqv), Mazursky and Nora Ephron. *The Ox* (92), a haunting tale of love and survival which he directed, was a critical success.

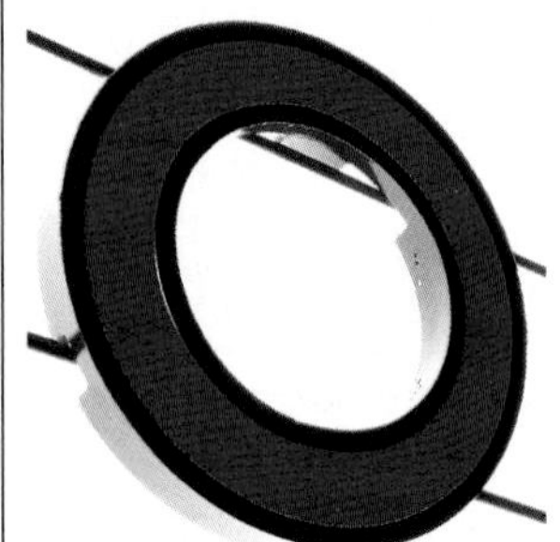

MERLE OBERON
British actress (1911-79)

Born in Tasmania and raised in India, Estelle Merle O'Brien Thompson was alleged to have Asian blood. While working as a

dance hostess and film extra under the name Queenie O'Brien she was discovered by Korda (qv), who gave her the role of Anne Boleyn in *The Private Life of Henry VIII* (33). It was followed by *The Private Life of Don Juan* (34) and *The Scarlet Pimpernel* (35). In the year she and Korda were married he sold part of her contract to Sam Goldwyn (qv) for whom she made *Wuthering Heights* (39). Her car accident aborted *I Claudius*. She chose later films, as she did her four husbands, indiscriminately.

MARGARET O'BRIEN
US actress (1938-)

The 1940s marked the departure of Shirley Temple (qv) and the arrival of O'Brien as America's most popular child star. In MGM's stable of children from the age of four, her emotional range was startling. Aged five she starred as a London war orphan in the tailor-made *Journey for Margaret* (42), at seven she joined Elizabeth Taylor (qv) on loan to Fox as an orphan in *Jane Eyre* (44), was top-billed as June Allyson's supportive sister in

Music for Millions (44), almost stole the show from Charles Laughton (qv) in *The Canterville Ghost* (44) and delighted as Judy Garland's (qv) baby sister in *Meet Me in St Louis* (44). She was central to *The Unfinished Dance* (47), *Little Women* and *The Secret Garden* (both 49). She left MGM for Columbia and made *Her First Romance* (51) but was unable to sustain popular appeal beyond adolescence. She made five unsuccessful comebacks; *Amy* (81) was the most recent.

DONALD O'CONNOR
US actor (1925-)

He was born into a circus family and made his debut in vaudeville before making *Melody for Two* (37) at the age of 11. Paramount films such as *Sing You Sinners* and *Tom Sawyer – Detective* (both 38) and *Boy Trouble* (39) preceded notable performances in a string of indifferent Universal musicals including *Mister Big* (43), *Chip off the Old Block* (44) and *Feudin' Fussin' and A-Fightin'* (48). He achieved fame with a talking mule in the surprise comedy hit *Francis* (50). His greatest film was *Singin' in the Rain* (52) with Gene Kelly

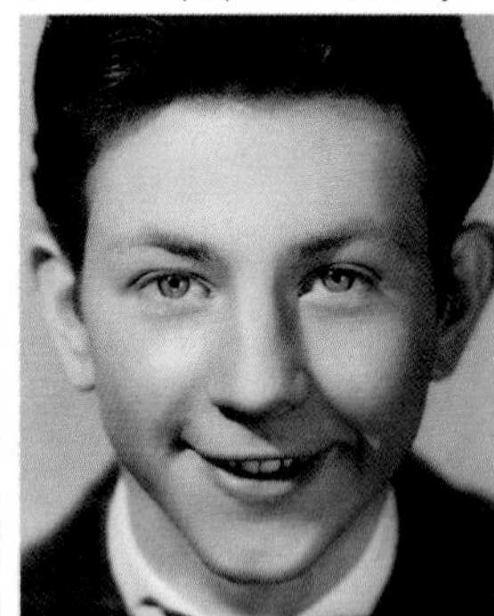

(qv) in which he performed Make 'Em Laugh. It was followed by *Walking My Baby Back Home* (53) and *There's No Business Like Show Business* (54). After playing the lead in *The Buster Keaton Story* (57) he made only a handful more films, including *That's Entertainment!* (74), *Ragtime* (81) and *Toys* (92).

MAUREEN O'HARA
US actress (1920-)

Irish born and educated in Dublin, she is best known for playing beautiful redheads in John Ford's (qv) *How Green Was My Valley* (41), *Rio Grande* (50) and *The Quiet Man* (52) with John Wayne (qv), *The Long Gray Line* (55) and *The Wings of Eagles* (57). Her first starring role was as Esmeralda in *The Hunchback of Notre Dame* (39) opposite Charles Laughton (qv), who took her to Hollywood from Britain where she had appeared with him in *Jamaica Inn*

(39). She was cast in swashbucklers and period romances, such as *The Black Swan* (42), *The Spanish Main* (45), *Sinbad the Sailor* (47), *Against All Flags* (52), *Lady Godiva* (55) and in westerns including *Ten Gentlemen From West Point* (42), *Buffalo Bill* (44), *The Redhead From Wyoming* (53), *McLintock!* (63), *The Rare Breed* (66) and *Big Jake* (71), her last with Wayne. She retired but made a well received comeback in *Only the Lonely* (91).

LAURENCE OLIVIER
British actor, director (1907-89)

The colossus of the acting profession, Olivier had three distinct periods to his film career: the early years of dandies and romantic leads, the middle period dominated by bringing three great Shakespeare characters to the

Olivier was the definitive Archie Rice in The Entertain

screen and his final cameo years. He won eight Oscar nominations. He was born in Dorking, Surrey, the son of a clergyman, and set sights on Hollywood during the New York run of Noël Coward's (qv) Private Lives. RKO were impressed by him and he made *Friends and Lovers* (31) and *Westward Passage* (32). MGM p him opposite Garbo (qv) in *Quee Christina* (33), but after a few da he was replaced by John Gilbert (qv). Back in London he was in Korda's (qv) *Moscow Nights* (35 and starred with his future wife Vivien Leigh (qv) in *Fire Over England* (37). He returned to Hollywood for *Wuthering Heights* (39) and stardom. *Rebecca* and *Pride and Prejudice* (both 40) ensued. After war service in the Fleet Air Arm he acted in and directed *Henry V* (44), which wo special Oscar. *Hamlet* (48) followed, winning best picture an actor awards. He was magnificer in *Carrie* (52) before his definitive *Richard III* (55). *The Prince and Showgirl* (57) with Marilyn Monr (qv) and *The Devil's Disciple* (59 followed. He entered an innovati phase with *The Entertainer* (60), made *Spartacus* (60) for the money and was ludicrously mad up for *Khartoum* (66). *Sleuth* (72 was a success as was *Marathon Man* (76) and *The Betsy* (78) wa written for him. In *The Boys Fro Brazil* (78) he was fine, but bega an undiscerning period with *The Jazz Singer* (80). *Wild Geese II* (85) was an ignominious end to film career.

MAX OPHULS
German director (1902-57)

Ophüls, or Opuls as he was bille in America, directed more than 200 stage plays in Germany and

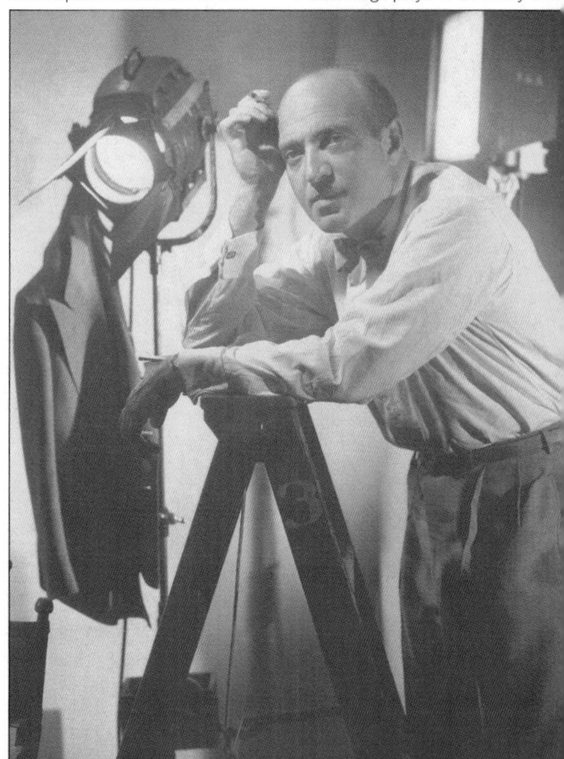

Austria before, aged 28, he first looked through a lens. His German films include *Die verkaufte Braut* (32) and *Liebelei* (33). Born into a Jewish family in Saarbrücken, he fled Nazism to France and directed films there before moving to Holland, then Italy. His Italian production of *La Signora di Tutti* (34) revealed the full lushly decorative and inviting Ophüls style, with its constant camera moves and intense music. In America he made *Letter From an Unknown Woman* (48) and the American-style melodramas *Caught* and *The Reckless Moment* (both 49). Returning to France he made *La Ronde* (50), *Le Plaisir* (52), *Madame de . . .* (53) and *Lola Montès* (55).

JOHN ORRY-KELLY
Australian costumer designer (1897-1964)

He left art college in Sydney for the New York stage where he designed the scenery and costumes for Broadway musical revues, before moving to Hollywood and Warner in 1931. He remained the studio's top designer until 1946, admired for his expertise in period detail and for making an impact in black and white. His contributions to lasting images of the screen range from Ginger Rogers (qv) and the chorus line clad in gold coins for We're In The Money from *Gold Diggers of 1933* (one of five Busby Berkeley (qv) extravaganzas he dressed) to Ingrid Bergman's (qv) chic in *Casablanca* (42). He is most famous for his creations for Bette Davis (qv), including the red ball gown in which she scandalised New Orleans amid the white-gowned debutantes in *Jezebel* (38) and her transformation from frump to sophisticate in *Now Voyager* (42). He received Oscars for *An American in Paris* (51), *Les Girls* (57) and *Some Like It Hot* (59).

OSCAR
US statuette (1927-)

The brainchild of a small group of Hollywood luminaries – to become the Academy of Motion Picture Arts and Sciences – who were looking for ways to thwart burgeoning union power, it was reputedly born on a tablecloth, sketched by the art director Cedric Gibbons (qv). It was

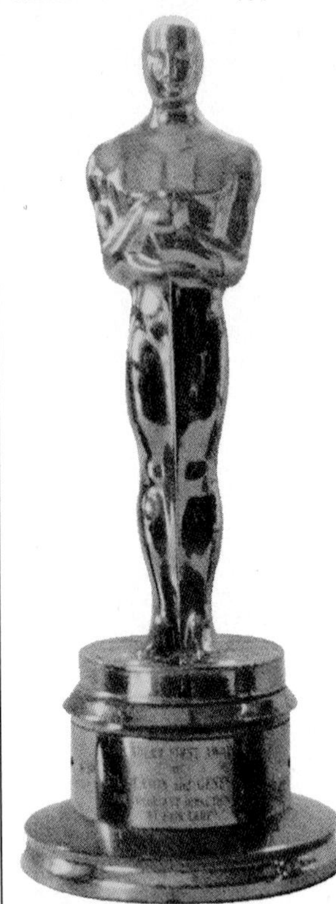

allegedly named, aged three, by Margaret Herrick, a secretary who went on to become a luminary of the academy, when she saw a resemblance to her Uncle Oscar. Made mostly of tin with a 14-carat gold coat, Oscar is 13½in tall and worth about $350 in materials, but millions more in box office bankability to the recipient. The first awards ceremony, hosted by Douglas Fairbanks (qv) and William C DeMille, took place in 1929 at the Roosevelt Hotel in Hollywood and handed out 11 Oscars in seven categories, reportedly in just 10 minutes. It has been growing ever since, adding categories, razzmatazz and voting members (now some 5,000) from all branches of the industry. In wartime a special statuette using cheaper materials was awarded, which ironically now have a greater rarity value. *Ben-Hur* (59) is still the biggest winner with 11 awards; Bob Hope (qv) holds the record for hosting 20 ceremonies.

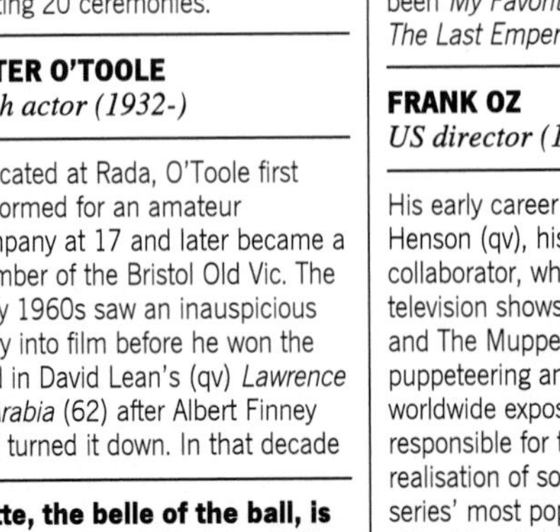

Bette, the belle of the ball, is appraised by John Orry-Kelly

PETER O'TOOLE
Irish actor (1932-)

Educated at Rada, O'Toole first performed for an amateur company at 17 and later became a member of the Bristol Old Vic. The early 1960s saw an inauspicious entry into film before he won the lead in David Lean's (qv) *Lawrence of Arabia* (62) after Albert Finney (qv) turned it down. In that decade *Becket* (64), *Lord Jim* (65) and *Goodbye Mr Chips* (69) established him. He was also adept at sniffing out offbeat roles, as with *The Ruling Class* (72) and *The Stunt Man* (80). The latter marked his return to better quality material after some rare and variable roles in the late 1970s, which it is widely believed were indicative of his chronic alcoholism. He continued to make disappointing or inappropriate choices, but each performance was none the less brightened by his idiosyncratic humour. His best recent films have been *My Favorite Year* (82) and *The Last Emperor* (87).

FRANK OZ
US director (1944-)

His early career runs parallel to Jim Henson (qv), his friend and collaborator, whose children's television shows Sesame Street and The Muppet Show gave his puppeteering and comedic talents worldwide exposure. Oz was responsible for the conception and realisation of some of the two series' most popular and enduring characters, including Fozzie Bear and Miss Piggy, both of which ca his unmistakable gravel voice. He also served as voice and manipulator of the character Yod in *The Empire Strikes Back* (80) and *Return of the Jedi* (83). He c directed the puppet feature *The Dark Crystal* (81) and has directe only live action comedies since *Little Shop of Horrors* (86), three them with Steve Martin (qv). His best film was *What About Bob?* (91). He has also acted cameos films by John Landis (qv).

W PABST
rman director (1885-1967)

; fluid camera and skilful editing
ught a fresh vitality to his art.
rn in Bohemia and raised in
nna, he began acting in
itzerland and America and
ned to directing German
guage plays in New York. After
war he directed theatre in
gue before making his first film,
e Treasure (23), in Germany.
:h *Joyless Street* (25) he
ected Garbo (qv) and established
nself as a film-maker of
ong naturalistic style. His most
nous picture is *Pandora's*
x (29), a spellbinding, erotic
n with Louise Brooks (qv). He
o distinguished himself with
stfront 1918 (30) and
meradschaft (31), which were
ndemned for their pacifism, and
his version of Brecht and Weill's
e Threepenny Opera (31).

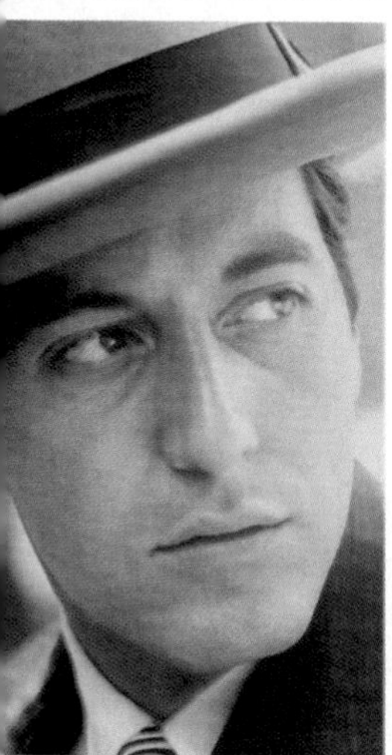

. PACINO
S actor (1940-)

scraped together enough
ney to attend drama school, where Charles Laughton (qv) was an early tutor, and moved on to Lee Strasberg's Actors Studio in 1966. He has given the cinema's most extended character study as Michael Corleone in *The Godfather* trilogy (72, 74, 90); he is, fittingly, of Sicilian descent. After only two films, *Me Natalie* (69) and *The Panic in Needle Park* (71), the first Godfather film launched him into a series of outsider portraits: the whistle-blowing cop *Serpico* (73), a bank robber in *Dog Day Afternoon* (75), the muckraking lawyer in *. . . And Justice for All* (79) and the urban terrorist of *Scarface* (83). He overacted in *Revolution* (86), but resurrected his career in *Sea of Love* (89), *Dick Tracy* (90) and *Frankie and Johnny* (91). He got his Oscar with *Scent of a Woman* (92), for a blistering performance as a cantankerous and suicidal former army colonel handicapped by blindness. He also directed the Shakespeare workshop film *Looking for Richard* (1996).

GERALDINE PAGE
US actress (1924-87)

A leading lady of American theatre and a proponent of Method acting, she chose an intermittent film career which brought eight Oscar nominations. Missouri-born and trained at the Chicago Academy of Fine Arts, she made her name in Tennessee Williams's Summer and Smoke on stage in 1952 and received a supporting Oscar nomination for her first big screen role as a frontier widow sparring with cavalry scout John Wayne (qv) in *Hondo* (53). Eight years later she reprised her Broadway triumphs in *Summer and Smoke* (61) and as the dissolute film star Alexandra Del Lago in Williams's *Sweet Bird of Youth* (62). She was the schoolmistress who destroyed Clint Eastwood (qv) in *The Beguiled* (71), the mother in Woody Allen's (qv) *Interiors* (78) and the widow on a last odyssey in *The Trip to Bountiful* (85), for which she received an Oscar.

MARCEL PAGNOL
French writer, director and producer (1895-1974)

Born near Marseille, he is a national institution. His films were distinguished by their warmth, depth of characterisation and magnificent acting from stars such as Raimu and Fernandel (qqv), whose careers he helped to build. He began writing plays before he was 20. Topaze, a tale of a shy teacher who gets the better of his disreputable boss, was filmed by Louis Gasnier in 1933 with Louis Jouvet, by Hollywood with John Barrymore (qv) and twice by Pagnol (36, 51). His films include *The Well-Digger's Daughter* (31), *Angèle* (34), *The Baker's Wife* and *Heartbeat* (both 38), but he is best known for his trilogy: *Marius* (30), directed by Alexander Korda (qv), *Fanny* (32), made by Marc Allégret (qv), and *César* (36), which he directed. In 1963 he turned his penultimate film, *Manon des Sources* (52), into a novel, adding a prequel, *Jean de Florette*, both filmed back-to-back by Claude Berri (qv) in 1986.

Marcel Pagnol, Provençal author of the Marius trilogy

ALAN J PAKULA
US producer, director (1928-)

Born in the Bronx of Polish-Jewish parents, he graduated from Yale Drama School before working in animation at Warner, serving an apprenticeship with MGM and becoming a production assistant at Paramount. He produced Robert Mulligan's *Fear Strikes Out* (57) and they went on to five more successes, from *To Kill a Mocking Bird* (62) to *The Stalking Moon* (69). Although his directorial debut, *The Sterile Cuckoo* (69), was unsuccessful at the box office, he soon established his reputation with *Klute* (71), a thriller noted for establishing the legitimacy of four-letter profanities in Hollywood. After directing the under-rated political thriller *The Parallax View* (74), he bounced back with *All the President's Men* (76), the highly acclaimed *Comes a Horseman* (78), the much-awarded *Sophie's Choice* (82) and the remarkable *Orphans* (87). Other films include *Presumed Innocent* (90) and *The Pelican Brief* (93).

GEORGE PAL
US producer, director (1908-80)

Born in Hungary, he studied architecture in Budapest then worked in Berlin as a set designer. He moved to Eindhoven, Holland, and created animated advertising shorts for the Philips electrical giant. He went to Hollywood at the start of the war and was awarded a contract to make *The Puppetoons* (41-47), a long-running series of stop-motion shorts, winning a special Oscar in 1943. In the early 1950s he began producing inventive sci-fi features using what for the time were astonishing special effects. They include *Destination Moon* (50), *When Worlds Collide* (51) and *War of the Worlds* (53). He won Oscars for all three and for *Tom Thumb* (58) and *The Time Machine* (60), which he also directed. Pal was one of the finest fantasists and pioneers to work in Hollywood.

George Pal and Tom Thumb, a miniature Russ Tamblyn

JACK PALANCE
US actor (1920-)

The son of Russian immigrants he was usually cast as a merciless villain. His gaunt face is the result of skin-tightening plastic surgery to injuries received as a boxer and in the second world war. He was an effective heavy in films from *Panic in the Streets* (50), through *Sudden Fear* (52) and *Shane* (53), both nominated for best supporting Oscars, to *The Lonely Man* (57). These were followed by several films in Europe and success on American TV with The Greatest Show on Earth series. Cinema character roles continued in such work as *The Professionals* (66), *They Came to Rob Las Vegas* (68), *Che!* (69), *Chato's Land* (72), *Oklahoma Crude* (73), *The Four Deuces* (75), *Dead on Arrival* (79), *Alone in the Dark* (82), *Young Guns* (88), *Batman* and *Tango and Cash* (both 89). *City Slickers* (91) brought an Oscar as best supporting actor and he played his twin brother in *City Slickers 2* (94).

HERMES PAN
US choreographer (1910-90)

He forged such a close relationship with Fred Astaire (qv) during the late 1930s and 1940s that their contributions to classics such as *Top Hat* (35) are indistinguishable; on occasion he even danced as a double for Astaire in long shots. Hermes Panagiotopolous was born in Nashville, Tennessee, left school at 12 and worked in the laboratories of the Edison Company before beginning his dance career in 10 cents-a-dance saloons. He met Ginger Rogers (qv) on Broadway in Top Speed and she introduced him to Astaire on the set of *Flying Down to Rio* (33). Astaire recognised his flair and his zeal for rehearsal and Pan subsequently choreographed nine of Astaire's 10 films with Rogers, including *Roberta* (35), *Follow the Fleet* (36) and *The Barkleys of Broadway* (49). He also choreographed several stage musicals that transferred to the screen, such as *Kiss Me Kate* (53), *Can-Can* (60) and *My Fair Lady* (64). He designed the staging for *Cleopatra* (63), provided the routines for 55 films and changed the face of the film musical. He died of a stroke in Beverly Hills.

ALAN PARKER
British director (1944-)

His films distance him from the leaden theatricality of much of British cinema. His trademark is a strong visual punch, which persists long after the picture is over. A copywriter, then a director in advertising, he chose *Bugsy Malone* (76) for his first feature film. A gangster spoof with children in the lead roles, it was produced by his former advertising associate David Puttnam (qv). *Midnight Express* (78) gave him a world stage and the first-time screenwriter Oliver Stone (qv) an Oscar. His films include *Fame* (80), *Pink Floyd – The Wall* (82), *Birdy* (85), *Angel Heart* (87), *Mississippi Burning* (88), *The Commitments* (91) and *Evita* (96). *The Commitments*, saw Parker harness his visuals to meaty characters and easy narrative flow. In 1997 he was appointed chairman of the British Film Institute, which he had earlier denounced as being run by "turnip heads".

LOUELLA PARSONS
US columnist (1893-1972)

Stars and studios lived in terror of her often malicious column, which could wreck films and careers. She summoned stars to lunch like flunkies, broke genuine personal revelations, such as Elizabeth Taylor's (qv) affair with Eddie Fisher, and made recommendations for parts which studio chiefs seriously considered. She could only have existed around a strong studio system. Parsons was born in Freeport, Illinois, and began her working life reading scripts at Essanay Studios, Chicago. She started the first film column for the Chicago Herald and then moved to the Morning Telegraph in New York. In 1922 she went to Hearst newspapers and began her reign of terror with a writing style brimming with hyperbole and exclamation marks, which addressed the stars directly. "Now see here Clarkie baby, whaddya think you were doing last night, huh?". Her second husband, Dr Harry Watson Martin, was physician to many stars and she shamelessly used the connection. She played herself in cameos, such as the forgettable *Hollywood Hotel* (37) and *Starlift* (51).

PIER PAOLO PASOLINI
Italian director, screenwriter (1922-75)

His blatant use of sex, violence and blasphemy outraged the Italian authorities, but *The Canterbury Tales* (72) and *Salo – the 120 Days of Sodom* (75)) proved he was no cinematic show-off out to shock. Clever juxtapositions on screen made his work fascinating. He had published poetry and novels by the time he turned to film. He contributed to the script of Fellini's (qv) *The Nights of Cabiria* (56) before making a resounding debut with *Accattone!* (61). The contradictions were already in place, while he owed a lot to the penchant of Italian neo-realism for location shooting and non-actors. Austerity, simplicity and dignity filtered through arid Italian landscapes characterised *The Gospel According to St Matthew* (64), a triumphant semi-documentary portrait of Christ as a rebel, again with non-actors. He even cast his mother as the Virgin Mary. Realism increasingly gave way to stylisation. Though *Oedipus Rex* (67) and *The Canterbury Tales* conveyed his enthusiasm for literature, he was not afraid to be direct and contemporary in *Theorem* (68) and *Pigsty* (69). A homosexual, he was murdered by a 17-year-old boy.

JOE PASTERNAK
US producer (1901-91)

Born in Transylvania, he emigrat to America and worked as a bus boy and waiter at Paramount, became an assistant director, moved to Universal in Europe ar then returned to find fame throu such Deanna Durbin (qv) music as *Three Smart Girls* (36), *100 Men and a Girl* (37) and *Mad About Music* (38). The mix of lollipop classics and ingénue act restored Universal's fortunes. *Destry Rides Again* (39) not only boosted Marlene Dietrich's (qv) career but also Pasternak's, whc progressed to such songs with schmaltz musicals for MGM as *Anchors Aweigh* (45), in which Gene Kelly (qv) danced with Jer MGM's cartoon mouse. *That Midnight Kiss* (49), *The Great Caruso* (51) and *The Student Prince* (54) were among his hits which he had to direct the temperamental tenor Mario Lan (qv). He retired in the late 1960

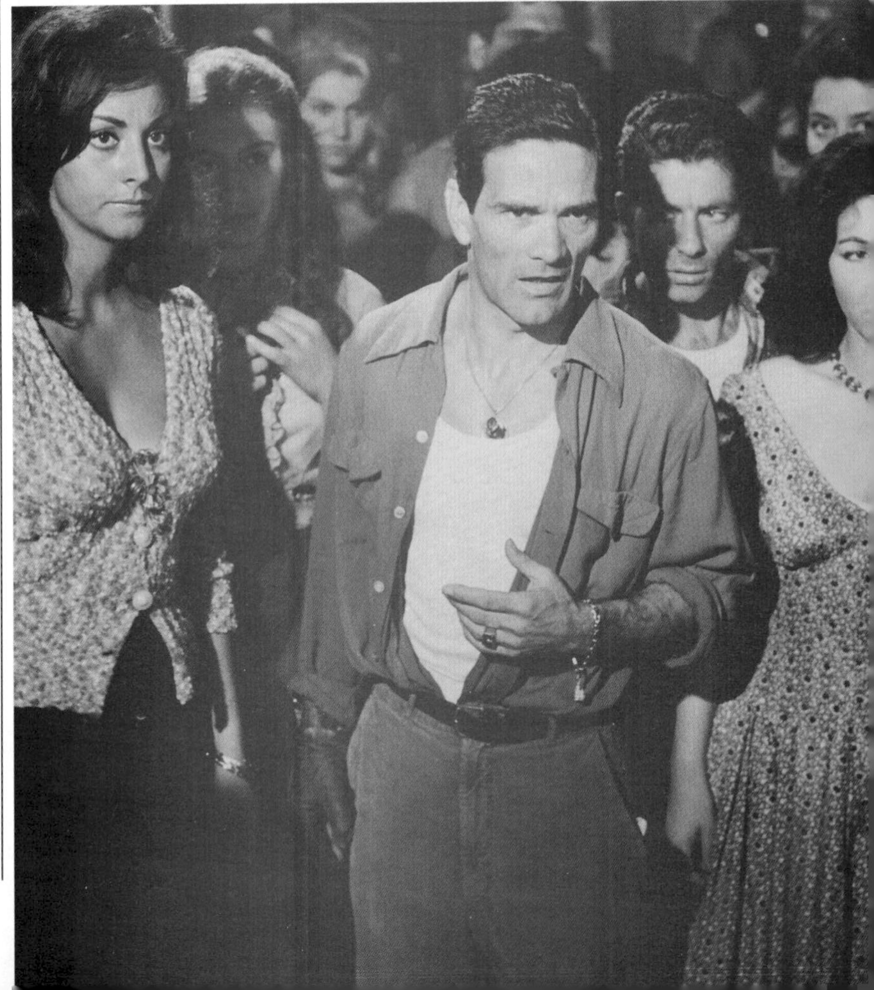

Pasolini directing action on Il Gobbo The Hunchback of Rome

HARLES PATHE
rench pioneer (1863-1957)

ne of the early entrepreneurial ants of the film industry, he ought and exhibited an Edison nonograph in 1894 and began elling phonographic machines. In 396 he formed Pathé Frères with s brothers Emile, Jacques and néophile, adding motion picture ojectors to his merchandise. In 901, leaving equipment sales to mile, he built a studio in ncennes and employed erdinand Zecca, who directed a ilestone series of dramas cluding *History of a Crime* (01) nd *The Victims of Alcoholism* 2). Pathé expanded further, anufacturing film stock, building udios, processing labs and nemas, developing Pathé Color nd launching Pathé Journal, the orld's first film newsreel. By 1908 had branches in London, New rk, Moscow and elsewhere and as selling more films to America an that country was making. After e first world war American films ined ascendancy and, over a riod of years, he was forced divest himself of his huge and verse empire. The remaining oduction and distribution strands ere bought by RKO in 1931.

OBERT PAUL
itish pioneer (1869-1943)

engineer by training and a entific instrument maker by ofession, he made copies of ison's (qv) Kinetoscope in 1894 d invented a camera to shoot films for it in collaboration with Birt Acres (qv). In 1895 they shot actuality footage, including *Rough Sea at Dover*. On the same day in 1896 that the Lumières (qv) had their first public display in Britain, Paul projected films at Finsbury Technical College in north London and the next month to a paying audience at Olympia. He showed the 1896 Derby at the Alhambra in London's Leicester Square on the night after the race and made the first British narrative film, *The Soldier's Courtship* (96), with a running time of one minute. He built the first British studio in north London and used it to create special effects. His *Voyage to the Arctic* (03) pre-dated Méliès's (qv) *The Conquest of the Pole* by nine years. He sold up in 1910 and returned to scientific instruments.

GEORGE PEARSON
British pioneer (1875-1973)

A trailblazer, he was successful because his films appealed to the growing working-class audiences during the 1920s, exemplified in *The Little People* (26). He was a headmaster before joining Pathé as an educational film scriptwriter because he believed cinema was the teacher's true medium. Appreciating the potential of film he switched to entertainment and established himself as one of Britain's leading silent directors. Credited with many innovations such as free-moving cameras, cross-cutting, specially equipped studios and location shooting, he discovered Betty Balfour and made her a star in the successful *Squibs* series. With the advent of sound he began producing quota quickies, the most successful of which was the waterfront drama *The River Wolves* (34), but was increasingly drawn to making documentaries, joining the GPO Film Unit in 1939 and then the Colonial Film Unit as head of production. He retired at the age of 81 and wrote his autobiography, Flashback.

GREGORY PECK
US actor, producer (1916-)

He unswervingly depicted men of reserve, integrity and dignity. Indeed, when David O Selznick (qv) cast him as a cold-blooded killer in the western *Duel in the Sun* (47), preview audiences were outraged. He became a star with his first picture, *Days of Glory* (44). Since then his track record has been remarkable, with roles in some of the most successful and critically applauded films of his time. His first notable success was his second film, *The Keys of the Kingdom* (45), in which his portrayal of a dedicated priest won him his first Oscar nomination. He was also nominated for *The Yearling* (46), *Gentleman's Agreement* (47) and *Twelve O'Clock High* (50). He won the award for his outstanding portrait of a liberal southern lawyer in *To Kill a Mockingbird* (62). In more recent years he has made *The Omen* (76), *The Boys From Brazil* (78) and switched roles for the remake of *Cape Fear* (91), having appeared in the 1962 original.

SAM PECKINPAH
US director (1926-84)

At school, military college and in the marines he was a notorious drinker with a foul temper. After studying drama he had minor jobs in television, then wrote for films and TV, sometimes with Don Siegel (qv). He began directing in 1961 and his first great work was *Major Dundee* (65). His abiding theme was the relationship between masculinity and violence, shot through with existential bleakness. It came to brutal fruition in *The Wild Bunch* (69), a bloody western that has gained notoriety, like the rest of his oeuvre, for its gore and

slow motion shoot-outs. *Straw Dogs* (71), shot in Britain, caused him trouble with British censors. His masterpiece is the thoughtful, evocative western *Pat Garrett and Billy the Kid* (73), although *Bring Me the Head of Alfredo Garcia* (74) should be regarded as the darkest example of his career. He made only five films in his last decade.

ARTHUR PENN
US director (1922-)

An actor and writer off and on Broadway, he came to the cinema via stage and television work. His film debut was *The Left-Handed Gun* (58) with Paul Newman (qv). He went back to Broadway notably with The Miracle Worker, a play about a therapist and her blind, deaf-mute patient, which he successfully directed for the screen. It won a best actress Oscar for Anne Bancroft (qv), best supporting actress for Patty Duke and a nomination for Penn as best director. More stage work was followed by *Mickey One* (65) with Warren Beatty (qv), *The Chase* (66) with Marlon Brando (qv) and *Bonnie and Clyde* (67). *Alice's Restaurant* (69) and *Little Big Man* (70) also won Oscar nominations. Since then, apart from *The Missouri Breaks* (76) with Brando and Jack Nicholson (qv), which divided critics, only the thrillers *Target* (85) and *Dead of Winter* (87) have kept his profile high.

S J PERELMAN
US screenwriter (1904-79)

One of the most celebrated American humourists of his time and a prolific author, he was wooed by Paramount to collaborate on the first Marx Brothers (qv) comedy soon after making his name with the bestseller, Dawn Ginsbergh's Revenge. The film was *Monkey Business* (31) and his chief contribution was rapid-fire gags and evil puns tailored to the leering, fast-talking Groucho: "Oh, why can't we break away from all this, just you and I, and lodge with my fleas in the hills, I mean flee to my lodge in the hills." He co-wrote *Horse Feathers* (32) and then

freelanced, writing story treatments, screenplays or plays, including his Broadway hit One Touch of Venus for screen adaptation. He and co-writers James Poe and John Farrow won the Oscar for their screenplay of Mike Todd's (qv) lavish *Around the World in 80 Days* (56).

GEORGES PERINAL
French cinematographer (1897-1965)

He was an outstanding lighting cameraman whose work enriched French and British cinema. A Parisian, his career in films began in 1913. He became a director of photography in the 1920s working on Jean Grémillon shorts. He then collaborated with René Clair (qv), shooting his first sound film, *Sous les Toits de Paris* (30) and *Le Million* and *A Nous la Liberté* (both 31). He was asked by Alexander Korda (qv) to work on *The Private Life of Henry VIII* (33) and stayed in Britain to shoot other Korda films, including *Things to Come* and *Rembrandt* (both 36), *The Four Feathers* (39) and *The Thief of Bagdad* (40). He lit Leslie Howard's (qv) *The First of the Few* (42) and Powell and Pressburger's (qqv) *The Life and Death of Colonel Blimp* (43) and later Korda's *An Ideal Husband* (48) and Carol Reed's (qv) *The Fallen Idol* (48). His last film was *Oscar Wilde* (60).

JOE PESCI
US actor (1943-)

So far he has established himself as a tough character actor. A child performer who became a musician and comedian, his Hollywood break came late with *Raging Bull* (80), for which he won an Oscar nomination. Steady but far-flung work since (with several films in Europe) has included *I'm Dancing as Fast as I Can* (82), *Eureka* and *Easy Money* (both 83), *Once Upon a Time in America* (84), *Moonwalker* (88), *Lethal Weapon 2* and *3* (89, 92) and *GoodFellas* (90), which won him a best supporting actor Oscar. *My Cousin Vinny* (92) confirmed his eminence as a character player and *The Public Eye* (92) saw him blossom as a newshound photographer. *Home Alone 2* (92) confirmed his box-office appeal..

WOLFGANG PETERSEN
German director (1941-)

He built a formidable reputation in theatre and television after training for four years at the Berlin Film and Television Academy. He made his film debut with *One of Us Two* (72), for which he was awarded the German national film prize as best new director. He then won excellent reviews for *The Consequence* (77), a stinging exploration of homosexual angst. However, it was his claustrophobic U-boat drama *Das Boot* (81) that won him worldwide recognition. At the time the most successful foreign language film released in America, it was nominated for six Oscars, including two for Petersen's direction and his screenplay. His next picture, *The Neverending Story* (84), was a big draw at the German box office and led to Hollywood offers. Although his first two American films were flops, his skill at orchestrating action set pieces turned *In the Line of Fire* (93) with Clint Eastwood (qv) and *Outbreak* (95) with Dustin Hoffman (qv) into potent hits.

MICHELLE PFEIFFER
US actress (1957-)

After work in a supermarket she studied journalism and went into television having won the Miss Orange County beauty contest, earning a regular role in a sitcom. Since *Grease 2* (82) and *Scarface* (83) she has gone from strength to strength, demonstrating a facility for light comedy in the otherwise unremarkable *Into the Night* (85) and making dramatic sparks fly with Jack Nicholson (qv) in *The Witches of Eastwick* (87). In just four years she collected three Oscar nominations, two of them for her best performances to date: as a nightclub singer in *The Fabulous Baker Boys* (89) and a Jackie Kennedy obsessive in *Love Field* (92). Her strength is versatility: the tragic innocent in *Dangerous Liaisons* (88), the seductive Catwoman in *Batman Returns* (92), a worn and weary waitress in *Frankie and Johnny* (91) and in Martin Scorsese's (qv) *The Age of Innocence* (93). She divorced actor Peter Horton in 1988 and married television producer David Kelley in 1993.

GERARD PHILIPE
French actor (1922-59)

The son of a hotel manager in the south of France he abandoned plans to become a doctor in favour of playing small parts on stage and screen in the early 1940s. He established himself in Dostoevsky's *The Idiot* (46) as the saintly Prince Mishkin. In *Le Diable au Corps* (47) he co-starred as a 17-year-old schoolboy in love with a married woman (Micheline Presle) whose soldier husband is fighting at the front. This sensual and sympathetic film provoked outrage, but rocketed Philipe to international stardom. A handsome actor, he displayed a range that encompassed the noble and the soulful, the dashing and the heroic and he became the most popular French romantic star of his generation. Other well-known films include Ophüls's (qv) *La Ronde* (50), the swashbuckling *Fanfan la Tulipe* (52) and *Montparnasse* (58). He became ill while filming *Republic of Sin* (60) in Mexico for Luis Buñuel (qv) and died of a heart attack at 37.

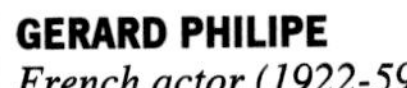

MICHEL PICCOLI
French actor (1925-)

A household name in France he has appeared in more than 100 films since the late 1940s. He was cast as a priest in *La Mort en ce Jardin* (56), but his career only began to prosper when he was offered a leading part in Melville's (qv) *Le Doulos* (63). His talent, which was to be spread across leading roles and character parts, was seized on by Godard (qv) for *Le Mépris* (63), Hitchcock (qv) for *Topaz* (69), Claude Chabrol (qv) for *La Décade prodigieuse* (72) and *Les Noces rouges* (73), and he made significant contributions to Buñuel's (qv) *Belle de Jour* (67) and *The Discreet Charm of the Bourgeoisie* (72). He was also well in tune with the anarchic satire of *Themroc* (73), which he produced and played the role of a rebel worker who puts the brakes on a dead-end life. *Leap Into the Void* (80) secured him the best actor award at Cannes and *A Strange Affair* (81) best actor at Berlin.

Pidgeon, handsome enough for musicals as well as dran

MARY PICKFORD
US actress (1893-1979)

She was America's sweetheart, more chaste than chased. The wonder was that she kept up her little girl lost guise until adulthood. Born in Toronto, Canada, she was trained for the theatre and made two-reelers for D W Griffith (qv), who patronised her as "Little Mary". He did not realise how great a force she was to be in early Hollywood, with films such as *H* *First Biscuits* (09) leading into *T* *Little Princess* and *Rebecca of Sunnybrook Farm* (both 17) anc *Pollyanna* (20). She commande huge fees and was a tough negotiator feared by tycoons suc as Adolph Zukor (qv) and Jesse Lasky. In 1919 she formed Unit Artists with Chaplin, Griffith and Douglas Fairbanks (qqv) and when she wed Fairbanks it was marriage made in box office heaven. *Little Lord Fauntleroy* (2 in which she played mother and son, kept her ideal aloft. When s retired she wrote: "I'm not exac satisfied, but I'm grateful."

WALTER PIDGEON
Canadian actor (1897-1984

He was one of the best loved Hollywood actors from his early career in silent films to the late ɔ70s. Born in East St John and ducated at the University of New 'unswick and the New England ɔnservatory of Music, Boston, he as wounded in France in the first ɔrld war. Returning to New York ɔping to become an actor he was tracted to Hollywood to appear in *'annequin* (26), the first of a ring of silent pictures. The advent the talkies increased his appeal. is resonant diction, baritone voice nd powerful bearing made him iitable for both drama and usicals. His best period came in e second world war as the ɔorting hero in Fritz Lang's (qv) riller *Man Hunt* (41), in John ɔrd's (qv) Welsh saga *How Green 'as My Valley* (41), as Greer arson's (qv) patient husband in *'rs Miniver* (42) and the eerie Dr orbius in the sci-fi classic *ɔrbidden Planet* (56). He worked t his later years in numerous ımeo roles, most notably *Funny 'rl* (68) and his last film *Sextette* '8), where he supported Mae est (qv) in her last role.

ASU PITTS
'S actress (1898-1963)

comic foil in countless films she as an accomplished screen tress with a range seldom ‹ploited once sound displaced ents. She was born in Kansas, ɘrived her name from her aunts iza and Susie and grew up in alifornia, entering films as a enager. She had appeared in everal pictures when her strange, stinctive mannerisms caught the 'e of King Vidor (qv), who wrote *ɘtter Times* (19) for her. Another re lead and her career landmark as an extraordinary performance Erich Von Stroheim's (qv) *Greed* 4), as a woman whose craving r wealth drives her husband mad. ıe made her last appearance in *'s a Mad Mad Mad Mad World* .3) before dying from cancer.

ONALD PLEASENCE
ritish actor (1919-95)

ıe of the most distinctively lainous faces, he was born in 'orksop, Nottinghamshire, and lucated at grammar school in ɔrkshire. He began his working life ı the railways before becoming stage manager of a theatre in Jersey in 1939. He made his London stage debut in 1942 in Twelfth Night. He was a wartime flight lieutenant in the RAF and resumed his stage career in 1946, taking on a variety of classical and avant-garde roles. He made his film debut in *The Beachcomber* (54). In 1963 he repeated his stage success in The Caretaker on screen and his career as a slightly

dangerous, edgy and unpredictable villain was born. Some of his most memorable films are *Dr Crippen* (63), *Cul-de-Sac* (66), *The Night of the Generals* (67), his magnificent Blofeld in *You Only Live Twice* (67) and *The Last Tycoon* (76). He was unforgettable as Loomis the psychiatrist in John Carpenter's (qv) *Halloween* (78).

SIDNEY POITIER
US actor (1927-)

Raised in the Bahamas he moved to Florida with his parents and made his Broadway debut by the age of 22. His film debut was in Joseph L Mankiewicz's (qv) *No Way Out* (50), but his intense power was first revealed in *The Blackboard Jungle* (55). *The Defiant Ones* (58) was the first of his films to examine racial issues as a central theme. He quickly became America's foremost black actor, winning an Oscar for *Lilies of the Field* (63) and much acclaim and recognition for his best performances: *In the Heat of the Night* and *Guess Who's Coming to Dinner* (both 67). The 1970s brought a series of bland roles. In *Little Nikita* (88), a silly thriller, he and River Phoenix played some affecting scenes together. As a director (he began in 1972 with *Buck and the Preacher*) he has not yet proved himself, though as an actor he still brings quiet dignity to his roles. In 1994 he was appointed president of Walt Disney.

ROMAN POLANSKI
Polish director (1933-)

Having watched his parents taken from the Cracow ghetto to concentration camps (his mother died in Auschwitz), he escaped and was shot at by German soldiers as he roamed the Polish countryside. Sharon Tate, his wife, was murdered in 1969 by the Manson family and in 1977 he fled America after being charged with raping a 13-year-old in the home of Jack Nicholson (qv). It is unsurprising that alienation, insecurity, obsession and violence form Polanski's dramatic centre, often framed by absurdity or irony. *Knife in the Water* (62), his only Polish-made feature, won him world acclaim. *Repulsion* (65) and *Rosemary's Baby* (68) followed in which, respectively, Catherine Deneuve (qv) and Mia Farrow flourished as never before. After *Cul-de-Sac* (66) he made *Macbeth* (71) in the wake of Tate's murder. Always a skilled technician, Polanski proved expert at ambiguity in *Chinatown* (74) and *The Tenant* (76). His version of *Death and the Maiden* (94) has typically sharp editing and fluid camera moves.

VAN NEST POLGLASE
US art director (1898-1968)

In Hollywood's heyday each studio's output had a distinctive look, attributable to the supervising art director. Polglase's vision at RKO, where he was in charge of decor, set construction and dressing throughout the 1930s, had a striking impact. Recognised for pristine, all-white, art deco interiors, his work set the mood for films such as *King Kong* (33), *Top Hat* (35) and *Citizen Kane* (41) and period spectacles including *The Hunchback of Notre Dame* (39). A New Yorker and initially an architecture student, he was made assistant art director in 1919 at Famous Players-Lasky (later

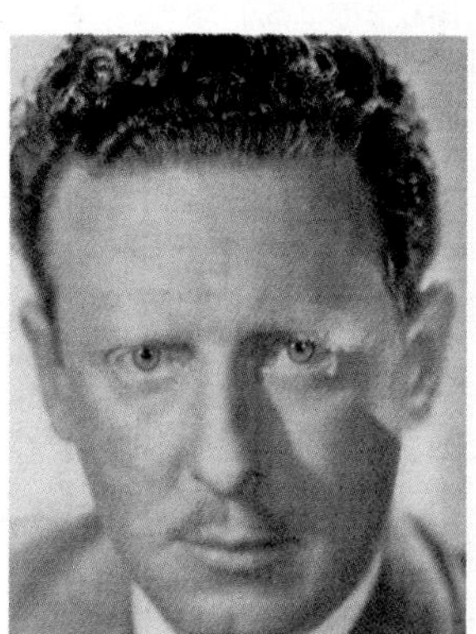

Paramount), which set the trend for art departments. In the 1920s he was among a remarkable group of talents working under Cedric Gibbons (qv) at MGM. From 1932 he led a team at RKO that included chief unit art director Carroll Clark, with whom he conceived the elegant look for Astaire and Rogers (qqv) musicals, and Perry Ferguson, whose ingenuity created wonders for *Citizen Kane*. Polglase was dropped by RKO in 1941 for heavy drinking and worked in the mid-1940s at Columbia, where he contributed to *Gilda* (46).

SYDNEY POLLACK
US director (1934-)

A Hollywood liberal whose films often use social issues as background, he is noted for his ability to elicit powerful performances from ordinary actors. He was born in Indiana and studied at the Neighborhood Playhouse, New York. When a television actor he was introduced to Burt Lancaster (qv), who remained a faithful mentor and friend influencing Pollack's early career. He moved to directing features with *The Slender Thread* (65), which opened with one of the aerial shots that was to become his hallmark. His first success was *They Shoot Horses, Don't They*

(69) for which he was nominated for a best director Oscar. *The Way We Were* (73) with Barbra Streisand and Robert Redford (qqv) was a box-office blockbuster and he has worked consistently with Redford ever since. Pollack's notable successes are *The Electric Horseman* (79), *Three Days of the Condor* (75), *Bobby Deerfield* (77) and *Tootsie* (82). He has also produced, including *Presumed Innocent* (90). He won the directing Oscar for *Out of Africa* (85), that year's best film.

ERICH POMMER
German producer (1889-1966)

At 18 he joined the Gaumont company in Paris and at 20 became the head of its central Europe office. He fought for the kaiser in the first world war and was badly wounded. In Germany he founded the Decla production company and made *The Cabinet of Dr Caligari* (19). He was in Hollywood briefly in the mid-1920s, but the bulk of his production output was German. He was responsible for such outstanding films as *The Last Laugh* (24), *Variety* (25), *Metropolis* (26), *The Blue Angel* (30) and *The Congress Dances* (31) and fostered the careers of Ernst Lubitsch, Fritz Lang and Josef von Sternberg (qqv). He left Germany when the Nazis came to power, working first in France then for Korda (qv) in Britain. He set up Mayflower with Charles Laughton (qv) and made

Vessel of Wrath (38), which he also directed, *St Martin's Lane* (38) and *Jamaica Inn* (39) and then moved to Hollywood. After the war he helped to restore the shattered German film industry.

COLE PORTER
US composer (1892-1964)

The only top American composer other than Irving Berlin (qv) to write his own lyrics, the Yale-educated heir to a fortune from Peru, Indiana, was a cosmopolitan sophisticate who spent the 1920s with his socialite wife in Paris, his favourite city. A superb and versatile melodist, he brought unique, sometimes risque wit to his non-romantic numbers. Many of his Broadway successes were filmed, among them *Anything Goes* (36, remade 56), which yielded the title song, I Get a Kick Out of You, All Through the Night and You're the Top, *Kiss Me Kate* (53) and *Silk Stockings* (57). Among scores specially composed for Hollywood were *Born to Dance* (36), *Broadway Melody of 1940* (40) and *High Society* (56). A riding accident in 1937 resulted, many operations later, in a leg amputation in 1958. Illness may explain the last and by a long way least of his enduring achievements, his film score for *Les Girls* (57), which Saul Chaplin had to complete.

Music and lyrics by Cole Porter graced High Society

EDWIN S PORTER
US pioneer (1869-1941)

The most innovative American before D W Griffith (qv), his most important picture was *The Great Train Robbery* (03), an 11-minute western for which he developed tracking and panning shots, intercutting and a famous close-up of a gun firing into the camera. He left school at 14 and took a variety of jobs before helping to develop a gunnery rangefinder while serving in the navy. He began making news films then worked at Edison, shooting much of the company's work. One of his early landmark films was *The Life of an American Fireman* (03). He gave Griffith his first job as an actor in *Rescued*

From an Eagle's Nest (07). In spite of making a number of social conscience films and special effects spectaculars, he was more interested in developing production techniques than film narrative, setting up Famous Players, which eventually became Paramount. Although he co-directed a number of features with John Ford (qv), notably *The Eternal City* (15), and worked on the development of sound, colour, widescreen and a 3-D process, he became a casualty of the 1929 Wall Street crash and died in obscurity.

ERIC PORTMAN
British actor (1903-69)

Portman never lost his Yorkshire accent and the stiff upper lip always had a curl of disdain even in such patriotic films as *49th*

Parallel (41) and *One of Our Aircraft Is Missing* (42). Most memorable was his class-conscious factory foreman in *Millions Like Us* (43) explaining to an upper-crust worker (Anne Crawford) why the likes of him is divided from the likes of her. *A Canterbury Tale* (44) gave him a more ambiguous role as a glue-thrower in Powell and Pressburger's (qqv) magical tribute to the mystery of Englishness. He was rarely out of work, his haughty presence giving much-needed weight to *The Spy With a Cold Nose* (66). More to his taste was the homosexual criminal, with Michael Caine (qv) as his partner, in Bryan Forbes's (qv) *Deadfall* (68). He was a camp character, but the accent never slipped.

DICK POWELL
US actor, director and producer (1904-63)

Few actors triumphed so completely in two such conflicting arenas as Powell. Typecast in the 1930s as the easygoing star of numerous Warner musicals, he re-emerged as a tough leading man in the Bogart (qv) tradition. Later on he changed gear again to become a successful producer, director and TV executive. He was a hit in *Blessed Event* (32), his first picture, and went on to appear in such popular musicals as *42nd Street* (33), *Gold Diggers of 1933* (33) and *Dames* (34), partnering Ruby Keeler (qv) in seven films. When his contract with Warner expired signed with Paramount and tried light comedy in Sturges's (qv) delightful *Christmas in July* (40), but he left for RKO after he was forced into more musicals. As Raymond Chandler's hard-boiled private eye Philip Marlowe in *Farewell My Lovely* (45) he hit his stride and starred in a series of noir thrillers. He was married t the actresses Joan Blondell (qv) and June Allyson.

DILYS POWELL
British critic (1901-95)

She was the doyenne of British film critics and had a career of unparalleled longevity, still producing a weekly column in he 94th year. Her childhood was spent in Bournemouth, Dorset, a she won a scholarship to Somerville College, Oxford, where she gained a first. She joined The Sunday Times literary staff and ir 1926 married Humfry Payne, wh became director of the British School of Archeology in Athens. H died suddenly in 1936 and she returned to The Sunday Times. Ir March 1939 she became the newspaper's film critic, a few months before the start of the second world war. She extended her audience through BBC radio, and in 1943 married Leonard Russell, then the newspaper's literary editor. She reviewed curre films until 1976 when she switch to writing about those on televisi but she continued to review for Punch magazine until its demise 1992. Her illuminating, generous wisdom inspired many film-make and actors; she was the most respected critic of her time.

ELEANOR POWELL
US dancer, actress (1910-82

She was a tap dancer supreme and although she made few film her memory lingers, particularly that of her smiling face as she clicked out the rhythm. She bega as a child performer and moved from the Broadway stage to (mainly) Hollywood re-creations Broadway in *George White's Scandals* and *Broadway Melody*

lichael Powell: Britain's isionary artist of the cinema

936 (both 35), *1938* (37) and *940* (40), in which she danced egin the Beguine with Astaire (qv). ight variations were drawn with *orn to Dance* (36), *Lady Be Good* 1), featuring Fascinatin' Rhythm nd The Last Time I Saw Paris, *hip Ahoy* (42), *I Dood It* (43) with

ed Skelton, *Sensations of 1945* 4), W C Fields's (qv) last film, nd *Duchess of Idaho* (50). The st was a guest role, because ter marrying Glenn Ford (qv) in 943 she effectively retired. vorce in 1959 brought a brief turn to the stage, but later she ecame a church minister.

ICHAEL POWELL

ritish producer, director and riter (1905-90)

e was born near Canterbury in ent and worked initially in a bank. siting his father, a French Riviera telkeeper, he acquired a job in ce as an assistant on Rex gram's (qv) *Mare Nostrum* (26). ter he worked at Elstree and entually became a writer and rector of quota quickies. He ade his name with *The Edge of e World* (37) and won a contract th Alexander Korda (qv). With neric Pressburger (qv) he formed e Archers, the most exciting eative partnership in British nema, beginning with *The Spy in ack* (39) and progressing through e works such as *49th Parallel* 1), *The Life and Death of Colonel mp* (43), *A Canterbury Tale* (44), *Know Where I'm Going* (45) and *Matter of Life and Death* (46). ter *Black Narcissus* (47) and *The d Shoes* (48) they made *The nall Back Room* (49) for Korda d the daring fusion of opera, llet and art, *Tales of Hoffman* 2). The partnership ended after *e Battle of the River Plate* (56) d in 1960 the reaction to his ntroversial psychological thriller, *eping Tom*, destroyed his putation. He was one of British nema's most original artists and spired giants such as Coppola, ielberg and Scorsese (qqv). elma Schoonmaker (qv), his dow, is Scorsese's editor.

WILLIAM POWELL

US actor (1892-1984)

He made nearly 100 films between 1922 and retirement in 1955, but Powell is for ever associated with the comedies and comic mysteries of the 1930s. Born in Pittsburgh, Pennsylvania, he made his Broadway debut at 20 and entered films at 30 in *Sherlock Holmes* (22). He was typecast as suave, sneering villains, notably the autocratic film director in *The Last Command* (28), before sound transformed his image. He played detective Philo Vance in four pictures and Dashiell Hammett's

sophisticate sleuth Nick Charles with Myrna Loy (qv) in the seven-film series of *The Thin Man* (34-47). He also shone as the flamboyant showman *The Great Ziegfeld* (36) with his former wife Carole Lombard (qv), in the screwball comedy classic *My Man Godfrey* (36) and as the eccentric patriarch in *Life With Father* (47). He is remembered best as Charles the smooth detective, a highball attached to his hand. He made his last appearance as the ship's doctor in *Mister Roberts* (55). Powell was engaged to Jean Harlow (qv) when she died and married the actress Diana Lewis.

TYRONE POWER

US actor (1913-58)

Even when it was *de rigueur* for leading men to have good looks, Power stood out and must have regretted that his long eyelashes and apologetic smile made him seem too lightweight for serious roles. He progressed from romantic leads in films such as *Ladies in Love* (36) and *Second Honeymoon* (37) to swashbucklers in *The Mark of Zorro* (40) and *Captain From Castile* (47), ending up as brow-furrowed heroes in *The Sun Also Rises* and *Witness for the Prosecution* (both 57). Career ▷

Tyrone Power: often better looking than his leading ladies

high points included *Alexander's Ragtime Band* (38) and *Jesse James (*39), the controversial western with good bad guys. His best performance was as the eventually degraded carnival geek in *Nightmare Alley* (47).

OTTO PREMINGER
US director, producer (1905-86)

The son of a Viennese lawyer who went on to become attorney-general of the Austro-Hungarian empire, he studied law before directing *Die Grosse Liebe* (32). He moved to Hollywood where his grand manner and short fuse did not endear him to Darryl F Zanuck (qv) at Fox, who had him replaced as director of *Kidnapped* (38). After Zanuck was called up to serve in the second world war, Preminger directed *Margin For Error* (43) and *Laura* (44), which was a critical and commercial hit, securing him an Oscar nomination. Now with the clout to shape his career he left Fox for independent production, relishing the controversy he created with *The Moon Is Blue* (53), which shocked by using words such as "pregnant" and "virgin". The all-black *Carmen Jones* (54) and *The Man With the Golden Arm* (55), Tinseltown's first attempt at understanding the drug addict. *Anatomy of a Murder* (59), *Advise and Consent* (62) and *The Cardinal* (63) are career highlights. He appeared in *The Pied Piper* (42) and *Margin For Error* (43).

ELVIS PRESLEY
US singer, actor (1935-77)

One of the most successful figures in the history of showbusiness, Presley was the survivor of twins to a poor white family in Tupelo, Mississippi. They moved to Tennessee when he was 13 where, after singing locally as The Hillbilly Cat, he won a recording contract. His film career began with *Love Me Tender* (56) and continued with *Jailhouse Rock* (57) and *King Creole* (58). From 1958 to 1960 his career was interrupted by army service in West Germany, where he met his future wife Priscilla. On discharge he continued with *GI Blues* (60), *Blue Hawaii* (61), *Girls! Girls! Girls!* (62), *Viva Las Vegas* (64), *Paradise Hawaiian Style* (66) and *Double Trouble* (67). He was not regarded as a great actor and his films were thin storylines with songs and girls. His film career nose-dived from 1969 and in his last years he became reclusive. His weight ballooned and his reliance on drugs got out of control. He died at 42 of an overdose-induced heart attack.

Elvis swings more than his pelvis in Girls! Girls! Girls!

EMERIC PRESSBURGER
British writer, director and producer (1902-88)

With his friend Michael Powell (qv) he wrote, produced and directed some of Britain's most prestigious films of the 1940s and 1950s, most notably *A Matter of Life and Death* (46), *Black Narcissus* (47) and *The Red Shoes* (48). Born in Hungary, he studied civil engineering at Prague University before shifting to journalism and then screenwriting German films, collaborating with Max Ophüls (qv) among others. With Hitler's rise he joined the exodus to France before arriving in Britain, making his debut with *The Challenge* (38). Contracted by Korda (qv) to write the *Spy in Black* (39) for Powell, it began an extraordinary collaboration that included *49th Parallel* (41) and *One of Our Aircraft Is Missing* (42). *The Life and Death of Colonel Blimp* (43) and *A Canterbury Tale* (44) evoked a romantic vision of Englishness while also stretching the boundaries between the surreal and the sublime. Other films include *The Small Back Room* (49) and *The Battle of the River Plate* (56) and *Tales of Hoffman* (52), their last collaboration. He continued writing under the name of Richard Imrie.

ROBERT PRESTON
US actor (1918-87)

For almost 20 years Preston was a reliable supporting actor or B-movie leading man. He secured a Paramount contract two years after leaving school, coasting amiably in many pictures until he became a hit on Broadway as the deceitful travelling salesman Harold

Hill in The Music Man, which won him a Tony and made him a star. After reprising *The Music Man* (62) on screen he was memorable as Jean Simmons's (qv) husband in *All the Way Home* (63) and as Steve McQueen's (qv) hard-drinking father in *Junior Bonner* (72). In the 1980s his career flourished again under the direction of Blake Edwards (qv), for whom he appeared in *S O B* (81) and in drag in *Victor/Victoria* (82), for which he received his sole Oscar nomination.

JACQUES PREVERT
French writer (1900-77)

He was drawn toward surrealism in the 1920s just as the scene was burgeoning and he became one of its most influential and imaginative intellectuals. It seemed a natural progression that he should turn to writing poetry, but less so that he should become a screenwriter, which he did in 1932 with *L'Affaire est dans le Sac*. It was the first of three of his works to be directed by his brother Pierre. In 1936

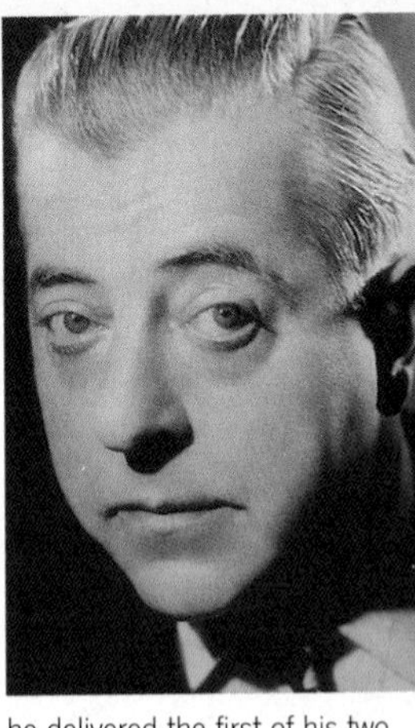

he delivered the first of his two masterpieces, *Le Crime de Monsieur Lange* directed by Jean Renoir (qv) and, for Marcel Carné (qv), *Les Enfants du Paradis* (45). Both films displayed immense emotional insight, marrying poetic fantasy to harsh, prosaic reality. His subsequent work included co-writing a ballet and writing lyrics for popular music. It brought him to a wider audience but never matched the depth of his best screenplays.

MARIE PREVOST
Canadian actress (1898-1937)

In a brief life she made many films starting as a celebrated Mack Sennett (qv) Bathing Beauty. A dark-haired coquette of fetching face and figure, her most notable films were three sophisticated social comedies for Ernst Lubitsch (qv). In *The Marriage Circle* (24) she was Adolphe Menjou's (qv) selfish, flirtatious wife, with May McAvoy and Pauline Frederick she was one of the *Three Women* (24) and as the lead in *Kiss Me Again* (25), the wife who takes a lover. In two bedroom farces, *Up in Mabel's Room* (26) and *Getting Gertie's Garter* (27), she was an asset in the title roles, cleverly skirting vulgarity, and played a hardened reformatory inmate in Cecil B DeMille's (qv) *The Godless Girl* (29). She made a successful transition to sound but, already a drug addict, her career dipped. She was relegated to supporting roles in forgotten titles or even lower down the cast in better vehicles for important actresses. She died of self-induced starvation in an effort to combat her weight problem.

NCENT PRICE
S actor (1911-93)

made his name as a romantic d in London and on Broadway, : became an archetypal villain st known for his horror films. ; first film was *Service de Luxe* 3). Period roles predominated, in *Tower of London* (39), *dson's Bay* (40), *Dragonwyck* 5) and *The Three Musketeers* 3). Contemporary roles, *Laura* 4), *Leave Her To Heaven* (45) d *While the City Sleeps* (56), and sterns were fewer. His horror out was *House of Wax* (53). *The* (58) and eight films for Roger rman (qv), including *The House Usher* (60), *The Pit and the ndulum* (61), *Tales of Terror* 2), *The Raven* (63), *The Masque the Red Death* and *The Tomb of eia* (both 64), established the pular image. He sent it up in *Dr ldfoot and the Bikini Machine* 5) and *The Abominable Dr ibes* (71). His last film was *ward Scissorhands* (90). He was expert in art and cookery and author. He was married to the ress Coral Browne.

CHARD PRYOR
S actor, writer (1940-)

rofane and penetrating social mmentator, he was also a sician, a versatile writer and or with a number of hits among 40 films he has appeared in, tten, produced or directed in 25 ars. After a poor childhood in nois and army service he came a nightclub entertainer and egular on TV talk shows in the 60s. He made his film debut in

1967 and impressed with occasional dramatic performances, notably in *Lady Sings the Blues* (72). He won an Emmy for material for Lily Tomlin (qv) and co-wrote Mel Brooks's (qv) *Blazing Saddles* (74). He was particularly successful with Gene Wilder (qv) in *Silver Streak* (76) and *Stir Crazy* (80) and was the inspiration for new talents, including Eddie Murphy (qv), with a series of audacious stage performances on film starting with *Richard Pryor Live in Concert* (79). Five times married, he was injured in a fire in 1980 and had suffered two heart attacks when multiple sclerosis cut his career short in the early 1990s.

VSEVOLOD I PUDOVKIN
Russian director (1893-1953)

His unique contribution married his theories on montage to traditional revolutionary romanticism, bringing together such disparate images as a workers' demonstration with a thawing river, to suggest revolution, as in his memorable adaptation of Gorky's *Mother* (26). Reluctant to depict the masses as the motive force of history, he centred the action on inspirational revolutionary heroes, most purposefully in such films as *The End of St Petersburg* (27) and *Storm over Asia* (28). Born in Penza, he dropped out of Moscow University to join the army and ended up as a prisoner during the first world war. He escaped to Moscow in 1918 where he became fascinated by the power of film after seeing D W Griffith's (qv) *Intolerance*. Joining Lev Kuleshov at the State Film School, where he developed the idea for *Mechanics of the Brain* (26), he made his debut as a director with *Hunger – Hunger – Hunger* (21). After recovering from a car crash he returned to make heroic films including *General Suvorov* (40) and *Admiral Nakhimov* (46).

DAVID PUTTNAM
British producer (1941-)

Born in London, the son of a newspaper photographer, he went into advertising at 16 as a messenger boy and became, at 20, an account director. He started his own business as a photographers' agent but in the late 1960s he

turned to films. His first production was *Melody* (71) and his first notable success was *That'll Be the Day* (74). He concentrated on low budget, cult successes including *Lisztomania* (75), *Bugsy Malone* (76) and *The Duellists* (77) until he received his first Oscar nomination for *Midnight Express* (78). *Chariots of Fire* (81) won him an Oscar, worldwide critical and commercial success. *The Killing Fields* (84) and *The Mission* (86) were both nominated for Oscars and in 1986 he was invited to head Columbia studios. His crisp approach to Hollywood egos and the ambitious financial demands of agents stepped on too many toes and after 13 months he was ousted. He has since produced films for Warner. *Memphis Belle* (90), *Meeting Venus* (91) and *War of the Buttons* (94) have appeared so far.

DENNIS QUAID
US actor (1954-)

Born in Houston, Texas, the younger brother of the actor Randy Quaid, he first attracted critical attention as the cycle-racing youth in *Breaking Away* (79). He and Randy played brothers and outlaws in *The Long Riders* (80) and he

was one of the test pilots trained as astronauts for *The Right Stuff* (83). After playing a spaceman in *Enemy Mine* (85) and a New Orleans cop in *The Big Easy* (86), he portrayed the legendary rocker Jerry Lee Lewis in *Great Balls of Fire* (89), a role enabling him to deploy his considerable musical skills. He was the unreliable stud in *Postcards from the Edge* (90) and gave an impressive performance in *Come See the Paradise* (90) as an American who marries into a Japanese-American family just before Pearl Harbor. More recently he distinguished himself playing Doc Holliday in *Wyatt Earp* (94). He is married to Meg Ryan (qv).

ANTHONY QUAYLE
British actor (1913-89)

He had a steely reserve and gracious charm which represented the kind of Englishness worldwide audiences understood. *Hamlet* (48), *The Battle of the River Plate* (56), *The Wrong Man* (57) and *Ice Cold in Alex* (58) gave him substantial roles, but he seemed content not to play leads. This contrasted markedly with his theatrical life; he often excelled at the Old Vic and on Broadway and ran the Shakespeare Memorial Theatre at Stratford-upon-Avon. He will be best remembered as Colonel Brighton in *Lawrence of Arabia* (62) and as Wolsey in *Anne of the Thousand Days* (69), which won him an Oscar nomination.

ANTHONY QUINN
Mexican actor (1915-)

His swarthy, craggy looks have graced more than 100 films to portray a bewildering array of nationalities, from native American to Greek. Typecast in ethnic roles he has been less fortunate with his scripts, although he won supporting actor Oscars in *Viva Zapata!* (52) and *Lust for Life* (56) and in the 1960s scored successes with *The Guns of Navarone* (61) and *Zorba the Greek* (64). Off-screen he is a passionate art and book collector whose ambition to star in a film about Picasso was recently frustrated. He has rarely been called on to engage an audience with the subtler skills he brought to bear on the tragically inarticulate Zampano the showman in Federico Fellini's (qv) *La Strada* (54).

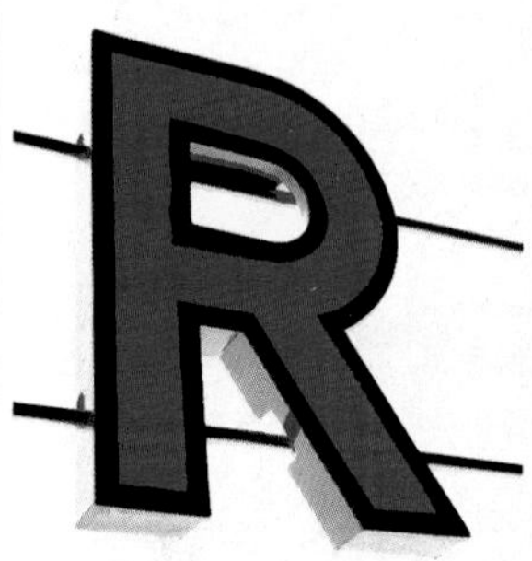

BOB RAFELSON
US director (1933-)

Before entering television as a story editor he had a number of different jobs: disc jockey, consultant to a Japanese film company and a musician in an Acapulco jazz band. In the mid-1960s he created the pop group the Monkees and was responsible for engineering its route to stardom. *Head* (68), the group's psychedelic film he directed and co-wrote with Jack Nicholson (qv), was a wacky but oddly sour depiction of fame and insanity. Although highly original it prepared nobody for *Five Easy Pieces* (70). A dark portrait of contemporary American disillusionment seen through the fashionable anti-hero (Nicholson), it marked Rafelson out as a startling talent. He was with Nicholson again on *The King of Marvin Gardens* (72), which was flawed but also incisive. He has directed only seven films in more than two decades, though his later choice of projects is uninspired – the bland thriller *Black Widow* (87) and the flaccid comedy *Man Trouble* (92), again with Nicholson.

GEORGE RAFT
US actor (1895-1980)

He was one of Hollywood's four favourite tough guys with Bogart, Cagney and Robinson (qqv). Virtually expressionless and often wearing gloves and spats with a trilby pulled over his eyes, he exuded a suave menace that was irresistible to 1930s audiences. Brought up in the tough Hell's Kitchen neighbourhood of New York, he was a boxer who reputedly won 15 of 22 professional fights. He was not shy with his gangland connections and claims he was working as a heavy at Texas Guinan's nightclub when she suggested he take a role in her film *Queen of the Night Clubs* (29). He played similar shady parts in other

films before the menacing hoodlum in *Scarface* (32) made his name. He was the steely nightclub owner in *Night After Night* (32) with Mae West (qv) and his hardline reputation was confirmed with roles in thrillers such as *Each Dawn I Die* (39), *They Drive by Night* (40) and *Broadway* (42). He was not averse to sending himself up and in *Some Like It Hot* (59) he asks a coin-flipping hood: "Where didya pick up that cheap trick?"

RAIMU
French actor (1883-1946)

Jules Muraire was in music hall at 16 and established himself in the theatre in the 1920s. His film career began in 1931 with Guitry's (qv) *Le Blanc et le Noir*, followed by Pagnol's (qv) *Marius*. It is with Pagnol's films that he will be for ever linked. His barrel organ voice and skilful switches from boisterous humour to dramatic intensity were particularly suited to Pagnol's characters. In Pagnol's Marseille trilogy as César, the crabby but lovable cafe owner whose son Marius runs away to sea, he repeated the role he brilliantly created on stage in *Marius* (31), *Fanny* (32) and *César* (36). Countless films followed, including *Gribouille* (37) for Marc Allégret (qv), a brief appearance in Duvivier's (qv) *Un Carnet de Bal* (37) and Pagnol's *The Well-Digger's Daughter* (40). His finest performance, though, is perhaps in *The Baker's Wife* (38) as the cuckolded husband who refuses to bake until his errant wife returns. He was one of France's greatest and best-loved actors.

LUISE RAINER
US actress (1910-)

The winner of best actress Oscar in consecutive years for *The Great Ziegfeld* (36) and *The Good Earth* (37), she was born in Vienna and was successful on stage and screen in Austria and Germany. Moving to America and a contract with MGM, she took Myrna Loy's (qv) place opposite William Powell (qv) in *Escapade* (35). She married the playwright Clifford Odets in 1937 and made only five more films for the studio: *The Emperor's Candlesticks* with Powell again and *Big City* (both 37) as Spencer Tracy's (qv) put-upon spouse, *The Toy Wife, The Great Waltz* as Johann Strauss's wronged wife, and *Dramatic School* (all 38). She retired from films, returning only for *Hostages* (43). Rarely seen since, her contribution to When the Lion Roars, the TV documentary on MGM, was a highlight.

CLAUDE RAINS
British actor (1889-1967)

A perfectly mannered Englishman whose polish was often employed for maximum irony, he was middle-aged before his film career took off, although he made his professional stage debut at the age of 10. His face somehow matched his urbane voice, although ironically he became a star entirely wrapped in bandages, playing the lead in *The Invisible Man* (33), a role Boris Karloff (qv) had turned down for that very reason. His outstanding later roles included the Bette Davis (qv) vehicles *Now Voyager* (42) and *Mr Skeffington* (44), a glossy Technicolor version of *The Phantom of the Opera* (43), *Caesar and Cleopatra* (45) and in Hitchcock's (qv) *Notorious* (46). His most memorable role was as the wily police chief who eventually begins a beautiful friendship with Bogart (qv) in *Casablanca* (42).

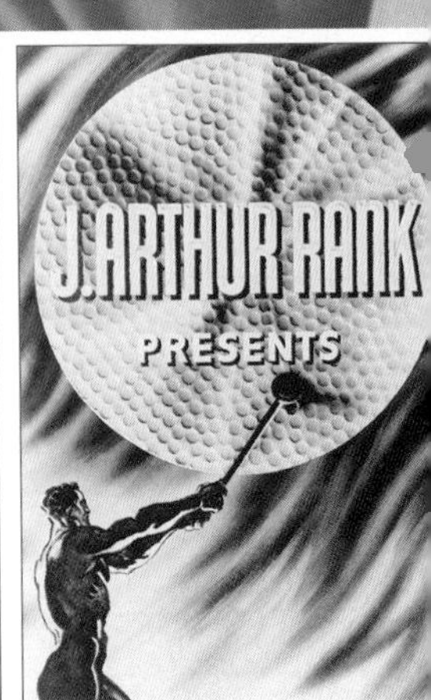

J ARTHUR RANK
British mogul (1888-1972)

As the heir to a prosperous flour business his financial future was already secure when in the early 1930s he began promoting religious features and acquired a taste for making and distributing

…p cop Rains and Ingrid …ergman in Casablanca

…ms. He built Pinewood Studios in …36, formed General Film …stributors and bought the Odeon …nema circuit, giving him a …mmanding position in each area …the film industry. Later Gaumont …nemas were added to the Rank …npire and other British studios …d production companies, …cluding Denham and …insborough. He had ambitions …Britain to rival Hollywood and …der his confident regime films …ch as *Henry V* (44), *Brief …counter* (45) and *Great …pectations* (46) were made. After …er-expansion, including a charm …hool, a monthly magazine on film …d a cartoon division, the …ganisation came under tough …cal control from John Davis, who …sured its survival. Rank was …nobled in 1957 and remained as …esident until his death.

JEAN-PAUL RAPPENEAU
French director, screenwriter (1932-)

It was as a screenwriter that he first gained repute, co-writing *Zazie dans le Métro* (60) and *La Vie privée* (62) with the director Louis Malle (qv) and, with three

collaborators, the international hit *That Man From Rio* (64), a spy spoof starring Jean-Paul Belmondo (qv). He made his directing debut with *La Vie de Château* (65), a light comedy in which a bored Catherine Deneuve (qv) gets mixed up with a Free French agent during the Nazi occupation, that he co-wrote with Alain Cavalier and Claude Sautet. Rappeneau only made four more films, but they included the swashbuckling romp *Les Mariées de l'An II* (70) and a homage to Hollywood comedies of the 1930s, *Le Sauvage* (75), starring Yves Montand (qv) and Deneuve. He capped his career with *Cyrano de Bergerac* (90), providing Gérard Depardieu (qv) with one of his greatest roles.

BASIL RATHBONE
British actor (1892-1967)

He was born in Johannesburg, the son of a British engineer, and brought to Britain at the age of four. His cousin, the actor Sir Frank Benson, persuaded him to

give up his insurance job for the stage. After winning the Military Cross in the first world war he appeared at Stratford-upon-Avon and in 1921 made his first film, *Innocent*. His American film career began in 1924 with *Trouping with Ellen*. Sound brought with it an MGM contract and his first talkie, *The Last of Mrs Cheyney* (29). In Selznick's (qv) *David Copperfield* (35) he played the cruel stepfather so successfully he became typecast as a fascinating villain. An expert swordsman, the most memorable of his duels was in *The Adventures of Robin Hood* (38) in which he fought Errol Flynn (qv). It was almost equalled by his encounter with Tyrone Power (qv) in *The Mark of Zorro* (40). His Holmes remains the definitive screen portrayal of the great detective first seen in *The Hound of the Baskervilles* (39), with Nigel Bruce as Watson.

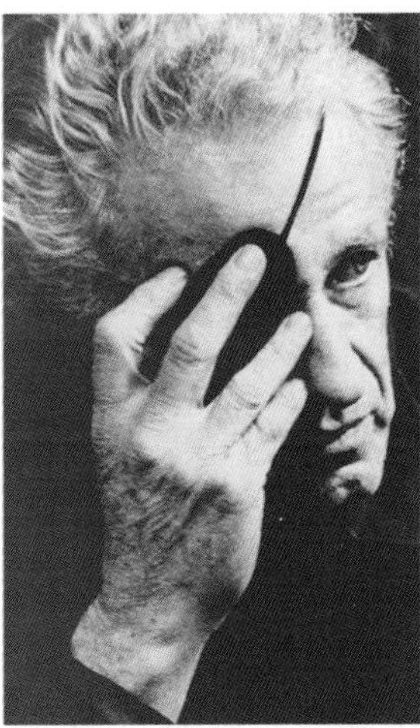

NICHOLAS RAY
US director (1911-79)

He studied architecture under Frank Lloyd Wright and worked in the theatre under the direction of Elia Kazan and John Houseman (qqv). His early pictures frequently focused on the outsider as hero. In his first, the lyrical *They Live by Night* (48), Farley Granger played a weak-natured bank robber on the run. *In a Lonely Place* (50) had Humphrey Bogart (qv) as a self-destructive screenwriter on a murder charge. *On Dangerous Ground* (51) featured Robert Ryan (qv) as an embittered city cop and *Johnny Guitar* (54) starred Joan Crawford (qv) as a conniving saloon owner. There was also James Dean (qv) as the *Rebel Without a Cause* (55). But it was not until his later years that his early prowess as a director was recognised. One admirer was Wim Wenders (qv) who cast him in an acting role in *The American Friend* (77) and with him co-directed *Lightning Over Water* (80).

SATYAJIT RAY
Indian director (1921-92)

Recognised as the director who introduced Indian cinema to the West, he was born into a well-to-do family prominent in the arts. He graduated with honours in economics and then enrolled at the Hindu poet Rabindranath Tagore's alternative university, where for two years he studied painting and art history. He worked as an art director and book illustrator, becoming so obsessed with one novel that, encouraged by Jean Renoir (qv) and his friends, he transformed it into his first film, *Pather Panchali* (55), which won a special jury prize at Cannes. Two sequels followed, *Aparajito* (56) and *The World of Apu* (59). Three memorable films of the 1960s focused on women, *Devi* (60), *Two Daughters* (61) and *The Lonely Wife* (64), while others explored Indian mythology, including *The Philosopher's Stone* (57) and *The Adventures of Goopy and Bagha* (68). Angered by the effects of the famine in Bengal he was moved to make *Distant Thunder* (73). His first film with Hindi and English versions was *The Chess Players* (77), starring Saeed Jaffrey and Richard Attenborough (qv). After several heart attacks in the 1980s he returned with *Branches of the Tree* (90) and *The Stranger* (92), which won him an honorary Oscar.

MARTHA RAYE
US actress, comedienne and singer (1916-94)

She was an iron-lunged belter of songs in the big band era and a brash comedienne. A striking contrast to velvet-voiced Bing Crosby (qv), with whom she made *Rhythm on the Range* (36), *Waikiki Wedding* and *Double or Nothing* (both 37), she appeared in a string of good-natured, undistinguished musicals of which the best known are the zany *Hellzapoppin* (41) and *Four Jills in a Jeep* (44), in which she played herself. She entertained the troops during the wars in Korea and Vietnam, earning the Jean Hersholt Humanitarian Award in 1969. A bouncy pleasure seeker whose husbands included musician David Rose and the make-up artist Bud Westmore (qv), she married her seventh and last when she was 75. She had her own TV show in the late 1950s, sang The Most Beautiful Girl in the World with Jimmy Durante (qv) in *Jumbo* (62) and was a passenger aboard *The Concorde – Airport '79* (79). Her most memorable was in Chaplin's (qv) *Monsieur Verdoux* (47).

RONALD REAGAN
US actor (1911-)

An Iowa sports broadcaster, he moved to California in his mid-twenties and signed with Warner. From *Love Is on the Air* (37) to *The Girl From Jones Beach* (49) he went virtually unnoticed until he played the brave, dying footballer in *Knute Rockne – All American* (40) with his then wife Jane Wyman (qv) and was the double amputee in *Kings Row* (42) saying: "Where's the rest of me?" He served as a captain in the USAAF, making wartime training films and became president of the Screen Actors Guild in 1947. He made *The Hasty Heart* (50) in Britain and *Bedtime for Bonzo* (51) memorably cast him opposite a chimpanzee. He married the actress Nancy Davis in 1952. Long-running television shows revived his career, but his final film was *The Killers* (64). By then his political ambitions were all-consuming and he became governor of California. He won the Republican nomination for president and the presidency in 1980 and a second term in 1984.

ROBERT REDFORD
US actor, director (1937-)

Born in Santa Monica, California, he attended the University of Colorado and the American Academy of Dramatic Arts, New York. His Broadway debut in Tall Story led to television and work as a jobbing actor until his film debut in *War Hunt* (62). His role in Neil Simon's (qv) play Barefoot in the Park won him the film role in 1967 and *Butch Cassidy and the Sundance Kid* (69) with Paul Newman (qv) catapulted him to stardom. *Downhill Racer* (69), *The Candidate* (72), *The Way We Were* (73) and *The Sting* (73), which brought an Oscar nomination, followed. After *The Great Gatsby* (74), *The Great Waldo Pepper* (75), *All the President's Men* (76) and *The Electric Horseman* (79), Redford made his directing debut with *Ordinary People* (80), which won the best picture Oscar. He acted in *The Natural* (84), *Out of Africa* (85) and returned to directing with *The Milagro Beanfield War* (87), *A River Runs Through It* (92) and *Quiz Show* (95). He resists the temptation to appear on screen when he is directing. He is the founder of the Sundance Institute, which stages an annual film festival for independents.

MICHAEL REDGRAVE
British actor (1908-85)

The son of the actor Roy Redgrave, he followed a successful foray into journalism and writing, and directing for the theatre with a part in Hitchcock's (qv) *The Lady Vanishes* (38). Before and after the war he had a variety of roles notable not only for his excellence but also for their unusual complexity. They include an episode in the supernatural thriller *Dead of Night* (45) and *The Captive Heart* (46). He also shone in *The Browning Version* (51), for which he won the Cannes Film Festival prize for best actor, and *The Importance of Being Earnest* (52). Thereafter, there was a decline in both his choice of parts and the intellectual prowess he brought to them, though he was on fine form in Welles's (qv) *Mr Arkadin* (55) and Losey's (qv) *Time Without Pity* (57). The ensuing decades were dry periods in which he found time for many performances with little inspiration, excepting *Uncle Vanya* (63). He was knighted in 1959. He died of Parkinson's disease.

VANESSA REDGRAVE
British actress (1937-)

The daughter of Michael Redgrave (qv) and Rachel Kempson and the sister of Lynn and Corin Redgrave, she is the highly theatrical and often controversial member of the distinguished acting dynasty. She was married to the director Tony Richardson (qv) and their daughters Joely and Natasha are successful actresses. Her stage career was outstanding, particularly with the Royal Shakespeare Company. Her film debut was *Behind the Mask* (58). With her brother, she became involved with the left-wing Workers' Revolutionary party, which led her to take many controversial stands. Her film career has been variable, but its highlights include *Morgan – A Suitable Case for Treatment* and *A Man for All Seasons* (both 66), *Camelot* (67), *Isadora* (68), *Mary Queen of Scots* (71), for which she was nominated for an Oscar, *The Bostonians* (84), *Wetherby* (85) and *Little Odessa* (95). Her finest role, in *Julia* (77), won her a best supporting actress Oscar.

CAROL REED
British director (1906-76)

Throughout the 1920s he appeared in minor stage roles. In the early 1930s he worked as assistant director on Basil Dean's *Autumn Crocus* (34) and made his directing debut with *Midshipman Easy* (35) followed by *Laburnum Grove* (36). His reputation was enhanced with *Bank Holiday* (38), *A Girl Must Live* and *The Stars Look Down* (both

A question of continuity for Carol Reed on location, right

, *Night Train to Munich* (40) *Kipps* (41). *The Way Ahead* evolved from an army training ‑cumentary into a distinguished ‑ish war film. He reached his ‑ative peak in the late 1940s ‑ a trio of outstanding films: *‑d Man Out* (47) with James ‑son (qv) as a hunted, wounded ‑fast gunman, *The Fallen Idol* ‑), in which a diplomat's son ‑eves the genial butler he ‑nires to be a murderer, and *The ‑rd Man* (49), Graham Greene's ‑ study of paranoia and despair ‑post-war Vienna. His talent often ‑wed through in the lesser films ‑t followed, although *Oliver!* (68) ‑s his biggest commercial ‑cess delivering him the ‑ector's Oscar and winning best ‑. He was knighted in 1952.

‑NNA REED
‑ actress (1921-86)

‑he 1940s and 1950s she was ‑dominantly cast as wholesome ‑friends and wives. It is ironic, ‑refore, that she won an Oscar ‑playing a prostitute in *From ‑e to Eternity* (53). Raised on a ‑n in Iowa, she had set her ‑ts on a secretarial career when, in 1941, she was given a screen test by MGM. In her first film, *The Get-Away* (41), she established her persona playing the innocent sister of an escaped convict and she made an impact as the army nurse who falls for John Wayne (qv) in *They Were Expendable* (45). Loaned out to RKO, she was luminous as James Stewart's (qv) wife in *It's a Wonderful Life* (46) and became a star. She signed with Columbia in 1951 but failed to escape her rosy-cheeked image. In 1958 she began a TV sitcom, The Donna Reed Show, playing an all-American housewife and mother.

KEANU REEVES
US actor (1964-)

Born in Beirut to a Chinese-Hawaiian father and English mother, he grew up in Australia and New York before enrolling at Toronto's High School for the Performing Arts. Effective as either a troubled youngster or idiotic teen, he convincingly inhabited one dimension for the multi-layered *River's Edge* (87), while he was at ease with the comedy of *The Prince of Pennsylvania* (88). It was the global triumph of *Bill and Ted's Excellent Adventure* (89) that won him the youth audience and put his face on many bedroom walls. Small, telling roles in *Dangerous Liaisons* (88) and *Parenthood* (89) finally gave way to *My Own Private Idaho* (91), his most substantial triumph. *Bram Stoker's Dracula* (92) and *Much Ado About Nothing* (93) followed, in which Reeves proved well in harmony with Elizabethan frivolity. *Speed* (94) saw him as a non-stop action man and he has since made non-mainstream films, the best of which is Van Sant's (qv) *Even Cowgirls Get the Blues* (94).

CARL REINER
US director (1923-)

Rob (qv), the son, may now overshadow the father, but in his day Reiner's brand of New York wit influenced many, not least Woody Allen (qv). A comic, writer, actor and later producer and director, he worked on TV's Your Show of Shows and appeared in *It's a Mad Mad Mad Mad World* (63) and *A Guide for the Married Man* (67) while he was assembling The Dick Van Dyke Show for television. His semi-autobiographical *Enter Laughing* (67) was written and directed by him from his own stage play. *Where's Poppa?* (70) on Jewish motherhood has won a cult following and he directed George Burns (qv) in *Oh, God* (77). One of his great achievements was bringing Steve Martin (qv) to the screen with *The Jerk* (79), *Dead Men Don't Wear Plaid* (82), *The Man With Two Brains* (83) and *All Of Me* (84). Martin has rarely been as good since.

ROB REINER
US actor, director (1945-)

One of the more versatile talents in contemporary Hollywood, he has had a string of directorial successes since his spoof rock film *This is Spinal Tap* (84) became a cult hit, including his satire on platonic friendship *When Harry Met Sally* (89) and his adaptation of Stephen King's novel *Misery* (90). Born in New York the son of actor-director Carl Reiner (qv), he attended UCLA before working in a number of improvisational theatre groups and writing comedy scripts for television. Making his acting debut in his father's film *Enter Laughing* (67), he won two Emmys

for his role as Meathead in the television sitcom All in the Family, before teaming up with his wife Penny Marshall (qv) in the comedy series More Than Friends and acting in films such as *Fire Sale* (77). After *Spinal Tap* he made the coming-of-age film *Stand By Me* (86) and *The Princess Bride* (87), before switching between romantic comedy, horror and melodrama. The courtroom saga *A Few Good Men* (92), in which Jack Nicholson (qv) stole the acting honours, received a clutch of Oscar nominations, including best picture. His acting credentials include parts in *Sleepless in Seattle* (93) and *Bullets Over Broadway* (94).

LOTTE REINIGER
German animator (1899-1981)

At the age of 17, while a theatre student at Max Reinhardt's school in Berlin, she designed silhouette intertitles for a film by the expressionist director, Paul Wegener, for whose *The Pied Piper of Hamelin* (18) she created the title sequence. Her main interest was in fairy tales and she adapted Chinese shadow theatre to film as well as inventing a special ▷

silhouette technique, first used in *Das Ornament des verliebten Herzens* (22). She won international renown for the world's first (and her only) feature length animated film, *The Adventures of Prince Achmed* (26), a charming tale with monsters, witches, a magic lamp and a rescued princess. With the coming of sound Reiniger, who settled in Britain in the mid-1930s, turned to developing animated films on musical themes – *Carmen* (33), *Papageno* (35), based on Mozart's The Magic Flute and *La Belle Hélène* (57). She also made the short silhouette sequence to Jean Renoir's (qv) *La Marseillaise* (38).

KAREL REISZ
British director (1926-)

An influential but intermittent film-maker, he was born in Czechoslovakia and came to Britain just before the Nazis invaded. He served with the RAF, read chemistry at Cambridge and taught before becoming a film journalist. His book The Technique of Film Editing is still admired and consulted. His first directorial credit was with Tony Richardson (qv) on the short, *Momma Don't Allow* (55). The documentary *We Are the Lambeth Boys* (59) was followed by his successful feature debut, *Saturday Night and Sunday Morning* (60). His films have been relatively few, however, and include *Night Must Fall* (64) with Albert Finney (qv), *Morgan – A Suitable Case for Treatment* (66), *Isadora* (68) with Vanessa Redgrave (qv), *The Gambler* (74) with James Caan, *The Dog Soldiers* (78) with Nick Nolte (qv), *The French Lieutenant's Woman* (81) with Meryl Streep (qv) and Jeremy Irons, *Sweet Dreams* (85) with Jessica Lange (qv) and *Everybody Wins* (90), again with Nolte. He has produced and co-produced films, including Lindsay Anderson's (qv) *This Sporting Life* (63).

IVAN REITMAN
Canadian director, producer (1946-)

He has directed and produced a phenomenal run of lucrative films since launching the National Lampoon series with *Animal House* (78) directed by John Landis (qv). Born in Czechoslovakia, he arrived

in Canada at the age of four, studied music and film and made a controversial debut producing *Columbus of Sex* (70), which earned him an obscenity conviction, and the early David Cronenberg (qv) films *Shivers* (76) and *Rabid* (77). His frequent collaborations with Harold Ramis and Bill Murray include *Ghostbusters* (86), which he directed and produced, and its sequel. He helped transform Schwarzenegger's (qv) image in *Twins* (88), *Kindergarten Cop* (90) and *Junior* (94). His films as a director include *Legal Eagles* (86) and *Dave* (93) and he produced *Beethoven* (92) and its sequel.

LEE REMICK
US actress (1935-91)

Born into a wealthy family in Quincy, Massachusetts, she studied ballet and modern dance and began her career as a member of the Music Circus Tent. She acted on stage and television for several years until her 1957 film debut in *A Face in the Crowd.* She spanned the genres from horror in *The Omen* (76) to the gentility of *The Europeans* (79) and made her reputation as a complex, sensual seductress in *Anatomy of a Murder* (59) and *Wild River* (60). Her films include *Days of Wine and Roses*

(62), for which she won an Oscar nomination, *The Running Man* (63), *No Way to Treat a Lady* (68) and *The Woman's Room* (80). When she married British director William Gowens in 1970 she moved temporarily to Britain. In the 1980s she turned to TV mini-series. She died from cancer at 55.

JEAN RENOIR
French director (1894-1979)

The son of Auguste Renoir, the Impressionist painter, he had a passion for cinema that led to him establishing his own production company. He directed his first film, *La Fille de L'Eau* (24), and made a minor classic in *Boudu Saved From Drowning* (32), a spiky social comedy with rich photography. Although *Le Crime de M Lange* (36) was an incisive political commentary, his first masterpiece was *La Grande Illusion* (37), a devastatingly human story of friendship and class. His second masterpiece, *La Règle de Jeu* (39), was a commercial failure on release, but a magnificent, poetic and deeply personal work. In the 1940s he set off for Hollywood where he worked under contract t Fox. Renoir could not recapture h former glory until his first colour film, *The River* (51). This America period led to commercial failure and he barely directed at all from 1960. He is cinema's most visionary poet, a perceptive direct widely regarded as one of the greatest of all time.

LAIN RESNAIS
'rench director (1922-)

he most intellectual of the New Vave directors to emerge in the ate 1950s and 1960s, he trained s an actor and film editor, then nade numerous documentary horts, many of them studies of rtists, and he gained public cclaim with *Nuit et Brouillard* (56) bout the Nazi concentration amps. Feature films followed, tarting with *Hiroshima Mon Amour* 59), which established his style of fractured narrative, surfing etween past and present, without enefit of a conventional plot and verlaid with gnomic utterances bout the nature of time, memory nd knowledge. The apotheosis 'as the plotless *Last Year at Aarienbad* (61), where characters ose among the topiary while trying) establish whether they have met efore. He has also made more onventional films, such as *La Guerre est finie* (66), *Stavisky* (74) nd *Providence* (77) about a tchy, terminally ill novelist, played y John Gielgud (qv).

ERNANDO REY
panish actor (1917-94)

he son of a republican army fficer, he studied architecture in ladrid and fought in the Spanish vil war before coasting into acting s a film extra, later dubbing nglish-language films into panish. His interpretations of yrone Power and Laurence Olivier qv) were a speciality. Spotted by uis Buñuel (qv) in the Mexican lm *Sonatas* (59) he was cast as e treacherous uncle in *Viridiana* 51), voted best film at Cannes but anned in Spain. Later, Rey and uñuel collaborated on three more utstanding features: *Tristana* (70), *he Discreet Charm of the*

'ourgeoisie (72) and *That Obscure bject of Desire* (77). As Spain's ost visible actor he appeared in ountless foreign films, most imously as the slippery drug ealer in *The French Connection* '1) and its sequel. For his omplex performance as a eclusive biographer in Saura's (qv) *Iisa, Vida mia* (77) he won the est actor award at Cannes.

lain Resnais, left, on the set f Mélo with Sabine Azéma

BURT REYNOLDS
US actor (1936-)

In the 1970s he was the first star since Shirley Temple (qv) to be ranked box office number one for five consecutive years. A southerner headed for a football career until injury sidelined him, he was a Universal contract player until he was dropped, along with Eastwood (qv), in 1956. He tenaciously made his way through the 1960s and 1970s in TV series including Gunsmoke and Dan August until

his breakthrough with a muscular performance in *Deliverance* (72). He posed nude for the centrefold of Cosmopolitan and became a top box office star in a string of macho action and bonehead comedy films, such as *The Mean Machine* (74) and *Smokey and the Bandit* (77), which capitalised on his stunt expertise and twinkly persona. His efforts in more sophisticated material were not appreciated and the long-awaited teaming of Reynolds with Eastwood in *City Heat* (84) disappointed. Evening Shade, a TV series, restored him. He has also directed.

RALPH RICHARDSON
British actor (1902-83)

Kenneth Tynan's essay in which he suggested that God was probably very like Richardson was cherished and decried by the man himself. He had a dislocated grace and his whimsical choice of roles made him seem an uncaring but brilliant amateur. Originally intended for the Catholic priesthood, he was an awesomely creative Shakespearean actor. In films he was a tinpot despot in H G Wells's *Things To Come* (36) and his patriotism drew him to wartime flag wavers such as *The Silver Fleet* (42). Three of his greatest screen performances were as Karenin in *Anna Karenina* (48), the butler in *The Fallen Idol* (48) and the father in *The Heiress* (49). He wandered into epics such as *Doctor Zhivago* (65) and *Battle of Britain* (69) and slid down the stairs on a silver tray as the grandfather in *Greystoke* (84), typical of a man who was a motorcyclist well into old age. His eccentricity enhanced all his roles.

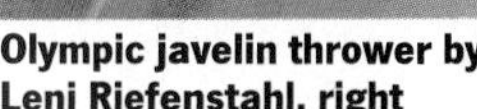

Olympic javelin thrower by Leni Riefenstahl, right

TONY RICHARDSON
British director (1928-91)

With the belated release of the anti-nuclear allegory *Blue Sky* (94), delayed by legal wrangles for three years and starring an Oscar-winning Jessica Lange (qv), reminded audiences of his powerful social dramas such as *A Taste of Honey* (61) and *The Loneliness of the Long Distance Runner* (62). A pharmacist's son from Yorkshire with an antipathy towards authority, he joined the Oxford University Dramatic Society before a successful career at the Royal Court Theatre and the Free Cinema group, where he teamed with Karel Reisz (qv) to co-direct *Momma Don't Allow* (55). He produced *Saturday Night and Sunday Morning* (60) and translated his stage production of John Osborne's *Look Back in Anger* (59) to film. Despite winning an Oscar for *Tom Jones* (63) he never recaptured acclaim with *The Charge of the Light Brigade* (68), *Ned Kelly* (70), *Joseph Andrews* (77) and *The Hotel New Hampshire* (84). Formerly married to Vanessa Redgrave (qv), he was the father of Natasha and Joely Richardson. He died of an Aids-related infection.

LENI RIEFENSTAHL
German director (1902-)

Her undoubted gifts as a film-maker and editor have been overshadowed by her association with and favoured status under Adolf Hitler, who commissioned her to make the hypnotic *Triumph of the Will* (35), a record of the Nazi party's rally at Nuremberg. This was followed by the two-part *Olympiad* (38), a celebration of the human body and the achievements of the 1936 Olympic Games in Berlin, the city of her birth. A striking blonde artist and dancer, she turned to film acting in her mid-twenties and absorbed sufficient technical knowledge to be able to direct, edit, produce, write (with Béla Balázs) and co-star in *The Blue Light* (32). Working as a photo-journalist during the second world war she was imprisoned by the allies for what was seen as her contribution to German propaganda and was not formally cleared until 1952. She was able then to release *Tiefland* (54), begun in 1939. She has since worked as a photo-journalist of striking and original talent, as was evidence by her coverage of the Munich Olympics in 1972.

N TIN TIN
S canine star (1916-32)

e first and arguably the greatest Hollywood's dog stars, he was e of a litter of German shepherd ppies found in a first world war nch by Lieutenant Lee Duncan, o took him home to California d trained him. He was in *The an From Hell's River* (22), but it s his contract with Warner and *here the North Begins* (23) that ade him a huge star. No mere ogrammed dog, but a sentient

d sensitive actor, Rin Tin Tin sibly weighed the odds, whether ndering his own fate, rescuing a ild or battling with a giant condor all of which he did in *The Night y* (26). He "introduced" acts in *e Show of Shows* (29) and, ccessfully making the transition sound, barked in the 12-episode rial *The Lone Defender* (30). arryl F Zanuck (qv) wrote several his screenplays – *Find Your Man* d *The Lighthouse by the Sea* oth 24) and *The Night Cry*. He as greatly mourned and his fans re not pleased by Jack Warner's /) revelation in his 1964 tobiography that the studio had nployed 18 understudies.

ARTIN RITT
S director (1919-90)

orn to Jewish immigrants on anhattan's lower East Side, he ecame identified with probing, ocially concerned films and the rong, sensitive performances he oaxed from his actors. A brief areer as an actor himself gave ay to directing where he learned economy, narrative drive and suspense from the 150 live dramas he directed for TV. Blacklisted for communist sympathies, he spent his time teaching at the Actors Studio. Paul Newman and Joanne Woodward (qqv) are identified with some of his best work, including *The Long Hot Summer* (58), *The Sound and the Fury* (59), *Paris Blues* (61) and *Hud* (63), for which he won an Oscar nomination. His career started with *Edge of the City* (57), which fairly thundered with resonance, while *The Spy Who Came in From the Cold* (65) is one of the best spy films ever made. He was still on top for *Sounder* (72), *The Front* (76) and *Norma Rae* (79), which won Sally Field (qv) the best actress Oscar. His last films, *Nuts* (87) and *Stanley & Iris* (90), were less successful.

Tex Ritter, left, sings for his long-time sidekick Syd Sayler

TEX RITTER
US cowboy (1905-74)

A student, first of political science then law, he rejected law school for music and became a moderately successful folk and country singer. Six years separated his theatrical debut in 1930 from his first film role in *Song of the Gringo* (36) but his growing number of fans, drawn to his rugged looks, wholesome image and inoffensive music, compensated for that. By the 1940s, which saw such box office hits as *The Cowboy From Sundown* (40), *King of Dodge City* (41) and *Deep in the Heart of Texas* (42), he was cinema's most successful professional cowboy. It was he who sang the title song over the credits in *High Noon* (52). Even when his popularity waned he continued to pursue a profitable singing career. His success is a testament to the power of the matinee idol and a bygone era of innocence. His influence on country musicians such as Garth Brooks is tangible.

THELMA RITTER
US actress (1905-69)

Nominated six times for a best supporting actress Oscar without winning, she was a stage and radio actress in her forties when she made her film debut in *Miracle on 34th Street* (47). Her forte was sharp-tongued, disillusioned characters, a range further narrowed by her unmistakable New York accent. She was most effective in her Oscar-nominated roles in *All About Eve* (50), *The Mating Season* (51), *With a Song in My Heart* (52), *Pickup on South Street* (53), *Pillow Talk* (59) and *Birdman of Alcatraz* (62). Her other films include *Rear Window* (54), *Move Over Darling* (63) and, by far the best, *Boeing Boeing* (65).

JACQUES RIVETTE
French director (1928-)

He always felt that his work could not be compressed into a standard length: his *Out One: Spectre* (72), is still unreleased in its original 13-hour version and even the abridged version was four hours long. This film underlined his desire to pick away at the glossy artifice of cinema convention and relies heavily on improvisation and chance. His taste for theatre was filtered through *Paris nous appartient* (61) and *L'Amour fou* (68). Only his first short film *Le Coup du Berger* (56) and *Céline and Julie Go Boating* (74) were at all light-hearted. He was a staff critic and later editor-in-chief of Cahiers du Cinéma. In between he was Renoir's (qv) assistant then cameraman on the 16mm shorts of Truffaut and Rohmer (qqv). His *La Bande des Quatre* (89) won the international critics prize at Berlin, while *La Belle Noiseuse* (91) was a study of the relationship between art and humanity.

The 10 best histories

All Quiet on the Western Front (1930)
Life in the German trenches, in a searing attack on war

Ben-Hur (1959)
Jew and Roman vie against each other in Biblical epic

Les Enfants du Paradis (1945)
Paris street and theatre life in the 1840s is vividly recreated

Gone With the Wind (1939)
Pre- and post-Civil War, Scarlett O'Hara lives another day

Henry V (1944)
Olivier's noble Shakespearean history parallels D-day landings

Lawrence of Arabia (1962)
David Lean's sweeping, epic study of a hero and his destiny

Mutiny on the Bounty (1935)
Captain Bligh became infamous after Charles Laughton's portrayal

Napoléon (1927)
Abel Gance's silent epic was to be an influential landmark

The Red Badge of Courage (1951)
John Huston's Civil War tale survived studio butchery

Seven Samurai (1954)
Kurosawa's classic inspired The Magnificent Seven

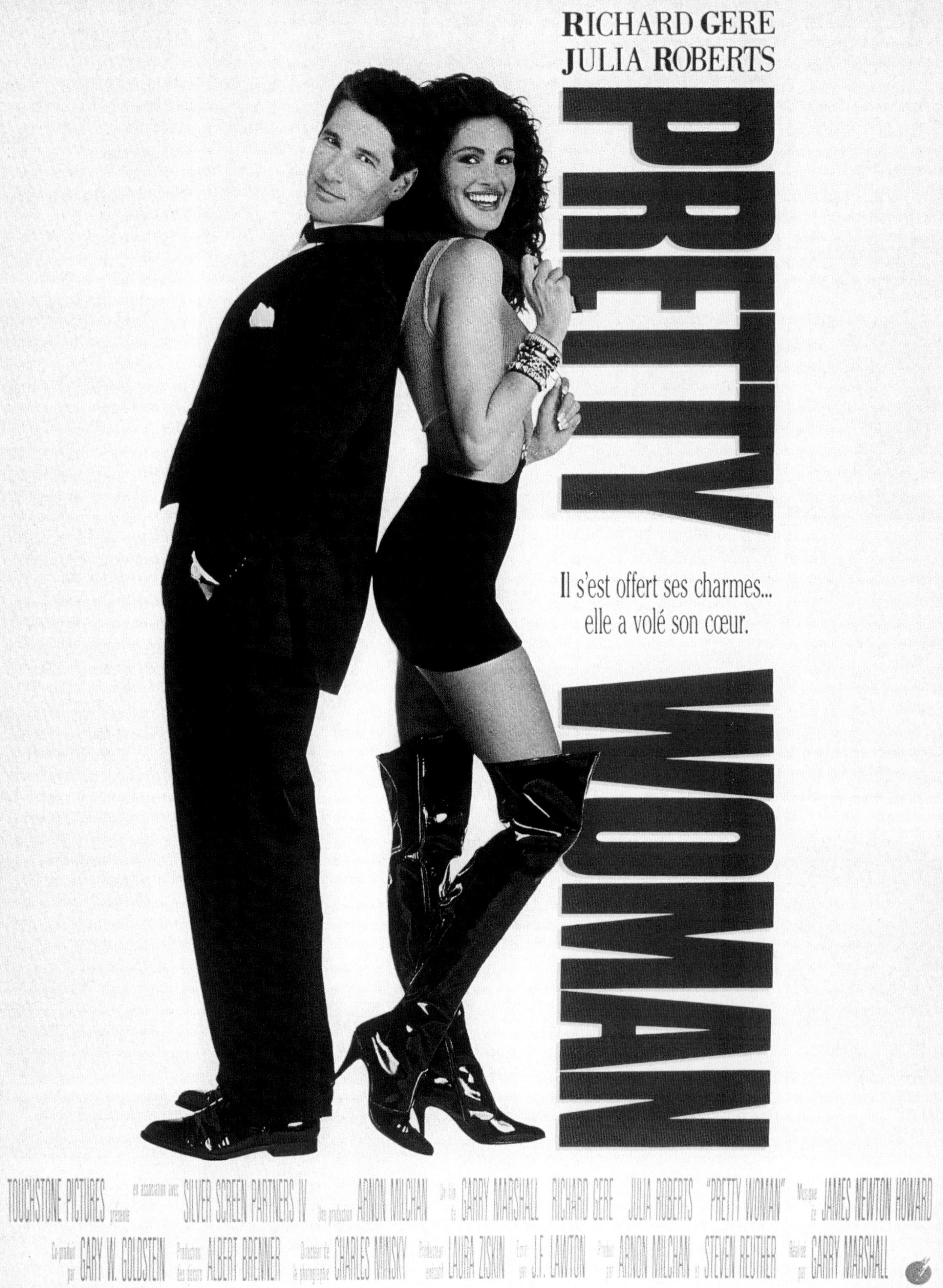

RICHARD GERE
JULIA ROBERTS
PRETTY
WOMAN
Il s'est offert ses charmes...
elle a volé son cœur.
TOUCHSTONE PICTURES présente en association avec SILVER SCREEN PARTNERS IV Une production ARNON MILCHAN Un film de GARRY MARSHALL RICHARD GERE JULIA ROBERTS "PRETTY WOMAN" Musique de JAMES NEWTON HOWARD
Co-produit par GARY W. GOLDSTEIN Production des décors ALBERT BRENNER Directeur de la photographie CHARLES MINSKY Producteur exécutif LAURA ZISKIN Ecrit par J.F. LAWTON Produit par ARNON MILCHAN et STEVEN REUTHER Réalisé par GARRY MARSHALL
DOLBY STEREO
DANS CERTAINES SALLES
Bande originale du film sur disques, cassettes et C.D. EMI
Touchstone Pictures

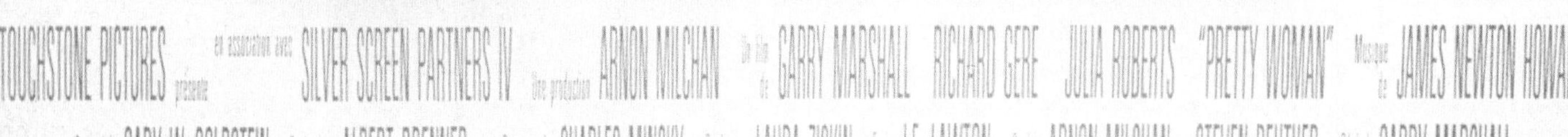

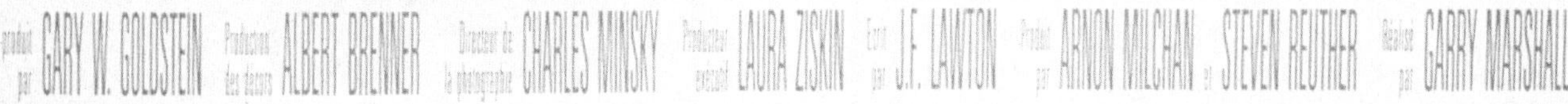

AL ROACH
S producer (1892-1992)

s 100-year lifespan is presentative of the history of the nema: going for laughs at the art, then sobering up as self-vareness grew. A New Yorker, he ospected for gold in Alaska then ent to Los Angeles where in 1912 became a cowboy extra. He amed with comedian Harold oyd (qv) and was soon producing o-reelers. His discoveries cluded Lloyd, Laurel & Hardy, ckey Rooney (qqv) and Charlie nase. Notably he made Lloyd's *afety Last* (23), Laurel & Hardy's *om Soup to Nuts* (28) and *Sons the Desert* (33) and created the *ur Gang* film series. *Topper* (37) as a comedy while *Of Mice and en* (39) showed that he could oduce drama. He came to terms th TV in 1948 with a series for reen directors and in 1983 he as awarded a special Oscar for is distinguished contributions to e motion picture art form".

ASON ROBARDS
'S actor (1922-)

ne son of a distinguished actor, e enlisted in the navy, saw action Pearl Harbor and won the Navy ross. Though initially unimpressed the acting profession he entered e American Academy of Dramatic ts in 1946, attaining star status Broadway in the 1950s, particularly for his interpretation of Eugene O'Neill. He made his film debut in *The Journey* (59) and has divided his career between theatre and films, notably the comedy *A Thousand Clowns* (65), and superior westerns including Leone's (qv) *Once Upon a Time in the West* (68) and Peckinpah's (qv) *The Ballad of Cable Hogue* (70). In maturity his authority and sandpapery voice have made him a distinctive actor, still active in his seventies. He has portrayed numerous roles from Al Capone and Franklin D Roosevelt to Howard Hughes and received consecutive supporting Oscars for his performances as Washington Post managing editor Ben Bradlee in *All the President's Men* (76) and writer Dashiell Hammett in *Julia* (77). Lauren Bacall (qv) was the third of his four wives.

TIM ROBBINS
US actor (1958-)

He lives with the actress Susan Sarandon (qv) and is the son of Greenwich Village folk singer Gill Robbins. He began acting at the age of 12 at a New York experimental theatre while attending high school. During drama studies at the UCLA theatre programme in 1981 he helped found the Actors Gang and later became its artistic director. He made his film debut in *No Small Affair* (84). His first success was in *Bull Durham* (88) with Sarandon. Many small but worthy roles followed, notably *Jacob's Ladder* (90), but Robert Altman's (qv) *The Player* (92) brought him the Cannes best actor award. He wrote, acted in and directed the political satire *Bob Roberts* (92) and has consolidated his career with *Short Cuts* (93), *The Hudsucker Proxy*, *The Shawshank Redemption* and *IQ* (all 94) and *Prêt à Porter* (95).

JULIA ROBERTS
US actress (1967-)

One of Hollywood's highest-paid actresses, she had no formal training beyond growing up in a theatrical family in Georgia. Eric, her actor brother, helped her land an early role in *Mystic Pizza* (88). She quickly moved out of his shadow and into another orbit, earning Oscar nominations for *Steel Magnolias* (89) and *Pretty Woman* (90). Her film portfolio is patchy and the emotional range of her roles rather monotone – variations on the basic theme of feisty but fragile – but she is a natural scene-stealer, being vulnerableand a gifted comedienne.

Her recent films include *Sleeping With the Enemy* and *Hook* (both 91) and *The Pelican Brief* (93), but her lust-consumed hack in Altman's *Prêt à Porter* (95) was a revelation. *My Best Friend's Wedding* (97) extended her range.

CLIFF ROBERTSON
US actor (1925-)

He is an earnest and reliable screen actor who, despite numerous leads, missed out on stardom. After wartime navy service and college he attended the Actors

Studio, carving a Broadway niche in the late 1940s. Joshua Logan cast him as Kim Novak's fiancé in *Picnic* (55) at Columbia and put him under contract, pairing him with Joan Crawford (qv) as her disturbed husband in *Autumn Leaves* (56). His films, many of them war stories, fluctuated between routine mediocrity, *Battle of the Coral Sea* (59), and excellence, *Underworld USA* (61). He was John F Kennedy's choice to portray the president as naval hero in *PT-109* (63), but his finest hour was his moving, Oscar-winning performance as the retarded *Charly* (68). He was director-actor of *J W Coop* (71) and *The Pilot* (80) and appeared in *Three Days of the Condor* (75) and *Midway* (76). He is best known for unmasking studio executive David Begelman as an embezzler – a brave act that earned him the Hollywood cold shoulder.

Paul Robeson in rare high spirits, captured by Karsh

PAUL ROBESON
US singer, actor (1898-1976)

Feted around the world for his rich bass baritone singing voice and praised for the simple dignity of his acting, he was the son of a runaway slave and a Methodist minister. He won a scholarship to Rutgers and played pro football while studying law at Columbia University. He was admitted to the bar in New York but decided on a stage career, achieving celebrity following appearances in All God's Chillun Got Wings and The Emperor Jones. Acclaimed for his portrayals of Joe in Show Boat and Othello, he made his film debut in the screen version of *The Emperor Jones* (33). He seemed happier in Britain where he starred in *Sanders of the River* (35) and *King Solomon's Mines* (37). In Hollywood he performed his signature song Ole Man River in *Show Boat* (36), but later returned to Europe after he was blacklisted in America for his left-wing politics and outspoken views on racism. He committed professional suicide by accepting a Stalin Peace Prize in 1952. His passport was revoked and he was not allowed to leave America for six years. He resumed touring Europe but was taken ill in the early 1960s and returned to New York to live his final years in bitter seclusion in Harlem.

EDWARD G ROBINSON
US actor (1893-1973)

Emmanuel Goldenberg was born in Bucharest, Romania, moving at the age of nine to New York's tough East Side. After winning a scholarship to the American Academy of Dramatic Arts, where he changed his name, he had a successful career on Broadway interrupted by a wartime stint in the navy. He made his film debut as an old man in *The Bright Shawl* (23) and his first talkie as a gangster in *A Hole in the Wall* (29). It was not until his success in Warner's *Little Caesar* (30) that he became a box office star. He played a crusading scientist in *Dr Erlich's Magic Bullet* (40) and an insurance detective in *Double Indemnity* (44) before returning to psychotic mode in *Key Largo* (48). He was in Hollywood's first anti-Nazi film *Confessions of a Nazi Spy* (39) and made propaganda broadcasts to Nazi-occupied Europe during the war, but his career was rocked after appearing in front of the House Un-American Activities Committee for alleged communist sympathies. After his death from cancer he was awarded a posthumous Oscar for his contribution to acting.

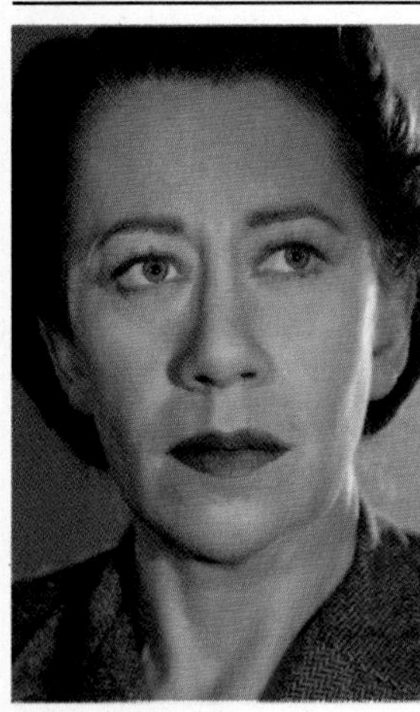

FLORA ROBSON
British actress (1902-84)

One of Britain's most celebrated stage actresses, she could play housemaids or queens. After studying at Rada she enjoyed a decade of intermittent stage appearances; for four years she retired from the stage to work as a welfare officer. She was offered her first screen role in *A Gentleman of Paris* (31) and for the next 50 years she made her mark in a wide variety of films, capitalising on her imperturbability in Britain and in Hollywood. She was a fine Empress Elizabeth in *Catherine the Great* (34) and a commanding yet vulnerable Elizabeth I in *Fire Over England* (37), a role she re-created opposite a swashbuckling Errol Flynn (qv) in *The Sea Hawk* (40). While she continued to be cast as royalty she was outstanding in *Wuthering Heights* (39), *Caesar and Cleopatra* and *Saratoga Trunk* (both 45) and *Black Narcissus* (46). She was created a Dame of the British Empire in 1960.

MARK ROBSON
US director (1913-78)

Born in Montreal, Canada, his first industry jobs after studying law at Pacific Coast University were minor ones, but they led to his appointment at RKO where he helped Robert Wise (qv) edit two Orson Welles (qv) films, *Citizen Kane* (41) and *The Magnificent Ambersons* (42). He did not receive a credit on either but attracted the attention of Val Lewton (qv), the producer-director who assigned him to direct a series of horror films. The most enduring and accomplished of his films with Lewton are *The Ghost Ship* (43) and his chilling classic *The Seventh Victim* (43). Both bear his unmistakable stylistic stamp and secured his name as a director, though he displayed a certain restlessness in the projects that followed. He competently switched quickly from the harsh realism of *Home of the Brave* (49) to the cloying *The Inn of the Sixth Happiness* (58) and the brash melodrama of *Valley of the Dolls* (67). He was also the executive producer on *Von Ryan's Express* (65). His penultimate film, *Earthquake* (74), was a commercial hit, but his artistic peak had passed. He suffered a fatal heart attack in 1978 while finishing *Avalanche Express* (79).

Richard Rodgers, at the piano, with lyricist Hart

RICHARD RODGERS
US composer (1902-79)

He was the creator of many of Broadway and Hollywood's most successful and familiar musicals, initially with lyrics provided by Lorenz Hart and then Oscar Hammerstein II. He had to wait until the advent of sound before *Spring Is Here* (30) marked his film debut. In a career that moved easily from stage to screen and back there were many outstanding individual songs, such as Isn't It Romantic? from *Love Me Tonight* (32), the Oscar-winning It Might As Well Be Spring from *State Fair* (45) and songs in *On Your Toes* and *Babes in Arms* (both 39) and *The Boys from Syracuse* (40). The incomparable run of *Oklahoma!* (55), *Carousel*, *The King and I* (both 56), *Pal Joey* (57), *South Pacific* (58), *Flower Drum Song* (61) and *Jumbo* (62) was topped with the very successful *The Sound of Music* (65). Tom Drake and Mickey Rooney (qv) portrayed Rodgers and Hart in *Words and Music* (48) and Rodgers appeared in *Main Street to Broadway* (53).

NICHOLAS ROEG
British director (1928-)

His directorial debut (with Donald Cammell) was the controversial *Performance* (70) starring Mick Jagger. A Londoner, Roeg entered the industry in his teens as an apprentice editor at MGM in London. He ascended from clapper boy to cinematographer and was the second unit photographer on *Lawrence Of Arabia* (62). He moved on to be director of photography on big budget productions including *Far From the Madding Crowd* (67). His most successful film was the thriller *Don't Look Now* (73), but his

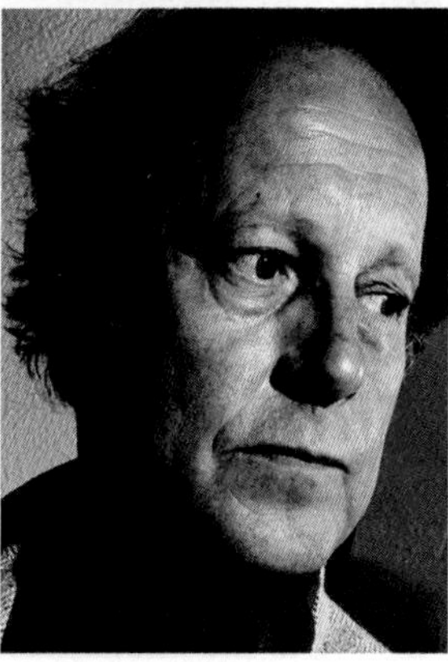

progressively more abstract intrigues of self-destruction, culminating in *Eureka* (83), were lost on all but a handful of mesmerised admirers. It was nearly a decade before he was considered to have "returned to form" with a playfully wicked adaptation of Roald Dahl's children's fantasy *The Witches* (90). In 1994 he tackled a project that had defeated Orson Welles and David Lean (qqv), the "impossible-to-film" *Heart of Darkness* by Joseph Conrad. Theresa Russell, his second wife, has starred in several of his films.

GINGER ROGERS
US actress, dancer (1911-95)

By her teens Missouri-born Virginia McMath, a feisty and versatile trouper, was in vaudeville, where she later formed Ginger and Pepper with Jack Pepper, the first of five husbands that included Lew Ayres (qv). During her Broadway debut in Top Speed she began making films and, in Hollywood from 1931, specialised in wisecracking blondes in such films as *42nd Street* and *Gold Diggers of 1933* (both 33). She teamed up with Fred Astaire (qv) at RKO and made *Flying Down to Rio* (33), which brought stardom. *The Gay Divorcee* (34), *Roberta* (35) and such gems of elegant light-hearted absurdity as *Top Hat* (35), *Swing Time* (36) and *Carefree* (38) followed, in which she lent the earthy touch to Astaire's wraithlike polish and sophistication. She

shone in comedy – *Bachelor Mother* (39), *The Major and the Minor* (42) – but more serious work won her a best actress Oscar for her heroine from the wrong side of the tracks in *Kitty Foyle* (40). Though reunited with Astaire in *The Barkleys of Broadway* (49), her best post-war film was *Monkey Business* (52). Her roles scaled down in the 1960s, but she enjoyed stage success, taking over the leads in both Hello Dolly! and Mame on Broadway.

ROY ROGERS
US cowboy (1911-)

With his palomino horse Trigger he was one of the cinema's most famous cowboys. Leonard Slye was born in Cincinnati and was a fruit picker in California before starting a singing duo with a cousin. He changed his name to Dick Weston when he formed The Sons of the Pioneers, which earned spots on radio and later in film. Bit roles and another name change followed. He appeared in B-movie oaters such as *Rhythm on the Range* (36) and *Days of Jesse James* (39) but in 1942, when Gene Autry (qv) left Republic, he was publicised as King of the Cowboys and became the top western box-office star with *The Yellow Rose of Texas* (44) and *Down Dakota Way* (49). He showed a talent for comedy when he was a foil to Bob Hope (qv) in *Son of Paleface* (52). With declining interest in B-oaters he switched his act to television. . He also proved to be a shrewd entrepreneur, investing in his own production company, real estate and a chain of restaurants. His personal fortune is reputed to exceed $100m. His wife since 1947 is Dale Evans.

Roy Rogers and his horse Trigger, which is now stuffed

VILL ROGERS
JS comedian (1879-1935)

· self-styled philosopher and omedian, he blurred the edges of vhere his plain-speaking cowboy topped and self-parody started. \merica went into deep mourning vhen he was killed in a plane rash. He made his debut in a wild vest show which found favour with airground and vaudeville patrons. le had already added satirical

ags to his show when he was igned for the Ziegfeld Follies. His rst film, a silent, was *Laughing Bill lyde* (18) and he lost a lot of noney striving to produce and irect. With the talkies he rose to tardom and he campaigned for ranklin D Roosevelt. His films ıcluded *One Glorious Day* (22), *A exas Steer* (27), *Connecticut ankee* (31) and *State Fair* (33). is son, Will Rogers Jr, played him ı *Look for the Silver Lining* (49), *he Story of Will Rogers* (52) and *he Eddie Cantor Story* (53).

KENNETH RIVE presents
JEAN-CLAUDE BRIALY IN A FILM BY ERIC ROHMER
CLAIRE'S KNEE (A) with AURORA CORNU BEATRICE ROMAND LAURENCE DE MONAGHAN
EASTMAN COLOUR
WINNER PRIX LOUIS DELLUC—BEST FRENCH PICTURE OF THE YEAR
SUBTITLED · A GALA RELEASE

ERIC ROHMER
French director (1920-)

A literature teacher who moved to film criticism, co-authoring a study of Hitchcock with Chabrol (qqv) in 1957 and editing Cahiers du Cinéma from 1957 to 1963, he turned to feature films in the 1960s. He grouped his work in cycles: the *contes moreaux* in the 1960s, the *comédies et proverbs* in the 1980s and the seasonal tales in the 1990s. He can register the most minuscule shifts in the emotional landscape and his literary background is reflected in his love of dialogue over action. His bourgeois characters — academics, professionals, self-employed artisans and students — live outwardly unsensational lives. They pursue their dreams, usually on parallel courses that rarely converge; they enter relationships, they leave them; they talk a lot. Rohmer has enjoyed considerable popularity with French television viewers for his biographical studies of Poe, Pascal and Lumière (qv).

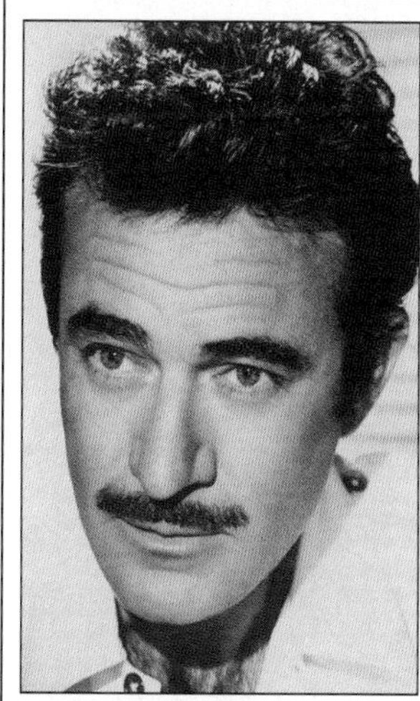

GILBERT ROLAND
Mexican actor (1905-94)

A tall, handsome Mexican with a fine moustache, he played swashbuckling pirates, macho matadors and cheroot-smoking gauchos. Luis Antonio Damaso de Alonso was the son of a Spanish bullfighter and it is rumoured he considered a future in the bullring before moving to America where he decided on a film career after appearing as an extra at the age of 13. Making his debut in *The Plastic Age* (25) he established himself as the handsome Armand in the silent version of *Camille* (27) before going on to appear in such films as *The Passionate Plumber* (32) with Buster Keaton (qv). Almost always a supporting star — Hollywood rarely featured Hispanics in starring roles — his credits include *Juarez* (39) with Paul Muni (qv) in the title role, *The Sea Hawk* (40) opposite Errol Flynn (qv) and most memorably as the matador in *The Bullfighter and the Lady* (51). Other films include Minnelli's (qv) Oscar-winning *The Bad and the Beautiful* (52), *Underwater!* (55) opposite Jane Russell (qv), *The Big Circus* (59) and *Barbarosa* (82).

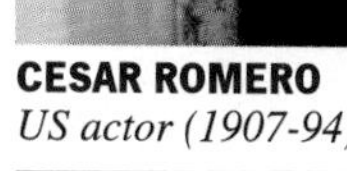

CESAR ROMERO
US actor (1907-94)

The archetypal Latin lover from the 1930s to the 1950s, he was born in New York of Cuban parents. He started out as a dime-a-dance ballroom dancer then graduated into musicals and a stint on Broadway until he came to notice playing the Cisco Kid in the light adventure screen series. His film debut was in *The Shadow Laughs* (33) and he served in the US Coastguard during the second world war. His roles include *Show Them No Mercy* and *The Devil Is a Woman* (both 35), *Romance of the Rio Grande* (40), *Weekend in Havana* (41), *Vera Cruz* (54), *Donovan's Reef* (63) and *The Proud and the Damned* (73). During the 1960s he appeared as The Joker in the Batman TV series and in the soap Falcon Crest in the late 1980s.

GEORGE A ROMERO
US director (1940-)

Since he virtually re-invented the horror film with his besieging zombies in *Night of the Living Dead* (68), he has enlivened the supernatural with explicit relish. A confessed addict of comics, he dragged horror kicking and screaming from its gothic vaults of decay and put his cannibalistic zombies on modern housing estates and shopping malls. Low budgets make his fictions seem like horrid documentaries, spiked as they are with social satire. *The Crazies* (73) had a community infected with a madness virus while *Martin* (78) was a brilliant re-working of the vampire. His collaboration with writer Stephen King includes *Creepshow* (82) and *The Dark Half* (93). He also acted in *The Silence of the Lambs* (91).

MICKEY ROONEY
US actor (1920-)

Joe Yule Jr was born into a vaudeville family and his career began when he was barely two years old. He can act, sing and dance, and has made more than 130 films, beginning with *Not to Be Trusted* (26) playing a midget. He made 40 Mickey McGuire shorts in the 1920s. Although only 5ft 3in he was a giant at the box office from 1939-41 and shared a special Oscar with Deanna Durbin (qv) in 1938. Brash and dynamic he delighted as Puck in Reinhardt's *A Midsummer Night's Dream* (35), but the peak years were at MGM: as Andy Hardy in 15 films; several with Judy Garland (qv), including the exuberant musicals *Babes in Arms* (39) and *Babes on Broadway* (41); tough cabin boy to Freddie Bartholomew's (qv) milksop in *Captains Courageous* (37); a reformed punk in *Boys Town* (38); Huckleberry Finn in *The Adventures of* (39); and as Elizabeth Taylor's (qv) stable companion in *National Velvet* (44). Thereafter, though maturing into a fine character actor, failures, notably directing efforts, outweighed successes and his private life was troubled. The fifth of his eight wives – Ava Gardner (qv) was his first – was murdered and, despite earning some $12m, he went bankrupt. He made his Broadway debut at the age of 60 in Sugar Babies and was nominated for a supporting Oscar for *The Black Stallion* (79).

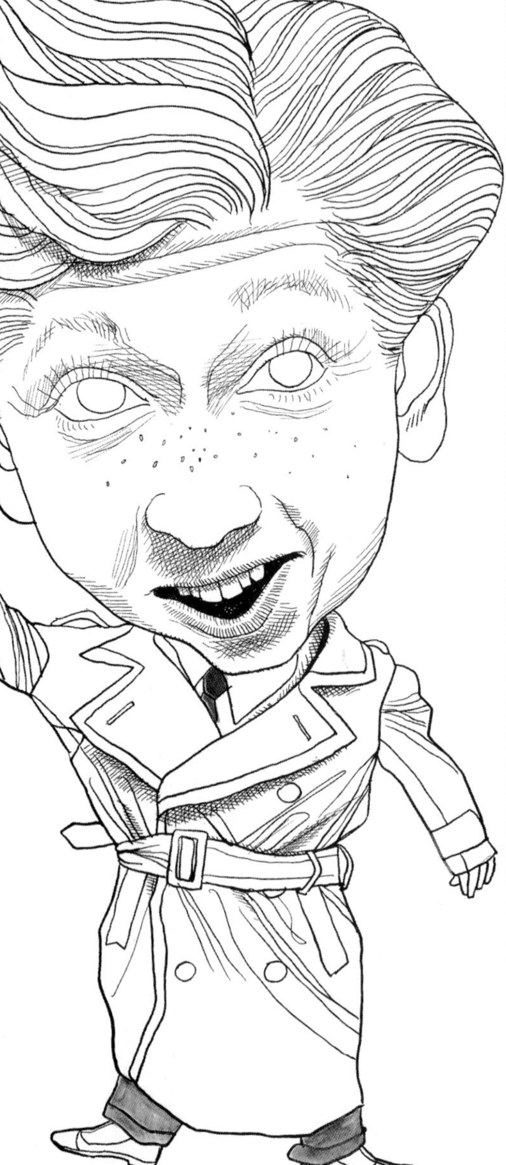

FRANCOISE ROSAY
French actress (1891-1974)

She was an actress who exported poised wit, knowing charm and ability around the world through an extraordinarily wide range of character roles. She acted and sang at the Conservatoire National de Déclamation in Paris and made *Falstaff* (13) before she gave up her career to marry the director Jacques Feyder (qv) in 1917. In 1923 she returned to the screen with even greater impact. Her career of more than 60 years and 100 films took off with *Crainquebille* (23), directed by her husband, while six years later she gained international acclaim with *The Trial of Mary Dugan* (29). She spent the war in Britain and Switzerland, teaching film acting at the Conservatoire de Genève. Her notable films include *La Kermesse héroïque* (35), *Un Carnet de Bal* (37), *Drôle de Drame* (37), her most successful collaboration with her husband, *Saraband for Dead Lovers* (48), *The Thirteenth Letter* (51), *The Sound and the Fury* (59) and *The Longest Day* (62).

FRANCESCO ROSI
Italian director, screenwriter (1922-)

A former law student and newspaper reporter, he has explored social themes such as poverty and corruption. He began his career as an assistant and script collaborator to directors including Visconti and Antonioni (qqv). His distinctive early work was acclaimed, particularly *Salvatore Giuliano* (62), which recounted the violent life and death of a Sicilian bandit, *Hands Over the City* (63), *Il Caso Mattei* (72), a Palme D'Or winner at Cannes, and *Illustrious Corpses* (76), an intriguing story of political conspiracy. *Christ Stopped at Eboli* (79) reflected his preoccupation with the conflicting characters that divide his country. His *The Moment of Truth* (65), starring the matador Miguelin, is arguably the greatest study of bullfighting and he has made a handsome adaptation of Bizet's *Carmen* (84). His late work includes a sombre adaptation of Gabriel Garcia Marquez's *Chronicle of a Death Foretold* (87).

HERBERT ROSS
US director, choreographer (1927-)

A dancer and actor who has directed on Broadway – Finian's Rainbow in 1960 and I Can Get It for You Wholesale in 1962 – he began working as a choreographer for the cinema with *Carmen Jones* (54). His first film as director was the musical remake of *Goodbye Mr Chips* (69). As choreographer he worked on *The Young Ones* (61), *Summer Holiday* (63), *Doctor Dolittle* (67) and *Funny Girl* (68). As director his strengths appear to lie in lighter material and sophisticated, bantering comedy, but his credits include the widely different *The Owl and the Pussyca* (70), *Play It Again Sam* (72), *Funny Lady* and *The Sunshine Boys* (both 75), *The Seven-Per-Cer Solution* (76), *The Turning Point* (77) – for which he was nominate for best picture and best director Oscars – *The Goodbye Girl* (77), *California Suite* (78), *Pennies Fron Heaven* (81), *Footloose* (84), *The Secret of My Success* (87), *Steel Magnolias* (89) and *Boys on the Side* (94). His first wife, the dancer Nora Kaye, co-produced many of his films, and his solo productions include *Soapdish* (91)

ROBERTO ROSSELLINI
Italian director (1906-77)

The father of Italian neo-realism, his gritty, naturalistic early pictures were much imitated by the French new wave. He primarily owes his standing to two of his earliest features, *Rome, Open City* (45) and *Paisà* (46). The first brings int dramatic focus the plight of ordinary people trapped in the political chaos of Nazi-occupied Italy. The second, which he co-wrote with Fellini (qv), illuminates six human stories leading up to th German surrender. By largely

ssellini and Ingrid Bergman
ere married for eight years

ploying non-professional actors d filming on location, he mmoned up an identifiable world almost documentary realism. A en amateur film-maker and entor in his youth, he never aptured his early acclaim, but did produce an impressive body work. In the early 1950s he ected Ingrid Bergman (qv) in six ns and — out of wedlock — toriously fathered her child, the tress Isabella Rosellini. The andal damaged their careers. ey were married for eight years.

OBERT ROSSEN
S director (1908-66)

ring his tough New York ldhood he boxed briefly before iting for the theatre. His play The dy Beautiful was not a success, t it did bring him to the attention Warner, for whom he began iting. His work was unusual for harshness and its potent, if ght, political subtexts; he was efly a member of the Communist rty. In the 1940s he began ecting in addition to writing and livered the powerful boxing drama *Body and Soul* (47), a sturdy and affecting work of personal significance, which ranks among his best. Another picture, *All the King's Men* (49), won a best picture Oscar. In the early 1950s he was blacklisted after appearing before the House Un-American Activities Committee. He later relented and named other communist sympathisers, but eschewed Hollywood. His two greatest films were yet to come: *The Hustler* (61) and *Lilith* (64) were uncompromising, hard-edged dramas that proved to be the culmination of a lifetime of troubles. They were his last films.

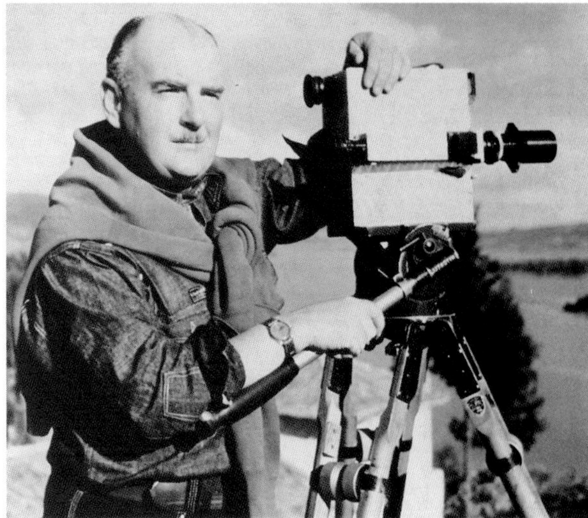

PAUL ROTHA
British director (1907-84)

A leading documentary film-maker who worked briefly with John Grierson (qv) in the early days of the Empire Marketing Board, he was also an incisive theoretician and film historian. His most notable books are The Film Till Now, Documentary Film and Rotha on the Film. Born in London of a medical family, he studied at the Slade School of Art and became an artist, stage designer and art critic before switching to films. Learning his craft with Hitchcock and Grierson (qqv), he was ostracised for writing a withering criticism of the British film industry. He believed that a film is good only if it represents the fundamental realities of today, which in his case meant the need for social reform. Setting up on his own in 1931 his work includes *Shipyards* (34), *Roads Across Britain* (39), a criticism of the world's food crisis in *World of Plenty* (43), *Land of Promise* (46) and *The World Is Rich* (47), which was nominated for an Oscar. He made three disappointing fiction features, *No Resting Place* (51), *Cat and Mouse* (58) and *The Silent Raid* (63).

SAMUEL LIONEL ROTHAFEL
US showman (1882-1936)

Of all the exhibitors "Roxy", S L Rothapfel (he later dropped the "p" to make his surname less Germanic), was the best. He started in 1908 with a screen at the back of his father's bar in Philadelphia and rose to become the emperor of opulence, constructing gilded pleasure domes that enticed patrons with films, accompanying glittering stage ▷

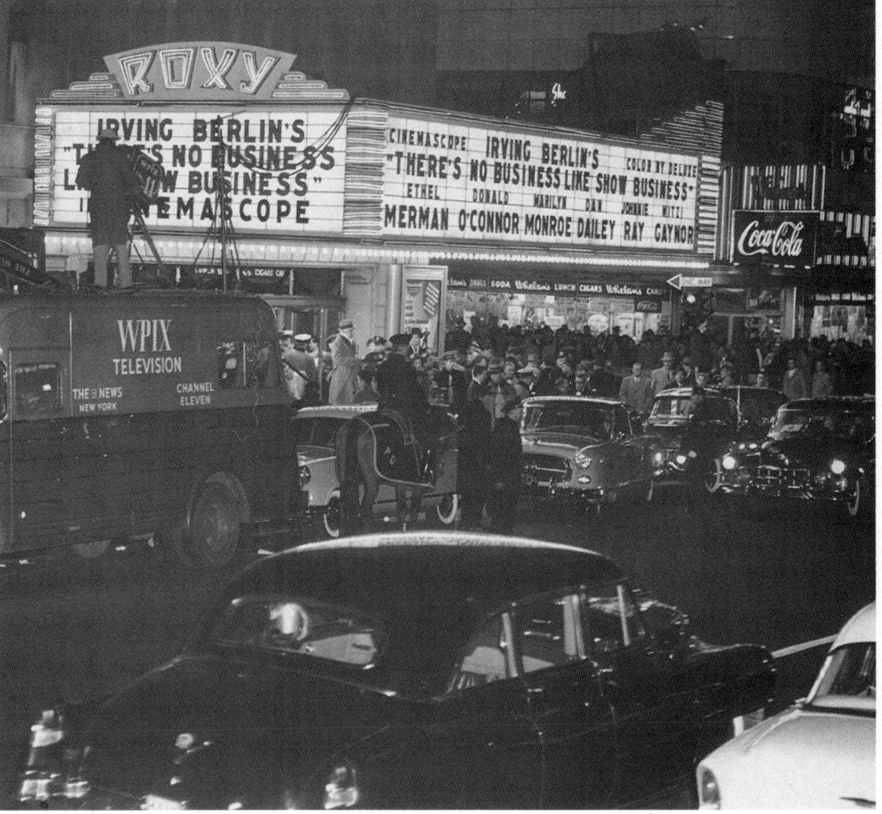

shows and immaculately uniformed usherettes. He had imitators around the world during the golden age of the picture palace. His most famous theatres were in New York: the Capitol on Broadway, which seated more than 5,000 and had a huge marble staircase dominating the lobby; the Roxy, known as the Cathedral of the Motion Picture, which held an audience of more than 6,000; and the only one that still stands, the magnificent art deco Radio City Music Hall, which opened in Rockefeller Center in 1932. By then he was ill and his touch was fading. The opening night gala was so chaotic it did not end until 2.30am.

GENA ROWLANDS
US actress (1934-)

A striking, eccentric actress, she is best known for her starring roles in the films of John Cassavetes (qv), her late husband. Virginia Cathryn Rowlands was born in Wisconsin and studied for two years at the American Academy of Dramatic Arts where she met Cassavetes. She appeared on the New York stage and brought up three children. After a successful run in Middle Of The Night on Broadway she was offered an MGM contract and made her debut in *The High Cost of Loving* (58). She was in the television series 187th Precinct and Peyton Place and in 1963 appeared in Cassavetes's *A Child Is Waiting*. The role for which she will be for ever associated is as the working-class woman suffering a nervous breakdown in *A Woman Under the Influence* (74), earning a nomination for a best actress Oscar. She eventually won for *Gloria* (80). She now acts only sporadically. *Once Around* (91) and *Unhook the Stars* (97) are welcome exceptions.

MIKLOS ROZSA
Hungarian composer (1907-95)

While most closely associated with his vigorous scores for *Quo Vadis?* (51), *Ben-Hur* (59) and *El Cid* (61), he composed a huge variety of music in a career spanning more than 50 years. Born in Budapest and the writer of neo-classical works from an early age, he composed ballets and symphonies in Paris and London before being contracted by fellow countryman Alexander Korda (qv) to his first film, *Knight Without Armour* (37). In 1940 Rozsa followed Korda to Hollywood to develop a jarring, driving style that enhanced the psychological impact of such *noir* thrillers as *Double Indemnity* (44), *Spellbound* (45) and *The Killers* (46). For the latter he introduced the dynamic chords that became the trademark of the television series Dragnet. In later years he scored such disparate films as Providence (77) and Fedora (78). He received 17 Oscar nominations and won the award for *Spellbound, A Double Life* (47) and *Ben-Hur.*

ALAN RUDOLPH
US director (1943-)

At the forefront of independent American film makers since the late 1970s and noted for the highly individual style he has achieved on consistently small budgets, he is the leading disciple of his mentor and sometime producer Robert Altman (qv). A native of Los Angeles and the son of an

actor/director, he dropped out of UCLA and trained in the Directors Guild of America programme before becoming Altman's assistant on several films including *Nashville* (75). He made his directorial debut with *Welcome to LA* (77), a portrait of lost souls which featured Keith Carradine and Geraldine Chaplin. He focuses on the intricacies of relationships, wittily or provocatively observed in such films as *Choose Me* (84), *Trouble In Mind* (85) and *Equinox* (93). *The Moderns* (88) and *Mrs Parker and the Vicious Circle* (94) were set, respectively, in the 1920s artistic cliques of Paris and New York and shared the qualities of handsome design and unusual narrative form.

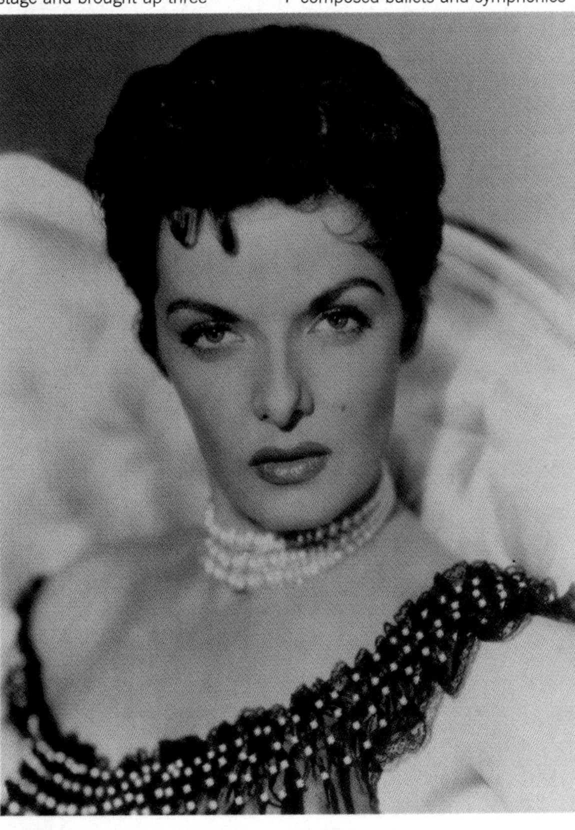

JANE RUSSELL
US actress (1921-)

In 1941 Howard Hughes (qv) conducted a nationwide hunt for the female lead in a western, insisting that the winner be well-endowed. Russell, then 19 years old, was the aspiring actress with the 38in bust who won. Hughes even designed a cantilevered bra for her, although she later confessed it was unwearable and her cleavage had been effected with one of her own. The film was *The Outlaw*, which was released in 1943 and immediately withdrawn, languishing for several years following outraged protests about sexual provocation. Russell's capacity for self-mockery enabled her to survive. She was a hit in *The Paleface* (48) with Bob Hope (qv) and its sequel *Son of Paleface* (52) and was teamed with Marilyn Monroe (qv) in *Gentlemen Prefer Blondes* (53). It was followed by *The French Line* (54), a musical which stirred more disapproving comments for her costumes. Her career then meandered into *The Revolt of Mamie Stover* (56) and *The Fuzzy Pink Nightgown* (57). Her autobiography reveals she never felt exploited but regarded it all with sly condescension.

Jane Russell in The Outlaw was too sexy for some

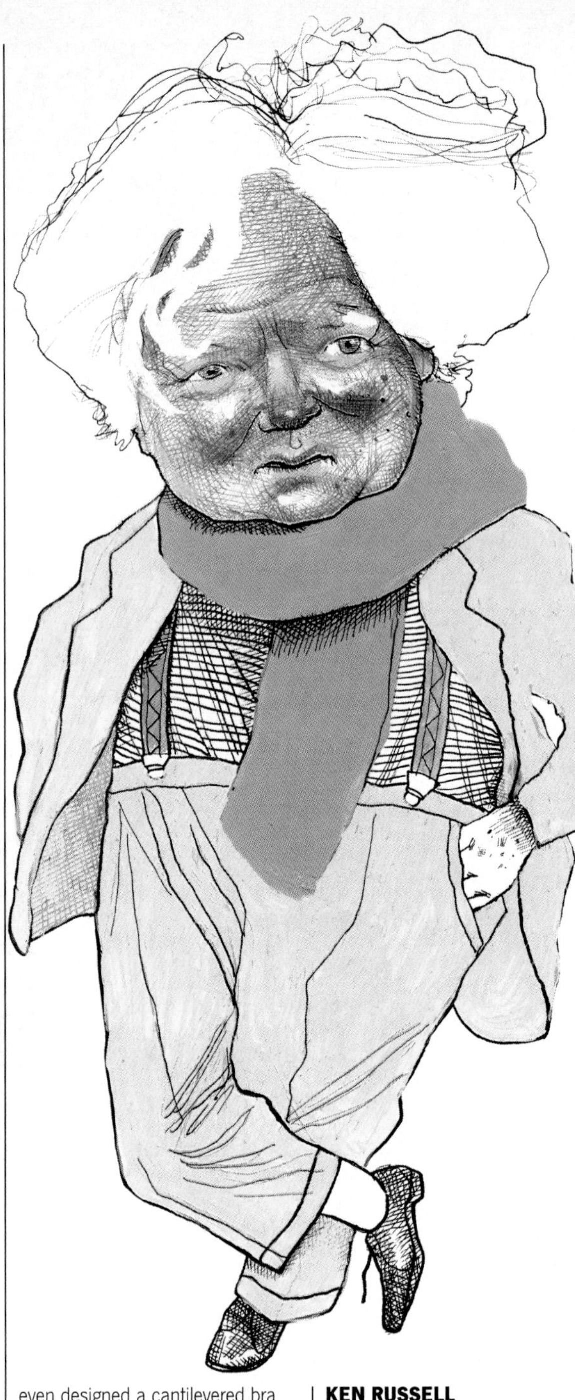

KEN RUSSELL
British director (1927-)

The *enfant terrible* of the British cinema, he made an indelible impression with his adaptation of D H Lawrence's *Women in Love* (69), a sensational biography of Tchaikovsky in *The Music Lovers* (71) and an almost satanic dramatisation of Aldous Huxley's *The Devils* (71). Henry Kenneth Alfred Russell was born in Southampton, Hampshire, and educated at the Nautical College. He spent time in the merchant navy and the RAF before careers as a ballet dancer, actor, photographer and film maker of sensational shorts. At the BBC he startled audiences with a series of flamboyant biopics on Elgar, Delius, Isadora Duncan and others His first feature was the uncharacteristic *French Dressing* (64). Brazenly flamboyant and a rn showman he has stayed ontentious: as in *Mahler* (74), *ommy* and *Lisztomania* (both 75), over-blown *Valentino* (77), *alome's Last Dance* (88) and an daptation of David Hines's *Whore* 1).

OSALIND RUSSELL

'S actress (1908-76)

itially a stage actress, her first m role came in *Evelyn Prentice* 4), one of three films she made at year. She signed a contract th MGM but was often hired out other studios as a popular lead. er first lead was in *The Casino urder Case* (35) and she went on establish herself as a witty and arming performer, particularly lept at comedy. It was a genre in nich she found her best-loved le, in Howard Hawks's (qv) asterpiece *His Girl Friday* (40). aying opposite Cary Grant (qv), eir partnership generated much the film's manic humour. It was er best film, although she received scar nominations for four others. er popularity withered with her cision to star in dramas, though *untie Mame* (58) was a success nd notched up one of her Oscar minations. Although she livered few performances of note ter her triumph in *Gypsy* (62), e remains one of the most eable actresses of the 1940s.

ARGARET RUTHERFORD

ritish actress (1892-1972)

reated a DBE in 1967, she is still ell loved almost 25 years after her eath, although she made only 40 m appearances. A speech and ano teacher, she was over 30 ars old before she made her age debut and although noticed *The Demi-Paradise* (43), it was Madame Arcati, another sessive eccentric, in *Blithe Spirit* 5) that she broke through. Down e cast list with Joyce Grenfell in *hile the Sun Shines* (47) and *The appiest Days of Your Life* (50), e stole the show. Her Miss Prism *The Importance of Being Earnest* 2) is near-definitive. Scene-ealing again in *The Smallest how on Earth* (57) she played gatha Christie's Miss Marple in *urder She Said* (61), *Murder at e Gallop* (63), *Murder Most Foul* and *Murder Ahoy* (both 64). She won a best supporting actress Oscar for *The VIPs* (63). Her husband was actor Stringer Davis.

Margaret Rutherford was a notorious scene-stealer

MEG RYAN

US actress (1961-)

An effervescent blue-eyed blonde, her career started due to the efforts of her mother, a casting director. She made her debut as Candice Bergen's (qv) daughter in *Rich and Famous* (81) before studying journalism at NYU, paying for her tuition with a two-year stint in the television soap As the World Turns. She decided, however, to stick to acting and impressed in the small but significant part of Anthony Edwards's wife (he was the flyer who was killed) in *Top Gun* (86). As the investigative journalist in the Spielberg (qv) produced sci-fi film *Innerspace* (87) she acted with Dennis Quaid (qv), whom she

married four years later and with whom she co-starred in *DOA* (88) and *Flesh and Bone* (93). She became a star with *When Harry Met Sally* (89); it was her idea to include the comical fake orgasm scene. Her next three films, *Joe Versus the Volcano* (90) with Tom Hanks (qv), Oliver Stone's (qv) *The Doors* (91) and *Prelude to a Kiss* (92) disappointed but she renewed her popularity with *Sleepless in Seattle* (93) and *Addicted to Love* (97).

ROBERT RYAN

US actor (1909-73)

Remembered for a range of maladjusted thugs and unyielding bigots, he was an active liberal who transformed himself for his screen roles. He electrified with the film noir claustrophobia of *The Woman on the Beach* (47), Jean Renoir's (qv) American swan-song, was the anti-semitic killer in *Crossfire* (47), the worn-out boxer in *The Set-Up* (49) and the icy, manipulative lover in *Clash By Night* (52). Ryan's impressive collection of heroes and

villains also took in *About Mrs Leslie* (54), *Bad Day at Black Rock* (55), *Billy Budd* (62) and *The Wild Bunch* (69). His early experiences are amusingly redolent of tough guy bravura. As a student he became the heavyweight boxing champ, while the jobs of ship's stoker, ranch hand and debt collector, not to mention a wartime stint with the marines, must have been a fertile breeding ground for his grim, leathery persona.

WINONA RYDER

US actress (1971-)

Winona Horowitz was born in Winona, Minnesota. Her parents worked as archivists for the 1960s hippie guru Timothy Leary; he is her godfather and Aldous Huxley was a close family friend. When she was seven years old the family moved to San Francisco and she spent the rest of her childhood in an agricultural commune. She began at the American Conservatory Theatre at 11 and was spotted there two years later. She made her film debut in *Lucas* (86). Since then she has worked consistently in such films as *Beetlejuice* (88), *Heathers* (89), *Mermaids* and *Edward Scissorhands* (both 90), *The Age of Innocence* and *The House of the Spirits* (both 93). Near-exhaustion in 1989 forced her to pull out of *The Godfather Part III* (90). She was nominated for a best actress Oscar for *Little Women* (94).

SABU
Indian actor (1924-63)

The documentarist Robert Flaherty (qv) discovered Sabu Dastagir, a stable boy from Mysore, when he was scouting for a lead for *Elephant Boy* (37). His impish intelligence entranced filmgoers

and Alexander Korda (qv) made sure he was featured in *The Drum* (38). He was selected to play the leading role in Korda's *The Thief of Bagdad* (40), an ambitious Arabian Nights epic that was started in Britain but because of the war completed in Hollywood. Sabu stayed in California to make *Jungle Book* (42) and several other escapist adventures with eastern settings, returning to Britain in 1946 to appear in Powell and Pressburger's (qqv) *Black Narcissus* (46) and *The End of the River* (47). His career slumped in post-war years as the taste for exotic adventures faded, and his later appearances were sporadic.

EVA MARIE SAINT
US actress (1924-)

Her delicate, pale beauty contributed to her distinction as a refined, sensitive actress, but she was seldom offered challenging roles. Born in New Jersey, she worked in radio and live TV drama before attracting serious notice on Broadway. She made her film debut in 1954, winning the supporting Oscar for her performance of fragile purity in Elia Kazan's (qv) *On the Waterfront*. She did not make many films but was memorable in *A Hatful of Rain* (57) and was selected by Alfred Hitchcock (qv) as his cool, enigmatic blonde foil to Cary Grant (qv) in *North by Northwest* (59). Her screen performances were

characterised by quiet awareness even when on the sidelines, such as in *Exodus* (60). In the 1970s and 1980s she returned to the stage and occasional films, such as *Cancel My Reservation* (72) and *Nothing in Common* (86).

GEORGE SANDERS
British actor (1906-72)

One of the screen's most urbane and cynical cads, his career reached its zenith in *All About Eve* (50), for which he won a best supporting actor Oscar for his viper-tongued drama critic. He was born in St Petersburg, Russia, of English parents who returned to Britain during the revolution. He attended Bedales school and technical college before a variety of jobs in textiles and tobacco. After spells in cabaret and as an understudy he made his first film, *Find the Lady* (36). Stardom came quickly for his roles as a sophisticated bounder. He spent the war playing glowering Nazis. His best parts were in *Rebecca* (40), *Man Hunt* (41), *The Moon and Sixpence* (42) and *The Picture of Dorian Gray* (45). After the war he floated through increasingly mediocre films. His third wife was Zsa Zsa Gabor, his fourth was her sister Magda. He committed suicide in a Barcelona hotel room, claiming he was bored.

MARK SANDRICH
US director (1900-45)

He was largely responsible for keeping RKO afloat in the 1930s. A consummate craftsman, he served his stars so well that his abilities as a director went largely unnoticed. Although versatile, he has mostly become associated with the films of Fred Astaire and Ginger Rogers (qqv). Starting out as a film electrician and prop man, he was directing two-reelers by 1926 and made his feature debut with the

Columbia melodrama *Runaway Girls* (28). However, it was his slick direction of Astaire and Rogers's first starring vehicle, *The Gay Divorcee* (34), and his ability to integrate musical numbers into the plot that built his reputation. While his most famous films remain *Top Hat* (35), *Follow the Fleet* (36), *Shall We Dance?* (37) and *Carefree* (38), Sandrich also guided noteworthy performances from Katharine Hepburn, Claudette Colbert, Paulette Goddard, Bing Crosby (qqv) and Jack Benny.

SUSAN SARANDON
US actress (1946-)

Susan Tomaling was born in New York and studied drama at Catholic University in Washington DC. Respected rather than idolised, she is also a vociferous campaigner for liberal causes. Her status has risen dramatically since her Oscar nomination as a naive would-be croupier in *Atlantic City* (80). Before that she appeared in a series of minor roles, most notably Janet in *The Rocky Horror Picture Show* (75). She has flourished in her forties, still able to exploit her been-round-the-block qualities in a range of juicy roles, from the groupie in *Bull Durham* (88) and the outspoken waitress in *White Palace* (90) to the fugitive in *Thelma & Louise* (91) and the mother in *Lorenzo's Oil* (92). The latter two roles won her best actress Oscar nominations, as did *The Client* (94). Sexy and sassy she also has a gritty integrity.

CARLOS SAURA
Spanish director (1932-)

He had already carved out a nich as a stills photographer when at the age of 21 he opted to enrol a film school. He directed shorts ar eventually taught film before completing his first full-length feature, *Los Golfos* (60), a scrapp but heartfelt drama about Spanis street children, which, like all his features, he also wrote. His third film, the thriller *La Caza* (66), wo acclaim and awards. Saura's wo is characterised by carefully measured tension, frequently concealing (necessarily, given the pressure of being an artist under Franco) political complexity. He h consistently attracted internation awards but although his later film – including the dance-orientated *Blood Wedding* (81) and *Carmen* (83) – have received the most feverish approbation, they lack th discreet pleasures of his earlier work. He is still, however, considered to be his country's most outstanding director who finds an unmatched exotic but troublesome beauty in Spain.

VICTOR SAVILLE
British director, producer (1897-1979)

Very much identified with popula British cinema of the 1930s, he had the knack of assessing publi taste and the entrepreneurial instincts to satisfy it on screen. H entered the film industry as a salesman in 1916. A spell as a production manager soon led to screenwriting for Gaumont-British for whom he directed or produce many successful films of the 1930s. After *Sunshine Susie* (31)

Carlos Saura, right, and crew on location with Ay Carmela

directed *Evergreen* (34), *First a* *rl* (35) and *It's Love Again* (36), showcasing the talent of Jessie atthews (qv). Proving his rsatility, he also directed the artime melodrama *I Was a Spy* 3) and *The Iron Duke* (35) arring George Arliss (qv). He next oved to Korda (qv) where he rected and produced among hers *Storm in a Teacup* (37) and *outh Riding* (38). He then oduced *The Citadel* (38) and *oodbye Mr Chips* (39) for MGM's itish studios, which were closed ring the second world war. He ntinued as a director and oducer in Hollywood, but his tput as a director was less riking than in Britain. His final m, produced in Britain, was *The reengage Summer* (61).

HN SAYLES
S director, screenwriter and tor (1950-)

rn in Schenectady, New York, d a graduate in psychology, his hievements include novels, ward-winning short stories, cult reenplays and an Oscar mination for his low-budget rectorial debut, *Return of the ecaucus 7* (80). Many of his reenplays, for *Piranha* (78), *The dy in Red* (79), *The Howling* (81) d *The Challenge* (82), were oduced by Roger Corman (qv). s own second film, *Lianna* (83), as about a married woman's sbian dalliance and *Baby It's You* 3) dealt with teenage romance. *e Brother From Another Planet* 4) was comic sci-fi, *Matewan* 7) about a 1920s miners' ike and *The Secret of Roan Inish* 4) a Celtic fantasy. His rapport th actors is outstanding.

Dore Schary made sure that MGM's lion continued to roar

FRANKLIN J SCHAFFNER
US director (1920-89)

Born in Japan, the son of missionaries, he was studying law when the United States entered the second world war. He joined the navy, then became an assistant director on The March of Time, the monthly news magazine, before working for the news department at CBS TV. Moving to drama, he won Emmy awards for Twelve Angry Men and The Caine Mutiny Court Martial, both later made into feature films by other directors. His big-screen debut was *The Stripper* (63) starring Joanne Woodward (qv), followed by Gore Vidal's *The Best Man* (64). With *The War Lord* (65) he embarked on his series of panoramic war, historical and adventure films – *Planet of the Apes* (68), *Patton* (70), which won seven Oscars, including best director, *Nicholas and Alexandra* (71) and *The Boys from Brazil* (78) with Laurence Olivier and Gregory Peck (qqv). A letdown, the risible *Yes Giorgio* (82) starred Luciano Pavarotti. He died from cancer after making *Welcome Home* (89).

DORE SCHARY
US writer, studio head (1905-80)

Beginning as a stock actor, he wrote biopics such as his Oscar-winning *Boys Town* (38), *Young Tom Edison* and *Edison The Man* (both 40) and produced *Lassie Come Home* (43). As an RKO producer he was responsible for such social awareness hits as *Crossfire* (47), *The Boy With Green Hair* and *They Live By Night* (both 48). After Louis B Mayer (qv) was ousted in 1951, Schary brought liberal convictions to MGM and resisted Hollywood blacklisting during the witch-hunting era. As head of production he had fought for John Huston's (qv) civil war movie *The Red Badge of Courage* (51) before he took over the hot seat for a five-year reign. He took a twin-track approach of making commercial hits and films with a message. Occasionally his conscience collided with commercial reality with such dullards as *Plymouth Adventure* (52), but *Bad Day at Black Rock* (55) was a striking early attack on prejudice. After he was fired by MGM in 1956, he made *Lonelyhearts* (58) and *Sunrise at Campobello* (60) about a young Roosevelt heading for presidential power, based on his stage play, which won five Tony awards.

MAXIMILIAN SCHELL
Austrian actor, director (1930-)

Best known to American and British audiences for his Oscar-winning performance as the defence lawyer in *Judgment at Nuremberg* (61), this handsome leading man also has a reputation

as a writer, producer and director on a number of critically acclaimed European films and documentaries. Born in Vienna, the younger brother of the actress Maria Schell, his family moved to Switzerland in 1938 after the Anschlüss. Making his professional debut on the stage in 1952 and his film debut with *Kinder, Mütter und ein General* (55), he travelled to America and played a German officer in *The Young Lions* (58). He produced and starred in a host of films from *Topkapi* (64) to *Counterpoint* (67) and made his directorial debut with Turgenev's *First Love* (70). He received Oscar nominations for his roles in *The Man in the Glass Booth* (75) and *Julia* (77). He also made *Marlene* (84), a striking documentary about Dietrich (qv).

FRED SCHEPISI
Australian director (1939-)

He is one of the Australian New Wave directors who has made his mark in Hollywood. Starting in advertising at the age of 15 in his native Melbourne, he graduated to directing commercials. He was well into his thirties when he made his first feature, *The Devil's Playground* (76), which he also had to distribute. The largely autobiographical story of sexual awakening in a Roman Catholic seminary, the film swept the Australian film awards. His next film, *The Chant of Jimmie Blacksmith* (78), a violent study of 19th-century racism, became the first Australian competition entry at Cannes. Leaving Australia shortly afterwards his career encompasses a mythic western *Barbarosa* (82), a sci-fi fable, *Iceman* (84), a psychological character study, *Plenty* (85), a romantic comedy, *Roxanne* (87), a real-life court case, *A Cry in the Dark* (88), a cold war thriller, *The Russia House* (90) and *Six Degrees of Separation* (94).

JOHN SCHLESINGER
British director (1926-)

After acting and television directing, he won first prize at the Venice Film Festival with the documentary *Terminus* (61). *A Kind of Loving* (62) was his first feature, followed by *Billy Liar* (63), which made a star of Julie Christie (qv). She won best actress Oscar for *Darling* (65) and he was nominated for best director. After *Far From the Madding Crowd* (67), the sexually adventurous *Midnight Cowboy* (69) brought him Oscars for best film and best director. *Sunday Bloody Sunday* (71) was frank in its portrayal of a bisexual, three-way split. He offered a sour study of Hollywood in *The Day of the Locust* (75) and scored a commercial success with *Marathon Man* (76). *Yanks* (79) was less popular and *Honky Tonk Freeway* (81) was one of the most expensive flops of all time. *The Falcon and the Snowman* (85), *The Believers* (87), *Madame Sousatzka* (88), *Pacific Heights* (90) and *The Innocent* (93) have kept his career ticking over, while TV films such as An Englishman Abroad, A Question of Attribution and Cold Comfort Farm (94) have been well received.

VOLKER SCHLONDORFF
German director (1939-)

The first top film-maker to emerge from the ruins of post-war ▷

German cinema, he was educated in Paris and studied film there, entering the industry as assistant to Louis Malle, Alain Resnais and most influentially, Jean-Pierre Melville (qqv). After documentary work in Algeria and Vietnam for French TV he based himself in Munich, making his name with *Young Torless* (66). German psychology and history have preoccupied him in films about conformity and moral bankruptcy, particularly *The Sudden Wealth of the Poor People of Komback* (70), *The Lost Honor of Katherina Blum* (75) and *The Tin Drum* (79), which shared the Palme D'Or at Cannes and won the foreign film Oscar. He has also focused on war-torn Beirut in *Circle of Deceit* (81) and he has adapted writers including Proust. His wife is Margarethe von Trotta, Germany's foremost woman director, who co-wrote and starred in their most personal work, *Summer Lightning* (72).

THELMA SCHOONMAKER
US editor (1945-)

A dedicated film editor most closely associated with director Martin Scorsese (qv), she has been nominated for three Oscars, winning with *Raging Bull* (80). She met Scorsese when they were studying film technique at New York University. Her first feature was as co-editor on *Passages From Finnegans Wake* (65) followed by *The Virgin President* and *Who's That Knocking at My Door?* (both 68). In 1970 she drew attention for her inventive editing of Michael Wadleigh's documentary *Woodstock* (70), her first Oscar nomination. She dropped out of editing for some time, never fully revealing her reasons, but re-emerged for *Raging Bull*. She collaborated with Scorsese on *The King of Comedy* (83), *After Hours* (85), *The Color of Money* (86), *The Last Temptation of Christ* (88), his segment of *New York Stories* (89) and *GoodFellas* (90), which brought her third Oscar nomination. *Cape Fear* (91) and *The Age of Innocence* (93) followed. She is the widow of the British director Michael Powell (qv).

Schoonmaker's editing gave Raging Bull its punch

PAUL SCHRADER
US screenwriter, director (1946-)

Unlike their European counterparts, American writers and directors are less likely to confront their own angst on screen. Like Scorsese (qv), his Catholic contemporary, Schrader's strict Calvinist upbringing in Grand Rapids, Michigan, has fuelled the best of his work. Because Calvinists considered cinema too worldly, he did not see his first film until he was 18 years old. He went on to study cinema, became a critic and found desperation and drink with his early attempts at screenwriting. It was in this fraught state that he wrote *Taxi Driver* (76) for Scorsese in two weeks. *Blue Collar* (78), his first work as a director, was followed by *Hardcore* (79), reportedly basing the character of George C Scott (qv), a man searching for his runaway daughter, on his father. He wrote and directed *American Gigolo* (80) and wrote Scorsese's *Raging Bull* (80) and *The Last Temptation of Christ* (88). His most accomplished film of recent years was *Mishima: A Life in Four Chapters* (85), written and directed with his mix of sharp intelligence and surging emotion.

BARBET SCHROEDER
French director (1941-)

One of the few contemporary French directors to make a successful transition to Hollywood, his most commercial film is *Single White Female* (92). Born in Tehran of German parentage and raised in Argentina, he settled in Paris after studying philosophy at the Sorbonne. He was a critic on Cahiers du Cinéma and a jazz musician before deciding on a career in films. He set up his own company producing works by Rohmer, Rivette (qqv) and others.

He made his directing debut with *More* (69), gaining attention with a documentary *Idi Amin Dada* (74) and the feature *Maîtresse* (76) with Gérard Depardieu (qv). Following a series of interviews, known as *The Charles Bukowski Tapes* (85), he made his Hollywood debut with *Barfly* (87) then *Reversal of Fortune* (90), which reflect an interest in self-obsessed individuals.

EUGEN SCHUFFTAN
German cinematographer (1893-1977)

His film work began in Germany in the early 1920s. Initially a technical specialist, he invented the Schüfftan process, a method of combining live action with paintings or models used brilliantly in Lang's (qv) *Metropolis* (27). Moving into cinematography he shot *People on Sunday* (29), a delightful documentary. He left Germany for France with the rise of Nazism in 1933. An inventive and poetic imagist, he photographed Carné's (qv) *Drôle de Drame* (37) and the melancholy *Quai des Brumes* (38). He went to America in 1940 where he was the technical director on René Clair's (qv) *It Happened Tomorrow* (44) and Siodmak's (qv) *The Dark Mirror* (46), and became Eugene Shuftan. In Europe he worked on Astruc's *The Crimson Curtain* (52) and Franju's (qv) *La Tête contre les Murs* (58). His best known achievement is his Oscar-winning cinematography for Rossen's (qv) *The Hustler* (61) starring Paul Newman (qv).

BUDD SCHULBERG
US writer (1914-)

He began as a Hollywood prince, went on to be court chronicler and ended as palace guard informant. The son of B P Schulberg, Paramount's foremost producer, he grew up surrounded by stars. As an apprentice screenwriter he was fired after a dire collaboration with the alcoholic writer F Scott Fitzgerald on *Winter Carnival* (39). His book about it, The Disenchanted, preceded another entitled What Makes Sammy Run?,

a sour study of a hustling produc[er]. After wartime documentaries with John Ford (qv) he won an Oscar [for] the screenplay of *On the Waterfr[ont]* (54), after which came *A Face in the Crowd* (57) about a flawed fo[lk] hero who becomes a demagogue. There was self-pity as well as ang[er] in his work; perhaps he could nev[er] come to terms with having name[d] old friends to the House Un-American Activities Committee. That is why *On The Waterfront* ca[n] be read as an apologia for betray[al].

ARNOLD SCHWARZENEGGE[R]
US actor (1947-)

Austrian-born, his teenage passio[n] for bodybuilding won him many titles, including Mr Universe five times. He moved to America in th[e] late 1960s and became an American citizen in 1983. He act[ed] in small film roles as Arnold Stro[ng] until Bob Rafelson's (qv) *Stay Hungry* (76), and the bodybuildin[g] documentary *Pumping Iron* (77). He then played the title role, a brutal mythical warrior, in *Conan the Barbarian* (82) and was at his chillingly hypnotic best in James Cameron's (qv) *The Terminator*

ƨchwarzenegger's passion for bodybuilding made him a star

84) as an unstoppable robot assassin. Between 1985 and 1988 he appeared in mediocre action thrillers. Ivan Reitman's (qv) *Twins* (88) was his first comedy. He played comedy twice more for Reitman, but his best recent work was in two sci-fi adventures, *Total Recall* (90) and *Terminator 2: Judgment Day* (91). He came unstuck with the inept action comedy *Last Action Hero* (93), but made amends in *True Lies* and *Junior* (both 94). He is one of the most popular actors of modern times and a shrewd businessman. He is married to Maria Shriver, a niece of the late John F Kennedy.

HANNA SCHYGULLA
German actress (1943-)

Born in Katowice, Poland, during the Nazi occupation, she was educated in Germany and at Munich University became involved in the Munich Action Theatre, taking time off to join the hippie trail backpacking across America in the 1960s. Her colleague was Rainer Werner Fassbinder (qv) and she became his leading lady in several plays and nearly a score of his films. She has a formidable

presence and a commanding beauty. Her outstanding films for Fassbinder are *The Bitter Tears of Petra von Kant* (73), *Effi Briest* (74), *The Marriage of Maria Braun* (78) and *Lili Marleen* (81). Among the many other directors she has worked with are Godard (qv) in *Passion* (82) and Wajda (qv) in *A Love in Germany* (84). She has also successfully maintained a parallel stage career.

ETTORE SCOLA
Italian director (1931-)

He entered the film industry aged 22 as a writer after studying law in Rome and established himself as a witty and humorous magazine writer. His first directorial assignments, which he also wrote, were broad comedies such as the frenzied satire *Dramma della Gelosia* (70), but he soon began to display considerable social and emotional depth. His films include *We All Loved Each Other So Much* (74), *Brutti sporchi e cattivi* (76), which won him best director at Cannes, *A Special Day* (77) with Marcello Mastroianni and Sophia Loren (qqv), which won an Oscar nomination, and *Macaroni* (85), which successfully paired Jack Lemmon (qv) with Mastroianni.

MARTIN SCORSESE
US director (1942-)

One of the most brilliant of contemporary film makers, he combines technique and emotion with a sustained visual punch. His Catholic background, seminary training and life-and-death obsession with film led to several student shorts. *The Big Shave* (67) is particularly striking in its use of imagery and menace. The outstanding *Mean Streets* (73) and *Taxi Driver* (76) depicted New York as a time bomb ready to explode and his highly mobile camera reflected the tension of his characters. He teamed again with Robert De Niro (qv) for *Raging Bull* (80). In *New York, New York* (77) he played with the conventions of the musical, *The King of Comedy* (83) spoke eloquently of the dark relationship between artist and audience. *The Last Temptation of Christ* (88) was controversial, and *GoodFellas* (90) and *Cape Fear* (91) were studies in alienation. *The Age of Innocence* (93) saw him tackle period literature. He followed with *Casino* (95), a study of the Las Vegas underworld.

GEORGE C SCOTT
US actor (1927-)

Few performers could match the power and authority Scott has brought to his roles. When cast as *Patton* (70), after numerous other actors had turned it down, he won an Oscar and refused to accept it, denouncing the Academy as a "meaningless, self-serving meat parade". A journalism graduate at the University of Missouri, he embarked on a stage career when he found he had little writing talent. After winning awards for Children of Darkness on Broadway he was cast in Otto Preminger's (qv) *Anatomy of a Murder* (59) the following year and was nominated for his first

Oscar. He continued to give commanding performances in *The Hustler* (61), *The List of Adrian Messenger* (63) and *Dr Strangelove* (64), emerging as a star in *Patton*. He has directed unsuccessfully with *Rage* (72) and *The Savage Is Loose* (74). He has made few films since, notably *Taps* (81) and *Malice* (93). His son Campbell is also an actor.

RANDOLPH SCOTT
US actor (1903-87)

Few cowboys walked taller or had a squarer jaw than the weatherbeaten tough guy in the white hat. The quintessential western hero, he starred in some of the finest matinee westerns in the 1940s and 1950s. George Randolph Crane was born to a well-to-do Virginian family. He lied about his age and fought in the first world war at the age of 14, before completing a degree in engineering at North Carolina University and working in his father's textile mill. He left to work as an extra in Hollywood then came into his own in ▷

westerns and as Hawkeye in *The Last of the Mohicans* (36). It was not until he set up Ranown with Harry Joe Brown in the 1950s that he produced his trademark and classy B-westerns, the best of which were directed by Budd Boetticher (qv) and confirmed him as a western legend. They included *Seven Men From Now* (56), *The Tall T* (57), *Buchanan Rides Alone* (58), *Ride Lonesome* (59), *Comanche Station* (60) and Peckinpah's (qv) *Ride the High Country* (62), the only film in which Scott plays a former lawman tempted to fall from grace.

RIDLEY SCOTT
British director (1937-)

He was one of the first graduates of the National Film and TV School. After making television commercials, his first feature, *The Duellists* (77), was a violent study in obsession, while *Alien* (79) was similarly a study in prolonged suspense. *Blade Runner* (82) has gained cult status. He was in a controversialist mode for *Thelma & Louise* (91) and made *1492: Conquest of Paradise* (92) with Gérard Depardieu (qv), which was the better of two celebratory Columbus films. In *GI Jane* (97) Demi Moore trained to become a Navy SEAL. In 1994 with his brother Tony he bought Shepperton studios near London, the Sound City of the 1930s, in the hope of boosting the British film industry.

JEAN SEBERG
US actress (1938-79)

At 17, while still at college, she was chosen by Otto Preminger (qv) to play *Saint Joan* (57). The film, however, was a critical and box office failure. After *Bonjour Tristesse* (58), again for Preminger, her career took a dive from which she was rescued by Godard (qv). He starred her opposite Belmondo (qv) in *Breathless* (59), leading to many French and international assignments. *Playtime* (62) was a bland melodrama directed by François Moreuil, her first husband, *Birds in Peru* (68) was a pretentious bore directed by her

second, novelist Romain Gary. In between she did her best work as the schizophrenic in *Lilith* (64), but roles in *Moment to Moment* and *A Fine Madness* (both 66), *Paint Your Wagon* (69), *Airport* (70) and the political thriller *L'Attentat* (73) failed to elevate her. Meanwhile, her life was disintegrating. Political sympathy with the Black Panthers was frowned upon, her third marriage ended after a miscarriage and a nervous breakdown and, a few months after marrying for the fourth time, she was found in her car in Paris, dead from a drug overdose at 40.

PETER SELLERS
British actor (1925-80)

The anarchic comic whose giggling outtakes have proved almost as popular as his films was born in Southsea, Hampshire. He joined his parents' comedy act as a teenager and went on to become an entertainer with the RAF. He came to prominence on the radio in the Goon Show, which displayed his talent for mimicry, then he made his mark on screen as the cello-playing young thug in *The Ladykillers* (55), the union leader in *I'm All Right Jack* (59) and as the lascivious Welsh librarian in *Only Two Can Play* (61). In 1964 *Dr Strangelove* and *The Pink Panther* propelled him into the international celebrity limelight, yet they confined him as a clown rather than fuelling his potential as an actor. At the same time he began his battle with heart disease. He reprised the cack-handed Clouseau in the 1970s, but only his uncharacteristically subdued performance in *Being There* (79) stands out among his later work.

DAVID O SELZNICK
US producer (1902-65)

He was born in Pittsburgh, the son of Lewis J Selznick the film mogul, and brother of the agent Myron Selznick, who introduced him to Vivien Leigh (qv), his future Scarlett O'Hara. After his father went bankrupt in 1923 he began producing documentaries, but lost money and moved to Hollywood. In 1926 he was hired by Louis B Mayer (qv), his father's former partner, as an assistant story editor and producer. RKO gave him his first successes with *A Bill Of Divorcement* and *What Price Hollywood* (both 32) and *King Kong* (33). At MGM he worked on big budget films such as *Dinner at Eight* (33), *David Copperfield* and *A Tale of Two Cities* (both 35). In 1936 he formed Selznick International and acquired Margaret Mitchell's civil war saga *Gone With the Wind* (39). He

brought Alfred Hitchcock (qv) to Hollywood to direct *Rebecca* (40) but through the 1940s only *Duel in the Sun* (47) captured the public's imagination. In the 1950s he turned to co-productions in Europe with little success. His last film was an unprepossessing version of *A Farewell to Arms* (57).

Ridley Scott casts his epic eye over a location for Black Rain

MACK SENNETT
US director, producer and actor (1880-1960)

The king of silent comedy was born in Canada and began as a performer in vaudeville, entering films as an actor and writer with Biograph working for D W Griffith (qv). He started directing in 1910 and in 1912 formed Keystone with Charles O Bauman and Adam Kessel. With actors such as Mabel Normand, Charlie Chaplin (for a year), Roscoe "Fatty" Arbuckle (qqv), the Keystone Cops, the Bathing Beauties and Kid Komedies, Keystone became the foremost comedy studio. It became part of the Triangle Film

Corporation in 1915 alongside Griffith and Thomas Ince (qv), but in 1917 he left and formed Mack Sennett Comedies, releasing films through other studios. Normand went with him and he discovered Harry Langdon (qv). Sound was initially inhibiting, but he worked with W C Fields, Bing Crosby and once with Buster Keaton (qqv). He retired in 1935 and received a special Oscar in 1937 "for his lasting contribution to the comedy technique of the screen". He appeared as himself in his experimental colour film *Movie Town* (31), *Hollywood Cavalcade* (39) and *Down Memory Lane* (49).

DELPHINE SEYRIG
French actress (1932-90)

Her graceful intensity and remote serenity made her a memorable leading lady of the 1960s and 1970s. Born in Lebanon, where her archeologist father was working, she made her theatre debut in Paris in 1952 but moved to New York in 1956 to train at the Actors Studio and appeared in an experimental film, *Pull My Daisy* (59). Back in France she appeared in Alain Resnais's (qv) haunting *Last Year at Marienbad* (61) and *Muriel* (63). Highly selective, she worked with Joseph Losey, Jacques Demy, Fred Zinnemann and Don Siegel (qqv), was enchanting in Truffaut's (qv) *Stolen Kisses* (68) and Buñuel's *The Discreet Charm of the Bourgeoisie* (72). Her passionate feminism was reflected in her collaborations with directors Marguerite Duras, Chantal Akerman and Ulrike Ottinger, notably in Duras's *India Song* (75). Seyrig also directed one feature, *Soi belle et tais-toi* (77).

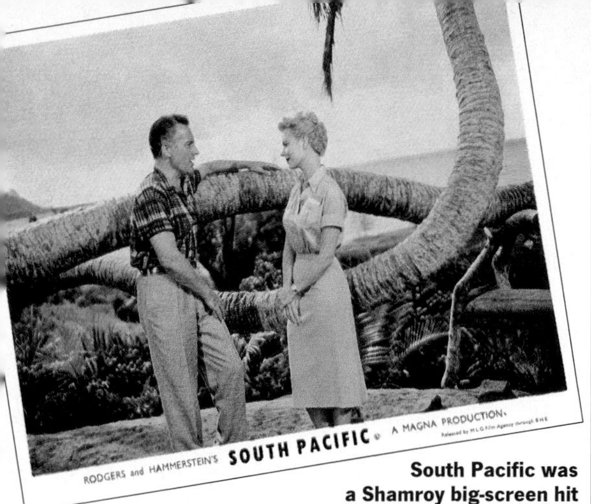

RODGERS and HAMMERSTEIN'S SOUTH PACIFIC A MAGNA PRODUCTION.

South Pacific was a Shamroy big-screen hit

:ON SHAMROY
S cinematographer (1901-74)

t can often only be guessed just w heavily a director has pended on his cameraman, it is rtain that Shamroy's deep derstanding of CinemaScope – shot *The Robe* (53), the first to released – and other descreen techniques was sential to directors working in at medium. His distinctive visual ilities first became apparent in o experimental films, *The Last oment* and *Acoma, the Sky City* oth 28), which attracted the ention of Paramount where he ade *Three-Cornered Moon* (33). was snapped up by Twentieth ntury Fox in 1940 where he ent the rest of his creative life, rking primarily on musicals and ics. Only Preminger (qv) tempted n away to shoot *Porgy and Bess* 9) and *The Cardinal* (63). *The* ack *Swan* (42), *Wilson* (44), ave *Her to Heaven* (45) and eopatra (63) all won him Oscars.

ENE SHARAFF
S costume designer (1910-93)

e received 16 Oscar nominations d won five. Born in Boston and ined in New York and Paris, she s a theatre designer when cruited for Arthur Freed's (qv) GM unit and contributed to many his musicals, including *Meet Me St Louis* (44). Later she worked other studios and made a rare nture into black and white drama *The Best Years of Our Lives* 5). She earned the first of her cars for the ballet in *An* nerican *in Paris* (51), the second for *The King and I* (55) and a third with *West Side Story* (61). At Fox in the 1960s she won Oscars for *Cleopatra* (63) and *Who's Afraid of Virginia Woolf?* (66). Barbra Streisand (qv) got the Sharaff touch for *Funny Girl* (68) and *Hello Dolly!* (69) and her final work was turning Faye Dunaway into Joan Crawford (qqv) as *Mommie Dearest* (81).

OMAR SHARIF
Egyptian actor (1932-)

He was ideal casting for the seemingly limitless exotic roles on offer in the 1960s and 1970s. Already a star in his native Egypt, he rode to international celebrity on a camel as the impulsive Sherif Ali in David Lean's (qv) *Lawrence of Arabia* (62). After playing an Armenian in *The Fall of the Roman Empire*, a Spanish priest in *Behold a Pale Horse* and a Yugoslav patriot in *The Yellow Rolls-Royce* (all 64), he landed his first international starring role in the lamentable *Genghis Khan* (65). His *Doctor Zhivago* (65) in Lean's star-laden epic saved him and *Funny Girl* (68), in which he played the dreamy eyed husband of Barbra Streisand's (qv) Fanny Brice, added to his bankability. But expensive flops such as *Mayerling* (68) and *Che!* (69) cut his career short. In the 1980s he was relegated to supporting roles in minor pictures.

ROBERT SHAW
British actor, writer (1927-78)

A stage actor who may be glimpsed in *The Lavender Hill Mob* (51), he worked in television, published novels and played supporting roles in films from *The Dam Busters* (55) to *From Russia With Love* (63). Given to impassioned, occasionally overwrought performances, often as a villain, he was nominated for a best supporting actor Oscar as King Henry VIII in *A Man for all Seasons* (65). He took leading roles in *Custer of the West* (68), *The Royal Hunt of the Sun* (69) and *Young Winston* (72) before *The Sting* (73) raised his profile to that of star. *The Taking of Pelham 1-2-3* (74), *Jaws* (75), *Robin and Marian* and *Swashbuckler* (both 76), *The Deep* and *Black Sunday* (both 77), *Force Ten From Navarone* (78) and *Avalanche Express* (79) kept his stock high. He died suddenly of a heart attack. His second wife was the actress Mary Ure.

NORMA SHEARER
US actress (1900-83)

Her route to 1930s stardom aroused the jealousy of actresses such as Joan Crawford (qv). Born in Canada, she became a model and then made several low-budget films, the high point being *He Who Gets Slapped* (24) with Lon Chaney (qv). At MGM she set her sights on Irving Thalberg (qv). Marriage to him elevated her, despite a slight squint and dullish acting. She even won an Oscar for *The Divorcee* (30) and Thalberg had her costumed elegantly in *The Barretts of Wimpole Street* (34) and *Romeo*

and Juliet (36). His death left her abandoned, even though she still had a large financial stake in MGM. *Marie Antoinette* (38) was an energetic display, while *The Women* (39) kept her centre stage. Retiring after *Her Cardboard Lover* (42) she married a ski instructor.

MARTIN SHEEN
US actor (1940-)

Born in Ohio of Spanish-Irish descent, he began his career in off-off-Broadway productions. He achieved widespread recognition in the lead of The Subject was Roses on Broadway in 1964 and then in various TV roles before appearing in films such as *The Incident* (67) and *Catch-22* (70). It was his performance as one of a pair of psychotic lovers in *Badlands* (73) that impressed and he displayed a menacing stillness and unfaltering intensity. He gave his second outstanding performance in ▷

Francis Ford Coppola's (qv) *Apocalypse Now* (79), during which he suffered a heart attack. *Apocalypse* was followed by *That Championship Season* (82), a small role in David Cronenberg's (qv) *The Dead Zone* (83) and *Da* (88), which he co-produced. His sons are the actors Emilio Estevez and Charlie Sheen; he appeared with the latter in *Wall Street* (87).

SAM SHEPARD
US actor, writer (1943-)

Playwright, rock'n'roller, reclusive rancher and all-round cool dude, the "Bob Dylan of theatre", Sam Shepard Rogers has become an icon without ever playing a conventional lead. His acting usually gives the impression that he has drifted on to the set from another life. In among unlikely bit parts – *Baby Boom* (87), *Steel Magnolias* (89), *The Pelican Brief* (93) – he stood out in *Days of Heaven* (78) as the doomed landowner and in *The Right Stuff* (83). As a writer he helped explode the myths of materialist America in Antonioni's (qv) *Zabriskie Point* (70) and reached deep into the emotional desert lands in Wenders's (qv) *Paris Texas* (84). Another non-American, Volker Schlöndorff (qv), drew his best performance, as a man who drifts round Europe and into a tragic encounter with his past in *Voyager* (91); for once Shepard broke sweat. He has three children, two with Jessica Lange (qv), his co-star in *Frances* (82).

ANN SHERIDAN
US actress (1915-67)

Clara Lou Sheridan was publicised as the "Oomph Girl" at Warner which raised her profile but did a disservice to her intrinsic intelligence and glamour, as did the many mediocre films and roles she was assigned. While training to teach she won a Texas beauty contest and a Paramount contract, beginning in 1934 with *Search for Beauty*. After some 20 films as an extra or bit player she joined Warner, which gave her featured parts in *Sing Me a Love Song* (36), *The Great O'Malley* (37), *Angels with Dirty Faces* (38) and *They Made Me a Criminal* (39). She impressed as the waitress in *They Drive by Night* (40). *Honeymoon for Three* (41) brought marriage to co-star George Brent (one of three husbands) and in the same year she was wonderfully witty in *The Man Who Came to Dinner*. Success followed opposite Ronald Reagan (qv) in *Kings Row* (42). After two leads, in *Nora Prentiss and The Unfaithful* (both 47), she went freelance, giving a brilliant performance in Hawks's (qv) *I Was a Male War Bride* (49). Her popularity waned in the 1950s and she made TV soaps before her early death from cancer.

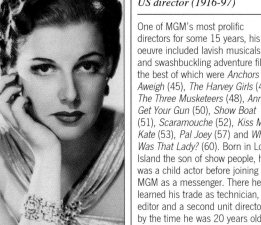

Sidney, right, with Debbie Reynolds and Cantinflas

GEORGE SIDNEY
US director (1916-97)

One of MGM's most prolific directors for some 15 years, his oeuvre included lavish musicals and swashbuckling adventure films, the best of which were *Anchors Aweigh* (45), *The Harvey Girls* (46), *The Three Musketeers* (48), *Annie Get Your Gun* (50), *Show Boat* (51), *Scaramouche* (52), *Kiss Me Kate* (53), *Pal Joey* (57) and *Who Was That Lady?* (60). Born in Long Island the son of show people, he was a child actor before joining MGM as a messenger. There he learned his trade as technician, editor and a second unit director by the time he was 20 years old. He learned his craft on a series of shorts, winning two Oscars – *Quicker 'n a Wink* (40) and *Of Pups and Puzzles* (41) – his first feature was *Free and Easy* (41). Following *Thousands Cheer* (43), his debut musical, he launched Esther Williams (qv) with *Bathing Beauty* (44). His stars included Gene Kelly, Frank Sinatra, Lana Turner, Ava Gardner, Stewart Granger and Elvis Presley (qqv).

SYLVIA SIDNEY
US actress (1910-97)

One of Paramount's biggest stars of the 1930s she played slight, vulnerable women and the public adored rooting for her. Sophia Kosow was born in the Bronx of Slavic parents and trained at the Theatre Guild School, making her professional stage debut in Washington at the age of 16. Her film debut was *Thru Different Eyes* (29). A portrait of her *Madame Butterfly* (32) was used on the packet of Japanese condoms which quickly became known as Sylvia Sidneys. Her films included *Jennie Gerhardt* (33), *Thirty Day Princess* (34) and *Mary Burns – Fugitive* (35). She hampered her career by turning down fluffy roles and by the 1940s she was disillusioned and turned increasingly to the stage. Some of her notable roles are in Lang's (qv) *Fury* (36),

Hitchcock's (qv) *Sabotage* (36) made in Britain, *Blood on the Su[n]* (45) and *The Searching Wind* (4[6]). After television she returned to fi[lm] with *Summer Wishes Winter Dreams* (73) for which she recei[ved] a best actress Oscar nomination.

DON SIEGEL
US director (1912-91)

When asked whether the zombie pod-people in his *Invasion of the Body Snatchers* (56), made at th[e] paranoid height of the cold war, represented a right or left takeov[er] Siegel would snarl: "Neither. They're the front office." To him the zombies did not represent revolutionaries or fascists but the money men who make decisions [in] the film industry. His fight with studio bureaucracy began early. Chicago born and Cambridge educated, he went to Warner to become head of montage, a position he claimed to have won because he pretended to be a relation of Jack Warner (qv). He won Oscars for two shorts and w[as] launched on features with *The Verdict* (46). Contemporary violence was his forte. *Riot in Ce[ll] Block 11* (54) was a prison dram[a] while *Flaming Star* (60) was Presley's (qv) best film. *The Kille[rs]* (64) outraged because of its cas[ual] acceptance of slaughter; and *Dir[ty] Harry* (71) hugely influenced Cli[nt] Eastwood (qv). *Charley Varrick* (7[3]) was another of his inventions.

SIMONE SIGNORET
French actress (1921-85)

A star for 36 years, she specialise[d] in portraying prostitutes – she enjoyed playing the role. One of t[he] beauties of the French cinema in the 1950s she put on weight in later years but continued to play leads, winning the César at the a[ge] of 56 for her performance as the bloated former prostitute *Madam[e] Rosa* (77). Yet she consistently maintained she was "a lazy actress" and was more intereste[d] in looking after her second

band Yves Montand (qv). The ghter of a French Jew who fled Britain during the second world , she supported her two thers in Paris by appearing as extra in films. After marrying the ctor Yves Allégret in 1945, she ame a star playing the dockside stitute *Dedée d'Anvers* (48). She on the game again in Max hüls's (qv) *La Ronde* (50), the dwide success of which blished her. She flourished in h films as *Casque d'Or* (52), *rèse Raquin* (53) and *Les boliques* (55) and won an Oscar Laurence Harvey's (qv) rejected r in *Room at the Top* (59).

EL SILVER
producer (1952-)

love of films began in dhood and he attended NYU School after which he assisted producer Lawrence Gordon on vehicles for the actor Burt nolds (qv). He worked as a ducer often alongside Gordon such Walter Hill (qv) films as *48* (82) and *Streets of Fire* (84). er he formed his own duction company, Silver ures, of which he remains the d. His reputation throughout 1980s and 1990s has been structed similarly to the actors old Schwarzenegger and ester Stallone (qv) with -profile, big-budget action entures. His involvement with *Lethal Weapon* trilogy (87, 89, s characteristic. He has thered a series of box-office s, notably the notorious Bruce s (qv) comedy *Hudson Hawk* but successes such as *Die d* (88) and *Die Hard 2* (90) n they have barely dented his tation as one of the most aciously commercial producers.

PHIL SILVERS
US comedian (1912-85)

Known the world over as the Machiavellian rogue Sergeant Bilko in the hit TV series The Phil Silvers Show, he promenaded his talents in musicals and light comedies on stage and screen. Philip Silversmith was born in Brooklyn, New York, the youngest of eight children of an immigrant Russian-Jewish family. He first went on stage at the age of 11, filling in when the projector broke down, before appearing in shorts for Warner. He made his feature debut in *Hit Parade of 1941* (40), but it was not until his

RKO film *Tom, Dick and Harry* (41) that his distinctive style brought rewards, with hits such as *Cover Girl* (44), *Summer Stock* (50) and *Top Banana* (54), which reprised his Tony-winning Broadway performance of 1951. With the success of Bilko in 1955, which won three Emmy awards, it was inevitable that it would colour future roles, such as in *It's a Mad Mad Mad Mad World* (63), *A Funny Thing Happened on the Way to the Forum* (66) and *Follow that Camel* (67), where he colluded with the Carry On team as a rascally sergeant in the Foreign Legion.

ALASTAIR SIM
British actor (1900-76)

Born and educated in Edinburgh, he worked briefly in the family tailoring firm and became an elocution teacher and amateur actor. The poet John Drinkwater advised him to turn professional. He was aged 30 when he made his stage debut and 35 for his first film, *Riverside Murder* (35). As the bumbling sidekick to *Inspector Hornleigh* (39) and its sequels he met Sidney Gilliat and Frank Launder (qqv), who gave him the starring role in the thriller *Green for Danger* (46) and a pedagogic role opposite the eccentric Margaret Rutherford (qv) in *The Happiest Days of Your Life* (50). Later he excelled in and out of drag as the headmistress of the notorious girl's school in *The Belles of St Trinian's* (55) and *Blue Murder at St Trinian's* (57). His other portrayals included the hoodwinked author of boys' serials in *Hue and Cry* (47), the bogus spiritualist in *London Belongs to Me* (48), the victim of a prankster in *Laughter in Paradise* (51) and the retired assassin in *The Green Man* (56). His last film was *Escape from the Dark* (76).

JEAN SIMMONS
British actress (1929-)

A vivacious pupil of the Aida Foster stage school in north London she was chosen to appear with Margaret Lockwood (qv) in *Give Us the Moon* (44). She was a hand maiden in the extravagant *Caesar and Cleopatra* (46) and sang Let Him Go, Let Him Tarry in *The Way to the Stars* (45). She was exceptional as the haughty young Estella in Lean's (qv) *Great Expectations* (46) and as a wayward native dancer in *Black Narcissus* (46). Olivier (qv) cast her as his Ophelia in *Hamlet* (48) and with Stewart Granger (qv), who became her husband, she appeared in *Adam and Evelyne* (49). Simmons moved to Hollywood and a frustrating period under contract to Howard Hughes (qv) appearing in spectaculars such as *The Robe* (53), *Guys and Dolls* (55) and *The Big Country* (58). Divorcing Granger she married the director Richard Brooks (qv) and was in his *Elmer Gantry* (60). Her later films were less interesting, although she won an Oscar nomination for *The Happy Ending* (69) and her best late appearance was in *The Dawning* (88).

MICHEL SIMON
Swiss actor (1895-1975)

A former photographer, boxer, music hall acrobat and stage actor he was at his peak during the 1930s and early 1940s and enjoyed a late life triumph as the anti-semitic peasant taking care of a Jewish boy in Claude Berri's (qv) *The Two of Us* (66). His Père Jules in Jean Vigo's (qv) *L'Atalante* (34), a drunken, independent-minded bargeman, was gross but tender. There was nothing lovable about his obscene tramp in Renoir's (qv) *Boudu Saved From Drowning* (32), spitting where he pleased and seducing the women of his benefactor's house. It was his most extrovert and outrageous performance. Also memorable were his portrayals of the clerk destroyed by passion for a prostitute in *La Chienne* (31), a thriller writer in the witty *Drôle de Drame* (37), Michèle Morgan's guardian in *Quai des Brumes* (38), both for Carné (qv), outstanding as a failed actor hiding behind jokiness in Duvivier's (qv) *The End of a Day* (39) and, as an ageing Faust, swapping identities with Gérard Philipe in Clair's (qqv) *Beauty and the Devil* (50).

NEIL SIMON
US playwright, screenwriter (1927-)

More financially successful than any playwright in the history of ▷

Frank Sinatra and 'friends', to keep the public at bay

American theatre, he is also known internationally as the creative exponent of New York Jewish wit. The comic twist and affectionate cynicism of his writing are perfectly captured by Walter Matthau (qv) in *The Odd Couple* (68). This film, still perhaps the writer's best known work for which he won an Oscar nomination, displays his ear for the absurdity of the everyday. It was preceded by *After the Fox* (66) which Simon co-wrote, and *Plaza Suite* (71). *The Prisoner of Second Avenue* (74), *The Sunshine Boys* (75) and *California Suite* (78) also had their first life on stage with the latter two nominated for Oscars, as was *The Goodbye Girl* (77). Recent work includes his trilogy *Brighton Beach Memoirs* (86), *Biloxi Blues* (88) and *Broadway Bound* (92).

FRANK SINATRA
US actor, singer (1915-)

Francis Albert Sinatra comes from Hoboken, New Jersey, the son of an immigrant fireman and became one of the century's greatest singing stars. He joined the Harry James band in 1939 but achieved fame with the Tommy Dorsey orchestra between 1940 and 1942. He made his solo debut in New York on New Year's Eve 1942 and drove the bobbysoxer audience wild. He was dubbed "The Voice". His film debut was with Dorsey in *Las Vegas Nights* (41) and his first acting part was in *Higher and Higher* (43). Most of his early films were indifferent, although *Anchors Aweigh* (45) and *On the Town* (49) were exceptions. His career slumped in the early 1950s, but he convinced Harry Cohn (qv), the head of Columbia, that he could play Maggio in *From Here to Eternity* (53). His fee was insulting, but he won the best supporting Oscar. Musically he struck up his partnership with Nelson Riddle. He was nominated for *The Man With the Golden Arm* (55) and co-starred with Bing Crosby and Grace Kelly (qqv) in *High Society* (56). Among his most notable films are *The Manchurian Candidate* (62) and *Von Ryan's Express* (65).

JOHN SINGLETON
US director (1967-)

He is both the youngest and the first African-American to be nominated for the directing Oscar. He won the New York Critics Award when he was 24 years old for his first feature, *Boyz N the Hood* (91), which he wrote (also receiving an Oscar nomination for his screenplay). The hard-hitting rites of passage story was informed by his youth in South Central Los Angeles. He studied film writing at the University of Southern California, graduating with the coveted Robert Riskin Award. He went on to win an unprecedented two Jack Nicholson Awards for his

screenplays. His second film, *Poetic Justice* (93), was a critical and commercial failure, but he was judged back on track with his third film, *Higher Learning* (95), a college drama of racial and sexual politics. Singleton is a member of the board of the Black Filmmakers Foundation and the American Library of Congress Film Preservation. He heads his own production and music companies.

ROBERT SIODMAK
German director (1900-73)

Following an ill-fated career as a banker in his native Germany, he was reduced to translating title cards of American films for a living. He became an editor in 1926 and directed his first film, *People On Sunday* (29), in collaboration with Edgar G Ulmer (qv) from a screenplay by Billy Wilder (qv) and his brother Curt. Schüfftan was the cinematographer and Zinnemann (qqv) an assistant. Although he made a number of features in Germany and France he is better known for his dark, atmospheric American films. Revealing a strong visual style (despite poor eyesight), he excelled at taut, psychological thrillers such as *The Spiral Staircase*, *The Killers* and *The Dark Mirror* (all 46) and *Criss Cross* (49). He was never at home in Hollywood and in 1951 returned to Europe. Of his several later films, *The Rats* (55) and *The Devil Strikes at Night* (57), both German, are noteworthy, as was his last film, *Der Kampf um Rom* (68-69)

DOUGLAS SIRK
German director (1900-87)

Claus Detlev Sierck was born t Danish parents and studied dr as a teenager before directing plays. Nazi rule imposed restrictions on theatrical work s moved to cinema with shorts a then features from 1935. Thes including the moving *Zu neuer Ufern* (37), were outstanding f the start, fluent and auspicious films which can easily be iden as stylistic precursors to his fir melodramatic work. In 1937 h emigrated to America, change name and worked on formulai low-budget features. He earne financial success with *Magnifi Obsession* (54) and went on t further acclaim with *All That Heaven Allows* (55) and his la hit *Imitation of Life* (59). He w one of the most appealing dire of romantic melodrama.

VICTOR SJOSTROM
Swedish director (1879-1960)

When his family moved to America his father turned into a religious zealot, which drove the young Sjöström back to Sweden alone. He began acting in Finland before joining Svenska Bio films where he met Mauritz Stiller (qv). They went on to galvanise the Swedish cinema. His *Ingeborg Holm* (13) drew admiration from intellectuals and critics while *A Man There Was* and *The Outlaw and his Wife* (both 17) and *The Phantom Carriage* ('21) also bore his original stamp. n Hollywood, as Victor Seastrom, he made his mark with *He Who Gets Slapped* (24), *The Tower of Lies* (25), *The Scarlet Letter* (26), *The Divine Woman* (28) with Garbo

qv) and his triumph, *The Wind* 28), with Lillian Gish (qv). He then eturned to Sweden and helped the lm industry make the transition to ound. He directed his last film, *Inder the Red Robe* (37), in ritain. His final bow was as the lderly scholar in Bergman's (qv) *Vild Strawberries* (57).

ERZY SKOLIMOWSKI
olish director (1938-)

ne of the few Polish actor-rectors to have pursued a ıccessful career on both sides of e former Iron Curtain, his films oncentrate on individuals caught an emotional and social ossroads, as in *Barrier* (66). He as a year old when the Nazis arched into Warsaw and one of e new generation after the war to ke advantage of expanded ucational opportunities, aduating from Warsaw University d the state film school at Lodz. A jazz player who published poems and short stories before collaborating as a screenwriter on Wajda's (qv) *Innocent Sorcerers* (59) and Polanski's (qv) *Knife in the Water* (60), he produced, wrote, directed and acted in his first feature, *Identification Marks: None* (64). Other successes led him to look for sponsorship abroad after *Hands Up!* (67) was delayed by the censors. He made a memorable impression with *Deep End* (70), an American-German co-production filmed in Britain, and won awards at Cannes for two British productions, *The Shout* (78) and *Moonlighting* (82). Other symbolically entitled films include *Success Is the Best Revenge* (84) and the Italian-French production *Torrents of Spring* (89).

EVERETT SLOANE
US actor (1909-65)

A strong, imposing character actor remembered for his portrayal of Bernstein in *Citizen Kane* (41), he was born in New York and educated at the University of Pennsylvania. He was a Wall Street runner until the 1929 crash left him penniless, so he decided to realise a boyhood acting ambition and turned to Broadway. He acted in thousands of radio dramas until he joined Orson Welles's (qv) Mercury Theatre in 1935. He went to Hollywood with Welles and made his impressive debut in *Citizen Kane*. A physically small man, he was never easy to cast, but he made many important films including *Journey Into Fear* (43), *The Lady From Shanghai* (48) and *Patterns* (56). His other films include *Somebody Up There Likes Me* (56) and *Home From the Hill* (60). He committed suicide.

Sloane, right, and Curtis in The Prince Who Was A Thief

DOUGLAS SLOCOMBE
British cinematographer (1913-)

A Londoner, he was originally a photo-journalist and gained his first experience of filming by shooting news and documentary footage during the second world war, including *Lights Out in Europe* (40), covering the German invasion of Poland. He subsequently went to Ealing Studios where he was a leading director of photography throughout the studio's heyday for dramas and comic classics such as *Kind Hearts and Coronets* (49) and *The Lavender Hill Mob* (51). His international reputation grew in the 1960s through his work on *The L-Shaped Room* and *The Servant* (both 63) and *The Lion in Winter* (68), after which he was in constant demand for expensive productions from *The Great Gatsby* (74) to numerous Steven Spielberg (qv) films, including the *Indiana Jones* trilogy (81, 84, 89). He has received three Oscar nominations.

ALEXIS SMITH
US actress (1921-93)

Born in Penticton, British Columbia, she was signed by Warner while a student and from 1940 until 1950 played often shrewd and decisive leading roles. Her performances in *Gentleman Jim* (42) with Errol Flynn (qv), *The Constant Nymph* (43), *The Doughgirls* (44) and *San Antonio* (45) are worth noting. Free from her contract, she scored with *Undercover Girl* (50), *Split Second* (53), *The Sleeping Tiger* (54) among others, but after *The Young Philadelphians* (59) she retired. Following success on Broadway in Stephen Sondheim's Follies she returned to films with *Once Is Not Enough* (75), *The Little Girl Who Lives Down the Lane* (76), *Casey's Shadow* (78) and *Tough Guys* (86). She was married to the actor Craig Stevens and they appeared together in *Dive Bomber* and *Steel Against the Sky* (both 41) and a French film, *La Truite* (82).

C AUBREY SMITH
British actor (1863-1948)

He was an upright, Cambridge-educated Victorian gentleman at large in Hollywood. An England cricketer before becoming an actor on stage and in silent American films, his imposing height, jutting jaw and bushy eyebrows made him a natural for noble and military roles. He was the Duke of Wellington twice, in *The House Of Rothschild* (34) and *Sixty Glorious Years* (38). His most famous role was probably Colonel Zapt in *The Prisoner of Zenda* (37). In *The Four Feathers* (39) he was the retired commander everyone had to live up to. Knighted in 1944, he was a one-note actor seemingly typecast for ever in period.

Douglas Slocombe, left, started in wartime newsreels

GEORGE ALBERT SMITH
British pioneer, inventor and director (1864-1959)

A portrait photographer and keen astronomer, he turned to film in 1896. Based in Brighton, along with several other pioneers, he became one of Britain's foremost innovators, particularly in special effects and trick photography. He patented double exposure, as seen in *Photographing a Ghost* (98), and his use of a second image superimposed in a circle on the main image can be seen in *Santa Claus* (98). He refined existing reverse-image techniques in *The House That Jack Built* (00) and developed the use of close-up as an inter-cutting device, as in *Grandma's Reading Glass* (00), where single objects, including her eye, are magnified. Forming a partnership with the American pioneer Charles Urban (qv) he patented Kinemacolor, the first successful colour process.

MAGGIE SMITH
British actress (1934-)

Her film appearances seem like incidental extras in a triumphant stage career, although they have earned her Oscars for *The Prime of Miss Jean Brodie* (69) and *California Suite* (78) as well as three nominations, for *Othello* (65), *Travels With My Aunt* (72) and *A Room With a View* (85). Born in Ilford, London, she trained at the Oxford Playhouse and made her stage debut in 1952. She has excelled in crisp comedic timing and eccentric delivery, particularly shining in roles that have the tortuousness of the British class system as their murky hinterland. She can seem to be coasting, as in *The Secret Garden* (93) and the *Sister Act* films (92, 93), relying on her armoury of comic tics to see her through. Few roles have capitalised on the capacity she showed in *The Lonely Passion of Judith Hearne* (87) to rise to darker material; too rarely has she let rip as in her keynote cameo in *Oh! What a Lovely War* (69), where her jaded showgirl recruiting volunteers "willing for a shilling" represents the moral bankruptcy of a moribund social order.

SISSY SPACEK
US actress (1949-)

She won a singer-songwriting contest in her native Texas, joined her cousins Rip Torn and Geraldine Page (qqv) in New York, studied with Lee Strasberg and abandoned music for films as an extra in Andy Warhol's (qv) *Trash* (70). She found fame at the age of 24 as the schoolgirl drawn into a runaway killing spree with Martin Sheen (qv) in *Badlands* (73). At 26 she was a high school ugly duckling turned telekinetic avenger in *Carrie* (76) and at 31 she portrayed singer Loretta Lynn, maturing from shy 13-year-old to adulthood in *Coal Miner's Daughter* (80), which won her a best actress Oscar. She was superb in *Missing* (82) and *The River* (84) and powerful in the underrated *Marie* (85). She won an Oscar nomination for *Crimes of the Heart* (86), but then attracted only a couple of feeble scripts before she accompanied Whoopi Goldberg (qv) on *The Long Walk Home* (90). Wasted as Costner's (qv) wife in *JFK* (91) she has since failed to find worthy vehicles.

SAM SPIEGEL
US producer (1903-85)

A spirited independent in the days of the studio system he was born in what was then Austria (now Poland) and began his career as a reader and translator at MGM in 1927. Universal sent him to Berlin where he produced French and German versions of its American films. Fleeing Hitler's Germany he lived in London, Paris, Vienna, Mexico City and New York before returning to Hollywood where *Tales of Manhattan* (42) was his first American production. His partnership with John Huston (qv) resulted in *The African Queen* (51) and he went solo for *On the Waterfront* (54), a superb work of intensity and imagination, while his feel for the epic sweep was realised with *The Bridge on the River Kwai* (57) and *Lawrence of Arabia* (62). All three won best picture Oscars.

Sam Spiegel on the set of The African Queen with Hepburn

STEVEN SPIELBERG
US director, producer (1947-)

He was making short films in his early teens in Phoenix, Arizona, and *Amblin'* (69) provided the name for his production company in 1984. It also landed him a Universal contract and his auspicious debut, *Duel* (71). One of his three greatest films is the shark thriller *Jaws* (75), a box-office success that whetted the public's appetite. *Close Encounters of the Third Kind* (77), his second hit, was followed by the flawed second world war comedy *1941* (79). He was on top again with *Raiders of the Lost Ark* (81), which spawned two sequels. His *ET The Extra-Terrestrial* (82), the story of a boy's friendship with an alien, was the most successful film of all time until he made *Jurassic Park* (93). In between he directed the likeable *The Color Purple* (85) and his most misjudged works, *Always* (89) and *Hook* (91). *Schindler's List* (93), a harrowing drama set in Nazi Germany, was a remarkable progression, its mature vision earning him board-sweeping recognition at the Academy Awards. He is possibly cinema's most astute businessman.

JOHN M STAHL
US director (1886-1950)

One of the key directors of stylish, melodramatic "women's pictures" it is unfortunate that much of his work has disappeared or been overshadowed by later remakes, particularly by Douglas Sirk (qv), his heir to the genre. Stahl was a[n] actor from New York who took up directing in 1914 at First National. He was a founding member of th[e] Academy of Motion Picture Arts and Sciences. After moving between studios and production partners he was a leading directo[r] from 1930 at Universal, where he made the first version of *Imitatio[n] of Life* (34) starring Claudette Colbert (qv), the original *Magnificent Obsession* (35), whic[h] made Robert Taylor (qv) a star, a[nd] *When Tomorrow Comes* (39), re-made as *Interlude* (57) by Sirk. A[t] Fox in the 1940s he delivered hit

John Stahl was renowned f[or] 'women's film[s]'

cluding *The Keys of the Kingdom* 4), propelling young Gregory ck (qv) to stardom and an Oscar mination, and the studio's gest Technicolor smash of the cade *Leave Her to Heaven* (45), ich showcases Gene Tierney (qv) the fiendish possessive wife.

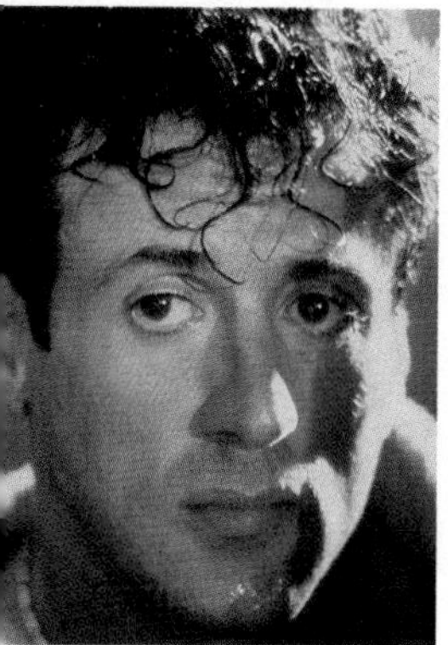

LVESTER STALLONE
actor, director (1946-)

actor and director who rose to minence on the tide of 1970s tosterone films, he transcended genre with pathos in his cessful *Rocky* series. Born in v York, he began his working life a pizza demonstrator, zoo cage eper and usher while trying to acting roles. His film debut was he porno film *Party at Kitty and ds* (71). *Bananas* (71), *The ds of Flatbush* (74), *No Place to le, Farewell, My Lovely* and one (all 75) followed in which played a series of hoods. In 6 he made *Rocky* from his own pt. The film was a worldwide hit four sequels (79, 82, 85, 90). r a series of lesser roles in the 1970s he hit on another racter who captured the public gination, the Vietnam veteran n Rambo in *First Blood* (82) its two bloody sequels (85, After a fallow period he rned to form with *Cliffhanger* *Demolition Man* (both 93).

RRY DEAN STANTON
actor (1926-)

was the alienated figure in a eball cap who wandered the eland of Wim Wenders's (qv) *s, Texas* (84), the role that ly helped him transcend his

Barbara Stanwyck, the chorus girl who made it to stardom

supporting status and become a cult international star. Born and educated in Kentucky, he followed his second world war naval service by joining the Pasadena Playhouse and made his film debut in *The Wrong Man* (57). Lean and gaunt with a southern drawl, he played western badmen, psychotic gangsters, manipulative conmen, sympathetic heroes and average Joes. Known as Dean Stanton throughout much of the 1960s, his credits include *Pork Chop Hill* (59), *Cool Hand Luke* (67), *The Godfather Part II* (74), *Alien* (79), *Escape From New York* (81), *Repo Man* (84), *The Last Temptation of Christ* (88), *The Fourth War* (90), the lovelorn detective in *Wild at Heart* (90), *Twin Peaks: Fire Walk With Me* (92) and *Hostages* (93).

BARBARA STANWYCK
US actress (1907-90)

An orphan who danced in a speakeasy, she was a Broadway chorus girl, a straight leading lady in her teens and worked almost solidly in Hollywood from *The Locked Door* (29) to the 1960s. She often played tough, outspoken characters whose spirit reflected her own. Although she won four Oscar nominations, for *Stella Dallas* (37), *Ball of Fire* (42), *Double Indemnity* (44) and *Sorry, Wrong Number* (48), her only Oscar was "for lifetime achievement" in 1981. Among her other films to be noted are *The Miracle Woman* and *Night Nurse* (both 31), *So Big* (32), *Baby Face* (33), *Annie Oakley* (35), *Remember the Night* (40), *The Strange Love of Martha Ivers* (46), *Thelma Jordon* (49), *The Furies* (50), *Executive Suite* (54) and *There's Always Tomorrow* (56). After a brief retirement came *Walk on the Wild Side* (62), *Roustabout* and *The Night Walker* (both 64). She was married to Frank Fay, a vaudeville star, and the actor Robert Taylor (qv).

ROD STEIGER
US actor (1925-)

He can shake a role until it rattles and has created memorable characters. His introduction to film was via the Actors Studio and a television version of Marty in 1952, which was painfully touching. He was Marlon Brando's (qv) corrupt elder brother in *On the Waterfront* (54), the film producer in *The Big Knife* (55), the boxing promoter in *The Harder They Fall* (56) and the pathetic Jud in *Oklahoma!* (55). His roles as a confederate Comanche in *Run of the Arrow* (57), *Al Capone* (59) and the emotionless Jew in *The Pawnbroker* (65) are authoritative. He won an Oscar for his portrayal of the redneck sheriff redeemed by Poitier (qv) in *In The Heat of the Night* (67), and his role as the mother's boy killer in *No Way to Treat a Lady* (68) is a notable treasure. Napoleon in *Waterloo* (71) was one of his flawed tyrants, but serious depression grounded him . *The Chosen* (81) was worth the wait, and in *Mars Attacks!* (96) he was a bellicose general.

MAX STEINER
US composer (1888-1971)

Born in Vienna into a prominent musical family, he was a child prodigy tutored by Gustav Mahler. He completed an eight-year course at the Viennese Imperial Academy of Music in one year and went on to compose his first operetta at the age of 14. By 16 he was a professional conductor. After writing much symphonic music he conducted musical comedies in Berlin, Paris and London then emigrated to America at Florenz Ziegfeld's invitation. After working in Ziegfeld's 6th Avenue Theater, he moved to Hollywood with the advent of sound. Steiner gave music a dramatic voice, his melodic and sweeping scores setting a pattern for film composition. He put his incomparable stamp on *King Kong* (33), *Gone With the Wind* (39), *Now Voyager* and *Casablanca* (both 42), *The Big Sleep* (46) and *The Treasure of the Sierra Madre* (48). In 42 years he scored more than 200 films, received 26 Oscar nominations and won three, for *The Informers* (35), *Now Voyager* and *Since You Went Away* (44).

JOSEF VON STERNBERG
US director (1894-69)

Rightly credited with creating Marlene Dietrich (qv) he pioneered the poetic film noir, using an imaginative interplay of light and shadow to create powerful atmospheric dramas. Sternberg was born in Vienna – the von was added to his credits allegedly without his knowledge as assistant director on *The Mystery of the Yellow Room* (19) – educated in Austria and America and worked as a film editor. After service in the first world war he was an assistant director before making *The Salvation Hunters* (25), his feature debut, which so impressed Chaplin (qv) that he hired him to make *The Sea Gull* (unreleased 26). The moody gangster film *Underworld* (27), *The Last Command* (28) and his first talkie *Thunderbolt* (29) led him to Germany to direct *The Blue Angel* (30). After six more magnificent films with Dietrich his career went into decline. An ambitious *I Claudius* (37) in Britain was never finished after its star Merle Oberon (qv) was injured in a car accident, but he made a magisterial return with *Anatahan* (52). He died of a heart attack after writing his autobiography Fun in a Chinese Laundry.

16 to become an actor, he worked as an assistant cameraman on Laurel & Hardy (qv) shorts, directing his first feature in 1933. Chosen by Katharine Hepburn (qv) to direct her in *Alice Adams* (35), he quickly made his mark. He was acknowledged by the Academy when he switched to epics, but his earlier films, from his comedy shorts to the polished sophistication of *Swing Time* (36) with Astaire and Rogers (qv) indicated a diverse talent. He encouraged excellent turns from Hepburn, Rogers, Barbara Stanwyck, Carole Lombard, Irene Dunne and Jean Arthur (qqv). Later he pushed perfectionism to extremes, blowing schedules and budgets. None the less, his films of the 1950s met with rapturous approval and he won Oscars for *A Place in the Sun* (51) and *Giant* (56). He received Oscar nominations for *Shane* (53) and *The Diary of Anne Frank* (59).

JAMES STEWART
US actor (1908-97)

He was arguably Hollywood's most liked leading man, working almost continuously from 1935 to *The Magic of Lassie* (78). At first he embodied innocence abroad, in Frank Capra's (qv) *You Can't Take It With You* (38), *Mr Smith Goes to Washington*, W S Van Dyke's (qv) *It's a Wonderful World* and *Destry Rides Again* (all 39) and *The Shop Around the Corner* (40). He won the best actor Oscar for *The Philadelphia Story* (40). After distinguished wartime service with the USAAF, a new assertiveness was apparent. *It's a Wonderful Life* (46) was balanced by *Call Northside 777* and Hitchcock's (qv) *Rope* (both 48) and tough roles in westerns such as *Winchester 73* (50) and *The Man From Laramie* (55). He worked with Hitchcock in *Rope* (48), *Rear Window* (54), *The Man Who Knew Too Much* (56) and *Vertigo* (58) and played popular American heroes in *The Glenn Miller Story* (54) and *The Spirit of St Louis* (57). Only films such as *Harvey* (50) and *Bell Book and Candle* (58) showcased his comic gifts. Later films included *Cheyenne Autumn* (64), *Shenandoah* (65), *Flight of the Phoenix* (66) and *The Shootist* (76). He received a special Oscar in 1985.

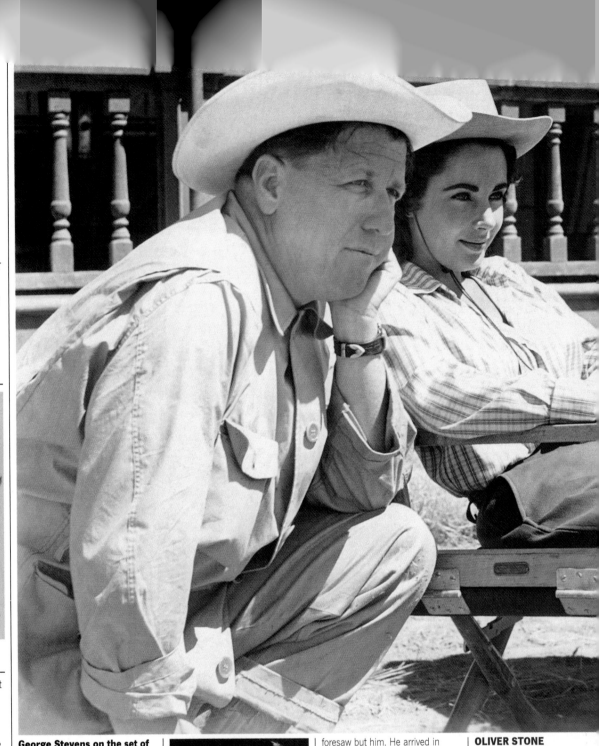

George Stevens on the set of Giant with Taylor and Hudson

MAURITZ STILLER
Swedish director (1883-1928)

Stiller's story, as the mentor of Greta Garbo (qv), is that of an artist deserted by his creation. It was, though, an outcome everyone

foresaw but him. He arrived in Sweden from Finland at the age of 27 with a considerable stage and film reputation, having made *The Modern Suffragette* (13). Graceful comedies of sexual intrigue were more his style and Ernst Lubitsch (qv) acknowledged his debt to *Erotikon* (20). His obsession with Garbo, whom he starred in *The Gösta Berling Saga* (24), led him in 1925 to follow her to Hollywood at the invitation of Louis B Mayer (qv). It was, however, the actress Mayer wanted and Stiller never completed an American film with her. His best work was with Pola Negri (qv) at Paramount in *Hotel Imperial* and *The Woman on Trial* (both 27). He returned to Sweden and died of a respiratory illness.

OLIVER STONE
US director, screenwriter a producer (1946-)

The most lionised American director of the late 1980s, he h consistently invited outrage with forceful visions of society. The s of a wealthy stockbroker – to whom he paid an ironic tribute *Wall Street* (87) – he dropped o of Yale and volunteered for serv in Vietnam, an experience that shaped his work and his interpretations of modern histo from *The Doors*, *JFK* (both 91) *Nixon* (95) to his Vietnam trilog *Platoon* (86), *Born on the Four July* (89) and *Heaven and Eart* (93). After NYU Film School he made his debut as

writer/director with a horror film, but made his reputation with visceral screenplays such as *Midnight Express* (78), for which he won an Oscar. His third and fourth directing efforts, *Salvador* (86) and *Platoon*, propelled him to the forefront, the latter winning four Oscars. He won another Oscar for *Born on the Fourth of July* but drew fire for flouting facts in the absorbing *JFK*. He went too far for many critics with his audacious and grotesque statement on violence and the media, *Natural Born Killers* (94). His next attempt at revisionist recent history was *Nixon* with Anthony Hopkins (qv) in the title role. He has also produced films, including *Reversal of Fortune* (90) and *The Joy Luck Club* (93).

SHARON STONE
US actress (1958-)

A strong-willed, icy actress who has emerged in the late 1980s with a reputation for explicit roles, she was born in Meadville, Pennsylvania, and educated at Edinboro State University. After winning a local beauty contest she worked consistently as a New York model in television commercials throughout the 1970s. She moved to Hollywood and won her first small role in *Stardust Memories* (80). She made a variety of mediocre films over the next few years including *Bolero* (82), *Irreconcilable Differences* (84), *Police Academy 4* (87) and *Action Jackson* (88) until her big break opposite Arnold Schwarzenegger (qv) in *Total Recall* (90). She became a top-flight name and the following year won international attention with her sexually explicit role in the controversial *Basic Instinct* (92). *Sliver* (93), *Intersection* (94) and *Casino* (95) have followed.

VITTORIO STORARO
Italian cinematographer (1940-)

A high-profile professional since he won Oscars for *Apocalypse Now* (79), *Reds* (81) and *The Last Emperor* (87), he is in constant demand for the irresistible rich gloss he brings to his work. His ability to express the sensuality of landscape, architecture and objects, his penchant for sweeping shots and an expressive style have lit up the films of Bertolucci, Coppola and Warren Beatty (qqv). His class was already evident in *The Spider's Strategem* (70) and *The Conformist* (71). *Last Tango in Paris* (73) outraged and he embraced the heart of darkness for *Apocalypse Now.* The stylisation of *One From the Heart* (82) and *Dick Tracy* (90) were quite different from the traditional photographic grandeur of *The Last Emperor* and *The Sheltering Sky* (90).

Keaton and Beatty in Reds, lit by Vittorio Storaro

Harry Stradling behind the camera, Eve Whitney in front

HARRY STRADLING
British cinematographer (1902-70)

In America from his teens he worked on run-of-the-mill silents, but his meticulous feel for the appropriate image flowered in France, notably with Feyder's (qv) mock-heroic *La Kermesse héroïque* (35). In Britain his films included *Pygmalion* (38) and the propaganda piece *The Lion Has Wings* (39). He returned to America and in almost 50 films over 30 years brought his impeccable judgment and a keen eye for colour to an extraordinary range of material: Hitchcock's (qv) *Suspicion* (41), the Esther Williams (qv) extravaganza *Bathing Beauty* (44), the inventive Gene Kelly-Judy Garland (qqv) musical *The Pirate* (48), *Easter Parade* (48) with Fred Astaire (qv), *A Streetcar Named Desire* (51), *Johnny Guitar* (54), *Guys and Dolls* (55), *A Face in the Crowd* (57), *Gypsy* (62), Taylor and Burton (qqv) in *Who's Afraid of Virginia Woolf?* (66), Streisand's (qv) debut film, *Funny Girl* (68) and many more. *The Picture of Dorian Gray* (45) and *My Fair Lady* (64) won him Oscars.

MERYL STREEP
US actress (1949-)

She graduated from Yale Drama School in 1975 and took leads in repertory before Broadway success. Her film debut was *Julia* (77) and recognition and an Oscar nomination came with *The Deer Hunter* (78), which was followed by *Manhattan* and *Kramer Vs Kramer* (both 79). She won an Oscar for *Sophie's Choice* (82) and was impressive in *Silkwood* (83), but some feel her performances were too mannered in *Out of Africa* (85) and *A Cry in the Dark* (88). Her versatility has become something of a millstone and though she gives excellent performances she is not an actress the public adores. She has tried to remedy a reputation for coldness with comedies including *She-Devil* (89), *Postcards from the Edge* (90), *Death Becomes Her* (92) and the action film *The River Wild* (94). More recently she was in *The Bridges of Madison County* (95) and *Marvin's Room* (96).

They fought like seven hundred...

THE MAGNIFICENT SEVEN

THE MIRISCH COMPANY PRESENTS

YUL BRYNNER CO-STARRING ELI WALLACH STEVE McQUEEN

IN

The Magnificent Seven

And Introducing HORST BUCHHOLZ

CO-STARRING CHARLES BRONSON • ROBERT VAUGHN

Screenplay by WILLIAM ROBERTS Produced and Directed by JOHN STURGES

A MIRISCH-ALPHA PICTURE Filmed in PANAVISION Colour by DeLuxe

Executive Producer WALTER MIRISCH

Music ELMER BERNSTEIN

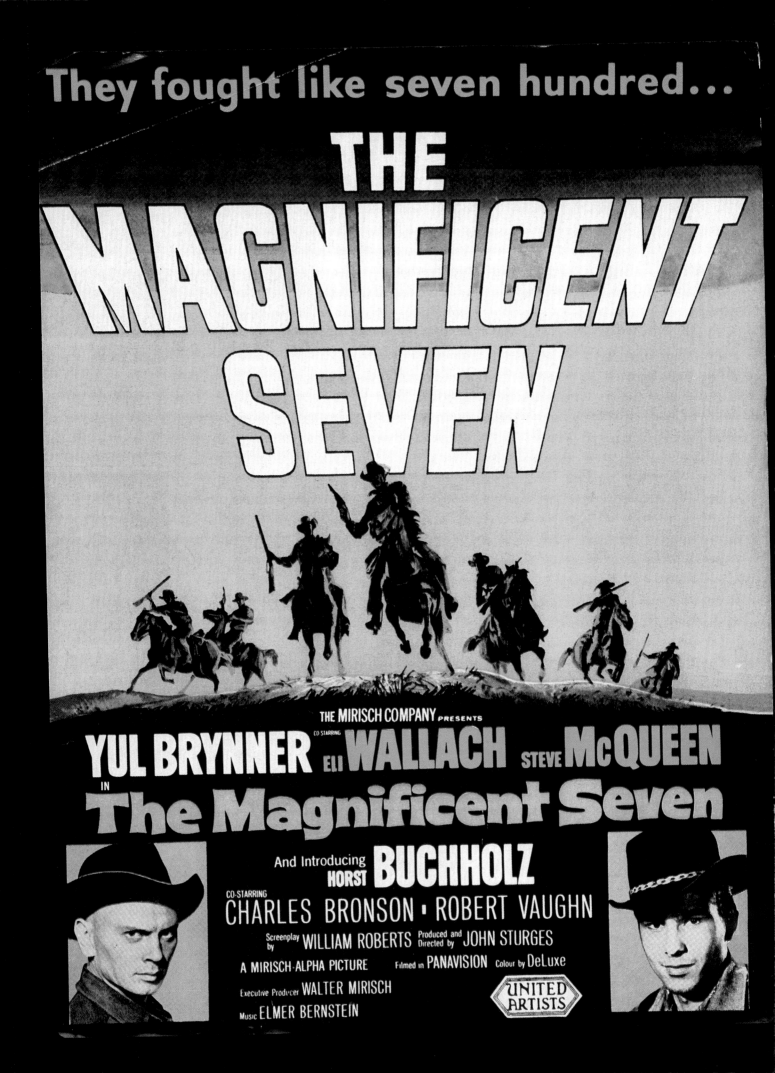

ARBRA STREISAND
JS director, actress and singer 1942-)

he is one of the greatest all-round ntertainers of the 20th century. A ewish kid from Brooklyn, she onquered Broadway, London's Vest End and Hollywood in turn nd won the best actress Oscar for er first film. She began in cabaret nd off-Broadway, then made her nternational mark with the musical unny Girl, a biography of Fanny rice. It made her a chart topper ho could entertain a multitude ve in New York's Central Park. Her tatus was high when she made ne film *Funny Girl* (68), followed y *Hello Dolly!* (69) and *On a Clear Day You Can See Forever* (70). Her omic performance in *What's Up Doc?* (72) and the sentimental *The Vay We Were* (73) confirmed her uperstar status. She won another scar for composing the song vergreen for *A Star is Born* (76) nd in 1983 directed and played the lead in *Yentl*, in which a girl disguises herself as a boy to receive a Jewish education. She also directed *The Prince of Tides* (91), in which her son Jason Gould had a small part, revealing further her considerable talents. She is committed to many social and ecological issues and continues to use her vast wealth to finance causes close to her heart.

JOSEPH STRICK
US director (1923-)

He is a classic case of how to alienate people and his integrity was often interpreted as obstinacy. He was a wartime airforce cameraman and then made *Muscle Beach* (48), a delightful short, with Irving Lerner. He spent several years compiling an acid documentary, *The Savage Eye* (60). His *The Balcony* (63) by Jean Genet was stagey and lurid, James Joyce's *Ulysses* (67) impossible but intriguing, while Henry Miller's *Tropic of Cancer* (70) was disjointed. He won an Oscar for *Interviews with My Lai Veterans* (70) and used the same face-to-face technique for *Criminals* (95), with footage of district attorneys grilling offenders. His inability to compromise had him fired from some projects.

ERICH VON STROHEIM
Austrian director, actor (1885-1957)

The archetypal tyrant director, his creative genius was thwarted by the monumental ambition of his projects – inevitably his films were butchered or taken out of his hands. In America from 1906, he worked as a journalist, bit player, designer, military adviser and assistant director until his acting-directing debut with *Blind Husbands* (19) followed by the even better *Foolish Wives* (22). His directorial masterpiece was the heavily cut *Greed* (24). It was followed by *The Merry Widow* (25) and his unfinished last work *Queen Kelly* (28) for Gloria Swanson (qv). He was then forcibly confined to acting where his stocky form, staring eyes and shaven bullet head made him an ideal brute or cad. Chilling in *The Great Gabbo* (29), he appeared opposite Garbo (qv) in *As You Desire Me* (32), was superb in Jean Renoir's (qv) *La Grande Illusion* (37), played Rommel in *Five Graves to Cairo* (43) and was curiously touching in *Sunset Boulevard* (49). Crushed and bitter, he died in France.

JOHN STURGES
US director (1910-92)

In the 1960s he emerged as one of Hollywood's most efficient action directors. He first worked as an editor for RKO in the 1930s and moved on to directing B-movies in the 1940s. At MGM 10 years later the scale of his pictures and his stars increased. *Bad Day at Black Rock* (55) was the most successful, followed by two superior westerns for Paramount, *Gunfight at the OK Corral* (57) and *Last Train From Gun Hill* (59). It was in the early 1960s that his knack for staging often extended action sequences put all-star casts at his disposal ▷

The 10 best dramas

The Bicycle Thief (1948)
An Italian neo-realist masterpiece, directed by Vittorio De Sica

Brief Encounter (1945)
Noël Coward's thwarted romance; a British masterpiece

Casablanca (1942)
An American classic, Bogart and Bergman as lovers who meet again

Citizen Kane (1941)
Often regarded as the greatest American film; by Orson Welles

La Dolce Vita (1960)
Federico Fellini's expose of the meretricious decadence of Rome society

La Grande Illusion (1937)
Jean Renoir's anti-war tract, with Jean Gabin, Pierre Fresnay, Erich von Stroheim

La Régle du Jeu (1939)
The French upper class disintegrates on the eve of war

One Flew Over the Cuckoo's Nest (1975)
Milos Forman's inspired cry for freedom for the human spirit, with Jack Nicholson

Tokyo Story (1953)
Ozu's masterpiece, old age as perceived by the young

Wild Strawberries (1957)
An old man on a journey recalls his life in Ingmar Bergman's classic

JANE RUSSELL ★ MARILYN MONROE

IN HOWARD HAWKS'

Gentlemen Prefer Blondes

TECHNICOLOR

CO-STARRING CHARLES COBURN

The Magnificent Seven (60) and ...e Great Escape (63). In the ...70s his touch was more prosaic, ...t he continued working with such ...ars as Clint Eastwood, John ...ayne and Michael Caine (qqv).

...RESTON STURGES
...S screenwriter, director (...898-1959)

...mous for his frenetic pacing and ...appy satires, his philosophy was ...mmed up in his masterpiece *...llivan's Travels* (41) in which a ...ccessful director tries to make a ...etentious social issue film and ...covers the hard way that the ...blic prefers entertainment to ...itics. Edmund Preston Biden ...s born into a well-off Chicago ...nily and was educated in ...erica and Europe before army ...vice in the first world war. Films ...owed Broadway and he ...pressed Hollywood with a series of sophisticated scripts before offering to direct *The Great McGinty* (40) for Paramount for a mere $10, which won him an Oscar. Six more sublimely witty satires followed, including *The Lady Eve* (41), *The Palm Beach Story* (42), *Hail the Conquering Hero* (44) and *The Miracle of Morgan's Creek* (44). His career went into decline after he signed a contract with Howard Hughes (qv) and he moved to Europe where his *Les Carnets du Major Thompson* (55) was not at all well received.

JULE STYNE
US composer (1905-94)

His family emigrated to America from Britain when he was a child. A piano prodigy, he performed with symphony orchestras at the age of eight. He formed a band in 1922 and found success by co-writing the song Sunday. In the 1930s he was the vocal coach to stars such as Shirley Temple (qv). Soon he was writing songs for Hollywood films including It's Magic for Doris Day's (qv) debut *Romance on the High Seas* (48) and in 1947 he worked with Sammy Cahn (qv) on the stage musical High Button Shoes. Later, with the lyricist Leo Robin, he wrote *Gentlemen Prefer Blondes* (53). His collaborations with lyricists Betty Comden and Adolph Green remain popular. He won an Oscar for the title song of *Three Coins in the Fountain* (54). His compositions were effervescent affairs — such as the scores of *Gypsy* (62) and *Funny Girl* (68).

Barbra Streisand belts out a Styne song in Funny Girl

MARGARET SULLAVAN
US actress (1911-60)

A striking personality, her determination was perceived as arrogance by studio heads and she would often seek escape on Broadway. She will be best remembered as the ingénue of melodramatic tear-jerkers. *Three Comrades* (38) cast her as a young woman in 1920s Germany dying of tuberculosis. She glowed as an unmarried mother in *Only Yesterday* (33), while her charismatic romantic innocence was fetching in *Little Man What Now?* (34), a quality repeated with more charm in *The Shop Around the Corner* (40). Despite her increasing deafness from the late 1940s, Sullavan continued with stage work, making her final film, *No Sad Songs for Me* (50), after a gap of seven years. Two of her four husbands were William Wyler and Henry Fonda (qqv). She committed suicide at the age of 49.

ROBERT L SURTEES
US cinematographer (1906-85)

The winner of Oscars for the cinematography of *King Solomon's Mines* (50), *The Bad and the Beautiful* (52) and *Ben-Hur* (59), he started in Hollywood in 1927 as an assistant cameraman to Gregg Toland (qv). By the 1940s he had revealed a unique skill in the handling of colour. Apart from the award winners, his work is seen at its best in *Thirty Seconds Over Tokyo* (44), *The Kissing Bandit* (48), *Intruder in the Dust* (49), *Quo Vadis* (51), *Mogambo* (53) alongside Freddie Young (qv), *Oklahoma!* (55), *Raintree County* (57), *Mutiny on the Bounty* (62), *The Collector* and *The Hallelujah Trail* (both 65), *Doctor Dolittle* and *The Graduate* (both 67), *Sweet Charity* (69), *Summer of '42* and *The Last Picture Show* (both 71), *Lost Horizon* and *The Sting* (both 73), *The Great Waldo Pepper* (75) and *The Turning Point* (77). His son is the cinematographer Bruce Surtees, who won an Oscar nomination for *Lenny* (74) and was responsible for many of Clint Eastwood's (qv) films including *The Outlaw Josey Wales* (76)

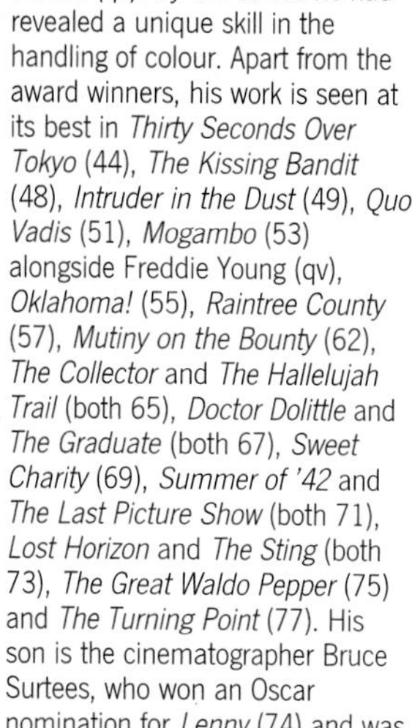

Preston Sturges with Rudy Vallee, left; Robert Surtees with one of his three Oscars

DONALD SUTHERLAND
Canadian actor (1935-)

An unpredictable chameleon with the ability to switch from freakishness to finesse, he was born in New Brunswick, Canada, studied at the University of Toronto and Lamda and made his stage debut in Scotland in 1958. Teased in his teens for his lanky, goofy looks he went on to portray a memorable goof of a more sinister kind in *The Dirty Dozen* (67) and made British cinema's most affectingly erotic love scene with Julie Christie (qv) in *Don't Look Now* (73). His numerous roles have ranged back and forth between these poles, with a speciality in grotesques, such as his fascist in Bertolucci's (qv) *1900* (77). He

was a gentler misfit as the anarchic Hawkeye in *MASH* (70) and the melancholy detective in *Klute* (71) opposite Jane Fonda (qv). He has popped up impressively in minor roles – *JFK* and *Backdraft* (both 91) and *Disclosure* (94) – but has had few meaty parts to rival *Ordinary People* (80). *Six Degrees of Separation* (94) was an exception. His son is the actor Keifer Sutherland.

GLORIA SWANSON
US actress (1897-1983)

She was the definitive 1920s star whose every marital development (she was married six times) was headline news. Born in Chicago, she accompanied the actor Wallace Beery (qv), her first husband, to Hollywood to make Mack Sennett (qv) comedies, then numerous weepies. For Cecil B DeMille (qv) from 1919 she became a star as a sophisticate in films such as *Male and Female* (19) and *The Affairs of Anatol* (21), her fame peaking in 1925. One of her biggest successes was as *Sadie Thompson* (28), but her undoing was producing – with her lover Joseph Kennedy – the ruinous, uncompleted Erich Von Stroheim (qv) epic *Queen Kelly* (29). She retired in 1934 and after an ill-fated comeback in 1941 triumphed as the forgotten silent screen star Norma Desmond in Billy Wilder's (qv) *Sunset Boulevard* (50). She endured as a health food advocate, raconteuse and autobiographer. Her final film was *Airport 75* (74).

MAX VON SYDOW
Swedish actor (1929-)

Born in Lund, Sweden, the son of a university professor, he has crossed the divide between distinguished European productions and Hollywood mainstream films. He was trained at Stockholm's Royal Dramatic Theatre School and made his screen debut in *Only a Mother* (49). A celebrated career on the Swedish stage was followed by a formative encounter with the director Ingmar Bergman (qv), which led to such classics as *The Seventh Seal* and *Wild Strawberries* (both 57). Tall, blond and gaunt he was perfect for Bergman's dark, brooding, psychologically intense films. His output has been prolific with such highlights as *Through a Glass Darkly* (63), *The Greatest Story Ever Told* (65), *The Quiller Memorandum* (66), *The Exorcist* (73), *Three Days of the Condor* (75), *Hannah and Her Sisters* (86), *Pelle the Conqueror* (88) and *Awakenings* (90). In 1988 he directed *Katinka*.

NORMA TALMADGE
US actress (1893-57)

Buster Keaton (qv) was her brother-in-law and Clarence Brown (qv) praised her comic talents. She was one of the silent cinema's biggest stars, her resolute chin and wounded stare setting the tradition for melodramatic screen acting. She was supremely elegant and her magnificent wardrobe was the envy of millions. The eldest of three sisters, she had appeared in 250 films at Vitagraph when she met and married the producer Joseph M Schenck. He resolved to turn her into a star (his wedding gift) and by the early 1920s she was the toast of Hollywood, thriving in such hits as Frank Borzage's (qv) *Secrets* (24) and Brown's *Kiki* (26). With the arrival of sound her nasal accent was exposed – cruelly in *DuBarry – Woman of Passion* (30) – and she retired, later turning to radio. Following a prolonged romance with Gilbert Roland (qv), she divorced Schenck in 1934. She later married the all-round entertainer George Jessel who, had he not turned down *The Jazz Singer* (27), could have been the man who started the talkies.

JESSICA TANDY
US actress (1909-94)

She made her stage debut at the age of 19 and won an Oscar at 80 for her crusty old southerner in *Driving Miss Daisy* (89). Born in London, she made a rapid rise as an actress, playing Ophelia to Gielgud's (qv) Hamlet in 1934. She married Jack Hawkins (qv) in 1932, but moved to New York eight years later when the marriage failed and met Hume Cronyn (qv), her second husband and regular co-star. Even though she was sensational as Blanche opposite Brando (qv) in the Broadway production of A Streetcar Named Desire in 1947, Warner opted for Vivien Leigh (qv) for the film, allegedly because at 5ft 4in Tanc was too small. She won three To awards and an Emmy, but made few films of note until the 1980s, although Hitchcock's (qv) *The B* (63) was an exception. Her last films, Benton's (qv) *Nobody's Fc* and *Camille* (both 94) were wort exits. She became an American citizen in 1954.

ALAIN TANNER
Swiss director (1929-)

One of the few Swiss directors tc achieve international fame, his work progressed from document to personal polemic to melanchc erotica. Born and educated in Geneva, he trained in film in London, co-directed an award-winning short and worked at BB(TV before joining Swiss television

Alain Tanner's reputation declined in the 1990s

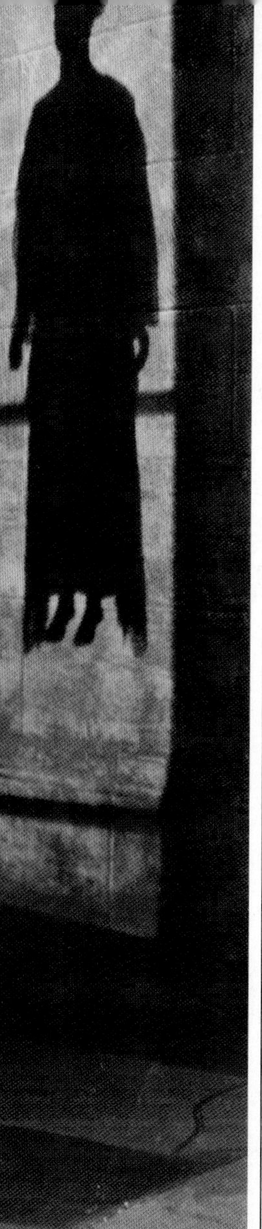

A grim prospect for Swanson in Bluebeard's Eighth Wife

He made his debut feature, *Charles – Dead or Alive* (69), with Groupe Cinq, a co-operative. His best received films were collaborations with writer and art critic John Berger – *The Salamander* (71), *Le Milieu du Monde* (74) and *Jonah Who Will Be 25 in the Year 2000* (76), a comedy of eight characters inspired by the 1968 student revolt in Paris. Two offshoots of Jonah followed, *Light Years Away* (81) and the drama *No Man's Land* (85). His most complex, evocative picture of alienation is *In The White City* (83), in which Bruno Ganz loses himself in Lisbon. Latterly Tanner has become an isolated figure with cool receptions for such work as *Diary of Lady M* (93).

QUENTIN TARANTINO
US writer, director (1963-)

He built up his knowledge of cinema while working in a video shop. His first screenplays were *True Romance* and *Natural Born Killers* but, unable to raise the money to shoot them, he lowered his sights and gathered funding for *Reservoir Dogs* (92). This tense and violent thriller was widely acclaimed and became a cult classic, though its British video release was suspended until mid-1995. Tony Scott managed to find funding for *True Romance* (93) and Oliver Stone (qv) for *Natural Born Killers* (94), although he rewrote the original and courted controversy over the film's violence. Tarantino's eagerly awaited second feature, *Pulp Fiction* (95), won the Palme D'Or at Cannes and a best screenplay Oscar. A sprawling, finely observed collection of crime stories, it has become a classic. His rise has been meteoric and his talent, particularly for dialogue, is undoubted; top stars ask to be considered for parts in his films. He also appears as an actor and was in *Destiny Turns On the Radio* (94). He was also executive producer for his friend Roger Avary's film *Killing Zoe* (94).

Quentin Tarantino in a rare moment of silent thought

ANDREI TARKOVSKY
Russian director (1932-86)

In voluntary exile from the Soviet Union for the last three years of his life, he died of lung cancer at the age of 54 leaving a towering reputation based on seven heavyweight features. A graduate of the Soviet State Film School, he established his reputation with *Ivan's Childhood* (62) about a 12-year-old boy who joins the partisans to fight the Nazis. His impressive epic *Andrei Rublev* (66) was shelved by the authorities for five years. Magnificently exploiting colour and CinemaScope, it explored the life of the great 15th-century icon painter. Thereafter, although undeniably haunting, the films, even the basic sci-fi epic *Solaris* (72) and the eerie *Stalker* (79), are bowed under the weight of rhetoric and philosophical discussion, while *The Mirror* (74), a dream-like evocation of the director's life, is impenetrable. His last films, *Nostalgia* (83) and *The Sacrifice* (86), were made in Italy and Sweden respectively.

JACQUES TATI
French director, writer and comedian (1908-82)

He directed only six features in a 60-year career, but left behind a comic hero as distinctive as Chaplin's (qv) tramp. If problems raising money reduced his output, so too did his obsessive preparations, which added years to projects. The grandson of the tsar's ambassador to France, Tati spurned his father's art restoration business in favour of cabaret and music hall. He appeared in several shorts, in particular *L'Ecole des Facteurs* (47), which he also directed. It was expanded into *Jour de Fête* (49), his first feature as an actor, writer and director, launching him as an important figure in the tradition of the great silent clowns. He made *Monsieur Hulot's Holiday* (53) and *Mon Oncle* (58). He employed many non-actors and though low on dialogue his films' comic lunacy was heightened by absurd soundtracks. *Playtime* (68) and *Traffic* (71) were uneven compared with earlier films.

BERTRAND TAVERNIER
French director (1941-)

He started as a critic for Cahiers du Cinéma and became ▷

Melville's (qv) assistant on *Leon Morin, Prête* (61). He still publishes books about film and he generally writes or co-writes his scripts. After a few shorts his first feature, *The Watchmaker* (73), adapted from Simenon, was an immediate success. An enthusiast for American cinema, his work is unmistakably French: the visual fluency may recall vintage Hollywood, but his favourite themes are good against evil and the unpredictability of people under pressure or in the grip of passion. His films include *Que La Fête Commence* (75), *Le Juge et l'Assassin* (76), *Deathwatch* and *Une Semaine de Vacances* (both 80), *Coup de Torchon* (81), *A Sunday in the Country* (84), *Round Midnight* (86), *Life and Nothing But* (92), *These Foolish Things* (91) and two documentaries, *Mississippi Blues* (83) with Robert Parrish, and *The Undeclared War* (92).

PAOLO AND VITTORIO TAVIANI

Italian directors, writers (1931- and 1929-)

The visual poets of Italian cinema, they established an international reputation when their austerely beautiful social drama *Padre Padrone* (77) won the Palme d'Or and the Critics Prize at Cannes. Educated at the University of Pisa, Paolo read liberal arts and Vittorio law. They graduated to shorts after being cinema club organisers, film critics and playwrights. They made documentaries for eight years before co-directing *A Man for Burning* (62) with Valentino Orsini. Writing and taking turns directing, their narratives, fused with a magical realism, were exemplified by *Padrone*, *La Notte di San Lorenzo* (81) and *Kaos* (84), before making more lyrical allegorical fantasies such as their American film *Good Morning Babylon* (87) and *Night Sun* (90), which reintroduced the theme of spiritual redemption. *Fiorile* (93) was a poignant drama about money, guilt, revenge and love in Tuscany.

Italy's visual poets: Vittorio, left, and Paolo Taviani

ELIZABETH TAYLOR

US actress (1932-)

A legendary and stunningly beautiful film star, she was born in London to wealthy American parents who introduced her to ballet and deportment classes. In 1939 the family returned to live in Beverly Hills. Her beauty soon came to the attention of film scouts and at the age of 10 she made her screen debut in *There's One Born Every Minute* (42). Under a long-term contract with MGM she made *Lassie Come Home* (43), *National Velvet* (44) and *Life With Father* (47). She matured quickly from diminutive star to seductress, with frothy comedies including the popular *Father of the Bride* (50). Her personal life was soon selling newspapers. She married hotel chain heir Nicky Hilton, the first of eight husbands, when only 18, and then the actor Michael Wilding. Her third marriage to entrepreneur Mike Todd (qv) coincided with some of her greatest roles, notably *Giant* (56) and Oscar nominations for *Raintree County* (57) *Cat on a Hot Tin Roof* (58) and *Suddenly Last Summer* (59). Todd was killed in a plane crash and Taylor was soon in a scandalous affair with Eddie Fisher, his best friend, whom she subsequently married. She won her first best actress Oscar for *Butterfield 8* (60) after almost dying of pneumonia – Taylor's dramatic bouts of ill-health are almost as famous as her marriages. The 1960s were characterised by her association with her fifth husband Richard Burton (qv), whom she met on the set of *Cleopatra* (63). She won her second Oscar for *Who's Afraid of Virginia Woolf?* (66). In the 1970s she became a sad, overweight, drug-addicted figure making the occasional forgettable film. After her marriage to the US senator John Warner ended in 1982, she entered the Betty Ford Clinic for the first of several visits to cure her many addictions, where she met Larry Fortensky, her present husband. As her film career fizzles out she has devoted herself to fund-raising for Aids research and launching a line of perfume.

ROBERT TAYLOR

US actor (1911-69)

MGM contracted the Nebraska-born Spangler Arlington Brugh straight from college, changed his name and touted him as "The Man With The Perfect Profile". His acting may have been too stolid, but he had a reputation for no-nonsense professionalism and the studio made him a headliner, putting him opposite Garbo (qv) in *Camille* (37) and against the English class system in *A Yank at Oxford* (38). He was the British officer in love with Vivien Leigh (qv) on *Waterloo Bridge* (40) and as he grew older he tried to toughen up his image. He served as a flight instructor in the American navy and directed 17 training films. Though he starred opposite Hollywood's most glamorous women, such as Jean Harlow, Ava Gardner and Elizabeth Taylor (qqv), his personal life was relatively scandal free. He made *Ivanhoe* (52), *Knights of the Round Table* (53) and *Quentin Durward* (55), but big roles dwindled along with his health and he was in mediocre films until his death.

SHIRLEY TEMPLE

US actress (1928-)

Winner of a special Oscar at the age of six, Temple was the saviour of Fox and Depression-era audiences. She was the top box office star between 1935 and 1938 and her eternal optimism and winning smile eclipsed even the popularity of Clark Gable and Fred Astaire (qqv). She was a phenomenon and no child star since has come near to equalling her success. Starting dancing lessons at three, she was cast in *Baby Burlesks*, a series of shorts that parodied adult stars, most famously Marlene Dietrich (qv). Signed up by Fox at six, she sang

Baby Take A Bow in *Stand Up an Cheer* (34) and stole the show. Loaned out for Paramount's *Littl Miss Marker* (34) she sealed her stardom. Her curls and dimples enchanted audiences in *Bright Eyes* (34), *Curly Top* (35), *Dimpl* (36) and *Rebecca of Sunnybrook Farm* (38). She played teenagers such hits as *Since You Went Awa* (44) and *Bachelor Knight* (47), b the innocent sparkle was waning. She retired in 1949 and re-entere the public arena in the late 1960 as a Republican politician and w Washington's ambassador to Ghana and Czechoslovakia.

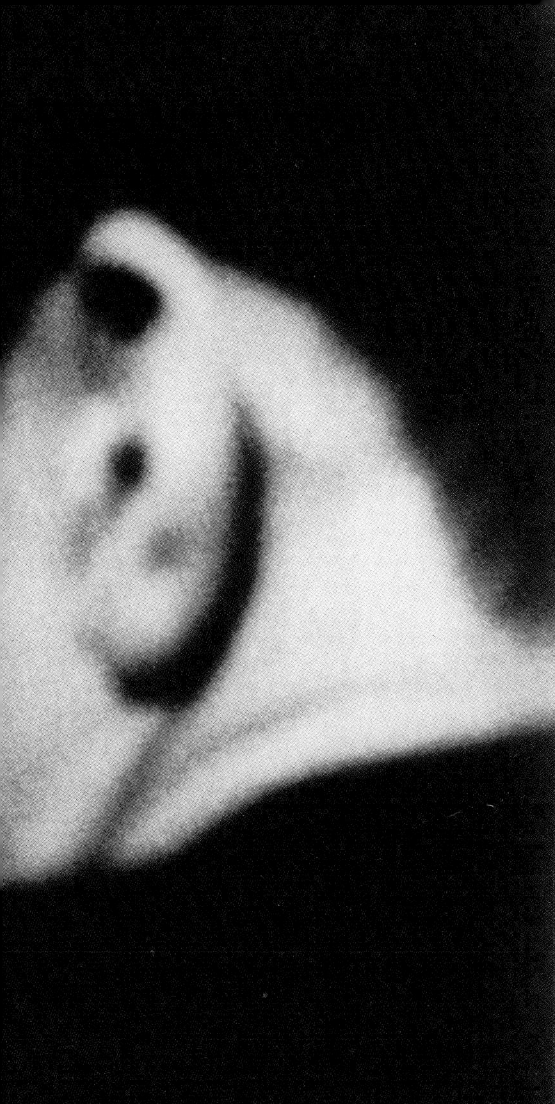

Taylor and Clift in A Place in the Sun; Scissorhands, right, was Caroline Thompson's idea

IRVING THALBERG
US producer (1899-1936)

Though Thalberg died young, it was not the only reason his reputation is still massive and mythic. He was, in short, MGM's golden boy from 1924 to 1933. When he was secretary to Universal boss Carl Laemmle (qv) he was entrusted with Universal City at the age of 20. One of his hits was Lon

Chaney's (qv) *The Hunchback of Notre Dame* (23). In 1923 Louis B Mayer (qv) made him studio vice-president at MGM and their relationship was a stormy "father and son" affair. He butchered Von Stroheim's (qv) *Greed* (25) but pushed through his *Merry Widow* (25). *Grand Hotel* (32) made money as did the Marx Brothers' (qv) films. Norma Shearer (qv), his wife, won an Oscar with *The Divorcee* (30) and he backed films such as *Freaks* (32). Fitzgerald celebrated his ruthless charm in The Last Tycoon. His only screen credit was posthumous and for *The Good Earth* (37).

RRY-THOMAS
tish actor (1911-90)

h his upper-crust accent, ustache, gap-toothed grin and rette holder, he featured in y of the better Boulting (qv) edies such as *Carlton-Browne he FO* (59), where he played a -witted diplomat sent to curry ur in a colonial backwater. mas Terry Hoar-Stevens was n into an upper-class family. He ked in a variety of jobs before nterest in amateur dramatics followed by music hall and o appearances. Making his film ut in Victor Saville's (qv) light sical comedy *It's Love Again* , it was not until *Private's gress* (56) and his womanising in *Blue Murder at St Trinian's* that he established himself as medy character actor. Other s include *I'm All Right Jack* , *School for Scoundrels* and *e Mine Mink* (both 60) and k-buster comedies such as *It's ad Mad Mad Mad World* (63) *Those Magnificent Men in r Flying Machines* (65). nosed with Parkinson's disease 970, he continued to make s. His last was *The Hound of Baskervilles* (77).

MIKIS THEODORAKIS
Greek composer (1925-)

He performed publicly in adolescence, but his studies at the Athens Conservatory were interrupted by the Nazi occupation, during which he was seized as a member of the resistance. He was again arrested and exiled in his early twenties during the Greek civil war. He began composing in Paris, writing for orchestra, dance and theatre and first received international recognition with his score for Powell and Pressburger's (qqv) war drama *Ill Met by Moonlight* (57). Back in Greece in the early 1960s he won a seat in parliament and began a fruitful collaboration with Michael Cacoyannis (qv) on the director's Euripidean trilogy, which started with *Electra* (62). He also provided the score for *Phaedra* (62), but is best known for his zesty music for *Zorba the Greek* (64). He composed for Costa-Gavras's (qv) acclaimed political thriller *Z* (69) and Sidney Lumet's (qv) *Serpico* (73), between which he was imprisoned by the colonels and exiled in France. He returned to Greece and Greek cinema in 1974.

CAROLINE THOMPSON
US writer, director (1956-)

She has emerged as a fine screenwriter with a particular gift for anthropomorphic animal dialogue, as in *Homeward Bound: The Incredible Journey* (93) and *Black Beauty* (94), which she also directed. Born and raised near Washington DC, the daughter of a lawyer and a teacher, she is a Harvard graduate. Her first novel, Firstborn, was published in 1983 and quickly optioned for filming. She later met Tim Burton (qv) and the idea for *Edward Scissorhands* (90) was formulated. The subsequent film was written by her, directed by Burton and starred Johnny Depp as an android boy whose inventor, Vincent Price (qv), dies before he can be given hands. She also scripted Burton's animated feature *The Nightmare Before Christmas* (93). Her screenplay of Frances Hodgson Burnett's classic children's story, *The Secret Garden* (93), directed by Agnieszka Holland (qv), breathed new life into an old work and led to her directing debut.

EMMA THOMPSON
British actress (1959-)

A likeable actress whom Hollywood has taken to its heart, she is part of an Oxbridge alternative comedy coterie which entered mainstream entertainment in the 1980s. Born in London, her parents are the actress Phyllida Law and Eric Thompson, creator of the BBC children's television series Magic Roundabout. She was educated at Cambridge where she joined the Footlights. After graduation she was briefly a stand-up club comic ▷

and came to the attention of television directors and writers. It was while making the well-received television drama series Fortunes of War that she met Kenneth Branagh (qv). She made her screen debut with *The Tall Guy* (89) and played Katherine in Branagh's *Henry V* (89). *Impromptu* (90) and *Dead Again* (91) followed, but it was *Howards End* (92) that brought her to international stardom and won her a best actress Oscar. *Peter's Friends* (92) and *Much Ado About Nothing* (93) were followed by *Remains of the Day* (93), and a second Oscar nomination. *In the Name of the Father* (93) won her a third . Later she made *Junior* (94), *Carrington* and *Sense and Sensibility* (both 95), winning an Oscar for the latter's screenplay.

RICHARD THORPE
US director (1896-1991)

At home with westerns, musicals, comedy and drama, he directed several hundred films. With a no-nonsense attitude that endeared him to the Hollywood studio system, he progressed from acting in vaudeville to directing a number of Charlie Murray comedy shorts. Following the transition from the silent era to sound he moved on to low-budget films. He joined MGM in the 1930s and was soon directing first division films. Retiring in 1967, his career as a director spanned almost 50 years. His enormously varied output includes *Rough Ridin'* (24), *White Pebbles* (27), *The Bachelor Girl* (29), *The Devil Plays* (31), *The Voice of Bugle Ann* (36), *The Adventures of Huckleberry Finn* (39), *Tarzan's New York Adventure* (42), *The Great Caruso* (51), *The Student Prince* (54) and Elvis Presley's (qv) *Jailhouse Rock* (57).

GENE TIERNEY
US actress (1920-91)

Well educated, and from a moneyed family, she was in The Male Animal on Broadway before making her screen debut in *The Return of Frank James* (40) with Henry Fonda (qv) at Twentieth Century Fox, where she did most of her subsequent work. She was hampered by miscasting, such as

the backwoods girl in *Tobacco Road* (41) or blandly decorative parts such as *The Razor's Edge* (46). Sleek and elegant, with a heart-shaped face and striking green-blue eyes, she was one of the great beauties of her era. Though always remembered as the mysterious *Laura* (44) and the tormented wife in *Whirlpool* (49) in black and white, she was at her best in Technicolor, as *Belle Starr* (41), in Lubitsch's (qv) *Heaven Can Wait* (43) and as the paranoid wife in John Stahl's (qv) melodrama *Leave Her to Heaven* (45), for which she won an Oscar nomination. Nervous breakdowns caused a seven-year absence from the screen, but she returned in *Advise and Consent* (62).

DMITRI TIOMKIN
US composer (1899-1979)

Active in Hollywood for 40 years, he was born in Russia and classically trained. Nominated for 22 Oscars, he won four, two for *High Noon* (52) and one each for *The High and the Mighty* (54) and *The Old Man and the Sea* (58). He was a concert pianist and conductor when he emigrated to America in 1925. His ballet music for *Devil-May-Care* (29) quickly led to full-blown scores from *Resurrection* (31) onwards. Any list of his film scores would have to include *Lost Horizon* (37), *The Westerner* (40), *The Moon and Sixpence* (42), *The Bridge of San Luis Rey* (44), *Duel in the Sun* (46), *Portrait of Jennie* and *Red River* (both 48), *Strangers on a Train* (51), *Giant* (56), *Wild Is the Wind* and *Gunfight at the OK Corral* (both 57), *Rio Bravo* (59), and *The Sundowners* (60), *Town Without Pity* and *The Guns of Navarone* (both 61), *55 Days at Peking* (63), *The Fall of the Roman Empire* (64) and *The War Wagon* (67).

EDWARD TISSE
Lithuanian cinematographer (1897-1961)

He was a newsreel cameraman during the Russian revolution and his early features include *Sickle and Hammer* and *Hunger Hunger Hunger* (both 21), but he is best known for his startling collaborations with Sergei Eisenstein (qv) in the 1920s. Eisenstein's disquieting images were perfectly shot by Tissé, who was integral in creating the harsh poetry and intensely manipulative propagandist images associated with the director. They worked together on all of Eisenstein's most important features – *Strike* and *Battleship Potemkin* (both 25), *October* (27), *The General Line* (29), *Alexander Nevsky* (38) and the two parts of *Ivan the Terrible* (43, 46). He also photographed Eisenstein's unfinished *Que Viva Mexico!* (31-32), which was released in 1939 as *Time in the Sun*, after re-editing. Though he later worked for other directors it is his association with Eisenstein that distinguishes him.

ANN TODD
British actress (1909-93)

Trained at the Central School in London, she made her screen debut in *Keepers of Youth* (31) and appeared in several films for Korda (qv), including *Things to Come* (36) and *South Riding* (38). Star status and international recognition came in 1945 with *The Seventh Veil* in which she starred as the young concert pianist in thrall to James Mason (qv), who played her brooding, violent guardian. Hitchcock (qv) invited her to America to play opposite Gregory Peck (qv) in *The Paradine Case* (48). She married David Lean (qv) in 1949, divorcing him in 1957. He directed her in *The Passionate Friends* (49) and as *Madeleine* (49), a well-to-do young woman on trial for murdering her lover. She returned as a test pilot's long-suffering wife in *The Sound Barrier* (52) and had her last interesting role as Leo McKern's wife in *Time Without Pity* (56). She produced, wrote and directed documentaries, notably *Thunder of the Gods* (57) about the island of Delphi.

MIKE TODD
US producer (1907-58)

A flamboyant showman, Avram Goldenbogen was born in Minneapolis. He became a Broadway producer in the 1930s and entered films after the second world war. Embracing widescreen technology, he was one of the backers who launched Fred Waller's unwieldy three-camera Cinerama format in 1952 with a national roadshow presentation, This is Cinerama. He financed Dr Brian O'Brien's single-camera process patented as Todd-AO, which he premiered in Rodgers and Hammerstein's *Oklahoma!* (55). He developed the process for *Around the World in 80 Days* (56), which won five Oscars including best picture. He also set a new rage for the "all-star cast" with 40 cameo appearances in the film, from Dietrich to Sinatra (qqv). A year after his marriage to Elizabeth Taylor (qv), he was killed in a plane crash. The Todd-AO process briefly outlived him and was used for *Cleopatra* (63) and *The Sound of Music* (65) among others.

GREGG TOLAND
US cinematographer (1904-48)

That Orson Welles (qv) shared a screen credit with him on *Citizen*

Kane (41) indicates the director's gratitude to Hollywood's pre-eminent cameraman. His deep focus, narrow aperture cinematography was pioneering and exceptional. After working wit experimenter Arthur Edeson, who photographed *All Quiet on the Western Front* (30), he signed a contract with Sam Goldwyn (qv). For *Mad Love* (35) he photographed Peter Lorre (qv) looking manic and sinister, while his Oscar-winning *Wuthering Heights* (39) for William Wyler (qv *The Grapes of Wrath* and *The Lon Voyage Home* (both 40) for Ford (qv) are visually impressive, as is *The Best Years of Our Lives* (46), although later films for Goldwyn, such as *Enchantment* (48), were less deserving of his talent.

LILY TOMLIN
US actress (1939-)

She brought comic exaggeration and eccentricity to the 1960s hit TV series Rowan and Martin's Laugh-In (particularly as Ernestin the withering telephone operator, and Edith Ann, the naughty five-year-old). It was these characters, her appearances in The Garry Moore Show and early cabaret ar coffee house performances that gave her her own TV show and roles in *Nashville* (75) and *The Late Show* (77). Born in Detroit s dropped out of pre-med school to concentrate on cabaret. She has made few films, but has a reputation for being a tough and uncompromising worker. Her wid range of comedy and dramatic skills have brought her numerous awards. Her films include *Nine tc Five* (80), *All of Me* (84), *Shadow and Fog* (92) and *Short Cuts* (93

RIP TORN
US actor (1931-)

A prolific theatre, screen and television actor, he is as adept at robust comedy as redneck villainy and has forged a formidable career as a stage director. A former oil field labourer and architectural draughtsman, he hitchhiked to Hollywood for a number of TV roles then moved to New York to study acting under Sanford Meisner and Lee Strasberg. Taking over from Ben Gazzara (qv) in Cat On a Hot Tin Roof on Broadway, he quickly established himself, making his

film debut in *Baby Doll* (56). Comfortable with Tennessee Williams material, he re-created his stage role of Tom Finley Jr in *Sweet Bird of Youth* (62) opposite his wife Geraldine Page (qv). In the 1970s he made an impact playing a self-destructive country singer in *Payday* (73) and a morose rancher in *Heartland* (79). More recently he has evolved into a gruff, watchable character actor and has enlivened films such as *Nadine* (87), *Defending Your Life* (91) and *Beautiful Dreamers* (92).

JACQUES TOURNEUR
US director (1904-77)

Born in Paris, the son of the distinguished silent film director Maurice, he became an American citizen in 1919, working as an actor and an assistant to his father. After a few French films he returned to Hollywood in 1934 and was a second unit director on *A Tale of Two Cities* (35). He rarely rose above B-movies, but he has a considerable reputation, principally based on three films made for RKO and the producer Val Lewton (qv): *Cat People* (42), *I Walked with a Zombie* and *The Leopard Man* (both 43). The masterly use of shadow, the slow and inexorable increase in tension and avoidance of obviously shocking material distinguish these from most horror films. Other important films include *Experiment Perilous* (44), *Build My Gallows High* (47) with Robert Mitchum (qv), *Berlin Express* (48), *The Flame and the Arrow* (50), *Way of a Gaucho* (52) and *Night of the Demon* (58). Latterly, he worked as much in TV as for the cinema.

ROBERT TOWNE
US writer (1936-)

He trained with Roger Corman (qv) and his screenplays include *The Last Woman on Earth* (60) and *The Creature From the Haunted Sea* (61). He has often not been credited for his contributions to scripts, but he has gained a reputation for being a great script doctor. In the same year that he wrote *Drive, He Said* (72) for Jack Nicholson (qv), he worked (uncredited) on *The Godfather*. The films that established him were *The Last Detail* (73), *Chinatown* (74) and *Shampoo* (75), which starred Warren Beatty (qv). Each earned

an Oscar nomination for best screenplay. More uncredited work, including *Marathon Man, The Missouri Breaks* (both 76) and *Heaven Can Wait* (78) followed, all more successful than work he has been credited for on films such as *The Bedroom Window* (87) and *Days of Thunder* (90). He directed *Tequila Sunrise* (88) and wrote the Chinatown sequel *The Two Jakes* (90), but although he is one of the toughest modern screenwriters he favours his friends, as with the Beatty vehicle *Love Affair* (94).

SPENCER TRACY
US actor (1900-67)

Often regarded as the greatest American film actor, his career spanned the genres. Tracy was born in Milwaukee, Wisconsin, the son of a strict Roman Catholic truck salesman and attended Ripon College, Wisconsin, before entering New York's American Academy of Dramatic Arts. He made his stage debut in 1922 and continued with a strong career on Broadway until his film debut *Up the*

River (30). From 1935-55 he was a mainstay at MGM. *Riff-Raff* and *It's a Small World* (both 35) confirmed his reputation, but it was two critical and commercial successes, *Captains Courageous* (37) and *Boys Town* (38), that thrust him to stardom and won him consecutive Oscars for best actor. He was nominated 10 times altogether. In 1942 he made *Woman of the Year*, his first film with Katharine Hepburn (qv), and so began a professional and personal relationship that produced *Keeper of the Flame* (42), *Adam's Rib* (49), *Pat and Mike* (52) and others. He went on to make *Bad Day at Black Rock* (55), *The Old Man and the Sea* (58), *Inherit the Wind* (60), *Judgment at Nuremberg* (61) and *Guess Who's Coming to Dinner?* (67). Though married to the actress Louise Treadwell from 1923 (they never divorced), his relationship with Hepburn was longstanding and kept out of the headlines by agreement with the press. Tracy died after a long period of ill health during which he was nursed by Hepburn.

ALEXANDER TRAUNER
French art director (1906-94)

His skills were demonstrated in the amazing theatrical exteriors of urban scenes in some of Marcel Carné's and Billy Wilder's (qqv) most memorable films. Born in Budapest, he studied art before moving to Paris to exhibit. As an assistant to art director Lazare Meerson, he learned to create moody working-class scenarios crammed full of shabby lodging houses in narrow cobblestoned streets. His first feature with Carné was *Drole de Drâme* (37), where he evoked a smog-bound London, before he conjured up the foggy environs of Le Havre in *Quai des Brumes* (38). Other films include *Hôtel du Nord* (38), *Le Jour se*

Gabin, Morgan on a Trauner set for Quai des Brumes

Leve (39), an uncredited *Les Visiteurs du Soir* (42) and *Les Enfants du Paradis* (45). He helped Orson Welles (qv) on *Othello* (52) and made his American debut on Howard Hawks's (qv) *Land of the Pharaohs* (55) before joining Wilder for *Love in the Afternoon* (57), *Witness for the Prosecution* (58) and *The Apartment* (60), which won him an Oscar. His other films included *Goodbye Again* and *One Two Three* (both 61) and *Irma La Douce* (63). His last film was *The Rainbow Thief* (90).

JOHN TRAVOLTA
US actor (1954-)

He was born in Englewood, New Jersey, and is of Irish-American descent. After leaving school at the age of 15 he worked in summer stock then off-Broadway. His mother was a professional singer who gave acting lessons. He hoofed his way swiftly from teen hero to international icon in *Saturday Night Fever* (77), then sat out most of the 1980s before hitting the cult jackpot again with *Pulp Fiction* (94). He was the partner until her death in 1977 of Diana Hyland, who had played his mother in the television film The Boy In The Plastic Bubble. As Vinnie Barbarino, the dim classroom peacock in the television series Welcome Back, Kotter, he found fame and his role as disco-dancing Tony Manero, which was followed by *Grease* (78) and *Urban Cowboy* (80). His film projects then started to flop. By the time he reprised Manero in *Staying Alive* (83) his career had headed into decline. He had, however, invested his earnings wisely and was already a successful businessman. He made a minor comeback in the *Look Who's Talking* films (89, 90, 93), but his Vincent Vega in *Pulp Fiction*, which won him an Academy Award nomination, reasserted his position as a surefire box-office hit.

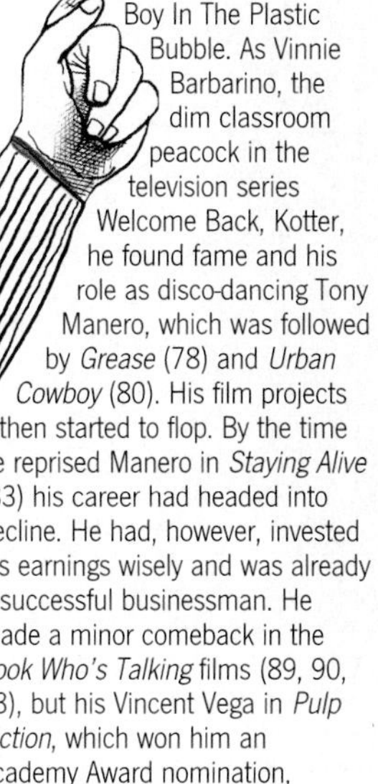

CLAIRE TREVOR
US actress (1909-)

An attractive blonde with a sympathetic personality and a tough streak, Claire Wemlinger was born in New York, studied at Columbia University and the American Academy of Dramatic Arts, worked on Broadway in the theatre and made Vitaphone shorts at Warner's east coast studio. In Hollywood she appeared in numerous Fox films including *The Mad Game* (33) with Spencer Tracy (qv), the first of her news reporter-career girl roles. Her performance as Bogart's (qv) hardboiled ex-girlfriend in *Dead End* (37) won her an Oscar nomination, her first western was *Valley of the Giants* (38) and her best was *Stagecoach*, (39). She was the tomboyish heroine of *Allegheny Uprising* (39) and the banker's daughter in *Dark Command* (40). In the mid-1940s she won a supporting Oscar for her ill-treated alcoholic mistress in *Key Largo* (48). She earned another Oscar nomination as an airline passenger in *The High and the Mighty* (54), won an Emmy for the TV remake of Dodsworth and played several mature roles in the 1960s, including Richard Beymer's mother in *The Stripper* (63).

JEAN-LOUS TRINTIGNANT
French actor (1930-)

In the 1960s and early 1970s he was in many European films of consequence, including *And Woman Was Created* (56), which was a romantic hit that should have taken him to Hollywood, but did not. The son of a famous racing driver, he was a lawyer who entered films via the stage and who became a star by sharing the erotic limelight of Roger Vadim's (qv) *And Woman Was Created* starring Brigitte Bardot (qv) with whom Trintignant had a much-publicised affair. Vadim's *Les Liaisons Dangereuses* (59) followed, but he was more assured in Costa-Gavras's (qv) *The Sleeping Car Murder* (65) and René Clement's (qv) *Is Paris Burning?* (66). *Z* (69) for Costa-Gavras showed him in political action, but his greatest role was as the fascist fantasist in Bertolucci's (qv) *The Conformist* (71). His international appeal dwindled with *A Man and a Woman: 20 Years Later* (86) until *Three Colours: Red* (94), which was nominated for an Oscar.

FRANCOIS TRUFFAUT
French director (1932-84)

He endured a childhood shaken by neglect and was dishonourably discharged for desertion from the army. But he had a passion for cinema and worked as a film critic for Cahiers du Cinéma, gaining acquaintance with Godard, Chabrol, Rivette and Rohmer (qqv). Hitchcock (qv) was his idol and he published a book of interviews with him, even hovering between marrying Hitchcock's daughter and Renoir's niece. He finally married an heiress, using her dowry to finance most of his productions. He provided the story for Godard's *Breathless* (60) and went on to co-produce the work of friends and colleagues. His first feature, *Les Quartre-cent Coups* (59), concerned a child as troubled and delinquent as he had been, but its passion, commitment and spontaneity marked it out as a cornerstone of the French New Wave. His abiding qualities can be found in *Jules et Jim* (61), *La Peau Douce* (64), *L'Enfant Sauvage* (70), *Les Deux Anglaises et le Continent* (71), *Day for Night* (73) and *The Green Room* (78).

DALTON TRUMBO
US screenwriter (1905-76)

He was responsible for a string of hits, achieving notoriety when he

Roman Holiday was scripted by Trumbo under an alias

was blacklisted by the House Un-American Activities Committee and jailed. A former newspaper reporter, he broke into films with a contribution to the treatment of *That Man's Here Again* (37). At his peak he was earning a then mighty $75,000 a script and his successes included *Kitty Foyle* (40) and *Thirty Seconds Over Tokyo* (44). In 1950 he was jailed for contempt, but he continued writing under pseudonyms. He won an Oscar for *Roman Holiday* (53) using the alias Ian McLellan Hunter and again for *The Brave One* (56) as Robert Rich. At the insistence of Kirk Douglas and Otto Preminger (qqv), he received full credit for *Spartacus* and *Exodus* (both 60). He made his directorial debut with a film version of his 1939 anti-war novel *Johnny Got His Gun* (71).

DOUGLAS TRUMBULL
US SFX creator (1942-)

A wizard of contemporary cinema and worshipped by science-fiction fans, he has created memorable images, including those for *2001: A Space Odyssey* (68), *Star Trek* (79) and *Blade Runner* (82). He studied architecture at El Camino College, California, before joining the Los Angeles-based Graphic Films as an educational and technical film-maker in the mid-1960s. His first film was the short *To the Moon and Beyond* (64) followed by *Candy* (68), but when Stanley Kubrick (qv) asked him to work on *2001* his career rocketed. He made *The Andromeda Strain* (71) and then directed the cult classic *Silent Running* (71). In 1974 he founded Future Generation Corporation and began work on his pet project Showscan, with film shot at 60 frames per second on 70mm (as opposed to 24 frames for conventional 35mm) to bombard the audience with 150% more visual information. He unveiled Showscan in a financial deal with the Brock Hotel Company, but ultimate success for the process is still elusive. Steven Spielberg (qv) turned to him for *Close Encounters of the Third Kind* (77) and Trumbull contributed to *Star Trek* while he was working on *Blade Runner*, which many believe to be his finest feature. His *Brainstorm* (83) was doomed; among other dramas its star Natalie Wood (qv) drowned during production.

FLORENCE TURNER
US actress (1885-1946)

In the early days of Hollywood the public did not know the stars' names. Turner joined Vitagraph in 1906, became the studio's leading lady and was known as the "Vitagraph Girl"; Florence Lawrence, her rival at Biograph, was the "Biograph Girl". Carl Laemmle (qv) lured Lawrence to his Independent Motion Picture Company to be the "Imp Girl" and in a notorious publicity stunt put it out that she had been killed by a streetcar, a rumour he later alleged was started by rivals. Meanwhile, Turner appeared opposite Maurice

Costello and other romantic actors, then in 1913 she moved to Britain, forming a production company. Her films included *My Old Dutch* and *Far From the Madding Crowd* (both 15). She went back to America in 1916 and returned to Britain from 1920 to 1924 for more starring roles. Her career dwindled in the 1930s.

KATHLEEN TURNER
US actress (1954-)

Statuesque, strong and sexy, Turner emerged as the 1980s leading lady. A diplomat's daughter and hence widely travelled, she trained at Missouri and Maryland universities and after television drama made it to Broadway. An arresting film debut in Lawrence Kasdan's (qv) steamy *Body Heat* (81) was followed by stardom in *Romancing the Stone* (84), the first of three films with Michael Douglas (qv). She was a prostitute in Ken Russell's (qv) *Crimes of Passion* (84), a hitwoman in Huston's (qv) *Prizzi's Honor* (85) and was nominated for an Oscar for Coppola's (qv) *Peggy Sue Got Married* (86). She was Jessica's voice in *Who Framed Roger Rabbit* (88) and more recently has dabbled in production and plumped for bold roles, such as in *The War of the Roses* (89) and as *Serial Mom* (94). She has also made several successful returns to the Broadway stage, and also played in Britain.

LANA TURNER
US actress (1921-95)

A contributor to several Hollywood myths, she was a well-developed teenager who was allegedly spotted while playing truant in a drugstore on Sunset Boulevard. Featured in *They Won't Forget* (37) and promoted as "the sweater girl", she became a wartime pin-up under contract to MGM. She found fame as a platinum blonde, principally in melodramatic roles and often playing promiscuous characters. She was married eight times (twice to the same man). In 1958 her private life made headlines when Cheryl Crane, her

ughter, stabbed her lover Johnny ampanato to death. She was nvincing as the errant, urderous wife in *The Postman ways Rings Twice* (46) and was minated for an Oscar for *Peyton ace* (57). Other important roles ere in *The Three Musketeers* (48), *Life of Her Own* (50), *The Bad d the Beautiful* (52), *Imitation of e* (59) and *Madame X* (66). casionally seen on television, her st film was *Witches' Brew* (79).

EN TURPIN
S comedian (1874-1940)

efore his film career began in 907 he was a vaudeville omedian. He signed to Essanay, n intensely productive film ompany specialising in comedies nd westerns, and was featured in nany of its short slapstick films ntil around 1910. He was isappointed, though, with his lack f success and decided to return to ne stage. He re-signed with ssanay in 1914 and had more ıck as Chaplin's (qv) stooge. He eft once more in 1916 and a year ater tasted fame under Mack ennett (qv). He put his vaudeville xperience to good use in his poofs of film stars and developed reputation for slapstick. His rademark was his crossed eyes. 3ut as with many silent-era stars e found his popularity diminished vith the advent of the talkies.

JOHN TURTURRO
US actor (1957-)

His brooding alienated roles are best exemplified as the haunted left-wing writer in *Barton Fink* (91), which won him the best actor award at the Cannes Film Festival. Born in Brooklyn, New York, of a working-class family he gained a masters degree in drama at Yale before establishing himself in a variety of off-Broadway

performances, most notably in John Patrick Shanley's Danny and the Deep Blue Sea. Making his film debut in *Raging Bull* (80), he appeared in films as diverse as *Desperately Seeking Susan* and *To Live and Die in LA* (both 85), *The Color of Money* and *Hannah and Her Sisters* (both 86) and *Five Corners* (88), where he impressed as a frightening but sympathetic psycho. Gaining critical acclaim for his bigoted pizza seller in Spike Lee's (qv) *Do the Right Thing* (89), he played the jazz club owner in *Mo' Better Blues*, before *Miller's Crossing* and *Jungle Fever* (all 90). His more recent successes include his directorial debut *Mac* (92), *Fearless* (93), *Being Human* (94) and *Quiz Show* (95).

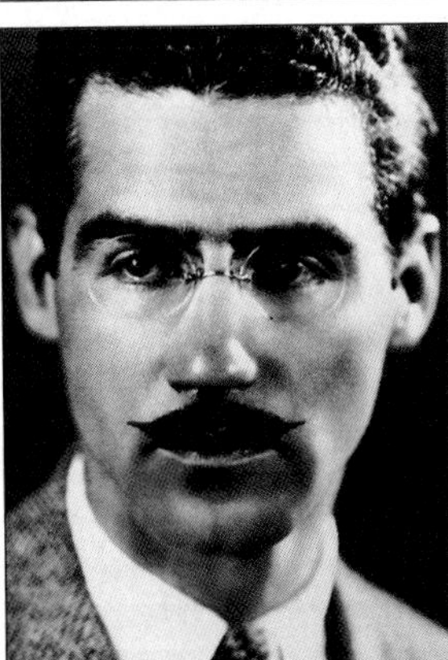

FRANK TUTTLE
US director (1892-1963)

As a key witness at the hearings of the House Un-American Activities Committee (admitting to his own communist background as well as naming names), Tuttle's revelations overshadowed his work as a director. Alan Ladd and Bing Crosby (qqv) were among the stars he employed on screen. He was a director who was at ease with a wide diversity of genres, delivering films of quality. When young he had shown competence in the amateur arena by directing and acting in student productions at Yale, while his assistant editorship of Vanity Fair magazine and screenwriting for Paramount – on films such as *The Cradle Buster* (22) and *Second Fiddle* (23) – helped shape his talent. *The Big Broadcast* (32), starring Crosby and George Burns (qv), *This Is the Night* (32), *Pleasure Cruise* and *Roman Scandals* (both 33) and *Waikiki Wedding* (37) illustrate his nimble touch. By contrast *Lucky Jordan* and *This Gun for Hire* (both 42) and *Hostages* (43) provide examples of his skill with suspense. Naming names ended his career.

CICELY TYSON
US actress (1933-)

Arguably the most award-laden African-American actress of all time, she conveys a marked nobility, wisdom and grace. She graduated from a successful modelling career to enrol at the Actors Studio, first appearing on stage in 1959. Cast by George C Scott (qv) to play the secretary Jane Porter in CBS TV's East Side West Side, she became the first black performer to appear regularly in a non-comedy series. It was her affecting performance in *The Heart Is a Lonely Hunter* (68) that made her mark in cinema. It led to a starring role as the sharecropper's wife in *Sounder* (72), for which she won an Oscar nomination. She then delivered a number of outstanding performances in TV films and mini-series, winning the Emmy for her portrayal of a 110-year-old slave in The Autobiography of Miss Jane Pittman. While her best work has been for the stage and TV, Tyson has distinguished a number of films, most recently *Fried Green Tomatoes* (91). She was co-founder of the Dance Theatre of Harlem and was married to the jazz musician Miles Davis.

LIV ULLMANN
Norwegian actress (1939-)

She was born in Japan but moved to Canada during the second world war. She finished high school in Norway, joined a theatre group and found stage work in Oslo, which led to work in Norwegian films. The turning point in her career came with *Persona* (66), the first film of a fruitful collaboration with the director Ingmar Bergman (qv). She played a mute, but her presence and movements were mesmeric. She went on to work with Bergman on *Hour of the Wolf* (68), *Cries and Whispers* (72) and *Face to Face* (76). The two became romantically linked and had a daughter. Unfortunately her American work, in *Lost Horizon* and *40 Carats* (both 73), were failures. She appeared sporadically in supporting roles in more British and American films, as well as directing *Sofie* (92), but it is her hypnotic performances for Bergman that define her achievement.

EDGAR G ULMER
US director (1900-72)

After working as a set designer and art director in Vienna and Berlin with Alexander Korda, Robert Siodmak, F W Murnau (qqv) and Max Reinhardt, he settled in Hollywood in 1930 and was soon turning out second feature, low budget films, almost exclusively for small companies; many of them were in Yiddish or Ukrainian. It is thought that only a fraction of his output has survived, but a handful have been enough to secure his reputation. The imagination, ingenuity and style of his best films, sometimes made in a matter of days, is unique. They include *The Black Cat* (34), *Bluebeard* (44), *Detour* (45), *The Strange Woman* (46), *The Man from Planet X* (51) and *The Naked Dawn* (55). He also made many films in Italy, Mexico, Germany and Spain.

Style marked out such Ulmer films as Ruthless

GEOFFREY UNSWORTH
British cinematographer (1914-78)

He entered the film industry in 1932 as a camera assistant and became an operator in 1937 on Korda (qv) films such as *The Four Feathers* (39) and Powell and Pressburger's (qqv) *The Life and Death of Colonel Blimp* (43). After working as Jack Cardiff's (qv) operator on *A Matter of Life and Death* (46) he became a director of photography and a master in filming colour, working in British films and in Hollywood. His achievements include *Scott of the Antarctic* (49), *A Night to Remember* (58), Stanley Kubrick's (qv) *2001: A Space Odyssey* (68), *Cabaret* (72), for which he won an Oscar, *Murder on the Orient Express* (74) and *A Bridge Too Far* (77). *Superman* (78), during which he died, was dedicated to him.

CHARLES URBAN
US pioneer (1871-1942)

An audacious entrepreneur, inventor (the Bioscope projector, the Biokam camera), manufacturer, producer and director, he based himself in Britain for many years, forming the Charles Urban Trading Company in 1902. He produced newsreels and documentaries for which he sent cameramen as far afield as Morocco (to film a revolution) and Mongolia, which yielded *The Execution of Li-Tang* (04), depicting the beheading of a bandit chief. Less authentic but apparently convincing was *The Coronation of Edward VII* (02), which he hired Georges Méliès (qv) to make in simulated sets with costumed stand-ins before the event, then inter-cut the real procession, releasing the film on coronation day. In partnership with British pioneer George Albert Smith (qv) he developed and marketed Kinemacolor, the first commercially successful colour process. He then made a number of shorts and a feature, *The Durbar at Delhi* (11), in colour. In America the next year he capitalised further on Kinemacolor, setting up studios on both coasts and producing a number of colour films. He later turned to directing and made several documentaries such as *Science of the Soap Bubbles* (21).

PETER USTINOV
British actor, writer and director (1921-)

An elder statesman of British stage and screen, he made his mark as a versatile raconteur, performer, writer and director long before playing the Belgian super-sleuth Hercule Poirot in three films. He was born in London of Anglo-Russian-French descent and was considered a child prodigy, training at the London Theatre Studio before making his acting debut at 16. His early films include *The Goose Steps Out* and *One of Our Aircraft Is Missing* (both 42).

Contributing to the screenplay of *The Way Ahead* (44) and then directing, writing and producing *School for Secrets* (46), he went on to work in multiple capacities as well as appearing in many comedies, such as *We're No Angels* (55), before triumphing with his first Oscar in *Spartacus* (60). Writing, producing, directing and acting in *Billy Budd* (62), he won another Oscar for *Topkapi* (64). He then featured in *The Comedians* (67), directed and acted in *Hammersmith Is Out* (72) before playing Poirot in *Death on the Nile* (78). He is also an art connoisseur and a witty after-dinner speaker.

ROGER VADIM
French director (1928-)

He represented erotic daring in 1950s and 1960s cinema, a modishness eclipsed by the legend of his Svengali-like relationships with screen goddesses Brigitte Bardot, Catherine Deneuve and Jane Fonda (qqv). A Parisian who always had an eye for beauty and its arrangement on the screen, he developed it during his eight years as assistant to Marc Allégret (qv) for whom he tested a 15-year-old Bardot. They embarked on a passionate affair, married in 1952 and he launched her as a sex kitten in his notorious *And Woman Was Created* (56). The film not only made St Tropez fashionable but created interest in a new generation of French film-makers. His oeuvre may be reduced to titillation, but he was an accomplished starmaker whose fantasy of his then wife Fonda as *Barbarella* (68) made her an icon. His work declined steeply from the satirical spectacle of Rock Hudson (qv) playing an athletics coach who seduces and murders notable students in *Pretty Maids All in a Row* (71) and persuading a weary Bardot into one last cavort as *Ms Don Juan* (73) and, eventually, a lamentable American remake, *And God Created Woman* (87).

Charles Urban in his office at his burgeoning film company

RUDOLPH VALENTINO
Italian actor (1895-1926)

It is difficult today to imagine the impact he had on the world's female population in the 1920s. Thousands of women lined his New York funeral route when he died, rioting to get near his coffin and collapsing grief-stricken in the streets. Rodolfo Alfonzo Raffaele Pierre Philibert Guglielmi was born in Castellaneta, Italy, and attended a military academy and agriculture college before leaving home for Paris in 1912, moving to America a year later. He worked in clubs, musicals and dance halls before becoming a film extra first in New York then Hollywood. He made his feature debut with *My Official Wife* (14) and worked steadily if unspectacularly until *The Four Horsemen Of The Apocalypse* and *The Sheik* (both 21) made him the fevered fantasy of women around the world. His career continued with *Blood and Sand* (22), *Cobra* (25) and *Son of the Sheik* (26). His personal life was as torrid as his screen performances and his marriage to Natasha Rambova, his second, volatile wife, kept gossip columnists in copy. He was not a great actor and had he lived he may well have gone out of fashion, but he died from peritonitis at the height of his popularity.

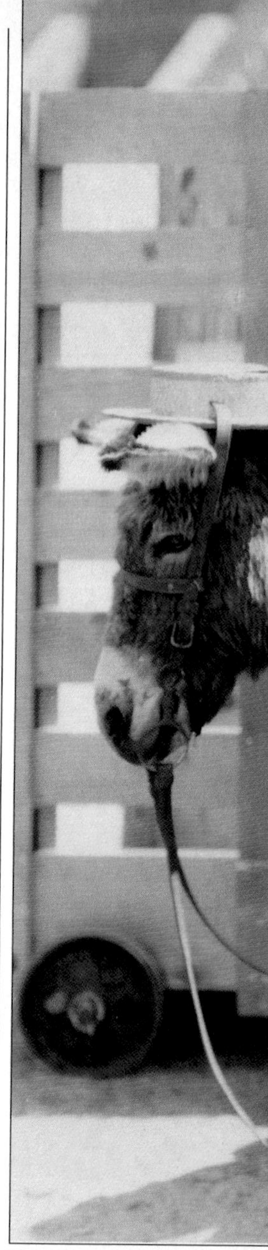

Valentino and Fred Niblo on the set of Blood and Sand

ALIDA VALLI
Italian actress (1921-)

Her beauty demonstrated a mysterious yearning. In the closing scene of *The Third Man* (49) when she walks past Joseph Cotten (qv) and out of shot, the lens, and the audience, strain to follow. She worked in films during the Italian fascist regime and when she turned down propaganda roles found herself unemployed. After the war she made *The Paradine Case* (47) in Hollywood for Hitchcock (qv) followed by *The Miracle of the Bells* (48). In Europe film roles suited her better: the sexually abandoned countess in Visconti's (qv) *Senso* (54) and the lover-abandoned woman in Antonioni's (qv) *Il Grido* (57). She was the procuress in Franju's (qv) shocker *Eyes Without a Face* (59) and in Pasolini's (qv) *Oedipus Rex* (67) an

ornament of mythical desire. In films with Bernardo Bertolucci (qv) – *The Spider's Stratagem* (70), *1900* (76) and *Luna* (79) – her allure was a scene-stealer.

W S VAN DYKE
US director (1889-1943)

He was called "One-Take Woody" for the speed with which he worked, but it in no way diminished

is films. Actors loved him for the ccomplished haste that allowed nem the luxury of spontaneity. The quick-change nature of his vaudeville origins contributed to his haste and versatility. He was D W Griffith's (qv) assistant on *Intolerance* (16) and his debut, *The Land of Long Shadows* (17), soon followed. He could craft adventures, such as *The Battling Fool* (24), or take over *White Shadows in the South Seas* (28), begun by Robert Flaherty. *Tarzan the Ape Man* (32) was the second of the jungle swingers and he was responsible for the dry-Martini repartee between Myrna Loy and William Powell (qqv) in *The Thin Man* (34). His work was as lush as *Marie Antoinette* (38) and as humdrum as *Andy Hardy Gets Spring Fever* (39).

JIMMY VAN HEUSEN
US songwriter (1913-90)

Edward Babcock was born in New York, studied music at Syracuse University and joined Paramount in 1940. He contributed to multi-composer films such as Suddenly It's Spring for *Lady in the Dark* (44) as well as complete scores for *A Connecticut Yankee at King Arthur's Court* (49) and six Crosby and Hope (qqv) *Road* films. They yielded songs of the calibre of Moonlight Becomes You, one of several hits for Bing Crosby. Adept at bouncy speciality numbers, such as It Hasn't Been Chilly In Chile for Betty Hutton in *Cross My Heart* (46) – he later added to Sinatra's (qv) hits with *Young at Heart* (54), *The Tender Trap* (55) and My Kind of Town from *Robin and the 7 Hoods* (64). Nominated 14 times for a best song Oscar, he won for Swinging on a Star from *Going My Way* (44), All the Way from *The Joker is Wild* (57), High Hopes from *A Hole in the Head* (59) and Call Me Irresponsible from *Papa's Delicate Condition* (63).

GUS VAN SANT
US director (1953-)

He spent much of his childhood on the road with his father, a travelling salesman. He graduated in art from the Rhode Island School of Design, directed commercials in Los Angeles and worked briefly with Roger Corman (qv). His first film was *Mala Noche* (85), a low-budget, grainy black and white feature about a tragic gay affair. It was an imaginative, auspicious debut and won a prize for best independent film at the Los Angeles Film Critics awards. His finest film to date is *Drugstore Cowboy* (89), a loose but darkly resonant story of a gang of junkies. It was particularly notable for Van Sant coaxing a revelatory performance from Matt Dillon (qv). He did much the same for River Phoenix in *My Own Private Idaho* (91), which was not a success but remains an important American film of the 1990s. However, his adaptation of Tom Robbins's novel *Even Cowgirls Get the Blues* (94) was a disaster which underwent severe recutting before its release.

AGNES VARDA
French director (1928-)

Born in Brussels to Greek-French parents, she grew up in France and

abandoned her plans to become a museum curator in favour of photography. She received her first break as the Théâtre National Populaire's official photographer. Her professional eye for detail and characteristic compositions have persisted in her work as a director. She first directed *La Pointe courte* (54) which, edited by Alain Resnais (qv) and inspiring his creative future, revealed Varda's keen interest in abstraction. She spent the next seven years making three shorts, all of which won awards. One of them, *L'Opéra Mouffe* (58), filtered the Mouffetard district of Paris through the perception of a pregnant woman. That same heightened reality characterised *Cléo de 5 à 7* (62). In *Le Bonheur* (65) the visual spectacle reflects the dreams of a young carpenter, while in *Vagabond* (85) alluring images of the Midi sit imaginatively alongside the electric performance of Sandrine Bonnaire. *Jacquot de Nantes* (91), an evocative, moving study in obsession, was a tribute following his death to her husband the director Jacques Demy (qv).

Van Heusen wrote music for six 'Road' films

CONRAD VEIDT
British actor (1893-1943)

Veidt was a stalwart of the great pre-Nazi period of German cinema who gave the screen the haunting and memorable image of the gaunt, white-faced murderer in *The Cabinet of Doctor Caligari* (19). Born in Berlin, he studied with Max Reinhardt before and after the first world war. He made his film debut in *The Spy* (17) and in 1919 stirred up controversy for his portrayal of a homosexual in *Anders Als Die* ▷

Anders. Caligari catapulted him to international attention and two years later he directed *Lord Byron.* He spent some time in Hollywood in the 1920s and on his return to Germany was detained by the Nazis because his wife was Jewish. He emigrated to Britain, where he took citizenship and appeared in many notable roles for Korda (qv), including *The Spy in Black* (39) and *Contraband* and *The Thief of Bagdad* (both 40) when he went to Hollywood. He dropped dead on a golf course at the age of 50, not long after making *Casablanca* (42), which stands as a fitting tribute.

PAUL VERHOEVEN
Dutch director (1938-)

Violent thrills are his speciality and his commercial success in Hollywood is exceptional among modern European directors. Born in Amsterdam and a young witness to wartime devastation, he began making films while studying for a PhD in maths and physics, subsequently shooting documentaries in the Dutch navy and forging a career in television. He received an Oscar nomination for his second feature, *Turkish Delight* (73), and apart from *Soldier of Orange* (79) – a drama about the Dutch resistance – all his films have displayed a distinctive obsession with sex and violence, notably *The Fourth Man* (79) and *Spetters* (80). His eye-catching work brought Verhoeven (and his featured actors, Rutger Hauer and Jeroen Krabbe) to America and, after an English-language debut with *Flesh + Blood* (85), he leaped from the art house with *Robocop* (87). Similar wit underpinned his work with Arnold Schwarzenegger (qv) for *Total Recall* (90), but *Basic Instinct* (92) and *Showgirls* (95) were unremitting nastiness.

VERA-ELLEN
US actress, dancer (1926-81)

Vera-Ellen Westmeyr Rohe was born in Cincinnati, Ohio, and

started dancing at the age of 10. Her Hollywood debut was in the Danny Kaye (qv) film *Wonder Man* (45), where her fresh-faced looks, sparkling smile and energetic hoofing attracted critical attention. She was in Kaye's *The Kid From Brooklyn* (46) and *Words and Music* (48), MGM's lavish and wholly inaccurate biopic of Rodgers (qv) and Hart, dancing the Slaughter On 10th Avenue ballet with Gene Kelly (qv) from the team's Broadway show On Your Toes. It was followed by *On the Town* (49), the high point of her career. She also appeared in *The Belle of New York* (52) with Astaire (qv), *Call Me Madam* (53), and *White Christmas* (54) with Bing Crosby (qv). She then bowed out of Hollywood, making a last film, *Let's Be Happy* (57), in Britain.

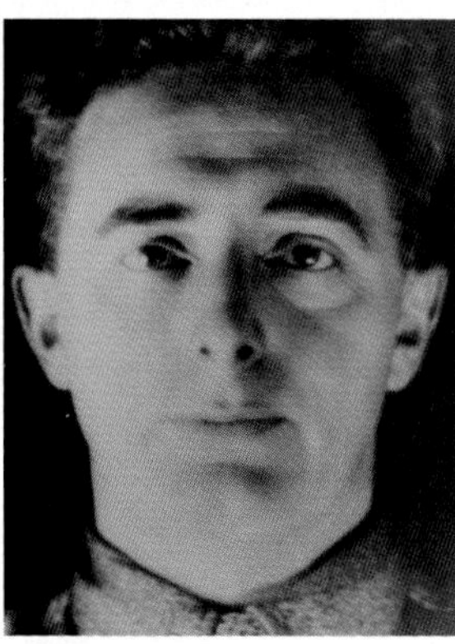

DZIGA VERTOV
Russian director (1896-1954)

Known as the *Man With a Movie Camera* (29), he was considered to be the cerebral artist of Soviet cinema, creating the modern documentary form Kino-Eye; to be later called cinéma vérité by the French. Denis Arkadievitch Kaufman was born in Poland – his nom de guerre literally meaning a spinning top. He studied music before moving to Moscow where he combined medical studies with working for Lev Kuleshov on Cinema Weekly. After producing his first feature, *Anniversary of the Revolution* (19), he directed *The Agit Train* (21) and a collection of newsreels called *Kino-Pravda* (25). After *A Sixth of the World* (26), he added sound to great effect to celebrate the miners in *Donbass Symphony* (31) and then honour his hero in *Three Songs About Lenin* (34). After the victory of Soviet realism during the 1930s he was characterised as a formalist, directing *Lullaby* (37), his last feature film, before working on newsreels and documentaries such as *The Oath of Youth* (47).

KING VIDOR
US director (1894-1982)

A childhood enthusiasm for film led to newsreel film-making in his native Texas and a move to Hollywood in 1915 with Florence, his actress wife. She became a star but he struggled. *The Turn in the Road* (19) was his first feature. At MGM he directed *Peg o' My Heart* (23) and others before *The Big Parade* (25) established him as a master of large scale sentimentality and iconic images. *The Crowd* (28), *Hallelujah* (29) and *The Champ* (31) won Oscar nominations as best director. *Show People* (28), a witty comedy of Hollywood, *Street Scene* (31) and *Our Daily Bread* (34) reinforced his reputation. Later films carried less overt messages but popular classics were *Stella Dallas* (37), *The Citadel* (38) – another Oscar nomination – *Northwest Passage* (40), *Duel in the Sun* (46), *The Fountainhead* (49) and *War and Peace* (56), his fifth Oscar nomination. In 1979 he received a well deserved honorary Oscar for lifetime achievement.

JEAN VIGO
French director (1905-34)

He died of leukaemia before his 30th birthday, but the impact of his sparse output lives on. The son of an anarchist who was found dead in a prison cell, Vigo had an unhappy childhood and was plagued by tuberculosis. On moving to Nice for his health he directed his first film, *A propos de Nice* (29), a daring and innovative satirical documentary. After *Taris Champion de Natation* (31), a playful 11-minute film about a champion swimmer, he directed his first fictional feature, *Zéro de Conduite* (33). Inspired by his own disconsolate days at boarding school, it ridiculed academic authority and was banned in France for 12 years. Yet it was to motivate film-makers from Godard to Truffaut (qqv). His fourth and last film, the anti-bourgeoisie *L'Atalante* (34), was butchered by its distributors to avoid giving offence. Only later was it released in its original version and recognised as a masterpiece.

LUCHINO VISCONTI
Italian director (1906-76)

His films are regarded as artistic classics. Count Don Luchino Visconti di Modrone was born in Milan into an ancient and noble family. He spent his youth building his vast knowledge of the arts and breeding horses. At 30 he joined the director Jean Renoir (qv) in Paris as costume designer on *A Day in the Country* (36). It was there that he became a communist, developing convictions he took to his grave. He returned to Italy and worked as assistant on *La Tosca* (40) before his first feature, *Ossessione* (42), which the fascist censors thought to be sexual rather than political. They cut it heavily for its gritty portrayal of working-class life. His second feature, *La Terra Trema* (48), a highly visual drama set in southern Italy, is now regarded as one of that country's greatest films. His other work includes *The Wanton Contessa* (54), *Rocco and His Brothers* (60), *Boccaccio '70* (62), *The Leopard* (63), *The Stranger* (67), *The Damned* (69), *Death In Venice* (71), *The Innocent* (76) and *Conversation Piece* (77). He was also a respected theatre and opera director who frequently worked with Maria Callas, the diva.

MONICA VITTI
Italian actress (1933-)

She was born Maria Louisa Ceciarelli. A sloe-eyed, husky-voiced and sensual Italian blonde, she eventually rivalled Sophia Loren (qv) for popularity in Italy, making dozens of films unfamiliar to English-speaking audiences. Although she was *Modesty Blaise* (66) and appeared in *An Almost Perfect Affair* (79), her international status comes from her association with Antonioni (qv), who directed her in the theatre after she graduated from Rome's drama academy. They established an intimate relationship on-screen and off and she became acknowledged as the perfect Antonioni heroine in *L'Avventura* (60), *La Notte* (61) and *L'Eclisse* (62). She co-starred with Richard Harris (qv) in *Red Desert* (64), after which she left her mentor until *The Mystery of Oberwald* (80), which was a failure. In 1989 she made her directing debut with *Scandolo Segreto.*

ANDRZEJ WAJDA
Polish director (1926-)

The father of the modern Polish cinema, his greatest films

ıtroversially explore the plight of ividuals caught up in social and itical events outside their ıtrol. The son of a cavalry officer ed by the Nazis, he was a istance fighter when he was 16 ırs old and an art student in ıkow after the liberation. rolling at the Lodz film school, worked as an assistant with ksander Ford before making *A neration* (54), the first in a ıtroversial trilogy completed with *nal* (56) and *Ashes and amonds* (58), which explored the cial and psychological pains of r. Disaffection was the theme of *ocent Sorcerers* (60) and his bsequent films reflected the owing unrest in Polish society, rticularly *Man of Marble* (77) and *an of Iron* (80), which supported lidarity. He moved to France ere he likened himself to the artyr *Danton* (82). Returning to land in 1989 he was appointed istic director of the Warsaw eatre and elected to parliament. s last film was *Miss Nobody* (96).

NTON WALBROOK
ritish actor (1900-67)

orn in Vienna, his ancestors were owns but he chose the legitimate age and worked with Max einhardt before making a name r himself in German cinema. His m career started in the 1920s nd he began to attract starring les in the 1930s. He fled the azis to Britain, where he played ince Albert in *Victoria the Great* 7) and *Sixty Glorious Years* (38). e made three of his best films ith Powell and Pressburger (qqv): *9th Parallel* (41), *The Life and eath of Colonel Blimp* (43) and *he Red Shoes* (48). In 1947 he ecame a British citizen. He was emorable in *The Queen of pades* (49), as the master of eremonies in Ophüls's (qv) *La onde* (50) and as King Ludwig in *he Sins of Lola Montès* (55).

OBERT WALKER
S actor (1918-51)

though he died in his early irties, Walker is remembered for handful of performances. He was so the father of the actors Robert and Michael from his marriage the actress Jennifer Jones (qv). is wholesome good looks were

exploited in *See Here Private Hargrove* (44) and *What Next Corporal Hargrove?* (45), *Since You Went Away* (44) with Jones, and *Under the Clock* (45) with Judy Garland (qv). He played the composer Jerome Kern (qv) in *Till the Clouds Roll By* (46) and the composer Brahms in *Song of Love* (47), but his divorce from Jones exacerbated a lifelong tendency to depression and he drank heavily. His marriage to Barbara Ford, daughter of the director John Ford (qv), lasted only weeks. He gave his finest performance in *Strangers on a Train* (51) for Hitchcock (qv). He was mistakenly prescribed sedatives that, combined with the alcohol in his system, killed him.

HAL B WALLIS
US producer (1898-1986)

Had he produced no other film than *Casablanca* (42) he would still be a film legend. He left Chicago for Los Angeles as a young man and worked as an exhibitor, which gave him an insight into public tastes. Warner hired him as a publicist, but after the arrival of the talkies he became a production executive. During the 1930s he devised the studio's policy for tough social-issue dramas, musicals with their dazzling Busby Berkeley (qv) choreography, romantic adventures starring Errol Flynn (qv), historical biographies with Paul Muni (qv) and women's dramas with Bette Davis (qv). His wartime successes were *Sergeant York* (41), *Yankee Doodle Dandy* and *Now Voyager* (both 42). In 1944 he formed his own company, releasing his films through Paramount. Highlights among the 400 films he was responsible for include *Gunfight at the OK Corral* (57) and *True Grit* (69).

RAOUL WALSH
US director (1887-1980)

He ran away to sea as a boy and worked on cattle drives, breaking horses before his first film in 1909. He worked for Pathé and later as an assistant to D W Griffith (qv), for whom he acted in *The Birth of a Nation* (15). His final acting job was in *Sadie Thompson* (28), which he wrote and directed. He lost an eye co-directing *In Old Arizona* (29) and wore a black

patch. The rest of his career was devoted to directing and he proved to be one of America's greatest and most sympathetic storytellers. He made westerns, including *The Big Trail* (30) with a young John Wayne (qv), gangster films including *White Heat* (49), period adventures such as *Blackbeard the Pirate* (52) and war films such as *The Naked and the Dead* (58). Despite his strong, consistent output he was never officially recognised by the academy. Advancing blindness forced him into retirement in 1964.

CHARLES WALTERS
US director (1911-82)

Although the golden age of the film musical was linked to Vincente Minnelli and Stanley Donen (qqv), Walters's work sparkled and strengthened the established duo at MGM. He was an actor and dancer when MGM sent him to work as a choreographer on musicals such as *DuBarry Was a Lady* (43), Minnelli's *Meet Me in St Louis* (44) and the portmanteau *Ziegfeld Follies* (46). His directorial debut, *Good News* (47), was followed by the excellent *Easter Parade* (48) in which Judy Garland and Fred Astaire (qqv) romped through A Couple Of Swells. *The Barkleys of Broadway* (49) was a witty re-teaming of Astaire and Rogers (qv) after 10 years and *Dangerous When Wet* (53) was one of Esther Williams's (qv) finest moments. The slightly bumpy *Torch Song* (53), in which Walters played Joan Crawford's (qv) clumsy dance partner, and *High Society* (56) with Bing Crosby and Grace Kelly (qqv), gave pleasure. *Please Don't Eat the Daisies* (60) and *Jumbo* (62) starring Doris Day (qv) were other successes.

ANDY WARHOL
US artist, film-maker (1927-87)

He was the defining exponent of pop art. His "factory" in Manhattan issued a stream of film work variously perceived as minimalism, conceptual art or improvisational documentary, such as *Sleep* (63), an eight-hour record of a man asleep. His collection of non-actors, dubbed Warhol Superstars, were an outlandish cluster of associates representing every sexual orientation and living up to his dictum that everyone should have "15 minutes of fame". Gradually his work became more technically competent and controversial, notably *Blue Movie* (69). After a former disciple shot him he turned over direction of the factory's output to his cameraman Paul Morrissey, who directed the tasteless but more conventional *Flesh* (68), *Trash* (70), and *Andy Warhol's Frankenstein* and *Andy Warhol's Dracula* (both 74).

JACK L WARNER
US mogul (1892-1978)

Along with Harry, Albert and Sam, his three older brothers, he established one of the leading Hollywood studios. A tough businessman and a cautious but even-handed boss, he was instrumental in structuring the careers of James Cagney, Bette Davis and Humphrey Bogart (qqv) and produced a series of forceful gangster films and popular musicals. After running a 90-seat nickelodeon in Pennsylvania, the brothers moved to Hollywood and set up their own company in 1923, with Jack heading production. Gambling on the introduction of sound with *The Jazz Singer* (27), over the next three decades the studio produced such memorable pictures as *Casablanca* (42) and *Rebel Without a Cause* (55). After the death of Sam and Harry, and with Albert's retirement in 1956, he forged on alone producing such productions as *My Fair Lady* (64) and *Camelot* (67). Following various takeovers and mergers, Warner remains one Hollywood's top studios with such hits as *Batman* (89) and *The Fugitive* (93).

HARRY WARREN
US composer (1893-1981)

Salvatore Guaragna was born in Brooklyn and made one of his ▷

Warren's Highland fling for Fred and Ginger

few errors in judgment by changing his name from mellifluous Italian to sober-sided American. His songs powered the Warner musicals of the 1930s and the Twentieth Century Fox showcases of the early 1940s. His lyricist partner was Al Dubin and they worked on such films as *42nd Street* and *Footlight Parade 1933* (both 33) and the three *Gold Diggers* musicals (33, 35, 36). Their songs ranged from the socio-romantic Lullaby of Broadway and Honeymoon Hotel to wish-fulfillers such as We're in the Money and I Only Have Eyes For You. With other partners he wrote two great train songs: Chattanooga Choo-Choo for *Sun Valley Serenade* (41) and The Atchison, Topeka and the Santa Fe for *The Harvey Girls* (46). He loved Verdi operas but never attempted anything more substantial himself. His range may have been narrow, but he lived up to the Italian reputation for tuneful melody.

DENZEL WASHINGTON
US actor (1954-)

A handsome and imposing leading man, he has already earned a best supporting actor Oscar for *Glory* (89) and nominations as best supporting actor in *Cry Freedom* (87) and best actor in *Malcolm X* (92). In his debut, *Carbon Copy* (81), he played the implausible son of George Segal. He was then in the television series St Elsewhere. Not all his subsequent films have been worthy. *For Queen and Country* (88) saw him miscast as a black Londoner and a veteran of the Falklands war; in *Heart Condition* (90) he was the ghost of a heart donor, haunting the racist policeman recipient of the organ. In Spike Lee's (qv) *Mo' Better Blues* (90), *Ricochet* (91) and *Mississippi Masala* (92) he was better than the material. Lee's *Malcolm X* owes its power to his playing, but only *Much Ado About Nothing* and *The Pelican Brief* (both 93) have so far offered him roles that do not hinge on the colour of his skin. He played Tom Hanks's (qv) initially reluctant lawyer in *Philadelphia* (93).

JOHN WATERS
US director (1946-)

He may have exchanged vulgarity for wit, but he has lost none of his

satirical edge. After a strict Catholic upbringing laced with secret visits to triple-X cinemas in his home town of Baltimore, he made such exploitation shorts as *Hag in a Black Leather Jacket* and *Eat Your Makeup*. He founded an acting troupe with the likes of Mink Stole and his grotesquely overweight schoolfriend Harris Glenn Milstead, better known as Divine. Both actors were at home with the obscene fun Waters brought to *Mondo Trasho* (70) and *Multiple Maniacs* (71), each a blunt, inventive if technically crude celebration of bad taste. *Pink Flamingos* (72), the most successful of his early films, continued the trend and Divine had no trouble at all fleshing out the role of most disgusting person alive. *Polyester* (81) was rather middle of the road, while *Hairspray* (88) made successful jabs at racism through the magnificent trivia of a television dance show. *Cry-Baby* (90) was less fluid than *Hairspray* and he fully entered the mainstream with *Serial Mom* (94) starring Kathleen Turner (qv).

FRANZ WAXMAN
German composer (1906-67)

One of the most ubiquitous and creative composers for three decades from the 1930s, his formidable range embraced the wild buffoonery of the Marx Brothers's (qv) *A Day at the Races*

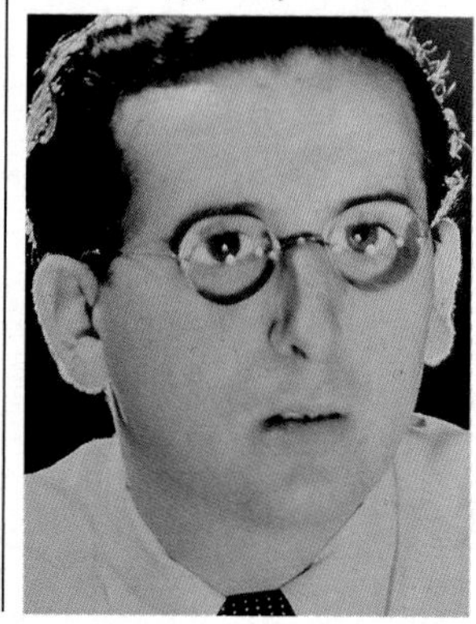

(37), the romantic comedy *The Philadelphia Story* (40) and the menacing thriller *Sorry Wrong Number* (48). After working as a bank clerk he played the piano in cafe dance bands to support his tuition at the Berlin Conservatory and the Dresden Music Academy. Breaking into films in 1930 arranging music for *The Blue Angel* (30) then scoring many German features, he left when the Nazis were attacking Jews. In Hollywood he headed Universal's music department and a year later signed with MGM as the studio's resident conductor. In 1942 he switched to Warner as music director and stayed there until 1946 when he founded the Los Angeles Music Festival. He is best remembered for his haunting scores to Hitchcock's (qv) *Rebecca* (40), *Suspicion* (41) and *Rear Window* (54). Composing countless film scores up until his death, he won Oscars for his work on *Sunset Boulevard* (50) and *A Place in the Sun* (51).

JOHN WAYNE
US actor (1907-79)

Born in Iowa, Marion Michael Morrison became an American icon. A college footballer, he graduated to bit parts in countless horse pictures as "Duke Morrison" before playing the lead in Raoul Walsh's (qv) *The Big Trail* (30). Years of B-movies followed until John Ford (qv) cast him as the Ringo Kid in *Stagecoach* (39). He dominated the western in its heyday, his rock-like 6ft 4in presence almost overshadowing his abilities. Ford and Hawks (qv) shrewdly drew on the darker side of his heroics, giving him characters such as Tom Dunson in *Red River* (48) and Ethan Edwards in *The Searchers* (56). Typically a man in uniform, whether a saddle weary cavalry man or mud-smeared marine, his real-life hawkish patriotism took him behind the camera for *The Green Berets* (68), a gung-ho film that alienated the anti-Vietnam generation, whose distrust had already been aroused by strong anti-communist beliefs voiced during the McCarthy era. To most filmgoers he is the western. He never hung up his cowboy hat, winning an Oscar for *True Grit* (69) and playing a retired gunslinger in *The Shootist* (76). In 1979 he lost his battle with cancer: he had a lung removed in 1963 and his stomach shortly before his death.

SIGOURNEY WEAVER
US actress (1949-)

Tall and striking, she began her career in avant-garde theatre, but broke the Hollywood gender barrier by carrying big action films. The daughter of an NBC television chief and a British actress, she attended Stanford and Yale and struggled through the 1970s constantly told she was too tall (5ft 11in) to be a leading lady. Plucked from off-Broadway for *Alien* (79) she became the indomitable Ripley, foe of the relentless, acid-drooling monster in three films. She went on to play strong, independent women across genres, with Mel Gibson (qv) in *The Year of Living Dangerously* (83), playing straight woman to the *Ghostbusters* (84), a super-bitch in *Working Girl* (88) and the murdered wildlife champion Dian Fossey in *Gorillas in the Mist* (88). More recently she was the harrowing lead in the adaptation of Ariel Dorfman's play *Death and The Maiden* (95).

CLIFTON WEBB
US actor (1891-1966)

A steady, largely undistinguished screen actor who was neverthele[s] nominated three times for an Oscar, he is known chiefly for one role in *Laura* (44), which he continually reprised. Webb Parmallee Hollenbeck was born in Indianapolis, Indiana, joined Palmer Cox's Lyceum Children's Theatre at the age of eight and made his stage debut in The Brownies at nine. His subsequent stage career eclipsed his screen performances, which started with *Polly With a Past* (20). *Laura* brought him fame and he went on to create Mr Belvedere in *Sitting Pretty* (48). He worked into his seventies and made *Satan Never Sleeps*, his last film, in 1962.

LOIS WEBER
US director (1881-1939)

Alternately writing, producing and acting, as well as directing, she was the highest paid director of the silent era after arriving at Universal in 1916. She consistentl[y] courted controversy, transmitting her moral messages through topic[s] considered sensationalist, attractin[g] opprobrium but finding box office favour. Corruption was treated in *Hypocrites* (15) and caused riots i[n] New York; the ballerina Pavlova starred (her only dramatic appearance) in the less inflammatory *The Dumb Girl of Portici* (16); *Where Are My Children?* (16) advocated birth control, condemned abortion and grossed $3m and *The People Vs John Doe* (16) attacked capital punishment. Her most successful film, *The Blot* (21), extolled pride over charity. Paramount seduced her in 1920 with $50,000 a film and 50% profits, but soon after she was divorced and suffered a

Lois Weber was the highest paid director in the silent era

vous breakdown. She recovered make *Sensation Seekers* (27) d her last silent, for DeMille (qv), e *Angel of Broadway* (27). her three talkies, *White Heat* 4) about inbreeding was hdrawn, ending the 400-film reer of a remarkable woman.

TER WEIR
stralian director (1944-)

e of the most successful stralian directors in Hollywood, best films have a deep sense of mospheric mystery, imagination d social concern, most vividly strated in *Picnic at Hanging ck* (75), *Gallipoli* (81) and *Dead ets Society* (89). Born in Sydney, e son of a real estate broker, he udied criminal law at Sydney iversity before leaving to work for s family and tripping around rope. After a stint on local evision he worked with the mmonwealth Film Institute in stralia, winning an award for *lmesdale* (71), before making s feature film debut with the ack comedy *The Cars That Ate aris* (74). Following it up with *cnic at Hanging Rock*, a sychological horror about a group schoolgirls who disappear during visit to an aboriginal site, he

onsolidated his success with *The ast Wave* (77) and his magnificent nti-war opus *Gallipoli*. Seduced to merica after *The Year of Living angerously* (83), he made *itness* (85) and *The Mosquito oast* (86) before winning critical cclaim with *Dead Poets Society* nd *Green Card* (90).

JOHNNY WEISSMULLER
US actor (1904-84)

After winning five gold swimming medals in the 1924 and 1928 Olympics, he was featured in a series of documentary shorts and had a cameo playing himself in *Glorifying the American Girl* (29). He landed his best known part, the role of Tarzan, when MGM was scouting for a lead. Between his first, *Tarzan the Ape Man* (32), and his last, *Tarzan and the Mermaids* (48), he played the role 12 times. The subsequent *Jungle Jim* series for Columbia was less successful, although its popularity can be attributed to his celebrity. He did some TV work as Jungle Jim but did not appear in any more films, apart from a cameo in *The Phynx* (70). Married five times, he worked as a Caesar's Palace compere in Las Vegas in the 1970s.

Welles as the mysterious Third Man in Vienna

ORSON WELLES
US actor, writer, director and producer (1915-85)

He is credited with influencing more directors than any other figure, largely with his first full-length film, *Citizen Kane* (41). Born in Wisconsin, he was orphaned at 12. He travelled the world, appeared on Broadway and, on radio, terrified America with his adaptation of The War of the Worlds in 1938. The next year he took up film-making. The technical brilliance of *Kane* – its Chinese box structure, expressionist visuals, innovative use of editing and sound, all dramatically packaged by Gregg Toland's (qv) deep-focus cinematography – makes the film a masterpiece. Its depiction of a golden boy's descent from fame and wealth into isolation provided a prophetic key to the rest of Welles's career. Touches of genius marked all his work, yet he was never a box office favourite and always struggled for financing. Between projects he did charismatic turns for others, most famously as a raging Mr Rochester and a chilling Harry Lime. As his physical bulk swelled, the roles grew slimmer – by *Catch-22* (70) he was grotesquely obese. Finally, TV commercials and voice-overs were all that were left, yet his reputation continues to grow as unfinished films are released and his curious career is reassembled.

WILLIAM A WELLMAN
US director (1896-1975)

"Wild Bill" was quite literally a high-flyer. In the early days when cinema was an adventure, it seemed natural that he should have been recruited as a director. He had flown for France in the first world war and his brilliant aviation epic *Wings* (27) about wartime pilots was the first film to win an Oscar. His autobiography admitted to a brawling personality and his films are male-orientated. *The Public Enemy* (31) was one of the first Warner gangster films and it set the house style. He made routine films but in some reached the heights. *Nothing Sacred* (37) was a satirical look at exploitative journalism and the first *A Star Is Born* (37) won him a screenplay Oscar. *Roxie Hart* (42) was a glorious exposé of what a showgirl would do for celebrity and *The Ox-bow Incident* (43) was an indictment of lynch mob rule.

High-flyer William Wellman's Wings won the first Oscar

WIM WENDERS
German director (1945-)

Born in Dusseldorf, he was a critic before making his first feature, *Summer in the City* (70). His work is questioning, forceful and ambivalent, with haunting, moody images. His protagonists are alienated from the world they inhabit and brood silently while searching for identity. In *The Anxiety of the Goalie at the Penalty Kick* (71) a goalkeeper leaves a soccer match and embarks on such a quest, while in *Alice in the Cities* (74) an ill-at-ease photographer follows suit, aided by a young girl who lends the film an unexpected charm. His ambivalence towards America (he frets about its colonisation of Germany, but loves its rock'n'roll), plays a key role in such films as *Kings of the Road* (76), *The American Friend* (77), a spiky homage to film noir, and the unfocused meandering of *Hammett* (83). *Paris, Texas* (84), his most successful film to date, and *Wings of Desire* (87), his return to Berlin, are redolent with meaning.

LINA WERTMULLER
Italian director (1928-)

She was a troublesome child expelled from many Catholic schools before becoming a teacher. Lured by the theatre, she began writing for a touring puppet show before launching herself as a ▷

playwright, actress and director. She worked in TV and radio and then assisted Fellini (qv) when he was making *8½* (63), directing her debut *The Lizards* in the same year. With her fifth film, *The Seduction of Mimi* (72), she won a best director prize at Cannes and continued to attract acclaim throughout that decade, particularly for *Seven Beauties* (76), a concentration camp drama which won her an Oscar nomination. She continues as an independent, her last being the splendid *Saturday Sunday and Monday* (90).

MAE WEST
US actress (1892-1980)

An archetypal sex goddess with languid delivery, voluptuous figure and verbal wit, West began as a vaudeville performer. She became a scandalously successful playwright – Sex, Drag, Diamond Lil and The Pleasure Man – and actress, making her film debut in *Night After Night* (32) at the age of 40. The censorship problems, which included a short jail term for obscenity, were mirrored in attitudes to her bawdy badinage, progressively toned down in successive films. Several of her remarks have entered the language: "It's not the men in my life that counts, it's the life in my men", "Beulah, peel me a grape" and, in response to the line "Goodness! What wonderful diamonds", "Goodness had nothing to do with it". She scripted or co-wrote her films including *She Done Him Wrong* and *I'm No Angel* (both 33), *Belle of the Nineties* (34) and *Goin' to Town* (35), by which time she was the highest paid woman in America, having rescued a floundering Paramount. After *The Heat's On* (43) she returned to the stage, subsequently making *Myra Breckinridge* (70) and *Sextette* (78), based on one of her plays.

THE WESTMORES
US make-up artists (founder George Westmore 1879-1931)

George Westmore was a British immigrant to Hollywood, a wigmaker who entered films in 1917 and pioneered make-up techniques. His six sons further developed the craft and set standards of expertise at every leading studio. One, Monte, was make-up supervisor on *Gone With the Wind* (39) at Warner. Perc made Rita Hayworth (qv) a redhead, transformed Bette Davis (qv) into Queen Elizabeth and beautified *Casablanca* (42). Ern worked on the famous faces of Twentieth Century Fox, Wally on those at Paramount for more than 40 years, from Fredric March's (qv) Oscar-winning duality as *Dr Jekyll and Mr Hyde* (32) to Elvis Presley (qv). Bud spent more than 20 years at Universal, creating famous monsters such as *The Creature From the Black Lagoon* (54). Frank worked on *The Ten Commandments* (56). George Westmores' descendants are still make-up artists in film and television, including Monte's son Michael who was the make-up supervisor on *Raging Bull* (80) and *Blade Runner* (82).

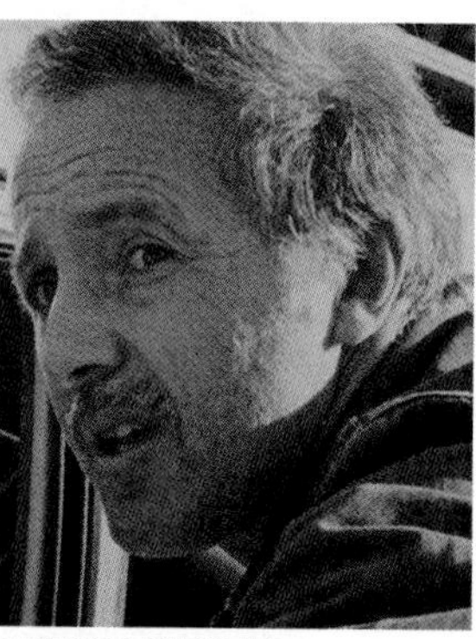

HASKELL WEXLER
US cinematographer, director (1926-)

Wexler insisted on projects that accorded with his radical sympathies. An admirer of cinéma vérité, which he exploited to great effect in countless documentaries, he commended himself to Hollywood for his ability to infuse his realism with high production values. Born in Chicago, he spent 10 years making documentaries before his Hollywood debut with *The Savage Eye* (59). He shot *The Loved One* (65) and won an Oscar for his cinematography on *Who's Afraid of Virginia Woolf?* (66). His other films include *In the Heat of the Night* (67), *Medium Cool* (69), *Interviews With My Lai Veterans* (70), for which he won a best documentary Oscar, Coppola's (qv) *The Conversation* and *American Graffiti* (both 73), *Bound for Glory* (76), which gained him a second cinematography Oscar, *One Flew Over the Cuckoo's Nest* (75), *Coming Home* and *Days of Heaven* (both 78) and *Latino* (85). He worked with John Sayles (qv) on *Matewan* (87) and Hopper's (qv) *Colors* (88).

Maria Carda, left, gets a Westmore makeover; Whale, centre, on Journey's End

JAMES WHALE
British director (1896-1957)

Despite a multi-faceted career as a newspaper cartoonist, army officer, actor, set designer, stage director and director of the film musical *Show Boat* (36), he is best known for bringing art and human complexity to the horror film. Moving to Hollywood to direct the screen version of his stage success *Journey's End* (30), he was snapped up by Universal to make *Frankenstein* (31) as a companion piece to *Dracula* (31). Selecting an unknown Boris Karloff over Bela Lugosi (qqv), he proceeded to redefine the material. Creating a visually poetic and chilling ambience, while serving Karloff's creature with a surprising dignity, Whale transformed Frankenstein into a horror classic. He did even better with his subsequent ventures into the genre bringing grace, invention and humour to *The Old Dark House* (32), *The Invisible Man* (33) and his greatest achievement *Bride of Frankenstein* (35). He quit the cinema in 1941 to pursue an artistic career. In 1957 he was found dead in his swimming pool.

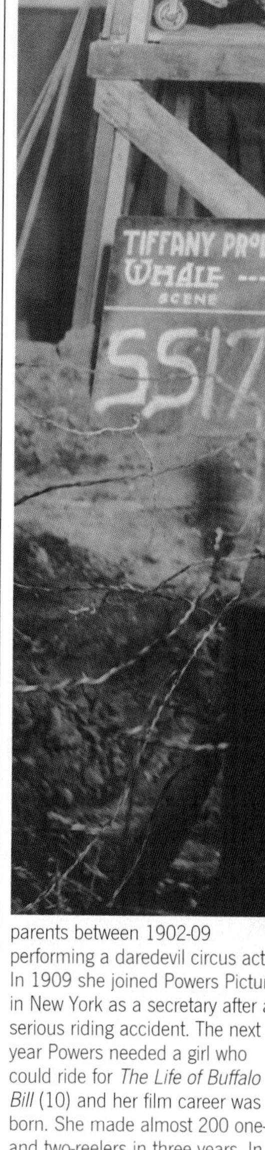

PEARL WHITE
US actress (1887-1938)

She was a phenomenally popular silent era star of frantic serials in which all she had to do was dash about reacting pop-eyed to the camera. The public loved her. She was "born in a trunk" to vaudeville parents in Green Ridge, Missouri, and made her stage debut at the age of six in Uncle Tom's Cabin. She toured America with her parents between 1902-09 performing a daredevil circus act. In 1909 she joined Powers Pictur in New York as a secretary after a serious riding accident. The next year Powers needed a girl who could ride for *The Life of Buffalo Bill* (10) and her film career was born. She made almost 200 one- and two-reelers in three years. In 1914 she made *The Perils of Pauline* serial for Pathé and international stardom came with *The Exploits of Elaine* serial in 1915. In 1920 she signed with Fox, but two years later had a bac fall during her acrobatic act at the Casino de Paris and retired to France. She died at her French estate after years of ill-health.

RICHARD WIDMARK
US actor (1914-)

A familiar figure in Hollywood film for three decades, he studied law but was diverted by drama and taught it for some years before becoming an actor. He made a la but striking entry into films and wa nominated for an Oscar for his debut as the psychopath who pushes crippled Mildred Dunnock down the stairs in *Kiss of Death* (47). His ability to convey all shades of viciousness, nastiness c pig-headed boorishness led to

many anti-heroic roles, such as in *Road House* (48) and *No Way Out* (50). More sympathetically, he was hounded in *Night and the City* (50), hunted the plague carriers in *Panic in the Streets* (50), was a complex petty criminal in *Pickup on South Street* (53) and enhanced many westerns including *Cheyenne Autumn* (64). A cop in *Madigan* (68), he prosecuted Nazis in *Judgment at Nuremberg* (61) and ventured into production – his wife, Jean Hazlewood, wrote the scripts – with the military courtroom drama *Time Limit* (57). He produced *The Bedford Incident* (65), but since *Coma* (78) his appearances have been infrequent.

HERBERT WILCOX

Irish director, producer (1892-1977)

He founded Elstree Studios in 1926, discovered and married Anna Neagle (qv) and made her a star. He was born in Cork, Ireland, and served in the Royal Flying Corps during the first world war. His talent for anticipating trends led him into the film industry in 1919. His directorial debut was *Chu Chin Chow* (23) followed by *Nell Gwyn* (26), which he remade in 1934 with Neagle, a success followed by *Peg of Old Drury* (35). Their triumph was *Victoria the Great* (37) and its sequel *Sixty Glorious Years*

(38). They went to Hollywood in 1939 with RKO, but their style was regarded as pompous and they returned to Britain. He enjoyed renewed success with *They Flew Alone* (42) *Piccadilly Incident* (46), *Spring in Park Lane* (48), *Odette* (50), *The Lady With the Lamp* (51) and *King's Rhapsody* (55), but he was bankrupted in 1964 and his career was ended.

BILLY WILDER

US director (1906-)

Born in Austria, he was a journalist in Berlin and claimed to have been a gigolo. With such future Hollywood luminaries as Robert Siodmak, Fred Zinnemann and Edgar Ulmer (qqv) he produced *People On Sunday* (29). In Hollywood his screenplay for Garbo's (qv) *Ninotchka* (39) was notable and he made his directorial debut with *The Major and the Minor* (42). His Oscar-winning *The Lost Weekend* (45) is the definitive study of alcoholism and *Sunset Boulevard* (50) is the best drama on Hollywood. He then made his soured classic, *Ace in the Hole* (51). His cold eye thawed with *Some Like It Hot* (59) and there was another Oscar for *The Apartment* (60), while *The Private Life of Sherlock Holmes* (70) was a bizarre epic. He still harbours hopes of making another film.

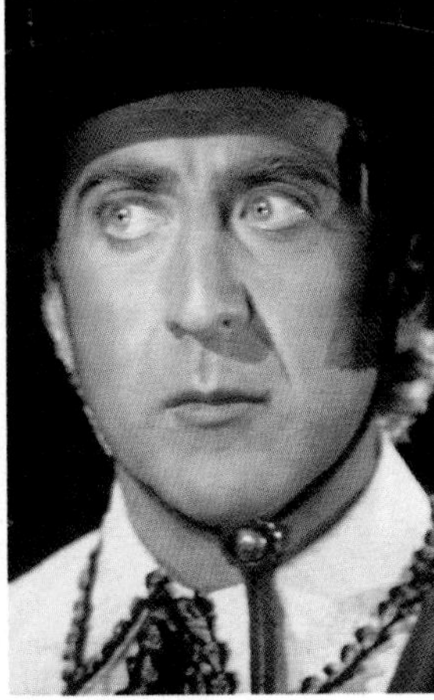

GENE WILDER

US actor (1935-)

Jerry Silberman was born in Milwaukee and attended the University of Iowa before training at the Bristol Old Vic and teaching fencing. He made his debut as an abductee of *Bonnie and Clyde* (67), but came to prominence with an Oscar nomination for the timid accountant in Mel Brooks's (qv) *The Producers* (68). Further performances for Brooks included the alcoholic gunfighter in *Blazing Saddles* (73) and the mad scientist's heir, *Young Frankenstein* (74). He made his debut as writer-director with *The Adventures of Sherlock Holmes' Smarter Brother* (75). He teamed with Richard Pryor (qv) four times, beginning with *Silver Streak* (76). When his wife, the comedienne Gilda Radner, died in 1989 after a long battle with cancer, he concentrated his energies on supporting the causes of cancer research.

EMLYN WILLIAMS

British actor, writer (1905-87)

His academic promise provided an escape route from a poverty stricken Welsh mining community. On leaving Oxford he graduated from small roles to respected stage actor in Britain and America and made his film debut in 1932 in *The Frightened Lady*. Within a few years he was also writing plays and screenplays and directing. In 1941 he won a New York Drama Critics

Award for his autobiographical play The Corn is Green, all the while continuing to act in and write films. His performances include *They Drive by Night* (40), *Ivanhoe* (52) and *I Accuse!* (58) as the writer Emile Zola. By the time he retired he had gained considerable acclaim in Britain and America, particularly for his incisive writing.

ESTHER WILLIAMS

US actress (1923-)

She put her stamp on the musical with song and dance numbers fashioned round her dazzling underwater routines. A champion swimmer at the age of 15 and a department store model, she joined Billy Rose's Aquacade where her exuberant swimming set pieces were praised by an MGM scout. Her career began with *Andy Hardy's Double Life* (42) and *A Guy Named Joe* (43) before *Bathing Beauty* (44) made her a star. The audience was mesmerised by her aquatic finale, in which fountains and flames shared the screen with a pool full of girls. "Hollywood's Mermaid" and the "Queen of the Surf", as she was billed, won fans with her gleaming good looks. *Thrill of a Romance* (45), *This Time for Keeps* (47), *Neptune's Daughter* (49), her best film, and *Million Dollar Mermaid* (52) all managed to mix swimming with romance. When she tried to dry off in the late 1950s her career ground to a halt. She played a schoolteacher, dry, in *The Unguarded Moment* (56).

JOHN WILLIAMS
US composer (1932-)

Few musical compositions have remained in the memory like the terrifying rhythm of Spielberg's (qv) *Jaws* (75). Born in Flushing, New York, and educated at UCLA, he graduated from Juilliard and became a jazz pianist before composing themes for television. He made his feature film debut on *I Passed for White* (60), following it with *The Killers* (64), *Valley of the Dolls* (67) and *The Reivers* (69). His musical arrangements for *Fiddler on the Roof* (71) won him his first Oscar. After more films, including Spielberg's *The Sugarland Express* (74), he won an Oscar for *Jaws* and *Star Wars* (77), but missed for *Close Encounters of the Third Kind* (77). He went on to win more statuettes for *Superman* (78), *The Empire Strikes Back* (80) and *ET – The Extra-Terrestrial* (82). His other credits include *The Big Chill* (83), *Indiana Jones and the Temple of Doom* (84), *The Witches of Eastwick* (87), *Accidental Tourist* (88), *JFK* (91), *Jurassic Park* (93) and *Schindler's List* (94).

RICHARD WILLIAMS
Canadian animator (1933-)

He has won more than 240 industry awards and an Oscar for his cartoon short *A Christmas Carol* (72), but it is his Oscar-winning work on *Who Framed Roger Rabbit* (88) that has brought him world renown. Following his studies at the Ontario College of Art, he joined Disney in 1948 but felt stifled by the company's regime. After moving to Britain in 1955 he made commercials while working on *The Little Island* (58), which won him a Bafta for best cartoon short. Setting up his own studio he created memorable credit sequences for such films as *What's New, Pussycat?* (65), *Casino Royale* (67), *The Charge of the Light Brigade* (68) and *The Return of the Pink Panther* (75). Sadly, he was unable to find distribution for his epic 30-year pet project, *The Thief and the Cobbler*.

ROBIN WILLIAMS
US actor (1952-)

An improvisational comedian of the highest rank, he moved into films after television success as the alien Mork from Ork in Happy Days and Mork and Mindy. His manically intense performances have only occasionally seemed attuned to his film roles, such as the radio disc jockey in *Good Morning, Vietnam* (87) and the inspirational teacher in *Dead Poets Society* (89); both films brought Oscar nominations. His skills came to the fore in *The World According to Garp* (82) and *Cadillac Man* (90), *The Fisher King* (91) – another best actor Oscar nomination – and the unabashed star vehicle *Mrs Doubtfire* (93). There have, though, been failures from *Popeye* (80), and *The Best of Times* (86) to *Toys* (92). He voiced the animated films *Aladdin* and *FernGully . . . The Last Rainforest* (both 92).

BRUCE WILLIS
US actor (1955-)

He provided a new kind of action hero for the jaded late 1980s, a cocky jester who filled the gap left by the flagging Bond machine. Born in Germany, he grew up in New Jersey, taking up acting at college and going on to stage roles in New York. His break came in 1984 in the quirky cult television series Moonlighting, where he and Cybill Shepherd revamped the screwball double act. He has been most successful in *Die Hard* (88) and *Die Hard 2* (90), while *Die Hard With a Vengeance* (95) proved to be one of the year's hits. When his bankability seemed to be matching the biggest names in Hollywood, his films began to flop, first with *The Bonfire of the Vanities* (90) then *Hudson Hawk* and *The Last Boy Scout* (both 91). As with John Travolta (qv), exposure in Tarantino's (qv) *Pulp Fiction* (94) – he reportedly begged for the part – has helped re-establish his credentials if not his bankability. He gave a thoughtful performance as the philandering builder in *Nobody's Fool* (94), but his decision to remove his name from the title credits may indicate that he is happier cruising in two-dimensional action roles. Married to Demi Moore (qv), he is a co-founder of the Planet Hollywood chain of restaurants.

DEBRA WINGER
US actress (1955-)

She spent two years in Israel, including three months in the Israeli defence force, before returning to America where she began acting after a serious accident while working in an amusement park. After a handful of undistinguished films she rode on a crest of critical and public acclaim for *Urban Cowboy* (80) opposite Travolta (qv), *An Officer and a Gentleman* (82), as Richard Gere's (qv) feisty love interest, and *Terms of Endearment* (83), as Shirley MacLaine's (qv) dying daughter. She won Oscar nominations for the last two. Her relatively sparse career has been dogged by bad choices such as *Legal Eagles* (86) and honourable failures such as *Cannery Row* (82), *Black Widow* (86) and Bertolucci's (qv) epic *The Sheltering Sky* (90). She has a reputation for being abrasive, but with her career seemingly in decline she came back triumphantly opposite Anthony Hopkins (qv) in *Shadowlands* (93).

MICHAEL WINNER
British director (1935-)

He has directed 30 feature films, producing and often writing them himself, but is best known for his urban vigilante film *Death Wish* (74) starring Charles Bronson. He was born in London and read law at Downing College, Cambridge, but began writing as a film critic and columnist at 16. He made shorts in the late 1950s, mainly for the BBC ("My first was This Is Belgium, filmed mostly in East Grinstead because it was raining in Belgium"), and made his feature debut with *Play It Cool* (62). He came to wider prominence with the Swinging Sixties film *I'll Never Forget What's 'is Name* (67), followed by *Hannibal Brooks* (69). After the western *Chato's Land* (72) and *Scorpio* (73) with Burt Lancaster (qv) he made *Death Wish*, which touched a raw public nerve. Sequels were made in 1981 and 1985. His other films include *The Big Sleep* (78), *The Wicked Lady* (83), *Appointment With Death* and *A Chorus of Disapproval* (both 88). His most recent film was the controversial *Dirty Weekend* (93).

ROBERT WISE
US director, producer (1914-)

As an apprentice editor he worked on *The Story of Vernon and Irene Castle* and *The Hunchback of Notre Dame* (both 39), *My Favorite Wife* (40) and *All That Money Can Buy* (41), but most notably with Orson Welles (qv) on *Citizen Kane* (41) and in Welles's absence on *The Magnificent Ambersons* (42). At short notice he was brought in as director to complete *The Curse of the Cat People* (44) for producer

ıe Marx Brothers with Sam ood on Night at the Opera

l Lewton (qv), for whom he ıade *Mademoiselle Fifi* (44) and ıe *Body Snatcher* (45). His work s sometimes been outstanding, in *The Set-Up* (49), *The Day the ırth Stood Still* (51), *Executive ıite* (54), *Somebody Up There kes Me* (56), *I Want to Live* (58) ıd *Odds Against Tomorrow* (59), s first production credit. He won ıst director Oscars for *West Side ɔry* (61) with Jerome Robbins d *The Sound of Music* (65). Only *ar Trek – The Motion Picture* 9) of his later films was a hit.

OHN WOO
hinese director (1946-)

principal of Hong Kong's operatic nema of violence, he became ıshionable internationally when his ıfluence on young western ırectors such as Quentin Tarantino ɥv) was acknowledged. Born in ıuangzho, but in Hong Kong from ıe age of four, he worked for ıeveral years as an assistant on the ıartial arts film assembly line. He ıade his directorial debut in 1973 ıith *The Young Dragons*. umerous films followed before he ıund his métier in the gangster ycle he began with *A Better omorrow* (86), which included *The ïller* (89) and *lard-Boiled* (92) and made Chow ıun Fat, his favourite actor, a ıperstar. The films are exciting, rtuoso set pieces of slaughter and ıayhem, counterpointed by ıligious motifs (Woo is devoutly Christian). His American debut *lard Target* (93) used visual style, nd has been followed by the xcellent *Face/Off* (97).

ATALIE WOOD
JS actress (1938-81)

latasha Gurdin was born in San rancisco to a Russian architect nd ballet dancer mother. She was ;iven dance lessons and made her rst screen appearance at the age f five. As a child star she charmed ı *Miracle on 34th Street* (47), vhile as a teenager she was a uitably sympathetic girlfriend for ames Dean (qv) in *Rebel Without Cause* (55), her first Oscar

nomination. For the relatively chaste 1950s and early 1960s she was ideal casting material as the acceptable face of nascent sexuality, her soulful dark eyes suggesting a smouldering temperament beneath a virginal exterior. The roles for which she won further Oscar nominations – *Splendor in the Grass* (61) and *Love With the Proper Stranger* (63) – drew on this quality, as did her performance as Maria, the ultimate star-crossed lover in *West Side Story* (61). Her six-year marriage to Robert Wagner ended in 1963 and she married producer Richard Gregson. She remarried Wagner in 1972 and took on less work, but was shooting *Brainstorm* (83) when she drowned in a boating accident.

SAM WOOD
US director (1883-1949)

A former real estate broker, actor and assistant to Cecil B DeMille (qv) before his directing debut at Paramount, he made four films, including *Excuse My Dust* (20) with Wallace Reid and nine with Gloria Swanson (qv), who considered him talentless. At MGM in the 1930s he directed *A Night at the Opera* (35) and *A Day at the Races* (37) for the Marx Brothers (qv), though Groucho considered him "a jerk". He went on to win five best picture and two best director Oscar nominations for films that included *Madame X* (37), *Goodbye Mr Chips* (39), *Kitty Foyle* (40), *The Devil and Miss Jones* (41), *Kings Row* and *The Pride of the Yankees* (both 42) and *For Whom the Bell Tolls* (43). Although notorious for his infamous support of the anti-communist witch-hunts in 1947, he made *Command Decision* (48) and *Ambush* (50) before his death.

JAMES WOODS
US actor (1947-)

He distinguished himself in a series of villainous roles before being nominated for an Oscar playing the single-minded journalist Richard Boyle in Oliver Stone's (qv) *Salvador* (86). Born in Utah and educated in political science at MIT, he was on stage in Boston before moving to New York where he established himself on Broadway. Typecast as a villain, he made his feature debut in Kazan's (qv) *The Visitors* (72) and played an anti-fascist in Pollack's (qv) *The Way We Were* (73). After Reisz's (qv) *The Gambler* (74) he made eight more films, including playing a stuntman in Penn's (qv) *Night Moves* (75), before his breakthrough as a police murderer in *The Onion Field* (79), playing a mercenary prison guard in *Fast-Walking* (82) and reprising the Kirk Douglas (qv) role in *Against All Odds* (84). He has created memorable characters in Cronenberg's (qv) *Videodrome* (83) and in *Once Upon a Time in America* (84), *The Hard Way* (91) and *The Getaway* (94) and has won two Emmys for television films.

JOANNE WOODWARD
US actress (1930-)

After acting at high school and university, she joined New York's Neighborhood Playhouse and the Actors Studio, combining Broadway appearances with TV roles. Her first film was *Count Three and Pray* (55) and in 1957 she won an Oscar for *The Three Faces of Eve*. In 1958 she married Paul Newman (qv) and has worked with him regularly. Her best performances have been in Lumet's (qv) *The Fugitive Kind* (59) and Schaffner's (qv) *The Stripper* (63). Her Oscar nominations include Newman's *Rachel Rachel* (68) and her role in *The Effect of Gamma Rays on Man-in-the-Moon Marigolds* (72), for which she won a best actress prize at Cannes. Since then her career has been less prolific. She appeared with Newman again in *Mr & Mrs Bridge* (90), had a small role in Jonathan Demme's (qv) *Philadelphia* (93) and provided the voice-over for Martin Scorsese's (qv) *The Age of Innocence* (93).

FAY WRAY
US actress (1907-)

Born in Alberta, Canada, she played the pretty half of the beauty and the beast partnership in *King Kong* (33). Her career began with Hal Roach (qv) comedies and Universal westerns before she became a star in Erich Von Stroheim's (qv) *The Wedding March* (28). *The Street of Sin* (28), *Thunderbolt* (29) and *Dirigible* (31) followed. Despite appearing with leading men such as William

Powell, Fredric March, Ronald Colman (qqv) and, in *The Legion of the Condemned* (28), Gary Cooper (qv), she existed most forcefully when she faced terror, as in *The Mystery of the Wax Museum* (33). She enjoyed a revival with *Queen Bee* and *Hell on Frisco Bay* (both 55) and *Summer Love* (58).

WILLIAM WYLER
US director (1902-81)

Even Laurence Olivier (qv) was exasperated by the number of times Wyler demanded he run through a scene: "He would crouch like a little bear at the side of the camera saying 'Just one more time, please'. No wonder he was known as Once-More Wyler." It paid off. He won Oscars for *Mrs Miniver* (42), *The Best Years of Our Lives* (46) and *Ben-Hur* (59). Born in Alsace, he became a Hollywood publicist and then made two-reeler westerns. *Dodsworth* (36) and *Dead End* (37) for Sam Goldwyn (qv), to whom he was contracted, established him and *Wuthering Heights* (39) was a respectful treatment of Brontë. His respectability was wide ranging, from *Detective Story* (51) to *Carrie* (52) and *Roman Holiday* (53). He worked well with women, getting the best from Bette Davis (qv) in *Jezebel* (38), *The Letter* (40) and *The Little Foxes* (41), and Barbra Streisand (qv) with *Funny Girl* (68).

JANE WYMAN
US actress (1914-)

She migrated from dumb blonde roles to Oscar winner as the deaf mute heroine of *Johnny Belinda* (48). A former hairdresser, model, blues singer and dancer, she moved up from film extra to her first line in *My Man Godfrey* (36), which was cut. She was trapped in bit parts until she showed dramatic mettle as Ray Milland's (qv) distraught fiancee in *The Lost Weekend* (45), which won an Oscar. Overnight she went from perky best friend to anguished drama queen, netting her first Oscar nomination as the long-suffering mother in *The Yearling*

(46). While in the throes of divorce from Ronald Reagan (qv), her second husband, she learned sign language and wore ear plugs to bring authenticity to her role in *Johnny Belinda*. Over the next few years she shone in a number of glossy films, notably *The Blue Veil* (51), *Magnificent Obsession* (54), which was her biggest commercial success, and *All That Heaven Allows* (55). But her allure quickly faded and she turned to TV, most recently starring as Angela Channing in the soap Falcon Crest.

FREDDIE YOUNG
British cinematographer (1902-)

He is one of the finest lighting cameramen in the world, admired by everyone. His career began during the first world war and he was still shooting TV commercials in his eighties. He learned his craft from the best practitioners in silent days – many pre-war British films carry the credit "F A Young" – and successfully switched when talkies arrived. He worked with Herbert Wilcox (qv) in the 1930s and with Powell and Pressburger (qqv), travelling across Canada in wartime to shoot *49th Parallel* (41). His post-war achievements include *Ivanhoe* (52), *Bhowani Junction* (56) and *Island in the Sun* (57), but his most celebrated partnership was with David Lean (qv) and he won the Oscar three times, for his breathtaking work on *Lawrence Of Arabia* (62), *Doctor Zhivago* (65) and *Ryan's Daughter* (70).

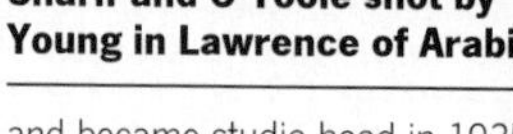

Sharif and O'Toole shot by Young in Lawrence of Arabi

LORETTA YOUNG
US actress (1913-)

She made almost 100 films and successfully moved to television at 40. She was more a fashion plate than a great actress, but won an Oscar for her role as a Swedish maid who stands for Congress in *The Farmer's Daughter* (47). Pushed into film extra work by her mother at the age of four – along with her three sisters – she won her first decent role in *Naughty But Nice* (27) as a schoolgirl, although the director wanted her sister Polly Ann, who was not available. At 16 she played a high-wire performer adored by Lon Chaney (qv) in *Laugh Clown Laugh* (28). She was extremely popular, but never made it to the top 10 box office stars of her time. Her knack was to stay in the public eye through her passion for fashion. Her range as an actress, however, was limited. Her better films included *Platinum Blonde* (31), *The Stranger* (46) and *Come to the Stable* (49).

ROBERT YOUNG
US actor (1907-)

Rarely given top billing, he played wholesome characters in 100 films over three decades before establishing himself on television in Father Knows Best. Born in Chicago and raised in California, he did odd jobs before acting in Carmel and Pasadena, then taking bit parts in films. Signed up by MGM to appear in the Charlie Chan vehicle *The Black Camel* (31), he played his first leading role in *New Morals for Old* (32). He was

in the shadow of Gary Cooper (qv) in *Today We Live* (33), Katharine Hepburn (qv) in *Spitfire* (34) and Barbara Stanwyck (qv) in *Red Salute* (35). He made a breakthrough with *Three Comrades* (38) and was excellent in *H M Pulman Esq* (41). Other films include *Journey for Margaret* (42), *The Canterville Ghost* (45), *The Enchanted Cottage* (45) and *Secret of the Incas* (54).

VICTOR YOUNG
US composer (1900-56)

Born in Chicago, he studied at the Warsaw Conservatory and toured Europe as a violinist with the Warsaw Philharmonic. In the 1920s he became a concert master, worked with the bandleader Ted Fio Rito and conducted for top artists such as Al Jolson (qv) in the 1930s. With his regular orchestra, he made a series of popular recordings. His hits included Who's Afraid of the Big Bad Wolf and Mona Lisa. When already established in film, his orchestra backed Judy Garland (qv) on Over the Rainbow from *The Wizard of Oz* (39) and Bing Crosby (qv) on Too-Ra-Loo-Ra-Loo-Ra from *Going My Way* (44). He had begun contributing scores in 1937 and among more than 300 were those for *Rio Grande* (50) and *Shane* (53). His Oscar for *Around the World in 80 Days* (56) was presented posthumously.

DARRYL F ZANUCK
US mogul (1902-79)

Fiercely energetic, his teeth clamped on a vast cigar, he used power to attract talent and women. David Niven (qv) recalled him as a master polo player, but his game plan was more ruthless. He started as an eight-year-old Indian boy in a silent film, lied about his age to serve in the first world war and later decided to be a writer, producing Rin Tin Tin (qv) scripts for Warner. He founded Twentieth Century Productions in 1933, merged with Fox two years later and became studio head in 193[illegible] His most interesting films include *The Grapes of Wrath* (40), *Gentleman's Agreement* (47), *All About Eve* (50), and *The Longest Day* (62). CinemaScope forced Zanuck out of Fox in 1952, thoug[illegible] he returned 10 years later to become its boss. He hired, and fired, his son Richard from the presidency during a bitter battle f[illegible] control. But the days of the seat-[illegible] pants mogul were over – his ord[illegible] "Don't say yes until I finish talkir[illegible] seemed out of date – and he wa[illegible] forced from power in 1971.

ROBERT ZEMECKIS
US director, screenwriter (1952-)

Riding high with a best director award for the multiple Oscar-winning *Forrest Gump* (94), which took more than $500m at the box office in less than a year, he has hardly put a foot wrong commercially since *Romancing th[illegible] Stone* (84). He scripted and directed *Back to the Future* (85) and went on to direct and provide the basic storylines for *Back to th[illegible] Future II* and *III* (90), meanwhile demonstrating that he was at eas[illegible] mixing live action and animation i[illegible] *Who Framed Roger Rabbit* (88). The fancy camera tricks in *Death Becomes Her* (92) and *Gump* would seem to confirm that he is [illegible] home with films relying heavily on special effects. His credits also include the endearing *I Wanna Hold Your Hand* (78) and the overlooked *Used Cars* (80).

Film score by Victor Youn[illegible] blarney by John Wayn[illegible]

Gong Li in Zhang Yimou's Raise the Red Lantern

MAI ZETTERLING
Swedish actress, director (1925-94)

A beautiful and literate actress, she was a blonde sex symbol until she decided to switch to directing in the early 1960s. She was born in Vasteras, Sweden, and trained at Stockholm's Royal Dramatic Theatre School before beginning a successful stage career. She made her screen debut at the age of 16 in *Frenzy* (44) from a script by Ingmar Bergman (qv), which brought her international stardom. She went on to make *Sunshine Follows Rain* (46), *Frieda* (47), *The Girl in the Painting* (48), *Desperate Moment* (53), *The Truth About Women* (58), *Only Two Can Play* (62) and *The Witches* (90). In 1963 she directed a short which won first prize at the Venice Film Festival. *Loving Couples* (64) was her first feature and *Night Games* (66) followed. Zetterling continued to direct films with feminism as a central theme, which include *The Girls* (68), *We Have Many Faces* (75) and *Scrubbers* (82).

ZHANG YIMOU
Chinese director (1950-)

He was Chen Kaige's (qv), cinematographer on two films, but is now foremost among China's fifth generation film makers – those admitted to the reopened Beijing Film Academy, which had been closed during the cultural revolution. A farm labourer in his youth, he became a skilled photographer: the land and a sense of composition figure strongly in his films. His directorial debut and the first of seven films starring his former partner Gong Li (qv) was *Red Sorghum* (87), an unconventional love story. His tragedy *Ju Dou* (90) was the first Chinese film nominated for the foreign film Oscar. That and *Raise the Red Lantern* (91) and *To Live* (94), were banned in China, then released after winning international awards, although officials applauded *The Story of Qiu Ju* (92), an inconsistency that mystified him. After *To Live,* Zhang was permitted to work only under a complicated agreement with the Guangxi state studio.

FRED ZINNEMANN
US director (1907-97)

Prosaic rather than inspired, efficient rather than inventive, he was technically accomplished, excellent with actors and responsible for the surging power of *High Noon* (52), *From Here to Eternity* (53) and *A Man For all Seasons* (66), winning Oscars for the latter films. *The Search* (48) was a moving moral tale with a welter of realistic detail. Born in Vienna, he began his film career as an assistant cameraman in Paris and Berlin, where he worked on Siodmak's (qv) *People on Sunday* (29). He was given an MGM contract and *The Wave* (35), which he co-directed. He won the first of four Oscars for *That Mothers Might Live* (38), but it was *The Seventh Cross* (44) that established him. He also directed *Act of Violence* (49), *The Men* (50), *Oklahoma!* (55), *The Nun's Story* (59) and *The Day of the Jackal* (73), retiring after *Five Days One Summer* (83).

ADOLPH ZUKOR
US mogul (1873-1976)

Leaving his humble Hungarian background for New York at the age of 15, he worked his way from floor sweeper in the fur business to prosperous Chicago furrier. Small and quietly spoken, but in pursuit of power and money, he had the instincts and acumen to achieve both. Entering the penny arcade business in 1903, he soon acquired, in partnership with Marcus Loew (qv), nickelodeon and theatre chains and started Hale's Tours – travel films shown in simulated moving railway carriages. In 1912 he bought and released the French four-reel *Queen Elizabeth* starring Sarah Bernhardt, formed Famous Players in Famous Plays with Edwin S Porter (qv) directing such films as *The Count of Monte Cristo* (13), and hired Mary Pickford (qv). In 1916 he masterminded a merger with Jesse L Lasky's Feature Play Company to become Famous Players-Lasky, whose officers included DeMille and Goldwyn (qqv), and Paramount was born. Famed for the sophistication of its films, the studio employed directors such as Lubitsch, von Sternberg and Billy Wilder (qqv) and stars ranging from Gary Cooper and Swanson to the Marx Brothers, Mae West and Jerry Lewis (qqv). President until 1936, then chairman, Zukor worked until his death at the age of 103.

Edited by Robin Morgan and George Perry

Executive Editor Tony Allaway

Art Direction Ivan Bulloch and Henry Nolan

Production Editor Steve Jezzard

Production Assistants Jeremy Vine, Digby Hildreth
Picture Editor Tracey King, Vince Page
Project Co-ordinator Danielle Willi
Illustrations John Springs
Chief Sub-editor Clive Graham-Ranger
Sub-editors Paul Sullivan, Janet Crumbie
Research Beth Porter
Imaging Rachel Jenkinson, Lee Banks, Andre Lockyer, Andrew McLeod, Bill Ward

Contributors
James Cameron-Wilson, Angie Errigo, Ryan Gilbey, Helen Hawkins, Sue Heal, Tom Hutchinson, Robyn Karney, John Marriott, Tony Patrick, Jeff Sawtell.

Photography
Agence France Presse, Ascap, Aquarius, British Film Institute, Kevin Brownlow, Cahiers du Cinéma, Canadian National Film Board, Gideon Cleary, Karen Davies, Deutsche Presse Agency, Disney Corporate Communications Ltd, Hugo Dixon, Freddie Francis, Jerry Goldsmith, Margaret Herrick Library of the Motion Picture Academy, Quincy Jones, Katz, Jeffrey Katzenberg, Kobal Collection, Geraint Lewis, Magnum, Francois Marie-Banier, William Morris Agency Los Angeles, Moviestore, Terry O'Neil, Retna, Rex, Ronald Grant Archive, John Springs, Sygma, Times Photo Library, Warner.

Booklist
The following books are among the hundreds consulted in the preparation of 1000 Makers of the Cinema:

Macmillan International Film Guide, ed Ephraim Katz; Biographical History Of Cinema, David Thomson; Movie and Video Guide, Leonard Maltin; Halliwell's Filmgoers Companion, ed John Walker; Halliwell's Film Guide, ed John Walker; Variety Movie Guide; Radio Times Film And Video, ed Derek Winnert; Virgin Film Guide (Baseline); Time Out Film Guide, ed Tom Milne; Oxford Companion To Film, ed Liz-Anne Bawden; Baseline Encyclopaedia Of Film, ed James Monaco; Macmillan Dictionary Of Film and Filmmakers; Chronicle of the Cinema, ed Robyn Karney; Film Review 1944- . . . , F Maurice Speed and James Cameron-Wilson; The Story Of Cinema Vols I II and III, David Shipman; The Illustrated Who's Who Of the Cinema (Orbis); The British Film Catalogue, Denis Gifford; Quinlan's Illustrated Directory Of Film Stars; History Of The Movies, ed Ann Lloyd; The Studio Series: MGM, Columbia, RKO, Universal, United Artists, Paramount, Disney etc (Octopus and Pyramid); The Hollywood Musical, Clive Hirschhorn; The Hollywood Story, Joel Finler; The Films Of . . . series (Citadel); Illustrated Encyclopaedia Of The World's Great Movie Stars and Their Films (Salamander); Bloomsbury Foreign Film Guide, ed Ronald Bergen and Robyn Karney; The BFI Companion To The Western, ed Edward Buscombe; Dilys Powell's The Golden Screen; Forever Ealing, George Perry; The Great British Picture Show, George Perry; British Sound Films, David Quinlan; Horror and Fantasy In The Cinema, Tom Hutchinson; Screen Goddesses, Tom Hutchinson.

CD-ROM: Film Index International (Chadwick-Healey); Cinemania (Microsoft).

Filmfinder

What was Meryl Streep's first movie? Was Richard Dreyfuss in The Graduate? When was Casablanca made? How many Bond films did Sean Connery nake? Want to rent a Demi Moore video but are unsure which movies you have missed? The answers are in this unique Filmfinder listing 40,000 films.

he Filmfinder catalogues every ignificant movie made by this election of the 1,000 most ıfluential names in the cinema. ook up a star or director arranged alphabetically) and you ill find a comprehensive list of ıeir notable feature films and the ear they were released to help you nd a video, settle an argument or imply jog your memory.

BBOTT & COSTELLO: Buck Privates, The Navy, Keep 'em Flying, **41**; Ride 'em owboy, Rio Rita, Who Done It?, **42**; Hit ıe Ice, It Ain't Hay, **43**; Lost In A Harem, **4**; Abbott & Costello In Hollywood, The aughty Nineties, **45**; Little Giant, The Time Their Lives, **46**; Buck Privates Come ome, **47**; Abbott & Costello Meet ankenstein, Mexican Hayride, The oose Hangs High, **48**; Abbott & Costello eet The Killer, Boris Karloff, **49**; Abbott Costello In The Foreign Legion, **50**; Abbott Costello Meet The Invisible Man, **51**; ck And The Beanstalk, Lost In Alaska, bott & Costello Meet Captain Kidd, **2**; Abbott & Costello Go To Mars, Abbott & ostello Meet Dr Jekyll And Mr Hyde, **3**; Abbott & Costello Meet The Keystone ops, Abbott & Costello Meet The ımmy, **55**; Dance With Me Henry, **56**.

DAM, KEN: The Brass Monkey, **47**; ssession, The Queen Of Spades, **49**; Your tness, **50**; Captain Horatio rnblower, **51**; The Crimson Pirate, **52**; The aster Of Ballantrae, **53**; Helen Of Troy, ound The World in 80 Days, **56**; Curse Of e Demon, **58**; The Trials Of Oscar lde, **60**; Dr No, Dr Strangelove, Sodom And morrah, **63**; Goldfinger, The Long Ships, **64**; The Ipcress File, Thunderball, **65**; Funeral In Berlin, **66**; You Only Live Twice, **67**; Chitty Chitty Bang Bang, **68**; Goodbye, Mr Chips, **69**; The Owl And The Pussycat, **70**; The Last Of Sheila, **73**; Barry Lyndon, Madam Kitty, **75**; The Seven Percent Solution, **76**; The Spy Who Loved Me, **77**; Moonraker, **79**; Pennies From Heaven, **81**; Agnes Of God, King David, **85**; Crimes Of The Heart, **86**; The Freshman, **90**; The Doctor, **91**; Addams Family Values, Undercover Blues, **93**; Boys On The Side, **95**; Bogus, **96** In and Out, **97**.

ADJANI, ISABELLE: Le Petit Bougnat, **69**; Faustine And The Beautiful Summer, **71**; The Slap, **74**; The Story Of Adele H, **75**; The Tenant, **76**; Violette Et François, **77**; The Driver, **78**; The Brontë Sisters, Nosferatu **79**; Possession, Quartet, **81**; Antonietta, Deadly Circuit, **82**; One Deadly Summer, **83**; Subway, **85**; Ishtar, **87**; Camille Claudel, **88**; Lung Ta: Les Cavaliers du Vent, **90**; Toxic Affair, **93**; La Reine Margot, **94**; Diabolique, **95**; Passionement, **97**..

ADLON, PERCY: Celeste, **81**; The Last Five Days, **82**; The Swing, **83**; Sugarbaby, **85**; Bagdad Cafe, **88**; Rosalie Goes Shopping, **89**; Salmonberries, **91**; Younger And Younger, **93**.

ADOREE, RENEE: Made In Heaven, **21**; Honor First, Monte Cristo, **22**; The Eternal Struggle, **23**; The Bandolero, A Man's Mate, Women Who Give, **24**; The Big Parade, Excuse Me, Man And Maid, Parisian Nights, Exchange Of Wives, **25**; The Black Bird, The Exquisite Sinner, La Boheme, Tin Gods, **26**; Back To God's Country, Heaven On Earth, Mr Wu, On Ze Boulevard, The Show, **27**; The Cossacks, Forbidden Hours, **28**; The Pagan, Tide Of Empire, **29**; Call Of The Flesh, Redemption, **30**.

AGUTTER, JENNY: East Of Sudan, **64**; Gates To Paradise, Star!, **68**; I Start Counting, **69**; The Railway Children, **70**; Walkabout, **71**; The Railway Children, **72**; Logan's Run, **76**; The Eagle Has Landed, Equus, **77**; China 9 Liberty 37, Dominique, **78**; The Riddle Of The Sands, **79**; Sweet William, **80**; An American Werewolf In London, The Survivor, **81**; Secret Places, **85**; Dark Tower, **87**; Child's Play 2, Darkman, King Of The Wind, **90**; Freddie As FRO7, **92**.

AIMEE, ANOUK: La Maison Sous La Mer, **46**; La Fleur De L'age, **47**; Les Amants De Vérone, **48**; Conquêtes Du Froid, **49**; The Golden Salamander, **50**; Le Rideau Cramoisi, **52**; The Paris Express, **53**; Forever My Heart, Happy Birthday, **54**; Ich Suche Dich, Les Mauvaises Rencontres, **55**; Nina, **56**; Lovers Of Paris, **57**; The Keepers, Montparnasse 19, **58**; The Chasers, The Journey, **59**; La Dolce Vita, Il Giudizio Universale, L'Imprevu, **60**; Lola, Quai Notre Dame, **61**; The Joker, Of Flesh And Blood, **62**; 8½, Il Terrorista, Sodom And Gomorrah, **63**; A Very Handy Man, Il Morbidone, La Fuga, **64**; La Stagioni Del Nostro Amore, Lo Scandalo, White Voices, **65**; A Man And A Woman, **66**; Un Soir Un Train, **68**; The Appointment, Justine, The Model Shop, **69**; Gumshoe, **71**; Second Chance, **76**; Leap Into The Void, **79**; Tragedy Of A Ridiculous Man, **81**; What Makes David Run?, **82**; Le Général De L'Armée Morte, **83**; Viva La Vie!, **84**; A Man And A Woman: 20 Years Later, **86**; Arrivederci E Grazie, **89**; La Table Tournante, **88**; Dr Bethune: The Making Of A Hero, **90**, Prêt-A-Porter, **95**.

ALDA, ALAN: Gone Are The Days, **63**; Paper Lion, **68**; The Extraordinary Seaman, **69**; Jenny, **70**; The Mephisto Waltz, **71**; To Kill A Clown, **72**; California Suite, Same Time, Next Year, **78**; The Seduction Of Joe Tynan, **79**; The Four Seasons, **81**; Sweet Liberty, **86**; A New Life, **88**; Crimes And Misdemeanors, **89**; Betsy's Wedding, **90**; Whispers In The Dark, **92**; Manhattan Murder Mystery, **93**, Canadian Bacon, **95**, Flirting with Disaster, **96**, Murder at 1600, **97**.

ALDRICH, ROBERT: The Southerner, The Story Of GI Joe, **45**; The Strange Love Of Martha Ivers, **46**; Body And Soul, **47**; Force Of Evil, So This Is New York, **48**; Caught, A Kiss For Corliss, The Red Pony, **49**; The White Tower, **50**; The Big Night, M, Of Men And Music, **51**; Abbott & Costello Meet Captain Kidd, The First Time, Limelight, **52**; Big Leaguer, **53**; Apache, Vera Cruz, **54**; The Big Knife, Kiss Me Deadly, **55**; Attack!, Autumn Leaves, **56**; The Angry Hills, Ten Seconds To Hell, **59**; The Last Sunset, **61**; Whatever Happened To Baby Jane?, **62**; Four For Texas, Sodom And Gomorrah, **63**; Hush . . . Hush Sweet Charlotte, Flight Of The Phoenix, **65**; The Dirty Dozen, **67**; The Killing Of Sister George, The Legend Of Lylah Clare, **68**; Whatever Happened To Aunt Alice?, **69**; Too Late The Hero, **70**; The Grissom Gang, **71**; Ulzana's Raid, **72**; Emperor Of The North, **73**; The Longest Yard, **74**; Hustle, **75**; The Choirboys, Twilight's Last Gleaming, **77**; The Frisco Kid, **79**; California Dolls, **81**.

ALLEGRET, MARC: Voyage Au Congo, **26**; Le Blanc Et Le Noir, **31**; Fanny, La Petite Chocolatière, **32**; L'hôtel Du Libre-èchange, **33**; Lac Aux Dames, Zou Zou, **34**; Aventure A Paris, Les Amants Terribles, Heart Of Paris, **35**; Les Beaux Jours, **36**; Orage, **38**; Le Corsaire, **39**; Parade En Sept Nuits, **41**; Felicie Nanteuil, L'Arlesienne, **42**; Twilight, **45**; Lunegarde, Petrus, **46**; Blanche Fury, **48**; Maria Chapdelaine, **49**; Blackmailed, **51**; Avec André Gide, **52**; Julietta, **53**; Lady Chatterley's Lover, **55**; Please! Mr Balzac, **56**; Be Beautiful But Shut Up, **57**; Un Drôle De Dimanche, **58**; Les Affreux, **59**; Les Parisiennes, **62**; L'Abominable Homme Des Douanes, **63**; Le Bal Du Cômte D'Orgel, **69**.

ALLEN, WOODY: What's New Pussycat?, **65**; What's Up Tiger Lily?, **66**; Casino Royale, **67**; Take The Money And Run, **69**; Bananas, **71**; Everything You Always Wanted To Know About Sex . . ., Play It Again Sam, **72**; Sleeper, **73**; Love And Death, **75**; The Front, **76**; Annie Hall, **77**; Interiors, **78**; Manhattan, **79**; Stardust Memories, **80**; A Midsummer Night's Sex Comedy, **82**; Zelig, **83**; Broadway Danny Rose, **84**; The Purple Rose Of Cairo, **85**; Hannah And Her Sisters, **86**; Radio Days, September, Another Woman, **88**; Crimes And Misdemeanors, New York Stories, **89**; Alice, **90**; Scenes From A Mall, **91**; Husbands And Wives, Shadows And Fog, **92**; Manhattan Murder Mystery, **93**; Bullets Over Broadway, **94**, Mighty Aphrodite, **95**; Everyone Says I Love You, **96**.

ALMENDROS, NESTOR: Six In Paris, **65**; More, My Night At Maud's, The Wild Child, **69**; Claire's Knee, La Collectionneuse, **71**; Chloe In The Afternoon, Two English Girls, **72**; Poil De Carotte, **73**; Femmes Au Soleil, General Idi Amin Dada, La Guêule Ouverte, **74**; The Story Of Adèle, **75**; I Want To Be A Woman, Mistress, The Marquise Of O, **76**; Madame Rosa, The Man Who Loved Women, **77**; Days Of Heaven, Goin' South, Koko A Talking Gorilla, Perceval, **78**; Kramer Vs Kramer, Love On The Run, **79**; The Blue Lagoon, The Last Metro, **80**; Sophie's Choice, Still Of The Night, **82**; Improper Conduct, Pauline At The Beach, **83**; Places In The Heart, **84**; Heartburn, **86**; Nadine, **87**; Nobody Listened, **88**; New York Stories, **89**; Billy Bathgate, **91**.

ALMODOVAR, PEDRO: Dos Putas, La Caida De Sodoma, **74**; El Sueno, Homenaje, **75**; El Estrella, **76**; Complementos, **77**; Folle Folle Folle Me, Tim, Salomé, **78**; Pepi Luci Bom, **80**; Labyrinth Of Passion, **82**; Dark Habits, What Have I Done To Deserve This?, **84**; Matador, **86**; Law Of Desire, **87**; Women On The Verge Of A Nervous Breakdown, **88**; Tie Me Up! Tie Me

wn!, **90**; High Heels, **91**; Mutante Action, ; Kika, **94**; Flower Of My Secret, **95**.

TMAN, ROBERT: Bodyguard, **48**; untdown, **68**; That Cold Day In The Park, ; Brewster McCloud, M*A*S*H, **70**; Cabe And Mrs Miller, **71**; Images, **72**; The ng Goodbye, **73**; California Split, eves Like Us, **74**; Nashville, **75**; Buffalo And The Indians, Three Women, The e Show, **76**; Welcome To LA, **77**; member My Name, A Wedding, **78**; .A.L.T.H., Quintet, Rich Kids, **79**; Popeye, ; Endless Love, **81**; Come Back To Five And Dime Jimmy Dean Jimmy Dean, ; Streamers, **83**; Secret Honor, **84**; l For Love, Lily In Love, Beyond Therapy, & Stiggs, **85**; Aria, **88**; Vincent And o, **90**; The Player, **92**; Short Cuts, **93**; s Parker and the Vicious Circle, Prêt-A-ter, **95**; Kansas City, **96**; The Gingerbread n, **97**.

IBLER, ERIC: Journey Into Fear, ; The Mask Of Dimitrios, The Way Ahead, The October Man, **47**; The ssionate Friends, **49**; The Magic Box, **51**; core, The Promoter, **52**; The Cruel , **53**; Lease Of Life, The Purple Plain, **54**; Yangtse Incident, **57**; A Night To member, **58**; The Wreck Of The Mary are, **59**; Mutiny On The Bounty, **62**; kapi, **64**.

IECHE, DON: Ladies In Love, One In Million, Ramona, **36**; Love Under Fire, You n't Have Everything, **37**; Alexander's gtime Band, In Old Chicago, Josette, **38**; llywood Cavalcade, Midnight, The ry Of Alexander Graham Bell, Swanee River, Three Musketeers, **39**; Down entine Way, **40**; Confirm Or Deny, Kiss The s Goodbye, Moon Over Miami, That ht In Rio, **41**; Girl Trouble, **42**; Happy d, Heaven Can Wait, **43**; Greenwich age, Wing And A Prayer, **44**; Guest Wife, ; So Goes My Love, **46**; That's My n, **47**; Sleep My Love, **48**; Slightly French, Phantom Caravan, **54**; Fire One, A Fever In The Blood, **61**; Picture mmy Dead, **66**; Suppose They Gave ar And Nobody Came?, **70**; Trading ces, **83**; Cocoon, **85**; Harry And The ndersons, **87**; Cocoon II: The Return, ngs Change, **88**; Oscar, **91**; Folks!, Homeward Bound: The Incredible rney, **93**; Corrina Corrina, **94**.

DERSON, G M: The Messenger 's Mistake, **02**; The Great Train Robbery, The Life Of An American Cowboy, ffles The American Cracksman, **05**; The ndit King, The Bandit Makes Good, stern Justice, **07**; The Black Sheep, The art Of A Cowboy, The Indian Trailer, A xican's Gratitude, A Tale Of The West, **09**; ay Out West, Broncho Billy's emption, The Cowboy And The Squaw, The sperado, The Forest Ranger, The Pony ress Rider, Take Me Out To The Ball Game, der Western Skies, **10**; Across The ns, Broncho Billy's Adventure, The Cowboy ward, The Faithful Indian, The Outlaw The Child, **11**; Alkali Ike's Boarding use, Broncho Billy Outwitted, An an's Friendship, **12**; Alkali Ike's fortunes, The Three Gamblers, **13**; ncho Billy's Indian Romance, The Calling lim Barton, The Good-for-Nothing, **14**; y Of The Royal Mounted, Broncho Billy's rriage, Broncho Billy's Revenge, The ampion, **15**; Broncho Billy And The enue Agent, **16**; Shootin' Mad, **18**; Night, **22**; The Bounty Killer, **65**.

DERSON, JUDITH: Blood Money, Rebecca, **40**; Free And Easy, Lady rface, **41**; All Through The Night, gs Row, **42**; Edge Of Darkness, **43**; Laura, And Then There Were None, **45**; ctre Of The Rose, The Strange Love Of tha Ivers, **46**; Pursued, The Red use, Tycoon, **47**; The Furies, **50**; Salomé, The Ten Commandments, **56**; Cat A Hot Tin Roof, **58**; Cinderfella, Macbeth, Don't Bother To Knock, **64**; A Man ed Horse, **70**; Inn Of The Damned, **74**; Trek III: The Search For Spock, **84**; vido Del Genio, Impure Thoughts, **85**.

DERSON, LINDSAY: Meet The neers, **48**; Idlers That Work, **49**; Three allations, Wakefield Express, **52**; O amland, Thursday's Children, **53**; Trunk veyor, **54**; The Children Upstairs, t And Mouth, Green And Pleasant Land, ry, A Hundred Thousand Children, Every Day Except Christmas, **57**; This rting Life, **63**; The White Bus, **67**; If . . ., **68**; O Lucky Man!, **73**; In Celebration, **75**; Britannia Hospital, **82**; The Whales Of August, **87**.

ANDREWS, DANA: Kit Carson, The Westerner, **40**; Ball Of Fire, Belle Starr , Swamp Water, Tobacco Road, **41**; Berlin Correspondent, **42**; The Ox-bow Incident, **43**; Laura, The Purple Heart, Up In Arms, Wing And A Prayer, **44**; Fallen Angel, State Fair, A Walk In The Sun, **45**; The Best Years Of Our Lives, Canyon Passage, **46**; Boomerang!, Daisy Kenyon, **47**; Deep Waters, The Iron Curtain, **48**; The Forbidden Street, My Foolish Heart, **49**; Edge Of Doom, Where The Sidewalk Ends, **50**; I Want You, Sealed Cargo, **51**; Assignment Paris, **52**; Duel In The Jungle, Elephant Walk, **54**; Smoke Signal, Strange Lady In Town, **55**; Beyond A Reasonable Doubt, Comanche, While The City Sleeps, **56**; Zero Hour, **57**; Night Of The Demon, Enchanted Island **58**; The Crowded Sky, **60**; Madison Avenue, **62**; Battle Of The Bulge, Brainstorm, In Harm's Way, The Loved One, The Satan Bug, **65**; The Frozen Dead, Johnny Reno, **66**; Hot Rods To Hell, **67**; The Devil's Brigade, **68**; Innocent Bystanders, **73**; Airport 75, **74**; Performer, **75**; The Last Tycoon, **76**; Born Again, **78**; Good Guys Wear Black, **79**; Prince Jack, **84**.

ANDREWS, JULIE: The Rose Of Bagdad, **49**; The Americanization Of Emily, Mary Poppins, **64**; The Sound Of Music, **65**; Hawaii, Torn Curtain, **66**; Thoroughly Modern Millie, **67**; Star!, **68**; Darling Lili, **70**; The Tamarind Seed, **74**; 10, Performer, **79**; Little Miss Marker, **80**; SOB, **81**; Victor/-Victoria, **82**; The Man Who Loved Women, **83**; Duet For One, That's Life!, **86**.

ANNAUD, JEAN-JACQUES: Black And White In Colour, **76**; Too Shy To Try, **78**; Hot Head, **79**; Quest For Fire, **81**; The Name Of The Rose, **86**; The Bear, **88**; The Lover, **92**; Wings Of Courage, **94**; Seven Years In Tibet, **95**.

ANN-MARGRET: Pocketful Of Miracles, **61**; State Fair, **62**; Bye Bye Birdie, **63**; Kitten With A Whip, The Pleasure Seekers, Viva Las Vegas, **64**; Bus Riley's Back In Town, The Cincinnati Kid, Once A Thief, **65**;Stagecoach, The Swinger, **66**; The Tiger And The Pussycat **70**; Carnal Knowledge, **71**; Tommy, **75**; Twist, Joseph Andrews, **76**; The Last Remake Of Beau Geste, **77**; Magic, **78**; The Villain, **79**; Middle Age Crazy, **80**; The Return Of The Soldier, **81**; I Ought To Be In Pictures, Vice Squad, **82**; Twice In A Lifetime, **85**; 52 Pick-Up, **86**; A Tiger's Tale, **87**; A New Life, **88**; Newsies, **93**; Grumpy Old Men, **94**; Grumpier Old Men, **95**; Seduced by Madness, **96**.

ANTONIONI, MICHELANGELO: Story Of A Love Affair, **50**; Camille Without Camellias, Love In The City, **53**; Girl Friends, **55**; Il Grido, **57**; Tempest, **59**; L'Avventura, **60**; La Notte, **61**; Eclipse, **62**; Red Desert, **64**; The Three Faces Of A Woman, **65**; Blow-Up, **66**; Zabriskie Point, **70**; The Passenger, **75**; The Mystery Of Oberwald, **80**; Chambre 666, Identification Of A Woman, **82**. Beyond The Clouds, **95**.

ARBUCKLE, ROSCOE 'FATTY': Selection of more than 100 films: The Sanitarium, **10**; Fatty's Day Off, **13**; The Alarm, **14**; The Moonshiners, **16**; Brewster's Millions, **21**; The Fighting Dude (first as William Goodrich), **25**; Niagara Falls, **32**.

ARDEN, EVE: Selection: The Song Of Love, **29**; Oh, Doctor!, Stage Door, **37**; Having A Wonderful Time, **38**; At The Circus, Eternally Yours, **39**; Comrade X, No No Nanette, **40**; Bedtime Story, Manpower, Ziegfeld Girl, **41**; Let's Face It, **43**; Cover Girl, **44**; Mildred Pierce, **45**; The Kid From Brooklyn, Night And Day, **46**; Song Of Scheherazade, The Unfaithful, The Voice Of The Turtle, **47**; One Touch Of Venus, **48**; My Dream Is Yours, **49**; Tea For Two, Three Husbands, **50**; Goodbye My Fancy, **51**; We're Not Married, **52**; The Lady Wants Mink, **53**; Our Miss Brooks, **56**; Anatomy Of A Murder, **59**; The Dark At The Top Of The Stairs, **60**; The Strongest Man In The World, **75**; Grease, **78**; Under The Rainbow, **81**; Grease 2, Pandemonium, **82**.

ARKIN, ALAN: The Last Mohican, The Russians Are Coming! The Russians Are Coming!, **66**; Wait Until Dark, **67**; The Heart Is A Lonely Hunter, Inspector Clouseau, **68**; Popi, **69**; Catch-22, **70**; Little Murders, **71**; Last Of The Red Hot Lovers, **72**; Freebie And The Bean, **74**; Hearts Of The West, Rafferty And The Gold Dust Twins, **75**; The Seven Percent Solution, **76**; The In-laws, The Magician Of Lublin, **78**; Simon, **80**; Improper Channels, **81**; The Last Unicorn, **82**; The Return Of Captain Invincible, **83**; Bad Medicine, Joshua Then And Now, **85**; Big Trouble, **86**; Coup De Ville, Edward Scissorhands, Havana, **90**; The Rocketeer, **91**; Glengarry Glen Ross, **92**; Indian Summer, So I Married An Axe Murderer, **93**; North, **94**; The Jerky Boys, Steal Big Steal Litte, **95**; Grosse Pointe Blank, **97**.

ARLEN, HAROLD: Let's Fall In Love, **33**; Gold Diggers Of 1937, The Singing Kid, Stage Struck, Strike Me Pink, **36**; At The Circus, The Wizard Of Oz, **39**; Blues In The Night, **41**; Cairo, Star Spangled Rhythm, **42**; Cabin In The Sky, The Sky's The Limit, **43**; Here Come The Waves, Up In Arms, **44**; Casbah, **48**; Dark City, The Petty Girl, **50**; Macao, **52**; The Farmer Takes A Wife, **53**; The Country Girl, A Star Is Born, **54**; Gay Purr-ee, **63**.

ARLEN, RICHARD: Vengeance Of The Deep, In The Name Of Love, **25**; Padlocked, **26**; The Blood Ship, Rolled Stocking, Wings, **27**; Beggars Of Life, Ladies Of The Mob, Manhattan Cocktail, **28**; Dangerous Curves, **29**; The Border Legion, Dangerous Paradise, Only Saps Work, The Santa Fe Trail, **30**; The Conquering Horde, Gunsmoke, The Lawyer's Secret, Touchdown!, **31**; The All American, Sky Bride, Tiger Shark, Wayward, Alice In Wonderland, College Humor, Island Of Lost Souls, Song Of The Eagle, Three-cornered Moon, **33**; Come On Marines!, **34**; Helldorado, The Calling Of Dan Matthews, **35**; Artists & Models, Murder In Greenwich Village, Silent Barriers, **37**; Call Of The Yukon, Legion Of Lost Flyers, Mutiny On The Blackhawk, **39**; The Devil's Pipeline, **40**; Raiders Of The Desert, **41**; Submarine Alert, **43**; The Lady And The Monster, Storm Over Lisbon, **44**; The Big Bonanza, **45**; When My Baby Smiles At Me, **48**; Hurricane Smith, **52**; Sabre Jet, **53**; The Mountain, **56**; Warlock, **59**; The Best Man, **64**; Apache Uprising, **66**; Buckskin, **68**; Sex And The College Girl, **70**; Won Ton Ton The Dog Who Saved Hollywood, **76**.

ARLETTY: Un Chien Qui Rapporte, La Belle Aventure, **32**; Waltz War, **33**; Pension Mimosas, **34**; La Garçonne, **36**; Les Perles De La Couronne, **37**; Hôtel Du Nord, **38**; Extenuating Circumstances, Fric-frac, Le Jour Se Leve, **39**; Madame Sans-gêne, **41**; Les Visiteurs du Soir, **42**; Les Enfants Du Paradis, **45**; Portrait D'Un Assassin, **49**; L'Amour Madame, **51**; Le Grand Jeu, Huis Clos, **54**; Maxime, Un Drôle De Dimanche, **58**; The Longest Day, **62**; Les Volets Clos **72**.

ARLISS, GEORGE: The Devil, Disraeli, **21**; The Man Who Played God, The Ruling Passion, **22**; The Green Goddess, **23**; Twenty Dollars A Week, **24**; Disraeli, **29**; The Green Goddess, Old English, **30**; Alexander Hamilton, The Millionaire, **31**; The Man Who Played God, A Successful Calamity, **32**; The King's Vacation, Voltaire, The Working Man, **33**; House Of Rothschild, The Last Gentleman, **34**; Cardinal Richelieu, The Iron Duke, The Guv'nor, Transatlantic Tunnel, **35**; East Meets West, His Lordship, His Lordship, **36**; Dr Syn, **37**.

ARMSTRONG, GILLIAN: My Brilliant Career, **79**; Starstruck, **82**; Having A Go, Not Just A Pretty Face, Mrs Soffel, **84**; High Tide, **87**; Bingo, Bridesmaids And Braces, **88**; Fires Within, **91**; The Last Days Of Chez Nous, **93**; Little Women, **94**; Oscar And Lucinda, **95**; Not Fourteen Again, **96**, Oscar & Lucinda **97**.

ARMSTRONG, LOUIS: Pennies From Heaven, **36**; Artists And Models, Every Day's A Holiday, **37**; Dr Rhythm, Going Places, **38**; Cabin In The Sky, **43**; Atlantic City, Hollywood Canteen, Jam Session, **44**; New Orleans, **47**; A Song Is Born, **48**; Here Comes The Groom, The Strip, **51**; Glory Alley, **52**; The Glenn Miller Story, **54**; High Society, **56**; The Five Pennies, Jazz On A Summer's Day, **59**; Paris Blues, **61**; When The Boys Meet The Girls, **65**; A Man Called Adam, **66**; Hello Dolly!, On Her Majesty's Secret Service, **69**.

ARTHUR, JEAN: Cameo Kirby, **23**; Biff Bang Buddy, Fast And Fearless, Thundering Romance, **24**; Drug Store Cowboy, A Man Of Nerve, Seven Chances, **25**; Born To Battle, The College Boob, The Cowboy Cop, Double Daring, Lightning Bill, Under Fire, **26**; Flying Luck, Husband Hunters, **27**; Sins Of The Fathers, Wallflowers, **28**; Canary Murder Case, Half Way To Heaven, The Mysterious Dr Fu Manchu, The Saturday Night Kid, **29**; Paramount On Parade, The Return Of Dr Fu Manchu, The Silver Horde, **30**; The Gang Buster, The Virtuous Husband, **31**; The Past Of Mary Holmes, **33**; The Defense Rests, Whirlpool, **34**; Diamond Jim, If You Could Only Cook, Public Hero, The Public Menace, The Whole Town's Talking, **35**; The Ex-Mrs Bradford, Mr Deeds Goes To Town, **36**; Easy Living, History Is Made At Night, The Plainsman, **37**; You Can't Take It With You, **38**; Mr Smith Goes To Washington, Only Angels Have Wings, **39**; Arizona, Too Many Husbands, **40**; The Devil And Miss Jones, **41**; The Talk Of The Town, **42**; A Lady Takes A Chance, The More The Merrier, **43**; The Impatient Years, **44**; Foreign Affair, **48**; Shane, **53**.

ARZNER, DOROTHY: Fashions For Women, Get Your Man, Ten Modern Commandments, **27**; Manhattan Cocktail, **28**; The Wild Party, **29**; Anybody's Woman, Paramount On Parade, Sarah And Son, **30**; Honor Among Lovers, Working Girls, **31**; Merrily We Go To Hell, **32**; Christopher Strong, **33**; Nana, **34**; Craig's Wife, **36**; The Bride Wore Red, The Last of Mrs Cheyney, **37**; Dance Girl Dance, **40**; First Comes Courage, **43**.

ASHBY, HAL: The Landlord, **70**; Harold And Maude, **71**; The Last Detail, **73**; Shampoo, **75**; Bound For Glory, **76**; Coming Home, **78**; Being There, **79**; Second-hand Hearts, **81**; Let's Spend The Night Together, **82**; The Slugger's Wife, **85**; 8 Million Ways To Die, **86**.

ASQUITH, ANTHONY: Shooting Stars, **27**; Underground, **28**; The Runaway Princess, **29**; A Cottage On Dartmoor, **30**; Tell England, **31**; Dance Pretty Lady, Marry Me, **32**; Letting In The Sunshine, The Lucky Number, **33**; The Unfinished Symphony, **34**; Brown On Resolution, Moscow Nights, **35**; Pygmalion, **38**; French Without Tears, **39**; Quiet Wedding, **40; Cottage To Let, **41**; Uncensored, **42**; The Demi-Paradise, We Dive At Dawn, **43**; Fanny By Gaslight, Two Fathers, **44**; The Way To The Stars, Johnny in the Clouds, **45**; While The Sun Shines, **47**; The Winslow Boy, The Woman In Question, The Browning Version, **50**; The Importance Of Being Earnest, **52**; The Final Test, The Net, **53**; The Young Lovers, Carrington VC, **54**; On Such A Night, **55**; Doctor's Dilemma, Orders To Kill, **58**; Libel, **59**; The Millionairess, **60**; Guns Of Darkness, **62**; An Evening With The Royal Ballet, The VIPs, **63**; The Yellow Rolls-Royce, **64**.

ASTAIRE, FRED: Dancing Lady, Flying Down To Rio, **33**; The Gay Divorcee, **34**; Roberta, Top Hat, **35**; Follow The Fleet, Swing Time, **36**; A Damsel In Distress, Shall We Dance, **37**; Carefree, **38**; The Story Of Vernon And Irene Castle, **39**; Broadway Melody Of 1940, **40**; Second Chorus, You'll Never Get Rich, **41**; Holiday Inn, You Were Never Lovelier, **42**; The Sky's The Limit, **43**; Yolanda And The Thief, **45**; Blue Skies, Ziegfeld Follies, **46**; Easter Parade, The Barkleys Of Broadway, **48**; Let's Dance, Three Little Words, **50**; Royal Wedding, **51**; The Belle Of New York, **52**; The Band Wagon, **53**; Daddy Long Legs, **55**; Funny Face, Silk Stockings, **57**; On The Beach, **59**; The Pleasure Of His Company, **61**; The Notorious Landlady, **62**; Finian's Rainbow, **68**; A Run On Gold, Midas Rule, **69**; That's Entertainment!, The Towering Inferno, **74**; The Amazing Dobermans, That's Entertainment, Part 2, **76**; The Purple Taxi, **77**; Imposters, **79**; Ghost Story, **81**.

ASTOR, MARY: John Smith, The Rapids, **22**; The Bright Shawl, Woman-Proof, **23**; Beau Brummell, The Fighting American, Inez From Hollywood, Unguarded Women, **24**; Don Q Son Of Zorro, Enticement, Playing With Souls, The Scarlet Saint, Oh Doctor!, **25**; The Wise Guy, **26**; Rose Of The Golden West, The Rough Riders, Two Arabian Knights, **27**; Dressed To Kill, Dry Martini, Heart To Heart, Romance And Bright Lights, **28**; New Year's Eve, Woman From Hell, **29**; Adios, Holiday, Ladies Love Brutes, **30**; Other Men's Women, The Royal Bed, **31**; The Lost Squadron, Red Dust, Those We Love, **32**; Convention City, The Little Giant, **33**; The Man With Two Faces, Return Of The Terror, Upperworld, Easy To Love, **34**; Dinky, I Am A Thief, The Man Of Iron, Red Hot Tires, **35**; Dodsworth, Lady From Nowhere, **36**; The Hurricane, The Prisoner Of Zenda, **37**; Listen Darling, Paradise For Three, Woman Against Woman, **38**; Midnight, **39**; Brigham Young, Turnabout, **40**; The Maltese Falcon, The Great Lie, **41**; Across The Pacific, The Palm Beach Story, **42**; Thousands Cheer, **43**; Meet Me In St Louis, **44**; Cass Timberlane, Cynthia, Desert Fury, Fiesta, **47**; Act Of Violence, Any Number Can Play, Little Women, **49**; A Kiss Before Dying, The Power And The Prize, **56**; The Devil's Hairpin, **57**; This Happy Feeling, **58**; Stranger In My Arms, **59**; Return To Peyton Place, **61**; Youngblood Hawke, **64**; Hush . . . Hush Sweet Charlotte, **65**.

ATTENBOROUGH, RICHARD: In Which We Serve, **42**; Schweik's New Adventures, **43**; Journey Together, **45**; School For Secrets, A Matter Of Life And Death, **46**; Brighton Rock, The Man Within, **47**; London Belongs To Me, The Guinea Pig, **48**; The Boys In Brown, The Lost People, **49**; The Magic Box, Morning Departure, **51**; Eight O'clock Walk, **52**; The Gift Horse, **53**; The Ship That Died Of Shame, **55**; The Baby And The Battleship, Brothers In Law, **56**; The Scamp, Sea Of Sand, Dunkirk, **57**; Danger Within, I'm All Right Jack, **59**; The Angry Silence, **60**; The League Of Gentlemen, S O S Pacific, Whistle Down The Wind, **61**; The Dock Brief, Only Two Can Play, **62**; The Great Escape, The L-shaped Room, **63**; Guns At Batasi, Seance On A Wet Afternoon, **64**; Flight Of The Phoenix, The Sand Pebbles, **66**; Doctor Dolittle, **67**; The Bliss Of Mrs Blossom, Only When I Larf, **68**; The Magic Christian, Oh! What A Lovely War, **69**; 10 Rillington Place, David Copperfield, Loot, **70**; A Severed Head, **71**; Young Winston, **72**; Brannigan, Conduct Unbecoming, Rosebud, Ten Little Indians, **75**; A Bridge Too Far, The Chess Players, **77**; Magic, **78**; The Human Factor, **79**; Gandhi, **82**; A Chorus Line, **85**; Cry Freedom, **87**; Chaplin, **92**; Jurassic Park, Shadowlands, **93**; Miracle On 34th Street, **94**; In Love and War, **96**.

AUDRAN, STEPHANE: The Cousins, The Sign Of Leo, **59**; Les Bonnes Femmes, **60**; Bluebeard, The Third Lover, **62**; Paris Vu Par, **65**; Line Of Demarcation, **66**; The Champagne Murders, **67**; Les Biches, **68**; La Femme Infidèle, Le Boucher, **69**; The Break Up, **70**; Just Before Nightfall, **71**; The Discreet Charm Of The Bourgeoisie, Un Meurtre Est Un Meurtre, **72**; Wedding In Blood, **73**; Comment Reussir Quand On Est Con Et Pleurnichard, Le Cri Du Coeur, Vincent François Paul And The Others, **74**; The Black Bird, Ten Little Indians, **75**; The Twist, **76**; Death Of A Corrupt Man, The Devil's Advocate, Violette Nozière, **77**; Eagle's Wing, **79**; The Big Red One, Clean Slate, **80**; Le Choc, **81**; Mortelle Randonnée, Paradis Pour Tous, La Scarlatine, **82**; The Blood Of Others, Cop Au Vin, Les Voleurs De La Nuit, **84**; La Cage Aux Folles **83:** The Wedding, La Gitane, Suivez Mon Regard, **85**; Babette's Feast, Les Prédateurs De La Nuit, The Seasons Of Pleasure, **87**; Manika, **88**; Sons, **89**; Mass In C Minor, Quiet Days In Clichy, **90**; Betty, **92;** Maximum Risk, **96**.

AURIC, GEORGES: Selection: Entr'acte, **24**; The Blood Of A Poet, **30**; A Nous La Liberté, **31**; Lac Aux Dames, **34**; Captain Blood, **35**; Midnight In Paris, **42**; The Eternal Return, **43**; Dead Of Night, Caesar And Cleopatra, **45**; Beauty And The Beast, La Symphonie Pastorale, **46**; It Always Rains On Sunday, **47**; Eagle With Two Heads, **48**; Orpheus, Passport To Pimlico, **49**; The Lavender Hill Mob, **51**; Moulin Rouge, The Wages Of Fear, **52**; Roman Holiday, The Titfield Thunderbolt, **53**; Rififi, **54**; Lola Montes, **55**; Heaven Knows Mr Allison, **57**; The Testament Of Orpheus, **59**; The Innocents, **61**.

AUTANT-LARA, CLAUDE: Selection: Construire Un Feu, **26**; Ciboulette, **33**; Le Mariage De Chiffon, **42**; Devil In The Flesh, Sylvie And The Phantom, **46**;

Occupe-toi D'Amélie, **49**; Seven Deadly Sins, **52**; Le Bon Dieu Sans Confession, **53**; The Game Of Love, Le Rouge Et Le Noir, **54**; Four Bags Full, Marguerite De La Nuit, A Pig Across Paris, **56**; Love Is My Profession, **58**; Le Bois Des Amants, Les Régates De San Francisco, **60**; The Count Of Monte Cristo, **61**.

AUTEUIL, DANIEL: La Nuit De Saint-Germain De Prés, Rape of Love, **77**; Les Heroes N'ont Pas Froid Aux Oreilles, **78**; Bête Mais Discipliné, **79**; Les Sous-doués Les Hommes Préferent Les Grosses, **80**; Pour 100 Briques, **82**; L'indic, **83**; L'amour En Douce, **85**; L'arbalete, Les Fauves, Palace, P'tit Con, Jean De Florette, Manon Des Sources, **86**; A Few Days With Me, **88**; Look Who's Talking, Romuald Et Juliette, **89**; Lacenaire, **90**; My Life Is Hell, **91**; Un Coeur En Hiver, **92**; Ma Saison Préférée, **93**; The Eighth Day, **95**.

AUTREY, GENE: Selection: In Old Santa Fe, **34**; Melody Trail, Tumblin' Tumbleweeds, **35**; Comin' Round The Mountain, The Singing Cowboy, **36**; Boots And Saddles, Git Along Little Dogies, Rootin' Tootin' Rhythm, **37**; In Old Monterey, Mexicali Rose, South Of The Border, **39**; Down Mexico Way, **41**; The Last Round-up, **47**; Riders In The Sky, **49**; Mule Train, **50**; Wagon Team, **52**; On Top Of Old Smoky, Winning Of The West, **53**.

AXELROD, GEORGE: Phffft! **54**; The Seven Year Itch, **55**; Bus Stop, **56**; Will Success Spoil Rock Hunter?, **57**; Breakfast At Tiffany's, **61**; The Manchurian Candidate, **62;** Paris When It Sizzles, **64**; How To Murder Your Wife, **65**; Lord Love A Duck, **66**; The Secret Life Of An American Wife, **68**; The Lady Vanishes, **79**; The Holcroft Covenant, **85**.

AYKROYD, DAN: Love At First Sight, **74**; 1941, **79**; The Blues Brothers, **80**; Neighbors, **81**; It Came From Hollywood, **82**; Doctor Detroit, Trading Places, Twilight Zone, **83**; Ghostbusters, Indiana Jones And The Temple Of Doom, Nothing Lasts Forever, Into The Night, **84**; Spies Like Us, **85**; Dragnet, **87**; Caddyshack II, The Couch Trip, The Great Outdoors, My Stepmother Is An Alien, **88**; Driving Miss Daisy, Ghostbusters II, **89**; Loose Cannons, **90**; My Girl, Nothing But Trouble, **91**; Sneakers, This Is My Life, **92**; My Girl 2, **94**; Getting Away With Murder, Tommy Boy, **95**; Sgt Bilko, **96**; Feeling Minnesota, **96**; Grosse Pointe Blank, **97**, Blues Brothers 2000, **97**.

AYRES, LEW: The Kiss, **29**; All Quiet On The Western Front, Common Clay, The Doorway To Hell, East Is West, **30**; The Iron Man, Many A Slip, Spirit Of Notre Dame, Up For Murder, **31**; Night World, **32**; Don't Bet On Love, State Fair, **33**; Let's Be Ritzy, Servant's Entrance. **34**; The Lottery Lover, Silk Hat Kid, Spring Tonic, **35**; Hearts In Bondage, Murder With Pictures, Shakedown, **36**; The Crime Nobody Saw, The Last Train From Madrid, **37**; Holiday, Rich Man Poor Girl, Scandal Street, Young Dr Kildare, **38**; Dr Kildare series, Broadway Serenade, Ice Follies Of 1939, Remember?, These Glamour Girls, **39**; The Golden Fleecing, **40**; Maisie Was A Lady, **41**; Fingers At The Window, **42**; The Dark Mirror, **46**; The Unfaithful, **47**; Johnny Belinda, **48**; The Capture, **50**; New Mexico, **51**; Donovan's Brain, No Escape, **53**; Advise And Consent, **62**; The Carpetbaggers, **64**; The Man, **72**; Battle For The Planet Of The Apes, **73**; End Of The World, **77**; Damien Omen II, Battlestar Galactica, **78.**

BACALL, LAUREN: To Have And Have Not, **44**; Confidential Agent, **45**; The Big Sleep, **46**; Dark Passage, **47**; Key Largo, **48**; Bright Leaf, Young Man With A Horn, **50**; How To Marry A Millionaire, **53**; Woman's World, **54**; Blood Alley, The Cobweb, **55**; Written On The Wind, **56**; Designing Woman, **57**; The Gift Of Love, **58**; Northwest Frontier, **59**; Sex And The Single Girl, Shock Treatment, **64**; Harper, **66**; Murder On The Orient Express, **74**; The Shootist, **76**; H.E.A.L.T.H., **80**; The Fan, **81**; Appointment With Death, Mr North, **88**; Tree Of Hands, **89**; Misery, **90**; Pret-A-Porter, **95**, The Mirror has Two Faces, **96**.

BACHARACH, BURT: Lizzie, **56**; The Blob, What's New Pussycat?, After The Fox, Alfie, **65**; The April Fools, Bob & Carol & Ted & Alice, Butch Cassidy And The Sundance Kid, **69**; Something Big, **71**; Lost Horizon, **73**; Arthur, **81**; Arthur 2, **88**; That Night, **92**; Alive, Dragon: The Bruce Lee Story, Matinee, Mr Wonderful, This Boy's Life, **93**, Austin Powers, **97**.

BADHAM, JOHN: Sunshine Part II, **75**; The Bingo Long Traveling All-Stars And Motor Kings, **76**; Saturday Night Fever, **77**; Dracula, **79**; Whose Life Is It Anyway?, **81**; Blue Thunder, Wargames, **83**; American Flyers, **85**; Short Circuit, **86**; Stakeout, **87**; Bird On A Wire, **90**; The Hard Way, **91**; Another Stakeout, Point Of No Return, The Assassin, **93**, Drop Zone, **95**; Nick of Time, **95**; Incognito, **96.**

BALCON, MICHAEL: Woman To Woman, The White Shadow, **23**; The Pleasure Garden, **25**; The Lodger, **26**; Woman To Woman, **29**; Man Of Aran, The Man Who Knew Too Much, **34**; The 39 Steps, **35**; Sabotage, Secret Agent, **36**; Goodbye Mr Chips, **38**; Next Of Kin, **42**; Champagne Charlie, **44**; Dead Of Night, **45**; The Captive Heart, The Overlanders, Hue And Cry, Nicholas Nickleby, **46**; Kind Hearts And Coronets, Passport To Pimlico, Whisky Galore, **49**; The Blue Lamp, **50**; The Lavender Hill Mob, The Man In The White Suit, **51**; The Cruel Sea, **53**; The Divided Heart, **54**; The Ladykillers, **55**; Dunkirk, **58**.

BALL, LUCILLE: Follow The Fleet, **36**; Stage Door, **37**; Annabel Takes A Tour, Having Wonderful Time, Joy Of Living, Next Time I Marry, Trailer Romances, Room Service, **38**; Five Came Back, That's Right – You're Wrong, **39**; Dance Girl Dance, Too Many Girls, **40**; Look Who's Laughing, **41**; The Big Street, **42**; Best Foot Forward, Dubarry Was A Lady, Thousands Cheer, **43**; Ziegfeld Follies, **44**; Without Love, **45**; Easy To Wed, Lover Come Back, **46**; Her Husband's Affairs, Lured, Personal Column, **47**; Easy Living, Sorrowful Jones, **49**; Fancy Pants, The Fuller Brush Girl, **50**; The Magic Carpet, **51**; The Long, Long Trailer, **54**; Forever Darling, **56**; The Facts Of Life, **60**; Critic's Choice, **63**; A Guide For The Married Man, **67**; Yours Mine And Ours, **68**; Mame, **74**.

BALLARD, LUCIEN: Morocco, **30**; Crime And Punishment, The Devil Is A Woman, **35**; Craig's Wife, The Shadow, **36**; Highway Patrol, Penitentiary, **38**; Blind Alley, **39**; Wild Geese Calling, **41**; Orchestra Wives, Whispering Ghosts, **42**; Holy Matrimony, Tonight We Raid Calais, **43**; The Lodger, Sweet And Lowdown, **44**; This Love Of Ours, **45**; Temptation, **46**; Night Song, **47**; Berlin Express, **48**; Fixed Bayonets, **51**; Diplomatic Courier, Don't Bother To Knock, O Henry's Full House, **52**; The Desert Rats, Inferno, **53**; New Faces, Prince Valiant, **54**; White Feather, **55**; The Killing, A Kiss Before Dying, The Proud Ones, **56**; Band Of Angels, **57**; Anna Lucasta, Murder By Contract, **58**; Al Capone, City Of Fear, **59**; Desire In The Dust, The Rise And Fall Of Legs Diamond, **60**; The Parent Trap, Susan Slade, **61**; Ride The High Country, **62**; The Caretakers, Take Her She's Mine, Wives And Lovers, **63**; The New Interns, **64**; Boeing Boeing, Dear Brigitte, The Sons Of Katie Elder, **65**; Nevada Smith, **66**; The Party, Will Penny, **68**; True Grit, The Wild Bunch, **69**; The Ballad Of Cable Hogue, The Hawaiians, **70**; A Time For Dying, **71**; The Getaway, Junior Bonner, **72**; Lady Ice, **73**; Three The Hard Way, **74**; Breakout, **75**; Drum, Mikey And Nicky, St Ives, **76**; Rabbit Test, **78**.

BALLHAUS, MICHAEL: Whity, **70**; Beware Of A Holy Whore, Sand, **71**; The Bitter Tears Of Petra Von Kant, **72**; Martha, **74**; Fox And His Friends **75**; Adolf & Marlene, Chinese Roulette, Satan's Brew, **76**; Frauen In New York, The Stationmaster's Wife, **77**; The Marriage Of Maria Braun, **78**; Despair, **79**; Dear Mr Wonderful, **82**; Baby It's You, **83**; After Hours, Private Conversations, **85**; The Color Of Money, Under The Cherry Moon, **86**; Broadcast News, The Glass Menagerie, **87**; Dirty Rotten Scoundrels, The House On Carroll Street, The Last Temptation Of Christ, Working Girl, **88**; The Fabulous Baker Boys, **89**; GoodFellas, Postcards From The Edge, **90**; Guilty By Suspicion, What About Bob?, **91**; Bram Stoker's Dracula, The Mambo Kings, **92**; The Age Of Innocence, **93**; I'll Do Anything, **94**, Sleepers, **96**; Primary Colors, **97**; Air Force One, **97**.

BANCROFT, ANNE: Don't Bother To Knock, **52**; Tonight We Sing, **53**; Demetrius And The Gladiators, Gorilla At Large, The Raid, **54**; The Naked Street, New York Confidential, **55**; Nightfall, **56**; The Girl In Black Stockings, **57**; The Miracle Worker, **62**; The Pumpkin Eater, **64**; The Slender Thread, **65**; Seven Women, **66**; The Graduate, **67**; Young Winston, **72**; The Hindenburg, The Prisoner Of Second Avenue, **75**; Lipstick, Silent Movie, **76**; The Turning Point, **77**; The Elephant Man, Fatso, **80**; To Be Or Not To Be, **83**; Garbo Talks, **84**; Agnes Of God, **85**; 84 Charing Cross Road, **87**; Torch Song Trilogy, **88**; Bert Rigby You're A Fool, **89**; Honeymoon In Vegas, **92**; Malice, Mr Jones, Point Of No Return, **93**, Home For The Holidays, How To Make An American Quit, **95**; Great Expectations, **97**; GI Jane, **97**.

BANKY, VILMA: Im Letzten Augenblick, **20**; Das Auge Des Toten, Galathea, **21**; Schattenkinder Des Glucks, **22**; Das Schone Abenteuer, Das Verbotene Land, Hotel Potemkin, King Of The Circus, **24**; The Dark Angel, The Eagle, **25**; The Son Of The Sheik, The Winning Of Barbara Worth, **26**; Magic Flame, The Night Of Love, **27**; The Awakening, Two Lovers, **28**; This Is Heaven, **29**; A Lady To Love, Sunkissed, **30.**

BARA, THEDA: A Fool There Was, **15**; Carmen, Romeo And Juliet, Serpent Of The Nile, The Vixen, **16**; The Tiger Woman, **17**; Camille, Cleopatra, Madame Du Barry, Salome, The She-Devil, The Soul Of Buddha, Under The Yoke, When A Woman Sins, Kathleen Mavourneen, La Belle Russe, The Light, The Lure Of Ambition, The Siren Song, When Men Desire, A Woman There Was, **18**; The Unchastened Woman, **25**; Madame Mystery, **26**.

BARBERA, JOSEPH, AND HANNA, WILLIAM: Selection: Yankee Doodle Mouse, **43**; Mouse Trouble, **44**; Quiet Please, **45**; The Cat Concerto, **46**; Kitty Foiled, **47**; The Little Orphan, Professor Tom, **48**; Two Mouseketeers, **51**; Dangerous When Wet, **53**; Good Will To Men, Mouse For Sale, **55**; Invitation To The Dance, **56**; Life With Loopy, **60**; Just A Wolf At Heart, **62**; Hey There It's Yogi Bear, **64**; Project X, **68**; Charlotte's Web, **73**; Mother, Jugs And Speed, **76**; Chomps, **79**; Attack Of The Phantoms, **80**; Heidi's Song, **82**; Escape From Grumble Gulch, **84**; Gobots: Battle Of The Rock Lords, **86**; Jetsons: The Movie, **90**; Tom And Jerry: The Movie, **92**; The Flintstones, **94**.

BARDEM, JUAN ANTONIO: The Happy Pair, **51**; Welcome Mr Marshall, **52**; Death Of A Cyclist, **55**; Calle Mayor, **56**; Pantaloons, **57**; Vengeance, **58**; Sonatas, **59**; A Las Cinco De La Tarde, **60**; Los Inocentes, **62**; Nunca Pasa Nada, **63**; The Uninhibited, **65**; El Ultimo Dia De La Guerra, **69**; Varietes, **71**; Behind The Shutters, La Corrupcion De Chris Miller, **73**; The Mysterious Island Of Captain Nemo, **74**; El Poder Del Deseo, **76**; The Long Weekend, **77**; Siete Dias De Enero, **79**; La Huela Delcrimen, **86**; Lorca La Muerte De Un Poeta, **87**.

BARDOT, BRIGITTE: The Girl In The Bikini, Manina La Fille Sans Voile, Act Of Love, **53**; Tradita, **54**; Doctor At Sea, Frou-frou, Futures Vedettes, **55**; And Woman Was Created, The Bride Is Much Too Beautiful, Mam'selle Pigalle, Nero's Mistress, Mam'selle Striptease, **56**; Une Parisienne, **57**; Love Is My Profession, **58**; Babette Goes To War, The Testament Of Orpheus, **59**; La Vérité, **60**; La Vie Privée, **62**; Le Mépris, **63**; Une Ravissante Idiote, **64**; Viva Maria!, **65**; Masculin-Féminin, **66**; Two Weeks In September, **67**; Shalako, Spirits Of The Dead, **68**; Les Femmes, **69**; The Bear And The Doll, Les Novices, **70**; Si Don Juan Etait Une Femme, **73**.

BARKER, W G: Selection: The Anarchist's Doom, Henry VIII, **11**; Hamlet **12**; East Lynne, The Great Bullion Robbery, Greater Love Hath No Man, London By Night, Sixty Years A Queen, **13**; The Fighting Parson, Lights Of London, **14**; Jane Shore, **15**; She, Trapped By London Sharks, **16**.

BARRAULT, JEAN-LOUIS: Les Beaux Jours, **35**; Jenny, The Life And Loves Of Beethoven, Mayerling, Street Of Shadows, **36**; Drôle De Drame, Mirages, The Pearls Of The Crown, **37**; Orage, **38**; La Symphonie Fantastique, **42**; Les Enfants Du Paradis, **45**; D'Homme A Hommes, **48**; La Ronde, **50**; The Longest Day, **62**; Chappaqua, **66**; La Nuit De Varennes **82**; Jean-Louis Barrault – A Man Of The Theatre, **84**; La Lumière Du Lac, **88**.

BARRYMORE, ETHEL: The Divorcée, **09**; The Nightingale, **14**; The Final Judgment, **15**; Our Mrs McChesney, **18**; Rasputin And The Empress **32**; None But The Lonely Heart, **44**; The Spiral Staircase, **46**; Night Song, **47**; Moonrise, The Paradine Case, Portrait Of Jennie, **48**; The Great Sinner, Pinky, **49**; It's A Big Country, Kind Lady, **51**; Deadline USA, Just For You, **52**; The Story Of Three Loves, **53**; Young At Heart, **54**; Johnny Trouble, **57**.

BARRYMORE, JOHN: An American Citizen, **13**; Raffles, Dr Jekyll And Mr Hyde, **20**; The Lotus Eater, **21**; Sherlock Holmes, **22**; Beau Brummell, **24**; Don Juan, The Sea Beast, **26**; When A Man Loves, **27**; Tempest, **28**; Eternal Love, The Show Of Shows, **29**; Moby Dick, **30**; The Mad Genius, Svengali, **31**; Arsene Lupin, A Bill Of Divorcement, Grand Hotel, Rasputin And The Empress, **32**; Dinner At Eight, Night Flight, Reunion In Vienna, Topaze, **33**; Twentieth Century, **34**; Romeo And Juliet, **36**; Bulldog Drummond Comes Back, Bulldog Drummond's Revenge, Maytime, True Confession, **37**; Bulldog Drummond's Peril, Hold That Co-ed, Marie Antoinette, Spawn Of The North, **38**; Midnight, **39**; The Great Profile, **40**; The Invisible Woman, Playmates, **41**.

BARRYMORE, LIONEL: Friends, **09**; Judith of Bethulia, **11**; Sadie Thompson, **28**; Fascination, **30**; A Free Soul, **31**; Mata Hari, **32**; Anna Karenina, David Copperfield, **35**; The Devil Is A Sissy, Little Lord Fauntleroy, Lloyd's Of London, Professional Soldier, **36**; Captains Courageous, **37**; Kidnapped, Young Dr Kildare plus all sequels, **38**; Swiss Family Robinson, Tom Brown's School Days, **40**; Naval Academy, **41**; Cadets On Parade, Junior Army, **42**; The Town Went Wild, **44**; Duel In The Sun, It's A Wonderful Life, **46**; Sarge Goes To College, Sepia Cinderella, **47**; Key Largo, **48**; Down To The Sea In Ships, **49**; Main Street To Broadway, **53.**

BARTHELMESS, RICHARD: Gloria's Romance, War Brides, Snow White, **16**; Bab's Diary, The Eternal Sin, For Valor, The Seven Swans, The Valentine Girl, **17**; Hit-the-trail Holliday, Rich Man Poor Man, **18**; Boots, Broken Blossoms, The Girl Who Stayed Home, Peppy Polly, Scarlet Days, Three Men And A Girl, The Hope Chest, **19**; The Idol Dancer, Way Down East, **20**; Experience, Tol'able David, **21**; The Bond Boy, Just A Song At Twilight, Sonny, **22**; The Bright Shawl, The Fighting Blade, Fury, Twenty-One, **23**; Classmates, The Enchanted Cottage, **24**; The Beautiful City, Shore Leave, Soul-fire, **25**; The Amateur Gentleman, Just Suppose, The White Black Sheep, **26**; The Drop Kick, The Patent Leather Kid, **27**; The Noose, Scarlet Seas, Wheel Of Chance, **28**; Drag, The Show Of Shows, Weary River, Young Nowheres, **29**; The Lash, The Dawn Patrol, Son Of The Gods, **30**; The Finger Points, The Last Flight, **31**; Alias The Doctor, The Cabin In The Cotton, **32**; Central Airport, Heroes For Sale, **33**; Midnight Alibi, A Modern Hero, **34**; Four Hours To Kill, **35**; Spy Of Napoleon, **36**; Only Angels Have Wings, **39**; The Man Who Talked Too Much, **40**; The Mayor Of 44th Street, The Spoilers, **42.**

BARTHOLOMEW, FREDDIE: Fascination, **30**; Lily Christine, **32**; Anna Karenina, David Copperfield, **35**; The Devil Is A Sissy, Little Lord Fauntleroy, Lloyd's Of London, Professional Soldier, **36**; Captains Courageous, **37**; Kidnapped, Listen Darling, Lord Jeff, **38**; Spirit Of Culver, Two Bright Boys, **39**; Swiss Family Robinson, Tom Brown's School Days **40**; Naval Academy, **41**; Cadets On Parade, A Yank At Eton, **42**; The Town Went Wild, **44**; Sarg Goes To College, Sepia Cinderella, **47**; St Benny The Dip, **51**.

BASEHART, RICHARD: Cry Wolf, Repeat Performance, **47**; He Walked By Night, **48**; Reign Of Terror, Roseanna McCoy, Tension, **49**; Outside The Wall, **50**; Decision Before Dawn, Fixed Bayonets, Fourteen Hours, The House On Telegraph H **51**; Titanic, **53**; Avanzi Di Galera, The Good Die Young, La Strada, La Mano Dello Straniero, **54**; Canyon Crossroads, La Vena D'Oro, Il Bidone, **55**; The Intimate Stranger, Moby Dick, **56**; Arrivederci Dimas, Time Limit, **57**; The Brothers Karamazov, **58**; Jons Und Erdme, **59**; 5 Branded Women, For The Love Of Mike, Portrait In Black, Visa To Canton, **60**; Hitler, The Savage Guns **62**; Kings Of The Sun, **63**; Four Days In November, **64**; The Satan Bug, **65**; Chato's Land, Rage, **7** And Millions Will Die, **73**; The Terror Of Dr Chancey, **75**; The Island Of Dr Moreau, Shenanigans, **77**; Being There, **79**; Bix, **81**.

BASINGER, KIM: Hard Country, **81**; Mother Lode **82**; The Man Who Loved Women, Never Say Never Again, **83**; The Natural, **84**; Fool For Love, **85**; 9½ Weeks, No Mercy, **86**; Blind Date, Nadine, **87**; My Stepmother Is An Alien, **88**; Batman, **8** The Marrying Man, **91**; Cool World, Final Analysis, **92**; The Real McCoy, Wayne's Wo 2, **93**; The Getaway, Prêt-A-Porter, **95**; LA Confidential, **97.**

BATES, ALAN: It's Never Too Late, **56**; The Entertainer, **60**; Whistle Down The Win **61**; A Kind Of Loving, **62**; The Running Man, **63**; The Guest/The Caretaker, Nothin But The Best, Zorba The Greek, **64**; Georgy Girl, King Of Hearts **66**; Far From Th Madding Crowd, Hands Up!, **67**; The Fixer, **68**; Women In Love, **69**; Three Sisters, **70**; The Go-Between, **71**; A Day In The Death Of Joe Egg, **72**; Butley, **74**; Ir Celebration, Royal Flash, **75**; The Shout, An Unmarried Woman, **78**; The Rose, **79**; Nijinsky, **80**; Quartet, The Return Of The Soldier, **81**; Britannia Hospital, **82**; Dr Fischer Of Geneva, An Englishman Abroad, The Wicked Lady, **83**; Duet For On **86**; A Prayer For The Dying, **87**; We Think The World Of You, **88**; Force Majeure **89**; 102 Boulevard Haussmann, Docteur M, Hamlet, Mister Frost, **90**; Entre Chien Et Loup, Secret Friends, **92**; Silent Tongue, **94**.

BAXTER, ANNE: Twenty-Mule Team, The Great Profile, **40**; Charley's Aunt, Swan Water, **41**; The Magnificent Ambersons, The Pied Piper, **42**; Crash Dive, Five Graves To Cairo, The North Star **43**; Guest In The House, The Fighting Sullivans, Sunday Dinner For A Soldier, **44**; A Royal Scandal, **45**; Angel On My Shoulder, The Razor's Edge, Smoky, **46**; Blaze Of Noon, Mother Wore Tights, **47**; Homecomir The Luck Of The Irish, The Walls Of Jericho, Yellow Sky, **48**; You're My Everythi **49**; All About Eve, A Ticket To Tomahawk, **50**; Follow The Sun, **51**; My Wife's Best Friend, O Henry's Full House, The Outcasts Of Poker Flat, **52**; The Blue Gardenia, I Confess, **53**; Carnival Story, **54**; Bedevilled, One Desire, The Spoilers, **5** The Come-on, The Ten Commandments, Three Violent People, **56**; Chase A Crooked Shadow, **58**; Cimarron, Summer Of The Seventeenth Doll, **60**; Walk On The Wild Sic **62**; The Family Jewels, **65**; Frauen, Die Durch Die Holle Gehen, **66**; The Busy Body **67**; Fools' Parade, The Late Liz, **71**; Jane Austen In Manhattan, **80**; The Architecture Of Frank Lloyd Wright, **83**; Hitchcock, The Thrill Of Genius, **85**.

BAXTER, WARNER: All Woman, **18**; Cheated Hearts, The Love Charm, **21**; If I Were Queen, **22**; In Search Of A Thrill, **23**; Alimony, The Female, The Garden Of Weeds, **24**; The Air Mail, The Awful Truth, The Golden Bed, **25**; The Great Gats Mannequin, Miss Brewster's Millions, **26**; The Coward, Drums Of The Desert, Singed, **27**; Craig's Wife, Ramona, Three Sinners, West Of Zanzibar, **28**; Behind That Curtain, Happy Days, In Old Arizona, Romance Of The Rio Grande, **29**; The Arizo d, Renegades, **30**; The Cisco Kid, addy Long Legs, The Squaw Man, **31**; Six ours To Live, **32**; 42nd Street, enthouse, **33**; Broadway Bill, **34**; King Of urlesque, One More Spring, **35**; The risoner Of Shark Island, The Road To Glory, he Robin Hood Of El Dorado, **36**; Slave hip, Vogues, Wife Doctor And Nurse, Daro Un ilione, Kidnapped, **38**; Barricade, The eturn Of The Cisco Kid, **39**; Earthbound, **0**; Adam Had Four Sons, **41**; Crime octor, **43**; Lady In The Dark, **44**; Just Before awn, **46**; Prison Warden, **49**; State enitentiary, **50**.

AYE, NATHALIE: Day For Night, Two eople, **73**; La Gueule Ouverte, The Slap, **74**; a Jalousie, Un Jour La Fête, **75**; La ernière Femme, Mado, **76**; The Man Who oved Women, Monsieur Papa, **77**; La hambre Verte, Mon Premier Amour, **78**; hort Memory, **79**; Sauve Qui Peut, The rl From Lorraine, Je Vais Craquer!, Une emaine De Vacances, **80**; Beau Père, ombre Rouge, **81**; I Married A Shadow, La alance, Le Retour De Martin Guerre, **2**; Notre Histoire, Rive Droite Rive Gauche, **4**; Beethoven's Nephew, Detective, une De Miel, **85**; De Guerre Lasse, **87**; En oute Innocence, **88**; Giocodi Massacro, a Baule Les Pins, The Man Inside, Un eekend Sur Deux, **90**; La Voix, **92**; e, **93**.

EART, EMMANUELLE: Demain Les ames, **76**; L'Enfant Trouvé, **84**; Manon es Sources, **86**; Date With An Angel, **7**; À Gauche En Sortant De L'ascenseur **88**; hildren Of Chaos, **89**; The Voyage Of aptain Fracassa, **90**; J'embrasse Pas, La elle Noiseuse, Divertimento, **91**; gainst Oblivion, Un Coeur En Hiver, **93**; Enfer, **94**, Nelly & Monsieur Arnaud , **5**; Mission: Impossible, **96**.

EATLES, THE: A Hard Day's Night, **4**; Help!, **65**; How I Won The War (Lennon), **7**; Candy (Starr), Yellow Submarine oices), **68**; The Magic Christian (Starr), **69**; et It Be, **70**; Blindman (Starr), Concert or Bangladesh (Starr and Harrison), Oh alcutta! (Lennon), **72**; Son Of Dracula tarr), That'll Be The Day (Starr), **74**; sztomania (Starr), **75**; The Last Waltz tarr), Sextette (Starr), **78**; Caveman tarr), **81**.

EATTY, WARREN: The Roman Spring f Mrs Stone, Splendor In The Grass, **61**; All all Down, **62**; Lilith, **64**; Mickey One, **5**; Kaleidoscope, Promise Her Anything, **66**; onnie And Clyde, **67**; The Only Game Town, **70**; McCabe And Mrs Miller, **71**; ollars, **72**; The Parallax View, **74**; The ortune, Shampoo, **75**; Heaven Can Wait, **8**; Reds, **81**; Ishtar, The Pick-up Artist, **7**; Dick Tracy, **90**; Bugsy, Madonna Truth Or are, **91**; Love Affair, **94**, Bulworth, **97**.

ECKER, JACQUES: L'or de Cristobal, **9**; Dernier Atout, **42**; Goupi Mains Rouges, **3**; Falbalas, **45**; Antoine Et Antoinette, **7**; Rendez-vous de Juillet, **48**; Edouard et aroline, **51**; Casque d'Or, **52**; Grisbi ue De L'Estrapade, Touchez Pas Au Grisbi, **3**; Ali Baba, **54**; Les Aventures Arsène Lupin, **57**; Modigliani Of ontparnasse, The Lovers of ontparnasse, **58**; Le Trou **60**.

EERY, WALLACE: The Fable Of The ush League Lover Who Failed To Qualify, The um Tree, Sweedie At The Fair (and the st of the Sweedie series), **14-15**; The roken Pledge, The Slim Princess, A ash Of Courage, Teddy At The Throttle, **16**; actus Nell, Patria, **17**; Johanna Enlists, **8**; The Life Line, The Love Burglar, Victory, **9**; The Last Of The Mohicans, The ollycoddle, **20**; The Four Horsemen Of The pocalypse, **21**; Robin Hood, The osary, **22**; Bavu, Drifting, The Flame Of Life, hite Tiger, **23**; The Sea Hawk, So Big, **4**; Adventure, The Lost World, The Pony xpress, **25**; Behind The Front, Old onsides, We're In The Navy Now, **26**; Casey The Bat, Now We're In The Air, **27**; he Big Killing, Partners In Crime, **28**; hinatown Nights, River Of Romance, **9**; The Big House, Billy The Kid, A Lady's orals, Min And Bill, Way For A Sailor, **0**; The Champ, The Secret Six, **31**; Flesh, rand Hotel, Hell Divers, **32**; The owery, Dinner At Eight, Tugboat Annie, **33**; he Mighty Barnum, Treasure Island, va Villa!, **34**; Ah Wilderness, China Seas, est Point Of The Air, **35**; A Message To arcia, **36**; Slave Ship, **37**; Bad Man Of rimstone, Port Of Seven Seas, Stablemates, **38**; Sergeant Madden, Stand Up And Fight, Thunder Afloat, **39**; Twenty-Mule Team, The Man From Dakota, Wyoming, **40**; The Bad Man, Barnacle Bill, The Bugle Sounds, **41**; Jackass Mail, **42**; Salute To The Marines, **43**; Barbary Coast Gent, Rationing, **44**; This Man's Navy, **45**; Bad Bascomb, The Mighty Mcgurk, **46**; Alias A Gentleman, A Date With Judy, **48**; Big Jack, **49**.

BEINEIX, JEAN-JACQUES: Diva, **81**; La Lune Dans Le Caniveau, **83**; Betty Blue **86**; Le Grand Cirque, Roselyne Et Les Lions, **89**; IP5: The Island Of Pachyderms, **92**; Otaku, **94**.

BELL, MONTA: The Pilgrim **23**; Broadway After Dark, How To Educate A Wife, The Snob **24**; Lady Of The Night, Pretty Ladies, The King On Main Street, Lights Of Old Broadway **25**; The Torrent, The Boy Friend, Upstage **26**; After Midnight, Man Woman and Sin **27**; Bellamy Trial, The Letter, **29**; Young Man Of Manhattan, East Is West **30**; The Fires Of Youth, Up For Murder, Personal Maid **31**; Downstairs **32**; The Worst Woman In Paris? **33**; China's Little Devils, **45.**

BELMONDO, JEAN-PAUL: Be Beautiful But Shut Up, **57**; Charlotte Et Son Jules, Les Tricheurs, Drôle De Dimanche, **58**; Ein Engel Auf Erden, Breathless/A Bout De Souffle, Web Of Passion/Leda, **59**; The Big Risk, Moderato Cantabile, Rita, Une Femme Est Une Femme, **60**; Backfire, La Rocca, Love And The Frenchwoman, Two Women, Léon Morin – Priest, **61**; La Viaccia, A Monkey In Winter, **62**; Le Doulos, L'Aine Des Ferchaux, Dragées Au Poivre, **63**; Cartouche, Cent Milles Dollars Au Soleil, Man Hunt, That Man From Rio, **64**; Banana Peel, Pierrot Le Fou, Les Tribulations D'Un Chinois En Chine, Weekend At Dunkirk, **65**; Is Paris Burning?, Tendre Voyou, **66**; Casino Royale, Le Voleur, **67**; The Brain, Un Homme Qui Me Plait, Mississippi Mermaid, **69**; Borsalino, Les Maries De L'An Deux, **70**; Le Casse, High Heels, The Inheritor, La Scoumoune, **72**; Le Magnifique, Stavisky **74**; L'Incorrigible, Night Caller, **75**; L'Alpageur, Le Corps De Mon Ennemi, **76**; L'Animal, **77**; Flic Ou Voyou, **79**; Le Marginal **83**; Joyeuses Paques, **84**; Hold-up, **85**; Le Solitaire, **87**; Itinéraire D'Un Enfant Gâté, **88**; Stranger In The House, **92**, Les Miserables, **95**; Desire, **96.**

BELUSHI, JOHN: Shame Of The Jungle, **75**; Goin' South, National Lampoon's Animal House, **78**; 1941, Old Boyfriends, **79**; The Blues Brothers, **80**; Continental Divide, Neighbors, **81**.

BENCHLEY, ROBERT: The Sex Life Of The Polyp, The Treasurer's Report, **28**; The Sport Parade, **32**; Dancing Lady, Headline Shooters, **33**; The Social Register, **34**; China Seas, Murder On A Honeymoon, **35**; Piccadilly Jim, **36**; Live Love And Learn, The Romance Of Digestion, **37**; How To Eat (and a series of How To shorts), **39**; Foreign Correspondent, Hired Wife, **40**; Bedtime Story, The Reluctant Dragon, Nice Girl?, You'll Never Get Rich, **41**; I Married A Witch, The Major And The Minor, Take A Letter Darling, **42**; Flesh And Fantasy, The Sky's The Limit, Song Of Russia, Young And Willing, **43**; Practically Yours, See Here Private Hargrove, **44**; It's In The Bag, Kiss And Tell, Road To Utopia, Weekend At The Waldorf, **45**; The Bride Wore Boots, Janie Gets Married, **46**.

BENJAMIN, RICHARD: Goodbye Columbus, **69**; Catch-22, Diary Of A Mad Housewife, **70**; The Marriage Of A Young Stockbroker, The Steagle, **71**; Portnoy's Complaint, **72**; The Last Of Sheila, Westworld, **73**; The Sunshine Boys, **75**; House Calls, **78**; Love At First Bite, Scavenger Hunt, **79**; First Family, How To Beat The High Co$t Of Living, The Last Married Couple In America, Witches' Brew, **80**; Saturday The 14th, **81**; My Favorite Year, **82**; City Heat, Racing With The Moon, **84**; The Money Pit, **86**; Little Nikita, My Stepmother Is An Alien, **88**; Mermaids, **90**; Made In America, **93**; Milk Money, **94**; Mrs Winterbourne, **96**.

BENNETT, JOAN: Power, **28**; Bulldog Drummond, Disraeli, The Mississippi Gambler, Three Live Ghosts, **29**; Crazy That Way, Maybe It's Love, Moby Dick, Puttin' On The Ritz, Scotland Yard, **30**; Doctors' Wives, Hush Money, Many A Slip, **31**; The Careless Lady, Me And My Gal, She Wanted A Millionaire, The Trial Of Vivienne Ware, Weekends Only, Wild Girl, **32**; Arizona To Broadway, Little Women, **33**; The Man Who Reclaimed His Head, The Pursuit Of Happiness, **34**; The Man Who Broke The Bank At Monte Carlo, Mississippi, Private Worlds, She Couldn't Take It, Two For Tonight, **35**; Big Brown Eyes, Thirteen Hours By Air, Two In A Crowd, Wedding Present, **36**; Vogues Of 38, **37**; Artists And Models Abroad, I Met My Love Again, The Texans, Trade Winds, **38**; The Housekeeper's Daughter, The Man In The Iron Mask, **39**; Green Hell, The House Across The Bay, The Man I Married, The Son Of Monte Cristo, **40**; Confirm Or Deny, Man Hunt, She Knew All The Answers, Wild Geese Calling, **41**; Girl Trouble, Twin Beds, The Wife Takes A Flyer, **42**; Margin For Error, **43**; The Woman In The Window, **44**; Colonel Effingham's Raid, Nob Hill, Scarlet Street, **45**; The Macomber Affair, The Woman On The Beach, **47**; Hollow Triumph, The Secret Beyond The Door, **48**; The Reckless Moment, **49**; Father Of The Bride, For Heaven's Sake, **50**; Father's Little Dividend, The Guy Who Came Back, **51**; Highway Dragnet, **54**; We're No Angels, **55**; Navy Wife, There's Always Tomorrow, **56**; Desire In The Dust, **60**; House Of Dark Shadows, **70**; Suspiria, **77**.

BENTON, ROBERT: Bonnie And Clyde, **67**; There Was A Crooked Man, **70**; Bad Company, Oh! Calcutta!, What's Up Doc?, **72**; The Late Show, **77**; Superman, **78**; Kramer Vs Kramer, **79**; Still Of The Night, **82**; Places In The Heart, **84**; Nadine, **87**; Billy Bathgate, **91**; Nobody's Fool, **95.**

BERESFORD, BRUCE: The Adventures Of Barry McKenzie, **72**; Barry McKenzie Holds His Own, **74**; Don's Party, **76**; The Getting Of Wisdom, **77**; Blue Fin, Money Movers, **78**; Breaker Morant, The Club, **80**; Fortress, Puberty Blues, **81**; Tender Mercies, **83**; King David, **85**; Crimes Of The Heart, The Fringe Dwellers, **86**; Aria, **88**; Driving Miss Daisy, Her Alibi, **89**; Black Robe, Mister Johnson, **91**; Rich In Love, **93**, Silent Fall, **95**; A Good man in Africa, **94**; Last Dance, **96**; Paradise Road, **97**.

BERGEN, CANDICE: The Group, The Sand Pebbles, **66**; The Day The Fish Came Out, Vivre Pour Vivre, **67**; The Magus, **68**; Getting Straight, Soldier Blue, **70**; Carnal Knowledge, The Hunting Party, T R Baskin, **71**; 11 Harrowhouse, **74**; Bite The Bullet, The Wind And The Lion, **75**; The Domino Principle, **77**; A Night Full Of Rain, Oliver's Story, **78**; Starting Over, **79**; Rich And Famous, **81**; Gandhi, **82**; Stick, **85**.

BERGMAN, INGMAR: Kris, **45**; Det Regnar Pa Var Karlek, **46**; Skepp Till India Land, **47**; Eva, Night Is My Future, Port Of Call, **48**; The Devil's Wanton, Three Strange Loves, Till Gladje, **49**; Sant Hander Inte Har, **50**; Divorced, Summer Interlude, **51**; Secrets Of Women, Summer With Monika, **52**; Sawdust And Tinsel, **53**; A Lesson In Love, **54**; Journey Into Autumn, Smiles Of A Summer Night, **55**; The Seventh Seal, Wild Strawberries, **57**; Brink Of Life, The Magician, **58**; The Virgin Spring, **59**; Brollopsdagen, The Devil's Eye, **60**; Through A Glass Darkly, Winter Light, **62**; The Silence, **63**; Now About All These Women, **64**; Persona, **66**; Stimulantia, **67**; Hour Of The Wolf, Shame, **68**; The Passion Of Anna, The Ritual, **69**; The Faro Documentary, **70**; The Touch, **71**; Cries And Whispers, **72**; Scenes From A Marriage, **73**; The Magic Flute, **74**; Face To Face, **76**; Autumn Sonata, The Serpent's Egg, **78**; Faro Document, **79**; From The Life Of The Marionettes **80**; Fanny And Alexander, **83**; After The Rehearsal, **84**; Dokument Fanny Och Alexander, **86.**

BERGMAN, INGRID: The Count From The Monk's Bridge, **34**; Branningar, Munkbrogreven, The Surf, Swedenhielms, Walpurgis Night, **35**; Intermezzo, On The Sunny Side, **36**; Die 4 Gesellen, Dollar, A Woman's Face, A Night In June, One Single Night, **38**; Intermezzo,**39**; Adam Had Four Sons, Dr Jekyll And Mr Hyde, Rage In Heaven, **41**; Casablanca, **42**; For Whom The Bell Tolls, **43**; Gaslight, Swedes In America, **44**; The Bells Of St Mary's, Saratoga Trunk, Spellbound, **45**; Notorious, **46**; Arch Of Triumph, Joan Of Arc, **48**; Under Capricorn, **49**; Stromboli, **50**; The Greatest Love, **51**; Strangers, We The Women, **53**; Joan At The Stake, **54**; Fear, **55**; Anastasia, Paris Does Strange Things, Elena Et Les Hommes, **56**; Indiscreet, The Inn Of The Sixth Happiness, **58**; Aimez-vous Brahms?, **61**; The Visit, **64**; The Yellow Rolls-Royce, **65**; Stimulantia, **67**; Cactus Flower, **69**; Langlois, Walk In The Spring Rain, **70**; From The Mixed-Up Files Of Mrs Basil E Frankweiler, **73**; Murder On The Orient Express, **74**; A Matter Of Time, **76**; Autumn Sonata, **78**.

BERGNER, ELISABETH: Der Evangelimann, **23**; Nju, **24**; Violinist Of Florence, **26**; Liebe, Königin Luise, **27**; Dona Juana, **28**; Fraulein Else, **29**; Ariane, **31**; Melo, **32**; The Rise Of Catherine The Great, **34**; Escape Me Never, **35**; As You Like It, **36**; Dreaming Lips, **37**; A Stolen Life, **39**; Paris Calling, **41**; Die Glückliche Jahre Der Thorwalds, **62**; Cry Of The Banshee, **70**; The Pedestrian, **74**; Der Pfingstausflug, **78**.

BERKELEY, BUSBY: Whoopee!, **30**; Palmy Days, **31**; Bird Of Paradise, The Kid From Spain, **32**; 42nd Street, Footlight Parade, Gold Diggers Of 1933, Roman Scandals, She Had To Say Yes, **33**; Dames, Fashions, **34**; Bright Lights, Gold Diggers Of 1935, I Live For Love, In Caliente, Stars Over Broadway, **35**; Gold Diggers Of 1937, Stage Struck, **36**; The Go Getter, Hollywood Hotel, The Singing Marine, Varsity Show, **37**; Comet Over Broadway, Garden Of The Moon, Gold Diggers In Paris, Men Are Such Fools, **38**; Babes In Arms, Fast And Furious, They Made Me A Criminal, **39**; Forty Little Mothers, Strike Up The Band, **40**; Babes On Broadway, Blonde Inspiration, **41**; For Me And My Gal, **42**; The Gang's All Here, **43**; Cinderella Jones, **46**; Take Me Out To The Ball Game, **49**; Million Dollar Mermaid, **52**; Easy To Love, Small Town Girl, **53**; Rose Marie, **54**; Jumbo, **62**.

BERLANGA, LUIS GARCIA: That Happy Pair, Welcome Mr Marshall, **51**;**52**; Novio A La Vista, **53**; Los Gancheros, **55**; Calabuig, **56**; Los Jueves Milagro, **58**; Placido, **61**; Les Quatre Vérités **62**; The Executioner/El Verdugo, **63**; Las Piranas, **67**; Vivan Los Novios!, **70**; Grandeur Nature/Life Size, **77**; The National Shotgun, **78**; The Heifer, **85**; Moros Y Cristianos, **87**; Todos A La Carcel/Everyone Off To Jail, **94**.

BERLIN, IRVING: Stop Look And Listen, **26**; The Jazz Singer, **27**; Hallelujah, **29**; Mammy, **30**; Reaching For The Moon, **31**; Top Hat, **35**; Follow The Fleet, **36**; On The Avenue, **37**; Alexander's Ragtime Band, Carefree, **38**; Second Fiddle, **39**; Louisiana Purchase, **41**; Holiday Inn, **42**; This Is The Army, **43**; Christmas Holiday, **44**; Blue Skies, **46**; Easter Parade, **48**; Annie Get Your Gun, **50**; Call Me Madam, **53**; There's No Business Like Show Business, White Christmas, **54**; Sayonara, **57**.

BERMAN, PANDRO S: Bad Company, **31**; Aggie Appleby, Maker Of Men, Ann Vickers, Morning Glory, One Man's Journey, **33**; The Age Of Innocence, By Your Leave, The Fountain, The Gay Divorcée, Gridiron Flash, The Life Of Vergie Winters, The Little Minister, Man Of Two Worlds, Of Human Bondage, The Richest Girl In The World, Romance In Manhattan, Spitfire, Stingaree, This Man Is Mine, **34**; Alice Adams, Break Of Hearts, Freckles, I Dream Too Much, In Person, Laddie, Roberta, Star Of Midnight, Sylvia Scarlett, Top Hat, **35**; The Big Game, Follow The Fleet, Mary Of Scotland, Muss 'em Up, Swing Time, That Girl From Paris, Winterset, A Woman Rebels, **36**; A Damsel In Distress, Quality Street, Shall We Dance, The Soldier And The Lady/Michael Strogoff, Stage Door, **37**; Carefree, Having Wonderful Time, The Mad Miss Manton, Mother Carey's Chickens, Room Service, **38**; The Flying Irishman, The Hunchback Of Notre Dame, The Story Of Vernon And Irene Castle, **39**; Honky Tonk, Love Crazy, Ziegfeld Girl, **41**; Rio Rita, Somewhere I'll Find You, **42**; Slightly Dangerous, **43**; Dragon Seed, Marriage Is A Private Affair, National Velvet, The Seventh Cross, **44**; The Picture Of Dorian Gray, **45**; Undercurrent, **46**; If Winter Comes, Living In A Big Way, The Sea Of Grass, **47**; The Three Musketeers, **48**; The Bribe, The Doctor And The Girl, Madame Bovary, **49**; Father Of The Bride **50**; Father's Little Dividend, The Light Touch, Soldiers Three, **51**; Ivanhoe, The Prisoner Of Zenda, **52**; All The Brothers Were Valiant, Battle Circus, Knights Of The Round Table, **53**; The Long Long Trailer, **54**; Blackboard Jungle, Quentin Durward **55**; Bhowani Junction, Tea And Sympathy, **56**; Jailhouse Rock, Something Of Value, **57**; The Brothers Karamazov, The Reluctant Debutante, **58**; All The Fine Young Cannibals, Butterfield 8, **60**; Sweet Bird Of Youth, **62**; The Prize, **63**; Honeymoon Hotel, **64**; A Patch Of Blue, **65**; Justine, **69**; Move, **70**.

BERNSTEIN, ELMER: Never Wave At A WAC, Sudden Fear, **52**; Cat Women Of The Moon, Make Haste To Live, Miss Robin Crusoe, Silent Raiders, **54**; The Eternal Sea, It's A Dog's Life, The Man With The Golden Arm, Storm Fear, The View From Pompey's Head, **55**; The Ten Commandments, **56**; Drango, Fear Strikes Out, Men In War, The Naked Eye, Sweet Smell Of Success, The Tin Star, **57**; Anna Lucasta, The Buccaneer, Desire Under The Elms, God's Little Acre, Kings Go Forth, Some Came Running, **58**; The Miracle, The Story On Page One, **59**; From The Terrace, The Magnificent Seven, The Rat Race, **60**; By Love Possessed, The Comancheros, Summer And Smoke, The Young Doctors, **61**; Birdman Of Alcatraz, A Girl Named Tamiko, To Kill A Mockingbird, Walk On The Wild Side, **62**; The Caretakers, The Great Escape, Hud, Kings Of The Sun, Love With The Proper Stranger, Rampage, **63**; The Carpetbaggers, Four Days In November, The World Of Henry Orient, **64**; Baby The Rain Must Fall, The Hallelujah Trail, The Reward, The Sons Of Katie Elder, **65**; Seven Women, Cast A Giant Shadow, Hawaii, Return Of The Magnificent Seven, The Silencers, **66**; Thoroughly Modern Millie, **67**; I Love You, Alice B Toklas, The Scalphunters, **68**; The Gypsy Moths, A Run On Gold, True Grit, Where's Jack?, **69**; Cannon For Cordoba, The Liberation Of LB Jones, Walk In The Spring Rain, **70**; Big Jake, Doctors' Wives, See No Evil, **71**; The Magnificent Seven Ride!, **72**; Cahill US Marshal, Nightmare Honeymoon, **73**; Gold, McQ, The Trial Of Billy Jack, **74**; Report To The Commissioner, **75**; From Noon Till Three, The Incredible Sarah, The Shootist, **76**; Billy Jack Goes To Washington, **77**; Bloodbrothers, Casey's Shadow, National Lampoon's Animal House, **78**; The Great Santini, Meatballs, Moonraker, Zulu Dawn, **79**; Airplane!, The Blues Brothers, Saturn 3, **80**; An American Werewolf In London, The Chosen, Genocide, Going Ape!, Heavy Metal, Honky Tonk Freeway, Stripes, **81**; Airplane II: The Sequel, **82**; Class, Five Days One Summer, Making Michael Jackson's Thriller, Spacehunter: Adventures In The Forbidden Zone, Trading Places, **83**; Bolero, Ghostbusters, Prince Jack, **84**; The Black Cauldron, Marie Ward, **85**; The Color Of Money, Three Amigos!, **86**; Da, Funny Farm, The Good Mother, **88**; My Left Foot, Slipstream, **89**; The Field, The Grifters, Life Is Cheap But Toilet Paper Is Expensive, **90**; Oscar, A Rage In Harlem, Rambling Rose, **91**; The Babe, The Cemetery Club, **92**; The Age Of Innocence, The Good Son, Mad Dog And Glory, Lost In Yonkers, **93**; Jimmy Hollywood, **94**; Devil in a Blue Dress, **95**; Bulletproof, **96**.

BERRI, CLAUDE: Les Baiser **63**; La Chance Et L'amour **64**; Le Vieil Homme Et L'Enfant, **66**; Mezel Tov Ou Le Mariage, **68**; The Man With Connections, **70**; Le Cinéma De La Papa, **71**; Le Sex Shop, **73**; The Male Of The Century, **75**; La Première Fois, **76**; In A Wild Moment, **77**; Je Vous Aime, **81**; Tchao Pantin, Waiter!, **83**; Blame It On Rio, **84**; Jean De Florette, Manon Des Sources, **86**; Germinal, **93**; Lucie Aubrac, **97**

BERTOLUCCI, BERNARDO: La Commare Secca, **62**; Prima Della Rivoluzione, **64**; Love And Anger, **67**; Partner, **68**; The Spider's Stratagem, The Conformist, **70**; Last Tango In Paris, **72**; 1900, **77**; La Luna, **79**; Tragedy Of A Ridiculous Man, **81**; The Last Emperor, **87**; The Sheltering Sky, **90**; The Ditvoorst Domains, **93**; Little Buddha, **94**; Steraling Beauty, **96**.

BESSON, LUC: Le Dernier Combat, **84**; Subway, **85**; The Big Blue, **88**; Nikita, **90**; Atlantis, **91**;Point Of No Return, **93**; Léon, **94**; The Fifth Element, **97.**

BITZER, BILLY: Interior New York Subway (and six further shorts), **05**; The

Informer, 12; Judith Of Bethulia, 13; The Battle Of The Sexes, The Escape, Home Sweet Home, 14; The Birth Of A Nation, 15; Intolerance, 16; The Great Love, The Greatest Thing In Life, Hearts Of The World, 18; Broken Blossoms, The Girl Who Stayed At Home, The Greatest Question, A Romance Of Happy Valley, Scarlet Days, True Heart Susie, 19; The Idol Dancer, The Love Flower, Way Down East, 20; Orphans Of The Storm, Sure Fire Flint, 22; The White Rose, 23; America, 24; The Midnight Girl, 25; The Battle Of The Sexes, Drums Of Love, 28; Lady Of The Pavements, 29; Hotel Variety, 33.

BLACKTON, J STUART: The Burglar On The Roof (and countless other five-minute films for Edison), Raffles The Amateur Cracksman, The Adventures of Sherlock Holmes, 05; Antony And Cleopatra, Barbara Fritchie, Julius Caesar, Macbeth, The Merchant Of Venice, Richard III, Romeo And Juliet, Salome, 08; King Lear, Les Misérables, The Life Of Moses, A Midsummer Night's Dream, Oliver Twist, Ruy Blas, Saul And David, 09; Elektra, A Modern Cinderella, Uncle Tom's Cabin, 10; As You Like It, Cardinal Wolsey, 12; The Christian, 14; The Battle Cry Of Peace, 15; The Judgment House, Womanhood, 17; Safe For Democracy, World For Sale, 18; Life's Greatest Problem, The Littlest Scout, My Husband's Other Wife, 19; Forbidden Valley, The House Of The Tolling Bell, 20; The Glorious Adventure, A Gypsy Cavalier, 22; On The Banks Of The Wabash, The Virgin Queen, 23; Behold This Woman, The Beloved Brute, Between Friends, The Clean Heart, Let Not Man Put Asunder, 24; The Happy Warrior, The Redeeming Sin, Tides Of Passion, 25; Bride Of The Storm, The Gilded Highway, Hell-Bent For Heaven, The Passionate Quest, 26.

BLANC, MEL: Neptune's Daughter, 49; Champagne For Caesar, 50; Gay Purr-ee, 62; Kiss Me Stupid, 64; Buck Rogers In The 25th Century, Great American Bugs Bunny – Road Runner Chase, 79; The Looney Looney Looney Bugs Bunny Movie, 81; 1,001 Rabbit Tales, 82; Daffy Duck's Movie: Fantastic Island, Strange Brew, 83; Heathcliff: The Movie, Howard The Duck, Porky Pig In Hollywood, 86; Night Of The Living Duck, Who Framed Roger Rabbit, Bugs V Daffy, 88; Daffy Duck's Quackbusters, Entertaining The Troops, 89; Jetsons: The Movie, 90.

BLIER, BERNARD: Troix-six-neuf, Heart Of Paris, 37; Entrée Des Artistes, Hôtel Du Nord, Altitude 3.200, 38; L'Enfer Des Anges, Le Jour Se Lève, Nuit De Décembre, 39; Carmen, 42; Le Café Du Cedran, 46; Quai Des Orfèvres, 47; Dedée D'Anvers, D'Homme A Hommes, 48; L'Ecole Buissonnière, Les Casse-pieds, 49; La Souricière, 50; Sans Laisser D'Adresse, 51; Je L'Ai Eté Trois Fois, 52; Secrets D'Alcove, 54; Les Hussards, 55; Crime And Punishment, 56; Les Misérables, The Man In The Raincoat, 57; Les Grandes Familles, Sans Famille, Retour De Manivelle, 58; The Cat, The Great War/La Grande Guerra, The Tramp/Archimede Le Clochard, Marie-Octobre, 59; The Hunchback Of Rome/Il Gobbo, 60; The Counterfeiters Of Paris, Le Président, Arrêtez Les Tambours, 61; Le Septième Juré, 62; Germinal, The Organizer, 63; A Killing In Monte Carlo, Crimen, La Bonne Soupe, Les Barbouzes, 64; Casanova '70, 65; The Stranger, To Commit A Murder, 67; Mon Oncle Benjamin, 69; Appellez-moi Mathilde, Elle Boit Pas, Elle Fume Pas, Elle Drague Pas . . . Mais Elle Cause!, Jo, Laisse Aller, 70; Le Cri Du Cormoran Le Soir Au-dessus Des Jonques, Le Tueur, Man Of The Year/Homo Eroticus, To Catch A Spy, Les Doigts Croisés 71; Moi Y'En A Vouloir Des Sous, The Tall Blond Man With One Black Shoe, Tout Le Monde Il Est Beau, 72; Par Le Sang Des Autres, Bon Baisers A Lundi, Il Piatto Piange, 74; C'est Dur Pour Tout Le Monde, Ce Cher Victor, Calmos, Le Faux-cul, 75; Le Corps De Mon Ennemi, 76; Le Compromis, 78; Buffet Froid, Série Noire, 79; Passion D'Amore, Petrole Petrole, 81; Ça N'Arrive Qu'A Moi, Cuore, 84; Scemo Di Guerra, 85; Je Hais Les Acteurs, Twist Again A Moscou, 86; The Possessed/Les Possédes, 87; Mangeclous, 88; Paganini, 89.

BLIER, BERTRAND: Hitler Connais Pas, 63; Si J'Etais Un Espion, 67; Les Valseuses, 74; Cool, Calm And Collected, 75; Get Out Your Handkerchiefs, 78; Buffet Froid, 79; Beau Père, 81; My Best Friend's Girl/La Femme De Mon Pôte, 83; Notre Histoire, 84; Tenue De Soirée, 86; Trop Belle Pour Toi!, 89; Merci La Vie, 91; 1 2 3 Soleil, 93; Grosse Fatigue, 94; Mon Homme, 96.

BLONDELL, JOAN: Sinners' Holiday, 30; Blonde Crazy, My Past, God's Gift To Women, Illicit, Millie, Night Nurse, The Public Enemy, The Reckless Hour, 31; Big City Blues, Central Park, The Crowd Roars, The Famous Ferguson Case, The Greeks Had A Word For Them, Lawyer Man, Make Me A Star, Miss Pinkerton, Three On A Match, Union Depot, 32; Blondie Johnson, Broadway Bad, Convention City, Footlight Parade, Gold Diggers Of 1933, Goodbye Again, Havana Widows, 33; Dames, He Was Her Man, I've Got Your Number, The Kansas City Princess, 34; Broadway Gondolier, Miss Pacific Fleet, Travelling Saleslady, We're In The Money, 35; Bullets Or Ballots, Colleen, Gold Diggers Of 1937, Sons O' Guns, Stage Struck, Three Men On A Horse, 36; Back In Circulation, The King And The Chorus Girl, The Perfect Specimen, Stand-in, 37; There's Always A Woman, 38; Amazing Mr Williams, East Side Of Heaven, Good Girls Go To Paris, The Kid From Kokomo, Off The Record, 39; I Want A Divorce, Two Girls On Broadway, 40; Model Wife, Three Girls About Town, Topper Returns, 41; Lady For A Night, 42; Cry Havoc, 43; Adventure, Don Juan Quilligan, A Tree Grows In Brooklyn, 45; Women In Love, The Corpse Came COD, Nightmare Alley, 47; For Heaven's Sake, 50; The Blue Veil, 51; The Opposite Sex, 56; Desk Set, Lizzie, This Could Be The Night, Will Success Spoil Rock Hunter?, 57; Angel Baby, 61; Advance To The Rear, 64; The Cincinnati Kid, 65; Ride Beyond Vengeance, 66; Waterhole 3, 67; Kona Coast, Stay Away Joe, 68; Big Daddy, 69; The Phynx, 70; Support Your Local Gunfighter, 71; Opening Night, 77; Grease, 78; The Champ, 79; The Woman Inside, 81.

BLOOM, CLAIRE: Limelight, 52; Innocents In Paris, The Man Between, 53; Richard III, 55; Alexander The Great, 56; The Brothers Karamazov, The Buccaneer, 58; Look Back In Anger, Die Schachnovelle, The Royal Game, 60; The Chapman Report, The Wonderful World Of The Brothers Grimm, 62; The Haunting, 63; The Outrage, 64; The Spy Who Came In From The Cold, 65; Charly, 68; The Illustrated Man, Three Into Two Won't Go, 69; Red Sky At Morning, 70; A Severed Head, 71; A Doll's House, 73; Islands In The Stream, 77; Clash Of The Titans, 81; Deja Vu, 85; Sammy And Rosie Get Laid, 87; Crimes And Misdemeanors, 89; The Princess And The Goblin, 91; Mighty Aphrodite, 95.

BLUTH, DON: Robin Hood, 73; Pete's Dragon, The Rescuers, 77; The Secret Of NIMH, 82; An American Tail, 86; The Land Before Time, 88; All Dogs Go To Heaven, 89; Rock-a-doodle, 92; Thumbelina, 94; The Pebble & the Penguin, 94.

BOETTICHER, BUDD: The Missing Juror, One Mysterious Night, 44; Escape In The Fog, A Guy A Gal And A Pal, Youth On Trial, 45; Assigned To Danger, Behind Locked Doors, 48; Black Midnight, The Wolf Hunters, 49; Killer Shark, 50; The Bullfighter And The Lady, The Cimarron Kid, 51; Bronco Buster, Horizons West, Red Ball Express, 52; City Beneath The Sea, East Of Sumatra, The Man From The Alamo, Seminole, Wings Of The Hawk, 53; The Magnificent Matador, 55; The Killer Is Loose, Seven Men From Now, 56; Decision At Sundown, The Tall T, 57; Buchanan Rides Alone, 58; Ride Lonesome, Westbound, 59; Comanche Station, The Rise And Fall Of Legs Diamond, 60; A Time For Dying, 69; Arruza, 72; My Kingdom For . . . , 85.

BOGARDE, DIRK: Dancing With Crime, 47; Esther Waters, Once A Jolly Swagman, 48; Boys In Brown, Dear Mr. Prohack, Quartet, 49; The Blue Lamp, So Long At The Fair, The Woman In Question, 50; Blackmailed, Penny Princess, 51; The Gentle Gunman, Hunted, 52; Appointment In London, Desperate Moment, They Who Dare, 53; Doctor In The House, For Better For Worse, The Sea Shall Not Have Them, The Sleeping Tiger, 54; Doctor At Sea, Simba, 55; The Spanish Gardener, 56; Cast A Dark Shadow, Doctor At Large, Ill Met By Moonlight, 57; Campbell's Kingdom, Doctor's Dilemma, A Tale Of Two Cities, The Wind Cannot Read, 58; Libel, 59; The Angel Wore Red, Song Without End, 60; The Singer Not The Song, Victim, 61; Damn The Defiant!, The Mind Benders, We Joined The Navy, 62; Doctor In Distress, I Could Go On Singing, The Password Is Courage, The Servant, 63; King And Country, 64; Hot Enough For June, Darling, 65; McGuire, Go Home! Modesty Blaise, 66; Accident, Our Mother's House, 67; The Fixer, Sebastian, 68; The Damned, Justine, Oh! What A Lovely War, 69; Upon This Rock, 70; Death In Venice, 71; The Serpent, 73; The Night Porter, 74; Permission To Kill, 75; A Bridge Too Far, Providence, 77; Despair, 79; The Vision, 87; Daddy Nostalgie, These Foolish Things, 90.

BOGART, HUMPHREY: A Devil With Women, Up The River, 30; Bad Sister, Body And Soul, A Holy Terror, Women Of All Nations, 31; Big City Blues, Love Affair, Three On A Match, 32; Midnight/Call It Murder, 34; Black Legion, Bullets Or Ballots, China Clipper, Isle Of Fury, The Petrified Forest, One Fatal Hour, 36; Dead End, The Great O'Malley, Kid Galahad, Marked Woman, San Quentin, Stand-in, 37; The Amazing Doctor Clitterhouse, Angels With Dirty Faces, Crime School, Men Are Such Fools, Racket Busters, Swing Your Lady, 38; Dark Victory, Invisible Stripes, King Of The Underworld, The Oklahoma Kid, The Return Of Dr X, The Roaring Twenties, You Can't Get Away With Murder, 39; Brother Orchid, It All Came True, They Drive By Night, Virginia City, 40; High Sierra, The Maltese Falcon, The Wagons Roll At Night, 41; Across The Pacific, All Through The Night, The Big Shot, Casablanca, 42; Action In The North Atlantic, Sahara, Thank Your Lucky Stars, 43; Passage To Marseille, To Have And Have Not, 44; Conflict, 45; The Big Sleep, Two Guys From Milwaukee, 46; Dark Passage, Dead Reckoning, The Two Mrs Carrolls, 47; Key Largo, The Treasure Of The Sierra Madre, 48; Knock On Any Door, Tokyo Joe, 49; Chain Lightning, In A Lonely Place, 50; The African Queen, The Enforcer, Sirocco, 51; Deadline USA, 52; Battle Circus, 53; The Barefoot Contessa, Beat The Devil, The Caine Mutiny, Sabrina, 54; The Desperate Hours, The Left Hand Of God, We're No Angels, 55; The Harder They Fall, 56.

BOGDANOVICH, PETER: Targets, Voyage To The Planet Of Prehistoric Women, 68; The Last Picture Show, 71; What's Up Doc?, 72; Paper Moon, 73; Daisy Miller, 74; At Long Last Love, 75; Nickelodeon, 76; Saint Jack, 79; They All Laughed, 81; City Girl, 84; Mask, 85; Illegally Yours, 88; Texasville, 90; Noises Off, 92; The Thing Called Love, 93.

BOLGER, RAY: The Great Ziegfeld, 36; Rosalie, 37; Sweethearts, 38; The Wizard Of Oz, 39; Sunny, 41; Four Jacks And A Jill, 42; Stage Door Canteen, 43; The Harvey Girls, 46; Look For The Silver Lining, Make Mine Laughs, 49; April In Paris, Where's Charley?, 52; Babes In Toyland, 61; The Daydreamer, 66; Just You And Me Kid, The Runner Stumbles, 79; That's Dancing!, 85.

BOLT, ROBERT: Lawrence Of Arabia, 62; Doctor Zhivago, 65; A Man For All Seasons, 66; Ryan's Daughter, 70; Lady Caroline Lamb, 72; The Bounty, 84; The Mission, 86.

BONDARCHUK, SERGEI: Young Guard 48; Dream Of A Cossack, 50; Taras Shevchenko, 51; Neokonchennaya Povest, Poprigunya, Othello, 55; Destiny Of A Man, The Soldiers Marched On, 59; A Summer To Remember, 60; War And Peace, 67; The Battle Of Neretva, 69; Waterloo, 70; Oni Srajalis Za Rodinou, 75; Vrhovi Zelengore, 76; Father Serge, The Steppe, 78; Autumn, 79; 10 Days That Shook The World, 82; Boris Godunov, 86; La Bataille des Trois Rois, 89.

BOORMAN, JOHN: Catch Us If You Can, 65; The Great Director, 66; Point Blank, 67; Hell In The Pacific, 68; Leo The Last, 70; Deliverance, 72; Zardoz, 74; Exorcist II: The Heretic, 77; Excalibur, Long Shot, 81; The Emerald Forest, 85; Hope And Glory, 87; Where The Heart Is, 90; I Dreamt I Woke Up, 91, Beyond Rangoon, 95; A Simple Plan, 98.

BORGNINE, ERNEST: China Corsair, The Mob, The Whistle At Eaton Falls, 51; From Here To Eternity, The Stranger Wore A Gun, 53; The Bounty Hunter, Demetrius And The Gladiators, Johnny Guitar, Vera Cruz, 54; Bad Day At Black Rock, The Last Command, Marty, Run For Cover, The Square Jungle, Violent Saturday, 55; The Best Things In Life Are Free, Wedding Breakfast, Jubal, 56; Three Brave Men, 57; The Badlanders, Torpedo Run, The Vikings, 58; The Rabbit Trap, 59; Man On A String, Pay Or Die, Summer Of The Seventeenth Doll, 60; Go Naked In The World, 61; Barabbas, 62; McHale's Navy, 64; Flight Of The Phoenix, The Oscar, 66; Chuka, The Dirty Dozen, 67; Ice Station Zebra, The Legend Of Lylah Clare, The Split, 68; The Wild Bunch, The Adventurers, A Bullet For Sandoval, Suppose They Gave A War And Nobody Came?, 70; Rain For A Dusty Summer, Willard, 71; Bunny O'Hare, Hannie Caulder, The Poseidon Adventure, The Revengers, 72; Emperor Of The North Pole, The Neptune Factor, 73; Law And Disorder, 74; The Devil's Rain, Hustle, 75; Shoot, 76; The Greatest, 77; Convoy, Prince And The Pauper, 78; The Black Hole, The Double McGuffin, Ravagers, 79; When Time Ran Out/Earth's Final Fury, 80; Deadly Blessing, Escape From New York, High Risk, Supersnooper, 81; Young Warriors, 83; Codename: Wildgeese, The Manhunt, 86; Moving Target, Skeleton Coast, Spike Of Bensonhurst, 88; Laser Mission, Turnaround, 89; Any Man's Death, 90; Mistress, 92; McHale's Navy, 97.

BORZAGE, FRANK: The Code Of Honor, The Courtin' Of Calliope Clew, 16 (and nearly 30 more melodramas and westerns for Universal;) Humoresque, 20; The Duke Of Chimney Butte, Get-Rich-Quick Wallingford, 21; Back Pay, Billy Jim, The Good Provider, The Pride Of Palomar, The Valley Of Silent Men, 22; The Age Of Desire, Children Of The Dust, The Nth Commandment, 23; Secrets, 24; The Circle, Daddy's Gone A-Hunting, The Lady, Lazybones, Wages For Wives, 25; The Dixie Merchant, Early To Wed, The First Year, Marriage License?, 26; Seventh Heaven, 27; Street Angel, 28; Lucky Star, The River, They Had To See Paris, 29; Liliom, Song O' My Heart, 30; Bad Girl, Doctors' Wives, Young As You Feel, 31; After Tomorrow, A Farewell To Arms, Young America, 32; Man's Castle, Secrets, 33; Flirtation Walk, Little Man What Now?, No Greater Glory, 34; Living On Velvet, Shipmates Forever, Stranded, 35; Desire, Hearts Divided, 36; The Big City, The Green Light, History Is Made At Night, Mannequin, 37; The Shining Hour, Three Comrades, 38; Disputed Passage, 39; Flight Command, The Mortal Storm, Strange Cargo, 40; Smilin' Through, 41; Seven Sweethearts, The Vanishing Virginian, 42; His Butler's Sister, Stage Door Canteen, 43; Till We Meet Again, 44; The Spanish Main, 45; I've Always Loved You, Magnificent Doll, 46; That's My Man, 47; Moonrise, 48; China Doll, 58; The Big Fisherman, 59.

BOSUSTOW, STEPHEN: Flip The Frog 32; Hell-Bent For Election 44; The Magic Fluke, 49; Trouble Indemnity, Gerald McBoing Boing 50; Rooty Toot Toot, 51; Man Alive, 52; The Tell-Tale Heart, 53; When Magoo Flew 54; Mister Magoo's Puddle Jumper 56; Trees And Jamaica Daddy, 57.

BOULTING, JOHN and ROY: Trunk Crime, 39; Inquest, Pastor Hall, 40; Thunder Rock, 42; Desert Victory, 43; Journey Together, Burma Victory, 45; Fame Is The Spur, 46; Brighton Rock, 47; The Guinea Pig, 48; Seven Days To Noon, 50; The Magic Box, 51; High Treason, 52; Single Handed, 53; Seagulls Over Sorrento, 54; Josephine And Men, 55; Private's Progress, Run For The Sun, 56; The Brothers In Law, Happy Is The Bride, Lucky Jim, 57; I'm All Right Jack, Carlton-Browne Of The FO, 59; A French Mistress, The Risk, 60; Heavens Above!, 63; Rotten To The Core, 65; The Family Way, 66; Twisted Nerve, 68; There's A Girl In My Soup, 70; Soft Beds And Hard Battles, 75; The Last Word, The Number, 79.

BOW, CLARA: Beyond The Rainbow, Down To The Sea In Ships, 22; The Daring Years, The Enemies Of Women, Maytime, 23; Black Lightning, Daughters Of Pleasure, Empty Hearts, Poisoned Paradise, 24; The Adventurous Sex, The Ancient Mariner, The Keeper Of The Bees, Kiss Me Again, Lawful Cheaters, Parisian Love, The Plastic Age, The Primrose Path, 25; Dancing Mothers, Mantrap, The Runaway, Two Can Play, 26; Children Of Divorce, Get Your Man, It, Rough House Rosie, Wings, 27; The Fleet's In, Red Hair, 28; Dangerous Curves, The Wild Party, 29; Her Wedding Night, Love Among The Millionaires, Paramount On Parade, True To The Navy, 30 Kick In, No Limit, 31; Call Her Savage, 32; Hoopla, 33.

BOYD, WILLIAM: Brewster's Millions, Exit The Vamp, 21; Manslaughter, Nice People, The Young Rajah, 22; Enemies Of Children, The Temple Of Venus, 23; Changing Husbands, 24; The Road To Yesterday, 25; Her Man O' War, The Volga Boatman, 26; Dress Parade, The King Of Kings, Two Arabian Knights, The Yankee Clipper, 27; The Cop, The Night Flyer, 28; The Flying Fool, High Voltage, Lady Of The Pavements, The Leatherneck, The Locked Door, 29; The Storm, Beyond Victory The Painted Desert, 31; Lucky Devils, Madison Square Garden, The Painted Womar Sky Devils, The Wiser Sex, 32; Emergency Call, 33; Cheaters, 34; Hopalong Cassidy, The Lost City, Night Life Of The Gods, 35; Call Of The Prairie, Federal Agent, Heart Of The West, Hopalong Cassidy Returns, 36; Borderland, Hopalong Rides Again, Texas Trail, 37; Cassidy Of Bar 20, The Frontiersman, Pride Of The West, 38 Range War, Santa Fe Marshal, The Showdown, 40; Border Vigilantes, Wide Oper Town, 41; Lost Canyon, Undercover Man, 42; Border Patrol, Hoppy Serves A Writ 43; Forty Thieves, Mystery Man, Texas Masquerade, 44; The Devil's Playground, 46 Dangerous Venture, The Marauders, 47; The Dead Don't Dream, False Paradise, Sinister Journey, 48; The Greatest Show On Earth, 52.

BOYER, CHARLES: L'homme Du Large, 20; Le Capitaine Fracasse, Le Proces Du Mary Dugan, 29; La Barcarolle D'Amour, Revolte Dans La Prison, 30; The Magnificent Lie, 31; The Man From Yesterday, Red-Headed Woman, 32; Heart Song, L'Epervier, Moi Et L'Imperatrice, 33; Caravan, La Bataille, Liliom, 34; Break C Hearts, Le Bonheur, Private Worlds, Shanghai, 35; The Garden Of Allah, Mayerling, 36; Conquest, History Is Made At Night, Tovarich, 37; Algiers, 38; Love Affair, When Tomorrow Comes, 39; All This And Heaven Too, 40; Appointment F Love, Back Street, Hold Back The Dawn, 41; Tales Of Manhattan, 42; Flesh And Fantasy, The Heart Of A Nation 43; Gaslight, Together Again, 44; Confidential Agent, 45; Cluny Brown, 46; A Woman's Vengeance, 47; Arch Of Triumph, 48; The 13th Letter, The First Legion, 51; The Happy Time, 52; Madame De . . ., Thunder In The East, 53; The Cobweb, Nana, 55; Around The World In 80 Days, 56; The Buccaneer, Maxime, 58; Fanny, 61; Four Horsemen Of The Apocalypse, 62; Love Is A Ball, 63; A Very Special Favor, 65; How To Steal A Million, Is Paris Burning?, 66 Barefoot In The Park, Casino Royale, 67; The April Fools, The Madwoman Of Chaillot, 69; Lost Horizon, 73; Stavisky, 74; A Matter Of Time, 76.

BRANAGH, KENNETH: A Month In The Country, 87; Henry V, 89; Dead Again, 91; Peter's Friends, Much Ado About Nothing, Swing Kids, 93; Mary Shelley's Frankenstein, 94; In the Bleak Midwinter, 95; Hamlet, 96.

BRANDAUER, KLAUS MARIA: The Salzburg Connection, 72; Die Babenberger In Osterreich, 76; Ein Sonntag Im Oktober, 79; Mephisto, 81; Der Weg Ins Freie, 82; Detskij Sad, Never Say Never Again, 83; Colonel Redl, 84; The Lightship, Out Of Africa, Quo Vadis?, 85; Streets Of Gold, 86; Burning Secret, Hanussen, 88; La Révolution Française, Seven Minutes, The Spider's Web, 89; The Russia House, Seven Minutes, 90; White Fang, 91; Becoming Colette, 92; Die Wand, 95.

BRANDO, MARLON: The Men, 50; A Streetcar Named Desire, 51; Viva Zapata!, 52; Julius Caesar, 53; Desirée, On The Waterfront, The Wild One, 54; Guys And Dolls 55; The Teahouse Of The August Moon, 56; Sayonara, 57; The Young Lions, 58; The Fugitive Kind, 59; One-Eyed Jacks, 61; Mutiny On The Bounty, 62; The Ugly American, 63; Bedtime Story, 64; The Saboteur Code Name Morituri, 65; The Appaloosa, The Chase, 66; A Countess

POWER · FACTOR
5-P-12

From Hong Kong, Reflections In A Golden Eye, **67**; Candy, **68**; Queimada!, **69**; The Godfather, The Nightcomers, Last Tango In Paris, **72**; The Missouri Breaks, **76**; Superman, **78**; Apocalypse Now, **79**; The Formula, **80**; A Dry White Season, **89**; The Freshman, **90**; Christopher Columbus, The Discovery, **92**; Don Juan de Marco, **95**; The Island of Dr Moreau, **96**.

BRASSEUR, PIERRE: La Fille De L'Eau, **24**; Madame Sans-Géne, **25**; Feu, **28**; Mon Ami Victor, **31**; Quick, **32**; Le Sexe Faible, **33**; Caravane, **34**; Les Pattes De Mouche, **36**; Mademoiselle Ma Mère, **37**; Claudine A L'Ecole, Giuseppe Verdi, Gosse De Riche, Quai Des Brumes, **38**; Dernière Jeunesse, **39**; The Corsican Brothers, **41**; Jeune Timides, Promesses A L'Inconnue, **42**; Adieu Léonard, Lumiére D'éte, **43**; Les Enfants Du Paradis, **45**; Les Portes De La Nuit, Jericho, Noah's Ark, Petrus, **46**; Les Amants De Verone, **48**; Portrait D'Un Assassin, **49**; Souvenirs Perdus, **50**; Bluebeard, Les Mains Sales, Le Plaisir, Skipper Next To God, **51**; La Tour De Nesle, Raspoutine, **54**; Napoleon, Oasis, **55**; Porte De Lilas, **57**; La Tete Contre Les Murs, Les Grandes Familles, Sans Famille, La Loi, **58**; Carthage In Flames, Les Yeux Sans Visage, **59**; Bell' Antonio, Candide, **60**; Les Amours Célèbres, **61**; Le Crime Ne Paie Pas, **62**; Les Bonnes Causes, **63**; A Very Handy Man, **64**; King Of Hearts, La Vie De Chateau, Un Monde Nouveau, **66**; Les Oiseaux Vont Mourir Au Perou, **68**; Fortuna, **69**; Les Maries De L'An Deux, **70**; La Sera Piu Bella Della Sua Vita, **72**.

BRESSON, ROBERT: Les Anges Du Péché, **43**; Les Dames Du Bois De Boulogne, **45**; Diary Of A Country Priest, **50**; A Man Escaped, **56**; Pickpocket, **59**; The Trial Of Joan Of Arc, **62**; Au Hasard Balthazar, Mouchette, **66**; Une Femme Douce, **69**; Four Nights Of A Dreamer, **71**; Lancelot Of The Lake, **73**; Le Diable Probablement, **77**; L'Argent, **83.**

BRIDGES, JEFF: The Yin And Yang of Mr Go, **69**; Halls Of Anger, **70**; The Last Picture Show, **71**; Bad Company, Fat City, **72**; The Iceman Cometh, The Last American Hero, Lolly Madonna War, **73**; Thunderbolt And Lightfoot, **74**; Hearts Of The West, Rancho Deluxe, **75**; King Kong, Stay Hungry, **76**; Somebody Killed Her Husband, **78**; The American Success Company, Winter Kills, **79**; Heaven's Gate, **80**; Cutter's Way, **81**; Kiss Me Goodbye, The Last Unicorn, Tron, **82**; Against All Odds, Starman, **84**; Jagged Edge, **85**; 8 Million Ways To Die, The Morning After, **86**; Nadine, **87**; Tucker: The Man And His Dream, 88; Cold Feet, The Fabulous Baker Boys, See You In The Morning, **89**; Texasville, **90**; The Fisher King, **91**; American Heart, Fearless, The Vanishing, **93**; Wild Bill, White Squall, **95**; The Mirror Has Two Faces, **96**.

BROCCOLI, ALBERT R: The Red Beret, **53**; The Black Knight, Hell Below Zero, **54**; A Prize Of Gold, **55**; The Cockleshell Heroes, Odongo, Safari, **56**; Fire Down Below, Pickup Alley, Zarak, **57**; High Flight, The Man Inside, No Time To Die, **58**; The Bandit Of Zhobe, Killers Of Kilimanjaro, **59**; The Trials Of Oscar Wilde, **60**; Dr No, **62**; Call Me Bwana, From Russia With Love, **63**; Goldfinger, **64**; Thunderball, **65**; You Only Live Twice, **67**; Chitty Chitty Bang Bang, **68**; On Her Majesty's Secret Service, **69**; Diamonds Are Forever, **71**; Live And Let Die, **73**; The Man With The Golden Gun, **74**; The Spy Who Loved Me, **77**; Moonraker, **79**; For Your Eyes Only, **81**; Octopussy, **83**; A View To A Kill, **85**; The Living Daylights, **87**; Licence To Kill, **89**; Golden Eye, **95**.

BROOK, PETER: Sentimental Journey, **43**; The Beggar's Opera, **53**; Moderato Cantabile, **60**; Lord Of The Flies, **63**; Marat-Sade, **66**; Tell Me Lies, **68**; King Lear, **70**; Meetings With Remarkable Men, **79**; La Tragédie De Carmen, **83.**

BROOKS, LOUISE: The Street Of Forgotten Men, **25**; The American Venus, It's The Old Army Game, Just Another Blonde, Love 'Em And Leave 'Em, The Show-Off, A Social Celebrity, **26**; The City Gone Wild, Evening Clothes, Now We're In The Air, Rolled Stockings, **27**; Beggars Of Life, A Girl In Every Port, Pandora's Box, **28**; Canary Murder Case, Diary Of A Lost Girl, **29**; Prix De Beauté, Windy Riley Goes To Hollywood, **30**; God's Gift To Women, It Pays To Advertise, The Public Enemy, The Steel Highway, **31**; Empty Saddles, **36**; King Of Gamblers, When You're In Love, **37**; Overland Stage Raiders, **38**.

BROOKS, MEL: The Producers, **68**; The Twelve Chairs, **70**; Blazing Saddles, Young Frankenstein, **74**; Silent Movie, **76**; High Anxiety, **77**; History Of The World Part 1, **81**; To Be Or Not To Be, **83**; Spaceballs, **87**; Life Stinks, **91**; The Vagrant, **92**; Robin Hood: Men In Tights, **93**, Dracula: Dead And Loving It, **95**.

BROOKS, RICHARD: Crisis, **50**; The Light Touch, **51**; Deadline USA, **52**; Battle Circus, Take The High Ground, **53**; The Flame And The Flesh, The Last Time I Saw Paris, **54**; Blackboard Jungle, **55**; The Catered Affair, The Last Hunt, **56**; Something Of Value, **57**; The Brothers Karamazov, Cat On A Hot Tin Roof, **58**; Elmer Gantry, **60**; Sweet Bird Of Youth, **62**; Lord Jim, **65**; The Professionals, **66**; In Cold Blood, **67**; The Happy Ending **69**; Dollars, **72**; Bite The Bullet, **75**; Looking For Mr Goodbar, **77**; Wrong Is Right, **82**; Fever Pitch, **85**.

BROWN, CLARENCE: The Great Redeemer, The Last Of The Mohicans, **20**; The Foolish Matrons, **21**; The Light In The Dark, **22**; The Acquittal, Don't Marry For Money, **23**; Butterfly, The Signal Tower, Smouldering Fires, **24**; The Eagle, The Goose Woman, **25**; Kiki, **26**; Flesh And The Devil, **27**; The Trail Of '98, A Woman Of Affairs, **28**; Navy Blues, Wonder Of Women, **29**; Anna Christie, Romance, **30**; A Free Soul, Inspiration, Possessed, **31**; Emma, Letty Lynton, The Son-Daughter, **32**; Looking Forward, Night Flight, **33**; Chained, Fifteen Wives, Sadie McKee, **34**; Ah Wilderness, Anna Karenina, **35**; The Gorgeous Hussy, Wife Vs Secretary, **36**; Conquest, **37**; Of Human Hearts, **38**; Idiot's Delight, The Rains Came, **39**; Edison The Man, **40**; Come Live With Me, They Met In Bombay, **41**; The Human Comedy, **43**; National Velvet, The White Cliffs Of Dover, **44**; The Yearling, **46**; Song Of Love, **47**; Intruder In The Dust, The Secret Garden, **49**; To Please A Lady, **50**; Angels In The Outfield, It's A Big Country, **51**; Plymouth Adventure, When In Rome, **52**; Never Let Me Go, **53**.

BROWNING, TOD: Jim Bludso, The Jury Of Fate, A Love Sublime, Peggy The Will O' The Wisp, **17**; The Brazen Beauty, The Deciding Kiss, The Eyes Of Mystery, The Legion Of Death, Revenge, Set Free, Which Woman, **18**; Bonnie Bonnie Lassie, The Exquisite Thief, A Petal On The Current, The Unpainted Woman, The Wicked Darling, **19**; The Virgin Of Stamboul, **20**; No Woman Knows, Outside The Law, **21**; Man Under Cover, Under Two Flags, The Wise Kid, **22**; Day Of Faith, Drifting, White Tiger, **23**; The Dangerous Flirt, Silk Stocking Sal, **24**; Dollar Down, The Mystic, The Unholy Three, **25**; The Black Bird, The Road To Mandalay, **26**; London After Midnight, The Show, The Unknown, **27**; The Big City, West Of Zanzibar, **28**; The Thirteenth Chair, Where East Is East, **29**; Outside The Law, **30**; Dracula, Iron Man, **31**; Freaks, **32**; Fast Workers, **33**; Mark Of The Vampire, **35**; The Devil Doll, **36**; Miracles For Sale, **39**.

BROWNLOW, KEVIN: The White Bus **65**; Red and Blue, It Happened Here **66**; The Charge Of The Light Brigade **68**; Winstanley, **75**; It Happened Here Again, **76**; Napoleon **52-79**.

BRYNNER, YUL: Port Of New York, **49**; Anastasia, The King And I, The Ten Commandments, **56**; The Brothers Karamazov, The Buccaneer, **58**; The Journey, Solomon And Sheba, The Sound And The Fury, Le Testament D'Orphée, **59**; The Magnificent Seven, Once More With Feeling, Surprise Package, **60**; Escape From Zahrain, Taras Bulba, **62**; Kings Of The Sun, **63**; Flight From Ashiya, Invitation To A Gunfighter, **64**; The Saboteur Code Name Morituri, **65**; Cast A Giant Shadow, The Poppy Is Also A Flower, Return Of The Magnificent Seven, **66**; The Double Man, The Long Duel, Triple Cross, **67**; Villa Rides, **68**; The File Of The Golden Goose, The Madwoman Of Chaillot, The Magic Christian, **69**; Adios, Sabata, The Battle Of Neretva, Catlow, The Light At The Edge Of The World, Romance Of A Horsethief, **71**; Fuzz, **72**; The Serpent, Westworld, **73**; The Ultimate Warrior, **75**; Futureworld, Gli Indesiderabili, It's Showtime, **76**.

BUCHANAN, JACK: Auld Lang Syne, **17**; Her Heritage, **19**; The Audacious Mr Squire, **23**; Bulldog Drummond's Third Round, **25**; Confetti, **27**; Toni, **28**; Paris, **29**; Monte Carlo, **30**; Man Of Mayfair, **31**; Goodnight Vienna, Yes Mr Brown, **33**; Brewster's Millions, That's A Good Girl, **35**; When Knights Were Bold, **36**; The Sky's The Limit, **37**; Break The News, Sweet Devil, **38**; Bulldog Sees It Through, **40**; The Gang's All Here, Happidrome, **43**; The Band Wagon, Josephine And Men, **53**; Les Carnets Du Major Thompson, **56**; As Long As They're Happy, **57**.

BUNNY, BUGS: Selection: Bunny Superstar, **75**; Great American Bugs Bunny, **79**; The Looney Looney Looney Bugs Bunny Movie, **81**; 1,001 Rabbit Tales, **82**; Gremlins 2: The New Batch, **83**.

BUNUEL, LUIS: Un Chien Andalou, **28**; L'Age D'Or, **30**; Land Without Bread, **32**; Gran Casino, **47**; The Great Madcap, **49**; Los Olvidados, **50**; Daughter Of Deceit, Susana, Una Mujer Sin Amor, **51**; Adventures Of Robinson Crusoe, El Bruto, Mexican Bus Ride, This Strange Passion, **52**; Illusion Travels By Streetcar, **53**; The River And Death, Wuthering Heights, **54**; The Criminal Life Of Archibaldo De La Cruz, **55**; Celà S'Appelle L'Aurore, La Mort En Ce Jardin, **56**; Nazarin, **58**; Republic Of Sin, La Fièvre Monte A El Pao, **59**;The Young One, **60**; Viridiana, **61**; The Exterminating Angel, **62**; Diary Of A Chambermaid, **64**; Simon Of The Desert, **65**; Belle De Jour, **67**; The Milky Way, Tristana, **70**; The Discreet Charm Of The Bourgeoisie, **72**; Le Moine, **73**; The Phantom Of Liberty, **74**; That Obscure Object Of Desire, **77**.

BURNS, GEORGE: The Big Broadcast, **32**; College Humor, International House, **33**; Many Happy Returns, Six Of A Kind, We're Not Dressing, **34**; The Big Broadcast Of 36, Here Comes Cookie, Love In Bloom, **35**; The Big Broadcast Of 37, College Holiday, **36**; A Damsel In Distress, **37**; College Swing, **38**; Honolulu, **39**; The Solid Gold Cadillac, **56**; The Sunshine Boys, **75**; Oh God!, **77**; Movie Movie, Sgt Pepper's Lonely Hearts Club Band, **78**; Going In Style, Just You And Me Kid, **79**; Oh God! **80**; Oh God! You Devil, **84**; 18 Again!, **88**; Wisecracks, **92**; Radioland Murders, **94**.

BURSTYN, ELLEN: For Those Who Think Young, Goodbye Charlie, **64**; Pit Stop, **69**; Alex In Wonderland, Tropic Of Cancer, **70**; The Last Picture Show, **71**; The King Of Marvin Gardens, **72**; The Exorcist, **73**; Alice Doesn't Live Here Anymore, **74**; Harry And Tonto, **75**; Providence, **77**; A Dream Of Passion, Same Time, Next Year, **78**; Resurrection, **80**; Silence Of The North, **81**; The Ambassador, In Our Hands, **84**; Twice In A Lifetime, **85**; Dear America, **87**; Hanna's War, **88**; Dying Young, **91**; The Cemetery Club, **92**; When A Man Loves A Woman, **94**; Roommates, **95**; The Spitfire Grill, **96.**

BURTON, RICHARD: The Last Days Of Dolwyn, Now Barabbas, **49**; Waterfront, The Woman With No Name, **50**; Green Grow The Rushes, **51**; My Cousin Rachel, **52**; The Desert Rats, The Robe, Thursday's Children, **53**; Demetrius And The Gladiators, **54**; Prince Of Players, The Rains Of Ranchipur, **55**; Alexander The Great, **56**; Bitter Victory, Sea Wife, **57**; Look Back In Anger, **58**; The Bramble Bush, Ice Palace, **60**; The Longest Day, **62**; Cleopatra, The VIPs, **63**; Becket, Hamlet, The Night Of The Iguana, Zulu, **64**; The Sandpiper, The Spy Who Came In From The Cold, **65**; Who's Afraid Of Virginia Woolf?, **66**; The Comedians, The Taming Of The Shrew, **67**; Boom!, Candy, Dr Faustus, **68**; Anne Of The Thousand Days, Staircase, Where Eagles Dare, **69**; Raid On Rommel, Villain, **71**; The Assassination Of Trotsky, Bluebeard, Hammersmith Is Out, **72**; Massacre In Rome, Sutjeska, Under Milk Wood, The Voyage, **73**; The Klansman, **74**; Volcano: An Inquiry Into The Life And Death Of Malcolm Lowry, **76**; Equus, Exorcist II: The Heretic, **77**; The Medusa Touch, The Wild Geese, **78**; Teil Steiner - Das Eiserne Kreuz 2 **79**; Circle Of Two, **80**; Absolution, Wagner, **81**; 1984, **84**.

BURTON, TIM: Pee-Wee's Big Adventure, **85**; Beetlejuice, **88**; Batman, **89**; Edward Scissorhands, **90**; Batman Returns, Singles, **92**; The Nightmare Before Christmas, **93**; Ed Wood, **94**; Batman Forever, **95**; Mars Attacks!, **96**.

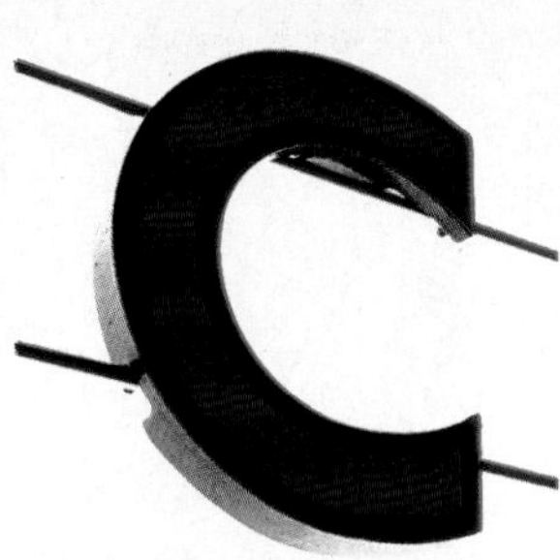

CACOYANNIS, MICHAEL: Windfall In Athens, **53**; Stella, **54**; The Girl In Black, **56**; A Matter Of Dignity, **57**; Our Last Spring, **59**; Eroica, **60**; Electra, The Wastrel, **61**; Zorba The Greek, **64**; The Day The Fish Came Out, **67**; The Trojan Women, **72**; The Story Of Jacob And Joseph, **74**; Attila 74, **75**; Iphigenia, **76**; Sweet Country, **86**; Up Down And Sideways, **93**.

CAGE, NICOLAS: Rumble Fish, Valley Girl, **83**; Birdy, The Cotton Club, Racing With The Moon, **84**; The Boy In Blue, Peggy Sue Got Married, **86**; Moonstruck, Raising Arizona, **87**; Never On Tuesday, Tempo Di Uccidere, Vampire's Kiss, **89**; Firebirds, Wild At Heart, **90**; Zandalee, **91**; Honeymoon In Vegas, **92**; Amos And Andrew, Deadfall, Red Rock West, **93**; Guarding Tess, It Could Happen to you, **94**; Kiss of Death, **95**; The Rock, **96**; Con Air, **97.**

CAGNEY, JAMES: Doorway To Hell, **30**; Sinner's Holiday, Blonde Crazy, The Millionaire, Other Men's Women, The Public Enemy, Smart Money, **31**; The Crowd Roars, Taxi!, Winner Take All, **32**, Footlight Parade, Hard To Handle, Lady Killer, The Mayor Of Hell, Picture Snatcher, **33**; He Was Her Man, Here Comes The Navy, Jimmy The Gent, St Louis Kid, **34**; Ceiling Zero, Devil Dogs Of The Air, Frisco Kid, 'G' Men, The Irish In Us, A Midsummer Night's Dream, **35**; Great Guy, **36**; Something To Sing About, **37**; Angels With Dirty Faces, Boy Meets Girl, **38**; Each Dawn I Die, The Oklahoma Kid, The Roaring Twenties, **39**; City For Conquest, The Fighting 69th, Torrid Zone, **40**; The Bride Came COD, The Strawberry Blonde, **41**; Captains Of The Clouds, Yankee Doodle Dandy, **42**; Johnny Come Lately, **43**; Blood On The Sun, **45**; 13 Rue Madeleine, **46**; The Time Of Your Life, **48**; White Heat, **49**; Kiss Tomorrow Goodbye, West Point Story, **50**; Come Fill The Cup, Starlift, **51**; What Price Glory?, **52**; A Lion Is In The Streets, **53**; Love Me Or Leave Me, Mister Roberts, Run For Cover, The Seven Little Foys, **55**; These Wilder Years, Tribute To A Bad Man, **56**; Man Of A Thousand Faces, Short Cut To Hell, **57**; Never Steal Anything Small, Shake Hands With The Devil, **59**; The Gallant Hours, **60**; One Two Three, **61**; Arizona Bushwhackers, **68**; Ragtime, **81**.

CAHN, SAMMY: Argentine Nights, **40**; Youth On Parade, **42**; Crazy House, Lady Of Burlesque, **43**; Follow The Boys, Knickerbocker Holiday, **44**; Anchors Aweigh, The Stork Club, **45**; The Kid From Brooklyn, The Sweetheart Of Sigma Chi, **46**; It Happened In Brooklyn, **47**; Romance On The High Seas, **48**; It's A Great Feeling, **49**; Rich Young And Pretty, **51**; April In Paris, Because You're Mine, **52**; Peter Pan, Three Sailors And A Girl, **53**; Three Coins In The Fountain, **54**; Love Me Or Leave Me, The Tender Trap, **55**; Anything Goes, The Court Jester, Meet Me In Las Vegas, **56**; The Joker Is Wild, Pal Joey, **57**; Indiscreet, The Long Hot Summer, Paris Holiday, **58**; A Hole In The Head, **59**; High Time, **60**; Pocketful Of Miracles, **61**; Boys' Night Out, How The West Was Won, **62**; Come Blow Your Horn, Papa's Delicate Condition, **63**; Robin And The Seven Hoods, **64**; The Oscar, **66**; Thoroughly Modern Millie, **67**; Star!, **68**; A Touch Of Class, **73**; Journey Back To Oz, **74**; Paper Tiger, **75**; The Duchess And The Dirtwater Fox, **76**; The Stud, **78**.

CAINE, MICHAEL: A Hill in Korea, Sailor Beware!, **56**; How To Murder A Rich Uncle, Steel Bayonet, **57**; Blind Spot, The Key, The Two-headed Spy, **58**; The Bulldog Breed, **60**; Foxhole In Cairo, **61**; The Day The Earth Caught Fire, Solo For Sparrow, The Wrong Arm Of The Law, **62**; Zulu, **64**; The Ipcress File, **65**; Alfie, Funeral In Berlin, Gambit, The Wrong Box, **66**; Billion Dollar Brain, Hurry Sundown, Woman Times Seven, **67**; Deadfall, The Magus, Play Dirty, **68**; Battle Of Britain, The Italian Job, **69**; The Last Valley, Too Late The Hero, **70**; Get Carter, Kidnapped, **71**; Pulp, Sleuth, Zed And Company, **72**; The Black Windmill, Marseilles Contract, **74**; The Man Who Would Be King, Peeper, The Romantic Englishwoman, The Wilby Conspiracy, **75**; Harry And Walter Go To New York, **76**; A Bridge Too Far, The Eagle Has Landed, **77**; California Suite, Silver Bears, The Swarm, **78**; Ashanti, Beyond The Poseidon Adventure, **79**; Dressed To Kill, The Island, **80**; Escape To Victory, The Hand, **81**; Deathtrap, **82**; Beyond The Limit, Educating Rita, **83**; Blame It On Rio, The Jigsaw Man, **84**; The Holcroft Covenant, Water, **85**; Half Moon Street, Hannah And Her Sisters, Mona Lisa, Sweet Liberty, The Whistle Blower, **86**; The Fourth Protocol, Jaws: The Revenge, Surrender, **87**; Dirty Rotten Scoundrels, Without A Clue, **88**; Bull's Eye!, **89**; Mr Destiny, A Shock To The System, **90**; Blue Ice, Death Becomes Her, The Muppet Christmas Carol, Noises Off, **92**; On Deadly Ground, **94**; Blood and Wine, **96.**

CAMERON, JAMES: Battle Beyond The Stars, Happy Birthday Gemini, **80**; Galaxy Of Terror, Planet Of Horrors, Piranha II: The Spawning, **81**; The Terminator, **84**; Rambo: First Blood Part II, **85**; Aliens, **86**; The Abyss, **89**; Point Break, Terminator 2: Judgment Day, **90**; True Lies, **94**; Titanic, **97**.

CAMPION, JANE: Sweetie, **89**; An Angel At My Table, **90**; The Piano, **94**, Portrait Of A Lady, **95**.

CANNON, DYAN: The Rise And Fall Of Legs Diamond, This Rebel Breed, **60**; Bob & Carol & Ted & Alice, **69**; Doctors' Wives, The Love Machine, Such Good Friends, **71**; The Anderson Tapes, The Burglars, **72**; The Last Of Sheila, Shamus, **73**; Child Under A Leaf, **74**; Heaven Can Wait, Revenge Of The Pink Panther, **78**; Honeysuckle Rose, **80**; Author! Author!, Deathtrap, **82**; Caddyshack II, **88**; The End Of Innocence, **90**; The Pickle, **93**.

CANTOR, EDDIE: Kid Boots, **26**; Special Delivery, **27**; Glorifying The American Girl, **29**; Whoopee!, **30**; Mr Lemon Of Orange, Palmy Days, **31**; The Kid From Spain **32**; Roman Scandals, **33**; Kid Millions, **34**; Strike Me Pink, **36**; Ali Baba Goes To Town, **37**; Forty Little Mothers, **40**; Thank Your Lucky Stars, **43**; Hollywood Canteen, Show Business, **44**; If You Knew Susie, **48**; The Story Of Will Rogers, **52**

CANUTT, YAKIMA: The Heart Of A Texan, (and more than 20 other silent westerns) **22**; Riders Of The Storm, The Three Outcasts, **29**; The Lonesome Trail, Westward Bound, **30**; Battling With Buffalo Bill, The Vanishing Legion, **31**; Guns For Hire, The Last Frontier, The Last Of The Mohicans, Two Fisted Justice, **32**; The Fighting Texans, **33**; Blue Steel, Man From Hell, The Star Packer, Texas Tornado, **34**; Branded A Coward, The Dawn Rider, Paradise Canyon, Westward Ho, **35**; The Black Coin, King Of The Pecos, The Lonely Trail, The Oregon Trail, Wildcat Trooper **36**; Gunsmoke Ranch, Hit The Saddle, Riders Of The Whistling Skull, **37**; The Mysterious Pilot, The Secret Of Treasure Island, **38**; Gone With The Wind, Stagecoach, **39**; The Great Train Robbery, The Ranger And The Lady, Under Texas Skies, **40**; Prairie Pioneers, **41**; Shadows On The Sage, **42**; Pride Of The Plains, **44**; Sheriff Of Cimarron, **45**; Wyoming, **47**; Adventures Of Frank And Jesse James, Oklahoma Badlands, **48**; The Doolins Of Oklahoma, **49**; Rocky Mountain, The Showdown, **50**; Ivanhoe, **52**; Knights Of The Round Table, **53**; The Lawless Rider, **54**; The Far Horizons, Helen Of Troy, **55**; Old Yeller, Zarak, **57**; Ben-Hur, **59**; Spartacus, Swiss Family Robinson, **60**; El Cid, **61**; How The West Was Won, **62**; The Fall Of The Roman Empire, **64**; Cat Ballou, **65**; Khartoum, **66**; The Flim Flam Man, **67**; Where Eagles Dare, **69**; A Man Called Horse, Rio Lobo, Song Of Norway, **70**; Breakheart Pass, Equus, **77**; High On The Range, **82**.

CAPRA, FRANK: The Strong Man, Tramp Tramp Tramp, **26**; For The Love Of Mike, Long Pants, **27**; The Matinee Idol, The Power Of The Press, Say It With Sables, o This Is Love, Submarine, That Certain hing, The Way Of The Strong, **28**; The onovan Affair, Flight, The Younger eneration, **29**; Ladies Of Leisure, Rain Or hine, **30**; Dirigible, The Miracle Woman, latinum Blonde, **31**; American Madness, orbidden, **32**; The Bitter Tea Of General en, Lady For A Day, **33**; Broadway Bill, It appened One Night, **34**; Mr Deeds oes To Town, **36**; Lost Horizon, **37**; You an't Take It With You, **38**; Mr Smith oes To Washington, **39**; Meet John Doe, **41**; unisian Victory, **43**; Arsenic And Old ace, **44**; It's A Wonderful Life, **47**; State Of he Union, **48**; Riding High, **50**; Here omes The Groom, **51**; A Hole In The Head, **9**; Pocketful Of Miracles, **61**.

ARDIFF, JACK: As You Like It, **36**; night Without Armour, Wings Of The Morning, **7**; The Four Feathers, **39**; Western pproaches, **44**; Black Narcissus, Caesar And leopatra, A Matter Of Life And Death, **6**; Black Narcissus, **47**; The Red Shoes, **48**; nder Capricorn, **49**; The Black Rose, **0**; The African Queen, The Magic Box, andora And The Flying Dutchman, **51**; he Master Of Ballantrae, **53**; The Barefoot ontessa, **54**; The Brave One, War And eace, **56**; Legend Of The Lost, The Prince nd The Showgirl, **57**; The Big Money, tent To Kill, The Vikings, **58**; The Diary Of nne Frank, Web Of Evidence, **59**; Scent f Mystery, Sons And Lovers, **60**; Fanny, **61**; he Lion, My Geisha, The Devil Never eeps, **62**; The Long Ships, **64**; Young assidy, **65**; The Liquidator, **66**; Dark Of he Sun, Girl On A Motorcycle, **68**; The utations, Scalawag, **73**; Ride A Wild ony, **76**; The Prince And The Pauper, Death n The Nile, **78**; Avalanche Express, The fth Musketeer, A Man A Woman And A Bank, **9**; The Awakening, The Dogs Of War, **0**; Ghost Story, **81**; The Wicked Lady, **83**; onan The Destroyer, Scandalous, **84**; at's Eye, Rambo: First Blood Part II, **85**; Tai-an, **86**; Million Dollar Mystery, **87**; Call om Space, **89**.

AREY, HARRY: Bill Sharkey's Last ame, **09**; The Informer, The Musketeers Of g Alley, My Hero, **12**; Broken Ways, ero Of Little Italy, Judith Of Bethulia, **13**; As Happened, **15**; Graft, **16**; Bucking roadway, The Secret Man, The Soul Herder, **7**; Hell Bent, The Phantom Riders, Wild omen, **18**; Bare Fists, The Outcasts Of oker Flat, Roped, **19**; Marked Men, est Is West, **20**; Desperate Trails, The Fox, **1**; Man To Man, **22**; Crashin' Thru, he Miracle Baby, **23**; The Flaming Forties, he Night Hawk, **24**; The Bad Lands, he Texas Trail, **25**; Satan Town, **26**; A Little urney, Slide Kelly Slide, **27**; The order Patrol, **28**; Bad Company, Trader orn, The Vanishing Legion, **31**; The ast Of The Mohicans, Law And Order, **32**; arbary Coast, The Last Outpost, **35**; he Prisoner Of Shark Island, Sutter's Gold, **6**; Kid Galahad, Souls At Sea, **37**; King f Alcatraz, You And Me, **38**; Mr Smith Goes o Washington, **39**; Beyond Tomorrow, hey Knew What They Wanted, **40**; Among he Living, Shepherd Of The Hills, undown, **41**; The Spoilers, **42**; Air Force, **3**; The Great Moment, **44**; Duel In The un, **46**; Angel And The Badman, The Sea Of rass, **47**; Red River, So Dear To My eart, **48**.

ARMICHAEL, HOAGY: Anything oes, **36**; Every Day's A Holiday, Topper, **37**; ollege Swing, Sing You Sinners, Thanks or The Memory, **38**; Road Show, **41**; True o Life, **43**; To Have And Have Not, **44**; ohnny Angel, The Stork Club, **45**; The Best ears Of Our Lives, Canyon Passage, **46**; ight Song, **47**; Johnny Holiday, **49**; Young an With A Horn, **50**; Here Comes The room, **51**; Belles On Their Toes, The Las egas Story, **52**; Gentlemen Prefer londes, **53**; Three For The Show, mberjack, **55**; Hey Boy! Hey Girl!, **59**; atari!, **62**; The Big TNT Show, **66**.

ARNE, MARCEL: Jenny, **36**; Drôle e Drame, **37**; Hôtel Du Nord, Le Quai Des rumes, **38**; Le Jour Se Lève, **39**; Les siteurs Du Soir, **42**; Les Enfants Du aradis, **45**; Les Portes De La Nuit, **46**; a Marie Du Port, **50**; Juliette Ou La lef Des Songes, **51**; Therèse Raquin, **3**; L'Air De Paris, **54**; Le Pays D'Où Je ens, **56**; Les Tricheurs, **58**; Terrain ague, **60**; Du Mouron Pour Les Petits seaux, **63**; Trois Chambres A anhattan, **65**; Les Jeunes Loups, **66**; Les ssasins De L'Ordre, **71**; La Merveilleuse site, **74**; La Bible, **84**.

CAROL, MARTINE: La Ferme Aux Loups, **43**; Voyage Surprise, **46**; Les Amants De Vérone, **48**; Caroline Chérie, **51**;Méfiez-Vous Des Blondes, Nous Irons A Paris, **50**; Le Desir Et L'Amour, **52**; La Spiaggia, Lucrezia Borgia, Un Caprice De Caroline Chérie, **53**; Les Belles De Nuit, Daughters Of Destiny, Madame Du Barry, The Bed, **54**; Sins Of Lola Montes, Nana, **55**; Adorables Créatures, Around The World In 80 Days, Foxiest Girl In Paris, Les Carnets Du Major Thompson, **56**; Action Of The Tiger, **57**; La Prima Notte, **58**; Ten Seconds To Hell, **59**; The Battle Of Austerlitz, **60**; Vanina Vanini, Love And The Frenchwoman, Un Soir Sur La Plage, **61**; Hell Is Empty, **67**.

CARON, LESLIE: An American In Paris, The Man With A Cloak, **51**; Glory Alley, **52**; Lili, The Story Of Three Loves, **53**; Daddy Long Legs, The Glass Slipper, **55**; Gaby, **56**; Doctor's Dilemma, Gigi, **58**; The Man Who Understood Women, **59**; The Subterraneans, **60**; Fanny, **61**; Guns Of Darkness, The L-Shaped Room, **62**; Father Goose, **64**; A Very Special Favor, **65**; Promise Her Anything, **66**; Madron, **70**; Chandler, **72**; Serail, **76**; The Man Who Loved Women, Valentino, **77**; Goldengirl, **79**; Contract, Tous Védettes, **80**; Die Unerreichbare, Imperative, **82**; Dangerous Moves, **84**; Courage Mountain, Guerriers Et Captives, **89**; Damage, **92**; That's Entertainment! III, **94**; Funny Bones, **95**.

CARPENTER, JOHN: The Resurrection Of Broncho Billy, **70**; Dark Star, **74**; Assault On Precinct 13, **76**; Halloween, **78**; The Fog, **80**; Escape From New York, Halloween II, **81**; The Thing, **82**; Christine, Halloween III: Season Of The Witch, **83**; Starman, **84**; Big Trouble In Little China, **86**; Prince Of Darkness, **87**; They Live, **88**; Memoirs Of An Invisible Man, **92**; In The Mouth Of Madness, Village Of The Damned, **95**; Escape from La, **96**.

CARRADINE, JOHN: Selection: Forgotten Commandments, The Sign Of The Cross, **32**; The Invisible Man, **33**; Bride Of Frankenstein, Les Misérables, **35**; Daniel Boone, The Garden Of Allah, Mary Of Scotland, The Prisoner Of Shark Island, Ramona, Under Two Flags, White Fang, Winterset, **36**; Captains Courageous, Danger – Love At Work, The Hurricane, The Last Gangster, Love Under Fire, **37**; Alexander's Ragtime Band, Four Men And A Prayer, Gateway, I'll Give A Million, Kidnapped, Of Human Hearts, Submarine Patrol, Thank You Mr Moto, **38**; Captain Fury, Drums Along The Mohawk, Five Came Back, The Hound Of The Baskervilles, Jesse James, Mr Moto's Last Warning, Stagecoach, The Three Musketeers, **39**; The Grapes Of Wrath, The Return Of Frank James, **40**; Blood And Sand, Man Hunt, Swamp Water, Western Union, **41**; Northwest Rangers, Son Of Fury, Whispering Ghosts, **42**; Hitler's Hangman, I Escaped From The Gestapo, Revenge Of The Zombies, **43**; The Adventures Of Mark Twain, Bluebeard, House Of Frankenstein, The Invisible Man's Revenge, The Mummy's Ghost, Return Of The Ape Man, Voodoo Man, **44**; Captain Kidd, Fallen Angel, House Of Dracula, **45**; Face Of Marble, **46**; C-Man, **49**; The Desert Song, **53**; The Egyptian, Johnny Guitar, Thunder Pass, **54**; Hidden Guns, Stranger On Horseback, **55**; Around The World In 80 Days, The Black Sleep, The Court Jester, The Ten Commandments, **56**; The Story Of Mankind, The True Story Of Jesse James, **57**; The Incredible Petrified World, **58**; Curse Of The Stone Hand, The Oregon Trail, **59**; The Adventures Of Huckleberry Finn, Sex Kittens Go To College, Tarzan The Magnificent, **60**; Cheyenne Autumn, The Patsy, **64**; House Of The Black Death, **65**; Billy The Kid Vs Dracula, Munster Go Home, **66**; Astro-Zombies, Blood Of Dracula's Castle, The Hostage, **67**; The Good Guys And The Bad Guys, The Lonely Man, The Trouble With Girls, **69**; Bigfoot, Cain's Way, Myra Breckinridge, **70**; The Seven Minutes, Shinbone Alley, **71**; Boxcar Bertha, Everything You Always Wanted To Know About Sex, Richard, **72**; Bad Charleston Charlie, Big Foot, The House Of Seven Corpses, Silent Night Bloody Night, Terror In The Wax Museum, **73**; Moon Child, **74**; Shock Waves, **75**; The Last Tycoon, The Shootist, **76**; Crash!, Satan's Cheerleaders, The Sentinel, The White Buffalo, **77**; The Bees, Nocturna, **78**; The Boogeyman, The Monster Club, **80**; The Howling, The Nesting, **81**; The Scarecrow, The Secret Of Nimh, **82**; Boogeyman II, House Of The Long Shadows, **83**; The Ice Pirates, **84**; Evils Of The Night, **85**; Monster In The Closet, Peggy Sue Got Married, Revenge, The Tomb, **86**.

CARRIERE, JEAN-CLAUDE: Le Soupirant, **63**; Diary Of A Chambermaid, **64**; Viva Maria!, Yoyo, **65**; Hôtel Paradiso, **66**; Belle De Jour, Le Voleur, **67**; La Piscine, **69**; Borsalino, L'Alliance, The Milky Way, **70**; Liza, Taking Off, Un Peu De Soleil Dans L'Eau Froide, **71**; The Discreet Charm Of The Bourgeoisie, **72**; Dorothea's Rache, Le Moine, Un Homme Est Mort, **73**; France Société Anonyme, La Chair De L'Orchidée, Un Amour De Pluie, The Phantom Of Liberty, **74**; La Faille, Léonor, Les Oeufs Brouillés, Serieux Comme Le Plaisir, **75**; Le Jardin Des Supplices, **76**; Julie Pôt De Colle, Le Diable Dans La Bôite, Le Gang, Photo Souvenir, That Obscure Object Of Desire, **77**; Chaussette Surprise, Un Papillon Sur L'Epaule, **78**; Ils Sont Grands Ces Petits, L'Associé, L'Homme En Colère, Retour A La Bien-aimée, The Tin Drum, **79**; Every Man For Himself, **80**; Circle Of Deceit, **81**; Antonietta, Danton, Itineraire Bis, The Return Of Martin Guerre, **82**; La Tragédie De Carmen, Le Général De L'Armée Morte, **83**; La Jeune Fille Et L'Enfer, Swann In Love, **84**; L'Unique, **85**; Max My Love, **86**; Les Exploits D'un Jeune Don Juan, The Possessed, Wolf At The Door, **87**; La Nuit Bengali, The Unbearable Lightness Of Being, **88**; Hard To Be A God, Hostage Of Europe, J'Ecris Dans L'Espace, The Mahabharata, Valmont, Milou In May, **89**; Cyrano De Bergerac, **90**; At Play In The Fields Of The Lord, **91**; L'Otage De L'Europe, The Return Of Casanova, **92**; Sommersby, **93**; The Horseman on the Roof, **95**.

CARROLL, MADELEINE: The First Born, The Guns Of Loos, What Money Can Buy, **28**; The American Prisoner, Atlantic, The Crooked Billet, L'Instinct, **29**; Escape, Fascination, French Leave, Madame Guillotine, School For Scandal, The W Plan, Young Woodley, **30**; The Kissing Cup Race, The Written Law, **31**; I Was A Spy, Sleeping Car, **33**; The World Moves On, **34**; The 39 Steps, The Dictator, **35**; The Case Against Mrs Ames, The General Died At Dawn, Lloyd's Of London, The Secret Agent, **36**; It's All Yours, On The Avenue, The Prisoner Of Zenda, **37**; Blockade, **38**; Cafe Society, Honeymoon In Bali, **39**; My Son My Son, Northwest Mounted Police, Safari, **40**; Bahama Passage, One Night In Lisbon, Virginia, **41**; My Favorite Blonde, **42**; White Cradle Inn, **47**; Don't Trust Your Husband, **48**; The Fan, **49**.

CASSAVETES, JOHN: Fourteen Hours, **51**; Taxi, **53**; The Night Holds Terror, **55**; Crime In The Streets, **56**; Affair In Havana, Edge Of The City, **57**; Saddle The Wind, **58**; Virgin Island, **59**; Shadows, **60**; Shadows, **61**; Too Late Blues, The Webster Boy, **62**; A Child Is Waiting, **63**; The Killers, **64**; Devil's Angels, The Dirty Dozen, **67**; Faces, Roma Come Chicago, Rosemary's Baby, **68**; If It's Tuesday This Must Be Belgium, **69**; Husbands, Machine Gun McCain, **70**; Minnie And Moskowitz, **71**; A Woman Under The Influence, **74**; Capone, **75**; The Killing Of A Chinese Bookie, Mikey And Nicky, Two Minute Warning, **76**; Opening Night, **77**; Brass Target, The Fury, **78**; Gloria, **80**; Whose Life Is It Anyway? **81**; The Haircut, The Incubus, Tempest, **82**; I'm Almost Not Crazy, Marvin And Tige, **83**; Love Streams, **84**; Big Trouble, **85**; Hollywood Mavericks, **95**.

CAVALCANTI, ALBERTO: Le Train Sans Yeux, **25**; Rien Que Les Heures, **26**; En Rade, Yvette, **27**; Le Capitaine Fracasse, Le Petit Chaperon Rouge, Vous Verrez La Semaine Prochaine, **29**; Toute Sa Vie, **30**; Dans Une Ile Perdue, Les Vacances Du Diable, A Mi-Chemin Du Ciel, **31**; Coralie Et Cie, Le Mari Garçon, **33**; The First Days, **39**; Went The Day Well?, Film And Reality, Greek Testament, **42**; Champagne Charlie, **44**; Dead Of Night, **45**; Nicholas Nickleby, They Made Me A Fugitive, **47**; The First Gentleman, **48**; For Them That Trespass, **49**; Simao O Caolho, **52**; Song Of The Sea, **53**; Mulher De Verdade, **54**; Herr Puntila And His Servant Matti, **55**; Castle In The Carpathians, **57**; La Prima Notte, **58**; The Monster Of Highgate Pond, **60**; Thus Spake Theodor Herzl, **67**.

CAYATTE, ANDRE: La Fausse Maitresse, **42**; Au Bonheur Des Dames, **43**; Serenade Aux Nuages, **45**; Roger La Honte, **46**; Le Chanteur Inconnu, Les Dessous Des Cartes, **47**; Les Amants De Vérone, **48**; Retour A La Vie, **49**; Justice Is Done, **50**; We Are All Murderers, **52**; Avant Le Déluge, **54**; Le Dossier Noir, **55**; Oeil Pour Oeil, **57**; The Mirror Has Two Faces, **59**; Le Glaive Et La Balance, **63**; La Vie Conjugale, **64**; Piege Pour Cendrillon, **65**; Les Risques Du Metier, **67**; Les Chemins De Katmandou, **69**; Mourir D'Aimer, Il N'Y A Pas De Fumée Sans Feu, **72**; Le Testament, **74**; A Chacun Son Enfer, **76**; L'Amour En Question, La Raison D'Etat, **78**.

CHABROL, CLAUDE: Le Beau Serge, **58**; Les Cousins, Leda, **59**; Les Bonnes Femmes, Les Godelureaux, **60**; Seven Deadly Sins, **61**; Bluebeard, Ophelia, The Third Lover, **62**; Les Plus Belles Escroqueries Du Monde, Le Tigre Aime La Chair Fraiche, **64**; Marie-Chantal Contre Le Docteur Kha, Le Tigre Se Parfume A La Dynamite, Paris Vu Par, **65**; La Ligne De Démarcation, The Champagne Murders, La Route De Corinthe, **67**; Les Biches, La Femme Infidèle, **68**; Le Boucher, **69**; La Rupture, Que La Bête Meure, **70**; Juste Avant La Nuit, **71**; High Heels, Scoundrel In White, Ten Days Wonder, **72**; Les Noces Rouges, **73**; The Nada Gang, **74**; Les Magiciens, **75**; Alice Or The Last Escapade, Les Innocents Aux Mains Sales, Folies Bourgeoises, **76**; L'Animal, Violette Nozière, **77**; Les Liens De Sang, **78**; Le Cheval D'Orgueil, **79**; Les Folies D'Elodie, **81**; Les Fantômes Du Chapelier, Polar, **82**; Le Sang Des Autres, Cop Au Vin, Les Voleurs De La Nuit, **84**; Suivez Mon Regard, **85**; Inspector Lavardin, Je Hais Les Acteurs, **86**; Jeux D'Artifices, L'Eté En Pente Douce, Le Bonheur Se Porte Large, Masques, Sale Destin! **87**; Alouette Je Te Plumerai, The Story Of Women, **88**; Dr M, Quiet Days In Clichy, **90**; Madame Bovary, **91**; Betty, The Cry Of The Owl, **92**; The Eye Of Vichy, **93**; L'Enfer, **94**; La Ceremonie, **95**.

CHANEY, LON: Poor Jake's Dreams, **13**; The Lion The Lamb And The Man, **15**; Hell Morgan's Girl, Anything Once, A Doll's House, Fires Of Rebellion, The Flashlight, The Girl In The Checkered Coat, Pay Me, The Rescue, The Scarlet Car, Triumph, The Vengeance Of The West, **17**; Broadway Love, A Broadway Scandal, Danger Go Slow, False Faces, Fast Company, The Grand Passion, The Kaiser, The Beast Of Berlin, Riddle Gawne, The Talk Of The Town, That Devil Bateese, **18**; A Man's Country, The Miracle Man, Paid In Advance, The Trap Victory, When Bearcat Went Dry, The Wicked Darling, **19**; The Gift Supreme, Nomads Of The North, The Penalty, Treasure Island, **20**; Bits Of Life, For Those We Love, Outside The Law, Night Rose, **21**; A Blind Bargain, Flesh And Blood, The Light In The Dark, Oliver Twist, Quincy Adams Sawyer, Shadows, The Trap, Voices, Of The City, **22**; All The Brothers Were Valiant, The Glory Of Love, The Hunchback Of Notre Dame, The Shock, **23**; He Who Gets Slapped, The Next Corner, **24**; The Monster, The Phantom Of The Opera, The Tower Of Lies, The Unholy Three, **25**; Outside The Law, The Black Bird, The Road To Mandalay, Tell It To The Marines, **26**; London After Midnight, Mockery, Mr Wu, The Unknown, **27**; The Big City, Laugh Clown Laugh, West Of Zanzibar, While The City Sleeps, **28**; Thunder, Where East Is East, **29**; The Unholy Three, **30**.

CHAPLIN, CHARLES: Selection: A Busy Day, The Face On The Barroom Floor, His Favorite Pastime, Kid Auto Races At Venice, The Knockout, Mabel's Busy Day, The Masquerader, Tillie's Punctured Romance, **14**; Shanghaied, The Tramp, **15**; Behind The Screen, The Fireman, The Floorwalker, The Pawnshop, The Rink, The Vagabond, **16**; The Cure, Easy Street, The Immigrant, **17**; A Dog's Life, Shoulder Arms, **18**; Sunnyside, **19**; The Idle Class, The Kid, **21**; Pay Day, **22**; The Pilgrim, A Woman Of Paris, **23**; The Gold Rush, **25**; The Circus, **28**; City Lights, **31**; Modern Times, **36**; The Great Dictator, **40**; Monsieur Verdoux, **47**; Limelight, **52**; A King In New York, **57**; The Countess From Hong Kong, **66**.

CHARISSE, CYD: Mission To Moscow, Something To Shout About, **43**; The Harvey Girls, Three Wise Fools, Till The Clouds Roll By, Ziegfeld Follies, **46**; Fiesta, The Unfinished Dance, **47**; The Kissing Bandit, On An Island With You, Words And Music, **48**; East Side West Side, Tension, **49**; Mark Of The Renegade, **51**; Singin' In The Rain, The Wild North, **52**; The Band Wagon, Easy To Love, Sombrero, **53**; Brigadoon, Deep In My Heart, **54**; It's Always Fair Weather, **55**; Meet Me In Las Vegas, **56**; Invitation To The Dance, Silk Stockings, **57**; Party Girl, Twilight For The Gods, **58**; Black Tights, **60**; Five Golden Hours, **61**; Two Weeks In Another Town, **62**; The Silencers, **66**; Maroc 7, **67**; Warlords Of Atlantis, **78**; That's Entertainment! III, **94**.

CHAYEFSKY, PADDY: As Young As You Feel, **51**; Marty, **55**; The Catered Affair, **56**; The Bachelor Party, **57**; The Goddess, **58**; Middle Of The Night, **59**; The Americanization Of Emily, **64**; Paint Your Wagon, **69**; The Hospital, **71**; Network, **76**; Altered States, **80**.

CHEN KAIGE: Yellow Earth, **84**; The Big Parade, **85**; King Of Children, **87**; Life On A String, **91**; Farewell My Concubine, **93**; Temptress Moon, **96**.

CHER: Wild On The Beach, **65**; Come Back To The Five And Dime Jimmy Dean Jimmy Dean, **82**; Silkwood, **83**; Mask, **85**; Moonstruck, Suspect, The Witches Of Eastwick, **87**; Mermaids, **90**; The Player, **92**; Faithful, **96**.

CHEVALIER, MAURICE: Trop Crédule (and other silent short films over 20 years), **08**; Innocents Of Paris, The Love Parade, **29**; The Big Pond, Paramount On Parade, Playboy Of Paris, **30**; The Smiling Lieutenant, **31**; Love Me Tonight, Make Me A Star, One Hour With You, **32**; A Bedtime Story, The Way To Love, **33**; The Merry Widow, **34**; Folies Bergères, **35**; Beloved Vagabond, **36**; The Man Of The Hour, With A Smile, **37**; Break The News, **38**; Pièges, **39**; Le Silence Est D'Or, **47**; Just Me, A Royal Affair, **50**; Schlager-parade, **53**; Cento Anni D'Amore, My Seven Little Sins, **54**; Love In The Afternoon, **57**; Gigi, **58**; Count Your Blessings, **59**; Black Tights, A Breath Of Scandal, Can-Can, Pépé, **60**; Fanny, **61**; In Search Of The Castaways, Jessica, **62**; A New Kind Of Love, **63**; I'd Rather Be Rich, Panic Button, **64**; Monkeys Go Home! **67.**

CHRISTIAN-JAQUE: Le Bidon D'Or, **32**; Adhemar Lampiot, Le Tendron d'Achille, Ça Colle, La Boeuf Sur La Langue, **33**; L'Hôtel Du Libre-Echange, **34**; Sous La Griffe, La Sonnette d'Alarme, **35**; Monsieur Personne, Rigolboche, Josette, **36**; La Maison D'en Face, A Venise Une Nuit, The Pearls Of The Crown, Francis The First, **37**; Les Pirates Du Rail, **38**; C'Etait Moi, L'Enfer Des Anges, **39**; Le Grand Elan, **40**; Who Killed Santa Claus?, Premier Bal, **41**; La Symphonie Fantastique, **42**; Voyage Sans Espoir, **43**; Carmen, Boule De Suif, **45**; Un Revenant, **46**; Man to Men **48**; The Wind Is My Lover, Souvenirs perdus, **50**; Bluebeard, **51**; Adorable Creatures, Fanfan La Tulipe, **52**; Lucrezia Borgia, **53**; Daughters Of Destiny, Madame Du Barry, **54**; Nana, **55**; If All The Guys In The World, **56**; The Law Is The Law, **58**; Babette Goes To War, **59**; Love And The Frenchwoman, **60**; Madame Sans-Gêne, **61**; The Black Tulip, **63**; Le Repas Des Fauves, **64**; The Dirty Game, Marco The Magnificent, **65**; La Seconde Verité, Le Saint Prend L'Affût, **66**; Dead Run, **67**; Lady Hamilton, **68**; The Legend of Frenchy King, **71**; Dr Justice, **75**; La Vie Parisienne, **78**; Carmé: L'Homme A La Camera, **80**.

CHRISTIE, JULIE: Crooks Anonymous, The Fast Lady, **62**; Billy Liar, **63**; Darling, Doctor Zhivago, Young Cassidy, **65**; Fahrenheit 451, **66**; Performer, Far From The Madding Crowd, **67**; Petulia, **68**; In Search Of Gregory, **70**; The Go-Between, McCabe And Mrs Miller, **71**; Don't Look Now, Nashville, **73**; Shampoo, **75**; Demon Seed, **77**; Heaven Can Wait, **78**; Memoirs Of A Survivor, **81**; The Return Of The Soldier, The Gold Diggers, Heat And Dust, **83**; Miss Mary, Power, **86**; Secret Obsession, **88**; Fools Of Fortune, **90**; Dragonheart, Hamlet, **96**.

CIMINO, MICHAEL: Magnum Force, **73**; Thunderbolt And Lightfoot, **74**; The Deer Hunter, **78**; Heaven's Gate, **80**; Year Of The Dragon, **85**; The Sicilian, **87**; Desperate Hours, **90**; The Sunchaser, **96**.

CLAIR, RENE: Entr'acte, Paris Qui Dort, **24**; Le Fantôme Du Moulin Rouge, **25**; Le Voyage Imaginaire, **26**; The Italian Straw Hat, La Proie Du Vent, **27**; Les Deux Timides, **28**; Sous Les Toits De Paris, **30**; A Nous La Liberté, Le Million, **31**; Quatorze Juillet, **32**; Le Dernier Milliardaire, **34**; The Ghost Goes West, **36**; Break The News, **38**; The Flame Of New Orleans, **41**; I Married A Witch, **42**; Forever And A Day, **43**; It Happened Tomorrow, **44**; And Then There Were None, **45**; Le Silence Est D'Or, **47**; La Beauté Du Diable, **50**; Les Belles De Nuit, **54**; Les Grandes Manoeuvres, **56**; Porte De Lilas, **57**; Love And The Frenchwoman, Tout L'Or Du Monde, **60**; Three Fables Of Love, **62**; Les Fêtes Galantes, **65**; Ladies And Gentlemen, **84**.

CLARKE, T E B: Champagne Charlie, **44**; Dead Of Night, Johnny Frenchman, **45**; Hue And Cry, **47**; Against The Wind, **48**; Passport To Pimlico, **49**; The Blue Lamp, **50**; The Lavender Hill Mob, The Magnet, **51**; Encore **52**; The Titfield Thunderbolt, **53**; Barnacle Bill, Gideon Of Scotland Yard, Law And Disorder, A Tale Of Two Cities, **58**; Sons And Lovers, **60**; The Horse Without A Head, **63**; A Man Could Get Killed, **66**; A Hitch In Time, **79**; High Rise Donkey, **80**.

CLAYTON, JACK: The Bespoke Overcoat, **55**; Room At The Top, **58**; The Innocents, **61**; The Pumpkin Eater, **64**; Our Mother's House, **67**; The Great Gatsby, **74**; Something Wicked This Way Comes, **83**; The Lonely Passion Of Judith Hearne, **87**.

CLEMENT, RENE: La Bataille Du Rail, Le Père Tranquille, **46**; Les Maudits, **47**; Au-dela Des Grilles, **49**; Le Château De Verre, **50**; Jeux Interdits, **52**; Knave Of Hearts, **54**; Monsieur Ripois, Gervaise, **56**; Barrage Contre Le Pacifique, **58**; Plein Soleil, **59**; Quelle Joie De Vivre, **61**; Jour Et L'Heure, **63**; Les Felins, **64**; Is Paris Burning?, **66**; Le Passager De La Pluie, **70**; La Maison Sous Les Arbres, **71**; La Course Du Lievre A Travers Les Champs, **72**; The Babysitter, **75**.

CLIFT, MONTGOMERY: Red River, The Search, **48**; The Heiress, **49**; The Big Lift, **50**; A Place In The Sun, **51**; From Here To Eternity, I Confess, Indiscretion Of An American Wife, **53**; Raintree County, **57**; Lonelyhearts, The Young Lions, **58**; Suddenly Last Summer **59**; Wild River, **60**; Judgment At Nuremberg, The Misfits, **61**; Freud, **62**; The Defector, **66**.

CLOSE, GLENN: The World According To Garp, **82**; The Big Chill, **83**; Greystoke: The Legend Of Tarzan Lord Of The Apes, The Natural **84**; Jagged Edge, Maxie, **85**; Fatal Attraction, **87**; Dangerous Liaisons, **88**; Immediate Family, **89**; Hamlet, Reversal Of Fortune, **90**; Hook, Meeting Venus, **91**; House Of The Spirits, **93**; The Paper, **94**; Mary Reilly, **95**; Mars Attacks!, 101 Dalmatians, **96**; Air Force One, **97**.

CLOUZOT, HENRI-GEORGES: La Terreur Des Batignolles, **31**; L'Assassin Habite Au 21, **42**; Le Corbeau, **43**; Quai Des Orfèvres, **47**; Manon, Retour A La Vie, **49**; Miquette, **50**; The Wages Of Fear, **53**; Les Diaboliques, **54**; Le Mystère Picasso, **56**; Les Espions, **57**; La Vérité, **60**; La Prisonnière, **69**.

COBB, LEE J: Ali Baba Goes To Town, North Of The Rio Grande, Rustler's Valley, **37**; Danger On The Air, **38**; Golden Boy, The Phantom Creeps, **39**; Men Of Boys Town, Paris Calling, This Thing Called Love, **41**; Buckskin Frontier, The Moon Is Down, The Song Of Bernadette, Tonight We Raid Calais, **43**; Winged Victory, **44**; Anna And The King Of Siam, **46**; Boomerang!, Captain From Castile, Johnny O'clock, **47**; Call Northside 777, Performer, The Dark Past, The Luck Of The Irish, The Miracle Of The Bells, **48**; Thieves' Highway, **49**; The Man Who Cheated Himself, **50**; The Family Secret, Sirocco, **51**; The Fighter, **52**; The Tall Texan, **53**; Day Of Triumph, Gorilla At Large, On The Waterfront, Yankee Pasha, **54**; The Left Hand Of God, The Racers, The Road To Denver, **55**; The Man In The Gray Flannel Suit, Miami Exposé, **56**; 12 Angry Men, The Garment Jungle, The Three Faces Of Eve, **57**; The Brothers Karamazov, Man Of The West, Party Girl, **58**; But Not For Me, Green Mansions, The Trap, **59**; Exodus, **60**; Four Horsemen Of The Apocalypse, How The West Was Won, **62**; Come Blow Your Horn, **63**; Our Man Flint, **66**; In Like Flint, **67**; Coogan's Bluff, Mafia, They Came To Rob Las Vegas, **68**; Mackenna's Gold, **69**; The Liberation Of LB Jones, Macho Callahan, **70**; Lawman, **71**; The Exorcist, The Man Who Loved Cat Dancing, **73**; Blood Sweat And Fear, Mork Il Poliziotto, The Nark, Ultimatum, **75**.

COBURN, JAMES: Face Of A Fugitive, **59**; The Magnificent Seven, **60**; Hell Is For Heroes, **62**; Charade, The Great Escape, **63**; The Americanization Of Emily, **64**; A High Wind In Jamaica, The Loved One, Major Dundee, **65**; Dead Heat On A Merry-Go-Round, Our Man Flint, What Did You Do In The War Daddy?, **66**; In Like Flint, The President's Analyst, Waterhole 3, **67**; Candy, Duffy, **68**; Hard Contract, **69**; The Carey Treatment, Fistful Of Dynamite, **72**; Harry In Your Pocket, The Last Of Sheila, Pat Garrett And Billy The Kid, **73**; The Internecine Project, **74**; Bite The Bullet, Hard Times, **75**; Midway, **76**; Cross Of Iron, **77**; Firepower, The Muppet Movie, **79**; The Baltimore Bullet, Mr Patman, **80**; High Risk, **81**; Martin's Day, **84**; Death Of A Soldier, **86**; Walking After Midnight, **88**; Young Guns II, **90**; Hudson Hawk, **91**; Deadfall, The Hit List, Sister Act 2: Back In The Habit, **93**; Maverick, **94**; Keys To Tulsa, **95**; Eraser, **96**; Affliction, **97**.

COCTEAU, JEAN: Le Sang D'Un Poète, **30**; L'Eternel Retour, **43**; Les Dames Du Bois De Boulogne, Beauty And The Beast, **45**; Eagle With Two Heads, Les Parents Terribles, **48**; Orphée, **49**; Les Enfants Terribles, **50**; Le Bel Indifferent, **57**; Le Testament D'Orphée, **60**.

CODY, LEW: Comrade John, **15**; many silent two-reelers such as The Broken Butterfly, **19**; Dangerous Pastime, **21**; The Valley Of Silent Men, **22**; Rupert Of Hentzau, **23**; The Shooting Of Dan McGrew, So This Is Marriage, **24**; The Sporting Venus, **25**; The Gay Deceiver, Monte Carlo, **26**; Adam And Evil, The Demi-Bride, **27**; Beau Broadway, Wickedness Preferred, **28**; What A Widow!, Divorce Amongst Friends, **30**; Dishonored, Beyond Victory, Sweepstakes, A Woman Of Experience, The Common Law, Sporting Blood, **31**; 70,000 Witnesses, The Common Law, A Parisian Romance, **32**; Sitting Pretty, Wine Women And Song, **33**; Shoot The Works, **34**.

COEN, JOEL & ETHAN: Blood Simple, **84**; Crimewave, Spies like us (Joel only), **85**; Raising Arizona, **87**; Miller's Crossing, **90**; Barton Fink, **91**; The Hudsucker Proxy, **94**; Fargo, **95**, The Big Liebowski, **97**.

COLBERT, CLAUDETTE: For The Love Of Mike, **27**; A Hole In The Wall, The Lady Lies, **29**; The Big Pond, L'Enigmatique M Parkes, Manslaughter, Young Man Of Manhattan, **30**; His Woman, Honor Among Lovers, Secrets Of A Secretary, The Smiling Lieutenant, **31**; The Man From Yesterday, The Misleading Lady, The Phantom President, The Sign Of The Cross, The Wiser Sex, **32**; I Cover The Waterfront, Three-cornered Moon, Tonight Is Ours, Torch Singer, **33**; Cleopatra, Four Frightened People, Imitation Of Life, It Happened One Night, **34**; The Bride Comes Home, The Gilded Lily, Private Worlds, She Married Her Boss, **35**; Under Two Flags, **36**; I Met Him In Paris, Maid Of Salem, Tovarich, **37**; Bluebeard's Eighth Wife, **38**; Drums Along The Mohawk, It's A Wonderful World, Midnight, Zaza, **39**; Arise My Love, Boom Town, **40**; Remember The Day, Skylark, **41**; The Palm Beach Story, **42**; No Time For Love, So Proudly We Hail!, **43**; Practically Yours, Since You Went Away, **44**; Guest Wife, **45**; The Secret Heart, Tomorrow Is Forever, Without Reservations, **46**; The Egg And I, **47**; Family Honeymoon, Sleep My Love, **48**; Bride For Sale, **49**; The Secret Fury, Three Came Home, **50**; Let's Make It Legal, Thunder On The Hill, **51**; The Planter's Wife, **52**; Daughters Of Destiny, Affairs In Versailles, **54**; Parrish, **55**; Texas Lady, **61**.

COLLINS, JOAN: Judgment Deferred, Lady Godiva Rides Again, **51**; I Believe In You, **52**; Cosh Boy, Decameron Nights, Turn The Key Softly, **53**; The Good Die Young, The Woman's Angle, **54**; The Adventures Of Sadie, The Girl In The Red Velvet Swing, Land Of The Pharaohs, The Square Ring, The Virgin Queen, **55**; The Opposite Sex, **56**; Island In The Sun, Sea Wife, Stopover Tokyo, The Wayward Bus, **57**; The Bravados, Rally Round The Flag Boys!, **58**; Esther And The King, Seven Thieves, **60**; The Road To Hong Kong, **62**; Warning Shot, **67**; Can Hieronymus Merkin Ever Forget Mercy Humppe And Find True Happiness?, If It's Tuesday This Must Be Belgium, Subterfuge, **69**; The Executioner, Up In The Cellar, **70**; Quest For Love, Revenge, **71**; Fear In The Night, Tales From The Crypt, **72**; Tales That Witness Madness, **73**; Dark Places, **74**; Alfie Darling, The Devil Within Her, **75**; Tom Jones, **76**; Empire Of The Ants, **77**; The Big Sleep, The Stud, Zero To Sixty, **78**; The Bitch, Game For Vultures, Sunburn, **79**; Homework, Nutcracker, **82**; Decadence, **94**; In the Bleak Midwinter, **95**.

COLMAN, RONALD: Sheba, **18**; Snow In The Desert, The Toilers, **19**; Anna The Adventuress, The Black Spider, **20**; Handcuffs Or Kisses, **21**; The Eternal City, The White Sister, **23**; $20 A Week, Her Night Of Romance, Romola, **24**; The Dark Angel, Lady Windermere's Fan, The Sporting Venus, Stella Dallas, **25**; Beau Geste, Kiki, **26**; Magic Flame, **27**; Two Lovers, **28**; Bulldog Drummond, Condemned, **29**; The Devil To Pay, Raffles, **30**; Arrowsmith, The Unholy Garden, **31**; Cynara, **32**; The Masquerader, **33**; Bulldog Drummond Strikes Back, **34**; Clive Of India, The Man Who Broke The Bank At Monte Carlo, A Tale Of Two Cities, **35**; Under Two Flags, **36**; Lost Horizon, The Prisoner Of Zenda, **37**; If I Were King, **38**; The Light That Failed, **39**; Lucky Partners, **40**; My Life With Caroline, **41**; Random Harvest, **42**; The Talk Of The Town, **43**; Kismet, **44**; The Late George Apley, **47**; A Double Life, **48**; Champagne For Caesar, **50**; Around The World In 80 Days, **56**; The Story Of Mankind, **57**.

CONKLIN, CHESTER: Tillie's Punctured Romance (and another dozen silent shorts with Chaplin), Uncle Tom's Cabin, **14**; Ambrose's Sour Grapes, The Best Of Enemies, A One Night Stand, **15**; Cinders Of Love, A Tugboat Romeo, **16**; A Clever Dummy, An International Sneak, **17**; It Pays To Exercise, Ladies First, Yankee Doodle In Berlin, **18**; Chicken A La Cabaret, **20**; Skirts, **21**; Anna Christie, Desire, **23**; Galloping Fish, Greed, **24**; The Masked Bride, The Phantom Of The Opera, A Woman Of The World, **25**; Behind The Front, The Duchess Of Buffalo, We're In The Navy Now, **26**; Cabaret, McFadden's Flats, Tell It To Sweeney, **27**; The Big Noise, Gentlemen Prefer Blondes, The Haunted House, Tillie's Punctured Romance, Varsity, **28**; Fast Company, The House Of Horror, The Studio Murder Mystery, The Virginian, **29**; Swing High, **30**; Her Majesty Love, **31**; Hallelujah I'm A Bum, **33**; Modern Times, **36**; Every Day's A Holiday, **37**; Hollywood Cavalcade, **39**; The Great Dictator, **40**; Hail The Conquering Hero, Knickerbocker Holiday, **44**; The Perils Of Pauline, **47**; The Beautiful Blonde From Bashful Bend, **49**; Paradise Alley, **61**; A Big Hand For The Little Lady, **66**.

CONNERY, SEAN: Action Of The Tiger, No Road Back, Time Lock, **57**; Another Time Another Place, Hell Drivers, **58**; Darby O'Gill And The Little People, Tarzan's Greatest Adventure, **59**; On The Fiddle, **61**; Dr No, The Frightened City, The Longest Day, **62**; From Russia With Love, **63**; Goldfinger, Marnie, Woman Of Straw, **64**; The Hill, Thunderball, **65**; A Fine Madness, **66**; You Only Live Twice, **67**; Shalako, **68**; La Tenda Rossa, The Molly Maguires, **70**; Diamonds Are Forever, **71**; The Anderson Tapes, **72**; The Offence, **73**; Murder On The Orient Express, Zardoz, **74**; The Man Who Would Be King, Ransom, The Wind And The Lion, **75**; The Next Man, Robin And Marian, **76**; A Bridge Too Far, **77**; Cuba, The Great Train Robbery, Meteor, **79**; Outland, Time Bandits, **81**; Five Days One Summer, Never Say Never Again, **83**; Highlander, The Name Of The Rose, **86**; The Untouchables, **87**; Memories Of Me, The Presidio, **88**; Family Business, Indiana Jones And The Last Crusade, **89**; The Hunt For Red October, The Russia House, **90**; Highlander II: The Quickening, Robin Hood: Prince Of Thieves, **91**; Medicine Man, **92**; Rising Sun, **93**; Just Cause, Dragonheart, **95**; First Knight, **95**; The Rock, **96**; The Avengers, **97**.

CONTE, RICHARD: Heaven With A Barbed Wire Fence, **39**; Guadalcanal Diary, **43**; The Purple Heart, **44**; A Bell For Adano, Captain Eddie, The Spider, A Walk In The Sun, **45**; 13 Rue Madeleine, Somewhere In The Night, **46**; The Other Love, **47**; Call Northside 777, Cry Of The City, **48**; House Of Strangers, Thieves' Highway, Whirlpool, **49**; The Sleeping City, Under The Gun, **50**; Hollywood Story, **51**; The Fighter, The Raiders, **52**; The Blue Gardenia, **53**; Highway Dragnet, **54**; Bengazi, The Big Combo, I'll Cry Tomorrow, New York Confidential, Target Zero, **55**; Full Of Life, **56**; The Brothers Rico, **57**; The Sea Wall, **58**; They Came To Cordura, **59**; Ocean's 11, **60**; Who's Been Sleeping In My Bed?, **63**; Circus World, **64**; The Greatest Story Ever Told, Synanon, **65**; Assault On A Queen, **66**; Hotel, Tony Rome, **67**; Lady In Cement, **68**; Explosion, **69**; The Godfather, No Way Out, **72**; Roma Violenta, **75**.

COOPER, GARY: The Thundering Herd, **25**; The Winning Of Barbara Worth, **26**; Arizona Bound, Children Of Divorce, It, The Last Outlaw, Nevada, Wings, **27**; Beau Sabreur, Doomsday, The First Kiss, Half A Bride, The Legion Of The Condemned, Lilac Time, **28**; Betrayal, The Shopworn Angel, The Virginian, Wolf Song, **29**; A Man From Wyoming, Morocco, Only The Brave, Paramount On Parade, Seven Days Leave, The Spoilers, The Texan, **30**; City Streets, Fighting Caravans, His Woman, I Take This Woman, **31**; Devil And The Deep, Farewell To Arms, If I Had A Million, Make Me A Star, **32**; Alice In Wonderland, Design For Living, One Sunday Afternoon, Today We Live, **33**; Now And Forever, Operator 13, **34**; The Lives Of A Bengal Lancer, Peter Ibbetson, The Wedding Night, **35**; Desire, The General Died At Dawn, Hollywood Boulevard, Mr Deeds Goes To Town, The Plainsman, **36**; Souls At Sea, **37**; The Adventures Of Marco Polo, Bluebeard's Eighth Wife, The Cowboy And The Lady, **38**; Beau Geste, The Real Glory, **39**; Northwest Mounted Police, The Westerner, **40**; Ball Of Fire, Meet John Doe, Sergeant York, **41**; The Pride Of The Yankees, **42**; For Whom The Bell Tolls, **43**; Casanova Brown, The Story Of Dr Wassell, **44**; Along Came Jones, Saratoga Trunk, **45**; Cloak And Dagger, **46**; Unconquered, Variety Girl, **47**; Good Sam, **48**; The Fountainhead, It's A Great Feeling, Task Force, **49**; Bright Leaf, Dallas, **50**; Distant Drums, It's A Big Country, Starlift, You're In The Navy Now, **51**; High Noon, Springfield Rifle, **52**; Blowing Wild, Return To Paradise, **53**; Garden Of Evil, Vera Cruz, **54**; The Court-martial Of Billy Mitchell, **55**; Friendly Persuasion, **56**; Love In The Afternoon, **57**; Man Of The West, Ten North Frederick, **58**; Alias Jesse James, The Hanging Tree, They Came To Cordura, The Wreck Of The Mary Deare, **59**; The Naked Edge, **61**.

COOPER, JACKIE: Sunny Side Up, **30**; The Champ, Skippy, Sooky, Young Donovan's Kid, **31**; Divorce In The Family, When A Feller Needs A Friend, **32**; The Bowery, Broadway To Hollywood, Lone Cowboy, **33**; Peck's Bad Boy, Treasure Island, **34**; Dinky, O'Shaughnessy's Boy, **35**; The Devil Is A Sissy, Tough Guy, **36**; Boy Of The Streets, **37**; Gangster's Boy, That Certain Age, White Banners, **38**; The Big Guy, Newsboys' Home, Scouts To The Rescue, Spirit Of Culver, Streets Of New York, Two Bright Boys, What A Life, **39**; Gallant Sons, The Return Of Frank James, Seventeen, **40**; Glamour Boy, Her First Beau, Life With Henry, Ziegfeld Girl, **41**; Men Of Texas, The Navy Comes Through, Syncopation, **42**; Where Are Your Children?, **43**; French Leave, Kilroy Was Here, Stork Bites Man, **47**; Everything's Ducky, **61**; The Love Machine, **71**; Stand Up And Be Counted, **72**; Chosen Survivors, **74**; The Pink Panther Strikes Again, **76**; Superman, **78**; Superman II, **80**; Superman III, **83**; Superman IV: The Quest For Peace, Surrender, **87**; Going Hollywood: The War Years, **88**.

COOPER, MERIAN C & SCHOEDSACK ERNEST B: Selection: Grass, **25**; Chang, **27**; Gow The Head Hunter, **28**; The Four Feathers, Lucky Devils, The Hounds Of Zaroff, The Phantom Of Crestwood, **32**; Ann Vickers, Flying Down To Rio, King Kong, Little Women, Morning Glory, The Son Of Kong, **33**; The Crime Doctor, The Lost Patrol, **34**; The Last Days Of Pompeii, She, **35**; The Toy Wife, **38**; The Four Feathers, **39**; The Fugitive, **47**; Three Godfathers, Fort Apache, **48**; Mighty Joe Young, She Wore A Yellow Ribbon, **49**; Rio Grande, Wagon Master, **50**; The Quiet Man, This Is Cinerama, **52**; The Sun Shines Bright, **53**; The Searchers, **56**; The Best Of Cinerama, **63**.

COPPOLA, FRANCIS FORD: Tonight For Sure, **62**; Battle Beyond The Sun, Dementia 13, **63**; Is Paris Burning?, You're A Big Boy Now, **66**; Finian's Rainbow, **68**; The Rain People, **69**; The Godfather, **72**; The Conversation, The Godfather Part II, **74**; Apocalypse Now, **79**; One From The Heart, **82**; The Outsiders, Rumble Fish, **83**; The Cotton Club, **84**; Captain Eo, Peggy Sue Got Married, **86**; Gardens Of Stone, **87**; Tucker: The Man And His Dream, **88**; New York Stories, **89**; The Godfather Part III, Hollywood Mavericks, **90**; Bram Stoker's Dracula, **92**; Jack, **96**; The Rainmaker, **97**.

CORMAN, ROGER: The Fast And The Furious, The Monster From The Ocean Floor, **54**; Apache Woman, **55**; The Day The World Ended, The Gunslinger, It Conquered The World, The Oklahoma Woman, **56**; Attack Of The Crab Monsters, Not Of This Earth, Rock All Night, Sorority Girl, **57**; The Cry Baby Killer, Machine-gun Kelly, Night Of The Blood Beast, **58**; Attack Of The Giant Leeches, A Bucket Of Blood, **59**; Fall Of The House Of Usher, The Last Woman On Earth, The Little Shop Of Horrors, **60**; Atlas, Creature From The Haunted Sea, The Pit And The Pendulum, **61**; Tales Of Terror, Tower Of London, **62**; Dementia 13, The Haunted Palace, The Raven, The Terror, The Young Racers, **63**; The Masque Of The Red Death, **64**; Tomb Of Ligeia, **65**; The Wild Angels, **66**; The St Valentine's Day Massacre, The Trip, **67**; Target, Bloody Mama, The Dunwich Horror, The Student Nurses, **70**; Von Richthofen And Brown, **71**; Boxcar Bertha, Unholy Rollers, **72**; I Escaped From Devil's Island, **73**; Big Bad Mama, **74**; Capone, Death Race 2000, Producer, **75**; Eat My Dust!, Fighting Mad, Lumiere, Moving Violation, **76**; Grand Theft Auto, I Never Promised You A Rose Garden, Thunder And Lightning, **77**; Avalanche, **78**; Fast Charlie, The Moonbeam Rider, Rock 'n' Roll High School, Saint Jack, **79**; Battle Beyond The Stars, **80**; Galaxy Of Terror, Smokey Bites The Dust, **81**; Forbidden World, **82**; Love Letters, Space Raiders, **83**; Amazons, Big Bad Mama II, Munchies, Slumber Party Massacre II, Daddy's Boys, Nightfall, The Terror Within, **88**; Bloodfist, Lords Of The Deep, Masque Of The Red Death, Time Trackers, Two To Tango, Wizards Of The Lost Kingdom II, **89**; Back To Back, Bloodfist II, Frankenstein Unbound, The Haunting Of Morella, Overexposed, Primary Target, Watchers 2, **90** Play Murder For Me, **91**; Bloodfist III: Forced To Fight, Field Of Fire, Final Embrace, Immortal Sins, **92**; Blackbelt II: Fatal Force, Dracula Rising, Dragon Fire, Eight Hundred Leagues Down The Amazon, Final Judgment, Little Miss Millions, Live By The Fist, Philadelphia, To Sleep With A Vampire, **93**; Threesome, **94**.

COSTA-GAVRAS, CONSTANTIN: The Sleeping Car Murders, **65**; Shock Troops, **67** Z, **68**; The Confession, **70**; State Of Siege, **73**; Special Section, **75**; Madame Rosa, **77**; Clair De Femme, **79**; Missing, **82**; Hanna K, **83**; Family Business, **86**; Betrayed, **88**; Music Box, **89**; Against Oblivion, **92**; Mad Cirty, **97**.

COSTNER, KEVIN: Chasing Dreams, Frances, Night Shift, **82**; Stacy's Knights, Table For Five, Testament, The Big Chill, **83**; The Gunrunner, **84**; American Flyers, Fandango, Silverado, **85**; Shadows Run Black, Sizzle Beach USA, **86**; No Way Out, The Untouchables, **87**; Bull Durham, **88**; Field Of Dreams, **89**; Dances With Wolves, Revenge, **90**; JFK, Robin Hood: Prince Of Thieves, **91**; The Bodyguard, **92**; A Perfect World, **93**; Wyatt Earp, The War, **94**; Waterworld, **95**; Tin Cup, **96**.

COTTEN, JOSEPH: Citizen Kane, Lydia, **41**; The Magnificent Ambersons, **42**; Hers To Hold, Shadow Of A Doubt, Journey Into Fear, **43**; Gaslight, I'll Be Seeing You, Since You Went Away, **44**; Love Letters, **45**; Duel In The Sun, **46**; The Farmer's Daughter, **47**; Portrait Of Jennie, **48**; Beyond The Forest, The Third Man, Under Capricorn, **49**; September Affair, Two Flags West, Walk Softly Stranger,

0; Half Angel, The Man With A Cloak, ›king Express, **51**; The Steel Trap, Untamed ›ontier, Othello, **52**; A Blueprint For ›urder, Niagara, **53**; Special Delivery, **55**; ›e Bottom Of The Bottle, The Killer Is ›oose, **56**; The Halliday Brand, **57**; From The ›arth To The Moon, Touch Of Evil, **58**; ›e Angel Wore Red, **60**; The Last Sunset, **1**; The Great Sioux Massacre, Hush . . Hush Sweet Charlotte, **65**; The Money ›ap, The Oscar, **66**; Brighty Of The ›and Canyon, Jack Of Diamonds, Some May ›ve, **67**; Petulia, **69**; The Grasshopper, ›ra! Tora! Tora!, **70**; The Abominable Dr ›ibes, Doomsday Voyage, **72**; A ›elicate Balance, Soylent Green, Timber ›amps, **73**; F For Fake, **74**; Airport 77, ›wilight's Last Gleaming, **77**; Caravans, **78**; ›uyana: Cult Of The Damned, The ›earse, Heaven's Gate, The House Where ›eath Lives, **80**; The Survivor, **81**.

›OURTENAY, TOM: The Loneliness Of ›e Long Distance Runner, Private Potter, **62**; ›lly Liar, **63**; King And Country, **64**; ›octor Zhivago, King Rat, Operation Crossbow, **5**; The Day The Fish Came Out, Night › The Generals, **67**; A Dandy In Aspic, **68**; ›tley, **69**; One Day In The Life Of Ivan ›enisovich, To Catch A Spy, **71**; The Dresser, **3**; Happy New Year, **87**; Let Him Have **91**; The Boy from Mercury, **96**.

›OUTARD, RAOUL: Paradiso Terrestre, **6**; Pêcheur D'Islande, **59**; Chronicle Of A ›ummer, Le Petit Soldat, Tirez Sur Le ›aniste, Une Femme Est Une Femme, A Bout ›e Souffle/Breathless, **60**; Jules Et Jim, ›ola, **61**; La Poupée, Love At Twenty, **62**; ›ontempt, Les Baisers, Les Carabiniers, ›vre Sa Vie, Bande A Part, **63**; Les Plus ›elles Escroqueries Du Monde, Male ›ompanion, La Peau Douce, Une Femme ›ariée, **64**; Alphaville, Pierrot Le Fou, **5**; Two Or Three Things I Know About Her, **6**; La Chinoise, The Sailor From ›braltar, Weekend, **67**; The Bride Wore ›ack, L'Etoile Du Sud, **68**; Z, **69**; The ›onfession, Hoa-Binh, **70**; Embassy, The ›erusalem File, **72**; Le Crabe Tambour, **7**; Passion, **82**; First Name: Carmen, **83**; ›angerous Moves, **84**; Max My Love, **6**; **87**; Blanc De Chine, Peaux De Vaches, **8**; Bethune: The Making Of A Hero, Les ›fants Volants, **91**; La Naissance De Amour, **93**; Le Cooeur Fantome, **96**..

›OWARD, NOEL: Hearts Of The World, **8**; The Queen Was In The Parlour, The ›ortex, **27**; The Scoundrel, **35**; In Which ›e Serve, **42**; This Happy Breed, **44**; Blithe ›pirit, Brief Encounter, **45**; The ›stonished Heart, **50**; Meet Me Tonight, **52**; ›ound The World In 80 Days, **56**; Our ›an In Havana, Surprise Package, **60**; Paris ›hen It Sizzles, **64**; Bunny Lake Is ›issing, **65**; A Matter Of Innocence, **67**; ›oom!, Star!, **68**; The Italian Job, **69**.

›RAVEN, WES: Last House On The ›eft, **72**; The Hills Have Eyes, Summer Of ›ear, **78**; Deadly Blessing, **81**; Swamp ›hing, **82**; A Nightmare On Elm Street, **84**; ›e Hills Have Eyes Part II, **85**; Deadly ›riend, **86**; Flowers In The Attic, A Nightmare ›n Elm Street 3: Dream Warriors, **87**; ›e Serpent And The Rainbow, **88**; Shocker, **9**; Bloodfist II, **90**; The People Under ›e Stairs, **91**; Wes Craven's New ›ightmare, **94**; Scream, **96**.

›RAWFORD, JOAN: Lady Of The ›ight, Old Clothes, The Only Thing, Pretty ›adies, Proud Flesh, Sally Irene And ›ary, **25**; The Boob, Paris, Tramp Tramp ›ramp, **26**; Spring Fever, The Taxi ›ancer, Twelve Miles Out, The Understanding ›eart, The Unknown, Winners Of The ›ilderness, **27**; Across To Singapore, Dream › Love, Four Walls, The Law Of The ›ange, Our Dancing Daughters, Rose Marie, ›est Point, **28**; The Duke Steps Out, The ›ollywood Revue Of 29, Our Modern Maidens, ›ntamed, **29**; Montana Moon, Our ›ushing Brides, **30**; Dance Fools Dance, ›aughing Sinners, Paid, Possessed, The ›tolen Jools, This Modern Age, **31**; Grand ›otel, Letty Lynton, Rain, **32**; Dancing ›ady, Today We Live, **33**; Chained, Forsaking › Others, Sadie McKee, **34**; I Live My ›fe, No More Ladies, **35**; The Gorgeous ›ussy, Love On The Run, **36**; The Bride ›ore Red, The Last Of Mrs Cheyney, ›annequin, **37**; The Shining Hour, **38**; ›e Follies Of 39, The Women, **39**; Strange ›argo, Susan And God, **40**; When Ladies ›eet, A Woman's Face, **41**; Reunion In ›rance, They All Kissed The Bride, **42**; ›bove Suspicion, **43**; Hollywood Canteen, **44**; Mildred Pierce, **45**; Humoresque, **46**; Daisy Kenyon, Possessed, **47**; Flamingo Road, It's A Great Feeling, **49**; The Damned Don't Cry, Harriet Craig, **50**; Goodbye, My Fancy, **51**; Sudden Fear, This Woman Is Dangerous, **52**; Torch Song, **53**; Johnny Guitar, **54**; Female On The Beach, Queen Bee, **55**; Autumn Leaves, **56**; The Story Of Esther Costello, **57**; The Best Of Everything, **59**; Whatever Happened To Baby Jane?, **62**; The Caretakers, **63**; Strait-Jacket, **64**; I Saw What You Did, **65**; Berserk, The Karate Killers, **67**; Trog, **70**.

CRICHTON, CHARLES: The Young Veterans, **41**; For Those In Peril, **44**; Dead Of Night, Painted Boats, **45**; Hue And Cry, **47**; Against The Wind, Another Shore, **48**; Train Of Events, **49**; Dance Hall, **50**; The Lavender Hill Mob, **51**; The Stranger In Between, **52**; The Titfield Thunderbolt, **53**; The Divided Heart, The Love Lottery, **54**; The Man In The Sky, **56**; Law And Disorder, **58**; Floods Of Fear, **59**; The Battle Of The Sexes, The Boy Who Stole A Million, **60**; The Third Secret, **64**; He Who Rides A Tiger, **66**; A Fish Called Wanda, **88**.

CRICHTON, MICHAEL: Extreme Close-up, Westworld, **73**; Coma, **78**; The Great Train Robbery, **79**; Looker, **81**; Runaway, **84**; Physical Evidence, **89**; Jurassic Park, Rising Sun, **93**; Disclosure, Congo, **95**.

CROMWELL, JOHN: Close Harmony, The Dance Of Life, The Mighty, The Dummy, **29**; For The Defense, Street Of Chance, The Texan, Tom Sawyer, **30**; Rich Man's Folly, Scandal Sheet, Unfaithful, Vice Squad, **31**; World And The Flesh, **32**; Ann Vickers, Double Harness, The Silver Cord, Sweepings, **33**; The Fountain, Of Human Bondage, Spitfire, This Man Is Mine, **34**; I Dream Too Much, Jalna, Village Tale, **35**; Banjo On My Knee, Little Lord Fauntleroy, To Mary With Love, **36**; The Prisoner Of Zenda, **37**; Algiers, **38**; In Name Only, Made For Each Other, **39**; Abe Lincoln In Illinois, Victory, **40**; So Ends Our Night, **41**; Son Of Fury, **42**; Since You Went Away, **44**; The Enchanted Cottage, **45**; Anna And The King Of Siam, **46**; Dead Reckoning, Night Song, **47**; Adventure In Baltimore, **49**; Caged, The Company She Keeps, **50**; The Racket, **51**; Top Secret Affair, **57**; The Goddess, **58**; The Scavengers, **59**; A Matter Of Morals, **60**; Three Women, **77**; A Wedding, **78**.

CRONENBERG, DAVID: They Came From Within, Shivers, **75**; Rabid, **77**; The Brood, Fast Company, **79**; Scanners, **81**; The Dead Zone, Videodrome, **82**; Into The Night, **85**; The Fly, **86**; Dead Ringers, **88**; Naked Lunch, **91**; M Butterfly, **93**; Crash, **96**.

CRONYN, HUME: The Cross Of Lorraine, Phantom Of The Opera, Shadow Of A Doubt, **43**; Blonde Fever, Lifeboat, Main Street After Dark, The Seventh Cross, **44**; A Letter For Evie, The Sailor Takes A Wife, **45**; The Green Years, The Postman Always Rings Twice, The Secret Heart, Ziegfeld Follies, **46**; The Beginning Or The End, Brute Force, **47**; The Bride Goes Wild, Rope, **48**; Top O' The Morning, Under Capricorn, **49**; People Will Talk, **51**; Crowded Paradise, **55**; Sunrise At Campobello, **60**; Cleopatra, **63**; Hamlet, **64**; The Arrangement, Gaily Gaily, **69**; There Was A Crooked Man, **70**; Conrack, The Parallax View, **74**; Honky Tonk Freeway, Rollover, **81**; The World According To Garp, **82**; Impulse, **84**; Brewster's Millions, Cocoon, **85**; Batteries Not Included, **87**; Cocoon: The Return, **88**; The Pelican Brief, **93**; Camille, **95**; Marvin's Room, **96**.

CROSBY, BING: The King Of Jazz, **30**; The Big Broadcast, **32**; College Humor, Going Hollywood, Too Much Harmony, **33**; Here Is My Heart, She Loves Me Not, We're Not Dressing, **34**; The Big Broadcast Of 36, Mississippi, Two For Tonight, **35**; Anything Goes, Pennies From Heaven, Rhythm On The Range, **36**; Double Or Nothing, Waikiki Wedding, **37**; Dr Rhythm, Sing You Sinners, **38**; East Side Of Heaven, Paris Honeymoon, The Star Maker, **39**; If I Had My Way, Rhythm On The River, Road To Singapore, **40**; Birth Of The Blues, Road To Zanzibar, **41**; Holiday Inn, Road To Morocco, Star Spangled Rhythm, **42**; Dixie, **43**; Going My Way, Here Come The Waves, **44**; The Bells Of St Mary's, Duffy's Tavern, Road To Utopia, **45**; Blue Skies, **46**; Road To Rio, Variety Girl, Welcome Stranger, **47**; The Emperor Waltz, **48**; A Connecticut Yankee In King Arthur's Court, Down Memory Lane, Top O' The Morning, **49**; Mr Music, Riding High, **50**; Here Comes The Groom, **51**; Just For You, Road To Bali, **52**; Little Boy Lost, **53**; The Country Girl, White Christmas, **54**; Anything Goes, High Society, **56**; Man On Fire, **57**; Alias Jesse James, Say One For Me, **59**; High Time, Let's Make Love, Pépé, **60**; The Road To Hong Kong, **62**; Robin And The Seven Hoods, **64**; Stagecoach, **66**; Ben, **72**; That's Entertainment!, **74**.

CRUISE, TOM: Endless Love, Taps, **81**; The Outsiders, Risky Business, **83**; Legend, **85**; The Color Of Money, Top Gun, **86**; Cocktail, Rain Man, **88**; Born On The Fourth Of July, **89**; Days Of Thunder, **90**; Far And Away, A Few Good Men, **92**; The Firm, **93**; Interview With The Vampire, **94**; Mission Impossible, **95**; Jerry Maguire, **96**; Eyes Wide Shut, **97**.

CRYSTAL, BILLY: Rabbit Test, **78**; Animalympics, **79**; This Is Spinal Tap, **84**; Running Scared, **86**; The Princess Bride, Throw Momma From The Train, **87**; Memories Of Me, **88**; When Harry Met Sally, **89**; City Slickers, **91**; Mr Saturday Night, **92**; City Slickers II: The Legend Of Curly's Gold, **94**; Forget Paris, **95**.

CUKOR, GEORGE: Grumpy, The Royal Family Of Broadway, The Virtuous Sin, **30**; Girls About Town, Tarnished Lady, **31**; A Bill Of Divorcement, What Price Hollywood?, **32**; Dinner At Eight, Little Women, Our Betters, Rockabye, **33**; David Copperfield, Sylvia Scarlett, **35**; Romeo And Juliet, **36**; Camille, **37**; Holiday, **38**; The Women, Zaza, **39**; The Philadelphia Story, Susan And God, **40**; Two-faced Woman, A Woman's Face, **41**; Her Cardboard Lover, Keeper Of The Flame, **42**; Gaslight, Winged Victory, **44**; Desire Me, A Double Life, **47**; Adam's Rib, Edward My Son, **49**; Born Yesterday, A Life Of Her Own, **50**; The Model And The Marriage Broker, **51**; The Marrying Kind, Pat And Mike, **52**; The Actress, **53**; It Should Happen To You, A Star Is Born, **54**; Bhowani Junction, **56**; Les Girls, Wild Is The Wind, **57**; Heller In Pink Tights, Let's Make Love, Song Without End, **60**; The Chapman Report, **62**; My Fair Lady, **64**; Justine, **69**; Travels With My Aunt, **72**; The Blue Bird, **76**; Rich And Famous, **81**.

CURTIS, JAMIE LEE: Halloween, **78**; The Fog, Prom Night, Terror Train, **80**; Halloween II, Road Games, **81**; Love Letters, Trading Places, **83**; The Adventures Of Buckaroo Banzai Across The Eighth Dimension, Grandview USA, **84**; Perfect, **85**; Amazing Grace And Chuck, A Man In Love, **87**; Dominick And Eugene, A Fish Called Wanda, **88**; Blue Steel, **90**; My Girl, Queen's Logic, **91**; Forever Young, **92**; Mother's Boys, My Girl 2, True Lies, **94**; Fierce Creatures, **97**.

CURTIS, TONY: City Across The River, Criss Cross, The Lady Gambles, **49**; Kansas Raiders, Sierra, **50**; The Prince Who Was A Thief, **51**; Flesh And Fury, Meet Danny Wilson, No Room For The Groom, Son Of Ali Baba, **52**; The All American, Houdini, **53**; Beachhead, Johnny Dark, So This Is Paris, **54**; The Purple Mask, Six Bridges To Cross, **55**; The Rawhide Years, Trapeze, **56**; The Midnight Story, Sweet Smell Of Success, **57**; The Defiant Ones, Kings Go Forth, The Perfect Furlough, The Vikings, **58**; Operation Petticoat, Some Like It Hot, **59**; The Great Impostor, Spartacus, Who Was That Lady?, **60**; The Outsider, **61**; Taras Bulba, **62**; Captain Newman MD, The List Of Adrian Messenger, **63**; Paris When It Sizzles, Sex And The Single Girl, **64**; Boeing Boeing, The Great Race, **65**; Arrivederci Baby, Not With My Wife You Don't!, **66**; Don't Make Waves, **67**; The Boston Strangler, **68**; Eye Of The Cat, Monte Carlo Or Bust!, **69**; Suppose They Gave A War And Nobody Came?, Jennifer On My Mind, **71**; That Man Bolt, **73**; Bucktown, Lepke, **75**; Casanova & Co, The Last Tycoon, **76**; The Bad News Bears Go To Japan, The Manitou, Sextette, **78**; Title Shot, **79**; Little Miss Marker, The Mirror Crack'd, **80**; Brainwaves, Othello, **82**; Where Is Parsifal?, **84**; Club Life, Insignificance, **85**; Balboa, The Fantasy Film World Of George Pal, The Last Of Philip Banter, **86**; Welcome To Germany, **88**; Lobster Man From Mars, Midnight, Walter & Carlo In America, **89**; Center Of The Web, **92**; Naked In New York, **94**; The Immortals, **95**.

CURTIZ, MICHAEL: Ma Es Holnap, **12**; Rablelek, **13**; As Ejszaka, Bank Ban, **14**; Akit Ketten Szeretnek, **15**; Doktor Ur, A Farkus, A Magyar Fold Ereje, Makkhetes, A Medikus, **16**; Ezredes Az, A Fold Embere, Tatarjaras, **17**; Alraune, Judas, Kilencvenkilenc, Lulu, **18**; Die Dame Mit Dem Schwarzen Handschuh, Die Gottesgeissel, Liliom, **19**; Boccaccio, Der Stern Von Damaskus, Die Dame Mit Den Sonnenblumen, Herzogin Satanella, Miss Tutti Frutti, **20**; Cherchez La Femme, Frau Dorothys Bekenntnis, Wege Des Schreckens, **21**; Der Junge Medardus, Die Lawine, Namenlos, Sodom Und Gomorrah, **23**; Eine Spiel Ums Leben, Harun Al Raschid, Die Sklavenkonigin, **24**; Celimene-La Poupée De Montmartre, **25**; Der Goldene Schmetterling, Fiaker Nr 13, **26**; The Desired Woman, Good Time Charley, A Million Bid, The Third Degree, **27**; Tenderloin, **28**; The Gamblers, The Glad Rag Doll, Hearts In Exile, The Madonna Of Avenue A, Noah's Ark, **29**; Bright Lights, Mammy, The Matrimonial Bed, Moby Dick, River's End, A Soldier's Plaything, Under A Texas Moon, **30**; God's Gift To Women, The Mad Genius, **31**; Alias The Doctor, The Cabin In The Cotton, Doctor X, The Strange Love Of Molly Louvain, The Woman From Monte Carlo, **32**; 20,000 Years In Sing Sing, Female, Goodbye Again, The Kennel Murder Case, The Keyhole, Private Detective 62; Mystery Of The Wax Museum, **33**; British Agent, Jimmy The Gent, The Key, Mandalay, **34**; Black Fury, Captain Blood, The Case Of The Curious Bride, Front Page Woman, Little Big Shot, **35**; The Charge Of The Light Brigade, Stolen Holiday, The Walking Dead, **36**; Kid Galahad, Mountain Justice, The Perfect Specimen, **37**; The Adventures Of Robin Hood, Angels With Dirty Faces, Four Daughters, Four's A Crowd, Gold Is Where You Find It, **38**; Daughters Courageous, Dodge City, Four Wives, The Private Lives Of Elizabeth And Essex, Sons Of Liberty, **39**; Santa Fe Trail, The Sea Hawk, Virginia City, **40**; Dive Bomber, The Sea Wolf, **41**; Captains Of The Clouds, Casablanca, Yankee Doodle Dandy, **42**; Mission To Moscow, This Is The Army, **43**; Janie, Passage To Marseilles, **44**; Mildred Pierce, Roughly Speaking, **45**; Night And Day, **46**; Life With Father, The Unsuspected, **47**; Romance On The High Seas, **48**; Flamingo Road, The Lady Takes A Sailor, My Dream Is Yours, **49**; The Breaking Point, Bright Leaf, Young Man With A Horn, **50**; Force Of Arms, I'll See You In My Dreams, Jim Thorpe All American, **51**; The Story Of Will Rogers, **52**; The Jazz Singer, Trouble Along The Way, **53**; The Boy From Oklahoma, The Egyptian, White Christmas, **54**; We're No Angels, **55**; The Best Things In Life Are Free, The Scarlet Hour, The Vagabond King, **56**; The Helen Morgan Story, **57**; King Creole, The Proud Rebel, **58**; The Hangman, The Man In The Net, **59**; The Adventures Of Huckleberry Finn, A Breath Of Scandal, **60**; The Comancheros, Francis Of Assisi, **61**.

CUSHING, PETER: The Man In The Iron Mask, **39**; A Chump At Oxford, Laddie, **40**; Hamlet, **48**; Moulin Rouge, **52**; The Black Knight, **54**; The End Of The Affair, **55**; Alexander The Great, Time Without Pity, **56**; Abominable Snowman, The Curse Of Frankenstein, **57**; Horror Of Dracula, The Revenge Of Frankenstein, **58**; The Hound Of The Baskervilles, John Paul Jones, Mania, The Psycho Killers, The Mummy, **59**; The Brides Of Dracula, Sword Of Sherwood Forest, **60**; The Naked Edge, **61**; The Man Who Finally Died, **62**; Evil Of Frankenstein, The Gorgon, Dr Terror's House Of Horrors, **64**; Dr Who And The Daleks, She, The Skull, **65**; Island Of Terror, Frankenstein Created Woman, **67**; Torture Garden, **68**; Frankenstein Must Be Destroyed, **69**; Scream And Scream Again, **70**; The House That Dripped Blood, The Vampire Lovers, **71**; Asylum, Dr Phibes Rises Again, Dracula AD 1972, Tales From The Crypt, Twins Of Evil, **72**; And Now The Screaming Starts!, Count Dracula And His Vampire Bride, The Creeping Flesh, From Beyond The Grave, **73**; The Beast Must Die, Frankenstein And The Monster From Hell, Madhouse, **74**; The Ghoul, **75**; At The Earth's Core, **76**; Star Wars, The Uncanny, **77**; Arabian Adventure, **79**; Monster Island, **81**; Sword Of The Valiant, **82**; House Of The Long Shadows, **83**; Top Secret!, **84**; Biggles: Adventures In Time, **86**; Innocent Blood, **92**.

Movie talk

Absolute film: images liberated from sequential narrative to create an alternative reality.

Action: the word spoken, usually by the director, to commence the take and signal the actors into motion. Hitchcock often added "please"

Animatics: animation used in place of live action.

Answer print: the first print in which picture and sound are synchronised.

Apple boxes: soapbox much used to elevate diminutive actors.

Aquarium: sound mixing booth.

Art director: visualises and provides detailed sketches for the decor and look of each set and scene from an aesthetic, period and technical viewpoint, with the budget firmly in mind.

Australian new wave: use of government support to finance new directors and regenerate stagnant film industry in mid-1970s, turning Australia into a leading English-speaking film-producing country.

Auteur: concept of the director as "author" or sole creator of a film, first mooted in 1948 and elaborated in 1960s. The "auteur theory" ignores film-making's collaborative consensus.

Back projection: occasionally used in multiplex cinemas with small viewing areas; in the past a means of simulating locations behind actors or sound stages.

Barn doors: hinged metal flaps on lights to control spread and spillage of beam.

Bazooka: tubular lighting support on a catwalk.

Best boy: senior apprentice or assistant to gaffer.

Biopic: film biography.

Blaxploitation: low budget films starring African-Americans.

Blimp: soundproof housing to deaden camera drive motor noise.

Boom: counterbalanced extendable arm for microphones and mobile camera mount capable of vertical and horizontal movement. Also on arm for supporting lighting.

B-movie: a shorter supporting picture in the double-bill era. Became extinct in 1960s.

CZINNER, PAUL: Homo Immanis, **19**; Inferno, **20**; Nju, **24**; Violinist Of Florence, **26**; Liebe, **27**; Dona Juana, **28**; Fraulein Else, The Woman He Scorned, **29**; Ariane, **31**; Melo, Der Traumende Mond, **32**; Catherine The Great, **34**; Escape Me Never, **35**; As You Like It, **36**; Dreaming Lips, **37**; Stolen Life, **39**; Die Traumende Mund, **53**; Don Giovanni, **55**; The Bolshoi Ballet, **57**; The Royal Ballet, **59**; Der Rosenkavalier, **62**; Romeo And Juliet, **66**.

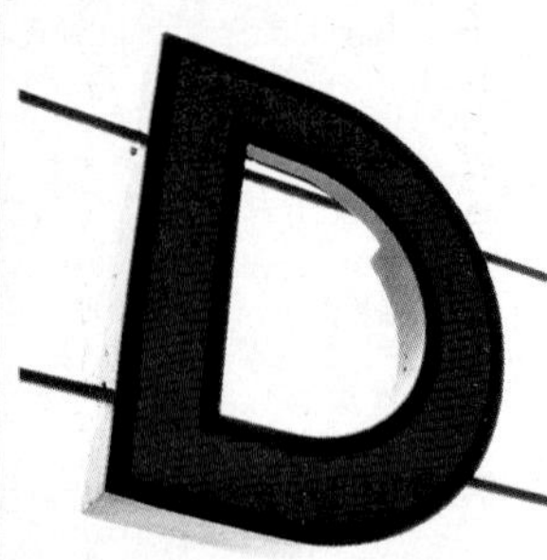

DAFOE, WILLEM: New York Nights, **82**; The Hunger, The Loveless, **83**; Roadhouse 66, Streets Of Fire, **84**; To Live And Die In LA, **85**; Platoon, **86**; The Last Temptation Of Christ, Mississippi Burning, Off Limits, **88**; Born On The Fourth Of July, Triumph Of The Spirit, **89**; Cry-Baby, Wild At Heart, **90**; Flight Of The Intruder, **91**;White Sands, **92**; Body Of Evidence, Faraway, So Close!, **93**; Tom & Viv, **94**; The English Patient, **96**; Speed 2: Cruise Control, **97**.

DANIELS, BEBE: The Common Enemy, **10** (and more than 30 early silent shorts); The Dancin' Fool, Why Change Your Wife? You Never Can Tell, **20**; The Affairs Of Anatol, Ducks And Drakes, The March Hare, One Wild Week, The Speed Girl, Two Weeks To Pay, **21**; Nancy From Nowhere, Nice People, North Of The Rio Grande, Pink Gods, Singed Wings, **22**; The Exciters, The Glimpses Of The Moon, His Children's Children, The World's Applause, **23**; Argentine Love, Dangerous Money, Daring Youth, The Heritage Of The Desert, Monsieur Beaucaire, Sinners In Heaven, Unguarded Women, **24**; The Crowded Hour, Lovers In Quarantine, The Manicure Girl, Miss Bluebeard, The Splendid Crime, Wild Wild Susan, **25**; The Campus Flirt, Miss Brewster's Millions, The Palm Beach Girl, Stranded In Paris, Volcano, **26**; Kiss In A Taxi, Senorita, She's A Sheik, Swim Girl Swim, **27**; Feel My Pulse, The Fifty-Fifty Girl, Hot News, Take Me Home, What A Night!, **28**; Rio Rita, **29**; Alias French Gertie, Dixiana, Lawful Larceny, Love Comes Along, **30**; My Past, The Maltese Falcon, Reaching For The Moon, **31**; Silver Dollar, 42nd Street, Cocktail Hour, Counsellor-At-Law, **33**; Registered Nurse, **34**; Music Is Magic, **35**; The Return Of Dean, **39**; Hi Gang!, **41**; Life With The Lyons, **53**; The Lyons In Paris, **55**.

DANIELS, WILLIAM H: Foolish Wives, **22**; Merry-Go-Round, **23**; Greed, **24**; Bardelys The Magnificent, The Boob, Dance Madness, **26**; Flesh And The Devil, **27**; The Actress, Bringing Up Father, **28**; The Kiss, Wild Orchids, **29**; Anna Christie, Romance, **30**; Susan Lenox: Her Fall And Rise, **31**; Grand Hotel, Mata Hari, **32**; Dinner At Eight, Queen Christina, **33**; The Barretts Of Wimpole Street, **34**; Anna Karenina, Naughty Marietta, **35**; Romeo And Juliet, Rose Marie, **36**; Broadway Melody Of 38, Camille, **37**; Marie Antoinette, **38**; Idiot's Delight, Ninotchka, **39**; The Mortal Storm, The Shop Around The Corner, **40**; Back Street, **41**; Girl Crazy, **43**; Brute Force, Lured, **47**; The Naked City, **48**; Harvey, Winchester **50**; Bright Victory, **51**; Pat And Mike, Plymouth Adventure, **52**; Thunder Bay, **53**; The Glenn Miller Story, **54**; The Far Country, The Shrike, Strategic Air Command, **55**; My Man Godfrey, Night Passage, **57**; Cat On A Hot Tin Roof, Some Came Running, **58**; A Hole In The Head, Never So Few, **59**; Can-Can, Ocean's Eleven, **60**; How The West Was Won, **62**; Come Blow Your Horn, The Prize, **63**; Marriage On The Rocks, Von Ryan's Express, **65**; Assault On A Queen, **66**; In Like Flint, Valley Of The Dolls, **67**; Marlowe, **68**; The Maltese Bippy, **69**; Move, **70**.

DANTE, JOE: Hollywood Boulevard, **76**; Piranha, **78**; The Howling, **81**; Twilight Zone The Movie, **83**; Gremlins, **84**; Explorers, **85**; Amazon Women On The Moon, Innerspace **87**; The 'Burbs, **89**; Gremlins 2 The New Batch, **90**; Matinee, **93**; Beverly Hills Cop III, Silence Of The Hams, **94**; Cat and Mouse, **95**.

DARRIEUX, DANIELLE: Le Bal, **31**; Château De Rêve, **33**; Dédé, La Crise Est Finie, Volga En Flammes, **34**; Quelle Drôle De Gosse!, **35**; Club De Femmes, I Give My Life, Mademoiselle Mozart, Mayerling, Taras Boulba, **36**; Mademoiselle Ma Mere, **37**; Katia, The Rage Of Paris, Retour A L'Aube, **38**; Battements De Coeur, **39**; Caprices, **41**; Adieu Chérie, **45**; Au Petit Bonheur, **46**; Ruy Blas, **47**; Jean De La Lune, **48**; Occupe-toi D'Amélie, **49**; La Ronde, **50**; Le Plaisir, Rich Young And Pretty, La Vérité Sur Bébé Donge, **51**; Five Fingers, **52**; The Earrings Of Madame De, **53**; Le Rouge Et Le Noir, Napoleon, **54**; Lady Chatterley's Lover, **55**; Alexander The Great, Typhon Sur Nagasaki, **56**; Un Drôle De Dimanche, **58**; Marie-Octobre, **59**; The Greengage Summer, **61**; Bluebeard **62**; Le Coup De Grâce, Les Oiseaux Vont Mourir Au Pérou, Vingt-Quatre Heures De La Vie D'Une Femme, Les Demoiselles De Rochefort, **68**; La Maison De Campagne, **69**; The Lonely Woman, **75**; L'Année Sainté, **76**; Le Cavaleur, **78**; Une Chambre En Ville, **82**; En Haut Des Marches, **83**; Scene Of The Crime, **86**; A Few Days With Me, **87**; Bille En Tête, **89**; Epiphany Sunday, **91**.

DASSIN, JULES: The Affairs Of Martha, Nazi Agent, Reunion In France, **42**; Young Ideas, **43**; The Canterville Ghost, **44**; A Letter For Evie, **45**; Two Smart People, **46**; Brute Force, **47**; The Naked City, **48**; Thieves' Highway, **49**; Night And The City, **50**; Rififi, **55**; He Who Must Die, **57**; Where The Hot Wind Blows!, **58**; Never On Sunday, **60**; Phaedra, **62**; Topkapi, **64**; 10:30pm Summer, **66**; Survival 1967, Up Tight, **68**; La Promesse De L'Aube, **70**; The Rehearsal, **74**; A Dream Of Passion, **78**; Circle Of Two, **80**; Not By Coincidence, **83**.

DAVES, DELMER: Destination Tokyo, **44**; Hollywood Canteen, The Very Thought Of You, **44**; Pride Of The Marines, **45**; Dark Passage, The Red House, **47**; To The Victor, **48**; A Kiss In The Dark, Task Force, **49**; Broken Arrow, **50**; Bird Of Paradise, **51**; Return Of The Texan, **52**; Never Let Me Go, Treasure Of The Golden Condor, **53**; Demetrius And The Gladiators, Drum Beat, **54**; Jubal, The Last Wagon, **56**; 3:10 To Yuma, **57**; The Badlanders, Cowboy, Kings Go Forth, **58**; The Hanging Tree, A Summer Place, **59**; Parrish, Susan Slade, **61**; Rome Adventure, **62**; Spencer's Mountain, **63**; Youngblood Hawke, **64**; The Battle Of The Villa Fiorita, **65**.

DAVIES, MARION: Runaway Romany, **17**; The Belle Of New York, When Knighthood Was In Flower, Little Old New York, **23**; Yolande, **24**; Lights Of Old Broadway, **25**; Quality Street, Tillie The Toiler, **27**; Show People, The Patsy, **28**; The Hollywood Revue Of 29, Marianne, **29**; The Florodora Girl, Not So Dumb, **30**; The Bachelor Father, Five And Ten, It's A Wise Child, **31**; Blondie Of The Follies, Polly Of The Circus, **32**; Going Hollywood, Peg O' My Heart, **33**; Operator 13, **34**; Page Miss Glory, **35**; Cain And Mabel, Hearts Divided, **36**; Ever Since Eve, **37**.

DAVIS, BETTE: Bad Sister, Seed, Waterloo Bridge, **31**; The Cabin In The Cotton, Dark Horse, Hell's House, The Man Who Played God, The Menace, The Rich Are Always With Us, So Big, Three On A Match, Way Back Home, **32**; 20,000 Years In Sing Sing, The Adopted Father, Bureau Of Missing Persons, Ex-Lady, Parachute Jumper, **33**; The Big Shakedown, Fashions, Fog Over Frisco, Housewife, Jimmy The Gent, Of Human Bondage, **34**; Bordertown, Dangerous, Front Page Woman, The Girl From 10th Avenue, Special Agent, **35**; The Golden Arrow, The Petrified Forest, Satan Met A Lady, **36**; It's Love I'm After, Kid Galahad, Marked Woman, That Certain Woman, **37**; Jezebel, The Sisters, **38**; Dark Victory, Juarez, The Old Maid, The Private Lives Of Elizabeth And Essex, **39**; All This And Heaven Too, The Letter, **40**; The Bride Came COD, The Great Lie, The Little Foxes, The Man Who Came To Dinner, Shining Victory, **41**; In This Our Life, Now Voyager, **42**; Old Acquaintance, Thank Your Lucky Stars, Watch On The Rhine, **43**; Hollywood Canteen, Mr Skeffington, **44**; The Corn Is Green, **45**; Deception, A Stolen Life, **46**; June Bride, Winter Meeting, **48**; Beyond The Forest, **49**; All About Eve, **50**; Another Man's Poison, Payment On Demand, **51**; Phone Call From A Stranger, The Star, **52**; The Virgin Queen, **55**; The Catered Affair, Storm Center, **56**; John Paul Jones, The Scapegoat, **59**; Pocketful Of Miracles, **61**; Whatever Happened To Baby Jane?, **62**; Dead Ringer, The Empty Canvas, Where Love Has Gone, **64**; Hush . . . Hush, Sweet Charlotte, The Nanny, **65**; The Anniversary, **68**; Connecting Rooms, **71**; Bunny O'Hare, Lo Scopone Scientifico, **72**; Burnt Offerings, **76**; Death On The Nile, Return From Witch Mountain, **78**; The Watcher In The Woods, **80**; The Whales Of August, **87**; Wicked Stepmother, **89**.

DAVIS, GEENA: Tootsie, **82**; Fletch, Transylvania 6-5000, **85**; The Fly, **86**; The Accidental Tourist, Beetlejuice, **88**; Earth Girls Are Easy, **89**; Quick Change, **90**; Thelma & Louise, **91**; Hero, A League Of Their Own, **92**; Angie, **94**; Cut-Throat Island, Speechless, **95**; The Long Kiss Goodnight, **96**.

DAVIS, JUDY: High Rolling, **77**; My Brilliant Career, **79**; The Winter Of Our Dreams, **81**; Who Dares Wins, **82**; Heatwave, **83**; A Passage To India, **84**; Kangaroo, **86**; High Tide, **87**; Georgia, **88**; Alice, **90**; Barton Fink, Impromptu, Naked Lunch, Where Angels Fear To Tread, **91**; Husbands And Wives, **92**; The Ref, **94**; On My Own, The New Age, **95**; Children of the Revolution, **96**; Absolute Power, **97**.

DAVIS JNR, SAMMY: The Benny Goodman Story, **56**; Anna Lucasta, **58**; Porgy And Bess, **59**; Ocean's 11, Pépé, **60**; Convicts Four, Sergeants 3, **62**; Johnny Cool, Die Dreigroschenoper, **63**; Nightmare In The Sun, Robin And The Seven Hoods, **64**; A Man Called Adam, **66**; Salt And Pepper, Sweet Charity, **68**; Man Without Mercy, **69**; One More Time, **70**; Save The Children, **73**; Little Moon & Jud McGraw, **78**; Sammy Stops The World, **79**; The Cannonball Run, **81**; Heidi's Song, **82**; Cannonball Run II, **84**; That's Dancing! **86**; The Perils Of PK, **86**; Moon Over Parador, **88**; Tap, **89**.

DAY, DORIS: Romance On The High Seas, **48**; It's A Great Feeling, My Dream Is Yours, **49**; Tea For Two, West Point Story, Young Man With A Horn, **50**; I'll See You In My Dreams, Lullaby Of Broadway, On Moonlight Bay, Starlift, Storm Warning, **51**; April In Paris, The Winning Team, **52**; By The Light Of The Silvery Moon, Calamity Jane, **53**; Lucky Me, Young At Heart, **54**; Love Me Or Leave Me, **55**; Julie, The Man Who Knew Too Much, **56**; The Pajama Game, **57**; Teacher's Pet, The Tunnel Of Love, **58**; It Happened To Jane, Pillow Talk, **59**; Midnight Lace, Please Don't Eat The Daisies, **60**; Lover Come Back, Jumbo, That Touch Of Mink, **62**; Move Over Darling, The Thrill Of It All, **63**; Send Me No Flowers, **64**; Do Not Disturb, **65**; The Glass Bottom Boat, **66**; The Ballad Of Josie, Caprice, **67**; Where Were You When The Lights Went Out?, With Six You Get Eggroll, **68**; Heart And Souls, **93**; That's Entertainment! III, **94**.

DAY-LEWIS, DANIEL: Sunday Bloody Sunday, **71**; Gandhi, **82**; The Bounty, **84**; The Insurance Man, My Beautiful Laundrette, A Room With A View, **85**; Nanou, **87**; Stars And Bars, The Unbearable Lightness Of Being, **88**; Eversmile New Jersey, My Left Foot, **89**; The Last Of The Mohicans, **92**; The Age Of Innocence, In The Name Of The Father, **93**; The Crucible, **95**; The Boxer, **97**.

DEAN, JAMES: Fixed Bayonets, Sailor Beware, **51**; Has Anybody Seen My Gal?, **52**; Trouble Along The Way, **53**; East Of Eden, Rebel Without A Cause, **55**; Giant, **56**.

DEARDEN, BASIL: The Black Sheep Of Whitehall, **41**; The Goose Steps Out, **42**; Bells Go Down, The Halfway House, My Learned Friend, **43**; They Came To A City, **44**; Dead Of Night, **45**; The Captive Heart, **46**; Frieda, **47**; Saraband For Dead Lovers, **48**; Train Of Events, **49**; The Blue Lamp, Cage Of Gold, Pool Of London, **50**; The Gentle Gunman, I Believe In You, **52**; The Rainbow Jacket, **54**; The Ship That Died Of Shame, The Square Ring, **55**; Who Done It?, **56**; Out Of The Clouds, The Smallest Show On Earth, **57**; Violent Playground, **58**; Sapphire, The League Of Gentlemen, **59**; All Night Long, Man In The Moon, The Secret Partner, Victim, **61**; The Mind Benders, **62**; A Place To Go, **63**; Woman Of Straw, **64**; Masquerade, **65**; Khartoum, Walk In The Shadow, **66**; Only When I Larf, **68**; The Assassination Bureau, **69**; The Man Who Haunted Himself, **70**.

DE HAVILLAND, OLIVIA: Alibi Ike, Captain Blood, The Irish In Us, A Midsummer Night's Dream, **35**; Anthony Adverse, The Charge Of The Light Brigade, **36**; Call It A Day, The Great Garrick, It's Love I'm After, **37**; Four's A Crowd, Gold Is Where You Find It, Hard To Get, The Private Lives Of Elizabeth And Essex, **38**; The Adventures Of Robin Hood, Dodge City, Gone With The Wind, Wings Of The Navy, **39**; My Love Came Back, Raffles, Santa Fe Trail, **40**; Hold Back The Dawn, The Strawberry Blonde, They Died With Their Boots On, **41**; In This Our Life, The Male Animal, **42**; Government Girl, Princess O'Rourke, Thank Your Lucky Stars, **43**; The Dark Mirror, Devotion, To Each His Own, The Well-Groomed Bride, **46**; The Snake Pit, **48**; The Heiress, **49**; My Cousin Rachel, **52**; Not As A Stranger, That Lady, **55**; The Ambassador's Daughter, **56**; The Proud Rebel, **58**; Libel, **59**; Light In The Piazza, **62**; Lady In A Cage, **64**; Hush . . . Hush, Sweet Charlotte, **65**; The Adventurers, **70**; Pope Joan, **72**; Airport 77, **77**; The Swarm, **78**; The Fifth Musketeer, **79**.

DE LAURENTIIS, DINO: L'Amore Canta, **41**; The Bandit, **44**; La Figlia Del Capitano, **47**; Bitter Rice, Molti Sogni Per Le Strade, **49**; Il Brigante Musolino, **50**; Anna, Europa '51, Guardie Ladri, **51**; Attila, La Lupa, La Strada, Mambo, **54**; Ulysses, **55**; War And Peace, **56**; Le Notti Di Cabiria , **57**; The Sea Wall, **58**; The Great War, Tempest, **59**; 5 Branded Women, **60**; Barabbas, **62**; Crimen, **64**; An Orchid For The Tiger, Pierrot Le Fou, The Three Faces Of A Woman, **65**; The Bible, Kiss The Girls And Make Them Die, **66**; Diabolik, The Stranger, **67**; Anzio, Barbarella, The Bride Wore Black, Romeo And Juliet, The Witches, **68**; Fraulein Doktor, Monte Carlo, Or Bust!, **69**; A Man Called Sledge, **70**; Waterloo, **71**; The Valachi Papers, **72**; Serpico, The Stone Killer, **73**; Crazy Joe, Three Tough Guys, **74**; Mandingo, **75**; Drum, Fellini's Casanova, King Kong, The Shootist, **76**; **77**; King Of The Gypsies, The Serpent's Egg, **78**; Hurricane, **79**; Flash Gordon, **80**; Ragtime, **81**; Conan The Destroyer, Dune, **84**; Year Of The Dragon, **85**; Blue Velvet, **86**; Desperate Hours, **90**; Once Upon A Crime, **92**; Body Of Evidence, **93**.

DELERUE, GEORGE: Nude In His Pocket, **57**; Hiroshima Mon Amour, **59**; The Joker, L'Amant de Cinq Jours, The Long Absence, Jules and Jim, Cartouche, **61**; Le Mépris, **63**; La Peau Douce, The Pumpkin Eater, Male Companion, That Man From Rio, **64**; Le Corniaud, Viva Maria, **65**; King Of Hearts, A Man For All Seasons, **66**; The Two Of Us, **67**; Women In Love, A Walk With Love And Death, Anne Of The Thousand Days, **69**; The Conformist, Promise At Dawn, **70**; Two English Girls, **71**; The Day Of The Jackal, Day For Night, The Day Of The Dolphin, **73**; The Slap, **74**; That Most Important Thing: Love, **75**; Femmes Fatales, **76**; Julie Pot de Colle, Julia, Le Point De Mire, Tendre Poulet, **77**; Va Voir Maman . . . Papa Travaille, La Petite Fille En Velours Bleu, Get Out Your Handkerchiefs, **78**; Le Cavaleur, L'Amour En Fuite, A Little Romance, **79**; The Last Metro, **80**; The Woman Next Door, Garde A Vue, True Confessions, Rich And Famous, **81**; A Little Sex, **82**; Man, Woman And Child, Confidentially Yours, Silkwood, **83**; Agnes Of God, **85**; Salvador, Platoon, Crimes Of The Heart, **86**; A Man In Love, The Lonely Passion Of Judith Hearne, **87**; Biloxi Blues, A Summer Story, Memories Of Me, **88**; Beaches, Heartbreak Hotel, Steel Magnolias, The French Revolution, **89**; Georg Elser, Joe Versus The Volcano, **90**.

DELON, ALAIN: Quand La Femme S'En Méle, **57**; Christine, Sois Belle Et Tais-Toi, **58**; Plein Soleil, Rocco And His Brothers, Women Are Weak, **60**; Amours Célèbres, **61**; The Devil And The Ten Commandments, L'Eclisse, **62**; Mélodie En Sous-Sol, The Black Tulip, The Leopard, **63**; Amour A La Mer, L'Insoumis, **64**; Once A Thief, The Yellow Rolls-Royce, **65**; Is Paris Burning?, Lost Command, Texas Across The River, **66**; Le Samourai, The Last Adventure, **67**; Girl On A Motorcycle, Spirits C The Dead, The Sicilian Clan, **68**; Jeff, The Swimming Pool, **69**; Borsalino, Le Cercle Rouge, The Love Mates, **70**; Il Etait Une Fois Un Flic, **71**; The Assassination Of Trotsky, Un Flic, La Prima Notte Di Quiete, Red Sun, Shock, **72**; La Race Des Seigneurs, Scorpio, Two Against The Law, **73**; Borsalino And Co, Creezy, Les Seins De Glace, The Slap, **74**; Flic Story, Zorro, **75**; Comme Un Boomerang, **76**; Death Of A Corrupt Man, Le Gang, Mr Klein, **77**; Attention, Les Enfants Regardent, **78**; The Concorde – Airport '79, **79**; Trois Hommes A Abattre, **80**; Pour La Peau D'Un Flic, Teheran '43, **81**; Le Choc, **82**; Le Battant, **83**; Notre Histoire, Swann In Love, **84**; Parole De Flic, **85**; Le Passage, **86**; Ne Reveillez Pas Un Flic Qui Dort, **88**; Dancing Machine, **90**; The Return Of Casanova, **92**; Un Crime, **93**; L'Orso Di Peluche, **94**.

DEL RIO, DOLORES: Joanna, **25**; What Price Glory?, **26**; Loves Of Carmen, Resurrection, **27**; The Gateway Of The Moon, Ramona, The Red Dance, Revenge, The Trail Of '98, **28**; Evangeline, **29**; Bird Of Paradise, Girl Of The Rio, **32**; Flying Down To Rio, **33**; Madame Du Barry, Wonder Bar, **34**; I Live For Love, In Caliente, **35**; Accused, The Widow From Monte Carlo, **36**; Devil's Playground, Lancer Spy, **37**; International Settlement, **38**; The Man From Dakota, **40**; Journey Into Fear, Flor Silvestre, **43**; Bugambilia, **45**; La Otra, **46**; The Fugitive, **47**; Historia De Una Mala Mujer, **48**; Dona Perfecta, **50**; La Cucaracha, **58**; Flaming Star, **60**; Cheyenne Autumn, **64**; More Than A Miracle, Rio Blanco, **67**; The Children Of Sanchez, **78**.

DEMILLE, CECIL: The Squaw Man, Brewster's Millions, The Only Son, The Call Of The North, The Virginian, The Ghost Breaker, **14**; The Girl Of The Golden West, Th Unafraid, The Captive, The Arab, Carmen, The Cheat **15**; The Golden Chance, Temptation, The Trail Of The Lonesome Pine, The Heart Of Nora Flynn, The Dream Girl, **16**; Joan The Woman, The Little American, The Devil Stone, **17**; We Can't Have Everything, The Squaw Man (remake), **18**; For Better For Worse, Male and Female, **19**; Something To Think About, **20**; Forbidden Fruit, The Affairs Of Anatol, Fool's Paradise, **21**; Saturday Night, Manslaughter, **22**; Adam's Rib, The Ten Commandments, **23**; Triumph, Feet Of Clay, **24**; The Golden Bed, The Road To Yesterday, **25**; Dynamite, **29**; Madame Satan, **30**; The Squaw Man (second remake) **31**; The Sign Of The Cross, **32**; This Day and Age, **33**; Cleopatra, **34**; The Crusades, **35**; The Plainsman, **37**; Union Pacific, **39**; North West Mounted Police, **40**; Reap The Wild Wind, **42**; The Story Of Dr Wassell, **44**; Unconquered, **47**; Samson and Delilah, **49**; Sunset Boulevard, **50**; The Greatest Show On Earth, **52**; The Ten Commandments, **56**.

DEMME, JONATHAN: Caged Heat, **74**; Crazy Mama, **75**; Fighting Mad, **76**; Citizens Band, **77**; Last Embrace, **79**; Melvin And Howard, **80**; Stop Making Sense, Swing Shift, **84**; Into The Night, **85**; Something Wild, **86**; Swimming To Cambodia **87**; Married To The Mob, **88**; The Silence Of The Lambs, **91**; Cousin Bobby, **92**; Philadelphia, **93**; Ulee's Gold, **97**.

DEMY, JACQUES: Le Sabotier Du Val De Loire, **56**; Le Bel Indifferent, **57**; Ars, Les Sept Péchés Capitaux, Lola, **61**; La Baie Des Anges, **63**; Les Parapluies De Cherbourg **64**; Les Demoiselles De Rochefort, **68**; The Model Shop, **69**; Peau D'Ane, **71**; The Pied Piper, **72**; L'Evénement Le Plus Important Depuis Que L'Homme A Marché Sur La Lune, **73**; Lady Oscar, **79**; Une Chambre En Ville, **82**; Parking, **85**; La Table Tournante, Trois Places Pour Le 26, **88**.

DENEUVE, CATHERINE: Les Collegiennes, **56**; L'Homme A Femmes, **60**; Les Parisiennes, Le Vice Et La Vertu, **62**; Vacances Portugaises, **63**; Les Plus Belles Escroqueries Du Monde, Les Parapluies De Cherbourg, **64**; Repulsion, **65**; Les Créatures, La Vie De Château, **66**; Belle De Jour, Manon 70, Les Demoiselles De Rochefort, **67**; Benjamin, La Chamade, Mayerling, **68**; The April Fools, La Sirène Du Mississippi, **69**; Tristana, **70**; Peau D'Ane, **71**; Dirty Money, **72**; Savage,

Evénement Le Plus Important Depuis ue L'Homme A Marche Sur La Lune, **73**; La rande Bourgeoise, La Femme Aux ottes Rouges, Zig-zag, **74**; Hustle, Le auvage, **75**; Anima Persa, Second hance, Si C'Etait A Refaire, **76**; March Or e, **77**; Ecoute Voir, L'Argent Des utres, **78**; A Nous Deux, Courage Fuyons, Ils ont Grands Ces Petits, **79**; The Last etro, **80**; Choice Of Arms, Je Vous Aime, **1**; Hôtel Des Ameriques, **82**; The unger, L'Africain, Le Bon Plaisir, **83**; Scene f The Crime, **86**; Agent Trouble, **87**; requence Meurtre, Drôle D'Endroit Pour Une encontre, **88**; La Reine Blanche, **91**; a Saison Preferée, **92**; Les Voleurs, **96**.

E NIRO, ROBERT: Greetings, **68**; am's Song, The Wedding Party, **69**; Bloody ama, Hi Mom!, **70**; Born To Win, The ang That Couldn't Shoot Straight, **71**; Bang e Drum Slowly, Mean Streets, **73**; The odfather Part II, **74**; The Last Tycoon, Taxi river, **76**; 1900, New York New York, **7**; The Deer Hunter, **78**; Raging Bull, **80**; ue Confessions, **81**; The King Of omedy, **83**; Falling In Love, Once Upon A me In America, **84**; Brazil, **85**; The ission, **86**; Angel Heart, The Untouchables, **7**; Midnight Run, **88**; Jacknife, We're o Angels, **89**; Awakenings, GoodFellas, tanley And Iris, **90**; Backdraft, Cape ear, Guilty By Suspicion, **91**; Mistress, Night nd The City, **92**; A Bronx Tale, Mad Dog nd Glory, This Boy's Life, **93**; Casino, eat, **95**; Sleepers, Marvin's Room, **96**.

E PALMA, BRIAN: Greetings, **68**; he Wedding Party, **69**; Hi Mom!, **70**; Get Know Your Rabbit, Sisters, **72**; hantom Of The Paradise, **74**; Carrie, bsession, **76**; The Fury, **78**; Home ovies, **79**; Dressed To Kill, **80**; Blow Out, **1**; Scarface, **83**; Body Double, **84**; ise Guys, **86**; The Untouchables, **87**; asualties Of War, **89**; The Bonfire Of e Vanities, **90**; Raising Cain, **92**; Carlito's ay, **93**; Mission: Impossible, **96**.

EPARDIEU, GERARD: Le Cri Du ormoran Le Soir Au-dessus Des Jonques, Le eur, Un Peu De Soleil Dans L'Eau oide, **71**; Au Rendez-vous De La Mort oyeuse, L'Affaire Dominici, La coumoune, Le Viager, Nathalie Granger, **72**; es Gaspards, Rude Journée Pour La eine, Two Against The Law, **73**; Les alseuses, La Femme Du Gange, tavisky, Vincent François Paul Et Les Autres, as Si Méchant Que Ca, **74**; Seven orts Sur Ordonnance, Je T'Aime Moi Non us, **75**; Barocco, La Nuit Tous Les hat Sont Gris, La Derniere Femme, aitresse, Rene La Canne, Violanta, **76**; axter, Vera Baxter, Dites-lui Que Je L'Aime, e Camion, **77**; Reve De Singe, Preparez os Mouchoirs, Le Sucre, The Left-handed oman, Les Chiens, **78**; Buffet Froid, osy La Bourrasque, Le Grand Embouteillage, **'9**; Inspecteur La Bavure, The Last etro, Loulou, Mon Oncle D'Amérique, **80**; e Choix Des Armes, Je Vous Aime, The oman Next Door, **81**; Danton, La Chèvre, Le rand Frère, The Return Of Martin uerre, **82**; La Lune Dans Le Caniveau, **83**; ort Saganne, Le Tartuffe, Les ompères, Police, Rive Droite Rive Gauche, **4**; One Woman Or Two, **85**; Jean De orette, Les Fugitifs, Ménage, Rue Du Départ, **6**; Under The Sun Of Satan, **87**; amille Claudel, Deux, Drôle D'Endroit Pour e Rencontre, **88**; I Want To Go Home, op Belle Pour Toi, **89**; Cyrano De Bergerac, reen Card, **90**; Shakha Proshakaco, erci La Vie, Mon Père Ce Héros, Tous Les atins Du Monde, Uranus, **91**; 1492: onquest Of Paradise, **92**; Germinal, Hélas our Moi, **93**; My Father The Hero, olonel Chabert, **94**, A Pure Formailty, Le arçu, **95**; The Secret Agent, **96**.

E SICA, VITTORIO: The Clemenceau ffair, **18**; La Vecchia Signora, **31**; Passa 'Amore, **33**; La Canzone Del Sole, **34**; mo Te Sola, Tempe Massimo, **35**; ohengrin, **36**; Napoli D'Altri Tempi, **37**; a Mazurka Di Papa, **38**; I Grandi Magazzini, **9**; Manon Lescaut, Rose Scarlatte, **40**; eresa Venerdi, Maddalena Zero In Condotta, **1**; The Children Are Watching Us, Un aribaldino Al Convento, **42**; Dieci Minuti Di ita, **43**; Porta Del Cielo, **45**; Rome pen City, Shoeshine, **46**; Bicycle Thieves, **8**; Miracle In Milan, **51**; Buongiorno efante!, Idea, Umberto D, **52**; The Earrings f Madame De, Stazione Termini, **53**; read Love And Dreams, L'Oro Di Napoli, Villa orghese, **54**; Bread, Love And Jealousy, oo Bad She's Bad, **55**; Pane Amore E . . . , The Roof/Il Tetto, **56**; A Farewell To Arms, The Monte Carlo Story, **57**; General Della Rovere, The Tailor's Maid, **59**; The Angel Wore Red, The Battle Of Austerlitz, It Started In Naples, The Millionairess, **60**; Il Giudizio Universale, Two Women, **61**; Boccaccio '70, **62**; The Condemned Of Altona, Il Boom, **63**; Marriage Italian-style, Yesterday Today And Tomorrow, **64**; After The Fox, A Young World, **66**; Woman Times Seven, **67**; The Shoes Of The Fisherman, The Witches, **68**; Amanti, **69**; I Girasoli, The Garden Of The Finzi-Continis, **70**; Lo Chiameremo Andrea, **72**; A Brief Vacation, The Voyage, **73**.

DE TOTH, ANDRE: Semmelweis, The Four Feathers, Toprini Nasz, **39**; Balalaika, Hat Het Buldogsag, Ket Lany Az Utcan, Ot Ora, The Thief Of Bagdad, **40**; The Jungle Book, **42**; Passport To Suez, **43**; Dark Waters, None Shall Escape, **44**; The Other Love, Ramrod, **47**; The Pitfall, **48**; Slattery's Hurricane, **49**; Man In The Saddle, **51**; Carson City, Last Of The Comanches, Springfield Rifle, **52**; House Of Wax, The Stranger Wore A Gun, Thunder Over The Plains, **53**; The Bounty Hunter, Crime Wave, Riding Shotgun, Tanganyika, **54**; The Indian Fighter, **55**; Hidden Fear, Monkey On My Back, **57**; The Two-headed Spy, **58**; Day Of The Outlaw, **59**; Man On A String, **60**; The Mongols, Morgan The Pirate, **61**; Gold For The Caesars, **64**; Play Dirty, **68**.

DE VITO, DANNY: Dreams Of Glass, **68**; One Flew Over The Cuckoo's Nest, **75**; The Van, **76**; The World's Greatest Lover, **77**; Goin' South, **78**; Going Ape!, **81**; Terms Of Endearment, **83**; Johnny Dangerously, Romancing The Stone, **84**; The Jewel Of The Nile, **85**; Head Office, My Little Pony, Ruthless People, Wise Guys, **86**; Throw Momma From The Train, Tin Men, **87**; Twins, **88**; The War Of The Roses, **89**; Other People's Money, **91**; Batman Returns, Hoffa, **92**; Jack The Bear, Last Action Hero, Look Who's Talking Now, **93**; 8 Seconds, Reality Bites, Renaissance Man, Junior, **94**; Get Shorty, **95**; Mars Attacks!, **96**; LA Confidential, **97**.

DICKINSON, THOROLD: The High Command, **37**; Spanish ABC, **38**; The Arsenal Stadium Mystery, **39**; Yesterday Is Over Your Shoulder, Gaslight, **40**; Next Of Kin, The Prime Minister, **42**; Men Of Two Worlds, **46**; The Queen Of Spades, **48**; Secret People, **52**; Hill 24 Doesn't Answer, **55**.

DIERTELE, WILLIAM: Faust, **26**; Geschlecht in Fesseln, Der Heilige und ihr Narr, **28**; Das Schweigen Im Walde, **29**; Kismet, Her Majesty Love, **31**; Jewel Robbery, The Crash, Six Hours To Live, Lawyer Man, **32**; Grand Slam, Adorable, The Devil's In Love, **33**; Fashions of 1934, Fog Over Frisco, Madame Du Barry, The Firebird, **34**; The Secret Bride, A Midsummer Night's Dream, Dr Socrates, **35**; The Story Of Louis Pasteur, The White Angel, Satan Met A Lady, **36**; The Great O'Malley, Another Dawn, The Life Of Emile Zola, **37**; Blockade, **38**; Juarez, The Hunchback Of Notre Dame, **39**; Dr Ehrlich's Magic Bullet, A Dispatch From Reuters, **40**; All That Money Can Buy, Tennessee Johnson, **41**; Kismet, I'll Be Seeing You, **44**; Love Letters, This Love Of Ours, **45**; The Searching Wind, **46**; The Accused, Portrait Of Jennie, **48**; Rope Of Sand, **49**; Paid In Full, Dark City, September Affair, **50**; Peking Express, Red Mountain, **51**; The Turning Point, Boots Malone, **52**; Salomé, **53**; Elephant Walk, **54**; Magic Fire, **56**; Omar Khayyam, **57**; Dubrowsky, **59**; Die Fastnachtsbeichte, Herrin der Welt, **60**.

DIETRICH, MARLENE: Der Kleine Napoleon, Der Mensch Am Wege, Tragodie Der Liebe, **23**; Der Sprung Ins Leben, **24**; The Joyless Street, **25**; Der Juxbaron, Kopf Hoch, Charly!, Madame Wonscht Keine Kinder, Manon Lescaut, Eine Dubarry Von Heute, **26**; Cafe Electric, Sein Grosster Bluff, **27**; Ich Kusse Ihre Hand Madame, Prinzessin in Olala, **28**; Die Frau Nach Der Man Sich Sehnt, Gefahren Der Brautzeit, Das Schiff Der Verlorenen Menschen, **29**; The Blue Angel, Morocco, **30**; Dishonored, **31**; Blonde Venus, Shanghai Express, **32**; Song Of Songs, **33**; The Scarlet Empress, **34**; The Devil Is A Woman, **35**; Desire, The Garden Of Allah, I Loved A Soldier, **36**; Angel, Knight Without Armour, **37**; Destry Rides Again, **39**; Seven Sinners, **40**; The Flame Of New Orleans, Manpower, **41**; The Lady Is Willing, Pittsburgh, The Spoilers, **42**; Follow The Boys, Kismet, **44**; Martin Roumagnac, **46**; Golden Earrings, **47**; A Foreign Affair, **48**; Jigsaw, **49**; Stage Fright, **50**; No Highway, **51**; Rancho Notorious, **52**; Around The World In 80 Days, **56**; The Monte Carlo Story, Witness For The Prosecution, **57**; Touch Of Evil, **58**; Judgment At Nuremberg, **61**; The Black Fox, **62**; Paris When It Sizzles, **64**; Just A Gigolo, **79**.

DIETZ, HOWARD: The Lottery Bride, **30**; Under Your Spell, **36**; Her Kind Of Man, **46**; Three Daring Daughters, **48**; Dancing In The Dark, **49**; The Band Wagon, Torch Song, **53**.

DILLON, MATT: Over The Edge, **79**; Little Darlings, My Bodyguard, **80**; Liar's Moon, **81**; Tex, **82**; The Outsiders, Rumble Fish, **83**; The Flamingo Kid, **84**; Rebel, Target, **85**; Native Son, **86**; The Big Town, Dear America, **87**; Kansas, **88**; Bloodhounds Of Broadway, Drugstore Cowboy, **89**; A Kiss Before Dying, **91**; Malcolm X, Singles, **92**; Golden Gate, Mr Wonderful, The Saint Of Fort Washington, **93**; Frankie Starlight, 2 Die 4, Frankie Starlight, **95**; Beautiful Girls, **96**.

DISNEY, WALT: Steamboat Willie, **28**; Snow White And The Seven Dwarfs, **37**; Fantasia, Pinocchio, **40**; Dumbo, The Reluctant Dragon, **41**; Bambi, **42**; The Three Caballeros, **45**; Make Mine Music, Song Of The South, **46**; Fun And Fancy Free, **47**; Melody Time, So Dear To My Heart, **48**; The Adventures Of Ichabod And Mr Toad, **49**; Cinderella, Treasure Island, **50**; Alice In Wonderland, **51**; The Story Of Robin Hood And His Merrie Men, **52**; The Living Desert, Peter Pan, The Sword And The Rose, **53**; 20,000 Leagues Under The Sea, Rob Roy, The Vanishing Prairie, **54**; The African Lion, Davy Crockett King Of The Wild Frontier, Lady And The Tramp, The Littlest Outlaw, **55**; Davy Crockett And The River Pirates, The Great Locomotive Chase, Secrets Of Life, Westward Ho, The Wagons, **56**; Johnny Tremain, Old Yeller, Perri, **57**; The Light In The Forest, Tonka, White Wilderness, **58**; Darby O'Gill And The Little People, Mysteries Of The Deep, The Shaggy Dog, Sleeping Beauty, Third Man On The Mountain, **59**; Jungle Cat, Kidnapped, Pollyanna, The Sign Of Zorro, Swiss Family Robinson, Ten Who Dared, Toby Tyler, **60**; The Absent-Minded Professor, Babes In Toyland, Greyfriars Bobby, Nikki Wild Dog Of The North, 101 Dalmatians, The Parent Trap, **61**; Almost Angels, Big Red, Bon Voyage!, In Search Of The Castaways, The Legend Of Lobo, Moon Pilot, **62**; The Incredible Journey, Miracle Of The White Stallions, Savage Sam, Son Of Flubber, Summer Magic, The Sword In The Stone, **63**; Emil And The Detectives, Mary Poppins, The Misadventures Of Merlin Jones, The Moon-Spinners, The Three Lives Of Thomasina, A Tiger Walks, **64**; The Monkey's Uncle, That Darn Cat, Those Calloways, **65**; The Fighting Prince Of Donegal, Follow Me Boys! Lt Robin Crusoe, The Ugly Dachshund, **66**; The Adventures Of Bullwhip Griffin, The Gnome-Mobile, The Happiest Millionaire, The Jungle Book, Monkeys Go Home!, **67**.

DIX, RICHARD: Dangerous Curve Ahead, The Sin Flood, **21**; Fools First, **22**; The Call Of The Canyon, The Christian, The Ten Commandments, **23**; Manhattan, The Woman With Four Faces, **24**; The Lucky Devil, Men And Women, Too Many Kisses, The Vanishing American, **25**; Let's Get Married, The Quarterback, Say It Again, **26**; The Gay Defender, Paradise For Two, Shanghai Bound, **27**; Easy Come Easy Go, Moran Of The Marines, Warming Up, **28**; Nothing But The Truth, Redskin, Seven Keys To Baldpate, The Wheel Of Life, **29**; Cimarron, **30**; Lovin' The Ladies, The Public Defender, Secret Service, **31**; The Conquerors, Hell's Highway, The Lost Squadron, **32**; Ace Of Aces, Day Of Reckoning, The Great Jasper, **33**; Stingaree, West Of The Pecos, **34**; The Arizonian, The Tunnel, **35**; Yellow Dust, **36**; Devil's Playground, It Happened In Hollywood, **37**; Blind Alibi, Sky Giant, **38**; Man Of Conquest, Reno, Twelve Crowded Hours, **39**; Cherokee Strip, The Marines Fly High, Men Against The Sky, **40**; The Roundup, **41**; Tombstone, **42**; Eyes Of The Underworld, The Ghost Ship, The Kansan, **43**; The Whistler, **44**; The Power Of The Whistler, **45**; Mysterious Intruder, **46**; The 13th Hour, **47**.

DMYTRYK, EDWARD: Television Spy, **39**; Emergency Squad, Golden Gloves, Her First Romance, Mystery Sea Raider, **40**; The Blonde From Singapore, Confessions Of Boston Blackie, The Devil Commands, Secrets Of The Lone Wolf, Sweetheart Of The Campus, Under Age, **41**; Counter-espionage, Seven Miles From Alcatraz, **42**; Behind The Rising Sun, Captive Wild Woman, The Falcon Strikes Back, Hitler's Children, Tender Comrade, **43**; Murder My Sweet, **44**; Back To Bataan, Cornered, **45**; Till The End Of Time, **46**; Crossfire, So Well Remembered, **47**; Give Us This Day, Obsession, **49**; Eight Iron Men, Mutiny, The Sniper, **52**; The Juggler, **53**; Broken Lance, The Caine Mutiny, **54**; The End Of The Affair, The Left Hand Of God, Soldier Of Fortune, **55**; The Mountain, **56**; Raintree County, **57**; The Young Lions, **58**; The Blue Angel, Warlock, **59**; The Reluctant Saint, Walk On The Wild Side, **62**; The Carpetbaggers, Where Love Has Gone, **64**; Mirage, **65**; Alvarez Kelly, **66**; Anzio, Shalako, **68**; Bluebeard, **72**; The Human Factor, **75**; He Is My Brother, **76**.

DONAT, ROBERT: Men Of Tomorrow, That Night In London, **32**; For Love Or Money, The Private Life Of Henry VIII, **33**; The Count Of Monte Cristo, **34**; The 39 Steps, **35**; The Ghost Goes West, **36**; Knight Without Armour, **37**; The Citadel, **38**; The 39 Steps, Goodbye Mr Chips, **39**; The Young Mr Pitt, **42**; Adventures Of Tartu, **43**; Perfect Strangers, **45**; Captain Boycott, **47**; The Cure For Love, **49**; The Winslow Boy, **50**; The Magic Box, **51**; Lease Of Life, **54**; The Inn Of The Sixth Happiness, **58**.

DONEN, STANLEY: Cover Girl, **44**; Holiday In Mexico, **46**; A Date With Judy, **48**; On The Town, Take Me Out To The Ball Game, **49**; Royal Wedding, **51**; Fearless Fagan, Love Is Better Than Ever, Singin' In The Rain, **52**; Give A Girl A Break, **53**; Deep In My Heart, Seven Brides For Seven Brothers, **54**; It's Always Fair Weather, **55**; Funny Face, Kiss Them For Me, The Pajama Game, **57**; Damn Yankees, Indiscreet, **58**; The Grass Is Greener, Once More With Feeling, Surprise Package, **60**; Charade, **63**; Arabesque, **66**; Bedazzled, Two For The Road, **67**; Staircase, **69**; The Little Prince, **74**; Lucky Lady, **75**; Movie Movie, **78**; Saturn 3, **80**; Blame It On Rio, **84**.

DONNER, RICHARD: X-15, **61**; The Omen, **76**; Superman The Movie, **78**; Inside Moves, **80**; The Final Conflict, **81**; The Toy, **82**; The Goonies, Ladyhawke, **85**; Lethal Weapon, The Lost Boys, **87**; Scrooged, **88**; Lethal Weapon 2, **89**; Delirious, **91**; Lethal Weapon 3, Radio Flyer, **92**; Free Willy, **93**; Maverick, **94**; Assassins, **95**; Conspiracy Theory, **97**.

DORS, DIANA: The Shop At Sly Corner, **46**; Here Come The Huggetts, Holiday Camp, Oliver Twist, **48**; Diamond City, **49**; Dance Hall, Good Time Girl, **50**; Lady Godiva Rides Again, **51**; The Saint's Return, The Weak And The Wicked, **53**; A Kid For Two Farthings, Value For Money, **55**; Yield To The Night, Blonde Sinner, **56**; An Alligator Named Daisy, As Long As They're Happy, The Long Haul, The Unholy Wife, **57**; I Married A Woman, Tread Softly Stranger, **58**; Passport To Shame, **59**; Scent Of Mystery, **60**; King Of The Roaring 20s, The Story Of Arnold Rothstein, On The Double, **61**; Allez France, **64**; The Sandwich Man, **66**; Berserk, **67**; Danger Route, Hammerhead, **68**; Baby Love, **69**; Deep End, There's A Girl In My Soup, **70**; Hannie Caulder, Nothing But The Night, The Pied Piper, The Amazing Mr Blunden, **72**; Craze, From Beyond The Grave, Theatre Of Blood, **73**; Keep It Up Downstairs, **76**; Adventures Of A Private Eye, The Groove Room, **77**; Confessions From The David Galaxy Affair, **79**; Steaming, **84**.

DOUGLAS, KIRK: The Strange Love Of Martha Ivers, **46**; I Walk Alone, Mourning Becomes Electra, Build My Gallows High, **47**; My Dear Secretary, The Walls Of Jericho, **48**; Champion, A Letter To Three Wives, **49**; The Glass Menagerie, Young Man With A Horn, **50**; Along The Great Divide, Ace In The Hole, Detective Story, **51**; The Bad And The Beautiful, The Big Sky, The Big Trees, **52**; Act Of Love, The Juggler, The Story Of Three Loves, **53**; 20,000 Leagues Under The Sea, **54**; The Indian Fighter, Man Without A Star, The Racers, Ulysses, **55**; Lust For Life, **56**; Gunfight At The OK Corral, Paths Of Glory, Top Secret Affair, **57**; The Vikings, **58**; The Devil's Disciple, Last Train From Gun Hill, **59**; Spartacus, **60**; Strangers When We Meet, The Last Sunset, Town Without Pity, **61**; Lonely Are The Brave, Two Weeks In Another Town, **62**; For Love Or Money, The Hook, The List Of Adrian Messenger, **63**; The Long Ships, Seven Days In May, **64**; The Heroes Of Telemark, In Harm's Way, **65**; Cast A Giant Shadow, Is Paris Burning?, The War Wagon, The Way West, **67**; The Brotherhood, A Lovely Way To Die, **68**; The Arrangement, **69**; There Was A Crooked Man, **70**; A Gunfight, The Light At The Edge Of The World, Summertree, To Catch A Spy, **71**; Scalawag, **73**; Once Is Not Enough, Posse, **75**; Victory At Entebbe, **76**; The Chosen, The Fury, **78**; Home Movies, The Villain, **79**; The Final Countdown, Saturn 3, **80**; The Man From Snowy River, **82**; Eddie Macon's Run, **83**; Tough Guys, **86**; Oscar, **91**; Welcome To Veraz, **92**; Greedy, **94**.

DOUGLAS, MELVYN: Tonight Or Never, **31**; As You Desire Me, The Broken Wing, The Old Dark House, Prestige, The Wiser Sex, **32**; Counsellor At Law, Nagana, The Vampire Bat, **33**; Dangerous Corner, Woman In The Dark, **34**; Annie Oakley, The Lone Wolf Returns, Mary Burns, Fugitive, The People's Enemy, She Married Her Boss, **35**; And So They Were Married, The Gorgeous Hussy, Theodora Goes Wild, **36**; Angel, Captains Courageous, I Met Him In Paris, I'll Take Romance, **37**; Arsene Lupin Returns, Fast Company, The Shining Hour, Tell No Tales, That Certain Age, There's Always A Woman, There's That Woman Again, The Toy Wife, **38**; Amazing Mr Williams, Good Girls Go To Paris, Ninotchka, **39**; He Stayed For Breakfast, Third Finger Left Hand, Too Many Husbands, **40**; Our Wife, That Uncertain Feeling, This Thing Called Love, Two-faced Woman, A Woman's Face, **41**; They All Kissed The Bride, We Were Dancing, **42**; Three Hearts For Julia, **43**; The Guilt Of Janet Ames, The Sea Of Grass, **47**; Mr Blandings Builds His Dream House, My Own True Love, **48**; The Great Sinner, A Woman's Secret, **49**; My Forbidden Past, On The Loose, **51**; Billy Budd, **62**; Hud, **63**; Advance To The Rear, The Americanization Of Emily, **64**; Rapture, **65**; Hotel, **67**; I Never Sang For My Father, **70**; The Candidate, One Is A Lonely Number, **72**; The Tenant, **76**; Twilight's Last Gleaming, **77**; Being There, The Changeling, The Seduction Of Joe Tynan, **79**; Tell Me A Riddle, **80**; Ghost Story, **81**; Hot Touch, **82**.

DOUGLAS, MICHAEL: Hail Hero!, **69**; Adam At 6am, **70**; One Flew Over The Cuckoo's Nest, **75**; Coma, **78**; The China Syndrome, Running, **79**; It's My Turn, **80**; The Star Chamber, **83**; Romancing The Stone, Starman, **84**; A Chorus Line, The Jewel Of The Nile, **85**; Fatal Attraction, Wall Street, **87**; Black Rain, The War Of The Roses, **89**; Basic Instinct, Shining Through, **92**; Falling Down, **93**; Disclosure, **95**; The American President, **95**; The Ghost and the Drakness, **96**.

DOVSCHENKO, ALEXANDER: Vasya The Reformer, Love's Berry, **26**; The Diplomatic Pouch, Zvenigora, **27**; Arsenal, **29**; Earth, **30**; Ivan, **32**; Air City, **35**; Shchors, **39**; Liberation, **40**; The Battle For Our Soviet Ukraine, **43**; Ukraine In Flames, **45**; Native Land, **46**; Life In Bloom, **49**; Poem Of The Sea, **58**; Story Of The Flaming Years, **61**; The Enchanted Desna, **65**; The Unforgettable, **68**.

DRESSLER, MARIE: Tillie's Punctured Romance, **14**; Tillie's Tomato Surprise, **15**; The Scrublady, Tillie Wakes Up, **17**; The Agonies Of Agnes, The Cross Red Nurse, **18**; Breakfast At Sunrise, **20**; The Callahans And The Murphys, The Joy Girl, The Patsy, **27**; Bringing Up Father, **28**; The Divine Lady, The Hollywood Revue Of 1929, Performer, The Vagabond Lover, **29**; Anna Christie, Caught Short, Chasing Rainbows, The Girl Said No, Let Us Be Gay, Min And Bill, One Romantic Night, **30**; Politics, Reducing, **31**; Emma, Prosperity, **32**; Christopher Bean, Dinner At Eight, Tugboat Annie, **33**.

DREYER, CARL: Leaves From Satan's Book, The President, **19**; The Parson's Widow, **20**; Love One Another, **21**; Once Upon A Time, **22**; Mikael, **24**; The Bride Of Glomdal, Master Of The House, **25**; The Passion Of Joan Of Arc, **28**; Vampyr, **32**; Day

Of Wrath, 43; Two People, 45; Ordet, 54; Gertrud, 64.

DREYFUSS, RICHARD: The Graduate, Valley Of The Dolls, 67; The Young Runaways, 68; Hello Down There, 69; American Graffiti, Dillinger, 73; The Apprenticeship Of Duddy Kravitz, The Second Coming Of Suzanne, 74; Jaws, 75; Inserts, Victory At Entebbe, 76; Close Encounters Of The Third Kind, The Goodbye Girl, 77; The Big Fix, 78; The Competition, 80; Whose Life Is It Anyway? 81; The Buddy System, 84; Down And Out In Beverly Hills, Stand By Me, 86; Nuts, Stakeout, Tin Men, 87; Moon Over Parador, 88; Always, Let It Ride, 89; Postcards From The Edge, Rosencrantz And Guildenstern Are Dead, 90; Once Around, What About Bob? 91; Another Stakeout, Lost In Yonkers, 93; Silent Fall, Mr Holland's Opus, 95.

DUNAWAY, FAYE: Bonnie And Clyde, The Happening, Hurry Sundown, 67; The Thomas Crown Affair, 68; The Arrangement, The Extraordinary Seaman, A Place For Lovers, 69; Little Big Man, Puzzle Of A Downfall Child, 70; The Deadly Trap, Doc, 71; Oklahoma Crude, 73; Chinatown, The Three Musketeers, The Towering Inferno, 74; The Four Musketeers, Three Days Of The Condor, 75; Voyage Of The Damned, Network, 76; Eyes Of Laura Mars, 78; The First Deadly Sin, 80; Mommie Dearest, 81; The Wicked Lady, 83; Ordeal By Innocence, Supergirl, 84; Barfly, 87; Burning Secret, The Gamble, Midnight Crossing, 88; Wait Until Spring, 89; The Handmaid's Tale, 90; Scorchers, 91; Arizona Dream, 92; The Temp, 93; Even Cowgirls Get The Blues, 94; Don Juan De Marco, Arizona Dreams, 95; The Chamber, Albino Alligator, 96.

DUNNE, IRENE: Leathernecking, 30; Bachelor Apartment, Cimarron, Consolation Marriage, The Great Lover, The Stolen Jools, 31; Back Street, Symphony Of Six Million, 13 Women, 32; Ann Vickers, If I Were Free, No Other Woman, The Secret Of Madame Blanche, The Silver Cord, 33; The Age Of Innocence, Stingaree, This Man Is Mine, 34; Magnificent Obsession, Roberta, Sweet Adeline, 35; Show Boat, Theodora Goes Wild, 36; The Awful Truth, High Wide And Handsome, 37; Joy Of Living, 38; Invitation To Happiness, Love Affair, When Tomorrow Comes, 39; My Favorite Wife, 40; Penny Serenade, Unfinished Business, 41; Lady In A Jam, 42; A Guy Named Joe, 43; Together Again, The White Cliffs Of Dover, 44; Over 21, 45; Anna And The King Of Siam, 46; Life With Father, 47; I Remember Mama, 48; The Mudlark, Never A Dull Moment, 50; It Grows On Trees, 52; It's Showtime, 76.

DURANTE, JIMMY: Roadhouse Nights, 30; The Cuban Love Song, New Adventures Of Get-Rich-Quick Wallingford, 31; Blondie Of The Follies, The Passionate Plumber, The Phantom President, Speak Easily, The Wet Parade, 32; Broadway To Hollywood, Hell Below, Meet The Baron, What! No Beer?, 33; George White's Scandals, Hollywood Party, Palooka, She Learned About Sailors, Strictly Dynamite, Student Tour, 34; Carnival, 35; Forbidden Music, Little Miss Broadway, Sally Irene And Mary, Start Cheering, 38; Melody Ranch, 40; The Man Who Came To Dinner, You're In The Army Now, 41; Music For Millions, Two Girls And A Sailor, 44; Two Sisters From Boston, 46; It Happened In Brooklyn, This Time For Keeps, 47; On An Island With You, 48; The Great Rupert, The Milkman, 50; Beau James, 57; Pépé, 60; Jumbo, 62; It's A Mad Mad Mad Mad World, 63.

DURBIN, DEANNA: Three Smart Girls, 36; One Hundred Men And A Girl, 37; Mad About Music, That Certain Age, 38; First Love, Three Smart Girls Grow Up, 39; It's A Date, Spring Parade, 40; It Started With Eve, Nice Girl?, 41; The Amazing Mrs Holliday, Hers To Hold, Her Butler's Sister, 43; Can't Help Singing, Christmas Holiday, 44; Lady On A Train, 45; Because Of Him, 46; I'll Be Yours, Something In The Wind, 47; For The Love Of Mary, Up In Central Park, 48.

DUVALL, ROBERT: To Kill A Mockingbird, 62; Captain Newman, MD, 63; Nightmare In The Sun, 64; The Chase, 66; Bullitt, Countdown, The Detective, 68; The Rain People, True Grit, 69; MASH, The Revolutionary, 70; Lawman, THX-1138, 71; The Godfather, The Great Northfield Minnesota Raid, Joe Kidd, Tomorrow, 72; Badge 373, Lady Ice, 73; The Conversation, The Godfather Part II, The Outfit, 74; Breakout, The Killer Elite, Network, 75; The Seven Percent Solution, 76; The Eagle Has Landed, The Greatest, 77; The Betsy, Invasion Of The Body Snatchers, 78; Apocalypse Now, The Great Santini, 79; The Pursuit Of DB Cooper, True Confessions, 81; Angelo My Love, Tender Mercies, 83; The Natural, 84; The Stone Boy, 85; The Lightship, Belizaire The Cajun, Let's Get Harry, 86; Hotel Colonial, 87; Colors, 88; Days Of Thunder, The Handmaid's Tale, A Show Of Force, 90; Convicts, The Plague, Rambling Rose, 91; Newsies, 92; Falling Down, Geronimo: An American Legend, Wrestling Ernest Hemingway, 93; The Paper, 94; The Scarlet Letter, Stars Fell On Henrietta, 95; Phenomenon, 96.

DUVIVIER, JULIEN: Le Prix Du Sang, 19; La Reincarnation De Serge Renaudier, 20; Der Unheimliche Gast, L'Ouragan Sur La Montagne, Les Roquevillard, 22; Le Reflet De Claude Mercoeur, 23; Coeurs Farouches, Credo Ou La Tragédie De Lourdes, L'Oeuvre Immortelle, L'Abbé Constantin, Poil De Carotte, 25; L'Agonie De Jerusalem, L'Homme A L'Hispano, 26; Le Mariage De Mademoiselle Beulemans, Le Mystère De La Tour Eiffel, 27; Le Tourbillon De Paris, 28; La Divine Croisière, La Vie Miraculeuse De Thérèse Martin, Maman Colibri, 29; Au Bonheur Des Dames, David Golder, 30; Allo Berlin? Ici Paris!, La Venus Du College, Poil De Carotte, Sous La Lune Du Maroc, 32; La Machine A Refaire La Vie, La Tête D'Un Homme, Le Petit Roi, 33; La Paquebot 'Tenacity', Maria Chapdelaine, 34; Escape From Yesterday, Golgotha, 35; The Golem, La Belle Equipe, The Man Of The Hour, 36; Pépé Le Moko, Un Carnet De Bal, 37; The Great Waltz, 38; The End Of A Day, La Charrette Fantôme, 39; Lydia, 41; Tales Of Manhattan, 42; Flesh And Fantasy, The Heart Of A Nation, 43; The Impostor, 44; Panique, 46; Anna Karenina, 47; The Sinners, 49; Captain Blackjack, The Little World Of Don Camillo, Sous Le Ciel De Paris, 51; La Fête A Henriette, On Trial, The Return Of Don Camillo, Marianne Of My Youth, Female, 56; Deadlier Than The Male, Lovers Of Paris, The Man In The Raincoat, 57; Marie Octobre, 59; Boulevard, La Grande Vie, 60; The Burning Court, The Devil And The Ten Commandments, 62; Highway Pickup, 63; Diabolically Yours, 67.

DWAN, ALLAN: Maiden And Men, 12; The County Chairman, Richelieu, 14; The Dancing Girl, David Harum, The Foundling, Jordan Is A Hard Road, The Pretty Sister Of Jose, 15; Betty Of Greystone, Fifty-Fifty, The Good Bad Man, The Habit Of Happiness, The Half-Breed, An Innocent Magdalene, Manhattan Madness, Intolerance, 16; Fighting Odds, A Modern Musketeer, Panthea, 17; Bound In Morocco, He Comes Up Smiling, Mr Fix-it, Society For Sale, 18; Cheating Cheaters, The Dark Star, Getting Mary Married, Soldiers Of Fortune, 19; The Forbidden Thing, In The Heart Of A Fool, The Luck Of The Irish, 20; A Broken Doll, A Perfect Crime, The Scoffer, The Sin Of Martha Queed, 21; The Hidden Woman, Robin Hood, Superstition, 22; Big Brother, The Glimpses Of The Moon, Lawful Larceny, Zaza, 23; Argentine Love, Her Love Story, Manhandled, A Society Scandal, Wages Of Virtue, 24; The Coast Of Folly, Night Life Of New York, Stage Struck, 25; Padlocked, Sea Horses, Summer Bachelors, Tin Gods, 26; East Side West Side, French Dressing, The Joy Girl, The Music Master, 27; The Big Noise, 28; The Far Call, Frozen Justice, The Iron Mask, South Sea Rose, Tide Of Empire, 29; Man To Man, What A Widow!, 30; Chances, Wicked, 31; Her First Affair, While Paris Sleeps, 32; Counsel's Opinion, I Spy, 33; Hollywood Party, 34; Black Sheep, Story, Navy Wife, 35; 15 Malden Lane, High Tension, Human Cargo, The Song And Dance Man, 36; Heidi, One Mile From Heaven, That I May Live, Woman-wise, 37; Josette, Rebecca Of Sunnybrook Farm, Suez, 38; Frontier Marshal, The Gorilla, The Three Musketeers, 39; Sailor's Lady, Trail Of The Vigilantes, Young People, 40; Look Who's Laughing, Rise And Shine, 41; Friendly Enemies, Here We Go Again, 42; Around The World, 43; Abroad With Two Yanks, Up In Mabel's Room, 44; Brewster's Millions, Getting Gertie's Garter, 45; Calendar Girl, Rendezvous With Annie, 46; Driftwood, Northwest Outpost, 47; Angel In Exile, The Inside Story, 48; Sands Of Iwo Jima, 49; Surrender, 50; Belle Le Grand, The Wild Blue Yonder, 51; I Dream Of Jeannie, Montana Belle, 52; Sweethearts On Parade, The Woman They Almost Lynched, 53; Cattle Queen Of Montana, Flight Nurse, Passion, Silver Lode, 54; Escape To Burma, Pearl Of The South Pacific, Tennessee's Partner, 55; Hold Back The Night, Slightly Scarlet, 56; The Restless Breed, The River's Edge, 57; Enchanted Island, 58; Most Dangerous Man Alive, 61.

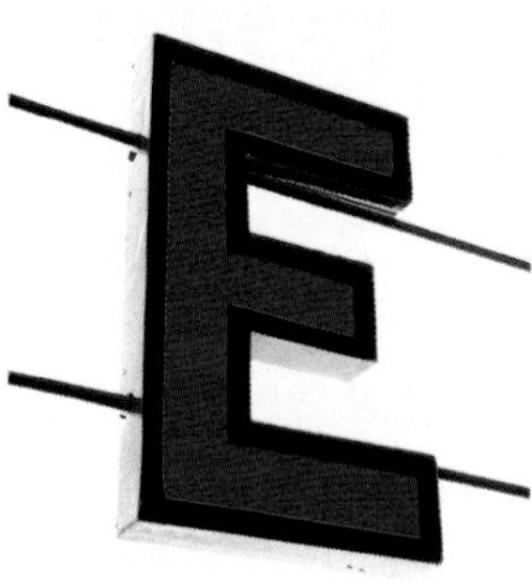

EASTWOOD, CLINT: Francis In The Navy, Lady Godiva, Revenge Of The Creature, Tarantula, 55; The First Traveling Saleslady, Never Say Goodbye,56; Escapade In Japan, 57; A Fistful Of Dollars, 64; For A Few Dollars More, 65; The Good The Bad And The Ugly, 66; The Witches, 67; Coogan's Bluff, Hang 'em High, 68; Paint Your Wagon, Where Eagles Dare, 69; Kelly's Heroes, Two Mules For Sister Sara, 70; The Beguiled, Dirty Harry, Play Misty For Me, 71; Joe Kid, 72; Breezy, High Plains Drifter, Magnum Force, 73; Thunderbolt And Lightfoot, 74; The Eiger Sanction, 75; The Enforcer, The Outlaw Josey Wales, 76; The Gauntlet, 77; Every Which Way But Loose, 78; Escape From Alcatraz, 79; Any Which Way You Can, Bronco Billy, 80; Firefox, Honkytonk Man, 82; Sudden Impact, 83; City Heat, Tightrope, 84; Pale Rider, 85; Heartbreak Ridge, 86; Bird, The Dead Pool, 88; Pink Cadillac, 89; The Rookie, White Hunter Black Heart, 90; Unforgiven, 92; In The Line Of Fire, A Perfect World, 93; The Bridges Of Madison County, 95; Midnight in the Garden of Good and Evil, Absolute Power, 97.

EDDY, NELSON: Broadway To Hollywood, Dancing Lady, 33; Student Tour, 34; Naughty Marietta, 35; Rose Marie, 36; Maytime, Rosalie, 37; The Girl Of The Golden West, Sweethearts, 38; Balalaika, Let Freedom Ring!, 39; Bitter Sweet, New Moon, 40; The Chocolate Soldier, 41; I Married An Angel, 42; Phantom Of The Opera, 43; Knickerbocker Holiday, 44; Make Mine Music, 46; Northwest Outpost, 47.

EDWARDS, BLAKE: Bring Your Smile Along, 55; He Laughed Last, 56; Mister Cory, 57; The Perfect Furlough, This Happy Feeling, 58; Operation Petticoat, 59; High Time, 60; Breakfast At Tiffany's, 61; Experiment In Terror, 62; Days Of Wine And Roses, 63; The Pink Panther, A Shot In The Dark, 64; The Great Race, 65; What Did You Do In The War, Daddy?, 66; Gunn, 67; The Party, 68; Darling Lili, 70; Wild Rovers, 71; The Carey Treatment, 72; The Tamarind Seed, 74; The Return Of The Pink Panther, 75; The Pink Panther Strikes Again, 76; Revenge Of The Pink Panther, 78; 10, 79; SOB, 81; Trail Of The Pink Panther, Victor/Victoria, 82; Curse Of The Pink Panther, The Man Who Loved Women, 83; City Heat, Micki And Maude 84; A Fine Mess, That's Life!, 86; Blind Date, 87; Sunset, 88; Skin Deep, 89; Switch, 91; Son Of The Pink Panther, 93.

EISENSTEIN, SERGEI: Glumov's Diary 23; Strike, 24; Battleship Potemkin, 25; Ten Days That Shook The World, October, 28; The General Line 29; Que Viva Mexico, 32; Bezhin Meadow, 37; Alexander Nevsky, 38; Ferghana Canal, 39; Ivan The Terrible Part One, Seeds Of Freedom, 43; Ivan The Terrible Part II, Ivan The Terrible Part III, 46.

ELFMAN, DANNY: Forbidden Zone, 80; Fast Times At Ridgemont High, 82; PeeWee's Big Adventure, 85; Back To School, Wisdom, 86; Summer School, 87; Beetlejuice, Midnight Run, Big Top PeeWee, Hot To Trot, Scrooged, 88; Batman, 89; Dick Tracy, Darkman, Edward Scissorhands, 90; Pure Luck, 91; Article 99, Batman Returns, 92, Sommersby, The Night Before Christmas, 92; Black Beauty, 94; Dolores Claiborne, 95.

ELLIOTT, DENHOLM: Dear Mr Prohack, 49; The Sound Barrier, The Ringer, 52; The Cruel Sea, The Heart Of The Matter, The Holly And The Ivy, They Who Dare, 53; Lease Of Life, 54; The Man Who Loved Redheads, The Night My Number Came Up, 55; Scent Of Mystery, 60; Nothing But The Best, Station Six-Sahara, 64; King Rat, 65; Alfie, The High Bright Sun, The Spy With A Cold Nose, 66; Maroc 7, Here We Go Round The Mulberry Bush, The Night They Raided Minsky's, The Seagull, 68; The Rise And Rise Of Michael Rimmer, Too Late The Hero, 70; The House That Dripped Blood, Percy, Quest For Love, 71; A Doll's House, Vault Of Horror, 73; The Apprenticeship Of Duddy Kravitz, Percy's Progress, 74; Russian Roulette, 75; Partners, Robin And Marian, To The Devil A Daughter, Voyage Of The Damned, 76; A Bridge Too Far, The Hound Of The Baskervilles, 77; The Boys From Brazil, La Petite Fille En Velours Bleu, Sweeney 2, Watership Down, 78; Cuba, Game For Vultures, Saint Jack, Zulu Dawn, 79; Bad Timing: A Sensual Obsession, Rising Damp, 80; Raiders Of The Lost Ark, 81; Brimstone And Treacle, The Missionary, 82; The Hound Of The Baskervilles, Trading Places, The Wicked Lady, 83; The Razor's Edge, 84; A Private Function, A Room With A View, Underworld, 85; The Whoopee Boys, Defence Of The Realm, 86; Maurice, September, 87; Stealing Heaven, 88; Indiana Jones And The Last Crusade, Killing Dad, Return To The River Kwai, 89; Scorchers, Toy Soldiers, 91; Noises Off, 92; To Die For, 95; Men in Black, 97.

EPSTEIN, JULIUS J: The Big Broadcast Of 1936, Broadway Gondolier, I Live For Love, In Caliente, Little Big Shot, Living On Velvet, Stars Over Broadway, 35; Sons O' Guns, 36; Confession, 37; Four Daughters, Secrets Of An Actress, 38; Daughters Courageous, Four Wives, 39; No Time For Comedy, Saturday's Children, 40; The Bride Came COD, Honeymoon For Three, The Strawberry Blonde, 41; The Man Who Came To Dinner, Casablanca, The Male Animal, 42; Arsenic And Old Lace, Mr Skeffington, 44; Chicken Every Sunday, Romance On The High Seas, 48; My Foolish Heart, 49; Take Care Of My Little Girl, 51; Forever Female, 53; The Last Time I Saw Paris, Young At Heart, 54; The Tender Trap, 55; Kiss Them For Me, 57; The Brothers Karamazov, 58; Take A Giant Step, 59; Tall Story, 60; Fanny, 61; Light In The Piazza, 62; Send Me No Flowers, 64; Return From The Ashes, 65; Any Wednesday, 66; Pete 'n' Tillie, 72; Once Is Not Enough, 75; Cross Of Iron, 77; House Calls, 78; Reuben Reuben, 83.

EVANS, EDITH: A Welsh Singer, 15; East Is East, 16; The Last Days Of Dolwyn, The Queen Of Spades, 48; The Importance Of Being Earnest, 52; Look Back In Anger, 58; The Nun's Story, 59; Tom Jones, 63; The Chalk Garden, 64; Young Cassidy, 65; The Whisperers, 66; Fitzwilly, 67; Prudence And The Pill, 68; Crooks And Coronets, The Madwoman Of Chaillot, 69; David Copperfield, Scrooge, Upon This Rock, 70; Craze, A Doll's House, 73; The Slipper And The Rose, 76; Nasty Habits, 77.

FAIRBANKS, DOUGLAS: Double Trouble, The Lamb, 15; American Aristocracy, Flirting With Fate, The Good Bad Man, The Habit Of Happiness, The Half-breed, His Picture In The Papers, Intolerance, Manhattan Madness, The Matrimoniac, Mystery Of The Leaping Fish, Reggie Mixes It 16; The Americano, Down To Earth, In Again Out Again, The Man From Painted Pos A Modern Musketeer, Reaching For The Moon, War Relief, Wild And Woolly, 17; Arizona, Bound In Morocco, Fire The Kaiser, He Comes Up Smiling, Headin' South Mr Fix-it, Say! Young Fellow, Sic 'em Sam, 18; His Majesty The American, The Knickerbocker Buckaroo, When The Clouds Roll By, 19; The Mark Of Zorro, The Mollycoddle, 20; The Nut, The Three Musketeers, 21; Robin Hood, 22; The Thief Of Bagdad, 24; Don Q Son Of Zorro, 25; The Black Pirate, 26; The Gaucho, Show People, 28; The Iron Mask, The Taming Of The Shrew, 29; Reaching For The Moon, 31; Mr Robinson Crusoe, 32; The Private Life Of Don Juan, 34.

FAIRBANKS JR, DOUGLAS: Stephen Steps Out, 23; The Air Mail, Stella Dallas, Wi Horse Mesa, 25; The American Venus, Broken Hearts Of Hollywood, Man Bait, Padlocked, 26; Is Zat So?, A Texas Steer, Women Love Diamonds, 27; The Barker, Dead Man's Curve, Modern Mothers, The Power Of The Press, The Toilers, A Woman O Affairs, 28; The Careless Age, Fast Life, The Forward Pass, The Jazz Age, Our Modern Maidens, The Show Of Shows, 29; The Dawn Patrol, Going Wild, The Little Accident, Little Caesar, Loose Ankles, One Night At Susie's, Outward Bound, Party Girl, The Way Of All Men, 30; Chances, I Like Your Nerve, Local Boy Makes Good, 31; It's Toug To Be Famous, Love Is A Racket, Scarlet Dawn, Union Depot, 32; Captured, The Life Of Jimmy Dolan, Morning Glory, The Narrow Corner, Parachute Jumper, 33; Catherine The Great, Success At Any Price, 34; Man Of The Moment, Mimi, Accused, The Amateur Gentleman, 36; The Prisoner Of Zenda, Jump For Glory, 37; Having Wonderful Time, Joy Of Living, The Rage Of Paris, The Young In Heart, 38; Gunga Din, Rulers Of The Sea, 39; Angels Over Broadway, Green Hell, Safari, 40 The Corsican Brothers, 41; The Exile, Sinbad The Sailor, 47; That Lady In Ermine, 48; The Fighting O'Flynn, 49; State Secret, Mister Drake's Duck, 50; Red And Blue, 67; The Funniest Man In The World, 69; Ghost Story, 81.

FASSBINDER, RAINER WERNER: Gods Of The Plague, Katzelmacher, Love Is Colder Than Death, 69; The American Soldier, Das Kaffeehaus, Die Niklashauser Fahrt, Matthias Kneissl, Recruits In Ingolstadt, Rio Das Mortes, Whity, Why Does Herr R Run Amok?, 70; Beware Of A Holy Whore, The Merchant Of Four Seasons, 71; Bremer Freiheit, Eight Hours Are Not A Day, Wildwechsel, The Bitter Tears Of Petra Von Kant, 72; Nora Helmer, Welt Am Draht, 73; 1 Berlin Harlem, Fear Eats The Soul, Effi Briest, Martha, 74; Angst Vor Der Angst, Fox And His Friends, Mother Kusters Goes To Heaven, Wie Ein Vogel Auf Dem Draht, 75; Chinese Roulette, I Only Want You To Love Me, Dass Ihr Mich Liebt, Satan's Brew, Schatten Der Engel, 76; Frauen In New York, The Stationmaster's Wife, 77; Der Kleine Godard, Germany In Autumn, In A Year Of Thirteen Moons, 78; Despair, The Third Generation, The Marriage Of Maria Braun, 79; Berlin Alexanderplatz, 80; Lili Marleen, 81; Lola, Querelle, Veronika Voss, 82.

FAYE, ALICE: 365 Nights In Hollywood, George White's Scandals, Now I'll Tell, She Learned About Sailors, 34; Every Night At Eight, George White's 1935 Scandals, King Of Burlesque, Music Is Magic, 35; Sing Baby Sing, Stowaway, 36; On The Avenue, Wake Up And Live, You Can't Have Everything, You're A Sweetheart, In Old Chicago, 37; Alexander's Ragtime Band, Sally Irene And Mary, 38; Barricade, Hollywood Cavalcade, Rose Of Washington Square, Tail Spin, 39; Lillian Russell, Little Old New York, Tin Pan Alley, 40; The Great American Broadcast, Tha Night In Rio, Weekend In Havana, 41; Hello Frisco Hello, 42; The Gang's All Here, 43; Four Jills In A Jeep, 44; Fallen Angel, 45; State Fair, 62; The Magic Of Lassie, 78.

FELLINI, FEDERICO: Rome Open City, 45; Luci del Varieta, 50; The White Sheik, 51; I Vitelloni, Love In The City, 53; La Strada, 54; The Swindle, 55; Nights Of Cabiria, 57; La Dolce Vita, 60; Boccaccio '70, 8½, 63; Juliet Of The Spirits, 65; Spirits Of The Dead, 68; Fellini

Satyricon, **70**; The Clowns, **71**; Fellini's Roma, **72**; Amarcord, **73**; Casanova, **76**; City Of Women, **81**; Il Tassinaro, **83**; And The Ship Sails On, **84**; Ginger And Fred, **86**; Intervista, **87**; The Voices Of The Moon, **90**.

FERNANDEL: Le Blanc Et Le Noir, Paris-Béguin, Le Rosier De Madame Husson, **31**; The Orderly, **33**; Adéma I Aviateur, Angele, La Porteuse De Pain, **34**; Ferdinand Le Noceur, **35**; Un De La Legion, **36**; Francis The First, Harvest, Hercule, Igance, Le Degourdis De Lo Onzième, Le Roi Du Sport, Un Carnet De Bal, Heartbeat, Josette, **38**; Fric-frac, **39**; The Italian Straw Hat, **40**; The Well-digger's Daughter, **41**; Simplet, **42**; Adrien, **43**; Nais, **45**; Hoboes In Paradise, Petrus, **46**; Botta E Riposta, The Cupboard Was Bare, Emile L'Africain, **49**; Three Sinners, Topaze, **50**; Adhemar, The Little World Of Don Camillo, The Red Inn, **51**; The French Touch, La Table Aux Crevés, **52**; The Most Wanted Man In The World, The Return Of Don Camillo, **53**; Ali Baba, Mam'zelle Nitouche, The Sheep Has Five Legs, **54**; Around The World In 80 Days, **56**; Fernandel The Dressmaker, The Man In The Raincoat, Pantaloons, The Virtuous Bigamist, **57**; The Easiest Profession, Paris Holiday, Senechal The Magnificent, **58**; Forbidden Fruit, Gangster Boss, The Law Is The Law, **59**; Cresus, Le Caid, **60**; Cocagne, Cow And I, Don Camillo Monseigneur, Dynamite Jack, **61**; The Devil And The Ten Commandments, **62**; My Wife's Husband, **63**; L'Age Ingrat, **64**; Don Camillo A Moscou, **65**; Le Voyage Du Pere, **66**; L'Homme A La Buick, **67**; Heureux Qui Comme Ulysse, **70**.

FERRER, JOSE: Joan Of Arc, **48**; Whirlpool, **49**; Crisis, Cyrano De Bergerac, **50**; Anything Can Happen, Moulin Rouge, **52**; Miss Sadie Thompson, **53**; The Caine Mutiny, Deep In My Heart, Twist Of Fate, **54**; The Shrike, The Cockleshell Heroes, **55**; The Great Man, **56**; Mayerling, **57**; The High Cost Of Loving, I Accuse!, **58**; Return To Peyton Place, **61**; Forbid Them Not, Lawrence Of Arabia, State Fair, **62**; Cyrano Et D'Artagnan, Nine Hours To Rama, **63**; The Greatest Story Ever Told, Ship Of Fools, **65**; Enter Laughing, **67**; The Little Drummer Boy, **69**; Merry-go-round, **74**; The Big Bus, Forever Young Forever Free, Paco, Voyage Of The Damned, **76**; Crash!, The Private Files Of J Edgar Hoover, The Sentinel, Who Has Seen The Wind, **77**; The Amazing Captain Nemo, Dracula's Dog, Fedora, The Swarm, **78**; The Fifth Musketeer, Natural Enemies, **79**; The Big Brawl, **80**; Blood Tide, A Midsummer Night's Sex Comedy, **82**; The Being, To Be Or Not To Be, **83**; Dune, The Evil That Men Do, **84**; Ingrid, **85**; Bloody Birthday, **86**; El Sol Y La Luna, **87**; Samson And Delilah, **88**; A Life Of Sin, Old Explorers, **90**; 1492: Conquest Of Paradise, Primary Motive, **92**.

FEUILLADE, LOUIS: Fantômas, Juve Contre Fantômas, Le Mort Qui Tue, **13**; Fantômas Contre Fantômas, Le Faux Magistrat, **14**; Les Vampires, **15**; Judex, L'Aventure Des Millions, Notre Pauvre Coeur, Un Mariage De Raison, **16**; La Deserteuse, La Nouvelle Mission De Judex, Le Passe De Monique, **17**; Les Petites Marionnettes, Tih Minh, Vendemiaire, **18**; Barrabas, L'Engrenage, L'Homme Sans Visage, **19**; Les Deux Gamines, **20**; L'Orpheline, Parisette, **21**; Le Fils Du Filibustier, **22**; L'Orphelin De Paris, La Gosseline, Le Gamin De Paris, Vindicta, **23**; La Fille Bien Gardée, Le Stigmate, Lucette, Pierrot Pierrette, **24**.

FEYDER, JACQUES: L'Homme De Compagnie, L'Instinct Est Maitre, Le Bluff, Le Frere De Lait, Le Pied Qui Etreintin, M Pinson Policier, Têtes De Femmes Femmes De Tête, Tiens Vous Etes A Poitiers?, Un Conseil D'Ami, **16**; Abrégeons Les Formalités!, La Trouvaille De Buchu, Le Billard Casse, Le Pardessus De Demi-saison, Le Ravin Sans Fond, Les Vieilles Femmes De L'Hospice, **17**; La Faute D'Orthographe, **19**; L'Atlantide, **21**; Crainquebille, **23**; Faces Of Children, Gribiche, L'Image, **25**; Carmen, **26**; Au Pays Du Roi Lepreux, **27**; The New Gentlemen, Thérèse Raquin, **28**; Gardiens De Phare, The Kiss, **29**; Anna Christie, Le Spectre Vert, Olympia, Si L'Empereur Savait Ca, **30**; Daybreak, Son Of India, **31**; Le Grand Jeu, **34**; Pension Mimosas, La Kermesse Héroïque, **35**; Knight Without Armour, **37**; Fahrendes Volk, **38**; La Loi Du Nord, A Woman Disappeared, **42**; Maturareise, **43**; Back Streets Of Paris, **46**.

FIELD, SALLY: The Way West, **67**; Stay Hungry, **76**; Heroes, Smokey And The Bandit, **77**; The End, Hooper, **78**; Beyond The Poseidon Adventure, Norma Rae, **79**; Smokey And The Bandit II, **80**; Absence Of Malice, Back Roads, **81**; Kiss Me Goodbye, **82**; Places In The Heart, **84**; Murphy's Romance, **85**; Surrender, **87**; Punchline, **88**; Steel Magnolias, **89**; Dying Young, Not Without My Daughter, Soapdish, **91**; Mrs Doubtfire, **93**; Forrest Gump, **94**; Eye for and Eye, **96**.

FIELDS, GRACIE: Sally In Our Alley, **31**; Looking On The Bright Side, **32**; This Week Of Grace, **33**; Love Life And Laughter, Sing As We Go, **34**; Look Up And Laugh, **35**; Queen Of Hearts, **36**; The Show Goes On, **37**; Keep Smiling, We're Going To Be Rich, **38**; Shipyard Sally, **39**; Holy Matrimony, Stage Door Canteen, **43**; Molly And Me, Paris Underground, **45**.

FIELDS, W C: Pool Sharks, **15**; Janice Meredith, **24**; Sally Of The Sawdust, That Royle Girl, **25**; It's The Old Army Game, So's Your Old Man, **26**; The Potters, Running Wild, Two Flaming Youths, **27**; Fools For Luck, Tillie's Punctured Romance, **28**; The Golf Specialist, **30**; Her Majesty, Love, **31**; If I Had A Million, Million Dollar Legs, **32**; Alice In Wonderland, The Fatal Glass Of Beer, International House, Tillie And Gus, **33**; It's A Gift, Mrs Wiggs Of The Cabbage Patch, The Old-fashioned Way, Six Of A Kind, You're Telling Me, **34**; David Copperfield, The Man On The Flying Trapeze, Mississippi, **35**; Poppy, **36**; The Big Broadcast Of 1938, **38**; You Can't Cheat An Honest Man, **39**; The Bank Dick, My Little Chickadee, **40**; Never Give A Sucker An Even Break, **41**; Follow The Boys, Sensations, Song Of The Open Road, **44**.

FINCH, PETER: Red Sky At Morning, **37**; Dave And Dad Come To Town, **38**; Mr Chedworth Steps Out, **39**; The Power And The Glory, **42**; The Rats Of Tobruk, **44**; A Son Is Born, **46**; Eureka Stockade, Train Of Events, **49**; The Miniver Story, The Wooden Horse, **50**; The Story Of Robin Hood And His Merrie Men, **52**; The Heart Of The Matter, The Story Of Gilbert And Sullivan, Elephant Walk, Father Brown, **53**; Josephine And Men, Make Me An Offer, Passage Home, The Dark Avenger, **55**; Battle Of The River Plate, Simon And Laura, A Town Like Alice, **56**; Robbery Under Arms, The Shiralee, Windom's Way, **57**; The Nun's Story, **58**; Kidnapped, Operation Amsterdam, The Trials Of Oscar Wilde, **60**; No Love For Johnnie, The Sins Of Rachel Cade, **61**; I Thank A Fool, **62**; In The Cool Of The Day, **63**; First Men In The Moon, Girl With Green Eyes, The Pumpkin Eater, **64**; Judith, **65**; Flight Of The Phoenix, **66**; Far From The Madding Crowd, **67**; The Legend Of Lylah Clare, **68**; The Red Tent, Sunday Bloody Sunday, **71**; Shattered, **72**; England Made Me, Lost Horizon, A Bequest To The Nation, **73**; The Abdication, **74**; Network, **76**; Raid On Entebbe, **77**; 10, **79**.

FINNEY, ALBERT: The Entertainer, Saturday Night And Sunday Morning, **60**; Tom Jones, The Victors, **63**; Night Must Fall, **64**; Two For The Road, **67**; Charlie Bubbles, **67**; The Picasso Summer, **69**; Scrooge, **70**; Gumshoe, **72**; Alpha Beta, **73**; Murder On The Orient Express, **74**; The Adventure Of Sherlock Holmes' Smarter Brother, **75**; The Duellists, **77**; Loophole, **80**; Looker, Wolfen, **81**; Annie, Shoot The Moon, **82**; The Dresser, **83**; Under The Volcano, **84**; Orphans, **87**; Miller's Crossing, **90**; The Playboys, **92**; Rich In Love, **93**; The Browning Version, **94**; A Man of No Importance, Run Of The Country, **95**; Washington Sqwuare, **97**.

FISHER, TERENCE: Colonel Bogey, Portrait From Life, A Song For Tomorrow, **48**; Marry Me, **49**; The Astonished Heart, So Long At The Fair, **50**; Home To Danger, **51**; Distant Trumpet, The Last Page, A Stolen Face, Wings Of Danger, **52**; Blood Orange, Four-Sided Triangle, Man In Hiding, Spaceways, A Stranger Came Home, **53**; Black Glove, Murder By Proxy, Children Galore, Final Appointment, Mask Of Dust, **54**; The Flaw, Stolen Assignment, **55**; The Gelignite Gang, The Last Man To Hang, **56**; The Curse Of Frankenstein, Kill Me Tomorrow, **57**; Dracula, Revenge Of Frankenstein, **58**; The Hound Of The Baskervilles, The Man Who Could Cheat Death, The Mummy, **59**; The Brides Of Dracula, The Stranglers Of Bombay, Sword Of Sherwood Forest, The Two Faces Of Dr Jekyll, **60**; The Curse Of The Werewolf, The Phantom Of The Opera, Sherlock Holmes And The Deadly Necklace, **62**; The Earth Dies Screaming, The Gorgon, The Horror Of It All, **64**; Dracula Prince Of Darkness, **65**; Island Of Terror, **66**; Frankenstein Created Woman, Night Of The Big Heat, **67**; The Devil Rides Out, **68**; Frankenstein Must Be Destroyed!, **70**; Frankenstein And The Monster From Hell, **74**.

FITZGERALD, BARRY: Juno And The Paycock, **30**; The Plough And The Stars, When Knights Were Bold, **36**; Ebb Tide, **37**; Bringing Up Baby, The Dawn Patrol, Four Men And A Prayer, Marie Antoinette, **38**; Full Confession, Pacific Liner, The Saint Strikes Back, **39**; The Long Voyage Home, **40**; How Green Was My Valley, San Francisco Docks, The Sea Wolf, Tarzan's Secret Treasure, **41**; The Amazing Mrs Holliday, Corvette K-225, Two Tickets To London, **43**; Going My Way, I Love A Soldier, None But The Lonely Heart, **44**; And Then There Were None, Duffy's Tavern, Incendiary Blonde, The Stork Club, **45**; California, Two Years Before The Mast, **46**; Easy Come Easy Go, Variety Girl, Welcome Stranger, **47**; Miss Tatlock's Millions, The Naked City, The Sainted Sisters, **48**; The Story Of Seabiscuit, Top O' The Morning, **49**; Union Station, **50**; Silver City, **51**; The Quiet Man, **52**; Happy Ever After, **54**; Wedding Breakfast, **56**; Rooney, **58**; Broth Of A Boy, **59**.

FLAHERTY, ROBERT: Nanook Of The North, **22**; Moana, The Pottery Maker, **25**; The Twenty-four Dollar Island, **27**; White Shadows In The South Seas, **28**; Tabu, **31**; The English Potter, The Glassmakers Of England, **33**; Man Of Aran, **34**; Elephant Boy, **37**; The Land, **42**; Louisiana Story, **48**.

FLEMING, VICTOR: When The Clouds Roll By, **19**; The Mollycoddle, **20**; Mamma's Affair, Woman's Place, **21**; Anna Ascends, The Lane That Had No Turning, Red Hot Romance, **22**; The Call Of The Canyon, Dark Secrets, The Law Of The Lawless, To The Last Man, **23**; The Code Of The Sea, Empty Hands, **24**; Adventure, The Devil's Cargo, Lord Jim, A Son Of His Father, **25**; The Blind Goddess, Mantrap, **26**; Hula, The Rough Riders, The Way Of All Flesh, **27**; The Awakening, **28**; Abie's Irish Rose, The Virginian, Wolf Song, **29**; Common Clay, Renegades, **30**; Around The World In 80 Minutes, **31**; Red Dust, The Wet Parade, **32**; Blonde Bombshell, The White Sister, **33**; Treasure Island, **34**; The Farmer Takes A Wife, Reckless, **35**; Captains Courageous, **37**; Test Pilot, **38**; Gone With The Wind, The Wizard Of Oz, **39**; Dr Jekyll And Mr Hyde, **41**; Tortilla Flat, **42**; A Guy Named Joe, **43**; Adventure, **45**; Joan Of Arc, **48**.

FLYNN, ERROL: In The Wake Of The Bounty, **33**; Murder At Monte Carlo, **34**; Captain Blood, The Case Of The Curious Bride, Don't Bet On Blondes, **35**; The Charge Of The Light Brigade, **36**; Another Dawn, The Green Light, The Perfect Specimen, The Prince And The Pauper, **37**; The Adventures Of Robin Hood, The Dawn Patrol, Four's A Crowd, The Sisters, **38**; Dodge City, The Private Lives Of Elizabeth And Essex, **39**; Santa Fe Trail, The Sea Hawk, Virginia City, **40**; Dive Bomber, Footsteps In The Dark, They Died With Their Boots On, **41**; Desperate Journey, Gentleman Jim, **42**; Edge Of Darkness, Northern Pursuit, Thank Your Lucky Stars, **43**; Uncertain Glory, Objective Burma!, San Antonio, **45**; Never Say Goodbye, **46**; Cry Wolf, Escape Me Never, **47**; Adventures Of Don Juan, Silver River, **48**; It's A Great Feeling, The Forsyte Saga, **49**; Kim, Montana, Rocky Mountain, **50**; Adventures Of Captain Fabian, **51**; Against All Flags, Mara Maru, **52**; The Master Of Ballantrae, **53**; Crossed Swords, Lilacs In The Spring, **54**; King's Rhapsody, The Dark Avenger, **55**; The Big Boodle, Istanbul, The Sun Also Rises, **57**; The Roots Of Heaven, Too Much Too Soon, **58**; Cuban Rebel Girls, **59**.

FONDA, HENRY: The Farmer Takes A Wife, I Dream Too Much, Way Down East, **35**; The Moon's Our Home, Spendthrift, Trail Of The Lonesome Pine, **36**; Slim, That Certain Woman, Wings Of The Morning, You Only Live Once, **37**; Blockade, I Met My Love Again, Jezebel, The Mad Miss Manton, Spawn Of The North, **38**; Drums Along The Mohawk, Jesse James, Let Us Live, The Story Of Alexander Graham Bell, Young Mr Lincoln, **39**; Chad Hanna, The Grapes Of Wrath, Lillian Russell, The Return Of Frank James, **40**; The Lady Eve, Wild Geese Calling, You Belong To Me, **41**; The Big Street, The Magnificent Dope, The Male Animal, Rings On Her Fingers, Tales Of Manhattan, **42**; The Immortal Sergeant, The Ox-Bow Incident, **43**; My Darling Clementine, **46**; Daisy Kenyon, The Fugitive, The Long Night, **47**; Fort Apache, On Our Merry Way, **48**; Jigsaw, **49**; Grant Wood, Home Of The Homeless, **50**; Benjy, Growing Years, **51**; The Impressionable Years, **52**; Mister Roberts, **55**; War And Peace, The Wrong Man, **56**; 12 Angry Men, The Tin Star, **57;** Reach For Tomorrow, Stage Struck, **58**; The Man Who Understood Women, Warlock, **59**; Advise And Consent, How The West Was Won, The Longest Day, **62**; Rangers Of Yellowstone, Spencer's Mountain, **63**; The Best Man, Fail-Safe, Sex And The Single Girl, **64**; Battle Of The Bulge, In Harm's Way, The Rounders, Big Deal at Dodge City, **65**; The Dirty Game, **66**; All About People, The Golden Flame, The Really Big Family, Welcome To Hard Times, **67**; Born To Buck, The Boston Strangler, Firecreek, Madigan, Once Upon A Time In The West, Yours, Mine And Ours, **68**; The Cheyenne Social Club, There Was A Crooked Man, Too Late The Hero, **70**; Sometimes A Great Notion, **71**; Ash Wednesday, Night Flight From Moscow, **73**; Mussolini: Ultimo Atto, My Name Is Nobody, **74**; The Great Smokey Roadblock, Midway, **76**; Il Grande Attacco, Rollercoaster, Tentacles, **77**; Big Yellow Schooner To Byzantium, Fedora, The Swarm, **78**; City On Fire, Meteor, Wanda Nevada, **79**; On Golden Pond, **81**.

FONDA, JANE: Tall Story, **60**; The Chapman Report, Period Of Adjustment, Walk On The Wild Side, **62**; In The Cool Of The Day, Sunday In New York, **63**; La Ronde, Les Félins, **64**; Cat Ballou, **65**; Any Wednesday, The Chase, The Game Is Over, **66**; Barefoot In The Park, Hurry Sundown, **67**; Barbarella, Spirits Of The Dead, **68**; They Shoot Horses Don't They?, **69**; Klute, **71**; Foxtrot Tango Alpha; Tout Va Bien, **72**; A Doll's House, Steelyard Blues, **73**; The Blue Bird, **76**; Fun With Dick And Jane, Julia, **77**; California Suite, Comes A Horseman, Coming Home, **78**; The China Syndrome, The Electric Horseman, **79**; 9 To 5, **80**; On Golden Pond, Rollover, **81**; The Doll Maker, **83**; Agnes Of God, **85**; The Morning After, **86**; Old Gringo, **89**; Stanley And Iris, **90**.

FONTAINE, JOAN: No More Ladies, **35**; A Damsel In Distress, The Man Who Found Himself, Music For Madame, Quality Street, You Can't Beat Love, **37**; Blonde Cheat, The Duke Of West Point, Maid's Night Out, Sky Giant, **38**; Gunga Din, Man Of Conquest, The Women, **39**; Rebecca, **40**; Suspicion, **41**; This Above All, The Constant Nymph, **42**; Frenchman's Creek, Jane Eyre, **44**; The Affairs Of Susan, **45**; From This Day Forward, **46**; Ivy, **47**; The Emperor Waltz, Kiss The Blood Off My Hands, Letter From An Unknown Woman, You Gotta Stay Happy, **48**; Born To Be Bad, September Affair, **50**; Darling How Could You, **51**; Ivanhoe, Othello, Something To Live For, **52**; The Bigamist, Decameron Nights, Flight To Tangier, **53**; Casanova's Big Night, **54**; Beyond A Reasonable Doubt, Serenade, **56**; Island In The Sun, Until They Sail, **57**; A Certain Smile, **58**; Voyage To The Bottom Of The Sea, **61**; Tender Is The Night, **62**; The Devil's Own, **66**.

FORBES, BRYAN: All Over The Town, Dear Mr Prohack, The Small Back Room, **48**; The Wooden Horse, **50**; Green Grow The Rushes, **51**; The World In His Arms, **52**; Appointment In London, Sea Devils, Wheel Of Fate, **53**; An Inspector Calls, The Million Pound Note, Up To His Neck, **54**; Now And Forever, Passage Home, Cockleshell Heroes, **55**; The Baby And The Battleship, The Extra Day, It's Great To Be Young, The Last Man To Hang, Satellite In The Sky, **56**; The Colditz Story, Quatermass 2, **57**; I Was Monty's Double, The Key, **58**; Yesterday's Enemy, **59**; The Angry Silence, The League Of Gentlemen, **60**; The Guns Of Navarone, Whistle Down The Wind, **61**; The L-Shaped Room, **62**; Of Human Bondage, Seance On A Wet Afternoon, A Shot In The Dark, **64**; King Rat, **65**; The Whisperers, The Wrong Box, **66**; Deadfall, The Madwoman Of Chaillot, **69**; Raging Moon, **70**; The Railway Children **71**; The Stepford Wives, **74**; The Slipper And The Rose, **76**; International Velvet, **78**; Sunday Lovers, **80**; Better Late Than Never, **82**; The Naked Face, Restless Natives, **85**.

FORD, GLENN: Heaven With A Barbed Wire Fence, My Son Is Guilty, **39**; Babies For Sale, Blondie Plays Cupid, Convicted Woman, The Lady In Question, **40**; Go West Young Lady, Texas, **41**; The Adventures Of Martin Eden, Flight Lieutenant, **42**; The Desperadoes, Destroyer, **43**; Gilda, A Stolen Life, **46**; Framed, **47**; The Loves Of Carmen, The Return Of October, The Man From Colorado, **48**; The Doctor And The Girl, Hollywood Goes To Church, Lust For Gold, The Undercover Man, **49**; Convicted, The Redhead And The Cowboy, The White Tower, **50**; Follow The Sun, The Secret Of Convict Lake, **51**; Affair In Trinidad, **52**; Appointment In Honduras, The Big Heat, The Man From The Alamo, **53**; City Story, Human Desire, **54**; The Americano, Blackboard Jungle, Trial, **55**; The Fastest Gun Alive, The Teahouse Of The August Moon, **56**; 3:10 To Yuma, Don't Go Near The Water, **57**; Cowboy, Imitation General, The Sheepman, **58**; The Gazebo, It Started With A Kiss, **59**; Cimarron, **60**; Cry For Happy, Pocketful Of Miracles, **61**; Experiment In Terror, Four Horsemen Of The Apocalypse, **62**; The Courtship Of Eddie's Father, **63**; Advance To The Rear, Dear Heart, Fate Is The Hunter, **64**; The Rounders, **65**; Is Paris Burning?, The Money Trap, Rage, **66**; The Last Challenge, **67**; Heaven With A Gun, Smith!, **69**; Santee, **73**; Midway, **76**; Superman, **78**; The Visitor, **79**; Happy Birthday To Me, **81**; Border Shootout, Casablanca Express, **90**.

FORD, HARRISON: Dead Heat On A Merry-Go-Round, **66**; Journey To Shiloh, **68**; Getting Straight, **70**; American Graffiti, **73**; The Conversation, **74**; Star Wars, **77**; Force 10 From Navarone, **78**; Apocalypse Now, Hanover Street, **79**; The Empire Strikes Back, **80**; Raiders Of The Lost Ark, **81**; Blade Runner, **82**; Return Of The Jedi, **83**; Indiana Jones And The Temple Of Doom, **84**; Witness, **85**; The Mosquito Coast, **86**; Frantic, Working Girl, **88**; Indiana Jones And The Last Crusade, **89**; Presumed Innocent, **90**; Regarding Henry, **91**; Patriot Games, **92**; The Fugitive, **93**; Clear And Present Danger, **94**; Sabrina, **95**; The Devil's Own, Air Force One, **97**.

FORD, JOHN: Bucking Broadway, Cheyenne's Pal, A Marked Man, The Scrapper, The Secret Man, The Soul Herder, The Tornado, **17**; Delirium, Hell Bent, The Phantom Riders, The Scarlet Drop, Thieves' Gold, Wild Women, A Woman's Fool, **18**; Bare Fists, A Fight For Love, A Gun Fightin' Gentleman, The Gun Pusher, The Outcasts Of Poker Flat, Riders Of Vengeance, Roped, The Rustlers, **19**; The Big Punch, Just Pals, The Prince Of Avenue A, **20**; Action, Desperate Trails, Sure Fire, **21**; Little Miss Smiles, Nero, Silver Wings, The Village Blacksmith, **22**; Cameo Kirby, The Face On The Barroom Floor, Three Jumps Ahead, **23**; Hearts Of Oak, The Iron Horse, **24**; The Fighting Heart, Kentucky Pride, **25**; The Blue Eagle, Three Bad Men, What Price Glory?, **26**; Seventh Heaven, Upstream, **27**; Four Sons, Mother Machree, Napoleon's Barber, **28**; Big Time, The Black Watch, **29**; Men Without Women, Up The River, **30**; Arrowsmith, The Brat, **31**; Air Mail, Flesh, **32**; Dr Bull, Pilgrimage, **33**; The Lost Patrol, **34**; The Informer, The Whole Town's Talking, **35**; Mary Of Scotland, The Plough And The Stars, The Prisoner Of Shark Island, **36**; The Hurricane, Wee Willie Winkie, **37**; Four Men And A Prayer, Submarine Patrol, **38**; Drums Along The Mohawk, Stagecoach, Young Mr Lincoln, **39**; The Grapes Of Wrath, The Long Voyage Home, **40**; How Green Was My Valley, Tobacco Road, **41**; They Were Expendable, **45**; My Darling Clementine, **46**; The Fugitive, **47**; Three Godfathers, Fort Apache, **48**; She Wore A Yellow Ribbon, **49**; Rio Grande, Wagon Master, When Willie Comes Marching Home, **50**; The Quiet Man, What Price Glory? **52**; Mogambo, The Sun Shines Bright, **53**; The Long Gray Line, Mister Roberts, **55**; The Searchers, **56**; The Wings Of Eagles, **57**; The Last Hurrah, **58**; Sergeant Rutledge, **60**; Two Rode Together, **61**; How The West Was Won, The Man Who Shot Liberty Valance, **62**;

onovan's Reef, **63**; Cheyenne Autumn, **4**; Young Cassidy, **65**; 7 Women, **66**.

OREMAN, CARL: Spooks Run Wild, **1**; Rhythm Parade, **42**; Dakota, **45**; So This New York, **48**; Champion, The Clay igeon, Home Of The Brave, **49**; Cyrano De ergerac, The Men, Young Man With A orn, **50**; High Noon, **52**; The Bridge On The iver Kwai, **57**; The Key, **58**; The Guns f Navarone, **61**; The Victors, **63**; 'ackenna's Gold, **69**; Young Winston, **2**; When Time Ran Out, **80**.

ORMAN, MILOS: Black Peter, **64**; A onde In Love, **65**; The Firemen's Ball, **7**; Taking Off, **71**; Visions Of Eight **73**; ne Flew Over The Cuckoo's Nest, **75**; air, **79**; Ragtime, **81**; Amadeus, **4**; Valmont, **89**; The People vs Larry lynt, **96**.

ORMBY, GEORGE: I See Ice, **34**; oots Boots, Off The Dole, No Limit, **35**; Keep our Seats Please, **36**; Keep Fit, Feather our Nest, **37**; It's In The Air, **38**; Trouble rewing, **39**; Let George Do It, Spare A opper, **40**; South American George, **41**; uch Too Shy, **42**; Get Cracking, **43**; e Snoops To Conquer, Bell-Bottom George, **4**; I Didn't Do It, **45**; George In Civvy treet, **46**.

ORSYTH, BILL: That Sinking Feeling, **9**; Gregory's Girl, **81**; Local Hero, **83**; omfort And Joy, **84**; Housekeeping, **7**; Breaking In, Being Human, **89**.

OSSE, BOB: Kiss Me Kate **53**; My ister Eileen, **55**; Sweet Charity, **69**; Cabaret, **2**; Lenny, **74**; All That Jazz, **79**; Star 0, **83**.

OSTER, JODIE: Kansas City Bomber, lenace On The Mountain, Napoleon And amantha, **72**; One Little Indian, Tom awyer, **73**; Alice Doesn't Live Here Anymore, **4**; Bugsy Malone, Echoes Of A ummer, The Little Girl Who Lives Down The ane, Taxi Driver, **76**; Candleshoe, reaky Friday, Il Casotto,Fleur Bleue, **77**; arny, Foxes, **80**; O'Hara's Wife, **82**; he Hotel New Hampshire, **84**; Mesmerized, **6**; Siesta, **87**; The Accused, Five orners, Stealing Home, **88**; Backtrack, **89**; ittle Man Tate, The Silence Of The ambs, **91**; Shadows And Fog, **92**; ommersby, **93**; Maverick, Nell, **94**; ome For The Holidays, **95**; Contact, **97**.

OX, JAMES: The Miniver Story, The lagnet, **50**; The Loneliness Of The Long istance Runner, **62**; The Servant, amahine, **63**; King Rat, Those Magnificent len In Their Flying Machines, **65**; The hase, **66**; Thoroughly Modern Millie, **67**; uffy, Isadora, **68**; Arabella, **69**; erformance, **70**; No Longer Alone, **78**; ountry, **81**; Pavlova, Runners, **83**; reystoke: The Legend Of Tarzan, Lord Of The pes, A Passage To India, **84**; Absolute eginners, New World, **86**; The Whistle lower, Comrades, High Season, **87**; oys In The Island, Farewell To The King, **89**; ne Russia House, **90**; Hostage, Patriot ames, **92**; The Remains Of The Day, **93**.

OX, MICHAEL J: Midnight Madness, **0**; Class Of 84, **82**; Back To The Future, een Wolf, **85**; Dear America, Light Of ay, The Secret Of My Success, **87**; Bright ights Big City, **88**; Back To The Future art II, Casualties Of War, **89**; Back To The uture Part III, **90**; Doc Hollywood, The ard Way, **91**; For Love Or Money, omeward Bound: The Incredible ourney, Life With Mikey, Where The ivers Flow North, **93**; Greedy, **94**; righteners, **95**; Mars Attacks!, **96**.

RANCIS, FREDDIE: Mine Own xecutioner, **47**; Moulin Rouge **53**; Beau rummell **54**; A Hill In Korea, Moby ick, Time Without Pity, **56**; The Scamp, **57**; ext To No Time, **58**; Room At The Top, irgin Island, **59**; The Battle Of The Sexes, lever Take Sweets From A Stranger, aturday Night And Sunday Morning, Sons nd Lovers, **60**; The Horsemasters, The nnocents, Two And Two Make Six, **61**; aranoiac, **63**; Evil Of Frankenstein, lysteria, Night Must Fall, Nightmare, Traitor's ate, **64**; Vengeance, Dr Terror's House f Horrors, The Skull, **65**; The Psychopath, **6**; The Deadly Bees, They Came From eyond Space, **67**; Dracula Has Risen From he Grave, Torture Garden, **68**; Mumsy lanny Sonny And Girly, Trog, **70**; Tales From he Crypt, **72**; Craze, The Creeping Flesh, Tales That Witness Madness, **73**; Son Of Dracula, Legend Of The Werewolf, **74**; The Ghoul, Legend Of The Werewolf, **75**; Golden Rendezvous, **77**; The Elephant Man, **80**; The French Lieutenant's Woman, **81**; Dune, **84**; The Doctor And The Devils, **85**; Dark Tower, Memed My Hawk, **87**; Clara's Heart, **88**; Glory, Her Alibi, **89**; Cape Fear, The Man In The Moon, **91**; School Ties, **92**; Princess Caraboo, **94**.

FRANCIS, KAY: The Cocoanuts, Dangerous Curves, Gentlemen Of The Press, Illusion, **29**; For The Defence, Let's Go Native, A Notorious Affair, Paramount On Parade, Passion Flower, Raffles, The Virtuous Sin, **30**; Girls About Town, Guilty Hands, Ladies' Man, Scandal Sheet, **31**; Cynara, Jewel Robbery, Man Wanted, Strangers In Love, Trouble In Paradise, **32**; Mary Stevens MD, Storm At Daybreak, **33**; British Agent, Doctor Monica, Mandalay, **34**; The Goose And The Gander, Living On Velvet, Stranded, **35**; Give Me Your Heart, The White Angel, **36**; Another Dawn, Confession, First Lady, **37**; Comet Over Broadway, My Bill, Secrets Of An Actress, **38**; In Name Only, King Of The Underworld, **39**; Little Men, Play Girl, When The Daltons Rode, **40**; Charley's Aunt, The Feminine Touch, **41**; Always In My Heart, Between Us Girls, **42**; Four Jills In A Jeep, **44**; Allotment Wives, Divorce, **45**; Wife Wanted, **46**.

FRANJU, GEORGES: Le Sang Des Bêtes, **49**; En Passant Par La Lorraine, **50**; Hôtel Des Invalides, **51**; Le Grand Melies, **52**; Monsieur Et Madame Curie, **53**; Les Poussières, Marine Marchande, **54**; Mon Chien, **55**; Le Theatre National Populaire, Sur Le Pont D'Avignon, **56**; Notre Dame Cathédrale De Paris, **57**; La Tête Contre Les Murs, La Première Nuit, **58**; Les Yeux Sans Visage, **59**; Pleins Feux Sur L'Assassin, **61**; Thérèse, **62**; Judex, **63**; Thomas The Impostor, **65**; La Faute De L'Abbé Mouret, **70**; Nuits Rouges, **73**; Le Dernier Mélodrame, **80**.

FRANKENHEIMER, JOHN: The Young Stranger, **57**; The Young Savages, **61**; All Fall Down, Birdman Of Alcatraz, The Manchurian Candidate, **62**; Seven Days In May, **64**; The Train, **65**; Grand Prix, Seconds, **66**; The Fixer, **68**; The Extraordinary Seaman, The Gypsy Moths, **69**; I Walk The Line, **70**; The Horsemen, **71**; The Iceman Cometh, Story Of A Love Story/Impossible Object, **73**; 99 And 44/100% Dead, **74**; French Connection II, **75**; Black Sunday, **77**; Prophecy, **79**; The Challenge, **82**; The Holcroft Covenant, **85**; 52 Pick-up, **86**; Dead-Bang, **89**; The Fourth War, **90**; Year Of The Gun, **91**.

FRANKLIN, SIDNEY: Let Katy Do It, **15** (and a dozen subsequent two-reelers co-directed with brother Chester); The Bride Of Fear, Confession, Forbidden City, Her Only Way, The Safety Curtain, Six Shooter Andy, **18**; Heart O' The Hills, The Hoodlum, The Probation Wife, **19**; Two Weeks, **20**; Courage, Not Guilty, Unseen Forces, **21**; East Is West, The Primitive Lover, Smilin' Through, **22**; Brass, Dulcy, Tiger Rose, **23**; Her Night Of Romance, **24**; Her Sister From Paris, Learning To Love, **25**; Beverly Of Graustark, The Duchess Of Buffalo, **26**; Quality Street, **27**; The Actress, **28**; Devil-May-Care, The Last Of Mrs Cheyney, Wild Orchids, **29**; The Lady Of Scandal, A Lady's Morals, **30**; The Guardsman, Private Lives, **31**; Smilin' Through, **32**; Reunion In Vienna, **33**; The Barretts Of Wimpole Street, **34**; The Dark Angel, **35**; The Good Earth, **37**; On Borrowed Time, The Barretts Of Wimpole Street, **57**.

FREARS, STEPHEN: The Burning, **67**; Gumshoe, **72**; The Hit, **84**; My Beautiful Laundrette, **85**; Prick Up Your Ears, Sammy And Rosie Get Laid, **87**; Dangerous Liaisons, **88**; The Grifters, **90**; Accidental Hero, **92**; The Snapper, **93**; Mary Reilly, **95**.

FREED, ARTHUR: Broadway Melody, **29**; The Wizard Of Oz, Babes In Arms, **39**; Little Nellie Kelly, Strike Up The Band, **40**; Babes On Broadway, Lady Be Good, **41**; For Me And My Gal, Panama Hattie, **42**; Best Foot Forward, Cabin In The Sky, DuBarry Was A Lady, Girl Crazy, **43**; Meet Me In St Louis, **44**; The Clock, Yolanda And The Thief, **45**; The Harvey Girls, Till The Clouds Roll By, Ziegfeld Follies, **46**; Good News, **47**; Easter Parade, The Pirate, Summer Holiday, Words And Music, **48**; Any Number Can Play, The Barkleys Of Broadway, On The Town, Take Me Out To The Ball Game, **49**; Annie Get Your Gun, Crisis, Pagan Love Song, **50**; An American In Paris, Royal Wedding, Show Boat, **51**; The Belle Of New York, Singin' In The Rain, **52**; The Band Wagon, **53**; Brigadoon, **54**; It's Always Fair Weather, Kismet, **55**; Invitation To The Dance, Silk Stockings, **57**; Gigi, **58**; Bells Are Ringing, The Subterraneans, **60**; Light In The Piazza, **62**.

FREEMAN, MORGAN: Who Says I Can't Ride A Rainbow? **71**; Brubaker, **80**; Eyewitness, **81**; Harry And Son, Teachers, **84**; Marie, **87**; Clean And Sober, **88**; Driving Miss Daisy, Glory, Johnny Handsome, Lean On Me, **89**; The Bonfire Of The Vanities, **90**; Robin Hood: Prince Of Thieves, **91**; The Power Of One, Unforgiven, **92**; Bopha!, **93**; The Shawshank Redemption, **94**; Outbreak, Moll Flanders, Seven, **95**; Chain Reaction, **96**.

FULLER, SAMUEL: I Shot Jesse James, **49**; The Baron Of Arizona, **50**; Fixed Bayonets, Steel Helmet, **51**; Park Row, **52**; Pickup On South Street, **53**; Hell And High Water, **54**; House Of Bamboo, **55**; China Gate, Forty Guns, Run Of The Arrow, **57**; The Crimson Kimono, Verboten!, **59**; Underworld, USA, **61**; Merrill's Marauders, **62**; Shock Corridor, **63**; The Naked Kiss, **64**; Shark!, **69**; Dead Pigeon On Beethoven Street, **72**; The Big Red One, **80**; White Dog, **82**; Street Of No Return, **88**.

GABIN, JEAN: Chacun Sa Chance, Mephisto, **30**; Paris-Béguin, **31**; Adieux Les Beaux Jours, **33**; Maria Chapdelaine, **34**; Zou Zou, Escape From Yesterday, La Bandera, Golgotha, **35**; The Lower Depths, La Belle Equipe, Pépé Le Moko, **36**; La Grande Illusion, Gueule D'Amour, **37**; La Bête Humaine, Judas Was A Woman, Quai Des Brumes, **38**; Le Jour Se Lève, **39**; Stormy Waters, **41**; Moontide, **42**; The Imposter, **44**; Martin Roumagnac, **46**; Les Murs De Malapaga, **49**; La Marie Du Port, **50**; Le Plaisir, The Night Is My Kingdom, **51**; The Moment Of Truth, **52**; Touchez Pas Au Grisbi, The House On The Waterfront, L'Air De Paris, Razzia, **54**; Gas-Oil, Napoleon, French Can Can, **55**; La Traversée De Paris, **56**; Deadlier Than The Male, Les Misérables, **57**; The Case Of Dr Laurent, Crime And Punishment, Most Dangerous Sin, Inspector Maigret, Love Is My Profession, Night Affair, The Possessors, **58**; Archimede Le Clochard, Rue De Paris, Le Rouge Est Mis, **59**; Le Baron De L'Ecluse, **60**; The Counterfeiters Of Paris, Le Président, **61**; A Monkey In Winter, **62**; Any Number Can Win, **63**; L'Age Ingrat, Monsieur, **64**; Action Man, The Upper Hand, **67**; The Sicilian Clan, **69**; The Cat, Le Drapeau Noir Flotte Sur La Marmite, Le Tueur, **71**; L'Affaire Dominici, **72**; Two Against The Law, **73**; Le Testament, **74**; L'Année Sainte, **76**.

GABLE, CLARK: Forbidden Paradise, White Man, **24**; Declasse, The Merry Widow, North Star, The Plastic Age, **25**; The Johnstown Flood, **26**; Dance Fools Dance, The Easiest Way, The Finger Points, A Free Soul, Laughing Sinners, Night Nurse, The Painted Desert, Possessed, The Secret Six, Sporting Blood, Susan Lenox: Her Fall And Rise, **31**; Hell Divers, No Man Of Her Own, Polly Of The Circus, Red Dust, Strange Interlude, **32**; Dancing Lady, Hold Your Man, Night Flight, The White Sister, **33**; Chained, Forsaking All Others, It Happened One Night, Manhattan Melodrama, Men In White, **34**; After Office Hours, Call Of The Wild, China Seas, Mutiny On The Bounty, **35**; Cain And Mabel, Love On The Run, San Francisco, Wife Vs Secretary, **36**; Parnell, Saratoga, **37**; Test Pilot, Too Hot To Handle, **38**; Gone With The Wind, Idiot's Delight, **39**; Boom Town, Comrade X, Strange Cargo, **40**; Honky Tonk, They Met In Bombay, **41**; Somewhere I'll Find You, **42**; Adventure, **45**; The Hucksters, **47**; Command Decision, Homecoming, **48**; Any Number Can Play, **49**; Key To The City, To Please A Lady, **50**; Across The Wide Missouri, Callaway Went Thataway, **51**; Lone Star, **52**; Mogambo, Never Let Me Go, **53**; Betrayed, **54**; Soldier Of Fortune, The Tall Men, **55**; The King And Four Queens, **56**; Band Of Angels, **57**; Run Silent Run Deep, Teacher's Pet, **58**; But Not For Me, **59**; It Started In Naples, **60**; The Misfits, **61**.

GANCE, ABEL: La Digue, Il Y A Des Pieds Au Plafond, Le Masque D'Horreur, Le Nègre Blanc, **12**; La Folie Du Docteur Tube, La Fleur Des Ruines, L'Enigma De Dix Heures, Strass Et Compagnie, Une Dame Au Château D'Acre, **15**; Barberousse, Ce Que Les Flots Racontent, Fioritures, L'Heroisme De Paddy, Le Fou De La Falaise, Le Périscope, Les Gaz Mortels, **16**; La Zone De La Mort, Le Droit A La Vie, Mater Dolorosa, **17**; La Dixième Symphonie, **18**; J'accuse, **19**; L'Atre, **20**; La Roue, **23**; Au Secours!, **24**; Napoléon, **27**; Napoléon Au St Helena, **29**; La Fin Du Monde, **31**; Mater Dolorosa, **32**; Le Maître De Forges, **33**; La Dame Aux Camélias, Poliche, **34**; Napoléon Bonaparte, Le Roman D'Un Jeune Homme Pauvre, Lucrezia Borgia, Jerome Perreau, **35**; Un Grand Amour De Beethoven, **36**; J'accuse, **38**; Louise, **39**; Le Paradis Perdu, **40**; La Vénus Aveugle, Le Capitaine Fracasse, **43**; Manolete, **44**; La Reine Margot, **53**; La Tour De Nesle, **54**; The Battle Of Austerlitz, **60**; Cyrano Et D'Artagnan, **63**; Bonaparte Et La Revolution, **71**.

GARBO, GRETA: En Lyckoriddare, **21**; Peter The Tramp, **22**; Gösta Berling's Saga, **24**; The Joyless Street, **25**; The Temptress, The Torrent, **26**; Flesh And The Devil, Love, **27**; The Divine Woman, Mysterious Lady, A Woman Of Affairs, **28**; The Kiss, A Man's Man, The Single Standard, Wild Orchids, **29**; Anna Christie, Romance, **30**; Inspiration, Susan Lenox: Her Fall And Rise, **31**; As You Desire Me, Grand Hotel, Mata Hari, **32**; Queen Christina, **33**; The Painted Veil, **34**; Anna Karenina, **35**; Camille, Conquest, **37**; Ninotchka, **39**; Two-Faced Woman, **41**.

GARDNER, AVA: Calling Dr Gillespie, Joe Smith, American, Kid Glove Killer, Sunday Punch, This Time For Keeps, We Were Dancing, **42**; Ghosts On The Loose, Hitler's Madman, Young Ideas, The Lost Angel, Swing Fever, **43**; Maisie Goes To Reno, **44**; She Went To The Races, **45**; The Killers, Whistle Stop, **46**; The Hucksters, Singapore, **47**; One Touch Of Venus, **48**; The Bribe, East Side West Side, The Great Sinner, **49**; My Forbidden Past, Pandora And The Flying Dutchman, Show Boat, **51**; Lone Star, The Snows Of Kilimanjaro, **52**; The Band Wagon, Mogambo, Ride, Vaquero, **53**; The Barefoot Contessa, Knights Of The Round Table, **54**; Bhowani Junction, **56**; The Little Hut, The Sun Also Rises, **57**; The Naked Maja, On The Beach, **59**; The Angel Wore Red, **60**; 55 Days At Peking, **63**; The Night Of The Iguana, Seven Days In May, **64**; The Bible, **66**; Mayerling, **68**; Tam Lin, The Life And Times Of Judge Roy Bean, **72**; Earthquake, Permission To Kill, **74**; The Blue Bird, **76**; The Cassandra Crossing, The Sentinel, **77**; City On Fire, **79**; The Kidnapping Of The President, **80**; Priest Of Love, **81**.

GARFIELD, JOHN: Four Daughters, **38**; Blackwell's Island, Daughters Courageous, Dust Be My Destiny, Four Wives, Juarez, They Made Me A Criminal, **39**; Castle On The Hudson, East Of The River, Flowing Gold, Saturday's Children, **40**; Out Of The Fog, The Sea Wolf, **41**; Dangerously They Live, Tortilla Flat, **42**; Air Force, Destination Tokyo, The Fallen Sparrow, Thank Your Lucky Stars, **43**; Between Two Worlds, Hollywood Canteen, **44**; Pride Of The Marines, **45**; Humoresque, Nobody Lives Forever, The Postman Always Rings Twice, **46**; Body And Soul, Difficult Years, Gentleman's Agreement, **47**; Force Of Evil, **48**; Jigsaw, We Were Strangers, **49**; The Breaking Point, Under My Skin, **50**; He Ran All The Way, **51**.

GARLAND, JUDY: Every Sunday, Pigskin Parade, **36**; Broadway Melody Of 38, Thoroughbreds Don't Cry, **37**; Everybody Sing, Listen Darling, Love Finds Andy Hardy, **38**; Babes In Arms, The Wizard Of Oz, **39**; Andy Hardy Meets Debutante, Little Nellie Kelly, Strike Up The Band, **40**; Babes On Broadway, Life Begins For Andy Hardy, Ziegfeld Girl, **41**; For Me And My Gal, **42**; Girl Crazy, Presenting Lily Mars, Thousands Cheer, **43**; Meet Me In St Louis, **44**; Under The Clock, **45**; The Harvey Girls, Till The Clouds Roll By, Ziegfeld Follies, **46**; Easter Parade, The Pirate, Words And Music, **48**; In The Good Old Summertime, **49**; Summer Stock, **50**; A Star Is Born, **54**; Pépé, **60**; Judgment At Nuremberg, **61**; A Child Is Waiting, I Could Go On Singing, **63**.

GARMES, LEE: The Garden Of Allah, The Private Life Of Helen Of Troy, **27**; The Yellow Lily, **28**; Disraeli, **29**; Bright Lights, Morocco, Whoopee!, **30**; An American Tragedy, Dishonored, **31**; Scarface, Shanghai Express, Strange Interlude, **32**; Shanghai Madness, Zoo In Budapest, **33**; Crime Without Passion, **34**; Once In A Blue Moon, The Scoundrel, **35**; Dreaming Lips, The Lilac Domino, The Sky's The Limit, **37**; Gone With The Wind, **39**; Angels Over Broadway, Beyond Tomorrow, **40**; Lydia, **41**; Footlight Serenade, Jungle Book, **42**; Forever And A Day, **43**; Guest In The House, Since You Went Away, **44**; Love Letters, **45**; Duel In The Sun, The Searching Wind, Spectre Of The Rose, **46**; Nightmare Alley, The Secret Life Of Walter Mitty, **47**; The Paradine Case, **48**; Caught, My Foolish Heart, **49**; Detective Story, **51**; Actors And Sin, The Captive City, The Lusty Men, **52**; Outlaw Territory/Hannah Lee, **53**; The Desperate Hours, Land Of The Pharaohs, **55**; D-Day The Sixth Of June, **56**; The Big Fisherman, **59**; Adventures Of A Young Man, **62**; A Big Hand For The Little Lady, **66**; How To Save A Marriage, **68**.

GARNER, JAMES: The Girl He Left Behind, Toward The Unknown, **56**; Sayonara, Shoot Out At Medicine Bend, **57**; Darby's Rangers, **58**; Cash McCall, Up Periscope, **59**; Boys' Night Out, The Children's Hour, **62**; The Great Escape, Move Over Darling, The Thrill Of It All, The Wheeler Dealers, **63**; 36 Hours, The Americanization Of Emily, **64**; The Art Of Love, **65**; Duel At Diablo, Grand Prix, A Man Could Get Killed, Mister Buddwing, **66**; Hour Of The Gun, **67**; How Sweet It Is!, The Pink Jungle, **68**; Marlowe, Support Your Local Sheriff, **69**; A Man Called Sledge, **70**; Skin Game, Support Your Local Gunfighter, **71**; They Only Kill Their Masters, **72**; One Little Indian, **73**; The Castaway Cowboy, **74**; H.E.A.L.T.H., **79**; The Fan, **81**; Victor/Victoria, **82**; Tank, **84**; Murphy's Romance, **85**; Sunset, **88**; The Distinguished Gentleman, **92**; Fire In The Sky, **93**; Maverick, **94**.

GARNETT, TAY: Celebrity, The Spieler, **28**; The Flying Fool, Oh Yeah!, **29**; Her Man, Officer O'Brien, **30**; Bad Company, **31**; Okay America, One Way Passage, Prestige, **32**; Destination Unknown, **33**; China Seas, She Couldn't Take It, **35**; Professional Soldier, **36**; Love Is News, Slave Ship, Stand-In, **37**; Joy Of Living, Trade Winds, **38**; Eternally Yours, **39**; Seven Sinners, Slightly Honorable, **40**; Cheers For Miss Bishop, **41**; My Favorite Spy, **42**; Bataan, The Cross Of Lorraine, **43**; Mrs Parkington, **44**; The Valley Of Decision, **45**; The Postman Always Rings Twice, **46**; Wild Harvest, **47**; A Connecticut Yankee In King Arthur's Court, **48**; The Fireball, **50**; Cause For Alarm, Soldiers Three, **51**; One Minute To Zero, **52**; Main Street To Broadway, **53**; The Black Knight, **54**; A Terrible Beauty, **60**; Cattle King, **63**; The Delta Factor, **70**; The Mad Trapper, 72; Timber Tramp, **73.**

GARSON, GREER: Goodbye Mr Chips, Remember?, **39**; Pride And Prejudice, **40**; Blossoms In The Dust, When Ladies Meet, **41**; Mrs Miniver, Random Harvest, **42**; Madame Curie, The Youngest Profession, **43**; Mrs Parkington, **44**; Adventure, The Valley Of Decision, **45**; Desire Me, **47**; Julia Misbehaves, **48**; The Forsyte Saga, **49**; The Miniver Story, **50**; The Law And The Lady, **51**; Julius Caesar, Scandal At Scourie, **53**; Her 12 Men, **54**; Strange Lady In Town, **55**; Pépé, Sunrise At Campobello, **60**; The Singing Nun, **66**; The Happiest Millionaire, **67**.

GAYNOR, JANET: The Blue Eagle, The Johnstown Flood, The Midnight Kiss, The Return Of Peter Grimm, The Shamrock

Handicap, **26**; Seventh Heaven, Sunrise, Two Girls Wanted, **27**; Four Devils, Street Angel, **28**; Christina, Happy Days, Lucky Star, Sunny Side Up, **29**; High Society Blues, **30**; Daddy Long Legs, Delicious, The Man Who Came Back, Merely Mary Ann, **31**; The First Year, Tess Of The Storm Country, **32**; Adorable, Paddy The Next Best Thing, State Fair, **33**; Carolina, Change Of Heart, La Ciudad De Carton, Servant's Entrance, **34**; The Farmer Takes A Wife, One More Spring, **35**; Ladies In Love, Small Town Girl, **36**; A Star Is Born, **37**; Three Loves Has Nancy, The Young In Heart, **38**; Bernardine, **57**.

GAZZARA, BEN: The Strange One, End As A Man, **57**; Anatomy Of A Murder, **59**; Risate Di Gioia, **60**; The Young Doctors, **61**; Citta Prigioniera, Convicts Four, **62**; A Rage To Live, **65**; The Big Mouth, **67**; The Bridge At Remagen, If It's Tuesday This Must Be Belgium, **69**; Husbands, **70**; The Sicilian Connection, **72**; The Neptune Factor, **73**; Capone, **75**; The Killing Of A Chinese Bookie, Voyage Of The Damned, **76**; High Velocity, Opening Night, **77**; Bloodline, Saint Jack, **79**; They All Laughed, **80**; Inchon, **82**; The Girl From Trieste, **83**; Uno Scandalo Perbene (and half a dozen other Italian films) **85**; Quicker Than The Eye, **88**; Road House, **89**; Oltre L'Oceano, **90**; Blindsided, Nefertiti: The Daughter Of The Sun, **93**.

GERE, RICHARD: Report To The Commissioner, **75**; Looking For Mr Goodbar, **77**; Bloodbrothers, Days Of Heaven, **78**; Yanks, **79**; American Gigolo, **80**; An Officer And A Gentleman, **82**; Beyond The Limit, Breathless, **83**; The Cotton Club, **84**; King David, **85**; No Mercy, Power, **86**; Miles From Home, **88**; Internal Affairs, Pretty Woman, **90**; Rhapsody In August, **91**; Final Analysis, Sommersby, **92**; Mr Jones, **93**; Intersection, **94**; Primal Fear, **95**; The Red Corner, The Jackal, **97**.

GERSHWIN, GEORGE: The King Of Jazz, **30**; Delicious, **31**; Girl Crazy, **32**; A Damsel In Distress, Shall We Dance?, **37**; The Goldwyn Follies, **38**; Lady Be Good, **41**; Girl Crazy, **43**; Broadway Rhythm, **44**; Rhapsody In Blue, **45**; Ziegfeld Follies, **46**; The Shocking Miss Pilgrim, **47**; The Barkleys Of Broadway, **49**; An American In Paris, Lullaby Of Broadway, **51**; Three For The Show, **55**; Funny Face, **57**; Porgy And Bess, **59**; Kiss Me Stupid, **64**; When The Boys Meet The Girls, **65**; Star!, **68**; A Matter Of Time, **76**.

GIBBONS, CEDRIC: The Bridge Of San Luis Rey, The Hollywood Revue Of 1929, **29**; When Ladies Meet, **33**; The Merry Widow, **34**; The Great Ziegfeld, Romeo And Juliet, **36**; Conquest, **37**; Marie Antoinette, **38**; The Wizard Of Oz, **39**; Bitter Sweet, Pride And Prejudice, **40**; Blossoms In The Dust, When Ladies Meet, **41**; Random Harvest, **42**; Madame Curie, Thousands Cheer, **43**; Gaslight, Kismet, National Velvet, **44**; The Picture Of Dorian Gray, **45**; The Yearling, **46**; Little Women, Madame Bovary, The Red Danube, **49**; Annie Get Your Gun, **50**; An American In Paris, Quo Vadis?, Too Young To Kiss, **51**; The Bad And The Beautiful, The Merry Widow, **52**; Julius Caesar, Lili, The Story Of Three Loves, Young Bess, **53**; Brigadoon, Executive Suite, **54**; Blackboard Jungle, I'll Cry Tomorrow, **55**; Lust For Life, Somebody Up There Likes Me, **56**.

GIBSON, MEL: Summer City, **76**; Mad Max, Tim, **79**; Gallipoli, Mad Max 2, **82**; The Year Of Living Dangerously, **83**; The Bounty, Mrs Soffel, The River, Mad Max Beyond Thunderdome, **84**; Lethal Weapon, **87**; Tequila Sunrise, **88**; Lethal Weapon 2, **89**; Air America, Bird On A Wire, Hamlet, **90**; Forever Young, Lethal Weapon 3, **92**; The Man Without A Face, **93**; Maverick, **94**; Braveheart, **95**; Conspiracy Theory, **97**.

GIELGUD, JOHN: Who Is The Man?, **24**; The Clue Of The New Pin, **29**; Insult, **32**; The Good Companions, **33**; The Secret Agent, **36**; The Prime Minister, **41**; Julius Caesar, **53**; Romeo And Juliet, **54**; Richard III, **55**; Around The World In 80 Days, **56**; The Barretts Of Wimpole Street, Saint Joan, **57**; The Immortal Land, **58**; Becket, Hamlet, **64**; The Loved One, To Die In Madrid, **65**; Chimes At Midnight, **66**; Revolution D'Octobre, **67**; Assignment To Kill, The Charge Of The Light Brigade, Sebastian, The Shoes Of The Fisherman, **68**; Oh! What A Lovely War, **69**; Julius Caesar, **70**; Eagle In A Cage, **71**; Galileo, Lost Horizon, **73**; 11 Harrowhouse, Gold, Murder On The Orient Express, **74**; Providence, **76**; Aces High, Joseph Andrews, **77**; The Human Factor, Murder By Decree, A Portrait Of The Artist As A Young Man, **79**; Caligula, The Elephant Man, The Formula, The Orchestra Conductor, **80**; Arthur, Chariots Of Fire, Lion Of The Desert, Priest Of Love, Sphinx, **81**; Gandhi, **82**; Invitation To The Wedding, Wagner, The Wicked Lady, **83**; Scandalous, The Shooting Party, **84**; Ingrid, Leave All Fair, Plenty, Time After Time, **85**; The Whistle Blower, **86**; Barbablu Barbablu, **87**; Appointment With Death, Arthur 2: On The Rocks, **88**; Getting It Right, **89**; Strike It Rich, **90**; Prospero's Books, **91**; The Power Of One, Shining Through, **92**, Shine **96**.

GILBERT, JOHN: The Apostle Of Vengeance, The Eye Of The Night, The Phantom, Shell 43, **16**; Golden Rule Kate, Happiness, Hater Of Men, The Millionaire Vagrant, The Mother Instinct, **17**; The Dawn Of Understanding, More Trouble, Shackled, Sons Of Men, Wedlock, **18**; Heart O' The Hills, The Red Viper Should Women Tell?, The White Heather, Widow By Proxy, **19**; Deep Waters, The Great Redeemer, The White Circle, **20**; Ladies Must Live, Love's Penalty, The Mask, Shame, **21**; Arabian Love, A California Romance, Calvert's Valley, Honor First, The Love Gambler, Monte Cristo, The Yellow Stain, **22**; Cameo Kirby, The Exiles, While Paris Sleeps, Saint Elmo, **23**; He Who Gets Slapped, His Hour, Just Off Broadway, The Lone Chance, The Snob, The Wolf Man, **24**; The Big Parade, The Merry Widow, **25**; La Boheme, **26**; Flesh And The Devil, Love, Man Woman And Sin, The Show, Anna Karenina, **27**; The Cossacks, Four Walls, A Woman Of Affairs, **28**; Desert Nights, The Hollywood Revue Of 29, **29**; Redemption, Way For A Sailor, **30**; Gentleman's Fate, The Phantom Of Paris, West Of Broadway, **31**; Downstairs, **32**; Fast Workers, Queen Christina, **33**; The Captain Hates The Sea, **34**.

GILBERT, LEWIS: The Little Ballerina, **47**; Once A Sinner, **50**; There Is Another Sun, The Scarlet Thread, **51**; Emergency Call, Johnny On The Run, Time Gentlemen Please!, **52**; Albert RN, Cosh Boy, **53**; The Good Die Young, The Sea Shall Not Have Them, **54**; Reach For The Sky, **56**; The Admirable Crichton, Cast A Dark Shadow, **57**; Carve Her Name With Pride, **58**; A Cry From The Streets, **59**; Light Up The Sky, Sink The Bismarck!, **60**; Ferry To Hong Kong, The Greengage Summer, **61**; HMS Defiant, **62**; The Seventh Dawn, **64**; Alfie, **66**; You Only Live Twice, **67**; The Adventurers, **70**; Friends, **71**; Paul And Michelle, **74**; Operation Daybreak, Seven Nights In Japan, **76**; The Spy Who Loved Me, **77**; Moonraker, **79**; Educating Rita, **83**; Not Quite Jerusalem, **84**; Shirley Valentine, **88**; Stepping Out, **90**.

GILLIAM, TERRY: Monty Python And The Holy Grail, **75**; Jabberwocky, **77**; Time Bandits, **81**; Brazil, **85**; The Adventures Of Baron Munchausen, **88**; The Fisher King, **90**; Twelve Monkeys, **95**; My Crazy Life, **97**.

GILLIAT, SIDNEY: Many solo credits. Champagne **28**; Rome Express, **32**; Friday The 13th, **33**; The Lady Vanishes, **38**; Jamaica Inn, **39**; Crooks' Tour, The Girl In The News, Night Train To Munich, They Came By Night, **40**; Kipps, **41**; The Young Mr Pitt, **42**; Millions Like Us, **43**; Waterloo Road, **44**; The Rake's Progress, **45**; I See A Dark Stranger, Green For Danger, **46**; London Belongs To Me, **48**; State Secret, **50**; The Story Of Gilbert And Sullivan, **53**; The Belles Of St Trinian's, The Constant Husband, **55**; Wee Geordie, **56**; Blue Murder At St Trinian's, The Green Man, **57**; Left Right And Centre, The Pure Hell Of St Trinian's, **61**; Only Two Can Play, **62**; The Great St Trinian's Train Robbery, **66**; Endless Night, **71**.

GISH, LILLIAN: The Burglar's Dilemma, A Cry For Help, Gold And Glitter, The Musketeers Of Pig Alley, My Baby, Two Daughters Of Eve, An Unseen Enemy, **12**; The Blue Or The Gray, The House Of Darkness, An Indian's Loyalty, Judith Of Bethulia, The Lady And The Mouse, The Left-handed Man, The Madonna Of The Storm, A Modest Hero, The Mothering Heart, Oil And Water, The Stolen Bride, The Unwelcome Guest, A Woman In The Ultimate, **13**; The Angel Of Contention, The Battle Of The Sexes, The Escape, The Green-eyed Devil, Home Sweet Home, The Hunchback, Man's Enemy, The Rebellion Of Kitty Belle, The Sisters, **14**; The Birth Of A Nation, Captain Macklin, Enoch Arden, The Lily And The Rose, **15**; The Children Pay, Daphne And The Pirate, Intolerance, Sold For Marriage, **16**; The House Built Upon Sand, **17**; The Great Love, Hearts Of The World, **18**; Broken Blossoms, A Romance Of Happy Valley, True Heart Susie, **19**; Way Down East, **20**; Orphans Of The Storm, **22**; The White Sister, **23**; Romola, **24**; La Boheme, The Scarlet Letter, **26**; Annie Laurie, The Enemy, The Wind, **28**; One Romantic Night, **30**; His Double Life, **33**; The Commandos Strike At Dawn, **42**; Duel In The Sun **47**; Portrait Of Jennie **49**; The Night Of The Hunter **55**; The Unforgiven **60**; Warning Shot, The Comedians, **67**; A Wedding, **78**; Hambone And Hillie, **84**; Sweet Liberty, **86**; The Whales Of August, **87**.

GODARD, JEAN-LUC: All Boys Are Called Patrick, **57**; Le Petit Soldat, Une Femme Est Une Femme, Breathless, **60**; Seven Capital Sins, **61**; Roggoppag, **62**; Le Mépris, Les Carabiniers, Vivre Sa Vie, **63**; Bande A Part, The Beautiful Swindlers, A Married Woman, **64**; Alphaville, Pierrot Le Fou, **65**; Made In USA, Masculine Feminine, Two Or Three Things I Know About Her, **66**; La Chinoise, **67**; Le Gai Savoir, Un Film Comme Les Autres, Weekend, **68**; British Sounds, Pravda, Struggle In Italy, Wind From The East, **69**; One Plus One, Vladimir Et Rosa, **70**; 1am, **71**; Tout Va Bien, **72**; Comment Ca Va, Ici Et Ailleurs, Number Two, **75**; Every Man For Himself, **80**; Passion, **82**; First Name: Carmen, **83**; Detective, Hail Mary, **85**; King Lear, Soigne Ta Droite, **87**; Aria, **88**; Against Oblivion, **92**; Woe Is Me, **93**; JLG by JLG, **94**; Forever Mozart, **96**.

GODDARD, PAULETTE: The Locked Door, **29**; City Streets, The Girl Habit, **31**; The Kid From Spain, The Mouthpiece, Pack Up Your Troubles, **32**; Roman Scandals, **33**; Kid Millions, **34**; Modern Times, **36**; Dramatic School, The Young In Heart, **38**; The Cat And The Canary, The Women, **39**; The Ghost Breakers, The Great Dictator, North West Mounted Police, Second Chorus, **40**; Hold Back The Dawn, Nothing But The Truth, Pot O' Gold, **41**; The Forest Rangers, The Lady Has Plans, Reap The Wild Wind, Star Spangled Rhythm, **42**; The Crystal Ball, So Proudly We Hail!, **43**; I Love A Soldier, Standing Room Only, **44**; Duffy's Tavern, Kitty, **45**; The Diary Of A Chambermaid, **46**; Suddenly It's Spring, Unconquered, Variety Girl, An Ideal Husband, **47**; Hazard, On Our Merry Way, **48**; Anna Lucasta, Bride Of Vengeance, **49**; The Torch, **50**; Babes In Bagdad, **52**; Paris Model, Sins Of Jezebel, The Unholy Four, Vice Squad, **53**; Charge Of The Lancers, **54**; Time Of Indifference, **64**.

GOLDBERG, WHOOPI: The Color Purple, **85**; Jumpin' Jack Flash, **86**; Burglar, Fatal Beauty, **87**; Clara's Heart, The Telephone, **88**; Ghost, Homer And Eddie, The Long Walk Home, **90**; House Party 2, Soapdish, **91**; The Player, Sister Act, Wisecracks, **92**; Made In America, National Lampoon's Loaded Weapon I, Sister Act 2: Back In The Habit, **93**; The Lion King, Naked In New York, Boys On The Side, Corrina Corrina, **94**; Moonlight And Valentino, T Rex, Bogus, **95**; The Associate, **96**.

GOLDBLUM, JEFF: California Split, **74**; Nashville, **75**; Next Stop Greenwich Village, Special Delivery, **76**; Annie Hall, Between The Lines, The Sentinel, **77**; Invasion Of The Body Snatchers, Remember My Name, Thank God It's Friday, **78**; Threshold, **81**; The Big Chill, The Right Stuff, **83**; The Adventures Of Buckaroo Banzai Across The Eighth Dimension, **84**; Into The Night, Silverado, Transylvania 6-5000, **85**; The Fly, **86**; Beyond Therapy, **87**; Vibes, **88**; Earth Girls Are Easy, The Tall Guy, **89**; Mister Frost, **90**; The Favor The Watch And The Very Big Fish, **91**; Deep Cover, Fathers And Sons, The Player, Shooting Elizabeth, **92**; Jurassic Park, **93**; Hideaway, **95**; Independence Day, **96**.

GOLDMAN, WILLIAM: Masquerade, **65**; Harper, **66**; Butch Cassidy And The Sundance Kid, **69**; The Hot Rock, **72**; The Great Waldo Pepper, The Stepford Wives, **75**; All The President's Men, Marathon Man, **76**; A Bridge Too Far, **77**; Magic, **78**; The Princess Bride, **87**; Misery, **90**; Chaplin, Memoirs Of An Invisible Man, **92**; Malice, **93**; Maverick, **94**; The Chamber, **96**; Absolute Poer, **97**.

GOLDSMITH, JERRY: Black Patch, **57**; City Of Fear, Face Of A Fugitive, **59**; Studs Lonigan, **60**; Freud, Lonely Are The Brave, **62**; Lilies Of The Field, The List Of Adrian Messenger, The Prize, Take Her, She's Mine, **63**; Fate Is The Hunter, Rio Conchos, Seven Days In May, Shock Treatment, **64**; In Harm's Way, A Patch Of Blue, The Saboteur Code Name Morituri, The Satan Bug, Von Ryan's Express, **65**; The Blue Max, Our Man Flint, The Sand Pebbles, Seconds, Stagecoach, **66**; The Flim Flam Man, In Like Flint, **67**; The Detective, Planet Of The Apes, **68**; 100 Rifles, The Illustrated Man, Justine, **69**; The Ballad Of Cable Hogue, The Magic Garden Of Stanley Sweetheart, Patton, Rio Lobo, Tora! Tora! Tora!, The Traveling Executioner, **70**; Escape From The Planet Of The Apes, The Last Run, The Mephisto Waltz, Wild Rovers, **71**; The Culpepper Cattle Company, The Man, The Other, **72**; Papillon, **73**; Chinatown, S*p*y*s, **74**; The Reincarnation Of Peter Proud, Take A Hard Ride, The Wind And The Lion, **75**; Logan's Run, The Omen, **76**; The Cassandra Crossing, High Velocity, Twilight's Last Gleaming, **77**; The Boys From Brazil, Capricorn One, Coma, Damien Omen II, Magic, The Swarm, **78**; Alien, The Great Train Robbery, Star Trek The Motion Picture, **79**; Outland, Raggedy Man, The Salamander, **81**; The Challenge, First Blood, Inchon, Poltergeist, The Secret Of Nimh, **82**; Psycho II, Twilight Zone The Movie, Under Fire, **83**; Gremlins, The Lonely Guy, Runaway, Supergirl, **84**; Baby . . . Secret Of The Lost Legend, Explorers, King Solomon's Mines, Legend, Rambo: First Blood Part II, **85**; Hoosiers, Link, Poltergeist II, **86**; Extreme Prejudice, Innerspace, Lionheart, **87**; Rambo III, Rent-a-cop, **88**; The 'Burbs, Criminal Law, Leviathan, Star Trek V: The Final Frontier, **89**; Gremlins 2: The New Batch, The Russia House, Total Recall, **90**; Not Without My Daughter, Sleeping With The Enemy, Warlock, **91**; Basic Instinct, Forever Young, Love Field, Medicine Man, Mom And Dad Save The World, Mr. Baseball, **92**; The Beverly Hillbillies, Dennis The Menace, Malice, Matinee, Rudy, Six Degrees Of Separation, The Vanishing, **93**; Angie, The River Wild, IQ, **94**; LA Confidential, Air Force One, **97**.

GOLDWYN, SAMUEL: The Squaw Man, **14**; Jubilo, **19**; The Highest Bidder, **21**; The Eternal City, Potash And Perlmutter, **23**; Tarnish, **24**; The Dark Angel, A Thief In Paradise, **25**; Stella Dallas, Ben-Hur, **26**; The Devil Dancer, Magic Flame, **27**; The Awakening, Two Lovers, **28**; Bulldog Drummond, Condemned, The Rescue, **29**; The Devil To Pay, Raffles, Whoopee!, **30**; Arrowsmith, One Heavenly Night, Street Scene, Tonight Or Never, The Unholy Garden, **31**; The Kid From Spain, **32**; Roman Scandals, **33**; Kid Millions, Nana, We Live Again, **34**; Barbary Coast, The Dark Angel, The Wedding Night, **35**; Dodsworth, Strike Me Pink, These Three, **36**; Dead End, The Hurricane, Stella Dallas, **37**; The Adventures Of Marco Polo, The Cowboy And The Lady, The Goldwyn Follies, **38**; The Real Glory, They Shall Have Music, Wuthering Heights, **39**; Raffles, The Westerner, **40**; Ball Of Fire, The Little Foxes, **41**; The Pride Of The Yankees, **42**; The North Star, They Got Me Covered, **43**; The Princess And The Pirate, Up In Arms, **44**; Wonder Man, **45**; The Best Years Of Our Lives, The Kid From Brooklyn, **46**; The Bishop's Wife, The Secret Life Of Walter Mitty, **47**; Enchantment, A Song Is Born, **48**; My Foolish Heart, Roseanna McCoy, **49**; Edge Of Doom, Our Very Own, **50**; I Want You, **51**; Hans Christian Andersen, **52**; Guys And Dolls, **55**; Porgy And Bess, **59**.

GONG LI: Red Sorghum, **87**; Empress Dowager, **88**; Ju Dou, **89**; The Terra-cotta Warrior, **90**; Raise The Red Lantern, **91**; The Story Of Qiu Ju, **92**; Farewell, My Concubine, Soul Of A Painter/Mary Of Beijing, **93**; Huozhe/To Live, **94**; Shanghai Triad, **95**; Temptress Moon, **96**.

GOODMAN, JOHN: CHUD, Maria's Lovers, Revenge Of The Nerds, **84**; Sweet Dreams, **85**; True Stories, The Big Easy, **86**; Burglar, Raising Arizona, **87**; Everybody' All-American, Punchline, The Wrong Guys, **88**; Always, Sea Of Love, **89**; Arachnophobia, Stella, **90**; King Ralph, **91**; The Babe, Barton Fink, **92**; Born Yesterday, Matinee, We're Back: A Dinosaur's Story, **93**; The Flintstones, **94**.

GORDON, RUTH: The Whirl Of Life, Camille, **15**; Abe Lincoln In Illinois, Dr Ehrlich's Magic Bullet, **40**; Two-Faced Woman, **41**; Action In The North Atlantic, **43** Over 21, **45**; A Double Life, **47**; Adam's Rib, **49**; The Marrying Kind, Pat And Mike, **52**; The Actress, **53**; Inside Daisy Clover, **65**; Lord Love A Duck, **66**; Rosie!, **67**; Rosemary's Baby, **68**; Whatever Happened To Aunt Alice?, **69**; Where's Poppa? **70**; Harold And Maude, **71**; The Big Bus, **76**; Every Which Way But Loose, **78** Boardwalk, **79**; Any Which Way You Can, My Bodyguard, **80**; Jimmy The Kid, **83**; Delt Pi, Maxie, **85**; Trouble With Spies, **87**.

GOULDING, EDMUND: The Bright Shawl, **23**; Dante's Inferno, **24**; The Beautifu City, Sally Irene And Mary, Sun-Up, **25**; Dancing Mothers, Paris, **26**; Love, **27**; Happiness Ahead, **28**; The Trespasser, **29**; The Devil's Holiday, Reaching For The Moon, **30**; The Night Angel, **31**; Blondie Of The Follies, Flesh, Grand Hotel, **32**; Riptide, **34**; The Flame Within, **35**; That Certain Woman, **37**; The Dawn Patrol, White Banners, **38**; Dark Victory, The Old Maid, We Are Not Alone, **39**; 'Til We Meet Again, **40**; The Great Lie, **41**; Claudia, The Constant Nymph, Forever And A Day, **43** Of Human Bondage, The Razor's Edge, **46**; Nightmare Alley, **47**; Everybody Does It, **49**; Mister 880, **50**; We're Not Married, **52**; Down Among The Sheltering Palms, **53**; Teenage Rebel, **56**; Mardi Gras, **58**.

GRABLE, BETTY: Hold 'em Jail, **32**; Child Of Manhattan, What Price Innocence?, **33**; By Your Leave, The Gay Divorcee, **34**; Collegiate, Don't Turn 'Em Loose, Follow The Fleet, Pigskin Parade, **36**; This Way Please, Thrill Of A Lifetime, **37**; Campus Confessions, College Swing, **38**; The Day The Bookies Wept, Man About Town, Million Dollar Legs, **39**; Down Argentine Way, Tin Pan Alley, **40**; I Wake Up Screaming, Moon Over Miami, A Yank In The RAF, **41**; Footlight Serenade, Song Of The Islands, Springtime In The Rockies, **42**; Coney Island, Sweet Rosie O'Grady, **43**; Four Jills In A Jeep, Pin-Up Girl, **44**; Billy Rose's Diamond Horseshoe, The Dolly Sisters, **45**; Mother Wore Tights, The Shocking Miss Pilgrim, **47**; That Lady In Ermine, When My Baby Smiles At Me, **48**; The Beautiful Blonde From Bashful Bend, **49**; My Blue Heaven, Wabash Avenue, **50**; Call Me Mister, Meet Me After The Show, **51**; The Farmer Takes A Wife, How To Marry A Millionaire, **53**; How To Be Very Very Popular Three For The Show, **55**.

GRAHAME, GLORIA: Blonde Fever, **44**; Without Love, **45**; It's A Wonderful Life, **46**; Crossfire, It Happened In Brooklyn, Merton Of The Movies, Song Of The Thin Man **47**; Roughshod, A Woman's Secret, **49**; The Bad And The Beautiful, The Greatest Sho On Earth, Macao, Sudden Fear, **52**; The Big Heat, Man On A Tightrope, In A Lonely Place, **53**; The Good Die Young, Human Desire, Naked Alibi, **54**; The Cobweb, Not As A Stranger, Oklahoma!, **55**; The Man Who Never Was, **56**; Odds Against Tomorrow **59**; Ride Beyond Vengeance, **66**; Blood And Lace, The Todd Killings, **71**; Chandler, The Loners, **72**; The Terror Of Dr Chancey, **75**; Head Over Heels, A Nightingale Sang In Berkeley Square, **79**; Melvin And Howard, **80**; The Nesting, **81**.

GRANGER, STEWART: A Southern Maid, **33**; Give Her A Ring, **34**; So This Is London, **39**; Convoy, **40**; Secret Mission, **42**; The Man In Grey, Thursday's Child, **43**; A Lady Surrenders, Fanny By Gaslight, Waterloo Road, **44**; Caesar And Cleopatra, Caravan, Madonna Of The Seven Moons, **46**; Captain Boycott, The Magic Bow, **47**; Blanche Fury, Saraband For Dead Lovers, **48**; Adam And Evelyne, Woman Hater, **49**; King Solomon's Mines, **50**; Soldiers Three, **51**; The Prisoner Of Zenda, Scaramouche, The Wild North, **52**; All The Brothers Were Valiant, Salome, Young Bess, **53**; Beau Brummel, Green Fire, **54**; Footsteps In The Fog, Moonfleet, **55**; Bhowani Junction, The Last Hunt, **56**; Gun Glory, The Little Hut, **57**; Harry Black And The Tiger, **58**; North To aska, **60**; The Secret Partner, **61**; Lo ɔadaccino Di Siena, Marcia O Crepa, **62**; Il iorno Piu Corto, Sodom And Gomorrah, **3**; The Secret Invasion, Unter Geiern, **64**; ıe Crooked Road, **65**; The Last Safari, ıe Trygon Factor, **67**; The Wild Geese, **78**; ell Hunters, **88**.

RANT, CARY: Blonde Venus, Devil ıd The Deep, Hot Saturday, Madame utterfly, Merrily We Go To Hell, Sinners The Sun, This Is The Night, **32**; Alice In Vonderland, The Eagle And The Hawk, ambling Ship, I'm No Angel, She Done Him rong, The Woman Accused, **33**; Born ɔ Be Bad, Kiss And Make Up, Ladies Should sten, Thirty Day Princess, **34**; Enter ladame, The Last Outpost, Wings In The ark, **35**; The Amazing Quest Of Ernest liss, **35**; Big Brown Eyes, Pirate Party On atalina Isle, Suzy, Wedding Present, ylvia Scarlett, **36**; The Awful Truth, The Toast f New York, Topper, When You're In ove, **37**; Bringing Up Baby, Holiday, **38**; unga Din, In Name Only, Only Angels lave Wings, **39**; His Girl Friday, The Howards f Virginia, My Favorite Wife, The hiladelphia Story, **40**; Penny Serenade, uspicion, **41**; Once Upon A loneymoon, The Talk Of The Town, **42**; estination Tokyo, Mr Lucky, **43**; Arsenic nd Old Lace, None But The Lonely Heart, nce Upon A Time, **44**; Night And Day, otorious, Without Reservations, **46**; The achelor And The Bobby-Soxer, The ishop's Wife, **47**; Every Girl Should Be larried, Mr Blandings Builds His Dream louse, **48**; I Was A Male War Bride, **49**; risis, **50**; People Will Talk, **51**; Monkey usiness, Room For One More, **52**; Dream /ife, **53**; To Catch A Thief, **55**; An Affair ɔ Remember, Kiss Them For Me, The Pride nd The Passion, **57**; Houseboat, ndiscreet, **58**; North By Northwest, Operation etticoat, **59**; The Grass Is Greener, **60**; hat Touch Of Mink, **62**; Charade, **63**; Father ɔoose, **64**; Walk Don't Run, **66**.

REENAWAY, PETER: The Falls, **80**; he Draughtsman's Contract, **82**; A Zed & wo Noughts, **85**; The Belly Of An rchitect, Drowning By Numbers, **87**; The ook The Thief His Wife And Her Lover, **9**; Prospero's Books, **91**; The Baby Of lacon, **93**; The Pillow Book, **95.**

REENE, GRAHAM: Orient Express, **4**; This Gun For Hire, **42**; Brighton Rock, **7**; The Fallen Idol, **48**; The Third Man, **9**; The Heart Of The Matter, **54**; Across The ridge, Saint Joan, **57**; Our Man In lavana, **59**; The Comedians, **67**; Travels /ith My Aunt, **72**; England Made Me, **3**; The Honorary Consul, **83**.

RIERSON, JOHN: Drifters, **29**; ıdustrial Britain, Upstream, **31**; So This Is ondon, **34**; Coalface, The Fishing anks Of Skye, Song Of Ceylon, **35**; Night lail, **36**; We Live In Two Worlds, **37**; he Face Of Scotland, **38**; A Yank Comes ack, **44**; The Brave Don't Cry, **52**; cotch On The Rocks, **54**; Man Of Africa, **56**.

RIFFITH, D W: The Adventures Of)ollie, **08** (first of 450 shorts); Judith Of ethulia, **13**; The Avenging Conscience, he Battle Of The Sexes, The Escape, Home, weet Home, **14**; The Birth Of A Nation, noch Arden, Jordan Is A Hard Road, The amb, The Lily And The Rose, **15**; Betty)f Greystone, Daphne And The Pirate, Fifty-ifty, The Good Bad Man, The Habit Of lappiness, Hoodoo Ann, An Innocent lagdalene, Intolerance, Let Katie Do It, lanhattan Madness, The Missing Links, **16**; he Great Love, The Greatest Thing In ife, **18**; Broken Blossoms, The Girl Who tayed At Home, The Greatest Question, Romance Of Happy Valley, Scarlet Days, rue Heart Susie, **19**; The Idol Dancer, he Love Flower, Way Down East, **20**; Dream treet, One Exciting Night, Orphans Of he Storm, **22**; The White Rose, **23**; America, sn't Life Wonderful?, **24**; Sally Of The awdust, That Royle Girl, **25**; The Sorrows Of atan, **26**; The Battle Of The Sexes, rums Of Love, **28**; Lady Of The avements, **29**; Abraham Lincoln, **30**; he Struggle, **31**.

UINNESS, ALEC: Evensong, **34**; reat Expectations, **46**; Oliver Twist, **48**; Kind learts And Coronets, A Run For Your loney, **49**; Last Holiday, The Mudlark, **50**; he Lavender Hill Mob, The Man In The Vhite Suit, **51**; The Card, **52**; The Captain's aradise, The Malta Story, The Square lile, **53**; Father Brown, **54**; The Ladykillers, The Prisoner, To Paris With Love, **55**; The Swan, **56**; The Bridge On The River Kwai, **57**; Barnacle Bill, The Horse's Mouth, **58**; The Scapegoat, Our Man In Havana, **59**; Tunes Of Glory, **60**; HMS Defiant, Lawrence Of Arabia, A Majority Of One, **62**; The Fall Of The Roman Empire, **64**; Doctor Zhivago, Situation Hopeless but Not Serious, **65**; Hotel Paradiso, The Quiller Memorandum, **66**; The Comedians, **67**; Cromwell, Scrooge, **70**; Brother Sun, Sister Moon, Hitler: The Last Ten Days, **73**; Murder By Death, **76**; Star Wars, **77**; The Empire Strikes Back, Raise The Titanic! **80**; Lovesick, Return Of The Jedi, **83**; A Passage To India, **84**; A Handful Of Dust, Little Dorrit, **88**; Kafka, **91**.

GUITRY, SACHA: Le Blanc Et Le Noir, **31**; Les Deux Couverts, **34**; Bonne Chance, Faisons Un Reve, Pasteur, **35**; Le Mot De Cambronne, Le Nouveau Testament, Mon Pere Avait Raison, The Story Of A Cheat, **36**; The Pearls Of The Crown, Quadrille, **37**; L'Accroche-coeur, Remontons Les Champs-Elysees, **38**; Nine Bachelors, **39**; Mlle Desirée, **42**; Donne-moi Tes Yeux, La Malibran, **43**; Le Diable Boiteaux, **48**; Aux Deux Colombes, Le Tresor De Cantenac, Toa, **49**; Deburau, Tu M'As Sauvé La Vie, **50**; Le Poison, **51**; Je L'ai Ete Trois Fois, **52**; The Virtuous Scoundrel, **53**; Royal Affairs In Versailles, **54**; Napoléon, Si Paris Nous Etait Conte, **55**; Le Trois Font La Paire, Lovers And Thieves, **57**.

GWENN, EDMUND: The Real Thing At Last, **16**; Hindle Wakes, How He Lied To Her Husband, The Skin Game, **31**; Condemned To Death, Love On Wheels, Money For Nothing, **32**; The Good Companions, **33**; For Love Or Money, Channel Crossing, Friday The 13th, I Was A Spy, **34**; Java Head, Strauss's Great Waltz, The Bishop Misbehaves, **35**; Sylvia Scarlett, Anthony Adverse, Early To Bed, Laburnum Grove, Mad Holiday, The Walking Dead, **36**; Parnell, **37**; A Yank At Oxford, **38**; Cheer Boys Cheer, An Englishman's Home, **39**; The Doctor Takes A Wife, The Earl Of Chicago, Foreign Correspondent, Pride And Prejudice, **40**; Charley's Aunt, The Devil And Miss Jones, One Night In Lisbon, Scotland Yard, **41**; A Yank At Eton, **42**; Forever And A Day, Lassie Come Home, The Meanest Man In The World, **43**; Between Two Worlds, The Keys Of The Kingdom, **44**; Bewitched, **45**; Of Human Bondage, Undercurrent, **46**; Green Dolphin Street, Life With Father, Miracle On 34th Street, **47**; Apartment For Peggy, Hills Of Home, **48**; Challenge To Lassie, **49**; Louisa, Mister 880, Pretty Baby, A Woman Of Distinction, **50**; Peking Express, **51**; Bonzo Goes To College, Les Misérables, Something For The Birds, **52**; The Bigamist, Mister Scoutmaster, **53**; The Student Prince, Them!, **54**; It's A Dog's Life, The Trouble With Harry, **55**; The Rocket From Calabuch, **56**.

HACKMAN, GENE: Lilith, **64**; Hawaii, **66**; Banning, Bonnie And Clyde, A Covenant With Death, **67**; The Split, **68**; Downhill Racer, The Gypsy Moths, Marooned, Riot, **69**; I Never Sang For My Father, **70**; The French Connection, The Hunting Party, **71**; Cisco Pike, The Poseidon Adventure, Prime Cut, **72**; Scarecrow, **73**; The Conversation, Young Frankenstein, **74**; Bite The Bullet, French Connection II, Lucky Lady, Night Moves, **75**; A Bridge Too Far, The Domino Principle, March Or Die, **77**; Superman, **78**; Superman II, **80**; All Night Long, Eureka, Reds, **81**; Two Of A Kind, Uncommon Valor, Under Fire, **83**; Misunderstood, **84**; Target, Twice In A Lifetime, **85**; Hoosiers, Power, **86**; No Way Out, Superman IV: The Quest For Peace, **87**; Another Woman, Bat 21, Full Moon In Blue Water, Mississippi Burning, Split Decisions, **88**; The Package, **89**; Loose Cannons, Narrow Margin, Postcards From The Edge, **90**; Class Action, Company Business, **91**; Unforgiven, **92**; The Firm, Geronimo: An American Legend, **93**; Wyatt Earp, **94**; Get Shorty, The Quick And The Dead, Crimson Tide, **95**; Extreme Measures, The Chamber, The Birdcage, **96**; Absolute Power, **97**.

HAMER, ROBERT: Pink String And Sealing Wax, Dead Of Night, **45**; It Always Rains On Sunday, **47**; Kind Hearts And Coronets, The Spider And The Fly, **49**; His Excellency, The Long Memory, **52**; Father Brown, **54**; To Paris With Love, **55**; The Scapegoat, **59**; School For Scoundrels, **60**.

HAMLISCH, MARVIN: Ski Party, **65**; The Swimmer, **68**; The April Fools, Take The Money And Run, **69**; Flap, Move, **70**; Bananas, Kotch, Something Big, **71**; Fat City, The War Between Men And Women, **72**; Save The Tiger, The Sting, The Way We Were, The World's Greatest Athlete, **73**; The Prisoner Of Second Avenue, **75**; The Spy Who Loved Me, **77**; Same Time Next Year, **78**; Chapter Two, Ice Castles, **79**; **80**; Pennies From Heaven, **81**; I Ought To Be In Pictures, Sophie's Choice, **82**; Romantic Comedy, **83**; A Chorus Line, DARYL, **85**; 3 Men And A Baby, **87**; Little Nikita, **88**; The Experts, The January Man, Shirley Valentine, Troop Beverly Hills, **89**; Frankie And Johnny, **91**; Missing Pieces, **92**; Angie, **94**; The Mirror Has Two Faces, **96**.

HANDL, IRENE: Missing – Believed Married, **37**; On The Night Of The Fire, **39**; Night Train To Munich, The Girl In The News, **40**; Pimpernel Smith, **41**; Mr. Emmanuel, **44**; Brief Encounter, **45**; Temptation Harbour, **47**; Silent Dust, The Perfect Woman, **49**; Stage Fright, **50**; Top Secret, **52**; The Case Of The Studio Payroll, **53**; The Belles Of St. Trinian's, Burnt Evidence, **54**; A Kid For Two Farthings, **55**; Brothers In Law, **57**; The Key, Carry On Nurse, **58**; I'm All Right Jack, **59**; School For Scoundrels, Doctor In Love, Two-Way Stretch, Make Mine Mink, A French Mistress, Carry On Constable, **60**; Double Bunk, A Weekend With Lulu, The Pure Hell Of St Trinian's, The Rebel, **61**; Heavens Above!, **63**; You Must Be Joking!, **65**; Morgan, The Wrong Box, **66**; Smashing Time, **67**; The Italian Job, **69**; On A Clear Day You Can See Forever, The Private Life Of Sherlock Holmes, **70**; Adventures Of A Private Eye, Come Play With Me, The Last Remake Of Beau Geste, **77**; The Hound Of The Baskervilles, **78**; The Great Rock 'n' Roll Swindle, **79**; Absolute Beginners, **86**.

HANKS, TOM: He Knows You're Alone, **81**; Bachelor Party, Splash, **84**; The Man With One Red Shoe, Volunteers, **85**; Every Time We Say Goodbye, The Money Pit, Nothing In Common, **86**; Dragnet, **87**; Big, Punchline, **88**; The 'Burbs, Turner & Hooch, **89**; The Bonfire Of The Vanities, Joe Versus The Volcano, **90**; A League Of Their Own, Radio Flyer, **92**; Philadelphia, Sleepless In Seattle, **93**; Forrest Gump, Apollo 13, **95**; That Thing You Do, **96**.

HARBURG, E Y (YIP): Applause, Glorifying The American Girl, Rio Rita, **29**; Follow The Leader, Roadhouse Nights, The Sap From Syracuse, **30**; Moonlight And Pretzels, Take A Chance, **33**; The Gold Diggers Of 37, The Singing Kid, Stage Struck, **36**; At The Circus, Babes In Arms, The Wizard Of Oz, **39**; Babes On Broadway, **41**; Cairo, Panama Hattie, Rio Rita, Ship Ahoy, **42**; Cabin In The Sky, Du Barry Was A Lady, Presenting Lily Mars, Song Of Russia, Thousands Cheer, **43**; Can't Help Singing, Meet The People, **44**; California, **46**; April In Paris, **52**; Gay Purr-ee, **62**; I Could Go On Singing, **63**; Finian's Rainbow, **68**; Alex In Wonderland, **70**.

HARDWICKE, CEDRIC: Nelson, **27**; Dreyfus, **31**; Rome Express, **32**; The Ghoul, Orders Is Orders, **33**; Bella Donna, King Of Paris, The Lady Is Willing, Nell Gwyn, Jew Süss, **34**; Becky Sharp, Les Misérables, Peg Of Old Drury, **35**; Calling The Tune, Laburnum Grove, Tudor Rose, Things To Come, **36**; The Green Light, King Solomon's Mines, **37**; The Hunchback Of Notre Dame, On Borrowed Timeas Death, Stanley And Livingstone, **39**; The Howards Of Virginia, The Invisible Man Returns, Tom Brown's School Days, Victory, **40**; Sundown, Suspicion, **41**; The Commandos Strike At Dawn, The Ghost Of Frankenstein, Invisible Agent, Valley Of The Sun, **42**; The Cross Of Lorraine, Forever And A Day, The Moon Is Down, **43**; The Keys Of The Kingdom, The Lodger, Wilson, Wing And A Prayer, **44**; Beware Of Pity, Sentimental Journey, **46**; The Imperfect Lady, Ivy, Lured, Nicholas Nickleby, Song Of My Heart, Tycoon, A Woman's Vengeance, **47**; I Remember Mama, Rope, **48**; A Connecticut Yankee In King Arthur's Court, Now Barabbas, **49**; The White Tower, The Winslow Boy, **50**; The Desert Fox, Mr Imperium, **51**; Caribbean, The Green Glove, **52**; Botany Bay, Salome, **53**; Bait, **54**; Helen Of Troy, Richard III, **55**; Around The World In 80 Days, Diane, Gaby, The Power And The Prize, The Ten Commandments, The Vagabond King, **56**; Baby Face Nelson, The Story Of Mankind, **57**; Five Weeks In A Balloon, **62**; The Pumpkin Eater, **64**.

HARE, DAVID: Plenty, Wetherby, **85**; Paris By Night, Strapless, **89**; Damage, **92**; The Secret Rapture, **93**.

HARLOW, JEAN: Double Whoopee, The Saturday Night Kid, **29**; Hell's Angels, **30**; Goldie, Iron Man, Platinum Blonde, The Public Enemy, The Secret Six, **31**; Three Wise Girls, The Beast Of The City, Red Dust, Red-Headed Woman, **32**; Bombshell, Hold Your Man, **33**; The Girl From Missouri, Dinner At Eight, **34**; China Seas, Reckless, **35**; Riffraff, Libeled Lady, Suzy, Wife Vs Secretary, **36**; Personal Property, Saratoga, **37**.

HARRIS, RICHARD: Shake Hands With The Devil, The Wreck Of The Mary Deare, **59**; A Terrible Beauty, **60**; The Guns Of Navarone, The Long And The Short And The Tall, **61**; Mutiny On The Bounty, **62**; This Sporting Life, **63**; The Red Desert, **64**; The Heroes Of Telemark, Major Dundee, The Three Faces Of A Woman, **65**; The Bible, Hawaii, **66**; Camelot, Caprice, **67**; Cromwell, A Man Called Horse, The Molly Maguires, **70**; Man In The Wilderness, **71**; The Hero, **72**; **73**; 99 And 44/100% Dead, Juggernaut, **74**; Echoes Of A Summer, The Return Of A Man Called Horse, Robin And Marian, **76**; The Cassandra Crossing, Golden Rendezvous, Gulliver's Travels, Orca, **77**; The Wild Geese, **78**; Game For Vultures, The Last Word, Ravagers, **79**; Highpoint, **80**; Tarzan, The Ape Man, **81**; Triumphs Of A Man Called Horse, **83**; Martin's Day, **84**; Mack The Knife, **89**; The Field, **90**; Patriot Games, Unforgiven, **92**; Wrestling Ernest Hemingway, **93**; Silent Tongue, **94**; Trojan Eddie, **96**.

HARRISON, REX: The Great Game, School For Scandal, **30**; All At Sea, **35**; Men Are Not Gods, **36**; Over The Moon, School For Husbands, Storm In A Teacup, **37**; The Citadel, St Martin's Lane, **38**; The Silent Battle, Ten Days In Paris, **39**; Night Train To Munich, **40**; Major Barbara, **41**; Blithe Spirit, The Rake's Progress, I Live In Grosvenor Square, **45**; Anna And The King Of Siam, **46**; The Foxes Of Harrow, The Ghost And Mrs Muir, **47**; Escape, Unfaithfully Yours, **48**; The Long Dark Hall, **51**; The Four Poster, **52**; Main Street To Broadway, **53**; King Richard And The Crusaders, **54**; The Constant Husband, **55**; The Reluctant Debutante, **58**; Midnight Lace, **60**; The Happy Thieves, **62**; Cleopatra, **63**; My Fair Lady, **64**; The Agony And The Ecstasy, The Yellow Rolls-Royce, **65**; Doctor Dolittle, The Honey Pot, **67**; A Flea In Her Ear, **68**; Staircase, **69**; Prince And The Pauper, Shalimar, **78**; Ashanti, **79**; A Time To Die, **83**.

HARRYHAUSEN, RAY: Mighty Joe Young, **49**; The Beast From 20,000 Fathoms, **53**; It Came From Beneath The Seas, **55**; The Animal World, **56**; 20 Million Miles To Earth, **57**; The Seventh Voyage Of Sinbad, **58**; The Three Worlds Of Gulliver, **60**; Jason And The Argonauts, **63**; One Million Years BC, **66**; The Golden Voyage Of Sinbad, **74**; Sinbad And The Eye Of The Tiger, **77**; Clash Of The Titans, **81**; Beverly Hills Cop III, **94**.

HART, WILLIAM S: The Bargain, His Hour Of Manhood, **14**; The Bad Buck Of Santa Ynez, The Conversion Of Frosty Blake, The Disciple, The Man From Nowhere, Pinto Ben, The Roughneck, Tools Of Providence, **15**; The Apostle Of Vengeance, The Captive God, The Patriot, The Return Of Draw Egan, Hell's Hinges, **16**; The Desert Man, Truthful Tulliver, The Aryan, **17**;

Movie talk

Breakaway: fragile and dispensable part of set that collapses during fight scenes.

British new wave: brief flourishing of British films 1958-63 when working classes, regional locations, florid language and normal sexuality replaced former gentility.

Brute: high-intensity arc spotlight.

Buzz track: ambient sound recorded on a set or location for use in final edit.

Cameo: producer's trick to enhance box office receipts for a film by including a small role for a big star.

Cel: sheets of transparent celluloid or plastic with progressive drawings to animate characters when filmed in sequence.

Change over: switch from one reel to the next in cinema's projection room.

Character role: from grouchy city editor to dotty spinster, often played by actors who make a comparable living as a character type.

Check the gate: camera gate is examined after every shot for any foreign body, such as a hair or dust, that would appear on exposed film. If anything is found a retake is necessary.

Choker: tight close up, usually of an actor's face.

Cinéma vérité: where the camera is an observer of unscripted events in search of truth.

Commissary: Hollywood studio restaurant where menu is often themed, as in *Jaws III* soup, *Little Shop of Horrors* salad and *Tootsie* jam tart.

Continuity supervisor: an assistant who notes down every shot and every detail of a scene to ensure that when shooting restarts everything from costume to actors' positions and even half-filled beer glasses match up.

Contract player: actor under contract to studio or production company.

Counterpoint: where action and sound create different but complementary emotion, often building to a dramatic climax.

Cyclorama: backdrop to represent sky or landscape in studio shoot.

Blue Blazes Rawden, Selfish Yates, Shark Monroe, Wolves Of The Trail, **18**; The Money Corporal, The Poppy Girl's Husband, **19**; The Cradle Of Courage, Sand, The Testing Block, The Toll Gate, **20**; O'Malley Of The Mounted, Three World Brand, The Whistle, White Oak, **21**; Travelin' On, **22**; Wild Bill Hickock, **23**; Singer Jim Mckee, **24**; Tumbleweeds, **25**.

HARVEY, LAURENCE: House Of Darkness, **48**; Landfall, The Man From Yesterday, Man On The Run, **49**; The Black Rose, Cairo Road, **50**; There Is Another Sun, The Scarlet Thread, **51**; I Believe In You, A Killer Walks, Women Of Twilight, **52**; Innocents In Paris, **53**; The Good Die Young, King Richard And The Crusaders, Romeo And Juliet, **54**; I Am A Camera, **55**; Storm Over The Nile, Three Men In A Boat, **56**; After The Ball, **57**; The Silent Enemy, The Truth About Women, **58**; Room At The Top, **59**; The Alamo, Butterfield 8, Expresso Bongo, **60**; The Long And The Short And The Tall, Summer And Smoke, Two Loves, **61**; A Girl Named Tamiko, The Manchurian Candidate, Walk On The Wild Side, The Wonderful World Of The Brothers Grimm, **62**; The Ceremony, The Running Man, **63**; Of Human Bondage, The Outrage, **64**; Darling, Life At The Top, **65**; The Spy With A Cold Nose, **66**; A Dandy In Aspic, Kampf Um Rom, **68**; L'Assoluto Naturale, The Magic Christian, **69**; Wusa, **70**; Escape To The Sun, **72**; Night Watch, **73**; Welcome To Arrow Beach, **74**.

HATHAWAY, HENRY: Heritage Of The Desert, **32**; Man Of The Forest, Sunset Pass, Under The Tonto Rim, **33**; Come On Marines!, The Last Round-up, Now And Forever, The Witching Hour, **34**; The Lives Of A Bengal Lancer, Peter Ibbetson, **35**; Go West Young Man, Trail Of The Lonesome Pine, **36**; Souls At Sea, **37**; Spawn Of The North, **38**; The Real Glory, **39**; Brigham Young – Frontiersman, Johnny Apollo, **40**; The Shepherd Of The Hills, Sundown, **41**; China Girl, Ten Gentlemen From West Point, **42**; Home In Indiana, Wing And A Prayer, **44**; The House On 92nd St, Nob Hill, **45**; The Dark Corner, **46**; Kiss Of Death, 13 Rue Madeleine, **47**; Call Northside 777, **48**; Down To The Sea In Ships, **49**; The Black Rose, **50**; The Desert Fox, Fourteen Hours, Rawhide, USS Tea Kettle, **51**; Diplomatic Courier, O Henry's Full House, Red Skies Of Montana, **52**; Niagara, White Witch Doctor, **53**; Garden Of Evil, Prince Valiant, **54**; The Racers, **55**; 23 Paces To Baker Street, The Bottom Of The Bottle, **56**; Legend Of The Lost, The Wayward Bus, **57**; From Hell To Texas, **58**; Woman Obsessed, **59**; North To Alaska, Seven Thieves, **60**; How The West Was Won, **62**; Rampage, **63**; Circus World, **64**; The Sons Of Katie Elder, **65**; Nevada Smith, **66**; Five Card Stud, **68**; True Grit, **69**; Raid On Rommel, Shootout, **71**; Hangup, **74**.

HAWKINS, JACK: The Perfect Alibi, **30**; The Good Companions, I Lived With You, The Lost Chord, A Shot In The Dark, **33**; Death At Broadcasting House, **34**; Peg Of Old Drury, **35**; Beauty And The Barge, **37**; Who Goes Next?, **38**; The Flying Squad, **40**; Next Of Kin, **42**; Bonnie Prince Charlie, The Fallen Idol, **48**; The Small Back Room, **49**; The Black Rose, The Elusive Pimpernel, State Secret, **50**; No Highway, **51**; The Adventurers, The Planter's Wife, Mandy, **52**; The Cruel Sea, Home At Seven, The Malta Story, Twice Upon A Time, **53**; Angels One Five, Front Page Story, The Seekers, **54**; The Intruder, Land Of The Pharaohs, The Prisoner, Touch And Go, **55**; The Man In The Sky, The Long Arm, **56**; The Bridge On The River Kwai, Fortune Is A Woman, **57**; Gideon's Day, The Two-headed Spy, **58**; Ben-Hur, **59**; The League Of Gentlemen, **60**; Two Loves, **61**; Five Finger Exercise, Lafayette, Lawrence Of Arabia, **62**; Rampage, **63**; Guns At Batasi, The Third Secret, Zulu, **64**; Lord Jim, Masquerade, **65**; Judith, The Opium Connection, **66**; Great Catherine, Shalako, **68**; Twinky, Oh! What A Lovely War, Monte Carlo Or Bust!, **69**; The Adventures Of Gerard, **70**; The Beloved, Kidnapped, Nicholas And Alexandra, Waterloo, When Eight Bells Toll, **71**; Escape To The Sun, The Ruling Class, Young Winston, **72**; Tales That Witness Madness, Theatre Of Blood, **73**.

HAWKS, HOWARD: The Road To Glory, Fig Leaves, **26**; The Cradle Snatchers, Paid To Love, Underworld, **27**; The Air Circus, Fazil, A Girl In Every Port, **28**; Trent's Last Case, **29**; The Dawn Patrol, **30**; The Criminal Code, **31**; The Crowd Roars, Scarface, Tiger Shark, **32**; Today We Live, **33**; Twentieth Century, **34**; Barbary Coast, Ceiling Zero, **35**; Come And Get It, The Road To Glory, **36**; Bringing Up Baby, **38**; Only Angels Have Wings, **39**; His Girl Friday, **40**; Ball Of Fire, Sergeant York, **41**; Air Force, **43**; To Have And Have Not, **44**; The Big Sleep, **46**; Red River, A Song Is Born, **48**; I Was A Male War Bride, **49**; The Big Sky, Monkey Business, O Henry's Full House, **52**; Gentlemen Prefer Blondes, **53**; Land Of The Pharaohs, **55**; Rio Bravo, **59**; Hatari!, **62**; Man's Favorite Sport?, **64**; Red Line 7000, **65**; El Dorado, **67**; Rio Lobo, **70**.

HAY, WILL: Those Were The Days, Radio Parade of 1935, **34**; Dandy Dick, Boys Will Be Boys, **35**; Where There's A Will, Windbag The Sailor, **36**; Good Morning Boys, Oh Mr Porter, **37**; Convict 99, Hey Hey USA, Old Bones Of The River, **38**; Ask A Policeman, Where's That Fire?, **39**; The Ghost Of St Michael's, **41**; The Black Sheep Of Whitehall, The Big Blockade, The Goose Steps Out, **42**; My Learned Friend, **43**.

HAYAKAWA, SESSUE: The Typhoon, The Wrath Of The Gods, **14**; The Cheat, **15**; Alien Souls, **16**; Hashimura Togo, The Jaguar's Claws, **17**; The Honor Of His House, The White Man's Law, The Bottle Imp, **18**; Bonds Of Honor, The Dragon Painter, The City Of Dim Faces, **19**; An Arabian Knight, The Cradle Of Courage, **20**; Black Roses, The First Born, Where Lights Are Low, **21**; Five Days To Live, The Vermilion Pencil, **22**; La Bataille, **23**; The Danger Line, Sen Yan's Devotion, The Great Prince Shan, **24**; J'ai Tué, **25**; Daughter Of The Dragon, **31**; Yoshiwara, **36**; Forfaiture, **37**; Macao, **40**; Tokyo Joe, **49**; Three Came Home, **50**; House Of Bamboo, **55**; The Bridge On The River Kwai, **57**; The Geisha Boy, **58**; Green Mansions, **59**; The Big Wave, Swiss Family Robinson, **60**.

HAYDEN, STERLING: Bahama Passage, Virginia, **41**; Blaze Of Noon, Variety Girl, **47**; El Paso, Manhandled, **49**; The Asphalt Jungle, **50**; Flaming Feather, Journey Into Light, **51**; The Denver And Rio Grande, Flat Top, The Golden Hawk, Hellgate, The Star, **52**; Fighter Attack, Kansas Pacific, So Big, Take Me To Town, **53**; Arrow In The Dust, Crime Wave, Johnny Guitar, Naked Alibi, Prince Valiant, Suddenly, **54**; Battle Taxi, The Eternal Sea, The Last Command, Shotgun, Timberjack, Top Gun, **55**; The Come-on, The Killing, **56**; Crime Of Passion, Five Steps To Danger, Gun Battle At Monterey, The Iron Sheriff, Valerie, Zero Hour, **57**; Ten Days To Tulara, Terror In A Texas Town, **58**; Dr Strangelove Or: How I Learned To Stop Worrying And Love The Bomb, **64**; Hard Contract, Sweet Hunters, **69**; Loving, **70**; Le Saut De L'Ange, **71**; The Godfather, Le Grand Départ, **72**; Final Programme, The Long Goodbye, **73**; 1900, **77**; King Of The Gypsies, **78**; The Outsider, Winter Kills, **79**; 9 To 5, **80**; Gas, **81**; Leuchtturm Des Chaos, Venom, **82**.

HAYWARD, SUSAN: Hollywood Hotel, **37**; Comet Over Broadway, Girls On Probation, The Sisters, **38**; $1,000 A Touchdown, Beau Geste, Our Leading Citizen, **39**; Adam Had Four Sons, Among The Living, Sis Hopkins, **41**; The Forest Rangers, I Married A Witch, Reap The Wild Wind, Star Spangled Rhythm, **42**; Hit Parade Of 1943, Jack London, Young And Willing, **43**; And Now Tomorrow, The Fighting Seabees, The Hairy Ape, **44**; Canyon Passage, Deadline At Dawn, **46**; The Lost Moment, Smash-up: The Story Of A Woman, They Won't Believe Me, **47**; The Saxon Charm, Tap Roots, **48**; House Of Strangers, My Foolish Heart, Tulsa, **49**; David And Bathsheba, I Can Get It For You Wholesale, I'd Climb The Highest Mountain, Rawhide, **51**; The Lusty Men, The Snows Of Kilimanjaro, With A Song In My Heart, **52**; The President's Lady, White Witch Doctor, **53**; Demetrius And The Gladiators, Garden Of Evil, **54**; I'll Cry Tomorrow, Soldier Of Fortune, Untamed, **55**; The Conqueror, **56**; Top Secret Affair, **57**; I Want To Live, **58**; Thunder In The Sun, Woman Obsessed, **59**; The Marriage-Go-Round, **60**; Ada, Back Street, **61**; I Thank A Fool, **62**; Stolen Hours, **63**; Where Love Has Gone, **64**; The Honey Pot, Valley Of The Dolls, **67**; The Revengers, **72**.

HAYWORTH, RITA: Charlie Chan In Egypt, Dante's Inferno, Paddy O'Day, Under The Pampas Moon, **35**; Human Cargo, Meet Nero Wolfe, Rebellion, A Message To Garcia, **36**; Criminals Of The Air, The Game That Kills, Girls Can Play, Hit The Saddle, Old Louisiana, Paid To Dance, The Shadow, Trouble In Texas, **37**; Convicted, Juvenile Court, Special Inspector, Who Killed Gail Preston?, **38**; Homicide Bureau, The Lone Wolf Spy Hunt, Only Angels Have Wings, The Renegade Ranger, **39**; Angels Over Broadway, Blondie On A Budget, The Lady In Question, Music In My Heart, Susan And God, **40**; Affectionately Yours, Blood And Sand, The Strawberry Blonde, You'll Never Get Rich, **41**; My Gal Sal, Tales Of Manhattan, You Were Never Lovelier, **42**; Cover Girl, **44**; Tonight And Every Night, **45**; Gilda, **46**; Down To Earth, **47**; The Lady From Shanghai, The Loves Of Carmen, **48**; Affair In Trinidad, **52**; Miss Sadie Thompson, Salome, **53**; Fire Down Below, Pal Joey, **57**; Separate Tables, **58**; The Story On Page One, They Came To Cordura, **59**; The Happy Thieves, **62**; Circus World, **64**; The Money Trap, **66**; The Opium Connection, L'Avventuriero, **67**; I Gatti, **68**; La Route De Salina, **69**; The Grove, The Wrath Of God, **72**.

HEAD, EDITH: Notorious, **46**; Selection: The Emperor Waltz, **48**; The File On Thelma Jordon, The Heiress, Samson And Delilah, **49**; All About Eve, **50**; A Place In The Sun, **51**; Carrie, The Greatest Show On Earth, **52**; Roman Holiday, **53**; Sabrina, **54**; The Rose Tattoo, To Catch A Thief, Proud And Profane, The Ten Commandments, Funny Face, The Buccaneer, Career, Don't Give Up The Ship, The Five Pennies, **59**; The Facts Of Life, Pépé, **60**; Pocketful Of Miracles, **61**; The Man Who Shot Liberty Valance, My Geisha, **62**; Love With The Proper Stranger, A New Kind Of Love, Wives And Lovers, **63**; A House Is Not A Home, What A Way To Go!, **64**; Inside Daisy Clover, The Slender Thread, **65**; The Oscar, Not With My Wife You Don't, **66**; Sweet Charity, **69**; Airport, **70**; The Sting, **73**; The Man Who Would Be King, **75**; Airport 77, **77**.

HECHT, BEN: Underworld, **27**; The Great Gabbo, The Unholy Night, **29**; Roadhouse Nights, **30**; The Front Page, The Unholy Garden, **31**; Scarface, **32**; Design For Living, Hallelujah I'm A Bum, Turn Back The Clock, **33**; Crime Without Passion, Twentieth Century, Upperworld, **34**; Barbary Coast, The Florentine Dagger, Once In A Blue Moon, The Scoundrel, **35**; Soak The Rich, **36**; Nothing Sacred, **37**; The Goldwyn Follies, **38**; Gunga Din, It's A Wonderful World, Lady Of The Tropics, Let Freedom Ring, Wuthering Heights, Gone With The Wind, **39**; Angels Over Broadway, Comrade X, **40**; Lydia, **41**; The Black Swan, China Girl, Tales Of Manhattan, Ten Gentlemen From West Point, **42**; Spellbound, **45**; Notorious, Specter Of The Rose, **46**; Her Husband's Affairs, Kiss Of Death, Ride The Pink Horse, **47**; The Miracle Of The Bells, Rope, **48**; Whirlpool, **49**; Where The Sidewalk Ends, **50**; Actors And Sin, Monkey Business, **52**; The Indian Fighter, Ulysses, **55**; Miracle In The Rain, **56**; A Farewell To Arms, Legend Of The Lost, **57**; Circus World, **64**.

HEFLIN, VAN: A Woman Rebels, **36**; Annapolis Salute, Flight From Glory, The Outcasts Of Poker Flat, Saturday's Heroes, **37**; Back Door To Heaven, **39**; Santa Fe Trail, **40**; The Feminine Touch, HM Pulham Esq, **41**; Grand Central Murder, Johnny Eager, Kid Glove Killer, Seven Sweethearts, Tennessee Johnson, **42**; Presenting Lily Mars, **43**; The Strange Love Of Martha Ivers, Till The Clouds Roll By, **46**; Green Dolphin Street, Possessed, **47**; BF's Daughter, Tap Roots, Act Of Violence, The Three Musketeers, **48**; East Side West Side, Madame Bovary, **49**; The Prowler, Tomahawk, Weekend With Father, **51**; My Son John, **52**; Shane, Wings Of The Hawk, **53**; Black Widow, The Golden Mask, The Raid, Tanganyika, Woman's World, **54**; Battle Cry, Count Three And Pray, **55**; Patterns, **56**; 3:10 To Yuma, **57**; Gunman's Walk, **58**; Tempest, They Came To Cordura, **59**; 5 Branded Women, Under Ten Flags, **60**; The Wastrel, **61**; Cry Of Battle, **63**; The Greatest Story Ever Told, Once A Thief, **65**; Stagecoach, **66**; The Man Outside, Sam Cooper's Gold, **68**; The Big Bounce, **69**; Airport, **70**.

HENIE, SONJA: Svy Dager For Elisabeth, **27**; One In A Million, **36**; Thin Ice, **37**; Happy Landing, My Lucky Star, **38**; Everything Happens At Night, Second Fiddle, **39**; Sun Valley Serenade, **41**; Iceland, **42**; Wintertime, **43**; It's A Pleasure!, **45**; The Countess Of Monte Cristo, **48**; London Calling, **58**.

HENREID, PAUL: Hohe Schule, **34**; Nur Ein Komodiant, Eva, **35**; Victoria The Great, **37**; An Englishman's Home, Goodbye Mr Chips, **39**; Night Train To Munich, Under Your Hat, **40**; Casablanca, Joan Of Paris, Now, Voyager, **42**; Between Two Worlds, The Conspirators, Hollywood Canteen, In Our Time, **44**; The Spanish Main, **45**; Deception, Devotion, Of Human Bondage, **46**; Song Of Love, **47**; Hollow Triumph, **48**; Rope Of Sand, **49**; Last Of The Buccaneers, So Young So Bad, **50**; Pardon My French, **51**; For Men Only, A Stolen Face, Thief Of Damascus, **52**; Mantrap, Siren Of Bagdad, **53**; Deep In My Heart, Kabarett, **54**; Pirates Of Tripoli, **55**; Meet Me In Las Vegas, A Woman's Devotion, **56**; Ten Thousand Bedrooms, **57**; Girls On The Loose, Live Fast Die Young, **58**; Holiday For Lovers, Never So Few, **59**; The Four Horsemen Of The Apocalypse, **62**; Dead Ringer, **64**; Operation Crossbow, **65**; Ballad In Blue, **66**; The Madwoman Of Chaillot, **69**; Exorcist II: The Heretic, **77**.

HENSON, JIM: Time Piece, **65**; The Muppet Movie, **79**; The Great Muppet Caper, **81**; The Dark Crystal, **82**; The Muppets Take Manhattan, **84**; Into The Night, Sesame Street Presents Follow That Bird, **85**; Labyrinth, **86**.

HEPBURN, AUDREY: Laughter In Paradise, The Lavender Hill Mob, Nous Irons A Monte Carlo, One Wild Oat, Young Wives' Tale, **51**; Secret People, **52**; Roman Holiday, **53**; Sabrina, **54**; War And Peace, **56**; Funny Face, Love In The Afternoon, **57**; Green Mansions, The Nun's Story, **59**; The Unforgiven, **60**; Breakfast At Tiffany's, **61**; The Children's Hour, **62**; Charade, **63**; My Fair Lady, Paris When It Sizzles, **64**; How To Steal A Million, **66**; Two For The Road, Wait Until Dark, **67**; Robin And Marian, **76**; Bloodline, **79**; They All Laughed, **81**; Always, **89**.

HEPBURN, KATHARINE: A Bill Of Divorcement, **32**; Christopher Strong, Little Women, Morning Glory, **33**; The Little Minister, Spitfire, **34**; Alice Adams, Break Of Hearts, **35**; Mary Of Scotland, A Woman Rebels, Sylvia Scarlett, **36**; Quality Street, Stage Door, **37**; Bringing Up Baby, Holiday, **38**; The Philadelphia Story, **40**; Keeper Of The Flame, Woman Of The Year, **42**; Stage Door Canteen, **43**; Dragon Seed, **44**; Without Love, **45**; Undercurrent, **46**; The Sea Of Grass, Song Of Love, **47**; State Of The Union, **48**; Adam's Rib, **49**; The African Queen, **51**; Pat And Mike, **52**; Summer Madness, **55**; The Iron Petticoat, The Rainmaker, **56**; Desk Set, **57**; Suddenly Last Summer, **59**; Long Day's Journey Into Night, **62**; Guess Who's Coming To Dinner, **67**; The Lion In Winter, **68**; The Madwoman Of Chaillot, **69**; The Trojan Women, **71**; A Delicate Balance, **73**; Rooster Cogburn, **75**; Olly Olly Oxen Free, **78**; On Golden Pond, **81**; The Ultimate Solution Of Grace Quigley, **85**; Love Affair, **94**.

HEPWORTH, CECIL: Selection: Express Train In A Railway Cutting, **99**; The Eccentric Dancer, The Explosion Of A Motor Car, How It Feels To Be Run Over, The Kiss, **00**; Coronation Of King Edward VII, Funeral Of Queen Victoria, The Glutton's Nightmare, How The Burglar Tricked The Bobby, **01**; The Call To Arms, How To Stop A Motor Car, **02**; Alice In Wonderland, Firemen To The Rescue, **03**; The Jonah Man, **04**; The Alien's Invasion, A Den Of Thieves, Falsely Accused, Rescued By Rover, **05**; A Seaside Girl, **07**; John Gilpin's Ride, **08**; Tilly The Tomboy, **09**; Rachel's Sin, **11**; Blind Fate, **12**; The Chimes, **14**; The Basilisk, The Battle, The Canker Of Jealousy, Iris, The Man Who Stayed At Home, The Outrage, Sweet Lavender, Time The Great Healer, Barnaby Rudge, The Bottle, **15**; Annie Laurie, The Cobweb, Comin Thro The Rye, Sowing The Wind, **16**; The American Heiress, Nearer My God To Thee, **17**; The Blindness Of Fortune, Boundary House, The Leopard's Spots, **18**; The Forest On The Hill, The Nature Of The Beast, Sheba, Broken In The Wars, **19**; Alf's Button, Anna The Adventuress, Helen Of Four Gates, The Amazing Quest Of Mr Edward Bliss, **20**; Narrow Valley, Tinted Venus, Wild Heather, Tansy, **21**; Mist In The Valley, Pipes Of Pan, **22**; Comin Thro The Rye, **24**; The House Of Marney, **27**.

HERRMANN, BERNARD: Citizen Kane, All That Money Can Buy, **41**; The Magnificent Ambersons, **42**; Anna And The King Of Siam, **46**; The Ghost And Mrs Muir, **47**; On Dangerous Ground, **51**; The Snows Of Kilimanjaro, **52**; The Egyptian, Garden Of Evil, **54**; The Kentuckian, Prince Of Players, The Trouble With Harry, **55** The Man In The Gray Flannel Suit, The Man Who Knew Too Much, The Wrong Man, **56**; A Hatful Of Rain, **57**; The 7th Voyage Of Sinbad, The Naked And The Dead, Vertigo, **58**; Blue Denim, Journey To The Centre Of The Earth, North By Northwest, **59** Psycho, **60**; Mysterious Island, **61**; Cape Fear, Tender Is The Night, **62**; The Birds, Jason And The Argonauts, **63**; Marnie, **64**; Joy In The Morning, **65**; Fahrenheit 451 **67**; The Bride Wore Black, Twisted Nerve, **68**; Bezetenhet Gat In De Muur, **69**; Endless Night, **71**; Sisters, **73**; It's Alive!, **74**; Obsession, Taxi Driver, **76**; It Lives Again, **78**; It's Alive III: Island Of The Alive, **87**; Cape Fear, **91**.

HERSHEY, BARBARA: With Six You Get Eggroll, **68**; Heaven With A Gun, Last Summer, **69**; The Baby Maker, The Liberation Of LB Jones, **70**; The Pursuit Of Happiness, **71**; Boxcar Bertha, Dealing: Or The Berkeley-To-Boston Forty-Brick Lost-Ba Blues, **72**; Angela, **73**; The Crazy World Of Julius Vrooder, **74**; Diamonds, You And Me, **75**; Trial By Combat, The Last Hard Men, **76**; The Stunt Man, **80**; Americana, Take This Job And Shove It, **81**; The Entity, The Right Stuff, **83**; The Natural, **84**; Hannah And Her Sisters, **86**; Shy People, Tin Men, **87**; Beaches, The Last Temptation Of Christ, A World Apart, **88**; Tune In Tomorrow, **90**; Paris Trout, The Publi Eye, **91**; A Dangerous Woman, Falling Down, Splitting Heirs, Swing Kids, **93**; Last Of The Dogmen, **95**; The Portrait of a Lady, **96**.

HERZOG, WERNER: Even Dwarfs Started Small, Signs Of Life, **68**; Aguirre: The Wrath Of God, **72**; The Enigma Of Kasper Hauser, **74**; Heart Of Glass, **76**; Stroszek, **77**; Woyzeck, **78**; Nosferatu The Vampyre, **79**; Fitzcarraldo, **82**; A Man Of Flowers, Where The Green Ants Dream, **84**; Cobra Verde, **88**; Gekauftes Gluck, Hard To Be A God, **89**; Scream Of Stone, **91**.

HESTON, CHARLTON: Peer Gynt, **41**; Julius Caesar, **49**; Dark City, **50**; The Greatest Show On Earth, Ruby Gentry, The Savage, **52**; Arrowhead, Bad For Each Other, Pony Express, The President's Lady, **53**; The Naked Jungle, Secret Of The Incas, **54**; The Far Horizons, Lucy Gallant, The Private War Of Major Benson, **55** The Ten Commandments, Three Violent People, **56**; The Big Country, The Buccaneer, Touch Of Evil, **58**; Ben-Hur, The Wreck Of The Mary Deare, **59**; El Cid, **61**; Diamond Head, The Pigeon That Took Rome, **62**; 55 Days At Peking, **63**; The Agony And The Ecstasy, The Greatest Story Ever Told, Major Dundee, The War Lord, **65**; Khartoum **66**; Counterpoint, Planet Of The Apes, Will Penny, **68**; Number One, **69**; Beneath The Planet Of The Apes, The Hawaiians, Julius Caesar, **70**; The Omega Man, **71**; Call Of The Wild, Skyjacked, **72**; Antony And Cleopatra, Soylent Green, **73**; Airport 75, Earthquake, The Three Musketeers, **74**; The Four Musketeers, **75**; The Last Hard Men, Midway, Two Minute Warning, **76**; The Prince And The Pauper, Gray Lady Down, **78**; The Awakening, The Mountain Men, **80**; Mother Lode, **82**; Almost An Angel, Solar Crisis, Treasure Island, **90**; Tombstone, True Lies, Wayne's World 2, **93**; In The Mouth Of Madness, **95**; Hamlet, **96**.

HILL, GEORGE ROY: Period Of Adjustment, **62**; Toys In The Attic, **63**; The World Of Henry Orient, **64**; Hawaii, **66**; Thoroughly Modern Millie, **67**; Butch Cassidy And The Sundance Kid, **69**; Slaughterhouse-Five, **72**; The Sting, **73**; The Great Waldo Pepper, **75**; Slap Shot, **77**; A Little Romance, **79**; The World According To Garp, **82**; The Little Drummer Girl, **84**; Funny Farm, **88**.

HILL, WALTER: Hard Times, **75**; The Driver, **78**; The Warriors, **79**; The Long Riders, **80**; Southern Comfort, **81**; 48HRS, **82**; Streets Of Fire, **84**; Brewster's Millions, **85**; Extreme Prejudice, **87**; Johnny Handsome, **89**; Another 48HRS, **90**;

espass, **92**; Geronimo **93**; Wild Bill, **5**; Last Man Standing, **96**.

TCHCOCK, ALFRED: The Pleasure rden, **25**; The Mountain Eagle, The Lodger, **6**; Downhill, Easy Virtue, The Ring, **27**; ampagne, The Farmer's Wife, **28**; ackmail, The Manxman, **29**; Elstree illing, Juno And The Paycock, Murder!, **30**; e Skin Game, **31**; Number Seventeen, ch And Strange, **32**; Waltzes From Vienna, **3**; The Man Who Knew Too Much, **34**; e 39 Steps, **35**; Sabotage, The Secret ent, **36**; Young And Innocent, **37**; The dy Vanishes, **38**; Jamaica Inn, **39**; becca, Foreign Correspondent, **40**; Mr Mrs Smith, Suspicion, **41**; Saboteur, **42**; adow Of A Doubt, **43**; Lifeboat, **44**; ellbound, **45**; Notorious, **46**; The Paradine se, Rope, **48**; Under Capricorn, **49**; ge Fright, **50**; Strangers On A Train, **51**; I nfess, **53**; Dial M For Murder, Rear ndow, **54**; To Catch A Thief, The Trouble th Harry, **55**; The Man Who Knew Too uch, The Wrong Man, **56**; Vertigo, **58**; rth By Northwest, **59**; Psycho, **60**; e Birds, **63**; Marnie, **64**; Torn Curtain, **66**; paz, **69**; Frenzy, **72**; Family Plot, **76**.

OFFMAN, DUSTIN: The Graduate, e Tiger Makes Out, **67**; John And Mary, dnight Cowboy, **69**; Little Big Man, **0**; Straw Dogs, Who Is Harry Kellerman And y Is He Saying Those Terrible Things out Me?, **71**; Alfredo Alfredo, **72**; Papillon, **3**; Lenny, **74**; All The President's Men, arathon Man, **76**; Straight Time, **78**; atha, Kramer Vs Kramer, **79**; Tootsie, **2**; Ishtar, **87**; Rain Man, **88**; Family siness, **89**; Dick Tracy, **90**; Billy athgate, Hook, **91**; Hero, **92**; Outbreak, nerican Buffalo, **95**; Sleepers, **96**.

OLDEN, WILLIAM: Three Weekends, **8**; Weary River, His Captive Woman, Fast e, The Trespasser, **29**; Not So Dumb, amed, Numbered Men, Holiday, Three aces East, What A Widow, **30**; The Man ho Came Back, Dance Fools Dance, Charlie an Carries On, **31**; Golden Boy, visible Stripes, **39**; Our Town, Those Were e Days, **40**; Arizona, I Wanted Wings, exas, **41**; The Fleet's In, Meet The Stewarts, e Remarkable Andrew, **42**; Young And lling, **43**; Blaze Of Noon, Dear Ruth, Variety rl, **47**; Apartment For Peggy, The Dark ast, Rachel And The Stranger, **48**; The Man om Colorado, Miss Grant Takes chmond, Streets Of Laredo, **49**; Born esterday, Father Is A Bachelor, Sunset oulevard, Union Station, **50**; Dear Wife, orce Of Arms, Submarine Command, **1**; Boots Malone, The Turning Point, **52**; scape From Fort Bravo, Forever Female, e Moon Is Blue, Stalag 17, **53**; The Bridges Toko-Ri, The Country Girl, Executive ite, Sabrina, **54**; Love Is A Many-plendored Thing, Picnic, **55**; The Proud d Profane, Toward The Unknown, **56**; The idge On The River Kwai, **57**; The Key, **8**; The Horse Soldiers, **59**; The World Of zie Wong, **60**; The Counterfeit Traitor, e Lion, Satan Never Sleeps, **62**; The 7th awn, Paris When It Sizzles, **64**; Alvarez elly, **66**; Casino Royale, **67**; The Devil's rigade, **68**; The Christmas Tree, The ild Bunch, **69**; Wild Rovers, **71**; The evengers, **72**; Breezy, **73**; Open eason, The Towering Inferno, **74**; Network, **6**; Damien Omen II, Fedora, **78**; shanti, Escape To Athena, **79**; The Earthling, hen Time Ran Out, **80**; SOB, **81**.

OLLAND, AGNIESZKA: Screen Test, **7**; Provincial Actors, **79**; Goraczka, **80**; obieta Samotna, **81**; A Woman Alone, **2**; Danton, **84**; Angry Harvest, **85**; La niga, To Kill A Priest, **88**; Europa uropa, **90**; Olivier Olivier, **92**; The Secret arden, **93**; Total Eclipse, **95**.

OLLIDAY, JUDY: Greenwich Village, omething For The Boys, Winged Victory, **44**; dam's Rib, **49**; Born Yesterday, **50**; e Marrying Kind, **52**; It Should Happen To ou, Phffft!, **54**; Full Of Life, The Solid old Cadillac, **56**; Bells Are Ringing, **60**.

OLLOWAY, STANLEY: The Rotters, **1**; The Co-optimists, **30**; Lily Of Killarney, ng As We Go, **34**; Squibs, **35**; The car Of Bray, **37**; Major Barbara, **41**; Salute hn Citizen, **42**; Champagne Charlie, his Happy Breed, The Way Ahead, **44**; Brief ncounter, The Way To The Stars, **45**; aesar And Cleopatra, **46**; Meet Me At Dawn, cholas Nickleby, **47**; Another Shore, amlet, **48**; Passport To Pimlico, The Perfect oman, **49**; Midnight Episode, The Winslow Boy, **50**; Lady Godiva Rides Again, The Lavender Hill Mob, The Magic Box, **51**; The Happy Family, Meet Me Tonight, **52**; The Beggar's Opera, Meet Mr Lucifer, The Titfield Thunderbolt, **53**; An Alligator Named Daisy, **57**; Hello London, No Trees In The Street, **58**; No Love For Johnnie, **61**; My Fair Lady, **64**; In Harm's Way, **65**; Ten Little Indians, **66**; Mrs Brown, You've Got A Lovely Daughter, **68**; Target: Harry, **69**; The Private Life Of Sherlock Holmes, **70**; Flight Of The Doves, **71**; Up The Front, **72**; Journey Into Fear, **75**.

HOPE, BOB: The Big Broadcast Of 38, College Swing, Give Me A Sailor, Thanks For The Memory, **38**; The Cat And The Canary, Never Say Die, Some Like It Hot, **39**; The Ghost Breakers, The Road To Singapore, **40**; Caught In The Draft, Louisiana Purchase, Nothing But The Truth, Road To Zanzibar, **41**; My Favorite Blonde, Road To Morocco, Star Spangled Rhythm, **42**; Let's Face It, They Got Me Covered, **43**; The Princess And The Pirate, **44**; Road To Utopia, **45**; Monsieur Beaucaire, **46**; My Favorite Brunette, Road To Rio, Variety Girl, Where There's Life, **47**; The Paleface, **48**; The Great Lover, Sorrowful Jones, **49**; Fancy Pants, **50**; The Lemon Drop Kid, My Favorite Spy, **51**; Road To Bali, Scared Stiff, Son Of Paleface, **52**; Here Come The Girls, Off Limits, **53**; Casanova's Big Night, **54**; The Seven Little Foys, **55**; The Iron Petticoat, That Certain Feeling, **56**; Beau James, **57**; Paris Holiday, **58**; Alias Jesse James, The Five Pennies, **59**; The Facts Of Life, **60**; Bachelor In Paradise, **61**; The Road To Hong Kong, **62**; Call Me Bwana, Critic's Choice, **63**; A Global Affair, **64**; I'll Take Sweden, **65**; Boy Did I Get A Wrong Number!, The Oscar, **66**; Eight On The Lam, **67**; The Private Navy Of Sgt O'Farrell, **68**; How To Commit Marriage, **69**; Cancel My Reservation, **72**; The Muppet Movie, **79**.

HOPKINS, ANTHONY: The White Bus, **67**; The Lion In Winter, **68**; Hamlet, **69**; The Looking Glass War, **70**; When Eight Bells Toll, **71**; Young Winston, **72**; A Doll's House, **73**; The Girl From Petrovka, Juggernaut, **74**; Audrey Rose, A Bridge Too Far, **77**; International Velvet, Magic, **78**; A Change Of Seasons, The Elephant Man, **80**; The Bounty, **84**; Blunt, **86**; 84 Charing Cross Road, The Good Father, **87**; A Chorus Of Disapproval, The Dawning, **88**; Desperate Hours, **90**; The Silence Of The Lambs, **91**; Bram Stoker's Dracula, Chaplin, Howards End, **92**; The Innocent, The Remains Of The Day, Shadowlands, The Trial, **93**; The Road To Wellville, Legends Of The Fall, **94**; Nixon, The Innocent, **95**; August, Surviving Picasso, **96**.

HOPPER, DENNIS: Jagged Edge, I Died A Thousand Times, Rebel Without A Cause, **55**; The Steel Jungle, Giant, **56**; Gunfight At The OK Corral, Sayonara, The Story Of Mankind, **57**; From Hell To Texas, **58**; The Young Land, **59**; Key Witness, **60**; Night Tide, **63**; Tarzan And Jane Regained, Sent Off, **64**; The Sons Of Katie Elder, **65**; Queen Of Blood, **66**; Cool Hand Luke, The Glory Stompers, The Trip, **67**; Hang 'Em High, Head, Panic In The City, **68**; Easy Rider, True Grit, **69**; The Last Movie, **71**; Crush Proof, **72**; Kid Blue, **73**; Mad Dog Morgan, **75**; The American Friend, Tracks, **77**; L'Ordre Et La Securite Du Monde, **78**; Apocalypse Now, **79**; Out Of The Blue, **80**; King Of The Mountain, Renacida, White Star, **81**; Human Highway, **82**; The Osterman Weekend, Rumble Fish, **83**; Slagskampen, **84**; My Science Project, **85**; Black Widow, Blue Velvet, Hoosiers, Riders Of The Storm, River's Edge, The Texas Chainsaw Massacre 2, **86**; OC & Stiggs, The Pick-up Artist, Straight To Hell, **87**; Blood Red, Colors, **88**; Backtrack, **89**; Chattahoochee, Flashback, The Hot Spot, **90**; Eye Of The Storm, The Indian Runner, Paris Trout, Catchfire, **91**; Boiling Point, Red Rock West, Super Mario Bros, True Romance, **93**; Chasers, Speed, **94**; Search And Destroy, Waterworld, **95**; Basquiat, **96**.

HORNE, LENA: The Duke Is Tops, **38**; Boogie Woogie Panama Hattie, **42**; Cabin In The Sky, I Dood It, Stormy Weather, Thousands Cheer, **43**; Broadway Rhythm, Swing Fever, Two Girls And A Sailor, **44**; Till The Clouds Roll By, Ziegfeld Follies, **46**; Words And Music, **48**; Duchess Of Idaho, **50**; Meet Me In Las Vegas, **56**; The Heart Of Show Business, **57**; Death Of A Gunfighter, **69**; The Wiz, **78**.

HORTON, EDWARD EVERETT: Too Much Business, **22**; Ruggles Of Red Gap, To The Ladies, **23**; The Man Who Fights Alone, **24**; Beggar On Horseback, Marry Me, **25**; La Boheme, Poker Faces, **26**; Taxi! Taxi!, **27**; The Terror, Miss Information, **28**; The Hottentot, The Sap, Sonny Boy, **29**; Once A Gentleman, Wide Open, The Aviator, **30**; The Age For Love, The Front Page, Kiss Me Again, Lonely Wives, Reaching For The Moon, Six Cylinder Love, Smart Woman, **31**; But The Flesh Is Weak, Trouble In Paradise, **32**; Alice In Wonderland, A Bedtime Story, Design For Living, It's A Boy, The Way To Love, Soldiers Of The King, **33**; Easy To Love, The Gay Divorcee, Kiss And Make-up, Ladies Should Listen, The Merry Widow, Success At Any Price, **34**; Biography Of A Bachelor Girl, The Devil Is A Woman, His Night Out, In Caliente, Top Hat, Your Uncle Dudley, The Night Is Young, $10 Raise, **35**; Hearts Divided, The Man In The Mirror, Nobody's Fool, The Singing Kid, **36**; Angel, The Great Garrick, The King And The Chorus Girl, Lost Horizon, Oh Doctor!, The Perfect Specimen, Shall We Dance, **37**; Bluebeard's Eighth Wife, Holiday, **38**; Paris Honeymoon, That's Right You're Wrong, **39**; Bachelor Daddy, The Body Disappears, Here Comes Mr Jordan, Sunny, Ziegfeld Girl, You're The One, **41**; I Married An Angel, The Magnificent Dope, Springtime In The Rockies, **42**; The Gang's All Here, Thank Your Lucky Stars, **43**; Arsenic And Old Lace, Brazil, Summer Storm, **44**; Lady On A Train, **45**; Cinderella Jones, Earl Carroll Sketchbook, **46**; Down To Earth, Her Husband's Affairs, **47**; The Story Of Mankind, **57**; Pocketful Of Miracles, **61**; It's A Mad Mad Mad Mad World, **63**; Sex And The Single Girl, **64**; The Perils Of Pauline, **67**; 2000 Years Later, **69**; Cold Turkey, **71**.

HOSKINS, BOB: The National Health, **73**; Royal Flash, **75**; Inserts, **76**; Zulu Dawn, **79**; The Long Good Friday, **81**; Pink Floyd The Wall, **82**; Beyond The Limit, **83**; The Cotton Club, Lassiter, **84**; Brazil, **85**; Mona Lisa, Sweet Liberty, **86**; The Lonely Passion Of Judith Hearne, A Prayer For The Dying, The Secret Policeman's Third Ball, **87**; Who Framed Roger Rabbit, **88**; Raggedy Rawney, **89**; Heart Condition, Mermaids, **90**; The Favor The Watch And The Very Big Fish, Hook, The Inner Circle, Shattered, **91**; Passed Away, **92**; Super Mario Bros, **93**; Nixon, **95**.

HOUSEMAN, JOHN: Jane Eyre, **44**; Miss Susie Slagle's, **45**; The Blue Dahlia, **46**; Letter From An Unknown Woman, **48**; They Live By Night, **49**; The Company She Keeps, **50**; On Dangerous Ground, **51**; The Bad And The Beautiful, Holiday For Sinners, **52**; Julius Caesar, **53**; Executive Suite, Her 12 Men, **54**; The Cobweb, Moonfleet, **55**; Lust For Life, **56**; All Fall Down, Two Weeks In Another Town, **62**; In The Cool Of The Day, **63**; Seven Days In May, **64**; This Property Is Condemned, **66**; Paper Chase, **73**; Rollerball, Three Days Of The Condor, **75**; St Ives, **76**; The Cheap Detective, **78**; Old Boyfriends, **79**; The Fog, Murder By Phone, My Bodyguard, Wholly Moses, **80**; Ghost Story, **81**; Another Woman, The Naked Gun: From The Files Of Police Squad!, Scrooged, **88**.

HOWARD, LESLIE: Outward Bound, **30**; Devotion, Five And Ten, A Free Soul, Never The Twain Shall Meet, **31**; The Animal Kingdom, Service For Ladies, Smilin' Through, **32**; Berkeley Square, Captured, Secrets, **33**; British Agent, The Lady Is Willing, Of Human Bondage, **34**; The Scarlet Pimpernel, **35**; The Petrified Forest, Romeo And Juliet, **36**; It's Love I'm After, Stand-In, **37**; Pygmalion, **38**; Gone With The Wind, Intermezzo: A Love Story, **39**; 49th Parallel, Pimpernel Smith, **41**; The First Of The Few, **42**; The Gentle Sex, **43**.

HOWARD, RON: Frontier Woman, **56**; The Journey, **59**; The Music Man, **62**; The Courtship Of Eddie's Father, **63**; Village Of The Giants, **65**; Five Minutes To Live, **66**; Smoke, **70**; The Wild Country, **71**; American Graffiti, Happy Mother's Day, Run Stranger Run, **73**; The Spikes Gang, **74**; Eat My Dust!, The First Nudie Musical, The Shootist, **76**; Grand Theft Auto, **77**; More American Graffiti, **79**; Night Shift, **82**; Splash, **84**; Cocoon, **85**; Gung Ho, **86**; No Man's Land, **87**; Willow, **88**; The 'Burbs, Parenthood, **89**; Backdraft, **91**; Far And Away, **92**; The Paper, **94**; Apollo 13, **95**.

HOWARD, TREVOR: The Way Ahead, **44**; Brief Encounter, The Way To The Stars, **45**; I See A Dark Stranger, Green For Danger, **46**; So Well Remembered, They Made Me A Fugitive, **47**; The Passionate Friends, The Third Man, **49**; Odette, The Clouded Yellow, The Golden Salamander, **50**; Outcast Of The Islands, **51**; The Gift Horse, **52**; The Heart Of The Matter, **53**; The Stranger's Hand, **54**; Les Amants Du Tage/Lovers' Net, **55**; Around The World In 80 Days, The Cockleshell Heroes, Run For The Sun, **56**; Interpol, Manuela, **57**; The Key, The Roots Of Heaven, **58**; Moment Of Danger, Sons And Lovers, **60**; The Lion, Mutiny On The Bounty, **62**; Father Goose, Man In The Middle, **64**; Operation Crossbow, Morituri, Von Ryan's Express, **65**; The Liquidator, **66**; The Long Duel, Pretty Polly, Triple Cross, **67**; The Charge Of The Light Brigade, **68**; Battle Of Britain, Twinky, **69**; The Night Visitor, Ryan's Daughter, **70**; Kidnapped, Mary Queen Of Scots, Catch Me A Spy, **71**; Pope Joan, **72**; Craze, A Doll's House, Ludwig, The Offence, **73**; 11 Harrowhouse, Persecution, Who?, **74**; Conduct Unbecoming, Hennessy, Whispering Death, **75**; The Bawdy Adventures Of Tom Jones, Eliza Fraser, The Count Of Monte Cristo, **76**; Aces High, The Last Remake Of Beau Geste, **77**; Flashpoint Africa, Slavers, Die Sklavenjäger; Stevie, Superman, **78**; Forbidden Paradise, Meteor, **79**; The Sea Wolves, Sir Henry At Rawlinson End, Windwalker, **80**; Les Années Lumières, **81**; Gandhi, The Missionary, **82**; Sword Of The Valiant, **84**; Dust, **85**; Foreign Body, **86**; White Mischief, **87**; The Unholy, **88**.

HOWE, JAMES WONG: The Trail Of The Lonesome Pine, **23**; The Alaskan, Peter Pan, **24**; The Best People, The Charmer, **25**; The Song And Dance Man, **26**; Sorrell And Son, **27**; Four Walls, **28**; Desert Nights, **29**; The Criminal Code, **31**; The Magician, **32**; The Thin Man, Viva Villa!, **34**; Mark Of The Vampire, **35**; Fire Over England, The Prisoner Of Zenda, **37**; The Adventures Of Tom Sawyer, Algiers, Comet Over Broadway, **38**; They Made Me A Criminal, In Name Only, It Might Be You!, **39**; Abe Lincoln In Illinois, City For Conquest, Dr Ehrlich's Magic Bullet, Saturday's Children, **40**; The Strawberry Blonde, **41**; Kings Row, Yankee Doodle Dandy, **42**; Passage To Marseille, **44**; Confidential Agent, Objective Burma!, **45**; My Reputation, **46**; Body And Soul, Pursued, **47**; Mr Blandings Builds His Dream House, The Time Of Your Life, **48**; The Baron Of Arizona, The Eagle And The Hawk, Tripoli, **50**; Behave Yourself, The Brave Bulls, He Ran All The Way, The Lady Says No, **51**; Come Back Little Sheba, The Fighter, **52**; Jennifer, Main Street To Broadway, **53**; Go Man Go, **54**; Dong Kingman, Picnic, The Rose Tattoo, **55**; Death Of A Scoundrel, **56**; Drango, Sweet Smell Of Success, **57**; Bell Book And Candle, The Invisible Avenger, The Old Man And The Sea, **58**; The Last Angry Man, The Story On Page One, **59**; Song Without End, Tess Of The Storm Country, **60**; Hud, **63**; The Outrage, **64**; The Glory Guys, This Property Is Condemned, Seconds, **66**; Hombre, **67**; The Heart Is A Lonely Hunter, **68**; The Molly Maguires, **70**; Funny Lady, **75**.

HUDSON, ROCK: Fighter Squadron, **48**; The Desert Hawk, Peggy, Winchester 73, **50**; Air Cadet, The Fat Man, Iron Man, Tomahawk, **51**; Bend Of The River, Has Anybody Seen My Gal?, Here Come The Nelsons, Horizons West, The Lawless Breed, Scarlet Angel, **52**; Back To God's Country, The Golden Blade, Gun Fury, Sea Devils, Seminole, Magnificent Obsession, **53**; Bengal Brigade, Taza Son Of Cochise, **54**; Captain Lightfoot, One Desire, **55**; Giant, All That Heaven Allows, Never Say Goodbye, Written On The Wind, **56**; Battle Hymn, Something Of Value, **57**; A Farewell To Arms, The Tarnished Angels, Twilight For The Gods, **58**; Pillow Talk, This Earth Is Mine, **59**; Come September, The Last Sunset, Lover Come Back, **61**; The Spiral Road, **62**; A Gathering Of Eagles, **63**; Man's Favorite Sport?, Send Me No Flowers, Strange Bedfellows, **64**; A Very Special Favor, **65**; Seconds, **66**; Tobruk, **67**; Ice Station Zebra, A Fine Pair, **68**; The Undefeated, **69**; Darling Lili, Hornets' Nest, **70**; Pretty Maids All In A Row, **71**; Showdown, **73**; Embryo, **76**; Avalanche, **78**; The Mirror Crack'd, **80**; The Ambassador, **84**.

HUGHES, HOWARD: Hell's Angels, **30**; The Age For Love, The Front Page, **31**; Cock Of The Air, Scarface, Sky Devils, **32**; The Outlaw, **43**; Outrage, Vendetta, **50**; His Kind Of Woman, Two Tickets To Broadway, The Racket, Flying Leathernecks, **51**; The Las Vegas Story, **52**; Angel Face, **53**; Affair With A Stranger, Underwater, **54**; Son Of Sinbad, **55**; The Conqueror, **56**; Jet Pilot, **57**.

HUGHES, JOHN: National Lampoon's Vacation, **83**; Sixteen Candles, **84**; The Breakfast Club, Weird Science, **85**; Ferris Bueller's Day Off, Pretty In Pink, **86**; Planes Trains & Automobiles, **87**; She's Having A Baby, **88**; Uncle Buck, **89**; Home Alone, **90**; Curly Sue, Dutch, **91**; Home Alone 2, **92**; Dennis The Menace, **93**.

HUNTER, HOLLY: The Burning, **81**; Swing Shift, **84**; Broadcast News, End Of The Line, Raising Arizona, **87**; Always, Animal Behavior, Miss Firecracker, **89**; Once Around, **91**; The Firm, The Piano, **93**; Home For The Holidays, Copy Cat, **95**; Crash, **96**.

HUPPERT, ISABELLE: Faustine And The Beautiful Summer, **71**; Cesar And Rosalie, **72**; L'ampelopede, **73**; Les Valseuses, **74**; Aloise, Je Suis Pierre Rivière, The Judge And The Assassin, Le Grand Delire, Le Petit Marcel, Docteur Françoise Gailland, Dupont Lajoie, Rosebud, **75**; Les Indiens Sont Encore Loin, The Lacemaker, Violette Nozière, **77**; The Bronte Sisters, **79**; Retour A La Bien-aimée, Sauve Qui Peut, Every Man For Himself, Heaven's Gate, Orokseg/The Inheritance, Loulou, **80**; Coup De Torchon, Eaux Profondes, Vera Storia Della Signora Delle Camelie, Wings Of The Dove, **81**; La Passion, The Trout, **82**; Coup De Foudre, My Best Friend's Girl, The Story Of Piera, **83**; La Garce, Sincerely Charlotte, **84**; Sac De Noeuds, **85**; Cactus, **86**; The Bedroom Window, The Possessed, **87**; Migrations, Milan Noir, The Story Of Women, **88**; A Woman's Revenge, **90**; Madame Bovary, Malina, **91**; After Love, Against Oblivion, **92**; The Flood, Amateur, **94**.

HURT, JOHN: The Wild And The Willing, **62**; This Is My Street, **63**; A Man For All Seasons, **66**; The Sailor From Gibraltar, **67**; Before Winter Comes, Sinful Davey, **69**; 10 Rillington Place, In Search Of Gregory, **70**; Mr Forbush And The Penguins, **71**; The Pied Piper, **72**; Little Malcolm, **74**; The Ghoul, **75**; The Island, **76**; The Disappearance, East Of Elephant Rock, **77**; The Lord Of The Rings, Midnight Express, The Shout, Watership Down, **78**; Alien, **79**; The Elephant Man, Heaven's Gate, **80**; History Of The World Part 1, Night Crossing, **81**; Partners, The Plague Dogs, **82**; Champions, The Osterman Weekend, **83**; The Hit, Observations Under The Volcano, Success Is The Best Revenge, 1984, **84**; After Darkness, The Black Cauldron, **85**; Jake Speed, Rocinante, **86**; From The Hip, Spaceballs, **87**; Aria, La Nuit Bengali, Little Sweetheart, White Mischief, **88**; Scandal, **89**; The Field, Frankenstein Unbound, Resident Alien, Romeo-Juliet, Windprints, **90**; I Dreamt I Woke Up, King Ralph, **91**; Dark At Noon, Lapse Of Memory, **92**; Even Cowgirls Get The Blues, Monolith, Thumbelina, Rob Roy, **94**; The Darkening, **96**.

HURT, WILLIAM: Altered States, **80**; Body Heat, Eyewitness, **81**; The Big Chill, Gorky Park, **83**; Kiss Of The Spider Woman, **85**; Children Of A Lesser God, **86**; Broadcast News, **87**; The Accidental Tourist, A Time Of Destiny, **88**; Alice, I Love You To Death, **90**; The Doctor, The Plague, Until The End Of The World, **91**; Mr Wonderful, **93**, Second Best, Trial By Jury, **94**; Smoke, Jane Eyre, **95**.

HUSTON, ANJELICA: Hamlet, Sinful Davey, A Walk With Love And Death, **69**; The Last Tycoon, Swashbuckler, **76**; The Postman Always Rings Twice, **81**; Frances, **82**; The Ice Pirates, This Is Spinal Tap, **84**; Prizzi's Honor, **85**; Good To Go, **86**; The Dead, Gardens Of Stone, **87**; A Handful Of Dust, Mr North, **88**; Crimes And Misdemeanors, Enemies A Love Story, **89**; The Grifters, The Witches, **90**; The Addams Family, **91**; The Player, Addams Family Values, Manhattan Murder Mystery, **93**, The Perez Family, **95**.

HUSTON, JOHN: The Acquittal, **23**; Murders In The Rue Morgue, **32**; The Amazing Doctor Clitterhouse, Jezebel, **38**; Juarez, **39**; Dr Ehrlich's Magic Bullet, **40**; High Sierra, The Maltese Falcon, **41**; Across The Pacific, In This Our Life, **42**; Three

Strangers, **46**; Key Largo, Treasure Of The Sierra Madre, **48**; We Were Strangers, **49**; The Asphalt Jungle, **50**; The African Queen, The Red Badge Of Courage, **51**; Moulin Rouge, **52**; Beat The Devil, **53**; Moby Dick, **56**; Heaven Knows Mr Allison, **57**; The Barbarian And The Geisha, The Roots Of Heaven, **58**; The Unforgiven, **60**; The Misfits, **61**; Freud, **62**; The Cardinal, The List Of Adrian Messenger, **63**; The Night Of The Iguana, **64**; The Bible, **66**; Casino Royale, Reflections In A Golden Eye, **67**; Candy, **68**; Sinful Davey, A Walk With Love And Death, **69**; The Kremlin Letter, **70**; Fat City, The Life And Times Of Judge Roy Bean, **72**; The Mackintosh Man, **73**; Chinatown, **74**; The Man Who Would Be King, The Wind And The Lion, **75**; Phobia, **80**; Victory, **81**; Annie, **82**; Under The Volcano, **84**; Prizzi's Honor, **85**; The Dead, **87**.

HUSTON, WALTER: Gentlemen Of The Press, The Lady Lies, The Virginian, **29**; Abraham Lincoln, The Bad Man, The Virtuous Sin, **30**; The Criminal Code, The Ruling Voice, Star Witness, Woman From Monte Carlo, **31**; American Madness, The Beast Of The City, A House Divided, Kongo, Law And Order, Night Court, Rain, The Wet Parade, **32**; Ann Vickers, Gabriel Over The White House, Hell Below, The Prizefighter And The Lady, Storm At Daybreak, **33**; Keep 'Em Rolling, **34**; Transatlantic Tunnel, **35**; Dodsworth, Rhodes, **36**; Of Human Hearts, **38**; The Light That Failed, **39**; All That Money Can Buy, The Maltese Falcon, The Shanghai Gesture, Swamp Water, **41**; Always In My Heart, In This Our Life, Yankee Doodle Dandy, **42**; Edge Of Darkness, Mission To Moscow, The North Star, **43**; Dragon Seed, **44**; And Then There Were None, **45**; Dragonwyck, Duel In The Sun, **46**; The Outlaw, **47**; Summer Holiday, The Treasure Of The Sierra Madre, **48**; The Great Sinner, The Furies, **50**.

HYAMS, PETER: Busting, Our Time, **74**; Peeper, **75**; Capricorn One, **78**; Hanover Street, **79**; Outland, **81**; The Star Chamber, **83**; 2010, **84**; Running Scared, **86**; The Presidio, **88**; Narrow Margin, **90**; Stay Tuned, **92**; The Relic, **97**.

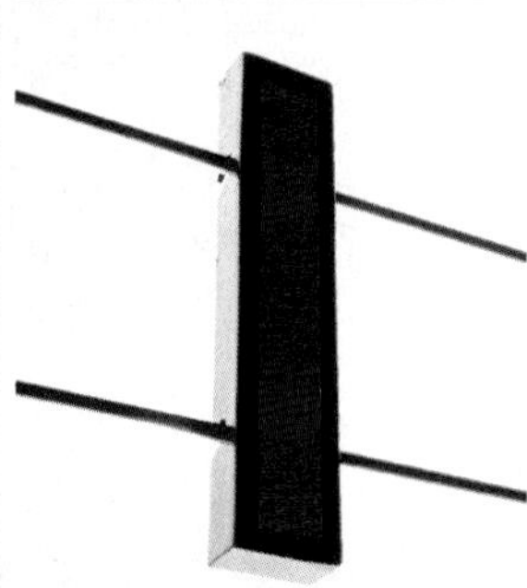

ICHIKAWA, KON: A Girl At Dojo Temple, **46**; Mr Poo, Ai-jin, **53**; The Heart, Okuman Choja, **54**; Seishun Kaidan, **55**; The Burmese Harp, Shokei No Heya, **56**; The Pit, Tohoku No Zunmu-tachi, **57**; Conflagration, **58**; Fires On The Plain, Jokyo, Nobi, Odd Obsession, The Key, **59**; Bonchi, **60**; Being Two Isn't Easy, The Outcast, **62**; An Actor's Revenge, Yukinojo Henge, Alone On The Pacific, My Enemy The Sea, **63**; Zeni No Odori, **64**; Tokyo Olympiad, **65**; Toppo Jijo No Botan Senso, **67**; Dodes'ka-den, **70**; Ai Futatabi, **71**; Matatabi, **73**; I Am A Cat, **75**; The Inugamis, Tsuma To Onna No Aida, **76**; Gokumonto, **77**; Jo-bachi, **78**; Hi No Tori, **80**; Kofuku, **82**; Sasame Yuki, **83**; Biruma No Tategoto, Ohan, **85**; Eiga Joyu, Taketori Monogatari, **87**; Amanogawa Densetsu Satsujin Jiken, Noh Mask Murders, **91**; Fusa, **93**; Yatsuhaka-mura, **96**.

INCE, THOMAS H: Custer's Last Fight, Across The Plains, The Deserter, **12**; The Italian, Typhoon, The Wrath Of The Gods, **14**; The Coward, Aloha, **15**; The Aryan, Civilization, Between Men, The Dawnmaker, **16**; The Thoroughbred, **17**; Blue Blazes, Rawden, Fuss And Feathers, String Beans, The Hired Man, Knight Of The Trail, **18**; The False Faces, The Busher, Hay Foot Straw Foot, Stepping Out, Egg Crate Wallop, 23½ Hours' Leave, **19**; Behind The Door, Black Is White, Let's Be Fashionable, Homer Comes Home, Hairpins, Home Spun Folks, **20**; Lying Lips, The Three Musketeers, Beau Revel, The Old Swimming Hole, The Cup Of Life, The Bronze Bell, **21**; Hail The Woman, Skin Deep, **22**; The Hottentott, Bell Boy 13, Human Wreckage, **23**; Christine Of The Hungry Heart, Barbara Fritchie, **24**; Free And Equal, Enticement, **25**.

INGRAM, REX: The Great Problem, **16**; Shore Acres, Hearts Are Trumps, **19**; The Conquering Power, Four Horsemen Of The Apocalypse, **21**; Trifling Women, The Prisoner Of Zenda, **22**; Where The Pavement Ends, Scaramouche, **23**; Mare Nostrum, The Magician, **26**; The Garden Of Allah, Belladonna, **27**; Baroud, **32**.

IVORY, JAMES: The Householder, **63**; Shakespeare Wallah, **65**; Bombay Talkie, **70**; Autobiography Of A Princess, The Wild Party, **75**; Roseland, **77**; The Europeans, Hullabaloo Over Georgie And Bonnie's Pictures, **78**; Jane Austen In Manhattan, **80**; Quartet, **81**; Heat And Dust, **83**; The Bostonians, **84**; A Room With A View, **86**; Maurice, **87**; Slaves Of New York, **89**; Mr & Mrs Bridge, **90**; Howards End, **92**; The Remains Of The Day, **93**, Jefferson In Paris, **95**; Surving Picasso, **96**.

IWERKS, UB: The Reluctant Dragon, **41**; The Three Caballeros, **45**; Song Of The South, **46**; Fun And Fancy Free, **47**; Melody Time, **48**; The Adventures Of Ichabod And Mr Toad, **49**; Cinderella, **50**; The Living Desert, **53**; 20,000 Leagues Under The Sea, The Vanishing Prairie, **54**; The African Lion, Davy Crockett, King Of The Wild Frontier, Lady And The Tramp, **55**; Davy Crockett And The River Pirates, The Great Locomotive Chase, **56**; 101 Dalmatians, The Parent Trap, **61**; The Birds, **63**; The Three Lives Of Thomasina, **64**.

JACKSON, GLENDA: This Sporting Life, **63**; Marat-Sade, **67**; Tell Me Lies, US, Negatives, **68**; Women In Love, **69**; The Boy Friend, Mary Queen Of Scots, The Music Lovers, Sunday Bloody Sunday, **71**; A Bequest To The Nation, A Touch Of Class, Triple Echo, **73**; The Maids, **74**; The Devil Is A Woman, Hedda, The Romantic Englishwoman, **75**; The Incredible Sarah, **76**; Nasty Habits, **77**; The Class Of Miss MacMichael, House Calls, Stevie, **78**; H.E.A.L.T.H., Lost And Found, **79**; Hopscotch, **80**; The Return Of The Soldier, **81**; Giro City, **82**; Turtle Diary, **85**; Beyond Therapy, Business As Usual, **87**; Salome's Last Dance, **88**; The Rainbow, **89**.

JANCSO, MIKLOS: A Varos Peremen, **57**; The Bells Have Gone To Rome, **58**; Izotopok A Gyogyaszatban, **59**; Az, Harom Csillag, **60**; Oldas Es Kotes, **63**; Igy Jottem, **64**; Jelenlet, **65**; The Roundup, **66**; Csend Es Kialtas, The Red And The White, Katonak, **67**; The Confrontation, Winter Wind, **69**; Il Giovane Attila, The Pacifist, Red Psalms, **71**; Meg Ker A Nep, **72**; Roma Rivuole Cesare, **73**; Szerelmem Elektra, **75**; Vizi Privati Pubbliche Virtu, **76**; Eletunket Es Verunket, **77**; Eletunket Es Verunket Part II, **79**; A Zsarnok Szive Avagy Boccaccio Magyarorszagon, **81**; Omega Omega, **82**; L'Aube, **86**; Szornyek Évadja, **87**; Jezus Krisztus Horoszkopia, **89**; God Walks Backwards, **91**.

JANNINGS, EMIL: Ossis, Tagebuch, Lulu, Wenn Vier Dasselbe Tun, **17**; The Eyes Of The Mummy, **18**; Madame Du Barry, Rose Bernd, **19**; The Brothers Karamazov, Anna Boleyn, Kohlhiesels Tochter, **20**; Danton, Loves Of Pharaoh, Vendetta, **21**; Othello, Peter The Great, **22**; Tragodie Der Liebe, **23**; Husbands Or Lovers, The Last Laugh, Quo Vadis?, Waxworks, NSU, **24**; Tartuffe, Variety, The Panther Of Paris, **25**; Faust, **26**; The Way Of All Flesh, **27**; The Last Command, The Patriot, Sins Of The Fathers, The Street Of Sin, **28**; Betrayal, **29**; The Blue Angel, Darling Of The Gods, **30**; Storms Of Passion, **31**; The Merry Monarch, **33**; Der Alte Und Der Junge Konig, **35**; Traumulus, **36**; Der Zerbrochene Krug, **37**; Robert Koch, **39**; Ohm Kruger, **41**; Die Entlassung, **42**; Altes Herz Wird Wieder Jung, **43**; Where Is Mr Belling?, **45**.

JARMAN, DEREK: Sebastiane, **76**; Jubilee, **78**; The Tempest, **79**; Caravaggio, **86**; The Last Of England, **87**; Aria, **88**; War Requiem, **89**; The Garden, **90**; Edward II, **91**; Blue, Wittgenstein, **93**.

JARMUSCH, JIM: Permanent Vacation, **82**; Stranger Than Paradise, **84**; Down By Law, **86**; Mystery Train, **89**; Night On Earth, **91**; Dead Man, **95**.

JARRE, MAURICE: The Keepers, **58**; Eyes Without A Face, Le Main Chaude, **59**; Crack In The Mirror, **60**; The Big Gamble, Le Président, **61**; Dragon Sky, Lawrence Of Arabia, The Longest Day, Sundays And Cybele, Thérèse Desqueyroux, **62**; Judex, Mort, Ou Est Ta Victoire?, Un Roi Sans Divertisement, **63**; Behold A Pale Horse, Weekend At Dunkirk, **64**; The Collector, Doctor Zhivago, To Die In Madrid, The Train, **65**; Gambit, Grand Prix, Is Paris Burning?, The Professionals, **66**; Night Of The Generals, **67**; Barbarella, Five Card Stud, The Fixer, Isadora **68**; The Damned, The Extraordinary Seaman, Topaz, **69**; El Condor, The Only Game In Town, Ryan's Daughter, **70**; Plaza Suite, Una Stagione All'Inferno, **71**; The Effect Of Gamma Rays On Man-in-the-Moon Marigolds, The Life And Times Of Judge Roy Bean, Pope Joan, Red Sun, **72**; Ash Wednesday, The Mackintosh Man, **73**; Grandeur Nature, Great Expectations, The Island At The Top Of The World, **74**; The Man Who Would Be King, Mandingo, Posse, **75**; The Last Tycoon, Shout At The Devil, **76**; March Or Die, Mohammad Messenger Of God, **77**; Prince And The Pauper, Two Solitudes, **78**; The American Success Company, **78**; The Magician Of Lublin, The Tin Drum, Winter Kills, **79**; The Black Marble, The Last Flight Of Noah's Ark, Resurrection, **80**; Circle Of Deceit, Lion Of The Desert, Taps, Shogun, **81**; Don't Cry It's Only Thunder, Firefox, Wrong Is Right, Young Doctors In Love, The Year Of Living Dangerously, **82**; Au Nom De Tous Les Miens, **83**; Dreamscape, A Passage To India, Top Secret!, **84**; The Bride, Enemy Mine, Mad Max Beyond Thunderdome, Witness, **85**; The Mosquito Coast, Solarbabies, Tai-pan, **86**; Fatal Attraction, Julia And Julia, No Way Out, **87**; Buster, Distant Thunder, Gorillas In The Mist, Moon Over Parador, Wildfire, **88**; Chances Are, Dead Poets Society, Enemies A Love Story, Prancer, **89**; After Dark My Sweet, Almost An Angel, Ghost, Jacob's Ladder, Solar Crisis, **90**; Fires Within, Only The Lonely, **91**; School Ties, The Setting Sun, **92**; Fearless, Mr Jones, **93**; The Mirror Has Two Faces, **96**.

JENNINGS, HUMPHREY: Post-haste, **34**; Story Of The Wheel, **35**; Farewell Topsails, **37**; Design For Spring, English Harvest, Penny Journey, Speaking From America, The Farm, Making Fashion, **38**; The First Days, SS Ionian, Spare Time, **39**; London Can Take It!, Spring Offensive, Welfare Of The Workers, **40**; The Heart Of Britain, Words For Battle, **41**; Listen To Britain, **42**; Fires Were Started, The Silent Village, **43**; The 80 Days, The True Story Of Lili Marlene, **44**; A Diary For Timothy, **45**; A Defeated People, **46**; The Cumberland Story, **47**; The Dim Little Island, **49**; Family Portrait, **50**.

JEWISON, NORMAN: Forty Pounds Of Trouble, The Thrill Of It All, **63**; Send Me No Flowers, **64**; The Art Of Love, The Cincinnati Kid, **65**; The Russians Are Coming!, The Russians Are Coming!, **66**; In The Heat Of The Night, **67**; The Thomas Crown Affair, **68**; Gaily Gaily, **69**; Fiddler On The Roof, **71**; Jesus Christ Superstar, **73**; Rollerball, **75**; FIST, **78**; And Justice For All, **79**; Best Friends, Fraulein Berlin, **82**; A Soldier's Story, **84**; Agnes Of God, **85**; Moonstruck, **87**; In Country, **89**; Other People's Money, **91**; Him, **93**; Only You, **94**; Bogus, **96**.

PRAWER JHABVALA, RUTH: The Householder, **63**; Shakespeare Wallah, **65**; The Guru, **69**; Bombay Talkie, **70**; Autobiography Of A Princess, **75**; Roseland, **77**; The Europeans, Hullabaloo Over Georgie And Bonnie's Pictures, **78**; Jane Austen In Manhattan, **80**; Quartet, **81**; The Courtesans Of Bombay, **82**; Heat And Dust, **83**; The Bostonians, **84**; A Room With A View, **85**; Madame Sousatzka, **88**; Mr & Mrs Bridge, **90**; Howards End, **92**; The Remains Of The Day **94**; Jefferson In Paris, **95**; Surviving Picasso, **96**.

JOFFE, ROLAND: The Killing Fields, **84**; The Mission, **86**; Fat Man And Little Boy, **89**; City Of Joy, **92**; The Scarlet Letter, **95**.

JOHNSON, CELIA: In Which We Serve, **42**; Dear Octopus, **43**; This Happy Breed, **44**; Brief Encounter, **45**; The Astonished Heart, **50**; I Believe In You, **51**; The Captain's Paradise, The Holly And The Ivy, **53**; A Kid For Two Farthings, **55**; The Good Companions, **57**; The Prime Of Miss Jean Brodie, **69**.

JOHNSON, NUNNALLY: Rough House Rosie, **27**; A Bedtime Story, **33**; Bulldog Drummond Strikes Back, Kid Millions, Moulin Rouge, **34**; The Man Who Broke The Bank At Monte Carlo; Thanks A Million, **35**; Banjo On My Knee, The Prisoner Of Shark Island, **36**; Jesse James, Rose Of Washington Square, Wife Husband And Friend, **39**; Chad Hanna, The Grapes Of Wrath, **40**; Tobacco Road, **41**; Life Begins At 8.30, The Pied Piper, Roxie Hart, **42**; Holy Matrimony, The Moon Is Down, **43**; Casanova Brown, The Keys Of The Kingdom, The Woman In The Window, **44**; Along Came Jones, **45**; The Dark Mirror, **46**; The Senator Was Indiscreet, **47**; Mr Peabody And The Mermaid, **48**; Everybody Does It, **49**; The Mudlark, Three Came Home, **50**; The Desert Fox, The Long Dark Hall, **51**; My Cousin Rachel, O Henry's Full House, Phone Call From A Stranger, We're Not Married, **52**; How To Marry A Millionaire, **53**; Black Widow, Night People, **54**; How To Be Very Very Popular, **55**; The Man In The Gray Flannel Suit, **56**; Oh Men! Oh Women!, The Three Faces Of Eve, The True Story Of Jesse James, **57**; The Man Who Understood Women, **59**; The Angel Wore Red, Flaming Star, **60**; Mr Hobbs Takes A Vacation, **62**; Take Her She's Mine, **63**; The World Of Henry Orient, **64**; The Dirty Dozen, **67**.

JOLSON, AL: The Jazz Singer, **27**; The Singing Fool, **28**; Say It With Songs, Sonny Boy, **29**; Big Boy, Mammy, **30**; Hallelujah I'm A Bum, **33**; Wonder Bar, **34**; Go Into Your Dance, **35**; The Singing Kid, **36**; Alexander's Ragtime Band, **38**; Hollywood Cavalcade, Rose Of Washington Square, Swanee River, **39**; Rhapsody In Blue, **45**.

JONES, CHUCK: Hell-bent For Election, **44**; For Sentimental Reasons, **49**; So Much So Little, **50**; Beep Prepared, Nelly's Folly, **61**; Gay Purr-ee, **63**; The Dot And The Line, **65**; The Phantom Tollbooth, **69**; Bugs Bunny Superstar, **75**; Great American Bugs Bunny Road Runner Chase, **79**; The Looney Looney Looney Bugs Bunny Movie, Uncensored Cartoons, **81**; Bugs Bunny's 3rd Movie: 1,001 Rabbit Tales, **82**; Daffy Duck's Movie: Fantastic Island, **83**; Porky Pig In Hollywood, **86**; Gremlins, **84**; Daffy Duck's Quackbusters, **89**; Gremlins 2 The New Batch, **90**.

JONES, JAMES EARL: Dr Strangelove Or: How I Learned To Stop Worrying And Love The Bomb, **64**; The Comedians, **67**; End Of The Road, The Great White Hope, **70**; The Man, **72**; Claudine, **74**; The Bingo Long Traveling All-Stars & Motor Kings, Deadly Hero, The River Niger, Swashbuckler, **76**; Exorcist II: The Heretic, The Greatest, The Last Remake Of Beau Geste, A Piece Of The Action, Star Wars, **77**; The Bushido Blade, **79**; The Empire Strikes Back, **80**; Blood Tide, Conan The Barbarian, **82**; Return Of The Jedi, **83**; City Limits, **85**; My Little Girl, Soul Man, **86**; Gardens Of Stone, Matewan, Pinocchio And The Emperor Of The Night, **87**; Coming To America, **88**; Best Of The Best, Field Of Dreams, Three Fugitives, **89**; The Ambulance, Grim Prairie Tales, The Hunt For Red October, **90**; Convicts, Scorchers, True Identity, **91**; Patriot Games, Sneakers, **92**; Excessive Force, The Meteor Man, The Sandlot, Sommersby, **93**; Clean Slate, The Lion King, **93**; Clear And Present Danger, **94**; Jefferson In Paris, **95**; Looking fro Richard, **96**.

JONES, JENNIFER: Dick Tracy's G-Men, New Frontier, **39**; The Song Of Bernadette, **43**; Since You Went Away, **44**; Love Letters, **45**; The American Creed, Cluny Brown, **46**; Duel In The Sun, **47**; Portrait Of Jennie, **48**; Madame Bovary, We Were Strangers, **49**; Gone To Earth, **50**; Carrie, Ruby Gentry, **52**; Terminal Station, Beat The Devil, **53**; Good Morning Miss Dove, Love Is A Many-Splendored Thing, **55**; The Man In The Gray Flannel Suit, **56**; The Barretts Of Wimpole Street, A Farewell To Arms, **57**; Tender Is The Night, **62**; The Idol, **66**; Angel Angel Down We Go, **69**; The Towering Inferno, **74**; Warm Nights Hot Pleasures, **80**.

JONES, QUINCY: The Boy In A Tree **60**; Mirage, The Pawnbroker, The Slender Thread, **65**; Made In Paris, Walk Don't Run, **66**; Banning, The Deadly Affair, Enter Laughing, In Cold Blood, In The Heat Of The Night, **67**; The Counterfeit Killer, A Dand[y] In Aspic, For Love Of Ivy, The Hell With Heroes, Jigsaw, Murder, The Split, **68**; Bob & Carol & Ted & Alice, Cactus Flower, The Italian Job, John And Mary, The Lost Man, Mackenna's Gold, **69**; Eggs, Last Of The Mobile Hot-Shots, Of Men And Demons, The Out-Of-Towners, They Call Me Mister Tibbs!, Up Your Teddy Bear, **70**; The Anderson Tapes, Brother John, Come Back, Charleston Blue, The Getaway, The Hot Rock, Man And Boy, The New Centurions, **72**; Toda Nudez Sera Castigada, **73**; The Wiz, **78**; The Color Purple, **85**; Boyz N The Hood, **91**.

JONES, TOMMY LEE: Love Story, **70**; Eliza's Horoscope, **72**; Jackson County Jail, **76**; Rolling Thunder, **77**; The Betsy, Eyes Of Laura Mars, **78**; Coal Miner's Daughter, **80**; Back Roads, **81**; **83**; The River Rat, **84**; Black Moon Rising, **86**; The B[ig] Town, **87**; Stormy Monday, **88**; The Package, **89**; Firebirds, **90**; Blue Sky, JFK, **91**; Under Siege, **92**; The Fugitive, Heaven And Earth, **93**; The Client, Natural Born Killers, Cobb **94**; Batman Forever, **95**, Men in Black, Volcano, **97**.

JORDAN, NEIL: Angel, **82**; The Company Of Wolves, **84**; Mona Lisa, **86**; High Spirits, **88**; We're No Angels, **89**; The Crying Game, **92**; Interview With The Vampire, **94**; Michael Collins, **96**.

KAHN, GUS: The Jazz Singer, **27**; Hit Of The Show, **28**; Whoopee!, **30**; Big City Blues, **32**; Flying Down To Rio, Storm At Daybreak, **33**; Bottoms Up, Caravan, Hollywood Party, Kid Millions, The Merry Widow, One Night Of Love, Stingaree, **34**; Escapade, Love Me Forever, Naughty Marietta, Reckless, Thanks A Million, **35**; Let'[s] Sing Again, Rose Marie, San Francisco, Three Smart Girls, **36**; Captains Courageous, A Day At The Races, The Firefly, Music For Madame, **37**; Everybody Sing, The Girl O[f] The Golden West, **38**; Balalaika, Broadway Serenade, Honolulu, Let Freedom Ring, **39**; Bitter Sweet, Marx Brothers Go West, Lillian Russell, Spring Parade, **40**; The Chocolate Soldier, Ziegfeld Girl, **41**; Broadway Rhythm, Show Business, **44**; I'll See You In My Dreams, **52**.

KAHN, MADELINE: The Dove, **68**; What's Up, Doc?, **72**; From The Mixed-Up Files Of Mrs Basil E Frankweiler, Paper Moon, **73**; Young Frankenstein, Blazing Saddles, **74**; The Adventure Of Sherlock Holmes's Smarter Brother, At Long Last Love **75**; Won Ton Ton The Dog Who Saved Hollywood, **76**; High Anxiety, **77**; The Cheap Detective, **78**; The Muppet Movie, **79**; First Family, Happy Birthday, Gemini, Simon, Wholly Moses, **80**; History Of The World Part 1, **81**; Yellowbeard, **83**; City Heat, Slapstick, **84**; Clue, **85**; Betsy's Wedding, **90**.

KANIN, GARSON: A Man To Remember, Next Time I Marry, **38**; Bachelor Mother, The Great Man Votes, They Made Her A Spy, **39**; My Favorite Wife, They Knew What They Wanted, **40**; Tom Dick And Harry, **41**; Ring Of Steel, **42**; A Lady Takes A Chance, The More The Merrier, **43**; Battle Stations, A Salute To France, **44**; The True Glory, From This Day Forward, **46**; A Double Life, **47**; Adam's Rib, **48**; Born Yesterday, **50**; The Marrying Kind, Pat And Mike, **52**; It Should Happen To You, **52**; The Girl Can't Help It, **56**; The Rat Race, **60**; The Right Approach, **61**; Dunku Cocuk, **65**; Walk Don't Run, **66**; Some Kind Of A Nut, Where It's At, **69**; Born Yesterday, **93**.

KARINA, ANNA: Le Petit Soldat, **60**; Une Femme Est Une Femme, **61**; Le Soleil Dans L'Oeil, Cleo From 5 To 7, Le Joli Mai, She'll Have To Go, Sheherazade, **62**; Three Fables Of Love, Vivre Sa Vie, Dragées Au Poivre, **63**; Un Mari A Prix Fixe, Bande A Part, La Ronde, De L'Amour, **64**; Le Voleur Du Tibidabo, Alphaville, Le Soldatesse, Suzanne Simonin, La Religieuse De Denis Diderot, Pierrot Le Fou, **65**; Made In USA, L'Amiel, The Oldest Profession, The Stranger, **67**; Tendres Requins, **68**; The Magus, Before Winter Comes, Justine, Laughter In The Dark, Le Temps De Mourir, **69**; Michael Kohlhaas – Der Rebell, **70**; L'Alliance, Rendezvous A Bray, **71**; The Salzburg Connection, Vivre Ensemble, **73**; L'Invenzione Di Morel, L'Assassin Musicien, **75**; Les Oeufs Brouillés, Also Es War So, **76**; Chinese Roulette, Bread And Chocolate, Chaussette Surprise, **78**; Just Like Home, **79**; The Story Of A Mother, **83**; L'Ami De Vincent, Hail Mary, **85**; Treasure Island, Cayenne Palace, Last Song, **87**; L'Eté Dernier A Tanger, **89**; The Abyss, The Man Who Would Be Guilty, **90**.

KARLOFF, BORIS: The Dumb Girl Of Portici, **16**; His Majesty The American, The Prince And Betty, **19**; The Courage Of Marge O'Doone, The Last Of The Mohicans, **20**; The Cave Girl, Cheated Hearts, The Hope Diamond Mystery, Without Benefit Of Clergy, **21**; The Altar Stairs, The Infidel, The Man From Downing Street, Omar The Tentmaker, A Woman Conquers, **22**; The Prisoner, **23**; Dynamite Dan, **24**; Forbidden Cargo, Lady Robin Hood, Never The Twain Shall Meet, Parisian Nights, The Prairie Wife, **25**; The Bells, The Eagle Of The Sea, Flames, Flaming Fury, The Golden Web, The Greater Glory, Her Honor The Governor, The Man In The Saddle, The Nicklehopper, Old Ironsides, **26**; Let It Rain, The Love Mart, The Meddlin' Stranger, The Phantom Buster, Soft Cushions, Tarzan And The Golden Lion, Two Arabian Knights, **27**; Burning The Wind, The Little Wild Girl, Vultures Of The Sea, **28**; Anne Against The World, Behind That Curtain, The Devil's Chaplain, The Fatal Warning, King Of The Kongo, Phantoms Of The North, Two Sisters, The Unholy Night, **29**; The Band One, Mother's Cry, The Sea Bat, The Utah Kid, **30**; Cracked Nuts, The Criminal Code, Donovan's Kid, Five Star Final, Frankenstein, Graft, Guilty Generation, I Like Your Nerve, King Of The Wild, The Mad Genius, The Public Defender, Smart Money, Tonight Or Never, Yellow Ticket, **31**; Alias The Doctor, Behind The Mask, Business And Pleasure, The Cohens And Kellys In Hollywood, The Mask Of Fu Manchu, The Miracle Man, The Mummy, Night World, The Old Dark House, Scarface, **32**; The Ghoul, **33**; The Black Cat, Gift Of Gab, House Of Rothschild, The Lost Patrol, **34**; The Black Room, The Bride Of Frankenstein, The Raven, **35**; Charlie Chan At The Opera, The Invisible Ray, Juggernaut, The Man Who Lived Again, The Walking Dead, **36**; The Man With 9 Heads, Night Key, West Of Shanghai, Mr Wong, **37**; The Invisible Menace, **38**; The Man They Could Not Hang, Mr Wong In Chinatown, Mystery Of Mr Wong, Son Of Frankenstein, Tower Of London, **39**; The Ape, Before I Hang, Black Friday, British Intelligence, Devil's Island, Doomed To Die, The Fatal Hour, The Man With Nine Lives, You'll Find Out, **40**; The Devil Commands, **41**; The Boogie Man Will Get You, **42**; The Climax, House Of Frankenstein, **44**; The Body Snatcher, Isle Of The Dead, **45**; Bedlam, **46**; Dick Tracy Meets Gruesome, Lured, The Secret Life Of Walter Mitty, Unconquered, **47**; Tap Roots, **48**; Abbott & Costello Meet The Killer Boris Karloff, **49**; The Strange Door, **51**; The Black Castle, **52**; Abbott & Costello Meet Dr Jekyll And Mr Hyde, The Hindu, Monster Of The Island, **53**; Voodoo Island, **57**; Corridors Of Blood, Frankenstein 70, Grip Of The Strangler, **58**; The Raven, The Terror, **63**; Bikini Beach, Black Sabbath, A Comedy Of Terrors, **64**; Die Monster Die!, **65**; The Ghost In The Invisible Bikini, **66**; Cauldron Of Blood, The Sorcerers, Venetian Affair, **67**; Curse Of The Crimson Altar, Targets, **68**; Isle Of The Snake People, **70**; The Fear Chamber, House Of Evil, Sinister Invasion, **71**.

KASDAN, LAWRENCE: The Empire Strikes Back, **80**; Body Heat, Raiders Of The Lost Ark, **81**; The Big Chill, Return Of The Jedi, **83**; The Accidental Tourist, **88**; I Love You To Death, **90**; Grand Canyon, **91**; Wyatt Earp, **94**; French Kiss, **95**.

KAUFMAN, PHILIP: Goldstein, **65**; Fearless Frank, **67**; The Great Northfield, Minnesota Raid, **72**; The White Dawn, **74**; The Outlaw Josie Wales, The Invasion Of The Body Snatchers, **78**; The Wanderers, **79**; Raiders Of The Lost Ark, **81**; The Right Stuff, **83**; The Unbearable Lightness Of Being, **88**; Henry And June, **90**; Rising Sun, **93**.

KAYE, DANNY: Up In Arms, **44**; Wonder Man, **45**; The Kid From Brooklyn, **46**; The Secret Life Of Walter Mitty, **47**; A Song Is Born, **48**; The Inspector General, It's A Great Feeling, **49**; On The Riviera, **51**; Hans Christian Andersen, **52**; Knock On Wood, White Christmas, **54**; The Court Jester, **56**; Me And The Colonel, Merry Andrew, **58**; The Five Pennies, **59**; On The Double, **61**; The Man From The Diner's Club, **63**; The Madwoman Of Chaillot, **69**.

KAZAN, ELIA: A Tree Grows In Brooklyn, **45**; Boomerang!, Gentleman's Agreement, The Sea Of Grass, **47**; Pinky, **49**; Panic In The Streets, **50**; A Streetcar Named Desire, **51**; Viva Zapata!, **52**; Man On A Tightrope, **53**; On The Waterfront, **54**; East Of Eden, **55**; Baby Doll, **56**; A Face In The Crowd, **57**; Wild River, **60**; Splendor In The Grass, **61**; America America, **63**; The Arrangement, **69**; The Visitors, **74**; The Last Tycoon, **76**.

KEATON, BUSTER: The Butcher Boy, Coney Island, **17**; The Cook, **18**; Convict 13, Neighbors, One Week, The Saphead, The Scarecrow, **20**; The Boat, The Goat, Hard Luck, The Haunted House, The High Sign, The Playhouse, **21**; The Paleface, The Blacksmith, Cops, Day Dreams, The Electric House, The Frozen North, My Wife's Relations, **22**; The Balloonatic, The Love Nest, Our Hospitality, The Three Ages, **23**; The Navigator, Sherlock Jr, **24**; Go West, Seven Chances, **25**; Battling Butler, **26**; College, The General, **27**; The Cameraman, Steamboat Bill Jr, **28**; The Hollywood Revue Of 1929, Spite Marriage, **29**; Doughboys, Free And Easy, **30**; Parlor Bedroom And Bath, Sidewalks Of New York, **31**; The Passionate Plumber, Speak Easily, **32**; What No Beer?, **33**; Allez Oop, Le Roi Des Champs-Elysées, **34**; The E-Flat Man, From Paducah, **35**; The Chemist, The Invader, Jail Bait, Mixed Magic, **36**; Hollywood Cavalcade, The Jones Family In Hollywood, The Jones Family And Quick Millions, Moochin' Through Georgia, Nothing But Pleasure, Pest From The West, **39**; Trouble Chaser, Li'l Abner, Pardon My Berth Marks, The Taming Of The Snood, The Villain Still Pursued Her, **40**; General Nuisance, His Ex Marks The Spot, She's Oil Mine, So You Won't Squawk, **41**; I Love You, **44**; That Night With You, That's The Spirit, El Moderno Barba Azul, **45**; God's Country, **46**; Un Duel A Mort, **48**; In The Good Old Summertime, The Lovable Cheat, You're My Everything, **49**; Sunset Boulevard, **50**; Limelight, **52**; L'Incantevole Nemica, **53**; Around The World In 80 Days, **56**; The Adventures Of Huckleberry Finn, **60**; Ten Girls Ago, **62**; It's A Mad Mad Mad Mad World, **63**; Pajama Party, The Triumph of Lester Snapwill, **64**; Beach Blanket Bingo, How To Stuff A Wild Bikini, The Railroader, Sergeant Deadhead, **65**; Due Marines E Un Generale, A Funny Thing Happened On The Way To The Forum, The Scribe, **66**.

KEATON, DIANE: Lovers And Other Strangers, **70**; The Godfather, Play It Again Sam, **72**; Sleeper, **73**; The Godfather Part II, **74**; Love And Death, **75**; Harry And Walter Go To New York, I Will I Will For Now, **76**; Annie Hall, Looking For Mr Goodbar, **77**; Interiors, **78**; Manhattan, **79**; Reds, **81**; Shoot The Moon, **82**; The Little Drummer Girl, Mrs Soffel, **84**; Crimes Of The Heart, **86**; Baby Boom, Heaven, Radio Days, **87**; The Good Mother, **88**; The GodfatherIII, **90**; Father Of The Bride, **91**; Look Who's Talking Now, Manhattan Murder Mystery, **93**; Father Of The Bride 2, **95**; First Wives Club, Marvin's Room, **96**.

KEELER, RUBY: 42nd Street, Footlight Parade, Gold Diggers Of 1933, **33**; Dames, Flirtation Walk, **34**; Go Into Your Dance, Shipmates Forever, **35**; Colleen, **36**; Ready Willing And Able, **37**; Mother Carey's Chickens, **38**; Sweetheart Of The Campus, **41**; The Phynx, **70**.

KEITEL, HARVEY: Who's That Knocking At My Door?, **68**; Street Scenes 1970, **70**; Mean Streets, **73**; Alice Doesn't Live Here Anymore, That's The Way Of The World, **75**; Buffalo Bill And The Indians, Mother Jugs & Speed, Taxi Driver, **76**; The Duellists, Welcome To LA, **77**; Blue Collar, **78**; Eagle's Wing, **79**; Bad Timing, Deathwatch, Saturn 3, **80**; The Border, That Night At Varennes, **82**; Corrupt, Exposed, Une Pierre Dans La Bouche, **83**; Falling In Love, Nemo, **84**; A Complex Plot About Women, Alleys And Crimes, **85**; The Men's Club, Off-Beat, Wise Guys, **86**; Blindside, The Inquiry, The Pick-Up Artist, **87**; The Last Temptation Of Christ, **88**; The January Man, **89**; Two Evil Eyes, The Two Jakes, **90**; Bugsy, Mortal Thoughts, Thelma & Louise, **91**; The Bad Lieutenant, Reservoir Dogs, Sister Act, **92**; Dangerous Game, The Piano, Point Of No Return, Rising Sun, The Young Americans, **93**; Monkey Trouble, Imaginary Crimes, **94**; Blue In The Face, Smoke, Clockers, **95**; From Dusk Till Dawn, **96**, City of Industry, **97**.

KELLY, GENE: For Me And My Gal, **42**; The Cross Of Lorraine, DuBarry Was A Lady, Pilot No 5, Thousands Cheer, **43**; Christmas Holiday, Cover Girl, **44**; Anchors Aweigh, **45**; Ziegfeld Follies, **46**; Living In A Big Way, **47**; The Pirate, The Three Musketeers, Words And Music, **48**; On The Town, Take Me Out To The Ball Game, **49**; Black Hand, Summer Stock, **50**; An American In Paris, It's A Big Country, **51**; The Devil Makes Three, Love Is Better Than Ever, Singin' In The Rain, **52**; Brigadoon, Seagulls Over Sorrento, Deep In My Heart, **54**; It's Always Fair Weather, **55**; Invitation To The Dance, **56**; The Happy Road, Les Girls, **57**; Marjorie Morningstar, Something For The Girls, The Tunnel Of Love, **58**; Inherit The Wind, Let's Make Love, **60**; Gigot, **62**; What A Way To Go!, **64**; A Guide For The Married Man, **67**; Les Demoiselles De Rochefort, **68**; Hello Dolly!, **69**; The Cheyenne Social Club, **70**; 40 Carats, **73**; That's Entertainment!, **74**; It's Showtime, That's Entertainment Part 2, **76**; Viva Knievel!, **77**; Xanadu, **80**; Reporters, **81**; That's Dancing!, **85**; That's Entertainment III, **94**.

KELLY, GRACE: Fourteen Hours, **51**; High Noon, **52**; Mogambo, **53**; The Bridges At Toko-ri, The Country Girl, Dial M For Murder, Green Fire, Rear Window, **54**; To Catch A Thief, **55**; High Society, The Swan, **56**; Invitation To Monte Carlo, **59**; The Poppy Is Also A Flower, **66**.

KERN, JEROME: Music In The Air, **34**; I Dream Too Much, Reckless, Roberta, Sweet Adeline, **35**; Show Boat, Swing Time, **36**; High Wide And Handsome, When You're In Love, **37**; Joy Of Living, **38**; One Night In The Tropics, **40**; Lady Be Good, Sunny, **41**; You Were Never Lovelier, **42**; Song Of Russia, **43**; Broadway Rhythm, Can't Help Singing, Cover Girl, **44**; Centennial Summer, Till The Clouds Roll By, **46**; Lovely To Look At, **52**.

KERR, DEBORAH: Penn Of Pennsylvania, Hatter's Castle, Love On The Dole, Major Barbara, **41**; The Day Will Dawn, **42**; The Life And Death Of Colonel Blimp, **43**; Perfect Strangers, **45**; I See A Dark Stranger, **46**; Black Narcissus, The Hucksters, If Winter Comes, **47**; Edward My Son, **49**; King Solomon's Mines, Please Believe Me, **50**; Quo Vadis?, **51**; The Prisoner Of Zenda, **52**; Dream Wife, From Here To Eternity, Julius Caesar, Thunder In The East, Young Bess, **53**; The End Of The Affair, **55**; The King And I, The Proud And Profane, Tea And Sympathy, **56**; An Affair To Remember, Heaven Knows Mr Allison, **57**; Bonjour Tristesse, Separate Tables, **58**; Beloved Infidel, Count Your Blessings, The Journey, **59**; The Grass Is Greener, The Sundowners, **60**; The Innocents, The Naked Edge, **61**; The Chalk Garden, The Night Of The Iguana, **64**; Marriage On The Rocks, **65**; Casino Royale, Eye Of The Devil, **67**; Prudence And The Pill, **68**; The Arrangement, The Gypsy Moths, **69**; The Assam Garden, **85**.

KIESLOWSKI, KRZYSZTOF: Personnel, **75**; Spokoj, **76**; Camera Buff, **79**; Blind Chance, **82**; Bez Konca, No End, **84**; A Short Film About Love, A Short Film About Killing, **88**; City Life, **90**; The Double Life Of Veronique, **91**; Our Hollywood Education, **92**; Three Colours: Blue, **93**; White, Red, **94**.

KING, HENRY: A Perilous Ride, **13**; Who Pays?, **15**; The Climber, **17**; Hobbs In A Hurry, **18**; 23½ Hours' Leave, A Fugitive From Matrimony, Haunting Shadows, A Sporting Chance, Where The West Begins, **19**; One Hour Before Dawn, Uncharted Channels, The White Dove, **20**; The Mistress Of Shenstone, Salvage, Tol'able David, The Sting Of The Lash, When We Were Twenty-one, **21**; The Bond Boy, The Seventh Day, Sonny, **22**; Fury, The White Sister, **23**; Romola, **24**; Any Woman, Sackcloth And Scarlet, Stella Dallas, **25**; Partners Again, With Potash And Perlmutter, The Winning Of Barbara Worth, **26**; Magic Flame, **27**; The Woman Disputed, **28**; She Goes To War, **29**; The Eyes Of The World, Hell Harbor, Lightnin', **30**; Merely Mary Ann, Over The Hill, **31**; The Woman In Room 13, **32**; I Loved You Wednesday, State Fair, **33**; Carolina, Marie Galante, **34**; One More Spring, Way Down East, **35**; The Country Doctor, Lloyd's Of London, Ramona, **36**; Seventh Heaven, **37**; Alexander's Ragtime Band, In Old Chicago, **38**; Jesse James, Stanley And Livingstone, **39**; Chad Hanna, Little Old New York, Maryland, **40**; Remember The Day, A Yank In The Raf, **41**; The Black Swan, **42**; The Song Of Bernadette, **43**; Wilson, **44**; A Bell For Adano, **45**; Margie, **46**; Captain From Castile, **47**; Deep Waters, **48**; Twelve O'Clock High, Prince Of Foxes, **49**; The Gunfighter, **50**; David And Bathsheba, I'd Climb The Highest Mountain, **51**; O Henry's Full House, The Snows Of Kilimanjaro, Wait 'Til The Sun Shines, Nellie, **52**; King Of The Khyber Rifles, **53**; Love Is A Many Splendored Thing, Untamed, **55**; Carousel, **56**; The Sun Also Rises, **57**; The Bravados, **58**; Beloved Infidel, This Earth Is Mine, **59**; Tender Is The Night, **62**.

KINGSLEY, BEN: Fear Is The Key, **72**; Gandhi, **82**; Betrayal, **83**; Sleeps Six, **84**; Harem, Turtle Diary, **85**; The Secret Of The Sahara, **86**; Maurice, Testimony, **87**; Pascali's Island, Without A Clue, **88**; Slipstream, **89**; The Children, The Fifth Monkey, A Violent Life, **90**; Bugsy, The Necessary Love, **91**; Sneakers, **92**; Dave, Schindler's List, Searching For Bobby Fischer, **93**; Death And The Maiden, **94**; Species, **95**.

KINSKI, KLAUS: Ludwig II, **55**; Das Geheimnis Der Gelben Narzissen, Die Toten Augen Von London, **61**; The Counterfeit Traitor, Das Gasthaus An Der Themse, Die Tur Mit Den Sieben Schlossen, **62**; Das Indische Tuch, Il Mistero Del Tempio Indiano, Kali-yug La Dea Della Vendetta, **63**; Der Letzte Ritt Nach Santa Cruz, Traitor's Gate, Wartezimmer Zum Jenseits, **64**; Doctor Zhivago, Estambul/The Man From Istanbul, Last Of The Renegades, The Pleasure Girls, **65**; Das Geheimnis Der Gelben Monche, For A Few Dollars More, Our Man In Marrakesh, **66**; A Bullet For The General, Five Golden Dragons, L'Uomo L'Orgoglio La Vendetta, The Million Eyes Of Su-muru, Mister Zehn Prozent Miezen Und Moneten, Circus Of Fear, **67**; Cinque Per L'Inferno, Coplan Sauve Sa Peau, Due Volte Giuda, Grand Slam, Marquis De Sade: Justine, Sam Cooper's Gold, Ognuno Per Se, **68**; E Dio Disse A Caino, I Bastardi, Il Dito Nella Piaga, La Legge Dei Gangsters, Sono Sartana Il Vostro Becchino, **69**; Appuntamente Col Disonore, Count Dracula, I Leopardi Di Churchill, La Peau De Torpedo, Wie Kommt Ein So Reizendes Madchen Zu Diesem Gewerbe?, **70**; La Bestia Uccide A Sangue Freddo, La Vendetta E Un Piatto Che Si Serve Freddo, Nella Stretta Morsa Del Ragno, **71**; Aguirre: The Wrath Of God, Il Venditore Di Morte, **72**; Il Mio Nome E Shanghai Joe, La Mano Spietata Della Legge, La Morte Ha Sorisso All'Assassino, Aguirre The Wrath Of God, **73**; Le Amanti Del Mostro, Le Orme, Who Stole The Shah's Jewels?, **74**; Das Netz, Lifespan, Un Genio Due Compari, Un Pollo, **75**; Jack The Ripper, **76**; Madame Claude, Operation Thunderbolt, **77**; Nosferatu The Vampyre, La Chanson De Roland, Woyzeck, Zoo-Zéro, **78**; Haine, **79**; La Femme-Enfant, Schizoid, **80**; Buddy Buddy, Les Fruits De La Passion, **81**; Andrc Burden Of Dreams, Fitzcarraldo, Love And Money, The Soldier, Venom, **82**; The Little Drummer Girl, The Secret Diary Of Sigmund Freud, **84**; Titan Find, Kommando Leopard, **85**; Codename: Wildgeese, Crawlspace, El Caballero Del Dragon, **86**; Nosferatu A Venezia, **87**; Slave Coast, **88**; Il Grande Cacciatore, **90**.

KLINE, KEVIN: Sophie's Choice, **82**; The Big Chill, The Pirates Of Penzance, **83**; Silverado, **85**; Violets Are Blue, **86**; Cry Freedom, **87**; A Fish Called Wanda, **88**; The January Man, **89**; I Love You To Death, **90**; Grand Canyon, Soapdish, **91**; Chaplin, Consenting Adults, **92**; Dave, The Nutcracker, **93**; Princess Caraboo, **94**; French Kiss, **95**; Fierce Creatures, In and OUT, The Ice Storm, **97**.

KONCHALOVSKY, ANDREI: The First Teacher, **65**; Asya's Happiness, **67**; Kotoray Lyubila Da Nie Vshla Zamuzh, **68**; A Nest Of Gentlefolk, **69**; Uncle Vanya, **71**; Romance For Lovers, **74**; Siberiade, **79**; Maria's Lovers, **84**; Runaway Train, **85**; Due For One, **86**; Shy People, **87**; Tango & Cash, **89**; Homer & Eddie, **90**; The Inner Circle, **91**; Raiba My Chicken, **94**.

KORDA, ALEXANDER: The Private Life Of Helen Of Troy, The Stolen Bride, Madam Wants No Children, **27**; A Modern Du Barry, The Night Watch, The Yellow Lily, **28**; Her Private Life, Love And The Devil, The Squall, **29**; Lilies Of The Field, The Princess And The Plumber, Women Everywhere, **30**; Marius, Die Manner Um Lucie, **31**; Service For Ladies, That Night In London, Wedding Rehearsal, **32**; Counsel's Opinion, The Girl From Maxim's, The Private Life Of Henry VIII, Strange Evidence, **33**; Catherine The Great, The Private Life Of Don Juan, **34**; Moscow Nights, Sanders Of The River, The Scarlet Pimpernel, The Ghost Goes West, **35**; The Man Who Could Work Miracles, Men Are Not Gods, Rembrandt, Things To Come, **36**; Elephant Boy, Farewell Again, Fire Over England, Knight Without Armour, Over The Moon, Paradise For Two, The Squeaker, 21 Days, A Storm In A Teacup, **37**; Action For Slander, The Challenge, The Divorce Of Lady X, The Drum, Prison Without Bars, The Return Of The Scarlet Pimpernel, South Riding, **38**; The Four Feathers, The Lion Has Wings, **39**; The Thief Of Bagdad, **40**; Lydia, Lady Hamilton, **41**; Jungle Book, To B Or Not To Be, **42**; Perfect Strangers, **45**; A Man About The House, Mine Own Executioner, Night Beat, **47**; Anna Karenina, Bonnie Prince Charlie, The Fallen Idol, An Ideal Husband, **48**; The Cure For Love, That Dangerous Age, Interrupted Journey, The Last Days Of Dolwyn, Saints And Sinners, The Small Back Room, The Thir Man, **49**; The Angel With The Trumpet, Seven Days To Noon, Gone To Earth, The Winslow Boy, The Wooden Horse, **50**; Cry The Beloved Country, Outcast Of The Islands, Tales Of Hoffman, **51**; The Sound Barrier, Folly To Be Wise, Who Goes There?, The Ringer, **52**; The Captain's Paradise, The Story Of Gilbert And Sullivan, The Holly And The Ivy, The Man Between, Mr Denning Drives North, Twice Upon A Time **53**; Aunt Clara, The Heart Of The Matter, Hobson's Choice, The Teckman Mystery, Three Cases Of Murder, **54**; The Belles Of St Trinians, The Constant Husband, The Deep Blue Sea, I Am A Camera, A Kid For Two Farthings, The Man Who Loved Redheads, Raising A Riot, Richard III, Summer Madness, **55**; Storm Over The Nile, **56**; Smiley, **57**.

KORDA, ZOLTAN: Women Everywhere, **30** Pa Puts His Foot Down, Cash/For Love Or Money, **34**; Sanders Of The River, **35**; Forge Me-Not, **36**; Elephant Boy, **37**; The Drum, **38**; The Four Feathers, **39**; The Thief Of Bagdad, **40**; Jungle Book, **42**; Sahara, **43**; Counter-Attack, **45**; The Macomber Affair, A Woman's Vengeance, **47**; Cry The Beloved Country, **51**; Storm Over The Nile, **56**.

KORNGOLD, ERICH WOLFGANG: Noah's Ark, **29**; Captain Blood, A Midsumme Night's Dream, **35**; Give Us This Night, Anthony Adverse, The Green Pastures, Rose C The Rancho, **36**; Another Dawn, The nce And The Pauper, **37**; The ventures Of Robin Hood, **38**; Juarez, The ivate Lives Of Elizabeth And Essex, **39**; e Sea Hawk, **40**; The Sea Wolf, **41**; Kings ɔw, **42**; The Constant Nymph, **43**; etween Two Worlds, **44**.

RASNA, NORMAN: Hollywood peaks, **32**; The Richest Girl In The World, **4**; Four Hours To Kill, Hands Across e Table, **35**; Wife Vs Secretary, **36**; Big ty, King And The Chorus Girl, **37**; The rst 100 Years, Three Loves Has Nancy, **38**; achelor Mother, **39**; It's A Date, **40**; Mr d Mrs Smith, The Flame Of New Orleans, e Devil And Miss Jones, It Started With e, **41**; Princess O'Rouke, **43**; Practically ours, **45**; The Big Hangover, **50**; The ue Veil, Behave Yourself, **51**; White hristmas, **54**; The Ambassador's aughter, Bundle Of Joy, **56**; Indiscreet, **58**; ho Was That Lady?, Let's Make Love, **0**; My Geisha, **62**; Sunday In New York, I'd ather Be Rich, **64**.

RAUSS, WERNER: The Cabinet Of Dr aligari, **19**; All For A Woman, Lady Hamilton, hattered, **21**; The Burning Earth, thello, **22**; The Treasure, **23**; Decameron ights, A Midsummer Night's Dream, axworks, **24**; Jealousy, The Joyless Street, artuffe, **25**; Nana, Secrets Of A Soul, e Student Of Prague, **26**; Looping The oop, **28**; Napoleon A St Hélène, **29**; orck, **31**; The Man Without A Name, **32**; enna Burgtheater, **36**; Robert Kochas, **9**; Jud Süss, **40**; Zwischen Himmel Und de, **42**; Paracelsus, **42**; Der Fallende ern, **50**; Sohn Ohne Heimat, **55**.

UBRICK, STANLEY: Fear And Desire, **3**; Killer's Kiss, **55**; The Killing, **56**; Paths Glory, **57**; Spartacus, **60**; Lolita, **62**; Strangelove Or: How I Learned To Stop orrying And Love The Bomb, **64**; 2001: Space Odyssey, **68**; A Clockwork Orange, **1**; Barry Lyndon, **75**; The Shining, **80**; ll Metal Jacket, **87**; Eyes Wide Shut, **97**.

UROSAWA, AKIRA: Judo Saga, **43**; do Saga II, **45**; No Regrets For Our Youth, **6**; Subarashiki Nichiyobi, **47**; Drunken ngel, **48**; The Silent Duel, Stray Dog, **49**; ashomon, Shuban, **50**; The Idiot, **51**; iru, **52**; The Seven Samurai, **54**; Live In ear, Record Of A Living Being, **55**; The ower Depths, Throne Of Blood, **57**; The dden Fortress, **58**; The Bad Sleep ell, **60**; Yojimbo, **61**; Sanjuro, **62**; The utrage, **64**; Red Beard, **65**; Dodes'ka- en, **70**; Dersu Uzala, **75**; Kagemusha, **80**; an, **85**; Dreams, **90**; Rhapsody In ugust, **91**; Madadayo, **93**.

A CAVA, GREGORY: Womanhandled, **5**; Let's Get Married, Say It Again, So's Your ld Man, **26**; The Gay Defender, aradise For Two, Running Wild, Tell It To weeney, **27**; Feel My Pulse, Half A ride, **28**; Big News, His First Command, aturday's Children, **29**; Laugh And Get ch, Smart Woman, **31**; The Age Of Consent, he Half-Naked Truth, Symphony Of Six illion, **32**; Bed Of Roses, Gabriel Over The hite House, **33**; Affairs Of Cellini, allant Lady, What Every Woman Knows, **34**; rivate Worlds, She Married Her Boss, **5**; My Man Godfrey, **36**; Stage Door, **37**; h Avenue Girl, **39**; The Primrose Path, **0**; Unfinished Business, **41**; Lady In A Jam, **2**; Living In A Big Way, **47**.

ADD, ALAN: The Goldwyn Follies, **38**; easts Of Berlin, Rulers Of The Sea, **39**; aptain Caution, Gangs Of Chicago, The reen Hornet, Her First Romance, The owards Of Virginia, In Old Missouri, ight Of The Western Stars, Meet The Missus, hose Were The Days, Wildcat Bus, **40**; he Black Cat, Cadet Girl, Citizen Kane, Paper Bullets, Great Guns, Petticoat Politics, The Reluctant Dragon, **41**; The Glass Key, Joan Of Paris, Lucky Jordan, Star Spangled Rhythm, This Gun For Hire, **42**; China, **43**; And Now Tomorrow, **44**; Duffy's Tavern, Salty O'Rourke, **45**; The Blue Dahlia, OSS, Two Years Before The Mast, **46**; Calcutta, My Favorite Brunette, Variety Girl, Wild Harvest, **47**; Beyond Glory, Saigon, Whispering Smith, **48**; Chicago Deadline, The Great Gatsby, **49**; Branded, Captain Carey USA, **50**; Appointment With Danger, Red Mountain, **51**; The Iron Mistress, **52**; Botany Bay, Desert Legion, The Red Beret, Shane, Thunder In The East, **53**; The Black Knight, Drum Beat, Hell Below Zero, Saskatchewan, **54**; Hell On Frisco Bay, The McConnell Story, **55**; Santiago, **56**; The Big Land, Boy On A Dolphin, **57**; The Badlanders, The Deep Six, The Proud Rebel, **58**; The Man In The Net, **59**; All The Young Men, Guns Of The Timberland, One Foot In Hell, **60**; Duel Of Champions, **61**; 13 West Street, **62**; The Carpetbaggers, **64**.

LAEMMLE, CARL: Blind Husbands, **19**; Colorada, **21**; The Flirt, Foolish Wives, The Altar Stairs, Another Man's Shoes, Broad Daylight, **22**; The Love Brand, The Hunchback Of Notre Dame, **23**; Fool's Highway, The Gaiety Girls, Excitement, **24**; The Phantom Of The Opera, Daring Days, **25**; The Fighting Peacemaker, **26**; Back To God's Country, Beware Of Widows, The Denver Dude, **27**; The Count Of Ten, The Cohens And The Kellys In Paris, **28**; Broadway, College Love, **29**; All Quiet On The Western Front, The Boudoir Diplomat, The King Of Jazz, A Lady Surrenders, **30**; Dracula, Frankenstein, **31**; The Mummy, **32**; The Invisible Man, Only Yesterday, **33**; Imitation Of Life, **34**; Bride Of Frankenstein, The Good Fairy, **35**; Show Boat, **36**.

LAKE, VERONICA: All Women Have Secrets, Sorority House, **39**; Forty Little Mothers, Young As You Feel, **40**; Hold Back The Dawn, I Wanted Wings, Sullivan's Travels, **41**; The Glass Key, I Married A Witch, Star Spangled Rhythm, This Gun For Hire, **42**; So Proudly We Hail!, **43**; The Hour Before The Dawn, **44**; Bring On The Girls, Duffy's Tavern, Hold That Blonde, Miss Susie Slagle's, Out Of This World, **45**; The Blue Dahlia, **46**; Ramrod, Variety Girl, **47**; Isn't It Romantic?, Saigon, The Sainted Sisters, **48**; Slattery's Hurricane, **49**; Stronghold, **51**; Footsteps In The Snow, **66**; Flesh Feast, **70**.

LAMARR, HEDY: Geld Auf Der Strasse, **30**; Die Koffer Des Herrn OF, Mein Brauchte Kein Geld, Sturm Im Wasserglas, **31**; Ecstasy, **33**; Algiers, **38**; Lady Of The Tropics, **39**; Boom Town, Comrade X, I Take This Woman, **40**; Come Live With Me, HM Pulham, Esq, Ziegfeld Girl, **41**; Crossroads, Tortilla Flat, White Cargo, **42**; The Heavenly Body, **43**; The Conspirators, Experiment Perilous, **44**; Her Highness And The Bellboy, **45**; Strange Woman, **46**; Dishonored Lady, **47**; Let's Live A Little, **48**; Samson And Delilah, **49**; Copper Canyon, A Lady Without Passport, **50**; My Favorite Spy, **51**; The Face That Launched A Thousand Ships, **53**; The Story Of Mankind, **57**; The Female Animal, **58**; Instant Karma, **90**.

LAMOUR, DOROTHY: The Jungle Princess, The Stars Can't Be Wrong, **36**; College Holiday, High Wide And Handsome, The Hurricane, The Last Train From Madrid, Swing High Swing Low, Thrill Of A Lifetime, **37**; The Big Broadcast Of 38, Her Jungle Love, Spawn Of The North, Tropic Holiday, **38**; Disputed Passage, Man About Town, St Louis Blues, **39**; Chad Hanna, Johnny Apollo, Moon Over Burma, Road To Singapore, Typhoon, **40**; Aloma Of The South Seas, Caught In The Draft, Road To Zanzibar, **41**; Beyond The Blue Horizon, The Fleet's In, Road To Morocco, Star Spangled Rhythm, **42**; Dixie, Riding High, They Got Me Covered, **43**; And The Angels Sing, Rainbow Island, **44**; Duffy's Tavern, Masquerade In Mexico, A Medal For Benny, **45**; Road To Utopia, **46**; My Favorite Brunette, Road To Rio, Variety Girl, Wild Harvest, **47**; The Girl From Manhattan, Lulu Belle, On Our Merry Way, **48**; The Lucky Stiff, Manhandled, Slightly French, **49**; Here Comes The Groom, **51**; The Greatest Show On Earth, **52**; Road To Bali, **53**; Road To Hong Kong, **62**; Donovan's Reef, **63**; Pajama Party, **64**; The Phynx, **70**; Won Ton Ton The Dog Who Saved Hollywood, **76**; Creepshow 2, **87**.

LANCASTER, BURT: The Killers, **46**; Brute Force, Desert Fury, I Walk Alone, Variety Girl, **47**; All My Sons, Kiss The Blood Off My Hands, Sorry Wrong Number, **48**; Criss Cross, Rope Of Sand, **49**; The Flame And The Arrow, Mister 880, **50**; Jim Thorpe All American, Ten Tall Men, Vengeance Valley, **51**; Come Back Little Sheba, The Crimson Pirate, The First Time, **52**; From Here To Eternity, His Majesty O'Keefe, South Sea Woman, **53**; Apache, Vera Cruz, **54**; The Kentuckian, The Rose Tattoo, **55**; The Rainmaker, Trapeze, **56**; Gunfight At The OK Corral, Sweet Smell Of Success, **57**; Run Silent Run Deep, Separate Tables, **58**; The Devil's Disciple, **59**; Elmer Gantry, The Unforgiven, **60**; Judgment At Nuremberg, The Young Savages, **61**; Birdman Of Alcatraz, **62**; A Child Is Waiting, The Leopard, The List Of Adrian Messenger, **63**; Seven Days In May, **64**; The Hallelujah Trail, The Train, **65**; The Professionals, **66**; The Scalphunters, The Swimmer, **68**; Castle Keep, The Gypsy Moths, **69**; Airport, **70**; Lawman, Valdez Is Coming, **71**; Ulzana's Raid, **72**; Executive Action, Scorpio, **73**; The Midnight Man, **74**; Buffalo Bill And The Indians, Victory At Entebbe, **76**; 1900, The Cassandra Crossing, Conversation Piece, The Island Of Dr Moreau, Twilight's Last Gleaming, **77**; Go Tell The Spartans, **78**; Zulu Dawn, **79**; Atlantic City, Cattle Annie And Little Britches, **80**; La Pelle, **81**; Local Hero, The Osterman Weekend, **83**; Little Treasure, **85**; Tough Guys, **86**; Il Giorno Prima, **87**; Rocket Gibraltar, **88**; Field Of Dreams, La Boutique De L'Orfèvre, **89**.

LANDIS, JOHN: Schlock, **73**; Kentucky Fried Movie, **77**; National Lampoon's Animal House, **78**; The Blues Brothers, **80**; An American Werewolf In London, **81**; Trading Places, Twilight Zone – The Movie, **83**; Into The Night, Spies Like Us, **85**; Three Amigos!, **86**; Coming To America, **88**; Oscar, **91**; Body Chemistry 2, Voice Of A Stranger, Innocent Blood, **92**; Beverly Hills Cop III, **94**; The Stupids, **96**; Blues Brothers 2000, **97**.

LANG, FRITZ: Der Herr Der Liebe, Die Frau Mit Den Orchideen, Die Pest In Florenz, The Half Caste, Harakiri, **19**; Das Wandernde Bild, **20**; Der Müde Tod/Destiny, The Indian Tomb, Vier Um Die Frau, **21**; Dr Mabuse, **22**; Die Nibelungen, **24**; Metropolis, **26**; Spies, **28**; Woman In The Moon, **29**; M, **31**; The Testament Of Dr Mabuse, **33**; Liliom, **34**; Fury, **36**; You Only Live Once, **37**; You And Me, **38**; The Return Of Frank James, **40**; Man Hunt, Western Union, **41**; Hangmen Also Die, **43**; Ministry Of Fear, The Woman In The Window, Scarlet Street, **45**; Cloak And Dagger, **46**; Secret Beyond The Door, **48**; American Guerrilla In The Philippines, The House By The River, **50**; Clash By Night, Rancho Notorious, **52**; The Big Heat, The Blue Gardenia, **53**; Human Desire, **54**; Moonfleet, **55**; Beyond A Reasonable Doubt, While The City Sleeps, **56**; Journey To The Lost City, **58**; The Indian Tomb, **59**; The Thousand Eyes Of Dr Mabuse, **60**; Contempt, **63**.

LANGDON, HARRY: Boobs In The Wood, Feet Of Mud, His Marriage Wow, The Luck O' The Foolish, Picking Peaches, The Sea Squawk, Shanghaied Lovers, **24**; There He Goes, **25**; Fiddlesticks, Soldier Man, The Strong Man, Tramp Tramp Tramp, **26**; His First Flame, Long Pants, Three's A Crowd, **27**; The Chaser, Heart Trouble, **28**; Hotter Than Hot, **29**; The Big Kick, The King, See America Thirst, A Soldier's Plaything, **30**; Hallelujah I'm A Bum, Hooks And Jabs, Knight Duty, My Weakness, Tired Feet, **33**; Atlantic Adventure, **35**; A Doggone Mixup, He Loved An Actress, Sue My Lawyer, There Goes My Heart, **38**; Zenobia, **39**; A Chump At Oxford, Misbehaving Saps At Sea, **40**; All American Co-Ed, Double Trouble, Road Show, **41**; House Of Errors, Piano Mooners, Tyreman Spare My Tyres, What Makes Lizzy Dizzy, **42**; Blonde And Groom, Here Comes Mr Zerk, Spotlight Scandals, **43**; Block Busters, Hot Rhythm, Mopey Dope, **44**; Snooper Service, Swingin' On A Rainbow, **45**.

LANGE, JESSICA: King Kong, **76**; All That Jazz, **79**; How To Beat The High Co$t Of Living, **80**; The Postman Always Rings Twice, **81**; Frances, Tootsie, **82**; Country, **84**; Sweet Dreams, Crimes Of The Heart, **85**; Everybody's All-American, Far North, **88**; Music Box, **89**; Men Don't Leave, **90**; Cape Fear, **91**; Night And The City, **92**; Blue Sky, **94**; Rob Roy, **95**; Losing Isaiah, **95**.

LANSBURY, ANGELA: Gaslight, National Velvet, **44**; The Picture Of Dorian Gray, **45**; The Harvey Girls, The Hoodlum Saint, Till The Clouds Roll By, **46**; If Winter Comes, The Private Affairs Of Bel Ami, **47**; State Of The Union, Tenth Avenue Angel, The Three Musketeers, **48**; The Red Danube, Samson And Delilah, **49**; Kind Lady, **51**; Mutiny, **52**; Remains To Be Seen, **53**; Key Man, **54**; A Lawless Street, The Purple Mask, **55**; The Court Jester, Please Murder Me, **56**; The Long Hot Summer, The Reluctant Debutante, **58**; Summer Of The 17th Doll, **59**; A Breath Of Scandal, The Dark At The Top Of The Stairs, **60**; Blue Hawaii, **61**; All Fall Down, The Manchurian Candidate, **62**; In The Cool Of The Day, **63**; Dear Heart, The World Of Henry Orient, **64**; The Amorous Adventures Of Moll Flanders, The Greatest Story Ever Told, Harlow, **65**; Mister Buddwing, **66**; Something For Everyone, **70**; Bedknobs And Broomsticks, **71**; Death On The Nile, **78**; The Lady Vanishes, **79**; The Mirror Crack'd, **80**; The Pirates Of Penzance, **83**; The Company Of Wolves, **84**.

LANSING, SHERRY: Kramer Vs Kramer, The China Syndrome, **79**; Firstborn, Racing With The Moon, **84**; Fatal Attraction, **87**; The Accused, **88**; Black Rain, **89**; School Ties, **92**; Indecent Proposal, **93**; Forrest Gump, **94**.

LANZA, MARIO: That Midnight Kiss, **49**; The Toast Of New Orleans, **50**; The Great Caruso, **51**; Because You're Mine, **52**; The Student Prince, **54**; Serenade, **56**; The Seven Hills Of Rome, **58**; For The First Time, **59**.

LASSALLY, WALTER: Thursday's Children, **54**; The Girl In Black, The Passing Stranger, **55**; Together, **56**; A Matter Of Dignity, **57**; Day Shall Dawn, We Are The Lambeth Boys, **59**; Beat Girl, **60**; Electra, A Taste Of Honey, **61**; The Loneliness Of The Long Distance Runner, **62**; Tom Jones, **63**; The Peaches, Psyche 59, Zorba The Greek, **64**; The Day The Fish Came Out, **67**; Joanna, Oedipus The King, **68**; The Adding Machine, Twinky, Three Into Two Won't Go, **69**; Something For Everyone, **70**; To Kill A Clown, Savages, **72**; The Seaweed Children, **73**; Autobiography Of A Princess, The Wild Party, **75**; Ansichten Eine Clowns, **76**; Die Frau Gegenüber, **78**; Hullabaloo Over Georgie And Bonnie's Pictures, Something Short Of Paradise, **79**; The Blood Of Hussain, **80**; Memoirs Of A Survivor, **81**; Heat And Dust, **82**; Private School, The Bostonians, **84**; The Perfect Murder, **88**; The Ballad Of The Sad Cafe, Diary Of A Madman, **91**.

LAUGHTON, CHARLES: Bluebottles, Day Dreams, **28**; Comets, Piccadilly, **29**; Wanted Men, **30**; Down River, **31**; Devil And The Deep, If I Had A Million, The Old Dark House, Payment Deferred, The Sign Of The Cross, **32**; Island Of Lost Souls, The Private Life Of Henry VIII, White Woman, **33**; The Barretts Of Wimpole Street, **34**; Les Misérables, Mutiny On The Bounty, Ruggles Of Red Gap, **35**; Rembrandt, **36**; St Martin's Lane, **38**; The Hunchback Of Notre Dame, Jamaica Inn, **39**; They Knew What They Wanted, **40**; It Started With Eve, **41**; Stand By For Action, Tales Of Manhattan, The Tuttles Of Tahiti, **42**; Forever And A Day, The Man From Down Under, This Land Is Mine, **43**; The Canterville Ghost, The Suspect, **44**; Captain Kidd, **45**; Because Of Him, **46**; Arch Of Triumph, The Big Clock, **47**; The Girl From Manhattan, The Paradine Case, **48**; The Bribe, The Man On The Eiffel Tower, **49**; The Blue Veil, The Strange Door, **51**; Abbott And Costello Meet Captain Kidd, O Henry's Full House, **52**; Salome, Young Bess, **53**; Hobson's Choice, **54**; Night Of The Hunter, **55**; Witness For The Prosecution, **57**; Spartacus, Under Ten Flags, **60**; Advise And Consent, **62**.

LAUNDER, FRANK: Children Of Chance, The W Plan, **30**; How He Lied To Her Husband, **31**; Josser In The Army, After Office Hours, **32**; Facing The Music, Happy, You Made Me Love You, **33**; Those Were The Days, **34**; Emil And The Detectives, Get Off My Foot, Educated Evans, **36**; Oh Mr Porter!, **37**; The Lady Vanishes, **38**; A Girl Must Live, **39**; Inspector Hornleigh Goes To It, Night Train To Munich, **40**; Partners In Crime, Uncensored, The Young Mr Pitt, **42**; Millions Like Us, We Dive At Dawn, **43**; Two Thousand Women, **44**; The Rake's Progress, **45**; I See A Dark Stranger, Green For Danger, **46**; Captain Boycott, **47**; London Belongs To Me, **48**; The Blue Lagoon, **49**; State Secret, The Happiest Days Of Your Life, **50**; Lady Godiva Rides Again, **51**; Folly To Be Wise, **52**; The Story Of Gilbert And Sullivan, **53**; The Belles Of St Trinian's, **54**; The Constant Husband, Wee Geordie, **55**; Blue Murder At St Trinians, The Green Man, **56**; Fortune Is A Woman, **57**; The Bridal Path, **59**; Left Right And Centre, The Pure Hell Of St Trinians, **60**; Only Two Can Play, **61**; Ring Of Spies, **64**; Joey Boy, **65**; The Great St Trinians Train Robbery, **66**; Endless Night **71**; Ooh You Are Awful, **73**; The Lady Vanishes, **79**; The Wildcats Of St Trinians, **80**.

LAUREL, STAN: films without Oliver Hardy: Madame Mystery, **16**; Nuts In May, **17**; The Egg, Mud And Sand, **22**; Roughest Africa, When Knights Were Cold, **23**; Smithy, Get 'Em Young, On The Front Page, **26**. Laurel And Hardy Films: A Lucky Dog **17**; The Battle Of The Century, Duck Soup, Hats Off, Love 'em And Weep, Putting Pants On Philip, Sailors Beware!, The Second Hundred Years, Slipping Wives, Sugar Daddies, With Love And Hisses, **27**; Early To Bed, The Finishing Touch, Flying Elephants, From Soup To Nuts, Habeas Corpus, Leave 'Em Laughing, Should Married Men Go Home?, Their Purple Moment, Two Tars, We Faw Down, You're Darn Tootin', **28**; Angora Love, Bacon Grabbers, Berth Marks, Big Business, Double Whoopee, The Hollywood Revue Of 29, The Hoose-gow, Liberty, Men O' War, Perfect Day, That's My Wife, They Go Boom, Unaccustomed As We Are, Wrong Again, **29**; Another Fine Mess, Below Zero, Blotto, Brats, Hog Wild, The Laurel And Hardy Murder Case, The Night Owls, The Rogue Song, Be Big, Beau Chumps, Laughing Gravy, **30**; One Good Turn, Our Wife, Pardon Us, The Stolen Jools, **31**; Come Clean, Any Old Port, The Chimp, County Hospital, Helpmates, The Music Box, Pack Up Your Troubles, Scram!, Their First Mistake, **32**; Towed In A Hole, Busy Bodies, Fra Diavolo, Dirty Work, Me And My Pal, The Midnight Patrol, Sons Of The Desert, Twice Two, **33**; Babes In Toyland, Going Bye-bye!, Hollywood Party, The Live Ghost, Oliver The Eighth, Them Thar Hills, **34**; The Fixer Uppers, Thicker Than Water, Tit For Tat, Bonnie Scotland, **35**; Our Relations, **36**; Pick A Star, Way Out West, **37**; Block-Heads, Swiss Miss, **38**; Flying Deuces, **39**; A Chump At Oxford, Saps At Sea, **40**; Great Guns, **41**; A-Haunting We Will Go, **42**; Air Raid Wardens, The Dancing Masters, Jitterbugs, **43**; The Big Noise, Nothing But Trouble, **44**; The Bullfighters, **45**; Atoll K, **50**.

LEAN, DAVID: In Which We Serve, **42**; This Happy Breed, **44**; Blithe Spirit, Brief Encounter, **45**; Great Expectations, **46**; Oliver Twist, **48**; Madeleine, The Passionate Friends, **49**; The Sound Barrier, **52**; Hobson's Choice, **54**; Summer Madness, **55**; The Bridge On The River Kwai, **57**; Lawrence Of Arabia, **62**; Doctor Zhivago, **65**; Ryan's Daughter, **70**; A Passage To India, **84**.

LEE, BRUCE: Marlowe, **69**; Fists Of Fury, **71**; The Chinese Connection, Fist Of Fury, **72**; Enter The Dragon, Return Of The Dragon, **73**; Game Of Death, **78**; Game Of Death II, **81**.

LEE, CHRISTOPHER: Corridor Of Mirrors, Hamlet, One Night With You, Scott Of The Antarctic, A Song For Tomorrow, **48**; The Gay Lady, **49**; Captain Horatio Hornblower, Valley Of The Eagles, **51**; Babes In Bagdad, The Crimson Pirate, Moulin Rouge, **52**; Innocents In Paris, **53**; The Death Of Michael Turbin, Destination Milan, The Final Column, **54**; Alias John Preston, Man In Demand, Police Dog, That Lady, **55**; The Cockleshell Heroes, Cross-Roads, Storm Over The Nile, **56**; Beyond Mombasa, The Curse Of Frankenstein, The Traitor, **57**; Corridors Of Blood, Battle Of The V-1, A Tale Of Two Cities, The Truth About Women, **58**; Dracula, The Hound Of The Baskervilles, The Man Who Could Cheat Death, The Mummy, Tempi Duri Per I Vampiri, **59**; The Hands Of Orlac, City Of The Dead, Too Hot To Handle, The Two Faces Of Dr Jekyll, **60**; Daffodil Killer, Das Geheimnis Der Gelben Narzissen, Hercules In The Haunted World, Taste Of Fear, Terror Of The Tongs, **61**; The Devil's Agent, The Pirates Of Blood River, Sherlock Holmes

And The Deadly Necklace, Beat Girl, **62**; Horror Castle, Night Is The Phantom, **63**; Castle Of The Living Dead, The Devil-Ship Pirates, The Gorgon, La Cripta E L'Incubo, **64**; Dr Terror's House Of Horrors, The Face Of Fu Manchu, She, The Skull, **65**; The Brides Of Fu Manchu, Dracula Prince Of Darkness, Rasputin The Mad Monk, **66**; Five Golden Dragons, Night Of The Big Heat, Circus Of Fear, Theatre Of Death, Blood Demon, **67**; The Blood Of Fu Manchu, The Castle Of Fu Manchu, Curse Of The Crimson Altar/Crimson Altar, The Devil Rides Out, Dracula Has Risen From The Grave, The Face Of Eve, The Vengeance Of Fu Manchu, Victims Of Terror, **68**; El Proceso De Las Brujas, The Magic Christian, The Oblong Box, Night Of The Blood Monster, **69**; Count Dracula, Cuadecuc, Eugenie, Julius Caesar, The Private Life Of Sherlock Holmes, Scars Of Dracula, Scream And Scream Again, Taste The Blood Of Dracula, The Keeper, **70**; The House That Dripped Blood, **71**; Dracula AD 1972, Hannie Caulder, Horror Express I Monster, Nothing But The Night, **72**; The Satanic Rites Of Dracula, The Creeping Flesh, Deathline, The Wicker Man, **73**; Dark Places, The Man With The Golden Gun, The Three Musketeers, **74**; The Diamond Mercenaries, The Four Musketeers, Killer Force, Whispering Death, Diagnosis: Murder, **75**; Dracula And Son, **76**; To The Devil Daughter, Airport 77, End Of The World, Starship Invasions, Meat Cleaver Massacre, **77**; The Passage, Caravans, Return From Witch Mountain, **78**; 1941, Arabian Adventure, The Silent Flute, Jaguar Lives!, Nutcracker Fantasy, Moon In Scorpio, **79**; Bear Island, Desperate Moves, Serial, **80**; An Eye For An Eye, The Salamander, **81**; The Last Unicorn, Safari 3000, **82**; House Of The Long Shadows, The Return Of Captain Invincible, **83**; The Rosebud Beach Hotel, **84**; The Mask Of Murder, The Howling II: Your Sister Is A Werewolf, **85**; The Girl, Jocks, Mio In The Land Of Faraway, **87**; Mask Of Murder Murder Story, The Return Of The Musketeers, **89**; Gremlins 2: The New Batch, Treasure Island, **90**; Journey Of Honor, **91**; Jackpot, **93**; Rough Diamonds, **94**; Clockers, **95**; Funny Man, A Feast at Midnight, **94**; The Stupids, **96**.

LEE, SPIKE: She's Gotta Have It, **86**; School Daze, **88**; Do The Right Thing, **89**; Mo' Better Blues, **90**; Malcolm X, **92**; Crooklyn, **94**; Clockers, **95**

LEGRAND, MICHEL: Charmants Garçons, **57**; The Screwball, Trap For A Killer, **58**; A Woman Is A Woman, 7 Capital Sins, The Counterfeiters Of Paris, Lola, **61**; Cleo From 5 To 7, Le Joli Mai, Eva, **62**; Bay Of Angels, Love Is A Ball, My Life To Live, **63**; Band Of Outsiders, Ravishing Idiot, The Umbrellas Of Cherbourg, **64**; Corrida, L'Or Et Le Plomb, Monnaie De Singe, **65**; A Matter Of Resistance, Who Are You Polly Maggoo?, **66**; A Matter Of Innocence, The Oldest Profession, **67**; How To Save A Marriage, Ice Station Zebra, Play Dirty, Sweet November, The Thomas Crown Affair, The Young Girls Of Rochefort, **68**; Castle Keep, The Happy Ending, The Picasso Summer, La Piscina, **69**; Darling Lili, The Lady In The Car With Glasses And A Gun, Les Maries De L'An Deux, Pieces Of Dreams, Wuthering Heights, Appelez-Moi Mathilde, **70**; The Magic Donkey, The Go-Between, Le Mans, Summer Of '42, A Time For Loving, Un Peu De Soleil Dans L'Eau Froide, **71**; Lady Sings The Blues, One Is A Lonely Number, Portnoy's Complaint, Un Homme Est Mort, **72**; 40 Carats, Breezy, Cops And Robbers, A Doll's House, F For Fake, A Bequest To The Nation, L'Evénment Le Plus Important Depuis Que L'Homme A Marché Sur La Lune, The Three Musketeers, **73**; Lovers Like Us, The Smurfs And The Magic Flute, **75**; Gable And Lombard, Le Voyage De Noces, Ode To Billy Joe, **76**; Gulliver's Travels, The Other Side Of Midnight, **77**; Lady Oscar, **79**; Atlantic City, The Hunter, The Mountain Men, **80**; The Phoenix, **81**; Best Friends, What Makes David Run?, **82**; Never Say Never Again, Yentl, **83**; A Love In Germany, Slapstick, **84**; As Someone Dies, Secret Places, **85**; Trois Places Pour Le 26, **88**; Five Days In June, **89**; The Pickle, **93**; Prêt-A-Porter, **95**; Les Miserables, **95**.

LEHMAN, ERNEST: Executive Suite, Sabrina, **54**; The King And I, Somebody Up There Likes Me, **56**; Sweet Smell Of Success, **57**; North By Northwest, **59**; From The Terrace, **60**; West Side Story, **61**; The Prize, **63**; The Sound Of Music, **65**; Who's Afraid Of Virginia Woolf?, **66**; Funny Girl, **68**; Hello Dolly!, **69**; Portnoy's Complaint, **72**; Family Plot, **76**; Black Sunday, **77**.

LEIGH, JANET: The Romance Of Rosy Ridge, If Winter Comes, **47**; Hills Of Home, Words And Music, **48**; Act Of Violence, The Doctor And The Girl, Holiday Affair, Little Women, The Red Danube, The Forsyte Saga, **49**; Angels In The Outfield, It's A Big Country, Strictly Dishonorable, Two Tickets To Broadway, **51**; Fearless Fagan, Just This Once, Scaramouche, **52**; Confidentially Connie, Houdini, The Naked Spur, Walking My Baby Back Home, **53**; The Black Shield Of Falworth, Living It Up, Prince Valiant, Rogue Cop, **54**; My Sister Eileen, Pete Kelly's Blues, **55**; Safari, **56**; Jet Pilot, **57**; The Perfect Furlough, Touch Of Evil, The Vikings, **58**; Pépé, Psycho, Who Was That Lady?, **60**; The Manchurian Candidate, **62**; Bye Bye Birdie, Wives And Lovers, **63**; An American Dream, Harper, Kid Rodelo, Three On A Couch, **66**; Grand Slam, **68**; Hello Down There, **69**; Night Of The Lepus, One Is A Lonely Number, **72**; Boardwalk, **79**; The Fog, **80**.

LEIGH, MIKE: Bleak Moments, **72**; Meantime, **83**; Four Days In July, **84**; The Short And Curlies, **87**; High Hopes, **88**; Life Is Sweet, **91**; A Sense Of History, **92**; Naked, **93**; Secrets and Lies, **96**.

LEIGH, VIVIEN: Things Are Looking Up, **34**; Look Up And Laugh, The Village Squire, **35**; Dark Journey, Fire Over England, Storm In A Teacup, **37**; St Martin's Lane, A Yank At Oxford, **38**; 21 Days Together, Gone With The Wind, **39**; Waterloo Bridge, **40**; Lady Hamilton, **41**; Caesar And Cleopatra, **45**; Gentleman's Agreement, **47**; Anna Karenina, **48**; A Streetcar Named Desire, **51**; The Deep Blue Sea, **55**; The Roman Spring Of Mrs Stone, **61**; Ship Of Fools, **65**.

LELOUCH, CLAUDE: The Right Of Man, **60**; L'Amour Avec Des Si, **63**; Night Women, Une Fille Et Des Fusils, **64**; Un Homme Et Une Femme, **66**; Vivre Pour Vivre, **67**; La Vie L'Amour La Mort, **68**; Un Homme Qui Me Plait, **69**; The Crook, Smic Smac Smoc, **71**; La Bonne Année, L'Aventure C'Est L'Aventure, Marriage, Toute Une Vie, **74**; Le Chat Et La Souris, Le Bon Et Les Méchants, **75**; Second Chance, **76**; Simon Et Sarah, **77**; Robert Et Robert, **78**; A Nous Deux, **79**; Bolero, **81**; Edith And Marcel, **83**; Partir Revenir, Viva La Vie!, **84**; Warning Bandits, A Man And A Woman: 20 Years Later, **86**; Itineraire D'Un Enfant Gâté, **88**; There Were Days And Moons, **90**; La Belle Histoire, **92**; Tout Ca Pour Ca!, **93**; The Thief And The Liar, **94**.

LEMMON, JACK: It Should Happen To You, Phffft!, **54**; Mister Roberts, My Sister Eileen, Three For The Show, **55**; You Can't Run Away From It, **56**; Fire Down Below, Operation Mad Ball, **57**; Bell Book And Candle, Cowboy, **58**; It Happened To Jane, Some Like It Hot, **59**; The Apartment, Pépé, The Wackiest Ship In The Army, **60**; Days Of Wine And Roses, The Notorious Landlady, **62**; Irma La Douce, Under The Yum Yum Tree, **63**; Good Neighbor Sam, **64**; The Great Race, How To Murder Your Wife, **65**; The Fortune Cookie, **66**; Luv, **67**; The Odd Couple, **68**; The April Fools, **69**; The Out-of-Towners, **70**; Kotch, **71**; Avanti!, The War Between Men And Women, **72**; Save The Tiger, **73**; The Front Page, **74**; The Prisoner Of Second Avenue, **75**; Alex And The Gypsy, **76**; Airport 77, **77**; The China Syndrome, **79**; Buddy Buddy, **81**; Missing, **82**; Mass Appeal, **84**; Macaroni, **85**; That's Life!, **86**; Dad, **89**; JFK, **91**; Glengarry Glen Ross, The Player, **92**; Grumpy Old Men, Short Cuts, **93**; Getting Away With Murder, Grumpier Old Men, **95**; Hamlet, **96**.

LEONE, SERGIO: The Colossus Of Rhodes, **61**; Sodom And Gomorrah, **63**; A Fistful Of Dollars, **64**; For A Few Dollars More, The Good The Bad And The Ugly, **66**; Once Upon A Time In The West, **68**; Fistful Of Dynamite, **72**; Once Upon A Time In America, **84**; Troppo Forte, **86**.

LeROY, MERVYN: No Place To Go, **27**; Flying Romeos, Harold Teen, Oh Kay!, **28**; Broadway Babies, Hot Stuff, Little Johnny Jones, Naughty Baby, **29**; Little Caesar, Numbered Men, Playing Around, Show Girl In Hollywood, Top Speed, **30**; Broad Minded, Five Star Final, Gentleman's Fate, Local Boy Makes Good, Tonight Or Never, Too Young To Marry, **31**; Big City Blues, The Heart Of New York, High Pressure, I Am A Fugitive From A Chain Gang, Three On A Match, Two Seconds, **32**; Elmer The Great, Gold Diggers Of 1933, Hard To Handle, Tugboat Annie, The World Changes, **33**; Happiness Ahead, Heat Lightning, Hi Nellie!, **34**; I Found Stella Parish, Oil For The Lamps Of China, Page Miss Glory, Sweet Adeline, **35**; Anthony Adverse, Three Men On A Horse, **36**; The King And The Chorus Girl, They Won't Forget, **37**; Fools For Scandal, **38**; The Wizard Of Oz, **39**; Escape, Waterloo Bridge, **40**; Blossoms In The Dust, Unholy Partners, **41**; Johnny Eager, Random Harvest, **42**; Madame Curie, **43**; Thirty Seconds Over Tokyo, **44**; Without Reservations, **46**; Homecoming, **48**; Any Number Can Play, East Side West Side, Little Women, **49**; Quo Vadis?, **51**; Lovely To Look At, Million Dollar Mermaid, **52**; Latin Lovers, **53**; Rose Marie, **54**; Mister Roberts, Strange Lady In Town, **55**; The Bad Seed, Toward The Unknown, **56**; Home Before Dark, No Time For Sergeants, **58**; The FBI Story, **59**; Wake Me When It's Over, **60**; The Devil At 4 O'Clock, **61**; Gypsy, A Majority Of One, **62**; Mary Mary, **63**; Moment To Moment, **66**.

LESTER, RICHARD: The Mouse On The Moon, **63**; A Hard Day's Night, **64**; Help!, The Knack And How To Get It, **65**; A Funny Thing Happened On The Way To The Forum, **66**; How I Won The War, **67**; Petulia, **68**; The Bed-Sitting Room, **69**; Juggernaut, The Three Musketeers, **74**; The Four Musketeers, Royal Flash, **75**; The Ritz, Robin And Marian, **76**; Butch And Sundance: The Early Days, Cuba, **79**; Superman II, **80**; Superman III, **83**; Finders Keepers, **84**; The Return Of The Musketeers, **89**.

LEVINSON, BARRY: The Internecine Project, **74**; Silent Movie, **76**; High Anxiety, **77**; And Justice For All, **79**; Inside Moves, **80**; History Of The World Part 1, **81**; Diner, **82**; The Natural, Unfaithfully Yours, **84**; Young Sherlock Holmes, **85**; Good Morning Vietnam, Tin Men, **87**; Rain Man, **88**; Avalon, **90**; Bugsy, **91**; Toys, **92**; Jimmy Hollywood, **94**; Disclosure, **95**; Mars Attacks!, Sleepers, **96**.

LEWIN, ALBERT: The Moon and Sixpence, **42**; The Picture Of Dorian Gray, **45**; The Private Affairs of Bel Ami, **47**; Pandora and the Flying Dutchman, **51**; Saadia, **54**; The Living Idol, **57**.

LEWIS, JERRY: My Friend Irma, **49**; At War With The Army, My Friend Irma Goes West, **50**; That's My Boy, **51**; Jumping Jacks, Sailor Beware, Road To Bali, **52**; The Caddy, Money From Home, Scared Stiff, The Stooge, **53**; Living It Up, Three Ring Circus, **54**; Artists And Models, You're Never Too Young, **55**; Hollywood Or Bust, Pardners, **56**; The Delicate Delinquent, The Sad Sack, **57**; The Geisha Boy, Rock-A-Bye Baby, **58**; Don't Give Up The Ship, Li'l Abner, **59**; The Bellboy, Cinderfella, Visit To A Small Planet, **60**; The Errand Boy, The Ladies' Man, **61**; It's Only Money, **62**; It's A Mad Mad Mad Mad World, The Nutty Professor, Who's Minding The Store?, **63**; The Disorderly Orderly, The Patsy, **64**; Boeing-Boeing, The Family Jewels, **65**; Three On A Couch, Way Way Out, **66**; The Big Mouth, **67**; Don't Raise The Bridge Lower The River, **68**; Hook Line And Sinker, **69**; One More Time, Which Way To The Front?, **70**; Hardly Working, **81**; Cracking Up, The King Of Comedy, **83**; Retenez Moi Ou Je Fais Un Malheur, To Catch A Cop, Par Ou T'Es Rentré? On T'As Vu Sortir, Slapstick, **84**; Cookie, **89**; Mr Saturday Night, **92**; Arizona Dream, **93**, Funny Bones, **95**.

LEWTON, VAL: Cat People, **42**; The Ghost Ship, I Walked With A Zombie, The Leopard Man, The Seventh Victim, **43**; The Curse Of The Cat People, Mademoiselle Fifi, **44**; The Body Snatcher, Isle Of The Dead, **45**; Bedlam, **46**; Please Believe Me, **49**; Apache Drums, **51**.

LINDER, MAX: Joe Says He Will Teach Max A Lesson, **05**; His First Air Trip, **07**; Un Veinele Bossu, **08**; Le Petit Jeune Homme, Un Mariage A L'Méricain, The Maniac Juggler, **09**; Max Aéronaute, Max Champion De Boxe, Max Se Marie, La Timidité Vaincu, **10**; Max Dans Sa Famille, Max Et Le Quinquina, **11**; Le Mal De Mer, Max Et Les Femmes, A Farm Idyll, Peintre Par Amour, Max And The Donkey, **12**; Max Asthmatique, Max Virtuose, Les Débuts D'Un Yachtman, Max Toreador, **13**; Max And The Lady Doctor, Max And The Jealous Husband, **14**; Max Et L'Espion, **15**; Max Comes Across, Max In A Taxi, Max Wants A Divorce, **17**; Le Petit Café, **19**; Le Feu Sacré, **20**; Be My Wife, Seven Years' Bad Luck, **21**; The Three Must-Get-Theres, **22**; Au Secours!, **23**; King Of The Circus, **24**.

LITVAK, ANATOLE: Dolly Macht Karriere, **30**; Nie Wieder Liebe, **31**; Be Mine Tonight, **32**; Chanson D'Une Nuit, Cette Vieille Canaille, Sleeping Car **33**; L'Equipage, **35**; Mayerling, **36**; Tovarich, The Woman I Love, **37**; The Amazing Doctor Clitterhouse, The Sisters, **38**; Confessions Of A Nazi Spy, **39**; All This And Heaven Too, Castle On The Hudson, City For Conquest, Years Without Days, **40**; Blues In The Night, Out Of The Fog, **41**; This Above All, **42**; The Long Night, **47**; The Snake Pit, Sorry Wrong Number, **48**; Decision Before Dawn, **51**; Act Of Love, The Girl On The Via Flammina **53**; The Deep Blue Sea, **55**; Anastasia, **56**; The Journey, **59**; Goodbye Again, **61**; Five Miles To Midnight, **63**; 10:30pm Summer, **66**; Night Of The Generals, **67**; The Lady In The Car With Glasses And A Gun, **70**.

LLOYD, HAROLD: Just Nuts, **15**; Over The Fence, **17**; Take A Chance, **18**; Bumping Into Broadway, Captain Kidd's Kids, From Hand To Mouth, His Royal Slyness, The Chef, Don't Shove, **19**; An Eastern Westerner, Get Out And Get Under, Haunted Spooks, High And Dizzy, From Hand To Mouth, **20**; Among Those Present, I Do, Never Weaken, Now Or Never, A Sailor-Made Man, **21**; Dr Jack, Grandma's Boy, **22**; Safety Last, Why Worry?, **23**; Girl Shy, Hot Water, **24**; The Freshman, **25**; For Heaven's Sake, **26**; The Kid Brother, **27**; Speedy, **28**; Welcome Danger, **29**; Feet First, **30**; Movie Crazy, **32**; The Cat's Paw, **34**; The Milky Way, **36**; Professor Beware, **38**; A Girl A Guy And A Gob, **41**; Mad Wednesday, **47**.

LOACH, KEN: Poor Cow, **68**; Kes, **69**; Family Life, **71**; Black Jack, **79**; **80**; Looks And Smiles, **81**; Fatherland, **86**; Hidden Agenda, **90**; Riff-Raff, **91**; Raining Stones, **93**; Ladybird Ladybird, **94**; Land And Freedom, **95**; Carla's Song, **97**.

LOCKWOOD, MARGARET: The Case Of Gabriel Perry, Honours Easy, Lorna Doone, Man Of The Moment, Midshipman Easy, Some Day, **35**; The Amateur Gentleman, Beloved Vagabond, Irish For Luck, Jury's Evidence, **36**; Doctor Syn, Melody And Romance, The Street Singer, Who's Your Lady Friend?, **37**; Bank Holiday, The Lady Vanishes, Owd Bob, **38**; A Girl Must Live, Rulers Of The Sea, Susannah Of The Mounties, **39**; The Girl In The News, Night Train To Munich, The Stars Look Down, **40**; Quiet Wedding, **41**; Alibi, **42**; Dear Octopus, The Man In Grey, **43**; Give Us The Moon, Love Story, **44**; I'll Be Your Sweetheart, A Place Of One's Own, The Wicked Lady, **45**; Bedelia, **46**; The White Unicorn, Hungry Hill, Jassy, **47**; Cardboard Cavalier, Look Before You Love, **48**; Madness Of The Heart, **49**; Highly Dangerous, **51**; Trent's Last Case, **52**; Laughing Anne, Trouble In The Glen, **53**; Cast A Dark Shadow, **55**; The Slipper And The Rose, **76**.

LOLLOBRIGIDA, GINA: I Pagliacci, **48**; Campane A Martello, **49**; Alina, Vita Da Cani, Cuori Senza Frontiere, **50**; Passport To Hell, Enrico Caruso, **51**; Fanfan The Tulip, Le Infedeli, Wife For A Night, Les Belles De Nuit, **52**; Le Grand Jeu, Beat The Devil, **53**; Bread Love And Dreams, Il Maestro Di Don Giovanni, **54**; Beautiful But Dangerous, Bread Love And Jealousy, The Wayward Wife, **55**; Trapeze, Woman Of Rome, **56**; The Hunchback Of Notre Dame, **57**; Anna Di Brooklyn, Where The Hot Wind Blows!, **58**; Never So Few, Solomon And Sheba, **59**; Come September, Go Naked In The World, **61**; Imperial Venus, **62**; Mare Matto, **63**; Strange Bedfellows, Woman Of Straw, **64**; The Dolls, **65**; Io Io Io E Gli Altri, Hotel Paradiso, Le Piacevoli Notti, Les Sultans, **66**; Plucked, Cervantes, **67**; Buona Sera Mrs Campbell, The Private Navy Of Sgt O'Farrell, That Splendid November, **68**; Bad Man's River, **71**; King Queen Knave, No Encontre Rosas Para Mi Madre, **72**.

LOM, HERBERT: Mein Kampf My Crimes, **40**; The Young Mr Pitt, **42**; The Dark Tower, **43**; Hotel Reserve, **44**; Night Boat To Dublin, The Seventh Veil, **46**; Appointment With Crime, Dual Alibi, Snowbound, **47**; The Brass Monkey, Portrait From Life, Good Time Girl, **48**; The Golden Salamander, **49**; Cage Of Gold, State Secret, Night And The City, **50**; Hell Is Sold Out, Two On The Tiles, Whispering Smith Hits London, Mr Dening Drives North, **51**; The Ringer, Rough Shoot, **52**; The Net, The Paris Express, **53**; The Love Lottery, Star Of India, The Beautiful Stranger, **54**; The Ladykillers, **55**; War And Peace, **56**; Action Of The Tiger, Fire Down Below, Helldrivers, **57**; Chase A Crooked Shadow, I Accuse!, Intent To Kill, No Trees In The Street, The Roots Of Heaven, **58**; The Big Fisherman, Northwest Frontier, Passport To Shame, Third Man On The Mountain, **59**; I Aim At The Stars, Spartacus, **60**; El Cid, Mysterious Island, **61**; The Frightened City, Mr Topaze, The Phantom Of The Opera, Tiara Tahiti, **62**; The Horse Without A Head, The Treasure Of Silver Lake **63**; A Shot In The Dark, **64**; Uncle Tom's Cabin, Return From The Ashes, **65**; Whom The Gods Wish To Destroy, Gambit, Our Man In Marrakesh, **66**; The Karate Killers, **67**; Assignment To Kill, The Face Of Eve, Villa Rides, **68**; 99 Women, Doppelganger, Mister Jerico, **69**; Burn Witch Burn, Count Dracula, The Secret Of Dorian Gray, **70**; Murders In The Rue Morgue, **71**; Asylum, **72**; And Now The Screaming Starts!, **73**; Dark Places, **74**; The Return Of The Pink Panther, And Then There Were None, **75**; The Pink Panther Strikes Again, **76**; Charleston, Revenge Of The Pink Panther, **78**; The Lady Vanishes, **79**; Hopscotch, The Man With Bogart's Face, **80**; Trail Of The Pink Panther, **82**; Curse Of The Pink Panther, The Dead Zone, **83**; King Solomon's Mines, **85**; Whoops Apocalypse, **86**; Memed My Hawk, **87**; Skeleton Coast, **88**; River Of Death, Ten Little Indians, **89**; Master of Dragonard Hill, **90**; The Pope Must Die, The Sect, **91**; Son Of The Pink Panther, **93**.

LOMBARD, CAROLE: A Perfect Crime, **21**; Durand Of The Bad Lands, Hearts And Spurs, Marriage In Transit, **25**; The Girl From Everywhere, **27**; His Unlucky Night, The Swan Princess, The Perfect Crime, The Divine Sinner, Me Gangster, Ned McCobb's Daughter, Power, Show Folks, **28**; Big News, High Voltage, The Racketeer, **29**; The Arizona Kid, Fast And Loose, Safety In Numbers, **30**; I Take This Woman, It Pays To Advertise, Ladies' Man, Man Of The World, Up Pops The Devil, **31**; No Man Of He Own, No More Orchids, No One Man, Sinners In The Sun, Virtue, **32**; Brief Moment The Eagle And The Hawk, From Hell To Heaven, Supernatural, White Woman, **33**; Bolero, The Gay Bride, Lady By Choice, Now And Forever, Twentieth Century, We're Not Dressing, **34**; Hands Across The Table, Rumba, **35**; Love Before Breakfast, My Man Godfrey, The Princess Comes Across, **36**; Nothing Sacred, Swing High Swing Low, True Confession, **37**; Fools For Scandal, **38**; In Name Only, Made For Each Other, **39**; They Knew What They Wanted, Vigil In The Night, **40**; Mr And Mrs Smith, **41**; To Be Or Not To Be, **42**.

LOOS, ANITA: American Aristocracy, The Half-breed, His Picture In The Papers, The Americano, Intolerance, **16**; Come On In, Under The Top, **18**; The Isle Of Conquest, A Temperamental Wife, A Virtuous Vamp, **19**; In Search Of A Sinner, **20**; Mama's Affai Woman's Place, **21**; Red Hot Romance, **22**; Dulcy, **23**; Learning To Love, **25**; Blondi Of The Follies, Red-Headed Woman, **32**; Biography Of A Bachelor Girl, **35**; San Francisco, **36**; Saratoga, **37**; The Women, **39**; Susan And God, **40**; Blossoms In The Dust, They Met In Bombay, When Ladies Meet, **41**; I Married An Angel, **42**.

LOREN, SOPHIA: Africa Sotto I Mari, La Tratta Delle Bianche, **52**; Aida, Due Notti Con Cleopatra, **53**; Attila, L'Oro Di Napoli, Miseria A Nobilta, Carosello Napoletano, Pellegrini D'Amore, **54**; The Miller's Beautiful Wife, Il Segno Di Venere, Peccato Che Sia Una Canaglia, La Donna Del Fiume, **55**; La Fortuna Di Essere Donna, **56**; Boy On A Dolphin, Legend Of The Lost, The Pride And The Passion, Scandal In Sorrento, **57**; Desire Under The Elms, Houseboat, The Key, **58**; The Blac Orchid, That Kind Of Woman, **59**; A Breath Of Scandal, Heller In Pink Tights, It Started In Naples, The Millionairess, Two omen, **60**; El Cid, Madame Sans-Gêne, **1**; Boccaccio '70, **62**; The Condemned Of ona, Five Miles To Midnight, Yesterday day And Tomorrow **63**; The Fall Of The man Empire, Marriage Italian-Style, **4**; Lady L, Operation Crossbow, **65**; abesque, Judith, **66**; A Countess From ong Kong, More Than A Miracle, **67**; Ghosts lian Style, **69**; I Girasoli, **70**; La oglie Del Prete, **71**; Man Of La Mancha, **2**; Il Viaggio, White Sister, **73**; Brief ncounter, The Verdict, La Pupa Del Gangster, **4**; Angela, The Cassandra Crossing, a Giornata Particolare, **77**; Brass Target, **8**; Revenge, Firepower, **79**; Running way, **89**; Saturday Sunday And Monday, **90**, êt-A-Porter**,** Grumpier Old Men, **95**.

ORRE, PETER: Bomben Auf Monte arlo, Die Koffer Des Herrn OF, M, **31**; FP1 twortet Nicht, **32**; The Man Who Knew o Much, **34**; Crime And Punishment, ands Of Orlac, **35**; Secret Agent, **36**; ack-up, Lancer Spy, Nancy Steel Is Missing, ink Fast Mr Moto, The Man With Nine eads, **37**; Mr Moto Takes A Chance, Mr oto's Gamble, Mysterious Mr Moto, ank You, Mr Moto, **38**; Mr Moto In Danger and, Mr Moto Takes A Vacation, Mr oto's Last Warning, **39**; I Was An dventuress, Island Of Doomed Men, range Cargo, The Stranger On The Third oor, You'll Find Out, **40**; The Face hind The Mask, The Maltese Falcon, Mr strict Attorney, They Met In Bombay, **1**; All Through The Night, The Boogie Man ll Get You, Casablanca, Invisible Agent, **2**; Background To Danger, The Cross Of rraine, **43**; Arsenic And Old Lace, The onspirators, Hollywood Canteen, The Mask Dimitrios, Passage To Marseille, **44**; onfidential Agent, Hotel Berlin, **45**; The east With Five Fingers, Black Angel, The nase, Three Strangers, The Verdict, **46**; My vorite Brunette, **47**; Casbah, **48**; **49**; uble Confession, **50**; Der Verlorene, **51**;),000 Leagues Under The Sea, Beat e Devil, **54**; Around The World In 80 Days, ngo Crossing, **56**; The Buster Keaton ory, Hell Ship Mutiny, The Sad Sack, Silk ockings, The Story Of Mankind, **57**; e Big Circus, **59**; The Cruel Day, Scent Of ystery, **60**; Voyage To The Bottom Of e Sea, **61**; Five Weeks In A Balloon, Tales Terror, **62**; The Raven, **63**; The medy Of Terrors, Muscle Beach Party, The atsy, **64**.

OSEY, JOSEPH: The Boy With Green air, **48**; The Lawless, **50**; The Big Night, M, e Prowler, The Tall Target, **51**; barco A Mezzanotte, **52**; The Sleeping ger, **54**; A Man On The Beach, **55**; e Intimate Stranger, Time Without Pity, **57**; e Gypsy And The Gentleman, **58**; nd Date, **59**; The Concrete Jungle, **60**; The amned, **62**; The Servant, **63**; King And untry, **64**; Eva, **65**; Modesty Blaise, cident, **67**; Boom!, Secret Ceremony, **8**; Figures In A Landscape, **70**; The Go- etween, **71**; The Assassination Of otsky, **72**; A Doll's House, **73**; alileo, The Romantic Englishwoman, **5**; Mr Klein, **77**; The Roads To The South, **8**; Don Giovanni, **79**; The Trout, **82**; eaming, **85**.

OVE, BESSIE: The Flying Torpedo, e Aryan, The Good Bad Man, Reggie Mixes The Mystery Of The Leaping Fish, randed, Love In The West, Intolerance, A ster Of Six, The Heiress At Coffee an's, **16**; Nina The Flower Girl, A Daughter The Poor, Cheerful Givers, The wdust Ring, Wee Lady Betty, Pernickety lly Ann, **17**; The Great Adventure, How uld You Caroline?, Carolyn Of The Corners, Little Sister Of Everybody, The Dawn Of nderstanding, **18**; The Enchanted Barn, The shing Ring Man, A Yankee Princess, e Little Boss, Cupid Forecloses, Over The rden Wall, A Fighting Colleen, Pegeen, **9**; Bonnie May, The Midlanders, **20**; Penny Top Hill Trail, The Honor Of Ramirez, e Spirit Of The Lake, The Swamp, The Sea on, **21**; The Vermilion Pencil, Forget- e-Not, Night Life In Hollywood, Bulldog ourage, Deserted At The Altar, **22**; The llage Blacksmith, The Adventures Of Prince ourageous, Three Who Paid, Ghost trol, Souls For Sale, Purple Dawn, Mary Of e Movies, Human Wreckage, St Elmo, e Eternal Three, Slaves Of Desire, Gentle lia, **23**; Torment, A Woman Of The ry, Those Who Dance, Dynamite Smith, The ent Watcher, Sundown, Tongues Of ame, **24**; Soul-Fire, New Brooms, A Son Of s Father, The King On Main Street, **25**; e Song And Dance Man, Young April, Going Crooked, **26**; Ten Thousand Reward, The Samaritan, Dress Parade, The American, **27**; The Matinee Idol, Anybody Here Seen Kelly?, Sally Of The Scandals, The Swell Head, **28**; The Broadway Melody, The Idle Rich, The Hollywood Revue Of 1929, The Girl In The Shadow, **29**; Chasing Rainbows, They Learned About Women, Conspiracy, Good News, See America Thirst, **30**; Farewell Party, **31**; I Live Again, **36**; Atlantic Ferry, **41**; London Scrapbook, **42**; Journey Together, **45**; The Magic Box, **50**; The Weak And The Wicked, **53**; The Barefoot Contessa, Beau Brummel, **54**; Tough And Go, **55**; The Story Of Esther Costello, **57**; Next To No Time, Nowhere To Go, **58**; Too Young To Love, **59**; The Greengage Summer, The Roman Spring Of Mrs Stone, **61**; The Wild Affair, Children Of The Damned, **63**; Promise Her Anything, **65**; Battle Beneath The Earth, **67**; Isadora, **68**; On Her Majesty's Secret Service, **69**; Sunday Bloody Sunday, **71**; Vampyres, Cat And Mouse, **74**; The Ritz, **76**; Ragtime, Lady Chatterley's Lover, Reds, **81**; The Hunger, **83**.

LOY, MYRNA: Ben-Hur, Pretty Ladies, **25**; Across The Pacific, The Cave Man, Don Juan, The Exquisite Sinner, The Gilded Highway, So This Is Paris, Why Girls Go Back Home, **26**; Bitter Apples, The Climbers, Finger Prints, Ham And Eggs At The Front, Heart Of Maryland, If I Were Single, The Jazz Singer, Simple Sis, **27**; Beware Of Married Men, The Crimson City, A Girl In Every Port, The Midnight Taxi, Pay As You Enter, State Street Sadie, Turn Back The Hours, What Price Beauty, **28**; The Black Watch, The Desert Song, Evidence, Fancy Baggage, The Great Divide, Hardboiled Rose, Noah's Ark, The Show Of Shows, The Squall, **29**; Bride Of The Regiment, Cameo Kirby, Cock O' The Walk, The Devil To Pay, Isle Of Escape, Jazz Cinderella, Last Of The Duanes, Renegades, Rogue Of The Rio Grande, The Truth About Youth, Under A Texas Moon, **30**; Arrowsmith, Body And Soul, A Connecticut Yankee, Consolation, Hush Money, The Naughty Flirt, Rebound, Skyline, Transatlantic, **31**; The Animal Kingdom, Emma, Love Me Tonight, The Mask Of Fu Manchu, New Morals For Old, Thirteen Women, Vanity Fair, The Wet Parade, The Woman In Room 13, **32**; The Barbarian, Night Flight, Penthouse, The Prizefighter And The Lady, Every Woman's Man, Scarlet River, Topaze, When Ladies Meet, **33**; Broadway Bill, Evelyn Prentice, Manhattan Melodrama, Men In White, Stamboul Quest, The Thin Man, **34**; Whipsaw, Wings In The Dark, **35**; After The Thin Man, The Great Ziegfeld, Libelled Lady, Petticoat Fever, To Mary With Love, Wife Vs Secretary, **36**; Double Wedding, Parnell, **37**; Manproof, Test Pilot, Too Hot To Handle, **38**; Another Thin Man, Lucky Night, The Rains Came, **39**; I Love You Again, Third Finger Left Hand, **40**; Love Crazy, Shadow Of The Thin Man, **41**; The Thin Man Goes Home, **44**; The Best Years Of Our Lives, So Goes My Love, **46**; Bachelor Knight, Song Of The Thin Man, **47**; Mr Blandings Builds His Dream House, **48**; That Dangerous Age, The Red Pony, **49**; Cheaper By The Dozen, **50**; Belles On Their Toes, **52**; The Ambassador's Daughter, **56**; Lonelyhearts, **58**; From The Terrace, Midnight Lace, **60**; The April Fools, **69**; Airport 75, **74**; The End, **78**; Just Tell Me What You Want, **80**.

LUBITSCH, ERNST: Auf Eis Gefuhrt, Blindekuh, Der Schwarze Moritz, Zucker Und Zimt, **15**; Der Gemischte Frauenchor, Shoe Salon Pinkus, **16**; Fideles Gefangnis, Der Blusenkonig, Ossi's Tagebuch, Prinz Sami, Wenn Vier Dasselbe Tun, **17**; Carmen, Das Madel Vom Ballett, Der Fall Rosentopf, Der Rodelkavalier, The Eyes Of The Mummy, Ich Mochte Kein Mann Sein, Meyer Aus Berlin, **18**; Die Austernprinzessin, Die Puppe, Madame DuBarry, **19**; Anne Boleyn, Die Wohnungsnot, Kolhiesels Tochter, One Arabian Night, Romeo Und Julia Im Schnee, **20**; Die Bergkatze, **21**; Das Weib Des Pharao, Montmartre/Die Flamme, **22**; Rosita, **23**; Forbidden Paradise, The Marriage Circle, Three Women, **24**; Kiss Me Again, Lady Windermere's Fan, **25**; So This Is Paris, **26**; The Student Prince In Old Heidelberg, **27**; Eternal Love, The Love Parade, **29**; Monte Carlo, Paramount On Parade, **30**; The Smiling Lieutenant, **31**; The Man I Killed, If I Had A Million, One Hour With You, Trouble In Paradise, **32**; Design For Living, **33**; The Merry Widow, **34**; Desire, **36**; Angel, Bluebeard's Eighth Wife, **38**; Ninotchka, **39**; The Shop Around The Corner, **40**; That Uncertain Feeling, **41**; To Be Or Not To Be, **42**; Heaven Can Wait, **43**; Where Do We Go From Here?, **45**; Cluny Brown, **46**; That Lady In Ermine, **48**.

LUCAS, GEORGE: THX-1138, **71**; American Graffiti, **73**; Star Wars, **77**; More American Graffiti, **79**; The Empire Strikes Back, Kagemusha, **80**; Raiders Of The Lost Ark, **81**; Return Of The Jedi, **83**; Indiana Jones And The Temple Of Doom, **84**; Mishima, **85**; Captain Eo, Howard The Duck, Labyrinth, **86**; Tucker: The Man And His Dream, Willow, **88**; Indiana Jones And The Last Crusade, **89**; Beverly Hills Cop III, **94**.

LUGOSI, BELA: Der Januskopf, **20**; Prisoners, The Thirteenth Chair, **29**; Such Men Are Dangerous, The Return of Chandu, **30**; The Black Camel, Dracula, **31**; Chandu The Magician, Murders In The Rue Morgue, White Zombie, **32**; The Death Kiss, International House, Island Of Lost Souls, Night Of Terror, The Whispering Shadow, **33**; The Black Cat, **34**; Phantom Ship, The Best Man Wins, Mark Of The Vampire, Murder By Television, The Mysterious Mr Wong, The Raven, **35**; The Invisible Ray, Shadow Of Chinatown, **36**; SOS Coast Guard, The Man With 9 Heads, **37**; The Gorilla, The Dark Eyes Of London, Ninotchka, The Phantom Creeps, Son Of Frankenstein, **39**; Black Friday, The Saint's Double Trouble, You'll Find Out, **40**; The Black Cat, The Devil Bat, The Invisible Ghost, Spooks Run Wild, The Wolf Man, **41**; Black Dragons, Bowery At Midnight, The Corpse Vanishes, The Ghost Of Frankenstein, Night Monster, **42**; House of Mystery, The Ape Man, Frankenstein Meets The Wolf Man, Ghosts On The Loose, The Return Of The Vampire, **43**; One Body Too Many, Return Of The Ape Man, Voodoo Man, **44**; The Body Snatcher, Zombies On Broadway, **45**; Genius At Work, **46**; Scared To Death, **47**; Abbott & Costello Meet Frankenstein, **48**; Bela Lugosi Meets A Brooklyn Gorilla, **50**; Mother Riley Meets The Vampire, **52**; Glen Or Glenda, **54**; Bride Of The Monster, **55**; The Black Sleep, Plan 9 From Outer Space, **56**.

LUMET, SIDNEY: Twelve Angry Men, **57**; Stage Struck, **58**; The Fugitive Kind, That Kind Of Woman, **59**; Long Day's Journey Into Night, A View From The Bridge, **62**; Fail-Safe, **64**; The Hill, The Pawnbroker, **65**; The Group, **66**; The Deadly Affair, **67**; Bye Bye Braverman, The Sea Gull, **68**; The Appointment, **69**; Last Of The Mobile Hot-Shots, **70**; The Anderson Tapes, Child's Play, **72**; The Offence, Serpico, **73**; Lovin' Molly, Murder On The Orient Express, **74**; Dog Day Afternoon, **75**; Network, **76**; Equus, **77**; The Wiz, **78**; Just Tell Me What You Want, **80**; Prince Of The City, **81**; Deathtrap, The Verdict, **82**; Daniel, **83**; Garbo Talks, **84**; The Morning After, Power, **86**; Running On Empty, **88**; Family Business, **89**; Close To Eden, A Stranger Among Us, **92**; Guilty As Sin, **93**; Night Falls on Manhattan, **97**.

LUPINO, IDA: Her First Affair, The Love Race, **32**; The Ghost Camera, High Finance, I Lived With You, Money For Speed, Prince Of Arcadia, **33**; Come On Marines, Ready For Love, Search For Beauty, **34**; Paris In Spring, Peter Ibbetson, Smart Girl, **35**; Anything Goes, The Gay Desperado, One Rainy Afternoon, Yours For The Asking, **36**; Artists And Models, Fight For Your Lady, Let's Get Married, Sea Devils, **37**; The Adventures Of Sherlock Holmes, The Lady And The Mob, The Light That Failed, The Lone Wolf Spy Hunt, **39**; They Drive By Night, **40**; High Sierra, Ladies In Retirement, Out Of The Fog, The Sea Wolf, **41**; Life Begins At 8.30, Moontide, **42**; The Hard Way, Forever And A Day, Thank Your Lucky Stars, **43**; Hollywood Canteen, In Our Time, **44**; Pillow To Post, **45**; Devotion, The Man I Love, Young Widow, **46**; Deep Valley, Escape Me Never, **47**; Road House, **48**; Lust For Gold, Not Wanted, Woman In Hiding, **49**; Never Fear, Outrage, **50**; On Dangerous Ground, **51**; Beware My Lovely, Hard Fast And Beautiful, **52**; The Bigamist, The Hitch-Hiker, Jennifer, **53**; Private Hell 36, **54**; The Big Knife, Women's Prison, **55**; Strange Intruder, While The City Sleeps, **56**; The Trouble With Angels, **66**; Junior Bonner, **72**; The Devil's Rain, **75**; Food Of The Gods, **76**; My Boys Are Good Boys, **78**; Deadhead Miles, **82**.

LYNCH, DAVID: Eraserhead, **77**; The Elephant Man, **80**; Dune, **85**; Blue Velvet, **86**; Weeds, **87**; Wild At Heart, **90**; The Cabinet Of Dr Ramirez, **91**; Twin Peaks: Fire Walk With Me, **92**; Lost Highway, **97**.

MCCAREY, LEO: Society Secrets, **21**; All Wet, **24**; Isn't Life Terrible, **25**; Long Live The King, Mighty Like A Moose, **26**; Should Men Walk Home, **27**; We Fall Down, Leave 'Em Laughing, **28**; Liberty, Red Hot Rhythm, The Sophomore, Wrong Again, **29**; Brats, Hog Wild, Let's Go Native, Part Time Wife, Wild Company, **30**; Indiscreet, **31**; The Kid From Spain, Duck Soup, **33**; Belle Of The Nineties, Six Of A Kind, **34**; Ruggles Of Red Gap, **35**; The Milky Way, **36**; The Awful Truth, Make Way For Tomorrow, **37**; Love Affair, **39**; My Favorite Wife, **40**; Once Upon A Honeymoon, **42**; Going My Way, **44**; The Bells Of St Mary's, **45**; Good Sam, **48**; My Son John, **52**; An Affair To Remember, **57**; Rally Round The Flag Boys!, **58**; The Devil Never Sleeps, **62**.

MCCAY, WINSOR: Gertie The Trained Dinosaur, **09**; Little Nemo, **11**; Jersey Skeeters, **16**; The Sinking Of The Lusitania, **18**; The Dream Of A Rarebit Fiend, **21**.

MCCREA, JOEL: Penrod And Sam, **23**; Dynamite, The Jazz Age, The Single Standard, **29**; Lightnin', The Silver Horde, **30**; Born To Love, The Common Law, Girls About Town, Kept Husbands, Once A Sinner, **31**; Bird Of Paradise, Business And Pleasure, The Lost Squadron, The Most Dangerous Game, The Sport Parade, Rockabye, **32**; Bed Of Roses, Chance At Heaven, One Man's Journey, The Silver Cord, **33**; Gambling Lady, Half A Sinner, The Richest Girl In The World, **34**; Barbary Coast, Our Little Girl, Private Worlds, Splendor, Woman Wanted, **35**; Adventure In Manhattan, Banjo On My Knee, Come And Get It, These Three, Two In A Crowd, **36**; Dead End, Interns Can't Take Money, Wells Fargo, Woman Chases Man, **37**; Three Blind Mice, Youth Takes A Fling, **38**; Espionage Agent, They Shall Have Music, Union Pacific, **39**; Foreign Correspondent, He Married His Wife, The Primrose Path, **40**; Reaching For The Sun, Sullivan's Travels, **41**; The Great Man's Lady, The Palm Beach Story, **42**; The More The Merrier, **43**; Buffalo Bill, The Great Moment, **44**; The Unseen, **45**; The Virginian, **46**; Ramrod, **47**; Four Faces West, **48**; Colorado Territory, South Of St Louis, **49**; The Outriders, Saddle Tramp, Stars In My Crown, **50**; Cattle Drive, **51**; Frenchie, The San Francisco Story, Rough Shoot, **52**; Lone Hand, **53**; Black Horse Canyon, Border River, **54**; Stranger On Horseback, Wichita, **55**; The First Texan, **56**; Gunsight Ridge, The Oklahoman, The Tall Stranger, Trooper Hook, **57**; Cattle Empire, Fort Massacre, **58**; The Gunfight At Dodge City, **59**; Ride The High Country, **62**; Cry Blood Apache, **68**; The Great American Cowboy, **74**; Mustang Country, **76**.

MACDONALD, JEANETTE: The Love Parade, **29**; Let's Go Native, The Lottery Bride, Monte Carlo, Oh For A Man!, The Vagabond King, **30**; Annabelle's Affairs, Don't Bet On Women, **31**; Love Me Tonight, One Hour With You, **32**; The Cat And The Fiddle, The Merry Widow, **34**; Naughty Marietta, **35**; Rose Marie, San Francisco, **36**; The Firefly, Maytime, **37**; The Girl Of The Golden West, Sweethearts, **38**; Broadway Serenade, **39**; Bitter Sweet, New Moon, **40**; Smilin' Through, **41**; Cairo, I Married An Angel, **42**; Follow The Boys, **44**; Three Daring Daughters, The Birds And The Bees, **48**; The Sun Comes Up, **49**.

MACKENDRICK, ALEXANDER: Midnight Menace, **37**; Love On The Range, **39**;

Movie talk

Dailies/rushes: day's scenes processed and rushed to director for viewing.

Director of photography: the creative boss responsible for style, atmosphere, lighting, composition, colour, lenses, filters, film stock and printing.

Distributor/renter: middle man between producer and exhibitor who markets, advertises and sells a film.

Executive producer: often a figurehead who lends his/her name to a project.

Exhibitor: cinema operator, whose booking power varies according to size. In Britain Odeon, MGM, UCI and Warner are principal cinema circuits.

Feature player: supporting rather than starring actor.

Fex: Russian avant-garde movement in the 1920s known as the Factory of the Eccentric Actor that took elements of theatre, circus and vaudeville and applied it to cinema.

Film noir: first used by French critics about bleak and fatalistically themed American urban suspense films of the 1940s and 1950s, which exuded disillusionment and moral corruption. Mostly shot against a bleak cityscape.

Final cut: completed edited film, usually the director's responsibility.

Flashback/forward: device for underpinning plot with past or future events.

Focus puller: usually first assistant cameraman who measures distance between lens and key points in scene for travelling shots.

Foley artist: creates sound effects not recorded on the set. After Jack Foley, a legendary practitioner of the craft.

Free cinema: 1950s British movement when some film-makers shunned portrayals of comfortable middle-class subjects for what they believed to be the reality of socially controversial subjects, often against bleak industrial backgrounds.

Front office: sanctions production and apportions a film's budget. Where the real power resides.

Gaffer: chief electrician responsible for lighting.

Saraband For Dead Lovers, 48; Whisky Galore, 49; The Blue Lamp, Dance Hall, 50; The Man In The White Suit, 51; Mandy, 52; The Maggie, 54; The Ladykillers, 55; Sweet Smell Of Success, 57; Sammy Going South, 63; A High Wind In Jamaica, 65; Don't Make Waves, Oh Dad Poor Dad Mama's Hung You In The Closet And I'm Feeling So Sad, 67.

MCLAGLEN, VICTOR: The Call Of The Road, 20; The Glorious Adventure, 22; Heartstrings, 23; The Beloved Brute, 24; The Fighting Heart, The Unholy Three, Winds Of Chance, 25; Beau Geste, What Price Glory?, 26; Mother Machree, Loves Of Carmenas Escamillo, 27; A Girl In Every Port, Hangman's House, The River Pirate, 28; Happy Days, Captain Lash, The Cock-Eyed World, Strong Boy, 29; A Devil With Women, 30; Annabelle's Affairs, Dishonored, Not Exactly Gentlemen, Wicked, Women Of All Nations, 31; While Paris Sleeps, Devil's Lottery, The Gay Caballero, Guilty As Hell, Rackety Rax, 32; Dick Turpin, Hot Pepper, Laughing At Life, 33; The Captain Hates The Sea, The Lost Patrol, Murder At The Vanities, No More Women, The Wharf Angel, 34; The Great Hotel Murder, The Informer, Under Pressure, 35; Klondike Annie, The Magnificent Brute, Professional Soldier, Under Two Flags, 36; Nancy Steel Is Missing, Sea Devils, This Is My Affair, Wee Willie Winkie, 37; The Battle Of Broadway, Pacific Liner, The Devil's Party, We're Going To Be Rich, 38; The Big Guy, Captain Fury, Ex-Champ, Full Confession, Gunga Din, Let Freedom Ring, Pacific Liner, Rio, 39; Diamond Frontier, South Of Pago Pago, 40; Broadway Limited, 41; Call Out The Marines, Powder Town, 42; The Princess And The Pirate, Roger Touhy Gangster, Tampico, 44; Rough Tough And Ready, The Last Gangster, 45; Whistle Stop, Love Honor And Goodbye, Calendar Girl, 46; The Foxes Of Harrow, The Michigan Kid, 47; Fort Apache, 48; She Wore A Yellow Ribbon, 49; Rio Grande, 50; The Quiet Man, 52; Fair Wind To Java, Trouble In The Glen, 53; Prince Valiant, 54; City Of Shadows, Lady Godiva, Many Rivers To Cross, Bengazi, 55; Around The World In 80 Days, 56; The Abductors, Secret Service, 57; Sea Fury, 58.

MACLAINE, SHIRLEY: The Trouble With Harry, Artists And Models, 55; Around The World In 80 Days, 56; Hot Spell, The Matchmaker, The Sheepman, 58; Some Came Running, Ask Any Girl, Career, 59; The Apartment, Can-Can, Ocean's Eleven, 60; All In A Night's Work, 61; The Children's Hour, My Geisha, Two For The Seesaw, 62; Irma La Douce, 63; What A Way To Go!, 64; John Goldfarb Please Come Home, The Yellow Rolls-Royce, 65; Gambit, 66; Woman Times Seven, 67; The Bliss Of Mrs Blossom, 68; Sweet Charity, 69; Two Mules For Sister Sara, 70; Desperate Characters, 71; The Possession Of Joel Delaney, 72; Sois Belle Et Tais-Toi, The Turning Point, 77; Being There, 79; A Change Of Seasons, Loving Couples, 80; Terms Of Endearment, 83; Cannonball Run II, 84; Madame Sousatzka, 88; Steel Magnolias, 89; Postcards From The Edge, Waiting For The Light, 90; Defending Your Life, 91; Used People, 92; Wrestling Ernest Hemingway, 93; Guarding Tess, 94; Mrs Winterbourne, Evening Star, 96.

MCLAREN, NORMAN: Love On The Wing, 38; Fiddle-De-Dee, 47; Begone Dull Care, Stars And Stripes, 49; Neighbors, 52; Blinkety Blank, 55; A Chairy Tale, 57; Pas De Deux, 67.

MACMURRAY, FRED: Girls Go Wild, 34; Alice Adams, The Bride Comes Home, Car 99, Grand Old Girl, Hands Across The Table, Men Without Names, The Gilded Lily, 35; The Princess Comes Across, The Texas Rangers, Thirteen Hours By Air, Trail Of The Lonesome Pine, 36; Champagne Waltz, Exclusive, Maid Of Salem, Swing High Swing Low, True Confession, 37; Cocoanut Grove, Men With Wings, Sing You Sinners, 38; Cafe Society, Honeymoon In Bali, Invitation To Happiness, 39; Little Old New York, Rangers Of Fortune, Remember The Night, Too Many Husbands, 40; Dive Bomber, New York Town, One Night In Lisbon, Virginia, 41; The Forest Rangers, The Lady Is Willing, Star Spangled Rhythm, Take A Letter Darling, 42; Above Suspicion, Flight For Freedom, No Time For Love, 43; And The Angels Sing, Double Indemnity, Practically Yours, Standing Room Only, Captain Eddie, Murder He Says, 44; Pardon My Past, Where Do We Go From Here?, 45; Smoky, 46; The Egg And I, Singapore, Suddenly It's Spring, 47; Family Honeymoon, Don't Trust Your Husband, The Miracle Of The Bells, On Our Merry Way, 48; Father Was A Fullback, 49; Borderline, Never A Dull Moment, 50; Callaway Went Thataway, A Millionaire For Christy, 51; Fair Wind To Java, The Moonlighter, 53; The Caine Mutiny, Pushover, A Woman's World, 54; At Gunpoint, The Far Horizons, The Rains Of Ranchipur, 55; There's Always Tomorrow, 56; Gun For A Coward, Quantez, 57; Day Of The Bad Man, Good Day For A Hanging, Face Of A Fugitive, 58; The Oregon Trail, The Shaggy Dog, 59; The Apartment, 60; The Absent-Minded Professor, 61; Bon Voyage!, 62; Son Of Flubber, 63; Kisses For My President, 64; Follow Me Boys!, 66; The Happiest Millionaire, 67; Charley And The Angel, 73; The Swarm, 78.

MCQUEEN, STEVE: Somebody Up There Likes Me, 56; The Blob, Never Love A Stranger, 58; The Great St Louis Bank Robbery, Never So Few, 59; The Magnificent Seven, 60; The Honeymoon Machine, 61; Hell Is For Heroes, 62; The War Lover, The Great Escape, Love With The Proper Stranger, Soldier In The Rain, 63; Baby The Rain Must Fall, The Cincinnati Kid, 65; Nevada Smith, The Sand Pebbles, 66; Bullitt, The Thomas Crown Affair, 68; The Reivers, 69; Le Mans, 71; The Getaway, Junior Bonner, 72; Papillon, 73; The Towering Inferno, 74; An Enemy Of The People, 77; Tom Horn, 79; The Hunter, 80.

MAGNANI, ANNA: Tempo Massimo, 34; Una Lampada Alla Finestra, 40; Teresa Venerdi, 41; Rome, Open City, 45; Abbasso La Ricchezza, The Bandit, 46; L'Onorevole Angelina, 47; L'Amore, 48; Molti Sogni Per Le Strade, 49; Bellissima, 51; Camicie Rosse, La Carosse D'Or, 52; The Rose Tattoo, 55; Suor Letizia, Wild Is The Wind, 57; Hell In The City, 58; The Fugitive Kind, Risate Di Gioia, 60; Mamma Roma, 62; Le Magot De Josefa, 63; The Secret Of Santa Vittoria, 69; Fellini's Roma, 72.

MAILER, NORMAN: The Naked And The Dead, 58; An American Dream, 66; Beyond The Law, Wild 90, 68; Maidstone, 71; Ragtime, 81; Tough Guys Don't Dance, 87.

MALICK, TERRENCE: Pocket Money, 72; Badlands, 73; The Gravy Train, 74; Days Of Heaven, 78.

MALKOVICH, JOHN: The Killing Fields, Places In The Heart, 84; Eleni, 85; Empire Of The Sun, The Glass Menagerie, Making Mr Right, 87; Dangerous Liaisons, Miles From Home, 88; The Sheltering Sky, 90; The Object Of Beauty, Queens Logic, 91; Jennifer 8, Of Mice And Men, Shadows And Fog, 92; In The Line Of Fire, 93; Heart Of Darkness, 94; Mulholland Falls, Mary Reilly, Beyond The Clouds, 95; Mary Reilly, 96; Con Air, 97.

MALLE, LOUIS: L'Ascenseur Pour L'Echafaud, 57; Les Amants, 58; Zazie Dans Le Metro, 60; A Very Private Affair, 62; Le Feu Follet, 63; Viva Maria!, 65; Young Torless, 66; Le Voleur, 67; Spirits Of The Dead, 68; La Souffle Au Coeur, 71; Place De La République, 73; Lacombe Lucien, 74; Black Moon, 75; Pretty Baby, 78; Atlantic City, 80; My Dinner With André, 81; Crackers, 84; Alamo Bay, 85; Au Revoir Les Enfants, 87; Milou En Mai, 90; Damage, 92; Vanya On 42nd Street, 94.

MAMET, DAVID: The Postman Always Rings Twice, 81; House Of Games, The Untouchables, 87; Things Change, 88; We're No Angels, 89; Homicide, 91; Glengarry Glen Ross, Hoffa, 92; Rising Sun, 93; Oleanna, 94; American Buffalo, 96.

MAMOULIAN, ROUBEN: Applause, 29; City Streets, 31; Dr Jekyll And Mr Hyde, Love Me Tonight, 32; Queen Christina, Song Of Songs, 33; We Live Again, 34; Becky Sharp, 35; The Gay Desperado, 36; High Wide And Handsome, 37; Golden Boy, 39; The Mark Of Zorro, 40; Blood And Sand, 41; Rings On Her Fingers, 42; Summer Holiday, 48; Silk Stockings, 57; Never Steal Anything Small, 59.

MANCINI, HENRY: Touch Of Evil, The Voice In The Mirror, 58; The Great Impostor, High Time, 60; Bachelor In Paradise, Breakfast At Tiffany's, 61; Days Of Wine And Roses, Experiment In Terror, Hatari!, Mr Hobbs Takes A Vacation, 62; Charade, Soldier In The Rain, 63; Dear Heart, The Killers, Man's Favorite Sport?, The Pink Panther, A Shot In The Dark, 64; The Great Race, 65; Arabesque, Moment To Moment, What Did You Do In The War Daddy?, 66; Gunn, Two For The Road, Wait Until Dark, 67; The Party, 68; Gaily Gaily, Me, Natalie, 69; Darling Lili, The Hawaiians, The Molly Maguires, I Girasoli, 70; Never Give An Inch, 71; Oklahoma Crude, The Thief Who Came To Dinner, Visions Of Eight, 73; 99 And 44/100% Dead, The Girl From Petrovka, The White Dawn, 74; The Great Waldo Pepper, Once Is Not Enough, The Return Of The Pink Panther, 75; Alex And The Gypsy, The Pink Panther Strikes Again, Silver Streak, W C Fields And Me, 76; House Calls, Revenge Of The Pink Panther, Who Is Killing The Great Chefs Of Europe?, 78; 10, More American Graffiti, Nightwing, The Prisoner Of Zenda, 79; A Change Of Seasons, Little Miss Marker, 80; Back Roads, Condorman, Mommie Dearest, SOB, 81; Trail Of The Pink Panther, Victor/Victoria, 82; Curse Of The Pink Panther, The Man Who Loved Women, Second Thoughts, 83; Harry And Son, 84; Life Force, Santa Claus, That's Dancing!, 85; A Fine Mess, The Great Mouse Detective, That's Life!, 86; Blind Date, The Glass Menagerie, 87; Sunset, Without A Clue, 88; Physical Evidence, Welcome Home, 89; Ghost Dad, 90; Switch, Married To It, 91; Tom And Jerry: The Movie, 92; Hexed, Son Of The Pink Panther, 93.

MANKIEWICZ, JOSEPH L: Fast Company, 29; If I Had A Million, 32; Alice In Wonderland, 33; Forsaking All Others, 35; Fury, 36; The Bride Wore Red, 37; Three Comrades, 38; The Philadelphia Story, Strange Cargo, 40; The Keys Of The Kingdom, 44; Somewhere In The Night, Dragonwyck, 46; The Ghost And Mrs Muir, The Late George Apley, 47; Escape, 48; House Of Strangers, A Letter To Three Wives, 49; All About Eve, No Way Out, 50; People Will Talk, 51; Five Fingers, 52; Julius Caesar, 53; The Barefoot Contessa, 54; Guys And Dolls, 55; The Quiet American, 58; Suddenly Last Summer, 59; Cleopatra, 63; The Honey Pot, 67; There Was A Crooked Man, 70; Sleuth, 72.

MANN, ANTHONY: Dr Broadway, Moonlight In Havana, 42; Nobody's Darling, 43; My Best Gal, Strangers In The Night, 44; The Great Flamarion, Sing Your Way Home, Two O'Clock Courage, 45; The Bamboo Blonde, Strange Impersonation, 46; Desperate, Railroaded, 47; T-Men, Raw Deal, 48; Border Incident, Reign Of Terror, Side Street, 49; It's A Big Country, Devil's Doorway, The Furies, Winchester '73, 50; The Tall Target, 51; Bend Of The River, 52; The Naked Spur, Thunder Bay, 53; The Glenn Miller Story, 54; The Far Country, The Man From Laramie, Strategic Air Command, 55; The Last Frontier, Serenade, 56; Men In War, The Tin Star, 57; God's Little Acre, Man Of The West, 58; Spartacus, Cimarron, 60; El Cid, 61; The Fall Of The Roman Empire, 64; The Heroes Of Telemark, 65; A Dandy In Aspic, 68.

MARAIS, JEAN: Bird Of Prey, 33; Le Pavillon Brûlé, Les Evades De L'An 4000, 41; Le Lit A Colonnes, 42; L'Eternel Retour, Voyage Sans Espoir, 43; La Belle Et La Bête, Carmen, Le Chouans, 46; Ruy Blas, The Eagle Has Two Heads, Au Yeux Du Souvenir, Les Parents Terribles, 48; Mayerling, 49; Orphée, Les Miracles N'Ont Lieu Qu'Une Fois, Nez De Cuir, 51; L'Appel Du Destin, La Maison Du Silence, L'Amour Madame, 52; Inside A Girls' Dormitory, Julietta, Les Amants De Minuit, 53; The Count Of Monte Cristo, Le Guerisseur, Versailles, 54; Futures Vedettes, Si Paris Nous Etait Conté, 55; Elena Et Les Hommes, Typhon Sur Nagasaki, Kiss Of Fire, 56; Le Tour Prends Garde!, Un Amour De Poche, White Nights, 57; La Vie A Deux, Chaque Jour A Son Secret, 58; SOS Noronha, Le Bossu, The Testament Of Orpheus, 59; The Battle Of Austerlitz, Le Capitan, La Princesse De Cleves, 60; Le Capitaine Fracasse, Napoleon II L'Aiglon, 61; Le Masque De Fer, Les Miracle Des Loups, Les Mystères De Paris, Pontius Pilate, 62; L'Honorable Stanislas Agent Secret, 63; Fantômas, Friend Of The Family, 64; Fantômas Se Déchaine, Le Gentleman De Cocody, Pleins Feux Sur Stanislas, Train D'Enfer, 65; Fantômas Vs Scotland Yard, Le Saint Prend L'Affût, Sept Hommes Et Une Garce, 66; Le Paria, 68; La Provocation, 69; Peau D'Ane, 71; Ombre Et Secrets, 83; Parking, 85; Next Of Kin, 86; Joan Of Arc Of Mongolia, 89; Shipwrecked Children, 92.

MARCH, FREDRIC: The Great Adventure, Paying The Piper, 21; The Dummy, Footlights And Fools, Jealousy, The Marriage Playground, Paris Bound, The Studio Murder Mystery, The Wild Party, 29; Ladies Love Brutes, Laughter, Manslaughter, Paramount On Parade, The Royal Family Of Broadway, Sarah And Son, True To The Navy, 30; Honor Among Lovers, My Sin, The Night Angel, 31; Dr Jekyll And Mr Hyde, Merrily We Go To Hell, The Sign Of The Cross, Smilin' Through, Strangers In Love, 32; Design For Living, The Eagle And The Hawk, Tonight Is Ours, 33; Affairs Of Cellini, All Of Me, The Barretts Of Wimpole Street, Death Takes A Holiday, Good Dame, We Live Again, 34; Anna Karenina, The Dark Angel, Les Misérables, 35; Anthony Adverse, Mary Of Scotland, The Road To Glory, 36; Nothing Sacred, A Star Is Born, 37; The Buccaneer, There Goes My Heart, Trade Winds, 38; Susan And God, Victory, 40; Bedtime Story, One Foot In Heaven, So Ends Our Night, 41; I Married A Witch, 42; The Adventures Of Mark Twain, Tomorrow The World, 44; The Best Years Of Our Lives, 46; An Act Of Murder, Another Part Of The Forest, 48; Christopher Columbus, 49; Death Of A Salesman, It's A Big Country, 51; Man On A Tightrope, 53; The Bridges At Toko-ri, Executive Suite, 54; The Desperate Hours, 55; Alexander The Great, The Man In The Grey Flannel Suit, 56; Middle Of The Night, 59; Inherit The Wind, 60; The Young Doctors, 61; The Condemned Of Altona, 63; Seven Days In May, 64; Hombre, 67; Tick Tick Tick, 70; The Iceman Cometh, 73.

MARSHALL, GEORGE: Prairie Trails, Ruth Of The Rockies, 20; After Your Own Heart, Hands Off, The Jolt, A Ridin' Romeo, Why Trust Your Husband?, 21; Smiles Are Trumps, 22; Don Quickshot Of The Rio Grande, Haunted Valley, Where Is This West?, 23; The Gay Retreat, 27; Pack Up Your Troubles, Their First Mistake, Towed In A Hole, 32; 365 Nights In Hollywood, She Learned About Sailors, Wild Gold, 34; In Old Kentucky, Life Begins At Forty, Music Is Magic, Show Them No Mercy!, Ten Dollar Raise, 35; Can This Be Dixie?, The Crime Of Dr Forbes, A Message To Garcia, 36; Ever Since Eve, Love Under Fire, Nancy Steel Is Missing, 37; The Battle Of Broadway, The Goldwyn Follies, Hold That Co-ed, 38; Destry Rides Again, You Can't Cheat An Honest Man, 39; The Ghost Breakers, When The Daltons Rode, 40; Pot O' Gold, Texas, 41; The Forest Rangers, Star Spangled Rhythm, Valley Of The Sun, 42; Riding High, True To Life, 43; And The Angels Sing, 44; Hold That Blonde, Incendiary Blonde, Murder He Says, 45; The Blue Dahlia, Monsieur Beaucaire, 46; The Perils Of Pauline, Variety Girl, 47; Hazard, Tap Roots, 48; My Friend Irma, 49; Fancy Pants, Never A Dull Moment, 50; A Millionaire For Christy, 51; The Savage, 52; Houdini, Money From Home, Off Limits, Scared Stiff, 53; Destry, Duel In The Jungle, Red Garters, 54; The Second Greatest Sex, 55; Pillars Of The Sky, 56; Beyond Mombasa, The Guns Of Fort Petticoat, 57; The Sad Sack, Imitation General, The Sheepman, 58; The Gazebo, It Started With A Kiss, The Mating Game, 59; Cry For Happy, 61; The Happy Thieves, How The West Was Won, 62; Papa's Delicate Condition, 63; Advance To The Rear, Dark Purpose, 64; Boy Did I Get A Wrong Number!, 66; Eight On The Lam, 67; The Wicked Dreams Of Paula Schultz, 68; Hook Line And Sinker, 69.

MARSHALL, HERBERT: Mumsie, 27; Dawn, 28; The Letter, 29; Murder, 30; The Calendar, Michael And Mary, Secrets Of A Secretary, 31; Blonde Venus, Evenings For Sale, The Faithful Heart, Trouble In Paradise, 32; Clear All Wires, I Was A Spy, The Solitaire Man, 33; Four Frightened People, Outcast Lady, The Painted Veil, Riptide, 34; Accent On Youth, The Dark Angel, The Flame Within, The Good Fairy, If You Could Only Cook, 35; Forgotten Faces, Girls' Dormitory, The Lady Consents, Make Way For A Lady, Till We Meet Again, A Woman Rebels, 36; Angel, Breakfast For Two, 37; Always Goodbye, Mad About Music, Woman Against Woman, 38; Zaza, 39; A Bill Of Divorcement, Foreign Correspondent, The Letter, 40; Adventure In Washington, Kathleen, The Litt[le] Foxes, When Ladies Meet, 41; The Moon And Sixpence, 42; Flight For Freedom, Forever And A Day, Young Ideas, 43; Andy Hardy's Blonde Trouble, 44; The Enchanted Cottage, The Unseen, 45; Crack-Up, Duel In The Sun, The Razor's Edg[e], 46; High Wall, Ivy, 47; The Secret Garden, 49; The Underworld Story, 50; An[ne] Of The Indies, Captain Blackjack, 51; Angel Face, 53; The Black Shield Of Falwor[th], Gog, Riders To The Stars, 54; The Virgin Queen, 55; The Weapon, 56; Wicked As Th[ey] Come, 57; The Fly, Stage Struck, 58; College Confidential, Midnight Lace, 60; A Fever In The Blood, 61; The Caretakers, The List Of Adrian Messenger, 63; The Thir[d] Day, 65.

MARSHALL, PENNY: Jumpin' Jack Flash, 86; Big, 88; Awakenings, 90; A League Of Their Own, 92; Renaissance Man, 94; The Preacher's Wife 96.

MARTIN, STEVE: Sgt Pepper's Lonely Hearts Club Band, 78; The Jerk, The Mupp[et] Movie, 79; Pennies From Heaven, 81; Dead Men Don't Wear Plaid, 82; The Man With Two Brains, 83; All Of Me, The Lonely Guy, 84; Movers And Shakers, 85; Little Shop Of Horrors, Three Amigos!, 86; Planes Trains And Automobiles, Roxann[e], 87; Dirty Rotten Scoundrels, 88; Parenthood, 89; My Blue Heaven, 90; Gra[nd] Canyon, LA Story, Father Of The Bride, 91; Housesitter, Leap Of Faith, 92; And Th[e] Band Played On, 93; Simple Twist Of Fate, 94; Mixed Nuts, Father Of The Bride 2, 95; Sgt Bilko, 96.

MARVIN, LEE: Diplomatic Courier, The Duel At Silver Creek, Eight Iron Men, Hangman's Knot, 52; The Big Heat, The Glory Brigade, Gun Fury, Seminole, The Stranger Wore A Gun, The Wild One, 53; The Caine Mutiny, Gorilla At Large, The Raic[ers], 54; Bad Day At Black Rock, I Died A Thousand Times, A Life In The Balance, Not As A Stranger, Pete Kelly's Blues, Shack Out On 101, Violent Saturday, 55; Attack!, Pillars Of The Sky, The Rack, Seven Men From Now, 56; Raintree County, 57; The Comancheros, 61; The Man Who Shot Liberty Valance, 62; Donovan's Reef, 63; T[he] Killers, 64; Cat Ballou, Ship Of Fools, 65; Our Time In Hell, The Professionals, 66; The Dirty Dozen, Point Blank, Tonight Let's All Make Love In London, 67; Hell In The Pacific, Sergeant Ryker, 68; Paint Your Wagon, 69; Monte Walsh, 70; Pocket Money, Prime Cut, 72; Emperor Of The North/Emperor Of The North Pole, The Iceman Cometh, 73; The Klansman, The Spikes Gang, 74; The Great Scout And Cathouse Thursday, Shout At The Devil, 76; Avalanche Express, 79; The Big Red O[ne], 80; Death Hunt, 81; Gorky Park, 83; Canicule, 84; The Delta Force, 85.

MARX BROTHERS: Chico, Groucho, Harpo, Zeppo: The Cocoanuts, 29; Animal Crackers, 30; Monkey Business, 31; Horse Feathers, 32; Duck Soup, 33. Witho[ut] Zeppo: A Night At The Opera, 35; A Day At The Races, 37; Room Service, 38; At Th[e] Circus, 39; Go West, 40; The Big Store, 41; A Night In Casablanca, Love Happy, 49; The Story Of Mankind, 57. Groucho only: Copacabana, 47; Mr Music, 50; Double Dynamite, 51; A Girl In Every Port, 52; Will Success Spoil Rock Hunter?, 57; Skido[o], 68. Harpo only: Too Many Kisses, 25; Stage Door Canteen, 43.

MASON, JAMES: Late Extra, 35; Blind Man's Bluff, Prison Breaker, The Secre[t] Of Stamboul, Troubled Waters, Twice Branded, 36; Catch As Catch Can, Fire Ove[r] England, The High Command, The Mill On The Floss, 37; The Return Of The Scarle[t] Pimpernel, 38; I Met A Murderer, 39; Hatter's Castle, This Man Is Dangerous, 41; The Night Has Eyes, Secret Mission, Thunder Rock, 42; The Alibi, The Bells Go Down, Candlelight In Algeria, The Man In Grey, They Met In The Dark, 43; Hotel Reserve, Fanny By Gaslight, 44; A Place Of One's Own, The Seventh Veil, They Were Sisters, The Wicked Lady, 45; Odd Man Out, The Upturned Glass, 47; Caught, East Side West Side, Madame Bovary, The Reckless Moment, 49; One-Way Street, 50; The Desert Fox, Pandora And The Flying Dutchman, 51; Face To Face, Five Fingers, Lady Possessed, The Prisoner Of Zenda, 52; Charade, Botany Bay, The Desert Rats, Julius Caesar, The Man Between, The Story Of Three Loves, 53; 20,000 Leagues

ıder The Sea, Prince Valiant, A Star Is
rn, 54; Bigger Than Life, Forever Darling,
5; Island In The Sun, 57; Cry Terror,
e Decks Ran Red, 58; Journey To The
entre Of The Earth, North By Northwest,
9; A Touch Of Larceny, The Marriage-Go-
und, The Trials Of Oscar Wilde, 60;
cape From Zahrain, Hero's Island, Lolita,
ara Tahiti, 62; The Fall Of The Roman
mpire, The Pumpkin Eater, Torpedo Bay, 64;
enghis Khan, Lord Jim, The
inhibited, 65; The Blue Max, Georgy Girl,
5; The Deadly Affair, 67; Stranger In
e House, Duffy, Mayerling, The Sea Gull,
8; Age Of Consent, 69; Spring And
rt Wine, The Yin And Yang Of Mr Go, 70;
d Man's River, Child's Play, Kill! Kill!
l!, 72; The Last Of Sheila, The Mackintosh
an, 73; 11 Harrowhouse, 74;
tobiography Of A Princess, Gente Di
spetto, Inside Out, Mandingo, 75;
yage Of The Damned, 76; Cross Of Iron,
7; The Boys From Brazil, Heaven Can
ait, The Water Babies, 78; Bloodline, Murder
Decree, The Passage, 79; North Sea
jack, 80; A Dangerous Summer, 81; Evil
der The Sun, The Verdict, 82;
exandre, Dr Fischer Of Geneva, Yellowbeard,
3; The Shooting Party, 84; The Assisi
derground, 85.

ASTROIANNI, MARCELLO: Sunday
August, 49; Atto Di Accusa, 51; The Girls
om The Spanish Steps, Penne Nere,
ensualita, 52; Altri Tempi, 53; Giorni
Amore, La Principessa Delle Canarie,
4; The Bigamist, 55; The Miller's Beautiful
fe, Too Bad She's Bad, 56; Lucky To
A Woman, The Most Wonderful Moment,
hite Nights, 57; Big Deal On Madonna
reet, Love On The Riviera, Tutti Innamorati,
8; Where The Hot Wind Blows!, 59; Il
ll'Antonio, La Dolce Vita, 60; Love A La
arte, The Assassin, Ghosts Of Rome,
1; La Notte, Divorce Italian Style, Family
ary, A Very Private Affair, 62; 8½, 63;
e Organiser, Marriage Italian Style,
sterday, Today And Tomorrow, 64;
asanova '70, Kiss The Other Sheikh, The
an With The Balloons, The Tenth
ctim, The Poppy Is Also A Flower, 66; Shoot
ud Louder I Don't Understand, 67;
e Stranger, 68; Diamonds For Breakfast,
osts Italian Style, A Place For Lovers,
9; Giochi Particolari, Leo The Last, The Pizza
angle, Scipione Detto Anche
Africano, 70; Il Girasole, It Only Happens To
hers, Liza, Permette Rocco Papaleo,
e Priest's Wife, 71; What?, Fellini's Roma,
2; La Grande Bouffe, Massacre In
me, Mordi E Fuggi, A Slightly Pregnant Man,
uche Pas La Femme Blanche!, 73; La
pa Del Gangster, The Bit Player, 74;
onsanfan, Down The Ancient Stairs,
5; Culastrise Nobile Veneziano, Signore E
gnori Buonanotte, The Sunday Woman,
e Divine Creature, 76; Todo Modo, Doppio
litto, A Special Day, 77; The Wife
stress, Bye Bye Monkey, 78; The Terrace,
ay As You Are, Revenge, Giallo
apoletano, L'Uomo Di Conseguenza, 79;
affic Jam, La Citta Delle Donne, 80;
ntasma D'Amore, 81; La Pelle, La Nuit De
rennes, 82; Oltre La Porta, Gabriela,
Général De L'Armée Morte, 83; The Story
Piera, Henry IV, 84; Macaroni, 85;
e Beekeeper, Ginger And Fred, I Soliti Ignoti
nt'anni Dopo, Big Deal On Madonna
reet 20 Years Later, A Beekeeper Dies, 86;
ark Eyes, 87; Splendor, Intervista, 88;
ss Arizona, What Time Is It?, 89; Verso
ra, 90; Everybody's Fine, Tchin-Tchin,
Voleur D'Enfants, 91; The Suspended Step
The Stork, Used People, 92; We Don't
lk About That, Un Deaux Trois Soleil, 93;
êt-A-Porter, Beyond The Clouds, 95.

ATTHAU, WALTER: The Indian
ghter, The Kentuckian, 55; Bigger Than Life,
6; A Face In The Crowd, Slaughter On
nth Avenue, 57; King Creole, Onionhead,
de A Crooked Trail, The Voice In The
rror, 58; Gangster Story, Strangers When
e Meet, 60; Lonely Are The Brave,
ho's Got The Action?, 62; Charade, Island
Love, 63; Ensign Pulver, Fail-Safe,
odbye Charlie, 64; Mirage, 65; The
rtune Cookie, 66; A Guide For The
arried Man, 67; Candy, The Odd Couple,
e Secret Life Of An American Wife, 68;
ctus Flower, Hello Dolly!, 69; Kotch, A New
af, Plaza Suite, 71; Pete 'n' Tillie, 72;
arley Varrick, The Laughing Policeman, 73;
rthquake, The Front Page, The Taking
Pelham One Two Three, 74; The Sunshine
ys, 75; The Bad News Bears,
ntleman Tramp, 76; California Suite,
sey's Shadow, House Calls, 78;
opscotch, Little Miss Marker, Portrait Of A
60% Perfect Man, 80; Buddy Buddy, First Monday In October, 81; I Ought To Be In Pictures, 82; The Survivors, 83; Movers And Shakers, 85; Pirates, 86; The Couch Trip, The Little Devil, 88; JFK, 91; Dennis The Menace, Grumpy Old Men, 93; IQ, 94; The Grass Harp, Grumpier Old Men, 95; I'm Not Rappaport, 96.

MATTHEWS, JESSIE: The Beloved Vagabond, 23; Straws In The Wind, 24; Out Of The Blue, 31; The Midshipmaid, There Goes The Bride, 32; Friday The 13th, The Good Companions, The Man From Toronto, 33; Evergreen, Waltzes From Vienna, 34; First A Girl, 35; It's Love Again, 36; Gangway, Head Over Heels, 37; Climbing High, Sailing Along, 38; Forever And A Day, 43; Candles At Nine, 44; Tom Thumb, 58.

MAYER, CARL: The Cabinet Of Dr Caligari, 19; Der Dummkopf, Der Gang In Der Nacht, The Hunchback And The Dancer, 20; The Haunted Castle, Shattered, 21; The Last Laugh, 24; Tartuffe, 25; Berlin: Symphony Of A Big City, Sunrise, 27; Four Devils, 29; 13 Men And A Girl, 30; Ariane, 31; Mélo, 32; Dreaming Lips, 36.

MELVILLE, JEAN-PIERRE: Le Silence De La Mer, 49; Les Enfants Terribles, 50; Quand Tu Lira Cette Lettre, 53; Bob Le Flambeur, 55; Deux Hommes Dans Manhattan, 59; Léon Morin – Priest, 61; Le Doulos, Magnet Of Doom, 63; Second Wind, 66; Le Samourai, 67; L'Armée Des Ombres, 69; Le Cercle Rouge, 70; Un Flic, 72.

MENJOU, ADOLPHE: Courage, The Faith Healer, The Sheik, The Three Musketeers, Through The Back Door, 21; Clarence, The Eternal Flame, Is Matrimony A Failure?, Pink Gods, Singed Wings, The Fast Mail, 22; Bella Donna, Rupert Of Hentzau, A Woman Of Paris, The World's Applause, 23; Broadway After Dark, Broken Barriers, The Fast Set, For Sale, Forbidden Paradise, The Marriage Cheat, The Marriage Circle, 24; Are Parents People?, The King On Main Street, A Kiss In The Dark, The Swan, 25; The Ace Of Cads, The Grand Duchess And The Waiter, Glorious Youth, A Social Celebrity, The Sorrows Of Satan, 26; Blonde Or Brunette, Evening Clothes, A Gentleman Of Paris, Serenade, Service For Ladies, 27; His Private Life, His Tiger Lady, A Night Of Mystery, 28; Fashions In Love, 29; Morocco, 30; The Easiest Way, Friends And Lovers, The Front Page, The Great Lover, Men Call It Love, The Parisian, 31; Bachelor's Affairs, Blame The Woman, A Farewell To Arms, Forbidden, The Night Club Lady, Prestige, The Great Lover, 32; Convention City, Morning Glory, The Circus Queen Murder, 33; Easy To Love, The Great Flirtation, The Human Side, Journal Of A Crime, Little Miss Marker, The Mighty Barnum, The Trumpet Blows, Morning Glory, 34; Broadway Gondolier, Gold Diggers Of 1935, 35; The Milky Way, One In A Million, Sing Baby Sing, Wives Never Know, 36; Cafe Metropole, One Hundred Men And A Girl, Stage Door, A Star Is Born, 37; The Goldwyn Follies, A Letter Of Introduction, Thanks For Everything, 38; Golden Boy, The Housekeeper's Daughter, King Of The Turf, 39; A Bill Of Divorcement, New Moon, Turnabout, 40; Father Takes A Wife, Road Show, 41; Roxie Hart, Syncopation, You Were Never Lovelier, 42; Hi Diddle Diddle, Sweet Rosie O'Grady, 43; Step Lively, 44; The Bachelor's Daughters, Heartbeat, A Man Alive, 46; The Hucksters, I'll Be Yours, Mr District Attorney, 47; State Of The Union, 48; Dancing In The Dark, My Dream Is Yours, 49; To Please A Lady, 50; Across The Wide Missouri, The Tall Target, 51; The Sniper, 52; Man On A Tightrope, 53; Timberjack, The Ambassador's Daughter, I Married A Woman, Bundle Of Joy, 56; Paths Of Glory, The Fuzzy Pink Nightgown, 57; Pollyanna, 60.

MENZIES, WILLIAM CAMERON: The Thief Of Bagdad, 24; Cobra, The Eagle The Bat, 25; The Bat, 27; Tempest, The Awakening, The Dove, The Garden Of Eden, 28; Alibi, Bulldog Drummond, The Iron Mask, The Taming Of The Shrew, 29; Du Barry, The Bad One, The Champ, Zampa, 30; Always Goodbye, The Spider, 31; Almost Married, Chandu The Magician, 32; Alice In Wonderland, I Loved You Wednesday, 33; The Wharf Angel, 34; Things To Come, 36; The Green Cockatoo, 37; Gone With The Wind, 39; Foreign Correspondent, 40; Address Unknown, The Devil And Miss Jones, Kings Row, 41; Address Unknown, 44; Ivy, 47; Reign Of Terror, 49; Drums In The Deep South, The Man He Found, 51; Invaders From Mars, The Maze, 53.

MERCER, JOHNNY: Merry-Go-Round, 34; To Beat The Band, 35; The Singing Marine, Hollywood Hotel, Ready Willing And Able, 37; The Cowboy From Brooklyn, Garden Of The Moon, 38; Naughty But Nice, 39; Second Chorus, 40; Blues In The Night, You're The One, 41; The Fleet's In, Star Spangled Rhythm, You Were Never Lovelier, 42; The Sky's The Limit, Riding High, 43; Here Come The Waves, 44; My Favourite Spy, Here Comes The Groom, Girl Of The Year, 51; The Belle Of New York, 52; Dangerous When Wet, Top Banana, 53; Seven Brides For Seven Brothers, 54; Daddy Long Legs, 55; You Can't Run Away From It, 56; That Certain Feeling, Bernardine, 57; Merry Andrew, 58; Breakfast At Tiffany's, 61; Charade, 63; The Pink Panther, 64; Darling Lili, 70.

MERCHANT, ISMAIL: Shakespeare Wallah, 65; The Guru, 69; Bombay Talkie, 70; Savages, 72; Autobiography Of A Princess, The Wild Party, 75; Roseland, 77; Hullabaloo Over Georgie And Bonnie's Pictures, The Europeans, 79; Quartet, 81; Heat And Dust, 83; The Bostonians, 84; A Room With A View, 86; Maurice, 87; The Deceivers, The Perfect Murder, 88; Slaves Of New York, 89; Mr And Mrs Bridge, 90; The Ballad Of The Sad Cafe, 91; Howards End, 92; The Remains Of The Day, 93; In Custody, 94; Jefferson In Paris, 95; The Proprietor, 96.

MERCOURI, MELINA: Stella, 55; He Who Must Die, 57; The Gypsy And The Gentleman, La Loi, 58; Never On Sunday, 60; Il Giudizio Universale, Vive Henri IV Vive L'Amour!, 61; Phaedra, 62; The Victors, 63; Topkapi, 64; The Uninhibited, 65; 10:30pm Summer, A Man Could Get Killed, 66; Gaily Gaily, 69; Promise At Dawn, 70; Once Is Not Enough, 75; Nasty Habits, 76; A Dream Of Passion, 78; Not By Coincidence, 83.

MEREDITH, BURGESS: Winterset, 36; There Goes The Groom, 37; Spring Madness, 38; Idiot's Delight, 39; Of Mice And Men, Castle On The Hudson, Second Chorus, 40; San Francisco Docks, That Uncertain Feeling, Tom Dick And Harry, 41; Street Of Chance, 42; The Story Of GI Joe, 45; Diary Of A Chambermaid, Magnificent Doll, 46; On Our Merry Way, Mine Own Executioner, 48; Jigsaw, The Man On The Eiffel Tower, 49; Golden Arrow, Joe Butterfly, 57; The Sorcerer's Village, 58; Advise And Consent, 62; The Cardinal, 63; In Harm's Way, 65; Batman, A Big Hand For The Little Lady, Madame X, The Crazy Quilt, 66; Hurry Sundown, 67; Skidoo, Stay Away Joe, 68; Hard Contract, MacKenna's Gold, 69; There Was A Crooked Man, 70; Clay Pigeon, Son Of Blob, 71; A Fan's Notes, The Man, 72; Golden Needles, 74; The Day Of The Locust, The Hindenburg, 75; Burnt Offerings, Rocky, 76; Golden Rendezvous, The Sentinel, Shenanigans, 77; The Amazing Captain Nemo, Foul Play, Magic, The Manitou, 78; Rocky II, 79; Final Assignment, When Time Ran Out, 80; Clash Of The Titans, The Last Chase, True Confessions, Mr Griffin And Me, 81; Rocky III, 82; Twilight Zone the Movie, 83; Santa Claus, 85; King Lear, 87; Full Moon In Blue Water, 88; Rocky V, State Of Grace, 90; Convicts, 91; Grumpy Old Men, 93.

MIFUNE, TOSHIRO: These Foolish Times, 46; Snow Trail/No Hate, 47; Drunken Angel, 48; Stray Dog, 49; Rashomon, Shuban, 50; The Idiot/Hakuchi, 51; The Life Of Oharu, 52; Miyamoto Musashi, The Seven Samurai, 54; Record Of A Living Being, 55; Ketto Ganryu Jima, 56; The Lower Depths, Throne Of Blood, The Hidden Fortress/Kakushi Toride No San-akunin, The Rickshaw Man, 57; The Bad Sleep Well, 60; The Man In The Storm, The Important Man, Yojimbo, 61; Chushingura, Ronin, Tatsu, Daitozoku, Heaven And Hell, Sanjuro, 62; Gojuman-Nin No Isan, 63; The Lost World Of Sinbad, The Legacy Of The Five Hundred Thousand, 64; Red Beard, 65; Grand Prix, Chi To Suna, A Bare Goemon, Sword Of Doom, 66; Rebellion/Joi-uchi, 67; Gionmatsuri, Admiral Yamamoto, 68; Hell In The Pacific, Nihonkai Daikaisen, Kage, Furin Kazan, 69; Machi-buse, Shinsengumi, 70; Zatoichi To Yojimbo, 71; Red Sun, 72; Paper Tiger, 75; Midway, 76; 1941, The Bushido Blade, Ogin-sama, Winter Kills, 79; The Challenge, Inchon, 81; Taketori Monogatari, 87; Shogun Mayeda, 91; Shadow Of The Wolf, 93.

MILES, BERNARD: The Love Test, 35; Everything Is Thunder, 36; 13 Men And A Gun, 38; One Of Our Aircraft Is Missing, The Big Blockade, In Which We Serve, 42; Tawny Pipit, 44; Great Expectations, 46; Nicholas Nickleby, Fame Is The Spur, 47; The Guinea Pig, 48; Chance Of A Lifetime, 50; The Magic Box, 51; Never Let Me Go, 53; The Man Who Knew Too Much, Moby Dick, Tiger In The Smoke, Zarak, 56; The Smallest Show On Earth, Saint Joan, 57; Tom Thumb, 58; Sapphire, 59; Heavens Above, Lock Up Your Daughters, 63; Run Wild Run Free, 69; The Lady And The Highwayman, 88.

MILESTONE, LEWIS: Seven Sinners, The Teaser, 25; The Caveman, The New Klondike, 26; Two Arabian Knights, 27; The Garden Of Eden, The Racket, 28; Betrayal, New York Nights, 29; All Quiet On The Western Front, 30; The Front Page, 31; Rain, 32; Hallelujah I'm A Bum, 33; The Captain Hates The Sea, 34; Paris In Spring, The Gilded Lily, 35; Anything Goes, The General Died At Dawn, 36; The Night Of Nights, 39; Of Mice And Men, Lucky Partners, 40; My Life With Caroline, 41; Edge Of Darkness, The North Star, 43; The Purple Heart, 44; A Walk In The Sun, 45; The Strange Love Of Martha Ivers, 46; Arch Of Triumph, No Minor Vices, 48; The Red Pony, 49; The Halls Of Montezuma, 51; Kangaroo, Les Misérables, 52; The Widow, Melba, They Who Dare, 53; Pork Chop Hill, 59; Ocean's Eleven, 60; Mutiny On The Bounty, 62.

MILLAND, RAY: The Lady From The Sea, The Flying Scotsman, 30; Payment Deferred, 32; Charlie Chan In London, We're Not Dressing, 34; Four Hours To Kill, The Gilded Lily, The Glass Key, 35; The Big Broadcast Of 37, The Jungle Princess, Next Time We Love, Three Smart Girls, 36; Bulldog Drummond Escapes, Easy Living, Ebb Tide, Wings Over Honolulu, Wise Girl, 37; Her Jungle Love, Men With Wings, Say It In French, Tropic Holiday, 38; Beau Geste, French Without Tears, Everything Happens At Night, Hotel Imperial, 39; Arise My Love, The Doctor Takes A Wife, Irene, Untamed, 40; I Wanted Wings, Skylark, 41; Are Husbands Necessary?, The Lady Has Plans, The Major And The Minor, Reap The Wild Wind, Star Spangled Rhythm, 42; The Crystal Ball, Forever And A Day, 43; Lady In The Dark, Ministry Of Fear, Till We Meet Again, The Uninvited, 44; Kitty, The Lost Weekend, 45; California, The Well-Groomed Bride, 46; Golden Earrings, The Imperfect Lady, The Trouble With Women, Variety Girl, 47; The Big Clock, Sealed Verdict, So Evil My Love, 48; Alias Nick Beal, It Happens Every Spring, 49; Copper Canyon, A Life Of Her Own, A Woman Of Distinction, 50; Circle Of Danger, Close To My Heart, Night Into Morning, Rhubarb, 51; Bugles In The Afternoon, Something To Live For, The Thief, 52; Jamaica Run, Let's Do It Again, 53; Dial M For Murder, 54; The Girl In The Red Velvet Swing, A Man Alone, 55; Lisbon, 56; The River's Edge, Three Brave Men, 57; High Flight, The Safecracker, 58; Panic In Year Zero!, The Premature Burial, 62; X – The Man With X-Ray Eyes, 63; The Confession, 64; Spree, 67; Hostile Witness, 68; Company Of Killers, Love Story, 70; Embassy, Frogs, The Thing With Two Heads, 72; Terror In The Wax Museum, 73; Gold, 74; Escape To Witch Mountain, The Swiss Conspiracy, 75; The Last Tycoon, 76; Aces High, La Ragazza Del Piagiame Gialle, The Uncanny, 77; Blackout, Oliver's Story, Slavers, 78; Battlestar: Galactica, Game For Vultures, 79; The Attic, 80; The Sea Serpent, 86.

MILLER, ANN: Ann Of Green Gables, 34; The Devil On Horseback, 36; The Life Of The Party, New Faces Of, Stage Door, 37; Having A Wonderful Time, Radio City Revels, Room Service, Tarnished Angel, You Can't Take It With You, 38; Hit Parade Of 41, Melody Ranch, Too Many Girls, 40; Go West Young Lady, Time Out For Rhythm, 41; Priorities On Parade, True To The Army, 42; Reveille With Beverly, What's Buzzin' Cousin?, 43; Carolina Blues, Hey Rookie, Jam Session, 44; Eadie Was A Lady, Eve Knew Her Apples, 45; The Thrill Of Brazil, 46; Easter Parade, The Kissing Bandit, 48; On The Town, 49; Watch The Birdie, 50; Texas Carnival, Two Tickets To Broadway, 51; Lovely To Look At, 52; Kiss Me Kate, Small Town Girl, 53; Deep In My Heart, 54; Hit The Deck, 55; The Great American Pastime, The Opposite Sex, 56; Won Ton Ton The Dog Who Saved Hollywood, 75.

MILLS, JOHN: The Midshipmaid, 32; Britannia Of Billingsgate, The Ghost Camera, 33; Blind Justice, Doctor's Orders, The Lash, A Political Party, River Wolves, Those Were The Days, 34; Forever England, Charing Cross Road, Royal Cavalcade, 35; First Offence, Tudor Rose, 36; The Green Cockatoo, You're In The Army Now, 37; Goodbye Mr Chips, 39; The Black Sheep Of Whitehall, Cottage To Let, Old Bill And Son, 41; The Big Blockade, In Which We Serve, The Young Mr Pitt, 42; We Dive At Dawn, 43; This Happy Breed, Waterloo Road, Victory Wedding, 44; The Way To The Stars, 45; Great Expectations, 46; The October Man, So Well Remembered, 47; Scott Of The Antarctic, 48; The History Of Mr Polly, The Rocking Horse Winner, 49; Morning Departure, 51; The Gentle Gunman, The Long Memory, 52; Mr Denning Drives North, 53; Hobson's Choice, 54; The End Of The Affair, Escapade, Above Us The Waves, The Colditz Story, 55; Around The World In 80 Days, The Baby And The Battleship, It's Great To Be Young, Town On Trial, War And Peace, 56; Dunkirk, I Was Monty's Double, 58; The Vicious Circle, Tiger Bay, 59; Ice Cold In Alex, Summer Of The Seventeenth Doll, Swiss Family Robinson, Tunes Of Glory, 60; The Singer Not The Song, 61; Flame In The Streets, Tiara Tahiti, The Valiant, 62; The Chalk Garden, 64; King Rat, Operation Crossbow, The Truth About Spring, Sky West And Crooked, 65; The Wrong Box, 66; Africa Texas Style!, Chuka, The Family Way, 67; A Black Veil For Lisa, Lady Hamilton, 68; Oh! What A Lovely War, Philip, Run Wild Run Free, 69; Adam's Woman, Ryan's Daughter, 70; Dulcima, 71; Lady Caroline Lamb, Young Winston, 72; Oklahoma Crude, 73; The Human Factor, 75; Trial By Combat, 76; The Devil's Advocate, 77; The Big Sleep, The 39 Steps, 78; Zulu Dawn, 79; The Quatermass Conclusion, 80; Gandhi, 82; Sahara, The Masks Of Death, 84; When The Wind Blows, 86; Who's That Girl?, 87; The Lady And The Highwayman, 88; The Last Straw, 91.

MINNELLI, LIZA: In The Good Old Summertime, 49; Charlie Bubbles, 67; The Sterile Cuckoo, 69; Tell Me That You Love Me Junie Moon, 70; Cabaret, 72; That's Entertainment!, 74; Lucky Lady, 75; A Matter Of Time, Silent Movie, 76; New York New York, 77; Arthur, 81; The Muppets Take Manhattan, 84; That's Dancing!, 85; Arthur 2: On The Rocks, Rent-a-Cop, 88; Stepping Out, 91; Parallel Lives, 94.

MINNELLI, VINCENTE: Cabin In The Sky, I Dood It, 43; Meet Me In St Louis, 44; The Clock, Yolanda And The Thief, 45; Ziegfeld Follies, Undercurrent, Till The Clouds Rolls By, 46; The Pirate, 48; Madame Bovary, 49; Father Of The Bride, 50; An American In Paris, Father's Little Dividend, 51; The Bad And The Beautiful, 52; The Band Wagon, The Story Of Three Loves, 53; Brigadoon, The Long Long Trailer, 54; The Cobweb, Kismet, 55; Lust For Life, Tea And Sympathy, 56; Designing Woman, 57; Gigi, The Reluctant Debutante, Some Came Running, 58; Bells Are Ringing, Home From The Hill, 60; Four Horsemen Of The Apocalypse, Two Weeks In Another Town, 62; The Courtship Of Eddie's Father, 63; Goodbye Charlie, 64; The Sandpiper, 65; On A Clear Day You Can See Forever, 70; A Matter Of Time, 76.

MIRREN, HELEN: Herostratus, 67; A Midsummer Night's Dream, 68; Age Of Consent, 69; Miss Julie, Savage Messiah, 72; O Lucky Man!, 73; Hamlet, 76; Caligula, 79; The Fiendish Plot Of Dr Fu Manchu, Hussy, The Long Good Friday, 80; Excalibur, 81; 2010, Cal, 84; Heavenly Pursuits, White Nights, 85; The Mosquito Coast, 86; Pascali's Island, People Of The Forest, 88; The Cook The Thief His Wife And Her Lover, When The Whales Came, 89; Bethune: The Making Of A Hero, 90; The Comfort Of Strangers, Where Angels Fear To Tread, 91; The Madness Of King George, 95; Some Mother's Son, 96.

MITCHUM, ROBERT: The Dancing Masters, The Human, Corvette K-225, Follow The Band, Gung Ho!, **43**; Nevada, Thirty Seconds Over Tokyo, **44**; The Story Of GI Joe, West Of The Pecos, **45**; The Locket, Till The End Of Time, Undercurrent, **46**; Crossfire, Desire Me, Out Of The Past, Pursued, **47**; Blood On The Moon, Rachel And The Stranger, **48**; The Big Steal, Holiday Affair, The Red Pony, **49**; Where Danger Lives, **50**; His Kind Of Woman, My Forbidden Past, The Racket, **51**; The Lusty Men, Macao, One Minute To Zero, **52**; Angel Face, Second Chance, White Witch Doctor, **53**; River Of No Return, She Couldn't Say No, Track Of The Cat, **54**; Man With The Gun, The Night Of The Hunter, Not As A Stranger, **55**; Bandido, Foreign Intrigue, **56**; The Enemy Below, Fire Down Below, Heaven Knows Mr Allison, **57**; The Hunters, Thunder Road, **58**; The Angry Hills, The Wonderful Country, **59**; The Grass Is Greener, Home From The Hill, Night Fighters, The Sundowners, **60**; The Last Time I Saw Archie, **61**; Cape Fear, The Longest Day, Two For The Seesaw, **62**; The List Of Adrian Messenger, Rampage, **63**; What A Way To Go!, Man In The Middle, **64**; Mister Moses, **65**; El Dorado, The Way West, **67**; Anzio, Five Card Stud, Secret Ceremony, Villa Rides, **68**; The Good Guys And The Bad Guys, Young Billy Young, **69**; Ryan's Daughter, **70**; Going Home, **71**; The Wrath Of God, **72**; The Friends Of Eddie Coyle, **73**; Farewell My Lovely, The Yakuza, **75**; The Last Tycoon, Midway, **77**; The Amsterdam Kill, The Big Sleep, Matilda, **78**; Breakthrough, **79**; Agency, **81**; That Championship Season, **82**; The Ambassador, Maria's Lovers, **84**; Mr North, Scrooged, **88**; The Informer, **89**; Presume Dangereux, **90**; Cape Fear, **91**; Les Sept Péchés Capitaux, Midnight Ride, **92**; Tombstone, Woman Of Desire, **93**.

MIX, TOM: On The Little Big Horn, **09**; The Long Trail, The Range Riders, **10**; An Arizona Wooing, Back To The Primitive, **11**; An Apache's Gratitude, The Escape Of Jim Dolan, The Law And The Outlaw, **13**; Cactus Jake Chip Of The Flying U, In The Days Of The Thundering Herd, The Moving Picture Cowboy, The Ranger's Romance, **14**; Cactus Jim's Shop Girl, A Child Of The Prairie, On The Eagle Trail, Pals In Blue, The Range Girl And The Cowboy, **15**; Local Color, The Taming Of Grouchy Bill, Twisted Trails, **16**; The Heart Of Texas Ryan, **17**; Ace High, Fame And Fortune, Six-Shooter Andy, Western Blood, **18**; The Feud, Fighting For Gold, Rough Riding Romance, Wilderness Trail, **19**; Hands Off, Desert Love, **20**; A Ridin' Romeo, After Your Own Heart, **21**; Catch My Smoke, Chasing The Moon, Do And Dare, Just Tony, Arabia, **22**; The Fighting Streak, Eyes Of The Forest, 3 Jumps Ahead, **23**; The Heart Buster, Teeth, The Trouble Shooter, **24**; The Best Bad Man, Dick Turpin, The Everlasting Whisper, The Lucky Horseshoe, The Rainbow Trail, Riders Of The Purple Sage, **25**; Hard Boiled, My Own Pal, Tony Runs Wild, The Great K & A Robbery, No Man's Gold, The Canyon of Light, The Yankee Senor, **26**; The Circus Ace, The Last Trail, **27**; The Arizona Wildcat, Daredevil's Reward, **28**; The Big Diamond Robbery, Outlawed, **29**; Under A Texas Moon, **30**; Destry Rides Again, My Pal The King, Flaming Guns, Hidden Gold, The Rider Of Death Valley, **32**; Rustler's Roundup, Terror Trail, **33**; The Miracle Rider, **35**.

MIZOGUCHI, KENJI: Haizan Nouta Wa Kanashi, **23**; Jin Kyo, **24**; Kami Ning Yo Haru No Sasayaki, **26**; Metropolitan Symphony, Tokyo March, Nihon Bashi, **29**; Gion Festival, The White Threads Of The Waterfall, **33**; The Poppies, The Virgin From Oyuki, **35**; Osaka Elegy, Sisters Of The Gion, **36**; Straits Of Love And Hate, **37**; The Story Of The Late Chrysanthemums, **39**; The 47 Ronin, **41**; The 47 Ronin, Part II, Musashi Miyamoto, Meito Bijomaru, **45**; Utamaro O Meguru Go-Nin No Onna, Women's Victory, **46**; The Love Of Actress Sumako, **47**; Women Of The Night, **48**; Waga Koi Wa Moenu, **49**; The Picture Of Madame Yuki, **50**; Woman Of Musashino, Oyusama, **51**; The Life Of Oharu, **52**; Gion Festival Music, Ugetsu Monogatari, **53**; Sansho The Bailiff, Chikamatzu Monogatari, The Woman In The Rumor, **54**; The Empress Yang Kwei-Fei, Princess Yang Kwei Fei, Shin Heike Monogatari, Tales Of The Taira Clan, **55**; Street Of Shame, **56**.

MONROE, MARILYN: Scudda Hoo! Scudda Hay!, Dangerous Years, Ladies Of The Chorus, **48**; Love Happy, **49**; All About Eve, The Asphalt Jungle, The Fireball, Right Cross, A Ticket To Tomahawk, **50**; As Young As You Feel, Hometown Story, Let's Make It Legal, Love Nest, **51**; Clash By Night, Don't Bother To Knock, Monkey Business, O Henry's Full House, We're Not Married, **52**; Gentlemen Prefer Blondes, How To Marry A Millionaire, Niagara, **53**; River Of No Return, There's No Business Like Show Business, **54**; The Seven Year Itch, **55**; Bus Stop, **56**; The Prince And The Showgirl, **57**; Some Like It Hot, **59**; Let's Make Love, **60**; The Misfits, **61**.

MONTAND, YVES: Les Portes De La Nuit, **46**; Souvenirs Perdus, **50**; L'Auberge Rouge, **51**; The Wages Of Fear, Tempi Nostri, **53**; Les Héros Sont Fatigués, Napoleon, **55**; Marguerite De La Nuit, The Wolves, **56**; Das Leben Der Frauen, The Crucible, **57**; La Grande Strada Azzura, Premier Mai, La Loi, **58**; Let's Make Love, **60**; Aimez-vous Brahms?, Sanctuary, **61**; Le Joli Mai, My Geisha, **62**; The Sleeping Car Murder, **65**; Grand Prix, Is Paris Burning?, La Guerre Est Finie, **66**; Vivre Pour Vivre, **67**; Mister Freedom, Un Soir Un Train, **68**; The Devil By The Tail, Z, **69**; L'Aveu, On A Clear Day You Can See Forever, **70**; La Folie Des Grandeurs, Le Cercle Rouge, **71**; César Et Rosalie, Le Fils, Tout Va Bien, **72**; Le Hasard Et La Violence, State Of Siege, **73**; Vincent, Francois, Paul And The Others, **74**; Le Sauvage, Police Python 357, **75**; La Menace, Le Fond De L'Air Est Rouge, Le Grand Escogriffe, **77**; The Roads To The South, **78**; Clair De Femme, I Comme Icare, **79**; All Fired Up, Le Choix Des Armes, **81**; Garçon!, **83**; Jean De Florette, Manon Des Sources, **86**; Trois Places Pour Les 26, **88**; Netchayev Is Back, **91**; IP5: The Island Of Pachyderms, **92**.

MONTGOMERY, ROBERT: So This Is College, Their Own Desire, Three Live Ghosts, Father's Day, Untamed, **29**; The Big House, The Divorcee, Free And Easy, Love In The Rough, Our Blushing Brides, The Richest Man In The World, War Nurse, **30**; The Easiest Way, Inspiration, The Man In Possession, Private Lives, Shipmates, Strangers May Kiss, Transatlantic, **31**; Blondie Of The Follies, But The Flesh Is Weak, Faithless, Letty Lynton, Lovers Courageous, **32**; Another Language, Hell Below, Made On Broadway, Night Flight, When Ladies Meet, **33**; Forsaking All Others, Fugitive Lovers, Hide-Out, The Mystery Of Mr X, Riptide, **34**; Biography Of A Bachelor Girl, No More Ladies, Vanessa Her Love Story, **35**; Petticoat Fever, Piccadilly Jim, Trouble For Two, **36**; Ever Since Eve, The Last Of Mrs Cheyney, Live Love And Learn, Night Must Fall, **37**; The First Hundred Years, Three Loves Has Nancy, Yellow Jack, **38**; Fast And Loose, **39**; Haunted Honeymoon, The Earl Of Chicago, **40**; Here Comes Mr Jordan, Mr & Mrs Smith, Rage In Heaven, Unfinished Business, **41**; They Were Expendable, **45**; Lady In The Lake, Ride The Pink Horse, **47**; June Bride, The Saxon Charm, **48**; Once More My Darling, **49**; Your Witness, **50**; The Gallant Hours, **60**.

MONTY PYTHON: And Now For Something Completely Different, **72**; Monty Python And The Holy Grail, **75**; The Life Of Brian, **79**; Monty Python Live At The Hollywood Bowl, **82**; Monty Python's The Meaning Of Life, **83**.

MOORE, COLLEEN: Intolerance, **16**; The Busher, The Egg Crate Wallop, **19**; The Devil's Claim, Dinty, **20**; The Sky Pilot, **21**; Broken Chains, Come On Over, His Nibs, The Wall Flower, **22**; Flaming Youth, Nth Commandment, **23**; Flirting With Love, Painted People, The Perfect Flapper, So Big, Through The Dark, **24**; The Desert Flower, Sally, We Moderns, **25**; Ella Cinders, Irene, It Must Be Love, Twinkletoes, **26**; Her Wild Oat, Naughty But Nice, Orchids And Ermine, **27**; Happiness Ahead, Lilac Time, Oh Kay!, Synthetic Sin, Footlights And Fools, Smiling Irish Eyes, So Long Letty, Why Be Good?, **29**; The Power And The Glory, **33**; The Social Register, Success At Any Price, **34**.

MOORE, DUDLEY: The Wrong Box, **66**; Bedazzled, Thirty Is A Dangerous Age Cynthia, **67**; Inadmissible Evidence, **68**; The Bed-Sitting Room, Staircase, Monte Carlo Or Bust!, **69**; Alice's Adventures In Wonderland, **72**; The Hound Of The Baskervilles, **77**; Foul Play, **78**; 10, **79**; Derek And Clive Get The Horn, Wholly Moses, **80**; Arthur, **81**; Six Weeks, **82**; Lovesick, Romantic Comedy, **83**; Best Defense, Micki & Maude, Unfaithfully Yours, **84**; Santa Claus, **85**; Like Father Like Son, **87**; Arthur 2: On The Rocks, **88**; Crazy People, **90**; The Pickle, Blame It On The Bell Boy, **92**; Fatal Instinct, **93**.

MOORE, ROGER: Paper Orchid, **49**; The Last Time I Saw Paris, **54**; Interrupted Melody, The King's Thief, Diane, **55**; Murder Is Announced, **56**; The Miracle, **59**; The Rape Of The Sabine Women, Gold Of The Seven Saints, The Sins Of Rachel Cade, **61**; Crossplot, **69**; The Man Who Haunted Himself, **70**; The Persuaders, **71**; Live And Let Die, **73**; Gold, The Man With The Golden Gun, **74**; That Lucky Touch, **75**; Shout At The Devil, Sicilian Cross, Street People, **76**; The Spy Who Loved Me, **77**; The Wild Geese, **78**; Escape To Athena, Moonraker, **79**; North Sea Hijack, The Sea Wolves, Sunday Lovers, **80**; The Cannonball Run, For Your Eyes Only, **81**; Curse Of The Pink Panther, Octopussy, **83**; The Naked Face, A View To A Kill, **85**; Bullseye!, Fire Ice And Dynamite, **90**; Bed And Breakfast, **92**.

MOOREHEAD, AGNES: Citizen Kane, The Big Street, **41**; Journey Into Fear, The Magnificent Ambersons, **42**; Government Girl, The Youngest Profession, Journey Into Fear, **43**; Dragon Seed, Jane Eyre, Mrs Parkington, The Seventh Cross, Since You Went Away, Tomorrow The World, **44**; Her Highness And The Bellboy, Keep Your Powder Dry, Our Vines Have Tender Grapes, **45**; Dark Passage, The Lost Moment, **47**; Johnny Belinda, Station West, Summer Holiday, The Woman In White, **48**; The Great Sinner, The Stratton Story, **49**; Without Honor, Caged, **50**; Adventures Of Captain Fabian, The Blue Veil, Captain Black Jack, Fourteen Hours, Show Boat, **51**; The Blazing Forest, **52**; Main Street To Broadway, Scandal At Scourie, The Story Of Three Loves, Those Redheads From Seattle, **53**; Magnificent Obsession, **54**; All That Heaven Allows, The Left Hand Of God, Untamed, **55**; The Conqueror, Meet Me In Las Vegas, The Opposite Sex, Pardners, The Revolt Of Mamie Stover, The Swan, **56**; Jeanne Eagels, Raintree County, The Story Of Mankind, The True Story Of Jesse James, **57**; The Bat, Night Of The Quarter Moon, Tempest, **59**; Pollyanna, **60**; Bachelor In Paradise, Twenty Plus One, **61**; How The West Was Won, Jessica, **62**; Who's Minding The Store?, **63**; Hush . . . Hush Sweet Charlotte, **64**; The Singing Nun, **66**; What's The Matter With Helen?, **71**; Dear Dead Delilah, **72**; Charlotte's Web, **73**.

MORE, KENNETH: Look Up And Laugh, **35**; Windmill Revels, **38**; Scott Of The Antarctic, **48**; Now Barabbas, Chance Of A Lifetime, **49**; Galloping Major, **50**; The Clouded Yellow, Appointment With Venus, No Highway, **51**; Brandy For The Parson, The Yellow Balloon, **52**; Genevieve, Never Let Me Go, **53**; Doctor In The House, **54**; Our Girl Friday, The Deep Blue Sea, Raising A Riot, **55**; Reach For The Sky, **56**; The Admirable Crichton, **57**; Next To No Time, A Night To Remember, **58**; The 39 Steps, North West Frontier, The Sheriff Of Fractured Jaw, **59**; Sink The Bismarck!, Man In The Moon, **60**; The Greengage Summer, **61**; The Longest Day, Some People, We Joined The Navy, **62**; The Comedy Man, **63**; The Mercenaries, **68**; Battle Of Britain, Fraulein Doktor, Oh! What A Lovely War, **69**; Scrooge, **70**; The Slipper And The Rose, **76**; Journey To The Center Of The Earth, **77**; Leopard In The Snow, **78**; The Spaceman And King Arthur, **79**.

MOREAU, JEANNE: Dernier Amour, **48**; Meurtres, **50**; Il Est Minuit Docteur Schweitzer, **52**; Touchez Pas Au Grisbi, Dortoir Des Grandes, Julietta, **53**; La Reine Margot, Les Intrigantes, Secrets D'Alcove, **54**; The Doctors, **55**; Le Salaire Du Péché, **56**; Frantic, Ascenseur Pour L'Echafaud, **57**; Les Louves, Les Amants, **58**; Le Dos Au Mur, Les Liaisons Dangereuses, **59**; 5 Branded Women, Moderato Cantabile, Une Femme Est Une Femme, **60**; Jules Et Jim, La Notte, Le Dialogue Des Carmelites, **61**; Eva, **62**; La Baie Des Anges, Le Feu Follet, The Trial, The Victors, Diary Of A Chambermaid, **63**; Mata Hari, **64**; Peau De Banane, The Train, Viva Maria!, The Yellow Rolls-Royce, **65**; Chimes At Midnight, Mademoiselle, **66**; The Oldest Profession, The Sailor From Gibraltar, **67**; The Bride Wore Black, Great Catherine, The Immortal Story, **68**; Alex In Wonderland, Langlois, Monte Walsh, **70**; Comptes A Rebours, L' Humeur Vagabonde, **71**; Chère Louise, Nathalie Granger, Admiral Benbow, **72**; Je T'Aime, La Race Des Seigneurs, Joana Francesa, **73**; Creezy, French Provincial, Les Valseuses, **74**; Hu-Man, Le Jardin Qui Bascule, **75**; The Last Tycoon, Lumière, **76**; Mr Klein, **77**; L'Adolescente, **79**; Plein Sud, **80**; Querelle, The Trout, The Wizard Of Babylon, **82**; Le Miraculé, Le Paltoquet, Sauve-Toi Lola, **86**; Calling The Shots, La Nuit De L'Océan, **88**; Alberto Express, La Femme Fardée, Nikita, **90**; Anna Karamazova, La Vieille Qui Marchait Dans La Mer, The Suspended Step Of The Stork, Until The End Of The World, **91**; See You Tomorrow, **92**; The Absence, Map Of The Human Heart, My Name Is Victor, The Summer House, **93**; Call Me Victor, **95**; The Proprietor, **96**.

MORRICONE, ENNIO: Selection: Il Federale, **61**; Before The Revolution, A Fistful Of Dollars, **64**; The Battle Of Algiers, Il Ritorno Di Ringo, **65**; El Greco, I Pugni In Tasca, For A Few Dollars More, The Good The Bad And The Ugly, La Resa Dei Conti, Navajo Joe, **66**; A Bullet For The General, Diabolik, Escalation, Faccia A Faccia, La Ragazza E Il Generale, Matchless, Grazie Zia, **67**; Galileo, Grand Slam, Guns For San Sebastian, The Mercenary, Once Upon A Time In The West, Il Sosia, A Quiet Place In The Country, Roma Come Chicago, Teorema, **68**; The Bird With The Crystal Plumage, Queimada!, Death Rides A Horse, Dirty Heroes, Ruba Al Prossimo Tuo, Fraulein Doktor, L'Assoluto Naturale, The Lady Of Monza, The Sicilian Clan, Un Esercito Di 5 Uomini, **69**; The Decameron, Violent City, I Cannibali, Investigation Of A Citizen Above Suspicion, La Tenda Rossa, Two Mules For Sister Sara, **70**; Addio Fratello Crudele, The Canterbury Tales, The Cat O' Nine Tails, Una Lucertola Con La Pelle Di Donna, **71**; La Tarantola Dal Ventre Nero, Bluebeard, The Burglars, Fistful Of Dynamite, Il Maestro E Margherita, Les Deux Saisons De La Vie, **72**; L'Attentat, Massacre In Rome, Le Serpent, **73**; The Flower Of The Arabian Nights, Un Uomo Da Rispettare, Fatti Di Gente Perbene, Le Trio Infernal, Le Secret, L'Anti Cristo, **74**; Allonsanfan, The Devil Is A Woman, Per Le Antiche Scale, The Human Factor, Night Caller, Salo, **75**; Autostop Rosso Sangue, The Inheritance, **76**; 1900, Exorcist II: The Heretic, Orca, **77**; Holocaust 2000, Days Of Heaven, La Cage Aux Folles, **78**; Bloodline, L'Umanoide, **79**; The Island, La Cage Aux Folles II, **80**; Butterfly, So Fine, Tragedy Of A Ridiculous Man, Vera Storia Della Signora Delle Camelie, **81**; White Dog, **82**; Nana, The Thing, Cop Killers, La Chiave, Treasure Of The Four Crowns, **83**; Hundra, Once Upon A Time In America, Sahara, **84**; Kommando Leopard, La Cage Aux Folles III: The Wedding, Red Sonja, Ginger And Fred, **85**; The Mission, **86**; The Untouchables, **87**; Cinema Paradiso, Frantic, **88**; Casualties Of War, **89**; Hamlet, State Of Grace, **90**; Bugsy, The Story Of Ilona And Kurti, Husbands And Lovers, **91**; City Of Joy, **92**; In The Line Of Fire, Années D'Enfance, La Scorta, **93**; Love Affair, Wolf, The Bachelor, **94**.

MUNI, PAUL: The Valiant, Seven Faces, **29**; I Am A Fugitive From A Chain Gang, Scarface, **32**; The World Changes, **33**; Hi Nellie!, **34**; Black Fury, Bordertown, Dr Socrates, **35**; The Story Of Louis Pasteur, **36**; The Good Earth, The Life Of Emile Zola, The Woman I Love, **37**; Juarez, We Are Not Alone, **39**; Hudson's Bay, **40**; The Commandos Strike At Dawn, **42**; Stage Door Canteen, **43**; Counter-Attack, A Song To Remember, **45**; Angel On My Shoulder, **46**; Stranger On The Prowl, **53**; The Last Angry Man, **59**.

MURNAU, FRIEDRICH WILHELM: Der Knabe In Blau, Satanas, **19**; The Hunchback And The Dancer, Der Januskopf, Journey Into The Night, Longing, **20**; The Haunted Castle, Marizza Gennant Die Schmuggler, **21**; Burning Earth, Nosferatu, Phantom, **22**; The Expulsion, Die Finanzen Des Grossherzogs, **23**; The Last Laugh, **24**; Tartuffe, Faust, **26**; Sunrise, **27**; Four Devils, **29**; City Girl, **30**; Tabu, **31**.

MURPHY, EDDIE: 48 HRS, **82**; Trading Places, **83**; Best Defense, Beverly Hills Cop, **84**; The Golden Child, **86**; Raw, Beverly Hills Cop II, Hollywood Shuffle, **87**; Coming To America, **88**; Harlem Nights, **89**; Another 48 Hrs, **90**; Boomerang, The Distinguished Gentleman, **92**; Beverly Hills Cop III, **94**; Vampire In Brooklyn, The Nutty Professor, **95**.

NAZIMOVA, ALLA: War Brides, **16**; Eye For Eye, Revelation, Toys Of Fate, **18**; The Brat, Out Of The Fog, The Red Lantern, **19**; The Heart Of A Child, Madame Peacock, Stronger Than Death, **20**; Camille, **21**; A Doll's House, **22**; Salome, **23**; Madonna Of The Streets, **24**; The Redeeming Sin, **25**; Escape, **40**; Blood And Sand, **41**; The Bridge Of San Luis Rey, In Our Time, Since You Went Away, **44**.

NEAGLE, ANNA: Should A Doctor Tell?, **31**; Goodnight Vienna, The Chinese Bungalow, **32**; Bitter Sweet, The Flag Lieutenant, The Little Damozel, **33**; The Queen's Affair, Nell Gwyn, **34**; Peg Of Old Drury, **35**; Limelight, **36**; London Melod[y] Victoria The Great, **37**; Sixty Glorious Years, **38**; Nurse Edith Cavell, **39**; Irene, No No Nanette, **40**; Sunny, **41**; They Flew Alone, **42**; Forever And A Day, **43**; I Live In Grosvenor Square, **45**; Piccadilly Incident, **46**; The Courtneys of Curzon Stree[t] **47**; Spring In Park Lane, **48**; Maytime In Mayfair, Elizabeth Of Ladymead, **49**; Odette, **50**; The Yellow Canary, The Lady With The Lamp, **51**; Derby Day, **52**; Lilacs In The Spring, **54**; My Teenage Daughter, **56**; No Time For Tears, **57**; The Man Who Wouldn't Talk, **58**; The Lady Is A Square, **59**

NEAME, RONALD: The Golden Salamander, **51**; The Card, **52**; The Million Pound Note, **54**; The Man Who Never Was, **56**; The Seventh Sin, Windom's Way, **57**; The Horse's Mouth, **58**; Tunes Of Glory, **60**; Escape From Zahrain, **62**; I Could Go On Singing, **63**; The Chalk Garden, **64**; Mister Moses, **65**; Gambit, A Man Could Get Killed, **66**; The Prime Of Miss Jean Brodie, **69**; Scrooge, **70**; The Poseidon Adventure, **72**; The Odessa File, **74**; Meteor, **79**; Hopscotch, **80**; First Monday In October, **81**; Foreign Body, **86**.

NEGRI, POLA: Love And Passion, **14**; Bestia, Czarna Ksiazka, Tajemnica Hotel, **15** Arabella, Jego Ostanti Czyn, Studfenci, Zona, **16**; Nicht Lange Tauschte Mich Das Gluck, Die Toten Augen, Rosen Die Der Sturm Entblattert, **17**; Gypsy Blood, The Eyes Of The Mummy, **18**; Madame DuBarry, Carousel Of Love, **19**; One Arabian Night, **2[0]** Die Bergkatze, Vendetta, Sappho, **21**; Montmartre, **22**; Bella Donna, The Cheat, Th[e] Spanish Dancer, **23**; Lily Of The Dust, Men, Shadows Of Paris, Forbidden Paradise, **24**; The Charmer, East Of Suez, Flower Of Night, A Woman Of The World, **25**; The Crown Of Lies, Good And Naughty, **26**; Barbed Wire, Hotel Imperial, The Woman On Trial, **27**; Loves Of An Actress, The Secret Hour, Three Sinners, The Woman Fro[m] Moscow, **28**; The Woman He Scorned, **29**; A Woman Commands, **32**; Fantasme, **34**; Mazurka, **35**; Moscow-Shanghai, **36**; Madame Bonary, Tango Notturno, Die Fromme Luge, **38**; Die Nacht Der Entsheidung, **39**; Hi Diddle Diddle, **43**; The Moon-Spinners, **64**.

NEWMAN, ALFRED: Whoopee!, **30**; Reaching For The Moon, **31**; Dodsworth, These Three, **36;** 52nd Street, Dead End, The Hurricane, The Prisoner Of Zenda, Wee Willie Winkie, You Only Live Once, **37**; Alexander's Ragtime Band, The Cowboy And The Lady, The Goldwyn Follies, **38**; Beau Geste, The Hunchback Of Notre Dame, The Rains Came, They Shall Have Music, Wuthering Heights, Young Mr Lincoln,

39; Broadway Melody Of 40, Foreign Correspondent, The Mark Of Zorro, Maryland, Public Deb No 1, They Knew What They Wanted, Tin Pan Alley, Vigil In The Night, **40**; Ball Of Fire, The Great American Broadcast, How Green Was My Valley, **41**; My Gal Sal, Roxie Hart, **42**; Coney Island, The Gang's All Here, The Song Of Bernadette, **43**; Irish Eyes Are Smiling, Wilson, **44**; State Fair, **45**; 13 Rue Madeleine, **46**; Boomerang!, Captain From Castile, Mother Wore Tights, **47**; The Snake Pit, When My Baby Smiles At Me, **48**; Oh You Beautiful Doll, Come To The Stable, Pinky, Prince Of Foxes, Thieves' Highway, You're My Everything **49**; All About Eve, My Blue Heaven, **50**; David And Bathsheba, Half Angel, On The Riviera, **51**; O Henry's Full House, The Prisoner Of Zenda, Stars And Stripes Forever, With A Song In My Heart, **52**; Call Me Madam, Tonight We Sing, **53**; Demetrius And The Gladiators, The Egyptian, There's No Business Like Show Business, **54**; Daddy Long Legs, Love Is A Many Splendored Thing, A Man Called Peter, The Seven Year Itch, **55**; Anastasia, Bus Stop, Carousel, The King And I, **56**; A Certain Smile, South Pacific, **58**; The Best Of Everything, The Diary Of Anne Frank, **59**; Flower Drum Song, The Pleasure Of His Company, **61**; The Counterfeit Traitor, How The West Was Won, State Fair, **62**; The Greatest Story Ever Told, **65**; Nevada Smith, **66**; Camelot, **67**; Firecreek, **68**; Airport, **70**; Players, **79**.

NEWMAN, PAUL: The Silver Chalice, **54**; The Rack, Somebody Up There Likes Me, **56**; The Helen Morgan Story, Until They Sail, **57**; The Left-Handed Gun, Cat On A Hot Tin Roof, The Long Hot Summer, Rally Round The Flag Boys!, **58**; The Young Philadelphians, **59**; Exodus, From The Terrace, **60**; The Hustler, Paris Blues, **61**; Adventures Of A Young Man, Sweet Bird Of Youth, **62**; Hud, A New Kind Of Love, The Prize, **63**; The Outrage, What A Way To Go!, **64**; Lady L, **65**; The Moving Target, Torn Curtain, **66**; Cool Hand Luke, Hombre, **67**; Rachel Rachel, The Secret War Of Harry Frigg, **68**; Butch Cassidy And The Sundance Kid, Winning, **69**; Wusa, **70**; Sometimes A Great Notion, **71**; The Effect Of Gamma Rays On Man-In-The-Moon Marigolds, The Life And Times Of Judge Roy Bean, Pocket Money, **72**; The Mackintosh Man, The Sting, **73**; The Towering Inferno, **74**; Buffalo Bill And The Indians, The Drowning Pool, **76**; Slap Shot, **77**; Quintet, **79**; When Time Ran Out, **80**; Absence Of Malice, Fort Apache The Bronx, **81**; The Verdict, **82**; Harry And Son, **84**; The Color Of Money, **86**; The Glass Menagerie, **87**; Blaze, Fat Man And Little Boy, **89**; Mr & Mrs Bridge, **90**; Why Havel?, **91**; The Hudsucker Proxy, Nobody's Fool, **94**.

NICHOLS, DUDLEY: Born Reckless, A Devil With Women, Men Without Women, **30**; Seas Beneath, **31**; The Lost Patrol, **34**; The Arizonian, The Crusades, The Informer, Steamboat Round The Bend, The Three Musketeers, **35**; Mary Of Scotland, The Plough And The Stars, **36**; The Hurricane, The Toast Of New York, **37**; Bringing Up Baby, **38**; Stagecoach, **39**; The Long Voyage Home, **40**; Man Hunt, Swamp Water, **41**; Air Force, For Whom The Bell Tolls, Government Girl, This Land Is Mine, **43**; It Happened Tomorrow, Sign Of The Cross, **44**; And Then There Were None, The Bells Of St. Mary's, Scarlet Street, **45**; Sister Kenny, **46**; The Fugitive, Mourning Becomes Electra, **47**; Pinky, **49**; Rawhide, **51**; Return Of The Texan, The Big Sky, **52**; Prince Valiant, **54**; Run For The Sun, **56**; The Tin Star, **57**; The Hangman, **59**; Heller In Pink Tights, **60**.

NICHOLS, MIKE: Who's Afraid Of Virginia Woolf?, **66**; The Graduate, **67**; Catch-22, **70**; Carnal Knowledge, **71**; The Day Of The Dolphin, **73**; The Fortune, **75**; Silkwood, **83**; Heartburn, **86**; Biloxi Blues, Working Girl, **88**; Postcards From The Edge, **90**; Regarding Henry, **91**; Wolf, **94**; The Birdcage, **96**.

NICHOLSON, JACK: The Cry Baby Killer, **58**; The Little Shop Of Horrors, Studs Lonigan, Too Soon To Love, The Wild Ride, **60**; The Broken Land, **62**; The Raven, The Terror, Thunder Island, **63**; Back Door To Hell, **64**; Ride In The Whirlwind, **65**; Hell's Angels On Wheels, The Shooting, The Trip, **67**; Head, Psych-Out, **68**; Easy Rider, **69**; Five Easy Pieces, On A Clear Day You Can See Forever, Rebel Rousers, **70**; Carnal Knowledge, A Safe Place, Drive He Said, **71**; The King Of Marvin Gardens, **72**; The Last Detail, **73**; Chinatown, **74**; The Fortune, One Flew Over The Cuckoo's Nest, The Passenger, Tommy, **75**; The Last Tycoon, The Missouri Breaks, **76**; Goin' South, **78**; The Shining, **80**; The Postman Always Rings Twice, Reds, **81**; The Border, Terms Of Endearment, **83**; Prizzi's Honor, **85**; Heartburn, **86**; Ironweed, The Witches Of Eastwick, **87**; Batman, **89**; The Two Jakes, **90**; A Few Good Men, Hoffa, Man Trouble, **92**; Wolf, **94**; The Crossing Guard, **95**; Mars Attacks!, **96**.

NIMOY, LEONARD: Queen For A Day, Rhubarb, **51**; Francis Goes To West Point, Kid Monk Baroni, **52**; Them!, **54**; The Brain Eaters, **58**; The Balcony, **63**; Deathwatch, **66**; Catlow, **71**; Invasion Of The Body Snatchers, **78**; Star Trek the Motion Picture, **79**; Star Trek II: The Wrath Of Khan, **82**; Star Trek III: The Search For Spock, **84**; Star Trek IV: The Voyage Home, The Transformers, **86**; 3 Men And A Baby, **87**; The Good Mother, **88**; Star Trek V: The Final Frontier, **89**; Funny About Love, **90**; Star Trek VI: The Undiscovered Country, **91**; Vincent, **92**; Holy Matrimony, Star Trek: Generations, **94**.

NIVEN, DAVID: Barbary Coast, Mutiny On The Bounty, **35**; Beloved Enemy, The Charge Of The Light Brigade, Dodsworth, Thank You Jeeves, **36**; Dinner At The Ritz, The Prisoner Of Zenda, **37**; Bluebeard's Eighth Wife, The Dawn Patrol, Four Men And A Prayer, Three Blind Mice, **38**; Bachelor Mother, Eternally Yours, The Real Glory, Wuthering Heights, **39**; Raffles, **40**; Spitfire, **42**; The Way Ahead, **44**; Magnificent Doll, The Perfect Marriage, A Matter Of Life And Death, **46**; The Bishop's Wife, The Other Love, **47**; Bonnie Prince Charlie, Enchantment, **48**; A Kiss For Corliss, A Kiss In The Dark, **49**; The Elusive Pimpernel, The Toast Of New Orleans, **50**; Happy Go Lovely, Appointment With Venus, The Lady Says No, Soldiers Three, **51**; The Moon Is Blue, **53**; The Love Lottery, Happy Ever After, **54**; Court Martial, The King's Thief, **55**; Around The World In 80 Days, The Birds And The Bees, The Silken Affair, **56**; The Little Hut, My Man Godfrey, Oh, Men! Oh Women!, **57**; Bonjour Tristesse, Separate Tables, **58**; Ask Any Girl, Happy Anniversary, **59**; Please Don't Eat The Daisies, **60**; The Best Of Enemies, The Guns Of Navarone, **61**; Citta Prigioniera, Guns Of Darkness, The Road To Hong Kong, **62**; 55 Days At Peking, **63**; Bedtime Story, The Pink Panther, **64**; Lady L, Where The Spies Are, **65**; Casino Royale, Eye Of The Devil, **67**; The Impossible Years, Prudence And The Pill, **68**; Before Winter Comes, The Brain, The Extraordinary Seaman, **69**; The Statue, **71**; King Queen Knave, **72**; Vampira, **74**; Paper Tiger, **75**; Murder By Death, No Deposit No Return, **76**; Candleshoe, **77**; Death On The Nile, **78**; Escape To Athena, **79**; Rough Cut, The Sea Wolves, The Biggest Bank Robbery, **80**; Better Late Than Never, Trail Of The Pink Panther, **82**; Curse Of The Pink Panther, **83**.

NOIRET, PHILIPPE: Gigi, **48**; Agence Matrimunaire, **53**; La Pointe Courte, **56**; Zazie Dans Le Métro, **60**; Tout L'Or Du Monde, **61**; Crime Does Not Pay, Thérèse Desqueyroux, **62**; Cyrano Et D'Artagnan, **63**; Monsieur, Les Copains, **64**; Lady L, **65**; La Vie De Château, Tendre Voyou, **66**; L'Une Et L'Autre, Night Of The Generals, Woman Times Seven, **67**; Adolphe Ou L'Age Tendre, Alexandre Le Bienheureux, Mister Freedom, **68**; The Assassination Bureau, Justine, Topaz, **69**; Caprices De Marie, **70**; La Mandarine, Le Vieille Fille, Les Aveux Les Plus Doux, Murphy's War, **71**; Le Trèfle A Cinq Feuilles, **72**; The Watchmaker, L'Attentat, La Grande Bouffe, Les Gaspards, Le Serpent, Day Of The Jackal, Poil De Carotte, Touche Pas A La Femme Blanche!, **73**; Le Jeu Avec Le Feu, Let Joy Reign Supreme/Que La Fête Commence, Le Secret, Un Nuage Entre Les Dents, **74**; Le Juge Et L'Assassin, My Friends, The Old Gun, **75**; A Woman At Her Window, **76**; Tendre Poulet, The Purple Taxi, **77**; La Barricade Du Point Du Jour, Le Témoin, Who Is Killing The Great Chefs Of Europe?, **78**; Due Pezzi Di Pane, On A Volé La Cuisse De Jupiter, Rue Du Pied-De-Grue, **79**; Pile Ou Face, Three Brothers, A Week's Vacation/Une Semaine De Vacances, **80**; Coup De Torchon, Kill Birgit Haas, **81**; L'Etoile Du Nord, **82**; Entre Nous, L'Africain, L'Ami De Vincent, Le Grand Carnival, Amici Miei Atto II, **83**; Fort Saganne, L'Eté Prochain, Les Ripoux, Souvenirs Souvenirs, Le Vol, **84**; Le Quatrième Pouvoir, Pourvu Que Ce Soit Une Fille, **85**; La Femme Secrete, Round Midnight, Twist Again A Moscou, **86**; The Family, The Gold-Rimmed Glasses, L'Homme Qui Plantait Des Arbres, Masques, Noyade Interdite, **87**; Chouans!, Cinema Paradiso, La Femme De Mes Amours, Young Toscanini, **88**; The Return Of The Musketeers, **89**; Dimenticare Palermo, Faux Et Usage De Faux, Life And Nothing But, Ripoux Contre Ripoux, **90**; Especially On Sunday, I Don't Kiss, Rossini Rossini!, Uranus, **91**; Against Oblivion, Fish Soup, Max And Jeremy, The Two Of Us, **92**; Tango, **93**; Grosse Fatigue, **94**; Il Postino, **95**.

NOLTE, NICK: Return To Macon County, **75**; The Deep, **77**; Dog Soldiers, Who'll Stop The Rain, **78**; North Dallas Forty, Heart Beat, **79**; 48 HRS, Cannery Row, **82**; Under Fire, **83**; Teachers, **84**; The Ultimate Solution Of Grace Quigley, **85**; Down And Out In Beverly Hills, **86**; Extreme Prejudice, Weeds, **87**; Farewell To The King, New York Stories, Three Fugitives, **89**; Another 48 HRS, Everybody Wins, Q & A, **90**; Cape Fear, The Prince Of Tides, **91**; Lorenzo's Oil, The Player, **92**; Blue Chips, I Love Trouble, **94**; Jefferson In Paris, Mulholland Falls, I'll Do Anything, **95**.

NORMAND, MABEL: The Diving Girl, **11**; The Fatal Chocolate, The Flirting Husband, Mabel's Adventures, Mabel's Stratagem, Oh Those Eyes!, Tomboy Bessie, The Water Nymph, The Brave Hunter, The Mender Of Nets, **12**; Cohen Saves The Flag, For Love Of Mabel, The Gusher, The Gypsy Queen, Her New Beau, Mabel's Awful Mistake, Mabel's Dramatic Career, Mabel's Heroes, The Mistaken Masher, A Red Hot Romance, The Speed Queen, A Misplaced Foot, A Muddy Romance, Barny Oldfield's Race For Life, **13**; Caught In A Cabaret, The Fatal Mallet, Gentlemen Of Nerve, Her Friend The Bandit, In The Clutches Of The Gang, Mabel At The Wheel, Mabel's Busy Day, Mabel's Married Life, Mabel's Nerve, Mabel's New Job, Mabel's Stormy Love Affair, Mabel's Strange Predicament, Tillie's Punctured Romance, Getting Acquainted, His Trysting Place, Won In A Closet, **14**; Fatty And Mabel Viewing The World's Fair At San Francisco, The Little Band Of Gold, The Little Teacher, Mabel's And Fatty's Simple Life, Mabel's And Fatty's Wash Day, My Valet, Stolen Magic, **15**; Bright Lights, Fatty And Mabel Adrift, **16**; The Floor Below, Jinx, Back To The Woods, Mickey, Peck's Bad Girl, The Venus Model, **18**; Sis Hopkins, Upstairs, **19**; The Slim Princess, **20**; Molly O, **21**; Oh Mabel Behave, Head Over Heels, **22**; Suzanna, **23**; The Extra Girl, **24**; One Hour Married, Raggedy Rose, **26**.

NORTH, ALEX: The 13th Letter, A Streetcar Named Desire, **51**; Les Misérables, Viva Zapata!, **52**; Desiree, Go Man Go, **54**; Daddy Long Legs, I'll Cry Tomorrow, The Racers, The Rose Tattoo, Unchained, **55**; The Bad Seed, The King And Four Queens, The Rainmaker, **56**; The Bachelor Party, **57**; Hot Spell, The Long Hot Summer, South Seas Adventure, Stage Struck, **58**; The Sound And The Fury, The Wonderful Country, **59**; Spartacus, **60**; The Misfits, Sanctuary, The Children's Hour, **61**; All Fall Down, **62**; Cleopatra, **63**; Cheyenne Autumn, The Outrage, **64**; The Agony And The Ecstasy, **65**; Who's Afraid Of Virginia Woolf?, **66**; The Devil's Brigade, The Shoes Of The Fisherman, **68**; A Dream Of Kings, Hard Contract, **69**; Willard, **71**; Pocket Money, **72**; Bite The Bullet, **75**; The Passover Plot, **76**; Somebody Killed Her Husband, **78**; Wise Blood, **79**; Carny, **80**; Dragonslayer, **81**; Under The Volcano, **84**; Prizzi's Honor, **85**; The Dead, Good Morning Vietnam, **87**; The Last Butterfly, **91**.

NOVARRO, RAMON: The Hostage, Joan The Woman, The Little American, **17**; The Goat, **18**; A Small Town Idol, **21**; Mr. Barnes Of New York, The Prisoner Of Zenda, Trifling Women, **22**; Scaramouche, Where The Pavement Ends, **23**; The Arab, The Red Lily, Thy Name Is Woman, **24**; A Lover's Oath, The Midshipman, **25**; Ben-Hur, **26**; Lovers?, The Road To Romance, The Student Prince, **27**; Across To Singapore, A Certain Young Man, Forbidden Hours, **28**; The Flying Fleet, The Pagan, **29**; Call Of The Flesh, Devil-May-Care, In Gay Madrid, **30**; Daybreak, Son Of India, **31**; Huddle, Mata Hari, The Son-Daughter, **32**; The Barbarian, A Night In Cairo, **33**; The Cat And The Fiddle, Laughing Boy, **34**; The Night Is Young, **35**; Contra La Corriente, **36**; The Sheik Steps Out, **37**; The Desperate Adventure, **38**; La Comédie Du Bonheur, **40**; La Virgen Que Forjo Una Patria, **42**; The Big Steal, We Were Strangers, **49**; Crisis, The Outriders, **50**; Heller In Pink Tights, **60**.

NOYCE, PHILLIP: Backroads, **77**; Newsfront, **78**; Heatwave, **82**; Echoes Of Paradise **87**; Dead Calm, **89**; Blind Fury, **90**; Patriot Games, **92**; Sliver, **93**; Clear And Present Danger, **94**; The Saint, **97**.

NYKVIST, SVEN: Baren Fran Frostmofjallet, **45**; Sawdust And Tinsel, **53**; Karin Mansdotter, Gorilla, **56**; The Virgin Spring, **59**; Through A Glass Darkly, **62**; The Silence, **63**; All These Women, Loving Couples, **64**; The Vine Bridge, **65**; Persona, **66**; Brant Barn, Roseanna, **67**; Hour Of The Wolf, Shame, **68**; The Ritual, **69**; The Last Run, One Day In The Life Of Ivan Denisovich, The Touch, **71**; Cries And Whispers, Och Rop, Summer Lightning, **72**; Scenes From A Marriage, Siddhartha, **73**; The Dove, The Magic Flute, **74**; Black Moon, **75**; Face To Face, The Tenant, **76**; King Of The Gypsies, One And One, Pretty Baby, The Serpent's Egg/Das Schlangenei, **77**; Autumn Sonata, **78**; Forbidden Paradise, Starting Over, **79**; From The Life Of The Marionettes, Marmeladupproret, Willie And Phil, **80**; The Postman Always Rings Twice, **81**; Cannery Row, **82**; Fanny And Alexander, La Tragédie De Carmen, Star 80, **83**; After The Rehearsal, Swann In Love, **84**; Agnes Of God, **85**; Dream Lover, The Sacrifice, **86**; Another Woman, Katinka, The Unbearable Lightness Of Being, **88**; Crimes And Misdemeanors, New York Stories, **89**; Buster's Bedroom, **91**; The Ox, Chaplin, **92**; Sleepless In Seattle, The Innocent, What's Eating Gilbert Grape, **93**; Only You, With Honors, **94**; Mixed Nuts, **95**.

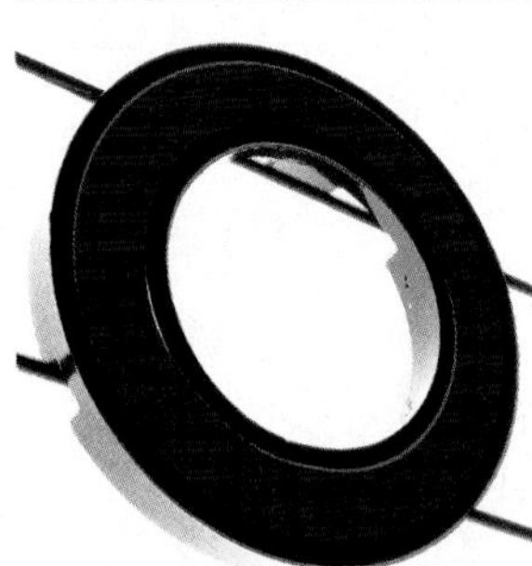

OBERON, MERLE: Alf's Button, Fascination, **30**; Never Trouble Trouble, **31**; Aren't We All?, Ebb Tide, For The Love Of Mike, Men Of Tomorrow, Service For Ladies, Wedding Rehearsal, **32**; The Private Life Of Henry VIII, **33**; The Broken Melody, The Battle, The Private Life Of Don Juan, **34**; The Dark Angel, Folies Bergère, The Scarlet Pimpernel, **35**; Beloved Enemy, These Three, **36**; I Claudius, Over The Moon, **37**; The Cowboy And The Lady, The Divorce Of Lady X, **38**; The Lion Has Wings, Wuthering Heights, **39**; Till We Meet Again, **40**; Affectionately Yours, Lydia, That Uncertain Feeling, **41**; First Comes Courage, Forever And A Day, Stage Door Canteen, **43**; Dark Waters, The Lodger, **44**; A Song To Remember, This Love Of Ours, **45**; A Night In Paradise, Temptation, **46**; Night Song, **47**; Berlin Express, **48**; Pardon My French, **51**; 24 Hours Of A Women's Life, **53**; Deep In My Heart, Desirée, Todo Es Posible En Granada, **54**; The Price Of Fear, **56**; Of Love And Desire, **63**; The Oscar, **66**; Hotel, **67**; Interval, **73**.

O'BRIEN, MARGARET: Babes On Broadway, **41**; Journey For Margaret, **42**; Dr Gillespie's Criminal Case, Madame Curie, Thousands Cheer, **43**; The Canterville Ghost, Jane Eyre, Lost Angel, Meet Me In St Louis, Music For Millions, **44**; Our Vines Have Tender Grapes, **45**; Bad Bascomb, Three Wise Fools, **46**; The Unfinished Dance, **47**; The Big City, Tenth Avenue Angel, **48**; Little Women, The Secret Garden, **49**; Her First Romance, **51**; Glory, **56**; Heller In Pink Tights, **60**; Diabolic Wedding, **71**; Annabelle Lee, **72**; Amy, **81**.

O'CONNOR, DONALD: Sing You Sinners, Sons Of The Legion, Tom Sawyer – Detective, **38**; Beau Geste, On Your Toes, Boy Trouble, **39**; What's Cookin', Sister Private **42**; Mister Big, Top Man, **43**; Chip Off The Old Block, The Merry Monahans, This Is The Life, Patrick The Great, **44**; Something In The Wind, **47**; Are You With It?, Feudin' Fussin' And A-Fightin', **48**; Yes Sir That's My Baby, **49**; Francis, Curtain Call At Cactus Creek, The Milkman, **50**; Double Crossbones, Francis Goes To The Races, **51**; Francis Goes To West Point, Singin' In The Rain, **52**; Call Me Madam, Francis Covers The Big Town, I Love Melvin, Walking My Baby Back Home, **53**; Francis Joins The Wacs, There's No Business Like Show Business, **54**; Francis In The Navy, **55**; Anything Goes, **56**; The Buster Keaton Story, **57**; Cry For Happy, The Wonders Of Aladdin, **61**; That Funny Feeling, **65**; That's Entertainment!, **74**; Ragtime, **81**; Pandemonium, **82**; A Time To Remember, **90**; Toys, **92**; That's Entertainment! III, **94**.

O'HARA, MAUREEN: Jamaica Inn, The Hunchback Of Notre Dame, **39**; A Bill Of Divorcement, Dance Girl Dance, **40**; How Green Was My Valley, They Met In Argentina, **41**; The Black Swan, Ten Gentlemen From West Point, To The Shores O Tripoli, **42**; The Fallen Sparrow, The Immortal Sergeant, This Land Is Mine, **43**; Buffalo Bill, **44**; The Spanish Main, **45**; Do You Love Me?, Sentimental Journey, **46**; The Foxes Of Harrow, The Homestretch, Miracle On 34th Street, Sinbad The Sailor, **47**; Sitting Pretty, **48**; Bagdad, Father Was A Fullback, Britannia Mews, A Woman's Secret, **49**; Comanche Territory, Rio Grande, Tripoli, **50**; Flame Of Araby, **51**; Against All Flags, At Sword's Point, Kangaroo, The Quiet Man, **52**; War Arrow, Th Redhead From Wyoming, **53**; Lady Godiva, The Long Gray Line, The Magnificent Matador, **55**; Everything But The Truth, Lisbon, **56**; The Wings Of Eagles, **57**; Malag Our Man In Havana, **60**; The Deadly Companions, The Parent Trap, **61**; Mr Hobbs Takes A Vacation, **62**; McLintock!, Spencer's Mountain, **63**; The Battle Of The Villa Fiorita, **65**; The Rare Breed, **66**; How Do I Love Thee?, **70**; Big Jake, **71**; Only The Lonely, **91**.

OLIVIER, LAURENCE: The Temporary Widow, Too Many Crooks, **30**; Friends And Lovers, Potiphar's Wife, Yellow Ticket, **31**; Westward Passage, **32**; No Funny Business, Perfect Understanding, **33**; Moscow Nights, **35**; As You Like It, **36**; Fire Over England, **37**; 21 Days, The Divorce Of Lady X, **38**; Q Planes, Wuthering Heights, **39**; The Conquest Of The Air, Pride And Prejudice, Rebecca, **40**; 49th Parallel, Lady Hamilton, **41**; The Demi-Paradise, **43**; Henry V, **44**; Hamlet, **48**; The Magic Box, **51**; Carrie, **52**; The Beggar's Opera, **53**; Richard III, **55**; The Prince And The Showgirl, **57**; The Devil's Disciple, **59**; The Entertainer, Spartacus, **60**; Term Of Trial, **62** Bunny Lake Is Missing, Othello, **65**; Khartoum, **66**; Dance Of Death, The Shoes The Fisherman, **68**; Battle Of Britain, Oh! What A Lovely War, **69**; David Copperfield, Three Sisters, **70**; Nicholas And Alexandra, **71**; Lady Caroline Lamb, Sleuth, **72**; The Gentleman Tramp, Marathon Man, The Seven Percent Solution, **76**; A Bridge Too Far, **77**; The Betsy, The Boys From Brazil, **78**; Dracula, A Little Romance, **79**; The Jazz Singer, **80**; Clash Of The Titans, Inchon, **81**; The Bounty The Jigsaw Man, **84**; Wild Geese II, **85**.

OPHULS, MAX: Die Verkaufte Braut, Die Verliebte Firma, **32**; Liebelei, Lachende Erben, **33**; La Signora Di Tutti, On A Vole Un Homme, **34**; Divine, **35**; Komedie Om Geld, La Tendre Ennemie, **36**; Yoshiwara, **37**; Le Roman De Werther, **38**; Sans Lendemain, Mayerling A Sarajevo, **40**; The Exile, **47**; Letter From An Unknown Woman, **48**; Caught, The Reckless Moment, **49**; La Ronde, **50**; Le Plaisir, **51**; Madame De . . ., **53**; Lola Montès, **55**.

ORRY-KELLY: I Am A Fugitive From A Chain Gang, **32**; Gold Diggers of 1933, **33**; Hollywood Hotel, Tovarich, **37**; Angels With Dirty Faces, Jezebel, **38**; The Private Lives Of Elizabeth And Essex, **39**; The Sea Hawk, The Letter, **40**; The Bride Came COD, The Maltese Falcon, The Strawberry Blonde, The Little Foxes, Kings Row, **41**; George Washington Slept Here, Casablanca, In This Our Life, Now Voyager, **42**; Mission To Moscow, **43**; Arsenic d Old Lace, **44**; The Corn Is Green, ; A Stolen Life, **46**; Caught, Berlin Express, ; An American In Paris, **51**; I Confess, ; Oklahoma!, **55**; Les Girls, **57**; Auntie me, **58**; Some Like It Hot, **59**; A jority Of One, Sweet Bird Of Youth, **61**; osy, **62**; Sunday In New York, Irma La uce, **63**.

TOOLE, PETER: Kidnapped, The vage Innocents, The Day They Robbed The nk Of England, **60**; Lawrence Of abia, **62**; Becket, **64**; Lord Jim, What's w Pussycat?, **65**; The Bible, How To al A Million, **66**; Night Of The Generals, sino Royale, **67**; Great Catherine, The n In Winter, **68**; Country Dance, Goodbye Chips, **69**; Murphy's War, **71**; Man La Mancha, The Ruling Class, **72**; Under k Wood, **73**; Rosebud, **75**; Foxtrot, n Friday, Rogue Male, **76**; Power Play, **78**; u Dawn, **79**; Caligula, The Stunt Man, ; My Favorite Year, **82**; Supergirl, **84**; ator, **85**; Club Paradise, **86**; The t Emperor, **87**; High Spirits, **88**; Crystal Or Fire Or Wind, As Long As It's Love, Di na, **89**; Buried Alive, The Nutcracker nce, The Rainbow Thief, Wings Of ne, **90**; King Ralph, Isabelle Eberhardt, ; Rebecca's Daughter, **92**; The enth Coin, **93**.

, FRANK: The Muppet Movie, **79**; Blues Brothers, The Empire Strikes Back, ; An American Werewolf In London, Dark Crystal, The Great Muppet Caper, ; Return Of The Jedi, Trading Places, The Muppets Take Manhattan, **84**; Spies e Us, **85**; Labyrinth, Little Shop Of rors, **86**; Dirty Rotten Scoundrels, **88**; at About Bob?, **91**; Housesitter, ocent Blood, The Muppet Christmas Carol, The Indian In The Cupboard, **95**.

BST, G W: Der Schatz, **23**; Grafin elli, **24**; The Joyless Street, **25**; Secrets Soul, Man Spielt Nicht Mit Der e!, **26**; The Love Of Jeanne Ney, **27**; s, **28**; Diary Of A Lost Girl, dora's Box, The White Hell Of Piz Palu, Westfront 1918, **30**; Skandalum Kameradschaft, The Threepenny Opera, L'Atlantide, **32**; De Haut En Bas, Don Quixote, A Modern Hero, **34**; emoiselle Docteur, **36**; Le Drame De nghai, **38**; Jeunes Filles En Détresse, **39**; acelsus, Komodianten, **43**; The /Der Prozess, **47**; Secret Shadows, **49**; Voice Of Silence, **52**; Cose Da Pazzi, Afraid To Live, **54**; The Jackboot Mutiny, Rosen Fur Bettina, Durch Die Walder ch Di Auen, Der Letzte Akt **56**.

INO, AL: Me Natalie, **69**; The Panic In dle Park, **71**; The Godfather, **72**; ecrow, Serpico, **73**; The Godfather Part II, Dog Day Afternoon, **75**; Bobby Deerfield, . . . And Justice For All, **79**; Cruising, **80**; or! Author!, **82**; Scarface, **83**; Revolution, Sea Of Love, **89**; Dick Tracy, The ather Part III, **90**; Frankie And Johnny, Glengarry Glen Ross, Scent Of A Woman, Carlito's Way, **93**, City Hall, Heat, **95**; king for Richard, **96**; Donnie Brasco, **97**.

E, GERALDINE: Hondo, **53**; mer And Smoke, **61**; Sweet Bird Of h, **62**; Toys In The Attic, **63**; Dear t, **64**; You're A Big Boy Now, **66**; The oiest Millionaire, Monday's Child, Trilogy, Whatever Happened To Aunt ?, The Bearding Of The President, The Beguiled, **71**; J W Coop, Pete 'n' **72**; Happy As The Grass Was n, **73**; The Day Of The Locust, **75**; Nasty ts, The Rescuers, **77**; Interiors, **78**; y's War, Honky Tonk Freeway, **81**; I'm cing As Fast As I Can, **82**; The Pope eenwich Village, **84**; The Bride, agan, The Trip To Bountiful, White ts, **85**; Walls Of Glass, **86**.

PAGNOL, MARCEL: Marius, **30**; The Well-Digger's Daughter, **31**; Fanny, **32**; Topaze, **33**; Tartarin De Tarascon, Angèle, Jofroi, **34**; Merlusse, **35**; Les Amours De Toni, César, **36**; Harvest, **37**; La Femme Du Boulanger, Le Schpountz, **38**; La Priére Aux Etoiles, La Fille Du Puisatier, **41**; Naïs, **47**; La Belle Meunière, **48**; Le Rosier De Mme Husson, Topaze, **50**; Manon Des Sources, **52**; Les Lettres De Mon Moulin, **54**.

PAKULA, ALAN J: Fear Strikes Out, **57**; To Kill A Mockingbird, **62**; Love With The Proper Stranger, **63**; Baby The Rain Must Fall, Inside Daisy Clover, **65**; Up The Down Staircase, **67**; The Stalking Moon, The Sterile Cuckoo, **69**; Klute, **71**; Love And Pain And The Whole Damn Thing, **72**; The Parallax View, **74**; All The President's Men, **76**; Comes A Horseman, **78**; Starting Over, **79**; Rollover, **81**; Sophie's Choice, **82**; Dream Lover, **86**; Orphans, **87**; See You In The Morning, **89**; Presumed Innocent, **90**; Consenting Adults, **92**; The Pelican Brief, **93**; The Devil's Own, **97**.

PAL, GEORGE: Dolly Follies, Ali Baba, In Lamplight Land, **35**; The Jasper Series, **42-45**; Destination Moon, The Great Rupert, **50**; When Worlds Collide, **51**; Houdini, War Of The Worlds, **53**; The Naked Jungle, **54**; Conquest Of Space, **55**; Tom Thumb, **58**; The Time Machine, **60**; Atlantis The Lost Continent, **61**; The Wonderful World Of The Brothers Grimm, **62**; Seven Faces Of Dr Lao, **64**; The Power, **68**; Doc Savage: The Man Of Bronze, **75**.

PALANCE, JACK: Panic In The Streets, Halls Of Montezuma, **50**; Sudden Fear, **52**; Arrowhead, Flight To Tangier, Second Chance, Shane, **53**; Man In The Attic, Sign Of The Pagan, The Silver Chalice **54**; The Big Knife, I Died A Thousand Times, Kiss Of Fire, **55**; Attack!, **56**; House Of Numbers, The Lonely Man, **57**; The Man Inside, **58**; Ten Seconds To Hell, **59**; Austerlitz, **60**; The Mongols, Rosmunda E Alboino, The Last Judgment **61**; Barabbas, **62**; Le Mépris, Il Criminale, **63**; Once A Thief, **65**; The Professionals, **66**; Kill A Dragon, Torture Garden, **67**; L'Urlo Dei Giganti, The Mercenary, They Came To Rob Las Vegas, The Marquis De Sade: Justine, **68**; Che!, The Desperados, **69**; The McMasters, Monte Walsh, Die Zum Teutel Gehen, **70**; The Horsemen, **71**; Chato's Land, **72**; Craze, Oklahoma Crude, **73**; Dracula, **74**; The Four Deuces, **75**; Eva Nera, Squadra Antiscippo, **76**; Il Padroni Della Citta, Safari Express, Welcome To Blood City, **77**; One Man Jury, **78**; Cocaine Cowboys, The Shape Of Things To Come, Dead On Arrival, **79**; Hawk The Slayer, Without Warning, **80**; Alone In The Dark, **82**; Bagdad Cafe, Young Guns, **88**; Batman, Outlaw Of Gor, Tango And Cash, **89**; Star Fire, **90**; City Slickers, **91**; Cyborg II: Glass Shadow, **93**; City Slickers II: The Legend Of Curly's Gold, Cops And Robbersons, **94**.

PAN, HERMES: Flying Down To Rio, **33**; The Gay Divorcee, **34**; Roberta, Top Hat, Follow The Fleet, **35**; Swing Time, **36**; A Damsel In Distress, Shall We Dance, **37**; Carefree, **38**; Second Chorus, **40**; Moon Over Miami, Dancer, Rise And Shine, Sun Valley Serenade, That Night In Rio, Weekend In Havana, **41**; Footlight Serenade, My Gal Sal, Dancer, Song Of The Islands, Springtime In The Rockies, Roxie Hart, **42**; Coney Island, Sweet Rosie O'Grady, Dancer, **43**; Irish Eyes Are Smiling, Pin Up Girl, Dancer, **44**; Diamond Horseshoe, **45**; Blue Skies, **46**; I Wonder Who's Kissing Her Now, **47**; That Lady In Ermine, **48**; The Barkleys Of Broadway, **49**; Let's Dance, A Life Of Her Own, Three Little Words, **50**; Texas Carnival, **51**; Lovely To Look At, **52**; Kiss Me Kate, **53**; The Student Prince, **54**; Jupiter's Darling, Hit The Deck, **55**; Meet Me In Las Vegas, **56**; Pal Joey, Silk Stockings, **57**; Porgy And Bess, The Blue Angel, **59**; Can-Can, **60**; Flower Drum Song, **61**; Cleopatra, **63**; My Fair Lady, **64**; The Great Race, **65**; Finian's Rainbow, **68**; Darling Lili, **70**; Lost Horizon, **73**.

PARKER, ALAN: Our Cissy, Footsteps, **74**; Bugsy Malone, **76**; Midnight Express, **78**; Fame, **80**; Pink Floyd The Wall, Shoot The Moon, **82**; Birdy, **85**; Angel Heart, **87**; Mississippi Burning, **88**; Come See The Paradise, **90**; The Commitments, **91**; The Road To Wellville, **94**; Evita, **97**.

PASOLINI, PIER PAOLO: Accatone!, **61**; Mama Roma, Rogopag, **62**; La Rabbia, **63**; The Gospel According To St Matthew, **64**; Uccellacci E Uccellini, **66**; Love And Anger, Oedipus Rex, The Witches **67**; Capriccio All'Italiana, Teorema, **68**; Pigsty/Porcile, **69**; The Decameron, Medea, **70**; The Canterbury Tales, **71**; Storie Scellerate, **73**; Arabian Nights, **74**; Salo – The 120 Days Of Sodom, **75**.

PASTERNAK, JOE: Three Smart Girls, **36**; One Hundred Men And A Girl, **37**; Mad About Music, That Certain Age, Youth Takes A Fling, **38**; Destry Rides Again, First Love, Three Smart Girls Grow Up, The Under-Pup, **39**; It's A Date, A Little Bit Of Heaven, Seven Sinners, Spring Parade, **40**; The Flame Of New Orleans, It Started With Eve, Nice Girl?, **41**; Seven Sweethearts, **42**; Presenting Lily Mars, Song Of Russia, Thousands Cheer, **43**; Music For Millions, Two Girls And A Sailor, **44**; Anchors Aweigh, Thrill Of A Romance, **45**; Holiday In Mexico, No Leave No Love, Two Sisters From Boston, **46**; This Time For Keeps, The Unfinished Dance, **47**; The Big City, A Date With Judy, The Kissing Bandit, Luxury Liner, On An Island With You, Three Daring Daughters, **48**; In The Good Old Summertime, That Midnight Kiss, **49**; Duchess Of Idaho, Nancy Goes To Rio, Summer Stock, The Toast Of New Orleans, **50**; The Great Caruso, Rich Young And Pretty, The Strip, **51**; Because You're Mine, The Merry Widow, Skirts Ahoy!, **52**; Easy To Love, Latin Lovers, Small Town Girl, **53**; Athena, The Flame And The Flesh, The Student Prince, **54**; Hit The Deck, Love Me Or Leave Me, **55**; Meet Me In Las Vegas, The Opposite Sex, **56**; Ten Thousand Bedrooms, This Could Be The Night, **57**; Party Girl, **58**; Ask Any Girl, **59**; Please Don't Eat The Daisies, Where The Boys Are, **60**; Jumbo, The Horizontal Lieutenant, **62**; The Courtship Of Eddie's Father, A Ticklish Affair, **63**; Looking For Love, **64**; Girl Happy, **65**; Made In Paris, Spinout, **66**; The Sweet Ride, **68**.

PECK, GREGORY: Days Of Glory, The Keys Of The Kingdom, **44**; Spellbound, The Valley Of Decision, **45**; Duel In The Sun, The Yearling, **46**; Gentleman's Agreement, The Macomber Affair, **47**; The Paradine Case, Yellow Sky, **48**; The Great Sinner, **49**; Twelve O'Clock High, **49**; The Gunfighter, **50**; Captain Horatio Hornblower, David And Bathsheba, Only The Valiant, **51**; The Snows Of Kilimanjaro, The World In His Arms, **52**; Roman Holiday, **53**; Man With A Million, Night People, The Purple Plain, **54**; The Man In The Gray Flannel Suit, Moby Dick, **56**; Designing Woman, **57**; The Big Country, The Bravados, **58**; Beloved Infidel, On The Beach, Pork Chop Hill, **59**; The Guns Of Navarone, **61**; Cape Fear, How The West Was Won, To Kill A Mockingbird, **62**; Captain Newman MD, **63**; Behold A Pale Horse, **64**; Mirage, **65**; Arabesque, **66**; Most Dangerous Man In The World, MacKenna's Gold, Marooned, The Stalking Moon, **69**; I Walk The Line, **70**; Shootout, **71**; The Trial Of The Catonsville Nine, **72**; Billy Two Hats, The Dove, **74**; The Omen, **76**; MacArthur, **77**; The Boys From Brazil, **78**; The Sea Wolves, **80**; Amazing Grace And Chuck, **87**; Old Gringo, **89**; Cape Fear, Other People's Money, **91**.

PECKINPAH, SAM: Invasion Of The Body Snatchers, **56**; The Deadly Companions, **61**; Ride The High Country, **62**; The Glory Guys, Major Dundee, **65**; Villa Rides, **68**; The Wild Bunch, **69**; The Ballad Of Cable Hogue, **70**; Straw Dogs, **71**; The Getaway, Junior Bonner, **72**; Pat Garrett And Billy The Kid, **73**; Bring Me The Head Of Alfredo Garcia, **74**; The Killer Elite, **75**; Cross Of Iron, **77**; China, Liberty 37, Convoy, **78**; The Osterman Weekend, **83**.

PENN, ARTHUR: The Left-Handed Gun, **58**; The Miracle Worker, **62**; Mickey One, **65**; The Chase, **66**; Bonnie And Clyde, **67**; Alice's Restaurant, **69**; Little Big Man, **70**; Night Moves, **75**; The Missouri Breaks, **76**; Four Friends, **81**; Target, **85**; Dead Of Winter, Hello Actors Studio, **87**; Penn & Teller Get Killed, **89**; Inside, **96**.

PERELMAN, SIDNEY JOSEPH: Monkey Business, **31**; Horse Feathers, **32**; Sitting Pretty, **33**; Florida Special, **36**; Ambush, **39**; The Golden Fleecing, **40**; One Touch Of Venus, **48**; Around The World In 80 Days, **56**.

PERINAL, GEORGES: Les Nouveaux Messieurs, **28**; Le Sang D'un Poète, Sous Les Toits De Paris, **30**; A Nous La Liberté, Jean De La Lune, Le Million, **31**; Quatorze Juillet, **32**; The Private Life Of Henry VIII, **33**; The Rise Of Catherine The Great, The Private Life Of Don Juan, **34**; Sanders Of The River, **35**; Rembrandt, Things To Come, **36**;The Drum, **38**; The Four Feathers, **39**; The Thief Of Bagdad, **40**; The Life And Death Of Colonel Blimp, **43**; Perfect Strangers, **45**; Nicholas Nickleby, **47**; The Fallen Idol, An Ideal Husband, **48**; The Mudlark, **50**; Three Cases Of Murder, **54**; Lady Chatterley's Lover, **55**; A King In New York, Saint Joan, **57**; Bonjour Tristesse, Tom Thumb, **58**; Once More With Feeling, Oscar Wilde, **60**.

PESCI, JOE: Death Collector, **75**; Raging Bull, **80**; I'm Dancing As Fast As I Can, **82**; Easy Money, Eureka, **83**; Once Upon A Time In America, Tutti Dentro, **84**; Man On Fire, **87**; Moonwalker, **88**; Lethal Weapon 2, **89**; Betsy's Wedding, GoodFellas, Home Alone, **90**; JFK, The Super, **91**; Home Alone 2: Lost In New York, Lethal Weapon 3, My Cousin Vinny, The Public Eye, **92**; A Bronx Tale, **93**; Jimmy Hollywood, With Honors, **94**; Casino, **95**; 8 Heads in a Duffel Bag, **97**.

PETERSEN, WOLFGANG: Stellenweise Glatteis, **70**; One Of Us Two, **72**; Einer Von Uns Beiden, **73**; Die Konsequenz, **77**; Schwarz Und Weiss Wie Tage Und Naechte, **78**; Das Boot, **81**; The Neverending Story, **84**; Enemy Mine, **85**; Shattered, **91**; In The Line Of Fire, **93**; Outbreak, **95**; Air Force One, **97**.

PFEIFFER, MICHELLE: Falling In Love Again, The Hollywood Knights, **80**; Charlie Chan And The Curse Of The Dragon Queen, **81**; Grease 2, **82**; Scarface, **83**; Into The Night, Ladyhawke, **85**; Sweet Liberty, **86**; Amazon Women On The Moon, The Witches Of Eastwick, **87**; Dangerous Liaisons, Married To The Mob, Tequila Sunrise, **88**; The Fabulous Baker Boys, **89**; The Russia House, **90**; Frankie And Johnny, **91**; Batman Returns, Love Field, **92**; The Age Of Innocence, **93**; Wolf, **94**; Dangerous Minds, My Posse Don't Do Homework, Up Close And Personal, **95**; One Fine Day, **96**.

PHILIPE, GERARD: The Idiot, Le Pays Sans Etoiles, **46**; Le Diable Au Corps, Candide, **47**; La Chartreuse De Parme, **48**; Une Si Jolie Petite Plage, Tous Les Chemins Menent A Rome, **49**; La Beauté Du Diable, La Ronde, Souvenirs Perdus, **50**; Juliette Ou La Clé Des Songes, **51**; Fanfan Le Tulipe, Seven Deadly Sins, **52**; Les Orgueilleux, **53**; Les Belles De Nuit, Villa Borghese, Le Rouge Et Le Noir, Knave Of Hearts, Affairs In Versailles, **54**; Si Paris Nous Etait Conté, **55**; Les Aventures De Till Eulenspiegel, Les Grandes Manoeuvres, La Meilleure Part, **56**; Pot-Bouille, **57**; La Vie A Deux, Le Joueur, Montparnasse, **58**; Les Liaisons Dangereuses, **59**; Republic Of Sin, **60**.

PICCOLI, MICHEL: Le Point Du Jour, **49**; French Can Can, **55**; La Mort En Ce Jardin, Nathalie, **56**; The Crucible, **57**; Rafles Sur La Ville, **58**; Le Mépris, Jour Et L'Heure, Le Doulos, **63**; De L'Amour, Diary Of A Chambermaid, **64**; Lady L, Le Coup De Grâce, Masquerade, The Sleeping Car Murder, **65**; Les Créatures, La Curée, Is Paris Burning?, La Guerre Est Finie, **66**; Belle De Jour, Diabolik, Mon Amour, Shock Troops/Un Homme De Trop, **67**; Benjamin, Ou Les Memoires D'Un Puceau, Dillinger Is Dead, La Chamade, The Young Girls Of Rochefort, **68**; La Prisonnière, Topaz, **69**; L'Amante, L'Invasion, Les Choses De La Vie, Max Et Les Ferrailleurs, The Milky Way, **70**; L'Udienza, Liza, La Poudre D'Escampette, **71**; The Discreet Charm Of The Bourgeoisie, Ten Days Wonder, **72**; L'Attentat, Themroc, La Grande Bouffe, Touche Pas A La Femme Blanche!, Blood Wedding, **73**; Grandeur Nature, Le Trio Infernal, Le Fanôme De La Liberté, Vincent François, Paul And The Others, **74**; Sept Morts Sur Ordonnance, La Faille, Leonor, **75**; F Comme Fairbanks, La Dernière Femme, Mado, René La Canne, Todo Modo, **76**; L'Imprécateur, Love Doll, L'Etat Sauvage, Spoiled Children, Strauberg Ist Da, **77**; La Part Du Feu, La Petite Fille En Velours Bleu, **78**; Le Divorcement, Le Mors Aux Dents, **79**; Leap Into The Void, Atlantic City, Der Preis Furs Uberleben, **80**; La Fille Prodigue, A Strange Affair, **81**; Oltre La Porta, Passion, Que Les Gros Salaires Levent Le Doigt!, Une Chambre En Ville, **82**; Le Général De L'Armée Morte, Le Prix Du Danger, **83**; Dangerous Moves, Partir Revenir, Peril En La Demeure, Success Is The Best Revenge, Viva La Vie!, **84**; Adieu Bonaparte, Mon Beau-Frere A Tué Ma Soeur, **85**; La Puritaine, La Rumba, Le Paltoquet, **86**; Mauvais Sang, L'Homme Voilé, Unknown Country, Y'A Bon Les Blancs, **87**; Blanc De Chine, **88**; Martha And I, Milou En Mai, **90**; Le Voleur D'Enfants, La Belle Noiseuse, Divertimento, Les Equilibristes, **91**; Archipelago, Le Bal Des Casse-Pieds, La Vie Crevée, **92**; Ruptures, La Cavale Des Fous, The Supper, **93**; Beaumarchais, **96**.

PICKFORD, MARY: Her First Biscuits, The Lonely Villa, The Violin Maker Of Cremona, In Old Kentucky, The Hessian Renegades, To Save Her Soul, Song Of The Wild, Wood Flute, Ramona, **09**; The Little Teacher, Their First Misunderstanding, **10**; The Courting Of Mary, The Italian Barber, The Way Of A Man, The New York Hat, The One She Loved, Wilful, Peggy, White Hills, In A Sultan's Garden, May To December, **11**; Lena And The Geese, Friends, **12**; In A Bishop's Carriage, A Good Little Devil, Caprice, Hearts Adrift, Tess Of The Storm Country, Such A Little Queen, The Eagle's Mate, Behind the Scenes, Fanchon The Cricket, **13**; Cinderella, Mistress Nell, **14**; A Dawn Of Tomorrow, The Diamond In The Sky, Little Pal, The Girl From Yesterday, **15**; The Foundling, The Eternal Grind, Hulda From Holland, Poor Little Peppina, Madame Butterfly, Less Than Dust, **16**; Pride Of The Clan, A Poor Little Rich Girl, Romance Of The Redwoods, The Little American, Rebecca Of Sunnybrook Farm, The Little Princess, **17**; Stella Maris, Amarilly Of Clothes Line Alley, M'liss, How Could You Jean?, **18**; Captain Kidd Junior, Joanna Enlists, Tess Of The Storm Country, Daddy Long Legs, The Hoodlum, Heart O' The Hills, **19**; Pollyana, Suds, **20**; The Love Light, Through The Back Door, Little Lord Fauntleroy, **21**; Tess Of The Storm Country, **22**; Rosita, **23**; Dorothy Vernon Of Haddon Hall, **24**; Little Annie Rooney, **25**; Sparrows, **26**; My Best Girl, **27**; Coquette, The Taming Of The Shrew, **29**; Kiki, **31**; Secrets, **33**.

PIDGEON, WALTER: Mannequin, Marriage License?, Miss Nobody, Old Loves For New, The Outsider, **26**; The Girl From Rio, The Gorilla, The Heart Of Salome, The Thirteenth Juror, **27**; Clothes Make The Woman, The Gateway Of The Moon, Melody Of Love, Turn Back The Hours, Woman Wise, **28**; Her Private Life, A Most Immoral Lady, **29**; Bride Of The Regiment, Going Wild, The Gorilla, Sweet Kitty Bellairs, Viennese Nights, **30**; The Hot Heiress, Kiss Me Again, **31**; The Kiss Before The Mirror, Rockabye, **33**; Journal Of A Crime, **34**; Big Brown Eyes, Fatal Lady, **36**; As Good As Married, Girl Overboard, A Girl With Ideas, My Dear Miss Aldrich, Saratoga, She's Dangerous, **37**; The Girl Of The Golden West, Listen Darling, Man-Proof, The Shopworn Angel, Too Hot To Handle, **38**; Nick Carter Master Detective, Six Thousand Enemies, Society Lawyer, Stronger Than Desire, **39**; Dark Command, Flight Command, The House Across The Bay, It's A Date, Sky Murder, **40**; Blossoms In The Dust, Design For Scandal, How Green Was My Valley, Man Hunt **41**; Mrs Miniver, Phantom Raiders, White Cargo, **42**; Madame Curie, The Youngest Profession, **43**; Mrs Parkington, **44**; Weekend At The Waldorf, **45**; Holiday In Mexico, The Secret Heart, **46**; If Winter Comes, **47**; Command Decision, Julia Misbehaves, **48**; The Red Danube, That Forsyte Woman, **49**; The Miniver Story, **50**; Calling Bulldog Drummond, Soldiers Three, The Unknown Man, **51**; The Bad And The Beautiful, Million-Dollar Mermaid, The Sellout, **52**; Dream Wife, Scandal At Scourie, **53**; Deep In My Heart, Executive Suite, The Last Time I Saw Paris, Men Of The Fighting Lady, **54**; Hit The Deck, **55**; Forbidden Planet, The Rack, These Wilder Years, **56**; Voyage To The Bottom Of The Sea, **61**; Advise And Consent, I Due Colonnelli, Big Red, **62**; Deadly Roulette, Casa Nostra: Arch Enemy Of The FBI, Warning Shot, **67**; Funny Girl, **68**; Rascal, **69**; Skyjacked/Sky Terror, **72**; Harry In Your Pocket, Won Ton Ton The Dog Who Saved Hollywood, **75**; Two-Minute Warning, **76**; Sextette, **78**.

PITTS, ZASU: A Little Princess, **17**; Better Times, **19**; Early to Wed, Patsy, **21**; Is Matrimony A Failure?, **22**; West Of The Water Tower, Poor Men's Wives, **23**; Daughters Of Today, The Fast Set, The Goldfish, Greed, **24**; Wine Of Youth, The Great Divide, Pretty Ladies, A Woman's Faith, **25**; Early To Wed, Her Big Night, Mannequin, Monte Carlo, What Happened To Jones, Risky Business, **26**; Casey At The Bat, Twin Beds, **27**; Buck Privates, 13 Washington Square, **28**; The Dummy, Oh Yeah!, Paris, This Thing Called Love, Sins Of The Fathers, The Squall, The Argyle Case, **29**; The Locked Door, Little Accident, The Squealer, War Nurse, Sin Takes A Holiday, Passion Flower, The Devil's Holiday, Honey, The Lottery Bride, Monte Carlo, No No Nanette, **30**; River's End, Bad Sister, Beyond Victory, Finn And Hattie, The Guardsman, Seed, A Woman of Experience, Penrod And Sam, **31**; Back Street, Blondie Of The Follies, The Man I Killed, Make Me A Star, Once In A Lifetime, Shopworn, Strangers Of The Evening, They Just Had To Get Married, Westward Passage, Is My Face Red, Roar Of The Dragon, Madison Square Garden, **32**; Hello Sister, Her First Mate, Love Honor And Oh Baby!, Meet The Baron, Mr Skitch, Out All Night, **33**; Dames, The Gay Bride, Love Birds, The Meanest Gal In Town, Mrs Wiggs Of The Cabbage Patch, Private Scandal, Sing And Like It, Their Big Moment, **34**; Ruggles Of Red Gap, **35**; The Plot Thickens, Thirteen Hours By Air, Sing Me A Love Song, **36**; 52nd Street, Forty Naughty Girls, **37**; Mickey The Kid, Eternally Yours, Nurse Edith Cavell, **39**; No No Nanette, **40**; Broadway Limited, Miss Polly, Weekend For Three, Mexican Spitfire At Sea, **41**; Tish, **42**; Life With Father, **47**; Francis, **50**; The Denver And Rio Grande, **52**; Francis Joins the WACS, **54**; This Could Be The Night, **57**; Teenage Millionaire, **62**; It's A Mad Mad Mad Mad World, The Thrill Of It All, **63**.

PLEASENCE, DONALD: The Beachcomber, **54**; Value For Money, 1984, **55**; The Black Tent, Manuela, **57**; Heart Of A Child, Look Back In Anger, The Man Inside, A Tale Of Two Cities, The Two-Headed Spy, **58**; Killers Of Kilimanjaro, The Shakedown, **59**; The Battle Of The Sexes, Circus Of Horrors, Sons And Lovers, **60**; The Inspector, **62**; The Great Escape, Dr Crippen, **63**; The Caretaker, **64**; The Greatest Story Ever Told, The Hallelujah Trail, **65**; Cul-de-Sac, Fantastic Voyage, **66**; Eye Of The Devil, Matchless, The Night Of The Generals, You Only Live Twice, **67**; Mister Freedom, Will Penny, **68**; The Madwoman Of Chaillot, **69**; Soldier Blue, **70**; Kidnapped, Outback, ThX-1138, **71**; The Jerusalem File, The Pied Piper, The Rainbow Boys, Wedding In White, **72**; Henry VIII And His Six Wives, Innocent Bystanders, La Loba Y La Paloma, The Mutations, Deathline, Tales That Witness Madness, **73**; Barry McKenzie Holds His Own, The Black Windmill, **74**; I Don't Want To Be Born, Escape To Witch Mountain, Hearts Of The West, Journey Into Fear, **75**; Trial By Combat, The Last Tycoon, The Passover Plot, **76**; The Eagle Has Landed, Oh God!, Telefon, Tomorrow Never Comes, The Uncanny, **77**; Blood Relatives, Halloween, L'Ordre Et La Sécurité Du Monde, Night Creature, Power Play, Sgt Pepper's Lonely Hearts Club Band, **78**; Dracula, Good Luck Miss Wyckoff, Jaguar Lives!, **79**; The Monster Club, **80**; Escape From New York, Halloween II, Race For The Yankee Zephyr, **81**; Alone In The Dark, **82**; The Devonsville Terror, **83**; The Ambassador, A Breed Apart, Creepers, Terror In The Aisles, Where Is Parsifal?, **84**; Frankenstein's Great-Aunt Tillie, Sotto Il Vestito Niente, To Kill A Stranger, The Treasure Of The Amazon, Warrior Of The Lost World, **85**; Cobra Mission, Ground Zero, Nosferatu A Venezia, Prince Of Darkness, Spettri, Warrior Queen, **87**; Halloween 4, Hanna's War, The House Of Usher, Phantom Of Death, **88**; Halloween 5, Paganini Horror, River Of Death, Ten Little Indians, **89**; American Rickshaw, Buried Alive, Casablanca Express, **90**; Millions, **91**; Dien Bien Phu, Shadows And Fog, **92**; The Advocate, **94**; Halloween 6: Dimension, **95**.

POITIER, SIDNEY: No Way Out, **50**; Cry The Beloved Country, Red Ball Express, **52**; Go Man Go, **54**; Blackboard Jungle, **55**; Goodbye My Lady, **56**; Band Of Angels, Edge Of The City, The Mark Of The Hawk, Something Of Value, **57**; The Defiant Ones, **58**; Porgy And Bess, Virgin Island, **59**; All The Young Men, **60**; Paris Blues, A Raisin In The Sun, **61**; Pressure Point, **62**; Lilies Of The Field, **63**; The Long Ships, **64**; The Bedford Incident, The Greatest Story Ever Told, A Patch Of Blue, The Slender Thread, **65**; Duel At Diablo, **66**; Guess Who's Coming To Dinner, In The Heat Of The Night, To Sir With Love, **67**; For Love Of Ivy, **68**; The Lost Man, **69**; They Call Me Mister Tibbs!, **70**; The Organization, Brother John, **71**; Buck And The Preacher, **72**; A Warm December, **73**; Uptown Saturday Night, **74**; Let's Do It Again, The Wilby Conspiracy, **75**; A Piece Of The Action, **77**; Stir Crazy, **80**; Hanky Panky, **82**; Fast Forward, **85**; Little Nikita, Shoot To Kill, **88**; Ghost Dad, **90**; Golden Gloves, **91**; Sneakers, **92**.

POLANSKI, ROMAN: Knife In The Water, **62**; Les Plus Belles Escroqueries Du Monde, **64**; Repulsion, **65**; Cul-de-Sac, **66**; Dance Of The Vampires, **67**; Rosemary's Baby, **68**; Macbeth, **71**; Che?, **73**; Chinatown, **74**; The Tenant, **76**; Tess, **79**; Pirates, **86**; Frantic, **88**; Bitter Moon, **92**; Grosse Fatigue, Una Pura Formalita, Death And The Maiden, **94**; The Raft, **97**.

POLGLASE, VAN NEST: Flying Down To Rio, King Kong, Ace Of Aces, **33**; The Little Minister, The Lost Patrol, Of Human Bondage, Son Of Kong, The Gay Divorcee, **34**; Alice Adams, The Informer, The Last Days Of Pompeii, Seven Keys To Baldpate, She, Sylvia Scarlett, Top Hat, **35**; Follow The Fleet, The Plough And The Stars, **36**; Stage Door, The Toast Of New York, **37**; Carefree, Room Service, Bringing Up Baby, **38**; Gunga Din, The Hunchback Of Notre Dame, Love Affair, 5th Avenue Girl, **39**; Kitty Foyle, My Favorite Wife, **40**; Citizen Kane, Suspicion, **41**; The Fallen Sparrow, **43**; Together Again, **44**; A Song To Remember, **45**; Gilda, **46**; The Crooked Way, **49**; The Admiral Was A Lady, **50**; Passion, **54**; Tennessee's Partner, **55**; Slightly Scarlet, **56**.

POLLACK, SYDNEY: The Slender Thread, **65**; This Property Is Condemned, **66**; The Scalphunters, **68**; Castle Keep, They Shoot Horses Don't They?, **69**; Jeremiah Johnson, **72**; The Way We Were, **73**; Three Days Of The Condor, The Yakuza, **75**; Bobby Deerfield, **77**; The Electric Horseman, **79**; Absence Of Malice, **81**; Tootsie, **82**; Out Of Africa, **85**; Havana, **91**; The Firm, **93**; Sabrina, **95**.

POMMER, ERICH: The Cabinet Of Dr Caligari, **19**; Der Müde Tod, **21**; Dr Mabuse, **22**; Die Nibelungen, The Last Laugh, **24**; Variété, **25**; Metropolis, **26**; Barbed Wire, Hotel Imperial, **27**; Die Wunderbare Luge Der Nina Petrowna, **29**; The Blue Angel, **30**; The Congress Dances, **31**; Monte Carlo Madness, **32**; Liliom, **34**; Farewell Again, Fire Over England, **37**; Vessel Of Wrath, St Martin's Lane, **38**; Jamaica Inn, **39**; Illusion In Moll, **52**.

PORTER, COLE: The Battle Of Paris, **29**; Fifty Million Frenchmen, **31**; The Gay Divorcee, **34**; Anything Goes, Born To Dance, **36**; Rosalie, **37**; Broadway Melody Of 1940, Love Thy Neighbour, **40**; Break The News, You'll Never Get Rich, **41**; Panama Hattie, **42**; DuBarry Was A Lady, Let's Face It, Something To Shout About, **43**; Something For The Boys, **44**; Night And Day, **46**; The Pirate, **48**; Lullaby Of Broadway, **51**; Kiss Me Kate, **53**; Anything Goes, High Society, **56**; Les Girls, Silk Stockings, **57**; Can-Can, **60**.

PORTER, EDWIN S: Smashing A Jersey Mosquito, Trapeze Disrobing Act, What Happened On 23rd Street, NYC, **01**; The Burning Of Durland's Riding Academy, The Messenger Boy's Mistake, **02**; Electrocuting An Elephant, Uncle Tom's Cabin, Rube And Mandy At Coney Island, The Great Train Robbery, What Happened In The Tunnel, **03**; The European Rest-Cure, Strenuous Life, **04**; Coney Island At Night, The Ex-Convict, The Miller's Daughter, **05**; Getting Evidence, Three American Beauties, Dream Of A Rarebit Fiend, **06**; Rescued From An Angel's Nest, **07**; Alice's Adventures in Wonderland, **13**; A Good Little Devil, Tess Of The Storm Country, **14**; Bella Donna, Sold, Zaza, The Eternal City, **15**; Lydia Gilmore, **16**.

PORTMAN, ERIC: Abdul The Damned, Hyde Park Corner, **35**; Hearts Of Humanity, The Cardinal, Maria Marten, Murder In The Old Red Barn, The Crimes Of Stephen Hawke, **36**; The Prince And The Pauper, **37**; Moonlight Sonata, **38**; 49th Parallel, **41**; One Of Our Aircraft Is Missing, Squadron Leader X, Uncensored, **42**; We Dive At Dawn, Millions Like Us, **43**; A Canterbury Tale, **44**; Great Day, **45**; Wanted For Murder, Men Of Two Worlds, **46**; Dear Murderer, The Mark Of Cain, **47**; Corridor of Mirrors, Daybreak, The Blind Goddess, **48**; The Spider And The Fly, **49**; Cairo Road, **50**; The Magic Box, His Excellency, **51**; South Of Algiers, **52**; The Colditz Story, **54**; The Deep Blue Sea, **55**; The Good Companions, **57**; The Naked Edge, **61**; Freud, **62**; The Man Who Finally Died, **63**; The Bedford Incident, **65**; The Spy With A Cold Nose, **66**; The Whisperers, **67**; Deadfall, Assignment To Kill, **68**.

POWELL, DICK: Blessed Event, Too Busy To Work, **32**; 42nd Street, College Coach, Convention City, Footlight Parade, Gold Diggers of 1933, The King's Vacation, **33**; Dames, Flirtation Walk, Happiness Ahead, Twenty Million Sweethearts, Wonder Bar, **34**; Broadway Gondolier, Gold Diggers Of 35, A Midsummer Night's Dream, Page Miss Glory, Shipmates Forever, Thanks A Million, **35**; Colleen, Gold Diggers Of 37, Hearts Divided, Stage Struck, **36**; Hollywood Hotel, On The Avenue, The Singing Marine, Varsity Show, **37**; The Cowboy From Brooklyn, Going Places, Hard To Get, **38**; Naughty But Nice, **39**; Christmas In July, I Want A Divorce, **40**; In The Navy, Model Wife, **41**; Star Spangled Rhythm, **42**; Happy Go Lucky, Riding High, True To Life, **43**; It Happened Tomorrow, Meet The People, Murder, **44**; Cornered, Farewell My Lovely, **45**; Johnny O'Clock, **47**; The Pitfall, Rogue's Regiment, Station West, To The Ends Of The Earth, **48**; Mrs Mike, **49**; The Reformer And The Redhead, Right Cross, **50**; Cry Danger, The Tall Target, You Never Can Tell, **51**; The Bad And The Beautiful, **52**; Split Second, **53**; Susan Slept Here, **54**; The Conqueror, You Can't Run Away From It, **56**; The Enemy Below, **57**; The Hunters, **58**.

POWELL, ELEANOR: George White's Scandals, Broadway Melody Of 1936, **35**; Born To Dance, **36**; Broadway Melody Of 1938, Rosalie, **37**; Honolulu, **39**; Broadway Melody Of 1940, **40**; Lady Be Good, **41**; Ship Ahoy, **42**; I Dood It, Thousands Cheer, **43**; Sensations Of 1945, **44**; Duchess Of Idaho, **50**.

POWELL, MICHAEL: The Fire Raisers, **33**; The Night Of The Party, Red Ensign, **34**; The Love Test, Some Day, **35**; The Edge Of The World, **37**; The Lion Has Wings, The Spy In Black, **39**; Contraband, The Thief Of Bagdad, **40**; 49th Parallel, **41**; One Of Our Aircraft Is Missing, **42**; The Life And Death Of Colonel Blimp, The Volunteer, **43**; A Canterbury Tale, **44**; I Know Where I'm Going!, **45**; A Matter Of Life And Death, **46**; Black Narcissus, **47**; The Red Shoes, **48**; The Small Back Room, **49**; The Elusive Pimpernel, Gone To Earth, **50**; Tales Of Hoffman, **52**; The Sorcerer's Apprentice, **55**; Battle Of The River Plate, **56**; Ill Met By Moonlight, **57**; Luna De Miel, **59**; Peeping Tom, The Queen's Guards, **60**; They're A Weird Mob, **66**; Sebastian, **68**; Age Of Consent, **69**; Pavlova, **83**.

POWELL, WILLIAM: Sherlock Holmes, Outcast, When Knighthood Was In Flower, **22**; The Bright Shawl, Under The Red Robe, **23**; Dangerous Money, Romola, **24**; The Beautiful City, Faint Perfume, My Lady's Lips, Too Many Kisses, **25**; Aloma Of The South Seas, Beau Geste, Desert Gold, The Great Gatsby, The Runaway, Sea Horses, Tin Gods, White Mice, **26**; Love's Greatest Mistake, Nevada, New York, Paid To Love, Senorita, She's A Sheik, Special Delivery, Time To Love, **27**; Beau Sabreur, The Dragnet, Feel My Pulse, Forgotten Faces, The Last Command, Partners In Crime, The Vanishing Pioneer, Interference, **28**; Canary Murder Case, Charming Sinners, The Four Feathers, The Greene Murder Case, Pointed Heels, **29**; Behind The Make-Up, Benson Murder Case, For The Defense, Paramount On Parade, Shadow Of The Law, Street Of Chance, **30**; Dishonored, Ladies' Man, Man Of The World, The Road To Singapore, **31**; High Pressure, Jewel Robbery, Lawyer Man, One Way Passage, **32**; Double Harness, The Kennel Murder Case, Private Detective 62, **33**; Evelyn Prentice, Fashions Of 1934, The Key, Manhattan Melodrama, The Thin Man, **34**; Escapade, Reckless, Rendezvous, Star Of Midnight, **35**; After The Thin Man, The Ex-Mrs Bradford, The Great Ziegfeld, Libeled Lady, My Man Godfrey, **36**; Double Wedding, The Emperor's Candlesticks, The Last Of Mrs Cheyney, **37**; The Baroness And The Butler, **38**; Another Thin Man, **39**; I Love You Again, **40**; Love Crazy, Shadow Of The Thin Man, **41**; Crossroads, **42**; The Heavenly Body, The Youngest Profession, **43**; The Thin Man Goes Home, **44**; The Hoodlum Saint, Ziegfeld Follies, **46**; Life With Father, The Senator Was Indiscreet, Song Of The Thin Man, **47**; Mr Peabody And The Mermaid, **48**; Dancing In The Dark, Take One False Step, **49**; It's A Big Country, **51**; The Treasure Of Lost Canyon, **52**; The Girl Who Had Everything, How To Marry A Millionaire, **53**; Mister Roberts, **55**.

POWER, TYRONE: Tom Brown Of Culver, **32**; Flirtation Walk, **34**; Girls' Dormitory, Ladies In Love, Lloyd's Of London, **36**; Cafe Metropole, Love Is News, Second Honeymoon, Thin Ice, **37**; Alexander's Ragtime Ban, In Old Chicago, Marie Antoinette, Suez, **38**; Day-Time Wife, Jesse James, The Rains Came, Rose Of Washington Square, Second Fiddle, **39**; Brigham Young – Frontiersman, Johnny Apollo, The Mark Of Zorro, **40**; Blood And Sand, A Yank In The RAF, **41**; The Black Swan, Son Of Fury, This Above All, **42**; Crash Dive, Daredevils Of The West, **43**; The Razor's Edge, **46**; Captain From Castile, Nightmare Alley, **47**; The Luck Of The Irish, That Wonderful Urge, **48**; Prince Of Foxes, **49**; American Guerilla In The Philippines, The Black Rose, The House In The Square, Rawhide, **51**; Diplomatic Courier, Pony Soldier, **52**; King Of The Khyber Rifles, Mississippi Gambler, **53**; The Long Gray Line, Untamed, **55**; The Eddy Duchin Story, **56**; Seven Waves Away, The Rising Of The Moon, The Sun Also Rises, Witness For The Prosecution, **57**.

PREMINGER, OTTO: Die Grosse Liebe, **32**; Under Your Spell, **36**; Danger Love At Work, **37**; Margin For Error, **43**; In The Meantime Darling, Laura, **44**; Fallen Angel, **45**; Centennial Summer, **46**; Daisy Kenyon, Forever Amber, **47**; The Fan, Whirlpool, **49**; Where The Sidewalk Ends, **50**; The 13th Letter, **51**; Angel Face, The Moon Is Blue, Stalag 17, **53**; Carmen Jones, River Of No Return, **54**; The Court-Martial Of Billy Mitchell, The Man With The Golden Arm, **55**; Saint Joan, **57**; Bonjour Tristesse, **58**; Anatomy Of A Murder, Porgy And Bess, **59**; Exodus, **60**; Advise And Consent, **62**; The Cardinal, **63**; Bunny Lake Is Missing, In Harm's Way, **65**; Hurry Sundown, **67**; Skidoo, **68**; Tell Me That You Love Me Junie Moon, **70**; Such Good Friends, **71**; Rosebud, **75**; The Human Factor, **79**.

PRESLEY, ELVIS: Love Me Tender, **56**; Jailhouse Rock, Loving You, **57**; King Creole, **58**; Flaming Star, GI Blues, **60**; Blue Hawaii, Wild In The Country, **61**; Follow That Dream, Girls! Girls! Girls!, Kid Galahad, **62**; Fun In Acapulco, It Happened At The World's Fair, Scorpio Rising, **63**; Kissin' Cousins, Roustabout, Viva Las Vegas, **64**; Girl Happy, Harum Scarum, Tickle Me, **65**; Frankie And Johnny, Paradise Hawaiian Style, Spinout, **66**; Clambake, Double Trouble, Easy Come Easy Go, **67**; Live A Little Love A Little, Speedway, Stay Away Joe, **68**; Charro!, The Trouble With Girls, **69**.

PRESSBURGER, EMERIC: One Rainy Afternoon, **36**; The Challenge, **38**; The Spy In Black, **39**; Contraband, **40**; 49th Parallel, **41**; One Of Our Aircraft Is Missing, **42**; The Volunteer, The Life And Death of Colonel Blimp, **43**; A Canterbury Tale, The Silent Fleet, **44**; I Know Where I'm Going!, **45**; A Matter Of Life And Death, **46**; Black Narcissus, **47**; The Red Shoes, **48**; The Small Back Room, **49**; The Elusive Pimpernel, Gone To Earth, **50**; Tales Of Hoffman, **52**; Twice Upon A Time, **53**; Die Fledermaus, **55**; Battle Of The River Plate, Miracle In Soho, **56**; Ill Met By Moonlight, **57**; Behold A Pale Horse, **64**; Operation Crossbow, **65**; They're A Weird Mob, **66**; The Boy Who Turned Yellow, **72**.

PRESTON, ROBERT: King Of Alcatraz, **38**; Beau Geste, Disbarred, Union Pacific, **39**; Moon Over Burma, Typhoon, **40**; Lady From Cheyenne, Midnight Angel, New York Town, The Night Of January 16, Parachute Battalion, **41**; Pacific Blackout, Reap The Wild Wind, This Gun For Hire, Wake Island, **42**; Night Plane From Chungking, **43**; The Macomber Affair, Variety Girl, Wild Harvest, **47**; The Big City, Blood On The Moon, Whispering Smith, **48**; The Lady Gamble, Tulsa, **49**; The Sundowners, **50**; Best Of The Badmen, My Outlaw Brother, When I Grow Up, Cloudburst, **51**; Face To Face, **52**; Crime In The Streets, **55**; The Last Frontie[r], **56**; The Dark At The Top Of The Stairs, **60**; How The West Was Won, The Music M[an], **62**; All The Way Home, Island Of Love, **63**; Child's Play, Junior Bonner, **72**; Mam[e], **74**; Semi-Tough, **77**; SOB, **81**; Victor/Victoria, **82**; The Last Starfighter, **8[4]**

PREVERT, JACQUES: L'Affaire Est Dans Le Sac, **32**; Le Crime De Monsieur Lange, Jenny, Une Partie De Campagne, **36**; Drôle De Drame, **37**; Port Of Shadows/Le Quai Des Brumes, **38**; Le Jour Se Lève, **39**; Remorques, **41**; Les Visiteurs Du Soir, **42**; Adieu Leonard, Lumière D'Eté, **43**; Les Enfants Du Paradi[s], **45**; Les Portes De La Nuit, Voyage Surprise, **46**; Aubervilliers, **47**; Les Amant[s] De Vérone, **48**; BIM, Souvenirs Perdus, **50**; La Bergere Et Le Ramoneur, **52**; The Hunchback Of Notre Dame, **57**.

PREVOST, MARIE: East Lynne With Variations, **19**; Don't Get Personal, Her Ni[ght] Of Nights, The Beautiful and the Damned, **22**; Brass, **23**; The Marriage Cir[cle], Cornered, Tarnished, Three Women, The Lover of Camille, The Dark Swan, **24**; Kiss Again, Bobbed Hair, Seven Sinners, **25**; The Caveman, Up In Mabel's Room, For W[ife] Only, **26**; Getting Gertie's Garter, The Night Bride, The Girl In The Pullman, **27**; Rush Hour, On To Reno, A Blonde For A Night, The Racket, The Sideshow, **28**; Divo[rce] Made Easy, The Flying Foul, The Godless Girl, **29**; Ladies Of Leisure, Paid, **30**; Spo[rting] Blood, Reckless Living, It's A Wise Child, The Good Bad Girl, **31**; Three Wise Girls, Slightly Married, **32**; Parole Girl, Only Yesterday, **33**; Hands Across The Table, **3[5]**; Tango, **36**.

PRICE, VINCENT: Service De Luxe, **38**; The Private Lives Of Elizabeth And Ess[ex], Tower Of London, **39**; Brigham Young – Frontiersman, Green Hell, The House Of S[even] Gables, Hudson's Bay, The Invisible Man Returns, **40**; The Song Of Bernadette, **43**; The Eve Of St Mark, The Keys Of The Kingdom, Laura, Wilson, **44**; Leave Her T[o] Heaven, A Royal Scandal, **45**; Dragonwyck, Shock, **46**; The Long Night, Moss Rose, The Web, **47**; Rogue's Regiment, The Three Musketeers, Up In Central Park, **48**; Bagdad, The Bribe, **49**; The Baron Of Arizona, Champagne F[or] Caesar, Curtain Call At Cactus Creek, **50**; Adventures Of Captain Fabian, His Ki[nd] Of Woman, **51**; The Las Vegas Story, **52**; House Of Wax, Dangerous Mission, **5[3]**; The Mad Magician, **54**; Son Of Sinbad, **55**; Serenade, The Ten Commandments, While The City Sleeps, **56**; The Story Of Mankind, **57**; The Fly, House On Haunte[d] Hill, **58**; The Bat, The Big Circus, The Return Of The Fly, The Tingler, **59**; Fall O[f the] House Of Usher, **60**; Master Of The World, The Pit And The Pendulum, **61**; Confessions Of An Opium Eater, Reprieve, Tales Of Terror, Tower Of Londo[n], **62**; Beach Party, Diary Of A Madman, The Haunted Palace, The Raven, Twice-To[ld] Tales, **63**; The Comedy Of Terrors, The Last Man On Earth, Tomb Of Ligeia, The Masque Of The Red Death, **64**; City Under The Sea, **65**; Dr Goldfoot And The Bikini Machine, **66**; The Jackals, **67**; Witchfinder General, **68**; More Dead Thar[n] Alive, The Oblong Box, The Trouble With Girls, **69**; Cry Of The Banshee, Scream A[nd] Scream Again, **70**; The Abominable Dr Phibes, **71**; Dr Phibes Rises Again, **72**; Theatre Of Blood, **73**; Percy's Progress, Madhouse, **74**; Journey Into Fear, **75**; Scavenger Hunt, **79**; The Monster Club, **80**; House Of The Long Shadows, Bloodb[ath] At The House Of Death, **83**; The Offspring, **86**; The Whales Of August, **87**; Dead Heat, **88**; Backtrack, **89**; Edward Scissorhands, **90**.

PRYOR, RICHARD: The Busy Body, **67**; Green Berets, Wild In The Streets, **6[8]**; The Phynx, Dynamite Chicken, **70**; You've Got To Walk It Like You Talk It Or Lose That Beat, **71**; Lady Sings The Blues, **72**; Hit, The Mack, Some Call It L[oving], Wattstax, **73**; Uptown Saturday Night, **74**; Adios Amigo, **75**; The Bingo Long Traveling All-Stars & Motor Kings, Car sh, Silver Streak, **76**; Greased htning, Which Way Is Up?, **77**; Blue Collar, ifornia Suite, The Wiz, **78**; The ppet Movie, Richard Pryor Live In Concert, ; In God We Tru$t, Stir Crazy, Wholly ses, **80**; Bustin' Loose, **81**; Richard Pryor e On The Sunset Strip, Some Kind Of 'o, The Toy, **82**; Richard Pryor Here And v, Superman III, **83**; Brewster's Millions, Jo Jo Dancer Your Life Is Calling, **86**; ical Condition, **87**; Moving, **88**; Harlem hts, See No Evil Hear No Evil, **89**; Look o's Talking Too, **90**; Another You, **91**.

OOVKIN, VSELOVOD: In Days Of iggle, **20**; Hunger Hunger Hunger, Sickle l Hammer, **21**; The Locksmith And Chancellor, **23**; Bricklayers, Chess Fever, Death Ray, **25**; Mechanics Of The in, Mother, **26**; The End Of St Petersburg, Storm Over Asia, **28**; Life's Just e, A Simple Case, The Deserter, **33**; ory, **38**; Minin And Pozharski, **39**; eral Suvorov, **40**; The Feast At Zhirmunka, In The Name Of The Homeland, Pir nirmunke, **43**; Admiral Nakhimov, Ivan The ible Part Two, **46**; Tri Vstrechi, **48**; kovsky, **50**; Vozvrashchenie Vasiliya nikova, **53**.

TTNAM, DAVID: Melody, **71**; The l Piper, **72**; The Final Programme, **73**; 'll Be The Day, Mahler, **74**; Brother You Spare A Dime?, Lisztomania, dust, **75**; Bugsy Malone, **76**; The llists, **77**; Midnight Express, **78**; Foxes, Chariots Of Fire, **81**; Local Hero, Red arch, **83**; Cal, The Killing Fields, **84**; ence Of The Realm, The Frog Prince, Mr e, **85**; The Mission, **86**; Memphis Belle, Meeting Venus, **91**; War Of The Buttons, ng Human, **94**; Le Confessional, **95**.

AID, DENNIS: I Never Promised You se Garden, Our Winning Season, Seniors, ember 30 1955, **78**; Breaking Away, GORP, The Long Riders, **80**; All Night , Caveman, The Night The Lights Out In Georgia, **81**; Jaws 3-D, The Right v, Tough Enough, **83**; Dreamscape, Enemy Mine, **85**; The Big Easy, **86**; space, Suspect, **87**; DOA, body's All-American, **88**; Great Balls Of **89**; Come See The Paradise, cards From The Edge, **90**; Flesh And , Undercover Blues, Wilder Napalm, Wyatt Earp, **94**; Dragonheart, The Game ve, **95**; Criminal Intent, **97**.

AYLE, ANTHONY: Hamlet, band, **48**; Oh Rosalinda!, **55**; Battle Of River Plate, **56**; Woman In A sing Gown, The Wrong Man, No Time For , **57**; The Man Who Wouldn't Talk, rt Attack, Ice Cold In Alex, **58**; Serious ge, Tarzan's Greatest Adventure, The Challenge, **60**; The Guns Of rone, **61**; HMS Defiant, Lawrence abia, **62**; The Fall Of The Roman Empire, Of Sudan, **64**; Operation Crossbow, dy In Terror, **65**; The Poppy Is Also A er, **66**; Misunderstood, **68**; Anne Of Thousand Days, Before Winter Comes, Kenna's Gold, **69**; Everything You vs Wanted To Know About Sex, **72**; A est To The Nation, **73**; The arind Seed, **74**; Moses, **75**; Great ctations, The Eagle Has Landed, Holocaust 2000, **78**; Murder By Decree, The Miracle, **85**; La Leggenda Del Bevitore, Silent Night, **88**; King Of The **90**.

NN, ANTHONY: Parole, The sman, **36**; Daughter Of Shanghai, River arest, The Last Train From Madrid, ers In Waikiki Wedding, **37**; The aneer, Bulldog Drummond In Africa, erous To Know, Hunted Men, King Of az, Tip-Off Girls, **38**; Island Of Lost Men, King Of Chinatown, Television Spy, Union Pacific, **39**; City For Conquest, The Ghost Breakers, Parole Fixer, Road To Singapore, Texas Rangers Ride Again, **40**; Blood And Sand, Bullets For O'Hara, They Died With Their Boots On, Thieves Fall Out, **41**; The Black Swan, Larceny Inc, Road To Morocco, **42**; Guadalcanal Diary, The Ox-Bow Incident, **43**; Buffalo Bill, Irish Eyes Are Smiling, Roger Touhy Gangster, **44**; Back To Bataan, China Sky, Where Do We Go From Here?, **45**; California, **46**; Black Gold, The Imperfect Lady, Sinbad The Sailor, Tycoon, **47**; The Brave Bulls, Mask Of The Avenger, **51**; Against All Flags, The Brigand, Viva Zapata!, The World In His Arms, **52**; Blowing Wild, City Beneath The Sea, East Of Sumatra, Ride, Vaquero, Seminole, **53**; La Strada, The Long Wait, **54**; The Beachcomber, The Magnificent Matador, The Naked Street, Seven Cities Of Gold, Attila, Ulysses, **55**; Angels Of Darkness, The Lust For Life, Man From Del Rio, The Wild Party, **56**; The Hunchback Of Notre Dame, The Ride Back, The Rising Of The Moon, The River's Edge, Wild Is The Wind, **57**; The Buccaneer, Hot Spell, **58**; The Black Orchid, Last Train From Gun Hill, The Savage Innocents, Warlock, **59**; Heller In Pink Tights, Portrait In Black, **60**; The Guns Of Navarone, **61**; Barabbas, Lawrence Of Arabia, Requiem For A Heavyweight, **62**; Behold A Pale Horse, Zorba The Greek, **64**; A High Wind In Jamaica, **65**; Lost Command, **66**; The Happening, **67**; Guns For San Sebastian, The Magus, The Shoes Of The Fisherman, **68**; A Dream Of Kings, The Secret Of Santa Vittoria, **69**; Flap, RPM, A Walk In The Spring Rain, **70**; Across 110th Street, Arruza, **72**; Los Amigos, The Don Is Dead, **73**; Marseilles Contract, **74**; The Inheritance, Tiger's Don't Cry, **76**; Mohammad Messenger Of God, **77**; Caravans, The Children Of Sanchez, The Greek Tycoon, **78**; The Passage, **79**; High Risk, Lion Of The Desert, The Salamander, **81**; Valentina, **82**; A Man Of Passion, Stradivari, **89**; Ghosts Can't Do It, Revenge, **90**; Jungle Fever, Mobsters, Only The Lonely, **91**; Last Action Hero, **93**; A Walk In The Clouds, **95**; Seven Servants, **97**.

RAFELSON, BOB: Head, **68**; Five Easy Pieces, **70**; The King Of Marvin Gardens, **72**; Stay Hungry, **76**; The Postman Always Rings Twice, **81**; Black Widow, **87**; Mountains Of The Moon, **90**; Blood & Wine, **96**.

RAFT, GEORGE: Queen Of The Night Clubs, **29**; Hush Money, Palmy Days, Quick Millions, **31**; Dancers In The Dark, If I Had A Million, Love Is A Racket, Madame Racketeer, Night After Night, Night World, Scarface, Taxi!, Under-Cover Man, **32**; The Bowery, Midnight Club, Pick-Up, **33**; All Of Me, Bolero, Limehouse Blues, Rhumba, Stolen Harmony, The Glass Key, Every Night At 8, She Couldn't Take It, **35**; It Had To Happen, Yours For The Asking, **36**; Souls At Sea, **37**; You And Me, Spawn Of The North, **38**; I Stole A Million, Invisible Stripes, The Lady's From Kentucky, Each Dawn I Die, **39**; The House Across The Bay, They Drive By Night, **40**; Manpower, **41**; Broadway, **42**; Background To Danger, Stage Door Canteen, **43**; Follow The Boys, **44**; Johnny Angel , Nob Hill, **45**; Mr Ace, Nocturne, Whistle Stop, **46**; Christmas Eve, Intrigue, **47**; Race Street, **48**; A Dangerous Profession, Johnny Allegro, Outpost In Morocco, Red Light, **49**; Nous Irons A Paris, I'll Get You For This, **50**; Lucky Nick Cain, **51**; Loan Shark, **52**; Man From Cairo, **53**; Black Widow, Rogue Cop, **54**; A Bullet For Joey, **55**; Around The World In 80 Days, **56**; Some Like It Hot, **59**; Jet Over The Atlantic, Ocean's Eleven, **60**; The Ladies' Man, **61**; Two Guys Abroad, **62**; For Those Who Think Young, The Patsy, **64**; Casino Royale, Five Golden Dragons, The Upper Hand, **67**; Skidoo, **68**; Deadhead Miles, Hammersmith Is Out, **72**; Sextette, **78**.

RAIMU: Le Blanc Et Le Noir, Mam'zelle Nitouche, Marius, **31**; Fanny, Les Gaites De L'Escadron, **32**; Charlemagne, Théodore Et Cie, Ces Messieurs De La Santé, J'Ai Une Idée, Tartarin De Tarascon, **34**; César, Le Roi, Les Jumeaux De Brighton, Faisons Un Rêve **36**; Gribouille, La Chaste Suzanne, Les Rois Du Sport, Les Perles De La Couronne, Un Carnet De Bal, Vous N'Avez Rien A Declarer?, **37**; The Baker's Wife/La Femme Du Boulanger, Heroes Of The Marne/Le Heros De La Marne, L'Etrange Monsieur Victor, Les Nouveaux Riches, **38**; Last Desire/Dernière Jeunesse, The Man Who Seeks The Truth, Monsieur Brotonneau, Noix De Coco, **39**; Le Duel, Parade En Sept Nuits, The Well-Digger's Daughter/La Fille Du Puisatier, Un Tel Père Et Fils, **40**; Les Petits Reins, L'Arlesienne, Le Bienfaiteur, Monsieur La Souris, Strangers In The House, **42**; The Heart Of A Nation, Le Colonel Chabert, **43**; L'Homme Au Chapeau Rond, Hoboes In Paradise/Les Gueux Au Paradis, **46**.

RAINER, LUISE: Ja Der Himmel Uber Wien, **30**; Sehnsucht 202, **32**; Heute Kommt's Drauf An, **33**; Escapade, **35**; The Great Ziegfeld, **36**; Big City, The Emperor's Candlesticks, The Good Earth, **37**; Dramatic School, The Great Waltz, The Toy Wife, **38**; Hostages, **43**.

RAINS, CLAUDE: The Invisible Man, **33**; The Clairvoyant, Crime Without Passion, The Man Who Reclaimed His Head, **34**; The Last Outpost, The Mystery Of Edwin Drood, **35**; Anthony Adverse, Hearts Divided, Stolen Holiday, **36**; The Prince And The Pauper, They Won't Forget, **37**; The Adventures Of Robin Hood, Four Daughters, Gold Is Where You Find It, White Banners, **38**; Daughters Courageous, Four Wives, Juarez, Mr Smith Goes To Washington, They Made Me A Criminal, **39**; The Lady With Red Hair, Saturday's Children, The Sea Hawk, **40**; Four Mothers, Here Comes Mr Jordan, The Wolf Man, **41**; Casablanca, Kings Row, Moontide, Now Voyager, **42**; Forever And A Day, The Phantom Of The Opera, **43**; Mr Skeffington, Passage To Marseille, **44**; This Love Of Ours, Caesar And Cleopatra, **45**; Angel On My Shoulder, Deception, Notorious, Strange Holiday, **46**; The Unsuspected, **47**; The Passionate Friends, Rope Of Sand, Song Of Surrender, **49**; Where Danger Lives, The White Tower, **50**; Sealed Cargo, **51**; The Man Who Watched Trains Go By, **53**; Lisbon, **56**; Pied Piper Of Hamelin, This Earth Is Mine, **59**; The Lost World, **60**; Battle Of The Worlds, **61**; Lawrence Of Arabia, **62**; Twilight Of Honor, **63**; The Greatest Story Ever Told, **65**.

RAPPENEAU, JEAN-PAUL: Signe Arsene Lupin, **59**; Zazie Dans Le Métro, Love And The Frenchwoman, **60**; La Vie Privée, **62**; That Man From Rio, **64**; La Fabuleuse Aventure De Marco Polo, La Vie De Château, **65**; Les Mariées De L'An II, **70**; Le Sauvage/The Savage, **75**; Tout Feu Tout Flamme, **82**; Cyrano De Bergerac, **90**.

RATHBONE, BASIL: The Fruitful Vine, Innocent, **21**; The Loves of Mary Queen Of Scots, The School For Scandal, **23**; Pity The Chorus Girl, **24**; The Masked Bride, **25**; The Great Deception, **26**; The Loves Of Sunya, **27**; The Last Of Mrs Cheyney, Barnum Was Right, **29**; The Bishop Murder Case, A Notorious Affair, The High Road, This Mad World, The Flirting Widow, A Lady Surrenders, Sin Takes a Holiday, **30**; A Woman Commands, **32**; One Precious Year, After The Ball, Loyalties, Just Smith, **33**; David Copperfield, Anna Karenina, The Last Days of Pompeii, A Feather In Her Hat, A Tale Of Two Cities, Captain Blood, Kind Lady, **35**; Private Number, Romeo And Juliet, The Garden of Allah, **36**; Confession, Love From A Stranger, Make A Wish, Tovarich, **37**; The Adventures Of Marco Polo, The Adventures Of Robin Hood, If I Were King, The Dawn Patrol, **38**; Son Of Frankenstein, The Hound Of The Baskervilles, The Sun Never Sets, The Adventures Of Sherlock Holmes, Rio, Tower Of London, **39**; Rhythm On The River, The Mark Of Zorro **40**; The Mad Doctor, The Black Cat, International Lady, **41**; Paris Calling, Fingers At The Window, Crossroads, Sherlock Holmes And The Voice Of Terror, **42**; Sherlock Holmes And The Secret Weapon, Sherlock Holmes In Washington, Above Suspicion, Sherlock Holmes Faces Death, Crazy House, **43**; Sherlock Holmes And The Spider Woman, The Scarlet Claw, Bathing Beauty, Pearl Of Death, Frenchman's Creek, **44**; The House Of Fear, The Woman In Green, Pursuit To Algiers, **45**; Terror By Night, Heartbeat, Dressed to Kill, **46**; Casanova's Big Night, **54**; We're No Angels, **55**; The Court Jester, The Black Sleep, **56**; The Last Hurrah, **58**; Ponzio Pilato, **61**; The Magic Sword, Tales Of Terror, Two Before Zero, **62**; Comedy Of Terrors, **63**; Voyage To A Prehistoric Planet, **65**; Queen Of Blood, **66**; The Ghost In The Invisible Bikini, Gill Women, Dr Rock And Mr Roll, Autopsia De Un Fantasma, **67**; Hillbillies In A Haunted House, **68**.

RAY, NICHOLAS: Knock On Any Door, They Live By Night, **48**; A Woman's Secret, **49**; Born To Be Bad, In A Lonely Place, **50**; Flying Leathernecks, On Dangerous Ground, **51**; The Lusty Men, **52**; Johnny Guitar, **54**; Rebel Without A Cause, Run For Cover, **55**; Bigger Than Life, Hot Blood, **56**; Bitter Victory, The True Story Of Jesse James, **57**; Party Girl, Wind Across The Everglades, **58**; The Savage Innocents, **60**; King Of Kings, **61**; 55 Days At Peking, **63**; Circus World, **64**; I'm A Stranger Here Myself, Wet Dreams, **74**; The American Friend, **77**; Lightning Over Water, **80**; Crystal Gazing, **82**.

RAY, SATYAJIT: Pather Panchali, **55**; Aparajito, **56**; Paras Pathar, **57**; The Music Room, **58**; The World Of Apu, **59**; Devi, **60**; Two Daughters, **61**; Expedition, **62**; Kanchanjangha, Mahanagar, **63**; The Lonely Wife, **64**; Shakespeare Wallah, **65**; Kapurush The Hero, **66**; Chidiakhana, **67**; The Adventures Of Goopy And Bagha, **68**; Days And Nights In The Forest, **69**; The Adversary, **71**; Company, **72**; Distant Thunder, **73**; The Middleman, **75**; The Chess Players, **77**; The Elephant God, **78**; Deliverance, **81**; The Home And The World, **84**; An Enemy Of The People, **89**; Branches Of The Tree, **90**; The Stranger, **92**.

RAYE, MARTHA: Rhythm On The Range, The Big Broadcast Of 1937, College Holiday, **36**; Artists & Models, Double Or Nothing, Mountain Music, Waikiki Wedding, Hideaway Girl, **37**; The Big Broadcast Of 1938, College Swing, Give Me A Sailor, Tropic Holiday, **38**; $1,000 A Touchdown, Never Say Die, **39**; The Boys From Syracuse, The Farmer's Daughter, **40**; Hellzapoppin, Keep 'em Flying, Navy Blues, **41**; Four Jills In A Jeep, Pin Up-Girl, **44**; Monsieur Verdoux, **47**; Jumbo, **62**; The Phynx, Puf'n'stuf, **70**; The Concorde – Airport 79, **79**.

REAGAN, RONALD: Hollywood Hotel, Love Is On The Air, **37**; Boy Meets Girl, Brother Rat, The Cowboy From Brooklyn, Girls On Probation, Going Places, Sergeant Murphy, Swing Your Lady, **38**; Accidents Will Happen, The Angels Wash Their Faces, Code Of The Secret Service, Dark Victory, Hell's Kitchen, Naughty But Nice, Secret Service Of The Air, Smashing The Money Ring, **39**; An Angel From Texas, Brother Rat And A Baby, Knute Rockne – All American, Murder In The Air, Santa Fe Trail, Tugboat Annie Sails Again, **40**; The Bad Man, International Squadron, Million Dollar Baby, Nine Lives Are Not Enough, **41**; Desperate Journey, Juke Girl, Kings Row, **42**; This Is The Army, **43**; Stallion Road, That Hagen Girl, The Voice Of The Turtle, **47**; The Girl From Jones Beach, John Loves Mary, Night Unto Night, **49**; Louisa, The Hasty Heart, **50**; Bedtime For Bonzo, Hong Kong, The Last Outpost, Storm Warning, **51**; She's Working Her Way Through College, The Winning Team, Tropic Zone, **52**; Law And Order, **53**; Cattle Queen Of Montana, Prisoner Of War, **54**; Tennessee's Partner, **55**; Hellcats Of The Navy, **57**; The Killers, **64**.

REDFORD, ROBERT: War Hunt, **62**; Inside Daisy Clover, Situation Hopeless But Not Serious, **65**; The Chase, This Property Is Condemned, **66**; Barefoot In The Park, **67**; Butch Cassidy And The Sundance Kid, Downhill Racer, Tell Them Willie Boy Is Here, **69**; Little Fauss And Big Halsy, **70**; The Candidate, The Hot Rock, Jeremiah Johnson, **72**; The Sting, The Way We Were, **73**; The Great Gatsby, **74**; The Great Waldo Pepper, Three Days Of The Condor, **75**; All The President's Men, **76**; A Bridge Too Far, **77**; The Electric Horseman, **79**; Brubaker, Ordinary People,

Movie talk

Gaffer tape: all-purpose black adhesive tape, a necessity on all film sets.

German new wave: left-wing reaction to the self-satisfied consumerism and affluence of West Germany.

Grip: stagehand and general purpose handyman.

The Hollywood 10: Herbert Biberman (prod/dir), Edward Dymytryk (dir), Adrian Scott (prod/writer), Alvah Bessie, Lester Cole, Ring Lardner Jr, John Howard Lawson, Albert Maltz, Samuel Ornitz and Dalton Trumbo (writers). Jailed for a year after refusing to reveal their political affiliations before the House Committee on Un-American Activities during anti-communist witch-hunt.

Honeywagon: portable lavatories used on location.

Horse opera/oater: western, usually a B-movie.

Independent/indie: low-cost production company that concentrates on particular genre for niche audience. A flourishing movement in America.

Italian neorealism: opposite of telefono blanco.

Key grip: most senior grip.

Keylight: main light on film set to create mood.

Leader: length of 35mm celluloid to top and tail finished film. Also used in splicing sections of exposed film.

Master: print of film from which duplicated negative is made.

Matte/travelling matte: tape or cut-out mask put over camera lens so that when blanked out section is exposed other images can be added.

Mixer: gathers dialogue, sound effects and music on to master soundtrack.

Nouvelle vague: tired of the conformity of the French industry, Truffaut, Resnais, Chabrol, Godard and Rohmer re-energised it with overt sexuality and vibrance of youth.

The pitch: brief resume of storyline for film upon which production chief decides on further development.

Playback: pre-recorded backing track for singers to mime to and dancers to dance to.

80; The Natural, **84**; Out Of Africa, **85**; Legal Eagles, **86**; The Milagro Beanfield War, **87**; To Protect Mother Earth, **89**; Havana, **90**; A River Runs Through It, Sneakers, **92**; Indecent Proposal, **93**; Quiz Show, **94**; Up Close And Present, **95**.

REDGRAVE, MICHAEL: The Lady Vanishes, Climbing High, **38**; Lady In Distress, Stolen Life, The Stars Look Down, **39**; Atlantic Ferry, Jeannie, Kipps, **41**; Thunder Rock, **42**; Dead Of Night, The Way To The Stars, **45**; The Captive Heart, The Years Between, **46**; Fame Is The Spur, Mourning Becomes Electra, The Man Within, **47**; Secret Beyond The Door, **48**; The Browning Version, The Magic Box, **51**; The Importance Of Being Earnest, **52**; The Sea Shall Not Have Them, The Green Scarf, **54**; The Dam Busters, Fledermaus, Mr Arkadin, The Night My Number Came Up, **55**; 1984, **56**; Time Without Pity, The Happy Road, **57**; Behind The Mask, Law And Disorder, The Quiet American, **58**; Shake Hands With The Devil, The Wreck Of The Mary Deare, **59**; The Innocents, No My Darling Daughter, **61**; The Loneliness Of The Long Distance Runner, **62**; Uncle Vanya, **63**; The Heroes Of Telemark, The Hill, Young Cassidy, **65**; Heidi Kehrt Heim, The 25th Hour, **67**; Assignment K, **68**; Battle Of Britain, Goodbye Mr Chips, Oh! What A Lovely War, **69**; David Copperfield, Goodbye Gemini, **70**; Connecting Rooms, The Go-Between, Nicholas And Alexander, **71**.

REDGRAVE, VANESSA: Behind The Mask, **58**; Blowup, A Man For All Seasons, Morgan, **66**; Camelot, Tonite Let's All Make Love In London, The Sailor From Gibraltar, **67**; The Charge Of The Light Brigade, Isadora, The Sea Gull, A Quiet Place In The Country, **68**; Oh! What A Lovely War, **69**; The Body, **70**; The Devils, La Vacanza, Dropout, Mary Queen Of Scots, The Trojan Women, **71**; Murder On The Orient Express, **74**; Out Of Season, **75**; The Seven Percent Solution, **76**; Julia, **77**; Agatha, Yanks, Bear Island, **79**; Wagner, **83**; The Bostonians, Sing Sing, **84**; Steaming, Wetherby, **85**; Comrades, **86**; Prick Up Your Ears, **87**; Consuming Passions, **88**; Diceria Dell'Untore, Romeo-Juliet, **90**; The Ballad Of The Sad Cafe, Stalin's Funeral, **91**; Howards End, **92**; House Of The Spirits, A Wall Of Silence, Sparrow, **93**; Mother's Boys, **94**; Little Odessa, A Month By The Lake, **95**; Wilde, **97**.

REED, CAROL: Midshipman Easy, It Happened In Paris, **35**; Laburnum Grove, **36**; Talk Of The Devil Who's Your Lady Friend?, **37**; Bank Holiday, Climbing High, Penny Paradise, **38**; A Girl Must Live, The Stars Look Down, **39**; The Girl In The News, Night Train To Munich, **40**; Kipps, Letter From Home, **41**; The Young Mr Pitt, The New Lot, **42**; The Way Ahead, **44**; The True Glory, **45**; Odd Man Out, **47**; The Fallen Idol, **48**; The Third Man, **49**; Outcast Of The Islands, **51**; The Man Between, **53**; A Kid For Two Farthings, **55**; Trapeze, **56**; The Key, **58**; Our Man In Havana, **59**; Mutiny On The Bounty, **62**; The Running Man, **63**; The Agony And The Ecstasy, **65**; Oliver!, **68**; Flap, **70**; Follow Me!, **72**.

REED, DONNA: The Get-Away, Babes On Broadway, The Bugle Sounds, Shadow Of The Thin Man, **41**; Apache Trail, Calling Dr Gillespie, The Courtship Of Andy Hardy, Eyes In The Night, Mokey, **42**; Dr. Gillespie's Criminal Case, The Human Comedy, The Man From Down Under, Thousands Cheer, **43**; Gentle Annie, Mrs. Parkington, See Here Private Hargrove, **44**; The Picture Of Dorian Gray, They Were Expendable, **45**; Faithful In My Fashion, It's A Wonderful Life, **46**; Green Dolphin Street, **47**; Beyond Glory, **48**; Chicago Deadline, **49**; Saturday's Hero, **51**; Hangman's Knot, Scandal Sheet, **52**; The Caddy, From Here To Eternity, Gun Fury, Raiders Of The Seven Seas, Trouble Along The Way, **53**; The Last Time I Saw Paris, They Rode West, Three Hours To Kill, **54**; The Benny Goodman Story, The Far Horizons, **55**; Backlash, Ransom, Beyond Mombasa, **56**; The Whole Truth, **58**; Pepe, **60**; Yellow-headed Summer, **74**.

REEVES, KEANU: Prodigal, Flying, Youngblood, **86**; River's Edge, **87**; Dangerous Liaisons, The Night Before, Permanent Record, The Prince Of Pennsylvania, **88**; Bill & Ted's Excellent Adventure, Parenthood, **89**; I Love You To Death, Aunt Julia And The Scriptwriter, Tune In Tomorrow, **90**; Bill And Ted's Bogus Journey, My Own Private Idaho, Point Break, **91**; Bram Stoker's Dracula, **92**; Freaked, Much Ado About Nothing, **93**; Little Buddha, Speed, Even Cowgirls Get The Blues, **94**; Johnny Mnemonic, Feeling Minnesota, A Walk In The Clouds, **95**; Chain Reaction, **96**.

REINER, CARL: The Gazebo, Happy Anniversary, **59**; Gidget Goes Hawaiian, **61**; It's A Mad Mad Mad Mad World, The Thrill Of It All, **63**; The Art Of Love, **65**; The Russians Are Coming! The Russians Are Coming!, **66**; Enter Laughing, A Guide For The Married Man, **67**; The Comic, Generation, **69**; Where's Poppa?, **70**; Oh God, **77**; The End, The One And Only, **78**; The Jerk, **79**; Dead Men Don't Wear Plaid, **82**; The Man With Two Brains, **83**; All Of Me, **84**; Summer Rental, **85**; Summer School, **87**; Bert Rigby You're A Fool, **89**; Sibling Rivalry, The Spirit Of 76, **90**; Fatal Instinct, **93**; That Old Feeling, **97**.

REINER, ROB: Enter Laughing, **67**; Halls Of Anger, Where's Poppa?, **70**; This Is Spinal Tap, **84**; The Sure Thing, **85**; Stand By Me, **86**; The Princess Bride, Throw Momma From The Train, **87**; When Harry Met Sally, **89**; Misery, Postcards From The Edge, **90**; Regarding Henry, The Spirit Of 76, **91**; A Few Good Men, **92**; Sleepless In Seattle, **93**; North, Mixed Nuts, Bullets Over Broadway, **94**; Bye Bye Love, **95** First Wives Club, Ghosts of Mississippi, **96**.

REINIGER, LOTTE: Der Rattenfanger Von Hamelin, **18**; Cinderella, Das Ornament Des Verliebten Herzens, Der Fliegende Koffer, Der Stern Von Bethlehem, **22**; The Adventures Of Prince Achmed, **26**; The Adventures Of Dr Dolittle, **28**; Die Jagd Nach Dem Gluck, Zehn Minuten Mozart, **30**; Harlekin, **31**; Sissi, **32**; Carmen, Don Quixote, **33**; The Stolen Heart, **34**; Galathea, The Little Chimney Sweep, Papageno, **35**; The King's Breakfast, **36**; Le Marseillaise, **38**; The Dancing Fleece, **50**; Mary's Birthday, **51**; Aladdin, The Magic Horse, Snow White And Rose Red, **53**; The Frog Prince, The Brave Little Tailor, The Grasshopper And The Ant, The Sleeping Beauty, The Three Wishes, **54**; Hansel And Gretel, Jack And The Beanstalk, Thumbelina, **55**; The Star Of Bethlehem, **56**; La Belle Hélène, Pied Piper Of Hamelin, **57**; The Seraglio, **58**; The Frog Prince, **61**; Cinderella, **63**.

REISZ, KAREL: Saturday Night And Sunday Morning, **60**; Night Must Fall, **64**; Morgan, **66**; Isadora, **68**; The Gambler, **74**; The Dog Soldiers, **78**; The French Lieutenant's Woman, **81**; Sweet Dreams, **85**; Everybody Wins, **90**.

REITMAN, IVAN: Columbus of Sex, **70**; Cannibal Girls, **73**; Shivers, **76**; Death Weekend, Rabid, **77**; Blackout, National Lampoon's Animal House, **78**; Meatballs, **79**; Heavy Metal, Stripes, **81**; Ghostbusters, Legal Eagles, **86**; Big Shots, **87**; Twins, **88**; Ghostbusters II, **89**; Kindergarten Cop, **90**; Beethoven, Stop! Or My Mom Will Shoot, **92**; Beethoven's 2nd, Dave, **93**, Junior, **94**; Father's Day, **97**.

REMICK, LEE: A Face In The Crowd, **57**; The Long Hot Summer, **58**; Anatomy Of A Murder, These Thousand Hills, **59**; Wild River, **60**; Sanctuary, **61**; Days Of Wine And Roses, Experiment In Terror, **62**; The Running Man, The Wheeler Dealers, **63**; Baby The Rain Must Fall, The Hallelujah Trail, **65**; The Detective, No Way To Treat A Lady, **68**; Hard Contract, **69**; Loot, **70**; A Severed Head, Never Give An Inch, **71**; A Delicate Balance, **73**; Hennessy, **75**; The Omen, **76**; Telefon, **77**; The Medusa Touch, **78**; The Europeans, **79**; The Women's Room, The Competition, Tribute, **80**; Emma's War, **86**; The Vision, **87**; Jesse, **88**.

RENOIR, JEAN: La Fille De L'Eau, **24**; Nana, **26**; Charleston, Marquitta, **27**; Le Tournoi, The Little Match Girl, Tire-au-Flanc, **28**; Le Bled, **29**; La Chienne, On Purge Bébé, **31**; Boudu Saved From Drowning, Chotard Et Compagnie, La Nuit Du Carrefour, **32**; Madame Bovary, **34**; Toni, **35**; Le Crime De Monsieur Lange, Une Partie De Campagne, The Lower Depths, La Vie Est A Nous, **36**; La Grande Illusion, La Marseillaise, **37**; La Bête Humaine, **38**; La Règle Du Jeu, **39**; Swamp Water, **41**; This Land Is Mine, **43**; The Southerner, **45**; Diary Of A Chambermaid, **46**; The Woman On The Beach, **47**; The River, **51**; La Carosse D'Or, **52**; French Can-Can, **55**; Elena Et Les Hommes, **56**; Le Testament Du Dr Cordelier, Le Déjeuner Sur L'Herbe, **59**; The Elusive Corporal, Il Fiore E La Violenza, **62**; Le Petit Théâtre De Jean Renoir, **69**.

RESNAIS, ALAIN: Nuit Et Brouillard, **55**; Hiroshima Mon Amour, **59**; Last Year At Marienbad, **61**; Muriel, **63**; La Guerre Est Finie, **66**; Je T'Aime Je T'Aime, **68**; The Year 01, **73**; Stavisky, **74**; Providence, **77**; Mon Oncle D'Amérique, **80**; La Vie Est Un Roman, **83**; L'Amour A Mort, **84**; Mélo, **86**; Je Veux Rentrer A La Maison, **89**; Contre L'Oubli, **92**; No Smoking Smoking, **93**; On connait la chanson, **97**.

REY, FERNANDO: Senora De Fatima, **51**; Comicos, **54**; Parque De Madrid, Sonatas, **59**; The Last Days Of Pompeii, **60**; La Rivolta Degli Schiavi, Viridiana, **61**; Face Of Terror/La Cara Del Terror, **62**; El Valle De Las Espadas, The Ceremony, **63**; Chimes At Midnight, El Greco, Navajo Joe, Return Of The Seven, Son Of A Gunfighter, **65**; The Viscount, Cervantes, **67**; Villa Rides, **68**; Guns Of The Magnificent Seven, **69**; The Adventurers, La Colera Del Viento, Land Raiders, Tristana, **70**; The French Connection, The Light At The Edge Of The World, A Town Called Hell, **71**; The Discreet Charm Of The Bourgeoisie, Antony And Cleopatra, White Sister **72**; La Duda, La Chute D'Un Corps, Questa Specie D'Amore, Rosso E, **73**; Corruzione Al Palazzo Di Giustizia, Dites-Le Avec Des Fleurs, Fatti Di Gente Perbene, La Femme Aux Bottes Rouges, **74**; French Connection II, Tarots, Illustrious Corpses, **75**; Striptease, A Matter Of Time, Seven Beauties, Voyage Of The Damned, **76**; Segundo Poder, Elisa Vida Mia, That Obscure Object Of Desire, **77**; El Crimen De Cuenca, Quintet, **79**; Vera Storia Della Signora Delle Camelie, **81**; Cercasi Gesu, La Straniera, Monsignor, **82**; The Hit, Una Strana Passione, **84**; Padre Nuestro, Rustlers' Rhapsody, **85**; El Caballero Del Dragon, Saving Grace, **86**; Hotel Du Paradis, Mi General, **87**; Diario De Invierno, El Tunel, Moon Over Parador, Pasodoble, **88**; Naked Tango, **91**; 1492: Conquest Of Paradise, After The Dream/Despues Del Sueno, Diceria Dell'Untore, **92**; Madregilda, **93**.

REYNOLDS, BURT: Angel Baby, Armored Command, **61**; Operation CIA, **65**; Navajo Joe, **66**; Fade-In, **68**; 100 Rifles, Sam Whiskey, Shark!, Impasse, **69**; Skullduggery, **70**; Deliverance, Everything You Always Wanted To Know About Sex, Fuzz, **72**; The Man Who Loved Cat Dancing, Shamus, White Lightning, **73**; The Longest Yard, The Mean Machine, **74**; At Long Last Love, Hustle, Lucky Lady, WW And The Dixie Dancekings, **75**; Gator, Nickelodeon, **76**; Semi-Tough, Smokey And The Bandit, **77**; The End, Hooper, **78**; Starting Over, **79**; Rough Cut, Smokey And The Bandit II, **80**; The Cannonball Run, Paternity, Sharky's Machine, **81**; Best Friends, The Best Little Whorehouse In Texas, **82**; The Man Who Loved Women, Smokey And The Bandit 3, Stroker Ace, **83**; Cannonball Run II, City Heat, **84**; Stick, **85**; Uphill All The Way, **86**; Heat, Malone, **87**; Rent-A-Cop, Switching Channels, **88**; All Dogs Go To Heaven, Breaking In, Physical Evidence, **89**; Modern Love, **90**; The Player, **92**; Cop And A Half, **93**, The Maddening, **95**; Bean, **97**.

RICHARDSON, RALPH: Friday The 13th, The Ghoul, **33**; Java Head, King Of Paris, The Return Of Bulldog Drummond, **34**; Bulldog Jack, **35**; The Man Who Could Work Miracles, Things To Come, **36**; Thunder In The City, **37**; The Citadel, The Divorce Of Lady X, South Riding, **38**; The Four Feathers, On The Night Of The Fire, The Lion Has Wings, Q Planes, **39**; The Day Will Dawn, **42**; The Silver Fleet, The Volunteer, **43**; School For Secrets, **46**; Anna Karenina, The Fallen Idol, **48**; The Heiress, **49**; Outcast Of The Islands, **51**; The Sound Barrier, **52**; The Holly And The Ivy, **53**; Richard III, **55**; The Passionate Stranger, Smiley, **54**; Exodus, Oscar Wilde, Our Man In Havana, **60**; The 300 Spartans, Long Day's Journey Into Night, **62**; Woman Of Straw, **64**; Doctor Zhivago, **65**; Khartoum, The Wrong Box, **66**; Battle Of Britain, The Bed-Sitting Room, The Looking Glass War, Midas Run, Oh! What A Lovely War, A Run On Gold, **69**; David Copperfield, Upon This Rock, **70**; Eagle In A Cage, Who Slew Auntie Roo?, **71**; Alice's Adventures In Wonderland, Lady Caroline Lamb, Tales From The Crypt, **72**; A Doll's House, O Lucky Man!, **73**; Rollerball, **75**; Charlie Muffin, **79**; Dragonslayer, Time Bandits, **81**; Invitation To The Wedding, Wagner, **83**; Give My Regards To Broad Street, Greystoke: The Legend Of Tarzan Lord Of The Apes, **84**.

RICHARDSON, TONY: Look Back In Anger, **59**; The Entertainer, Saturday Night And Sunday Morning, **60**; Sanctuary, A Taste Of Honey, **61**; The Loneliness Of The Long Distance Runner, **62**; Tom Jones, **63**; The Loved One, **65**; Red And Blue, Mademoiselle, **66**; The Sailor From Gibraltar, **67**; The Charge Of The Light Brigade, **68**; Hamlet, Laughter In The Dark, **69**; Ned Kelly, **70**; A Delicate Balance, **73**; Joseph Andrews, **77**; The Border, **82**; The Hotel New Hampshire, **84**; Blue Sky, **94**.

RIEFENSTAHL, LENI: The Blue Light, **32**; Victory Of Faith, **33**; Day Of Freedom, Berchtes Garden Uber Salzburg, Triumph Of The Will, **35**; Olympiad, **38**; Tiefland, **54**.

RIN TIN TIN: Where The North Begins, **23**; The Lighthouse By The Sea, Tracked In The Snow Country, Below The Lines, Find Your Man, **24**; Clash Of The Wolves, **25**; The Night Cry, **26**; Dog Of The Regiment, Jaws Of Steel, The Hills Of Kentucky, **27**; Rinty Of The Desert, **28**; Frozen River, The Million Dollar Collar, The Show Of Shows, Tiger Rose, **29**; The Lone Defender, On The Border, The Man Hunter, **30**.

RITT, MARTIN: Winged Victory, **44**; Edge Of The City, No Down Payment, **57**; The Long Hot Summer, **58**; The Black Orchid, The Sound And The Fury, **59**; 5 Branded Women, **60**; Paris Blues, **61**; Adventures Of A Young Man, **62**; Hud, **63**; The Outrage, **64**; The Spy Who Came In From The Cold, **65**; Hombre, **67**; The Brotherhood, **68**; The Great White Hope, The Molly Maguires, **70**; Pete 'n' Tillie, Sounder, **72**; Conrack, **74**; The Front, **76**; Casey's Shadow, **78**; Norma Rae, **79**; Back Roads, **81**; Cross Creek, **83**; Murphy's Romance, **85**; Nuts, **87**; Stanley & Iris, **90**.

RITTER, TEX: Heading For The Rio Grande, The Old Corral, **36**; Mystery Of The Hooded Horsemen, Sing Cowboy Sing, Trouble In Texas, Arizona Days, **37**; Frontier Town, Starlight Over Texas, Where The Buffalo Roam, Hittin' The Trail, **38**; Song Of The Buckaroo, Sundown On The Prairie, **39**; The Cowboy From Sundown, The Golden Trail, **40**; King Of Dodge City, Roaring Frontiers, The Devil's Price, Marshal Of Santa Fe, **41**; Little Joe The Wrangler, Deep In The Heart Of Texas, The Old Chisholm Trail, **42**; Arizona Trail, Oklahoma Raiders, **43**; Dead Or Alive, Marshall Of Gunsmoke, Cheyenne Roundup, Gangsters Of The Frontier, **44**; Enemy Of The Law, Bullets, **45**; The Cowboy, **53**; Apache Ambush, **55**; What Am I Bid?, **67**.

RITTER, THELMA: Miracle On 34th Street, **47**; City Across The River, Father Was A Fullback, A Letter To Three Wives, **49**; All About Eve, I'll Get By, Perfect Strangers, **50**; As Young As You Feel, The Mating Season, The Model And The Marriage Broker, **51**; With A Song In My Heart, **52**; The Farmer Takes A Wife, Pickup On South Street, Titanic, **53**; Rear Window, **54**; Daddy Long Legs, Lucy Gallant, **55**; The Proud And Profane, **56**; A Hole In The Head, Pillow Talk, **59**; The Misfits, The Second Time Around, **61**; Birdman Of Alcatraz, How The West Was Won, **62**; For Love Or Money, Move Over Darling, A New Kind Of Love, **63**; Boeing Boeing, **65**; The Incident, **67**.

RIVETTE, JACQUES: Aux Quatre Coins, **49**; Le Quadrille, **50**; Le Divertissement, **52**; Le Coup Du Berger, **56**; Paris Belongs To Us, **60**; La Religieuse **65**; L'Amour Fou, **68**; Noli Me Tangere, **71**; Spectre, **72**; Céline And Julie Go Boating, **74**; Northwest Wind, **76**; Le Pont Du Nord, **81**; Merry Go Round, **83**; L'Amour Par Terre, **84**; Hurlevent, **85**; La Bande Des Quatre, **89**; La Belle Noiseuse, Divertimento, **91**; Jeanne La Pucelle, **94** Haut bas fragile, **97**.

ROACH, HAL: Luke's Movie Muddle, **16**; On The Fire, **18**; Captain Kidd's Kids, His Royal Slyness, Hoot Mon, **19**; An Eastern Westerner, Get Out And Get Under, High And Dizzy, **20**; A Sailor-Made Man, **21**; Doctor Jack, Grandma's Boy, **22**; Safety Last, Why Worry?, **23**; The Battling Orioles, The King Of The Wild Horses, The White Sheep, **24**; Black Cyclone, **25**; Devil Horse, **26**; From Soup To Nuts, **28**; Men Of The North, **30**; On The Loose, Pardon Us, **31**; The Music Box, **32**; Fra Diavolo, **33**; Heroes Of The Regiment, Tit F Tat, **35**; The Bohemian Girl, General Spanky, Kelly The Second, Mr Cinderella, Neighborhood House, Our Relations, **36**; Nobody's Baby, Pick A Star, Topper, Way C West, **37**; There Goes My Heart, **38**; Captain Fury, Of Mice And Men, Topper Ta A Trip, **39**; Captain Caution, A Chump At Oxford, One Million BC, Saps At Sea, Turnabout, **40**; All American Co-ed, Broadway Limited, Miss Polly, Niagara Fal Road Show, Tanks A Million, Topper Returns, **41**; Brooklyn Orchid, Calaboose, Flying With Music, **42**; As You Were, **51**.

ROBARDS, JASON: The Journey, **59**; By Love Possessed, **61**; Long Day's Journ Into Night, Tender Is The Night, **62**; Act One, **63**; A Thousand Clowns, **65**; Any Wednesday, A Big Hand For The Little Lady, **66**; Divorce American Style, Hour O The Gun, The St Valentine's Day Massacre, **67**; Isadora, The Night They Ra Minsky's, Once Upon A Time In The West, **68**; The Ballad Of Cable Hogue, Foo Julius Caesar, Tora! Tora! Tora!, **70**; Johnny Got His Gun, Murders In The Rue Morgue, **71**; The War Between Men And Women, **72**; Pat Garrett And Billy The Kid **73**; Mr Sycamore, A Boy And His Dog, **75**; Adie And The King Of Hearts, All The President's Men, **76**; Julia, **77**; Comes A Horseman, **78**; Hurricane, **79**; Cabo Blar Melvin And Howard, Raise The Titanic!, **80**; The Legend Of The Lone Ranger, **81** Burden Of Dreams, **82**; Max Dugan Returns, Something Wicked This Way Com **83**; The World Of Tomorrow, **84**; Square Dance, **87**; Bright Lights Big City, The Go Mother, **88**; Dream A Little Dream, Parenthood, Black Rainbow, Reunion, **89**; Quick Change, **90**; Storyville, **92**; The Adventures Of Huck Finn, Philadelphia, **9** The Paper, **94**, Crimson Tide, **95**.

ROBBINS, TIM: No Small Affair, **84**; Fraternity Vacation, The Sure Thing, **85**; Howard The Duck, Top Gun, **86**; Bull Durham, Five Corners, Tapeheads, **88**; E The Viking, Miss Firecracker, **89**; Cadillac Man, Jacob's Ladder, **90**; Jungle Fever, **91**; Bob Roberts, The Player, **92**; Short Cuts, **93**; The Hudsucker Proxy, IQ, Shawshank Redemption, **94**, Prêt A Porter, Dead Man Walking, IQ, **95**.

ROBERTS, JULIA: Blood Red, Mystic Pizza, **88**; Steel Magnolias, **89**; Flatliners Pretty Woman, **90**; Dying Young, Hook, Sleeping With The Enemy, **91**; The Player **92**; The Pelican Brief, **93**; I Love Trouble, Prêt-A-Porter, **95;** Mary Reilly, Th Game Of Love, **95**; My Best Friend's Wedding, **97**.

ROBERTSON, CLIFF: Picnic, **55**; Autumn Leaves, **56**; The Girl Most Likely, The Naked And The Dead, **58**; Battle Of The Coral Sea, Gidget, **59**; All In A Night' Work, The Big Show, Underworld USA, **61**; The Interns, **62**; My Six Loves, PT-10 Sunday In New York, **63**; 633 Squadron, The Best Man, **64**; Love Has Many Faces From The Beach, Masquerade, **65**; The Honey Pot, **67**; Charly, The Devil's Brigad **68**; Too Late The Hero, **70**; The Great Northfield Minnesota Raid, J W Coop, **71** Eli And Rodger Of The Skies, **73**; Man On A Swing, **74**; Out Of Season, Three D Of The Condor, **75**; Midway, Obsession, Shoot, **76**; Dominique, **78**; The Pilot, **80** Brainstorm, Class, Star 80, **83**; Shaker Run, **85**; Malone, **87**; Wild Hearts Can't Broken, **91**; Wind, **92**; Renaissance Man, **94**; Escape from LA, **96**.

ROBESON, PAUL: Body And Soul, **25**; The Emperor Jones, **33**; Sanders Of The River, **35**; Show Boat, Song Of Freedom, **36**; Big Fella, Jericho, King Solomon's M **37**; The Proud Valley, **40**; Native Land, Tales Of Manhattan, **42**.

ROBINSON, EDWARD G: The Bright Shawl, **23**; A Hole In The Wall, **29**; East West, A Lady To Love, Little Caesar, Night Ride, Outside The Law, The Widow Chicago, **30**; Five Star Final, Smart Money, **31**; The Hatchet Man, Silver Dol Tiger Shark, Two Seconds, **32**; I Loved A Woman, The Little Giant, **33**; Dark Haza The Man With Two Faces, **34**; Barbary

st, The Whole Town's Talking, **35**;
ets Or Ballots, **36**; Kid Galahad, The Last
gster, Thunder In The City, **37**; The
zing Doctor Clitterhouse, I Am The Law, A
t Case Of Murder, **38**; Blackmail,
fessions Of A Nazi Spy, **39**; Brother
hid, A Dispatch From Reuters, Dr
ch's Magic Bullet, **40**; Manpower, The
Wolf, Unholy Partners, **41**; Larceny
Tales Of Manhattan, **42**; Destroyer, Flesh
Fantasy, **43**; Double Indemnity, Mr
kle Goes To War, Tampico, The Woman In
Window, **44**; Journey Together, Our
s Have Tender Grapes, Scarlet Street, **45**;
Stranger, **46**; The Red House, **47**;
My Sons, Key Largo, The Night Has A
usand Eyes, **48**; House Of Strangers,
A Great Feeling, **49**; My Daughter Joy, **50**;
rs And Sin, **52**; Big Leaguer, The
s Web, Vice Squad, **53**; Black Tuesday,
A Bullet For Joey, Hell On Frisco
Illegal, Tight Spot, The Violent Men, **55**;
tmare, The Ten Commandments,
A Hole In The Head, **59**; Pépé, Seven
ves, **60**; My Geisha, Two Weeks In
her Town, **62**; Sammy Going South, The
, **63**; Cheyenne Autumn, Good
hbor Sam, The Outrage, Robin And The
n Hoods, **64**; The Cincinnati Kid,
Grand Slam, **67**; The Blonde From
ng, The Biggest Bundle Of Them All,
ckmate, Never A Dull Moment, Operation
eter, MacKenna's Gold, **69**; Song Of
way, **70**; Neither By Day Or Night, Soylent
n, **73**.

SON, FLORA: A Gentlemen Of
s, **31**; Dance Pretty Lady, **32**; Catherine
Great, **34**; Farewell Again, Fire Over
and, **37**; Invisible Stripes, We Are Not
e, Wuthering Heights, **39**; The Sea
k, **40**; Bahama Passage, **41**; 2000
nen, **44**; Great Day, Invisible Stripes,
Years Between, Caesar And Cleopatra,
toga Trunk, **45**; Black Narcissus,
Frieda, Holiday Camp, **47**; Saraband,
d Time Girl, The Tall Headlines, The
a Story, **53**; Romeo And Juliet, **54**; The
y And The Gentleman, **58**; Murder
e Gallop, 55 Days At Peking, **63**; Guns At
si, **64**; Those Magnificent Men In
Flying Machines, Young Cassidy, **65**; 7
nen, Cry In The Wind, **66**; Eye Of The
, **67**; The Shuttered Room, **68**; Fragment
ear, The Cellar, **70**; Alice's
ntures In Wonderland, **72**; Dominique,
Clash Of The Titans, **81**.

SON, MARK: The Seventh Victim,
Ghost Ship, **43**; Youth Runs Wild, **44**;
Of The Dead, **45**; Bedlam, **46**;
mpion, Home Of The Brave, My Foolish
t, Roughshod, **49**; Edge Of Doom,
Bright Victory, I Want You, **51**; Return To
dise, Hell Below Zero, **53**; The
es At Toko-Ri, Phffft!, **54**; A Prize Of
Trial, **55**; The Harder They Fall,
The Little Hut, Peyton Place, **57**; The Inn
e Sixth Happiness, **58**; From The
ce, **60**; The Inspector, **62**; Nine Hours
ama, The Prize, **63**; Von Ryan's
ess, **65**; Lost Command, **66**; Valley Of
Dolls, **67**; Daddy's Gone A-Hunting,
Happy Birthday Wanda June, **71**;
o, **72**; Earthquake, **74**; Avalanche
ess, **79**.

GERS, RICHARD: Follow Through,
g Is Here, **30**; The Hot Heiress, **31**; Love
onight, **32**; Dancing Lady,
lujah I'm A Bum, **33**; Manhattan
drama, **34**; Mississippi, Evergreen,
The Dancing Pirate, **36**; Fools For
dal, **38**; Babes In Arms, On Your
39; The Boys From Syracuse, Too Many
40; I Married An Angel, **42**; Higher
Higher, Stage Door Canteen, **43**; State
45; Victory At Sea, **54**; Oklahoma!,
Carousel, The King And I, **56**; Pal Joey,
South Pacific, **58**; Flower Drum
, **61**; Jumbo, **62**; The Sound Of
c, **65**.

G, NICHOLAS: Far From The
ding Crowd, **67**; Performance, **70**;
about, **71**; Don't Look Now, **73**;
Man Who Fell To Earth, **76**; Bad Timing,
Eureka, **83**; Insignificance, **85**;
way, **86**; Aria, **87**; Track 29, **88**; The
es, **90**; Cold Heaven, **92**; Heart Of
ness, **94**; Hotel Paradise, **96**.

ERS, GINGER: Campus
thearts, **28**; Follow The Leader, Queen
The Sap From Syracuse, Young
Of Manhattan, **30**; Honor Among Lovers,
de Fleet, The Tip Off, **31**; Carnival
Hat Check Girl, The Tenderfoot, The
enth Guest, You Said A Mouthful,
32; 42nd Street, Broadway Bad, Chance At Heaven, Don't Bet On Love, Flying Down To Rio, Gold Diggers Of 33, Professional Sweetheart, Rafter Romance, A Shriek In The Night, Sitting Pretty, **33**; Change Of Heart, Finishing School, The Gay Divorcee, Romance In Manhattan, Twenty Million Sweethearts, Upper World, **34**; In Person, Roberta, Star Of Midnight, Top Hat, **35**; Follow The Fleet, Swing Time, **36**; Shall We Dance, Stage Door, **37**; Carefree, Having Wonderful Time, Vivacious Lady, **38**; Bachelor Mother, Fifth Avenue Girl, The Story Of Vernon & Irene Castle, **39**; Kitty Foyle, Lucky Partners, The Primrose Path, **40**; Tom Dick And Harry, **41**; The Major And The Minor, Once Upon A Honeymoon, Roxie Hart, Tales Of Manhattan, **42**; Tender Comrade, Lady In The Dark, **44**; I'll Be Seeing You, Weekend At The Waldorf, **45**; Heartbeat, Magnificent Doll, **46**; It Had To Be You, **47**; The Barkleys Of Broadway, **49**; Perfect Strangers, **50**; The Groom Wore Spurs, Storm Warning, **51**; Dreamboat, Monkey Business, We're Not Married, **52**; Forever Female, **53**; Black Widow, Twist Of Fate, **54**; Tight Spot, **55**; The First Traveling Saleslady, Teenage Rebel, **56**; Oh Men! Oh Women!, **57**; Quick Let's Get Married, **64**; Harlow, **65**.

ROGERS, ROY: Gallant Defender, **35**; Rhythm On The Range, California Mail, **36**; The Old Wyoming Trail, **37**; Billy The Kid Returns, Come On Rangers, Under Western Stars, **38**; Days Of Jesse James, Frontier Pony Express, In Old Caliente, Jeepers Creepers, Wall Street Cowboy, **39**; The Border Legion, The Carson City Kid, Colorado, Dark Command, The Ranger And The Lady, Young Bill Hickok, Young Buffalo Bill, **40**; Arkansas Judge, Bad Man Of Deadwood, In Old Cheyenne, Jesse James At Bay, Nevada City, Red River Valley, Robin Hood Of The Pecos, Sheriff Of Tombstone, **41**; Heart Of The Golden West, Man From Cheyenne, Ridin' Down The Canyon, Romance On The Range, Sons Of The Pioneers, South Of Santa Fe, Sunset On The Desert, Sunset Serenade, **42**; Hands Across The Border, Idaho, King Of The Cowboys, The Man From Music Mountain, Silver Spurs, Song Of Texas, **43**; The Cowboy And The Senorita, Hollywood Canteen, Lights Of Old Santa Fe, San Fernando Valley, Song Of Nevada, The Yellow Rose Of Texas, **44**; Along The Navajo Trail, Bells Of Rosarita, Don't Fence Me In, The Man From Oklahoma, Sunset In El Dorado, Utah, **45**; Heldorado, Home In Oklahoma, My Pal Trigger, Out California Way, Rainbow Over Texas, Roll On Texas Moon, Song Of Arizona, Under Nevada Skies, **46**; Apache Rose, Bells Of San Angelo, The Gay Ranchero, Hit Parade Of 47, On The Old Spanish Trail, Springtime In The Sierras, **47**; Eyes Of Texas, The Far Frontier, Grand Canyon Trail, Melody Time, Night Time In Nevada, Under Under California Skies, **48**; Down Dakota Way, The Golden Stallion, Susanna Pass, **49**; Bells Of Coronado, North Of The Great Divide, Sunset In The West, Trail Of Robin Hood, Trigger Jr, Twilight In The Sierras, **50**; Heart Of The Rockies, In Old Amarillo, Pals Of The Golden West, South Of Caliente, Spoilers Of The Plains, **51**; Son Of Paleface, **52**; Alias Jesse James, **59**; Mackintosh And TJ, **75**.

ROGERS, WILL: Laughing Bill Hyde, **18**; Almost A Husband, Jubilo, **19**; Water Water Everywhere, Cupid The Cowpuncher, Honest Hutch, Jes' Call Me Jim, **20**; Boys Will Be Boys, Doubling For Romeo, Guile Of Women, A Poor Relation, An Unwilling Hero, **21**; The Headless Horseman, One Glorious Day, **22**; Fruits Of Faith, The Roping Fool, One Day In 365, Hollywood, **23**; Two Wagons Both Covered, Truthful Liar, **24**; A Texas Steer, Tip Toes, **27**; Happy Days, They Had To See Paris, **29**; Lightnin', So This Is London, Happy Days, **30**; Ambassador Bill, A Connecticut Yankee, Young As You Feel, **31**; Business And Pleasure, Down To Earth, Too Busy To Work, **32**; Dr Bull, Mr Skitch, State Fair, **33**; David Harum, Handy Andy, Judge Priest, **34**; The Country Chairman, Doubting Thomas, In Old Kentucky, Life Begins At Forty, Steamboat Round The Bend, **35**.

ROHMER, ERIC: Le Signe Du Lion, **60**; La Boulangère De Monceau, **62**; La Carrière De Suzanne, **63**; Paris Vu Par, **65**; La Collectionneuse, **67**; Ma Nuit Chez Maud, **69**; Claire's Knee, **71**; L'Amour, L'Après-midi, **72**; Die Marquise Von O, **76**; Perceval **78**; The Aviator's Wife, **81**; Le Beau Mariage, **82**; Pauline A La Plage, **83**; Les Nuits De La Pleine Lune, **84**; Quatre Aventures De Reinette Et Mirabelle, Le Rayon Vert, **86**; L'Ami De Mon Amie, **87**; A Tale Of Springtime, **89**; A Winter's Tale, **91**; L'Arbe, Le Maire Et La Mediatheque, **93**.

ROLAND, GILBERT: The Plastic Age, **25**; The Campus Flirt, **26**; Camille, The Dove, The Love Mart, Rose Of The Golden West, **27**; The Woman Disputed, **28**; New York Nights, Men Of The North, Monsieur Le Fox, **30**; Call Her Savage, Life Begins, No Living Witness, The Passionate Plumber, The Woman In Room 13, **32**; After Tonight, Our Betters, She Done Him Wrong, La Viuda Romantica, I Thou And She, **33**; Elinor Norton, **34**; The Mystery Woman, Juliette Buys A Baby, **35**; The Last Train From Madrid, Thunder Trail, **37**; Gateway, **38**; Juarez, La Vida Bohemia, **39**; The Sea Hawk, **40**; The Desert Hawk, **44**; Captain Kidd, **45**; Beauty And The Bandit, The Gay Cavalier, South Of Monterey, King Of The Bandits, Robin Hood Of Monterey, **47**; We Were Strangers, **49**; Crisis, The Furies, The Torch, Malaya, **50**; The Bullfighter And The Lady, Mark Of The Renegade, Ten Tall Men, **51**; Apache War Smoke, The Bad And The Beautiful, Glory Alley, The Miracle Of Our Lady Of Fatima, My Six Convicts, **52**; Beneath The 12 Mile Reef, Thunder Bay, **53**; The French Line, **54**; The Racers, The Treasure Of Pancho Villa, That Lady, Underwater!, **55**; Bandido, Around The World In 80 Days, **56**; The Midnight Story, Three Violent People, **57**; The Big Circus, **59**; Guns Of The Timberland, **60**; Samar, **62**; Cheyenne Autumn, **64**; The Reward, **65**; Any Gun Can Play, The Poppy Is Also A Flower, **67**; The Christian Licorice Store, **71**; The Black Pearl, Islands In The Stream, **77**; Caboblanco, **80**; Barbarosa, **82**.

ROMERO, CESAR: The Shadow Laughs, **33**; The Thin Man, British Agent, Cheating Cheaters, **34**; Cardinal Richelieu, Clive Of India, The Devil Is A Woman, Diamond Jim, The Good Fairy, Hold 'Em Yale, Metropolitan, Rendezvous, Show Them No Mercy, **35**; 15 Malden Lane, Love Before Breakfast, Public Enemy's Wife, **36**; Dangerously Yours, Wee Willie Winkie, **37**; Always Goodbye, Five Of A Kind, Happy Landing, My Lucky Star, **38**; Charlie Chan At Treasure Island, The Cisco Kid And The Lady, Frontier Marshal, The Little Princess, The Return Of The Cisco Kid, Wife Husband And Friend, **39**; The Gay Caballero, He Married His Wife, Lucky Cisco Kid, Viva Cisco Kid, Romance Of The Rio Grande, **40**; Dance Hall, The Great American Broadcast, Ride On Vaquero, Tall Dark And Handsome, Weekend In Havana, **41**; A Gentleman At Heart, Orchestra Wives, Springtime In The Rockies, Tales Of Manhattan, **42**; Coney Island, Wintertime, **43**; Captain From Castil, Carnival In Costa Rica, **47**; Deep Waters, Julia Misbehaves, That Lady In Ermine, **48**; The Beautiful Blonde From Bashful Bend, **49**; Love That Brute, Once A Thief, **50**; FBI Girl, Happy Go Lovely, The Lost Continent, **51**; The Jungle, Scotland Yard Inspector, **52**; The Shadow Man, **53**; Vera Cruz, **54**; The Americano, The Racers, **55**; Around The World In 80 Days, The Leather Saint, **56**; The Story Of Mankind, **57**; Villa!, **58**; Ocean's 11, **60**; If A Man Answers, Seven Women From Hell, **62**; The Castillan, Donovan's Reef, We Shall Return, **63**; A House Is Not A Home, **64**; Marriage On The Rocks, Two On A Guillotine, Broken Sabre, Sergeant Deadhead, **65**; Batman, **66**; Hot Millions, Madigan's Million, Skidoo, **68**; Crooks And Coronets, Latitude Zero, Midas Run, A Talent For Loving, How To Make It, **69**; The Computer Wore Tennis Shoes, **70**; Now You See Him Now You Don't, **72**; The Proud And The Damned, The Spectre Of Edgar Allan Poe, **73**; The Strongest Man In The World, **75**; Carlucca Tiger, **76**; Flesh And Bullets, **85**; The Mortuary Academy, **88**; Judgment Day, **89**.

ROMERO, GEORGE A: Night Of The Living Dead, **68**; There's Always Vanilla, **71**; Hungry Wives, **72**; The Crazies, Jack's Wife, **73**; Dawn Of The Dead, Martin, **78**; Knightriders, **81**; Creepshow, **82**; Day Of The Dead, **85**; Monkey Shines, **88**; Two Evil Eyes, **90**; **91**; The Dark Half, **93**.

ROONEY, MICKEY: Not To Be Trusted, **26**; Orchids And Ermine, **27**; The Beast Of The City, Fast Companions, My Pal The King, Sins Per Day, High Speed, **32**; The Big Cage, The Big Chance, Broadway To Hollywood, The Chief, The Life Of Jimmy Dolan, **33**; Beloved, Blind Date, Chained, Death On The Diamond, Half A Sinner, Hide-Out, I Like It That Way, The Lost Jungle, Love Birds, Manhattan Melodrama, **34**; Ah Wilderness, The County Chairman, The Healer, A Midsummer Night's Dream, Riff-Raff, **35**; The Devil Is A Sissy, Down The Stretch, Little Lord Fauntleroy, **36**; Captains Courageous, A Family Affair, The Hoosier Schoolboy, Live Love And Learn, Slave Ship, Thoroughbreds Don't Cry, **37**; Boys Town, Hold That Kiss, Judge Hardy's Children, Lord Jeff, Love Finds Andy Hardy, Love Is A Headache, Out West With The Hardys, Stablemates, You're Only Young Once, **38**; Andy Hardy Gets Spring Fever, Babes In Arms, The Hardys Ride High, The Adventures Of Huckleberry Finn, Judge Hardy And Son, **39**; Andy Hardy Meets Debutante, Strike Up The Band, Young Tom Edison, **40**; Andy Hardy's Private Secretary, Babes On Broadway, Life Begins For Andy Hardy, Men Of Boys Town, **41**; Andy Hardy's Double Life, The Courtship Of Andy Hardy, A Yank At Eton, **42**; Girl Crazy, The Human Comedy, Thousands Cheer, **43**; Andy Hardy's Blonde Trouble, National Velvet, **44**; Love Laughs At Andy Hardy, **46**; Killer McCoy, **47**; Summer Holiday, Words And Music, **48**; The Big Wheel, **49**; The Fireball, He's A Cockeyed Wonder, Quicksand, **50**; My Outlaw Brother, My True Story, The Strip, **51**; Sound Off, **52**; All Ashore, Off Limits, A Slight Case Of Larceny, **53**; The Atomic Kid, The Bridges At Toko-Ri, Drive A Crooked Road, **54**; The Twinkle In God's Eye, **55**; The Bold And The Brave, Francis In The Haunted House, Magnificent Roughnecks, **56**; Baby Face Nelson, Operation Mad Ball, **57**; Andy Hardy Comes Home, A Nice Little Bank That Should Be Robbed, **58**; The Big Operator, The Last Mile, **59**; Platinum High School, The Private Lives Of Adam And Eve, **60**; Breakfast At Tiffany's, Everything's Ducky, King Of The Roaring 20s, **61**; Requiem For A Heavyweight, **62**; It's A Mad Mad Mad Mad World, **63**; The Secret Invasion, **64**; How To Stuff A Wild Bikini, **65**; Ambush Bay, **66**; The Devil In Love, Skidoo, **68**; 80 Steps To Jonah, The Comic, The Extraordinary Seaman, **69**; Cockeyed Cowboys Of Calico County, **70**; B J Lang Presents, **71**; Pulp, Richard, **72**; That's Entertainment!, **74**; Bon Baisers De Hong Kong, **75**; The Domino Killings, Pete's Dragon, **77**; The Magic Of Lassie, **78**; Arabian Adventure, The Black Stallion, **79**; La Traversée De La Pacific, The Emperor Of Peru, **82**; The Care Bears Movie, **85**; Lightning The White Stallion, **86**; Erik The Viking, **89**; My Heroes Have Always Been Cowboys, **91**; The Legend Of Wolf Mountain, **92**; La Vida Lactea, **93**; The Adventures Of The Red Baron, **94**.

ROSAY, FRANCOISE: Crainquebille, **23**; Gribiche, **25**; Les Deux Timides, **28**; The Trial Of Mary Dugan, The One Woman Idea, **29**; Si L'Empereur Savait Ca!, **30**; La Chance, The Magnificent Lie, **31**; He, Le Rosier De Madame Husson, **32**; Le Grand Jeu, **33**; Maternité, Pension Mimosas, Whirlpool, **34**; La Kermesse Héroique, **35**; Jenny, **36**; Drôle De Drame, Un Carnet De Bal, **37**; Le Joueur D'Echecs, Les Gens Du Voyage, Paix Sur Le Rhin, Ramuntcho, **38**; Die Hochzeitsreise, **39**; Elles Etaient Douze Femmes, **40**; Une Femme Disparait, **42**; The Halfway House, **43**; Johnny Frenchman, **45**; Back Streets Of Paris, **46**; Saraband For Dead Lovers, **48**; Maria Chapdelaine, Quartet, Donne Senza Nome, **49**; September Affair, **50**; The Thirteenth Letter, L'Auberge Rouge, **51**; Seven Deadly Sins, **52**; La Reine Margot, **54**; That Lady, Young Girls Today, **55**; Interlude, The Seventh Sin, **57**; Le Joueur, Me And The Colonel, **58**; The Sound And The Fury, **59**; Le Cave Se Rebiffe, Frau Cheney's Ende, Stop Me Before I Kill!, **61**; The Longest Day, Du Rififi Chez Les Femmes, **62**; Up From The Beach, **65**; The 25th Hour, **67**; Operation Léontine, **68**; Un Merveilleux Parfum D'Oseille, **69**; Pas Folle La Guêpe, **72**; The Pedestrian, **74**.

ROSI, FRANCESCO: Camicie Rosse, Bellissima, **51**; La Sfida/The Challenge, **57**; I Magliare, **59**; Salvatore Giuliano, **62**; Le Mani Sulla Citta, **63**; The Moment Of Truth, **65**; C'Era Una Volta, **67**; Uomini Contro, **70**; The Mattei Affair, **73**; Lucky Luciano, **74**; Illustrious Corpses, **76**; Christ Stopped At Eboli, **79**; I Tre Fratelli, **80**; Carmen, **84**; Chronicle Of A Death Foretold, **87**; Dimenticare Palermo, **90**.

ROSS, HERBERT: Goodbye Mr Chips, **69**; The Owl And The Pussycat, **70**; T R Baskin, **71**; Play It Again Sam, **72**; The Last Of Sheila, **73**; Funny Lady, The Sunshine Boys, **75**; The Seven-Per-Cent Solution, **76**; The Goodbye Girl, The Turning Point, **77**; California Suite, **78**; Nijinsky, **80**; Pennies From Heaven, **81**; I Ought To Be In Pictures, **82**; Max Dugan Returns, **83**; Footloose, Protocol, **84**; Dancers, The Secret Of My Success, **87**; Steel Magnolias, **89**; My Blue Heaven, **90**; Soapdish, True Colors, **91**; Undercover Blues, **93**; Cloak And Dagger, Boys On The Side, **94**.

ROSSELLINI, ROBERTO: La Nave Bianca, **41**; Una Pilota Ritorna, **42**; Open City, **45**; Paisan, **46**; Germany Year Zero, **47**; La Macchina Ammazzacattivi, L'Amore, **48**; The Miracle, **49**; Flowers Of St Francis, Stromboli, **50**; Europa '51, **51**; Les Sept Péchés Capitaux, **52**; Viaggio In Italia, We The Women, **53**; Giovanna D'Arco Al Rogo, **54**; Fear, **55**; Il Generale Della Rovere, **59**; Era Notte A Roma, **60**; Vanina Vanini, **61**; Anima Nera, RoGoPag, **62**; The Age Of Iron, **64**; The Rise Of Louis XIV, **66**; The Acts Of The Apostles, **68**; The Night Of Counting The Years, **70**; Socrates, **71**; Agostino D'Ippona, Cozimo De'Medici, **72**; Anno Uno, Blaise Pascal, **74**; The Messiah, **78**.

ROSSEN, ROBERT: Body And Soul, Johnny O'Clock, **47**; All The King's Men, The Undercover Man, **49**; The Brave Bulls, **51**; Mambo, **54**; Alexander The Great, **56**; Island In The Sun, **57**; They Came To Cordura, **59**; The Hustler, **61**; Billy Budd, **62**; Lilith, **64**.

ROTHA, PAUL: Australian Wine, **31**; Roadways, **33**; Ship Yards, **34**; Ship Steel, **35**; People Of Britain, **36**; Eastern Valley, **37**; Road Across Britain, **39**; You're Telling Me, A Few Ounces A Day, The Fourth Estate, Mr Borland Thinks Again, **40**; World Of Plenty, **43**; Total War In Britain, **45**; Land Of Promise, **46**; The World Is Rich, The Centre, **47**; No Resting Place, **51**; World Without End, **53**; Cat And Mouse, **58**; Cradle Of Genius, **59**; The Life Of Adolf Hitler, Resistance, The Silent Raid, **62**.

ROWLANDS, GENA: The High Cost Of Loving, **58**; Lonely Are The Brave, **62**; A Child Is Waiting, **63**; Tony Rome, **67**; Faces, **68**; Gli Intoccabili, **70**; Minnie And Moskowitz, **71**; A Woman Under The Influence, **74**; Two Minute Warning, **76**; Opening Night, **77**; The Brink's Job, **78**; Gloria, **80**; Tempest, **82**; Love Streams, **84**; Light Of Day, **87**; Another Woman, **88**; Night On Earth, Once Around, Ted & Venus, **91**; Unhook the Stars, **96**.

ROZSA, MIKLOS: Knight Without Armour, The Squeaker, **37**; The Spy In Black, The Four Feathers, **39**; The Thief Of Bagdad, **40**; Lydia, Sundown, That Hamilton Woman, **41**; Jacare, Jungle Book, **42**; Five Graves To Cairo, Sahara, So Proudly We Hail, **43**; Double Indemnity, The Man In Half-Moon Street, **44**; Blood On The Sun, Lady On A Train, The Lost Weekend, A Song To Remember, Spellbound, **45**; Because Of Him, The Killers, The Strange Love Of Martha Ivers, **46**; Brute Force, A Double Life, The Macomber Affair, The Red House, Song Of Scheherazade, **47**; Command Decision, Kiss The Blood Off My Hands, The Naked City, Secret Beyond The Door, **48**; Adam's Rib, Criss Cross, Madame Bovary, The Red Danube, **49**; The Asphalt Jungle, Crisis, The Miniver Story, **50**; The Light Touch, Quo Vadis?, **51**; Ivanhoe, Plymouth Adventure, **52**; Julius Caesar, Knights Of The Round Table, **53**; Green Fire, **54**; Diane, The King's Thief, Moonfleet, **55**; Bhowani Junction, Lust For Life, Tribute To A Bad Man, **56**; The Seventh Sin, Something Of Value, Tip On A Dead Jockey, **57**; A Time To Love And A Time To Die, **58**; Ben-Hur, The World The Flesh And The Devil, **59**; El Cid, King Of Kings, **61**; Sodom And Gomorrah, The VIP, **63**; The Green Berets, The Power, **68**; The Private Life Of Sherlock Holmes, **70**; The Golden Voyage Of Sinbad, **73**; The Private Files Of J Edgar Hoover, Providence, **77**; Fedora, **78**; Last Embrace, Time After Time, **79**; Eye Of The Needle, **81**; Dead Men Don't Wear Plaid, **82**; Manhattan Murder Mystery, **93**.

RUDOLPH, ALAN: Welcome To LA, **77**; Remember My Name, **78**; Roadie, **80**; Endangered Species, **82**; Return

Engagement, 83; Choose Me, Songwriter, 84; Trouble In Mind, 85; Made In Heaven, 87; The Moderns, 88; Undercover, Love At Large, 90; Mortal Thoughts, 91; Equinox, 93; Mrs Parker And The Vicious Circle, 94.

RUSSELL, JANE: The Outlaw, 43; Young Widow, 46; The Paleface, 48; Double Dynamite, His Kind Of Woman, 51; The Las Vegas Story, Macao, Montana Belle, Road To Bali, Son Of Paleface, 52; Gentlemen Prefer Blondes, 53; The French Line, 54; Foxfire, Gentlemen Marry Brunettes, The Tall Men, Underwater!, 55; Hot Blood, The Revolt Of Mamie Stover, 56; The Fuzzy Pink Nightgown, 57; Fate Is The Hunter, 64; Johnny Reno, Waco, 66; Born Losers, 67; Darker Than Amber, 70.

RUSSELL, KEN: French Dressing, 64; Billion Dollar Brain, 67; Women In Love, 69; The Boy Friend, The Devils, The Music Lovers, 71; Savage Messiah, 72; Mahler, 74; Lisztomania, Tommy, 75; Valentino, 77; Altered States, 80; Crimes Of Passion, 84; Gothic, 86; Aria, The Lair Of The White Worm, Salome's Last Dance, 88; The Rainbow, 89; Whore, 91; Mindbender, 95.

RUSSELL, ROSALIND: Evelyn Prentice, Forsaking All Others, The President Vanishes, 34; Casino Murder Case, China Seas, The Night Is Young, Reckless, Rendezvous, West Point Of The Air, 35; Craig's Wife, It Had To Happen, Trouble For Two, Under Two Flags, 36; Live Love And Learn, Night Must Fall, 37; The Citadel, Four's A Crowd, Man-proof, 38; Fast And Loose, The Women, 39; Hired Wife, His Girl Friday, No Time For Comedy, 40; Design For Scandal, The Feminine Touch, They Met In Bombay, This Thing Called Love, 41; My Sister Eileen, Take A Letter Darling, 42; Flight For Freedom, What A Woman!, 43; Roughly Speaking, She Wouldn't Say Yes, 45; Sister Kenny, 46; The Guilt Of Janet Ames, Mourning Becomes Electra, The Velvet Touch, 47; Tell It To The Judge, 49; A Woman Of Distinction, Never Wave At A WAC, 50; The Girl Rush, Picnic, 55; Auntie Mame, 58; Five Finger Exercise, Gypsy, A Majority Of One, 62; The Trouble With Angels, 66; Oh Dad Poor Dad Mama's Hung You In The Closet And I'm Feeling So Sad, Rosie!, 67; Where Angels Go Trouble Follows, 68; The Unexpected Mrs Pollifax, 71.

RUTHERFORD, MARGARET: Dusty Ermine, Talk Of The Devil, 36; The Demi-Paradise, The Yellow Canary, 43; Blithe Spirit, 45; Meet Me At Dawn, While The Sun Shines, 47; English Without Tears, Miranda, 48; Passport To Pimlico, 49; The Happiest Days Of Your Life, Her Favourite Husband, 50; The Magic Box, 51; Castle In The Air, Curtain Up, The Importance Of Being Earnest, Miss Robin Hood, 52; Innocents In Paris, Trouble In Store, The Runaway Bus, 53; Aunt Clara, Mad About Men, 54; An Alligator Named Daisy, Just My Luck, The Smallest Show On Earth, 57; I'm All Right Jack, 59; On The Double, Murder She Said, 61; The Mouse On The Moon, Murder At The Gallop, The VIPs, 63; Murder Ahoy, Murder Most Foul, 64; Chimes At Midnight, 66; A Countess From Hong Kong, Arabella, 67; The Virgin And The Gypsy, 70.

RYAN, MEG: Rich And Famous, 81; Amityville: The Demon, 83; Top Gun, 86; Innerspace, 87; DOA, The Presidio, 88; When Harry Met Sally, 89; Joe Versus The Volcano, 90; The Doors, 91; Prelude To A Kiss, 92; Flesh And Bone, Sleepless In Seattle, 93; When A Man Loves A Woman, IQ, 94; French Kiss, Restoration, 95; Courage Under Fire, 96; Addicted to Love, 97.

RYAN, ROBERT: College Widow, 27; Strong Boy, 29; Golden Gloves, Northwest Mounted Police, 40; Behind The Rising Sun, Bombardier, Gangway For Tomorrow, The Iron Major, The Sky's The Limit, 43; Tender Comrade, Marine Raiders, 44; Crossfire, Trail Street, The Woman On The Beach, 47; Berlin Express, The Boy With Green Hair, Return Of The Bad Men, 48; Act Of Violence, Caught, The Set-Up, 49; Born To Be Bad, Woman On Pier 13, The Secret Fury, 50; Best Of The Bad Men, Flying Leathernecks, The Racket, 51; Beware My Lovely, Clash By Night, Horizons West, On Dangerous Ground, 52; City Beneath The Sea, Inferno, The Naked Spur, 53; About Mrs. Leslie, Alaska Seas, Her 12 Men, 54; Bad Day At Black Rock, Escape To Burma, House Of Bamboo, The Tall Men, 55; Back From Eternity, The Proud Ones, 56; Men In War, 57; God's Little Acre, 58; Lonelyhearts, Day Of The Outlaw, Odds Against Tomorrow, 59; Ice Palace, 60; The Canadians, King Of Kings, 61; Billy Budd, The Longest Day, 62; Battle Of The Bulge, The Crooked Road, 65; The Professionals, 66; The Busy Body, The Dirty Dozen, Hour Of The Gun, 67; A Minute To Pray A Second To Die, Anzio, Custer Of The West, 68; The Wild Bunch, 69; Captain Nemo And The Underwater City, 70; Lawman, The Love Machine, 71; And Hope To Die, 72; Executive Action, The Iceman Cometh, Lolly-madonna War, The Outfit, 73.

RYDER, WINONA: Lucas, 86; Square Dance, 87; 1969, Beetlejuice, 88; Great Balls Of Fire!, Heathers, 89; Edward Scissorhands, Mermaids, Welcome Home Roxy Carmichael, 90; Night On Earth, 91; Bram Stoker's Dracula, 92; The Age Of Innocence, House Of The Spirits, 93; Reality Bites, Little Women, 94; How To Make An American Quilt, Boys, 95; Boys, 96.

SABU: Elephant Boy, 37; The Drum, 38; The Thief Of Bagdad, 40; Arabian Nights, Jungle Book, 42; White Captive, 43; Cobra Woman, 44; Black Narcissus, Tangier, 46; The End Of The River, 47; Man-Eater Of Kumaon, 48; Song Of India, 49; Savage Drums, 51; Hello Elephant, 52; Il Tesoro Del Bengala, 53; Jaguar, 56; Sabu And The Magic Ring, 57; Herrin Der Welt, 59; Ankor-Vat, 60; Rampage, 63; A Tiger Walks, 64.

SAINT, EVA MARIE: On The Waterfront, 54; That Certain Feeling, 56; A Hatful Of Rain, Raintree County, 57; North By Northwest, 59; Exodus, 60; All Fall Down, 62; 36 Hours, 64; The Sandpiper, 65; Grand Prix, The Russians Are Coming! The Russians Are Coming!, 66; The Stalking Moon, 69; Loving, 70; Cancel My Reservation, 72; Nothing In Common, 86.

SANDERS, GEORGE: Find The Lady, Dishonour Bright, Lloyd's Of London, The Man Who Could Work Miracles, Strange Cargo, 36; The Lady Escapes, Lancer Spy, Love Is News, Slave Ship, 37; Four Men And A Prayer, International Settlement, 38; Allegheny Uprising, Confessions Of A Nazi Spy, Mr Moto's Last Warning, Nurse Edith Cavell, The Outsider, The Saint In London, The Saint Strikes Back, So This Is London, 39; Bitter Sweet, Foreign Correspondent, Green Hell, The House Of Seven Gables, Rebecca, The Saint Takes Over, The Saint's Double Trouble, The Son Of Monte Cristo, 40; A Date With The Falcon, The Gay Falcon, Man Hunt, Rage In Heaven, The Saint In Palm Springs, Sundown, 41; The Black Swan, The Falcon Takes Over, The Falcon's Brother, Her Cardboard Lover, The Moon And Sixpence, Quiet Please – Murder, Son Of Fury, Tales Of Manhattan, 42; Appointment In Berlin, Paris After Dark, They Came To Blow Up America, This Land Is Mine, 43; Action In Arabia, The Lodger, Summer Storm, 44; Hangover Square, The Picture Of Dorian Gray, The Strange Affair Of Uncle Harry, 45; The Strange Woman, Scandal In Paris, 46; Forever Amber, The Ghost And Mrs Muir, Lured, The Private Affairs Of Bel Ami, 47; The Fan, Samson And Delilah, 49; All About Eve, 50; Captain Blackjack, I Can Get It For You Wholesale, The Light Touch, 51; Assignment Paris, Ivanhoe, 52; Call Me Madam, Voyage In Italy, 53; King Richard And The Crusaders, Witness To Murder, 54; Jupiter's Darling, The King's Thief, Moonfleet, The Scarlet Coat, 55; Death Of A Scoundrel, Never Say Goodbye, That Certain Feeling, While The City Sleeps, 56; The Seventh Sin, 57; From The Earth To The Moon, The Whole Truth, 58; Solomon And Sheba, That Kind Of Woman, A Touch Of Larceny, 59; Bluebeard's 10 Honeymoons, The Last Voyage, Cone Of Silence, Village Of The Damned, 60; La Rendezvous, Call Me Genius, Five Golden Hours, 61; In Search Of The Castaways, Operation Snatch, 62; Cairo, 63; The Cracksman, Dark Purpose, A Shot In The Dark, 64; The Amorous Adventures Of Moll Flanders, 65; The Quiller Memorandum, Trunk To Cairo, 66; The Golden Head, Good Times, The Jungle Book, Warning Shot, 67; Rey De Africa, 68; The Best House In London , The Candy Man, The Body Stealers, 69; The Kremlin Letter, 70; Psychomania, Wheelers, 72.

SANDRICH, MARK: Napoleon Jnr, 26; Night Owls, 27; Runaway Girls, Bear Knees, 28; The Talk Of Hollywood, 29; Hot Bridge, The Way Of All Fish, The Strife Of The Party, False Rumours, 31; Hurry Call, 32; Aggie Appleby Maker Of Men, Melody Cruise, 33; Cockeyed Cavaliers, The Gay Divorcee, Hips Hips Hooray, 34; Top Hat, 35; Follow The Fleet, A Woman Rebels, 36; Shall We Dance?, 37; Carefree, 38; Man About Town, 39; Buck Benny Rides Again, 40; Love Thy Neighbor, Skylark, 41; Holiday Inn, 42; So Proudly We Hail!, 43; Here Come The Waves, I Love A Soldier, 44.

SARANDON, SUSAN: Joe, 70; Fleur Bleue, 71; Lady Liberty, 72; The Front Page, Lovin' Molly, 74; The Great Waldo Pepper, The Rocky Horror Picture Show, 75; The Great Smokey Roadblock, Dragonfly, 76; Checkered Flag Or Crash, The Other Side Of Midnight, 77; Washington Story, Westward The Women, King Of The Gypsies, Pretty Baby, 78; Something Short Of Paradise, 79; Atlantic City, Loving Couples, 80; Tempest, 82; The Hunger, 83; The Buddy System, In Our Hands, 84; Compromising Positions, 85; The Witches Of Eastwick, 87; Bull Durham, Sweet Hearts Dance, 88; A Dry White Season, The January Man, 89; White Palace, 90; Thelma & Louise, 91; Bob Roberts, Light Sleeper, Lorenzo's Oil, The Player, 92; Little Women, The Client, 94; Safe Passage, Dead Man Walking, 95.

SAURA, CARLOS: Los Golfos, 60; Llanto Por Un Bandido, 64; La Caza, 66; Peppermint Frappé, 67; El Jardin De Las Delicias, 70; Ana Y Los Lobos, La Prima Angelica, 74; Cria Cuervos, 76; Elisa Vida Mia, 77; Los Ojos Vendados, 78; Mama Cumple 100 Anos, 79; Deprisa Deprisa, 80; Blood Wedding, 81; Antonieta, Sweet Hours/Dulces Horas, 82; Carmen, 83; Los Zancos, 84; El Amor Brujo, 86; El Dorado, 88; La Noche Oscura, 89; Ay Carmela, 90; Sevillanas, Shoot, The South, 92.

SAVILLE, VICTOR: Conquest Of Oil, The Liquid Sunshine, 21; Mademoiselle From Armentières, 26; The Arcadians, Hindle Wakes, Roses Of Picardy, 27; Tesha, 28; Kitty, Woman To Woman, 29; The W Plan, A Warm Corner, 30; Hindle Wakes, Michael And Mary, Sunshine Susie, The Sport Of Kings, 31; The Faithful Heart, Love On Wheels, 32; Friday The 13th, The Good Companions, I Was A Spy, 33; Evensong, Evergreen, 34; First A Girl, The Iron Duke, The Dictator, Me And Marlborough, 35; It's Love Again, 36; Dark Journey, Storm In A Teacup, Action For Slander, 37; The Citadel, South Riding, 38; Goodbye Mr Chips, 39; Bitter Sweet, The Earl Of Chicago, The Mortal Storm, 40; Dr Jekyll And Mr Hyde, A Woman's Face, 41; White Cargo, 42; Forever And A Day, 43; Tonight And Every Night, 45; The Green Years, 46; Green Dolphin Street, If Winter Comes, 47; Conspirator, 49; Kim, 50; Calling Bulldog Drummond, 51; Affair In Monte Carlo, I The Jury, 53; The Long Wait, The Silver Chalice, 54; Kiss Me Deadly, 55; The Greengage Summer, 61; Mix Me A Person, 62.

SAYLES, JOHN: Piranha, 78; The Lady In Red, 79; Alligator, Battle Beyond The Stars, Story, Return Of The Secaucus 7, 80; The Howling, 81; The Challenge, 82; Baby It's You, Enormous Changes At The Last Minute, Lianna, 83; The Brother From Another Planet, 84; The Clan Of The Cave Bear, 86; Matewan, Wild Thing, 87; Eight Men Out, 88; Breaking In, 89; City Of Hope, 91; Passion Fish, 92; The Secret Of Roan Inish, 95; Lone Star, 96.

SCHAFFNER, FRANKLIN J: Dino, 55; The Stripper, 63; The Best Man, 64; The War Lord, 65; The Double Man, 67; Planet Of The Apes, 68; Patton, 70; Nicholas And Alexandra, 71; Papillon, 73; Islands In The Stream, 77; The Boys From Brazil, 78; Sphinx, 81; Yes Giorgio, 82; Lionheart, 87; Welcome Home, 89.

SCHARY, DORE: Murder In The Clouds, 34; Your Uncle Dudly, Chinatown Squad, Silk Hat Kid, 35; The Big City, Outcast, The Girls From Scotland Yard, 37; Boys Town, 38; Young Tom Edison, Edison The Man, 40; Married Bachelor, 41; I'll Be Seeing You, 45; The Spiral Staircase, Till The End Of Time, 46; The Bachelor And The Bobby-Soxer, The Farmer's Daughter, 47; Mr Blandings Builds His Dream House, 48; Battleground, 49; The Next Voice You Hear, 50; It's A Big Country, 51; Go For Broke, The Hoaxters, Plymouth Adventure, 52; Dream Wife, Take The High Ground, 53; Bad Day At Black Rock, The Battle Of Gettysburg, The Last Hunt, 55; The Swan, 56; Designing Woman, 57; Lonelyhearts, 58; Sunrise At Campobello, 60; Act One, 63.

SCHELL, MAXIMILIAN: Kinder, Mutter Und Ein General, 55; The Young Lions, 58; Judgment At Nuremberg, 61; Five Finger Exercise, The Reluctant Saint, 62; The Condemned Of Altona, 63; Topkapi, 64; Return From The Ashes, 65; The Deadly Affair, Counterpoint, 67; The Desperate Ones, 68; Krakatoa, East Of Java, 69; First Love, 70; Trotta, 71; Paulina 1880, Pope Joan, 72; The Odessa File, The Pedestrian, 74; The Man In The Glass Booth, 75; Der Richter Und Sein Henker, St Ives, 76; A Bridge Too Far, Cross Of Iron, Assassination, Julia, 77; Geschichten Aus Dem Wienerwald, Amo Non Amo, Avalanche Express, The Black Hole, Players, 79; The Chosen, 81; Marlene, Morgen In Alabama, 84; The Rose Garden, 89; The Freshman, 90; A Far Off Place, 93; Little Odessa, 95; Left Luggage, 97.

SCHEPISI, FRED: Libido, 73; The Devil's Playground, 76; The Chant Of Jimmy Blacksmith, 78; Barbarosa, 82; Iceman, 84; Plenty, 85; Roxanne, 87; A Cry In The Dark, 88; The Russia House, 90; Mr Baseball, 92; IQ, 94; Six Degrees Of Separation, 95.

SCHLESINGER, JOHN: A Kind Of Loving, 62; Billy Liar, 63; Darling, 65; Far From The Madding Crowd, 67; Midnight Cowboy, 69; Sunday Bloody Sunday, 71; The Day Of The Locust , 75; Marathon Man, 76; Yanks, 79; Honky Tonk Freeway, 81; The Falcon And The Snowman, 85; The Believers, 87; Madame Sousatzka, 88; Pacific Heights, 90; The Innocent, 93; Eye For An Eye, 95.

SCHLONDORFF, VOLKER: Young Torless, 66; A Degree Of Murder, 67; Baal, Michael Kohlhaas – Der Rebell, 69; Der Plotzliche Reichtum Der Armen Leute Von Kombach, 70; Die Moral Der Ruth Halbfass, 71; A Free Woman, Summer Lightning, 72; The Lost Honor Of Katharina Blum, 75; Der Fangschus, 76; The Tin Drum, 79; Circle Of Deceit, 81; Swann In Love, 84; The Handmaid's Tale, 90; Voyager, 91; The Film Narrator, 93.

SCHOONMAKER, THELMA: Finnegans Wake, 65; The Virgin President, Who's That Knocking At My Door?, 68; Woodstock, 70; The Kids Are Alright, 79; Raging Bull, 80; The King Of Comedy, 83; After Hours, 85; The Color Of Money, 86; The Last Temptation Of Christ, 88; New York Stories, 89; GoodFellas, 90; Cape Fear, 91; The Age Of Innocence, 93.

SCHRADER, PAUL: The Yakuza, 75; Obsession, Taxi Driver, 76; Rolling Thunder, 77; Blue Collar, 78; Hardcore, Old Boyfriends, 79; American Gigolo, Raging Bull, 80; Cat People, 82; Mishima: A Life In Four Chapters, 85; The Mosquito Coast, 86; Light Of Day, 87; The Last Temptation Of Christ, Patty Hearst, 88; The Comfort Of Strangers, 91; Light Sleeper, 92.

SCHROEDER, BARBET: The Valley, 72; Maitresse, 76; Koko A Talking Gorilla, 78; Les Tricheurs, 83; Barfly, 87; Reversal Of Fortune, 90; Single White Female, 92; Kiss Of Death, 95; Before and After, 96.

SCHUFFTAN, EUGEN: People On Sunday, 29; Farewell, 30; Das Ekel, 31; L'Atlantide/Die Herrin Von Atlantis, 32; 33; La Crise Est Finie, Le Scandale, 34; The Tender Enemy, 36; Drôle De Drame, 37; Hatred, Quai Des Brumes, Le Drame De Shanghai, 38; L'Emigrante, Sans Landmain, 39; Gunman In The Streets, 50; La Tête Contre Les Murs, 58; Eyes Without A Face, 59; Un Couple, 60; The Hustler, 61; Captain Sinbad, 63; Lilith, 64; The Doctor Says, 66.

SCHULBERG, BUDD: Little Orphan Annie, 38; Winter Carnival, 39; Weekend For Three, 41; City Without Men, Government Girl, 43; On The Waterfront, 54; A Face In The Crowd, 57; Wind Across The Everglades, 58.

SCHWARZENEGGER, ARNOLD: Hercules In New York, 70; The Long Goodbye, 73; Stay Hungry, 76; The Villain, 79; Conan The Barbarian, 82; Conan The Destroyer, The Terminator, 84; Commando, Red Sonja, 85; Raw Deal, 86; Predator, The Running Man, 87; Red Heat, Twins, 88; Kindergarten Cop, Total Recall, 90; Terminator 2: Judgment Day, 91; Last Action Hero, 93; True Lies, Junior, 94; Eraser, 96; Batman & Robin, 97.

SCHYGULLA, HANNA: Die Komodiantin Und Der Zuhalter, 68; Gotter D Pest, Katzelmacher, Liebe Ist Kalter Als Der Tod, 69; Die Niklashauser Fahrt, Recrui In Pioniere In Ingolstadt, Rio Das Mortes, Warum Lauft Herr R Amok?, 70; Warnung V Einer Heiligen Nutte, Der Handler Der Vier Jahreszeiten, 71; Wildwechsel, 72; The Bitter Tears Of Petra Von Kant, 73; Effi Briest, 74; Ansichten Eines Clowns, Falsche Bewegung, 75; The Marriage Of Maria Braun, 78; Die Dritte Generation, 79; Die Falschung, Lili Marlene, 81; Antonieta, Heller Wahn, La Nuit De Varennes, Passion, 82; Storia Di Piera, 83; Il Futuro E Donna, Eine Liebe In Deutschland, 84; The Delta Force, 86; Forever Lulu, 87; El Verano De La Senora Forbes, Miss Arizona, 88; Abraham's Gold, Aventure De Catherine C, 90; Dead Again, 91; Warszawa, Golem, 92; I Don't Just Want You To Love Me, The Blue Exile, Petrified Garden, 93.

SCOLA, ETTORE: La Congiuntura, Let's Talk About Women, 64; Thrilling, 65; Follie D'Estate, The Magnificent Cuckold, 66; Il Profeta, Made In Italy, Il Diavolo Innamorato, 67; Anyone Can Play, Riusciranno I Nostri Eroi A Ritrovare L'Amico Misteriosamente Scomparso In Africa?, 68; Il Commissario Pepe, 69; The Pizza Triangle, 70; Noi Donne Siamo Fatte Cosi, Permette? Rocco Papaleo, 71; La Piu Bella Serata Della Mia Vita, Torino, 72; We All Loved Each Other So Much, 74; Brutti Sporchi E Cattivi, Signore E Signori Buonanotte, 76; Una Giornata Particolare, I Nuovi Mostri, 77; Che Si Dice A Roma, 79; La Terrazza, 80; Passion D'Amore, 81 La Nuit De Varennes, Le Bal, 82; Macaroni, 85; La Famiglia, 87; Che Ora E, Splendor, 89; Il Viaggio Di Capitan Fracass, 90.

SCORSESE, MARTIN: Who's That Knocking At My Door?, 68; Boxcar Bertha, Elvis On Tour, 72; Mean Streets, 73; Alice Doesn't Live Here Anymore, 74; Taxi Driver, 76; New York New York, 77; The Last Waltz, 78; Raging Bull, 80; The King Of Comedy, 83; After Hours, 85; The Color Of Money, 86; The Last Temptation Of Christ, 88; New York Stories, 89; GoodFellas, 90; Cape Fear, 91; The Age Of Innocence, 93; Casino, 95 Kundun, 97.

SCOTT, GEORGE C: The Hanging Tree, Anatomy Of A Murder, 59; The Hustler, 61; The List Of Adrian Messenger, 63; Dr Strangelove Or: How I Learned To Stop Worrying And Love The Bomb, 64; The Bible, Not With My Wife You Don't!, 66; The Flim Flam Man, 67; Petulia, 68; Patton, 70; The Hospital, The Last Run, They Might Be Giants, 71; The New Centurions, Rage, 72; The Day Of The Dolphin, Oklahoma Crude, 73; Bank Shot, The Savage Is Loose, 74; The Hindenburg, 75; Islands In The Stream, Prince And The Pauper, 77; Movie Movie, 78; The Changeling, Hardcore, 79; The Formula, 80; Taps, 81; Firestarter, 84; The Exorcist III, The Rescuers Down Under, 90; Malice, 93; Angus, 95.

SCOTT, RANDOLPH: Women Men Marry, 31; Heritage Of The Desert, Hot Saturday, Wild Horse Mesa, 32; Broken

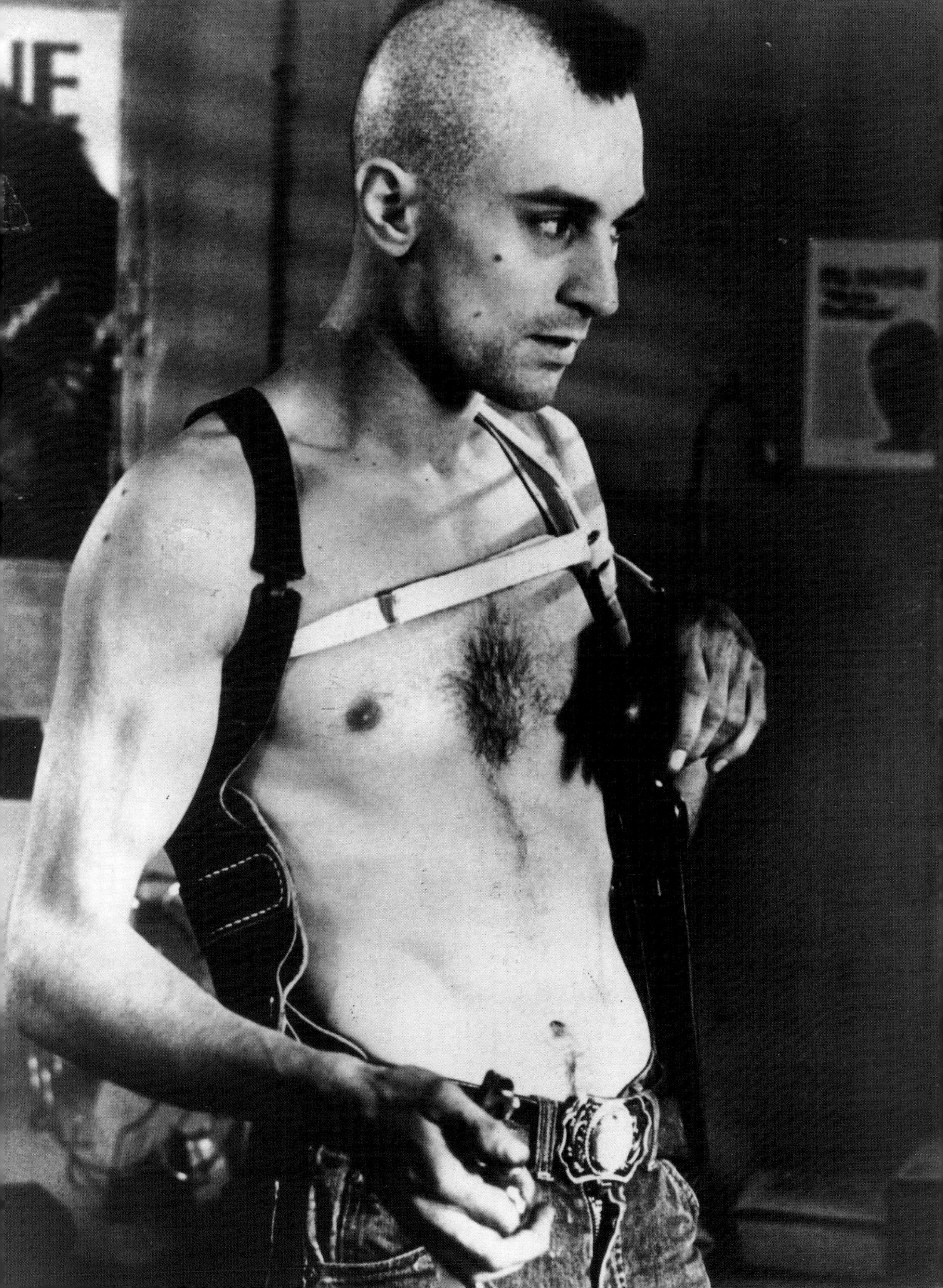

Dreams, Cocktail Hour, Hello Everybody!, Man Of The Forest, Murders In The Zoo, Sunset Pass, Supernatural, The Thundering Herd, To The Last Man, **33**; The Last Round-Up, Wagon Wheels, **34**; Home On The Range, Roberta, Mystery, She, So Red The Rose, Village Tale, **35**; And Sudden Death, Follow The Fleet, Go West Young Man, The Last Of The Mohicans, **36**; High Wide, And Handsome, **37**; Rebecca Of Sunnybrook Farm, The Road To Reno, The Texans, **38**; Coast Guard, Frontier Marshal, Jesse James, Susannah Of The Mounties, **39**; My Favorite Wife, Virginia City, When The Daltons Rode, **40**; Belle Starr, Paris Calling, Western Union, **41**; Pittsburgh, The Spoilers, To The Shores Of Tripoli, **42**; Bombardier, Corvette K-225, The Desperadoes, Gung Ho!, **43**; Belle Of The Yukon, **44**; Captain Kidd, China Sky, **45**; Abilene Town, Badman's Territory, Home Sweet Homicide, **46**; Christmas Eve, Gunfighters, Trail Street, **47**; Albuquerque, Coroner Creek, Return Of The Bad Men, **48**; Canadian Pacific, The Doolins Of Oklahoma, Fighting Man Of The Plains, The Walking Hills, **49**; Cariboo Trail, Colt 45, The Nevadan, **50**; Fort Worth, Man In The Saddle, Santa Fe, Starlift, Sugarfoot, **51**; Carson City, Hangman's Knot, The Man Behind The Gun, **52**; The Stranger Wore A Gun, Thunder Over The Plains, **53**; The Bounty Hunter, Riding Shotgun, **54**; A Lawless Street, Rage At Dawn, Tall Man Riding, Ten Wanted Men, **55**; Seven Men From Now, Seventh Cavalry, **56**; Decision At Sundown, Shoot Out At Medicine Bend, The Tall T, **57**; Buchanan Rides Alone, **58**; Ride Lonesome, Westbound, **59**; Comanche Station, **60**; Ride The High Country, **62**.

SCOTT, RIDLEY: The Duellists, **77**; Alien, **79**; Blade Runner, **82**; Legend, **85**; Someone To Watch Over Me, **87**; Black Rain, **89**; Thelma & Louise, **91**; 1492: Conquest Of Paradise, **92**; Monkey Trouble, **94**; White Squall, **95**.

SEBERG, JEAN: Saint Joan, **57**; Bonjour Tristesse, **58**; A Bout De Souffle, The Mouse That Roared, **59**; Let No Man Write My Epitaph, **60**; L'Amant De Cinq Jours, Playtime, **62**; A La Française, **63**; Les Plus Belles Escroqueries Du Monde, Echappement Libre, Lilith, **64**; Un Milliard Dans Un Billiard, **65**; Estouffade A La Caraibe, A Fine Madness, La Ligne De Démarcation, Moment To Moment, **66**; La Route De Corinthe, **67**; Birds In Peru, **68**; Paint Your Wagon, Pendulum, **69**; Airport, Macho Callahan, Ondata Di Calore, **70**; Kill, **71**; Questa, **72**; L'Attentat, La Corrupcion De Chris Miller, Specie D'Amore, Camorra, **73**; Cat And Mouse, **74**; The Wild Duck, **76**.

SELLERS, PETER: Orders Are Orders, **54**; The Ladykillers, **55**; The Naked Truth, The Smallest Show On Earth, **57**; Tom Thumb, Up The Creek, **58**; I'm All Right Jack, Carlton-Browne Of The FO, The Mouse That Roared, **59**; The Battle Of The Sexes, The Millionairess, Two-Way Stretch, Never Let Go, **60**; The Road To Hong Kong, Only Two Can Play, **61**; The Dock Brief, Mr Topaze, Lolita, Waltz Of The Toreadors, The Wrong Arm Of The Law, **62**; Heavens Above!, **63**; Dr Strangelove Or: How I Learned To Stop Worrying And Love The Bomb, The Pink Panther, A Shot In The Dark, The World Of Henry Orient, **64**; What's New Pussycat?, **65**; The Wrong Box, After The Fox, **66**; The Bobo, Casino Royale, Woman Times Seven, **67**; I Love You Alice B Toklas, The Party, **68**; The Magic Christian, **69**; Hoffman, There's A Girl In My Soup, **70**; Alice's Adventures In Wonderland, Where Does It Hurt?, **72**; The Blockhouse, Ghost In The Noonday Sun, The Optimists, **73**; The Great McGonagall, **74**; The Return Of The Pink Panther, Soft Beds And Hard Battles, **75**; Murder By Death, The Pink Panther Strikes Again, **76**; Revenge Of The Pink Panther, **78**; Being There, The Prisoner Of Zenda, **79**; The Fiendish Plot Of Dr Fu Manchu, **80**; Trail Of The Pink Panther, **82**.

SELZNICK, DAVID O: Forgotten Faces, **28**; 4 Feathers, Dance Of Life, **29**; The Conquerors, Is My Face Red?, The Age Of Consent, A Bill Of Divorcement, The Half-Naked Truth, Lucky Devils, The Roadhouse Murder, Symphony Of Six Million, What Price Hollywood?, **32**; Christopher Strong, Dancing Lady, Meet The Baron, No Other Woman, Our Betters, Topaze, King Kong, Dinner At Eight, **33**; Anna Karenina, David Copperfield, Reckless, A Tale Of Two Cities, **35**; Little Lord Fauntleroy, **36**; Nothing Sacred, The Prisoner Of Zenda, A Star Is Born, **37**; The Adventures Of Tom Sawyer, The Young In Heart, **38**; Gone With The Wind, Made For Each Other, **39**; Rebecca, **40**; Since You Went Away, **44**; Spellbound, **45**; Duel In The Sun, **47**; The Paradine Case, Portrait Of Jennie, **48**; The Third Man, **49**; Gone To Earth, **50**; Indiscretion, **51**; A Farewell To Arms, **57**; Tender Is The Night, **62**.

SENNETT, MACK: The Vaquero's Vow, **08**; Those Animal Hats, **09**; The Water Nymph, **12**; Mabel's Dramatic Career, A Misplaced Foot, In The Clutches Of The Gang, **13**; A Film Johnnie, Mabel At The Wheel, Mabel's Strange Predicament, Tango Tangles, Tillie's Punctured Romance, **14**; The Surf Girl, The Hunt, **16**; No Mother To Guide Him, The Submarine Pilot, Uncle Tom Without The Cabin, **19**; Down On The Farm, **20**; Home Talent, Molly O', A Small Town Idol, The Crossroads Of New York, Oh Mabel Behave, **22**; The Extra Girl, The Shriek Of Araby, Suzanna, **23**; The Goodbye Kiss, The Old Barn, **28**; Midnight Daddies, **30**; Movie Town, I Surrender Dear, The Loud Mouth, One More Chance, Wrestling Swordfish, **31**; Hypnotized, **32**; The Timid Young Man, **35**; Hollywood Cavalcade, **39**; Down Memory Lane, **49**.

SEYRIG, DELPHINE: Pull My Daisy, **59**; Last Year At Marienbad, **61**; Muriel, **63**; La Musica, Who Are You Polly Magou?, **66**; Accident, **67**; Mister Freedom, Stolen Kisses, **68**; The Milky Way, **70**; Lily Of The Valley, Daughters Of Darkness, Peau D'Ane, **71**; The Discreet Charm Of The Bourgeoisie, Diary Of A Suicide, **72**; The Day Of The Jackal, A Doll's House, **73**; The Black Windmill, Dites-Le Avec Des Fleurs, Le Cri Du Coeur, **74**; Aloise, India Song, Jeanne Dielman, Le Jardin Qui Bascule, **75**; Caro Michele, Der Letzte Schrei, **76**; Baxter Vera Baxter, Réperages, Sois Belle Et Tais-toi, **77**; Utközben, **79**; Le Chemin Perdu, **80**; Freak Orlando, Chère Inconnue, **81**; Le Grain De Sable, **83**; Dorian Gray Im Speigel Der Boulevardpresse, **84**; Golden Eighties, Letters Home, **86**; Seven Women Seven Sins, **87**; Joan Of Arc Of Mongolia, **89**.

SHAMROY, LEON: Bitter Sweets, **28**; Alma De Gaucho, **30**; Stowaway, **32**; Jennie Gerhardt, Three-Cornered Moon, **33**; You Only Live Once, **37**; The Young In Heart, **38**; The Adventures Of Sherlock Holmes, Down Argentine Way, Tin Pan Alley, **40**; The Great American Broadcast, The Black Swan, Roxie Hart, Ten Gentlemen From West Point, **42**; Stormy Weather, **43**; Wilson, **44**; Leave Her To Heaven, State Fair, A Tree Grows In Brooklyn, **45**; Daisy Kenyon, Forever Amber, **47**; That Lady In Ermine, **48**; Prince Of Foxes, Twelve O'Clock High, **49**; David And Bathsheba, The Snows Of Kilimanjaro, With A Song In My Heart, **52**; Call Me Madam, The Robe, **53**; The Egyptian, **54**; Daddy Long Legs, Love Is A Many Splendored Thing, **55**; The King And I, **56**; South Pacific, **58**; The Blue Angel, Porgy And Bess, **59**; The Cardinal, Cleopatra, **63**; The Agony And The Ecstasy, **65**; The Glass Bottom Boat, **66**; Caprice, **67**; Planet Of The Apes, **68**; Justine, **69**.

SHARAFF, IRENE: Meet Me In St Louis, **44**; The Best Years Of Our Lives, **46**; An American In Paris, **51**; Call Me Madam, **53**; Brigadoon, A Star Is Born, **54**; Guys And Dolls, The King And I, **55**; Porgy And Bess, **59**; Can-Can, **60**; Flower Drum Song, West Side Story, **61**; Cleopatra, **63**; Who's Afraid Of Virginia Woolf?, **66**; The Taming Of The Shrew, **67**; Funny Girl, **68**; Hello Dolly!, **69**; The Great White Hope, **70**; The Other Side Of Midnight, **77**; Mommie Dearest, **81**.

SHARIF, OMAR: Lawrence Of Arabia, **62**; Behold A Pale Horse, The Fall Of The Roman Empire, The Yellow Rolls-Royce, **64**; Doctor Zhivago, Genghis Khan, **65**; The Poppy Is Also A Flower, **66**; C'Era Una Volta, **67**; Funny Girl, Mayerling, **68**; Che!, MacKenna's Gold, **69**; The Last Valley, **70**; Le Casse, **71**; Juggernaut, L'Ile Mysterieuse, The Tamarind Seed, **74**; Funny Lady, An Ace Up My Sleeve, **75**; Ashanti, Bloodline, **79**; The Baltimore Bullet, Oh Heavenly Dog, **80**; Green Ice, **81**; Top Secret, **84**; The Possessed, **87**; The Novice, **88**; Mountains Of The Moon, The Rainbow Thief, Viaggio D'Amore, **90**; Mother, War In The Land Of Egypt, **91**; 588 Rue Paradis, Beyond Justice, Tengoku No Taizai, **92**.

SHAW, ROBERT: The Lavender Hill Mob, **51**; The Dam Busters, **55**; Hell In Korea, **56**; Sea Fury, **58**; The Valiant, **62**; From Russia With Love, **63**; The Caretaker, The Luck Of Ginger Coffey, **64**; Battle Of The Bulge, A Man For All Seasons, **65**; The Birthday Party, Custer Of The West, **68**; Battle Of Britain, Royal Hunt Of The Sun, **69**; Figures In A Landscape, **70**; A Town Called Bastard, **71**; Young Winston, **72**; The Hireling, A Reflection Of Fear, The Sting, **73**; The Taking Of Pelham One-Two-Three, **74**; Diamonds, Jaws, **75**; Der Richter Und Sein Henker, Robin And Marian, Swashbuckler, **76**; Black Sunday, The Deep, **77**; Force Ten From Navarone, **78**; Avalanche Express, **79**.

SHEARER, NORMA: Way Down East, The Restless Sex, The Leather Pushers, The Flapper, The Stealers, **20**; Channing Of The Northwest, The Man Who Paid, **22**; A Clouded Name, The Devil's Partner, Lucretia Lombard, Man And Wife, Pleasure Mad, The Wanters, **23**; The End Of The World, Broadway After Dark, Broken Barriers, Empty Hands, He Who Gets Slapped, The Snob, The Wolf Man, **24**; Excuse Me, His Secretary, Lady Of The Night, Pretty Ladies, A Slave Of Fashion, The Tower Of Lies, Waking Up The Town, **25**; The Devil's Circus, Upstage, The Waning Sex, **26**; After Midnight, The Demi-Bride, The Student Prince, **27**; The Actress, A Lady Of Chance, The Latest From Paris, **28**; The Hollywood Revue Of 29, The Last Of Mrs Cheyney, Their Own Desire, The Trial Of Mary Dugan, **29**; The Divorcee, Let Us Be Gay, **30**; A Free Soul, Private Lives, Strangers May Kiss, **31**; Smilin' Through, Strange Interlude, **32**; The Barretts Of Wimpole Street, Riptide, **34**; Romeo And Juliet, **36**; Marie Antoinette, **38**; Idiot's Delight, The Women, **39**; Escape, **40**; Her Cardboard Lover, We Were Dancing, **42**.

SHEEN, MARTIN: The Incident, **67**; The Subject Was Roses, **68**; Catch-22, **70**; Pickup On 101, Rage, **72**; Badlands, **73**; The Legend Of Earl Dunrand, **75**; The Little Girl Who Lives Down The Lane, **76**; The Cassandra Crossing, **77**; Apocalypse Now, Eagle's Wing, **79**; The Final Countdown, Loophole, **80**; Enigma, Gandhi, That Championship Season, **82**; The Dead Zone, Man Woman And Child, **83**; Firestarter, A State Of Emergency, **86**; The Believers, Siesta, Wall Street, **87**; Da, Judgment In Berlin, Personal Choice, Walking After Midnight, **88**; Beverly Hills Brats, Beyond The Stars, Cold Front, **89**; Cadence, Touch And Die, **91**; Original Intent, **92**; Gettysburg, Hear No Evil, **93**; Trigger Fast, **94**; The American President, **95**.

SHEPARD, SAM: Me And My Brother, **67**; Bronco Bullfrog, Zabriskie Point, **70**; Days Of Heaven, Renaldo And Clara, **78**; Resurrection, **80**; Raggedy Man, **81**; Frances, Tongues, **82**; The Right Stuff, **83**; Country, Paris Texas, **84**; Fool For Love, **85**; Crimes Of The Heart, **86**; Baby Boom, **87**; Far North, **88**; Steel Magnolias, **89**; Bright Angel, Defenseless, Voyager, **91**; Thunderheart, **92**; The Pelican Brief, **93**; Silent Tongue, **94**; Safe Passage, **95**.

SHERIDAN, ANN: Search For Beauty, Bolero, Come On Marines!, Murder At The Vanities, **34**; Behold My Wife, Car 99, The Crusades, Enter Madame, Fighting Youth, The Glass Key, Home On The Range, Mississippi, Red Blood Of Courage, Rocky Mountain Mystery, Rumba, **35**; Black Legion, Sing Me A Love Song, **36**; Alcatraz Island, The Footloose Heiress, The Great O'Malley, San Quentin, Wine Women And Horses, **37**; Angels With Dirty Faces, Broadway Musketeers, The Cowboy From Brooklyn, A Letter Of Introduction, Little Miss Thoroughbred, Mystery House, The Patient In Room 18, She Loved A Fireman, **38**; The Angels Wash Their Faces, Dodge City, Indianapolis Speedway, Naughty But Nice, They Made Me A Criminal, Winter Carnival, **39**; Castle On The Hudson, City For Conquest, It All Came True, They Drive By Night, Torrid Zone, **40**; Honeymoon For Three, The Man Who Came To Dinner, Navy Blues, **41**; George Washington Slept Here, Juke Girl, Kings Row, Wings For The Eagle, **42**; Edge Of Darkness, Thank Your Lucky Stars, **43**; The Doughgirls, Shine On, Harvest Moon, **44**; One More Tomorrow, **46**; Nora Prentiss, The Unfaithful, **47**; Good Sam, Silver River, The Treasure Of The Sierra Madre, **48**; I Was A Male War Bride, **49**; Stella, Woman On The Run, **50**; Just Across The Street, Steel Town, **52**; Appointment In Honduras, Take Me To Town, **53**; Come Next Spring, The Opposite Sex, **56**; The Woman And The Hunter, **57**.

SIDNEY, GEORGE: Of Pups And Puzzles, Free And Easy, The Third Dimensional Murder **41**; Pacific Rendezvous, **42**; Pilot No 5, Thousands Cheer, **43**; Bathing Beauty, **44**; Anchors Aweigh, **45**; The Harvey Girls, Holiday In Mexico, **46**; Cass Timberlane, **47**; The Three Musketeers, **48**; The Red Danube, **49**; Annie Get Your Gun, Key To The City, **50**; Show Boat, **51**; Scaramouche, **52**; Kiss Me Kate, Young Bess, **53**; Jupiter's Darling, **55**; The Eddy Duchin Story, **56**; Jeanne Eagels, Pal Joey, **57**; Pépé, Who Was That Lady?, **60**; Bye Bye Birdie, A Ticklish Affair, **63**; Viva Las Vegas, **64**; The Swinger, **66**; Half A Sixpence, **67**.

SIDNEY, SYLVIA: Thru Different Eyes, **29**; An American Tragedy, City Streets, Confessions Of A Co-ed, Ladies Of The Big House, Street Scene, **31**; Madame Butterfly, Merrily We Go To Hell, The Miracle Man, **32**; Jennie Gerhardt, Pick-Up, **33**; Good Dame, Thirty Day Princess, **34**; Accent On Youth, Behold My Wife, Mary Burns – Fugitive, **35**; Fury, Sabotage, Trail Of The Lonesome Pine, **36**; Dead End, You Only Live Once, **37**; You And Me, **38**; One Third Of A Nation, **39**; The Wagons Roll At Night, **41**; Blood On The Sun, **45**; Mr Ace, The Searching Wind, **46**; Love From A Stranger, **47**; Les Misérables, **52**; Violent Saturday, **55**; Behind The High Wall, **56**; Summer Wishes Winter Dreams, **73**; I Never Promised You A Rose Garden, Raid On Entebbe, **77**; Damien Omen II, **78**; Corrupt, Hammett, **83**; Beetlejuice, **88**; Exorcist III, **90**; Used People, **92**.

SIEGEL, DON: Hitler Lives?, Star In The Night, **45**; The Verdict, **46**; The Big Steal, Night Unto Night, **49**; The Duel At Silver Creek, No Time For Flowers, **52**; China Venture, Count The Hours, **53**; Private Hell, Riot In Cell Block 11, **54**; An Annapolis Story, **55**; Crime In The Streets, Invasion Of The Body Snatchers, **56**; Baby Face Nelson, **57**; The Gun Runners, The Lineup, Spanish Affair, **58**; Edge Of Eternity, Hound-dog Man, **59**; Flaming Star, **60**; Hell Is For Heroes, **62**; The Killers, **64**; Coogan's Bluff, Madigan, **68**; Death Of A Gunfighter, **69**; Two Mules For Sister Sara, **70**; The Beguiled, Dirty Harry, Play Misty For Me, **71**; Charley Varrick, **73**; The Black Windmill, **74**; The Shootist, **76**; Telefon, **77**; Escape From Alcatraz, **79**; Rough Cut, **80**; Jinxed!, **82**.

SIGNORET, SIMONE: Back Streets Of Paris, **46**; Against The Wind, Dedée D'Anvers, L'Impasse Des Deux Anges, **48**; Manèges, Swiss Tour, Le Traqué, La Ronde, **50**; Casque D'Or, **52**; Thérèse Raquin, **53**; Diabolique, **55**; La Mort En Ce Jardin, **56**; Les Sorcières De Salem, **57**; Room At The Top, **59**; Adua E Le Compagne, **60**; Les Amours Célèbres, Le Mauvais Coup, **61**; Term Of Trial, **62**; Le Jour Et L'Heure, Dragées Au Poivre, **63**; Ship Of Fools, Compartiment Tueurs, **65**; Is Paris Burning?, **66**; The Deadly Affair, Games, **67**; The Sea Gull, **68**; L'Américain, L'Armée Des Ombres, **69**; The Confession, **70**; Le Chat, Comptes A Rebours, La Veuve Couderc, **71**; Les Granges Brulées, Rude Journée Pour La Reine, Police Python.357, **75**; Le Fond De L'Air Est Rouge, Madame Rosa, **77**; L'Adolescente, **79**; Chère Inconnue, **81**.

SILVER, JOEL: The Warriors, **79**; Xanadu, **80**; 48 HRS, Jekyll & Hyde Together Again, **82**; Streets Of Fire, **84**; Brewster's Millions, Commando, Weird Science, **85**; Jumpin' Jack Flash, **86**; Lethal Weapon, Predator, **87**; Action Jackson, Die Hard, Who Framed Roger Rabbit, **88**; Lethal Weapon 2, Road House, **89**; The Adventures Of Ford Fairlane, Die Hard 2, Predator 2, **90**; Hudson Hawk, The Last Boy Scout, Ricochet, **91**; Lethal Weapon 3, **92**; Demolition Man, **93**.

SILVERS, PHIL: Hit Parade Of 1941, **40**; Ice-Capades, Lady Be Good, The Penalty, Tom Dick And Harry, You're In The Army Now, **41**; All Through The Night, Footlight Serenade, Just Off Broadway, My Gal Sal, Roxie Hart, **42**; Coney Island, A Lady Takes A Chance, **43**; Cover Girl, Four Jills In A Jeep, Something For The Boys, **44**; Diamond Horseshoe, Don Juan Quilligan, A Thousand And One Nights, Where Do We Go From Here, **45**; If I'm Lucky, **46**; Summe Stock, **50**; Lucky Me, Top Banana, **54**; Forty Pounds Of Trouble, It's A Mad Mad Ma Mad World, **63**; A Funny Thing Happened On The Way To The Forum, **66**; Follow That Camel, A Guide For The Married Man, **67**; Buona Sera Mrs Campbel **68**; The Boatniks, **70**; The Strongest Man In The World, **75**; Won Ton Ton The Do Who Saved Hollywood, **76**; The Chicken Chronicles, **77**; The Cheap Detective, **78**; Racquet, **79**.

SIM, ALASTAIR: A Fire Has Been Arranged, Late Extra, The Private Secretary, Riverside Murder, **35**; The Man In The Mirror, The Mysterious Mr Davis, Troubled Waters, Wedding Group, **36**; Gangway, Melody And Romance, The Squeaker, Strang Experiment, **37**; The Terror, Alf's Button Afloat, Climbing High, Sailing Along, This Ma Is News, **38**; Inspector Hornleigh, Inspector Hornleigh On Holiday, This Man In Paris, **39**; Nero, Inspector Hornleigh Goes To It, Law And Disorder, **40**; Her Father's Daughter, Cottage To Let, **41**; Let The People Sing, **42**; Waterloo Road, **44** Green For Danger, **46**; Captain Boycott, Hue And Cry, **47**; London Belongs To Me, **48**; The Happiest Days Of Your Life, Stage Fright, **50**; Scrooge, Lady Godiva Ride Again, Laughter In Paradise, **51**; Folly To Be Wise, **52**; Innocents In Paris, **53**; An Inspector Calls, **54**; The Belles Of St Trinian's, Escapade, **55**; Wee Geordie, The Green Man, **56**; Blue Murder At St Trinian's, **57**; Doctor's Dilemma, **58**; Left Right And Centre, **59**; The Millionairess, School For Scoundrels, **60**; The Anatomist, **61**; The Ruling Class, **72**; Royal Flash, The Prodigal Daughter, **75**; Escape From Th Dark, Rogue Male, **76**.

SIMMONS, JEAN: Give Us The Moon, Meet Sexton Blake, Emmanuel, Kiss The Brid Goodbye, **44**; The Way To The Stars, **45**; Black Narcissus, Caesar And Cleopatra, Great Expectations, **46**; Hungry Hill, The Woman In The Wall, Uncle Silas, **47**; Hamlet **48**; Adam And Evelyne, The Blue Lagoon, **49**; Cage Of Gold, So Long At The Fair, Trio, **50**; The Clouded Yellow, **51**; Androcles And The Lion, **52**; The Actress, Affair With A Stranger, Angel Face, The Robe, Young Bess, **53**; A Bullet Is Waiting, Desiree, The Egyptian, She Couldn't Say No, **54**; Footsteps In The Fog, Guys And Dol **55**; Hilda Crane, **56**; This Could Be The Night, Until They Sail, **57**; The Big Country, Home Before Dark, **58**; This Earth Is Mine, **59**; Elmer Gantry, The Grass Is Greene Spartacus, **60**; All The Way Home, **63**; Life At The Top, **65**; Mister Buddwing, **66**; Divorce American Style, Rough Night In Jericho, **67**; The Happy Ending, **69**; Say Hello To Yesterday, **71**; Mr Sycamore, **74**; Dominique, **78**; The Dawning, Going Undercover, **88**; King Ralph, **91**.

SIMON, MICHEL: Feu Mathias Pascal, **25**; Casanova, **27**; La Passion De Jeanne D'Arc, Tire-au-Flanc, **28**; L'Enfant De L'Amour, **30**; Jean De La Lune, La Chienne, On Purge Bébé, **31**; Boudu Saved From Drowning, **32**; L'Atalante, Lac Aux Dames, **34**; Sous Les Yeux De L'Occident, **36**; Drôle De Drame, Naples Au Baiser De Feu, **37**; Les Disparus De Saint-Agil, La Belle Etoile, Quai Des Brumes, **38**; Le Dernier Tournaut Belle Etoile, 32 Rue Montmartre, Eusebe Député, La Fin Du Jour, **39**; Circonstances Attenuantes, La Comédie Du Bonheur, Les Musiciens Du Cie **40**; The King's Jester, La Tosca, **41**; Au Bonheur Des Dames, **43**; Un Ami Viendra C Soir, Panique, Vautrin, **46**; Non Coupable, **47**; Fabiola, Fric-Frac, L'Escape D'Un Matin, **49**; La Beauté Du Diable, **50**; Le Poison, **51**; The Merchant Of Venice Ce Rideau Rouge, **52**; Saadia, La Vie D'Un Honnête Homme, **53**; L'Etrange Désir De M Bard, **54**; M Pipelet, **55**; Un Certain M Jo, **57**; It Happened In Broad Daylight, Les Trois Font La Paire, **58**; Austerlitz, Candide, **60**; Cyrano Et D'Artagna World At Night No.3, **63**; The Train, **64**; Le Vieil Homme Et L'Enfant, **67**; The Marria Came Tumbling Down, **68**; La Maison, **70**; Blanche, **71**; La Piu Bella Serata Della Mia Vita, **72**; L'Ibis Rouge, **75**.

SIMON, NEIL: After The Fox, **66**; Barefoot In The Park, **67**; The Odd Couple, **68**; The Out-Of-Towners, **70**; Plaza Suite, **71**; The Heartbreak Kid, Last Of The Red Hot Lovers, **72**; The Prisoner Of

Second Avenue, 74; The Sunshine Boys, 75; Murder By Death, 76; The Goodbye Girl, 77; California Suite, The Cheap Detective, 78; Chapter Two, 79; Seems Like Old Times, 80; Only When I Laugh, 81; I Ought To Be In Pictures, 82; Max Dugan Returns, 83; The Slugger's Wife, 85; Brighton Beach Memoirs, 86; Biloxi Blues, 88; The Marrying Man, 91; Broadway Bound, 92; Lost In Yonkers, 93.

SINATRA, FRANK: Las Vegas Nights, 41; Ship Ahoy, 42; Higher And Higher, Reveille With Beverly, 43; Step Lively, 44; Anchors Aweigh, The House I Live In, 45; Till The Clouds Roll By, 46; It Happened In Brooklyn, 47; The Kissing Bandit, The Miracle Of The Bells, 48; On The Town, Take Me Out To The Ball Game, 49; Double Dynamite, 51; Meet Danny Wilson, 52; From Here To Eternity, 53; Suddenly, Three Coins In The Fountain, Young At Heart, 54; Guys And Dolls, The Man With The Golden Arm, Not As A Stranger, The Tender Trap, 55; Around The World In 80 Days, High Society, Johnny Concho, 56; The Joker Is Wild, Pal Joey, The Pride And The Passion, 57; Kings Go Forth, Some Came Running, 58; A Hole In The Head, Never So Few, 59; Can-Can, Ocean's Eleven, Pepe, 60; The Devil At 4 O'Clock, 61; Advise And Consent, The Manchurian Candidate, Sergeants 3, 62; Come Blow Your Horn, Four For Texas, The List Of Adrian Messenger, 63; Robin And The Seven Hoods, 64; Marriage On The Rock, None But The Brave, Von Ryan's Express, 65; Assault On A Queen, Cast A Giant Shadow, 66; The Naked Runner, Tony Rome, 67; The Detective, Lady In Cement, 68; Dirty Dingus Magee, 70; That's Entertainment!, 74; The First Deadly Sin, 80; Cannonball Run II, 84.

SINGLETON, JOHN: Boyz N The Hood, 91; Poetic Justice, 93; Higher Learning, 95; Rosewood, 97.

SIODMAK, ROBERT: People On Sunday, 29; Farewell, 30; Der Mann, Voruntersuchung, Tumultes, 31; Quick, La Crise Est Finie, 32; Brennendes Geheimnis, Le Sexe Faible, 33; La Vie Parisienne, 35; Mr Flow, 36; Cargaison Blanche, 37; Mollenard, 38; Pièges, 39; West Point Widow, 41; Fly By Night, My Heart Belongs To Daddy, The Night Before The Divorce, 42; Someone To Remember, Son Of Dracula 43; Christmas Holiday, Cobra Woman, Phantom Lady, The Suspect, 44; Conflict, The Strange Affair Of Uncle Harry, 45; The Dark Mirror, The Killers, The Spiral Staircase, 46; Time Out Of Mind, 47; Cry Of The City, 48; Criss Cross, The File On Thelma Jordon, The Great Sinner, 49; Deported, 50; The Whistle At Eaton Falls, 51; The Crimson Pirate, 52; Le Grand Jeu, 53; The Rats, 55; Mein Vater Der Schauspieler, 56; Nachts Wenn Der Teufel Kam, 57; Dorothea Angermann, 58; Katia, The Rough And The Smooth, 59; Mein Schulefreund, 60; L'Affaire Nina B, 61; Tunnel 28, 62; Der Schatz Der Azteken, 65; Custer Of The West, Kampf Um Rom, 68; Kampf Um Rom II: Der Verrat, 69.

SIRK, DOUGLAS: Das Madchen Vom Moorhof, Stutzen Der Gesellschaft, 35; Das Hofkonzert, La Chanson Du Souvenir, Schlussakkord, 36; La Habanera, Zu Neuen Ufern, 37; Boefje, 39; Hitler's Madman, 43; Summer Storm, 44; Scandal In Paris, 46; Lured, 47; Sleep My Love, 48; Shockproof, Slightly French, 49; Mystery Submarine, 50; The First Legion, The Lady Pays Off, Thunder On The Hill, Weekend With Father, 51; Has Anybody Seen My Gal?, Meet Me At The Fair, No Room For The Groom, 52; All I Desire, Take Me To Town, 53; Magnificent Obsession, Sign Of The Pagan, Taza Son Of Cochise, 54; All That Heaven Allows, Captain Lightfoot, 55; There's Always Tomorrow, Written On The Wind, 56; Battle Hymn, Interlude, 57; The Tarnished Angels, A Time To Love And A Time To Die, 58; Imitation Of Life, 59; My Life For Zarah Leander, 86.

SJOSTROM, VICTOR: Halvblod, Ingeborg Holm, Miraklet, 13; Hogfjallets Dotter, Havsgamar, The Strike, 15; Tosen Fran Stormyrtorpet, The Outlaw And His Wife, Thomas Graal's Best Film, 17; Jerusalem, Sons Of Ingmar, Thomas Graal's Best Child, 18; Hans Nads Testamente, Karin Ingmarsdotter, Klostret I Sendomir, 19; Masterman, Korkarlen, 20; Ordet, The Phantom Carriage, 21; Fire On Board, The Surrounded House, 22; Name The Man, 23; He Who Gets Slapped, 24; Confessions Of A Queen, The Tower Of Lies, 25; The Scarlet Letter, 26; The Divine Woman, The Masks Of The Devil, The Wind, 28; Father And Son, A Lady To Love, 30; Markurells I Wadkoping, 31; Synnove Solbakken, 34; Under The Red Robe, 37; Rallare, 47; To Mennesker, 50; Hard Klang, Karlek, 52; Mannen I Morker, 55; Wild Strawberries, 57.

SKOLIMOWSKI, JERZY: Identification Marks: None, 64; Walkover, 65; Barrier, 66; Hands Up!, Le Départ, 67; Dialog, 68; The Adventures Of Gerard, Deep End, 70; King Queen, Knave, Poslizg, 72; The Shout, 78; Moonlighting, 82; Success Is The Best Revenge, 84; The Lightship, 85; Mesmerized, 86; Torrents Of Spring, 89; Ferdydurke, 91; Before And After Death, 92.

SLOANE, EVERETT: Citizen Kane, 41; Journey Into Fear, 43; The Lady From Shanghai, 48; Prince Of Foxes, 49; The Men, 50; Bird Of Paradise, The Blue Veil, The Desert Fox, The Enforcer, The Prince Who Was A Thief, Sirocco, The Sellout, 51; Way Of A Gaucho, 52; The Big Knife, 55; Lust For Life, Patterns, Somebody Up There Likes Me, 56; The Gun Runners, Marjorie Morningstar, 58; Home From The Hill, 60; By Love Possessed, 61; Brushfire!, 62; The Man From The Diner's Club, 63; The Disorderly Orderly, The Patsy, Ready For The People, 64.

SLOCOMBE, DOUGLAS: Lights Out In Europe, 40; Saraband For Dead Lovers, 48; Kind Hearts And Coronets, 49; The Lavender Hill Mob, The Man In The White Suit, 51; Barnacle Bill, Tread Softly Stranger, 58; The Mark, 61; Freud, 62; The L-Shaped Room, The Servant, 63; Guns At Batasi, 64; A High Wind In Jamaica, The Blue Max, Promise Her Anything, 65; Fathom, Dance Of The Vampires, Robbery, 67; Boom!, The Lion In Winter, 68; The Italian Job, 69; The Buttercup Chain, 70; Murphy's War, The Music Lovers, 71; Travels With My Aunt, 72; Jesus Christ Superstar, 73; Marseilles Contract, The Great Gatsby, 74; Hedda, The Maids, Rollerball, That Lucky Touch, 75; The Bawdy Adventures Of Tom Jones, The Sailor Who Fell From Grace With The Sea, 76; Close Encounters Of The Third Kind, Julia, Nasty Habits, 77; Caravans, 78; The Lady Vanishes, Lost And Found, 79; Close Encounters Of The Third Kind, Nijinsky, 80; Raiders Of The Lost Ark, 81; Never Say Never Again, The Pirates Of Penzance, 83; Indiana Jones And The Temple Of Doom, 84; Lady Jane, Water, 85; Indiana Jones And The Last Crusade, 89.

SMITH, ALEXIS: Dive Bomber, The Smiling Ghost, Steel Against The Sky, 41; Gentleman Jim, 42; The Constant Nymph, Thank Your Lucky Stars, 43; The Adventures Of Mark Twain, The Doughgirls, Hollywood Canteen, 44; Conflict, The Horn Blows At Midnight, Rhapsody In Blue, San Antonio, 45; Night And Day, Of Human Bondage, One More Tomorrow, 46; Stallion Road, The Two Mrs Carrolls, 47; The Decision Of Christopher Blake, Whiplash, The Woman In White, 48; Any Number Can Play, One Last Fling, South Of St Louis, 49; Montana, Undercover Girl, Wyoming Mail, 50; Cave Of Outlaws, Here Comes The Groom, 51; The Turning Point, 52; Split Second, 53; The Sleeping Tiger, 54; The Eternal Sea, 55; Beau James, 57; This Happy Feeling, 58; The Young Philadelphians, 59; Once Is Not Enough, 75; The Little Girl Who Lives Down The Lane, 76; Casey's Shadow, 78; The Trout, 82; Tough Guys, 86; The Age Of Innocence, 93.

SMITH, C AUBREY: Builder Of Bridges, 15; The Witching Hour, 16; Castles In Spain, 20; Bohemian Girl, 23; The Rejected Woman, 24; The Perfect Alibi, 30; The Bachelor Father, Daybreak, Just A Gigolo, Never The Twain Shall Meet, Son Of India, Surrender, Trader Horn, Guilty Hands, The Man In Possession, The Phantom Of Paris, 31; Love Me Tonight, But The Flesh Is Weak, Polly Of The Circus, Tarzan The Ape Man, Trouble In Paradise, 32; Adorable, The Barbarian, Bombshell, Morning Glory, Queen Christina, Secrets, 33; Bulldog Drummond Strikes Back, Caravan, Cleopatra, House Of Rothschild, One More River, The Scarlet Empress, We Live Again, 34; China Seas, Clive Of India, The Crusades, The Gilded Lily, Jalna, The Lives Of A Bengal Lancer, The Tunnel, 35; The Garden Of Allah, Little Lord Fauntleroy, Lloyd's Of London, Romeo And Juliet, 36; The Hurricane, The Prisoner Of Zenda, Wee Willie Winkie, 37; Four Men And A Prayer, Kidnapped, Sixty Glorious Years, 38; Another Thin Man, Balalaika, The Four Feathers, The Sun Never Sets, The Under-Pup, 39; Rebecca, Bill Of Divorcement, A Little Bit Of Heaven, Waterloo Bridge, 40; Dr Jekyll And Mr Hyde, 41; Flesh And Fantasy, Forever And A Day, Madame Curie, 43; The Adventures Of Mark Twain, The White Cliffs Of Dover, 44; And Then There Were None, 45; Cluny Brown, 46; Unconquered, 47; An Ideal Husband, 48; Little Women, 49.

SMITH, GEORGE ALBERT: The Corsican Brothers, The Haunted Castle, 97; Cinderella, Faust And Mephistopheles, The Miller And The Sweep, Waves And Spray, Santa Claus, Photographing A Ghost, 98; Aladdin And The Wonderful Lamp, The Legacy, 99; A Big Swallow, Grandma's Reading Glass, The House That Jack Built, 00; Mother Goose Nursery Rhymes, 02; Dorothy's Dream, 03; Kinemacolor Puzzle, 09.

SMITH, MAGGIE: Nowhere To Go, 58; The VIPs, 63; The Pumpkin Eater, 64; Othello, Young Cassidy, 65; The Honey Pot, 67; Hot Millions, Oh! What A Lovely War, The Prime Of Miss Jean Brodie, 69; Travels With My Aunt, 72; Murder By Death, 76; California Suite, Death On The Nile, 78; Clash Of The Titans, Quartet, 81; Better Late Than Never, Evil Under The Sun, The Missionary, 82; Lily In Love, A Private Function, A Room With A View, 85; The Lonely Passion Of Judith Hearne, 87; Hook, 91; Sister Act, 92; The Secret Garden, Sister Act 2: Back In The Habit, 93; First Wives Club, 96.

SPACEK, SISSY: Prime Cut, 72; Badlands, Ginger In The Morning, 73; Phantom Of The Paradise, 74; Carrie, Welcome To LA, 76; 3 Women, 77; Heart Beat, 79; Coal Miner's Daughter, 80; Raggedy Man, 81; Missing, 82; The River, 84; Marie, 85; Crimes Of The Heart, 'Night Mother, Violets Are Blue, 86; The Long Walk Home, 90; Hard Promises, JFK, 91; Trading Mom, 94; Beyond the Call, 96.

SPIEGEL, SAM: Tales Of Manhattan, 42; The Stranger, 46; We Were Strangers, 49; The African Queen, The Prowler, When I Grow Up, 51; Melba, 53; On The Waterfront, 54; The Bridge On The River Kwai, The Strange One, 57; Suddenly Last Summer, 59; Lawrence Of Arabia, 62; The Chase, 66; Night Of The Generals, 67; Nicholas And Alexandra, 71; The Last Tycoon, 76; Betrayal, 83.

SPIELBERG, STEVEN: Duel, 71; The Sugarland Express, 74; Jaws, 75; Close Encounters Of The Third Kind, 77; I Wanna Hold Your Hand, 78; 1941, 79; Raiders Of The Lost Ark, 81; ET The Extra-Terrestrial, 82; Twilight Zone The Movie, 83; Indiana Jones And The Temple Of Doom, 84; The Color Purple, 85; Empire Of The Sun, 87; Always, Indiana Jones And The Last Crusade, 89; Back To The Future Part III, Gremlins 2 The New Batch, 90; Hook, 91; Jurassic Park, Schindler's List, 93.

STAHL, JOHN M: Wives Of Men, 18; Her Code Of Honor, A Woman Under Oath, 19; The Woman In His House, Women Men Forget, 20; The Child Thou Gavest Me, Sowing The Wind, 21; The Dangerous Age, One Clear Call, The Song Of Life, Suspicious Wives, 22; The Wanters, 23; Husbands And Lovers, Why Men Leave Home, 24; Fine Clothes, 25; The Gay Deceiver, Memory Lane, 26; In Old Kentucky, Lovers?, 27; Marriage By Contract, 28; A Lady Surrenders, 30; Seed, Strictly Dishonorable, 31; Back Street, 32; Only Yesterday, 33; Imitation Of Life, 34; Magnificent Obsession, 35; Parnell, 37; A Letter Of Introduction, 38; When Tomorrow Comes, 39; Our Wife, 41; Holy Matrimony, The Immortal Sergeant, 43; The Eve Of St Mark, The Keys Of The Kingdom, 44; Leave Her To Heaven, 45; The Foxes Of Harrow, 47; The Walls Of Jericho, 48; Father Was A Fullback, Oh You Beautiful Doll, 49.

STALLONE, SYLVESTER: Party At Kitty And Studs, Bananas, 71; Rebel, 73; The Lords Of Flatbush, 74; Capone, Death Race 2000, Farewell My Lovely, No Place To Hide, The Prisoner Of Second Avenue, 75; Cannonball, Rocky, 76; FIST, Paradise Alley, 78; Rocky II, 79; Nighthawks, Victory, 81; First Blood, Rocky III, 82; Staying Alive, 83; Rhinestone, 84; Rambo: First Blood Part II, Rocky IV, 85; Cobra, 86; Over The Top, 87; Rambo III, 88; Lock Up, Tango & Cash, 89; Rocky V, 90; Oscar, 91; Stop! Or My Mom Will Shoot, 92; Cliffhanger, Demolition Man, 93; The Specialist, 94; Judge Dredd, Assassins, 95.

STANTON, HARRY DEAN: Revolt At Fort Laramie, The Wrong Man, Tomahawk Trail, 57; The Proud Rebel, 58; Pork Chop Hill, 59; The Adventures Of Huckleberry Finn, Dog's Best Friend, 60; Hero's Island, 62; The Man From The Diner's Club, 63; Ride In The Whirlwind, 65; Cool Hand Luke, The Hostage, A Time For Killing, 67; Day Of The Evil Gun, The Miniskirt Mob, 68; Rebel Rousers, 70; Two-Lane Blacktop, Cisco Pike, 71; Count Your Bullets, 72; Dillinger, Pat Garrett And Billy The Kid, 73; Cockfighter, The Godfather Part II, Where The Lilies Bloom, Zandy's Bride, 74; 92 In The Shade, Farewell My Lovely, Rafferty And The Gold Dust Twins, Rancho Deluxe, Win Place Or Steal, 75; The Missouri Breaks, 76; Renaldo And Clara, Straight Time, 78; Alien, The Rose, Wise Blood, 79; The Black Marble, La Mort En Direct, Private Benjamin, Uforia, 80; Escape From New York, 81; One From The Heart, Young Doctors In Love, 82; Christine, 83; The Bear, Paris Texas, Red Dawn, Repo Man, 84; The Care Bears Movie, Fool For Love, One Magic Christmas, 85; Pretty In Pink, 86; Slamdance, 87; The Last Temptation Of Christ, Mr North, Stars And Bars, 88; Twister, Dream A Little Dream, 89; The Fourth War, Wild At Heart, 90; Man Trouble, Twin Peaks: Fire Walk With Me, 92; Hostages, 93.

STANWYCK, BARBARA: Broadway Nights, 27; The Locked Door, Mexicali Rose, 29; Ladies Of Leisure, 30; Illicit, The Miracle Woman, Night Nurse, Ten Cents A Dance, 31; Forbidden, The Purchase Price, Shopworn, So Big, 32; Baby Face, The Bitter Tea Of General Yen, Ever In My Heart, Ladies They Talk About, 33; Gambling Lady, A Lost Lady, 34; Annie Oakley, Red Salute, The Secret Bride, Woman In Red, 35; Banjo On My Knee, The Bride Walks Out, His Brother's Wife, A Message To Garcia, The Plough And The Stars, 36; Breakfast For Two, Internes Can't Take Money, Stella Dallas, This Is My Affair, 37; Always Goodbye, The Mad Miss Manton, 38; Golden Boy, Union Pacific, 39; Remember The Night, 40; Ball Of Fire, The Lady Eve, Meet John Doe, You Belong To Me, 41; The Gay Sisters, The Great Man's Lady, Ball Of Fire, 42; Flesh And Fantasy, Lady Of Burlesque, 43; Double Indemnity, Hollywood Canteen, 44; Christmas In Connecticut, 45; The Bride Wore Boots, California, My Reputation, The Strange Love Of Martha Ivers, 46; Cry Wolf, The Other Love, The Two Mrs Carrolls, 47; BF's Daughter, Sorry Wrong Number, 48; East Side West Side, The File On Thelma Jordon, The Lady Gambles, 49; The Furies, No Man Of Her Own, To Please A Lady, 50; The Man With A Cloak, 51; Clash By Night, 52; All I Desire, Blowing Wild, Jeopardy, The Moonlighter, Titanic, 53; Cattle Queen Of Montana, Executive Suite, Witness To Murder, 54; Escape To Burma, The Violent Men, 55; The Maverick Queen, There's Always Tomorrow, These Wilder Years, 56; Crime Of Passion, Forty Guns, Trooper Hook, 57; Walk On The Wild Side, 62; The Night Walker, Roustabout, 64.

STEIGER, ROD: Teresa, 51; On The Waterfront, 54; The Big Knife, The Court-Martial Of Billy Mitchell, Oklahoma!, 55; Back From Eternity, The Harder They Fall, Jubal, 56; Across The Bridge, Run Of The Arrow, 57; The Unholy Wife, Cry Terror, 58; Al Capone, 59; Seven Thieves, 60; The Mark, 61; The World In My Pocket, 13 West Street, Convicts Four, The Longest Day, 62; Hands Over The City, 63; Time Of Indifference, 64; And There Came A Man, Doctor Zhivago, The Loved One, The Pawnbroker, 65; The Girl And The General, In The Heat Of The Night, 67; No Way To Treat A Lady, The Sergeant, 68; The Illustrated Man, Three Into Two Won't Go, 69; Happy Birthday Wanda June, Waterloo, 71; Duck You Sucker, Gli Eroi, 72; Lolly-Madonna War, Lucky Luciano, 73; Mussolini: Ultimo Atto, 74; Hennessy, 75; Les Innocents Aux Mains Sales, W C Fields And Me, 76; FIST, 78; Wolf Lake, The Amityville Horror, Love And Bullets, 79; Cattle Annie And Little Britches, Klondike Fever, The Lucky Star, 80; The Chosen, Lion Of The Desert, 81; Der Zauberberg, 82; The Naked Face, 84; Catch The Heat, The Kindred, American Gothic, 87; The January Man, Sauf Votre Respect, Tennessee Nights, That Summer Of White Roses, 89; Men Of Respect, 90; The Ballad Of The Sad Cafe, Guilty As Charged, 91; The Player, 92; The Neighbor, 93; The Specialist, 94; Incognito, 97.

STEINER, MAX: Rio Rita, 29; Dixiana, 30; Cimarron, 31; A Bill Of Divorcement, Symphony Of Six Million, 32; Bed Of Roses, Ace of Aces, King Kong, Little Women, Morning Glory, 33; Stingaree, Down to Their Last Yacht, The Lost Patrol, Of Human Bondage, 34; Alice Adams, The Informer, She, Top Hat, 35; The Charge Of The Light Brigade, Follow The Fleet, 36; The Life Of Emile Zola, A Star Is Born, 37; That Certain Woman, Tovarich, The Dawn Patrol, Four Daughters, Jezebel, The Sisters, White Banners, Gold Is Where You Find It, The Amazing Dr Clitterhouse, Angels With Dirty Faces, 38; Dark Victory, Dodge City, Gone With The Wind, 39; The Letter, 40; Sergeant York, They Died With Their Boots On, 41; Casablanca, Now Voyager, 42; Arsenic And Old Lace, Since You Went Away, 44; Mildred Pierce, Rhapsody In Blue, 45; The Big Sleep, 46; Johnny Belinda, Key Largo, The Treasure Of The Sierra Madre, 48; White Heat, 49; The Glass Menagerie, 50; The Desert Song, 52; So Big, By The Light Of The Silvery Moon, 53; The Caine Mutiny, 54; The Searchers, 56; Band Of Angels, A Summer Place, 59; The Dark At The Top Of The Stairs, 60; Parrish, Susan Slade, 61; A Majority Of One, Rome Adventure, 62; Spencer's Mountain, 63; A Distant Trumpet, Youngblood Hawke, 64; Two On A Guillotine, 65.

STERNBERG, JOSEPH VON: The Masked Bride, The Salvation Hunters, 25; The Exquisite Sinner, A Woman Of The Sea, 26; Underworld, 27; Docks Of New York, The Dragnet, The Last Command, The Street Of Sin, 28; The Case Of Lena Smith, Thunderbolt, 29; The Blue Angel, Morocco, 30; An American Tragedy, Dishonored, 31; Blonde Venus, Shanghai Express, 32; The Scarlet Empress, 34; Crime And Punishment, The Devil Is A Woman, 35; The King Steps Out, 36; The Great Waltz, 38; Sergeant Madden, 39; The Shanghai Gesture, 41; The Town, 44; Macao, The Saga Of Anatahan, 52; Jet Pilot, 57; The Epic That Never Was, 63.

STEVENS, GEORGE: Black Cyclone, 25; The Desert's Toll, 26; Wrong Again!, 29; Walking Back Home, Grin And Bear It, Flirting In The Park, Ladies Last, Hog Wild, Brats, Blood And Thunder, 30; Call A Cop, 31;The Cohens And Kellys In Trouble, 33; Bachelor Bait, Hollywood Party, Kentucky Kernels, The Undie-World, Roughnecking, Waht Fur, 34; Alice Adams, Annie Oakley, Laddie, The Nitwits, 35; Swing Time, 36; A Damsel In Distress, Quality Street, 37; Vivacious Lady, 38; Gunga Din, 39; Vigil In The Night, 40; Penny Serenade, 41; The Talk Of The Town, Woman Of The Year, 42; This Is The Army!, The More The Merrier, 43; I Remember Mama, On Our Merry Way, 48; A Place In The Sun, 51; Something To Live For, 52; Shane, 53; Giant, 56; The Diary Of Anne Frank, 59; The Greatest Story Ever Told, 65; The Only Game In Town, 70.

STEWART, JAMES: The Murder Man, 35; After The Thin Man, Born To Dance, The Gorgeous Hussy, Next Time We Love, Rose Marie, Small Town Girl, Speed, Wife Vs Secretary, 36; The Last Gangster, Navy Blue And Gold, Seventh Heaven, 37; Of Human Hearts, The Shopworn Angel, Vivacious Lady, You Can't Take It With You, 38; Destry Rides Again, Ice Follies Of 1939, It's A Wonderful World, Made For Each Other, Mr Smith Goes To Washington, 39; The Mortal Storm, No Time For Comedy, The Philadelphia Story, The Shop Around The Corner, 40; Come Live With Me, Pot O' Gold, Ziegfeld Girl, 41; It's A Wonderful Life, 46; Magic Town, 47; Call Northside 777, A Miracle Can Happen, Rope, You Gotta Stay Happy, 48; The Stratton Story, 49; Broken Arrow, Harvey, The Jackpot, Winchester 73, Malaya, 50; No Highway, 51; Bend Of The River, Carbine Williams, The Greatest Show On Earth, 52; The Naked Spur, Thunder Bay, 53; The Glenn Miller Story, Rear Window, 54; The Far Country, The Man From Laramie, Strategic Air Command,

55; The Man Who Knew Too Much, **56**; Night Passage, The Spirit Of St Louis, **57**; Bell Book And Candle, Vertigo, **58**; Anatomy Of A Murder, The FBI Story, **59**; The Mountain Road, **60**; Two Rode Together, **61**; How The West Was Won, The Man Who Shot Liberty Valance, Mr Hobbs Takes A Vacation, **62**; Take Her She's Mine, **63**; Cheyenne Autumn, **64**; Dear Brigitte, Shenandoah, **65**; Flight Of The Phoenix, The Rare Breed, **66**; Bandolero!, Firecreek, **68**; The Cheyenne Social Club, **70**; Fools' Parade, **71**; That's Entertainment!, **74**; The Shootist, **76**; Airport 77, **77**; The Big Sleep, The Magic Of Lassie, **78**; Afurika Monogatari, **81**.

STILLER, MAURITZ: Vampyren, **12**; Madame De Thebes, **15**; Anjuta The Dancer, Love And Journalism, **16**; Thomas Graal's Best Film, **17**; Thomas Graal's Best Child, **18**; The Three Who Were Doomed, Song Of The Scarlet Flower, **19**; Erotikon, **20**; The Exiles, **21**; Gunnar Hede's Saga, **22**; The Atonement Of Gosta Berling, **24**; The Temptress, The Blizzard, **26**; Hotel Imperial, The Woman On Trial, **27**; The Street Of Sin, **28**.

STONE, OLIVER: Seizure, **74**; Midnight Express, **78**; The Hand, **81**; Conan The Barbarian, **82**; Scarface, **83**; Year Of The Dragon, **85**; 8 Million Ways To Die, Platoon, Salvador, **86**; Wall Street, **87**; Talk Radio, **88**; Born On The Fourth Of July, **89**; Reversal Of Fortune, **90**; The Doors, JFK, **91**; Heaven And Earth, **93**; Natural Born Killers, **94**; Nixon, **95**.

STONE, SHARON: Stardust Memories, **80**; Deadly Blessing, **81**; Bolero, **82**; Irreconcilable Differences, **84**; King Solomon's Mines, **85**; Allan Quatermain And The Lost City Of Gold, Cold Steel, Police Academy 4, **87**; Above The Law, Action Jackson, **88**; Personal Choice, Blood And Sand, **89**; Total Recall, **90**; He Said She Said, Scissors, Year Of The Gun, **91**; Basic Instinct, Diary Of A Hitman, **92**; Where Sleeping Dogs Lie, Sliver, **93**; Intersection, The Specialist, **94**; The Quick And The Dead, Last Dance, Casino, **95**.

STORARO, VITTORIO: The Bird With The Crystal Plumage, Delitto Al Circolo Del Tennis, **69**; Giovinezza Giovinezza, The Spider's Stratagem, Orlando Furioso, **70**; Addio Fratello Crudele, Il Conformista, **71**; Corpo D'Amore, **72**; Giordano Bruno, Last Tango In Paris, Malizia, **73**; Submission, **77**; Agatha, Apocalypse Now, La Luna, **79**; Reds, **81**; One From The Heart, **82**; Wagner, **83**; Ladyhawke, **85**; Ishtar, The Last Emperor, **87**; Tucker: The Man And His Dream, **88**; New York Stories, **89**; Dick Tracy, The Sheltering Sky, The Last Emperor, **90**; Little Buddha, **94**; Taxi, **96**, Tango, **97**.

STRADLING, HARRY: La Kermesse Héroique, **35**; Knight Without Armour, **37**; The Citadel, Pygmalion, South Riding, **38**; The Lion Has Wings, Jamaica Inn, **39**; The Corsican Brothers, The Devil And Miss Jones, Mr & Mrs Smith, Suspicion, **41**; Her Cardboard Lover, White Cargo, **42**; Bathing Beauty, **44**; The Picture Of Dorian Gray, **45**; Till The Clouds Roll By, **46**; Easter Parade, The Pirate, Words And Music, **48**; The Barkleys Of Broadway, In The Good Old Summertime, Tension, **49**; Edge Of Doom, **50**; I Want You, A Millionaire For Christy, A Streetcar Named Desire, Valentino, **51**; Androcles And The Lion, Hans Christian Andersen, My Son John, Angel Face, **52**; Forever Female, A Lion Is In The Streets, **53**; Johnny Guitar, **54**; Guys And Dolls, Helen Of Troy, **55**; The Eddy Duchin Story, **56**; A Face In The Crowd, The Pajama Game, **57**; Auntie Mame, Marjorie Morningstar, **58**; A Summer Place, The Young Philadelphians, **59**; The Crowded Sky, The Dark At The Top Of The Stairs, Who Was That Lady?, **60**; A Majority Of One, On The Double, Parrish, **61**; Five Finger Exercise, Gypsy, **62**; Island Of Love, Mary Mary, **63**; My Fair Lady, **64**; How To Murder Your Wife, Synanon, **65**; Moment To Moment, Penelope, Walk Don't Run, Who's Afraid Of Virginia Woolf?, **66**; Funny Girl, Support Your Local Sheriff, **68**; Hello Dolly!, **69**; On A Clear Day You Can See Forever, The Owl And The Pussycat, **70**.

STREEP, MERYL: Julia, **77**; The Deer Hunter, **78**; Kramer Vs Kramer, Manhattan, The Seduction Of Joe Tynan, **79**; The French Lieutenant's Woman, **81**; Sophie's Choice, Still Of The Night, **82**; Silkwood, **83**; Falling In Love, **84**; Out Of Africa, Plenty, **85**; Heartburn, **86**; Ironweed, **87**; A Cry In The Dark, **88**; She-Devil, **89**; Postcards From The Edge, **90**; Death Becomes Her, **92**; House Of The Spirits, **93**; The River Wild, **94**; The Bridges Of Madison County, **95**; Marvin's Room, **96**.

STREISAND, BARBRA: Funny Girl, **68**; Hello Dolly!, **69**; On A Clear Day You Can See Forever, The Owl And The Pussycat, **70**; What's Up Doc?, **72**; The Way We Were, **73**; For Pete's Sake, **74**; Funny Lady, **75**; A Star Is Born, **76**; The Main Event, **79**; Yentl, **83**; Nuts, **87**; The Prince Of Tides, **91**; The Mirror Has Two Faces, **96**.

STRICK, JOSEPH: Muscle Beach, **48**; The Big Break, **53**; The Savage Eye, **60**; An Affair Of The Skin, The Balcony, **63**; The Hecklers, **66**; Ulysses, The Legend Of The Boy And The Eagle, **67**; Ring Of Bright Water, **69**; Tropic Of Cancer, Interviews With My Lai Veterans, **70**; Road Movie, **74**; A Portrait Of The Artist As A Young Man, **77**; Criminals, **95**.

STROHEIM, ERICH VON: The Birth Of A Nation, Ghosts, Old Heidelberg, **15**; Intolerance, The Social Secretary, **16**; Sylvia Of The Secret Service, **17**; Hearts Of The World, The Heart Of Humanity, **18**; Blind Husbands, **19**; The Devil's Pass Key, Foolish Wives, **20**; Merry-Go-Round, **23**; Greed, **23-25**; The Merry Widow, **25**; The Wedding March, Queen Kelly, **28**; The Great Gabbo, **29**; Three Faces East, **30**; Friends And Lovers, **31**; The Lost Squadron, As You Desire Me, **32**; Crimson Romance, Fugitive Road, **34**; The Crime Of Dr Crespi, **35**; The Devil Doll, **36**; La Grande Illusion, Mademoiselle Docteur, L'Alibi, **37**; Les Pirates de Rail, L'Affaire Lafargé, Les Disparus De Saint-Agil, Ultimatum, It Happened In Gibraltar, **38**; 32 Rue De Montmartre, **39**; Menaces, I Was An Adventuress, **40**; So Ends Our Night, **41**; Five Graves To Cairo, The North Star, **43**; The Lady And The Monster, Storm Over Lisbon, **44**; The Great Flammarion, Scotland Yard Investigator, **45**; The Mask Of Dijon, **46**; La Danse De Mort, Le Signal Rouge, **48**; Sunset Boulevard, **49**; Alraune, **52**; Minuit – Quai De Bercy, L'Envers Du Paradis, Alerte Au Sud, **53**; Serie Noire, **55**.

STURGES, JOHN: Thunderbolt, **45**; Alias Mr Twilight, The Man Who Dared, Shadowed, **46**; For The Love Of Rusty, Keeper Of The Bees, **47**; The Best Man Wins, Sign Of The Ram, **48**; The Walking Hills, **49**; The Capture, The Magnificent Yankee, Mystery Street, Right Cross, **50**; It's A Big Country, Kind Lady, The People Against O'Hara, **51**; The Girl In White, **52**; Escape From Fort Bravo, Fast Company, Jeopardy, **53**; Bad Day At Black Rock, The Scarlet Coat, Underwater!, **55**; Backlash, **56**; Gunfight At The OK Corral, **57**; The Law And Jake Wade, The Old Man And The Sea, **58**; Last Train From Gun Hill, Never So Few, **59**; The Magnificent Seven, **60**; By Love Possessed, **61**; A Girl Named Tamiko, Sergeants 3, **62**; The Great Escape, **63**; The Hallelujah Trail, The Satan Bug, **65**; Hour Of The Gun, **67**; Ice Station Zebra, **68**; Marooned, **69**; Joe Kidd, **72**; Valdez Il Mezzosangue, **73**; McQ, **74**; The Eagle Has Landed, **76**.

STURGES, PRESTON: Christmas In July, The Great McGinty, Remember The Night, **40**; The Lady Eve, Sullivan's Travels, **41**; The Palm Beach Story, Star Spangled Rhythm, **42**; The Great Moment, Hail The Conquering Hero, The Miracle Of Morgan's Creek, **44**; I'll Be Yours, The Sin Of Harold Diddlebock, **47**; Unfaithfully Yours, **48**; The Beautiful Blonde From Bashful Bend, **49**; Vendetta, **50**; The French They Are A Funny Race, **56**.

STYNE, JULE: Hold That Co-Ed, **38**; Hit Parade Of 1941, **40**; Rookies On Parade, **41**; Priorities On Parade, Youth On Parade, **42**; Hit Parade Of 43, The Heat's On, Let's Face It, Thumbs Up, **43**; Knickerbocker Holiday, Carolina Blues, **44**; Anchors Aweigh, Tonight And Every Night, **45**; The Kid From Brooklyn, Tars And Spars, **46**; Earl Carroll, Sketchbook, It Happened In Brooklyn, **47**; Romance On The High Seas, Two Guys From Texas, **48**; It's A Great Feeling, **49**; West Point Story, **50**; Meet Me After The Show, **51**; Macao, **52**; Gentlemen Prefer Blondes, **53**; Living It Up, Three Coins In The Fountain, **54**; How To Be Very Very Popular, My Sister Eileen, **55**; Bells Are Ringing, **60**; Gypsy, **62**; What A Way To Go, **64**; Funny Girl, **68**; The Fisher King, **91**.

SULLAVAN, MARGARET: Only Yesterday, **33**; Little Man What Now?, **34**; The Good Fairy, So Red The Roses, **35**; The Moon's Our Home, Next Time We Love, **36**; The Shining Hour, The Shopworn Angel, Three Comrades, **38**; The Mortal Storm, The Shop Around The Corner, **40**; Appointment For Love, Back Street, So Ends Our Night, **41**; Cry Havoc, **43**; No Sad Songs For Me, **50**.

SURTEES, ROBERT L: Heavenly Music, **43**; Thirty Seconds Over Tokyo, **44**; Strange Holiday, **45**; The Kissing Bandit, **48**; Intruder In The Dust, That Midnight Kiss, **49**; King Solomon's Mines, **50**; The Light Touch, Quo Vadis, The Strip, **51**; The Bad And The Beautiful, The Merry Widow, The Wild North, **52**; Escape From Fort Bravo, Mogambo, Ride Vaquero, **53**; The Long Long Trailer, Valley Of The Kings, **54**; Oklahoma!, Trial, **55**; The Swan, Tribute To A Bad Man, **56**; Les Girls, Raintree County, **57**; The Law And Jake Wade, Merry Andrew, **58**; Ben-Hur, **59**; Cimarron, It Started In Naples, **60**; Mutiny On The Bounty, **62**; PT 109, **63**; Kisses For My President, **64**; The Collector, The Hallelujah Trail, The Satan Bug, The Third Day, **65**; Lost Command, **66**; Doctor Dolittle, The Graduate, **67**; The Arrangement, Sweet Charity, **69**; The Liberation Of LB Jones, **70**; The Last Picture Show, Summer Of 42, **71**; The Cowboys, The Other, **72**; Lost Horizon, Oklahoma Crude, The Sting, **73**; The Great Waldo Pepper, The Hindenburg, **75**; A Star Is Born, **76**; The Turning Point, **77**; Bloodbrothers, Same Time Next Year, **78**.

SUTHERLAND, DONALD: Castle Of The Living Dead, **64**; The Bedford Incident, Fanatic, Dr. Terror's House Of Horrors, **65**; Promise Her Anything, **66**; The Dirty Dozen, **67**; Joanna, Oedipus The King, Sebastian, The Split, **68**; Act Of The Heart, Alex In Wonderland, Kelly's Heroes, MASH, Start The Revolution Without Me, **70**; Johnny Got His Gun, Klute, Little Murders, **71**; FTA, **72**; Don't Look Now, Lady Ice, Steelyard Blues, **73**; S*p*y*s, **74**; The Day Of The Locust, **75**; Fellini's Casanova, The Eagle Has Landed, **76**; 1900, The Disappearance, The Kentucky Fried Movie, **77**; Blood Relatives, Invasion Of The Body Snatchers, National Lampoon's Animal House, **78**; The Great Train Robbery, A Man A Woman And A Bank, Murder By Decree, **79**; Bear Island, Nothing Personal, Ordinary People, **80**; Eye Of The Needle, Gas, Threshold, **81**; Max Dugan Returns, **83**; Crackers, Ordeal By Innocence, **84**; Catholic Boys, Revolution, **85**; The Rosary Murders, The Trouble With Spies, Wolf At The Door, **87**; A Dry White Season, Lock Up, Lost Angels, Bethune, **89**; Backdraft, Buster's Bedroom, Eminent Domain, JFK, Schrei Aus Stein, **91**; Buffy The Vampire Slayer, **92**; Benefit Of The Doubt, Shadow Of The Wolf, Six Degrees Of Separation, Younger And Younger, **93**; Disclosure, **94**; Outbreak, Six Degrees Of Separation, **95**.

SWANSON, GLORIA: The Fable Of Elvira And Farina And The Meal Ticket, Sweedie Goes To College, The Broken Pledge, **15**; A Dash Of Courage, Hearts And Sparks, Dangers Of A Bride, The Sultan's Wife, Teddy At The Throttle, **16**; Every Woman's Husband, Her Decision, The Secret Code, Shifting Sands, Society For Sale, Station Content, Wife Or Country, You Can't Believe Everything, **18**; Don't Change Your Husband, For Better For Worse, Male And Female, **19**; Something To Think About, Why Change Your Wife?, **20**; The Affairs Of Anatol, Don't Tell Everything, The Great Moment, Under The Lash, **21**; Beyond The Rocks, Her Gilded Cage, Her Husband's Trademark, The Impossible Mrs Bellew, **22**; Bluebeard's Eighth Wife, Hollywood, My American Wife, Prodigal Daughters, Zaza, **23**; Her Love Story, The Humming Bird, Manhandled, A Society Scandal, Wages Of Virtue, **24**; The Coast Of Folly, Madame Sans-Gêne, Stage Struck, **25**; Fine Manners, The Untamed Lady, **26**; The Love Of Sunya, **27**; Sadie Thompson, **28**; Queen Kelly, The Trespasser, **29**; What A Widow!, **30**; Indiscreet, Tonight Or Never, **31**; Perfect Understanding, **33**; Music In The Air, **34**; Father Takes A Wife, **41**; Sunset Boulevard, **50**; Three For Bedroom C, **52**; Nero's Weekend, **56**; Airport 75, **74**.

SYDOW, MAX VON: Only A Mother, **49**; Miss Julie, **51**; No Man's Woman, **55**; The Seventh Seal, Wild Strawberries, **57**; Nara Livet, Ansiktet, **58**; The Virgin Spring, **59**; Through A Glass Darkly, Winter Light, **63**; The Greatest Story Ever Told, The Reward, **65**; Hawaii, Har Har Du Ditt Liv, The Quiller Memorandum, Made In Sweden, **66**; Hour Of The Wolf, Shame, **68**; The Passion Of Anna, **69**; The Kremlin Letter, The Night Visitor, **70**; Utvandrarna, Beroringen, Appelkriget, Embassy, Nybyggarna, **72**; The Exorcist, **73**; Steppenwolf, **74**; Agget Ar Lost!, Cuore Di Cane, Il Contesto, Three Days Of The Condor, Trompe L'Oeil, The Ultimate Warrior, **75**; Foxtrot, Le Désert Des Tartares, Voyage Of The Damned, **76**; Exorcist II: The Heretic, Gran Bollito, March Or Die, **77**; Brass Target, **78**; Hurricane, **79**; La Mort En Direct, Flash Gordon, **80**; Victory, She Dances Alone, **81**; Conan The Barbarian, The Flight Of The Eagle, Target Eagle, **82**; Le Cercle Des Passions, Never Say Never Again, Strange Brew, **83**; Dreamscape, Dune, **84**; Code Name: Emerald, Il Pentito, Quo Vadis, **85**; Duet For One, Hannah And Her Sisters, The Second Victory, **86**; Wolf At The Door, **87**; Katinka, Pelle The Conqueror, **88**; Awakenings, Father, **90**; The Bachelor, A Kiss Before Dying, The Ox, Until The End Of The World, **91**; The Best Intentions, Europa, **92**; Needful Things, **93**; Hamsun, **96**.

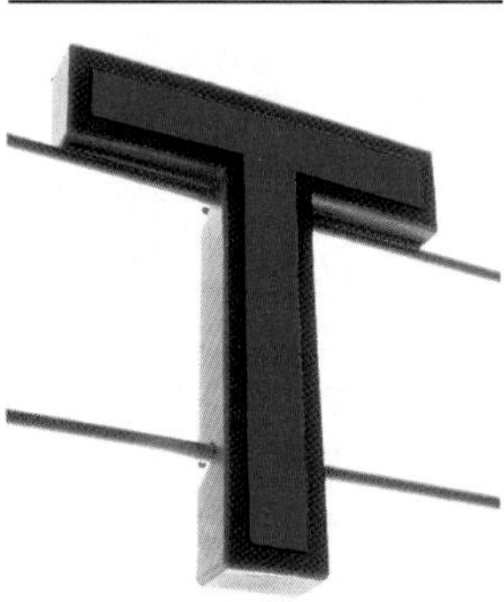

TALMADGE, NORMA: A Broken Spell, A Dixie Mother, In Neighboring Kingdoms, Love Of Chrysanthemum, Uncle Tom's Cabin, **10**; The Child Crusoes, The General's Daughter, Her Hero, The Sky Pilot, A Tale Of Two Cities, The Thumb Print, **11**; Captain Barnacle's Messmate, Casey At The Bat, The First Violin, Fortunes Of A Composer, Mrs 'enry 'awkins, The Troublesome Stepdaughters, **12**; Harriet's Baby, The Blue Rose, The Doctor's Secret, Extremities, Fanny's Conspiracy, His Silver Bachelorhood, The Midget's Revenge, An Old Man's Love Story, Omens And Oracles, The Other Woman, Solitaires, Under The Daisies, **13**; Cupid Versus Money, A Daughter Of Israel, Goodbye Summer, A Helpful Sisterhood, John Rance Gentleman, The Mill Of Life, The Peacemaker, The Sacrifice Of Kathleen, Sawdust And Salome, Sunshine And Shadows, **14**; The Barrier Of Faith, The Battle Cry Of Peace, **15**; The Children In The House, Going Straight, The Devil's Needle, Fifty-Fifty, The Missing Links, The Social Secretary, Martha's Vindication, **16**; Panthea, **17**; De Luxe Annie, Forbidden City, Her Own Way, **18**; The Isle Of Conquest, The Heart Of Wetona, The New Moon, The Probation Wife, The Way Of A Woman, **19**; The Branded Woman, Yes Or No, **20**; Love's Redemption, The Passion Flower, The Sign On The Door, The Wonderful Thing, Foolish Wives, **21**; The Eternal Flame, Smilin' Through, **22**; Ashes Of Vengeance, The Song Of Love, The Voice From The Minaret, Within The Law, **23**; The Of All The World, Secrets, **24**; Graustark, The Lady, **25**; Kiki, **26**; Camille, The Dove, **27**; The Woman Disputed, **28**; New York Nights, **29**; DuBarry Woman Of Passion, **30**.

TANDY, JESSICA: The Indiscretions Of Eve, Murder In The Family, **38**; The Seventh Cross, **44**; The Valley Of Decision, **45**; Dragonwyck, The Green Years, **46**; Forever Amber, A Woman's Vengeance, **47**; September Affair, **50**; The Desert Fox, **51**; The Light In The Forest, **58**; Adventures Of A Young Man, **62**; The Birds, **63**; Butley, **74**; Honky Tonk Freeway, **81**; Best Friends, Still Of The Night, The World According To Garp, **82**; The Bostonians, **84**; Cocoon, **85**; Batteries Not Included, **87**; Cocoon: The Return, The House On Carroll Street, **88**; Driving Miss Daisy, **89**; Fried Green Tomatoes, **91**; Used People, **92**; Camilla, Nobody's Fool, **95**.

TANNER, ALAIN: La Salamandre, **71**; Le Retour D'Afrique, **73**; Le Milieu Du Monde, **74**; Jonas Qui Aura 25 Ans En L'An 2000, **76**; Messidor, **78**; Les Années Lumières, **81**; Dans La Ville Blanche, **83**; No Man's Land, **85**; La Vallée Fantôme, Une Flamme Dans Mon Coeur, **87**; La Femme De Rose Hill, **89**; L'Homme Qui A Perdu Son Ombre, **92**; Le Journal De Lady M, **93**.

TARANTINO, QUENTIN: Reservoir Dogs, **92**; True Romance, **93**; Pulp Fiction, Four Rooms, Destiny Turn On The Radio, **95**; Jackie Brown, **97**.

TARKOVSKY, ANDREI: The Steamroller And The Violin, **61**; My Name Is Ivan, Ivanovo Detstvo, **62**; Andrei Rublev, **66**; Solaris, **72**; The Mirror, **74**; Stalker, **79**; Nostalgia, **83**; Offret, **86**.

TATI, JACQUES: On Demande Une Brute, **34**; Gai Dimanche, **35**; Soigne Ton Gauche, **36**; Le Diable Au Corps, Sylvie Et Le Fantôme, **46**; L'Ecole De Facteurs, **47**; Jour De Fête, **49**; Mr Hulot's Holiday, **53**; Mon Oncle, **58**; Playtime, **68**; Traffic, **71**; Parade, **74**.

TAVERNIER, BERTRAND: Les Baisers, **63**; The Watchmaker, **73**; Que La Fete Commence, Le Juge Et L'Assassin, **75**; Des Enfants Gâtés, **77**; La Mort En Direct, Une Semaine De Vacances, **80**; Coup De Torchon, **81**; Mississippi Blues, **83**; A Sunday In The Country, **84**; Round Midnight, **86**; Béatrice, **87**; Daddy Nostalgia, Life And Nothing But, The Undeclared War, **92**; D'Artagnan's Daughter, **96**.

TAVIANI, PAOLO & VITTORIO: Un Uomo Da Bruciare, **62**; I Fuorilegge Del Matrimonio, **63**; Sovversivi, **67**; Sotto Il Segno Dello Scorpione, **69**; San Michele Aveva Un Gallo, **71**; Allonsanfan, **74**; Padre Padrone, **77**; Il Prato, **79**; The Night Of San Lorenzo, **81**; Kaos, **84**; Good Morning Babylon, **87**; Night Sun, **90**; Fiorile, **93**.

TAYLOR, ELIZABETH: There's One Born Every Minute, **42**; Lassie Come Home, **43**; Jane Eyre, National Velvet, The White Cliffs Of Dover, **44**; Courage Of Lassie, **46**; Cynthia, Life With Father, **47**; A Date With Judy, Julia Misbehaves, Conspirator, Little Women, **49**; The Big Hangover, Father Of The Bride, **50**; Father's Little Dividend, A Place In The Sun, **51**; Ivanhoe, Love Is Better Than Ever, **52**; The Girl Who Had Everything, **53**; Beau Brummel, Elephant Walk, The Last Time I Saw Paris, Rhapsody, **54**; Giant, **56**; Raintree County, **57**; Cat On A Hot Tin Roof, **58**; Suddenly Last Summer, **59**; Butterfield 8, **60**; Cleopatra, The VIPs, **63**; The Sandpiper, **65**; Who's Afraid Of Virginia Woolf?, **66**; The Comedians, The Comedians In Africa, Reflections In A Golden Eye, The Taming Of The Shrew, **67**; Boom!, Dr. Faustus, Secret Ceremony, **68**; The Only Game In Town, **70**; Under Milk Wood, **71**; Hammersmith Is Out, Zed And Co, **72**; Ash Wednesday, Night Watch, **73**; Identikit, That's Entertainment!, **74**; The Blue Bird, **76**; A Little Night Music, **78**; Winter Kills, **79**; The Mirror Crack'd, **80**; Young Toscanini, **88**; The Flintstones, **94**.

TAYLOR, ROBERT: Handy Andy, There's Always Tomorrow, A Wicked Woman, **34**; Broadway Melody Of 1936, Magnificent Obsession, Murder In The Fleet, Society Doctor, Times Square Lady, West Point Of The Air, **35**; The Gorgeous Hussy, His Brother's Wife, Private Number, Small Town Girl, **36**; Broadway Melody Of 1938, Camille, Lest We Forget, Personal Property, This Is My Affair, **37**; The Crowd Roars, Three Comrades, A Yank At Oxford, **38**; Lady Of The Tropics, Lucky Night, Remember?, Stand Up And Fight, **39**; Escape, Flight Command, Waterloo Bridge, **40**; Billy The Kid, When Ladies Meet, **41**; Her Cardboard Lover, Stand By For Action, Johnny Eager, **42**; Bataan, Song Of Russia, The Youngest Profession, **43**; Undercurrent, **46**; High Wall, **47**; The Bribe, Conspirator, **49**; Ambush, Devil's Doorway, **50**; Quo Vadis, Westward The Women, **51**; Ivanhoe, **52**; All The Brothers Were Valiant, I Love Melvin, Knights Of The Round Table, Ride Vaquero, **53**; Rogue Cop, Valley Of The Kings, **54**; Many Rivers To Cross, Quentin Durward, **55**; D-Day The Sixth Of June, The Last Hunt, The Power And The Prize, **56**; Tip On A Dead Jockey, **57**; The Law And Jake Wade,

Party Girl, Saddle The Wind, **58**; The Hangman, The House Of The Seven Hawks, **59**; Killers Of Kilimanjaro, **60**; Cattle King, Miracle Of The White Stallions, **63**; The Glass Sphinx, **65**; Return Of The Gunfighter, **66**; A House Is Not A Home, The Night Walker, Johnny Tiger, Savage Pampas, Where Angels Go Trouble Follows, **68**; The Day The Hot Line Got Hot, **69**.

TEMPLE, SHIRLEY: The Red Haired Alibi, **32**; Baby Take A Bow, Bright Eyes, Change Of Heart, Little Miss Marker, Now And Forever, Now I'll Tell, Stand Up And Cheer, **34**; Curly Top, The Little Colonel, The Littlest Rebel, Our Little Girl, **35**; Captain January, Dimples, Poor Little Rich Girl, Stowaway, **36**; Heidi, Wee Willie Winkie, **37**; Just Around The Corner, Little Miss Broadway, Rebecca Of Sunnybrook Farm, **38**; The Little Princess, Susannah Of The Mounties, **39**; The Blue Bird, Young People, **40**; Kathleen, **41**; Miss Annie Rooney, **42**; I'll Be Seeing You, Since You Went Away, **44**; Kiss And Tell, **45**; Bachelor Knight, Honeymoon, That Hagen Girl, **47**; Fort Apache, **48**; Adventure In Baltimore, Almost A Bride, Mr Belvedere Goes To College, The Story Of Seabiscuit, **49**.

TERRY-THOMAS: The Brass Monkey, **48**; Private's Progress, **56**; Blue Murder At St Trinian's, Happy Is The Bride, Lucky Jim, The Naked Truth, **57**; Tom Thumb, Too Many Crooks, **58**; I'm All Right Jack, Carlton-Browne Of The FO, **59**; School For Scoundrels, Make Mine Mink, **60**; Bachelor Flat, **61**; The Wonderful World Of The Brothers Grimm, **62**; It's A Mad Mad Mad Mad World, **63**; Strange Bedfellows, **64**; How To Murder Your Wife, Those Magnificent Men In Their Flying Machines, **65**; Kiss The Girls And Make Them Die, Munster, Go Home, Our Man In Marrakesh, **66**; Danger: Diabolik, A Guide For The Married Man, The Karate Killers, The Perils Of Pauline, **67**; Don't Raise The Bridge Lower The River, How Sweet It Is!, It's Your Move, Where Were You When The Lights Went Out?, **68**; 2000 Years Later, Arabella, Monte Carlo Or Bust!, **69**; Le Mur De L'Atlantique, **70**; The Abominable Dr Phibes, **71**; Dr Phibes Rises Again, Gli Eroi, **72**; Robin Hood, Vault Of Horror/Tales From The Crypt Part II, **73**; Who Stole The Shah's Jewels?, **74**; Side By Side, **75**; The Bawdy Adventures Of Tom Jones, The Mysterious House Of Dr C, Spanish Fly, **76**; The Hound Of The Baskervilles, The Last Remake Of Beau Geste, **77**.

THALBERG, IRVING: He Who Gets Slapped, **24**; The Merry Widow, The Big Parade, **25**; Ben-Hur, **26**; Flesh and the Devil, **27**; The Crowd, **28**; Hallelujah, **29**; Anna Christie, The Big House, **30**; Private Lives, **31**; Grand Hotel, Freaks, Strange Interlude, **32**; The Merry Widow, The Barretts Of Wimpole Street, **34**; Mutiny On The Bounty, China Seas, A Night At The Opera, **35**; Romeo And Juliet, **36**; The Good Earth, **37**.

THEODORAKIS, MIKIS: The Barefoot Battalion, **54**; Ill Met By Moonlight, **57**; Honeymoon, **59**; Electra, Shadow Of The Cat, **61**; The Lovers Of Teruel, Phaedra, **62**; Five Miles To Midnight, **63**; Zorba The Greek, **64**; The Day The Fish Came Out, **67**; Z71 Biribi, **69**; The Trojan Women, **72**; Serpico, State Of Siege, **73**; Actas De Marusia, **76**; Iphigenia, **77**; Hell River, **78**; Easy Road, Kostas, **79**; Nela, O Anthropos Me To Garyfallo, **80**; Belladonna, The Savage Hunt, **81**; Mod Att Leva, **83**; Les Clowns De Dieu, **86**; Sis, **89**.

THOMPSON, CAROLINE: Edward Scissorhands, **90**; The Addams Family, **91**; The Incredible Journey: Homeward Bound, The Secret Garden, Tim Burton's Nightmare Before Christmas, **93**; Black Beauty, **94**.

THOMPSON, EMMA: Henry V, The Tall Guy, **89**; Dead Again, Impromptu, **91**; Howards End, Peter's Friends, **92**; In The Name Of The Father, Much Ado About Nothing, The Remains Of The Day, **93**; My Father, The Hero, Junior, **94**, Carrington, Sense And Sensibility, **95**.

THORPE, RICHARD: Burn 'em Up Barnes, **21**; Battling Buddy, Bringin' Home The Bacon, Fast And Fearless, Flames Of Desire, Hard Hittin' Hamilton, Rarin' To Go, Restless Wives, Rip Roarin' Roberts, Rough Ridin', Three O'Clock In The Morning, Thundering Romance, Walloping Wallace, **24**; The Desert Demon, Double Action Daniels, Fast Fightin', Full Speed, Galloping On, Gold And Grit, On The Go, Quicker'n Lightnin', Tearin' Loose, **25**; The Bandit Buster, The Bonanza Buckaroo, College Days, Coming An' Going, The Dangerous Dub, Deuce High, Double Daring, Easy Going, The Fighting Cheat, Josselyn's Wife, Rawhide, Riding Rivals, The Roaring Rider, The Saddle Cyclone, Speedy Spurs, A Streak Of Luck, Trumpin' Trouble, Twin Triggers, Twisted Triggers, **26**; Between Dangers, The Cyclone Cowboy, The Desert Of The Lost, The First Night, The Galloping Gobs, The Interferin' Gent, The Meddlin' Stranger, The Obligin' Buckaroo, Pals In Peril, Ride 'em High, The Ridin' Rowdy, Roarin' Broncs, Skedaddle Gold, Soda Water Cowboy, Tearin' Into Trouble, White Pebbles, **27**; The Ballyhoo Buster, The Cowboy Cavalier, Desperate Courage, The Flying Buckaroo, Saddle Mates, The Valley Of Hunted Men, The Vanishing West, Vultures Of The Sea, **28**; The Bachelor Girl, The Fatal Warning, King Of The Kongo, **29**; Border Romance, The Dude Wrangler, The Lone Defender, The Thoroughbred, Under Montana Skies, The Utah Kid, Wings Of Adventure, **30**; The Devil Plays, Grief Street, King Of The Wild, The Lady From Nowhere, The Lawless Woman, Neck And Neck, The Sky Spider, Wild Horse, **31**; The Beauty Parlor, Cross Examination, Escapade, Forbidden Company, Forgotten Women, The King Murder, The Midnight Lady, Murder At Dawn, Probation, Editor, The Secrets Of Wu Sin, Slightly Married, The Thrill Of Youth, Women Won't Tell, **32**; Forgotten, I Have Lived, Love Is Dangerous, A Man Of Sentiment, Notorious But Nice, Rainbow Over Broadway, Strange People, **33**; Cheating Cheaters, City Park, Editor, Green Eyes, Murder On The Campus, The Quitter, Secret Of The Château, Stolen Sweets, **34**; Last Of The Pagans, Strange Wives, **35**; Tarzan Escapes, The Voice Of Bugle Ann, **36**; Dangerous Number, Double Wedding, Night Must Fall, **37**; The Crowd Roars, The First Hundred Years, Love Is A Headache, Man-proof, Three Loves Has Nancy, The Toy Wife, **38**; The Adventures Of Huckleberry Finn, Tarzan Finds A Son!, **39**; 20 Mule Team, The Earl Of Chicago, Wyoming, **40**; The Bad Man, Barnacle Bill, Tarzan's Secret Treasure, **41**; Joe Smith, American, Tarzan's New York Adventure, White Cargo, **42**; Above Suspicion, Apache Trail, Cry Havoc, Three Hearts For Julia, **43**; The Thin Man Goes Home, Two Girls And A Sailor, **44**; Her Highness And The Bellboy, Thrill Of A Romance, What Next Corporal Hargrove?, **45**; Fiesta, This Time For Keeps, **47**; A Date With Judy, On An Island With You, **48**; Big Jack, Challenge To Lassie, Malaya, The Sun Comes Up, **49**; Black Hand, Three Little Words, **50**; The Great Caruso, It's A Big Country, The Unknown Man, Vengeance Valley, **51**; Carbine Williams, Ivanhoe, The Prisoner Of Zenda, **52**; All The Brothers Were Valiant, The Girl Who Had Everything, Knights Of The Round Table, **53**; Athena, The Student Prince, **54**; The Prodigal, The Adventures Of Quentin Durward, **55**; Jailhouse Rock, Ten Thousand Bedrooms, Tip On A Dead Jockey, **57**; The House Of The Seven Hawks, Killers Of Kilimanjaro, **59**; The Honeymoon Machine, **61**; The Horizontal Lieutenant, The Tartars, **62**; Follow The Boys, Fun In Acapulco, **63**; That Funny Feeling, The Truth About Spring, **65**; The Golden Head, The Last Challenge, **67**.

TIERNEY, GENE: Hudson's Bay, The Return Of Frank James, **40**; Belle Starr, The Shanghai Gesture, Sundown, Tobacco Road, **41**; China Girl, Rings On Her Fingers, Son Of Fury, Thunder Birds, **42**; Heaven Can Wait, **43**; Laura, **44**; A Bell For Adano, Leave Her To Heaven, **45**; Dragonwyck, The Razor's Edge, **46**; The Ghost And Mrs Muir, **47**; The Iron Curtain, That Wonderful Urge, **48**; Whirlpool, **49**; Night And The City, Where The Sidewalk Ends, **50**; Close To My Heart, The Mating Season, On The Riviera, The Secret Of Convict Lake, **51**; Plymouth Adventure, Way Of A Gaucho, **52**; Never Let Me Go, **53**; Black Widow, The Egyptian, Personal Affair, **54**; The Left Hand Of God, **55**; Advise And Consent, **62**; Toys In The Attic, **63**; The Pleasure Seekers, **64**.

TIOMKIN, DMITRI: Devil-May-Care, **29**; Lord Byron Of Broadway, The Rogue Song, **30**; Resurrection, **31**; Alice In Wonderland, **33**; Mad Love, **35**; Lost Horizon, **37**; The Great Waltz, Spawn Of The North, You Can't Take It With You, **38**; Mr Smith Goes To Washington, Only Angels Have Wings, **39**; The Westerner, **40**; The Corsican Brothers, Meet John Doe, **41**; The Moon And Sixpence, **42**; Shadow Of A Doubt, **43**; The Battle Of St Pietro, The Bridge Of San Luis Rey, **44**; Dillinger, **45**; The Dark Mirror, Duel In The Sun, It's A Wonderful Life, **46**; The Long Night, **47**; Portrait Of Jennie, Red River, **48**; Champion, Home Of The Brave, **49**; Cyrano De Bergerac, DOA, The Men, **50**; Strangers On A Train, The Thing, **51**; The Big Sky, High Noon, **52**; Blowing Wild, I Confess, **53**; Dial M For Murder, The High And The Mighty, **54**; Friendly Persuasion, Giant, **56**; Gunfight At The OK Corral, Wild Is The Wind, **57**; The Old Man And The Sea, **58**; Rio Bravo, **59**; The Alamo, The Sundowners, The Unforgiven, **60**; The Guns Of Navarone, Town Without Pity, **61**; 55 Days At Peking, **63**; The Fall Of The Roman Empire, **64**; The War Wagon, **67**; Mackenna's Gold, **69**; Tchaikovsky, **70**.

TISSE, EDWARD: Signal, **18**; Hammer, Hunger Hunger Hunger, **21**; Strike, Battleship Potemkin, **25**; October, **28**; Woman Happy Woman Unhappy, The General Line, **29**; Romance Sentimentale, **30**; Que Viva Mexico, **32**; Aerograd, **35**; Bezhin Meadow, **37**; Alexander Nevsky, **38**; Ivan The Terrible Part One, **43**; In The Mountains Of Yugoslavia, Ivan The Terrible Part Two, **46**; Meeting On The Elbe, **49**; Glinka, **52**.

TODD, ANN: Keepers Of Youth, The Ghost Train, **31**; The Squeaker, **37**; Action For Slander, South Riding, **38**; All This And Heaven Too, **40**; Bad Men Of Missouri, Blood And Sand, **41**; The Seventh Veil, Perfect Strangers, **45**; The Paradine Case, So Evil My Love, **48**; Madeleine, The Passionate Friends, **49**; The Sound Barrier, **52**; The Green Scarf, **55**; Time Without Pity, **56**; The Son Of Captain Blood, **62**; The Human Factor, **79**.

TODD, MIKE: Oklahoma!, **55**; Around The World In 80 Days, **56**.

TOLAND, GREGG: Bulldog Drummond, Condemned, The Trespasser, **29**; The Devil To Pay, Raffles, Whoopee!, **30**; Indiscreet, One Heavenly Night, Palmy Days, Tonight Or Never, The Unholy Garden, **31**; The Kid From Spain, Man Wanted, Play Girl, The Tenderfoot, The Washington Masquerade, **32**; The Masquerader, The Nuisance, Roman Scandals, Tugboat Annie, **33**; Forsaking All Others, Lazy River, Nana, We Live Again, **34**; The Dark Angel, Les Miserables, Mad Love, Public Hero Number One, Splendor, The Wedding Night, **35**; Beloved Enemy, Come And Get It, The Road To Glory, Strike Me Pink, These Three, **36**; Dead End, History Is Made At Night, Woman Chases Man, **37**; The Cowboy And The Lady, The Goldwyn Follies, Kidnapped, **38**; Intermezzo, They Shall Have Music, Wuthering Heights, **39**; The Grapes Of Wrath, The Long Voyage Home, Raffles, The Westerner, **40**; Ball Of Fire, Citizen Kane, The Little Foxes, **41**; December 7th, The Outlaw, **43**; The Best Years Of Our Lives, The Kid From Brooklyn, Song Of The South, **46**; The Bishop's Wife, **47**; Enchantment, A Song Is Born, **48**.

TOMLIN, LILY: Nashville, Songs, **75**; The Late Show, **77**; Moment By Moment, **78**; Nine To Five, **80**; The Incredible Shrinking Woman, **81**; All Of Me, **84**; Big Business, **88**; The Search For Signs Of Intelligent Life In The Universe, **91**; The Player, Shadows And Fog, **92**; The Beverly Hillbillies, Short Cuts, **93**, Blue In The Face, Getting Away With Murder, **95**.

TORN, RIP: Baby Doll, **56**; A Face In The Crowd, Time Limit, **57**; Pork Chop Hill, **59**; King Of Kings, **61**; Hero's Island, Sweet Bird Of Youth, **62**; Critic's Choice, **63**; The Cincinnati Kid, **65**; One Spy Too Many, You're A Big Boy Now, **66**; Beach Red, **67**; Beyond The Law, The Heroin Gang, Coming Apart, **69**; Maidstone, Tropic Of Cancer, **70**; 1AM, **71**; Slaughter, **72**; Payday, **73**; Crazy Joe, **74**; The Man Who Fell To Earth, **76**; Birch Interval, Nasty Habits, The Private Files Of J Edgar Hoover, **77**; Coma, **78**; Heartland, The Seduction Of Joe Tynan, The Wobblies, **79**; First Family, One-trick Pony, **80**; Airplane II: The Sequel, The Beastmaster, Jinxed!, A Stranger Is Watching, **82**; Cross Creek, **83**; City Heat, Flashpoint, Misunderstood, Songwriter, **84**; Beer, Summer Rental, **85**; Extreme Prejudice, Nadine, **87**; The Telephone, **88**; Cold Feet, Hit List, Silence Like Glass, **89**; Defending Your Life, **91**; Beautiful Dreamers, Dolly Dearest, **92**; Robocop 3, Where The Rivers Flow North, **93**.

TOURNEUR, JACQUES: Accusée, Levez-vous, Maison De Danses, **30**; Partir, Tout Ca Ne Vaut Pas L'Amour, Un Vieux Garçon, **31**; Au Nom De La Loi, Les Gaietés De L'Escadron, **32**; La Fusée, Les Deux Orphelines, Pour Etre Aimé, Toto, **33**; Le Voleur, Les Filles De La Concierge, **34**; A Tale Of Two Cities, **35**; Nick Cartermaster Detective, They All Came Out, **39**; Doctors Don't Tell, **41**; Cat People, Phantom Raiders, **42**; I Walked With A Zombie, The Leopard Man, **43**; Days Of Glory, Experiment Perilous, **44**; Canyon Passage, **46**; Out Of The Past, **47**; Berlin Express, **48**; Easy Living, **49**; The Flame And The Arrow, Stars In My Crown, **50**; Anne Of The Indies, Circle Of Danger, **51**; Way Of A Gaucho, **52**; Appointment In Honduras, **53**; Stranger On Horseback, Wichita, **55**; Great Day In The Morning, Nightfall, **56**; Curse Of The Demon, The Fearmakers, Fury River, **58**; Mission Of Danger, Timbuktu, **59**; The Giant Of Marathon, **60**; The Comedy Of Terrors, **64**; City Under The Sea, **65**.

TOWNE, ROBERT: The Last Woman On Earth, **60**; Creature From The Haunted Sea, **61**; Tomb Of Ligeia, **65**; Bonnie And Clyde, **67**; Villa Rides, **68**; Drive He Said, **72**; The Last Detail, **73**; Chinatown, **74**; Shampoo, The Yakuza, **75**; Personal Best, **82**; Greystoke: The Legend Of Tarzan, Lord Of The Apes, **84**; The Bedroom Window, The Pick-up Artist, Tough Guys Don't Dance, **87**; Tequila Sunrise, **88**; Days Of Thunder, The Two Jakes, **90**; The Firm, **93**; Love Affair, **94**; Mission: Impossible, **96**.

TRACY, SPENCER: Up The River, **30**; Goldie, Quick Millions, Six Cylinder Love, **31**; Disorderly Conduct, Me And My Gal, The Painted Woman, She Wanted A Millionaire, Sky Devils, Society Girl, Young America, **32**; 20,000 Years In Sing Sing, The Face In The Sky, The Mad Game, Man's Castle, The Power And The Glory, Shanghai Madness, **33**; Bottoms Up, Looking For Trouble, Marie Galante, Now I'll Tell, The Show-off, **34**; Dante's Inferno, It's A Small World, The Murder Man, Riffraff, Whipsaw, **35**; Fury, Libeled Lady, San Francisco, **36**; The Big City, Captains Courageous, Mannequin, They Gave Him A Gun, **37**; Boys Town, Test Pilot, **38**; Stanley And Livingstone, **39**; Boom Town, Edison The Man, I Take This Woman, Northwest Passage, **40**; Dr Jekyll And Mr Hyde, Men Of Boys Town, **41**; Keeper Of The Flame, Tortilla Flat, Woman Of The Year, **42**; A Guy Named Joe, **43**; The Seventh Cross, Thirty Seconds Over Tokyo, **44**; Without Love, **45**; Cass Timberlane, The Sea Of Grass, **47**; State Of The Union, **48**; Adam's Rib, Edward My Son, Malaya, **49**; Father Of The Bride, **50**; Father's Little Dividend, The People Against O'Hara, **51**; Pat And Mike, Plymouth Adventure, **52**; The Actress, **53**; Broken Lance, **54**; Bad Day At Black Rock, **55**; The Mountain, **56**; Desk Set, **57**; The Last Hurrah, The Old Man And The Sea, **58**; Inherit The Wind, **60**; The Devil At 4 O'Clock, Judgment At Nuremberg, **61**; How The West Was Won, **62**; It's A Mad Mad Mad Mad World, **63**; Guess Who's Coming To Dinner, **67**.

TRAUNER, ALEXANDER: A Nous La Liberté, **31**; Quai Des Brumes, **38**; Le Jour Se Lève, **39**; Othello, **52**; Land Of The Pharaohs, Lady Chatterley's Lover, **55**; The Nun's Story, **59**; The Apartment, **60**; Romanoff And Juliet, **61**; Irma La Douce, **63**; Behold A Pale Horse, **64**; Up Tight, **68**; Les Maries De L'An Deux, **70**; Impossible Object, **73**; Grandeur Nature, **74**; The Man Who Would Be King, **75**; La Première Fois, **76**; Mr Klein, **77**; Fedora, The Roads To The South, **78**; Don Giovanni, **79**; The Fiendish Plot Of Dr Fu Manchu, **80**; Coup De Torchon, **81**; Tchao Pantin, **83**; Vive Les Femmes!, **84**; Harem, Subway, **85**; Round Midnight, **86**; Le Moustachu, **87**; La Nuit Bengali, **88**; Comédie D'Amour, Reunion, **89**; The Rainbow Thief, **90**.

TRAVOLTA, JOHN: The Devil's Rain, **75**; Carrie, **76**; Saturday Night Fever, **77**; Grease, Moment By Moment, **78**; Urban Cowboy, **80**; Blow Out, **81**; Staying Alive, Two Of A Kind, **83**; Perfect, **85**; The Experts, Look Who's Talking, **89**; Look Who's Talking Too, **90**; Eyes Of An Angel, Shout, **91**; Look Who's Talking Now, **93**; Pulp Fiction, **94**; Get Shorty, White Man's Burden, Broken Arrow, **95**; Face/Off, **97**.

TREVOR, CLAIRE: Jimmy And Sally, The Last Trail, Life In The Raw, The Mad Game, **33**; Baby Take A Bow, Elinor

Movie talk

Post-production: the editing, adding of opticals and special effects and sound mixing.

Poverty row: Columbia grew out of this area around Sunset and Gower in Hollywood, also known as Gower Gulch because cowboys lingered around there waiting for film work.

Premiere: media-grabbing first night for film, often in aid of high-profile charity, in front of glossy invited audience.

Press show: pre-release screening for critics and other journalists.

Producer: in overall charge of administration and budgeting a film, often from concept to distributor.

Production designer: responsible for visual concept of a film and senior to art director.

Quota quickies: British low budget films made in 1930s to fulfil quota decreed by Cinematograph Act, which stipulated that 30% of films shown in Britain be British made. Michael Powell was originally a quickie director.

Rembrandt lighting: dramatic lighting with pronounced shadows, as in Rembrandt's The Night Watch, attributed to Cecil B DeMille.

Running: confirmation that film is moving through camera gate.

Save the red: instruction to turn off stage door signal warning that a scene is being shot. While red light is on no admission is allowed.

Second unit: autonomous production unit assigned to sequences not covered by main crew, with second unit director.

Short: two or three-reel film seldom of more than 30 minutes.

Allen or **Alan Smithee**: any film with this director's credit means that the director is either so ashamed or unhappy with the finished film that he refuses to put his name to it.

Sneak preview: pre-release screening in obscure location to gauge reaction of cinemagoers.

Spaghetti western: Italian-made western pioneered by Sergio Leone with Clint Eastwood, followed by paella western co-productions filmed in and around Almeria, southern Spain.

Norton, Hold That Girl, Wild Gold, **34**; Black Sheep, Dante's Inferno, My Marriage, Navy Wife, Spring Tonic, **35**; 15 Malden Lane, Career Woman, Human Cargo, The Song And Dance Man, Star For A Night, To Mary With Love, **36**; Big Town Girl, Dead End, King Of Gamblers, One Mile From Heaven, Second Honeymoon, Time Out For Romance, **37**; The Amazing Doctor Clitterhouse, Five Of A Kind, Valley Of The Giants, Walking Down Broadway, **38**; Allegheny Uprising, I Stole A Million, Stagecoach, **39**; Dark Command, **40**; Honky Tonk Texas, **41**; The Adventures Of Martin Eden, Crossroads, Street Of Chance, **42**; The Desperadoes, Good Luck Mr Yates, The Woman Of The Town, **43**; Farewell My Lovely, **44**; Johnny Angel, **45**; The Bachelor's Daughters, Crack-up, **46**; Born To Kill, **47**; The Babe Ruth Story, Key Largo, Raw Deal, The Velvet Touch, **48**; The Lucky Stiff, **49**; Borderline, **50**; Best Of The Badmen, Hard Fast And Beautiful, **51**; Hoodlum Empire, My Man And I, Stop You're Killing Me, **52**; The Stranger Wore A Gun, **53**; The High And The Mighty, **54**; Lucy Gallant, Man Without A Star, **55**; The Mountain, **56**; Marjorie Morningstar, **59**; Two Weeks In Another Town, **62**; The Stripper, **63**; How To Murder Your Wife, **65**; The Cape Town Affair, **67**; Kiss Me Goodbye, **82**.

TRINTIGNANT, JEAN-LOUIS: And Woman Was Created, If All The Guys In The World, **56**; Les Liaisons Dangereuses, **59**; Austerlitz, **60**; 7 Capital Sins, Antinea, L'Amante Della Citta Sepolta, Journey Beneath The Desert, Una Vita Difficile, Violent Summer, **61**; Il Sorpasso, Le Coeur Battant, The Success, **63**; Mata Hari, Agent H-21, Château En Suede, **64**; The Sleeping Car Murder, **65**; Is Paris Burning?, La Longue Marche, Un Homme Et Une Femme, Trans-Europ-Express, **66**; Deadly Sweet, Mon Amour, **67**; Les Biches, The Libertine, **68**; L'Américain 69 Metti, Una Sera A Cena, My Night At Maud's, Z, **69**; Las Secretas Intenciones, The Man Who Lies, **70**; The Conformist, The Crook, **71**; And Hope To Die, Without Apparent Motive, **72**; Défense De Savoir, L'Attentat, L'Escapade, Les Violons Du Bal, Un Homme Est Mort, The Train, A Well-filled Day, **73**; Act Of Aggression, Le Jeu Avec Le Feu, Love At The Top, The Secret, **74**; Flic Story, Il Pleut Sur Santiago, **75**; L'Ordinateur Des Pompes Funebres, Le Désert Des Tartares, Le Voyage De Noces, Lifeguard, The Sunday Woman, **76**; Faces Of Love, Les Passagers, **77**; L'Argent Des Autres, **78**; Le Maitre-nageur, Melancolie Baby, **79**; La Banquiere, The Terrace, **80**; Eaux Profondes, Je Vous Aime, Le Grand Pardon, Passion D'Amore, Une Affaire D'Hommes, **81**; Colpire Al Cuore, La Nuit De Varennes, **82**; Confidentially Yours, Femmes De Personne, La Crime, Le Bon Plaisir, Under Fire, **83**; L'Eté Prochain, Partir Revenir, Volley For A Black Buffalo, Viva La Vie!, **84**; L'Homme Aux Yeux D'Argent, Rendez-vous, **85**; La Femme De Ma Vie, A Man And A Woman: 20 Years Later, Quinze Aout, **86**; La Vallée Fantôme, Le Moustachu, **87**; Bunker Palace Hotel, **89**; Merci La Vie, **91**; L'Instinct De L'Ange, **93**; Regarde Les Hommes Tomber, Three Colours: Red, **94**.

TRUFFAUT, FRANCOIS: Les Quatre Cents Coups, **59**; Paris Nous Appartient, Tirez Sur Le Pianiste, **60**; Tire Au Flanc, Jules Et Jim, **61**; L'Amour A Vingt Ans, **62**; La Peau Douce, **64**; Fahrenheit 451, **67**; The Bride Wore Black, Baisers Volés, **68**; Mississippi Mermaid, L'Enfant Sauvage, **69**; Domicile Conjugal, Langlois, **70**; Two English Girls, **72**; Day For Night, Such A Gorgeous Kid Like Me, **73**; The Story Of Adèle H, **75**; Small Change, **76**; Close Encounters Of The Third Kind, The Man Who Loved Women, **77**; The Green Room, **78**; Love On The Run, **79**; Close Encounters Of The Third Kind: Special Edition, The Last Metro, **80**; The Woman Next Door, **81**; Vivement Dimanche!, The Man Who Loved Women, **83**.

TRUMBO, DALTON: Love Begins At 20, Road Gang, Tugboat Princess, **36**; Devil's Playground, **37**; Fugitives For A Night, A Man To Remember, **38**; Career, Five Came Back, The Flying Irishman, Heaven With A Barbed Wire Fence, The Kid From Kokomo, Sorority House, **39**; A Bill Of Divorcement, Curtain Call, Half A Sinner, Kitty Foyle, The Lone Wolf Strikes, We Who Are Young, **40**; Accent On Love, You Belong To Me, **41**; The Remarkable Andrew, **42**; A Guy Named Joe, Tender Comrade, **43**; Thirty Seconds Over Tokyo, **44**; Jealousy, Our Vines Have Tender Grapes, **45**; Emergency Wedding, **50**; The Brave One, **56**; Exodus, Spartacus, **60**; The Last Sunset, **61**; Lonely Are The Brave, **62**; The Sandpiper, **65**; Hawaii, **66**; The Fixer, **68**; The Horsemen, Johnny Got His Gun, **71**; Executive Action, Papillon, **73**; Always, **89**.

TRUMBULL, DOUGLAS: 2001: A Space Odyssey, Candy, **68**; The Andromeda Strain, Silent Running, **71**; Close Encounters Of The Third Kind, **77**; Star Trek The Motion Picture, **79**; Blade Runner, **82**; Brainstorm, **83**.

TURNER, FLORENCE: How To Cure A Cold, **07**; The Merchant Of Venice, The New Stenographer, Richard III, **08**; His Masterpiece, **09**; A Dixie Mother, Francesca Da Rimini, How Championships Are Won And Lost, St Elmo, Twelfth Night, **10**; Answer Of The Roses, Cherry Blossoms, Jealousy, Jean Rescues, The New Stenographer, The Path Of True Love, The Prejudice Of Pierre Marie, The Show Girl, A Tale Of Two Cities, **11**; Aunty's Romance, An Indian Romeo And Juliet, Jean Intervenes, She Cried, **12**; Checkmated, The Deerslayer, The Harper Mystery, The House In Suburbia, The Rose Of Surrey, Under The Make-up, **13**; Flotilla The Flirt, For Her People, The Murdock Trial, Polly's Progress, Through The Valley Of Shadows, **14**; Alone In London, Far From The Madding Crowd, Grim Justice, My Old Dutch, Snobs, **15**; East Is East, **16**; Auld Lang Syne, **17**; Fool's Gold, **19**; The Brand Of Lopez, **20**; All Dolled Up, The Old Wives' Tale, Passion Fruit, The Ugly Duckling, **21**; The Little Mother, **22**; Sally Bishop, **23**; Women And Diamonds, **24**; The Dark Angel, The Mad Marriage, Never The Twain Shall Meet, **25**; The Gilded Highway, The Last Alarm, Padlocked, **26**; The Chinese Parrot, College, Stranded, **27**; Jazzland, The Road To Ruin, **28**; The Kid's Clever, **29**; The Rampant Age, **30**; Ridin' Fool, **31**.

TURNER, KATHLEEN: Body Heat, **81**; The Man With Two Brains, **83**; A Breed Apart, Crimes Of Passion, Romancing The Stone, **84**; The Jewel Of The Nile, Prizzi's Honor, **85**; Peggy Sue Got Married, **86**; Dear America, Julia And Julia, **87**; The Accidental Tourist, Switching Channels, Who Framed Roger Rabbit, **88**; Tummy Trouble, The War Of The Roses, **89**; Rollercoaster Rabbit, **90**; VI Warshawski, **91**; Trail Mix-up, Undercover Blues, **93**; Naked In New York, Serial Mom, **94**; Moonlight And Valentino **95**.

TURNER, LANA: They Won't Forget, The Great Garrick, **37**; The Adventures Of Marco Polo, Dramatic School, Love Finds Andy Hardy, Rich Man Poor Girl, **38**; Calling Dr Kildare, Dancing Co-ed, These Glamour Girls, **39**; Two Girls On Broadway, We Who Are Young, **40**; Dr Jekyll And Mr Hyde, Honky Tonk, Johnny Eager, Ziegfeld Girl, **41**; Somewhere I'll Find You, **42**; Slightly Dangerous, The Youngest Profession, **43**; Marriage Is A Private Affair, **44**; Keep Your Powder Dry, Weekend At The Waldorf, **45**; The Postman Always Rings Twice, **46**; Cass Timberlane, Green Dolphin Street, **47**; Homecoming, The Three Musketeers, **48**; A Life Of Her Own, **50**; Mr Imperium, **51**; The Bad And The Beautiful, The Merry Widow, **52**; Latin Lovers, **53**; Betrayed, The Flame And The Flesh, **54**; The Prodigal, The Rains Of Ranchipur, The Sea Chase, **55**; Diane, **56**; Peyton Place, **57**; Another Time Another Place, The Lady Takes A Flyer, **58**; Imitation Of Life, **59**; Portrait In Black, **60**; Bachelor In Paradise, By Love Possessed, **61**; Who's Got The Action?, **62**; Love Has Many Faces, **65**; Madame X, **66**; The Big Cube, **69**; Persecution, **74**; Bittersweet Love, **76**; Witches' Brew, **80**.

TURPIN, BEN: Midnight Disturbance, Mr Flip, **09**; Evans Links With Sweedie, Golf Champion Chick, **14**; Carmen, His New Job, A Night Out, Snakeville's Hen Medic, **15**; Hired And Fired, The Wicked City, **16**; The Butcher's Nightmare, Caught In The End, A Clever Dummy, Lost And Found, The Pawnbroker's Heart, Roping Her Romeo, A Studio Stampede, **17**; The Battle Royal, Hide And Seek Detectives, She Loved Him Plenty, **18**; Cupid's Day Off, Sleuths, Uncle Tom Without The Cabin, When Love Is Blind, Yankee Doodle In Berlin, **19**; The Daredevil, Down On The Farm, Married Life, The Star Boarder, **20**; Home Talent, Love And Doughnuts, A Small Town Idol, **21**; Bright Eyes, Home Made Movies, **22**; Hollywood, The Shriek Of Araby, **23**; The Reel Virginian, Romeo And Juliet, Yukon Jake, **24**; Hogan's Alley, The Marriage Circus, Wild Goose Chaser, **25**; A Harem Knight, A Prodigal Bridegroom, Steel Preferred, When A Man's A Prince, **26**; Broke In China, The College Hero, A Hollywood Hero, Love's Languid Lure, Pride Of Pikeville, **27**; The Wife's Relations, **28**; The Love Parade, The Show Of Shows, **29**; Swing High, **30**; Cracked Nuts, **31**; Make Me A Star, Million Dollar Legs, **32**; Hollywood Cavalcade, **39**; Saps At Sea, **40**.

TURTURRO, JOHN: Raging Bull, **80**; Exterminator II, The Flamingo Kid, **84**; Desperately Seeking Susan, To Live And Die In LA, **85**; The Color Of Money, Gung Ho, Hannah And Her Sisters, Off Beat, **86**; The Sicilian, **87**; Five Corners, **88**; Backtrack, Do The Right Thing, **89**; Miller's Crossing, Mo' Better Blues, State Of Grace, **90**; Barton Fink, Jungle Fever, Men Of Respect, **91**; Brain Donors, Mac, **92**; Fearless, **93**; Being Human, Quiz Show, **94**.

TUTTLE, FRANK: The Cradle Buster, **22**; Puritan Passions, Second Fiddle, Youthful Cheaters, **23**; Dangerous Money, Grit, **24**; A Kiss In The Dark, Lovers In Quarantine, The Lucky Devil, The Manicure Girl, Miss Bluebeard, **25**; The American Venus, Kid Boots, Love 'em And Leave 'em, The Untamed Lady, **26**; Blind Alleys, One Woman To Another, The Spotlight, Time To Love, **27**; Easy Come Easy Go, His Private Life, Love And Learn, Something Always Happens, Varsity, **28**; The Green Murder Case, Marquis Preferred, The Studio Murder Mystery, Sweetie, **29**; Benson Murder Case, Her Wedding Night, Love Among The Millionaires, Men Are Like That, Only The Brave, Paramount On Parade, True To The Navy, **30**; Dude Ranch, It Pays To Advertise, No Limit, **31**; The Big Broadcast, This Is The Night, This Reckless Age, **32**; Pleasure Cruise, Dangerously Yours, Roman Scandals, **33**; All The King's Horses, Here Is My Heart, Ladies Should Listen, Springtime For Henry, **34**; The Glass Key, Two For Tonight, **35**; College Holiday, **36**; Waikiki Wedding, **37**; Dr Rhythm, **38**; Charlie McCarthy, Detective, I Stole A Million, Paris Honeymoon, **39**; Lucky Jordan, This Gun For Hire, **42**; Hostages, **43**; The Hour Before The Dawn, **44**; Don Juan Quilligan, The Great John L, **45**; Suspense, Swell Guy, **46**; Gunman In The Streets, **50**; The Magic Face, **51**; Hell On Frisco Bay, **55**; A Cry In The Night, **56**; Island Of Lost Women, **59**.

TYSON, CICELY: Odds Against Tomorrow, **59**; A Man Called Adam, **66**; The Comedians, **67**; The Heart Is A Lonely Hunter, **68**; Sounder, **72**; The Blue Bird, The River Niger, **76**; A Hero Ain't Nothin' But A Sandwich, **78**; The Concorde: Airport 79, **79**; Bustin' Loose, **81**; Fried Green Tomatoes, **91**.

ULLMANN, LIV: Fjols Til Fjells, **57**; Short Is The Summer, Tonny, **62**; De Kalte Ham Skarven, **64**; Persona, Ung Flukt, **66**; Hour Of The Wolf, Shame, **68**; Ann-magritt, The Passion Of Anna, **69**; The Night Visitor, **70**; Cold Sweat, The Emigrants, **71**; Cries And Whispers, The New Land, Pope Joan, **72**; 40 Carats, Lost Horizon, Scenes From A Marriage, **73**; The Abdication, Zandy's Bride **74**; Leonor, **75**; Face To Face, **76**; A Bridge Too Far, Couleur Chair, **77**; Autumn Sonata, The Serpent's Egg, **78**; Players, **79**; Richard's Things, **80**; Love, **81**; The Wild Duck, **83**; The Bad Boy, Dangerous Moves, **84**; Ingrid, Let's Hope It's A Girl, **85**; Gabya True Story, Mosca Addio, **87**; La Amiga, **88**; The Rose Garden, **89**; Mindwalk, The Ox, **91**; The Long Shadow, Sophie, **92**.

ULMER, EDGAR G: People On Sunday, **29**; The Black Cat, **34**; From Nine To Nine, **35**; Damaged Lives, Green Fields, **37**; Yankel Dem Schmidt, **38**; Cossacks In Exile, Die Klatsche, Moon Over Harlem, **39**; Americaner Schadchen, **40**; Prisoner Of Japan, Tomorrow We Live, **42**; Corregidor, Danger! Women At Work, Girls In Chains, Isle Of Forgotten Sins, Jive Junction, **43**; Bluebeard, **44**; Club Havana, Detour, Strange Illusion, **45**; Her Sister's Secret, The Strange Woman, The Wife Of Monte Cristo, **46**; Carnegie Hall, **47**; Ruthless, **48**; The Pirates Of Capri, **49**; The Man From Planet X, St Benny The Dip, **51**; Babes In Bagdad, **52**; Eterna Femmina, **54**; Murder Is My Beat, The Naked Dawn, **55**; Daughter Of Dr Jekyll, **57**; The Amazing Transparent Man, Beyond The Time Barrier, Hannibal, **60**; Antinea, L'Amante Della Citta Sepolta, **61**; The Cavern, **66**.

UNSWORTH, GEOFFREY: Scott Of The Antarctic, **49**; Trio, **50**; The Million Pound Note, The Purple Plain, **54**; A Town Like Alice, **56**; Hell Divers, **57**; Bachelor Of Hearts, Dangerous Exile, A Night To Remember, **58**; The World Of Suzie Wong, **60**; Don't Bother To Knock, **61**; The 300 Spartans, The Main Attraction, **62**; Becket, **64**; Genghis Khan, Othello, **65**; Half A Sixpence, Oh Dad Poor Dad Mama's Hung You In The Closet And I'm Feeling So Sad, **67**; 2001: A Space Odyssey, The Bliss Of Mrs Blossom, Dance Of Death, **68**; The Assassination Bureau, The Magic Christian, The Reckoning, **69**; Cromwell, Goodbye Gemini, Three Sisters, **70**; Say Hello To Yesterday, Umman Wittering And Zigo, **71**; Alice's Adventures In Wonderland, Cabaret, **72**; Baxter, Don Quixote, Liebe, Schmerz Und Das Danze Verdammte Zeug, **73**; The Abdication, The Internecine Project, Murder On The Orient Express, Zardoz, **74**; Lucky Lady Of Phopink Panther, Royal Flash, **75**; A Matter Of Time, **76**; A Bridge Too Far, **77**; Superman, **78**; The First Great Train Robbery, Tess, **79**; Superman II, **80**.

USTINOV, PETER: Hullo Fame, **40**; One Of Our Aircraft Is Missing, The Goose Steps Out, **42**; The Way Ahead, **44**; The True Glory, **45**; School For Secrets, **46**; Vice Versa, **48**; Private Angelo, **49**; Le Plaisir, Quo Vadis?, **51**; Beau Brummel, The Egyptian, **54**; Lola Montès, We're No Angels, **55**; I Girovaghi, **56**; The Man Who Wagged His Tail, **57**; Spartacus, The Sundowners, **60**; Romanoff And Juliet, **61**; Billy Budd, **62**; Topkapi, **64**; John Goldfarb Please Come Home, Lady L, **65**; The Comedians, **67**; Blackbeard's Ghost, Hot Millions, **68**; Viva Max!, **69**; Hammersmith Is Out, **72**; Robin Hood, **73**; Logan's Run, One Of Our Dinosaurs Is Missing, Treasure Of Matecumbe, **76**; Doppio Delitto, The Last Remake Of Beau Geste, The Mouse And His Child, The Purple Taxi, **77**; Death On The Nile, The Thief Of Baghdad, **78**; Ashanti, Nous Maigrirons Ensemble, Players, Tarka The Otter, **79**; Charlie Chan And The Curse Of The Dragon Queen, The Great Muppet Caper, **81**; Evil Under The Sun, **82**; Memed My Hawk, **87**; Appointment With Death, Peep And The Big Wide World, **88**; La Révolution Française, **89**; C'era Un Castello Con 40 Cani, **90**; Lorenzo's Oil, **92**; Stiff Upper Lips, **97**.

VADIM, ROGER: Blackmailed, **51**; And Woman Was Created, Mam'zelle Pigalle, Mademoiselle Striptease, **56**; No Sun In Venice, **57**; The Night Heaven Fell, **58**; Dangerous Liaisons, **59**; Les Liaisons Dangereuses, 7 Capital Sins, Et Mourir De Plaisir, Please Not Now!, **61**; Le Repos Du Guerrier, Les Parisiennes, Vice And Virtue, **62**; Dragées Au Poivre, **63**; La Ronde, Nutty, Château En Suede, **64**; La Curée, **66**; Barbarella, Spirits Of The Dead, **68**; Pretty Maids All In A Row, **71**; Ciao! Manhattan, Helle, **72**; Ms Don Juan, **73**; La Jeune Fille Assassinée, **74**; Une Femme Fidèle, **76**; Night Games, **80**; Rich And Famous, **81**; Hot Touch, **82**; Surprise Party, **83**; Into The Night, **85**; And God Created Woman, **87**; L'Amour Necessaire, **91**.

VALENTINO, RUDOLPH: My Official Wife, **14**; Alimony, **17**; All Night, A Society Sensation, **18**; The Big Little Person, The Delicious Little Devil, The Eyes Of Youth, The Home Breaker, Out Of Luck, A Rogue's Romance, Virtuous Sinners, **19**; An Adventuress, The Cheater, The Married Virgin, Once To Every Woman, Passion's Playground, Stolen Moments, The Wonderful Chance, **20**; Camille, The Conquering Power, The Four Horsemen Of The Apocalypse, The Sheik, Uncharted Seas, **21**; Beyond The Rocks, Blood And Sand, Moran Of The Lady Letty, The Young Rajah, **22**; Monsieur Beaucaire, A Sainted Devil, **24**; Cobra, The Eagle, **25**; Son Of The Sheik, **26**.

VALLI, ALIDA: We The Living, **42**; The Miracle Of The Bells, The Paradine Case, **48**; The Third Man, **49**; Walk Softly Stranger, The White Tower, **50**; Senso, The Stranger's Hand, **54**; Il Grido, **57**; The Night Heaven Fell, The Sea Wall, **58**; Eyes Without A Face, **59**; Une Aussi Longue Absence, **61**; Disorder, The Happy Thieves, Ophelia, **62**; El Valle De Las Espadas, **63**; Oedipus Rex, **67**; The Spider's Stratagem, **70**; Diario Di Un Italiano, La Prima Notte Di Quiete, **72**; La Chair De L'Orchidée, La Grande Trouille, The Tempter, **74**; Ce Cher Victor, Le Jeu De Solitaire, Lisa And The Devil, **75**; Novecento, The Cassandra Crossing, Suspiria, **77**; Un Cuore Semplice, Zoo-Zero, **78**; Der Landvogt Von Griefensee, Luna, **79**; Aquella Casa En Las Afueras, Inferno, **80**; Aspern, **81**; Sogni Mostruosamente Proibiti, **83**; Secrets Secrets, **84**; Le Jupon Rouge, **87**; A Notre Regrettable Epoux, **88**; The Party Is Over, Silent Love, **91**; Il Lungo Silenzio, **93**.

VAN DYKE, W S: Gift O' Gab, The Land Of Long Shadows, The Men Of The Desert, The Open Places, The Range Boss, Sadie Goes To Heaven, Lady Of The Dugout, **17**; Daredevil Jack, The Hawk's Trail, **20**; The Avenging Arrow, Double Adventure, **21**; According To Hoyle, The Boss Of Camp 4 Director, Forget Me Not, White Eagle, **22**; The Destroying Angel, The Little Girl Next Door, The Miracle Makers, **23**; Barriers Burned Away, The Battling Fool, The Beautiful Sinner, Half-A-Dollar Bill, Loving Lies, Winner Take All, **24**; The Desert's Price, Gold Heels, Hearts And Spurs, Ranger Of The Big Pines, Timber Wolf, The Trail Rider, **25**; The Gentle Cyclone, War Paint, **26**; California, Eyes Of The Totem, Foreign Devils, The Heart Of The Yukon, Spoilers Of The West, Winners Of The Wilderness, **27**; Story, Under The Black Eagle, White Shadows In The South Seas, Wyoming, Story, **28**; The Pagan, **29**; The Cuban Love Song, Guilty Hands, Never The Twain Shall Meet, Trader Horn, **31**; Night Court, Tarzan The Ape Man, **32**; Eskimo, Penthouse, The Prizefighter And The Lady, **33**; Forsaking All Others, Hide-Out, Laughing Boy, Manhattan Melodrama, The Thin Man, **34**; I Live My Life, Naughty Marietta, **35**; After The Thin Man, The Devil Is A Sissy, His Brother's Wife, Love On The Run, Rose Marie, San Francisco, **36**; The Good Earth, Personal Property, Rosalie, They Gave Him A Gun, **37**; Marie Antoinette, Sweethearts, **38**; Andy Hardy Gets Spring Fever, Another Thin Man, It's A Wonderful World, Stand Up And Fight, **39**; Bitter Sweet, I Love You Again, I Take This Woman, **40**; The Feminine Touch, Rage In Heaven, Shadow Of The Thin Man, **41**; Cairo, Dr Kildare's Victory, I Married An Angel, Journey For Margaret, **42**.

VAN HEUSEN, JIMMY: Playmates, **41**; My Favorite Spy, Road To Morocco, **42**; Dixie, **43**; Lady In The Dark, Belle Of The Yukon, Going My Way, **44**; The Bells Of St Mary's, **45**; Cross My Heart, **46**; Road To Bali, **52**; Young At Heart, **54**; Not As A Stranger, The Tender Trap, **55**; Anything Goes, Pardners, **56**; The Joker Is Wild, **57**; Indiscreet, Some Came Running, **58**; Career, A Hole In The Head, Holiday For Lovers, Journey To The Centre Of The Earth, Night Of The Quarter Moon, Say One For Me, This Earth Is Mine, **59**; High Time, Ocean's Eleven, **60**; Pocketful Of Miracles, **61**; The Road To Hong Kong, **62**; Papa's Delicate Condition, **63**;

Honeymoon Hotel, The Pleasure Seekers, Robin And The Seven Hoods, Where Love Has Gone, **64**; Thoroughly Modern Millie, **67**; Star!, **68**; The Great Bank Robbery, **69**.

VAN SANT, GUS: Property, **78**; Mala Noche, **85**; Five Ways To Kill Yourself, Ken Death Gets Out Of Jail, My New Friends, **87**; Junior, **88**; Drugstore Cowboy, **89**; My Own Private Idaho, **91**; Even Cowgirls Get The Blues, **94**; 2 Die 4, **95**.

VARDA, AGNES: La Pointe Courte, **54**; Toute La Mémoire Du Monde, **56**; O Saisons O Châteaux, **57**; Du Cote De La Cote, L'Opéra Mouffe, **58**; La Cocotte D'Azur, **59**; Les Fiancés Du Pont Macdonald, **61**; Cleo From 5 To 7, **62**; Salut Les Cubains, **63**; Christmas Carol, Le Bonheur, **65**; The Creatures, **66**; Elsa, Far From Vietnam, **67**; Black Panthers, Uncle Yanco, **68**; Lions Love, **69**; Nausicaa, **70**; Daguerreotypes, Responses De Femmes, **75**; One Sings The Other Doesn't, **77**; Vagabond, **85**; Jane B By Agnes V, **88**; La Petit Amour, **89**; Jacquot De Nantes, **91**.

VEIDT, CONRAD: The Spy, **17**; The Cabinet Of Dr Caligari, Different From The Others, **19**; Love Makes Us Blind, **23**; The Beloved Rogue, The Last Performance, A Man's Past, **27**; The Man Who Laughs, **28**; 13 Men And A Girl, **30**; Der Mann, Der Den Mord Beging, **31**; I Was A Spy, **33**; Bella Donna, Jew Suss, **34**; Dark Journey, **37**; The Spy In Black **39**; Contraband, Escape, The Thief Of Bagdad, **40**; The Men In Her Life, Whistling In The Dark, A Woman's Face, **41**; All Through The Night, Casablanca, Nazi Agent, **42**; Above Suspicion, **43**.

VERHOEVEN, PAUL: Business Is Business, **71**; Oh Jonathan Oh Jonathan, Turkish Delight, **73**; Katie's Passion, **75**; The Fourth Man, Soldier Of Orange, **79**; Spetters, **80**; Flesh + Blood, **85**; Robocop, **87**; Total Recall, **90**; Basic Instinct, **92**, Showgirls, **95**; Starship Troopers, **97**.

VERA-ELLEN: Wonder Man, **45**; The Kid From Brooklyn, Three Little Girls In Blue, **46**; Carnival In Costa Rica, **47**; Words And Music, **48**; On The Town, Love Happy, **49**; Three Little Words, Happy Go Lovely, **50**; The Belle Of New York, **52**; Big Leaguer, Call Me Madam, **53**; White Christmas, **54**; Let's Be Happy, **57**.

VERTOV, DZIGA: Anniversary Of The Revolution, Cinema Week, **19**; History Of The Civil War, **22**; Kino-Eyelife Caught Unawares, **24**; Cinema-truth, **25**; A Sixth Of The World, Stride Soviet!, Soviet, **26**; The Eleventh Year, **28**; The Man With A Movie Camera, **29**; Enthusiasm: Donbass Symphony, **31**; Three Songs Of Lenin, **34**; Lullaby, Serge Ordjonikidze, **37**; Three Heroines, **38**; The Oath Of Youth, **47**; News Of The Day, **54**.

VIDOR, KING: Better Times, The Other Half, Poor Relations, The Turn In The Road, **19**; The Family Honor, The Jack-knife Man, **20**; Love Never Dies, The Sky Pilot, **21**; Conquering The Woman, Dusk To Dawn, Peg O' My Heart, The Real Adventure, **22**; Three Wise Fools, The Woman Of Bronze, **23**; Happiness, His Hour, Wife Of The Centaur, Wild Oranges, Wine Of Youth, **24**; The Big Parade, Proud Flesh, **25**; Bardelys The Magnificent, La Boheme, **26**; The Patsy, **27**; The Crowd, Show People, **28**; Hallelujah, **29**; Billy The Kid, Not So Dumb, **30**; The Champ, Street Scene, **31**; Bird Of Paradise, Cynara, **32**; The Stranger's Return, **33**; Our Daily Bread, **34**; So Red The Rose, The Wedding Night, **35**; The Texas Rangers, **36**; Stella Dallas, **37**; The Citadel, **38**; Comrade X, Northwest Passage, **40**; H M Pulham Esq, **41**; An American Romance, **44**; Duel In The Sun, **46**; On Our Merry Way, **48**; Beyond The Forest, The Fountainhead, **49**; Lightning Strikes Twice, **51**; Japanese War Bride, Ruby Gentry, **52**; Man Without A Star, **55**; War And Peace, **56**; Solomon And Sheba, **59**.

VIGO, JEAN: A Propos De Nice, **29**; Taris Champion De Natation, **31**; Zéro De Conduite, **33**; L'Atalante, **34**.

VISCONTI, LUCHINO: Ossessione, **42**; Giorni Di Gloria, **45**; La Terra Trema, **48**; Bellissima, **51**; Appunti Su Un Fatto Di Cronaca, We The Women, **53**; Senso, **54**; Of Life And Love, White Nights, **57**; Rocco And His Brothers, **60**; Boccaccio 70, **62**; The Leopard, **63**; Sandra, **65**; The Stranger, **67**; The Witches, **68**; The Damned, **69**; Death In Venice, **71**; Ludwig, **73**; The Innocent, **76**; Conversation Piece, **77**.

VITTI, MONICA: Ridere Ridere Ridere, **55**; L'Avventura, **60**; La Notte, **61**; L'Eclisse, Three Fables Of Love, **62**; Dragées Au Poivre, **63**; High Infidelity, Château En Suede, Il Deserto Rosso, **64**; Four Kinds Of Love, **65**; Modesty Blaise, The Queens, **66**; I Married You For Fun, **67**; La Femme Ecarlate, La Ragazza Con La Pistola, On My Way To The Crusades I Met A Girl Who, **68**; Nini Tirabuscle, The Pizza Triangle, **70**; Gli Ordini Sono Ordini, The Pacifist, **71**; Polvere Di Stelle, Teresa La Ladra, Tosca, **73**; The Phantom Of Liberty, **74**; Midnight Pleasures, **75**; L'Anatra All'Arancia, La Goduria, Mimi Bluette, **76**; L'Alta Meta Del Cielo, **77**; Amore Miei, La Raison D'Etat, Letti Selvaggi, **78**; An Almost Perfect Affair, Per Vivere Meglio, Take Two, Tigers In Lipstick, **79**; The Mystery Of Oberwald, **80**; Il Tango Della Gelosia, **81**; Io So Che Tu Sai Che Io So, **82**; The Flirt, Scusa Se E Poco, Trenta Minuti D'Amore, **83**; Secret Scandal, **89**.

WAJDA, ANDRZEJ: Ceramika Ilzecka, **51**; A Generation, **54**; Ide Ku Sloncu, **55**; Kanal, **56**; Ashes And Diamonds, **58**; Lotna, **59**; Innocent Sorcerers, **60**; Samson, **61**; Love At Twenty, Siberian Lady Macbeth, **62**; Ashes, **65**; Gates To Paradise, **67**; Everything For Sale, Przekladaniec, **68**; Hunting Flies, **69**; The Birchwood, **70**; Pilatus Und Andere, The Wedding, **72**; Land Of Promise, **75**; Man Of Marble, Screen Tests, **77**; Without Anaesthesia, The Young Girls Of Wilko, **79**; Man Of Iron, The Orchestra Conductor, **80**; Danton, Interrogation, **82**; A Love In Germany, **84**; Visage De Chien, **85**; A Chronicle Of Amorous Accidents, **86**; The Possessed, **87**; Dr Korczak, **90**; Holy Week, **96**.

WALBROOK, ANTON: Michael Strogoff, Victoria The Great, **37**; Sixty Glorious Years, **38**; Gaslight, **40**; 49th Parallel, Dangerous Moonlight, **41**; The Life And Death Of Colonel Blimp, **43**; The Red Shoes, **48**; The Queen Of Spades, **49**; La Ronde, **50**; On Trial, **53**; Lola Montès, **55**; Saint Joan, **57**; I Accuse!, **58**.

WALKER, ROBERT: I'll Sell My Wife, **41**; Bataan, Madame Curie, Slightly Dangerous, **43**; See Here Private Hargrove, Since You Went Away, Thirty Seconds Over Tokyo, **44**; Under The Clock, Her Highness And The Bellboy, The Sailor Takes A Wife, What Next Corporal Hargrove?, **45**; Till The Clouds Roll By, **46**; The Beginning Or The End, Song Of Love, **47**; One Touch Of Venus, **48**; Please Believe Me, The Skipper Surprised His Wife, **50**; Strangers On A Train, Vengeance Valley, **51**; My Son John, **52**.

WALLIS, HAL B: The Dawn Patrol, Little Caesar, **30**; Five Star Final, **31**; I Am A Fugitive From A Chain Gang, **32**; Mystery Of The Wax Museum, Gold Diggers Of 1933, Footlight Parade, **33**; G-Men, A Midsummer Night's Dream, Captain Blood, **35**; The Story Of Louis Pasteur, Anthony Adverse, The Charge Of The Light Brigade, Green Pastures, **36**; Marked Woman, Kid Galahad, The Life Of Emile Zola, **37**; A Slight Case Of Murder, Jezebel, The Adventures Of Robin Hood, Boy Meets Girl, Four Daughters, The Sisters, Brother Rat, **38**; Dark Victory, Juarez, The Old Maid, The Private Lives Of Elizabeth and Essex, The Roaring Twenties, **39**; Dr Erlich's Magic Bullet, Torrid Zone, They Drive By Night, The Sea Hawk, A Dispatch From Reuters, The Letter, **40**; High Sierra, The Sea Wolf, The Great Lie, Sergeant York, The Maltese Falcon, **41**; The Man Who Came to Dinner, Kings Row, Yankee Doodle Dandy, Now Voyager, Casablanca, **42**; Air Force, Watch On The Rhine, Princess O'Rourke, **43**; Passage To Marseille, **44**; Love Letters, **45**; The Strange Love Of Martha Ivers, **46**; I Walk Alone, **47**; So Evil My Love, Sorry Wrong Number, The Accused, **48**; Rope Of Sand, **49**; Paid In Full, The Furies, Dark City, **50**; September Affair, That's My Boy, **51**; Come Back Little Sheba, **52**; About Mrs Leslie, **54**; The Rose Tattoo, **55**; Artists And Models, The Rainmaker, **56**; Gunfight At The OK Corral, **57**; King Creole, Hot Spell, **58**; Last Train From Gun Hill, Career, **59**; GI Blues, **60**; Summer And Smoke, **61**; Becket, **64**; The Sons Of Katie Elder, Boeing Boeing, **65**; Barefoot In The Park, **67**; True Grit, Anne Of The Thousand Days, **69**; Norwood, **70**; Red Sky At Morning, Shoot Out, Mary Queen Of Scots, **71**; Follow Me, **72**; A Bequest To The Nation, The Don Is Dead, **73**; Rooster Cogburn, **75**.

WALSH, RAOUL: Carmen, The Regeneration, The Birth Of A Nation, **15**; Blue Blood And Red, The Honor System, The Serpent, **16**; Betrayed, The Conqueror, The Innocent Sinner, The Pride Of New York, The Silent Lie, This Is The Life, **17**; I'll Say So, On The Jump, The Prussian Cur, Woman And The Law, **18**; Evangeline, Every Mother's Son, Should A Husband Forgive?, **19**; The Deep Purple, From Now On, The Strongest, **20**; The Oath, Serenade, **21**; Kindred Of The Dust, **22**; Lost And Found On A South Sea Island, **23**; The Thief Of Bagdad, **24**; East Of Suez, The Spaniard, **25**; The Lady Of The Harem, The Lucky Lady, The Wanderer, What Price Glory?, **26**; Loves Of Carmen, The Monkey Talks, **27**; Me Gangster, The Red Dance, Sadie Thompson, **28**; The Cockeyed World, Hot For Paris, In Old Arizona, **29**; The Big Trail, **30**; The Man Who Came Back, Women Of All Nations, Yellow Ticket, **31**; Me And My Gal, Walking Down Broadway, Wild Girl, **32**; The Bowery, Going Hollywood, Sailor's Luck, **33**; Baby Face Harrington, Every Night At Eight, Under Pressure, **35**; Big Brown Eyes, Klondike Annie, Spendthrift, **36**; Artists & Models, Hitting A New High, When Thief Meets Thief, You're In, The Army Now, **37**; College Swing, **38**; The Roaring Twenties, St Louis Blues, **39**; Dark Command, They Drive By Night, **40**; High Sierra, Manpower, The Strawberry Blonde, They Died With Their Boots On, **41**; Desperate Journey, Gentleman Jim, **42**; Background To Danger, Northern Pursuit, **43**; Uncertain Glory, **44**; The Horn Blows At Midnight, Objective Burma!, Salty O'Rourke, **45**; The Man I Love, **46**; Cheyenne, Pursued, **47**; Fighter Squadron, One Sunday Afternoon, Silver River, **48**; Colorado Territory, White Heat, **49**; Along The Great Divide, Captain Horatio Hornblower, Distant Drums, The Enforcer, **51**; Blackbeard The Pirate, Glory Alley, The Lawless Breed, The World In His Arms, **52**; Gun Fury, A Lion Is In The Streets, Sea Devils, **53**; Saskatchewan, **54**; Battle Cry, The Tall Men, **55**; The King And Four Queens, The Revolt Of Mamie Stover, **56**; Band Of Angels, **57**; The Naked And The Dead, **58**; A Private's Affair, The Sheriff Of Fractured Jaw, **59**; Esther And The King, **60**; Marines, Let's Go, **61**; A Distant Trumpet, **64**.

WALTERS, CHARLES: Good News, **47**; Easter Parade, **48**; The Barkleys Of Broadway, **49**; Summer Stock, **50**; Texas Carnival, Three Guys Named Mike, **51**; The Belle Of New York, **52**; Dangerous When Wet, Easy To Love, Lili, Torch Song, **53**; The Glass Slipper, The Tender Trap, **55**; High Society, **56**; Don't Go Near The Water, **57**; Ask Any Girl, **59**; Please Don't Eat The Daisies, **60**; Two Loves, **61**; Jumbo, **62**; The Unsinkable Molly Brown, **64**; Walk Don't Run, **66**.

WARHOL, ANDY: The Couch, **62**; Blow Job, Dance Movie, Eat, Kiss, Sleep, **63**; Batman Dracula, Empire, Harlot, Henry Geldzahler, Soap Opera, Tarzan And Jane Regained Sort Of, Taylor Mead's Ass, The Thirteen Most Beautiful Women, **64**; Afternoon, Beauty No Bitch, Camp, Drunk, Face, Hedy, Horse, Kitchen, The Life Of Juanita Castro, Lupe, More Milk Yvette, My Hustler, Outer And Inner Space, Paul Swan, Poor Little Rich Girl, Prison, Restaurant, Screen Test No Screen Test No Space, Suicide, The Thirteen Most Beautiful Boys, Vinyl, **65**; The Chelsea Girls, Eating Too Fast, The Velvet Underground And Nico, **66**; Bike Boy, Four Stars, I A Man, The Loves Of Ondine, Nude Restaurant, **67**; Flesh, Lonesome Cowboys, The Queen, **68**; Diaries Notes And Sketches, Blue Movie, **69**; Imitation Of Christ, Trash, **70**; Andy Warhol's Bad, Andy Warhol's Women, Dynamite Chicken, **71**; CS Blues, Heat, L'Amour, **72**; Painters Painting, **73**; Andy Warhol's Dracula, Andy Warhol's Frankenstein, **74**.

WARNER, JACK L : A Dangerous Adventure, **22**; This Is The Army, **43**; My Fair Lady, **64**; Camelot, **67**; 1776, Dirty Little Billy, **72**.

WARREN, HARRY: Spring Is Here, **30**; 42nd Street, Footlight Parade 1933, Gold Diggers Of 1933, Roman Scandals, **33**; Dames, Wonder Bar, **34**; Broadway Gondolier, Go Into Your Dance, Gold Diggers Of Broadway, In Caliente, Stars Over Broadway, **35**; Gold Diggers Of 1937, **36**; Going Places, Hard To Get, **38**; Down Argentine Way, Tin Pan Alley, **40**; The Great American Broadcast, Sun Valley Serenade, That Night In Rio, Week-end In Havana, **41**; Iceland, Orchestra Wives, Song Of The Islands, **42**; Hello Frisco Hello, Sweet Rosie O'Grady, **43**; Diamond Horseshoe, Yolanda And The Thief, **45**; The Harvey Girls, Ziegfeld Follies, **46**; Summer Holiday, **48**; The Barkleys Of Broadway, My Dream Is Yours, **49**; Summer Stock, **50**; The Belle Of New York, Skirts Ahoy!, **52**; The Caddy, **53**; Artists And Models, **55**; The Ladies' Man, **61**; Satan Never Sleeps, **62**; Fate Is The Hunter, **64**; Rosie!, **67**.

WATERS, JOHN: Mondo Trasho, **70**; Multiple Maniacs, **71**; Pink Flamingos, **72**; Female Trouble, **75**; Desperate Living, **77**; Polyester, **81**; Something Wild, **86**; Hairspray, **88**; Cry-baby, Homer & Eddie, **90**; Serial Mom, **94**.

WASHINGTON, DENZEL: Carbon Copy, **81**; A Soldier's Story, **84**; Power, **86**; Cry Freedom, **87**; For Queen And Country, **88**; Glory, The Mighty Quinn, Reunion, **89**; Mo' Better Blues, **90**; Ricochet, **91**; Malcolm X, Mississippi Masala, **92**; Much Ado About Nothing, The Pelican Brief, Philadelphia, **93**; Crimson Tide, Virtuosity, Devil In A Blue Dress, **95**; Courage Under Fire, The Preacher's Wife, **96.**

WAXMAN, FRANZ: The Blue Angel, **30**; Liliom, **34**; Bride Of Frankenstein, Magnificent Obsession, **35**; Fury, Sutter's Gold, **36**; Captains Courageous, A Day At The Races, **37**; A Christmas Carol, Three Comrades, **38**; At The Circus, **39**; Boom Town, The Philadelphia Story, Rebecca, Strange Cargo, **40**; Dr Jekyll And Mr Hyde, Suspicion, **41**; Tortilla Flat, Woman Of The Year, **42**; Air Force, Destination Tokyo, Edge Of Darkness, Old Acquaintance, **43**; Objective Burma!, Pride Of The Marines, **45**; Humoresque, **46**; Dark Passage, Nora Prentiss, Possessed, The Two Mrs Carrolls, The Unsuspected, **47**; The Paradine Case, Sorry Wrong Number, **48**; Night And The City, Sunset Boulevard, **50**; The Blue Veil, He Ran All The Way, A Place In The Sun, **51**; Little Sheba, My Cousin Rachel, **52**; Stalag 17, **53**; Prince Valiant, Rear Window, The Silver Chalice, **54**; Mister Roberts, **55**; Crime In The Streets, **56**; Love In The Afternoon, Peyton Place, Sayonara, The Spirit Of St Louis, **57**; The Nun's Story, **59**; Cimarron, The Story Of Ruth, King Of The Roaring 20s: The Story Of Arnold Rothstein, **60**; Taras Bulba, **62**; Lost Command, **66**.

WAYNE, JOHN: Salute, Words And Music, **29**; The Big Trail, Men Are Like That, Men Without Women, **30**; Arizona, Girls Demand Excitement, Maker Of Men, The Range Feud, Three Girls Lost, **31**; The Big Stampede, Haunted Gold, Lady And Gent, Ride Him Cowboy, The Shadow Of The Eagle, Texas Cyclone, **32**; Baby Face, His Private Secretary, The Life Of Jimmy Dolan, The Man From Monterey, Riders Of Destiny, Sagebrush Trail, **33**; Neath The Arizona Skies, Blue Steel, The Lucky Texan, The Man From Utah, Randy Rides Alone, The Star Packer, The Trail Beyond, West Of The Divide, **34**; The Dawn Rider, The Desert Trail, The Lawless Frontier, Lawless Range, The New Frontier, Paradise Canyon, Rainbow Valley, Texas Terror, The Three Musketeers, Westward Ho, **35**; Conflict, King Of The Pecos, The Lawless Nineties, The Lonely Trail, The Oregon Trail, Sea Spoilers, Winds Of The Wasteland, **36**; I Cover The War, Idol Of The Crowds, **37**; Born To The West, Overland Stage Raiders, Pals Of The Saddle, Red River Range, Santa Fe Stampede, **38**; Allegheny Uprising, The New Frontier, The Night Riders, Stagecoach, Three Texas Steers, Wyoming Outlaw, **39**; Dark Command, The Long Voyage Home, Seven Sinners, Three Faces West, **40**; Lady From Louisiana, Shepherd Of The Hills, **41**; Flying Tigers, In Old California, Lady For A Night, Pittsburgh, Reap The Wild Wind, Reunion In France, The Spoilers, **42**; A Lady Takes A Chance, In Old Oklahoma, **43**; The Fighting Seabees, Tall In The Saddle, **44**; Back To Bataan, Dakota, Flame Of Barbary Coast, They Were Expendable, **45**; Without Reservations, **46**; Angel And The Badman, Tycoon, **47**; 3 Godfathers, Fort Apache, Red River, Wake Of The Red Witch, **48**; The Fighting Kentuckian, Sands Of Iwo Jima, She Wore A Yellow Ribbon, **49**; Rio Grande, **50**; Bullfighter And The Lady, Flying Leathernecks, Operation Pacific, **51**; Big Jim Mclain, The Quiet Man, **52**; Hondo, Island In The Sky, Trouble Along The Way, **53**; The High And The Mighty, **54**; Blood Alley, The Sea Chase, **55**; The Conqueror, The Searchers, **56**; Jet Pilot, Legend Of The Lost, The Wings Of Eagles, **57**; The Barbarian And The Geisha, China Doll, I Married A Woman, **58**; The Horse Soldiers, Rio Bravo, **59**; The Alamo, North To Alaska, **60**; The Comancheros, **61**; Hatari!, How The West Was Won, The Longest Day, The Man Who Shot Liberty Valance, **62**; Donovan's Reef, Mclintock!, **63**; Circus World, **64**; The Greatest Story Ever Told, In Harm's Way, The Sons Of Katie Elder, **65**; Cast A Giant Shadow, **66**; El Dorado, The War Wagon, **67**; The Green Berets, **68**; True Grit, The Undefeated, **69**; Chisum, Rio Lobo, **70**; Big Jake, **71**; The Cowboys, **72**; Cahill, The Train Robbers, **73**; McQ, **74**; Brannigan, Rooster Cogburn, **75**; The Shootist, **76**.

WEAVER, SIGOURNEY: Annie Hall, **77**; Madman, **78**; Alien, **79**; Eyewitness, **81**; Deal Of The Century, The Year Of Living Dangerously, **83**; Ghostbusters, **84**; One Woman Or Two, **85**; Aliens, Half Moon Street, **86**; Gorillas In The Mist, Working Girl, **88**; Ghostbusters II, **89**; 1492: Conquest Of Paradise, Alien, **92**; Dave, **93**; Death And The Maiden, **95**.

WEBB, CLIFTON: Polly With A Past, **20**; Let Not Man Put Asunder, **24**; Heart Of A Siren, New Toys, **25**; Laura, **44**; The Dark Corner, The Razor's Edge, **46**; Sitting Pretty, **48**; Mr Belvedere Goes To College, **49**; Cheaper By The Dozen, For Heaven's Sake, **50**; Elopement, Mr Belvedere Rings The Bell, **51**; Dreamboat, Stars And Stripes Forever, **52**; Mister Scoutmaster, Titanic, **53**; Three Coins In The Fountain, Woman's World, **54**; The Man Who Never Was, **56**; Boy On A Dolphin, **57**; Holiday For Lovers, The Remarkable Mr Pennypacker, **59**; Satan Never Sleeps, **62**.

WEBER, LOIS: The Heiress, On The Brink, **11**; The Troubadour's Triumph, **12**; The Female Of The Species, The Jew's Christmas, **13**; Behind The Veil, False Colors, A Fool And His Money, The Merchant Of Venice, **14**; A Cigarette That's All, Hypocrites, It's No Laughing Matter, Scandal, Sunshine Molly, **15**; The Devil's Brew, The Dumb Girl Of Portici, Idle Wives, The People Vs John Doe, Saving The Family Name, Where Are My Children?, **16**; Even As You And I, The Flirt, The Hand That Rocks The Cradle, The Mysterious Mrs M, The Price Of A Good Time, **17**; Borrowed Clothes, The Doctor And The Woman, For Husbands Only, **18**; Home, Mary Regan, A Midnight Romance, When A Girl Loves, **19**; Forbidden, To Please One Woman, **20**; The Blot, Too Wise Wives, What Do Men Want?, What's Worth While?, **21**; A Chapter In Her Life, **23**; The Marriage Clause, **26**; The Angel Of Broadway, Sensation Seekers, **27**; White Heat, **34**.

WEIR, PETER: Three To Go, **70**; Holmesdale, **71**; Whatever Happened To Green Valley?, **73**; The Cars That Ate Paris, **74**; Picnic At Hanging Rock, **75**; The Last Wave, **77**; The Plumber, **80**; Gallipoli, **81**; The Year Of Living Dangerously, **83**; Witness, **85**; The Mosquito Coast, **86**; Dead Poets Society, **89**; Green Card, **90**; Fearless, **93**; The Ruman Show, **97**.

WEISSMULLER, JOHNNY: Glorifying The American Girl, **29**; Tarzan The Ape Man, **32**; Tarzan And His Mate, **34**; Tarzan

Escapes, **36**; Tarzan Finds A Son!, **39**; Tarzan's Secret Treasure, **41**; Tarzan's New York Adventure, **42**; Stage Door Canteen, Tarzan Triumphs, Tarzan's Desert Mystery, **43**; Tarzan And The Amazons, **45**; Swamp Fire, Tarzan And The Leopard Woman, **46**; Tarzan And The Huntress, **47**; Jungle Jim, Tarzan And The Mermaids, **48**; The Lost Tribe, **49**; Captive Girl, Mark Of The Gorilla, Pygmy Island, **50**; Fury Of The Congo, Jungle Manhunt, **51**; Jungle Jim In The Forbidden Land, Voodoo Tiger, **52**; Killer Ape, Savage Mutiny, Valley Of The Headhunters, **53**; Cannibal Attack, Jungle Man-Eaters, **54**; Devil Goddess, Jungle Moon Men, **55**; The Phynx, **70**.

WELLES, ORSON: Citizen Kane, **41**; It's All True, Journey Into Fear, The Magnificent Ambersons, **42**; Jane Eyre, **44**; The Stranger, Tomorrow Is Forever, **46**; The Lady From Shanghai, Macbeth, **48**; Black Magic, Prince Of Foxes, The Third Man, **49**; The Black Rose, **50**; Othello, Trent's Last Case, **52**; Trouble In The Glen, **53**; Royal Affairs In Versailles, Three Cases Of Murder, **54**; Don Quixote, Confidential Report, **55**; Moby Dick, **56**; Man In The Shadow, **57**; The Long Hot Summer, The Roots Of Heaven, South Seas Adventure, Touch Of Evil, **58**; Compulsion, **59**; The Battle Of Austerlitz, Crack In The Mirror, **60**; Rogopag, The Tartars, **62**; The Trial, The VIPs, **63**; Chimes At Midnight, A Man For All Seasons, **66**; Casino Royale, I'll Never Forget What's 'is Name, The Sailor From Gibraltar, **67**; The Immortal Story, Oedipus The King, **68**; Catch-22, The Kremlin Letter, Start The Revolution Without Me, Upon This Rock, **70**; The Battle Of Neretva, A Safe Place, Waterloo, **71**; Get To Know Your Rabbit, Malpertuis: Histoire D'Une Maison Maudite, Necromancy, The Other Side Of The Wind, Ten Days Wonder, Treasure Island, **72**; F For Fake, **73**; Challenge, **74**; Ten Little Indians/And Then There Were None, **75**; Voyage Of The Damned, **76**; Rime Of The Ancient Mariner, **77**; The Late Great Planet Earth, **78**; The Muppet Movie, **79**; Butterfly, Genocide, History Of The World Part 1, The Man Who Saw Tomorrow, **81**; Almonds And Raisins, **83**; In Our Hands, Slapstick, Where Is Parsifal?, **84**; The Transformers, **86**; Someone To Love, **87**; Hot Money, **89**.

WELLMAN, WILLIAM A: Big Dan, Cupid's Fireman, The Man Who Won, Second Hand Love, **23**; The Circus Cowboy, Not A Drum Was Heard, Vagabond Trail, **24**; When Husbands Flirt, **25**; The Boob, The Cat's Pajamas, You Never Know Women, **26**; Wings, **27**; Beggars Of Life, Ladies Of The Mob, The Legion Of The Condemned, **28**; Chinatown Nights, The Man I Love, Woman Trap, **29**; Dangerous Paradise, Maybe It's Love, Young Eagles, **30**; Night Nurse, Other Men's Women, The Public Enemy, Safe In Hell, Star Witness, **31**; The Conquerors, The Hatchet Man, Love Is A Racket, The Purchase Price, So Big, **32**; Central Airport, College Coach, Frisco Jenny, Heroes For Sale, Lilly Turner, Midnight Mary, Wild Boys Of The Road, **33**; Looking For Trouble, The President Vanishes, Stingaree, **34**; Call Of The Wild, **35**; The Robin Hood Of El Dorado, Small Town Girl, **36**; Nothing Sacred, A Star Is Born, **37**; Men With Wings, **38**; Beau Geste, The Light That Failed, **39**; Reaching For The Sun, **41**; The Great Man's Lady, Roxie Hart, Thunder Birds, **42**; Lady Of Burlesque, The Ox-Bow Incident, **43**; Buffalo Bill, **44**; The Story Of GI Joe, This Man's Navy, **45**; Gallant Journey, **46**; Magic Town, **47**; The Iron Curtain, Yellow Sky, **48**; Battleground, **49**; The Happy Years, The Next Voice You Hear, **50**; Across The Wide Missouri, It's A Big Country, Westward The Women, **51**; My Man And I, **52**; Island In The Sky, **53**; The High And The Mighty, Track Of The Cat, **54**; Blood Alley, **55**; Goodbye My Lady, **56**; Darby's Rangers, Lafayette Escadrille, **58**.

WENDERS, WIM: Summer In The City, **70**; The Goalkeeper's Fear Of The Penalty Kick, **71**; The Scarlet Letter, **73**; Alice In The Cities, **74**; Wrong Move, **75**; Kings Of The Road, **76**; The American Friend, **77**; The Left-handed Woman, **78**; Lightning Over Water, **80**; Long Shot, **81**; Chambre 666, The State Of Things, **82**; Hammett, **83**; Aus Der Familie Der Panzereschen, Paris Texas, **84**; Tokyo-ga, **85**; Wings Of Desire, **87**; Until The End Of The World, **91**; Faraway So Close!, **93**, Beyond The Clouds, **95**; The End of Violence, **97**.

WERTMULLER, LINA: The Lizards, **63**; Let's Talk About Men, **65**; Rita The Mosquito, **66**; Don't Sting The Mosquito, **67**; The Family, **70**; The Seduction Of Mimi, **72**; All Screwed Up, Love And Anarchy, **73**; Swept Away By An Unusual Destiny In The Blue Sea Of August, **75**; Seven Beauties, **76**; A Night Full Of Rain, **78**; Blood Feud, **79**; A Joke Of Destiny, **83**; Sotto Sotto, **84**; A Complex Plot About Women, Alleys And Crimes, Vicoli E Delitti, **85**; Summer Night With Greek Profile, Almond Eyes And Scent Of Basil, **87**; Of Crystal Or Cinders, Fire Or Wind, As Long As It's Love, O Di Cristallo O Ol Genere, O Fuoco O Di Vento, Purche Sia Amore, The Tenth One In Hiding, **89**; Saturday Sunday And Monday, **90**; Me Let's Hope That I Make It, **92**; Ciao Professore, **94**.

WEST, MAE: Night After Night, **32**; I'm No Angel, She Done Him Wrong, **33**; Belle Of The Nineties, **34**; Goin' To Town, **35**; Go West Young Man, Klondike Annie, **36**; Every Day's A Holiday, **37**; My Little Chickadee, **40**; The Heat's On, **43**; Myra Breckinridge, **70**; It's Showtime, **76**; Sextette, **78**.

WEXLER, HASKELL: The Savage Eye, Five Bold Women, **59**; Angel Baby, The Hoodlum Priest, **61**; America America, A Face In The Rain, **63**; The Best Man, **64**; The Bus, The Loved One, **65**; Who's Afraid Of Virginia Woolf?, **66**; In The Heat Of The Night, **67**; The Thomas Crown Affair, **68**; Medium Cool, **69**; Gimme Shelter, Interviews With My Lai Veterans, **70**; The Trial Of The Catonsville Nine, **72**; American Graffiti, **73**; One Flew Over The Cuckoo's Nest, **75**; Bound For Glory, Underground, **76**; Coming Home, Days Of Heaven, **78**; The Rose, **79**; No Nukes, **80**; Second-hand Hearts, **81**; Lookin' To Get Out, Richard Pryor Live On The Sunset Strip, **82**; The Black Stallion Returns, Bus II, The Man Who Loved Women, **83**; Latino, **85**; Matewan, **87**; Colors, **88**; Blaze, Three Fugitives, **89**; Through The Wire, To The Moon, Alice, **90**; At The Max, Other People's Money, **91**; The Babe, **92**, The Secret Of Ronan Inish, **95**.

WHALE, JAMES: Journey's End, **30**; Frankenstein, Waterloo Bridge, **31**; The Impatient Maiden, The Old Dark House, **32**; The Invisible Man, The Kiss Before The Mirror, **33**; By Candlelight, One More River, **34**; Bride Of Frankenstein, Remember Last Night?, **35**; Show Boat, **36**; The Great Garrick, The Road Back, **37**; Port Of Seven Seas, Sinners In Paradise, Wives Under Suspicion, **38**; The Man In The Iron Mask, **39**; Green Hell, **40**; They Dare Not Love, **41**.

WHITE, PEARL: The Girl From Arizona, The Hoodoo, The Life Of Buffalo Bill, The Maid Of Niagara, The New Magdalene, A Summer Flirtation, The Woman Hater, **10**; The Angel Of The Slums, For The Honor Of The Name, The Lost Necklace, **11**; Bella's Beau, The Chorus Girl, The Girl In The Next Room, Oh Such A Night!, Pals, **12**; Accident Insurance, The Girl Reporter, Heroic Harold, Pearl As A Detective, **13**; Home Sweet Home, Lizzie And The Iceman, The Perils Of Pauline, The Ring, Shadowed, Willie's Disguise, **14**; The Exploits Of Elaine, The New Exploits Of Elaine, The Romance Of Elaine, **15**; The Iron Claw, The King's Game, Pearl Of The Army, **16**; The Fatal Ring, **17**; The House Of Hate, The Lightning Raider, **18**; The Black Secret, **19**; Black Is White, The Dark Mirror, The Thief, The White Moll, **20**; Beyond Price, Know Your Men, The Mountain Woman, A Virgin Paradise, **21**; Any Wife, Broadway Peacock, Without Fear, **22**; Plunder, **23**; Perils Of Paris, **24**.

WIDMARK, RICHARD: Kiss Of Death, **47**; Road House, The Street With No Name, Yellow Sky, **48**; Down To The Sea In Ships, Slattery's Hurricane, **49**; Halls Of Montezuma, Night And The City, No Way Out, Panic In The Streets, **50**; The Frogmen, **51**; Don't Bother To Knock, My Pal Gus, O Henry's Full House, Red Skies Of Montana, **52**; Destination Gobi, Pickup On South Street, Take The High Ground, **53**; Broken Lance, Garden Of Evil, Hell And High Water, Cheyenne Autumn, **54**; The Cobweb, A Prize Of Gold, **55**; Backlash, The Last Wagon, Run For The Sun, **56**; Saint Joan, Time Limit, **57**; The Law And Jake Wade, The Tunnel Of Love, **58**; The Trap, Warlock, **59**; The Alamo, **60**; Judgment At Nuremberg, The Secret Ways, Two Rode Together, **61**; How The West Was Won, **62**; Cheyenne Autumn, Flight From Ashiya, **64**; The Bedford Incident, **65**; Alvarez Kelly, **66**; The Way West, **67**; Madigan, **68**; Death Of A Gunfighter, A Talent For Loving, **69**; The Moonshine War, **70**; When The Legends Die, **72**; Murder On The Orient Express, **74**; The Sell Out, To The Devil A Daughter, **76**; The Domino Killings, Rollercoaster, Twilight's Last Gleaming, **77**; Coma, The Swarm, **78**; Bear Island, **80**; National Lampoon Goes To The Movies, **81**; Who Dares Wins, Hanky Panky, **82**; Against All Odds, **84**; True Colors, **91**.

WILCOX, HERBERT: Flames Of Passion, The Wonderful Story, **22**; Chu Chin Chow, **23**; Decameron Nights, Southern Love, **24**; The Only Way, **25**; Limehouse, Nell Gwyn, **26**; The Luck Of The Navy, Madame Pompadour, Mumsie, Tiptoes, **27**; The Bondman, Dawn, **28**; When Knights Were Bold, The Woman In White, **29**; The Loves Of Robert Burns, Rookery Nook, Wanted Men, **30**; Carnival, Chance Of The Night-time, The Rosary, **31**; The Blue Danube, The Flag Lieutenant, The Love Contract, Say It With Music, Thark, **32**; Bitter Sweet, The King's Cup, The Little Damozel, Goodnight Vienna, Sorrell And Son, That's A Good Girl, Yes Mr Brown, **33**; The Queen's Affair, **34**; Brewster's Millions, Escape Me Never, Nell Gwyn, Peg Of Old Drury, **35**; Limelight, This'll Make You Whistle, The Three Maxims, **36**; The Frog, The Gang Show, London Melody, The Rat, Suicide Legion, Our Fighting Navy, Victoria The Great, **37**; Blondes For Danger, Sixty Glorious Years, **38**; Nurse Edith Cavell, **39**; Irene, No No Nanette, **40**; Sunny, **41**; They Flew Alone, **42**; Forever And A Day, The Yellow Canary, **43**; I Live In Grosvenor Square, **45**; Piccadilly Incident, **46**; The Courtneys Of Curzon Street, **47**; Elizabeth Of Ladymead, Spring In Park Lane, **48**; Maytime In Mayfair, **49**; Into The Blue, Odette, **50**; The Lady With The Lamp, **51**; Derby Day, Trent's Last Case, **52**; The Beggar's Opera, Laughing Anne, Trouble In The Glen, **53**; Lilacs In The Spring, **54**; King's Rhapsody, **55**; My Teenage Daughter, **56**; The Dangerous Years, **57**; The Man Who Wouldn't Talk, Wonderful Things, **58**; The Heart Of A Man, The Lady Is A Square, **59**.

WILDER, BILLY: People On Sunday, Der Teufelsreporter, **29**; Seitensprunge, **30**; Der Falsche Ehemann, Emil And The Detectives, Der Mann Der Seinen Morder sucht, Ihre Hoheit Befiehlt, **31**; Das Blaue Vom Himmel, Ein Blonder Traum, Es War Einmal Ein Walzer, Scampolo – Ein Kind Der Strasse, **32**; Was Frauen Traumen, Madame Wunscht Keine Kinder, Mauvaise Graine, **33**; Music In The Air, **34**; Lottery Lover, **35**; Bluebeard's Eighth Wife, **38**; Midnight, What A Life, Ninotchka, **39**; Arise My Love, **40**; Hold Back The Dawn, **41**; Ball Of Fire, The Major And The Minor, **42**; Five Graves To Cairo, **43**; Double Indemnity, **44**; The Lost Weekend, **45**; The Emperor Waltz, A Foreign Affair, A Song Is Born, **48**; Sunset Boulevard, **50**; Ace In The Hole, **51**; Stalag 17, **53**; Sabrina, **54**; The Seven Year Itch, **55**; The Spirit Of St Louis, Love In The Afternoon, **57**; Witness For The Prosecution, **58**; Some Like It Hot, **59**; The Apartment, **60**; One Two Three, **61**; Irma La Douce, **63**; Kiss Me Stupid, **64**; The Fortune Cookie, **66**; The Private Life Of Sherlock Holmes, **70**; Avanti!, **72**; The Front Page, **74**; Fedora, **78**; Buddy, Buddy, **81**.

WILDER, GENE: Bonnie And Clyde, **67**; The Producers, **68**; Quackser Fortune Has A Cousin In The Bronx, Start The Revolution Without Me, **70**; Willy Wonka And The Chocolate Factory, **71**; Everything You Always Wanted To Know About Sex, **72**; Blazing Saddles, **73**; The Little Prince, Rhinoceros, Young Frankenstein, **74**; The Adventure Of Sherlock Holmes's Smarter Brother, **75**; Silver Streak, **76**; The World's Greatest Lover, **77**; The Frisco Kid, **79**; Stir Crazy, Sunday Lovers, **80**; Hanky Panky, **82**; The Woman In Red, **84**; Haunted Honeymoon, **86**; Hello Actors Studio, **87**; See No Evil Hear No Evil, **89**; Funny About Love, **90**.

WILLIAMS, EMLYN: The Frightened Lady, Men Of Tomorrow, Sally Bishop, **32**; Friday The 13th, **33**; Evensong, Evergreen, The Man Who Knew Too Much, My Song For You, Roadhouse, **34**; City Of Beautiful Nonsense, The Divine Spark, The Iron Duke, The Dictator, **35**; Broken Blossoms, **36**; I Claudius, Night Must Fall, **37**; The Citadel, Dead Men Tell No Tales, A Night Alone, **38**; Jamaica Inn, The Stars Look Down, **39**; The Girl In The News, They Drive By Night, You Will Remember, **40**; Hatter's Castle, Major Barbara, This England, **41**; Life Begins At 8.30, **42**; The Corn Is Green, **45**; The Last Days Of Dolwyn, **49**; Three Husbands, **50**; Another Man's Poison, The Magic Box, The Scarf, **51**; Ivanhoe, **52**; The Deep Blue Sea, **55**; I Accuse!, **58**; Beyond This Place, The Wreck Of The Mary Deare, **59**; The L-Shaped Room, **63**; Night Must Fall, **64**; Eye Of The Devil, **67**; David Copperfield, The Walking Stick, **70**.

WILLIAMS, ESTHER: Andy Hardy's Double Life, **42**; A Guy Named Joe, **43**; Bathing Beauty, **44**; Thrill Of A Romance, **45**; Easy To Wed, The Hoodlum Saint, Ziegfeld Follies, **46**; Fiesta, This Time For Keeps, **47**; On An Island With You, **48**; Neptune's Daughter, Take Me Out To The Ball Game, **49**; Duchess Of Idaho, Pagan Love Song, **50**; Texas Carnival, **51**; Million Dollar Mermaid, **52**; Dangerous When Wet, Easy To Love, **53**; Jupiter's Darling, **55**; The Unguarded Moment, **56**; Raw Wind In Eden, **58**; The Big Show, **61**; That's Entertainment! III, **94**.

WILLIAMS, JOHN: Daddy-O, **59**; Because They're Young, I Passed For White, **60**; Bachelor Flat, The Secret Ways, **61**; Diamond Head, **62**; Gidget Goes To Rome, **63**; The Killers, **64**; John Goldfarb Please Come Home, None But The Brave, **65**; How To Steal A Million, Not With My Wife You Don't, Penelope, The Plainsman, **66**; Fitzwilly, Valley Of The Dolls, **67**; Sergeant Ryker, **68**; Daddy's Gone A-Hunting, The Reivers, **69**; Fiddler On The Roof, **71**; Cinderella Liberty, The Long Goodbye, The Man Who Loved Cat Dancing, The Paperchase, **73**; Conrack, Earthquake, The Sugarland Express, The Towering Inferno, **74**; The Eiger Sanction, Jaws, **75**; Family Plot, Midway, The Missouri Breaks, **76**; Black Sunday, Close Encounters Of The Third Kind, Star Wars, **77**; The Fury, Jaws 2, The Stud, Superman, **78**; 1941, Dracula, **79**; Airplane!, The Empire Strikes Back, Superman II, **80**; Heartbeeps, Raiders Of The Lost Ark, **81**; ET The Extra-Terrestrial, Monsignor, Yes Giorgio, **82**; Beyond The Limit, The Big Chill, Jaws 3D, Return Of The Jedi, Superman III, **83**; Indiana Jones And The Temple Of Doom, The River, Terror In The Aisles, Top Secret!, **84**; Emma's War, Ferris Bueller's Day Off, Space Camp, **86**; Empire Of The Sun, Jaws The Revenge, Superman IV: The Quest For Peace, The Witches of Eastwick, **87**; Accidental Tourist, **88**; Always, Born On The Fourth Of July, Indiana Jones And The Last Crusade, **89**; Home Alone, Presumed Innocent, Stanley and Iris, **90**; JFK, **91**; Far And Away, Home Alone 2, Lost In New York, **92**; Jurassic Park, **93**; Schindler's List, **94**; Sleepers, **96**.

WILLIAMS, RICHARD: The Little Island, **58**; A Lecture On Man, Love Me Love Me Love Me, **62**; Circus Drawings, **64**; Diary Of A Madman, **65**; The Dermis Probe, **66**; A Christmas Carol, **71**; Nasrudin, **72**; Raggedy Ann & Andy, **77**; Who Framed Roger Rabbit, **88**; Arabian Knight, **95**.

WILLIAMS, ROBIN: Can I Do It Till I Need Glasses?, **77**; Popeye, **80**; The World According To Garp, **82**; The Survivors, **83**; Moscow On The Hudson, **84**; The Best Of Times, Club Paradise, Seize The Day, **86**; Dear America, Good Morning Vietnam, **87**; The Adventures Of Baron Munchausen, Dead Poets Society, **89**; Awakenings, Cadillac Man, **90**; Dead Again, The Fisher King, Hook, Shakes The Clown, **91**; Aladdin, Fern Gully . . . The Last Rainforest, Toys, **92**; Mrs Doubtfire, **93**; Being Human, **94**; Birds Of A Feather, Jumanji, **95**; Father's Day, **97**.

WILLIS, BRUCE: Blind Date, **87**; Die Hard, Sunset, **88**; In Country, Look Who's Talking, That's Adequate, **89**; The Bonfire Of The Vanities, Die Hard 2, Look Who's Talking Too, **90**; Billy Bathgate, Hudson Hawk, The Last Boy Scout, Mortal Thoughts, **91**; Death Becomes Her, The Player, **92**; National Lampoon's Loaded Weapon I, Striking Distance, **93**; Color Of Night, Nobody's Fool, Pulp Fiction, **94**; Die Hard With A Vengeance, **95**.

WINGER, DEBRA: Slumber Party 57, **77**; Thank God It's Friday, **78**; French Postcards, **79**; Urban Cowboy, **80**; Cannery Row, An Officer And A Gentleman, **82**; Terms Of Endearment, **83**; Mike's Murder, **84**; Black Widow, Legal Eagles, **86**; Made In Heaven, **87**; Betrayed, **88**; Everybody Wins, The Sheltering Sky, **90**; Leap Of Faith, **92**; A Dangerous Woman, Shadowlands, Wilder Napalm, **93**; Forget Paris, **95**.

WINNER, MICHAEL: Play It Cool, **62**; West 11, **63**; System, The Jokers, **66**; I'll Never Forget What's 'is Name, **67**; Hannibal Brooks, **69**; The Games, **70**; Lawman, **71**; Chato's Land, The Mechanic, The Nightcomer, **72**; The Stone Killer, Scorpio, **73**; Death Wish, **74**; Won Ton Ton The Dog Who Saved Hollywood, **76**; The Sentinel, **77**; The Big Sleep, **78**; Firepower, **79**; Death Wish II, **82**; The Wicked Lady, **83**; Scream For Help, **84**; Death Wish 3, **85**; Appointment With Death, A Chorus Of Disapproval, **88**; Bullseye!, **89**; Decadence, Dirty Weekend, **93**.

WISE, ROBERT: Bachelor Mother, Fifth Avenue Girl, The Hunchback Of Notre Dame, **39**; Dance Girl Dance, My Favorite Wife, **40**; Citizen Kane, The Devil And Daniel Webster, **41**; The Magnificent Ambersons, Seven Days' Leave, **42**; Bombardier, **43**; The Curse Of The Cat People, Mademoiselle Fifi, **44**; The Body Snatcher, **45**; Criminal Court, A Game Of Death, **46**; Born To Kill, **47**; Blood On The Moon, Mystery In Mexico, **48**; The Set-up, **49**; Three Secrets, Two Flags West, **50**; The Day The Earth Stood Still, The House On Telegraph Hill, **51**; The Captive City, Something For The Birds, **52**; The Desert Rats, Destination Gobi, So Big, **53**; Executive Suite, **54**; Helen Of Troy, **55**; Somebody Up There Likes Me, Tribute To A Bad Man, **56**; This Could Be The Night, Until They Sail, **57**; I Want To Live, Run Silent Run Deep, **58**; Odds Against Tomorrow, **59**; West Side Story, **61**; Two For The Seesaw, **62**; The Haunting, **63**; The Sound Of Music, **65**; The Sand Pebbles, **66**; Star!, **68**; The Andromeda Strain, **71**; Two People, **73**; The Hindenburg, **75**; Audrey Rose, **77**; Star Trek The Motion Picture, **79**; Rooftops, **89**.

WOO, JOHN: The Young Dragons, **73**; The Dragon Tamers, **74**; Countdown to Kung Fu, Princess Chang Ping, **75**; Money Crazy, Follow The Star, **77**; Last Hurrah For Chivalry, **78**; From Rags To Riches, **79**; To Hell With The Devil, Laughing Times, **81**; Plain Jane To The Rescue, **82**; The Sunset Warrior, **83**; The Time You Need A Friend, **84**; Run Tiger Run, **85**; A Better Tomorrow, **86**; A Better Tomorrow II, **87**; The Killer, **89**; Bullet In The Head, **90**; Once A Thief, **91**; Hard-Boiled, **92**; Hard Target, **93**; Broken Arrow, **96**; Face/Off, **97**.

WOOD, NATALIE: The Bride Wore Boots, Tomorrow Is Forever, **46**; Driftwood, The Ghost And Mrs Muir, Miracle On 34th Street, **47**; Chicken Every Sunday, Scudda Hoo! Scudda Hay!, **48**; Father Was A Fullback, The Green Promise, **49**; The Jackpot, Never A Dull Moment, No Sad Songs For Me, Our Very Own, **50**; The Blue Veil, Dear Brat, **51**; Just For You, The Rose Bowl Story, The Star, **52**; The Silver Chalice, **54**; One Desire, Rebel Without A Cause, **55**; The Burning Hills, A Cry In The Night, The Girl He Left Behind, The Searchers, **56**; Bombers B-52, **57**; Kings Go Forth, Marjorie Morningstar, **58**; Cash McCall, **59**; All The Fine Young Cannibals, **60**; Splendor In The Grass, West Side Story, **61**; Gypsy, **62**; Love With The Proper Stranger, **63**; Sex And The Single Girl, **64**; The Great Race, Inside Daisy Clover, **65**; Penelope, This Property Is Condemned, **66**; Bob & Carol & Ted & Alice, **69**; Peeper, **75**; Meteor, **79**; The Last Married Couple In America, Willie And Phil, **80**; Brainstorm, **83**.

WOOD, SAM: A City Sparrow, The Dancin' Fool, Double Speed, Excuse My Dust, Her Beloved Villain, Her First Elopement, Sick Abed, What's Your Hurry?, **20**; Don't Tell Everything, The Great Moment, Peck's Bad Boy, The Snob, Under The Lash, **21**; Beyond The Rocks, Her Gilded Cage, Her Husband's Trademark, The Impossible Mrs Bellew, **22**; Bluebeard's Eighth Wife, His Children's Children, My American Wife, Prodigal Daughters, **23**; Bluff, The Female, The Mine With The Iron Door, The Next Corner, **24**; The Re-creation Of Brian Kent, **25**; Fascinating Youth, One Minute To Play, **26**; The Fair Co-ed, A Racing Romeo, Rookies, **27**; The Latest From Paris, Telling The World, **28**; It's A Great

Life, So This Is College, **29**; The Girl Said No, The Richest Man In The World, They Learned About Women, Way For A Sailor, **30**; The Man In Possession, New Adventures Of Get-Rich-Quick Wallingford, Paid, A Tailor-made Man, **31**; Huddle, Prosperity, **32**; The Barbarian, Christopher Bean, Hold Your Man, **33**; Stamboul Quest, **34**; Let 'em Have It, A Night At The Opera, Whipsaw, **35**; The Unguarded Hour, **36**; A Day At The Races, Madame X, Navy Blue And Gold, **37**; Lord Jeff, Stablemates, **38**; Gone With The Wind, Goodbye Mr Chips, **39**; Kitty Foyle, Our Town, Raffles, Rangers Of Fortune, **40**; The Devil And Miss Jones, **41**; Kings Row, The Pride Of The Yankees, **42**; For Whom The Bell Tolls, The Land Is Bright, **43**; Address Unknown, Casanova Brown, **44**; Guest Wife, Saratoga Trunk, **45**; Heartbeat, **46**; Ivy, **47**; Command Decision, **48**; Ambush, The Stratton Story, **49**.

WOODS, JAMES: Hickey And Boggs, The Visitors, **72**; The Way We Were, **73**; The Gambler, **74**; Distance, Night Moves, **75**; Alex And The Gypsy, **76**; The Choirboys, Raid On Entebbe, **77**; The Onion Field, **79**; The Black Marble, **80**; Eyewitness, **81**; Fast-Walking, Split Image, **82**; Videodrome, **83**; Against All Odds, Once Upon A Time In America, **84**; Cat's Eye, Joshua Then And Now, **85**; Salvador, **86**; Best Seller, Cop, **87**; The Boost, **88**; Immediate Family, True Believer, **89**; The Hard Way, **91**; Chaplin, **92**; The Getaway, **94**; Contact, **97**.

WOODWARD, JOANNE: Count Three And Pray, **55**; A Kiss Before Dying, **56**; No Down Payment, The Three Faces Of Eve, **57**; The Long Hot Summer, Rally Round The Flag Boys!, **58**; The Fugitive Kind, The Sound And The Fury, **59**; From The Terrace, **60**; Paris Blues, **61**; A New Kind Of Love, The Stripper, **63**; Signpost To Murder, **65**; A Big Hand For The Little Lady, A Fine Madness, **66**; Rachel Rachel, **68**; Winning, **69**; Wusa, **70**; They Might Be Giants, **71**; The Effect Of Gamma Rays On Man-In-The-Moon Marigolds, **72**; Summer Wishes Winter Dreams, **73**; The Drowning Pool, **76**; The End, **78**; Harry And Son, **84**; The Glass Menagerie, **87**; Mr & Mrs Bridge, **90**; The Age Of Innocence, Philadelphia, **93**.

WRAY, FAY: Gasoline Love, **23**; The Coast Patrol, **25**; Lazy Lightning, The Man In The Saddle, The Wild Horse Stampede, **26**; Loco Luck, A One Man Game, Spurs And Saddles, **27**; The First Kiss, The Legion Of The Condemned, The Street Of Sin, The Wedding March, **28**; The Four Feathers, Pointed Heels, Thunderbolt, **29**; Behind The Makeup, The Border Legion, Captain Thunder, Paramount On Parade, The Sea God, **30**; The Conquering Horde, Dirigible, The Finger Points, The Lawyer's Secret, Three Rogues, The Unholy Garden, **31**; Doctor X, The Most Dangerous Game, Stowaway, **32**; Ann Carver's Profession, Below The Sea, The Big Brain, The Bowery, King Kong, Master Of Men, Mystery Of The Wax Museum, One Sunday Afternoon, Shanghai Madness, The Vampire Bat, The Woman I Stole, **33**; Affairs Of Cellini, Black Moon, Bulldog Jack, The Captain Hates The Sea, Cheating Cheaters, The Clairvoyant, The Countess Of Monte Cristo, Madame Spy, Once To Every Woman, The Richest Girl In The World, Viva Villa!, White Lies, Woman In The Dark, **34**; Come Out Of The Pantry, Mills Of The Gods, **35**; Roaming Lady, They Met In A Taxi, When Knights Were Bold, **36**; It Happened In Hollywood, Murder In Greenwich Village, Once A Hero, **37**; The Jury's Secret, **38**; Navy Secrets, Smashing The Spy Ring, **39**; Wildcat Bus, **40**; Adam Had Four Sons, Melody For Three, **41**; Not A Ladies' Man, **42**; Small Town Girl, Treasure Of The Golden Condor, **53**; The Cobweb, Hell On Frisco Bay, Queen Bee, **55**; Rock, Pretty Baby, **56**; Crime Of Passion, Tammy And The Bachelor, **57**; Dragstrip Riot, Summer Love, **58**.

WYLER, WILLIAM: Lazy Lightning, The Stolen Ranch, **26**; Blazing Days, The Border Cavalier, Desert Dust, Hard Fists, Straight Shootin', **27**; Anybody Here Seen Kelly?, Thunder Riders, **28**; Hell's Heroes, The Love Trap, The Shakedown, **29**; The Storm, **30**; A House Divided, Tom Brown Of Culver, **32**; Counsellor-At-Law, Her First Mate, **33**; Glamour, **34**; The Gay Deception, The Good Fairy, **35**; Come And Get It, Dodsworth, These Three, **36**; Dead End, **37**; Jezebel, **38**; Wuthering Heights, **39**; The Letter, The Westerner, **40**; The Little Foxes, **41**; Mrs Miniver, **42**; The Fighting Lady, **44**; Thunderbolt, **45**; The Best Years Of Our Lives, **46**; The Heiress, **49**; Detective Story, **51**; Carrie, **52**; Roman Holiday, **53**; The Desperate Hours, **55**; Friendly Persuasion, **56**; The Big Country, **58**; Ben-Hur, **59**; The Children's Hour, **62**; The Collector, **65**; How To Steal A Million, **66**; Funny Girl, **68**; The Liberation Of LB Jones, **70**.

WYMAN, JANE: Gold Diggers Of 1937, My Man Godfrey, Smart Blonde, **36**; The King And The Chorus Girl, Mr Dodd Takes The Air, Public Wedding, Ready Willing And Able, The Singing Marine, Slim, **37**; Brother Rat, The Lion Roars, He Couldn't Say No, International Spy, Wide Open Faces, **38**; The Kid From Kokomo, Kid Nightingale, Private Detective, Tail Spin, Torchy Plays With Dynamite, **39**; An Angel From Texas, Brother Rat And A Baby, Flight Angels, Gambling On The High Seas, My Love Came Back, Tugboat Annie Sails Again, **40**; Bad Men Of Missouri, The Body Disappears, Honeymoon For Three, You're In The Army Now, **41**; Footlight Serenade, Larceny Inc, My Favorite Spy, **42**; Princess O'Rourke, **43**; Crime By Night, The Doughgirls, Hollywood Canteen, Make Your Own Bed, **44**; The Lost Weekend, **45**; Night And Day, One More Tomorrow, The Yearling, **46**; Cheyenne, Magic Town, **47**; Johnny Belinda, **48**; It's A Great Feeling, A Kiss In The Dark, The Lady Takes A Sailor, **49**; The Glass Menagerie, Stage Fright, **50**; The Blue Veil, Here Comes The Groom, Starlift, Three Guys Named Mike, **51**; Just For You, The Story Of Will Rogers, **52**; Let's Do It Again, So Big, **53**; Magnificent Obsession, **54**; All That Heaven Allows, Lucy Gallant, **55**; Miracle In The Rain, **56**; Holiday For Lovers, **59**; Pollyanna, **60**; Bon Voyage!, **62**; How To Commit Marriage, **69**.

YOUNG, FREDDIE: Escape Me Never, **35**; Goodbye Mr Chips, Nurse Edith Cavell, **39**; 49th Parallel, **41**; So Well Remembered, **47**; Escape, **48**; Conspirator, Edward My Son, **49**; Treasure Island, The Winslow Boy, **50**; Calling Bulldog Drummond, **51**; Ivanhoe, **52**; Knights Of The Round Table, Mogambo, Terror On A Train, **53**; Betrayed, **54**; Bedevilled, **55**; Bhowani Junction, Lust For Life, **56**; Beyond Mombasa, Invitation To The Dance, Island In The Sun, The Little Hut, **57**; I Accuse!, Indiscreet, The Inn Of The Sixth Happiness, **58**; Solomon And Sheba, The Wreck Of The Mary Deare, **59**; Macbeth, **60**; Lawrence Of Arabia, **62**; Doctor Zhivago, Lord Jim, **65**; The Deadly Affair, You Only Live Twice, **67**; Battle Of Britain, Sinful Davey, **69**; Ryan's Daughter, **70**; Nicholas And Alexandra, **71**; The Asphyx, **72**; Luther, The Tamarind Seed, **74**; Permission To Kill, **75**; The Blue Bird, **76**; Stevie, **78**; Sidney Sheldon's Bloodline, **79**; Richard's Things, Rough Cut, **80**; Sword Of The Valiant, **82**; Invitation To The Wedding, **83**; Arthur's Hallowed Ground, **85**.

YOUNG, LORETTA: Sweet Kitty Bellairs, **16**; Naughty But Nice, **27**; The Head Man, Laugh Clown Laugh, The Magnificent Flirt, Scarlet Seas, The Whip Woman, **28**; The Careless Age, Fast Life, The Forward Pass, The Girl In The Glass Cage, The Show Of Shows, The Squall, **29**; The Devil To Pay, Loose Ankles, The Man From Blankley's, Road To Paradise, The Second Story Murder, The Truth About Youth, **30**; Beau Ideal, Big Business Girl, I Like Your Nerve, Kismet, Platinum Blonde, The Right Of Way, The Ruling Voice, Three Girls Lost, Too Young To Marry, **31**; The Hatchet Man, Life Begins, Play Girl, Taxi!, They Call It Sin, Weekend Marriage, **32**; The Devil's In Love, Employees' Entrance, Grand Slam, Heroes For Sale, The Life Of Jimmy Dolan, Man's Castle, Midnight Mary, She Had To Say Yes, Zoo In Budapest, **33**; Born To Be Bad, Bulldog Drummond Strikes Back, Caravan, House Of Rothschild, The White Parade, **34**; Call Of The Wild, Clive Of India, The Crusades, Shanghai, **35**; Ladies In Love, Private Number, Ramona, The Unguarded Hour, **36**; Cafe Metropole, Love Is News, Love Under Fire, Second Honeymoon, Wife Doctor And Nurse, **37**; Four Men And A Prayer, Kentucky, Suez, **38**; Eternally Yours, The Story Of Alexander Graham Bell, Wife Husband And Friend, **39**; The Doctor Takes A Wife, He Stayed For Breakfast, **40**; Bedtime Story, Lady From Cheyenne, The Men In Her Life, **41**; China, A Night To Remember, **43**; And Now Tomorrow, Ladies Courageous, **44**; Along Came Jones, **45**; The Perfect Marriage, The Stranger, **46**; The Bishop's Wife, The Farmer's Daughter, **47**; The Accused, Rachel And The Stranger, **48**; Come To The Stable, Mother Is A Freshman, **49**; Key To The City, **50**; Cause For Alarm, Half Angel, **51**; Because Of You, Paula, **52**; It Happens Every Thursday, **53**.

YOUNG, ROBERT: The Black Camel, Guilty Generation, The Sin Of Madelon Claudet, **31**; The Kid From Spain, New Morals For Old, Strange Interlude, Unashamed, The Wet Parade, **32**; Hell Below, Men Must Fight, The Right To Romance, Saturday's Millions, Today We Live, Tugboat Annie, **33**; The Band Plays On, Carolina, Death On The Diamond, House Of Rothschild, Lazy River, Paris Interlude, Spitfire, Whom The Gods Destroy, **34**; The Bride Comes Home, Calm Yourself, Red Salute, Remember Last Night?, Vagabond Lady, West Point Of The Air, **35**; The Bride Walks Out, It's Love Again, The Longest Night, Secret Agent, Stowaway, Sworn Enemy, The Three Wise Guys, **36**; The Bride Wore Red, Dangerous Number, The Emperor's Candlesticks, I Met Him In Paris, Married Before Breakfast, Navy Blue And Gold, **37**; Josette, Paradise For Three, Rich Man Poor Girl, The Shining Hour, Three Comrades, The Toy Wife, **38**; Bridal Suite, Honolulu, Maisie, Miracles For Sale, **39**; Dr Kildare's Crisis, Florian, The Mortal Storm, Northwest Passage, Sporting Blood, **40**; HM Pulham Esq, Lady Be Good, Married Bachelor, The Trial Of Mary Dugan, Western Union, **41**; Cairo, Joe Smith American, Journey For Margaret, **42**; Claudia, Sweet Rosie O'Grady, **43**; The Canterville Ghost, The Enchanted Cottage, Those Endearing Young Charms, **45**; Claudia And David, Lady Luck, The Searching Wind, **46**; Crossfire, They Won't Believe Me, **47**; Relentless, Sitting Pretty, **48**; Adventure In Baltimore, And Baby Makes Three, Bride For Sale, The Forsyte Saga, **49**; Goodbye My Fancy, The Second Woman, **51**; The Half-Breed, **52**; Secret Of The Incas, **54**.

YOUNG, VICTOR: Anything Goes, The Big Broadcast Of 1937, Klondike Annie, **36**; Artists & Models, Maid Of Salem, Make Way For Tomorrow, **37**; Golden Boy, The Light That Failed, **39**; Northwest Mounted Police, **40**; I Wanted Wings, **41**; The Palm Beach Story, Reap The Wild Wind, **42**; For Whom The Bell Tolls, **43**; Frenchman's Creek, Ministry Of Fear, **44**; Kitty, Love Letters, **45**; The Searching Wind, Two Years Before The Mast, **46**; Golden Earrings, I Walk Alone, **47**; The Big Clock, The Emperor Waltz, The Paleface, State Of The Union, **48**; My Foolish Heart, Samson And Delilah, **49**; Rio Grande, **50**; The Greatest Show On Earth, The Quiet Man, Scaramouche, **52**; Shane, **53**; Johnny Guitar, Three Coins In The Fountain, **54**; Strategic Air Command, **55**; Around The World In 80 Days, **56**; Run Of The Arrow, **57**.

ZETTERLING, MAI: Lasse-maja, **41**; Frenzy, **44**; Iris And The Lieutenant, Sunshine Follows Rain, **46**; Frieda, **47**; Portrait From Life, Night Is My Future, **48**; The Lost People, Quartet, **49**; The Bad Lord Byron, Blackmailed, **51**; The Ringer, **52**; Desperate Moment, The Tall Headlines, **53**; Knock On Wood, **54**; Of Love And Lust, A Prize Of Gold, **55**; Seven Waves Away, **57**; The Truth About Women, **58**; Jet Storm, **59**; Offbeat, **61**; The Main Attraction, Only Two Can Play, **62**; The War Game, **63**; Loving Couples, **64**; The Vine Bridge, **65**; Night Games, **66**; Doctor Glas, The Girls, Vincent The Dutchman, **72**; Visions Of Eight, **73**; We Have Many Faces, **75**; Of Seals And Man, **78**; Love, **81**; Scrubbers, **82**; Amarosa, **86**; Hidden Agenda, The Witches, **90**.

ZHANG YIMOU: Red Sorghum, **87**; Ju Dou, **89**; Raise The Red Lantern, **91**; The Story Of Qiu Ju, **92**; To Live, **94**, Shanghai Triad, **95**; Keep Cool, **97**.

ZEMECKIS, ROBERT: I Wanna Hold Your Hand, **78**; 1941, **79**; Used Cars, **80**; Romancing The Stone, **84**; Back To The Future, **85**; Who Framed Roger Rabbit, **88**; Back To The Future Part II, Back To The Future Part III, **90**; Death Becomes Her, The Public Eye, Trespass, **92**; Forrest Gump, **94**.

ZINNEMANN, FRED: The Wave, **35**; That Mothers Might Live, **38**; Eyes In The Night, Kid Glove Killer, **42**; The Seventh Cross, **44**; Little Mr Jim, My Brother Talks To Horses, **46**; The Search, **48**; Act Of Violence, **49**; The Men, **50**; Benjy, Teresa, **51**; High Noon, The Member Of The Wedding, **52**; From Here To Eternity, **53**; Oklahoma!, **55**; A Hatful Of Rain, **57**; The Nun's Story, **59**; The Sundowners, Behold A Pale Horse, **60**; A Man For All Seasons, **66**; The Day Of The Jackal, **73**; Julia, **77**; Five Days One Summer, **83**.

Movie talk

Speed: normal speed of sound recording equipment.

Stand in: doubles for star when scene is being set up preparatory to shoot, enabling the performer to rest.

Star system: regular casting of unknown actors to create box office appeal. Started in early 1900s with Florence Lawrence, then Pickford, Chaplin and Fairbanks.

Stop motion: an object is moved between single frame exposures, thus appearing to move fluidly when the resulting film is projected.

Strike the set: dismantlement of studio set after director calls out "check the gate" and "it's a wrap".

Stunt double: stunt man or woman who performs in particularly dangerous stunts on behalf of the star.

Telefono blanco: 1930s Italian films, usually romantic comedies set against sumptuously upholstered surroundings and replete with white telephones. Such frothy extravagance was guaranteed not to upset Mussolini.

3D: various techniques for creating three-dimensional projected images have been tried out but never quite caught on, except in theme parks such as Disneyland.

Turn over: start camera and sound recording.

Undercrank: slow down camera speed from 24 frames per second for difficult stunts which, when projected at normal speed make the action appear faster. Similarly, overcranking produces slow motion effect.

Widescreen: variations on "Academy ratio", the 1.33:1 screen shape still standard on television. The widescreen aspect ratio is 1.66:1 in Europe and 1.85:1 in America. Optical (anamorphic) squeezed images produce a 2.35:1 screen shape.

Wrangler: animal, usually horse, expert. Some films have had a "cockroach wrangler".

Wrap: as in "it's a wrap" to signify successful shooting of scene or film.

Wrap party: final booze-up at end of shooting.

Who's who in the Filmfinder pictures

Page 193: (from top) Buster Keaton, Warren Beatty and Faye Dunaway, Marlon Brando, Vivien Leigh, Keanu Reeves, Lillian Gish

Page 194: Ben Kingsley in *Gandhi*, 1982

Page 199: Charlie Chaplin in *Modern Times*, 1936

Page 207: Ingrid Bergman and Humphrey Bogart in *Casablanca*, 1942

Page 215: Glenda Jackson in *Mary Queen Of Scots*, 1971

Page 223: Jeanne Moreau and Henri Serre in *Jules et Jim*, 1961

Page 231: Robert De Niro in *Taxi Driver*, 1976